# THE NEW HANDBOOK OF SECOND LANGUAGE ACQUISITION

SECOND EDITION

# THE NEW HANDBOOK OF SECOND LANGUAGE ACQUISITION

Edited by

## William C. Ritchie
*Syracuse University, USA*

**and**

## Tej K. Bhatia
*Syracuse University, USA*

2009

Emerald

United Kingdom • North America • Japan
India • Malaysia • China

Emerald Group Publishing Limited
Howard House, Wagon Lane, Bingley BD16 1WA, UK

First edition 2009

Copyright © 2009 Emerald Group Publishing Limited

**Reprints and permission service**
Contact: booksandseries@emeraldinsight.com

**British Library Cataloguing in Publication Data**
A catalogue record for this book is available from the British Library

ISBN: 978-1-84855-240-1

Awarded in recognition of
Emerald's production
department's adherence to
quality systems and processes
when preparing scholarly
journals for print

# CONTENTS

## 2 Research Methodology in Second Language Acquisition from a Linguistic Perspective

Suzanne Flynn
Claire Foley

## II APPROACHES TO THE STUDY OF SECOND LANGUAGE ACQUISITION

## 3 Grammatical Theory: Interfaces and L2 Knowledge

Lydia White

## 4  Emergentism and Second Language Acquisition

William O'Grady
Miseon Lee
Hye-Young Kwak

## 5  Variationist Linguistics and Second Language Acquisition

Dennis R. Preston
Robert Bayley

## 6 An Information-Processing Approach to Second Language Acquisition

Jeanette Altarriba
Dana M. Basnight-Brown

## 7 The Artificial Development of Second Language Ability: a Sociocultural Approach

James P. Lantolf
Matthew E. Poehner

## 8 Cognitive Linguistics and Second Language Learning

Marjolijn Verspoor
Andrea Tyler

# III COMPONENTS OF LINGUISTIC REPRESENTATION AND PROCESSING IN SECOND LANGUAGE ACQUISITION

## 9 Second Language Acquisition of the Lexicon
Alan Juffs

## 10 Second Language Acquisition of Morphosyntax
Roger Hawkins

## 11  Second Language Phonology

John Archibald

## 12  L2 Pragmatic Development

Gabriele Kasper

## 13 Sentence Parsing in L2 Learners: Linguistic and Experience-Based Factors

Paola E. Dussias
Pilar Piñar

## 14 Implicit Learning in Second Language Acquisition

John N. Williams

## IV NEUROPSYCHOLOGY AND COGNITIVE DEVELOPMENT

## 15 Neuropsychology of Second Language Acquisition

Cosimo Urgesi
Franco Fabbro

## 16 Child Second Language Acquisition

Usha Lakshmanan

## 17 Age and the End State of Second Language Acquisition

David Birdsong

# 18 Multilingualism and Aging

Kees de Bot

# V MODALITY AND THE CONTRIBUTION OF THE ENVIRONMENT

# 19 Input and Second Language Processing

Kira Gor

Michael H. Long

## 20 Second Language Acquisition in the Instructional Environment

Teresa Pica

## 21 Untutored Second Language Acquisition

Wolfgang Klein
Christine Dimroth

## 22 The Interlanguage Development of Deaf and Hearing Learners of L2 English: Parallelism via Minimalism

Gerald P. Berent

## 23 Second Language Acquisition: Research and Application in the Information Age

Tej K. Bhatia
William C. Ritchie

**VI** SOCIAL PSYCHOLOGY AND SECOND LANGUAGE
ACQUISITION

**24** Language Contact and Second Language
Acquisition

Jeff Siegel

**25** Language Mixing, Universal Grammar and Second
Language Acquisition

Tej K. Bhatia
William C. Ritchie

# CONTRIBUTORS

*Numbers in parentheses indicate the pages on which the authors' contributions begin.*

**Jeanette Altarriba** (115), Department of Psychology, University at Albany, State University of New York, Albany, NY 12222, USA

**John Archibald** (237), Department of Linguistics, University of Calgary, Calgary, Alta., Canada T2N 1N4

**Dana M. Basnight-Brown** (115), Department of Psychology, University at Albany, State University of New York, Albany, NY 12222, USA

**Robert Bayley** (89), Department of Linguistics, University of California, Davis, CA 95616, USA

**Gerald P. Berent** (523), Department of Research and Teacher Education, National Technical Institute for the Deaf, Rochester Institute of Technology, Rochester, NY 14623, USA

**Tej K. Bhatia** (545, 591), Department of Languages, Literatures, and Linguistics, Syracuse University, Syracuse, NY 13244, USA

**David Birdsong** (401), Department of French and Italian, University of Texas, Austin, TX 78712, USA

**Kees de Bot** (425), Department of Applied Linguistics, University of Groningen, 9700 AB Groningen, The Netherlands

**Jean-Marc Dewaele** (623), Department of Applied Linguistics and Communication, Birkbeck College, University of London, London WC1 H 0PD, UK

**Christine Dimroth** (503), Language Acquisition Group, Max Planck Institute for Psycholinguistics, 6500 AH Nijmegen, The Netherlands

**Paola E. Dussias** (295), Department of Spanish, Italian, and Portuguese, Pennsylvania State University, University Park, PA 16802, USA

**Franco Fabbro** (357), IRCCS "E. Medea," Polo Friuli Venezia Giulia and Department of Philosophy, University of Udine, 33100 Udine, Italy

**Suzanne Flynn** (29), Department of Linguistics and Philosophy, Massachusetts Institute of Technology, Cambridge, MA 02467, USA

**Claire Foley** (29), Program in Linguistics, Boston College, Chestnut Hill, MA 02467, USA

**Susan Gass** (3), English Language Center, Michigan State University, East Lansing, MI 48824, USA

**Howard Giles** (647), Department of Communication, University of California/Santa Barbara, Santa Barbara, CA 93106, USA

**Kira Gor** (445), Second Language Acquisition Program, School of Languages, Literatures, and Cultures, University of Maryland, College Park, MD 20742, USA

**Roger Hawkins** (211), Department of Language and Linguistics, University of Essex, Colchester CO4 3SQ, UK

**Alan Juffs** (181), Department of Linguistics, University of Pittsburgh, Pittsburgh, PA 15260, USA

**Gabriele Kasper** (259), Department of Second Language Studies, University of Hawaii at Manoa, Honolulu, HI 96822, USA

**Wolfgang Klein** (503), Language Acquisition Group, Max Planck Institute of Psycholinguistics, 6500 AH Nijmegen, The Netherlands

**Hye-Young Kwak** (69), Department of Linguistics, University of Hawaii at Manoa, Honolulu, HI 96822, USA

**Usha Lakshmanan** (377), Department of Psychology, Program in Brain and Cognitive Sciences, Southern Illinois University/Carbondale, Carbondale, IL 62901, USA

**James P. Lantolf** (137), Department of Applied Linguistics, Pennsylvania State University, University Park, PA 16802, USA

**Miseon Lee** (69), Division of English Language and Literature, Hanyang University, Seoul 133-791, South Korea

**Michael H. Long** (445), Second Language Acquisition Program, School of Languages, Literatures, and Cultures, University of Maryland, College Park, MD 20742, USA

**Kimberly A. Noels** (647), Department of Psychology, University of Alberta, Edmonton, Alta., Canada T6G 2E9

**William O'Grady** (69), Department of Linguistics, University of Hawaii at Manoa, Honolulu, HI 96822, USA

**Teresa Pica** (473), Graduate School of Education, University of Pennsylvania, Philadelphia, PA 19104, USA

**Pilar Piñar** (295), Department of Foreign Languages, Literatures, and Cultures, Gallaudet University, Washington, DC 20002, USA

**Matthew E. Poehner** (137), Department of Curriculum and Instruction, Pennsylvania State University, University Park, PA 16802, USA

**Dennis R. Preston** (89), Department of English, Oklahoma State University, Stillwater, OK 74078, USA

**William C. Ritchie** (545, 591), Department of Languages, Literatures, and Linguistics, Syracuse University, Syracuse, NY 13244, USA

**Jeff Siegel** (569), School of Behavioural, Cognitive, and Social Sciences, University of New England, Armidale, NSW 2351, Australia

**Andrea Tyler** (159), Department of Linguistics, Georgetown University, Washington, DC 20057, USA

**Cosimo Urgesi** (357), IRCCS "E. Medea," Polo Friuli Venezia Giulia and Department of Philosophy, University of Udine, 33100 Udine, Italy

**Marjolijn Verspoor** (159), Department of English Linguistics, University of Groningen, 9712 Groningen, The Netherlands

**Lydia White** (49), Department of Linguistics, McGill University, Montreal, Que., Canada H3A 1A7

**John N. Williams** (319), Research Centre for English and Applied Linguistics, University of Cambridge, Cambridge CB2 1QY, UK

# PREFACE

The present volume is the second edition of a book, the first edition of which was entitled merely *Handbook of Second Language Acquisition*; one might wonder what warrants the addition of "new" to the title of this edition. The major purpose of this preface is to give evidence that the addition of "new" to the title is well justified.

As might be expected of any living field of inquiry, research on second-language acquisition (SLA) and use has changed quite radically since the first edition was published 13 years ago. Publication has flourished; conferences have grown in interdisciplinarity, length, number, and attendance; and the field is even more widely recognized as an important area of scholarly research than it was in 1996. While building on the strengths of the first edition, this volume reflects the changes in the field in several ways.

Several scholars who provided outstanding chapters to the first volume have also contributed to this edition either as single authors or as coauthors. These include Gerald Berent, Suzanne Flynn, Susan Gass, Michael Long, Dennis Preston, and Lydia White as well as the two coeditors. Each of the other 31 authors who contributed to the volume is either already a well-established scholar in the research area about which he or she has written, or is a young and highly promising scholar in that area.

The topics covered in this book fall into three categories in relation to those covered in the first edition. First, there are topics covered in both editions, but have received thorough updating in the contributions to this edition—all in the form of completely new chapters. Second, there are topics that have become centrally important because of changes in the field and its relationships with other disciplines. Third, there are topics that were not covered in the first edition, but have been suggested by published reviews of the first edition or, less formally, by scholars in the field and by readers of the first volume. We begin our discussion by describing these categories in the order given.

Research methodology is reviewed in this edition as it was in the first, but by authors who bring a different perspective from that represented in the earlier edition—Suzanne Flynn and Claire Foley (chapter 2). The first edition provided a chapter on each of several general approaches to the study of SLA including the generative, variatonist, and information-processing approaches. This edition retains these as the topics of entirely new chapters, specifically chapter 3 by Lydia White, chapter 5 by Dennis Preston and Robert Bayley, and chapter 6 by Jeanette Altarriba and Dana Basnight-Brown. With respect to components of linguistic knowledge/representation, there was a chapter on phonology in SLA in the first edition as well as scattered treatments of morphology and syntax in a number of different chapters. In the present edition, John Archibald has contributed an entirely new, updated chapter (chapter 11), and Roger Hawkins has provided a treatment of morphosyntax in chapter 10. A new treatment of the neuropsychology of SLA (chapter 15) was contributed by new authors Cosimo Urgesi and Franco Fabbro. The material in Michael Long's classic treatment of input and interaction in the 1996 edition is updated here in his chapter 19 coauthored with Kira Gor. Gerald Berent, who contributed a chapter on the acquisition of English by the deaf to the first edition, gives a completely new account of these phenomena in chapter 22 of the present edition. There has been a new synthesis of work on bilingual code-switching and code-mixing, including work on related perceptions of grammaticality in second-language learners, since the first edition appeared, and Tej Bhatia and William Ritchie review these developments in chapter 25.

In the second category—topics that have become important because of changes in the field—a prominent place must go to new general approaches to the study of SLA. The growth of new positions on the question of the innateness of principles of grammar has given rise to a general approach to the study of language referred to as "emergentism," and this approach has influenced thinking in the study of SLA. Chapter 4 by William O'Grady, Miseon Lee, and Hye-Young Kwak provides a review of work done within this approach. Another approach that has become prominent since 1996 is that referred to as sociocultural theory grounded in Vygotskian psychology, and chapter 7 by James Lantolf and Matthew Poehner provide an overview of that approach. The general research program referred to as cognitive linguistics has gained prominence since 1996, and the extension of that approach to the study of SLA receives a treatment in chapter 8 by Marjolijn Verspoor and Andrea Tyler. An area of research that has grown in recent years is the study of the processing of speech and writing in second-language learners, and Paola Dussias and Pilar Piñar give an overview of work in that area in chapter 13. A distinction that has played a greater role in recent work on SLA is that between implicit and explicit learning, and chapter 14 is included here on that topic by John Williams. The huge growth of publicly accessible electronic information processing of various kinds—including the Internet—has opened new avenues of opportunity for SLA and SLA research, and a new chapter on this topic (chapter 23 by Tej Bhatia and William Ritchie) is included in this edition. Finally, there is a growing rapprochement between researchers in language contact and SLA researchers, and Jeff Siegel's chapter 24 reviews SLA from the point of view of contact linguistics.

As mentioned above, we have benefited greatly from reviews and comments about the first edition by reviewers and other readers of the first edition. One of the joys of producing the second edition of a work is that one has a chance to include material in the second edition that was, for whatever reason, missing from the first. The topics in the third category above—topics that were not covered in the first edition but would have been if there had been room—include a number of important subjects. The first edition did not include a free-standing history of the field; Susan Gass' chapter 1 fills that gap in this edition. There was no treatment of the increasingly important work on the lexicon and SLA, and chapter 9 by Alan Juffs corrects this omission. Another area of research that was not treated in the first edition was SLA and pragmatics, and Gabriele Kasper's chapter 12 fills this function in the current edition. Another important topic missing from the first edition was child SLA; chapter 16 by Usha Lakshmanan now corrects this situation. Although there was much discussion of age and SLA (including critical/sensitive period phenomena) scattered through the first edition, there was no single chapter on the topic, but the chapters by David Birdsong (chapter 17) and Kees de Bot (chapter 18) now fill this function. Teresa Pica's chapter 20 now eliminates the lack of a chapter on SLA in the instructional environment, and Wolfgang Klein and Christine Dimroth's chapter 21 provides some insight into untutored acquisition. The study of individual differences in SLA is also an important area lacking treatment in the first edition; Jean-Marc Dewaele's chapter 26 now fills that gap. Finally, there was no separate chapter on social factors in SLA, and there is now a rich discussion of these issues in chapter 27 by Kimberly Noels and Howard Giles.

From the above it should be clear that this book is in no sense simply a revision of the first edition but is, rather, a thorough reworking with a new organization, new topics, and, where advantageous, new authors. We hope that it is as useful, if not more so, than the first edition seems to have been.

The book is divided into six parts, each containing chapters that are related in function or in topic. Part I establishes a background for the rest of the book by providing a history of the field and an overview of methods employed in SLA research. Part II covers six different approaches currently adopted in SLA research. Part III treats three areas of linguistic knowledge in SLA—lexicon, morphosyntax, and pragmatics—as well as sentence parsing in SLA and the important distinction between implicit and explicit learning/knowledge. Part IV examines neuropsychology and the problem of SLA and age. Part V is concerned with the role of the environment in SLA, and Part VI treats the social dimension of SLA.

# ACKNOWLEDGMENTS

We have contracted many debts of gratitude in developing this volume. We are grateful first and foremost to the contributors, without whom, after all, the volume would have been impossible and without whose cooperation and assistance this undertaking would have been considerably less pleasant than it was. Their patience in waiting for the final product has been nothing short of remarkable.

We gratefully acknowledge the support of the Department of Languages, Literatures, and Linguistics, the College of Arts and Sciences, and the Office of the Vice Chancellor for Academic Affairs of Syracuse University.

The previous volume benefited immeasurably from the advice and the counsel of a number of valued colleagues in the field—most prominently Suzanne Flynn, Susan Gass, Michael Long, Barbara Lust, Teresa Pica, Dennis Preston, and Lydia White. In addition, the following have offered both moral support and valuable advice in the development of the previous and the present volume: Roger W. Andersen, Elizabeth Bates, Jerry Berent, Derek Bickerton, Noam Chomsky, Kevin Gregg, Jeff MacSwan, Peter Robinson, Jackie Schachter, Dan Slobin, Jackie Toribio, and Ken Wexler.

We are also grateful to our friends, colleagues, and teachers like Braj and Yamuna Kachru, Jamees Gair, Barbara Lust, Hans Hock, Salikoko Mufwerne, Rajeshwari Pandharipande, Meena and S. N. Sridhar. Their support, inspiration, and scholarship mean a great deal to us and have directly influenced this work.

Our very special thanks are also due to Rachel Brown and Cristina Irving at Emerald for their professional assistance, patience, and consideration.

Finally, we could not have completed the work without the constant support of our families: Laurie, Jane, and Peter; Shobha, Kanika, Ankit; no words can express our deepest appreciation for them.

# PART I

# HISTORY AND RESEARCH METHODOLOGY

## INTRODUCTION TO PART I

Part I provides the historical and methodological setting for the remainder of the volume. It consists of two chapters: First, chapter 1 ("A Historical Survey of SLA Research") is a new historical survey of research on second language acquisition (SLA) by Susan Gass and, second, chapter 2 ("Research Methodology in Second Language Acquisition from a Linguistic Perspective") by Suzanne Flynn and Claire Foley is a discussion of central methodological notions in SLA research—particularly in the tradition of linguistics-oriented work.

After a brief discussion of recent issues raised in the literature concerning the origins of the field, Gass provides an analysis of changes in the character of SLA research as reflected in the articles published between 1950 and 2006 in four leading journals in the field—*Language Learning, Studies in Second Language Acquisition, Second Language Research,* and *Applied Linguistics.* She reviews these significant changes quantitatively in terms of three dimensions: (1) overall type of article, (2) data elicitation type, and (3) statistical procedure(s) used.

After an overview of distinctions central to experimental design in general—quantitative versus qualitative and longitudinal versus cross-sectional research, reliability, and validity—Flynn and Foley differentiate among three prominent approaches to the study of SLA, which they refer to as the linguistic, psychological, and sociolinguistic, and then, while acknowledging that there is a wide variety of data elicitation techniques used within the linguistics tradition of SLA research, they focus specifically on two methods of data elicitation that they associate with that tradition—elicited imitation and act-out tasks.

C H A P T E R  I

# A HISTORICAL SURVEY OF SLA RESEARCH

Susan Gass

## I. INTRODUCTION: SCOPE OF INQUIRY

This paper is an attempt to chronicle the history of second language acquisition (SLA) research. I felt it would be more useful to approach history by looking at the type of research conducted rather than by considering details of what is known about SLA, that is, the findings of SLA research over the years. There are books that are concerned with overviews (e.g., Doughty & Long, 2003; Gass & Selinker, 2008; Ritchie & Bhatia, 1996) and those that deal with specific areas of SLA (e.g., Bardovi-Harlig, 2000; Gass, 1997; Gass & Houck, 1999; Lantolf, 2000; Lantolf & Thorne, 2006; White, 2003). However, to my knowledge there are no treatises that deal with the field by the type of research orientation. Research orientation subsumes a type of data analysis, the types of measures used to collect data, and the statistics used to analyze data.

When I agreed to write this article, I did not anticipate what a daunting task this would be. As soon as I began to delve into the literature, I realized immediately that I would have to restrict the sources that I was working with to make this a minimally manageable task. There were a number of initial decisions that had to be made, the first of which involved the beginnings of the field.

## II. WHERE DOES THE FIELD BEGIN?

The answer to this question is, of course, somewhat arbitrary. In fact, M. Thomas (1998) claimed that "Second language acquisition theory conventionally represents itself as having been invented *ex nihilo* in the last decades of the twentieth century" (p. 387). She points out that the conventional wisdom is that the field began in the late 1960s or early 1970s. She cites a number of individuals who support this view. Support

3

for this belief, which in her view is mistaken, is presented below:

- Serious research in SLA has a relatively short history. L2 acquisition study would be difficult to trace back more than perhaps 15 years (Rutherford, 1988, p. 404).
- Early SLA research goes back to about 1953 (Cook, 1993).
- R. Ellis (1994) has only seven articles cited before 1950.
- F. Newmeyer and S. Weinberger state that SLA research has come "from total non-existence" in the past 50 years (1988, pp. 40–41).

Thomas's main point is that there is a great deal of SLA history before the so-called beginnings that are outlined in numerous places; she refers to works by Augustine (4th century) and Wittgenstein (early 20th century) and Roger Bacon (13th century), all of whom showed a theoretical interest in language. Gass, Fleck, Leder, and Svetics (1998), in a reply to Thomas, make the following counter-arguments:

> ... the attitude of most scholars in SLA toward the past is reasonable given that no significant work in SLA from antiquity has been discovered—by Thomas or anyone else—and that if such work exists Thomas has the burden to bring it to light before declaring the field guilty of ahistoricity. ... [We argue] that [the field of SLA] should be defined theoretically first, and historically second. We claim that the point at which SLA separated itself from language teaching is a logical point from which to date the beginnings of SLA as a true discipline. We ... reject Thomas's comparison of SLA and its history to various other scientific disciplines and their histories, arguing that these disciplines have true milestones to point to in the distant past, whereas SLA does not. (p. 407)

It is clear from this brief summary of the debate that the choice of the beginning of the field is not straightforward. Despite Thomas's arguments, scholars today still consider SLA a discipline that does not go back much earlier than the 1960s or 1970s, and some would even take a later date. For example, de Bot, Lowie, and Verspoor (2005) imply a much later beginning to the field than is generally assumed. "The field of Second Language Acquisition ... research focuses on how languages are learned. Even though a great deal of research has been conducted on this topic over the last *two decades*, we are still far from understanding all the details of that process" (emphasis mine, p. 3). In a similar vein, M. Long (2007) states in the preface of his book *Problems in SLA*, "Second language acquisition ... is a young science, to the extent that it deserves the name at all, struggling to emerge and differentiate itself from such fields as education and applied linguistics. It shows many signs of scientific youth, including disagreements as to the proper scope of inquiry and, not unrelated, an intemperate rush to theory" (p. vii).

Thus, there is some controversy and clear disagreement as to what constitutes a beginning point of SLA research. In conducting research reported in this paper, I decided to go back approximately 57 years, certainly not far enough to satisfy Thomas, but further back than others would agree was an appropriate starting point. I adopted this position based on the early literature in the field and, in particular, on the beginning of the first journal exclusively devoted to the discipline, namely, *Language Learning*.

## III.  WHAT SOURCES TO USE

The next question that I was confronted with was how to limit the sources I was going to use for the survey. Clearly, the consequence of this decision dictated the breadth of the survey. It became almost immediately obvious that it would be virtually impossible to survey anything other than journals; books were far too numerous, and there would be too many choices—should book *x* be included? Should book *y* be included? Importantly, there were few objective criteria to be used to delimit the category of books.

But even the selection of journals was fraught with difficulty because the implication of using some journals, but not others, entails an implicit definition of the field. In order to be as objective as possible, I consulted the only survey that I was aware of that emanated from the field itself and that had a ranking of journals as part of its domain (VanPatten & Williams, 2002). The authors were interested in determining tenure criteria for the field, particularly given that so many people conducting SLA research are located in different departments. They distributed a survey to 72 SLA researchers and received 45 responses from leading scholars in the United States and Canada.[1]

The respondents were scholars in a variety of departments (English, linguistics, foreign languages, combined departments of modern languages, and second language studies). All respondents held the rank of associate or full professor at a Canadian or US postsecondary institution and had published research in the field of SLA. One of the questions concerned rankings of the top journals in the field; 15 journals appeared on their list. A first decision was to consider only those journals that were ranked in the top half of the list (those that received a 4.3 or higher out of a total possible score of 5).[2] This resulted in a list of the following journals in order of ranking (they listed 11 on the survey itself with room to write in other journals): *Studies in Second Language Acquisition*; *Language Learning*; *Applied Psycholinguistics*; *Second Language Research*; *Bilingualism, Language & Cognition*; *Applied Linguistics*; *The Modern Language Journal*; and *TESOL Quarterly*. Given that this list was still far too large to be manageable, I therefore decided to further limit the scope of the journals to be included in the present survey to only those journals that seemed to have the greatest focus on second language learning: *Studies in Second Language Acquisition, Language Learning, Second Language Research*, and *Applied Linguistics*. The others had a broader scope (e.g., language disabilities, language teaching). Some will disagree with this choice because, of course, any selection of this sort biases the survey in some way because each journal has its own orientation. This will become apparent as I report the results. My goal, however, was to come up with an objective means of reducing the scope to a set of articles that could be analyzed.

---

[1]We are aware of the limits of using a survey based only on North American respondents (the purpose of the survey was to address tenure issues in North American universities), but we are unaware of another faculty-based, objective means to determine the significance of journals in the field.

[2]The specific question asked was: The following journals publish research of high quality and represent the best in the field of SLA. There were five possible responses, ranging from 1 (strongly disagree) to 5 (strongly agree).

## IV. THE EXTENT OF THE SURVEY

As discussed earlier, another decision concerned how far back to go. This decision was relatively easy because most of the journals (with the exception of *Language Learning*) go back only 25–30 years. I therefore decided to go back to the beginning of each of these journals, which ranged from 1948 (*Language Learning*) to 1985 (*Second Language Research*). This yielded a total of 2285 articles, as can be seen in Table I.

Because each of these journals has a slightly different orientation, it is important to provide a brief background on each. The most revealing and objective way is to present their mission statements.

## V. BACKGROUND INFORMATION ON JOURNALS

### A. *Language Learning*

In the case of *Language Learning* the mission statement and even subtitle of the journal have changed over the years. The various versions are presented in Table II.

### B. *Studies in Second Language Acquisition*

A mission statement does not appear in the journal itself. The website gives the following as the scope:

> *Studies in Second Language Acquisition* is a refereed journal of international scope devoted to the scientific discussion of issues in second and foreign language acquisition of any language (Retrieved April 19, 2009, from http://journals.cambridge.org/action/displayJournal?jid = SLA).

There is no way of knowing if this has changed since the inception of the journal.

### C. *Second Language Research*

The following editorial policy appears in *Second Language Research*. This is the same policy that has been in effect since the first issue in 1985 (January 2006, Vol. 22, issue 1).

> *SLR* will publish theoretical and experimental papers in second language acquisition and second language performance. Preference will be for contributions that explore the links between these areas and related, non-applied fields such as theoretical linguistics, neurolinguistics and first language developmental psycholinguistics.

TABLE I

**Articles Surveyed in Four Second Language Journals**

| Name of Journal | Language Learning | Studies in Second Language Acquisition | Second Language Research | Applied Linguistics |
|---|---|---|---|---|
| Number of articles surveyed | 974 | 534 | 263 | 514 |
| Year of first issue | 1948 | 1978 | 1985 | 1980 |

TABLE II

**Mission Statements from *Language Learning***

| | | |
|---|---|---|
| Subtitle | 1948–1993 | *A Journal of Applied Linguistics* |
| | 1993–present | *A Journal of Research in Language Studies* |
| Mission statement | 1948–1978 | None |
| | 1978–1992 | *Language Learning* publishes articles in applied linguistics of potential interest to those concerned with the learning of language. Applied Linguistics is understood as the application of linguistic method and philosophical perspective to problem areas that are usually viewed as lying outside the narrower, more traditional concerns of linguistics proper. *Language Learning* welcomes studies in psycholinguistics, anthropological linguistics, sociolinguistics, language pedagogy, second language acquisition. |
| | 1993–1998 | *Language Learning* publishes research articles that systematically apply methods of inquiry and theories from linguistics, psycholinguistics, cognitive science, ethnography, ethnomethodology, sociolinguistics, sociology, semiotics, educational inquiry, and cultural or historical studies to address fundamental issues in language learning, such as bilingualism, language acquisition, second and foreign language education, literacy, culture, cognition, pragmatics, and intergroup relations. |
| | 1999–December, 2008 | *Language Learning* is a scientific journal dedicated to the understanding of language learning, broadly defined. It publishes research articles that systematically apply methods of inquiry from disciplines including psychology, linguistics, cognitive science, educational inquiry, neuroscience, ethnography, sociolinguistics, sociology, and semiotics. It is concerned with fundamental theoretical issues in language learning such as child, second, and foreign language acquisition, language education, bilingualism, literacy, language representation in mind and brain, culture, cognition, pragmatics, and intergroup relations (Retrieved April 19, 2009, from http://www.wiley.com/bw/journal.asp?ref = 0023-8333). |
| Comment | | The change from the first subtitle to today's subtitle was intended to open "the focus to cater for the ever-widening range of disciplines and methodologies that contribute to our understanding of language" (editorial comment, p. v, Vol. 49, issue 1). |
| | | The biggest change was from the first mission statement to the second. Most notably, the term applied linguistics was removed. From the second to the third mission statement, smaller changes are noted. For example, ethnomethodology and cultural or historical studies disappeared and neuroscience arrived on the scene. |
| | | With regard to the actual disciplines covered, there is overlap from the second to the third statement (e.g., pragmatics, bilingualism, language learning, cognition, culture, intergroup relations), but there is a new addition in the representation in mind and brain. |

Information on the *SLR* website is substantially the same: "In addition to providing a forum for investigators in the field of non-native language learning, it seeks to promote interdisciplinary research which links acquisition studies to related non-applied fields such as:

- Neurolinguistics
- Theoretical linguistics
- First language developmental psycholinguistics" (Retrieved April 19, 2009, from http://www.sagepub.com/journalsProdDesc.nav?prodId = Journal201828).

D. *Applied Linguistics*

Like *Language Learning*, the "Aims" statement has changed over the years. In addition, the relationship of contributing organizations (the American Association for Applied Linguistics, the British Association for Applied Linguistics, and the International Association of Applied Linguistics) to the journal has changed in subtle ways, although one would be hard-pressed to see an actual change in policy as a result of the changing relationships. Table III presents the sponsoring relationships and the different *Aims* statements.

## VI. CODING OF THE DATA

The survey of articles in these four journals left me with an overwhelming amount of data. To begin to sort through the data, I used six coding categories to analyze the type of article that was published and hence trace the change over time:

- Theoretical/position paper
- Quantitative research
- Qualitative research
- Combined qualitative and quantitative research
- Introductory (introducing something new, such as a new teaching method)
- Descriptive (used for a description of two languages, as was the case with contrastive analyses)

In the present analysis, I did not include either responses or papers that appeared in special issues. Therefore, what follows is based on 1824 articles distributed as follows: *Language Learning*—964, *Studies in Second Language Acquisition*—285, *Second Language Research*—164, and *Applied Linguistics*—411.

The first statistic of note is the steady increase in the number of articles. This information is presented in Table IV. The circles represent the beginnings of new journals (*Studies in Second Language Acquisition* 1978, *Applied Linguistics* 1980, *Second Language Research* 1985). As can be seen, there is a steady increase (with the exception of 1961–1965) in the quantity of articles published in these journals. In fact, *Language Learning* moved from two issues a year to four in 1983 (although the 1983 editorial announcing this change reminds the reader that the journal began as a quarterly journal in 1948); *Studies in Second Language Acquisition* moved to three issues a year in 1984 (coinciding with the move to being published by Cambridge University Press) and to four issues a year in 1989; *Applied Linguistics* moved from three issues to four in 1988; *Second Language Research* (a journal that actually grew out of an earlier journal *Interlanguage Studies Bulletin*, which began in 1976) moved from three to four issues a year in 1996.

Table V shows the historical results using the six categories from the four journals together, and in Figure 1 these are represented in graphic format. This was done in five-year increments.

TABLE III

**Historical Information About** *Applied Linguistics*

| | | |
|---|---|---|
| Sponsorship | 1980–1984 | Sponsored by the American Association for Applied Linguistics and the British Association for Applied Linguistics |
| | 1985–1997 | Sponsored by the American Association for Applied Linguistics and the British Association for Applied Linguistics and published in cooperation with the International Association of Applied Linguistics (AILA) |
| | 1998–present | Published in cooperation with the American Association for Applied Linguistics, International Association of Applied Linguistics, and the British Association for Applied Linguistics |
| Aims | 1980–1997 | The aim of this journal is to promote a principled approach to language education and other language related concerns by encouraging inquiry into the relationship between theoretical and practical studies. The journal is less interested in the ad hoc solution of particular problems and more interested in the handling of problems in a principled way by reference to theoretical studies. |
| | | Viewing applied linguistics as a relation between theory and practice the editors give priority to papers which develop specific links between theoretical linguistic studies, educational research, and the planning and implementation of practical programmes. Within this framework the journal welcomes contributions in such areas of current inquiry as first and second language learning and teaching, bilingualism and bilingual education, discourse analysis, translation, language testing, language teaching methodology, language planning, the study of interlanguages, stylistics and lexicography. |
| | 1998–September 2006 | *Applied Linguistics* seeks to promote principled and multidisciplinary approaches to language related concerns in all areas of social life. Areas of interest include bilingualism and multilingualism; computer-mediated communication; conversation analysis; deaf linguistics; discourse analysis and pragmatics; corpus linguistics; critical discourse analysis; first and additional language learning, teaching, and use; forensic linguistics; language assessment; language planning and policies; language for special purposes; literacies; multimodal communication; rhetoric and stylistics; and translation. |
| | December 2006– March 2009 | *Applied Linguistics* publishes research into language with relevance to real-world problems. The journal is keen to help make connections between fields, theories, research methods, and scholarly discourses, and welcomes contributions which critically reflect on current practices in applied linguistics research. It promotes scholarly and scientific discussion of issues that unite or divide scholars in applied linguistics. It is less interested in the *ad hoc* solution of particular problems and more interested in the handling of problems in a principled way by reference to theoretical studies. |
| | | *Applied Linguistics* is viewed not only as the relation between theory and practice, but also as the study of language and language-related problems in specific situations in which people use and learn languages. Within this framework the journal welcomes contributions in such areas of current enquiry as: bilingualism and multilingualism; computer-mediated communication; conversation analysis, deaf linguistics; discourse analysis and pragmatics; corpus linguistics; critical discourse analysis; first and additional language learning, teaching and use; forensic linguistics; language assessment; language planning and policies; language for special purposes; literacies; multimodal communication; rhetoric and stylistics; and translation (Retrieved April 19, 2009, from http://www.oxfordjournals.org/our_journals/applij/about.html). |

### TABLE III. (*Continued*)

| | |
|---|---|
| Comment | The major change from the first *Aims* statement to the second is the emphasis on multi-disciplinary work and the removal of the heavy emphasis on language education. The seeds of multidisciplinary work were present in the first statement "viewing applied linguistics as a relation between theory and practice the editors give priority to papers which develop specific links between theoretical linguistic studies, educational research, and the planning and implementation of practical programmes," but this emphasis is made clearer with the explicit words "multidisciplinary work" in the second statement. Implicit in the first sentence of the second statement is the view of language as part of social life. In other words, a focus on theoretical linguistics devoid from social context is not within the purview of the journal.<br><br>The list of research areas is expanded and updated in the second statement (e.g., the term *second* is expanded to *additional*, nonnative language use is added to language learning and teaching, language policies is added to language planning), and new disciplinary areas are added, reflecting a change in the disciplinary scope of applied linguistics (e.g., literacies, multimodal communication, pragmatics, corpus linguistics). The third version of *Aims* statement expands on the interconnections of disciplines and the problem-centered nature of applied linguistics as well as provides a definition of *Applied Linguistics*. |

### TABLE IV
### Total Number of Articles Per Five-Year Period

|           | Total |
|-----------|-------|
| 1948–1950 | 48    |
| 1951–1955 | 38    |
| 1956–1960 | 71    |
| 1961–1965 | 96    |
| 1966–1970 | 83    |
| 1971–1975 | 85    |
| 1976–1980 | 139   |
| 1981–1985 | 190   |
| 1986–1990 | 270   |
| 1991–1995 | 253   |
| 1996–2000 | 261   |
| 2001–2006 | 290   |

There are a few important changes to note. First, the field has become less descriptive and more theoretical. This is not surprising as one would expect this pattern from a developing field. The second striking pattern is the almost steady increase in quantitative studies starting from 2% in the early years of the field (or at least as these journals represent the field) to more than 61% currently.

What is more interesting is to look at these patterns by journal because, as will be seen, each journal has developed its own orientation. The data are presented in Table VI and Figure 2 for *Language Learning*, Table VII and Figure 3 for *Studies in Second Language Acquisition*, Table VIII and Figure 4 for *Second Language Research*, and Table IX and Figure 5 for *Applied Linguistics*.

TABLE V

**Article Types in All Journals Surveyed in the Present Study**

|           | Quantitative | Qualitative | Theory    | Introductory | Quantitative+ Qualitative | Descriptive |
|-----------|--------------|-------------|-----------|--------------|---------------------------|-------------|
| 1948–1950 | 0.02 (1)     | 0.13 (6)    | 0.25 (12) | 0.23 (11)    | 0.00 (0)                  | 0.38 (18)   |
| 1951–1955 | 0.00 (0)     | 0.21 (8)    | 0.55 (21) | 0.13 (5)     | 0.00 (0)                  | 0.11 (4)    |
| 1956–1960 | 0.04 (3)     | 0.17 (12)   | 0.41 (29) | 0.18 (13)    | 0.00 (0)                  | 0.20 (14)   |
| 1961–1965 | 0.07 (7)     | 0.15 (14)   | 0.24 (23) | 0.22 (21)    | 0.00 (0)                  | 0.32 (31)   |
| 1966–1970 | 0.17 (14)    | 0.08 (7)    | 0.48 (40) | 0.12 (10)    | 0.00 (0)                  | 0.14 (12)   |
| 1971–1975 | 0.47 (40)    | 0.08 (7)    | 0.34 (29) | 0.07 (6)     | 0.01 (1)                  | 0.02 (2)    |
| 1976–1980 | 0.45 (63)    | 0.04 (6)    | 0.46 (64) | 0.02 (3)     | 0.01 (2)                  | 0.01 (1)    |
| 1981–1985 | 0.42 (79)    | 0.15 (29)   | 0.40 (76) | 0.01 (2)     | 0.02 (4)                  | 0.00 (0)    |
| 1986–1990 | 0.45 (122)   | 0.14 (38)   | 0.31 (84) | 0.03 (7)     | 0.06 (17)                 | 0.01 (2)    |
| 1991–1995 | 0.57 (144)   | 0.15 (38)   | 0.21 (53) | 0.02 (4)     | 0.06 (14)                 | 0.00 (0)    |
| 1996–2000 | 0.56 (145)   | 0.16 (41)   | 0.21 (55) | 0.00 (0)     | 0.08(20)                  | 0.00 (0)    |
| 2001–2006 | 0.61 (177)   | 0.17 (48)   | 0.15 (44) | 0.00 (1)     | 0.07 (20)                 | 0.00 (0)    |

*Note:* Data are presented as a percentage of total with raw numbers in ( ).

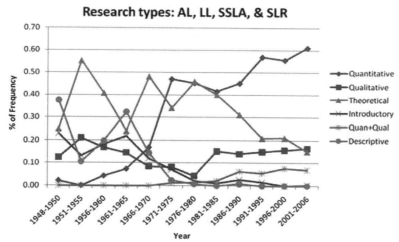

**Figure 1**   A chronological view of research types for all journals combined.

In *Language Learning*, the most dramatic change is the increase in quantitative studies and the decrease in purely theoretical articles, which include position papers. This suggests that the field of SLA is increasingly a data-driven field.

A similar situation to what was seen with *Language Learning* can be seen with *Studies in Second Language Acquisition*, the second oldest of the journals surveyed here. Results are shown in Table VII and Figure 3. As can be seen, there is a dramatic increase in quantitative studies. In fact, it is the journal with the highest percentage of quantitative studies of all of the journals surveyed here.

The next journal to be considered is *Second Language Research*. The results for this journal (the youngest journal that was surveyed) are different from the previous two.

TABLE VI

**Article Types in Language Learning**

|  | Quantitative | Qualitative | Theory | Introductory | Quantitative+ Qualitative | Descriptive |
|---|---|---|---|---|---|---|
| 1948–1950 | 0.02 (1) | 0.13 (6) | 0.25 (12) | 0.23 (11) | 0.00 (0) | 0.38 (18) |
| 1951–1955 | 0.00 (0) | 0.21 (8) | 0.55 (21) | 0.13 (5) | 0.00 (0) | 0.11 (4) |
| 1956–1960 | 0.04 (3) | 0.17 (12) | 0.41(29) | 0.18 (13) | 0.00 (0) | 0.20 (14) |
| 1961–1965 | 0.07 (7) | 0.15 (14) | 0.24 (23) | 0.22 (21) | 0.00 (0) | 0.32 (31) |
| 1966–1970 | 0.17 (14) | 0.08 (7) | 0.48 (40) | 0.12 (10) | 0.00 (0) | 0.14 (12) |
| 1971–1975 | 0.47 (40) | 0.08 (7) | 0.34 (29) | 0.07 (6) | 0.01 (1) | 0.02 (2) |
| 1976–1980 | 0.54 (57) | 0.06 (6) | 0.35 (37) | 0.03 (3) | 0.02 (2) | 0.00 (0) |
| 1981–1985 | 0.57 (58) | 0.17 (17) | 0.22 (22) | 0.01 (1) | 0.04 (4) | 0.00 (0) |
| 1986–1990 | 0.56 (52) | 0.17 (16) | 0.19 (18) | 0.00 (0) | 0.08 (7) | 0.00 (0) |
| 1991–1995 | 0.83 (62) | 0.08 (6) | 0.07 (5) | 0.00 (0) | 0.03 (2) | 0.00 (0) |
| 1996–2000 | 0.82 (59) | 0.07 (5) | 0.00 (0) | 0.00 (0) | 0.11 (8) | 0.00 (0) |
| 2001–2006 | 0.77 (74) | 0.13 (12) | 0.04 (4) | 0.00 (0) | 0.06 (6) | 0.00 (0) |

*Note:* Data are presented as a percentage of total with raw numbers in ( ).

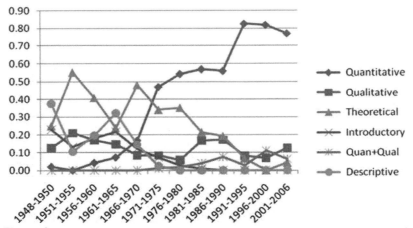

**Figure 2**  A chronological view of research articles in *Language Learning* (percentage).

In essence, there has not been as dramatic a shift from the beginning of this journal (1985) until today. Its main focus is quantitative/empirical studies and theoretical statements. There appears to be little room for other kinds of studies. This is seen in Table VIII and Figure 4.

The final journal that we looked at from the perspective of article types is *Applied Linguistics*. With the exception of the decrease in theoretical articles, the other types have remained relatively steady. This journal, however, differs from the others in the relatively low percentage of quantitative studies and relatively high percentage of qualitative studies.

TABLE VII
**Article Types in *Studies in Second Language Acquisition***

| | Quantitative | Qualitative | Theory | Introductory | Quantitative+ Qualitative | Descriptive |
|---|---|---|---|---|---|---|
| 1978–1980 | 0.18 (6) | 0.00 (0) | 0.79 (27) | 0.00 (0) | 0.00 (1) | 0.03 (1) |
| 1981–1985 | 0.40 (12) | 0.00 (0) | 0.60 (18) | 0.00 (0) | 0.00 (0) | 0.00 (0) |
| 1986–1990 | 0.63 (32) | 0.08 (4) | 0.22 (11) | 0.00 (0) | 0.08 (4) | 0.00 (0) |
| 1991–1995 | 0.61 (31) | 0.12 (6) | 0.18 (9) | 0.00 (0) | 0.10 (5) | 0.00 (0) |
| 1996–2000 | 0.67 (37) | 0.07 (4) | 0.20 (11) | 0.00 (0) | 0.05 (3) | 0.00 (0) |
| 2001–2006 | 0.83 (53) | 0.03 (2) | 0.06 (4) | 0.00 (0) | 0.08 (5) | 0.00 (0) |

*Note:* Data are presented as a percentage of total with raw numbers in ( ).

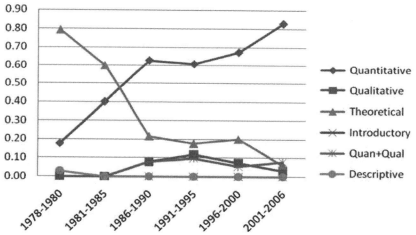

**Figure 3**　A chronological view of research articles in *Studies in Second Language Acquisition* (percentage).

TABLE VIII
**Article Types in *Second Language Research***

| | Quantitative | Qualitative | Theory | Introductory | Quantitative+ Qualitative | Descriptive |
|---|---|---|---|---|---|---|
| 1985–1990 | 0.43 (19) | 0.00 (0) | 0.52 (23) | 0.00 (0) | 0.02 (1) | 0.02 (1) |
| 1991–1995 | 0.53 (21) | 0.03 (1) | 0.40 (16) | 0.05 (2) | 0.00 (0) | 0.00 (0) |
| 1996–2000 | 0.64 (25) | 0.05 (2) | 0.28 (11) | 0.00 (0) | 0.03 (1) | 0.00 (0) |
| 2001–2006 | 0.61 (25) | 0.00 (0) | 0.37 (15) | 0.02 (1) | 0.00 (0) | 0.00 (0) |

*Note:* Data are presented as a percentage of total with raw numbers in ( ).

## VII. DATA ELICITATION TYPES

As a field changes and matures, the modes of eliciting data also change and mature. This section considers the same four journals, looking at how data are elicited. For convenience sake, with some modifications, I followed the data elicitation types laid

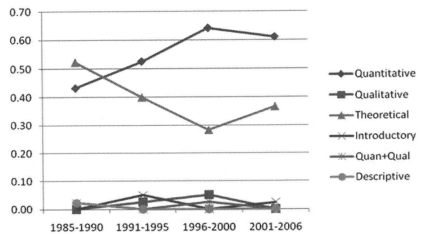

**Figure 4**  A chronological view of research articles in *Second Language Research* (percentage).

TABLE IX
**Article Types in *Applied Linguistics***

|           | Quantitative | Qualitative | Theory    | Introductory | Quantitative+ Qualitative | Descriptive |
|-----------|--------------|-------------|-----------|--------------|---------------------------|-------------|
| 1980–1985 | 0.16 (9)     | 0.21 (12)   | 0.62 (36) | 0.02 (1)     | 0.00 (0)                  | 0.00 (0)    |
| 1986–1990 | 0.23 (19)    | 0.22 (18)   | 0.39 (32) | 0.09 (7)     | 0.06 (5)                  | 0.01 (1)    |
| 1991–1995 | 0.34 (30)    | 0.29 (25)   | 0.26 (23) | 0.02 (2)     | 0.08 (7)                  | 0.00 (0)    |
| 1996–2000 | 0.25 (24)    | 0.32 (30)   | 0.35 (33) | 0.00 (0)     | 0.08 (8)                  | 0.00 (0)    |
| 2001–2006 | 0.28 (25)    | 0.38 (34)   | 0.24 (21) | 0.00 (0)     | 0.10 (9)                  | 0.00 (0)    |

*Note:* Data are presented as a percentage of total with raw numbers in ( ).

out by A. Mackey and S. Gass (2005) and more recently in Gass and Mackey (2007). Seven categories were developed: (1) judgment, (2) production, (3) proficiency tests and language skills, (4) individual differences and cognitive processes, (5) observations and interviews, (6) existing databases, and (7) questionnaires and surveys (see Appendix A.1). The results of this analysis are presented by journal in Figures 6–9 (see Appendix B.1).

With regard to *Language Learning*, in the first 20 years or so of the journal, most data collection came from existing databases, questionnaires, and observations and interviews, suggesting little in the way of originally elicited data. Beginning in the early 1970s, there was little fluctuation in elicitation types with existing databases being low and overall proficiency measures and specific skill measures being high.

Probably because of the year in which *Studies in Second Language Acquisition* was founded, a time in which researchers approached SLA from a linguistic orientation, judgment data—a common elicitation tool in linguistics—were used at a high rate in the early years. To this day, they are still the most commonly used elicitation measures in this journal. Existing databases, as with *Language Learning*, are infrequently used.

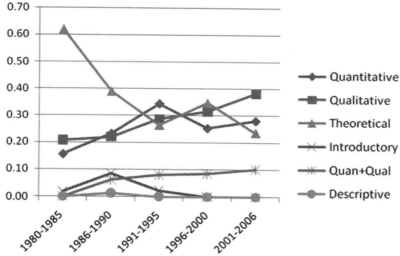

**Figure 5** A chronological view of research articles in *Applied Linguistics* (percentage).

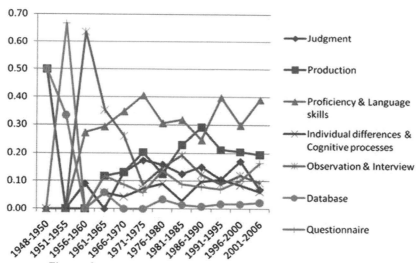

**Figure 6** Data elicitation types for *Language Learning* (percentage).

*Second Language Research*, the journal with the greatest focus on linguistic issues, not surprisingly, reflects that orientation with a high percentage of articles eliciting data with some sort of judgment data. With the exception of a reduction over time in production data and a slight increase in judgment data, from the 1980s to the 1990s, the type of data elicitation has remained stable across the years.

*Applied Linguistics* appears to be different from the other three journals, a fact that is consistent with the orientation of research noted in the previous section. Given the greater emphasis on qualitative analyses, it is not surprising to see that existing

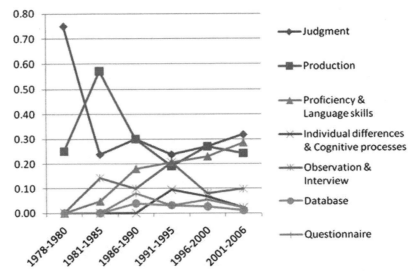

**Figure 7**  Data elicitation types for *Studies in Second Language Acquisition* (percentage).

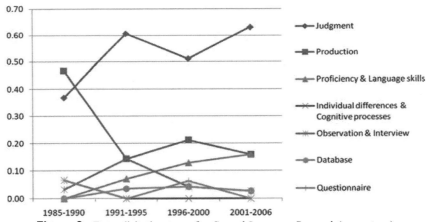

**Figure 8**  Data elicitation types for *Second Language Research* (percentage).

databases as a source of data analysis are and have been high. Judgment data, on the other hand, following a precipitous drop from the early to the mid-1980s, have remained relatively low. The greater emphasis on sociolinguistic-oriented articles (including areas such as discourse analysis) is reflected in these data.

## VIII. STATISTICAL PROCEDURES

In this final section are presented data reflecting some of the most commonly used statistics in second language research. They have been divided into seven categories for

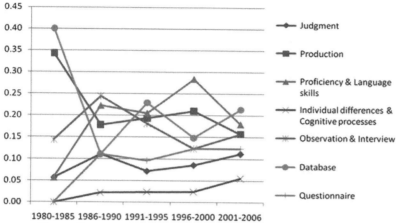

**Figure 9** Data elicitation types for *Applied Linguistics* (percentage).

TABLE X

**Articles Using Comparison of Means (Across All Journals)**

| Summary | 1961–1965 | 1966–1970 | 1971–1975 | 1976–1980 | 1981–1985 | 1986–1990 | 1991–1995 | 1996–2000 | 2001–2006 |
|---|---|---|---|---|---|---|---|---|---|
| *t* test | 1 | 3 | 7 | 9 | 14 | 32 | 18 | 20 | 19 |
| ANOVA | 1 | 2 | 14 | 20 | 32 | 52 | 79 | 83 | 114 |
| MANOVA | 0 | 0 | 0 | 0 | 0 | 5 | 4 | 6 | 5 |
| ANCOVA | 0 | 3 | 3 | 0 | 1 | 3 | 2 | 4 | 7 |
| MANCOVA | 0 | 0 | 0 | 0 | 0 | 0 | 1 | 0 | 1 |
| Repeated measure | 0 | 0 | 0 | 1 | 2 | 4 | 6 | 10 | 18 |

ease of explication: (1) comparison of means, (2) nonparametric tests, (3) descriptive statistics, (4) correlation and regression analysis, (5) confirmatory factor analysis (CFA) and structural equational modeling (SEM), (6) explanatory factor analysis (EFA) and principal component analysis (PCA), and (7) other.

## A. Comparison of Means

Within the category of comparison of means are included analyses of variance including ANOVA, MANOVA, ANCOVA, and MANCOVA as well as *t* tests (including paired) and repeated measures. In Table X are the totals from all journals combined from 1961 until 2006 (before 1961 there were very few articles that had any statistics reported).

As can be seen, the bulk of these comparisons are ANOVAs with a steady increase over time. Another area of increase can be seen in the number of studies using repeated measures.

## B. Nonparametric Tests

Nonparametric tests include chi-square, Wilcoxon, Mann–Whitney U, and Kruskal–Wallis Tests. Within this category, the vast majority are chi-square, as can be seen in Table XI, again beginning with 1961.

## C. Descriptive Statistics

Articles in this category used only descriptive statistics. The trends can be seen in Table XII. The decrease in numbers in recent years is not surprising as more and more researchers are including inferential statistics along with descriptive statistics. These were not included in this category.

## D. Correlation and Regression Analysis

As can be seen in Table XIII, beginning in the early 1970s, the use of these statistics has remained common and relatively stable.

TABLE XI
**Articles Using Nonparametric Tests (Across All Journals)**

|  | 1961– 1965 | 1966– 1970 | 1971– 1975 | 1976– 1980 | 1981– 1985 | 1986– 1990 | 1991– 1995 | 1996– 2000 | 2001– 2006 |
|---|---|---|---|---|---|---|---|---|---|
| Chi-square | 1 | 2 | 2 | 2 | 16 | 23 | 24 | 27 | 24 |
| Other nonparametric | 0 | 0 | 0 | 0 | 1 | 5 | 5 | 2 | 7 |

TABLE XII
**Articles Using Descriptive Statistics (Across All Journals)**

| 1961–1965 | 1966–1970 | 1971–1975 | 1976–1980 | 1981–1985 | 1986–1990 | 1991–1995 | 1996–2000 | 2001–2006 |
|---|---|---|---|---|---|---|---|---|
| 3 | 3 | 6 | 13 | 8 | 14 | 7 | 8 | 5 |

TABLE XIII
**Articles Using Correlation and Regression Analysis (Across All Journals)**

| 1961–1965 | 1966–1970 | 1971–1975 | 1976–1980 | 1981–1985 | 1986–1990 | 1991–1995 | 1996–2000 | 2001–2006 |
|---|---|---|---|---|---|---|---|---|
| 4 | 5 | 24 | 32 | 29 | 22 | 30 | 21 | 31 |

TABLE XIV

**Articles Using EFA, SEM, CFA, and PCA (Across All Journals)**

|              | 1976–1980 | 1981–1985 | 1986–1990 | 1991–1995 | 1996–2000 | 2001–2006 |
|--------------|-----------|-----------|-----------|-----------|-----------|-----------|
| EFA and PCA  | 6         | 3         | 3         | 6         | 5         | 1         |
| CFA and SEM  | 0         | 1         | 1         | 5         | 3         | 6         |

TABLE XV

**Articles Using Other Statistical Procedures (Across All Journals)**

|       | 1971–1975 | 1976–1980 | 1981–1985 | 1986–1990 | 1991–1995 | 1996–2000 | 2001–2006 |
|-------|-----------|-----------|-----------|-----------|-----------|-----------|-----------|
| Other | 2         | 3         | 8         | 8         | 7         | 8         | 6         |

## E. Confirmatory Factor Analysis and Structural Equational Modeling and Explanatory Factor Analysis and Principal Component Analysis

These statistics did not appear in the SLA literature until the mid-1970s; their use is still relatively uncommon, and in fact, the frequency of use has not changed appreciably in the past 30 years. The figures can be seen in Table XIV.

## F. Other

Within the other category were discriminant analysis, cluster analysis, and item analysis (including generalizabilty theory, differential item functioning, multidimensional scaling). With the exception of *Language Learning*, which had articles using item analysis from 1971 onward, this category across all journals had very few instances. This is seen in Table XV.

In Figures 10–13 the results of the statistical analyses by journal can be seen. In most of the journals, there has been an increase in the general use of statistics, with means comparisons being the most common. Only in *Language Learning* are correlations and regressions frequently used. All other statistical analyses are low in number. The most interesting pattern, and one that differentiates itself from the other patterns, is that found for *Applied Linguistics*, where means comparisons do not dominate to the extent that they do in the other journals. As can be seen in Figure 13, there seems to be less of a statistical identity for *Applied Linguistics* than there is for other journals.

In considering these results as a whole, there is indication that the field has become more sophisticated in its use of statistics. For example, the category of descriptive statistics is used for those studies that have only descriptive statistics with no inferential statistics. In looking at the category of most growth (comparison of means), we see that as this category increases, the number of studies with descriptive statistics only decreases. This is seen in Figure 14. If we include the nonparametric category, the picture remains largely the same, as can be seen in Figure 15.

The final analysis that I consider is the use of multiple statistical analyses within a single article. This is considered with data from the field as a whole (see Table XVI and

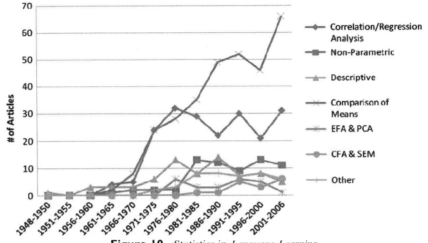

**Figure 10**  Statistics in *Language Learning.*

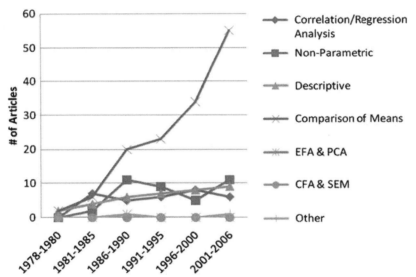

**Figure 11**  Statistics in *Studies in Second Language Acquisition.*

a graphic representation in Figure 16). The data are presented as a percentage of the total number of articles in a given five-year period. As is clear, the number of articles with no statistics has decreased over the years, with those using descriptive only remaining relatively steady, although there seems to be a decrease in the recent past. Articles using single or multiple inferential statistics have seen an increase in recent years.

The changes in the use of statistical analyses are to be expected in a field that is and has been heavily reliant on social science models where empirical and experimental

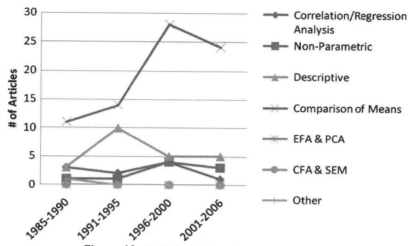

**Figure 12**  Statistics in *Second Language Research.*

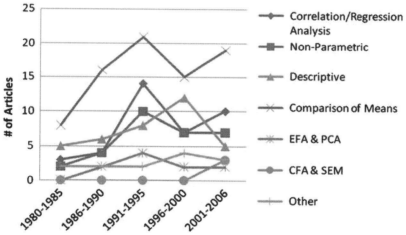

**Figure 13**  Statistics in *Applied Linguistics.*

research is valued. My preconceived notions as I began this survey were that we would see an even greater diversity of statistical procedures used, but that will have to await similar analyses in the future.

## IX. CONCLUSION

This paper has used four prominent journals in the field of SLA to chronicle how research has taken place over the past six decades with a greater emphasis on the past two to three decades. There are as many limitations to this analysis as there are

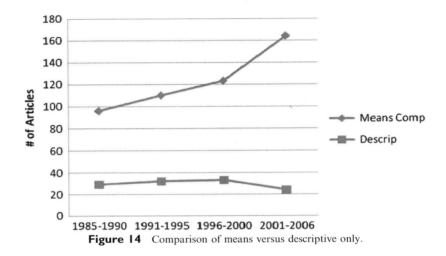

**Figure 14**   Comparison of means versus descriptive only.

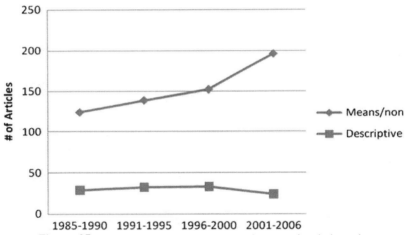

**Figure 15**   Means comparison/nonparametric versus descriptive only.

advantages. The main limitation is that the analysis was based on a small and select number of journals. And furthermore, these journals represent a certain bias in delineating the scope of the field. On the positive side, the journals analyzed in this article were those that were objectively determined to be among the most prestigious in the field and did have second language research as their scope of inquiry. Many second language researchers publish in journals that are not solely dedicated to SLA. This in and of itself is a positive indication of the value of the discipline outside of its parochial borders. I did not use those publications as part of this survey because it was more likely that the type of research published outside of the four journals surveyed here may be shaped by factors external to the field of SLA. My goal, on the other hand, was

TABLE XVI
**Distribution of Articles With and Without Statistics**

|  | No statistics | Descriptives | Single inferential statistics | Multiple inferential statistics | Sum |
|---|---|---|---|---|---|
| 1948–1950 | 0.98 | 0.02 | 0.00 | 0.00 | 48 |
| 1951–1955 | 1.00 | 0.00 | 0.00 | 0.00 | 38 |
| 1956–1960 | 0.96 | 0.04 | 0.00 | 0.00 | 71 |
| 1961–1965 | 0.93 | 0.02 | 0.03 | 0.02 | 96 |
| 1966–1970 | 0.84 | 0.04 | 0.06 | 0.06 | 83 |
| 1971–1975 | 0.53 | 0.06 | 0.26 | 0.15 | 85 |
| 1976–1980 | 0.53 | 0.08 | 0.29 | 0.10 | 139 |
| 1981–1985 | 0.52 | 0.08 | 0.21 | 0.19 | 190 |
| 1986–1990 | 0.46 | 0.11 | 0.27 | 0.16 | 270 |
| 1991–1995 | 0.34 | 0.10 | 0.35 | 0.21 | 253 |
| 1996–2000 | 0.32 | 0.09 | 0.41 | 0.18 | 261 |
| 2001–2006 | 0.30 | 0.04 | 0.43 | 0.22 | 290 |
| Sum | 0.50 | 0.07 | 0.28 | 0.15 | 1824 |

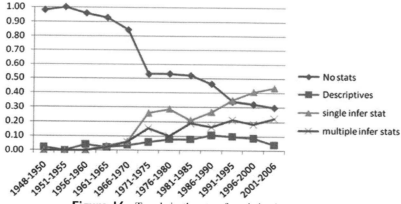

**Figure 16**  Trends in the use of statistics (percentage).

to determine how the field shaped itself over time. To accomplish that goal, I needed to look inward.

What we have seen is a discipline that started as a descriptive discipline and slowly moved to being more theoretical. This supports the appearance of books and articles in the recent past that have focused on theoretical debates (see, e.g., Jordan, 2005; Long, 2007, among others). As the discipline has grown over the past 60 years and particularly in the past 25 years, we have also witnessed a greater diversity of elicitation types (although certain journals have their "preferred" type) and an increase in the sophistication of statistical analyses.

All of these areas put together show the dynamic and changing nature of the way research is and has been conducted in the field of SLA.

## ACKNOWLEDGMENT

I am grateful to my research assistant, Junkyu Lee, who did the tedious task of going through numerous articles. Each time I asked, "what about *x*?" he came back quickly with a cogent summary of *x*. His work on this article was exemplary.

## REFERENCES

Bardovi-Harlig, K. (2000). *Tense and aspect in second language acquisition: Form, meaning, and use*. Malden, MA: Blackwell.

Cook, V. (1993). *Linguistics and second language acquisition*. New York: St. Martin's Press.

de Bot, K., Lowie, W., & Verspoor, M. (2005). *Second language acquisition: An advanced resource book*. London: Routledge.

Doughty, C., & Long, M. (Eds.). (2003). *The handbook of second language acquisition*. Oxford: Blackwell.

Ellis, R. (1994). *The study of second language acquisition*. Oxford: Oxford University Press.

Gass, S. (1997). *Input, interaction, and the second language learner*. Mahwah, NJ: Lawrence Erlbaum Associates.

Gass, S., Fleck, C., Leder, N., & Svetics, I. (1998). Ahistoricity revisited: Does SLA have a history? *Studies in second language acquisition, 20*, 407–421.

Gass, S., & Houck, N. (1999). *Interlanguage refusals: A cross-cultural study of Japanese-English*. Berlin: Mouton de Gruyter.

Gass, S., & Mackey, A. (2007). *Data elicitation for second and foreign language research*. Mahwah, NJ: Lawrence Erlbaum Associates.

Gass, S., & Selinker, L. (2008). *Second language acquisition: An introductory course* (3rd ed.). New York: Taylor and Francis.

Jordan, G. (2005). *Theory construction in second language acquisition*. Amsterdam: John Benjamins.

Lantolf, J. (2000). *Sociocultural theory and second language learning*. Oxford: Oxford University Press.

Lantolf, J., & Thorne, S. (2006). *Sociocultural theory and the genesis of second language development*. Oxford: Oxford University Press.

Long, M. (2007). *Problems in SLA*. Mahwah, NJ: Lawrence Erlbaum Associates.

Mackey, A., & Gass, S. (2005). *Second language research: Methodology and design*. Mahwah, NJ: Lawrence Erlbaum Associates.

Newmeyer, F. J., & Weinberger, S. (1988). The ontogenesis of the field of second language learning research. In S. Flynn & W. O'Neil (Eds.), *Linguistic theory in second language acquisition* (pp. 34–45). Dordrecht: Kluwer.

Ritchie, W., & Bhatia, T. K. (1996). *Handbook of second language acquisition*. San Diego: Academic Press.

Rutherford, W. (1988). Grammatical theory and L2 acquisition: A brief overview. In S. Flynn & W. O'Neil (Eds.), *Linguistic theory in second language acquisition* (pp. 404–416). Dordrecht: Kluwer.

Thomas, M. (1998). Programmatic ahistoricity in second language acquisition theory. *Studies in Second Language Acquisition, 20*, 387–405.

VanPatten, B., & Williams, J. (2002). Research criteria for tenure in second language acquisition: Results from a survey of the field. Retrieved May 12, 2007, from http://www.uic.edu/depts/sfip/news/slatenurestudy.html

White, L. (2003). *Second language acquisition and universal grammar*. Cambridge, UK: Cambridge University Press.

## A.1. APPENDIX

Examples of the type of elicitation measure considered in each category can be seen below:

### A.1.1. Judgment

Acceptability/grammaticality judgment
Magnitude estimation
Truth-value judgment
Other interpretation tasks (e.g., comprehension ability, not necessarily reading)
Sentence matching
Preference task
Matching tasks
Metalinguistic knowledge
Picture judgment
Other judgment (frequency/idiom)
Processing research
   Online sentence interpretations
   Moving window
   Reaction time (speed)
   Lexical decision/word naming
   Cross-modal priming
Video playback for interpretation
Culture-pair test
Multiple choice
(Sound) perception/recognition
Grammar test
Bilingual syntax measure
Discrimination

### A.1.2. Production

Elicited imitation (repetition, dictation)
Sentence combining
Production of grammar structure/sentence manipulation task

Sentence completion
Sociolinguistic/pragmatics-based research
  Elicited narratives
  Discourse completion task
  Role play
Recall/story-retelling
Cloze
Feedback
  Error correction
  Teachers'/parents' feedback/evaluation
  Peers' revision/comments
Interaction-based research
  Spot the difference
  Jigsaw tasks
  Picture description tasks
Story-telling
Other communicative tasks

### A.1.3. Proficiency Test and Language Skills

Vocabulary
Speaking/speech production
Writing/written production/essay
Reading
Listening
Translation
Inferencing
Summary test

### A.1.4. Individual Differences and Cognitive Process

Anxiety/personality measures
Introspective measures
Retrospective measures
MLAT (aptitude)
WM/memory
Other cognitive measure
IQ (+reasoning)
Memorization

### A.1.5. Observation and Interview

Case study
Naturalistic (without prompt)

Case study and ethnography and experience
Spontaneous speech
Report

### A.1.6. Database

Corpus/existing database
Entrance/grade score
Computer simulation

## B.1. APPENDIX

Raw data corresponding to Figures 6–9 are given below
Raw data for Figure 6

| LL | Judgment | Production | Proficiency and Language Skills | Individual Differences and Cognitive Processes | Observation and Interview | Database | Questionnaire |
|---|---|---|---|---|---|---|---|
| 1948–1950 | 0 | 1 | 0 | 0 | 0 | 1 | 0 |
| 1951–1955 | 0 | 0 | 0 | 0 | 0 | 1 | 2 |
| 1956–1960 | 1 | 0 | 3 | 0 | 7 | 0 | 0 |
| 1961–1965 | 0 | 2 | 5 | 1 | 6 | 1 | 2 |
| 1966–1970 | 3 | 3 | 8 | 1 | 6 | 0 | 2 |
| 1971–1975 | 12 | 14 | 28 | 5 | 6 | 0 | 4 |
| 1976–1980 | 14 | 11 | 27 | 8 | 13 | 3 | 12 |
| 1981–1985 | 17 | 31 | 43 | 4 | 26 | 2 | 12 |
| 1986–1990 | 17 | 33 | 28 | 11 | 14 | 1 | 9 |
| 1991–1995 | 12 | 24 | 45 | 12 | 10 | 2 | 8 |
| 1996–2000 | 20 | 24 | 35 | 10 | 14 | 2 | 12 |
| 2001–2006 | 9 | 25 | 50 | 8 | 12 | 3 | 21 |

Raw data for Figure 7

| SSLA | Judgment | Production | Proficiency and Language Skills | Individual Differences and Cognitive Processes | Observation and Interview | Database | Questionnaire |
|---|---|---|---|---|---|---|---|
| 1978–1980 | 6 | 2 | 0 | 0 | 0 | 0 | 0 |
| 1981–1985 | 5 | 12 | 1 | 0 | 3 | 0 | 0 |
| 1986–1990 | 15 | 15 | 9 | 0 | 5 | 2 | 4 |
| 1991–1995 | 15 | 12 | 13 | 6 | 13 | 2 | 2 |
| 1996–2000 | 20 | 20 | 17 | 5 | 6 | 2 | 4 |
| 2001–2006 | 29 | 22 | 26 | 2 | 9 | 1 | 2 |

Raw data for Figure 8

| *SLR* | Judgment | Production | Proficiency and Language Skills | Individual Differences and Cognitive Processes | Observation and Interview | Database | Questionnaire |
|---|---|---|---|---|---|---|---|
| 1985–1990 | 11 | 14 | 0 | 2 | 1 | 0 | 2 |
| 1991–1995 | 17 | 4 | 2 | 0 | 4 | 1 | 0 |
| 1996–2000 | 24 | 10 | 6 | 0 | 2 | 2 | 3 |
| 2001–2006 | 24 | 6 | 6 | 0 | 1 | 1 | 0 |

Raw data for Figure 9

| AL | Judgment | Production | Proficiency and Language Skills | Individual Differences and Cognitive Processes | Observation and Interview | Database | Questionnaire |
|---|---|---|---|---|---|---|---|
| 1980–1985 | 2 | 12 | 2 | 0 | 5 | 14 | 0 |
| 1986–1990 | 5 | 8 | 10 | 1 | 11 | 5 | 5 |
| 1991–1995 | 6 | 16 | 17 | 2 | 15 | 19 | 8 |
| 1996–2000 | 7 | 17 | 23 | 2 | 10 | 12 | 10 |
| 2001–2006 | 10 | 14 | 16 | 5 | 14 | 19 | 11 |

CHAPTER 2

# RESEARCH METHODOLOGY IN SECOND LANGUAGE ACQUISITION FROM A LINGUISTIC PERSPECTIVE

Suzanne Flynn and Claire Foley

## I. INTRODUCTION

In the field of research on multilingualism, methodology has been the subject of changing scrutiny over a period of decades. In this chapter, first, we aim to introduce several key concepts and distinctions in discussions of research methods, and at the same time provide a partial guide to existing surveys on methodology in second language acquisition (SLA). Second, we review methods that have developed in linguistic approaches to SLA, attempting to fill a gap in the survey literature. Throughout the chapter, we use SLA to refer to the acquisition of a language or more than one language beyond the first, and also to bilingual (or multilingual) acquisition. (For a historical treatment of methods in SLA research, see Gass, this volume.)

## II. SOME KEY CONCEPTS AND DISTINCTIONS IN METHODOLOGY IN SLA

### A. Overview

Several key concepts and distinctions have remained central to discussions of methodology over time. Approaches to data collection have often been classified as *quantitative* or *qualitative*. A different set of distinctions applying to research design is the three-way contrast among *qualitative*, *descriptive*, and *experimental* work. Sampling can be characterized as *longitudinal* or *cross-sectional*. The concepts of *reliability* and *validity* remain central to the development of particular methods.

*The New Handbook of Second Language Acquisition*

Finally, the distinctions among three fundamental approaches to SLA, *linguistic*, *psychological*, and *sociolinguistic*, serve to organize particular data gathering methods. At the end of this section, we draw on these final categories to identify the specific methods to be discussed in this chapter.

## B. Quantitative vs. Qualitative Work

A basic difference between *quantitative* and *qualitative* work is that quantitative research involves numeric data, while qualitative work involves data that are non-numeric. We turn first to characteristics and particular methodologies associated with each category, and next to the fact that the difference is not always clear-cut.

Qualitative work may often be synthetic, pulling together observations to develop generalizations or hypotheses. Adams, Fujii, and Mackey (2005) point out that in many cases, researchers using qualitative methods derive categories for analysis from the data or participants themselves, instead of applying them from the outset. They note that studies using qualitative methods often take into account the sociocultural context of language use. Larsen-Freeman and Long (1991) view a "prototypical" qualitative study as one where "researchers do not set out to test hypotheses, but rather to observe what is present with their focus, and consequently the data, free to vary during the course of the observation" (11). A limitation of this general approach to data collection is that conclusions often cannot be generalized; an advantage is that a richer picture of the course and context of acquisition may be possible. Case studies and ethnographies are commonly viewed as "qualitative" approaches to data collection.[1]

Quantitative approaches often begin with, rather than develop, a hypothesis. Rather than exploring a wide range of factors and contexts, they systematically examine a narrower set of variables, often with a view to statistical analysis that will permit results to be generalized. Lazaraton (2005) traces some of the history of views on quantitative methods in the study of SLA, beginning in the early 1980s. She develops a picture of how changes in scholarship have defined and redefined quantitative research, drawing on meta-studies of published research, such as Nunan (1991), and also discussing surveys of the views of scholars in the field and changes in standards for submissions to applied linguistics journals. Brown (1988) provides a guide to research design and analysis under quantitative approaches. A commonly noted limitation to this general approach is that the narrow focus risks missing important contextual information or other variables (e.g., Johnson, 1992, p. 34); advantages include precise targeting of particular factors, and often the possibility that conclusions may be generalized. Experiments and survey research are approaches to data collection commonly identified as "quantitative."

Many projects cannot be classified as purely quantitative or purely qualitative. For example, a study with a qualitative approach to observation may ultimately lead to counting of categories or tokens, leading to a quantitative analysis. A study with a quantitative approach may include details or descriptions that are qualitative. Brown and Rodgers (2002) (citing Grotjahn and others) further discuss some of the ways in

---

[1]Seliger and Shohamy (1989) distinguish between qualitative work, which is "heuristic" and "not deductive," and descriptive work, which "can be heuristic or deductive," but which still may have an overall synthetic approach. (They also include a discussion of multivariate and correlational designs.)

which the qualitative/quantitative split is overly simple. Larsen-Freeman and Long (1991, pp. 10–24) summarize characteristics that various researchers have attributed to qualitative (e.g., observations in natural settings; subjective) and quantitative (e.g., controlled observations; objective), concluding that a useful way to understand methodologies is to situate them on a continuum from qualitative to quantitative.

Finally, the difference between qualitative and quantitative approaches often stems from epistemology. Adams, Fujii, and Mackey (2005) and Johnson (1992) discuss some of the philosophical assumptions underlying the two general approaches.

## C. Longitudinal vs. Cross-Sectional Work

A second distinction in methods concerns sampling. *Longitudinal* studies collect data from a relatively small number of participants at multiple points in time. *Cross-sectional* studies collect data from a larger number of participants at the same single point (or in some cases, two or three specific points) in time.

Longitudinal studies can offer a picture of development over time, and observations have a kind of context unavailable in cross-sectional studies. Particular interactions may reveal more to a researcher because of the researcher's knowledge of the subject and of the earlier stages of development. Longitudinal studies permit the kind of in-depth knowledge of participants that may allow researchers to probe particular factors influencing language acquisition, such as personal or social background.

Cross-sectional studies offer different advantages. Their results may be susceptible to statistical analysis, and it may be possible to draw general conclusions from cross-sectional studies that cannot be drawn from studies with a smaller number of participants.

Larsen-Freeman and Long (1991, pp. 11–14) discuss these two approaches, including ways in which they can be combined. Although the mapping is not exact, studies with the characteristics of qualitative work (see above) often adopt longitudinal approaches (e.g., see the discussion of case studies in Brown & Rodgers, 2002; van Lier, 2005), while studies with a more quantitative approach may use cross-sectional sampling (e.g., examples in Brown, 1988). Also see Nunan (1996) for a discussion of longitudinal and cross-sectional work.

## D. Reliability

Research is increasingly "reliable" as the measures it uses more truly reflect the targeted knowledge, rather than errors in administration or analysis. Reliability is thus connected to consistency in data collection procedures and in scoring data. Brown and Rodgers (2002, p. 241) note that studies are reliable to the degree that other researchers could analyze the same data and obtain the same results (internal reliability) or replicate the study (external reliability). To increase reliability, researchers can work to standardize both administration of the research method and scoring (or coding) of participant responses. Norris and Ortega (2003) note that the American Educational Research Association standards for educational and psychological measurement specify that research reports should include information that will help readers assess reliability, including details on procedures, scoring or coding guidelines, training that coders underwent, and the consistency of coders' judgments. (See Norris & Ortega, 2003, pp. 740–746.)

### E. Validity

The "validity" of a study refers to the extent to which results genuinely test the claims of the study. Thus, if a range of different studies addressing different theoretical proposals are able to employ the method to obtain results shedding light on the proposal, the method gains evidence of validity. Further, as Lust, Flynn, and Chien (1987, p. 274) point out, converging evidence across tasks supports validity.

"Internal validity" refers to factors internal to a study that may affect whether the data collection procedures are truly measuring what the study claims they measure. Seliger and Shohamy (1989, p. 95) list factors affecting internal validity of a study, including sample size, time allotted for the study, and the effect of the task itself (e.g., practice effects).

"External validity" refers to generalizability. As Johnson (1992, pp. 176–177) notes, details about the study in the research report will help readers assess the degree to which findings can apply to other settings.

Validity is related to the "strength" of a method. Lust, Flynn, and Foley (1996, p. 63) argue that "[t]he best test of the strength of a particular method lies in whether or not the evidence it provides converges with evidence from other methods." Debates over the strength of methods in SLA date back many years. For example, discussions of the findings from studies of order of acquisition of English inflectional morphology (Dulay & Burt, 1973) led to debates over the Bilingual Syntax Measure, and to claims that evidence from this elicited production method converged with findings from natural speech.

### F. Disciplinary Differences

A choice of methods will reflect assumptions about the nature of the subject, and about which dimensions of the subject are central or essential (Seliger & Shohamy, 1989, p. 115). In studies of SLA, these assumptions can be directed by a basic orientation to the field—often either linguistic, psychological, or sociological. These three categories do not reflect the only way to partition approaches to SLA, but they correspond to distinctions that many researchers make. They also often correspond to other ways of partitioning the field: for example, in a discussion of the conceptual basis for "measurement" in SLA, Norris and Ortega identify three central conceptual approaches to SLA: generative, interactionist, and emergentist. These three categories relate (although they do not map perfectly) to the contrasts among linguistic, psychological, and sociolinguistic approaches to SLA.

In this chapter, we limit our discussion to the linguistic category. In linguistic research on SLA, many studies have used grammaticality judgments as a data collection method (Sorace, 1996). In a discussion of studies that have probed features of Universal Grammar, Ellis (1994) states that "the main method used to date is the grammaticality judgment task" (441). The centrality of grammaticality judgment tasks is echoed by Norris and Ortega (2003): in a chart listing methods for different approaches to SLA, under generative approaches, they list "grammaticality judgment tasks of various kinds."

Since there are other excellent discussions of acceptability judgments in the literature (e.g., Chaudron, 2003; Sorace, 1996), one of our aims in this chapter is to explore more fully other tasks that probe SLA from a linguistic perspective. While other surveys of methods have discussed these tasks, our goal is somewhat different from that of other surveys. First, we list and briefly describe other sources on methodology that have commented on a wider range of methods. Second, we discuss in depth a production method (elicited imitation, EI) and a comprehension method (act-out, AO) whose particular advantages make them useful for linguistic approaches to SLA.

## III. SOME SOURCES COMMENTING ON DATA COLLECTION METHODS

Earlier chapters in anthologies or books on methodology have described and commented on a range of methods. Ellis (1994, pp. 669–674) includes an overview of various methods for data collection, as do Larsen-Freeman and Long (1991, pp. 26–38) and Seliger and Shohamy (1989, pp. 158–580). Chaudron (2003) discusses 18 specific data collection methods, classified as either naturalistic, elicited production, or experimental procedures. Sanz (2005) provides a set of articles on research adopting quantitative and/or qualitative approaches to SLA from an information-processing perspective. Hinkel (2005) includes chapters on ethnography (Harklau, 2005), case studies (van Lier, 2005), and classroom research (Nunan, 2005).

See Bachman and Cohen (1998) for a set of articles on the interface between research on SLA and language testing.

## IV. METHODS FOR LINGUISTIC APPROACHES TO SLA

### A. Overview

Because most studies of SLA from a linguistic perspective are guided by a particular theoretical approach to language, most test a specific hypothesis. This section includes some design considerations that apply to studies adopting any method, and then turns to a discussion of three specific methods: EI, AO, and technical methods for brain imaging.

### B. Design Considerations

As noted above, the choice of a method depends on the nature of the subject matter. For particular areas of inquiry, either production or comprehension studies may target and partially reveal underlying linguistic knowledge.

Researchers need to collect certain background information about participants. Such information may include, among other things, the items in the list below:

Background information on research participants
- Age
- Months or years of formal study of L2

- Age at which formal study began
- Months or years of residence in country where L2 is spoken natively
- If living in a country where L2 is spoken natively, age at arrival
- L2 proficiency
- Information about social context (e.g., use of L2 in job, with family members or friends, in other interactions)
- Information on attitude or motivation
- Other language(s) spoken, and information on the above for other languages

Scholars have struggled with both defining and measuring L2 proficiency. Larsen-Freeman and Long (1991, pp. 38–44) discuss attempts to define proficiency, and also describe efforts to establish and use indices of development in a language. Thomas (1994) surveys published articles to see how researchers define and measure proficiency. The choice of a development index that can provide independent information on the proficiency of participants in a research study is an important design decision.

## C. Rationale

In the remainder of this chapter, we provide details on two specific methods for L2 acquisition: EI and comprehension. Our rationale for including only a small set of methods is that (i) length constraints preclude an in-depth discussion of an extensive set of methods, (ii) other existing sources discuss a wider range of methods (see section III), and (iii) small set permits discussion of principles for choosing a method that extend to other methods. Our rationale for including these specific methods is that (i) the methods represent production and comprehension, (ii) the methods are particularly susceptible to measures for enhancing reliability, and (iii) the methods have been used independently to study the same linguistic questions, permitting discussions of their strength and validity.

In each of the following sections, we provide an overview of the method, a discussion of its advantages and limitations (including a discussion of reliability) and citations of studies that have used the method.

## D. Elicited Imitation

Elicited imitation is a production method that asks participants to listen to a sentence or structure from the L2 and repeat it exactly as they heard it. The method has been used for decades for both first language acquisition and SLA studies. Lust et al. (1996) discuss some of the history of the method and provide details on its use in L1 studies.

When the sentence is long enough to tax memory, the respondent must consult the developing grammatical system to reconstruct the target sentence and produce a response.[2] The task usually begins with an explanation of the procedure, followed by a

---

[2]See Lust et al. (1996) for a defense of this claim.

practice or pretraining battery of structures, which begins with short structures and works its way up to practice structures that have the same length (in terms of both words and syllables) as the sentences to be included in the test batteries, but simpler structure. If the respondent can complete the pretraining battery, the process is repeated for a set of test batteries.

Each battery reflects the experimental design, including a token corresponding to each of several structures to be tested. For example, (1)–(3) illustrate a three-way contrast tested in Flynn (1989a, 1989b).[3]

(1) *Headed RC, lexically specified head*
The boss introduced the gentleman who questioned the lawyer.
(2) *Headed RC, unspecified head*
The boss introduced the person who instructed the lawyer.
(3) *Free relative*
The professor introduced whoever greeted the lawyer.

Aside from lexical differences, the structures in (1)–(3) differ only in relative clause type.[4] An EI experiment usually includes multiple batteries which instantiate the same set of structures. The order of tokens within a battery is independently randomized.

Responses are first transcribed and then analyzed. Each response may be described as either matching or not matching the target utterance. The research group develops criteria for classifying responses into one category or another. For example, guidelines may specify that a response be scored "correct" if it reflects no changes at all in the sentence as it was originally read, as in (4), and also if it reflects changes that the research group has decided to term insignificant.[5] The same guidelines may also specify that a change be scored as "incorrect" if it reflects significant changes, such as the lexical change in (5) or the structural change in (6).

(4) *Response with no change*
Experimenter: The gentleman greeted the person who answered the lawyer.
Respondent: The gentleman greeted the person who answered the lawyer.
(5) *Response with lexical change*
Experimenter: The owner questioned the businessman who greeted the worker.
Respondent: The **man** questioned the businessman who greeted the worker.
(6) *Response with structural change (specifically, conversion to coordinate structure)*
Experimenter: The janitor criticized the person who called the lawyer.
Respondent: The janitor criticized the person **and he** called the lawyer.

---

[3]Flynn's design included other factors not presented here.
[4]In developing the test batteries, a set of similar noun and verb items would be randomly distributed across appropriate syntactic positions, except that shorter or longer words might be chosen to standardize syllable length.
[5]Examples of changes the research group might decide to code as "insignificant" include pauses, or in a study investigating grammar, phonetic changes that are not linked to grammar, such as substitution of the segment [r] for [l] in "lawyer."

These results can be analyzed both quantitatively and qualitatively. In a quantitative analysis, the percentage of responses that match or do not match the target for each structure can shed light on the hypothesis (see below). In a qualitative analysis, the type of changes that participants make can be studied, and may reveal features of the developing grammar. (This qualitative analysis may in turn include a quantitative component: particular changes, such as conversion to coordinate structure, as in (6), may be tallied, and percentages of responses that included that particular change may be computed for different structural types in the design.)

Some writers and researchers have expressed a degree of uncertainty about EI. For example, Gass and Selinker (2001, p. 40) ask, "Precisely what type of knowledge is reflected in an EI task is controversial. Do the results reflect a learner's underlying competence? Or are there task-performance issues . . . ?" Two considerations shed some light on these questions.

First, the power of EI lies in comparative results, rather than in absolute results. That is, a particular percentage "correct" on a particular linguistic construction in EI is not especially meaningful. What is meaningful is the relative percentage "correct" across two structural types, when the two types differ only in experimentally controlled factors. In the design reflected in (4)–(6) above, for example, the percentage "correct" for free relatives means less than the contrast between the percentage "correct" across the three types.

Second, EI certainly does reflect what Gass and Selinker (2001) term "task-performance issues," and can be affected by features of all physiological and cognitive systems for speech and hearing. The precise nature of the process by which a sentence is heard and reconstructed is not fully visible and not fully understood. The criticism is further validated by recent research that reveals the ways in which particular design choices, such as lexical choices, can affect performance in EI (e.g., Valian & Aubry, 2005; Valian, Prasada, & Scarpa, 2006). However, all use of language, natural or experimental, is behavior, and all behavior is subject to "performance issues." For no type of language use, including natural speech, is the psycholinguistic process fully understood.

For example, the interface between pragmatics and grammar is complex and important in natural speech (see Kasper, this volume). Studies of natural speech must take into account the unknown interactions between the pragmatic context, including physical, social, and linguistic features, and the language use being studied. Even studies that specifically probe these interactions can rarely investigate, much less control, the full range of relevant pragmatic factors. Natural speech also involves features of auditory and articulatory systems, just as EI does. EI differs, for example, in the requirement that a sentence be represented in short-term memory as it is reconstructed for production—but short-term memory plays a role in natural speech as well, just a less-clearly-defined role. EI may in fact be more frequently or easily targeted by the valid criticism that we don't fully understand the psycholinguistic process because EI is more controlled and standardized than many other methods; thus, the fact that poorly understood processes are at work is more transparent.

The controls in design and administration mean that any performance factors influencing results exert an influence on all structures being tested. This means that significant differences across structures in an EI design are meaningful, even though the performance factors are not fully understood.

An advantage EI offers is that its procedures lend themselves to reliability. Instructions for an EI task are simple, and as sentences are read and repeated back, experimenters can confine their comments to brief, encouraging remarks (e.g., "Great. Let's try another one.") Thus, administration can be standardized, increasing reliability. Guidelines for transcription and coding can be developed and recorded so that other parties can apply them, yielding the same results from analysis. Reliability in transcription and coding can thus be verified easily.

Another advantage EI offers is that it can target particular linguistic questions with precision, by controlling all other factors in a design except the linguistic feature under investigation (e.g., relative clause type in (4)–(6) above).

A third advantage is that EI tasks can be administered fairly efficiently. This means that larger cross-sectional samples can be gathered than would be possible with lengthier methods.

At the same time, in its precise targeting of linguistic features, EI is limited. Its narrow focus means that other interesting features of SLA development cannot be probed at the same time. Another limitation is that both transcription and coding require linguistic sophistication, which may add significantly to the time required for training transcribers and coders.

While all production tasks are influenced by pragmatic and cognitive factors, EI reduces the influence, possibly as far as any production task could. Holland, Holyoak, Nisbett, and Thagard (1986) in fact assert that "one can imagine few tasks in the cognitive domain that have more stimulus guidance and stimulus constraint than repeating a sentence" (p. 173). EI offers this advantage at the same time that it allows precise control over factors to be tested. The power of this combination has led to EI's use not only in adult SLA (e.g., Flynn, 1989a, 1989b; Pacheco, 2007) but also in studies of conduction aphasia (e.g., Odell, Bonkoski, & Mello, 1995) and Alzheimer's disease (e.g., Small, Kemper, & Lyons, 2000), and in diagnostic work (e.g., Johnson, Weston, & Bain, 2004).

## E. Act-Out

The AO task is a comprehension method whose use extends back over 30 years in the field of first language acquisition. (For early L1 examples, see Bever, 1970; Lust, 1986; Sinclair, 1976; Shorr & Dale, 1981.) As used in studies of both L1 and L2 acquisition, the method asks participants in a study to use a set of character figures and/or props to show their interpretation of a sentence. The conceptual grounding for the method and its use in first language acquisition is discussed at greater length in Lust et al.(1987) and Lust, Flynn, Foley, and Chien (1999).

Like the EI task, the AO task usually begins with an explanation of the procedure. An initial set of character figures (dolls) and/or props are introduced, and next, the participant is quizzed to test for lexical knowledge (e.g., "Can you show me the tiger? Can you show me a cup?") Next, a pretraining battery of structures is presented. Once again, these begin with short structures and gradually lead to practice structures that have the same length (in terms of both words and syllables) as the sentences to be included in the test batteries, but that have simpler structure. If the respondent can complete the pretraining battery, the process is repeated for a set of test batteries. While respondents may be coached in their AOs during pretraining, administration of the test batteries involves no dialog or coaching; for every AO, the experimenter offers a brief word of praise and moves on.

In studies of L1 acquisition, the AO task has played a particularly prominent role over many years in studies of the acquisition of relative clauses (e.g., Flynn & Lust, 1981; Goodluck & Tavakolian, 1982; Hamburger & Crain, 1982; Kidd & Bavin, 2002; Tavakolian, 1981). Its use in the study of relative clauses was extended to L2 acquisition in Flynn's (1983) study of comprehension of structures like (7)–(9):

(7)  *Headed RC, lexically specified head*
     The triangle bumped the circle which touched the square.
(8)  *Headed RC, unspecified head*
     The square hit the thing that touched the circle.
(9)  *Free relative*
     The triangle touched whatever bumped the square.

Like results in EI, responses to structures like (7)–(9) (and other items replicating these structures) can be analyzed both quantitatively and qualitatively. In a quantitative analysis, the percentage of responses that match or do not match the target for each structure can shed light on hypothesized differences in the grammatical representation underlying knowledge of these structures.[6] In a qualitative analysis, the type of changes that participants make can be studied, and may reveal features of the developing grammar. For example, in the AO task, the interpretation of empty elements like the gap in a relative clause can be probed. A response to sentence (7) in which the triangle bumps the circle and then the triangle touches the square might (if replicated systematically) generate hypotheses about L2 learners' hypotheses concerning the establishment of the antecedent for the relative clause gap.

Because the AO task can be designed in a controlled way, it offers the advantage of being able to systematically test precise syntactic factors (as in the relative clause examples in (7)–(9)). Sutton (1996) argues that probing sensitivity to structural contrasts is important to understanding language acquisition, because it can shed light on the process of development. While other comprehension methods, such as picture-judgment or picture-choice tasks, can be used in designs that test sensitivity to contrasts, the AO task can potentially yield more information on the nature of the sensitivity, because the response is much richer than a simple yes/no response, which cannot yield qualitative findings in addition to basic quantitative results. Thus, it can test for sensitivity to structural contrasts in a way that takes fuller advantage of the knowledge in the developing mind.

A second advantage noted by Goodluck (1996) for L1 studies applies to L2 studies as well: relative to some other comprehension methods, such as picture-choice methods or methods using online stimuli, the AO task requires less time and fewer costs to

---

[6]For example, a response that did not match the target sentence might have included a prop not named in the stimulus sentence, or demonstrated an action that could not correspond to the predicate of the target sentence.

develop. The time required to create controlled picture stimuli, for example, is not needed in the AO task, where respondents use props to show their own interpretation.

A third advantage is the freedom the AO task provides for respondents to demonstrate interpretations the experimental designers might not have anticipated. (See Goodluck, 1996; Lust et al., 1999.) While choice methods limit possible responses to what the experimenters have thought of, in the AO task, the respondent may provide a window into interpretation that had not been previously considered. (See Lust et al., 1987 for further discussion of the assumptions underlying the method and the interaction between behavior and interpretation.)

A limitation of the AO method is the extensive time needed for planning the design. While care in design is obviously important in all methods, the number of factors other than those being tested that can influence behavior is particularly large in an AO task. For example, until pilot participants test the setup, pragmatic difficulties with using particular props and toys, with the arrangement of items, with the demonstration of particular actions, or with capture of the action by video camera may not be anticipated. Often, several refinements of pilot batteries are necessary before all unanticipated difficulties can be resolved.

A second limitation is the need for careful administration. Keeping the position of props uniform and maintaining level intonation in sentence batteries require training and checks on consistency over the course of a project. Experimenters also need to refrain from moving or commenting more on one prop than another, to avoid inadvertently increasing the saliency of one prop.

A second limitation concerns data coding. Depending on the complexity of the structures being tested, a range of factors may need to be captured, including choice of props, type of action, action sequence or simultaneity, and commentary the participant may voluntarily offer. Video recording is usually essential, and both initial coding and reliability measures take time. A coding form for data capture may take time to develop and refine.

Because it is susceptible to controlled administration, the AO task is easily subject to checks on reliability. Its advantages have led to its use in some studies of L2 acquisition (e.g., Finney, 1997, 2002; Pacheco, 2007) and also in studies of language comprehension and aphasia (e.g., Caplan & Futter, 1986; Hickok & Avrutin, 1996; Inglis, 1999; Thompson, Tait, Ballard, & Fix, 1999). The AO task's ability to precisely target grammatical features that can be investigated using other measures of comprehension and production suggests that it could be much more widely used in L2 studies than it has been to date.

# V. CONCLUSION

In this chapter we have attempted to clarify certain general assumptions regarding research methodology in the field of SLA. We sought to do this by first introducing several critical concepts and distinctions made in discussions of research methods. In this context, we also provided a partial guide to existing surveys on methodology in the field. We next focused on two specific methodologies—EI as an oral production task and AO as a comprehension task. These two methods are often overlooked in surveys of the field, and when they are not overlooked, they are often misunderstood. We argue that, given their advantages, they are underused. Because of the specific advantages outlined in section IV, we believe that clarifying the assumptions underlying these methods "can significantly move the field to a more developed scientific status where experiment and theory can most fruitfully interact" (Lust et al., 1999, p. 450).

A goal of SLA and of all language acquisition research is to establish measures of a learner's developing language competence in the target language. This is achieved principally through the measurement and analysis of various modes of language behavior, primarily speaking (production) and listening (comprehension). Each task used for this purpose assumes (1) that the developing competence for each language learner does not yet match that of an adult native speaker, and (2) that the linguistic behavior elicited from each language learner with each task maps the territory lying between the target language grammar and the learner's developing grammar (see additional discussion in Flynn, 1986; Lust et al., 1999). In this way, assessment of the variance in the learner's elicited behavior vis-à-vis the target grammar provides a window into developing linguistic competence. Crucially, while each experimental task involves accessing language knowledge in some way, the different task demands specific to each test mean that each task assesses this knowledge in unique ways. It may also mean that other aspects of language knowledge related to the specific function and to the specific behavioral mode of the task are also tapped. The differences in task requirements for different types of experimental tasks modulate the nature of the data elicited in language acquisition studies.

In the case of EI and AO, these specific task requirements have been probed through decades of work on L1 acquisition. In a scholarly context where grammaticality judgments are the prevailing method used for linguistic approaches to SLA (see the discussion of Ellis, 1994; Norris & Ortega, 2003 in section II), it is worth further exploring the light these two methods can shed on developing linguistic competence in the acquisition of languages beyond the first. We have argued in this chapter that these two methods are susceptible to tests of reliability and validity; furthermore, the tasks offer richer data than tasks calling for a yes/no answer. This richer data (in the form of the utterances a participant constructs in EI and a set of actions in AO) can expose factors that also characterize other types of production and comprehension tasks. As findings from the two methods are compared and contrasted, the specific set of factors that differentiate the methods can be examined. The degree to which these factors also characterize other types of production and comprehension tasks demands systematic empirical validation (see, e.g., Munnich, Flynn, & Martohardjono, 1994). Grammaticality judgment tasks (see, e.g., Birsdong, 1989), sentence combining tasks, yes/no answers to comprehension questions, truth-value judgment tasks (see discussion in Crain & Thornton, 1998), and others are all mediated by a set of both linguistic and nonlinguistic factors that affect access to a learner's knowledge of the target language or yield results seriously confounded by the task (see Flynn, 1986).

As in all science, we seek converging sets of results across a wide set of tasks and replication of these results. The choice of task(s) used in any one study will result in important and significant differences both in terms of the data elicited and the conclusions derived from these results.

# REFERENCES

Adams, R., Fujii, A., & Mackey, A. (2005). Research methodology: Qualitative research. In C. Sanz (Ed.), *Mind and context in adult second language acquisition: Methods, theory and practice* (pp. 69–101). Washington, DC: Georgetown University Press.

Bachman, L. F., & Cohen, A. D. (1998). *Interfaces between second language acquisition and language testing research*. New York: Cambridge University Press.

Bever, T. (1970). The cognitive basis for linguistic structures. In J. Hayes (Ed.), *Cognition and the development of language* (pp. 279–352). New York: Wiley.

Birsdong, D. (1989). *Metalinguistic performance and interlanguage competence*. Berlin: Springer Press.

Brown, J. D. (1988). *Understanding research in second language learning*. New York: Cambridge University Press.

Brown, J. D., & Rodgers, T. S. (2002). *Doing second language research*. New York: Oxford University Press.

Caplan, D., & Futter, C. (1986). Assignment of thematic roles to nouns in sentence comprehension by an agrammatic patient. *Brain and Language*, *27*, 117–134.

Chaudron, C. (2003). Data collection in SLA research. In C. Doughty & M. Long (Eds.), *The handbook of second language acquisition* (pp. 762–830). Malden, MA: Blackwell Publishing.

Crain, S., & Thornton, R. (1998). *Investigations in universal grammar: A guide to experiments on the acquisition of syntax and semantics*. Cambridge, MA: MIT Press.

Dulay, H., & Burt, M. (1973). Should we teach children syntax? *Language Learning*, *23*(2), 245–258.

Ellis, R. (1994). *The study of second language acquisition*. New York: Oxford University Press.

Finney, M. A. (1997). Markedness, operator movement and discourse effects in the acquisition of purpose clause constructions in a second language. *Second Language Research*, *13*(1), 10–33.

Finney, M. A. (2002). Effects of Spanish pragmatic and lexical constraints in the interpretation of L2 English anaphora. *Pragmatics*, *12*(3), 297–328.

Flynn, S. (1983). *A study of principal branching direction in second language acquisition: The generalization of a parameter of universal grammar from first to second language acquisition*. Ph.D. dissertation, Cornell University, Ithaca, New York.

Flynn, S. (1986). Production vs. comprehension: Differences in underlying competences. *Studies in Second Language Acquisition*, *8*, 135–164.

Flynn, S. (1989a). Spanish, Japanese, and Chinese speakers' acquisition of English relative clauses: New evidence for the head-direction parameter. In K. Hyltenstam & L. Obler (Eds.), *Bilingualism across the lifespan* (pp. 116–131). Cambridge, UK: Cambridge University Press.

Flynn, S. (1989b). The role of the head-initial/head-final parameter in the acquisition of English relative clauses by adult Spanish and Japanese speakers. In S. Gass & J. Schachter (Eds.), *Linguistic perspectives on second language acquisition* (pp. 89–108). Cambridge, UK: Cambridge University Press.

Flynn, S., & Lust, B. (1981). Acquisition of relative clauses: Developmental changes in their heads. In W. Harbert & J. Herchensohn (Eds.), *Cornell working papers in linguistics* (Vol. 1). Ithaca, NY: Department of Modern Languages and Linguistics, Cornell University.

Gass, S., & Selinker, L. (2001). *Second language acquisition: An introductory course* (2nd ed.). Mahwah, NJ: Lawrence Erlbaum Associates.

Goodluck, H. (1996). The act-out task. In D. McDaniel, H. S. Cairns, & C. McKee (Eds.), *Methods for assessing children's syntax* (pp. 147–162). Cambridge, MA: MIT Press.

Goodluck, H., & Tavakolian, S. (1982). Competence and processing in children's grammar of relative clauses. *Cognition, 11*, 1–27.

Hamburger, H., & Crain, S. (1982). Relative acquisition. In S. A. Kuczaj (Ed.), *Language development: Syntax and semantics*. Hillsdale, NJ: Lawrence Erlbaum.

Harklau, L. (2005). Ethnography and ethnographic research on second language teaching and learning. In E. Hinkel (Ed.), *Handbook of research in second language teaching and learning* (pp. 179–194). Mahwah, NJ: Lawrence Erlbaum Associates.

Hickok, G., & Avrutin, S. (1996). Comprehension of wh-questions in two Broca's aphasics. *Brain and Language, 52*, 314–327.

Hinkel, E. (Ed.). (2005). *Handbook of research in second language teaching and learning.* Mahwah, NJ: Lawrence Erlbaum Associates.

Holland, J. H., Holyoak, K. J., Nisbett, R. E., & Thagard, P. R. (1986). *Induction: Processes of inference, learning and discovery*. Cambridge, MA: MIT Press.

Inglis, A. L. (1999). The complexity of 'Asyntactic' comprehension: Investigations of an unusual dissociation between passives and object relatives. *Journal of Neurolinguistics, 12*, 41–77.

Johnson, C. A., Weston, A. D., & Bain, B. A. (2004). An objective and time-efficient method for determining severity of childhood speech delay. *American Journal of Speech-Language Pathology, 13*, 55–65.

Johnson, D. M. (1992). *Approaches to research in second language acquisition*. New York: Longman.

Kidd, E., & Bavin, E. L. (2002). English-speaking children's comprehension of relative clauses: Evidence for general-cognitive and language-specific constraints on development. *Journal of Psycholinguistic Research, 31*, 599–617.

Larsen-Freeman, D., & Long, M. (1991). *An introduction to second language acquisition research.* New York: Longman.

Lazaraton, A. (2005). Quantitative research methods. In E. Hinkel (Ed.), *Handbook of research in second language teaching and learning* (pp. 209–224). Mahwah, NJ: Lawrence Erlbaum Associates.

Lust, B. (Ed.). (1986). *Studies in the acquisition of anaphora. Volume I: Defining the constraints.* Dordrecht: Reidel.

Lust, B., Flynn, S., & Chien, Y.-C. (1987). What children know: Methods for the study of first language acquisition. In B. Lust (Ed.), *Studies in the acquisition of anaphora. Volume II: Applying the constraints* (pp. 271–356). Dordrecht: Reidel.

Lust, B., Flynn, S., & Foley, C. (1996). What children know about what they say: Elicited imitation as a research method for assessing children's syntax. In D. McDaniel, C. McKee, & H. Cairns (Eds.), *Methods for assessing children's syntax* (pp. 55–76). Cambridge, MA: MIT Press.

Lust, B., Flynn, S., Foley, C., & Chien, Y.-C. (1999). How do we know what children know? Problems and advances in establishing scientific methods for the study of language acquisition and linguistic theory. In W. C. Ritchie & T. K. Bhatia (Eds.), *Handbook of child language acquisition* (pp. 427–456). New York: Academic Press.

Munnich, E., Flynn, S., & Martohardjono, G. (1994). Grammaticality judgment task and elicited imitation: Differences and similarities in evaluating linguistic competence. In E. Tarone, S. Gass, & A. Cohen (Eds.), *Research methodology in second language acquisition* (pp. 319–337). Mahwah, NJ: Lawrence Erlbaum Associates.

Norris, J., & Ortega, L. (2003). Defining and measuring SLA. In C. Doughty & M. Long (Eds.), *The handbook of second language acquisition* (pp. 717–761). Malden, MA: Blackwell Publishing.

Nunan, D. (1991). Methods in second language classroom-oriented research: A critical review. *Studies in Second Language Acquisition, 13*, 249–274.

Nunan, D. (1996). Issues in second language acquisition research: Examining substance and procedure. In W. C. Ritchie & T. K. Bhatia (Eds.), *Handbook of second language acquisition* (pp. 349–374). Boston, MA: Academic Press.

Nunan, D. (2005). Classroom research. In E. Hinkel (Ed.), *Handbook of research in second language teaching and learning* (pp. 225–240). Mahwah, NJ: Lawrence Erlbaum Associates.

Odell, K. H., Bonkoski, J., & Mello, J. (1995). Repetition of self-generated utterances in conduction aphasia. *American Journal of Speech-Language Pathology, 4*, 169–173.

Pacheco, S. (2007). *Syntax-pragmatics interface: Brazilian-Portuguese L2 acquisition of English.* Ph.D. dissertation, PURS/Porto Alegre, Brazil.

Sanz, C. (Ed.). (2005). *Mind and context in adult second language acquisition.* Washington, DC: Georgetown University Press.

Seliger, H. W., & Shohamy, E. (1989). *Second language research methods.* New York: Oxford University Press.

Shorr, D. N., & Dale, P. S. (1981). Prepositional marking of source-goal structure and children's comprehension of English passives. *Journal of Speech and Hearing Research, 24*, 179–184.

Sinclair, H. (1976). Developmental psycholinguistics. In B. Inhelder & H. Chipman (Eds.), *Piaget and his school* (pp. 189–204). Berlin: Springer-Verlag.

Small, J., Kemper, S., & Lyons, K. (2000). Sentence repetition and processing resources in Alzheimer's disease. *Brain and Language, 75*, 232–258.

Sorace, A. (1996). The use of acceptability judgments in second language acquisition research. In W. Ritchie & T. K. Bhatia (Eds.), *Handbook of second language acquisition* (pp. 375–409). San Diego, CA: Academic Press.

Sutton, A. (1996). Evidence of sensitivity to structural constraints in the literature on children's language comprehension. *Journal of Speech and Hearing Research, 39*, 1304–1314.

Tavakolian, S. (1981). The conjoined-clause analysis of relative clauses. In S. Tavakolian (Ed.), *Language acquisition and linguistic theory* (pp. 167–187). Cambridge, MA: MIT Press.

Thomas, M. (1994). Assessment of L2 proficiency in second language acquisition research. *Language Learning, 44*, 307–336.

Thompson, C. K., Tait, M. E., Ballard, K. J., & Fix, S. C. (1999). Agrammatic aphasic subjects comprehension of subject and object extracted wh questions. *Brain and Language, 67*, 169–187.

Valian, V., & Aubry, S. (2005). When opportunity knocks twice: Two-year-olds' repetition of sentence subjects. *Journal of Child Language, 32*, 617–641.

Valian, V., Prasada, S., & Scarpa, J. (2006). Direct object predictability: Effects on young children's imitation of sentences. *Journal of Child Language, 33*, 247–269.

van Lier, L. (2005). Case study. In E. Hinkel (Ed.), *Handbook of research in second language teaching and learning* (pp. 195–208). Mahwah, NJ: Lawrence Erlbaum Associates.

# APPROACHES TO THE STUDY OF SECOND LANGUAGE ACQUISITION

## INTRODUCTION TO PART II

As Susan Gass has argued in chapter 1, the systematic study of second language acquisition (SLA) is a relatively young enterprise, dating back only to the 1960s or 1970s. In part as a consequence of this state of affairs and of the fact that the phenomena of SLA fall naturally within the scope of a number of established disciplines, there is no single, universally accepted approach to the study of SLA. Researchers from the disciplines of linguistics (including variationist sociolinguistics), psychology (including social psychology), and sociology and the various research traditions and schools within these disciplines and subdisciplines have undertaken research on SLA. The purpose of this part of the volume is to provide insight into some of the current major approaches to the study of SLA through a series of chapters, each of which provides a general characterization of a given approach by a leading scholar (or scholars) working within the approach and a summary of recent research conducted within its purview. Chapters 3–5 and 8 are concerned with approaches that originated in linguistics, and chapters 6 and 7 are dedicated to more psychological approaches.

Chapter 3 by Lydia White ("Grammatical Theory: Interfaces and L2 Knowledge") provides both an overall characterization of the generative paradigm (sometimes referred to as "the UG approach") and a report of recent research within this approach that bears on a number of central issues in the field. A number of well-known empirical claims have come out of this general research program—that knowledge of grammatical form (the language user's mental grammar of his/her language) is highly abstract; that it constitutes a distinct, special module of the mind (including internal modular structure) with properties that distinguish it from, say, knowledge of semantics or of pragmatics or of social categories; and that it is, to a large extent, innate rather than acquired on the basis of experience. One problem that language learners have been found to have lies at the interfaces between the grammar and other modules of the mind and among the modules internal to the grammar. It is this problem that White focuses on in her chapter.

The remainder of the chapters in this part of the volume either explicitly reject one or more of the results of work in the generative framework or simply pursue a different research tradition. In any case, taken together they represent the richness of existing approaches to the study of SLA.

In chapter 4 ("Emergentism and Second Language Acquisition"), William O'Grady, Miseon Lee, and Hye-Young Kwak adopt a view of SLA that proposes an alternative to the claim that grammatical knowledge has a distinct status or that it is largely innate and pursues a program in which the core properties of language are claimed to be derivable from the application of a processor that does not presuppose a system of rules, as does the account of grammatical knowledge within the generative framework, but rather applies to a sentence left to right and minimizes the burden on working memory. O'Grady et al. provide an account of the interaction of universal quantification and negation using their processor for both English and Korean. They then report an empirical study of L1 Korean speakers learning L2 English and find that predictions based on their position are generally borne out by the results.

The study of social determinants of linguistic performance within sociolinguistics gave rise in the 1960s to an approach to the study of language focused on the relative frequency of occurrence of features of speech as they appear in performance under a variety of conditions—both grammar internal and grammar external (i.e., social). This variationist approach to the study of language was extended to the study of second language phenomena in the 1970s and has been pursued since then. Chapter 5 by Dennis R. Preston and Robert Bayley ("Variationist Linguistics and Second Language Acquisition") reviews work done within this approach. After providing brief historical background on both L1 and L2 use, Preston and Bayley answer a series of criticisms of variationist work in SLA, some based on misunderstandings of the goals of the approach, and then review recent work within the paradigm. Finally, they propose an interpretation of variationist results in terms of underlying psycholinguistic processing based on the standard competence/performance distinction, thus meeting those criticisms of variationism that have seen it as limited to generalizations over performance with no psycholinguistic content.

There is a considerable body of research on SLA conducted within the information-processing approach to the study of behavior grounded in cognitive psychology. Work in this paradigm is based on the view that language use is a cognitive skill that, like any other such skill, consists in mechanisms such as working (short-term) and long-term memory, information storage and retrieval, controlled and automatic processing, restructuring in the process of acquisition, and so on. Chapter 6 by Jeanette Altarriba and Dana M. Basnight-Brown ("An Information-Processing Approach to Second Language Acquisition") reviews basic concepts and research conducted within this approach. They address a number of general issues in the study of SLA in terms of this approach, including the nature of a putative critical period for language acquisition, the multi-mechanism nature of SLA in general, the passage from controlled to automatic processing as acquisition takes place, and the kind of cognitive restructuring involved in acquisition.

While chapters 3–6 are concerned with basic research specific to SLA, both chapter 7 and chapter 8 are more concerned with the direct classroom application of principles derived from approaches to the study of the mind in general as they apply to SLA.

The approaches addressed in chapters 3–6 (and, in fact, chapter 8 as well) treat the process and consequences of SLA independent of the social context in which they occur. In chapter 7 ("The Artificial Development of Second Language Ability: A Sociocultural Approach"), James P. Lantolf and Matthew E. Poehner present an approach grounded in Vygotsky's sociocultural theory of mind under which social context is claimed to be the very source of human mental abilities. After a general presentation of the Vygotskian framework, the authors analyze in some detail the mediated attainment of clitic placement and the use of the perfect auxiliary in the L2 French of L1 English speakers.

A number of linguists who originally worked within the generative tradition have, in the last 20 years, adopted a more psychological approach to the study of language based on human categorization, metaphor, and metonymy in cognitive psychology, which they designate *cognitive linguistics*. Chapter 8 ("Cognitive Linguistics and Second Language Learning") by Marjolijn Verspoor and Andrea Tyler outlines this general approach and reports recent results of research on the classroom application of the framework to instruction on lexicon and grammar, the latter including the teaching of definite articles and modal auxiliaries in English.

# GRAMMATICAL THEORY: INTERFACES AND L2 KNOWLEDGE

Lydia White

In this chapter, recent second language (L2) research on linguistic interfaces is discussed. The interfaces include external ones (where the grammar interfaces with the conceptual–intentional system and with the articulatory–perceptual system), as well as internal ones (where different modules of the grammar interface with each other, such as syntax with semantics, or phonology with morphology). Researchers currently seek to account for well-known difficulties of L2 learners and L2 speakers (henceforth L2ers) by consideration of interface phenomena.

## I. INTRODUCTION

Various instantiations of grammatical theory (e.g. Chomsky, 1965, 1981, 1993) have as their goal to provide a model of the linguistic competence of native speakers, a characterization of their unconscious knowledge of language. This knowledge is assumed to be mentally represented by means of an abstract linguistic system, or grammar, which consists of a number of components (or modules), encompassing syntax, phonology, morphology and semantics. The grammar underlies our language use, both comprehension and production.

Grammatical theory is grounded in concerns about first language (L1) acquisition, particularly the so-called *logical problem of language acquisition*. The crucial observation is that the ultimate attainment of native speakers, their unconscious knowledge, goes far beyond what is provided in the linguistic input to children in the process of acquiring language (e.g. Chomsky, 1986; Hornstein & Lightfoot, 1981). In other words, there is a mismatch between the primary linguistic data that children are exposed to and their ultimate attainment. The solution offered to this problem is

*The New Handbook of Second Language Acquisition*

the postulation of an innate universal grammar (UG), including abstract principles and parameters which provide constraints on linguistic representations. The claim, then, is that certain aspects of our linguistic knowledge do not have to be learned; rather, they are derived from UG, which limits the choices children can make in acquiring the grammar of their L1.

Grammatical theory, of course, says nothing directly about L2 acquisition. At a descriptive level, it offers a model of the linguistic competence of native speakers; at an explanatory level, it seeks to explain how L1 acquisition comes about. Nevertheless, we may be able to characterize non-native competence in similar ways, assuming that interlanguage grammars also involve unconscious representations which can be characterized in terms of a grammar. Furthermore, if it can be shown that L2ers exhibit unconscious knowledge of the target language which could not be derived solely from the L2 input, or from the L1, then this motivates claims for the continuing operation of UG in second language acquisition (SLA).

This question was in fact the focus of generative SLA research in the 1980s and 1990s. Much of this research typically concentrated on the syntactic component of the interlanguage grammar, with a particular consideration of whether interlanguage grammars are constrained by principles of UG and whether transfer from the L1 can be accounted for in terms of initial adoption of L1 parameter settings. Debate centred on questions such as whether or not L2ers have access to UG and whether or not they are able to reset parameters (see White, 1989, 2003b).

## II. INTERFACES

In earlier generative L2 research, there was relatively little consideration of how syntactic knowledge might interact with other components of the grammar. More recently, however, there has been a shift in emphasis. Research has moved on from rather global questions about UG accessibility and parameter resetting to an intricate consideration not only of L2 successes in the domain of abstract syntax but also to areas where problems are evident even when UG access can be demonstrated. An area of current concern involves the so-called interfaces, with investigation centering on how different modules of the interlanguage grammar relate to each other. In particular, there is active consideration of whether failure to acquire a fully native-like L2 grammar can be attributed to problems integrating material at the interfaces and whether this is an area where cross-linguistic influence is likely to be persistent.

The grammar itself consists of a lexicon and a computational system (or, more likely, a collection of computational systems, for syntax, phonology and semantics). As Jackendoff (2002, p. 111) puts it: 'language comprises a number of independent combinatorial systems, which are aligned with each other by means of a collection of interface systems'. In other words, different modules of the grammar must interface with each other: these, then, are grammar-internal interfaces. But the grammar as a whole must also be outward looking: the linguistic system mediates between sounds and meanings; hence, the grammar must interface with grammar-external domains, including with the articulatory–perceptual system at phonetic form (PF) and with the conceptual–intentional system at logical form (LF) (e.g. Chomsky, 1993), as shown in (1).

(1)

| Articulatory–perceptual system | PF | Lexicon and computational system | LF | Conceptual–intentional system |
|---|---|---|---|---|

In this paper, I will discuss how recent SLA research addresses the linguistic interfaces and attempts to account for well-known L2 difficulties by a consideration of various interface phenomena. While the current assumption (often implicit) appears to be that interfaces are necessarily problematic, we will see that there is no reason to assume that all interfaces are alike; some grammatical interfaces do not cause problems to L2ers, others do. We turn first to a consideration of how the grammar interfaces with external domains.

## III. EXTERNAL INTERFACES

### A. Conceptual–Intentional

Utterances do not occur in a vacuum; rather, sentences are uttered in context. Syntactic means of expression may vary because of the context. While discourse, pragmatics and information structure are usually treated as being outside the grammar proper (i.e. not part of the computational system), they, nevertheless, can have significant effects on how we use language, in particular on how speakers and hearers convey meanings and interpret sentences. The interface between syntax and discourse/pragmatics is probably the one that has been most investigated in SLA.

For illustration, two discourse/pragmatic phenomena will be considered, namely topic (the conveying of old information, known to speaker and hearer) and focus (new information, which the speaker wishes to present or contrast with what has gone before). Topic and focus have well-known grammatical effects, some syntactic, some prosodic, which differ somewhat from language to language. We begin with a consideration of how the topic of discourse is realized syntactically.

In null subject languages like Italian or Spanish, subject pronouns can be overt or null. Even though null subjects are licensed syntactically, the choice between overt and null is not optional. Rather, discourse constraints are implicated: in particular, null subjects are strongly preferred when there is no change in topic, while overt pronouns are infelicitous in such contexts; instead they are required when there is a change of topic. In languages like English, which do not license null subjects, overt subject pronouns convey either old or new information (i.e. same topic or different topic).

In fact, null subjects can be seen as constituting the original interface phenomenon investigated in SLA research (though not identified as such at the time). For L2 Spanish, Liceras (1988) pointed out that the syntactic [+ null subject] setting of the null subject parameter does not fully account for when subjects may be dropped. In addition, there are discourse (in her terms, *stylistic*) constraints which L2ers may not fully acquire, even though they have successfully reset the parameter from a syntactic point of view. Interestingly, Liceras's data reveal exactly the same problem that has since been investigated in more detail by other researchers, namely overuse of overt subjects in discourse contexts where a null pronoun would be appropriate. The interlanguage grammar, then, does not interface with discourse/pragmatic requirements in the same way that the native speaker grammar does.

More recently, there has been considerable research on this issue pointing in the same direction: the syntactic properties of subjects in null subject languages are acquired relatively easily, the discourse/pragmatic ones take longer (or are not acquired at all). For example, Sorace (2003) suggests that Italian L2ers will have persistent difficulties in determining when overt subjects should be used. She argues that there will be overuse of overt pronouns in Italian, under the influence of English, in contexts where they are infelicitous because there has not been a topic change. In the exchange in (2) (examples from Sorace, 2003), the answer to the question in (2a) involves old information (since Lucia has already been mentioned); hence, a null subject would be appropriate in (2b), whereas an overt pronoun would not.

(2)   a. Perchè Lucia non ha preso le chiavi?
         Why Lucia not has taken the keys
         'Why didn't Lucia take her keys?'
      b. Perchè *lei/∅ pensava di trovarti a casa
         Because (she) thought of find-you at home
         'Because she thought she would find you at home'

Belletti, Bennati, and Sorace (2007) show that near-native speakers of L2 Italian sometimes produce overt subjects in contexts where null subjects would be more appropriate; although the error is not extensive, they do this to a significantly greater extent than native speakers. At the same time, their use of null subjects in general indicates that they have otherwise acquired the [+ null subject] setting of the parameter. Similar findings have been reported by Tsimpli and Sorace (2006) for Russian-speaking learners of Greek.

However, there are other studies which report occasional overuse of null pronouns in contexts where overt pronouns would be expected, for L2 Turkish (Gürel, 2006) and L2 Spanish (Montrul & Louro, 2006). Overuse of null subjects when there has been a topic change indicates a different problem at the syntax/discourse interface, namely failure to realize constraints on focus, since a focused subject must be overt. Indeed, L2ers have other problems in the realization of focus, pertaining to word order, to which we now turn.

In addition to influencing subject choice in null subject languages, there are a variety of discourse/pragmatic constraints on word order. In languages which allow word-order alternations, these alternations are not necessarily in free variation. Rather, there are circumstances in which one order will be preferred over another. In many cases, this relates to focus. In null subject languages, for example subjects can appear postverbally (word order is VS), as well as preverbally (SV). Choice of VS order is determined by discourse conditions which L2ers may not fully master. As with null subjects, research suggests that acquisition of syntax (in this case, word order) is in advance of acquisition of the discourse-related constraints on word-order alternations.

In Italian and Spanish, postverbal subjects are permitted on syntactic grounds and under certain discourse conditions. Syntactically, VS word order is a consequence of the unaccusative/unergative distinction, as shown in (3) (Spanish examples from Lozano 2006).[1] In (3a), the verb is unergative and the preferred word order is SV, whereas in (3b), the verb is unaccusative and the preferred word order is VS.

(3)  a. Una mujer gritó
         A woman shouted
     b. Vino la policia
         Arrived the police
         'The police arrived'

However, when the subject is presentationally focused, it must appear in final position, yielding VS order even for unergative verbs. In response to a question like (4a), the appropriate answer focuses the subject, yielding VS order, as in (4b) (capitals indicate focus). In other words, for unaccusative verbs, the syntactic and discourse requirements line up, such that VS order is always preferred, whereas for unergatives they differ: SV is appropriate under neutral conditions, while VS is required under focus.

(4)  a. ¿Quién gritó anoche en la calle?
         Who shouted last-night in the street?
     b. Gritó UNA MUJER (unergative VS; focused subject)
         Shouted a woman

Several recent studies have examined such word alternations in L2, comparing syntactic and discourse properties. Belletti and Leonini (2004) report that L2 learners of Italian fail to produce VS order under focus, instead using L1 orders. Hertel (2003) found that advanced L2 learners of Spanish had acquired the syntax of unaccusativity, hence VS order, as well as the use of VS order under focus, while learners at lower levels of proficiency acquired neither. Most interesting is Lozano's (2006) finding of a dissociation between syntax and discourse: his subjects (advanced learners of Spanish) in unfocused contexts made the same word-order distinctions as native speakers, preferring SV with unergatives and VS with unaccusatives. However, in focused contexts involving unergative verbs, they accepted VS and SV in equal proportion, unlike the native speakers, who accepted only VS. Belletti et al. (2007) further show that failure to consistently produce VS order in focused contexts persists even for near-native L2 speakers of Italian. Instead, when VS order is not produced, the predominant response (around 60% of the time) is to use the L1 English way of indicating focus, namely SV order with stress on the subject, something that the Italian controls hardly ever do.

Other relevant examples come from German, where subtle word-order alternations are subject to conditions relating to focus and information structure. German is a verb second (V2) language: in main clauses, the finite verb must appear in the second position, where it can in principle be preceded by any constituent (subject, object,

---

[1]Unaccusatives are intransitive verbs whose sole argument is a theme; unergatives are intransitive verbs whose sole argument is an agent. The subject of an unaccusative verb, being a theme, is generated in object position, where it can remain in certain languages (Burzio, 1986), whereas the subject of an unergative verb is an agent, generated in subject position.

adjunct) and any projection (NP, PP, CP, etc.). Swedish is also a V2 language; however, German and Swedish differ in terms of the information structure of the constituent appearing in the first position in the clause (the so-called *prefield*). Bohnacker and Rosén (2007) present corpus data showing differences between German and Swedish native speakers in terms of what occurs in the prefield. Swedish speakers use a higher proportion of subjects in this position than German speakers, and correspondingly fewer objects and adjuncts. Furthermore, expletive subjects, which are low in information content, are commoner in the Swedish prefield than in German. Bohnacker and Rosén show that L2 speakers of German whose L1 is Swedish acquire appropriate German V2 syntax as beginners; they argue that this is due to syntactic transfer from the L1. At the same time, L2ers fail to acquire appropriate German information structure determining what constituents are felicitous in the prefield; even advanced German L2ers continue to transfer information structure from the L1, in some sense underusing the preverbal position.

Hopp (2004) also seeks to disentangle syntactic from information structure properties in L2 German, investigating L2ers' knowledge of scrambling, a syntactic phenomenon whereby objects can surface outside of their canonical position. In embedded clauses, the normal word order is SOV, as in (5a) (from Hopp, 2004). In cases involving scrambling, the object can precede the subject, as in (5b). However, scrambling is subject to an information-structure-related restriction: scrambled NPs typically involve old information rather than being new or focused—compare (5b) with the infelicitous (5c) (capitals indicate focus).

(5)  a.  ... ... dass John gestern das Buch kaufte
        ... ... that John yesterday the book bought
      b.  ... ... dass das Buch JOHN gestern kaufte
      c.  ... ... *dass DAS BUCH John gestern kaufte

Hopp found that high intermediate, advanced and near-native L2 speakers of German—L1s Japanese, an SOV language which also allows scrambling, and English, an SVO language with no scrambling—are sensitive to syntactic properties of German word order, distinguishing grammatical from ungrammatical sentences in a variety of sentence types. However, they were less target-like on information structure. Furthermore, there were clear L1 effects, with the Japanese groups observing the focusing constraint on scrambling and the English groups failing to do so. Once again, then, we see a disjunction between the L2ers' syntactic knowledge, which is target-like in the relevant respects, and knowledge of interface conditions, which is subject to protracted L1 effects.[2]

To summarize, the results of recent research point fairly consistently to L2 problems associated with external interface phenomena involving a relationship between syntax and discourse/pragmatics/information structure. In some of the research discussed so far, it is suggested that the problem involves the integration of syntactic and discourse properties. In other words, while appropriate L2 syntax is acquired, 'external'

---

[2]The syntax/semantics interface is also implicated in scrambling, which is subject to a definiteness restriction: only definite NPs can be scrambled. Both groups had problems with this aspect of scrambling.

constraints on the syntax are acquired late (or not at all). However, some researchers have argued that such interface problems arise within the computational system itself, that is they reflect non-native representations associated with the CP, or C-domain, as discussed in the next section.

## B. Problems on the Grammar Side (C-Domain)

CP is the syntactic level that interfaces with discourse. Platzack (2001) proposes that the syntax of the C-domain is vulnerable in language acquisition. In other words, problems at the syntax/discourse interface, such as those described above, are attributable to representational problems involving CP, assuming the articulated type of CP proposed by Rizzi and colleagues (e.g. Rizzi, 1997), where CP is divided into a number of functional categories, such as ForceP, FiniteP, TopicP, FocusP, etc. as shown in (6).[3]

(6)

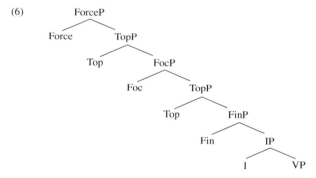

A number of proposals have been made that L2 interface problems are located either in the functional categories or in the features associated with the expanded C-domain, and that some kind of representational deficit is possibly implicated. Returning to the use of VS order to express focus in languages like Spanish and Italian, Belletti and Leonini (2004) report that Italian L2ers (with various L1s, the majority German) fail to associate VS order with focus. They point out the L2ers' behaviour is such as to suggest that they are indeed sensitive to the pragmatic content of the constructions in question, since they use equivalent L1 means to express focus, for example via stress on the focused element. In other words, the problem is not that L2ers fail to appreciate the discourse context. Instead, Belletti and Leonini maintain that the interface problem is grammatical in nature; in particular, L2ers have difficulties in consistently projecting the functional category (FocP), required in the L2 representation but absent in the L1.

As well as relating interface problems to functional categories, others have suggested that the problem resides with features of functional categories, particularly interpretive features. Topic shift is such a feature (see Sorace, 2003) explaining the overuse of overt subjects in null subject languages, discussed above. Along these lines, Valenzuela

---

[3]Rizzi (1997) argues that there can be more than one topic position in the clause, but only one focus position.

(2006) identifies L2 problems associated with the articulated CP structure, attributable to a specificity feature. Once again, the issue is topic constructions, this time as they relate to clitic pronouns. Valenzuela looks at properties of clitic left dislocation (CLLD) in L2 Spanish. In CLLD, the topic occurs in the left periphery of the clause, and a clitic marks the position in which the topic must be interpreted, as in (7a). This contrasts with contrastive left dislocation (CLD) as found in Germanic languages, where no clitic is involved, as in (7b) (examples from Valenzuela, 2006).

(7)   a. El libro, lo leí
         the book, it read-1S
      b. The book, I read
      c. Un libro, leí
         a book, read-1S
      d. *Un libro, lo leí
         a book, it read-1S

   Crucially, there is a specificity requirement on CLLD, which is permitted only when the topic is [+ specific]; if the topic is non-specific, Spanish in fact uses the CLD construction; hence, (7c) is grammatical and (7d) is not. In other words, there is a specificity feature associated with TopicP (and also with the clitic itself). Valenzuela shows that near-native speakers of Spanish whose L1 is English have little difficulty in acquiring the syntax of CLLD, including the fact that CLLD can occur in embedded clauses, unlike CLD. On the other hand, they do not robustly acquire the interpretive constraint which determines that when the topic is non-specific, a clitic is not permitted. For non-specific topics, the L2ers produce and accept both CLD and CLLD. Valenzuela takes this to be an interface issue, of the kind proposed by Sorace, showing problems with features implicated in interpretation, in this case specificity.

   In sum, there is convergence on the proposal that the syntax/discourse/pragmatics interface is particularly problematic in L2. There is less agreement on whether the problems are in some sense grammar external, allowing the claim that L2 grammars as such are not defective, or whether there are in fact problems with representation in the C-domain (either functional categories or features associated with them). Nevertheless, under either kind of analysis, the assumption is that interfaces are vulnerable to cross-linguistic influence: how topic and focus are realized in the L1 continues to influence how they are realized in the interlanguage, leading to overuse of overt subjects, overuse of SV word order, problems with realization of specificity and inappropriate use of scrambling, amongst other things.

### C. Articulatory–Perceptual

   We now turn, more briefly, to the other traditional external interface, namely the articulatory–perceptual system, mediated by PF. While there has been considerable research on L2 speech perception and production over the years, there is little that explicitly addresses interface issues. Research that is relevant in this context is found in a series of experiments by Brown (2000). She examines how the L2er's L1 phonological representations inhibit or facilitate perception of L2 speech sounds. Where perception is inhibited, acquisition of new phonological contrasts proves to be impossible.

Brown hypothesizes that L2 speech perception is constrained by the L1 feature inventory. If a contrastive feature is absent in the L1, learners will be unable to perceive, hence unable to acquire, L2 contrasts that depend on that feature. In other words, they will fail to distinguish between two L2 phonemes that depend on a distinctive feature not present in the L1 feature inventory. This explains difficulties that Japanese speakers have with English /l/ versus /r/. In Japanese, these sounds are allophones, because Japanese lacks the coronal feature which distinguishes between them. Brown's claim is that, in the absence of the relevant contrastive feature in the L1, it is impossible to discriminate between the two sounds in the L2, where they are separate phonemes. In other words, there is no motivation to construct a new representation for English. In a series of experiments, Brown shows that Japanese speakers are indeed unable to perceive the English l/r contrast. In sum, the L1 phonology (in particular, the feature inventory) blocks perception of certain phonetic properties of the L2 input. The existing grammar leads to a total block at a crucial interface.

## D. Sentence Processing

There is another grammar-external interface which has recently begun to receive considerable attention in the L2 literature (Clahsen & Felser, 2006; see also Dussias & Piñar, this volume). This is the interface between the grammar and the parser. When listening to sentences, speakers must assign a structural representation to each utterance; this is known as *parsing*. Hence, the computational system must interface with the parser (and with the production system as well, although this will not be addressed here). Of particular interest is the fact that, in some cases, there appear to be cross-linguistic differences as to parsing procedures or preferences.

Considering the relationship between the grammar and the parser, there are at least two possibilities for a breakdown at this interface: (i) L2ers might acquire a grammar appropriate to the L2 but have problems specific to L2 parsing, sometimes resorting to inappropriate parsing routines or (ii) L2ers might fail to acquire a grammar appropriate to the L2, resulting in an inability to assign native-like structural representations, with consequences for L2 parsing.[4] Another possibility, of course, is that neither the grammar nor the parser is in any way disrupted, at least in very advanced L2ers; in consequence, L2ers manifest no parsing problems, behaving instead like native speakers (Hopp, 2006).

One way of addressing such issues has been to consider how the parser deals with ambiguity resolution, including cases such as (8), which involves relative clause attachment. In (8), the relative clause *who went to a private clinic* could potentially be interpreted as modifying the first NP (*the daughter*) (known as *high attachment*) or the second NP (*the actor*) (known as *low attachment*). The grammar permits both interpretations but native speakers of English show a parsing preference for low

---

[4]Sorace and Filiaci (2006) offer another possibility: the grammar and parsing procedures may both be appropriate for the L2 but integrating them causes difficulties.

attachment, whereas native speakers of Spanish prefer high attachment in equivalent sentences in Spanish.

(8)   Someone shot the daughter of the actor who went to a private clinic

Fernández (2002) and Dussias (2003) have investigated how bilingual English/ Spanish speakers parse such sentences and report that they do not behave like monolinguals. Fernández found that bilinguals use the parsing routines of their dominant language: English-dominant speakers preferred low attachment in both languages, Spanish-dominant chose high attachment in both languages. Dussias, on the other hand, found a preference for low attachment, regardless of dominance or language being tested. Both these studies assume that a grammar appropriate for the L2 has been acquired; nevertheless, parsing preferences appropriate for one language are sometimes implemented in the other language, resulting in interpretations which are not ungrammatical but which differ from monolingual preferences.

Other research has focused on the parsing of long-distance (filler/gap) dependencies, where some constituent (the filler), such as a wh-phrase, appears early in the sentence but has to be associated with a gap (*e*) later in the sentence, as in (9). In (9a), *who* is associated with a subject gap—it must be interpreted as the subject of the embedded verb—whereas in (9b), it is associated with an object gap and is interpreted as the object of the embedded verb. Note that in (9b), the wh-phrase is associated with two gaps, one in the position in which it must be interpreted (as the object of *fire*), as well as an intermediate gap. In (9c), on the other hand, the wh-phrase, *who*, cannot be associated with the gap in the embedded clause; there is no position for an intermediate gap (since this position is filled by *whether*) and the sentence is ungrammatical, due to a violation of the subjacency constraint.

(9)   a. [Who$_i$ does Jane expect [$e_i$ to win]]?
      b. [Who$_i$ does Bill think [$e_i$ Jane will fire $e_i$]]?
      c. *[Who$_i$ does Bill wonder [whether Jane will fire $e_i$]]?

In recent work, Clahsen and Felser (2006) have advanced the Shallow Parsing Hypothesis, which claims that the syntactic component of the L2 grammar is defective. As a result, when the parser interfaces with the L2 grammar, certain syntactic analyses—including the postulation of intermediate gaps—are unavailable. Instead, L2ers rely heavily on lexical, semantic and pragmatic information when processing sentences. According to Clahsen and Felser, sentences involving long-distance dependencies cannot be parsed in a native-like way: while native speakers show an activation effect (manifested as shorter reading times) in sentences with intermediate gaps, L2ers fail to do so. Clahsen and Felser maintain that this means that something is missing from the interlanguage syntactic structure. In fact, this claim cannot be entirely correct. According to the Shallow Parsing Hypothesis, in the absence of intermediate gaps, sentences like (9b) and (9c) should be equally grammatical, and equally parsable. But in fact, there is ample evidence that L2ers observe syntactic constraints on long-distance dependencies, such as subjacency (Juffs & Harrington,

1995; White & Juffs, 1998), judging sentences like (9b) differently from (9c), something which is unexpected on the Shallow Parsing Hypothesis.[5]

To conclude this section, with respect to the interface between grammar and parser, there are considerable discrepancies in results, and disagreements as to how to interpret them. In a number of cases, it does indeed appear that L2ers behave differently from native speakers: some studies report native-like grammar but non-native parsing; some report effects of L1 parsing strategies; some report serious grammatical defects which impinge on L2 parsing. While the issues are by no means resolved, this interface is one which is stimulating fruitful lines of investigation.[6]

## IV. INTERNAL INTERFACES

We now turn to interfaces between different modules internal to the grammar, particularly the relationships between syntax, semantics, morphology and phonology. In addition, the lexicon interfaces with all these domains.

### A. Syntax/Semantics

The syntax/semantics interface potentially overlaps with the external conceptual structure interface. Here, however, we will concentrate on research that examines grammar-internal interface issues. Dekydtspotter and colleagues, in a number of papers on L2 French, have explored the syntax/semantics interface, with a particular emphasis on situations where word-order alternations in the L2 syntax result in subtle interpretative differences (not due to discourse), and where the L1 and L2 differ in the relevant respects.

For example Dekydtspotter, Sprouse, and Swanson (2001) investigate interpretive properties of French continuous (10a) and discontinuous (10b) *combien* (how many) (examples from Dekydtspotter et al., 2001). In particular, they investigate whether L2ers are sensitive to very subtle interactions between scope and syntactic position when indefinite objects (*combien de livres*, 'how many books') and quantified subjects *(les étudiants tous*, 'the students all'*)* are involved.

(10)   a.  <u>Combien de livres</u> est-ce que les étudiants achètent tous?
           How-many of books is it that the students buy all?
           'How many books are the students all buying?'
     b.  <u>Combien</u> est-ce que les étudiants achètent tous <u>de livres</u>?

---

[5]Note that the research that Clahsen and Felser (2006) report on involves gaps in sentences more complex than those in (9), including extraction within relative clauses, as in (i):

(i)  The nurse [*who*$_i$ the doctor argued [$e_i$ that the rude patient had angered $e_i$]] is refusing to work late.

[6]Fodor (2002) suggests that an internal interface is implicated in parsing as well. She points out that many of the syntactic ambiguities traditionally investigated in the parsing literature become unambiguous once prosody (including silent prosody) is taken into account.

To understand what is under consideration, imagine a scenario in which there are several students, each of who is buying four books at the beginning of the semester. All of them buy the required text for the class and then each of them buys three other books, but they do not buy the same books as each other. Following such a scenario, one can ask the question in (10a) or the question in (10b). It should be noted that (10a), where *combien* is contiguous with *de livres*, is the more usual way of phrasing such a question.

Both questions can be answered in terms of the number of books bought by each student (namely, four), the narrow scope reading. (10a) can also be answered in terms of the number of books in common (in this case, one), the wide scope reading (even though this may not be the interpretation that springs immediately to mind). However, one sentence is not a simple permutation of the other: (10b) cannot have the wide scope interpretation. In other words, there is a scope ambiguity with continuous *combien* which disappears with the discontinuous version of the sentence. The change in word order (syntax) results in the loss of an interpretation (semantics).

*How many* in English behaves like continuous *combien* in French; in other words, the scopal ambiguity is there, though, again, one of the readings (the narrow scope reading) is more prominent. Dekydtspotter et al. demonstrate that advanced L2ers (like native speakers and unlike intermediate L2ers) accept the wide scope answer (number in common, i.e. one) significantly less with discontinuous *combien* than with continuous, whereas the narrow scope interpretation (answer, four books) was accepted equally, regardless of word order. (The intermediate group differed from the advanced group and the native speakers in disliking the discontinuous construction altogether.)

Dekydtspotter and colleagues have investigated a number of other cases where French (the L2) exhibits alternations not found in English (the L1), and where these alternations result in interpretative differences. These include result and process nominals and multiple de-phrases (*la version de la 9e de Karajan* vs. *\*la destruction de Tokyo de Godzilla*) (Dekydtspotter, Sprouse, & Anderson, 1997), as well as *wh*-quantifiers with adjectival restrictions (*qui de célèbre fumait* vs. *qui fumait de célèbre*) (Dekydtspotter & Sprouse, 2001). In these cases, just like the case of continuous versus discontinuous *combien*, L2ers, like native speakers, show a clear pattern of contrasting judgments indicating sensitivity to interpretive contrasts.

In sum, the syntax/semantics interface is NOT generally a problem area: once L2ers get beyond L1 transfer, they do in fact acquire the relevant subtle interpretive distinctions that hold only for the L2. In the example involving *combien*, it was the fact that the syntax of the L2 permits a discontinuous construction, unlike the L1, that caused problems to the intermediate proficiency group. Once this syntactic property was acquired, the interpretive contrasts fell into place.

## B. Syntax/Morphology

The finding of relative success at the syntax/semantics interface contrasts with other internal interfaces, including the interface between syntax and morphology. L2ers are well known to have difficulties in realizing bound inflectional morphology and free function words, which may be omitted or supplied variably. For example, tense marking is sometimes omitted and sometimes supplied by the same speaker (compare (11a) and (11b), from Lardiere, 1998); the same is true for articles (compare (11c) and (11d), from White, 2003a).

(11)   a. He call me last night
       b. We spoke English to her
       c. I'm expecting telephone call
       d. And she cleans the house

Sometimes morphology is produced but the form is inappropriate. For example non-finite verbs may be used where a finite verb should appear, as in (12a) (Prévost & White, 2000), or masculine gender may be used in feminine contexts, as in (12b) (from White, Valenzuela, Kozlowska-Macgregor, & Leung, 2004).

(12)   a. möchten ma du ein Kaffee?
          want-INF then you a coffee
          'Would you like a coffee?'
       b. la barba rojo
          the-F beard-F red-M
          'the red beard'

A fruitful line of investigation has attempted to explain such behaviour in terms of an interface problem between the morphosyntactic representation and the lexicon.[7] A number of researchers have suggested that when variable or missing inflection is observed in L2, it is missing only at a surface level (Haznedar & Schwartz, 1997; Lardiere, 1998, 2000; Prévost & White, 2000; amongst others). The idea is that failure to produce verbs inflected for tense, for example is not indicative of a defective or impaired grammatical representation. Rather, an abstract tense feature is represented in the syntax but the learner fails to consistently link this feature to the particular form /-ed/ by which it is realized in English. Lardiere (2000) sees this as a problem mapping between interlanguage syntax and lexicon; Prévost and White (2000) attribute the problem to difficulties in accessing inflected lexical items, particularly when speaking.

The theory of distributed morphology (DM) (Halle & Marantz, 1993) can accommodate such accounts, assuming the (late) insertion of underspecified vocabulary items. In DM, the features of a syntactic node (such as tense, person, number and gender) are fully specified, while features of lexical items are not necessarily fully specified, some being underspecified (on theory internal grounds). For lexical insertion to take place, the features of the vocabulary item must be consistent with the features of the relevant terminal node in the syntax, but there does not have to be an exact match: it is sufficient that the features of the vocabulary item form a proper subset of the features of the syntactic node. L2ers, it appears, have a tendency to insert underspecified forms (often uninflected) in contexts where a more fully specified form is required. Accounts

---

[7]Other accounts (e.g. Hawkins, this volume) attribute morphological difficulties to absence of features in the syntactic representation; in other words, a syntactic problem is implicated, rather than an interface problem.

along these lines have been offered for L2 tense and agreement (Prévost & White, 2000) and gender (Bruhn de Garavito & White, 2002; Hulk & Cornips, 2006; White et al., 2004).

In recent work, McCarthy (2007) proposes various refinements to this idea. In particular, she argues that a theory of morphological underspecification can predict the defaults chosen by L2ers. She notes that defaults are not the same across languages and that they do not necessarily involve uninflected forms; in Spanish, for example finite third person singular is independently motivated as the underspecified form for agreement. This contrasts with English, where the default is the bare form of the verb. In principle, the L2er could make two types of errors: underspecification (use of a non-target form whose features are underspecified) or feature clash (use of a non-target form whose features clash with those required by the syntax). In a context like (13), where the syntactic representation requires first person singular, the only incorrect form that avoids a feature clash is the default form-*a* (as in 13a), rather than faulty inflection involving feature clash (as in 13b) (examples from McCarthy, 2007).

(13)   a. yo habla (underspecification)
          I speak-3s
        b. yo hablas (feature clash)
          I speak-2s

Experimental research confirms her proposal: agreement errors in L2 Spanish almost invariably involve overuse of third person singular. Furthermore, McCarthy finds that use of underspecified defaults affects comprehension as well as production. Importantly the morphologically underspecified forms that surface in L2 are exactly the same as those representations would be in the grammar of a monolingual adult native speaker. What is different from native speakers is that, for some as yet not fully understood reason, the underspecified forms surface in contexts where a more fully specified form would be appropriate.

To summarize, problems with realization of inflectional morphology are common, going along with success in corresponding syntax (see Lardiere, 1998; White, 2003a; White et al., 2004). Morphological errors do not, however, suggest total absence of the relevant morphology, nor of the associated morphosyntactic properties. Rather, in certain circumstances, there appear to be difficulties in accessing lexical items that are in fact represented in the grammar/lexicon, allowing defaults to surface. This is an interface issue: the syntax 'wants' one thing, but the lexicon supplies something else.

## C. Phonology/Morphology

The final interface domain to be considered here concerns the relationship between the phonological component of the grammar and morphology (and syntax). In recent work, Goad and White propose a prosodic account of L2ers' omission or mispronunciation of inflectional morphology and function words, couched within a theory of prosodic transfer (Goad & White, 2004, 2006; Goad, White, & Steele, 2003). According to the Prosodic Transfer Hypothesis (PTH), L1 prosodic structure constrains interlanguage production of material typically associated with syntactic functional categories, such as tense, agreement, number and determiners. In particular,

L2ers have difficulties constructing prosodic representations which are disallowed in the L1.

Consider English past tense as an example. As far as the morphosyntactic representation is concerned, it makes no difference whether past tense is realized as regular or irregular; rather, the issue is that there is a functional head, T, with a ±past feature, as shown in (14).

(14) Regular vs. irregular inflection: syntactic representation

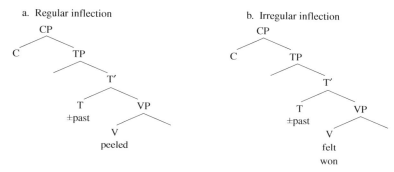

The prosodic representation, on the other hand, makes a crucial distinction between regular and irregular inflection, as shown in (15). In particular, regular inflection (e.g. *peeled*) is realized by adjunction to the prosodic word (PWd) (see 15a), whereas pseudo-inflection (*felt*) and suppletion (*won*) are realized PWd internally (see 15b). Hence, the appropriate pronunciation of English past tense requires integration of syntactic and phonological representations: if L2ers have acquired the appropriate syntactic representation but not the appropriate prosodic one, they may be unable to pronounce certain inflections, or they may pronounce them in ways which circumvent the relevant prosodic representation.

(15) Regular vs. irregular inflection: prosodic representation

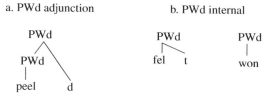

Goad et al. (2003) and White (2007) investigate the L2 English of Mandarin speakers. Mandarin lacks overt morphological realization of tense and agreement, as well as PWd adjunction in general. Goad and colleagues show that Mandarin speakers have a morphosyntactic tense feature in their interlanguage English, as shown by their behaviour on a variety of tasks, including sentence completion and grammaticality judgments. At the same time, some learners have problems in organizing inflection into the prosodic structure (PWd adjunction) required for target-like production in English. In consequence, they delete regular inflection across the board in production, or they use an L1 structure (involving a PWd-internal representation) in so far as this is possible. Goad and White (2006) show that PWd adjunction is eventually acquired.

In a related vein, Bruhn de Garavito (2007) examines the acquisition of Spanish by native speakers of French, with a focus on plural morphology. Given that French and Spanish are similar with respect to morphosyntactic realization of plural, it might be expected that French speakers would have no difficulties in realizing the L2 Spanish morphology. But, in fact, at lower proficiency levels, French speakers (unlike English speakers) omit the Spanish plural (-s/-es) 38% of the time in obligatory contexts. Bruhn de Garavito attributes this to transfer of French syllable structure, in particular, to the fact that French (unlike Spanish and English) does not license a syllable final [s].

## V. CONCLUSION

We have seen that recent approaches to SLA from the perspective of grammatical theory have focused on linguistic interfaces, both external and internal. Well-known L2 phenomena, such as variability, optionality, transfer and fossilization, have been explained in terms of interfaces or have been claimed to be more likely to occur at interfaces.

One important point to bear in mind is that the need to integrate different kinds of linguistic material at the interfaces is not something unique to L2 acquisition. On the contrary, the interface between syntax and discourse/pragmatics has received considerable attention elsewhere and has been identified as an area of difficulty in L1 acquisition (e.g. Schaeffer, 2000), in simultaneous bilingual acquisition, for a variety of language combinations (e.g. Haznedar, 2007; Hulk & Müller, 2000; Paradis & Navarro, 2003; Serratrice, Sorace, & Paoli, 2004), in cases of heritage language acquisition (Montrul, 2004) as well as in L1 attrition (Tsimpli, Sorace, Heycock, & Filiaci, 2004). Hence, what happens in L2 acquisition must be understood in a wider context.

Much of the research reviewed above has suggested that interface areas are potentially problematic and that the problems are not (necessarily) on the side of the computational system as such. Rather, they are the result of how external domains impinge on the grammar (or vice versa) or how one area of the grammar impinges on another. This does not, however, imply that all interfaces are equally problematic. Indeed, Tsimpli and Sorace (2006) suggest that grammar-internal interfaces, such as the syntax/semantics interface, cause fewer problems than grammar-external interfaces, such as the syntax/discourse interface. Some of the results reviewed above support such a proposal. For example, Dekydtspotter and colleagues have found that L2ers are successful in acquiring subtle properties relating to the syntax/semantics interface. In other words, the L2ers showed no difficulties attributable to the interface as such. Nevertheless, it is clear that other internal interfaces do create difficulties, for example the syntax/morphology interface or the phonology/morphology interface. What remains unresolved is to what extent underlying interlanguage representations are implicated; this may prove to be something that differs from interface to interface.

# REFERENCES

Belletti, A., Bennati, E., & Sorace, A. (2007). Theoretical and developmental issues in the syntax of subjects: Evidence from near-native Italian. *Natural Language and Linguistic Theory*, 25, 657–689.

Belletti, A., & Leonini, C. (2004). Subject inversion in L2 Italian. In S. Foster-Cohen, M. Sharwood Smith, A. Sorace, & M. Ota (Eds.), *Eurosla Yearbook 4* (pp. 95–118). Amsterdam: John Benjamins.

Bohnacker, U., & Rosén, C. (2007). Transferring information-structural patterns from Swedish to German. In A. Belikova, L. Meroni & M. Umeda (Eds.), *Proceedings of Generative Approaches to Language Acquisition North America 2*. Somerville, MA: Cascadilla Proceedings Project.

Brown, C. (2000). The interrelation between speech perception and phonological acquisition from infant to adult. In J. Archibald (Ed.), *Second language acquisition and linguistic theory* (pp. 4–63). Oxford: Blackwell.

Bruhn de Garavito, J. (2007). Acquisition of the Spanish plural by French L1 speakers: The role of transfer. In J. Liceras, H. Zobl, & H. Goodluck (Eds.), *The role of features in second language acquisition* (pp. 271–298). Mahweh, NJ: Lawrence Erlbaum.

Bruhn de Garavito, J., & White, L. (2002). L2 acquisition of Spanish DPs: The status of grammatical features. In A. T. Pérez-Leroux & J. Liceras (Eds.), *The acquisition of Spanish morphosyntax: The L1/L2 connection* (pp. 153–178). Dordrecht: Kluwer.

Burzio, L. (1986). *Italian syntax: A government-binding approach*. Dordrecht: Reidel.

Chomsky, N. (1965). *Aspects of the theory of syntax*. Cambridge, MA: MIT Press.

Chomsky, N. (1981). *Lectures on government and binding*. Dordrecht: Foris.

Chomsky, N. (1986). *Knowledge of language: Its nature, origin, and use*. New York: Praeger.

Chomsky, N. (1993). A minimalist program for linguistic theory. In K. Hale & S. J. Keyser (Eds.), *The view from building 20: Essays in linguistics in honor of Sylvain Bromberger* (pp. 1–52). Cambridge, MA: M.I.T. Press.

Clahsen, H., & Felser, C. (2006). Grammatical processing in language learners. *Applied Psycholinguistics*, 27, 3–42.

Dekydtspotter, L., & Sprouse, R. (2001). Mental design and (second) language epistemology: Adjectival restrictions of wh-quantifiers and tense in English–French interlanguage. *Second Language Research*, 17, 1–35.

Dekydtspotter, L., Sprouse, R., & Anderson, B. (1997). The interpretive interface in L2 acquisition: The process-result distinction in English-French interlanguage grammars. *Language Acquisition*, 6, 297–332.

Dekydtspotter, L., Sprouse, R., & Swanson, K. (2001). Reflexes of mental architecture in second-language acquisition: The interpretation of *combien* extractions in English-French interlanguage. *Language Acquisition*, 9, 175–227.

Dussias, P. (2003). Syntactic ambiguity resolution in L2 learners: Some effects of bilinguality on L1 and L2 processing strategies. *Studies in Second Language Acquisition*, 25, 529–557.

Dussias, P., & Piñar, P. (This volume). Second language acquisition and sentence processing. In W. C. Ritchie & T. K. Bhatia (Eds.), *The new handbook of second language acquisition*. Bingley, UK: Emerald Group Publishing Limited.

Fernández, E. (2002). *Bilingual sentence processing: Relative clause attachment in English and Spanish*. Amsterdam: John Benjamins.

Fodor, J. (2002). Prosodic disambiguation in silent reading. In M. Hirotani (Ed.), *Proceedings of the Thirty-Second Annual Meeting of the North-Eastern Linguistic Society* (pp. 113–137). Amherst, MA: GLSA.

Goad, H., & White, L. (2004). Ultimate attainment of L2 inflection: Effects of L1 prosodic structure. In S. Foster-Cohen, M. Sharwood Smith, A. Sorace, & M. Ota (Eds.), *Eurosla Yearbook, 4* (pp. 119–145). Amsterdam: John Benjamins.

Goad, H., & White, L. (2006). Ultimate attainment in interlanguage grammars: A prosodic approach. *Second Language Research, 22,* 243–268.

Goad, H., White, L., & Steele, J. (2003). Missing inflection in L2 acquisition: Defective syntax or L1-constrained prosodic representations? *Canadian Journal of Linguistics, 48,* 243–263.

Gürel, A. (2006). L2 acquisition of pragmatic and syntactic constraints in the use of overt and null subject pronouns. In R. Slabakova, S. Montrul, & P. Prévost (Eds.), *Inquiries in linguistic development: in honor of Lydia White* (pp. 259–282). Amsterdam: John Benjamins.

Halle, M., & Marantz, A. (1993). Distributed morphology and the pieces of inflection. In K. Hale & S. J. Keyser (Eds.), *The view from building* (Vol. 20, pp. 111–176). Cambridge, MA: MIT Press.

Hawkins, R. (this volume). Second language acquisition of morphosyntax. In W. C. Ritchie & T. K. Bhatia (Eds.), *The new handbook of second language acquisition.* Bingley, UK: Emerald Group Publishing Limited.

Haznedar, B. (2007). Crosslinguistic interference in Turkish-English bilingual first language acquisition: The overuse of subjects in. In A. Belikova, L. Meroni, & M. Umeda (Eds.), *Proceedings of Generative Approaches to Language Acquisition North America 2.* Somerville, MA: Cascadilla Proceedings Project.

Haznedar, B., & Schwartz, B. D. (1997). Are there optional infinitives in child L2 acquisition? In E. Hughes, M. Hughes, & A. Greenhill (Eds.), *Proceedings of the 21st Annual Boston University Conference on Language Development,* Somerville (pp. 257–268). MA: Cascadilla Press.

Hertel, T. J. (2003). Lexical and discourse factors in the second language acquisition of Spanish word order. *Second Language Research, 19,* 273–304.

Hopp, H. (2004). Syntactic and interface knowledge in advanced and near-native interlanguage grammars. In S. Foster-Cohen, M. Sharwood Smith, A. Sorace, & M. Ota (Eds.), *Eurosla Yearbook 4* (pp. 67–94). Amsterdam: John Benjamins.

Hopp, H. (2006). Syntactic features and reanalysis in near-native processing. *Second Language Research, 22,* 369–397.

Hornstein, N., & Lightfoot, D. (Eds.). (1981). *Explanation in linguistics: The logical problem of language acquisition.* London: Longman.

Hulk, A., & Cornips, L. (2006). Neuter gender and interface vulnerability in child L2/2L1 Dutch. In S. Unsworth, T. Parodi, A. Sorace, & M. Young-Scholten (Eds.), *Paths of development in L1 and L2 acquisition* (pp. 107–134). Amsterdam: John Benjamins.

Hulk, A., & Müller, N. (2000). Bilingual first language acquisition at the interface between syntax and pragmatics. *Bilingualism: Language and Cognition, 3,* 227–244.

Jackendoff, R. (2002). *Foundations of language.* Oxford: Oxford University Press.

Juffs, A., & Harrington, M. (1995). Parsing effects in second language sentence processing: Subject and object asymmetries in wh-extraction. *Studies in Second Language Acquisition, 17,* 483–516.

Lardiere, D. (1998). Case and tense in the 'fossilized' steady state. *Second Language Research, 14,* 1–26.

Lardiere, D. (2000). Mapping features to forms in second language acquisition. In J. Archibald (Ed.), *Second language acquisition and linguistic theory* (pp. 102–129). Oxford: Blackwell.

Liceras, J. (1988). Syntax and stylistics: More on the pro-drop parameter. In J. Pankhurst, M. Sharwood Smith, & P. Van Buren (Eds.), *Learnability and second languages: A book of readings* (pp. 71–93). Dordrecht: Foris.

Lozano, C. (2006). Focus and split-intransitivity: The acquisition of word order alternations in non-native Spanish. *Second Language Research, 22,* 145–187.

McCarthy, C. (2007). *Morphological variability in second language Spanish.* Ph.D. dissertation, McGill University.

Montrul, S. (2004). Subject and object expression in Spanish heritage speakers: A case of morphosyntactic convergence. *Bilingualism: Language and Cognition, 7,* 125–142.

Montrul, S., & Louro, C. R. (2006). Beyond the syntax of the null subject parameter. In V. Torrens & L. Escobar (Eds.), *The acquisition of syntax in Romance languages* (pp. 401–418). Amsterdam: John Benjamins.

Paradis, J., & Navarro, S. (2003). Subject realization and crosslinguistic interference in the bilingual acquisition of Spanish and English: What is the role of input? *Journal of Child Language, 30,* 371–393.

Platzack, C. (2001). The vulnerable C-domain. *Brain and Language, 77,* 364–377.

Prévost, P., & White, L. (2000). Missing surface inflection or impairment in second language acquisition? Evidence from tense and agreement. *Second Language Research, 16,* 103–133.

Rizzi, L. (1997). The fine structure of the left periphery. In L. Haegeman (Ed.), *Elements of grammar: Handbook in generative syntax* (pp. 281–337). Dordrecht: Kluwer.

Schaeffer, J. (2000). *Direct object scrambling and clitic placement: Syntax and pragmatics.* Amsterdam: John Benjamins.

Serratrice, L., Sorace, A., & Paoli, S. (2004). Crosslinguistic influence at the syntax-pragmatics interface: Subjects and objects in English-Italian bilingual and monolingual acquisition. *Bilingualism: Language and Cognition, 7,* 183–205.

Sorace, A. (2003). Near-nativeness. In C. Doughty & M. Long (Eds.), *Handbook of second language acquisition* (pp. 130–151). Oxford: Blackwell.

Sorace, A., & Filiaci, F. (2006). Anaphora resolution in near-native speakers of Italian. *Second Language Research, 22,* 339–368.

Tsimpli, I., Sorace, A., Heycock, C., & Filiaci, F. (2004). First language attrition and syntactic subjects: A study of Greek and Italian near-native speakers of English. *International Journal of Bilingualism, 8,* 257–277.

Tsimpli, I.-M., & Sorace, A. (2006). Differentiating interfaces: L2 performance in syntax-semantics and syntax-discourse phenomena. In D. Bamman, T. Magnitskaia, & C. Zaller (Eds.), *Proceedings of the 30th Annual Boston University Conference on Language Development (BU)* (pp. 653–664). Somerville, MA: Cascadilla Press.

Valenzuela, E. (2006). L2 end state grammars and incomplete acquisition of the Spanish CLLD constructions. In R. Slabakova, S. Montrul, & P. Prévost (Eds.), *Inquiries in linguistic development: In honor of Lydia White* (pp. 283–304). Amsterdam: John Benjamins.

White, L. (1989). *Universal grammar and second language acquisition.* Amsterdam: John Benjamins.

White, L. (2003a). Fossilization in steady state L2 grammars: Persistent problems with inflectional morphology. *Bilingualism: Language and Cognition, 6,* 129–141.

White, L. (2003b). *Second language acquisition and universal grammar.* Cambridge, UK: Cambridge University Press.

White, L. (2007). Some puzzling features of L2 features. In J. Liceras, H. Zobl, & H. Goodluck (Eds.), *The role of features in second language acquisition* (pp. 301–326). Mahwah, NJ: Lawrence Erlbaum.

White, L., & Juffs, A. (1998). Constraints on wh-movement in two different contexts of non-native language acquisition: Competence and processing. In S. Flynn, G. Martohardjono, & W. O'Neil (Eds.), *The generative study of second language acquisition* (pp. 111–129). Mahweh, NJ: Lawrence Erlbaum.

White, L., Valenzuela, E., Kozlowska-Macgregor, M., & Leung, Y.-K. I. (2004). Gender agreement in nonnative Spanish: Evidence against failed features. *Applied Psycholinguistics, 25,* 105–133.

CHAPTER 4

# EMERGENTISM AND SECOND LANGUAGE ACQUISITION

William O'Grady, Miseon Lee and Hye-Young Kwak

## I. INTRODUCTION

Language presents us with many puzzles. Why does it have the particular properties that it does? Why does it vary and change in certain ways, but not in others? How is it acquired so quickly and with so little effort by preschool children despite its apparent complexity? And why is the acquisition of a second language so difficult for adults, despite their intellectual sophistication and their access to carefully designed educational programs?

An attractive feature of approaches to language based on universal grammar (UG) is that they offer an integrated account of these puzzles—an inborn system of grammatical categories and principles gives language its defining properties, places limits on the ways in which it can vary and change, and explains how even the most complex phenomena are acquired with such ease by children. With the help of additional assumptions, it even appears possible to offer insights into why the acquisition of a second language proves so challenging.

Yet the UG-based program has encountered deep suspicion and resistance from many quarters during the half century that it has dominated explanatory work on language. For a significant segment of the professional linguistic community, it simply does not ring true. The objections vary with the commentator—UG principles are too abstract (Tomasello, 2003, pp. 3–7), the type of nativism that UG seems to presuppose is biologically implausible (Elman et al., 1996; MacWhinney, 2000), a focus on faculty-specific principles distances the study of language from the rest of cognitive science (Jackendoff, 1988, 2002, pp. xi–xii), the phenomena purportedly accounted for by UG theories are better explained in other ways (Haspelmath, 2008; Hawkins, 2004; O'Grady, 2005), and so forth. But is there an alternative?

69

In recent years, much of the opposition to the UG program has coalesced around a loosely associated set of ideas that have come to be grouped together under the rubric of emergentism. Despite the very considerable diversity of emergentist thought, there seems to be at least one central thesis to which all of its various proponents adhere: The complexity of language must be understood in terms of the interaction of simpler and more basic nonlinguistic factors.

In the case of language, it has been suggested that those factors include features of human physiology (the vocal tract, for instance), the nature of the perceptual mechanisms, the effect of pragmatic principles, the role of social interaction in communication, the character of the learning mechanisms, and limitations on working memory and processing capacity, but not inborn grammatical principles.

The earliest emergentist work focused on the important problem of how children acquire a language in response to the sorts of experience typical of childhood. More recently, there has been growing interest in the relevance of emergentism to understanding second language acquisition (SLA) as well, marked in part by the fact that three major journals have devoted special issues to the examination and evaluation of emergentist work on SLA—*Applied Linguistics* (2006), under the editorship of Nick Ellis and Diane Larsen-Freeman; *Lingua* (2008), edited by Roger Hawkins; and *The Modern Language Journal* (2008), under the editorship of Kees de Bot. Although modest in comparison to work in the UG framework, the emergentist literature on SLA offers analyses for a representative range of phenomena, including grammatical morphology (Ellis, 2006b), competition-based processing (MacWhinney, 2008, and the references cited there), quantifier scope (O'Grady, 2007), and *want to* contraction (O'Grady, Nakamura, & Ito, 2008). See Ellis and Larsen-Freeman (2006) for some general discussion.

## II. EMERGENTIST APPROACHES TO LANGUAGE ACQUISITION

Emergentist approaches to language acquisition can be divided into two types, depending on the dominant explanatory strategy that they adopt. On the one hand, there is a very influential and impressive body of research that focuses on the importance of the input (or usage) for understanding how language acquisition works. Ellis (2002, 2006a) provides a far-reaching discussion of this approach. On the other hand, a smaller body of research explores the role of the processor–working memory interface in language acquisition, addressing problems of learnability and development that have traditionally been the exclusive domain of UG-based work. O'Grady (2008a, 2008c) offers an introduction to this approach. Let us consider each program in more detail.

### A. Input-Based Emergentism

One of the earliest examples of a systematic input-based approach to language learning is the Competition Model put forward by Brian MacWhinney (MacWhinney, 1987; Bates & MacWhinney, 1987). This approach, which remains highly influential, offers a theory of how language learners come to identify and prioritize the various competing cues (word order, animacy, case, agreement, and so on) that are relevant to sentence comprehension. The key variables, MacWhinney suggests, are to be found in the input: How often the cue is present when a particular pattern is being interpreted (cue availability), and how often it points to a particular interpretation (cue reliability). In the case of English, for instance, word order is a highly available and reliable cue for identifying a sentence's subject—which almost always occurs preverbally. In contrast, agreement is highly reliable (only subjects trigger agreement), but is often unavailable since there is so little inflection in English. The situation could well be reversed in a free word order language, where agreement (or case) might be both more available and more reliable than word order.

Pioneering work of a different sort in the input-oriented tradition has been carried out by Jeffrey Elman (e.g., 1993, 2002, 2005), who has employed the techniques of connectionist modeling to investigate the language acquisition process. This has led to a number of intriguing findings, including Lewis and Elman's (2001) demonstration that a simple recurrent network (SRN)[1] can simulate the acquisition of agreement in English from data similar to the input available to children.

A focus on the input is also characteristic of many other scholars working in an emergentist framework. A recurring intuition is that the frequency with which particular phenomena are encountered plays a key role in shaping the developmental process. One of the strongest advocates of this view is Nick Ellis (e.g., 2002, 2006a, 2006b), who holds that language learning is, in essence, "the gathering of information about the relative frequency of form-function mappings" (2006a, p. 1)—with provisos concerning perceptibility (see below), attention, interference from other languages, and the like.

Frequency also has an important role to play in the view of language acquisition associated with Construction Grammar and other usage-based theories. As Michael Tomasello observes (2003, p. 327), language acquisition in such theories "depends crucially on the type and token frequency with which certain structures appear in the input"—an idea that has been put forward and developed in promising ways by Goldberg (1998), Goldberg and Casenhiser (2008), and Ambridge, Theakston, Lieven, and Tomasello (2006), among many others. A similar attention to frequency guides research in other areas of cognitive science too, including psycholinguistics and neurolinguistics (e.g., Chater & Manning, 2006; Chang, Dell, & Bock, 2006; Dick et al., 2001; Ferreira, 2003) as well as the study of language change (e.g., Bybee & Hopper, 2001).

## In Defense of Frequency Factors

In considering the role of input frequency in language acquisition (first or second), it is vital to bear in mind a key point: What counts is not how many times learners hear a particular form—it is how many times they encounter *mappings* between a form and its meaning. An illustration of why this distinction is important comes from the English determiner *the*.

Although *the* is the most frequent word in the English language, it is mastered relatively late, both in first language acquisition and second language learning. How

---

[1]An SRN processes patterns of sequentially ordered elements, producing outputs that are a function of both the current input and the SRN's own internal state. SRNs are especially good at noticing local co-occurrence relationships—given the word X, what's the likelihood that the next word will be Y?

can this fact be reconciled with the claim that frequency has a major role in shaping the language acquisition process? Two observations are crucial.

First, as noted by Ellis (2006b, p. 171), grammatical functors are frequently difficult to perceive on the basis of "bottom-up" (purely acoustic) evidence. Herron and Bates (1997) had subjects identify semi-homophonous function words and content words (the pronoun *I* and the noun *eye*, the auxiliary verb *will* and the noun *will*, and so on) that had been spliced into various contexts—some neutral, some appropriate for just the content word, and some appropriate for just the function word. They found that even adult native speakers of English were able to recognize the word out of its normal context as little as half the time.

Second, contextual indeterminacy often undermines the association of a form with its intended meaning. As Ionin, Zubizarreta, and Maldonado (2008) observe, for example, it is no small matter to determine that the *the–a* contrast in English turns on definiteness rather than specificity. Language learners must confront two sorts of problems. Not only is the contrast between definiteness and specificity a subtle one, definites are often specific, as in the following example from Ionin et al.

(1)   [+definite, +specific]
      I want to talk to the owner of this store—she is my neighbor, and I have an urgent message for her.

Is *the* used here because of definiteness—the speaker is referring to someone whose existence and uniqueness are established by general world knowledge (typically a store has a unique owner)? Or is it because of specificity—the speaker intends to refer to someone known to her (a neighbor for whom she has an urgent message)?

This is not to say that the function of *the* as a definiteness marker is never clear. Sometimes it is (as in *I want to talk to the owner, whoever that is*), but as Ionin et al. observe (pp. 573–574):

> Given the subtlety of the discourse triggers related to speaker and hearer knowledge, generalizing from them is likely to be a fairly long and difficult process.

In the final analysis then, although *the* may indeed occur very frequently, the transparent mappings between form and meaning that are needed by the acquisition device occur far less often—perhaps even quite rarely.

In the case of SLA, the learner's sensitivity to frequency effects can be obscured by yet another set of considerations—transfer from the native language. Ellis (2006b) develops this point at considerable length, examining the effects of L1-related cue competition, salience, attentional tuning, overshadowing, and blocking.

## B. Processor-Based Emergentism

The starting point for processor-based emergentism is the view, put forward by Hawkins (2004) and O'Grady (2005), that key properties of the syntactic phenomena that have long been used as support for UG-based approaches to language are in fact better explained in terms of processing factors. Hawkins develops this idea for a number of phenomena central to typology, such as Greenbergian universals and cross-linguistic variation in the syntax of filler-gap dependencies (including the body of relativization facts traditionally described by the Keenan–Comrie markedness hierarchy). O'Grady's work focuses more directly on the problem of language acquisition—hence its relevance to this chapter.

The central thesis of that work, which we also adopt here, is that a simple processor, committed to reducing the burden on working memory, lies at the heart of the human language faculty. Although such a processor makes no use of grammatical principles, its operation plays a key role in explaining the properties of many core syntactic phenomena—binding, control, agreement, island constraints, scope, and so forth. It is also crucial to the account of how those properties can be acquired in response to the limited sorts of experience available in the early years of life. We return to this idea and its implications for SLA in section III, where we present a detailed illustration of this approach.

It is vital to note that there is no inherent incompatibility between input-based research and the processor-based program. To the contrary, the proponents of input-based emergentism are strongly committed to the existence of a processor—their central point is in fact a claim about the processor, namely, that it is highly sensitive to the relative frequency of form–meaning mappings and distributional contingencies (Chang et al., 2006; Seidenberg & MacDonald, 1999).

Likewise, the processor-based approach does not deny the relevance of the input to understanding language acquisition and use. To the contrary, it insists that frequency of occurrence is extremely important (e.g., O'Grady, 2008a, 2008b)—although not more important than the calculus that assesses the burden that computational operations of various sorts place on working memory. The acquisition of relative clauses is a case in point: Direct object relatives are more frequent in the input than subject relatives (Diessel & Tomasello, 2005, pp. 898–899), but are nonetheless mastered later due to their well-documented processing burden (e.g., Caplan & Waters, 2002; Gibson, 1998).

To the extent that there is a major point of dispute between input-based and processor-based approaches to language, it lies in the question of whether the input provides learners with enough information to support induction of the full language. The dominant view of those committed to input-based emergentism seems to be that the input is sufficient in this regard (e.g., MacWhinney, 2004). This is of course consistent with the opposition of many emergentists to the long-standing assumption, heavily promoted in the literature on formal syntax, that input deficiencies constitute a *prima facie* argument for UG (the so-called poverty-of-stimulus claim).

A different view is put forward by O'Grady (2005, 2008a), who holds that there is in fact a poverty-of-stimulus problem, but that it does not support the case for UG. Instead, he proposes that the gap between experience and a speaker's linguistic knowledge is bridged with the help of the processor, which directs learners to particular options that are not evident from information available in the input. We return to this point in sections III and IV.

In his critique of emergentist work on SLA, Gregg (2003, p. 122) raises a point with which we agree: Emergentism is badly in need of a "property theory" of linguistic competence—that is, a theory of the language faculty and of language itself—that can rival UG-based theories. We believe that processor-based emergentism offers the promise of just such a theory in that it is able to address the three issues that rightly lie at the heart of contemporary linguistic theory:

   i. Why does language have the particular properties that it does?
   ii. Why is typological variation involving those properties restricted in particular ways?
   iii. How are those properties acquired by children, based on experience that is limited in particular ways?

We believe that the explanations needed to address these questions within an emergentist framework also shed light on the problems associated with understanding why SLA follows the particular course that it does.

A program devoted to the exploration of these matters obviously requires very specific proposals—and very specific types of evidence in support of those proposals. With that in mind, we will devote the remainder of this chapter to a relatively detailed case study of a subtle phenomenon involving the interaction between negation and quantification exemplified in English and Korean constructions such as the following.

(2)   English
      Mary didn't read all the books.

(3)   Korean
      Mary-ka      motun    chayk-ul    ilk-ci        anh-ass-ta.
      Mary-Nom     all       book-Acc    read-Comp    Neg-Pst-Decl
      'Mary didn't read all the books.'

We begin, in the next section, by considering how the processor goes about assigning interpretations to sentences of this type and how its operation contributes to an account both of language acquisition and of typological variation. Section IV reports on new experimental work that we have done on the acquisition of English scope by native speakers of Korean, illustrating the sorts of insights that an emergentist approach can offer to the classic problems of second language learning.

## III. SCOPE

Our starting point is the proposal outlined in detail by O'Grady (2005), which holds that the core properties of language are best explained by reference to an "efficiency-driven" processor whose primary objective is not to implement grammatical rules but simply to minimize the burden on working memory.[2] In the case of scope, two simple ideas come into play. Because each implies a strategy that minimizes the burden on

---

[2]Following Carpenter, Miyake, and Just (1994), we take working memory to be a pool of operational resources that both holds representations and supports computations on them. See also Jackendoff (2002, p. 200).

working memory by avoiding delays and revisions, we will refer to them as "efficiency assumptions."

  i. As the processor works its way through a sentence, it immediately assigns each NP an interpretation, based on available clues such as position, determiner type, case marker, context, and so forth.
  ii. The revision of a previously assigned interpretation is costly since it disrupts the normal linear operation of the processor, which forms and interprets sentences in real time under conditions that value quickness.

These assumptions can be represented schematically as follows:

(4)  a. An NP is encountered and assigned an interpretation "x," based on its position and other local properties:

NP
[x]

  b. Based on the properties of a subsequently encountered element, the NP's interpretation is recomputed:

NP . . . . . . . .Z. . .
[x]--->[y]

The latter procedure adds to the burden on working memory resources by requiring both the recovery of the earlier interpreted NP and its recomputation.

Now let us consider a concrete example involving a universally quantified NP such as *all the men*. In a typical case, such an NP has a "full set" interpretation, grouping together each and every man in the relevant discourse context so that some property can be attributed to them all. We can depict this as follows for expository purposes (Figure 1).

*all the men*

**Figure I**  "Full set" interpretation of *all the men*; the set includes each and every man in the relevant discourse context.

Thus, in a sentence such as *All the men arrived on time*, it is understood that the property of having arrived on time applies to the entire group of men—anyone in the relevant domain of discourse who is a man must have arrived on time. Likewise, in a pattern such as *The committee interviewed all the men*, it is understood that the property of having been interviewed by the committee holds for each man.

The negative operator *not* interacts with *all* in a variety of intricate ways. Perhaps the simplest interaction occurs in sentences such as the following, in which *not* combines directly with the quantified NP and unambiguously has scope over it. (That is, the interpretation of *all* is modified under the influence of the negative.)

(5)  [Not all the men] arrived on time.

Here the set denoted by the quantified NP is partitioned, so that the property of having arrived on time applies to only some of its members. We can depict this type of interpretation of the NP as follows (Figure 2). (The actual proportion of men in the excluded subset can, of course, vary.)

*not all the men*

**Figure 2**   Interpretation of *all the men* when it is in the scope of negation; the set of men is partitioned, so that the property of having arrived on time applies to only some of its members.

Although this interpretation requires a computational operation (the partitioning of the set) not found in the absence of negation, it at least does not run afoul of the efficiency assumptions outlined earlier. By the time the processor encounters the quantified NP, it has already come upon the negation. It is thus able to consider a partitioned set interpretation for the NP right away, without having to abandon or modify a *previously* computed interpretation.

Matters are different in the case of a sentence such as the following, in which the quantified NP serves as subject and the negative occurs to its right.

(6)   All the men didn't arrive on time.

Here, there are two interpretations. On the first interpretation, traditionally called the "universal wide scope reading" (*all > not*), all members of the discoursally relevant set of men behave alike with respect to the property of having arrived on time—they fail to do so. We will henceforth refer to this as the "full set interpretation."

On the second interpretation, traditionally labeled the "negation wide scope reading" (*not > all*), the set of men differ internally with respect to the property at hand—it is understood that some men arrived on time and some didn't. We will call this the "partitioned set interpretation."

The two readings differ with respect to their compliance with our efficiency assumptions. Consider first the full set interpretation, which can be derived as follows.

(7)   a.   <u>First:</u> Formation of the NP *all the men* and assignment of the full set interpretation:

        [All the men]

       b.   <u>Subsequently:</u> Formation and interpretation of the rest of the sentence, with no change to the interpretation of the subject NP.

        [All the men didn't arrive on time]

Now consider the partitioned set interpretation.

(8) a. <u>First</u>: Formation of the NP *all the men* and assignment of the usual full set interpretation:

[All the men]

b. <u>Subsequently</u>: The negative operator is encountered and assigned wide scope, forcing recomputation of the subject NP by partitioning the previously formed set.

[All the men didn't ...]

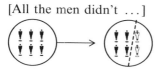

According to the second of our efficiency assumptions, this interpretation should be more difficult since the processor has to depart from its normal linear course and revise an earlier assigned interpretation—creating a significant extra burden on working memory.

If these ideas are on the right track, we would expect to find supporting evidence for the difficulty of the partitioned set interpretation both in the developmental profile observed in language acquisition and in the facts of typological variation.

## A. Acquisition

Musolino and Lidz (2006) report on the results of a truth-value judgment task that they carried out with 20 five-years-olds, following up on earlier work by Musolino, Crain, and Thornton (2000). The children watched an experimenter use props to act out a scenario in which two of three horses succeed in jumping over a fence. The children were then asked to judge the truth of *Every horse didn't jump over the fence*. Given the scenario presented by the experimenter, the sentence is true on the partitioned set interpretation (since not every horse jumped over the fence) and false on the full set interpretation (since two of the three horses did in fact jump over the fence) (Figure 3).

The children opted for the full set interpretation 85% of the time, accepting the sentences as true just 15% of the time.[3]

---

[3]The acceptance rate increased to as high as 60% when children were presented with "contextual support" in the form of a contrastive sentence such as (i).

(i) Every horse jumped over the log, but every horse didn't jump over the fence.

This suggests a dispreference for the partitioned set interpretation rather than its absolute rejection.

**Figure 3**   Scenario used to test the truth of *Every horse didn't jump over the fence.*

In the studies just mentioned, adults manifested no difficulty with the partitioned set interpretation. However, more recent work by Conroy and Lidz (2007)
involving a different experimental paradigm suggests that they too prefer the full set
interpretation.

Could the interpretive preferences manifested by children (and adults) be the result
of exposure to the relevant sentences during the language acquisition process? It seems
not. Based on an examination of maternal speech to a total of 42 children in the
CHILDES database, Gennari and MacDonald (2005/2006) report finding no instances
of either *every* or *all* in the subject position of a negated sentence. Evidently then,
children hear few if any sentences like *Every horse didn't jump over the fence*, with
either interpretation.[4]

This is of course precisely the sort of situation typically used to make the case for
UG—a subtle and abstract syntactic fact is underdetermined by experience. However,
processor-based emergentism offers an alternative: Children are directed toward the
full set interpretation of sentences such as *Every horse didn't jump over the fence* not by
prior experience, but rather by a processor dedicated to minimizing the burden on
working memory. As we have already seen (example (8)), the partitioned set
interpretation in sentences such as these requires the processor to depart from its
normal linear course in order to revise the interpretation previously assigned to the
quantified NP, creating a burden not associated with the full set interpretation.

## B. Typology

The processing effects that contribute to interpretive preferences in scope seem to
have typological consequences as well. Particularly relevant in this regard is Chinese,
in which sentences such as the following have only the full set interpretation in which
the property of not having jumped over the fence is attributed to the entire group of
horses (Musolino et al., 2000, p. 22).

(9)   Mei-pi ma dou mei tiao-guo langan.
      Every horse all not jump over fence
      'Every horse didn't jump over the fence.'

Crucially, however, we know of no language in which the reverse situation holds and
negation MUST have scope over a universally quantified subject NP to its left. That is,
there are no languages that are just like English or Chinese in their syntax, except that

---

[4]Musolino and Lidz (2006, pp. 841–842) have collected examples of negated sentences with a universally
quantified subject in adult-to-adult speech, but these sentence all have the partitioned set interpretation that
children disprefer (e.g., *All the birds don't seem to be the same*)—the exact opposite of what the input-based
account would predict.

a sentence such as *Every horse didn't jump over the fence* can ONLY mean "Not every horse jumped over the fence."

All of this makes sense if we assume, following Hawkins (2004) and O'Grady (2005), that processing considerations define degrees of computational difficulty and that individual languages can differ in terms of the burden they are willing to accept—with the proviso that if the interpretation that is harder to process is permitted, then the easier interpretation must also be allowed. This yields two possibilities:

i. The computationally costly pattern, in which the processor has to revise the interpretation of a previously interpreted NP, is disallowed; the pattern in which the NP retains its full set interpretation is permitted. Chinese works this way; as we have just seen, a sentence such as (9) permits only the full set interpretation for the quantified NP.

ii. The computationally costly pattern is allowed, but is disfavored compared to its less-difficult-to-process counterpart. English works this way—a sentence such as *Every horse didn't jump over the fence* permits two readings, but the computationally easier full set interpretation is preferred, as we have seen.

Similar sorts of implicational relationships are widely acknowledged in phonology. For instance, to take a simple example, it is a matter of consensus among phonologists that a CVC syllable is articulatorily more difficult than a CV syllable. Predictably, this leads to two options:

i. languages in which syllable-final consonants are prohibited—for example, Hawaiian

ii. languages in which a syllable-final consonant is permitted, but there are indications that it is articulatorily difficult—for example, English, in which children initially drop syllable-final consonants

We propose that comparable asymmetries, motivated by processing difficulty rather than articulatory factors, are pervasive in syntax.

## IV. SCOPE IN KOREAN-SPEAKING ESL LEARNERS

Because Korean is an SOV language with negation adjacent to the verb, a universally quantified NP precedes the negative operator even when it functions as direct object.

(10)  John-i    **motun**   salam-ul      po-ci       anh-ass-ta.
      John-NOM  all         person-ACC    see-COMP    NEG-PST-DECL
      'John didn't see all the people.'

The two potential interpretations of this sentence therefore differ with respect to the efficiency assumptions that we have proposed. Whereas the full set reading is built without modifying the interpretation that is initially assigned to the quantified

NP, the partitioned set reading requires this interpretation to be revised, as illustrated below.

(11)   a.   <u>First</u>: Formation of the NP *motun salam* "all people" and assignment of the default full set interpretation:

John-i        **motun**    salam-ul        po-ci        anh-ass-ta.
John-Nom    all           person-Acc     see-Comp   Neg-Pst-Decl

b.   <u>Subsequently</u>: The negative operator is encountered and assigned wide scope, forcing recomputation of the quantified NP by partitioning the previously formed set.

John-i        **motun**    salam-ul        po-ci        anh-ass-ta.
John-NOM    all           person-ACC     see-Comp   Neg-Pst-Decl

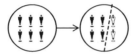

Consistent with the second of our efficiency assumptions, we expect the partitioned set interpretation to be accompanied by an increase in the burden on working memory as the processor abandons its normal linear course to revise an earlier assigned interpretation.

We therefore predict that Korean speakers will manifest just two types of acceptability judgments: They will permit either only the full set reading or both the full set reading and the more demanding partitioned set reading. Under no circumstances should they permit only the more difficult partitioned set reading (Table 1).

TABLE I

**Predictions for Scope Interpretation in Korean**

|               | Full set reading | Partitioned set reading |
|---------------|------------------|--------------------------|
| Possibility 1 | Accept           | Reject                   |
| Possibility 2 | Accept           | Accept (but dispreferred) |
| Impossible    | Reject           | Accept                   |

These predictions seem to be at least partially borne out in the study conducted by Han, Lidz, and Musolino (2007). Using a truth-value judgment task, they found an acceptance rate by their adult subjects of 98% for the full set interpretation in the type of negative pattern we are considering. In contrast, the acceptance rate for the partitioned set interpretation was just 46%, with 7 of the 20 subjects rejecting it on all the test items.[5]

---

[5]Because of Han et al.'s between-participants design, their results do not allow us to ascertain the correctness of our prediction that no Koreans will permit *only* the partitioned set interpretation.

A parallel preference was manifested among Han et al.'s child subjects (all four-year-olds), who accepted the full set interpretation 86.67% of the time, compared to just 33.33% for the partitioned set reading. Indeed, many child subjects rejected the partitioned set interpretation on all test items.

These preferences are very different from those associated with English patterns such as *John didn't see all the men* or *John didn't see everyone*, in which the partitioned set interpretation is dominant. As observed earlier, such a preference is fully consistent with our efficiency assumptions. This is because the occurrence of the negative to the left of the quantified direct object in English allows the processor to partition the set immediately, instead of first building a full set interpretation and then revising it.[6]

(12)  John didn't see all the men.

This brings us to the question of what happens when a speaker of Korean learns English. In order to get at this issue, we conducted the experiment described below.

## A. Participants

Forty-two native speakers of Korean participated in our experiment, all of whom were students in a linguistics class at Hanyang University in Seoul, Korea. Based on their previous English-language courses, their proficiency in English was estimated to be at the intermediate or high-intermediate level. They had received no formal training in semantics, but anecdotal reports suggest that at least some may have received instruction in high school or college English courses about the preferred interpretation for sentences such as (12). We return to this matter below.

## B. Procedure and Materials

Subjects were presented with a total of eight test items, preceded by two practice items and interspersed with 10 fillers. There were two conditions for the test items—one with a context favoring the full set interpretation and another with a context supporting a partitioned set reading (see below). A Latin square design was employed, so that every subject was exposed to each of the eight test items, but no test item was encountered in more than one context.

---

[6]Of course, this does not explain why the partitioned set interpretation is not only possible, but also preferred in this case. Interestingly, Musolino and Lidz (2006) present evidence that five-year-olds accept the full set interpretation about 75% of the time, in contrast with adults whose acceptance rate in basic descriptive contexts is just 20%. We agree with Musolino and Lidz that these preferences can be traced to an implicature that children are slow to learn: Use of the *not ... every/all* pattern rather than the *not ... any* pattern (e.g., *John didn't see anyone*) implicates that the stronger statement is inappropriate and that John must in fact have seen some of the people. It is also important to note that the full set interpretation is actually preferred in certain cases, as in *Max didn't consider all the people who would be inconvenienced by his decision*, brought to our attention by Kevin R. Gregg.

The stories were presented orally (via a pre-made recording) as the subjects read a written version in their individual test booklets. A sample story favoring the partitioned set interpretation of the sentence *Tom didn't fix all the computers* follows:

> Tom is at his uncle's repair shop.
>
> Tom's uncle is about to go out for lunch. He asks Tom to fix three radios and three computers before he returns. Tom promises to do so.
>
> Tom fixes the three radios easily.
>
> Then, Tom examines the first computer. But, he can't fix it. He decides to wait until his uncle comes back.
>
> Then, Tom looks at the second computer. There is something wrong with the sound, but he can't fix it.
>
> Finally, Tom comes to the third computer. There is something wrong with the screen. Screens are very hard to fix. But, Tom manages to fix it.

The context favoring the full set interpretation begins in the same manner, but the final paragraph goes as follows:

> Finally, Tom comes to the third computer. There is something wrong with the screen. He thinks that he can fix it quickly. However, after Tom works on it for a while, he gives up.

Each story was accompanied by a picture that summarized the end result—one repaired computer and two still-broken computers in the case of the partitioned set context, and three still-broken computers in the case of the full set context.

At the end of the story, the subjects were asked to judge the truth of a summary sentence in the test booklet. Each such sentence contained a negated verb with a universally quantified direct object phrase of the form *all the N*.

(13)  Tom didn't fix all the computers.

Subjects were given 10 seconds to make their selection before presentation of the next item.

In order to gather data relevant to the assessment of possible transfer effects and ascertain how Korean speakers judge scope in their native language, subjects participated in both an English version of the experiment and a Korean version (written only). As a precaution against the possibility that rendering judgments about scope in Korean might influence the judgments given for English, all subjects were tested first on English and then on the corresponding Korean materials a week later.

The subjects were tested as a group in a classroom at their university under the supervision of one of the experimenters. Each session took approximately 30 minutes to complete.

### C.  Results and Discussion

Table 2 summarizes the results from the truth-value judgment portion of our experiment for Korean.

TABLE 2
**Percentage of "True" Responses (Korean Version)**

| Context favoring | |
| --- | --- |
| Full set reading | Partitioned set reading |
| 97% (163/168) | 21% (36/168) |

TABLE 3
**Percentage of "True" Responses (English Version)**

| Context favoring | |
| --- | --- |
| Full set reading | Partitioned set reading |
| 93% (157/168) | 28% (47/168) |

As can be seen here, our subjects exhibit a very strong preference for the full set interpretation, accepting it as true in the matching contexts 97% of the time; in contrast, the partitioned set interpretation was judged to be true in contexts that favored it just 21% of the time. This difference is statistically significant ($t$ (41) = 12.49, $p < .05$).

This is just what we would expect. As explained above, the partitioned set interpretation in Korean involves a higher level of computational difficulty than the full set reading and should therefore be less accessible.

Now consider the truth-value judgments given by the same subjects on the English version of our experiment.[7] Here again, the preference for the full set interpretation is statistically significant ($t$ (41) = 9.06, $p < .05$).

As the contrast in Table 3 makes clear, our subjects exhibited a very strong preference for the full set interpretation of the quantified NP in English. Indeed the preference is not significantly different from the one manifested in Korean, despite the subjects' relatively high proficiency in English and the fact that at least some had probably received instruction concerning the preferred partitioned set interpretation of the English test items. What should we make of this result?

It has sometimes been suggested, notably by Pienemann (1998), that processing considerations play a major role in determining whether and when particular properties of the L1 are transferred to the L2. We adopt a similar idea here, although we do not of course adopt the grammatical mechanisms that typically accompany such proposals. Our hypothesis can be stated as follows.

(14)   The preferred interpretation in the L1 will be favored in the L2 if and only if it does not have a greater processing cost in the L2.

---

[7] A control group of six native English speakers judged the test items to be true in the partitioned set context 100% of the time, compared to just 67% in the full set context. In a follow-up questionnaire, one of these subjects observed that although the test sentence was "technically accurate" in the full set context, it was a "slightly confusing way of describing what happened" and that it would be clearer to say (for example) *Tom didn't fix any of the computers.*

As we have already seen, the full set interpretation of the universally quantified NP is preferred in Korean. Since that interpretation has a comparable low cost in English, our hypothesis predicts that it should also be favored in that language by Korean L2 learners, which is indeed what our results show.

An independent test for our hypothesis comes from the acquisition of Korean by native speakers of English—the reverse of the situation we have been focusing on. As already observed, native speakers of English prefer the partitioned set interpretation of *negated V + all N* patterns in their first language. Crucially, the corresponding interpretation in Korean has a much higher computational cost since the processor is forced to revise its initial interpretation of the quantified NP.

(15)   The partitioned set interpretation in Korean:

John-i          **motun**   salam-ul        po-ci           anh-ass-ta.
John-Nom    all           person-Acc    see-Comp    Neg-Pst-Decl
'John didn't see all the people.'

a. First: Formation of the NP *motun salam* "all people" and assignment of the default full set interpretation:

John-i          **motun**   salam-ul ...
John-NOM    all           person-ACC

b. Subsequently: The negative operator is encountered and assigned wide scope, forcing recomputation of the quantified NP by partitioning the previously formed set.

John-i          **motun**   salam-ul        po-ci           anh-ass-ta.
John-NOM    all           person-Acc    see-Comp    Neg-Pst-Decl

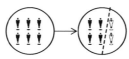

In English, in contrast, the partitioned set interpretation of a direct object NP places no special burden on working memory, since it does not require the recomputation of a previously determined interpretation. (Because *not* precedes the quantified NP, the option of forming the partitioned set interpretation is available from the outset.)

(16)   The partitioned set interpretation in English:

John didn't see all the people.

Which interpretation do English-speaking L2 learners prefer in Korean? Is it the partitioned set reading that is favored in English? Or is it, as our hypothesis predicts, the less costly full set reading?

In order to address this issue, we conducted a small pilot study involving five relatively advanced English-speaking learners of Korean as a second language by having them take the Korean version of our test. The full set interpretation in Korean was accepted 100% of the time, compared to just 50% for the partitioned set interpretation that is preferred in English. Three of the subjects accepted both interpretations in Korean (as do some native speakers of Korean), and two accepted only the full set reading. Crucially, no one showed a preference for the partitioned set reading that is favored in English.

Although no more than mildly suggestive, these results are consistent with what we predict: the preferred interpretation in the L1 is not carried over to the L2 when it has a higher processing cost in the second language. We hope that work currently underway with beginning and intermediate subjects will allow us to deepen our understanding of the role of processing cost in the acquisition of scopal patterns.

## V. CONCLUDING REMARKS

After a brief introductory survey of emergentist work in SLA, we focused our attention on a phenomenon that exemplifies the challenges confronting contemporary linguistic theory. Negative-quantifier scope manifests a subtle form–meaning mapping that is underdetermined by the input and yet is acquired with apparent effortlessness. Moreover, although it exhibits significant variation across languages, that variation is strictly limited. For these reasons, the phenomenon is a classic candidate for treatment in a UG-type framework.

In fact though, such a treatment is unnecessary; there is an emergentist alternative. A simple efficiency-driven processor, committed to minimizing the burden on working memory, explains why scope has the properties that it does, how language learners come to acquire those properties, and why typological variation is constrained in the way that it is. The key insight, as we have tried to show, is simply that the processor resists revisions to previously computed interpretations—a procedure that requires the recovery of the earlier interpreted NP from memory and the use of additional working memory resources to support its reinterpretation. The aversion to such reinterpretations and to the computational cost that they incur offers insights into key typological and developmental facts—and into why SLA follows the particular course that it does.

## ACKNOWLEDGMENT

We are grateful for the helpful and insightful comments of Kevin R. Gregg on an earlier version of this chapter.

## REFERENCES

Ambridge, B., Theakston, A., Lieven, E., & Tomasello, M. (2006). The distributed learning effect for children's acquisition of an abstract syntactic construction. *Cognitive Development, 21*, 174–193.

Bates, E., & MacWhinney, B. (1987). Competition, variation, and language learning. In B. MacWhinney (Ed.), *Mechanisms of language acquisition* (pp. 157–193). Mahwah, NJ: Erlbaum.

Bybee, J., & Hopper, P. (2001). *Frequency and the emergence of linguistic structure.* Amsterdam: John Benjamins.

Caplan, D., & Waters, G. (2002). Working memory and connectionist models of parsing: A reply to MacDonald and Christiansen (2002). *Psychological Review, 109*, 66–74.

Carpenter, P., Miyake, A., & Just, M. (1994). Working memory constraints in comprehension: Evidence from individual differences, aphasia, and aging. In M. Gernsbacher (Ed.), *Handbook of Psycholinguistics* (pp. 1075–1122). San Diego: Academic Press.

Chang, F., Dell, G., & Bock, K. (2006). Becoming syntactic. *Psychological Review, 113*, 234–272.

Chater, N., & Manning, C. (2006). Probabilistic models of language processing and acquisition. *Trends in Cognitive Sciences, 10*, 335–344.

Conroy, A., & Lidz, J. (2007). *Seriality in LF processing.* Ms. Department of Linguistics, University of Maryland.

Dick, F., Bates, E., Wulfeck, B., Aydelott Utman, J., Dronkers, N., & Gernsbacher, M. (2001). Language deficits, localization, and grammar: Evidence for a distributive model of language breakdown in aphasic patients and neurologically intact individuals. *Psychological Review, 108*, 759–788.

Diessel, H., & Tomasello, M. (2005). A new look at the acquisition of relative clauses. *Language, 81*, 882–906.

Ellis, N. (2002). Frequency effects in language processing. *Studies in Second Language Acquisition, 24*, 143–188.

Ellis, N. (2006a). Language acquisition as rational contingency learning. *Applied Linguistics, 27*, 1–24.

Ellis, N. (2006b). Selective attention and transfer phenomena in L2 acquisition: Contingency, cue competition, salience, interference, overshadowing, blocking, and perceptual learning. *Applied Linguistics, 27*, 164–194.

Ellis, N., & Larsen-Freeman, D. (2006). Language emergence: Implications for applied linguistics. *Applied Linguistics, 27*, 558–589.

Elman, J. (1993). Learning and development in neural networks: The importance of starting small. *Cognition, 48*, 71–99.

Elman, J. (2002). Generalization from sparse input. *Proceedings of the 38th Regional Meeting of the Chicago Linguistic Society* (pp. 175–200). Chicago: Chicago Linguistics Society.

Elman, J. (2005). Computational approaches to language acquisition. In K. Brown (Ed.), *Encyclopedia of language and linguistics* (2nd ed., pp. 726–732). Oxford, UK: Elsevier.

Elman, J., Bates, E., Johnson, M., Karmiloff-Smith, A., Parisi, D., & Plunkett, K. (1996). *Rethinking innateness: A connectionist perspective on development.* Cambridge, MA: MIT Press.

Ferreira, F. (2003). The misinterpretation of noncanonical sentences. *Cognitive Psychology, 47*, 164–203.

Gennari, S., & MacDonald, M. (2005/2006). Acquisition of negation and quantification: Insights from adult production and comprehension. *Language Acquisition, 13*, 125–168.

Goldberg, A. (1998). The emergence of the semantics of argument structures. In B. MacWhinney (Ed.), *The Emergence of Language* (pp. 197–212). Mahwah, NJ: Erlbaum.

Goldberg, A., & Casenhiser, D. (2008). Construction learning and second language acquisition. In P. Robinson & N. Ellis (Eds.), *Handbook of cognitive linguistics and second language acquisition* (pp. 197–215). New York: Routledge.

Gibson, E. (1998). Linguistic complexity: Locality of syntactic dependencies. *Cognition, 68*, 1–76.

Gregg, K. (2003). The state of emergentism in second language acquisition. *Second Language Research, 19*, 95–128.

Han, C., Lidz, J., & Musolino, J. (2007). V-raising and grammar competition in Korean: Evidence from negation and quantifier scope. *Linguistic Inquiry, 38*, 1–48.

Hawkins, J. (2004). *Efficiency and complexity in grammars*. Oxford, UK: Oxford University Press.

Haspelmath, M. (2008). Parametric versus functional explanations of syntactic universals. In T. Biberauer (Ed.), *The limits of syntactic variation* (pp. 75–107). Amsterdam: John Benjamins.

Herron, D., & Bates, E. (1997). Sentential and acoustic factors in the recognition of open- and closed-class words. *Journal of Memory and Language, 37*, 217–239.

Ionin, T., Zubizarreta, M., & Maldonado, S. (2008). Sources of linguistic knowledge in the second language acquisition of English articles. *Lingua, 118*, 554–576.

Jackendoff, R. (1988). Why are they saying these things about us? *Natural Language and Linguistic Theory, 6*, 435–442.

Jackendoff, R. (2002). *Foundations of language*. Oxford, UK: Oxford University Press.

Lewis, J., & Elman, J. (2001). Learnability and the statistical structure of language: Poverty of stimulus arguments revisited. *Proceedings of the 26th Annual Boston University Conference on Language Development* (pp. 359–370). Somerville, MA: Cascadilla Press.

MacWhinney, B. (1987). The competition model. In B. MacWhinney (Ed.), *Mechanisms of language acquisition* (pp. 249–308). Mahwah, NJ: Erlbaum.

MacWhinney, B. (2000). Emergence from what? Comments on Sabbagh & Gelman. *Journal of Child Language, 27*, 727–733.

MacWhinney, B. (2004). A multiple process solution to the logical problem of language acquisition. *Journal of Child Language, 31*, 883–914.

MacWhinney, B. (2008). A unified model. In P. Robinson & N. Ellis (Eds.), *Handbook of cognitive linguistics and second language acquisition* (pp. 341–371). New York: Routledge.

Musolino, J., Crain, S., & Thornton, R. (2000). Navigating negative quantificational space. *Linguistics, 38*, 1–32.

Musolino, J., & Lidz, J. (2006). Why children aren't universally successful with quantification. *Linguistics, 44*, 817–852.

O'Grady, W. (2005). *Syntactic carpentry: An emergentist approach to syntax*. Mahwah, NJ: Erlbaum.

O'Grady, W. (2007). The syntax of quantification in SLA: An emergentist approach. In M. O'Brien, C. Shea, & J. Archibald (Eds.), *Proceedings of the 8th generative approaches to second language acquisition conference (GASLA 2006): The Banff conference* (pp. 98–113). Somerville, MA: Cascadilla Press.

O'Grady, W. (2008a). Does emergentism have a chance? In H. Chan, H. Jacob, & E. Kapia (Eds.), *Proceedings of 32nd Annual Boston University Conference on Language Development* (pp. 16–35). Somerville, MA: Cascadilla Press.

O'Grady, W. (2008b). Innateness, universal grammar, and emergentism. *Lingua, 118*, 620–631.

O'Grady, W. (2008c). The emergentist program. *Lingua, 118*, 447–464.

O'Grady, W., Nakamura, N., & Ito, Y. (2008). Want-to contraction in second language acquisition: An emergentist approach. *Lingua, 118*, 478–498.

Pienemann, M. (1998). *Language processing and second language development: Processability theory*. Amsterdam: John Benjamins.

Seidenberg, M., & MacDonald, M. (1999). A probabilistic constraints approach to language acquisition and processing. *Cognitive Science, 23*, 569–588.

Tomasello, M. (2003). *Constructing a language: A usage-based theory of language acquisition*. Cambridge, MA: Harvard University Press.

CHAPTER 5

# VARIATIONIST LINGUISTICS AND SECOND LANGUAGE ACQUISITION

Dennis R. Preston and Robert Bayley

The relevance of sociolinguistics to second language acquisition (SLA) is twofold. First, it is concerned with variation in language—the product, process, acquisition, and cognitive location of such variation; these matters are the focus of this chapter. Second, it concerns itself with sociological and social–psychological aspects of language. To the extent that those aspects are crucial to account for variation of the first sort, they are included here. Similar concerns are, however, independently surveyed in other chapters of this volume, particularly from socio-political and affective points of view.

## I. A BRIEF HISTORY OF LANGUAGE VARIATION STUDY

The earliest work on variable language focused on geographical distribution, but not for its own sake; historical linguists investigated areal diversity in order to test the major tenet of the late nineteenth-century European Neogrammarians—that sound change was without exception (e.g., Osthoff & Brugmann, 1878). If each region displayed an exceptionless application of a sound change that had operated in its territory, the interpretation of such changes as *laws* would be strengthened. Even though initial surveys found exceptions, suggesting that the Neogrammarian view was an exaggeration, dialect study continued to have a historical bias. Respondents were selected from older, less well-educated, rural segments of the population, indicating a focus on locating and recording older forms before they disappeared. Eventually, early- and mid-twentieth-century dialect study, particularly in the United States, settled into a period in which its findings appeared to be of greater relevance to cultural geography or even folklore than to general linguistics and the study of linguistic change in particular (e.g., McDavid, 1979). In early US dialect studies, subgroups of

89

the population were identified, but methods for respondent selection and categorization were inconsistent with generally accepted social science procedures (Pickford, 1956). Nevertheless, these studies have provided a wealth of information on regional language distribution that has well served later sociolinguistic work.

That work, which began in the early 1960s in studies such as Labov's on the lower east side of New York City (1966), refocused the study of variation on linguistic change and on variables other than locale. The quantitative paradigm pioneered by Labov has had considerable influence on SLA research and is reviewed in the next section.

## II. THE QUANTITATIVE PARADIGM

Labov (1966, 1972) established a specific approach to quantitative studies of language variation. Its central claim is that the alternative forms do not occur randomly. The frequency of their occurrences is predicted by (1) the shape and identity of the element itself and its linguistic context, (2) stylistic level (defined operationally), (3) social identity, and (4) historical position (assuming that one form is on the way in and the other on the way out).

The collection of data is especially crucial in this paradigm, for Labov claims there is an *observer's paradox* (Labov, 1972, p. 113)—the more aware respondents are that their speech is being observed, the less natural their performances will be. Since self-monitored speech is less casual, that is a major drawback to a crucial assumption: less casual speech is also less systematic, and thus less revealing of a speaker's basic language system, or vernacular. That assumption suggests that sociolinguists seek a systematicity significantly different from Chomskyan competence, and we discuss below questions of the Labovian and Chomskyan research programs in SLA.

Since surreptitious recording strikes most as unethical, eliciting natural samples is a serious problem, but a number of techniques have been developed to overcome the observer's paradox. In one, the familiarity of the collector is taken advantage of. Milroy (1980) shows that a fieldworker who becomes a member of a social network is not only allowed collection that insures more authentic and representative data, but is also provided with insights into the norms and values of the community that aid later interpretation.

The degree to which data-recording equipment and activities (e.g., audio recorders, experimental settings) influence language behavior should not be minimized, but many investigators report that, after a brief period of nervousness and comment, instruments have little effect. Milroy goes so far as to suggest that "... the presence of the tape-recorder in itself ... seemed less likely to produce a shift away from the vernacular than did conversation with a higher-status participant ..." (1980, p. 60).

Accidental opportunities for the collection of natural data may also arise. During interviews, interaction among respondents, interaction between a respondent and another person not a part of the interview, or interaction between the fieldworker and the respondent outside the interview focus or topic may occur. In all these cases, respondents may shift from a relatively formal interview style to a more relaxed one.

The formality of the interview may also be reduced by topic. Such questions as "Did you ever have a dream that really scared you?" or "Were you ever in a situation where you were in serious danger of getting killed?" (Labov, 1984, p. 33) and those that ask about childhood games (Labov, 1972, pp. 91–92) have been effective in eliciting less careful speech.

Finally, the focus of a study may be so precise that observation (not recording) may suffice. In a study of /r/-deletion in New York City department stores, Labov determined what goods were located on the fourth floor and asked a clerk for directions. Then Labov leaned forward slightly and said "Excuse me?" to elicit a more emphatic version (Labov, 1966, Chapter III). Though the procedure was simple, it allowed investigation of the linguistic variable in preconsonantal (*fourth*) and final (*floor*) positions, in two ethnic groups, in two stylistic varieties (ordinary and emphatic), and in three different social status groups—inferred from the reputation of the stores where the survey was conducted.

His concern for the vernacular has led Labov to suggest that there is a stylistic continuum reaching from the most formal (carefully monitored, often elicited through written stimuli) to the most casual (unmonitored); the casual end of the continuum exemplifies vernacular style.

The special status of an interview itself may produce suspect data. A continuum based on data derived from variation in one setting may not be a good indication of general conversational styles. Briggs (1986), for example, notes that the interview is a type of speech event that may have different associations for lower-class speakers than for university-trained researchers. An additional criticism of the operational distinctions used in studying the continuum addresses the problem of reading. Romaine (1980) claims that one cannot assume that speaking and reading form a continuous dimension, and Milroy and Milroy (1977) note that in some speech communities skills in reading aloud might be so weak as to make the reading of a continuous passage require even more attention than the reading of word lists. Finally, Irvine (1979), although not specifically critical of the stylistic continuum, raises questions about types of formality and their meaning and distribution of use in different speech communities.

## A. Background

To illustrate the Labovian treatment of variation, or what Eckert (2005) has referred to as *first wave* studies, the simplification of final consonant clusters in English that end in /t/ and /d/ will be used. Table I shows the percentage of such deletion under four different linguistic conditions and for four social classes of African–American speakers from Detroit.

These data show patterned variability; both linguistic facts (whether the cluster is followed by a vowel or a consonant, and whether the final member of the cluster is itself the past-tense morpheme or not) and social facts (class, i.e., socioeconomic status) have an effect on deletion.

Labov first attempted to deal with such facts in terms of a variable rule. Normally, linguistic rules are categorical—they always work whenever the conditions for their application are met.

$$X \longrightarrow Y \mid \underline{\quad} Z$$

TABLE I
**Deletion of t/d in Detroit African–American Speech**

| | Social classes | | | |
| Environments | Upper middle | Lower middle | Upper working | Lower working |
|---|---|---|---|---|
| Following vowel: | | | | |
| t/d is past morpheme (e.g., missed in) | 0.07 | 0.13 | 0.24 | 0.34 |
| t/d is not past morpheme (e.g., mist in) | 0.28 | 0.43 | 0.65 | 0.72 |
| Following consonant: | | | | |
| t/d is past morpheme (e.g., missed by) | 0.49 | 0.62 | 0.73 | 0.76 |
| t/d is not past morpheme (e.g., mist by) | 0.79 | 0.87 | 0.94 | 0.97 |

*Source:* Wolfram and Fasold (1974, p. 132).

X becomes (or is realized as) Y whenever Z follows. For example, in the first author's phonological system, the following vowel-raising rule is categorical.

$$[\varepsilon] \longrightarrow [\mathrm{I}] \underline{\quad\quad} +nas$$

That is, /ɛ/ is realized as [I] if a nasal follows, causing *pin* and *pen* to be homophones. (The first author says *ball-point* when he wants something to write with rather than to stick with.)

The t/d data in Table I cannot be displayed in such a rule. If the rule is written categorically,

$$t/d \longrightarrow \varnothing \mid C \; \{\varnothing,\#\}\underline{\quad}\#\# \; \{C,V\}$$

t/d would be deleted every time it followed a consonant and appeared at the end of a word—that is, before a word boundary (##). Whether t/d was or was not a separate morpheme (∅,#) and whether a consonant or vowel did or did not follow (C, V) have no influence on this rule, for curly brackets simply indicate that one condition or the other must be present for the rule to operate. The data in Table I show that even when all the best conditions for deletion are met (lower working class, t/d is not the past-tense morpheme, and the following word begins with a consonant), the deletion rate, although 0.97, is still not categorical.

One solution is to make such rules optional. The mechanism for this shows the product of the rule and the constraining factors in parentheses.

$$t/d \longrightarrow (\varnothing) \mid C \; (\#) \underline{\quad} \#\# \; \{C,V\}$$

Here t/d may be deleted word-finally after a consonant, whether t/d is a separate morpheme or not (#). The product of the rule (∅ = "nothing") and the morpheme boundary are indicated as options by enclosing them in parentheses.

This solution, however, provides no quantitative information about morpheme status, following segment, and social class. If social class constituted the only source of variation, one might be justified in claiming that variation should be represented in rules of language use or implementation only (e.g., Kiparsky, 1972). Table I data show, however, that the variation is as much or more influenced by morpheme status and following segment as it is by social class. A variable rule allows the incorporation of such probabilistic information:

$$
\text{t/d} \longrightarrow <\varnothing> \mid C \begin{pmatrix} \varnothing \\ \\ \# \end{pmatrix} \underline{\hspace{1cm}} \#\# \begin{pmatrix} C \\ \\ V \end{pmatrix}
$$

Angle brackets replace parentheses around both the variable output of the rule and constraints on it. To insert the probabilistic information, an alternative to Table I must be prepared in which one can see the pooled contribution of each of the elements studied (Table II).

With these figures keyed to the variable rule, one may determine the likelihood of the rule's application in a particular case. For example, if an upper-middle-status speaker (0.41) uses a nonpast (0.71) in front of a vowel (0.36), we know the various weights that influence consonant cluster simplification. Note that the social status likelihood is associated with the overall application of the rule, and that one might add the probability for the entire speech community (0.57) or for a subgroup (as we have done above). Note also that the linguistic influences are usually numbered according to their relative strengths. In this case, a following consonant is the strongest promoter of cluster reduction and is assigned a "1." Finally, the exact probability for the example cited above is not an average of the probabilities for all the influencing factors. There is an interesting mathematical history to this problem in variable rule analysis, but the details are not provided here since they are extensively covered in the recent literature on variation analysis (Bayley, 2002; Paolillo, 2002; Tagliamonte, 2006).

Finally, we note that the variable of age provides the principal variationist means for studying linguistic change: the use of apparent time (Bailey, 2002). The pattern in Figure 1, taken from Trudgill's study of Norwich variation (1972, p. 191), is typical of linguistic change; the 10–19 age group has radically increased the instance of lowered and centralized (e) even in their most formal styles. It appears that RP-like [ɛ], in such

TABLE II

**Deletion of t/d in Detroit African–American Speech (Combined Deletion Percentages)**

| | |
|---|---|
| Following sound: | |
| Consonant | 0.77 (1) |
| Vowel | 0.36 (4) |
| Morpheme status: | |
| Nonpast | 0.71 (2) |
| Past | 0.42 (3) |
| Social status: (5) | 0.57 |
| Upper middle | 0.41 |
| Lower middle | 0.51 |
| Upper working | 0.64 |
| Lower working | 0.70 |

*Source:* Wolfram and Fasold (1974, p. 132).

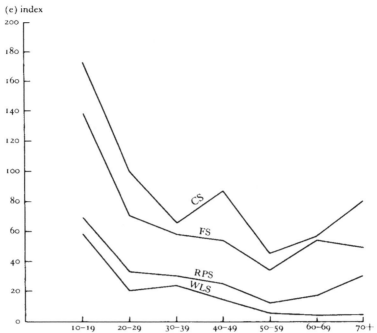

**Figure I**   Norwich (e) by age and style (0 = total [ ] pronunciation; 200 = total [ ] pronunciation; WLS, word list style; RPS, reading passage style; FS, formal style; CS, casual style). (Taken from Chambers and Trudgill, 1998, p. 80. Reprinted with the permission of Cambridge University Press.)

words as *bell* and *tell*, is giving way to [3] and even [Λ]. Apparent time study, however, may confuse age-grading (in which linguistic forms are appropriate to a chronological age) with language change.[1] Since change of language forms within the individual rather than change that has a lasting influence on the language itself is usually the focus in SLA; this important sociolinguistic distinction will not be of such great concern here, although groups of learners with similarly developing interlanguages could obviously be considered a parallel to historical change in a monolingual setting.

## B.  The Early Labovian Paradigm in SLA Research

L. Dickerson (1974) first applied the Labovian style of variationist analysis to SLA, and W. Dickerson (1976) more explicitly drew the parallel between stages in inter-language development and linguistic change and noted that the use of the variable rule model was appropriate to such study. Their work showed that two variationist rubrics

---

[1]The older descriptive work of dialectologists is often of particular help here in determining whether or not a feature is undergoing change or represents age grading. Labov made just such use of the Linguistic Atlas of New England in his study of Martha's Vineyard (summarized in Labov, 1972) and of the Linguistic Atlas of the Middle and South Atlantic States and other historical data in his work on New York City (1966). Other clues to the progress of linguistic change, particularly as it is influenced by sex and social status, are comprehensively outlined in Labov (1972).

could be applied to SLA data: (1) the linguistic environment is a predictor of variable occurrence, and (2) longitudinal (or apparent-time) treatment of data reveals the progress of linguistic change (in SLA, usually in the individual rather than in the system of groups of learners). Moreover, the relationship between the linguistic environment and time shows that the environments are important conditioning factors in the progress of the change itself.

The studies of L. Dickerson and W. Dickerson were followed by a number of studies of variation in the acquisition of English that illustrated the systematic nature of interlanguage variation. These studies included Adamson and Kovacs' (1981) reanalysis of Schumann's (1978) data on the acquisition of negation by a Spanish-speaking immigrant and Wolfram's (1985) study of past-tense marking by Vietnamese in the Washington DC area.

Early on, Tarone (1982) proposed the *continuous competence model*, which suggests that the stylistic continuum of the language acquirer operates much like that of the native speaker. The more attention the learner pays to speech, the more prestige forms are likely to occur (where prestige forms are construed to be target language forms or learners' understandings of what those forms are).

Tarone's characterization of style borrows heavily from the sociolinguists' operational devices used to elicit this dimension rather than from its underlying causes (e.g., degree of formality). Stylistic fluctuation, in her account, is due to the degree of monitoring or attention to form, and varying degrees of attention to form are by-products of the amount of time that various language tasks allow the language user for monitoring (e.g., writing perhaps the most, spontaneous conversation the least). According to Tarone, this variation takes place for the early language acquirer within only one envelope or register. Only more advanced learners acquire different registers that entail such matters as genre and other complex norms of interaction and use that, in turn, contribute to the positioning of a task on the stylistic continuum.

## III.  MORE RECENT TRENDS

### A.  Objections

If sociolinguistics had such a promising beginning in SLA research, why is it that SLA and sociolinguistics have not had a better friendship until relatively recently? We will discuss four impediments, most already hinted at:

(1) the apparent reluctance or inability of variationists to advance plausible psycholinguistic models;
(2) the mistaken understanding of sociolinguistic aims as only sociological, social–psychological, and anthropological (including ethnomethodological) ones;
(3) misunderstandings of concepts, findings, and research tools developed in variationist linguistics; and
(4) the recent relative hegemony of the generative program in SLA research.

We will proceed backwards and defer comment on (1) until we have had the opportunity to say even more positive things about what the interaction has done and what potential it holds.

## Variationist Linguistics and the Generative Paradigm in the Study of SLA

We will first be concerned with the way in which sociolinguistic accounts of language are or are not compatible with those given by Universal Grammar (UG). In the long run, we believe that a more careful specification of the domain of relevance of sociolinguistic inquiry will have direct bearing on the more general question of the relationship of variationist work to linguistic (and, therefore, SLA) theory, but we begin the account of such matters squarely in the territory of the dominant paradigm.

Without detailing why things have gone this way, let us observe that for much of the generativist enterprise grammars was rather more negatively than positively conceived. The earlier language of the enterprise suggested the general thrust—barriers, filters, control, bounding nodes—and this trend continues in even more recent formulations' use of the term constraint. With regard to UG in SLA, for example, Dekydtspotter, Sprouse, and Anderson (1998, p. 341) suggest the following: "Given that the sole 'role' of UG is to restrict the hypothesis space available to the language acquirer, *Full Restriction* might be a more perspicuous name than *Full Access*." We seem to have been a good deal more concerned with mapping out the territory where human language could not go than with where it does, but let us avoid caricature. Generative grammars are not at all uninterested in what a language does, for some of what happens follows from the existence and settings of the various constraints of the model and from interactions between and among them. Additionally, the UG research program has made some specific claims about what a grammar must be, and those claims have had interesting repercussions in the area of SLA.

Consider first the relationship of a perennially hot topic to UG. If the critical age hypothesis turns out to hold,[2] then other factors, namely the complex cognitive abilities of adults in general (and learners of foreign and second languages in particular) will emerge as the linguistic research areas of greatest interest in SLA.

Lurking behind that scenario, of course, is the question of the relationship between UG and the learner, but no matter which of the logically possible forms of adult access to UG turns out to be the case, the results will not make UG a general theory of SLA:

(1) If adults have no access to UG, then the same conclusions hold as those of a strong critical age hypothesis; that is, adults learn languages through so-called nonlinguistic cognitive abilities.

(2) If adults have access to the shape of UG only as it is instantiated in L1, then the same conclusions hold for everything not hit in L2 by those settings, for any re-settings will have to appeal to nonlinguistic sorts of learning abilities.

---

[2]It is clear what some UG proponents believe about this:

> For the language teacher, [the critical period] means that you simply cannot teach a language to an adult the way a child learns a language. That's why it's such a hard job (Chomsky, 1988, p. 179).

(3) If adults have full access to the conditions of UG (or even manipulative access through the settings of L1), it is still the chore of SLA research to explain those aspects of learners' language ability that do not fall out of those conditions.

Let us be clear about what we mean by those things that do not fall out. We are not concerned with the fact that some kinds of information highlighting, staging, and referencing may not fall out. Nor are we concerned that language-processing facts do not automatically fall out. Nor are we the least concerned that gender, status, age, formality, and other socially distinguishing characteristics do not fall out. What we mean to focus on is the fact that although generally autonomous or modular theories have (or are capable of developing) adequate ways of characterizing the structures of utterances as they reside in competence, they admit to having no way of predicting why a grammar has one form or another. For example, nothing predicts why Standard English embedded questions like to undo auxiliary movement:[3]

(1) Why did George leave?
(2) *I know why did George leave.
(3) I know why George left.

Although UG accounts can precisely describe the difference between (2) and (3), they cannot use any general settings for English to show that (3) not (2) will be the well-formed alternative.[4]

Many errors like those of (2) above appear in L2 performance. In fact, a large list of syntactic features (as well as features from other levels of the grammar) of only passing descriptive interest to UG (i.e., not predicted by its features) could be made from any error inventory of learner use—e.g., complement types (infinitive versus gerund "I'm interested to go"), verb valences (missing obligatory objects—"I put on the table").

Additionally, many variable data are without significance to UG. For example, once it is shown that English is a language that (under certain circumstances) can delete complementizers,

I decided that/∅ I would go,

then UG has done its chore. The fact, for example, that the complementizer is more likely to occur after main verbs that have an auxiliary than those without (Thompson & Mulac, 1991) is perhaps rightly ignored by UG. Gregg (1990, p. 374) is certainly correct when he notes that, in a territory that UG regards as linguistic competence,

---

[3]We ignore the fact that many varieties of English do not obey this rule and carefully avoid the fact that all speakers of English have this rule as a variable one, although those who believe their English is "standard" will often not admit it, even though there is ample evidence in even the written English of well-educated native speakers.

[4]Briefly, the facts are these. Since WH moves to [Spec,CP], [C,C'] is an available landing site for I, but there is nothing in the parameters set for English that predict whether I will or will not move to C. Put more specifically, there is nothing in the embedding of a question sentence which predicts I-to-C movement. Note that when C is full, as it is in embedded yes–no questions when "if" or "whether" is base-generated, one cannot get I-to-C: *I don't know if did he go. Varieties that consistently move I in embedded questions simply do not base-generate anything into C: I don't know did he go.

items are either in or out (and, quite clearly, since *that* and Ø are options for the complementizer, they are both in).

But from a broader psycholinguistic perspective, particularly one concerned with language change within the individual, the mechanisms that govern the choice of forms that are unquestionably there in linguistic competence are of considerable interest, perhaps even of crucial importance in a dynamic environment when one of the forms is doomed (if the learner is to achieve anything like a native-speaker's competence). Therefore, what SLA researchers learn from and teach those who are concerned with shoring up, tightening, and extending the agenda of UG may be limited, particularly if the goal of a relatively comprehensive SLA theory is to account for the general linguistic ability of post-critical-period second and foreign language acquirers. In short, SLA interests are much broader than the goals of UG. Doubtless, and to the benefit of both research efforts, some SLA researchers will want to test the tenets of UG and offer alternative representations of it in its own terms based on findings from SLA data, but if SLA limits its attention to those relatively narrow boundaries, it will miss many boats. Many SLA research efforts that have grammaticality as the central concern, quite aside from social and/or discoursal concerns, make that clear. In short, if a great deal of what is to be learned requires an understanding of the cognitive procedures involved in acquisitional territory beyond the fallout of certain settings of the grammar, then a theory of SLA that does not include such territory will be paucal. On to the next impediment.

## Misunderstandings of Variationist Linguistics by SLA Researchers

No mode of inquiry has ownership rights to its concepts and procedures, so variationists can expect to have what they have found out (and what they have found out about finding out) to be used by others. Unfortunately, errors in SLA characterizations of variation have developed that concern the subtypes of variation and even how variation itself is identified. Since these misunderstandings have been evident in the work of leading SLA practitioners, they are worth dwelling on. For example, Ellis (1985) defines the variable rule as follows:

> If it is accepted that learners perform differently in different situations, but that it is possible to predict how they will behave in specific situations, then the systematicity of their behavior can be captured by means of variable rules. These are "if...then" rules. They state that if x conditions apply, then y language forms will occur. (Ellis, 1985, p. 9)

That is simply not so. Ellis' description is an apt characterization of a categorical (albeit context-sensitive) rule (described above), not a variable one. Although he later recognizes the proportional rather than categorical nature of variable rules, one wonders how many were confused by this earlier definition.

Indeed, misunderstandings of variationist linguistics reach even farther, into the methodology itself. Ellis (1987) explains how he quantified past-tense form occurrences by non-native speakers of English in a variety of tasks.

> Each verb was scored as correct or deviant in contexts requiring the use of the past tense. Repetitions of any verb (common in the oral tasks, particularly in Task 3) were not counted. (Ellis, 1987, p. 7)

There are good reasons not to count some forms (e.g., categorical occurrences that exaggerate the influence of the set of factors they belong to), but not to count repetitions in general simply means that opportunities to discover the forces on variation have been ignored. If free variation exists, it is established by showing that plausible influencing factors have been subjected to a quantitative analysis and have been found to have no effect on the occurrences of the dependent variable. We are suspicious that language variation that is influenced by nothing at all is a chimera, but we would be happy to admit to such variability if we were shown that a careful search of the environment had been made and that no such influencing factors had been found. We are adamant about this since we believe that the discovery and weighting of influencing factors is the most valuable area of interaction between variation linguistics and SLA.

## The Mistaken Understanding of the Aims of Sociolinguistics

The third impediment is a much more general misunderstanding of what sociolinguistics is, and it partly stems from the label itself. This misunderstanding limits sociolinguistic interests to what might be called socially sensitive pragmatics. The focus of such work has to do with how various linguistic tasks are appropriately done—part of the ethnography of communication. A learner of American English will want to know under what circumstances her professor ought to be greeted with "Hello you ol' sumbitch" or with "Good morning Professor." Although we believe that studies of who says what to whom, when, where, why, and even how often are very interesting, they are not the central stuff of variationist linguistics. Even Gregg (1990), who seems to have a fair grasp of what variationists are about, is willing to caricature by suggesting that his (apparently conscious) decision to avoid second verb ellipsis (e.g., Tuffy thwacked Throckmorton and Spike Beauregard) is based on a rule that he calls "Try not to sound like a twit" (p. 375). In many variationist studies, the list of factors that determine probabilities of occurrence includes no so-called social features (or twit-avoidance rules). Since such weighted rather than categorical factors are part of a speaker's language ability, the study of the influence of just such factors is most typical of the variationist's concern.

It is also perhaps the case that so-called social concerns are often much-loved, for they seem to get away from the hard stuff of linguistics. Asking a number of respondents to rate samples for their politeness, aggressiveness, or some other factor is doable almost anywhere, involves straightforward statistical analyses (if any), and seems to require little or no theoretical surroundings or even training. (Often a mention of Grice, 1975 will do, although even that is often filtered through Brown and Levinson, 1987.) Thereby the hard stuff of phonology, morphology, syntax, and semantics is avoided; worse, the hard stuff of pragmatics, ethnography, statistics, data collection, and the like is often also not in evidence.

## B. More Recent Work

Before we turn to the psycholinguistic problem, let us provide some examples of variationist SLA work that examines both learner variation in target language features

TABLE III

**Influence of Perfectivity on Past-Tense Marking in Chinese English Learners**

| | Respondent proficiency level | | | | | |
| | Lower | | | Higher | | |
| Verb type | $p_i$ | % | N | $p_i$ | % | N |
|---|---|---|---|---|---|---|
| Perfective | 0.67 | 42 | 856 | 0.69 | 73 | 1406 |
| Imperfective | 0.33 | 15 | 964 | 0.31 | 38 | 1691 |
| Input | 0.22 | 22 | 1820 | 0.58 | 54 | 3097 |

*Source:* Bayley (1994, p. 175).

that are usually considered obligatory (e.g., past-tense marking in English) and learner success or failure with target language patterns of variability (e.g., t/d deletion in English).

Bayley (1994) examines past-tense marking by Chinese learners of English; one factor taken into consideration is perfectivity[5] (Table III).

The "Input," represents the tendency for the rule to work overall (i.e., for pasts to be marked in general). The lower- and higher-proficiency learners represent both sides of that possibility. Overall, there is a considerable probability that a lower-proficiency speaker will not mark past tense in English (0.22) while there is some probability that a higher-level proficiency speaker will (0.58).

When one investigates the linguistic factor under consideration, however, although the percentages of correct forms are dramatically different for the lower- and higher-proficiency speakers (e.g., 15–38% correct for imperfectives), the probabilistic weights are stable (0.33 and 0.31, respectively, in the same category). The same is true of the relationship of percentages versus weights for the perfectives.

These results imply a model in which the factor of perfectivity has a stable pattern of influence throughout the learning process. That is, perfective verbs encourage past-tense marking and imperfectives discourage it with nearly the same weight at both proficiency levels. That suggests two things. First, the path of acquisition for this feature is tied to markedness. Second, and more interesting, the relatively level influence of past-tense marking according to perfectivity across proficiency levels suggests that no radical restructuring of the grammar as regards this feature has taken place. In other words, although the high-proficiency respondents in this investigation mark more pasts, the probabilistic weight assigned to one of the factors (perfectivity) that significantly influences this marking is nearly equal to the weight assigned the same factor for lower-proficiency speakers from the same group of learners.

[5]It is a rule of thumb in both first and second language acquisition studies that perfectives are typically past. Bayley (1994) reviews evidence from earlier studies.

TABLE IV

**Effect of the Preceding Segment (of the Verb Stem) on Past-Tense Marking in Chinese English Learners**

| Preceding segment | Respondent proficiency level | | | | | |
|---|---|---|---|---|---|---|
| | Lower | | | Higher | | |
| | $p_i$ | % | N | $p_i$ | % | N |
| Vowel | 0.47 | 23 | 128 | 0.66 | 61 | 80 |
| Liquid | 0.57 | 31 | 29 | 0.46 | 45 | 65 |
| Obstruent | 0.46 | 23 | 213 | 0.38 | 36 | 340 |

*Source:* Bayley (1994, p. 175).

Perhaps, therefore, we should collect evidence that shows that, for some factors,

(1) all learners from the same language background make up learner communities,[6] and
(2) all learners from all language backgrounds belong to the same learner community, and
(3) subgroups of learners even from the same language background make up distinct communities.

The implications of those three categories for transfer, universals, and some more individual notion of learning should be clear.

We do encounter just such patterns (and ones of even greater complexity), but before we turn to issues of cross-linguistic patterning, let us look at a case that satisfies category (3). In Table IV, Bayley (1994) provides an example from another of the factors studied, in this case the influence of the preceding segment (i.e., the verb's stem-final segment).

As promised, these data reflect the conditions of (3), that is, the higher- and lower-proficiency respondents do not belong to the same community of learners in spite of their shared L1. In fact, the regression test tells us that the preceding segment is not even a significant contributor to the probability of past-tense realization for the lower-proficiency learners, making the difference between the two groups even more dramatic. That learning from exposure has gone on here, specifically in terms of the weights associated with the different environments, seems unquestionable. (The same order of influence of preceding segments as that seen in the higher-level-proficiency learners is to be found in the performances of native speakers, e.g., Guy, 1980). This factor, unlike the one of verbal aspect, acquires significance in its influence on past-tense marking as learners advance in proficiency.

The implication of the contrast between the two factors is relatively clear. Some categories that have an influence on the dependent variable appear to be a stable part of the learner's machinery. One might almost say that the successful learner learns

---

[6]The first author has tried to suggest (e.g., Preston 1989, p. 257) the metaphor that groups of learners belong to the same speech community when these probabilistic values are not significantly different, but that was apparently misunderstood and taken in the Bloomfieldian sense by some (e.g., Williams 1990, p. 499).

TABLE V

**Effect of the Features of the Preceding Segment on Plural Marking by Chinese, Czech, and Slovak English Learners**

|                       | Czech/Slovak | Chinese |
|-----------------------|--------------|---------|
| Vowel                 | 0.31         | 0.52    |
| /r/                   | 0.60         | 0.58    |
| Sibilant              | 0.54         | 0.28    |
| Nonsibilant fricative | 0.44         | NA      |
| Nasal                 | 0.50         | 0.46    |
| Stop                  | 0.60         | 0.60    |
| Lateral               | 0.24         | 0.05    |

*Source:* Young (1993, p. 90).

around them, but is not likely to do away with them. Other categories develop in the learner, and appear to take their shape from the surrounding evidence.

We have waffled in attributing L1 or universal influence to perfectivity in the above account, for we have not yet represented a study that separates learners from (radically) different L1s, an obvious condition for the examination of (2). Young's (1993) study of Czech and Slovak learners' noun plural marking in English in which he compares those data with his earlier studies of Chinese learners, however, offers appropriate examples.

Although the Czech and Slovak learners are more proficient overall in their marking of noun plurals than the Chinese, the influence of redundant plural marking in discourse is very close (0.78 and 0.71 for redundant marking, and 0.46 and 0.43 for nonredundant marking, respectively). In other words, redundant plural marking in discourse fits the specifications outlined in (2) as a factor that has similar influence, in spite of radically different L1s.[7]

It is relatively easy, of course, to find cases where the factor group influences on respondents from different L1s do not match up. In the same study that compares Czech and Slovak learners of English with Chinese learners, the data in Table V presents the effects of the preceding segment on plural marking.

For some subcategories of this factor group (vowels, sibilants), the two L1 groups are on the opposite sides of the 0.50 watershed. That is, features of the preceding segment that promote plural marking for Czech and Slovak learners of English retard it for Chinese learners and vice versa. While some factors do have similar influence, the overall patterns are very different. These are obviously two radically different learner communities as regards this factor.

Aside from t/d deletion, we have focused so far on forms that are categorical in L1. However, in recent years, L2 researchers, recognizing that fully acquiring a second language involves acquiring the ability to style shift appropriately as well as to interpret native-speaker patterns of variation, have investigated the acquisition of

---

[7]Of course, more learners from other language groups should be investigated before any claim is made that this is a universal. The point made here lies in the use of the model in investigating such relationships, not in the breadth of the claim.

target language patterns of variability in great detail. Much of this work has involved French, both Canadian and continental. Mougeon and his colleagues, for example, studied variation in the language of students in a French immersion program in Toronto (Mougeon, Rehner, & Nadasdi, 2004). Their studies of more than a dozen morphosyntactic, lexical, and phonological variables showed that the immersion students' development of sociolinguistic competence was considerably below that of native speakers of Quebec French on several levels including frequency of variant use and mastery of the linguistic and external constraints on variant use. Findings also indicated that immersion speakers' lack of use of both vernacular and mildly marked variants was related to educational input from teachers and textbooks, where vernacular forms were rarely, if ever, found.

Other Canadian studies include the work of Sankoff and her colleagues, who investigated the use of discourse markers by Anglophone adolescents in Montreal. As expected, they found that the use of a variety of discourse markers correlated with the extent to which speakers participated in Francophone peer groups. Sankoff et al. (1997) concluded that the use of discourse markers provided a useful indication both of French fluency and participation in the Francophone community. Similarly, Nagy, Blondeau, and Auger (2003), in a study of the constraints on subject doubling by Montreal Anglophones, found that learners who had more exposure to native French speakers exhibited a higher rate of subject doubling and thus more closely resembled Montreal French speakers than speakers whose social networks consisted primarily of other Anglophones.

A number of studies of the acquisition of continental French have focused on variable deletion of *ne*, the first particle of negation. Regan (1996), for example, studied Irish learners of French before and after year-long sojourns in France. She found that students, like native speakers, deleted *ne* more frequently after their time abroad. In addition, some students overgeneralized *ne* deletion, which may be interpreted as evidence that they were eager to adopt native-like patterns of variability. In a recent study, Dewaele (2004) examined the effects of extralinguistic factors on *ne* deletion in a study of 73 L2 French speakers. He found that gender and age had little effect, but that both degree of extroversion and frequency of French use had significant effects.

Researchers have also examined the acquisition of target language patterns of variability in languages other than French. In an early study, Adamson and Regan (1991) studied the variable alveolarization of /ŋ/ in the English of Cambodian and Vietnamese immigrants in Philadelphia. Contrary to expectations, they found that males were more likely to use the nonstandard variant in more careful speech. Presumably, for these speakers, projecting a masculine image was more important than the effect of style. In a recent study of variation in the speech of Japanese- and Spanish-speaking learners of English, Major (2004) examined several phonological variables including the (ING) variable, palatalization in four linguistic environments (e.g., *got you, did you, this year,* and *raise your*), deletion of [v] from *of* (e.g., *can o' beans),* and *n* assimilation in *can* (e.g., [n] → [m] in *I* ca[m] *be here*). Major's results also suggest that gender differences are more important for L2 learners than stylistic differences. Both the Japanese and the Spanish L1 groups showed gender differences, but only the Spanish L1 group showed evidence of style-shifting.

Many scholars are accustomed to distinguishing between the acquisition of categorical and variable L1 forms. However, in some cases, forms are categorically required in some environments, categorically prohibited in others, and variable in still others. One such form is the Chinese morphosyntactic particle *de* (的), which serves a variety of grammatical functions. *De* can function as a genitive marker (e.g., *tā de lí* "his pear"), an attributive marker (e.g., *xīnqín de lǎonóng* "hardworking farmer"), and a nominalization marker (e.g., *wǒ bǐjiào xǐhuān de shì yóuyǒng* "What I like very much is swimming"). Used in combination with *huà* (话), *de* can also indicate a conditional clause. In a study of native speakers of Mandarin and advanced learners who were living in China, Li (2007) showed that in native speech *de* is always used in conditional clauses and never in lexicalized terms. For other functions, however, native speakers sometimes omit *de*, including from relative clauses. And, as is the case with other instances of morphosyntactic variation, presence or absence of *de* is systematically conditioned by linguistic factors, including grammatical function, and by social factors, with men more likely than women to omit *de*. In addition, as we might expect from the fact that omission of *de* is characteristic of informal speech, *de* is more likely to be present in teachers' classroom discourse and in language teaching materials than in casual conversation.

Li's (2007) results for Chinese L2 speakers provide additional information that allows us to generalize some of the findings from studies of the acquisition of European languages. First, as in Adamson and Regan (1991) and Major (2004), gender played a significant role. Men tended to omit *de* more frequently than women did. Second, as with the French immersion speakers studied by Mougeon et al. (2004), the Chinese L2 speakers tended to follow prescriptive norms more closely than their native-speaking contemporaries, even though the learners had spent up to four years in China and interacted with native speakers on a daily basis. In fact, the learners' use of *de* more closely matched *de* use in their teachers' classroom discourse and in their textbooks than in the speech of their Chinese contemporaries. Third, with some exceptions, the L2 speakers matched the native-speaker pattern for grammatical function fairly closely. Figure 2 shows Li's results for grammatical function of variable *de* in both native and L2 Chinese. Table VI shows the rates of optional *de* use by Chinese native speakers, Chinese teachers in classroom contexts, Chinese textbooks, and L2 Chinese.

In addition to these research examples, it would be possible to put variationist techniques to use at even finer levels of discrimination. Preston (1989) shows, for example, through an examination of research data (Tarone, 1985) that such carefully monitored performances as test-taking do and do not form a part of the well-attested stylistic continuum. Such results confirm that Krashen's (1987) monitor theory is about one-half correct. When certain simple rule facts (e.g., third singular present marking on verbs in English) get super-monitored (e.g., in a grammar test), they fall in place at the top end (i.e., the heavily monitored) of the variationist's stylistic continuum. When certain hard rule facts (e.g., English articles) are tested, however, a variable rule analysis shows that not only do they not fall in place at the top end of the continuum, but also that the statistical model cannot even understand them as a part of that continuum. That would appear to be confirmed by Johnson and Newport (1989), where the older subjects were most dramatically opposed to the younger

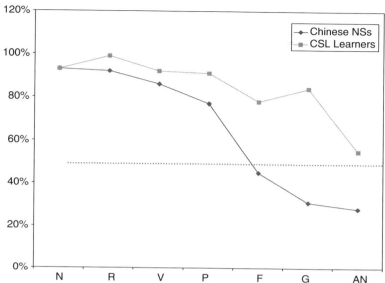

**Figure 2** Optional cases: Frequency of *de* use by Chinese native-speakers (NSs) and Chinese as a second language (CSL) learners. N, nominalization; R, relative clause; V, verb; P, phrase; F, DE constructions followed by determiner or number-classifier phrase; G, genitive; AN, adjective+noun. (Taken with permission from Li, 2007, p. 134.)

TABLE VI

**Use of *de* by Chinese Native Speakers, Chinese Learners, Teachers, and Textbooks**

|  | Chinese NSs | CSL learners | Teachers' speech | Textbooks |
|---|---|---|---|---|
| Frequency (%) | 56 | 78 | 76 | 75 |
| Input | 0.64 | 0.84 | 0.84 | 0.85 |
| *N* | 3290 | 9549 | 2145 | 2270 |

*Source:* Li (2007, p. 92, 122, 141).

subjects in precisely this grammatical domain. A monitor theory may be correct, therefore, in assuming that some sort of switched-on rule-learning program may be effective in promoting L2-like performance of some easy rules when there is time for overt extraction of that knowledge but that it is no help at all for hard rules.

Note how these findings constitute a two-way street between variation studies and SLA. The direction or slope of performances along a stylistic continuum, suggested to SLA from variation studies, gives researchers in SLA a tool to approach the question of what grammar a learner has internalized at various levels of monitoring. On the other hand, the super-monitored items that do not fit into a stylistic continuum discovered in SLA data help confirm the suspicions mentioned above that some tasks (e.g., reading) may not position themselves appropriately on the stylistic continuum and may, therefore, represent questionable means of data gathering in sociolinguistics itself.

SLA is in some ways dramatically positioned to contribute to variationist under-standing of language. Its respondents are on a fast-track language change, allowing real—rather than apparent—time studies. Moreover, the variants of an item undergoing change (particularly in the early stages of acquisition) are not as likely to take on socially symbolic meanings, an influence that may confound the rate and even nature of change in monolingual settings.

From a selfish variationist perspective, we hope that multivariate analyses of SLA data will allow us to look forward to productive, cross-fertilizing clarification of such notions as change from above and change from below (already hinted at above in the discussion of the stylistic continuum), hyper- (and hypo-) correction, linguistic insecurity, convergence and divergence, age-grading versus change, specific strategies in incorporating variable evidence (e.g., fudged lects [Chambers & Trudgill, 1998]), and the more general role of markedness. Preston (1989), for example, claims that marked forms develop more quickly in monitored interlanguage performances, and that unmarked ones are acquired earlier in less-monitored styles—a parallel between interlanguage development and the variationist notions of change from above and below.

Taking SLA notions first, however, we would also like to see a variationist perspective taken on such constructs as fossilization, an area that will parallel developments on the so-called creole continuum, making those data interpretable as something other than socially motivated preservations of older forms.

We hope this discussion so far clarifies how variationist techniques can aid SLA, and how SLA data can shed light on proposals from UG and other areas of linguistics by sorting out influences rather than trying to isolate them. Many a good study seems foolishly criticized by the post-hoc recriminations the investigators have directed towards their own work when they note that other variables may have confounded the one they set out to study. Of course they have! Why not deal realistically with this inevitable variety, while focusing on how the factor one delights most in does (or does not) influence the data.

## C. The Psycholinguistics of Sociolinguistics in SLA

We hope this discussion will also serve to clarify the fact that the unfortunately-named variable rule is not a challenge to UG models of either native or second/foreign language linguistic competence. On the other hand, acknowledgment of serious claims from a variationist perspective leads us to consider (1) the position in the linguistic makeup of the mechanisms that guide variation and (2) their possible contribution to questions of linguistic change in the individual (i.e., learning). Such attacks as Gregg's (1990) on studies that assign selection devices to the domain of competence (e.g., Tarone's work) or that misrepresent commonplaces in the sociolinguistic tradition (illustrated above from Ellis' work) may be helpful in letting SLA practitioners know that variationists have not been well represented in "SLA-variation" literature, but these attacks overlook the serious challenges to minimally elaborated psycholinguistic theories posed by careful attempts to build a variable psycholinguistic model (not necessarily a model of variable competence).

But VARBRUL, or any form of logistic regression, does not come completely theory-free. One must be interested in identifying and weighing the factors that promote the occurrence of one form or another. One must assume that those factors are connected in some way to individual language change. If variation in a developing interlanguage is viewed as simply a waffling back and forth between one grammar and another (for no apparent reason), then there will be little or no interest in a program that seeks the causes and mechanisms of variation itself. Perhaps for some that is simply the case.

> ... every human being speaks a variety of languages. We sometimes call them different styles or different dialects, but they are really different languages, and somehow we know when to use them, one in one place and another in another place. Now each of these languages involves a different switch setting. In the case of [different languages] it is a rather dramatically different switch setting, more so than in the case of the different styles of [one language] .... (Chomsky 1988, p. 188)

This view, which assumes that there are as many grammars as there are styles (e.g., Bickerton, 1971), is rather easily cut up with Occam's razor, and we are surprised to find it still strongly asserted in 1988. More importantly, it fails in the face of more plausible variable psycholinguistic models, which, as suggested above, do not necessarily locate the key to variability exclusively in linguistic competence. Here is one attempt at such a model, adjusted to fit SLA data.

For a two-way variable, imagine that one is equipped with a coin that is flipped before the product appears. Taking Bayley's (1994) study of past-tense marking by Chinese learners of English as our representative data, let heads represent the (L1-like) marking of the past tense and tails represent no marking. This model does not deny the possibility that there might be cases where apparent alternatives are actually instantiations of different grammars, that is, different competences. In this case, however, "mark" and "don't mark" might be taken to be options in a single competence, quite a different claim from one that asserts the existence of a variable competence.

This model overlooks dynamic questions of two sorts. First, it ignores the issue of how two ways to do one thing arose (although some of the research samples outlined above indirectly address that question). Second, it avoids the more immediate (though not unrelated) question of the longevity of variation in the system (a problem, again, not ignored by the research efforts outlined above). The model advanced will, however, provide openings for such dynamic considerations.

The coin proposed for the respondents is fair (so far). When flipped, it is as likely to turn up heads as tails. Bayley has shown, however, that aspect, the final segment of the verb stem, respondent proficiency, verb type (e.g., strong vs. weak), the following segment, and interview type all influence the probability of past-tense marking.

Assuming that the reader does not have experience in petty-cash crooked gambling devices, let us explain that unfair coins are well established as a possibility in gamblers' lore. The belief goes that if one adds weight to the tails side of a coin and flips it, it is more likely to come up heads; the more weight added, the greater the probability it will come up heads. Back to our data (Table VII).

As we see in Table VII, the input weight (0.38, higher- and lower-proficiency levels combined) reflects the overall performance of the dependent variable itself—in this

TABLE VII

**Effect of Verb Type, Aspect, Proficiency, and Interview Type
on Past-Tense Marking in Chinese English Learners**

| | |
|---|---|
| Verb type: | |
| Suppletive | 0.75 |
| Weak syllabic | 0.27 |
| Aspect | |
| Perfective | 0.67 |
| Imperfective | 0.33 |
| Proficiency | |
| High | 0.65 |
| Low, intermediate | 0.34 |
| Participant structure | |
| Paired interview | 0.53 |
| Individual interview | 0.47 |
| Input | 0.38 |

*Source:* Bayley (1994, p. 170).

case, the past-tense marker. It is precisely this sort of combined statistical product that fired Bickerton's (1971) suspicion that an individual's psycholinguistic makeup was poorly represented in such studies. He is right, of course, if one tries to build this 0.38 weight into the coin-flipping mechanism of the individual, for we have already seen that the input probability of high-proficiency learners on this past-tense marking feature is 0.58 while that for lower- and intermediate-proficiency learners is 0.22. Even if we limit the preparation of our unfair coin to one for a high-proficiency learner (and we shall), Bickerton may still be right, for this input weight represents the overall likelihood of past-tense marking and may be just a statistical ploy (a constant or correction device) to help in the calculation of each single factor group's influence. So far as an individual's linguistic competence is concerned, therefore, it may play no role, and that is the position taken here (although not in Preston, 1989).

The factors that constrain past marking are treated as part of the individual's overall linguistic ability, and the following characterizes their influences on the coin-flip and offers suggestions for their entry points (or abodes) in the mechanism. For the purposes of this illustration, let's assume that our respondent is about to blurt out "I loved everything the linguist said." Whether *love* will be marked for past or not is our focus.

(1) We have already seen that verbal aspect is important, and we will take our sample sentence to be imperfective. Since imperfectives retard past-tense attachment by a weight of 0.31, we must activate a device that sticks an appropriate amount of weight on the heads side, giving tails side (i.e., no past-tense marking) a greater likelihood of occurrence.

Let's be careful about the cognitive workshop where this operation was done. In the case of an independent influence on past-tense marking by aspect, it is safe to assume that the options are there in the learner's competence. That is, the two-sided coin is available in competence. (There are of course one-sided coins [marbles?] that, when taken from competence and readied for performance instantiation, don't need to be flipped at all.) When the fair past-tense-marking coin is engaged by the performance readying mechanism, a weight attachment device from the temporal–aspectual readyroom jumps out and sticks the weight predicted by 0.31 on the heads side. If nothing else influenced past-tense marking, this weight could be read as a simple probability, but there is more.

(2) The salience of the difference between present and past forms is significant. It ranges from a low of 0.27 for modals and weak syllabics (e.g., *paint+ed*) to a high of 0.75 for suppletives (e.g., *go-went*).

We shall have to add the weight contributed by a weak nonsyllabic (love) to the heads side of the coin. That is, a factor of 0.42 will contribute to the continuing decline of the probability for past-tense marking. It is still fairly clear that the two-sided coin about to be flipped has been plucked from linguistic competence. That is, both past-tense marker = "something" and past-tense marker = ∅ have been handed to us on the coin, and a mechanism that we might call the salience of morpho(phono)logical alteration has rushed in with the appropriate weight.

(3) Also significant (although, as noted above, not for lower-proficiency learners) is the preceding segment. The phonemic shape of *love* places an obstruent (/v/) before the past marker, and the weight contributed by that factor is 0.38 (see Table IV). Add a weight determined by that factor to (again!) the heads side of the coin.

Here, we believe, is the first significantly different operation, for the influence of this factor on performance would have occurred even if no coin (i.e., the options) had been minted in competence. So as not to incur the wrath of phonologists, we will not suggest that the operations that are at work here have nothing to do with matters that are perhaps very much a part of linguistic competence in another component of it. In fact, this weight reflects an operation shared with native speakers for whom the variability of past-tense marking is never influenced by the first two factors considered (i.e., aspect and salience). The reason should be clear; native speakers do not have past-tense-marking coins with "mark" and "don't mark" sides in their competences; therefore, such guiding factors on past-tense marking for Chinese learners of English as aspect and salience have no effect on native speakers.

Native speakers (and advanced Chinese learners of English) do have a rule, however, that influences the likelihood of consonant cluster reduction in word-final position (as elaborated on earlier). In short, a consonant cluster simplifier adds the weight determined by 0.38 to the heads side of our increasingly unfair coin, but it is only a serendipitous fact that there is a "don't flip" side to the coin at all.

We see here how a carefully constructed variation study teases out and shows the independence of factors that govern (i.e., predict) performance variation, noting that two factors appear to depend on an underlying option in linguistic competence (as regards the variable feature itself) while another depends on a phonological operation unrelated to any option in competence.

We believe such a model is psycholinguistically plausible, for it specifically shows how another of Bickerton's (1971) objections to inherent variability is, in fact, not an issue. When respondents issue 20%, 40%, or 60% of one form of a variable, they are not monitoring their overall performance with some daylong tallying device. They are simply evidencing the influence of a set of probabilistic weights that come to bear on each occurrence. Since this is Bickerton's principal psychostatistical objection to the notion of variation, we assume that we may put it aside, and that a variable rule account is preferable to the claim that variation is the result of moving back and forth between alternative grammars—such movement triggered by essentially unstudiable, low-level social factors.

The attachment of weights of the sorts described above is surely not part of what has been advanced profitably in generative grammar under the label of competence, even if some of the motivating factors behind such probabilistic influences have their origins in such competence (as, e.g., optimal syllable-structure rules might), and such claims as Gregg's (1990) that variation linguistics is not helpful in the SLA enterprise may be rejected.

## IV. CONCLUSIONS

We know so little yet about language and mind that it is premature to rule out linguistic research areas on the basis of their failure to deal directly and uniquely with the ramifications of linguistic competence. Even more frankly, we do not know where the elements of a variable psycholinguistic model fit, nor do we know where the linguistic levels fit into it, but we do know that native languages as well as interlanguages display facts that can be captured by a device that includes such variable weightings and offers the opportunity for appropriate interpretations of these various forces. Pending stupendous advances elsewhere in our general field of inquiry, the data from every subarea of investigation—SLA and use, first language acquisition and use, pidgin–creole varieties, permanent and short-term language disability, alternative modalities (e.g., sign), and more—will contribute to and be informed by the study of language in its broader perspective. The theories that develop from such attention need not be naively data-driven, but eventually they will want to address some of the complexities of the data, and in some areas (perhaps especially SLA), the complexities demand such attention for even early-stage, metaphoric characterizations of theory.

## REFERENCES

Adamson, H. D., & Kovac, C. (1981). Variation theory and second language acquisition data: An analysis of Schumann's data. In D. Sankoff & H. Cedergren (Eds.), *Variation omnibus* (pp. 285–292). Edmonton: Linguistic Research, Inc.

Adamson, H. D., & Regan, V. (1991). The acquisition of community speech norms by Asian immigrants learning English as a second language. *Studies in Second Language Acquisition*, *13*, 1–22.

Bailey, G. (2002). Real and apparent time. In J. K. Chambers, P. Trudgill, & N. Schilling-Estes (Eds.), *The handbook of language variation and change* (pp. 312–332). Oxford: Blackwell.

Bayley, R. (1994). Interlanguage variation and the quantitative paradigm: Past-tense marking in Chinese–English. In E. Tarone, S. Gass, & A. Cohen (Eds.), *Research methodology in second-language acquisition* (pp. 157–181). Hillsdale, NJ: Lawrence Erlbaum.

Bayley, R. (2002). The quantitative paradigm. In J. K. Chambers, P. Trudgill, & N. Schilling-Estes (Eds.), *The handbook of language variation and change* (pp. 117–141). Oxford: Blackwell.

Bickerton, D. (1971). Inherent variability and variable rules. *Foundations of Language*, 7, 457–492.

Briggs, C. (1986). *Learning how to ask: A sociolinguistic appraisal of the role of the interview in social science research.* Cambridge: Cambridge University Press.

Brown, P., & Levinson, S. (1987). *Politeness.* Cambridge: Cambridge University Press.

Chambers, J., & Trudgill, P. (1998). *Dialectology* (2nd ed.). Cambridge: Cambridge University Press.

Chomsky, N. (1988). *Language and problems of knowledge: The Managua lectures.* Cambridge, MA: MIT Press.

Dekydtspotter, L., Sprouse, R., & Anderson, B. (1998). Interlanguage A-bar dependencies: Binding, construals, null prepositions and Universal Grammar. *Second Language Research*, 14, 331–358.

Dewaele, J.-M. (2004). Retension or omission of the *ne* in advanced French interlanguage: The variable effect of extralinguistic factors. *Journal of Sociolinguistics*, 8, 433–450.

Dickerson, L. (1974). *Internal and external patterning of phonological variability in the speech of Japanese learners of English: Toward a theory of second language acquisition.* Ph.D. dissertation, University of Illinois, Urbana-Champaign.

Dickerson, W. (1976). The psycholinguistic unity of language learning and language change. *Language Learning*, 26, 215–231.

Eckert, P. (2005). *Variation, convention, and social meaning.* Plenary address presented at the annual meeting of the Linguistic Society of America, January 7.

Ellis, R. (1985). *Understanding second language acquisition.* Oxford: Oxford University Press.

Ellis, R. (1987). Interlanguage variability in narrative discourse: Style shifting in the use of past tense. *Studies in Second Language Acquisition*, 9, 1–20.

Gregg, K. (1990). The Variable Competence Model of second language acquisition and why it isn't. *Applied Linguistics*, 11(4), 364–383.

Grice, W. (1975). Logic and conversation. In P. Cole & J. Morgan (Eds.), *Syntax and semantics 3: Speech acts* (pp. 41–58). New York: Academic Press.

Guy, G. (1980). Variation in the group and the individual: The case of final stop deletion. In W. Labov (Ed.), *Locating language in time and space* (pp. 1–36). New York: Academic.

Irvine, J. (1979). Formality and informality in communicative events. *American Anthropologist*, 81, 773–790.

Johnson, J. S., & Newport, E. (1989). Critical period effects in second language learning: The influence of maturational state on the acquisition of English as a second language. *Cognitive Psychology*, 21, 60–99.

Kiparsky, P. (1972). Explanation in phonology. In S. Peters (Ed.), *Goals of linguistic theory* (pp. 189–227). Englewood Cliffs, NJ: Prentice-Hall.

Krashen, S. (1987). *Principles and practice in second language acquisition.* Englewood Cliffs, NJ: Prentice-Hall.

Labov, W. (1966). *The social stratification of English in New York City*. Arlington, VA: Center for Applied Linguistics.

Labov, W. (1972). *Sociolinguistic patterns*. Philadelphia, PA: University of Pennsylvania Press.

Labov, W. (1984). Field methods of the project on linguistic change and variation. In J. Baugh & J. Sherzer (Eds.), *Language in use: Readings in sociolinguistics* (pp. 28–53). Englewood Cliffs, NJ: Prentice-Hall.

Li, X. (2007). T*he acquisition of sociolinguistic competence by learners of Chinese as a second language: A variationist perspective*. Ph.D. dissertation, University of Texas at San Antonio.

Major, R. (2004). Gender and stylistic variation in second language phonology. *Language Variation and Change, 16*, 169–188.

McDavid, R. I., Jr. (1979). *Dialects in culture*. Tuscaloosa: University of Alabama Press.

Milroy, L. (1980). *Language and social networks*. Oxford: Blackwell.

Milroy, L., & Milroy, J. (1977). *Speech and context in an urban setting*. Belfast Working Papers in Language and Linguistics 2(1).

Mougeon, R., Rehner, K., & Nadasdi, T. (2004). The learning of spoken French by immersion students from Toronto, Canada. *Journal of Sociolinguistics, 8*, 408–432.

Nagy, N., Blondeau, H., & Auger, J. (2003). Second language acquisition and "real" French: An investigation of subject doubling in the French of Montreal Anglophones. *Language Variation and Change, 15*, 73–103.

Osthoff, H., & Brugmann, K. (1878). *Einleitung to Morphologische Untersuchungen auf dem Gebiete der indogermanischen Sprachen I* (pp. iii-xx). Leipzig: S. Hirzel; English translation in W. P. Lehmann. (1967). *A reader in nineteenth century historical Indo-European linguistics* (Chapter 14). Bloomington, IN: Indiana University Press.

Paolillo, J. (2002). *Analyzing linguistic variation*. Stanford, CA: CSLI.

Pickford, G. (1956). American linguistic geography: A sociological appraisal. *Word, 12*, 211–233.

Preston, D. (1989). *Sociolinguistics and second language acquisition*. Oxford: Blackwell.

Regan, V. (1996). Variation in French interlanguage: A longitudinal study of sociolinguistic competence. In R. Bayley & D. R. Preston (Eds.), *Second language acquisition and linguistic variation* (pp. 177–202). Amsterdam: John Benjamins.

Romaine, S. (1980). A critical overview of the methodology of urban British sociolinguistics. *English World Wide, 1*, 163–198.

Sankoff, G., Thibault, P., Nagy, N., Blondeau, H., Fonollosa, M.-O., & Gagnon, L. (1997). Variation in the use of discourse markers in a contact situation. *Language Variation and Change, 9*, 191–217.

Schumann, J. (1978). *The pidginization process*. Rowley, MA: Newbury House.

Tagliamonte, S. (2006). *Analysing sociolinguistic variation*. Cambridge: Cambridge University Press.

Tarone, E. (1982). Systematicity and attention in interlanguage. *Language Learning, 32*, 69–84.

Tarone, E. (1985). Variability in interlanguage use: A study of style-shifting in morphology and syntax. *Language Learning, 35*, 373–404.

Thompson, S. A., & Mulac, A. (1991). The discourse conditions for the use of the complementizer *that* in conversational English. *Journal of Pragmatics, 15*, 237–251.

Trudgill, P. (1972). Sex, covert prestige and linguistic change in the urban English of Norwich. *Language in Society, 1*, 179–195.

Williams, J. (1990). Review of D. Preston, sociolinguistics and second language acquisition. *TESOL Quarterly, 24*, 497–500.

Wolfram, W. (1985). Variability in tense marking: A case for the obvious. *Language Learning, 35*, 229–253.

Wolfram, W., & Fasold, R. (1974). *The study of social dialects in American English*. Englewood Cliffs, NJ: Prentice-Hall.

Young, R. (1993). Functional constraints on variation in interlanguage morphology. *Applied Linguistics, 14*, 76–97.

CHAPTER 6

# AN INFORMATION-PROCESSING APPROACH TO SECOND LANGUAGE ACQUISITION

Jeanette Altarriba and Dana M. Basnight-Brown

An information-processing approach to the acquisition of a second language (L2) would suggest that several basic processes are involved in the learning of a new language. Attention, encoding, rehearsal, storage, retrieval, etc., are all facets that lead to grasping those mental representations that allow one to process information in a new language. McLaughlin and Heredia (1996), in an earlier edition of this handbook, outlined the extant literature on L2 learning that would bolster an information-processing framework as a way of lending structure to the existing research on the acquisition of a new language. The present chapter is an attempt to update that knowledge and expand upon their framework with the current literature and the theories and data that have been developed since that earlier work.

In line with the earlier chapter, we view humans as active and engaged problem solvers and maintain that the various components that direct and drive language behavior can be examined independently, though at some level, these components may interact, moderating overall behavior. It is also maintained that the processes that occur as one acquires a new language—a new symbol set—take time, and certain paradigms and tasks in the cognitive domain have been developed to measure response time. Finally, automatic processing, processing that occurs with little or no conscious awareness (Shiffrin & Schneider, 1977) is considered the cornerstone of the development of proficiency and expertise in an L2.

The following sections will examine the components involved in L2 acquisition from the above perspectives and highlight the role of automaticity, practice, cognitive restructuring, and individual differences in the learning of a new language. Finally, implications drawn from the above approach on pedagogical and instructional strategies will be discussed.

*The New Handbook of Second Language Acquisition*

## I. PROCESSING-BASED EXPLANATIONS FOR LANGUAGE LEARNING

What basic processes in language development either facilitate or hinder language learning? An information-processing approach to language development provides for an analysis of those processes broken down by levels of language representation. Phonology, orthography, and syntax, for example, are just a few of the levels of language that can moderate the pace and ease with which an individual learns aspects of a new language. These basic processes may be influenced, in turn, by other factors such as age of acquisition (AoA), memory span, context, and the environment. However, research has revealed that the basic processes that govern linguistic ability as applied at *any* age can vastly determine language learning.

One theory that at first glance appears to rest purely upon developmental mechanisms for language learning is the critical period hypothesis (Lenneberg, 1967). This idea implies that there is a critical period in human maturation beyond which language can never truly be acquired with native-like proficiency. A strict view of this hypothesis would imply that the proposed "cut off" applies to everyone, and as such, so long as learning takes place within this period of time, everyone is capable of equal mastery. Several researchers have applied this notion of critical periods to the learning of an L2 and have reported supporting data, particularly with regard to syntax and phonology (see e.g., Birdsong, 1992; this volume). Johnson and Newport (1989), for example, reported that individuals who learned English as an L2 by age seven performed as well as native English speakers on grammaticality judgment tasks. In contrast, they found that those who had acquired English later performed differently than native speakers and exhibited a decline in their performance on the above tasks as age of L2 acquisition increased. Moreover, neurological research indicates that late learners exhibit wave-forms as measured via event related potentials that suggest less left-hemispheric specialization in syntactic processing for late learners (cf., Weber-Fox & Neville, 1996).

In recent work, McDonald (2000) further challenged a strict interpretation of the critical period hypothesis, and in a more information-processing vein, delimited a basic level of language processing for which this hypothesis appears unsupported. In her work, native, early, and late Spanish learners of English and similar groups of Vietnamese speakers were asked to make grammaticality judgments for sentences in their L2.

Spanish speakers began learning English either at age 3, or in the case of late learners, at age 14. In the case of the Vietnamese participants, the early learners acquired English by age 5, while the late learners acquired English between the ages of 6 and 10 years. All groups were presented with English sentences orally and were asked to determine whether or not they were grammatical or ungrammatical. Of particular interest was performance on specific grammatical rules.

The results indicated that for Spanish speakers who were early learners of English, their performance was identical to that of native English speakers. Late learners demonstrated difficulties with all aspects of grammaticality (with the exception of syntax), as compared to native English speakers. For Vietnamese speakers, difficulties arose for early learners of English particularly for those grammatical rules that differed markedly from Vietnamese. The late learners, among the Vietnamese, had difficulties with English along the lines of the more general problems exhibited by late learners in the Spanish group. The author contends that the structure of the native language can moderate the degree to which L2 learning is accomplished in an expert manner. That is, to the extent that a non-native learner acquires a language that is quite distinct in terms of its phonology, orthography, etc., difficulties in decoding surface features can hinder the degree to which native-like fluency is ultimately acquired in the L2. Thus, it is important to examine such learning theories across a set of component processes for while the notion of critical periods may hold for some levels of linguistic processing, it may not hold across *all* basic components involved in the mastery of a new language.

In more recent work, McDonald (2006) extends her previous work and suggests that the difficulties experienced by late learners of an L2 can best be accounted for by the following processing issues: low L2 working memory capacity, poor L2 decoding, and inefficient processing speed in L2. As mentioned earlier, late L2 learners are often more likely to accept ungrammatical statements as grammatical, in their L2, as compared to native speakers. However, rather than relying on explanations that are merely linguistic, per se, McDonald notes that some of the difficulty lies with basic level, cognitive processes. Inherent in the grammaticality judgment task is the need to tax memory load as participants must perceive and analyze sentential content, semantics, pragmatics, etc., while performing a decision. In addition, phonological decoding must take place with the various components of the sentence or utterance. These tasks are typically time constrained as the participant must decide upon the current stimulus within a particular temporal framework and be prepared to process subsequent trials.

McDonald (2006) examined the relative contribution of the information-processing limitations noted above on a group of late learners of English with varying native language backgrounds (e.g., Chinese, German, Hindi, Japanese, etc.). All tasks were performed in English. Participants' working memory spans were measured. That is, they heard lists of words and were asked to report those words in order from smallest to largest—a size judgment task. Next, participants were administered a gating task wherein they heard an initial sound for a word and were required to report the entire word. Parts of the word were subsequently presented, and participants were asked to guess the word at each stage of the task until the word was accurately reported. Finally, participants were presented with one of two tasks: a word detection task, or a grammaticality judgment task. For the word detection task, participants were shown a visual fixation point on a computer screen for 2000 ms. This fixation point was replaced by a target word for 1000 ms. Then, a sentence was presented auditorily that either contained the word or did not contain the word. As soon as the word was heard in the condition in which it was present in the sentence, the participant was instructed to press the space bar as quickly as possible. The grammaticality judgment task included the oral presentation of sentences that were either grammatical or ungrammatical, in random order. Participants were asked to listen to each sentence and then to press one key on the computer keyboard if the sentence was grammatical and a different key if the sentence was ungrammatical. As with the word detection task, participants were asked to respond as quickly as possible, as responses were timed.

The results revealed some very important processing differences between the late learners of English and a comparable group of native English speakers. This latter group of participants had no exposure to a language other than English except within a classroom. Late learners of English had significantly lower memory span scores than their monolingual counterparts. It is important to note that this task involved the presentation and recollection of single words, and thus, was not overtly influenced by syntactic processing issues (i.e., an insufficient knowledge of basic English grammar). In the gating task, late L2 learners required more gates, on average, in order to correctly retrieve words, as compared to English monolingual speakers. Thus, the former group demonstrated greater word decoding difficulties than the latter. In the word detection task, late learners were significantly slower to detect target words in subsequent sentences than their matched controls. Thus, processing speed differences emerged across the two groups. Finally, the native speakers outperformed the late learners in the grammaticality judgment task. That is, native speakers were more accurate at judging grammatical versus ungrammatical sentences in English than the late learners of English. Overall, it appears that the difficulties that late L2 learners encounter in processing L2 words and sentences may lie at very basic levels of memory and cognitive processing—levels that are engendered in information-processing accounts of learning and memory—and not in aspects of the languages themselves. Thus, linguistic characteristics such as morphology, semantics, and the like may moderate various aspects of overall language knowledge, but actual comprehension may be influenced to a greater extent by basic memory processes.

While cognitive factors play an influential role in the process of acquiring the basic rules of a language, the actual *production* of language utterances may also be affected by these basic processes. One of those processes involves the planning process. McLaughlin and Heredia (1996) noted that, "Procedural knowledge is thought to be acquired through extensive practice and feedback, and once learned, is more easily activated in memory than declarative knowledge" (p. 218). The question arises then as to how one obtains a degree of fluency in language learning—a factor that does not merely suggest a speeding up of processes but rather a type of reconfiguration into newer and more economical processing structures. The question of fluency in language and the levels of mental representation that govern its development were recently explored by Derwing, Rossiter, Munro, and Thomson (2004). Their work was concerned with the underlying variables that represent the level of effort speakers must exert in the L2 in order to produce fluent utterances under a variety of conditions. In addition, they were interested in how those factors were perceived and interpreted by listeners. A main focus of their work was on language planning time and its effects on accuracy, syntactic and morphological complexity, and fluency. It has been reported that planning time is directly related to greater grammatical complexity as well as increased fluency (see e.g., Crookes, 1989; Yuan & Ellis, 2003). Moreover, in line with the earlier studies described above, planning by its very nature involves the use of memory capacity and memory retrieval in order to "program" forthcoming utterances.

In their work, Derwing et al. (2004) examined judges' rated fluency of speech samples that were collected from a group of Mandarin learners of English. These samples included picture descriptions, monologues on specific topics, and other dialogue tasks. The key difference across these different tasks was the degree to which specific planning had to take place that was more or less constrained in terms of time. For example, the picture description task included never-before-seen photos of people and objects that had to be verbally described by the participant immediately after viewing the picture. In the conversational tasks, participants were asked to discuss the happiest moment in their lives and were given about 30 seconds before their responses were recorded (monologue task). In the dialogue task, the participant was asked to question the researcher about their happiest moment, and a conversation between the researcher and the participant quickly ensued. All responses were tape-recorded. A set of untrained judges rated fluency, comprehensibility, and accentedness, while a number of trained judges rated outputs for "goodness of prosody" and other temporal factors of speech. Rated fluency measures included features such as amount of self-repetition, word selection errors, number of pruned or truncated syllables, prosodic factors, and other measurable speech characteristics.

The results indicated that ratings of fluency for participants differed as a function of the type of task. Ratings on the picture description task were significantly lower than on the other two, more conversational tasks—those for which planning time was provided and the information being elicited was, in part, already known by the participants. Planning time allows for greater accuracy in choosing lexical items, structures, and content, in general. Judgments of "goodness of prosody," however, did not vary across tasks. Overall fluency was more highly correlated to comprehensibility than to accentedness. Thus, one important component of production in an L2 relates to the degree to which time is available to plan utterances and access the grammatical rules and constraints in the lesser-known language. Additionally, it is important to note that the concept of language fluency is not unidimensional. That is, a speaker of a new language may exhibit perceived fluency for certain topics or in certain linguistic settings but not in others. Thus, one may conclude that other environmental features of the particular linguistic setting may moderate a basic process that governs the development of language proficiency or language fluency, such as planning. More will be said about the development of proficiency in L2, in a later section.

In the following section, we will turn to a discussion of whether the processes involved in second language acquisition (SLA) stem from a single mechanism or are the result of multiple cognitive processes.

## II. UNDERLYING MECHANISMS IN THE ACQUISITION OF LANGUAGE SKILLS

This section will review research that describes the process of learning a new language as one that involves a set of basic components that when aligned in certain ways, set the stage for the development of language proficiency in that new language. Historically, information-processing and cognitive approaches to SLA have focused on whether the process involves a single versus multiple mechanisms. As discussed in the previous section, much of the cognitive research on bilingualism has led modern theorists to favor a multimechanism account. This suggests that L2 learning consists of several processes rather than a single process (see McLaughlin & Heredia, 1996). In addition, these authors explain that there is "evidence for the importance of data-driven and conceptually driven processes in the acquisition of any cognitive skill as complex as L2 learning" (p. 222), which suggests that both top-down and bottom-up processes are involved in SLA.

One aspect of human memory and perception that appears to be extremely important in the language acquisition process is the working memory system (i.e., previously referred to as the short-term memory system). Working memory is best defined as the active, mental workplace for storing or rehearsing visual or auditory information. One of the main features characterizing this system is that it has limited capacity in terms of storage. With regard to the linguistic functions that involve working memory, Ashcraft (2005) explains, "... when word meanings are retrieved from long-term memory and put together to understand a sentence, working memory is where this putting together happens. It is the location of conscious, attention-consuming mental effort" (p. 165). Working memory has been shown to be extremely important in general language abilities, in areas of speech processing (ambiguous words, context effects, etc.) and in production. Variability in working memory capacity has also been shown to be responsible for individual differences in L2 learning ability (see e.g., van den Noort, Bosch, & Hugdahl, 2006), an issue that will be discussed in more detail in the following section.

Another cognitive process reported to be essential to L2 acquisition, and specifically involved in L2 speech production, is phonological memory (PM). PM is part of the working memory system and is specifically responsible for retaining verbal information in short-term memory. Typically, information in this system is only retained for a couple seconds; however, continuous rehearsal by the articulatory system can allow the information to be held for longer periods of time (Baddeley & Hitch, 1974). In order to examine the role that this cognitive process plays in L2 speech production, O'Brien, Segalowitz, Collentine, and Freed (2006) examined PM abilities in native English speakers who had low levels of proficiency in Spanish. The authors reported individual differences in PM capacity, such that individuals with better PM improved their narrative abilities in the L2 (over a 13-week testing period) as compared to those L2 learners with lower PM capacity. Most interestingly, O'Brien et al. (2006) concluded that during the early stages of L2 acquisition much of the individual's PM capacity is consumed with the learning of content words and vocabulary, in general. However, as proficiency increases, more PM capacity can be allocated to the acquisition of complex grammar. Lastly, once the bilingual has reached a high level of proficiency in the L2, PM will not play as large a role, mostly because speech production has become automatic (O'Brien et al., 2006, p. 399).

Therefore, it is evident that *multiple* cognitive processes and memory stores are essential for L2 learning (long-term memory, working memory, PM, etc.); however, specific dimensions of language (phonology, orthography, etc.) also determine whether (and to what extent) multiple mechanisms and processes are utilized. For example, a bilingual's first language structure and the degree to which it overlaps with the L2, will determine whether multiple processes are allocated to a greater degree (e.g., languages which differ in orthographic structure, such as Chinese and English, will require the use of additional and/or different perceptual and cognitive functions during word recognition). As explained by Wang, Koda, and Perfetti (2003), one of the primary goals of L2 learners is to acquire the orthography of the new language and successfully map it to spoken language. However, when first language (L1) structure differs greatly, the "new orthography has different mapping principles" (p. 133), which in turn place different cognitive demands on those L2 learners.

Recently, Basnight-Brown, Chen, Hua, Kostic, and Feldman (2007) have shown that L1 structure, particularly alphabetic (Serbian) versus nonalphabetic (Chinese) experience, influences cognitive processing in the L2 (i.e., English). In this study, Chinese–English and Serbian–English bilinguals (matched on proficiency) processed regular and irregular verb forms (e.g., *talked-talk*, *bought-buy*, respectively). The results indicated that the Serbian bilinguals, who had experience with an alphabetic language (and a highly inflected language), were more sensitive to form overlap between the past and present tense verb forms. Chinese–English bilinguals, in contrast, relied on different perceptual mechanisms and were therefore, less analytic when processing the verbs.

In the same vein, the impact of different writing systems on the mechanisms responsible for L2 processing has also been recently reported in Korean–English and Chinese–English bilinguals (Wang et al., 2003). In category judgment and phoneme deletion tasks, these authors observed that experience with an alphabetic language allowed the Korean–English bilinguals to be more sensitive to both phonological and orthographic information in the L2 (English). Native Chinese speakers, in contrast, were less sensitive to the phonological codes in English. Overall, the results from these studies provide compelling evidence that orthographic and phonological character-istics of a bilingual's L1 can play a critical role in the L2 acquisition process and the mechanisms employed in learning a new language. However, the question still remains as to whether or not the influence of certain linguistic features is the result of automatic processing or strategic processing on the part of the emerging bilingual. The role of automaticity in the acquisition of an L2 will be the focus of our next section.


## III. AUTOMATIC AND CONTROLLED PROCESSES

McLaughlin and Heredia (1996) described a process by which strategic processing and learning of certain linguistic building blocks are seen as a conduit to the development of automatic processes and the execution of complex tasks. The development of language skills may be viewed as a complex task that is driven by a number of subtasks and their various, smaller components. The current section summarizes the role of automaticity in the acquisition of language skills and focuses on the tasks that have been used to demonstrate automatic processing within the course of language development. Various studies are reviewed that capture the progression from strategic to automatic processing in the course of acquiring a new language and the importance of general cognitive functions such as rehearsal, repetition, and elaboration in L2 learning. In this way, one might view the development of automaticity as a function of the agility with which aspects of a new language are processed in an information-processing scheme.

In their review of the literature on automaticity and L2 learning, Segalowitz and Hulstijn (2005) emphasize the role of repetition, frequency, and practice in the process of gaining proficiency in an L2. In general, one can conceive of automatic processes as those that require little or no attentional control or attentional resources. The acquisition of any new skill may begin with effortful, controlled and strategic processing, but over time, and with practice and greater frequency of occurrence and use, these skills eventually become automatized. In an early study by Favreau and Segalowitz (1983, as cited in Segalowitz & Hulstijn, 2005), the importance of automatic processing in understanding proficiency in an L2 was demonstrated. Two groups of participants were included in their study. The stronger bilinguals were able to read text in L1 and L2 equally fast to achieve the same level of comprehension in each language. The weaker group read L2 more slowly than L1 to achieve the same level of understanding. Favreau and Segalowitz presented these groups with a primed lexical decision task in which prime words were followed by target words. Prime words were names of categories, such as "Fruit." Target words were either words from the same category, "Orange," words from a different category, "Chair," or nonwords. Participants were asked to read the prime words and to judge whether or not the target words were real words in a given language. Participants received pairs in both the L1 and the L2. Both the stronger and the weaker participants demonstrated facilitation in responding to targets that were preceded by related primes, in the L1. However, only the stronger participants showed this type of ease of responding when pairs were presented in the L2. Moreover, of interest was the finding that the weaker bilinguals were not overall slower than the stronger bilinguals—they merely showed less automatic activation of prime words. This type of task, the word priming task, assumes that once a prime word has been accessed and its characteristics have been retrieved, activation spreads to related words in one's mental representation for these words/concepts. When a target word is processed and that word happens to be related to the preceding prime, response times to that target word are facilitated due to the spread of activation from the prime (Collins & Loftus, 1975). Thus, for more proficient bilinguals, it appears that the automatic activation of meaning occurs similarly for both languages.

While automatic processing is important to the development of language skills in both an L1 and an L2, Segalowitz and Hulstijn (2005) note the importance of controlled processes, as well, in overall cognitive processing (particularly of a new language). For example, it is clear that individuals must focus on a language itself, its structure, phonology, morphology, orthography, etc., while learning the language, and this focus is required at any point in language acquisition since one never really reaches a stop-point with regards to language learning. In the comprehension of spoken languages, selective attention is involved in the process of filtering out extraneous information, noise, etc., in order to focus on those parts of spoken communication that provide the important details of the message being communicated. One must pay attention to various acoustic cues such as prosody, intonation, and the like, in order to properly comprehend the meaning of the communication. Thus, controlled processing is also inherent in the processes that one undertakes in order to fully acquire a new language.

In a recent study, Segalowitz and Frenkiel-Fishman (2005) demonstrated the role of attentional control and attention shifting in the development of proficiency in an L2. Participants were English–French bilinguals with varying degrees of proficiency in the French language. However, all participants were more proficient in English than in French. Participants performed a noun judgment task in which they were asked to judge whether or not particular words depicted animate or inanimate objects (e.g., a horse vs. a hammer). Trials were presented in English and in French. Participants' responses were timed. The results indicated that reaction times were significantly slower in L2 than in L1 for these participants. Thus, although the words were always highly familiar and the participants were extremely accurate, the L2 took longer to activate and to process therefore leading to longer reaction times in that language. A second study was aimed directly at the question of cognitive control. Participants were asked to perform two tasks. The first was a temporal judgment task in which they had to judge whether a word depicting time was close to or far from the present time. For example, "I'll do it soon," would be an example of a "close" judgment while "I'll do it later," would be an example of a distant judgment. In the second task, participants had to decide whether or not a conjunction indicated the presence or absence of a causal connection between two phrases. For example, in the phrase, "She gained weight because she overate," the word "because" indicates a causal connection between the two events mentioned in the phrase. In contrast, in "He passed the exam despite the fact that he never read the book," indicates that there is no apparent, causal connection between performing at a satisfactory level on the exam and reading the book.

Participants in the above study were provided with a cue on a computer screen as to the type of trial (i.e., temporal judgment or causal judgment) that would appear next. Over a series of trials, participants had to switch back and forth between these different types of tasks, in an unpredictable fashion. Trials were presented in the L1, the stronger language for these bilinguals, and in the L2, their weaker language. Results indicated that the cost in time involved in switching between tasks was larger in the L2 than in the L1. That is, the amount of time required to prepare and execute a trial in L2 when the preceding trial required a different type of task was longer than when the same type of switch occurred in L1. Switching between tasks simply took longer to accomplish in the L2 than in the L1. One might predict that had these bilinguals been more balanced in their knowledge of their languages, that the costs involved in switching between tasks would have been relatively equal in both languages. Thus, these types of task switching paradigms indicate that at once, some aspects of language processing are automatic, as when one retrieves knowledge of time and causal relations; however, these tasks also demand conscious and effortful processing particularly when planning to provide a new type of response. In this way, the use of language skills by emerging bilinguals can be viewed as a combination of automatic and controlled processing depending upon the demands of the current task.

While automaticity is an important feature of cognitive processing in that it allows humans to be more efficient and economical information processors, it is also the case that ingrained automatic responses may interfere with the acquisition of new linguistic rules in the L2 that are distinct from what has been automatized in the L1. For example, Zyzik (2006) examined a set of Spanish verbs that had been newly acquired by English–Spanish bilinguals. Verbs such as "*pesarse*" (to weigh) were used as they included the addition of "*se*" to the base verb "*pesar*." In a different form, this verb may be used to describe the situation where someone is weighing themselves, "*se pesa*." Participants viewed pictures that described a particular activity and were then given a cue sentence that contained the base verb along with a question or prompt requiring a response from the participant. In English, one might say, "He would like to weigh himself," (*El quiere pesarse*), or "He weighs himself every day," (*El se pesa todos los dias*). Thus, the distinction is between "weigh" and "weighs" in English whereas in Spanish, the issue involves proper use of the reflexive form. The results of this study indicated that early learners of Spanish often incorrectly attached "*se*" to particular lexical items overgeneralizing the use of this particular clitic. That is, whereas the English language makes these transitions by the simple addition of an affix in a single location, Spanish requires the knowledge of how to contrive the verb appropriately for a particular instance, and this task might involve placing the affix before the base verb or after the base verb. Thus, the grammatical rules governing these transitions as they are known in the L1 may be well ingrained in the participant, so much so that learning a variation of these rules in L2 takes quite a bit of effort and time. In this particular study, early learners were compared to groups of participants with greater levels of proficiency in Spanish. Although errors still existed, they were somewhat diminished in the more practiced groups of participants. That is, bilinguals with greater expertise in their L2 are able to recover from this type of linguistic error, as the frequency with which they encounter the proper uses of these verbs increases.

Other recent studies have documented the progressive integration of grammatical rules in L2 as a bilingual speaker becomes more proficient in that language. Jiang (2007) timed participants' reading of grammatical and ungrammatical sentences in their L2. The idea was to measure participants' sensitivity to grammatical errors in a self-paced reading task and to observe whether or not a delay in reading would occur when particular errors were included in the ungrammatical condition. Participants were native Chinese speakers who spoke English as an L2. An interesting aspect of this study was the fact that the errors that were included in the ungrammatical sentences were of varying kinds: errors in pluralization or errors of verb categorization. While there were no appreciable differences in participants' reading of grammatical and ungrammatical sentences when the errors were in pluralization, changes in verb structure produced slower reading times for ungrammatical sentences as compared to grammatical sentences.

Thus, knowledge regarding verb structure in the English language was much more highly integrated in the linguistic knowledge of these Chinese speakers than was the knowledge of pluralization. What this finding indicates from an information-processing point of view is that linguistic knowledge is decidedly parsed into various subcategories of knowledge, and to say that someone is fluent or proficient in a new language may be a misnomer if one does not specify the level at which the individual is proficient (morphological, syntactic, etc.). Clearly, not all language abilities evolve at the same time in either an L1 or an L2. It would be useful to investigate the progression of linguistic knowledge in an emerging bilingual and to document just what linguistic devices emerge over time and in what order. Moreover, results like this would lend support to the notion that the acquisition of an L2 is componential and not entirely "monolithic" (McLaughlin & Heredia, 1996).

## A. The Role of Practice

The preceding section emphasized the dynamic nature of L2 learning in that the process of learning requires controlled, attentional processing, but over time, automatic processing develops, as well. All the while, it is still the case, of course, that some attentional focus is needed in the face of new linguistic features of an L2, learning new syntactic structures, or new uses for already familiar words in an L2. However, just what are the means through which a strategic or controlled process becomes more automatic? One of the responses to this question is practice. With the frequent repetition of the same or similar processes comes the ability to perform a task much more easily and sometimes more quickly, as well. Gatbonton (1994), as cited in Segalowitz and Hulstijn (2005) "... advocated repetition to promote automaticity of basic communicative utterances within a context that requires the learner to coordinate these learning activities with the control of attention, decision making, and other higher level aspects of language processing" (p. 383). In fact, she coined the term "creative automatization" to denote the act of creating utterances that were effective and repeating those utterances over and over again.

Craik and Lockhart (1972) in their classic paper on levels of processing noted at least two types of practice or rehearsal: maintenance rehearsal and elaborative rehearsal. Maintenance rehearsal involves the repetition of the same, basic analyses that we perform on an incoming stimulus in a repeated fashion. According to Craik and Lockhart, this type of rehearsal may be useful to maintain information in short-term memory but may not be sufficient to transfer that information into long-term memory. In contrast, elaborative rehearsal, the kind of rehearsal that involves a combination of repeating the same processes one engages in when acquiring information as well as an attempt to re-organize, re-code, or otherwise elaborate upon information particularly in more meaningful (i.e., semantic) ways leads to the notion of "deeper" levels of encoding, the strengthening of memory traces, and longer-lasting memories. Thus, if true "practice" is to be involved as controlled processes become more automatic, they need to be of a certain level of depth in order to effectively lead to automatization.

In the case of learning a new language, to merely say that "practice makes perfect" would lead to an overgeneralization of just what is needed in order to become a fluent speaker of an L2. Sullivan and Perigoe (2004) discussed a method of language learning that has been applied to certain populations of L1 language learners. Their Association Method is described as an "... incremental, phonetically based, multi-sensory approach designed to increase the understanding and use of spoken language; improve articulation, co-articulation, and speech fluency; and teach reading and written composition skills" (p. 339). This is an information-processing approach to learning a language that focuses on attention, retention, and recall and views these processing venues as both separate and as integrated or "associated" with one another in very important ways. The language learning system that follows this particular view contains both structured learning tasks as well as the element of repetition or practice in the acquisition of new language skills. More will be said about this method of learning in a later section of this chapter. However, for the current section, the issue is that one of the guiding principles of this method is the idea that structure, repetition, and similarity in how specific linguistic examples are experienced leads to effective learning of a new language.

The next section takes these ideas one step further and explores the ways in which language learning leads to a mental restructuring in terms of a learners' cognitive framework to be better able to incorporate higher levels of linguistic information as one becomes more and more proficient in an L2.

## B. Restructuring in the Acquisition Process

When an individual begins to learn a new skill, or L2 for that matter, there are cognitive shifts and representational changes that take place during the acquisition process. For this reason, much of the cognitive research on SLA has focused on the restructuring or reorganization of information that occurs as skills proceed from novice to expert (i.e., or from low to high proficiency in an L2). Obviously, experts in any arena have usually had more practice and time to hone their skills, but of particular interest to the current discussion are the cognitive skills that are acquired during this time. For example, nonlinguistic research designed to examine differences between expert and novice chess players has suggested that experts perform faster and with less extensive searches of possible moves as compared with novices (de Groot, 1965, as cited in Holyoak, 1995). In addition, experts learned to perceptually encode larger and more meaningful chunks of information from the chessboard, suggesting that a restructuring of certain cognitive processes had occurred (Chase & Simon, 1973). In a different analytical problem-solving domain, the study of expert and novice physics problem solvers revealed that experts developed schemas that allowed them to categorize problems faster than novices (Chi, Feltovich, & Glaser, 1981). This in turn allowed them to minimize the time spent searching for a solution, similar to the cognitive shifting observed in expert chess players. Overall, research in these disciplines suggests that cognitive restructuring occurs because experts are more efficient at combining multiple rules into one rule (or fewer rules) (Holyoak, 1995).

In the domain of SLA, a similar restructuring of certain cognitive skills (i.e., and linguistic rules) has been observed as a bilingual's proficiency level increases. In their original chapter, McLaughlin and Heredia (1996) explained that "more expert language learners show greater plasticity in restructuring their internal representations of the rules governing linguistic input" (p. 217), which implies that greater proficiency occurs when linguistic rules are combined or reorganized in a more efficient manner (as evidenced by the novice/expert differences reported in the other skill areas previously discussed). The restructuring of L2 skills has often been described as a *U-shaped* function, the developmental phenomena characterized by a loss (or regression) of a specific skill. Once again, McLaughlin and Heredia (1996) reported that "various phenomena in the L2 literature suggest that performance declines as more complex internal representations replace less complex ones, and increases again as skill becomes expertise" (p. 217). For example, evidence of this occurs in the developmental process of phonological discrimination abilities. In L1 acquisition, infants are reported to reach a developmental stage where they begin to confuse words that have similar sounds, words that they previously had no difficulty with at earlier stages in the acquisition process. However, once their vocabulary improves, the confusion between these sounds diminishes and they are able to discriminate the sounds without difficulty (Stager & Werker, 1997). This apparent U-shaped developmental process has been reported to occur in SLA as well, although Werker, Hall, and Fais (2004) argue that this shift does not exhibit a true loss, but rather it is the result of a "restructuring or reorganization" that occurs when the individual begins to process the input (i.e., L1 or L2) differently.

In SLA, restructuring is necessary and occurs at different levels and across modalities—in speech production and perception, as well as in visual word recognition. It is quite evident to anyone who has interacted with early bilinguals or who has tried to learn an L2 later in life, that those who learn their L2 as children typically obtain native-like skills with regards to L2 phonology (Flege, Yeni-Komshian, & Liu, 1999). In order to test for similarities/differences in the restructuring of speech recognition and production in early and late bilinguals, MacKay, Flege, Piske, and Schirru (2001) examined the formation and reorganization of phoneme categories. It was hypothesized that if L2 sounds differed greatly from L1 sounds, the bilinguals would form separate perceptual categories, and would therefore, not be as influenced by L1 pronunciations. In contrast, L2 sound categories that were perceptually *merged* with L1 sounds and were not represented as separate perceptual entries, would not be perceived in as native-like a manner (i.e., first language pronunciation would taint perception of the L2 phonemes). In this specific study, MacKay et al. (2001) examined whether early and late Italian–English bilinguals formed categories for the English /b/, /d/, and /g/ phonemes, phonemes that are pronounced with a short lag voice onset time (VOT) in English, but which have prevoiced VOTs in Italian. It was expected that if merging (or restructuring) of the two categories occurred, the bilinguals would produce different results from both the English and the Italian monolinguals. In the experiment, the bilinguals were presented with words on a computer screen and were instructed to pronounce each word aloud. It was expected that when producing the English phonemes, the bilinguals would show (1) less prevoicing as compared to when they spoke in their native Italian, as well as, (2) more prevoicing when compared with native English speakers. The results appeared to support these hypotheses and also showed differences between early and late bilinguals. The early bilinguals revealed less prevoicing than the late bilinguals, suggesting that those who learned the language at a younger age had more native-like speech. Most interestingly, the results indicated that overall, the bilinguals did not form separate phonetic categories for the English /b d g/ phonemes. As MacKay et al. (2001) concluded, "the internal category structure of the bilingual participants existing (Italian) /b/ category evolved to encompass the phonetic properties of *both* Italian and English /b/ tokens" (p. 526), which suggests that phonetic restructuring produced a merging of the two perceptual categories.

In addition to speech production and perception, cognitive restructuring (or remapping of orthographic, phonological, and semantic codes) has also been reported in bilingual word recognition (e.g., Silverberg & Samuel, 2004; Talamas, Kroll, & Dufour, 1999). In a translation recognition task (i.e., bilinguals must determine if two words presented are correct translations of each other), less proficient English–Spanish bilinguals were more likely to confuse words that were similar orthographically (e.g., *ajo*, the Spanish translation of *garlic*, and *ojo*, the Spanish translation of *eye*), but not semantically. In contrast, the more proficient bilinguals made more errors to those words that shared semantic meaning, suggesting that as proficiency increases, linguistic restructuring causes the meaning of L2 words to be activated faster.

In the same vein, Silverberg and Samuel (2004) examined whether differences in proficiency and/or AoA of the L2 were responsible for changes in semantic and orthographic processing. Three groups of Spanish–English bilinguals: early bilinguals (i.e., those who they determined learned their L2 before the age of seven), and late bilinguals who were either highly proficient or less proficient in English (as measured by accuracy on a naming test), participated in a priming task. This traditional cognitive paradigm allows one to examine language processing under automatic conditions, if the correct experimental constraints are in place (see Altarriba & Basnight-Brown, 2007, for a review of those variables in the bilingual literature). This task involves the presentation of two words (usually in sequential order), to which the individual must determine if the second word is a real word or a fake word in the test language. In Silverberg and Samuel's study, word pairs consisted of semantically similar (*nail-tornillo*, the Spanish translation of *screw*) and orthographically similar items (*torture-tornillo*). Analogous to the findings reported by Talamas et al. (1999), it was observed that the early bilinguals showed sensitivity to semantic overlap (i.e., as evidenced by a significant semantic priming effect), but not to words that were orthographically similar (i.e., the absence of an orthographic priming effect). Late bilinguals with high levels of proficiency (i.e., matched on proficiency to the early bilinguals), however, showed no sensitivity to the semantic overlap between items, suggesting that AoA also plays a role in the restructuring process. Most interesting, is the fact that the high and low proficiency late learners (matched on AoA) did not show identical patterns in word recognition and processing, which suggests that AoA and proficiency both play a role in the cognitive and developmental shifts that occur in SLA.

Lastly, in addition to the developmental factors discussed, McLaughlin and Heredia (1996) point out that practice with the L2 also leads to restructuring, caused by the increase in automaticity of certain L2 linguistic skills (as described earlier). In summary, it is evident that as one becomes more proficient in an L2, the restructuring of linguistic rules and apparent shifts in cognitive processing play a large role in how L2 skills progress.

In the following section, we will turn to a discussion of individual differences in L2 learning and the cognitive processes that are thought to be responsible for why some individuals acquire higher levels of proficiency in an L2 than others.

## IV. INDIVIDUAL DIFFERENCES IN SECOND LANGUAGE ACQUISITION

Research, as well as personal experience for many, consistently reveals that it is easier to learn a foreign language as a child. In the past, much of the empirical work has focused on the critical period, or the specific window of time in which children are able to obtain native-like skills (i.e., specifically phonology) in an L2 (Lenneberg, 1967). However, one of the remaining questions driving current research is why some individuals are able to learn an L2 better than others. Naturally, certain personality characteristics and environmental factors, such as language aptitude (i.e., a talent for language learning), motivation, and learning strategies, have all been shown to influence the level of proficiency that an individual obtains (see Segalowitz, 1997 for a review). However, the goal of the current section is to explore cognitive differences across individuals that appear to modulate the acquisition process.

Several case studies conducted on multilingual individuals have revealed that overall intelligence is not the driving factor responsible for L2 abilities. For example, Smith and Tsimpli (1991) observed a male with below average IQ who was able to successfully learn more than one dozen languages. In addition, Novoa, Fein, and Obler (1988, as cited in Obler & Gjerlow, 2002) reported data from an American teenager (C.J.) who acquired several foreign languages in adulthood and obtained a very high level of proficiency and native-like abilities in several of them, despite the fact that his I.Q. was not particularly high (i.e., average to slightly above average). However, it is noted that he performed well on "Raven's progressive matrices", a nonverbal task that is specifically concerned with pattern recognition, suggesting that individuals with an affinity for L2 learning may have certain cognitive or perceptual abilities that differ from others.

One specific talent, or perceptual ability, that does appear to play a role in the acquisition of L2 phonology is musical ability. Even though this ability does not appear to be a *necessary* prerequisite for L2 learning (i.e., case study data from the individual C.J., discussed previously, revealed that he did not have superior musical ability, Novoa et al., 1988), it does appear to be a factor that influences L2 skills to some degree. Recent research designed to explore the role that musical ability plays in SLA successfully examined this factor in a larger sample size, as opposed to a single individual. Slevc and Miyake (2006) studied several dimensions of L2 skills (i.e., vocabulary and grammatical knowledge, phonological production, and perception) in native Japanese speakers who had all learned the L2, English, during adolescence. All participants were tested on the Wing Measures of Musical Talents (Wing, 1968), a series of tests that examine an individual's ability to perceive and produce accurate note and pitch changes in music. The results from regression analyses conducted on the L2 linguistic and musical skill data revealed that musical ability accounted for variance in how the bilinguals perceived and pronounced phonemes in English. However, it did not appear to influence lexical or grammatical knowledge in the L2. Overall, these findings from a larger population suggest that musical ability can predict L2 proficiency, specifically phonological skills in the foreign language. Interestingly, Slevc and Miyake (2006) suggest that this skill may be particularly important for late L2 learners who typically have a more difficult time acquiring native-like skills, a disadvantage that may require late learners "to rely on other, nonlinguistic mechanisms and abilities to aid in L2 acquisition" (p. 679).

In McLaughlin and Heredia's (1996) original chapter, they explain that an individual's ability to learn an L2 is influenced by several linguistic skills: phonetic coding ability, grammatical sensitivity, rote learning ability, and inductive language learning ability (Carroll, 1981, see McLaughlin & Heredia, 1996 for a review of these individual factors). Of particular interest to the current discussion is Carroll's analyses suggesting that individual differences in L2 acquisition stem from individual variation in cognitive functioning, or more specifically, differences in "executive" working memory (see also Segalowitz, 1997). As discussed in the previous section, working memory is defined as the active, mental workplace for storing or rehearsing visual, and/or auditory information (Ashcraft, 2005). The capacity of an individual's working memory store is often measured by having participants process and later retrieve lists of words (sometimes while performing another cognitive task). For example, individuals may be presented with two to six sentences (depending on the set size), and at the end of each set, they are asked to recall the last word in each sentence (Daneman & Carpenter, 1980). Using a slightly different method, Michael and Gollan (2005) described a typical memory span test where participants are asked to solve sets of math problems (2–6 problems per set). After each problem, a word is presented, and at the end of each set, all of the presented words are recalled. The number of correctly recalled items is used to determine the individual's memory span. Research that has used memory span to explore processing differences in a bilingual's first and second language has revealed that performance on memory span tasks is better in the L1, as compared to the L2. This most likely occurs because processing in an L1 is more automatic, and therefore, does not exploit working memory capacity to the same degree as it does in L2 processing (van den Noort et al., 2006).

Research examining the influence of individual memory span and SLA has revealed that working memory capacity can predict Test of English as a Foreign Language (TOEFL) scores in Japanese–English bilinguals (Harrington & Sawyer, 1992). More recently, Michael, Tokowicz, and Kroll (2003, as cited in Michael & Gollan, 2005), observed that Spanish–English bilinguals with higher memory spans were able to translate words in both language directions (L1–L2 and L2–L1) faster than those with lower memory spans. However, when the experimental task was changed so that only activation of the L2 was necessary (i.e., L2 picture naming), the memory span advantage disappeared. This led the authors to conclude that, "... higher working memory capacity is particularly beneficial for bilingual tasks that necessitate the activation of both languages" (Michael & Gollan, 2005, p. 401).

Perhaps even more interesting is the reported interaction between memory span, proficiency in the L2, and degree of orthographic overlap between a bilingual's two languages (Kroll, Michael, Tokowicz, & Dufour, 2002). In this study, native English speakers who were novice learners of Spanish and French, translated words in both language directions. Surprisingly, those with lower memory spans appeared to translate cognate words (i.e., words with similar orthography in both languages, for example, *music* and *musica* in Spanish and English) faster than those with higher working memory spans (Kroll et al., 2002). This pattern suggests that higher span learners were not as sensitive to form overlap between the two words, and may have been more concerned with the semantic meaning of the words. Overall, this implies that higher span learners may have actually reached a higher level of proficiency in the L2 (Michael & Gollan, 2005).

Lastly, a series of interesting experiments conducted by Christoffels, de Groot, and Kroll (2006) examined the role of proficiency and working memory span in three groups of Dutch–English bilinguals: (1) university students, (2) foreign language teachers of English, and (3) professional translators. All three types of bilinguals participated in picture naming and word translation tasks. The results revealed that the teachers and professional translators, who were matched on proficiency (as measured by educational background with the L2, a vocabulary test, and measures of response latencies in the L2), showed similar patterns of processing in both tasks.

As expected, the students, who had lower levels of proficiency, were significantly slower than these more proficient bilinguals (Christoffels et al., 2006).

Of greater interest to the current discussion is that data collected on three different tasks designed to measure working memory capacity revealed that the teachers and the students performed similarly, regardless of the fact that they differed in proficiency. In contrast, the professional translators performed significantly better than both groups, revealing that this group of bilinguals had greater working memory capacity. Overall, these findings suggest that lexical retrieval and L2 processing speed are skills that improve as proficiency increases, but that working memory span is a cognitive component independent of proficiency (Christoffels et al., 2006).

It is evident from the current discussion that certain cognitive components (i.e., specifically working memory capacity) appear to be responsible for some of the individual differences observed in SLA (aside from those that involve environmental and instructional differences in L2 learning). In addition to this component, it was mentioned previously that individual differences in PM could modulate the acquisition process as well (O'Brien et al., 2006). Lastly, transfer appropriate learning, the cognitive term used to describe why memory retrieval is more successful when the context (i.e., psychological state) of the to-be-remembered material matches the context in which it was learned, has also been thought to be responsible for individual variability in L2 learning. Segalowitz (1997) suggests that L2 learners differ in this cognitive ability, such that some individuals are better at transferring this linguistic information (between learning and retrieval) than others. Overall, it appears that several cognitive processes (i.e., perceptual and memory related) can determine why some individuals obtain more native-like abilities in a foreign language than others. Given what we now know regarding information processing when acquiring a new language, how can the underlying mechanisms that govern this process inform methods of teaching and learning a new language? It is precisely this question that is the focus of the next section.

## V. PEDAGOGICAL IMPLICATIONS AND INSTRUCTIONAL STRATEGIES

Thus far, it has been argued in the current chapter that L2 learning typically involves all of the basic mechanisms that are part of an information-processing approach to learning—attention, encoding, representation, practice and rehearsal, storage, and retrieval. These are the basic processes that characterize the processing of new knowledge from sensory store, to short-term store, and ultimately to long-term store. Working memory and the capacity of working memory are also important features of this approach, as is the ability to transform processes from controlled or strategic modes to automatized ones.

If these features are all aligned within a model or theory of language acquisition, what might that theory suggest as an effective approach for learning an L2? Sparks and Ganschow (1991) note that difficulties arise with language learning when individuals fail to perceive the individual components of a new language—components such as morphology, phonology, orthography, semantics, and pragmatics. Basically, this Linguistic Coding Differences Hypothesis sees the ultimate goal of attaining fluency in a new language as based on success at mastering the individual units of grammar of that language. Along these lines, Altarriba and Mathis (1997) taught English speaking monolinguals a set of common nouns in Spanish. Training occurred as a series of study-test phases in which participants were shown a pair of English–Spanish translations on a computer screen while hearing the words pronounced twice over headphones. The idea here was to emphasize the phonology of the two words providing for a possible auditory link between each word and its Spanish translation. Translations were also presented visually to emphasize the orthographic structure of the words. No cognates were used. In the test phases, participants were asked to match Spanish words to their English definitions, emphasizing the semantic characteristics of the words, as well as the pragmatics surrounding the uses of the words. Other tests had participants write the Spanish words they selected from a list to match a set of English definitions or sentences. Thus, participants practiced the orthography of the newly acquired Spanish words, as well. Even though participants experienced just a single learning session, they exhibited knowledge of the semantics and the orthography of the Spanish words in subsequent tests of their ability to recognize accurate translation pairs as compared to foils. Though performance was not at the level of a fluent set of Spanish–English bilinguals who served as controls, the evidence did indicate that the training methods positively contributed to the learning of Spanish vocabulary. Thus, "… there is an important need to use a variety of tasks that draw upon different skills to enhance fluency …" when acquiring an L2 (Derwing et al., 2004, p. 674).

In a classroom setting, Sullivan and Perigoe (2004) as referenced earlier suggest the use of the Association Method of language learning. In this approach, there are 10 basic tenets:

(1) Receptive language learning follows expressive instruction and production.
(2) Incremental teaching or component learning is important.
(3) Success at learning a language should be encouraged.
(4) Building on previously learned material is also highly relevant.
(5) The written form should accompany all language learning.
(6) Speech rate should be modified and started out slowly when learning to emphasize all phonological components of the new language.
(7) Spoken examples are always accompanied by their visual representations.
(8) Ultimately, it is expected that the learner will produce complete and accurate recall of all that is learned.
(9) Structure, practice, repetition, rehearsal, and similarity across items should all be incorporated into the learning environment.
(10) Teaching should incorporate all of the senses as learners are expected to pronounce, read, listen to, and write information acquired in the new language.

Thus, this method clearly embodies an information-processing approach to acquiring an L2 by emphasizing what some might call a "bottom-up" method of learning accompanied by an approach that emphasizes learning all of the components of a new grammar in a very systematic way.

In addition to learning the so-called "mechanics" of a new language, other factors influence the efficiency with which a new grammar is learned. For example, motivational and social cues may affect the way in which an L2 is acquired. The surrounding language context or language environment might likewise support, or perhaps hinder, the acquisition of language skills and abilities. Contexts such as formal classrooms, family settings, and cultural venues (e.g., study abroad programs) may also influence the ways in which languages are experienced, encoded, and ultimately stored in memory. Freed, Segalowitz, and Dewey (2004) performed a study that investigated the degree to which oral fluency differed as a function of studying a foreign language abroad versus studying it in a formal classroom setting. These two settings were compared to an intensive immersion program. They were also interested in finding out whether the amount of time spent on particular language-related tasks differed across settings. Finally, they asked whether or not any learning differences in the three aforementioned contexts were a direct result of any task-time differences reported across settings.

Freed et al. (2004) compared three different learning environments: formal language classrooms at a home institution, an extensive summer immersion program, and a study abroad program. Students were administered oral proficiency assessments both before and after participating in one of the above learning experiences. All of the students were involved in the study and learning of the French language. Participants were evaluated for the level of gain in language proficiency made over the course of a summer session in one of the three environments, particularly as a function of the time spent engaged in various learning tasks. Results indicated that the immersion group made significant improvements in their oral performance in French in terms of the total number of words spoken, the length of the longest turn taken, speech rate, and measures of fluidity. The study abroad group made significant gains only in terms of the fluidity of speech, as compared to the "at home" group, but neither improved as much as the immersion group. One factor that might account for the above difference was the fact that the immersion group reported having spent the greatest amount of time per day writing and speaking in French, while the study abroad group, for example, stated that they engaged in spoken English more than they did in spoken French. Thus, the results of a study such as this one indicate that it is the act of rehearsing, practicing, and repeating the language that strengthens the mental representations needed in order to gain oral fluency, and to the extent that an environment emphasizes those features in the course of their language learning exercises, speakers of a new language will progress to fluency at a much faster rate than their less-practiced counterparts. Again, features that are consistent with an information-processing paradigm are seen to contribute to an overall improvement in performance in a new, foreign language.

## VI. CONCLUSIONS

The current chapter builds upon the original work of McLaughlin and Heredia (1996) and explores the ways in which research and theory on L2 development has continued to be informed by an information-processing approach. Issues involving the role of memory, practice, automaticity, and strategic processing, attention, and retrieval have all played a role in shaping the direction of the past decade of research on L2 learning. It still remains as a reasonable conclusion that the acquisition of L2 skills is at once the function of learning the component parts of a language and of putting all those parts together to form a holistic knowledge base regarding that language. The acquisition of a grammar and all its features still informs the research paradigms that have been used since the publication of the earlier review, but additionally, one can observe the attempts to formulate new ways of language instruction and education based on those principles derived from an information-processing analysis of the factors contributing to successful language learning.

Future directions in research and thinking about this topic will likely focus on the ways in which people incorporate new knowledge or new schemas for language into memory through a more technologically advanced means of learning, in general, as well as focusing a bit more on the diversity of languages in terms of their structure and form and the relation between that diversity and new modes of learning.

## REFERENCES

Altarriba, J., & Basnight-Brown, D. M. (2007). Methodological considerations in performing semantic and translation priming experiments across languages. *Behavior Research Methods, 39*, 1–18.

Altarriba, J., & Mathis, K. M. (1997). Conceptual and lexical development in second language acquisition. *Journal of Memory and Language, 36*, 550–568.

Ashcraft, M. H. (2005). *Cognition* (4th ed.). Saddle River, NJ: Pearson Education, Inc.

Baddeley, A., & Hitch, G. (1974). Working memory. In G. A. Bower (Ed.), *The psychology of learning and motivation* (pp. 47–89). New York: Academic Press.

Basnight-Brown, D. M., Chen, H., Hua, S., Kostic, A., & Feldman, L. B. (2007). Monolingual and bilingual recognition of regular and irregular English verbs: Does sensitivity to orthographic similarity vary with language experience? *Journal of Memory and Language, 57*, 65–80.

Birdsong, D. (1992). Ultimate attainment in second language acquisition. *Language, 68*, 706–755.

Carroll, J. B. (1981). Twenty five years of research on foreign language aptitude. In K. C. Diller (Ed.), *Individual differences and universals in language learning aptitude*. Rowling, MA: Newbury House.

Chase, W. G., & Simon, H. A. (1973). The mind's eye in chess. In W. G. Chase (Ed.), *Visual information processing*. New York: Academic Press.

Chi, M. T. H., Feltovich, P. J., & Glaser, R. (1981). Categorization and representation of physics problems by experts and novices. *Cognitive Science, 5*, 121–152.

Christoffels, I. K., de Groot, A. M. B., & Kroll, J. F. (2006). Memory and language skills in simultaneous interpreters: The role of expertise and language proficiency. *Journal of Memory and Language, 54*, 324–345.

Collins, A. M., & Loftus, E. F. (1975). A spreading activation theory of semantic processing. *Psychological Review, 82*, 407–428.

Craik, F. I., & Lockhart, R. S. (1972). Levels of processing: A framework for memory research. *Journal of Verbal Learning and Verbal Behavior, 11*, 671–684.

Crookes, G. (1989). Planning and interlanguage variation. *Studies in Second Language Acquisition, 11*, 367–383.

Daneman, M., & Carpenter, P. A. (1980). Individual differences in working memory and reading. *Journal of Verbal Learning and Verbal Behavior, 19*, 450–466.

de Groot, A. D. (1965). *Thought and choice in chess*. The Hague, UK: Mouton.

Derwing, T. M., Rossiter, M. J., Munro, M. J., & Thomson, R. I. (2004). Second language fluency: Judgments on different tasks. *Language Learning, 54*, 655–679.

Favreau, M., & Segalowitz, N. S. (1983). Automatic and controlled processes in the first- and second-language reading of fluent bilinguals. *Memory & Cognition, 11*, 565–574.

Flege, J. E., Yeni-Komshian, G. H., & Liu, S. (1999). Age constraints on second-language acquisition. *Journal of Memory and Language, 41*, 78–104.

Freed, B. F., Segalowitz, N., & Dewey, D. P. (2004). Context of learning and second language fluency in French. *Studies in Second Language Acquisition, 26*, 275–301.

Gatbonton, E. (1994). *Bridge to fluency: Speaking*. Scarborough, ON: Prentice Hall Canada.

Harrington, M., & Sawyer, M. (1992). L2 working memory capacity and L2 reading skill. *Studies in Second Language Acquisition, 14*, 25–38.

Holyoak, K. J. (1995). Problem solving. In E. E. Smith & D. N. Osherson (Eds.), *Thinking*. Cambridge, MA: MIT Press.

Jiang, N. (2007). Selective integration of linguistic knowledge in adult second language learning. *Language Learning, 57*, 1–33.

Johnson, J. S., & Newport, E. L. (1989). Critical period effects in second language learning: The influence of maturational state on the acquisition of English as a second language. *Cognitive Psychology, 21*, 60–99.

Kroll, J. F., Michael, E., Tokowicz, N., & Dufour, R. (2002). The development of lexical fluency in a second language. *Second Language Research, 18*, 137–171.

Lenneberg, E. (1967). *Biological foundations of language*. New York: Wiley.

MacKay, I. R. A., Flege, J. E., Piske, T., & Schirru, C. (2001). Category restructuring during second language speech acquisition. *Journal of the Acoustical Society of America, 110*, 516–528.

McLaughlin, B., & Heredia, R. (1996). Information-processing approaches to research on second language acquisition. In W. C. Ritchie & T. K. Bhatia (Eds.), *Handbook of second language acquisition* (pp. 213–228). San Diego, CA: Academic Press.

McDonald, J. L. (2000). Grammaticality judgments in a second language: Influences of age of acquisition and native language. *Applied Psycholinguistics, 21*, 395–423.

McDonald, J. L. (2006). Beyond the critical period: Processing-based explanations for poor grammaticality judgment performance by late second language learners. *Journal of Memory and Language, 55*, 381–401.

Michael, E. B., & Gollan, T. H. (2005). Being and becoming bilingual. In J. F. Kroll & A. M. B. de Groot (Eds.), *Handbook of bilingualism* (pp. 389–407). Oxford: Oxford University Press.

Michael, E. B., Tokowicz, N., & Kroll, J. F. (2003, April). *Modulating access of L2 words: The role of individual differences and language immersion experience*. Paper presented at the Fourth International Symposium on Bilingualism, Tempe, AZ.

Novoa, L., Fein, D., & Obler, L. K. (1988). Talent in foreign languages: A case study. In L. K. Obler & D. Fein (Eds.), *The exceptional brain: Neuropsychology of talent and special abilities* (pp. 294–302). New York, NY: Guilford.

Obler, L. K., & Gjerlow, K. (2002). *Language and the brain*. Cambridge, UK: Cambridge University Press.

O'Brien, I., Segalowitz, N., Collentine, J., & Freed, B. (2006). Phonological memory and lexical, narrative, and grammatical skills in second language oral production by adult learners. *Applied Psycholinguistics*, *27*, 377–402.

Segalowitz, N. (1997). Individual differences in second language acquisition. In J. F. Kroll & A. M. B. de Groot (Eds.), *Tutorials in bilingualism: Psycholinguistic perspectives* (pp. 85–112). Mahwah, NJ: Lawrence Erlbaum Associates.

Segalowitz, N., & Frenkiel-Fishman, S. (2005). Attention control and ability level in a complex cognitive skill: Attention shifting and second-language proficiency. *Memory & Cognition*, *33*, 644–653.

Segalowitz, N., & Hulstijn, J. (2005). Automaticity in bilingualism and second language learning. In J. F. Kroll & A. M. B. de Groot (Eds.), *Handbook of bilingualism: Psycholinguistic approaches* (pp. 371–388). Oxford: Oxford University Press.

Shiffrin, R. M., & Schneider, W. (1977). Controlled and automatic human information processing: II. Perceptual learning, automatic attending, and a general theory. *Psychological Review*, *84*, 127–190.

Silverberg, S., & Samuel, A. G. (2004). The effect of age of second language acquisition on the representation and processing of second language words. *Journal of Memory and Language*, *51*, 381–398.

Slevc, L. R., & Miyake, A. (2006). Individual differences in second-language proficiency. *Psychological Science*, *17*(8), 675–681.

Smith, N., & Tsimpli, I. M. (1991). Linguistic modularity: A case study of a "savant" linguist. *Lingua*, *84*, 315–351.

Sparks, R., & Ganschow, L. (1991). Foreign language learning difficulties: Affective or native language aptitude differences? *Modern Language Journal*, *75*, 3–16.

Stager, C. L., & Werker, J. F. (1997). Infants listen for more phonetic detail in speech perception than in word learning tasks. *Nature*, *388*, 381–382.

Sullivan, A., & Perigoe, C. B. (2004). The association method for children with hearing loss and special needs. *The Volta Review*, *104*, 339–348.

Talamas, A., Kroll, J. F., & Dufour, R. (1999). From form to meaning: Stages in the acquisition of second-language vocabulary. *Bilingualism: Language and Cognition*, *2*, 45–58.

Van den Noort, M. W. M. L., Bosch, P., & Hugdahl, K. (2006). Foreign language proficiency and working memory capacity. *European Psychologist*, *11*, 289–296.

Wang, M., Koda, K., & Perfetti, C. A. (2003). Alphabetic and nonalphabetic L1 effects in English word identification: A comparison of Korean and Chinese English L2 learners. *Cognition*, *87*, 129–149.

Weber-Fox, C. M., & Neville, H. J. (1996). Maturational constraints on functional specializations for language processing: ERP and behavioral evidence in bilingual speakers. *Journal of Cognitive Neuroscience*, *8*, 231–256.

Werker, J. F., Hall, D. G., & Fais, L. (2004). Reconstruing U-shaped functions. *Journal of Cognition and Development*, *5*, 147–151.

Wing, H. D. (1968). *Tests of musical ability and appreciation: An investigation into the measurement, distribution, and development of musical capacity* (2nd ed.). London, UK: Cambridge University Press.

Yuan, F., & Ellis, R. (2003). The effects of pre-task planning and on-line planning on fluency, complexity and accuracy in L2 monologic oral production. *Applied Linguistics*, *24*, 1–27.

Zyzik, E. (2006). Transitivity alternations and sequence learning: Insights from L2 Spanish production data. *Studies in Second Language Acquisition*, *28*, 449–485.

CHAPTER 7

# THE ARTIFICIAL DEVELOPMENT OF SECOND LANGUAGE ABILITY: A SOCIOCULTURAL APPROACH

James P. Lantolf and Matthew E. Poehner

A general assumption of second language acquisition (SLA) research is that acquiring a language comprises the same cognitive process regardless of the social settings involved. Gass (1990) for instance notes that the fundamental psycholinguistic process of SLA is the same whether it occurs in classrooms or outside of them. Long (1998, p. 93) argues this position forcefully:

> change the social setting altogether, e.g., from street to classroom, or from a foreign to a second language environment, and as far as we know, the way the learner acquires does not change much either, as suggested, e.g., by a comparison of error types, developmental sequences, processing constraints, and other aspects of the acquisition process in and out of classrooms.

Given what we call the "cognitive identity assumption" (CIA), it is not too surprising that researchers and educators would call for the instantiation of instructional practices which more or less replicate the so-called "'natural' language learning experiences" of the outside world in the classroom setting, whereby among other things form-focused teaching with all of its accoutrements, including explicit error correction and grammar explanations, would be minimized (Larsen-Freeman & Long, 1991, p. 299).

At least one SLA researcher (Tarone, 1998, 2000, 2007), however, has challenged the CIA perspective. Tarone has argued, for example, that several SLA theories limit the scope of their research—and by implication, the claims derived from it—to "decontextualized learner cognition" (2007, p. 839). She insightfully reminds us that unlike computers, the human mind is not "impervious to social context" (2007, p. 839) and as such not only do learners receive different types of input and corrective

*The New Handbook of Second Language Acquisition*

feedback in different settings, but they also orient differently to input and feedback as settings change.

Although we do not agree that cognition can ever be decontextualized, since all human settings (including the experimental laboratory) are fundamentally social, and therefore contextual (see Harre & Gillett, 1994; Lave, 1997), we are in fundamental agreement with Tarone's position that context affects processing in profound ways. In fact, because our perspective is grounded in Vygotsky's sociocultural theory of mind, our position is not that context *influences* cognitive processes but that it is, as Leont'ev (1978) proposes, the very *source* of the human mind.

In the present chapter, we will consider some of the implications for language acquisition of Vygotsky's theoretical claim that the educational setting is a radically different cognitive space from other social circumstances in which people develop knowledge about the objective world. Space does not permit a full account of the theory and the evidence supporting its principles. Our focus will be two central aspects of the theory that pertain directly to development in educational settings: systemically organized (or what Vygotsky (1987) calls *scientific*) knowledge and mediation in the zone of proximal development (ZPD). The former provides the cognitive content while the latter is the metacognitive process through which social interaction takes on psychological status and becomes internalized (see Karpov & Haywood, 1998).

## I. THE SYMBOLIC BASIS OF MIND

Although the argument for the symbolic organization of mind has been widely discussed in the general psychological and, more recently, in the second language (L2) literature (see Lantolf & Thorne, 2006), we nevertheless believe it will be helpful to briefly review this position. The basis of the argument is that human thinking, like human labor activity, is mediated through auxiliary means. The auxiliary means in the case of thinking are variously referred to as symbolic tools or artifacts, which find their analogy in the technical tools that humans produce and deploy in order to operate on, and indeed change, the natural world. Just as technical tools (e.g., hammer, saw, shovels, bull dozers, computers, cell phones, etc.) directed toward the natural world modify and enhance the activity of our body, symbolic tools directed at our psychological world modify and enhance the activity of our brain. In both cases, what would otherwise be natural processes that humans share with other animals are restructured as a consequence of mediation.

Symbolic artifacts, as with technical tools, are produced by cultures with a specific intention in mind and to satisfy particular needs. Numbers and mathematics, for example, were originally created to meet specific concrete practical needs, such as keeping track of quantities of items exchanged in the market place. Geometry arose out of the need to control land areas covered by silt when the Nile flooded (Sanchez Vazquez, 1977, p. 175). Language originally served the communicative needs humans experienced as they engaged in collective work activity, such as hunting to obtain food. Eventually, of course, this resulted in human societal organization and the rise of culture.

Vygotsky argued that unlike with technical tools, the representational quality of symbols imbues them with *bi-directionality*. In other words, symbols can be outwardly directed as when we communicate our ideas and intentions to others in order to influence them in some way; or they can be inwardly directed for the purpose of influencing our own thinking processes. Here, it is essential to recognize that the primary, or original, function of symbolic activity is social with the secondary, psychological, function deriving from the social function. This is the root of Leont'ev's claim that the source of mind resides in the social (see Lantolf & Thorne, 2006; Vygotsky, 1987 for a full discussion).

As mentioned, the relationship between animals and the world is direct and unmediated, while that of humans is regulated through (linguistic) symbols that are self-generated but socially derived. Thus, when an animal is hungry, it immediately begins the process of searching out food to satisfy its physical need for nourishment while humans are able to inhibit such impulses. This would have proved advantageous in the case of our early ancestors, for instance, whose hunting endeavors were rendered far more efficacious through construction of appropriate weapons and enlistment of conspecifics than they would have been had individuals attempted to instinctively bring down prey on their own and using only their bodies (Arievitch & van der Veer, 2004).

Inhibiting what would otherwise be automatic instinctive behavior is a necessary precondition for planning, which involves carrying out an activity on the ideal plane through symbolic means prior to acting. Thus, while spiders simply weave webs, architects plan out buildings symbolically using language, numbers, and drawings before objectivizing them in concrete activity. Planning is a cognitive process that occurs not only internally in an architect's mind but also externally in the plans, which are simultaneously symbolic and material. The important feature of the planning process is that inclusion of symbolic artifacts changes the nature of the process itself. As Vygotsky cogently puts it:

> the inclusion of a tool in the behavioral process, first, sets to work a number of new functions connected with the use and control of the given tool; second, abolishes and makes unnecessary a number of natural processes, whose work is [now] done by the tool; third, modifies the course and the various aspects (intensity, duration, order, etc.) of all mental processes included in the instrumental act, replacing some functions with others, i.e., it recreates, reconstructs the whole structure of behavior just like a technical tool recreates the entire system of labor operations. (Vygotsky, 1997, p. 87)

Although the structure of mental activity changes with the insertion of symbolic artifacts into the thinking process, natural processes, endowed by human biology, are not eliminated. On the contrary, "they join the instrumental act, but they turn out to be functionally dependent in their structure on the instrument being used" (Vygotsky, 1997, p. 89). Just as with technical tools, which mediate and therefore alter the structure of our bodily movements when we use them (e.g., a hammer compels us to use a different physical motion than does a saw or a screwdriver), the integration of different symbolic tools into mental processing mediates and modifies the structure of mental operations.

## II. CONCEPTUAL MEDIATION: SPONTANEOUS AND SCIENTIFIC KNOWLEDGE

The principle of symbolic mediation has profound consequences for Vygotsky's conceptualization of the relationship between language and thinking. According to Lee (1985, p. 77), Vygotsky drew from the work of Sapir (1921/1949) to explicate how linguistic representation and communication (with others and with the self) relate to the thinking process. Here, he was primarily interested in the notion that words, as symbols, represent concepts that are themselves culturally organized generalizations with regard to the objects they denote in the real world. In this regard, Sapir (1921/1949, p. 15) wrote (a sentiment echoed by Vygotsky, 1987) "but what if language is not so much a garment [for finished thought] as a prepared road or groove?" and "as soon as the word is at hand, we instinctively feel, with something of a sigh of relief, that the concept is ours for the handling. Not until we own the symbol do we feel that we hold a key to the immediate knowledge or understanding of the concept" (Sapir 1921/1949, p. 17).

The concept represented by the English word "tree" is a culturally created generalization for an abstract object that in fact does not materially exist in the natural world. What exists are lindens, maples, willows, pines, etc. Vygotsky (2004, p. 171) relates the case of a child without much formal education, who when presented with the question "How do a tree and a log differ?" responded with "I haven't seen a tree, I swear I haven't seen one" and when the researcher pointed to a tree that was directly outside the window where the interaction happened and asked "And what is this?" she received the answer "It's a linden." Vygotsky points out that "the boy was correct: none of us has seen a tree. We've seen birches, willows, pines, and so forth." (*ibid.*). Culture has created the abstract and general concept "tree" represented linguistically in the English word *tree* and in the Spanish word *árbol*, or the German word *Baum*. Yet the child, because of the impoverished cultural circumstances in which he had been raised, had not mastered the concept "tree" and his response was based on his belief that "tree" was yet another concrete object on a par with linden, willow, and birch. Sapir (1921/1949, p. 14) argues that in our daily lives, we are normally not as concerned with concepts represented in language as we are "with concrete particularities and specific relations." Thus, when a speaker points out to a listener that "a dog is running through the flowerbed," it is not likely that either interlocutor is much focused on "dog" as a general concept and is instead much more concerned with the concrete entity that is likely to damage the flowers.

### A. Spontaneous and Scientific Concepts

Vygotsky captures the difference between conceptual representation and concrete use of language in his distinction between *spontaneous* and *scientific concepts*. Spontaneous concepts are formed during concrete practical experience and largely based on "an immediate observable property of an object" (Kozulin, 1995, p. 123). At the very core of our lived experience as human beings, spontaneous concepts are empirical, developed over time, and generally more than adequate for carrying out daily activities. In spite of their functionality, however, they are often incomplete or not fully accurate. For instance, in the prescientific era, our visual senses informed us that the sun moved across the sky, and even though we now know better we continue to talk, think, and behave in our everyday world as if we lived in a geocentric universe where the sun rises, sets, and moves across the sky.

In general, the meanings of words acquired during childhood socialization constitute spontaneous knowledge. Children's understanding of a kinship term such as "uncle" normally arises spontaneously and unconsciously, and it, along with other kinship terms, is something children have a hard time systematically explaining through definition, relying instead on explanation through concrete reference. Words such as "rose" and the general categorical term "flower" often are understood by children to be synonymous and to refer to specific concrete objects. As Vygotsky (1987) argues and Luria (1982) demonstrates through empirical research, children eventually develop a more conceptual understanding of flower as a generalization and of "rose" as an instantiation of the more general notion. Indeed, for Vygotsky, this process is the very foundation of the role of language in thinking.

Some types of everyday knowledge are not spontaneously acquired but are nonetheless not on a par with scientific knowledge (see below). This type of knowledge is intentionally learned, often involving some form of explicit instruction. Included within what we might call "non-spontaneous" everyday knowledge are such capacities as baking cakes, driving cars, repairing engines, carpentry, butchery, etc. Such knowledge is, in large part, and like spontaneous knowledge, grounded in direct empirical observation. One does not need a deep understanding of chemistry to bake a cake, or of the physics of motion to drive a car, or of animal biology to butcher a carcass.

Empirical knowledge, as Karpov (2003, pp. 69–71) points out, "may work if the common salient characteristics of objects or events reflect their significant, essential characteristics," but it runs into problems when observable features of an object or set of objects are not essential features. Consider, for example, why clothes dry when hung out of doors. An empirical, and perfectly adequate, response would be "because of the sun." Below we will present a scientific response to the question based on more abstract and systematically organized knowledge. In many ways, non-spontaneous empirical knowledge is similar to the rule-of-thumb explanations of grammatical features provided in typical language instruction. Hammerly (1982) characterizes rule of thumb as "*simple, nontechnical, close to popular/traditional notions*" (p. 421, italics in original) and recommends that grammar explanations be "short and to the point" because if they are complex and extensive, "it is too much for the students to absorb" (p. 421). A common explanation for use of preterit aspect in Spanish found in many textbooks is that if a sentence contains a temporal adverb indicating past (e.g., *ayer* "yesterday"), the preterit should be used. Such an account does reflect use of preterit in some concrete circumstances, but it fails to capture the general principle of verbal aspect explained later in the chapter.

## B. Scientific Concepts

Scientific concepts "represent the generalizations of the experience of humankind that is fixed in science, understood in the broadest sense of the term to include both natural and social science as well as the humanities" (Karpov, 2003, p. 66). These concepts arise as a consequence of *theoretical learning*, which is domain specific and "aimed at selecting the essential characteristics of objects or events of a certain class and presenting these characteristics in the form of symbolic and graphic models" (Karpov, 2003, p. 71). The developmental value of theoretical knowledge is that it liberates us from the constraints of everyday experiences, allowing us to function appropriately in a wide array of concrete circumstances. This is because theoretical knowledge empowers individuals to "reproduce the essence of an object [physical or symbolic] in the mental plane" (Kozulin, 1995, p. 124).

Earlier we mentioned the everyday understanding of the clothes-drying process. Scientifically, however, the explanation of evaporation is that light energy is absorbed by clothing, which increases the kinetic energy of water molecules to the point where they overcome the adhesive forces binding them to the clothing causing them to release into the atmosphere (Ratner, 2006). As a further example, consider the difference between the everyday understanding of circle as a property of objects that share the common feature of roundness—a wheel, a pancake, a bracelet—and the scientific concept of a circle as "a figure that appears as the result of the movement of a line with one free and one fixed end" (Kozulin, 1995, p. 124). The scientific definition encompasses all possible circles and "requires no previous knowledge of round objects to understand" (p. 195). According to Kozulin (p. 195), teachers often introduce the concept of circle to their students through empirical observation by showing them examples of round objects, much in the way spontaneous learning happens in the everyday world.

## III. METACOGNITION: THE ZONE OF PROXIMAL DEVELOPMENT AND SELF-REGULATION

In articulating the relevance of joint activity for subsequent independent functioning, Vygotsky outlined a theoretical framework for understanding the full range of individuals' abilities as well as a grounded approach for optimally supporting their development. Both of these functions—diagnosis and intervention—are expressed in his well-known concept, the ZPD. The ZPD initially appears in Vygotsky's writings in the context of IQ testing among students entering primary school (for details, see van der Veer & Valsiner, 1991, pp. 336–341). Vygotsky noted that only children with low IQs at the start of schooling improved their scores when retested later, while students with high scores tended to remain at the same level. Vygotsky's research with special needs children led him to suspect that the explanation might be that school instruction was not uniform in its impact on the children's development.

Following his understanding of the relation between intermental and intramental functioning, Vygotsky proposed a double method of assessment in which the children were offered mediation as their independent performance began to break down. He reasoned that their responsiveness provided important clues to their level of development. He explained the approach with examples such as the following:

> Imagine that we have examined two children and have determined that the mental age of both is seven years. This means that both children solve tasks accessible to seven

year olds. However, when we attempt to push these children further in carrying out the tests, there turns out to be an essential difference between them. With the help of leading questions, examples, and demonstrations, one of them easily solves test items taken from two years above the child's level of [actual] development. The other solves test items that are only a half-year above his or her level of [actual] development. (Vygotsky, 1956, pp. 446–447; cited in Wertsch, 1985, p. 68)

In this way, Vygotsky was able to obtain a view of the children's abilities that encompassed both their independent performance as well as the level of performance they reached when offered mediation. The former he described as their *zone of actual development* and the latter their *ZPD*. Vygotsky forcefully argued that failure to take account of an individual's ZPD means failure to fully understand the range of his/her abilities:

... with the help of this method, we can take stock not only of today's completed process of development, not only the cycles that are already concluded and done, not only the processes of maturation that are completed; we can also take stock of processes that are now in the state of coming into being, that are only ripening, or only developing. (Vygotsky, 1956, pp. 447–448; cited in Wertsch, 1985, p. 68)

Vygotsky found that the children's degree of responsiveness to mediation during the IQ test was a better predictor of subsequent academic performance than was solo performance. Learners who improved their performance substantially with mediation were assumed to have a larger ZPD than those whose improvement was more modest, and the large ZPD group made greater gains in schooling. Vygotsky further reasoned that learners with initially high IQ scores who failed to show marked improvement during the first year of school were not being adequately challenged by the school curriculum. In a sense, their ZPD lay beyond what was offered in school and as a result they stagnated. From this, Vygotsky concluded that teaching has the greatest impact on learner development when it is focused just beyond their current level of ability, that is, when it targets their ZPD. Thus, Vygotsky came to conceptualize teaching and assessment as a dialectic: fully understanding an individual's abilities entails offering mediation in order to co-construct a ZPD, while mediation, as a form of support aimed at helping the individual exceed his/her current abilities, constitutes teaching in support of development; conversely, teaching to promote development demands sensitivity to individuals' emergent needs and abilities, that is, to their ZPD. This integration of teaching and assessment as a unified activity was subsequently taken up by researchers and educators under the rubric *Dynamic Assessment* (DA).

## IV. EDUCATION AS ARTIFICIAL DEVELOPMENT

According to Vygotsky (1997, p. 88) "education may be defined as the artificial development of the child" and as such it is seen as "the artificial mastery of natural processes of development."

We are not making an argument that supports a return to grammar-translation pedagogy; nor are we arguing in support of memorization of abstract grammatical formulae. Theoretical knowledge, whether it be of a circle, evaporation, or grammatical aspect, in and of itself, is essentially useless. Indeed, Vygotsky (1987, p. 169) recognized this in commenting that theoretical concepts "detached from reality" constitute *verbalism* that is highly unlikely to result in any meaningful development on the part of the student. The key to educational development is to connect theoretical understanding with concrete practical activity. This process is referred to as *praxis* (see Sanchez Vazquez, 1977). Ilyenkov (1974) suggests that knowledge not connected to concrete activity is not knowledge in the true sense and at best is a "substitute" for real knowledge. Following Vygotsky, he argues that verbalism—"the chronic disease of school education"—can only be overcome if students are guided to connect theoretical concepts to the object of study as it exists in the real world. In this way, learners can assess the effectiveness of the concept itself and if necessary challenge it, or the efficacy of how they may be using it, to guide their activity. Connecting the concept and object of study is not likely to occur through rehearsal of the object in prefabricated activities designed to illustrate the correctness of a given explanation. This not only means that traditional pattern drills and other grammatical exercises that illustrate how given rule-of-thumb function are counter-productive to genuine understanding and mastery, but it also calls into question the idea that tasks should be designed to elicit specific features of language (see Ellis, 2003) or that input should be structured "so that learners are pushed away from the less-than-optimal strategies" (e.g., assign agent role to first noun in a sentence) (Wong, 2004, p. 37).[1] As will be documented in the next section, learners have a difficult time overcoming the consequences of such approaches when they are eventually confronted with the real object, in the present case, language.

## A. Conceptual Knowledge in the Language Classroom: Aspect in L2 Spanish

In this section, we briefly discuss data from an extensive study on the teaching of Spanish as a foreign language conducted by Yáñez Prieto (2008) built around concept-based principles. To our knowledge, Negueruela (2003) was the first to design an L2 course using concept-based instruction as its pedagogical centerpiece. Like Yáñez Prieto, Negueruela also approached Spanish verbal aspect from a conceptual per-spective, although he worked with lower, intermediate-level learners and relied on a somewhat dated (Bull, 1971) explanation of the function of aspect. Yáñez Prieto, in contrast, relied upon more current theoretical discussions of aspect as emerging from research in cognitive linguistics (see Castañeda, 2006a, 2006b; Doiz-Bienzobas, 2002; Rothstein, 2004; Salaberry, 2000). In addition, while Negueruela attempted to link theoretical knowledge with practical activity by engaging learners in mini-dramas and scenarios to stimulate interaction, Yáñez Prieto's (2008) study made use of literary

---

[1]Van Patten and Sanz (1995, p. 173) recognize that at some point, learners must be exposed to discursive input, but they argue against this in the early stages of instruction as it risks using up processing time and it may also diminish the chances of noticing the relevant feature. This goes to the heart of Ilyenkov's point that manipulating the object of study to illustrate the veracity of the rule or explanation given is a distortion of the goal of education, which is to connect theoretical knowledge with the real object of study rather than a contrived version of it.

texts, which students read, discussed, analyzed for content and language, and used as the basis for writing activities. Neguereula's study has been considered in numerous other venues and therefore we will forego further analysis here (see Lantolf, 2007; Lantolf & Thorne, 2006; Negueruela & Lantolf, 2006).

Yáñez Prieto's study was carried out in an advanced university-level Spanish course with the researcher serving as the instructor. The course was conducted over a 16-week period in the spring semester of 2004 at a major US research university. The focus of the course was teaching language and literature as a unity in order to promote learner development in both domains: that is, the ability to read Spanish literary texts and to use this ability to enhance proficiency in speaking and writing the language. Among the topics covered was the connection between figurative language in everyday interaction and its use in literature—a surprising topic to many students, who associated figurative language with literature and viewed everyday spoken language as "highly literal" (see Littlemore & Low, 2006). We limit our discussion to instruction in verbal aspect, a notoriously difficult feature of Romance languages for speakers of English.

Concept-based instruction requires presenting learners with a coherent verbal statement of the theoretical concept under study, and more importantly, it calls for the development of a material representation of the concept in a form that both guides learner performance and is also internalizable (Gal'perin, 1967; Talyzina, 1981). The materialization can be in the form of concrete everyday objects, as for instance, when Karpova (1977) used colored dishes to materialize words to teach young (3–4-year olds) children the concept of words and syntax in L1 Russian.

According to Whitley (1986), the following is representative of how the aspectual distinction in Spanish is presented to English-speaking learners: imperfect "tells what was happening; recalls what used to happen; describes a physical, mental emotion; tells time in the past; describes the background; and sets the stage upon which another action occurred," while the preterit "records, reports, and narrates" and in the case of certain verbs, "causes a change of meaning," which is relative to English and not a component of the concept of aspect. Yáñez Prieto, adopting a conceptual approach, first explained lexical aspect whereby verbs (or events) have inherent aspect. That is, some events or states are by nature perfective or imperfective and this is encoded in words such as "jump," "throw," "hit," and "shoot," which are inherently perfective because the beginning and the end of the event coincide, while "walk," "study," and "talk" as well as "like," "resemble," and "believe" encode inherently imperfective events or states, that once initiated may continue indefinitely. Following Salaberry (2000, p. 19), Yáñez Prieto explained that the distinction in lexical aspect can be made more fine grained through use of a set of semantic features. Accordingly, *dynamicity* distinguishes states from events, whereby the former lack and the latter possess this quality. Events in turn are distinguished as *activities*, which have no specified end point (e.g., run, walk, swim, etc.); *accomplishments*, which extend over time but have a goal or end point (e.g., paint a picture, make a chair, build a house, etc.); or *achievements*, which have an inherent end point (e.g., jump, throw, find, lose, etc.). Activities and states, because they have no clear end point, lack *telicity* and are therefore classified as *atelic*, while accomplishments and achievements have a clear end point and possess the quality of telicity. Finally, *durativity* serves to distinguish achievements, which as punctual events are non-durative, from accomplishments and activities, which, because they extend over time, are durative.

Once students understood lexical aspect, the instructor explained how morphology allows users to override lexical aspect in order to adopt a particular temporal perspective on a given event or state. For example, the stative verb *estar* (to be at a place) is inherently non-dynamic, durative, and atelic, but can be brought into discourse as a telic event, as in *Estuvo en Madrid en siete días* (It took him/her seven days to get to Madrid).

The concept of grammatical aspect was then materialized for the learners in the schemas presented in Figures 1 and 2 for preterit and imperfect, respectively.

The figures take account of user perspective and focus. The image of an eye represents the user's (speaker or writer) position in time. $P_1$ and $F_1$ indicate, respectively, the initial perspective and focus of the speaker or writer. The possibility of a second perspective with an accompanying focus is represented in the image of a person holding a camera. The initial perspective in both figures places initial focus on the past in contrast to the present or future as the time frame under consideration. This may bring a second perspective into play with its own focus. The second focus may be on the inception or termination of an event, which would in either case call for preterit morphology. Thus, a second focus on the inception of Jazmin's running would yield an utterance such as *En ese momento, Jazmín corrió hacia la estación de trenes* (At that moment, Jazmin ran (launched off running) toward the train station). A second focus on the termination of the event, as in *Jazmín corrió a la estación de trenes* (Jazmin ran to the train station), could also be brought into discourse using preterit morphology. Notice that the verb *correr* (to run) is lexically categorized as an atelic activity. If there is no secondary perspective, then the initial focus $F_1$ is on the event in its entirety as bounded; that is, having a beginning, middle, and end point. Thus, *ayer corrí* (yesterday I ran) and *el año pasado corrí todos los días* (last year I ran every day) illustrate the use of grammatical morphology to treat an inherently atelic activity as if it were a telic accomplishment.

With regard to imperfective aspect, as with preterit, the initial perspective $P_1$ and focus $F_1$ is past. However, when the secondary perspective $P_2$ and accompanying focus $F_2$ orients toward the portion of the event that unfolds between the initial and terminal points (i.e., its boundaries), imperfective meaning is intended and therefore the corresponding morphological markers must be suffixed to the verb. Notice that this situation holds irrespective of whether a temporal expression such as *ayer* (yesterday) or *el año pasado* (last year) is used. Thus, a secondary shift in focus from an event's "boundedness" to its "ongoingness," yields an imperfective utterance, as in *el año pasado corría todos los días* (last year I [would or used to] run every day). In this case, an inherently durative, atelic activity is brought into discourse as such and only its past temporal quality is in focus. On the other hand, an inherently telic accomplishment, such as *construir una casa* (to build a house), rendered in the imperfect is talked about as if it were atelic and therefore unbounded *el año pasado construía una casa* (last year I was in the process of building a house).

Of course, one can say much more about Spanish aspect than is illustrated in the foregoing brief discussion. However, we hope it gives the reader an idea of how the instructor presented the theoretical concept. Yáñez Prieto (personal communication to

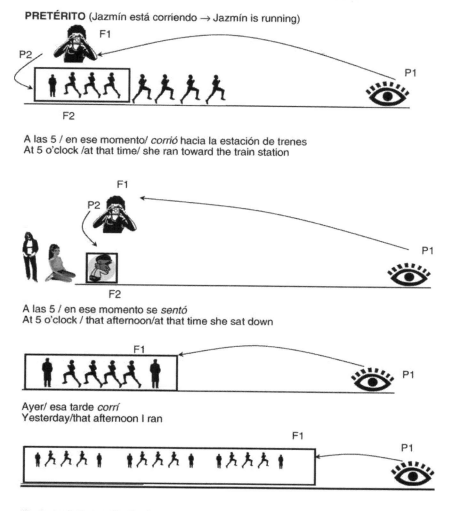

**PRETÉRITO** (Jazmín está corriendo → Jazmín is running)

A las 5 / en ese momento/ *corrió* hacia la estación de trenes
At 5 o'clock /at that time/ she ran toward the train station

A las 5 / en ese momento se *sentó*
At 5 o'clock / that afternoon/at that time she sat down

Ayer/ esa tarde *corrí*
Yesterday/that afternoon I ran

El año pasado *corrí* todos los días
Last year I ran every day

*Corrí* en un equipo de atletismo por dos años
I ran on a sports team for two years

**Figure 1**   Materialization of perfective aspect (based on Yáñez Prieto, 2008).

Lantolf, April 14, 2008) has since indicated that she would revise the materialization schema presented in Figures 1 and 2 in the future, because some students experienced problems fully grasping its significance. Nevertheless, most of the students benefited from the conceptualization and materialization of aspect and were therefore able to understand that use of aspect in Spanish depends on the meanings a user wishes to bring into discourse and not on some empirically based notion of what is correct or incorrect.

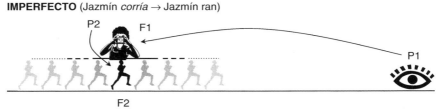

Ayer/ en ese momento/ esa tarde *corría*
Yesterday/at that time/that afternoon he was running

**Figure 2**   Materialization schema for imperfect aspect (Yáñez Prieto, 2008).

Yáñez Prieto brought conceptual knowledge into contact with practice through the reading, analysis, and discussion (oral and written) of literary texts. To be sure, she engaged her students in a wide array of additional communicative activities, but the central purpose of the course, as already mentioned, was the integration of language and literature. The catalyst for the "experiencing of aspect" was a short story written by one of the most famous literary figures of the Hispanic world, the Argentine writer Julio Cortázar. The story *Continuidad de los parques* "Continuity of the parks" was selected for three reasons, according to Yañez Prieto: the vocabulary is relatively simple, the story is short (one page in length), and the writer's use of aspect challenged the typical rule-of-thumb approach. In Cortázar's story, the author plays with aspect in ways that obviously contradict rule-of-thumb pedagogy. For example, instead of using preterit to indicate that a character in the story entered a room or arrived on the scene, Cortázar casts these actions in the imperfect: "*Primero **entraba** la mujer, recelosa; ahora **llegaba** el amante, lastimada la cara por el chicotazo de una rama*" ["First, the woman entered-*imperfect* fearfully; now, the lover arrived-*imperfect* with his face slashed from an encounter with a branch"] (Yáñez Prieto, 2008) [bold and italics in original].

The story was contrasted with a scene from a Spanish-language soap opera which used aspect shifts in a very different way from Cortázar. The point was to raise the learners' awareness of "free direct speech" represented in the soap opera with "free indirect speech" represented in the stream of consciousness depicted in Cortázar's story (Yáñez Prieto, 2008). The instructor believed that the difference between the story and the soap opera would create cognitive dissonance for the students that could be used to promote development. The students were then provided with activities where they had to transition between free direct and free indirect speech and explain the shifts in meanings that occurred in each case.

The example that follows documents the cognitive dissonance experienced by a learner, whose pseudonym is Dulcinea, when conceptual understanding of aspect was brought into conflict with her previous rule-of-thumb learning. The excerpt is taken from Dulcinea's dialogue journal during the seventh week (roughly the mid point) of the course:

(1)   This week we learned about aspect and perspective. I feel that I am starting to understand that there are many more uses for the preterit and imperfect than those introduced in textbooks. **It is confusing however to grasp the idea that the**

**preterit can be used to describe something in the past, when we have been taught the "rules" that the imperfect is used for description in the past**. (Yáñez Prieto, 2008) [Bold in original]

As Yáñez Prieto points out, Dulcinea's comments do not reflect a reorientation toward a conceptual approach to aspect, according to which user meaning arises from perspective and focus; instead, they indicate an attempt to expand the original rule of thumb to include preterit as an option for description in the past.

The conflict created by clash of concept-based and rule-of-thumb pedagogies, also well documented in Negueruela's (2003) study, is seen not only in the students' understanding of aspect, as Dulcinea's remarks show, but also in the learners' performance and their explanation of the aspectual choices they make in this performance. The following is an excerpt from the discussion between the instructor and Juliet (also a pseudonym) about Juliet's reasons for using imperfect aspect in one of the sentences in a composition written in the early part of the course. The topic of the conversation is the sentence: *esto era la verdad para nuestra heroína* (this was [imperfect] the truth for our heroine). Juliet explains her choice in (2):

(2)   ... now that I think, I think that it should be *"fue"* [was-preterit] ? ... **Because I'm talking about the teenage years,** but, like, I think I was just thinking about, like, the **confusing nature of the years which is more like an emotional thing, which is more like imperfect because it's a state of mind**. (Yáñez Prieto, 2008) [bold in the original]

The rule of thumb states that imperfect is used to describe emotion or state of mind in the past. It is unclear why Juliet first assumes her initial formulation is incorrect and should instead be rendered as preterit. However, she does not seem to be fully committed to the change, given her interrogative intonation in the initial segment of her discourse. She then reverts to the rule of thumb, which leads her to settle on the imperfect and which, in this case, makes sense. Nevertheless, Juliet has clearly not yet internalized the new, concept-based, understanding of how aspect can serve a speaker's meaning-making intentions.

As the students gradually became more attuned to Cortázar's manipulation of aspect in his story and its contrast with the soap opera excerpt, they began to experiment with it in their own writing activity. In recounting the night when her parents announced to the family that their mother had developed a serious illness, Emma (pseudonym) used aspect to tell her story much in the style of Cortázar. The learner's commentary in (3) speaks for itself:

(3)   **Although a lot of my paper could have been written in either imperfect or preterit, I tried to use each tense strategically to convey different meanings**. For example, when I was talking about the moments when we were in the dining room in silence, **I used imperfect to depict everything as if the reader was there in the middle of the action, seeing everything as it was happening**:
*Pero esa noche, mi papá no nos molestaba con sus preguntas y mi mama ni siquiera levantaba la vista de su plato. Esa noche, el silencio no era cómodo; era pesado y fuerte. Llenaba el cuarto, hundiendo a mi familia, y mis hermanas y yo cruzábamos miradas preocupadas. Algo no estaba bien.*

[But that night, my dad did-imperfect not bother us with his questions and my mom did-imperfect not even raise her eyes from her plate. That night silence was-imperfect not comfortable; it was-imperfect heavy and strong. It filled-imperfect the room, sinking my family, and my sisters and I crossed-imperfect worried glances. Something was-imperfect not right.]

When I went to my mom's room to see her after I found out that she was sick, **I used preterit for all the verbs. This time I wanted to show each action as a complete act**: *Descendí la escalera lentamente, sin sentir los escalones bajo los pies. Con cada paso hacia su cuarto mi corazón latió más alto. Cuando llegué a su cuarto, era oscuro y callado y mi mamá estaba en la cama, los ojos cerrados.*

[I went-preterit down the stairs slowly, without feeling the treads under my feet. With each footstep towards her room my heart beat-preterit louder. When I arrived-preterit at her room, it was-imperfect dark and quiet and my mom was-imperfect in bed, with her eyes closed.] (Yáñez Prieto, 2008)

According to Yáñez Prieto, Emma's aspectual choices go against the rule of thumb for this feature of the language. For instance, her use of imperfect to describe completed actions on the powerfully emotional evening related in her story runs squarely counter to what the rule of thumb states requiring preterit to recount completed actions in the past. Her intent was to emphasize how that particular evening was radically different from all other evenings for the family and "how the piece of news [on her mother's health] forever altered the family routine" (Yáñez Prieto, 2008). Based on her appreciation of Cortazar's story, Emma realized the potential aspect manipulation has for achieving her intended effect: "**I, like, went back and looked at the stories that we read** and I tried to like **mix up the tenses** and, like, put in **imperfect** where I could, where I was, like, trying to like talk about **the middle of the moment** and, like, ... like, **let the reader see up-close**" (Yáñez Prieto, 2008) [bold in original].

Shifting from a rule of thumb to a conceptual understanding of the object of learning can be a difficult process resulting in tensions, particularly when the two forms of understanding conflict (see Negueruela, 2003). The quality of mediation offered to learners, both in the form of materialized artifacts, as already described, as well as dialogic support, is crucial to facilitating their reorientation. In the next section, we turn to the ZPD as a metacognitive process through which learning as social interaction becomes psychological with internalized forms of mediation enabling learners to gain greater autonomy.

## V. DYNAMIC ASSESSMENT

In educational settings, the process of actualizing the ZPD is often achieved through DA. Of course, while Vygotsky described formal schooling as a leading activity of development, he himself did not limit the ZPD to educational contexts. For instance, he also discussed the ZPD in relation to play, which he regarded as crucial to development, especially during childhood (Vygotsky, 1978, and for a contemporary study of play integrated into language classrooms, see Haught & McCafferty, 2008).

Despite DA's relatively long history in the general psycho-educational research literature originating with the work of Vygotsky's colleague, Luria (1961), it has only recently appeared in research relating to language instruction (see Ableeva, 2008; Kozulin & Garb, 2002; Lantolf & Poehner, 2004; Poehner, 2008; Poehner & Lantolf, 2005). Luria first introduced DA to researchers outside Russia as a diagnostic procedure for differentiating among low-performing students, arguing that taking account of learners' ZPD by offering mediation during assessments helps to reveal the underlying sources of poor performance, thereby providing valuable information for instructional decisions. Most DA proponents have paid greater attention to the diagnostic potential of Luria's research than they have to attempts to actually promote development during the assessment process itself. Consequently, they have focused their efforts on designing DA procedures for the administration of existing test instruments. For example, Budoff's *Learning Potential Assessment* (Budoff, 1968) and Brown's *Graduated Prompt Approach* (Brown & Ferrara, 1985) both attempt to uncover learners' abilities that might otherwise remain hidden during non-dynamic assessments. Budoff's approach follows a pretest—intervention—posttest model which presents mediation as a type of coaching to teach learners strategies for solving problems on the tests. In Brown's approach, hints, prompts, and leading questions for each test item are scripted and arranged in accordance with an implicit to explicit hierarchy prior to the administration of the assessment. Learner scores include not only a tally of items answered correctly and incorrectly, but also an indication of the level (i.e., implicit to explicit) of mediation required for each item.

Although Reuven Feuerstein's (e.g., Feuerstein, Rand, & Hoffman, 1979) approach to DA, known as the mediated learning experience (MLE), appears to be only indirectly influenced by Vygotsky's theory, it nevertheless shares strikingly similar views on cognitive development and the importance of mediation attuned to learners' emergent abilities (Kozulin, 2003).[2] Methodologically, Feuerstein's approach is characterized by dialogic interaction and negotiation of support as mediator and learner are together "bowed over the same task, engaged in a common quest for mastery" (Feuerstein et al., 1979, p. 102). As Minick (1987) explains, teaching and assessment in Feuerstein's MLE are fully integrated, with both elements at play in every interaction.

The L2 DA research to date has focused on classroom rather than large-scale testing contexts and has consequently remained closer to Feuerstein's clinical model, which we have referred to as *interactionist DA* (Lantolf & Poehner, 2004). In our view, DA has much to offer formal language testing, and indeed some preliminary work implementing DA on a large scale has already begun (Erben, Ban, & Summers, 2008). That said, the dialectic integration of teaching and assessment is a powerful framework for L2 pedagogy, where assessments are typically planned to be in support of learner development rather than tightly integrated with it. In this regard, DA represents a systematic approach to formative assessment driven by a theoretical understanding of the processes of development that arise in social interaction (Poehner, 2008; Poehner & Lantolf, 2005).

---

[2]Interestingly, Feuerstein attributes various features of his work to the influence of his mentor, André Rey, who was a colleague of Piaget and no doubt acquainted with Vygotsky's research.

In order for the reader to better understand how DA might be implemented with L2 classroom learners, we offer the following example taken from a larger study of L2 DA reported by Poehner (2008). This program was linked to a seventh-semester undergraduate French course focused on developing learners' oral proficiency. Learners were asked to orally recount narratives presented in two formats: video clips from popular movies and excerpts from French literary texts. In (4) below, a learner (N) is narrating a scene from the film *Nine Months* in which two characters, Rebecca and Samuel, are arguing. N encounters difficulty in expressing that Rebecca suspected Samuel of making an accusation. The French construction N tries to produce, *il l'a accusée* (he accused her), is relatively complex as it involves the past tense of the verb *accuser* as well as the clitic *le*. Note in this exchange that the mediator (M) does not simply correct the learner but instead provides increasingly explicit support in order to determine the point at which she is able to take over the performance.

(4)   1. N: ... et à ce moment Rebecca a pensé que Sam a accusé elle* a accusé elle* de
         ne pas ( ... )
         *... and at that moment Rebecca thought that Sam accused her* accused her* of*
         *not ( ... )*
      2. M: a accusé elle*?
         *accused her*?*
      3. N: ( ... ) elle a lui accusé*? I guess that would be wrong a accusé elle* can you
         say that?
         ( ... ) *accused her*?*                                        *accused her**
      4. M: well usually you would use the elle as an object right
      5. N: right
      6. M: so like he accused [her
      7. N: her

In line 1, N stumbles as she produces the incorrect construction *a accusé elle*, and her response to M's repetition of this formulation is to attempt to self-correct, resulting in the equally problematic *elle a lui accusé*. Her move to change the original construction rather than simply to repeat it suggests she is aware that it is not correct, and she similarly comments that she knows her second attempt also contains errors. Even at this point, when M has done nothing more than repeat N's utterance, insight has been gained into her level of ability: she is not able to produce the necessary construction but has sufficient knowledge of the language to evaluate her own performance and recognize mistakes. Her attempt, however, is incorrect as N herself points out. She returns in line 3 to her original construction but poses it as a question to M, seeking his approval.

Beginning in line 4, M offers a series of hints and prompts to help N think through the performance. He first reminds her of the need to identify a direct object in the construction and then offers a translation of the utterance in English (line 6). Their discussion then turns to the appropriate placement of the object pronoun, a topic that often poses challenges to English-speaking learners of French because the two languages follow different patterns (in French perfective constructions, the clitic precedes the conjugated auxiliary verb).

8. M: so you'd have to insert it like a direct object
9. N: so a elle accusé* a elle accusé*?
            *accused her\*   accused her\*?*
10. M: well remember the objects usually go before the verb
11. N: but if it's in past tense is it after after the avoir and then before the past participle
12. M: actually they go before the before the avoir
13. N: but I'm saying it's Sam accused her
14. M: right
15. N: so how would I ...
16. M: it's just the order of the words would be different in French so instead of Sam accused her it would be Sam her accused
17. N: Sam her accused so uh Sam elle a accusée*?
18. M: except the elle would be switched to l'a accusée
19. N: l'accusé*! Uh [l'a accusée
               [*accused her*
20. M: l'a accusée
21. N: (laughs) okay so Sam l'a accusée (...) okay so uh Rebecca a pensé...
            *Sam accused her ( ...) okay so uh Rebecca thought...*

Here again, M proceeds from more implicit (line 10) to more explicit (line 12) mediation. Neither of these prompts are sufficient to help N, and so in line 16, M offers an English translation of the structure, and finally in line 18, he provides the correct construction. Although the mediation does not lead N to produce the construction herself, the exchange does reveal that she has some knowledge of French clitics and perfective constructions. Importantly, had she arrived at the solution following a more implicit hint, for instance M's general comment about clitic placement in line 10, this would have suggested that she was nearer to successful independent performance. As a diagnostic then, this type of interaction moves well beyond a classification of performance as correct or incorrect and yields a highly detailed portrait of learners' abilities.

Given the dialectic relationship between teaching and assessment in this model, the mediation offered in DA interactions simultaneously supports learner development. N's later performance during this same session suggests that she indeed profited from M's support during the exchange above. In (5) below, N is describing a scene from the film in which the characters Sean and Christine have broken up. Sean's character is devastated that Christine left him, a point N tries to relate through use of a clitic in a perfective construction (she left him, *elle l'a quitté*). While N still experiences difficulties, her performance is markedly improved from the earlier interaction.

(5) 1. N: she left him ah (...) I'm trying to think of how you would say she left
    2. him uh (...) elle est partie de sa vie (laughs)
               *she departed his life*
    3. M: (?)

4. N: I don't know how you say she left him
5. M: you can use the verb quitter
               *to leave*
6. N: oh quitter! so elle l'a elle l'a quitté?
               *oh to leave! So she him she left him?*
7. M: voilà

N's initial way of framing the break up in line 2 is unusual, and her laughter indicates that she is aware that it sounds melodramatic. Switching to English, she confesses to not knowing how to express the idea of one person leaving another (line 4). M begins by offering the lexical item *quitter* (to leave), and this proves to be sufficient for N to continue her narrative. She recognizes this infinitive and then produces the needed construction, *elle l'a quitté*. In contrast to their earlier discussion, N had no trouble inserting the clitic into the present perfective construction in (5). Her response to M's provision of the infinitive *quitter* revealed that the problem at this point was purely lexical in nature.

The interaction in (5) then shows strong evidence that N had begun to internalize the mediation M offered earlier. Their initial dialoguing targeted an ability that was forming within N's ZPD and as a result, the interaction had an impact on her development. In other words, N had developed *through* the teaching–assessment. Of course, N's performance in (5) still required external support, but it is difficult to see how such a noticable change would have been promoted and brought to the surface in a traditional assessment. Again, from the perspective of a diagnosis, DA underscores the fact that two performances that might both be marked "unsatisfactory" or "incorrect" may represent two very different levels of ability. Thus, just as Vygotsky's example of two children who differed with regard to their ZPD, it is also the case that the same individual may exhibit problematic independent performance at two points in time but may have developed nonetheless.

## VI. CONCLUSION

As with the broader field of education, SLA has arrived at a point where researchers are moving beyond applications of Vygotsky's ideas as a framework for understanding processes of development and are pursuing his more powerful proposal that pedagogy itself can be organized to lead development. Daniels (2007, pp. 330–331) surveys a range of contemporary Vygotsky-inspired pedagogies and notes that while each acknowledges the importance of appropriately organized interaction and the selection and quality of content, approaches differ regarding the relative emphasis these two elements are given. For instance, he points out that in Russia, Germany, and Scandinavia, greater attention has been paid to instructional content while programs in the United States, Latin America, and Iberia have tended to prioritize dialogic interaction. While we appreciate Daniels' suggestion of possible cultural and political explanations for these preferences, it is important to bear in mind that for Vygotsky content and interaction are interrelated and defining elements of development-oriented pedagogy.

In this chapter, we have focused on both cognitive (i.e., scientific knowledge) and metacognitive (i.e., collaboration in the ZPD) factors in organizing and promoting the artificial development of language ability in the educational context—the context where consciousness plays a central role in acquisition. In the educational setting, development is guided by well-organized scientific knowledge that preserves the integrity of the object of learning and brings this knowledge into the service of communicative activity. Conceptual knowledge has the potential to qualitatively transform learners' ability to understand and act in the world because it frees them from specific empirical experiences and enables them to generalize their use of language across an array of contexts. This ability requires more than memorizing definitions of concepts. Learners must be given the opportunity to explore the possibilities for meaning making through the relevant concepts. Their explorations are most effective when mediated in dialogic interaction with a more knowledgeable other. This allows them to stretch beyond their current level of independent functioning and push their abilities toward future development. As Daniels (2007, p. 307) insightfully observes, Vygotsky viewed formal education neither as a "naturalistic" (i.e., mirroring empirically based development in non-school settings) nor as a "common sense" endeavor. Rather, education for Vygotsky concerned nothing less than engineering the mediational means through which individuals can overcome the limitations of here-and-now circumstances to develop the abilities needed to solve problems that are not yet known and to function in a world that has not yet been created. In the current era of globalization and rapidly changing linguistic landscapes, Vygotsky's vision has perhaps even greater relevance than in his own day.

# REFERENCES

Ableeva, R. (2008). *Dynamic assessment of listening comprehension in L2 French.* Unpublished Ph.D. dissertation, The Pennsylvania State University, University Park, PA.

Arievitch, I. M., & van der Veer, R. (2004). The role of nonautomatic processes in activity regulation: From Lipps to Galperin. *History of Psychology, 7,* 154–182.

Brown, A., & Ferrara, R. A. (1985). Diagnosing zones of proximal development. In J. V. Wertsch (Ed.), *Culture, communication and cognition. Vygotskian perspectives.* Cambridge: Cambridge University Press.

Budoff, M. (1968). Learning potential as a supplementary testing procedure. In J. Hellmuth (Ed.), *Learning disorders* (Vol. 3). Seattle, WA: Special Child.

Bull, W. E. (1971). *Time, tense, and the verb. A study in theoretical and applied linguistics with particular attention to Spanish.* Berkeley, CA: University of California Press.

Castañeda, A. (2006a). Aspecto, perspectiva y tiempo de procesamiento en la oposición imperfecto/indefinido en español. Ventajas explicativas y aplicaciones pedagógicas. *RAEL: Revista Electrónica de Lingüística Aplicada, 5,* 107–140.

Castañeda, A. (2006b). Perspectiva en las representaciones gramaticales. Aportaciones de la Gramática Cognitiva a la enseñanza de español LE. *Boletín ELE, 34*(mayo), 11–28.

Daniels, H. (2007). Pedagogy. In H. Daniels, M. Cole, & J. V. Wertsch (Eds.), *The Cambridge Companion to Vygotsky* (pp. 307–331). Cambridge: Cambridge University Press.

Doiz-Bienzobas, A. (2002). The preterit and the imperfect as grounding predications. In F. Brisard (Ed.), *Grounding. The epistemic footing of deixis and reference* (pp. 299–347). Berlin, NY: Mouton de Gruyerter.

Ellis, R. (2003). *Task-based language learning and teaching*. Oxford: Oxford University Press.

Erben, T., Ban, R., & Summers, R. (2008). Changing examination structures within a college of education: The application of dynamic assessment in pre-service ESOL endorsement courses in Florida. In J. P. Lantolf & M. E. Poehner (Eds.), *Sociocultural theory and the teaching of second languages*. London: Equinox Publishing.

Feuerstein, R., Rand, Y., & Hoffman, M. B. (1979). *The dynamic assessment of retarded performers: The learning potential assessment device, theory, instruments, and techniques*. Baltimore, MD: University Park Press.

Gal'perin, P. Ya. (1967). On the notion of internalization. *Soviet Psychology, 5*(3), 28–33.

Gass, S. M. (1990). Second and foreign language learning: Same, different or none of the above? In B. VanPatten & J. Lee (Eds.), *Second and foreign language learning* (pp. 34–45). Clevedon: Multilingual Matters.

Hammerly, H. (1982). *Synthesis in language teaching: An introduction to linguistics*. Blaine, WA: Second Language Publications.

Haught, J., & McCafferty, S. G. (2008). Embodied language performance: Drama and the ZPD in the second language classroom. In J. P. Lantolf & M. E. Poehner (Eds.), *Sociocultural theory and the teaching of second languages*. London: Equinox Publishing.

Harre, R., & Gillett, G. (1994). *The discursive mind*. London: Sage.

Ilyenkov, E. V. (1974). Activity and knowledge. In E. V. Ilyenkov (Ed.), *Filosofiya I Kul'tura [Philosophy and Culture]*. Moscos: Plitizdat. http://www.marxists.org/archive/ilyenkov/works/activity/index.htm

Karpov, Y. B., & Haywood, H. C. (1998). Two ways to elaborate Vygotsky's concept of mediation: Implications for instruction. *American Psychologist, 53*, 27–36.

Karpov, Y. V. (2003). Vygotsky's doctrine of scientific concepts. Its role in contemporary education. In A. Kozulin, B. Gindis, V. S. Ageyev, & S. M. Miller (Eds.), *Vygotsky's educational theory in cultural context* (pp. 65–82). Cambridge: Cambridge University Press.

Karpova, S. N. (1977). *The realization of language in children*. Paris: Mouton.

Kozulin, A. (1995). The learning process: Vygotsky's theory in the mirror of its interpretations. *School Psychology International, 16*, 117–129.

Kozulin, A. (2003). Psychological tools and mediated learning. In A. Kozulin, B. Gindis, V. S. Ageyev, & S. M. Miller (Eds.), *Vygotsky's educational theory in cultural context*. Cambridge: Cambridge University Press.

Kozulin, A., & Garb, E. (2002). Dynamic assessment of EFL text comprehension of at-risk students. *School Psychology International, 23*, 112–127.

Lantolf, J. P. (2007). Conceptual knowledge and instructed second language learning: A sociocultural perspective. In S. Fotos & H. Nassaji (Eds.), *Form focused instruction and teacher education. Studies in honour of Rod Ellis* (pp. 35–54). Oxford: Oxford University Press.

Lantolf, J. P., & Poehner, M. E. (2004). Dynamic assessment: Bringing the past into the future. *Journal of Applied Linguistics, 1*, 49–74.

Lantolf, J. P., & Thorne, S. L. (2006). *Sociocultural theory and the genesis of second language development*. Oxford: Oxford University Press.

Larsen-Freeman, D., & Long, M. H. (1991). *An introduction to second language acquisition research*. London: Longman.

Lave, J. (1997). What's special about experiments as contexts for thinking. In M. Cole, Y. Engeström, & O. Vasquez (Eds.), *Mind, culture, and activity: Seminal paper from the laboratory of comparative human cognition* (pp. 57–69). Cambridge, UK: Cambridge University Press.

Lee, B. (1985). Intellectual origins of Vygotsky's semiotic analysis. In J. V. Wertsch (Ed.), *Culture, communication and cognition. Vygotskian perspectives* (pp. 66–93). Cambridge: Cambridge University Press.

Leont'ev, A. N. (1978). *Activity, consciousness and personality*. Englewood Cliffs, NJ: Prentice Hall.

Littlemore, J., & Low, G. (2006). *Figurative thinking and foreign language learning*. Houndmills, UK: Palgrave MacMillan.

Long, M. H. (1998). SLA: Breaking the siege. *University of Hawai'i Working Papers in ESL, 17*: 174–191. [Problems in SLA. Mahwah, NJ: Erlbaum. 2006].

Luria, A. R. (1961). Study of the abnormal child. *American Journal of Orthopsychiatry. A Journal of Human Behavior, 31*, 1–16.

Luria, A. R. (1982). *Language and cognition*. New York: Wiley.

Minick, N. (1987). Implications of Vygotsky's theories for dynamic assessment. In C. S. Lidz (Ed.), *Dynamic assessment: An interactive approach to evaluating learning potential*. New York: The Guilford Press.

Negueruela, E. (2003). *A sociocultural approach to the teaching and learning of second languages: Systemic-theoretical instruction and L2 development*. Unpublished Ph.D. dissertation, The Pennsylvania State University, University Park, PA.

Negueruela, E., & Lantolf, J. P. (2006). Concept-based instruction and the acquisition of L2 Spanish. In R. Salaberry & B. A. Lafford (Eds.), *The art of teaching Spanish. Second language acquisition from research to praxis* (pp. 79–102). Washington, DC: Georgetown University Press.

Poehner, M. E. (2008). *Dynamic assessment. A Vygotskian approach to understanding and promoting l2 development*. Berlin, NY: Springer.

Poehner, M. E., & Lantolf, J. P. (2005). Dynamic assessment in the language classroom. *Language Teaching Research, 9*, 233–265.

Ratner, C. (2006). *Cultural psychology. A perspective on psychological functioning and social reform*. Mahwah, NJ: Erlbaum.

Rothstein, S. (2004). *Structuring events: A study in the semantics of aspect*. Oxford: Blackwell.

Salaberry, M. R. (2000). *The development of past tense morphology in L2 Spanish*. Amsterdam: John Benjamins.

Sanchez Vazquez, A. (1977). *The philosophy of Praxis*. London: Merlin Press.

Sapir, E. (1921/1949). *Language*. New York: Harcourt, Brace & World.

Talyzina, N. (1981). *The psychology of learning*. Moscow: Progress Publishers.

Tarone, E. (1998). A sociolinguistic perspective on an SLA theory of mind. *Studia Anglica Posnaniensa, 23*, 431–444.

Tarone, E. (2000). Still wrestling with 'context' in interlanguage theory. *Annual Review of Applied Linguistics, 20*, 182–198.

Tarone, E. (2007). Sociolinguistic approaches to second language acquisition research—1997–2007. *The Modern Language Journal, 91*, 837–848.

Van der Veer, R., & Valsiner, J. (1991). *Understanding Vygotsky*. Oxford: Blackwell.

Van Patten, B., & Sanz, C. (1995). From input to output: Processing instruction and communicative tasks. In F. R. Eckman, D. Highland, P. W. Lee, J. Mileham, &

R. R. Weber (Eds.), *Second language acquisition theory and pedagogy* (pp. 169–186). Mahwah, NJ: Erlbaum.

Vygotsky, L. S. (1956). *Isbrannye psikhologicheskie issledovaniya [Selected psychological investigations]*. Moscow: Izdatel'stvo Akademii Pedagogischeskikh Nauk SSSR.

Vygotsky, L. S. (1978). *Mind in society: The development of higher psychological processes.* Cambridge, MA: Harvard University Press.

Vygotsky, L. S. (1987). *The collected works of L. S. Vygotsky. Volume 1. Problems in General Psychology. Including the Volume Thinking and Speech.* New York: Plenum.

Vygotsky, L. S. (1997). *The collected works of L. S. Vygotsky. Volume 3. Problems of the theory and history of psychology.* New York: Plenum.

Vygotsky, L. S. (2004). The fundamental problems of defectology. In R. W. Rieber & D. K. Robinson (Eds.), *The essential Vygotsky* (pp. 153–176). New York: Kluwer/Plenum.

Wertsch, J. V. (1985). *Vygotsky and the social formation of mind.* Cambridge, MA: Harvard University Press.

Whitley, M. S. (1986). *Spanish/English contrasts.* Washington, DC: Georgetown University Press.

Wong, W. (2004). The nature of processing instruction. In B. Van Patten (Ed.), *Processing instruction. Theory, research, and commentary* (pp. 33–64). Mahwah, NJ: Erlbaum.

Yáñez Prieto, M. del. C. (2008). *On literature and the secret art of (im)possible worlds: Teaching/learning literature through language.* Unpublished Ph.D. dissertation, The Pennsylvania State University, University Park, PA.

CHAPTER 8

# COGNITIVE LINGUISTICS AND SECOND LANGUAGE LEARNING

Marjolijn Verspoor and Andrea Tyler

Cognitive Linguistics (henceforth CL) holds that language is a reflection of human cognition and conceptualization. Based on the premise that human perceptions of the world are always filtered through our particular physical and neurological architecture, cognitive linguists argue that humans do not have direct access to an objective, external reality. Rather, what we do have direct access to is our humanly subjective conceptualizations. Conceptualization arises from the complex interactions of our rich cognitive abilities and species-specific interactions with the external spatial–physical–social world. Crucially, while claiming that human access to the external world is indirect and filtered, cognitive linguists also argue that our interactions with the social–physical world are fundamental to how our cognition is shaped. Basic force dynamics, such as our understanding of gravity or motion along a path, provide foundational schemata that give structure to our understanding of many other domains of experience. This is the notion of embodied meaning. Finally, the primary function of language is communication. Language is a tool used by humans, who are fundamentally social in character, to interact with other humans; one key aspect of social interaction involves externalizing internal conceptualizations—for instance, ideas about entities and events that are not immediately present—in order to make them available to other humans. We learn language by using it in communicative contexts. Thus, linguistic meaning is not referential and objective, but subjective, dynamic, flexible, encyclopaedic, and usage based. Since language is understood to reflect conceptualization, it is all about meaning. Not only words and expressions but also the grammar, or morphosyntax, of a language reflects conceptualization and is therefore meaningful. It is argued in this chapter that a cognitive linguistic approach to language is in line with modern strands of education-oriented applied linguistics and useful to second language (SL) pedagogy, especially because of its focus on the

*The New Handbook of Second Language Acquisition*

motivated, meaningful connections between forms that are often ignored by other theories of language.

## I. WHAT IS DIFFERENT ABOUT COGNITIVE LINGUISTICS?

In traditional approaches to language, language is seen as an autonomous system, independent of other human cognitive and social abilities. In recent years, the dominant view has held that a basic part of the human endowment is an independent language module that is genetically programmed to develop with minimal linguistic input. In generativist terms, language is acquired with virtually no effort on the part of the acquirer. This is a mathematically based model in which abstract rules are understood to manipulate strings of symbols, thus generating forms at different levels of the language system, such as phonology, syntax, and semantics (which are separate from the lexicon and general human memory). The syntactic patterns are meaningless. These levels or subcomponents are also viewed as largely independent of each other. Under this view, languages share a set of universal properties (in the areas of syntax, semantics, and phonology) because of the genetically engineered language module; the model predicts that languages will be quite similar to one another, largely regular and rule governed. More recently, pragmatics and speech act theory have been acknowledged as an additional layer important in the interpretation of contextualized utterances, but separate from language proper. Such a model of language explicitly portrays the lexicon as largely arbitrary and represents metaphors and other figurative language as mere stylistic elements, disconnected from syntax and the lexicon. Extended to SL learning, the idea seems to be that if a learner just learns the sounds and vocabulary items, masters the grammar rules and memorizes their (supposedly rather limited) exceptions, and learns the appropriate match between forms and speech acts, he or she can master the language.

A distinct, alternative view of language is offered by a cognitive linguistic approach. CL rejects the idea that language is the product of an abstract, encapsulated, computational system. Rather, language is seen as a natural outcome of humans with social and cultural needs to communicate, who have exploited their rich cognitive resources—such as the ability to focus attention, to automatize, to categorize, to form generalizations, to detach from the immediate here-and-now, and to infer—to develop language, that is, to express meaning. Language is seen as a reflection of human cognition and conceptualization. Instead of an emphasis on rules or abstract principles particular to language, CL focuses on established cognitive and perceptual principles (such as figure and ground organization) that are manifested throughout human cognition, including language. Such a view of language entails that morphosyntactic patterns are not meaningless, as they reflect, albeit in rather abstract form, human conceptualizations. Moreover, human conceptualizations are grounded in human experience and interaction with the world. For instance, human understanding of animate beings and their ability to apply force to other entities is reflected in basic transitive clauses, which involve not only syntactic ordering patterns of nouns and verbs, but also linking of participant roles, such as agent and patient, to syntactic slots (e.g., Goldberg, 1995; Langacker, 1987). CL has revealed that much that has traditionally been assumed to be idiosyncratic and arbitrary is systematic. For instance, much of metaphoric language has been shown to systematically reflect basic human experience with the physical–spatial world and is consistent with patterns found in the syntax and discourse. Thus, CL provides a more comprehensive, coherent account of how grammatical constructions, lexical items, and discourse patterns work. Although all languages are naturally constrained by general human cognitive abilities and general human experiences with the world (e.g., all humans experience basic force dynamics in the same way), languages may differ rather radically in the culturally or environmentally determined conceptualizations they express.

The CL view also entails that language is learned, not acquired. Language learning is an interactive process involving bottom–up processing, driven by linguistic experience and specific interactions with the world, as well as top–down processing, reflecting general learning and cognitive mechanisms such as generalization over instances and expectation-driven processing of new information involving organized background knowledge. Language knowledge is dependent on human memory, and human memory is highly sensitive to frequency of the input (Ellis, 2008). Generally speaking, the more one uses or is exposed to a particular form, the more "entrenched" it will become; the more entrenched a form, the easier it will be to retrieve and produce, a view that is very much in line with the Rumelhart and McClelland model of activation (1986). Additionally, human memory is patterned. The mind appears to develop highly complex schemata which, in Tannen's (1993) terms act as flexible, structured expectations. When new entities and experiences are encountered, they are interpreted in relationship to established schemata, which are thus constantly changing and adapting to new information. Like all other aspects of the social–physical world we encounter, when new linguistic expressions and patterns are encountered, they may be added to a speaker's store of linguistic representations. In other words, knowledge of a language is dynamic and evolves through a person's experience with the language and his or her social–physical environment.

## II. COGNITIVE LINGUISTIC THEORY AND ITS IMPLICATIONS FOR SLA

CL began to develop in the 1970s from the work of a number of different researchers and has been influenced by many linguists, but it would be safe to say that Talmy (1981), Lakoff (1987), and Langacker (1987) are widely recognized as key founders. CL is a theory of language that is in many respects compatible with current SL teaching practices and findings in SL research. Over the last 10 years, several publications have appeared that suggest how CL may benefit SL teaching. Even though Nick Ellis pointed out that CL insights were potentially useful for the field of SLA in 1998 and 1999, SLA researchers are only now beginning to discover CL; thus, research applying CL insights to L2 teaching is in its infancy. The purpose of this chapter is to begin to show how CL insights might be incorporated in L2 research and teaching. Rather than explaining all aspects of CL theory, which would be well beyond the scope of a single chapter, we will give a few examples of how select CL tenets, such as the linguistic importance of categorization by prototype with motivated meaning extensions, the ubiquity of metaphor and metonymy at all "levels" of language, how these CL insights help make clear differences between languages, and how awareness of such differences may be used insightfully in the L2 classroom.

## A. Prototypes and Centrality Effects

Our ability to function in the physical and social world depends on our ability to categorize other entities, processes, events, and social relations. When we categorize, we show how we recognize, differentiate, and understand persons, things, situations, activities, and events in our world. No theory of language denies the importance of categorization; however, different linguistic models take different theoretical approaches to categorization. CL holds that categorization is based on context-sensitive prototypes (Gibbs, 1994; Rosch, 1975; Taylor, 2003 (originally 1989)), as opposed to categorization based on innate semantic features or necessary and sufficient conditions. Consistent with the notion that human conceptualization is not based on a "God's eye" view or direct access to a veridical, referential world, CL rejects that systems of categories are objectively "out there" in the world. Rather, they are rooted in people's embodied experience with the social–physical world and are conceptual in nature. Thus, conceptual categories are expected to vary across individuals and cultures. Importantly, human categorization is not based only on perceptual resemblance, but also on functional aspects.

Categorization based on prototypes is the process of conceptually grouping entities, events, and experiences around the "best examples" or "central members" of a category. For example, the category FRUIT (CL holds that words are labels for categories) may have an apple as its prototype. In Western cultures, we encounter apples relatively frequently; they are not too big or too small compared to other kinds of fruit, and they are not overly sweet or sour compared to the other members of the category. Fruits such as oranges, pears, and bananas are also central members of this category, but berries, lemons, and watermelons are less prototypical because of their relatively odd size, lack of sweetness, or relative infrequency. In other words, natural categories are graded with some more central and some more peripheral members. The very periphery of the category may be fuzzy in that some members could be considered members of other categories as well, which makes it possible that a tomato may be categorized as a fruit technically but as a vegetable in its everyday use. Categorization is also dynamic in that it depends on use and context. If you are having breakfast and getting ready to eat a bowl of cereal, the prototypical spoon you would think about is likely to be made of metal and about 8 inches long. If you are cooking soup and want to stir it, the prototypical spoon you would think about is likely to be made of wood and considerably larger.

Because categorization depends on our everyday interaction with our environment, things may be categorized differently depending on the function they have within a particular context, environment, or culture. It is therefore not surprising that students from different linguistic and cultural backgrounds will have somewhat different categories with different prototypes. For instance, they may consider different types of fruits as more prototypical. The idea that words are labels for categories and that these categories have emerged through human interaction with the environment also entails that there are rarely real translation equivalents across languages. For example, a typical house in a rather cold climate will have different architectural features, functions, and associations than a house in a rather warm climate. Another difference that may occur between two languages is the degree to which words refer to similar entities. For example, in English there are two labels (categories) shade and shadow, where Dutch has only one: schaduw. Such differences in categorization may cause problems for the L2 learner, who may have trouble discerning and understanding the differences between the two categories and may therefore use an incorrect label. A notoriously difficult problem that results from differences in linguistic categorization is the use of articles and determiners in Western languages such as English versus the use of classifiers in languages such as Chinese, Korean, and Japanese. In English discourse, all entities are categorized as definite (indicating that the speaker assumes the hearer can identify the object) or indefinite. In Chinese, however, definiteness does not have to be marked. Instead, a classifier, when used, may give information about the animacy, shape, or structure of an entity, expressing distinctions that a nonnative speaker may not recognize easily.

Moreover, often it is possible to identify a central attribute that the noun classifier is labeling, such as "long, thin object," but many members of the category do not share that attribute. For instance in Japanese and Korean, the same classifier is used for long, thin objects and phone calls. To the SL learner, the classifer system may seem highly arbitrary, and therefore difficult to master. Cognitive linguists, such as Lakoff (1987) have studied noun classifiers and identified motivated, systematic processes, including metaphor and metonymy, by which the categories have been extended from a central sense. In the example above, "phone calls" may be a metonymic extension from "telephone lines," which are long, thin objects. This kind of analysis offers great potential for presenting the classifier system as principled and motivated, thus relieving learners of the burden of rote memorization.

Cognitive linguists argue that all linguistic forms (words, morphemes, syntactic constructions, and so on) are labels for categories. These categories also have the organization of a central or core member with less central but related members.

A core sense is usually understood as the most basic sense with the other senses relating to it by motivated, semantic extensions. At the word level, this is perhaps most easily illustrated with nouns that depict physical objects. According to an Internet dictionary (http://dict.die.net/house/), the noun *house* has 12 distinct senses, ranging from a particular building that serves as a dwelling for one or more families to the management of a gambling house or casino. Below, the original definitions have been reordered and grouped to illustrate how more central, concrete senses may be related to more peripheral senses.

1. A dwelling that serves as living quarters for one or more families: "he has a house on Cape Cod." (1a) A social unit living together: "I waited until the whole house was asleep." (1b) Play in which children take the roles of father or mother or children and pretend to interact like adults: "the children were playing house." (1c) Aristocratic family line: "the House of York."
2. A building in which something is sheltered or located: "they had a large carriage house." (2a) A building where theatrical performances or motion-picture shows can be presented: "the house was full." (2b) The audience gathered together in a theatre or cinema: "the house applauded." (2c) An official assembly having legislative powers: "the legislature has two houses." (2d) Members of a business

organization: "he worked for a brokerage house." (2e) The members of a religious community living together. (2f) The management of a gambling house or casino: "the house gets a percentage of every bet."

3. One of 12 equal areas into which the zodiac is divided.

In this example, the "core" sense is "a dwelling that serves as living quarters for one or more families." The other senses of *house* are not random or arbitrary. Almost all the different senses are related to the physical sense of house in some way. A house is a building in which families live, and the people living in the house may also be referred to as *house*. The word house may also refer to some institutions that have organizations that have some similarities to families. The way these meaning extensions may take place through image schemas, metonymy, and metaphor will be discussed in the next section, but suffice it to say here that of all the senses of *house*, some are more central (e.g., in 1), some are more peripheral (e.g., in 2), and one seems even odd (3). But even (3) is not random if one takes into consideration that each constellation is construed as a figure of terrestrial origin, such as a ram (Aries), or weighing scales (Libra), or the water carrier (Aquarius), and these figures reside in certain areas, metaphorically called their houses. To summarize, in retrospect it is possible to see that the more central senses may have motivated language users to use the same word in an associated sense.

Similar centrality effects may occur at the morphological, syntactic, pragmatic, and discourse levels. The central sense of the suffix *-er* in English refers to an agent who does something regularly or by profession as in *teacher*. Less central uses can be found in *villager* (a person who lives in a particular place), a *toaster* (an instrument), and a *go-getter* (an attribute). The present progressive is another example at the morphological level, with a central sense of "event in progress" and an extended sense using the same construction to indicate recurring events.

1. *He is talking on the phone right now* (event in progress, imperfect, i.e., process construed as constant throughout the designated temporal frame).
2. *He is always arriving late* (re-occurring event, imperfect, here part of the speaker's existing, ongoing belief about the state of the world).

Sentence patterns or syntactic constructions also evidence various centrality effects. Importantly, whereas the traditional view assumes that each verb is lexically designated for a particular set of argument structures, which determine the sentential patterns in which the verb occurs, a CL view holds that the sentence pattern itself is meaningful and designates the argument structure as a reflection of how a situation or event is construed. For instance, the verb *give* is traditionally represented as having two possible argument structures, the prepositional dative (*Mary gave the cake to Francis*) and the double object (*Mary gave Francis the cake*). These two "versions" are represented as semantically equivalent; the prepositional dative structure is typically considered basic and the double object construction as derived from it. However, subtle differences in interpretation between the two patterns do exist (e.g., *I taught John French* entails that John learned French, whereas *I taught French to John* does not have this entailment). Moreover, not all transitive verbs have these two alternations. Following Goldberg (2006), the syntactic patterns (or constructions) themselves are meaningful and designate the argument structure. For instance, the double object construction is represented as meaning "X causes Y to receive Z," for example, *Mary gave Francis the cake* means roughly *Mary caused Francis to receive the cake*. Corpus analysis shows that *give*, whose lexical semantics closely match the meaning of this construction, is the most frequently occurring verb to appear in the construction. It represents the central member for the construction. Thus, a matching occurs between the semantics of the verb and the meaning of the constructions in which it occurs. Another type of syntactic centrality-extension effect involves extension of the meaning of the construction itself. Returning to the double object construction, the English sentence "Michael gave Claire a book" is an instance of the central sense in which an agent physically transferred some entity to another person. A less central example of the pattern would be "Sharon knitted Michael a sweater" where the action of knitting is understood as having been undertaken with the intention of transferring the patient (here the sweater) to the recipient (here Michael). Unlike in the sentence "Michael gave Claire a book," in the "knitting" sentence, we don't know if the transfer actually took place.

Centrality effects can also be found at other linguistic levels such as at the pragmatic level in ways of greeting or ways of thanking in a particular culture and at the discourse level in ways of organizing a narrative, a letter, or a research paper. Centrality effects can also account for nonverbal behavior such as how close to stand to another person when speaking, how to behave in a classroom, or what time to arrive at a party.

## B. Motivated Meaning Extensions

When we refer back to the HOUSE example, we can see that almost all entries have to do either with the physical-structural properties (the building) or the persons associated with such a structure. The relation between a central sense and the less central senses of a word is one of motivated meaning extension. Cognitive linguists argue that these meaning extensions reflect regular cognitive processes, such as metaphoric and metonymic thinking. Many of the conventional uses of a form reflect historical extensions that have become conventionalized. At one time these were new senses of linguistic expressions that reflect a conceptual link speakers made between an original sense and a novel sense; these extensions have subsequently become an established part of the language.

The motivation to extend a meaning in the past may still hold and be easily recognized in some cases, but in other cases the newer sense may have been conventionalized to such an extent that the original relation is not self-evident and native speakers themselves are unaware of it. Let's take the English word "bread" as an example. In English culture, bread, that is, "food made from dough of flour or meal and usually raised with yeast or baking powder and then baked," has long been an important staple. At some point, the notion of "bread" seems to have been extended metonymically to stand for "the food one needs to survive" as in the ritualized "give us our daily bread." Cognitive linguists argue that this metonymical sense has in turn been extended metaphorically to the related sense of "money" as in *He has to work for his bread* and *to take the bread out of one's mouth*, meaning to take away someone's livelihood. If the language learner is alerted to principles of extension such as metaphor and metonymy and knows that "bread" stands for the staple food in Western culture, then he or she has potentially valuable tools that might allow him or her to work out that "dry bread" stands for a meager meal and that "bread with butter" stands for a rich meal. Similarly, a learner might be able to work out that an expression such as *to know on which side one's bread is buttered* stems from a metaphoric extension and means "having the sense to know where one's interest lies" and *bread buttered on both sides* for "great good fortune, lucky circumstances." We are not claiming that working out these relationships will be an easy process for the language learner. However, the informed language teacher might be able to point out a few instances of such patterns in order to make learners more aware that they are common in all languages. Knowledge of such principled extensions may provide learners with important strategies for interpreting extended uses and thus facilitate the learning process.

Let's consider conceptual metaphor, one of the key processes of meaning extension, a bit more closely. In CL, language is understood as being grounded in lived human experience with the real world and as crucially reflecting the human perceptual system and human understanding of the spatial–physical–social world we inhabit. Moreover, our understanding of the spatial–physical–social world provides structure for our understanding of less external, less perceptually based experiences. This is the heart of "conceptual metaphor," which is seen as pervasive in terms of how humans understand the world and how all aspects of language are structured. For example, the use of *up* in the sentence *The price of gas is up* is a result of humans regularly observing real world situations in which an increase in amount is correlated with an increase in vertical elevation, such as the level of liquid in a glass rising (the vertical elevation) as the amount of liquid increases. Because these two physical phenomena are so closely correlated in real world experience, speakers of English use language from the domain of vertical elevation, *up*, to talk about increases in amount.

*Up* is associated not only with "increase" but also with our physical and cultural experience. In the *up* and *down* pair, *up* is seen as positive and *down* is seen as negative, probably motivated by a variety of experiences such as the fact that when one is standing up, one is in a less vulnerable position than when one is lying down. An erect posture is associated with a positive emotional state and a drooping posture typically goes along with sadness and depression motivating the conceptual metaphor *happy is up; sad is down* as illustrated by the following expressions.

> I'm feeling up.
> That lifted my spirits.
> I'm depressed.
> I feel really low these days.

Conceptual metaphors that are based on very basic human experience are likely to be universal. We hypothesize that it may be helpful to point out possible similarities between languages where appropriate. Anecdotally, we have had success presenting such information to SL learners, but this hypothesis has yet to be tested in a controlled experiment.

Conceptual metaphors motivate meaning extensions not only in words and expressions but also in grammatical constructions. We will illustrate this with the *now is here—then is there* conceptual metaphor as it may apply to the use of tenses in English. This discussion draws heavily from Tyler and Evans (2001). Prototypically, a present tense in English will refer to something that is happening now and a past tense to something that has happened in the past. According to Sweetser (1990), the *now is here—then is there* conceptual metaphor can be applied to the use of tenses in that it maps proximal and distal spatial phenomena and their real world consequences to different examples of temporal language. One example is a tense shift in discourse when an author may foreground ideas with the present tense and background ideas with past tense (Riddle, 1985; Tyler & Evans, 2001):

> In November 1859, Charles Darwin's The Origin of Species ... **was** published in London. The central idea in this book **is** the principle of natural selection. In the sixth edition Darwin **wrote** "This principle of preservation of the survival of the fittest, I have called Natural Selection." (Eigen & Winkler, 1983, p. 53)

We can understand this use of the present tense to indicate what is in focus in a text as drawing on our physical experience in the world. Events that are occurring at the present moment tend to be our focus of attention, rather than events that happened in the past. Similarly, entities and activities that are occurring proximal to us tend to be in our vision and are therefore more likely to be the focus of our attention than those occurring at a distance.

Another aspect of entities being proximal is that they are potentially under our physical control. For example, if a parent wants to control a child, physical constraint and therefore physical closeness is often required. Instead of using physical control, humans can also use language to exert control. Following the logic of the *now is here— then is there* metaphor, a present tense would indicate more proximity and therefore more control than a past tense. Therefore, in situations of possible imposition, where the speaker wants to indicate that he or she has no control over the addressee, English speakers tend to use the past tense when they make requests or offer invitations. Using the past tense implies that the speaker is physically distant from the addressee and therefore cannot exercise physical control over the addressee. The further implication is that the addressee is free to agree to or reject the imposition. (Note this analysis is consistent with Brown and Levinson's (1987) insights into politeness theory and the notion of negative face.) The same metaphor accounts for the use of the past tense in the following example.

> Patient calling a doctor's office:
> Receptionist: Good morning, Doctor X's office.
> Patient: Yes, I **wanted** to ask you a question. (Davies, personal communication)

Here the patient is clearly getting ready to ask a question and the wanting is continuing into the present moment. The choice of past tense is a conventionalized polite way to pose the question. This example exploits the implication of physical distance, cued by the use of past tense, which gives a nod to the polite fiction that the addressee is freer to accept or reject the request. The modal verbs also reflect this systematic pattern in that the historically past tense modals *could* and *would* are the polite forms of *can* and *will* to make requests, suggestions, and the like.

Another important reflex of the proximal–distal metaphor involves the use of the present tense form of a modal to indicate a higher degree of certainty, realis, and speaker force in contrast to the use of past tense to indicate a lower degree of certainty, realis, and an attenuation of speaker force or control. Experientially, humans are much surer of the reality of that which they can immediately perceive with their physical senses than that which is out of range of their physical senses. This includes being surer of that which is experienced in the immediate moment than that which we remember. Thus, present tense is used to express higher degrees of certainty, realis, and force than past tense. The metaphor explains the systematic lessening of certainty and realis indicated by the use of historically past tense modals. Thus, in the present/past pairs will/would, can/could, and shall/should, we find the past tense forms consistently indicating less certainty on the part of the speaker or less social and/or physical force. For example, in legal discourse, *shall* indicates a legally binding circumstance while *should* indicates a preferred, but nonbinding circumstance.

In the next section, we will consider more closely how a CL view may be implemented in L2 learning and teaching.

### C. Cognitive Linguistics and L2 Teaching

A number of negative consequences for L2 learning arise from assuming a traditional model of language. Vocabulary, set expressions, and figurative language are seen as rather arbitrary and must be learned item per item. Grammar and syntax are represented as a set of rules to be mastered, but the rules are inevitably plagued with seemingly arbitrary exceptions. Moreover, the syntactic rules are represented as being unique to a language component whose organizing principles are divorced from general principles found in other areas of human cognition. The result is a fragmented picture of language in which important interactions among syntax, the lexicon, figurative language, and discourse are not represented.

Many L2 researchers have grown dissatisfied with such accounts of language. Some have even advocated abandoning linguistic theory and focusing solely on psychological aspects of L2 learning, such as the role of attention or learner motivation (e.g., Larsen-Freeman, 1996). While recognizing that research with a psychological focus has contributed much to our understanding of L2 learning, we argue that a full understanding will not be achieved without careful consideration of the model of language assumed by L2 researchers and teachers. We posit that CL, with its commitment to finding recurring cognitive principles reflected in all levels of language, can provide important insights for L2 research and enrich L2 pedagogy.

The advantage of recognizing that language is usage based in conjunction with the principle of centrality effects in language, culture and behavior in teaching an SL is manifold. First of all, students can be made aware of the fact that textbooks may present only "typical" examples, but that uses in language are never so fixed because the precise interpretation of language forms shift with the context in which they are used. Without having to learn lists of exceptions, learners can be alert to how native speakers may extend meaning senses and use words and constructions in a range of nonprototypical senses. For example, even though *bike* is normally a count noun in English, it is possible to use *bike* in a noncount sense as in *All I saw on the road was bike* to emphasize (or overstate) that there were so many bikes that they were difficult to keep apart, just like grains of sand or blades of grass. Being sensitized to the possibility of such noncentral uses, L2 learners may be better able to appropriately interpret and notice the input and eventually integrate it with their existing knowledge base. A CL approach emphasizes that language is usage based and that speakers choose among an array of linguistic resources to convey a particular perspective. The exact way these resources are used to create a particular interpretation is largely conventionalized and so likely to vary from language to language. Taking a usage-based perspective might help students realize that even though their word choice, sentence structure, or essay organization may not be incorrect in a technical sense, it may vary enough from the target L2 prototype that native speakers may find it difficult to comprehend.

Cognitive linguistic insights can also help in developing materials for SL learners or in encouraging learners to use strategies to make the learning burden of vocabulary, expressions, and grammatical constructions lighter. The main reason for this hypothesis is our belief that learners will usually understand and remember items that are thematically or meaningfully related more easily than arbitrary items. This view is amply supported by work in psychology, which has long established that humans learn new information more easily and reliably when they can relate it to established schemas (e.g., Rumelhart & Norman, 1981; Wilson & Anderson, 1986). There is now sufficient empirical evidence that such a CL approach works at the lexical level and empirical work is being conducted at this time at the grammatical and syntactic levels.

Judging from publications over the last three decades, SLA theory occupied itself to a great extent with the acquisition of grammar and syntax up to about the 1990s, and it was assumed that vocabulary would be learned on its own mainly through the input (cf. Krashen, 1981). However, more recently the idea of focused attention to vocabulary has come in vogue again, and there is now a consensus that a vocabulary-learning program needs both intentional and incidental components (cf. Coady & Huckin, 1997; Ellis, 1994; Schmitt & McCarthy, 1997). According to Bensoussan and Laufer (1984), it is especially difficult for learners to understand and learn different senses of one word. They observed that learners did not tend to give up one particular meaning of a word they were familiar with, even though that word did not make sense in the context in which it occurred (Laufer, 1997, p. 152). Also, Schmitt (2000) found that even advanced learners seldom know all the meaning senses of a polysemous word and that learning them was a slow and patchy process.

Especially with this renewed interest in vocabulary learning, CL offers a potent set of learning tools. Numerous CL-inspired studies have demonstrated that the multiple senses and uses of a polysemous word are systematic. For example, seemingly unrelated uses of prepositions are actually connected in explainable ways (e.g., Boers, 1996; Brugman, 1981; Tyler & Evans, 2003). Lindstromberg (1997) has applied a cognitive approach to understanding English prepositions and Rudzka-Ostyn (2003) to teaching English phrasal verbs. As Verspoor and Lowie (2003) among others have shown, these insights can be usefully applied to the L2 classroom in vocabulary learning. In their experiment with 78 Dutch learners of English, they showed that offering a core meaning rather than a noncore sense has helped not only to guess the meaning of these words but also to retain them. They chose 18 polysemous words whose core sense had given rise to a meaning extension that is still relatively close to the core sense, and also to a meaning extension occupying a more peripheral position in the network. They offered learners the items in two different conditions. In the experimental condition, a core sense with Dutch translation was provided and learners had to guess the more peripheral sense:

1. *His father originally sent him solid golden <u>nuggets</u> (goudklompje).*
2. *The new LSS does that with a choice of V6 engines and with a body, interior and suspension that make the car a true <u>nugget</u> in today's rushing stream of the fancy cars.*

In the control condition, the learners were provided with the translation of a more peripheral sense and had to guess the other peripheral sense.

1. *They came up with the <u>nugget</u> that he had been involved in dubious business speculations (interessante informatie).*
2. *The new LSS does that with a choice of V6 engines and with a body, interior and suspension that make the car a true <u>nugget</u> in today's rushing stream of the fancy cars.*

The experimental students were found to be significantly more likely to interpret the relatively closely connected meaning extension correctly and also to remember its exact meaning in a delayed posttest (after two weeks). The same principle has been empirically tested and proven useful in idiomatic expressions.

In another experiment, Boers (2000) presented common expressions relating to anger to Flemish-speaking learners of English. Drawing on Kövecses' (1986) work on metaphors of emotion, Boers developed language lessons that pointed out English has many expressions to describe anger that are motivated by overarching conceptual metaphors. For instance, the conceptual metaphor *anger as a hot fluid in a container* has given rise to expressions such as *anger welled up inside me, I was boiling with anger, she was all steamed up, she erupted, simmer down, he flipped his lid, I was fuming,* and *he blew up at me.* The *anger as fire* conceptual metaphor gives rise to expressions such as an *inflammatory remark, adding fuel to the fire, He kept smoldering for days, She was breathing fire, She exploded,* and *He's hot under the collar.* And the *angry people as dangerous animals* conceptual metaphor gives rise to expressions such as *He has a ferocious temper, Don't snap at me, She unleashed her anger,* and *Don't bite my head off.* In a controlled experiment, an experimental group was presented with anger expressions organized according to their common conceptual metaphors; a control group was presented the same expressions organized randomly. This experiment and several others (e.g., Boers, 2000; Boers & Demecheleer, 1998; Boers, Demecheleer, & Eyckmans, 2004; Kövecses & Szabó, 1996; MacLennan, 1994) showed that alerting learners to such metaphors helps language learners better retain vocabulary and more accurately interpret previously unseen metaphors.

These studies have shown that, at least at the lexical level, meaningful connections help the learner remember. In their article surveying the available evidence in the effectiveness of CL applications to SL teaching, Boers and Lindstromberg (2006) conclude that the studies taken collectively constitute "a fairly robust body of evidence in favour of CL-inspired language pedagogy" (p. 31).

For grammar learning, fewer experiments that attempt to apply CL to L2 learning have been undertaken. In part this may be because with both the communicative approach and task-based approaches, the dominant paradigms in recent SLA research, there has been an emphasis on psychological factors in learning and on implicit learning through rich input, meaning negotiation, and pushed output. These L2 teaching methodologies do not overtly relate to any particular model of language and do not overtly attempt to explain the patterns of the target language. Moreover, as we mentioned above, many SLA researchers have grown disillusioned with formal linguistic theories that seem to have little application to SL learning or teaching. Thus, most researchers have remained unaware of CL.

One early attempt at providing empirical evidence for a cognitive approach to grammar teaching was undertaken by Huong and Verspoor (2008). They report on a controlled experiment to see whether CL principles can be applied effectively in the teaching of the use of articles in English to Vietnamese students. The effects of a cognitive lesson were compared to a lesson based on a commonly used ESL book using a notional functional approach. In the experimental condition, students are made aware of the conceptual bases for definiteness and countability before they are presented with actual examples. The examples and explanations are arranged in order of prototypicality, and the meaning relations between the different uses are shown. The outcome of the experiment is that the cognitive approach is significantly more effective in the short term, but not quite significantly more in the long term. The results, however, are promising enough to motivate further study.

Tyler (2008) tested the efficacy of using a CL approach to teaching modal verbs to advanced language learners. The subjects were all non-English L1 lawyers who were enrolled in a master of laws (LL.M) program in the United States. All had taken English for many years and scored at least 620 TOEFL. In spite of their advanced level of English proficiency, they experienced considerable difficulty using English modals appropriately. Drawing on Sweetser's (1990) force dynamics analysis of the semantics of modal verbs, Tyler developed a set of teaching materials that aimed to translate the theoretical insights of the CL analysis into an accessible format for nonlinguists.

Sweetser specifically argued that the root meanings, that is, "real world" physical and social meanings, of modals have to do with physical forces, barriers, and paths. The semantics of each of the modals is represented as being based on either external or internal force and with a particular level of compulsion that compel forward motion along a path. Further, the analysis motivates a mapping between our understanding of these physical forces and our understanding of mental "forces, barriers, and paths," which is reflected in the epistemic uses. As an illustration, consider Sweeter's representation of *may*.

*May is* represented as a situation in which an authority figure takes away or keeps away a potential barrier to the doer undertaking some action. The action of keeping the barrier at bay has the result of allowing the doer to undertake the action. Thus, the meaning focuses on lack of restriction imposed on the doer by someone else who has the authority or power to impose the restriction, and hence the interpretation of permission granted by an authority who could potentially block the doer's action. In terms of the extension from the root to the epistemic meaning, Sweetser argues,

> we can see why general sociophysical potentiality, and specifically social permission, should be ... chosen as analogous to possibility in the world of reasoning. *May* is an absent potential barrier in the sociophysical world, and the epistemic *may* is a force-dynamically parallel case in the world of reasoning. The meaning of epistemic *may* would thus be that there is no barrier to the speaker's process of reasoning from the available premises to the conclusion expressed in the sentence qualified by *may* ....
> (Sweetser, 1990, p. 59)

Tyler developed a set of diagrams to represent these force dynamics. In these scenes, the larger figure represents the external authority or force; the smaller, bolded figure represents the doer or entity moving along the path. The root meaning of *may* is depicted as an authority figure opening a door for the doer.

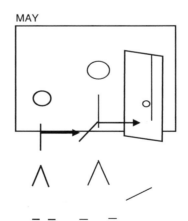

MAY

A piece of legal writing produced for a required LL.M class was assessed for appropriate use of modals. Forty subjects who matched for proficiency in modals use were selected. One group of 20 LL.M students was given a 30-min, teacher-fronted CL explanation of the modals using the diagrams just described. The explanation was followed by pair work in which the subjects discussed how the meaning of several short passages changed with choice of modal. The subjects were given no further formal instruction on modals. The control group continued in the immersion environment in which they were required to read many documents illustrating appropriate use of modals, but received no focused instruction on modals. Four weeks later, all subjects produced a second piece of legal writing. Again, modal production was assessed. The subjects in the experimental group showed significant improvement, $p < 0.01$, over the four-week period; the subjects in the control group showed no gain in appropriate use of modals.

Tyler and her colleagues have also undertaken a series of experiments focusing on the efficacy of using a CL approach to teach the multiple meanings of the prepositions *over, above, to, for*, and *at*. Drawing on the principled polysemy model of the semantics of English prepositions developed by Tyler and Evans (2003), these researchers developed two sets of teaching materials. The experimental materials incorporated a cognitive approach emphasizing polysemy networks, experiential correlation, multiple construals on a spatial scene, and other basic tenets from CL. The presentation emphasized the systematic relations among the various meanings associated with each preposition. The control materials presented the same prepositions with the same set of extended meanings, but there was no explanation concerning how the central meaning and additional meanings might be systematically related. The sets of materials for both groups were identical, except for the presence of the cognitive explanation. The materials consisted of a teacher-fronted presentation that contained pictures, cartoons, and videoclips illustrating the various meanings of the prepositions. The teacher-fronted presentations were followed by two task-based activities. The goal was to provide both groups with materials that were matched for interestingness and instructional techniques. The only difference was the presence of an underlying CL analysis in the organization of the materials and in the explanations of how various meanings related to each other in the experimental materials. Proficiency level of the participants and time on task were carefully controlled. The preliminary results indicate that subjects receiving the CL treatment consistently outperformed the control groups. For instance, on an experiment focusing on *over* and *above*, the experimental group outperformed the control group on six out of seven target items, $p < 0.05$.

To conclude, we argue that a CL approach may be particularly useful for L2 learners. By viewing language as a function of general interaction with other cognitive abilities and our interaction with the world, CL offers explanations that draw on learners' everyday real world experience by tapping into an intuitive reservoir of knowledge that facilitates an understanding of the systematic relationships among the units of language. This is the same reservoir of experiential knowledge of the world that underpins the human conceptual system and, hence, language itself. This is not to say that CL will magically make learning an SL easy. Learning any language requires committing a vast array of lexical items to memory. All languages have "irregularities," such as irregular past tense marking in English, which will have to be memorized. All languages have certain conventionalized uses that are not straightforwardly open to a systematic explanation. Moreover, each language potentially highlights slightly different aspects of human experience and conceptualization of the spatial–physical world, and thus learners will face certain challenges mapping the differences between their L1 and the L2. Nevertheless, CL offers important advances in our understanding of language that would appear to be of real benefit to L2 learners.

## III. FURTHER READING

There are a number of good introductions to the field of CL that language teachers may be interested in exploring for further details of the theoretical underpinnings of this approach. Two early introductions are provided in Ungerer and Schmid (1996) and Dirven and Verspoor (1998). A more comprehensive introduction of CL currently available is Evans and Green (2006). Another good, although brief, introduction is provided by Lee (2001). Croft and Cruse (2004) provide an overview of the field, although their book is more technical and less user-friendly than the previous ones mentioned. A good introduction to English grammar that adopts a CL framework is Radden and Dirven (2007). Taylor (2002) provides an excellent introduction to Langacker's *Cognitive Grammar*.

In addition, there are a number of pioneering theoretical works in CL that SLA specialists interested in CL may wish to explore. For those who want to have quick access, we recommend Geeraerts' (2006) collection of 12 seminal articles in CL and an introduction that summarizes CL theory. For those who are interested in reading the complete foundational works, we recommend Ronald Langacker's two-volume set *Foundations of Cognitive Grammar* (Langacker, 1987, 1991), Eve Sweetser's influential monograph *From Etymology to Pragmatics* (1990), George Lakoff's book on categorization and experientialism *Women, Fire and Dangerous Things* (Lakoff, 1987), Leonard Talmy's two-volume set *Toward a Cognitive Semantics* (Talmy, 2000), George Lakoff and Mark Johnson's pioneering work on metaphor and the experiential basis of meaning *Metaphors We Live By* (Lakoff & Johnson, 1980), Adele Goldberg's landmark study on the syntax of verbal argument structure *Constructions* (Goldberg, 1995), and *The Semantics of English Prepositions* (Tyler & Evans, 2003), which presents the most complete account of the polysemy networks of English prepositions to date.

Finally, several volumes address issues of CL and SL learning: Pütz, Niemeier, and Dirven (2001a, 2001b), Achard and Niemeier (2004), Ellis and Robinson (2008), and Tyler, Kim, and Takada (2008). There is a fine pedagogical volume on English prepositions within CL, *English Prepositions Explained* (Lindstromberg, 1997).

## REFERENCES

Achard, M., & Niemeier, S. (Eds.). (2004). *Cognitive linguistics, second language acquisition, and foreign language teaching*. Berlin: Mouton de Gruyter.

Bensoussan, M., & Laufer, B. (1984). Lexical guessing in context in EFL reading comprehension. *Journal of Research in Reading, 7*, 15–32.

Boers, F. (1996). *Spatial prepositions and metaphor*. Tübingen: Günter Narr Verlag.

Boers, F. (2000). Metaphor awareness and vocabulary retention. *Applied Linguistics, 21*, 553–571.

Boers, F., & Demecheleer, M. (1998). A cognitive semantic approach to teaching prepositions. *English Language Teaching Journal, 53*, 197–204.

Boers, F., Demecheleer, M., & Eyckmans, J. (2004). Cultural variation as a variable in comprehending and remembering figurative idioms. *European Journal for English Studies, 8,* 375–388.

Boers, F., & Lindstromberg, S. (Eds.). (2006). *Not so arbitrary: Cognitive linguistic approaches to teaching vocabulary and phraseology*. Berlin: Mouton de Gruyter.

Brown, P., & Levinson, S. (1987). *Politeness: Some universals in language use*. Cambridge: Cambridge University Press.

Brugman, C. (1981). *The Story of Over*. M.A. thesis, University of California, Berkeley, Available from the Indiana Linguistics Club.

Coady, J., & Huckin, T. (1997). *Second language vocabulary acquisition*. Cambridge: Cambridge University Press.

Croft, W., & Cruse, D. A. (2004). *Cognitive linguistics*. Cambridge: Cambridge University Press.

Dirven, R., & Verspoor, M. (1998). *Cognitive exploration of language and linguistics*. Amsterdam: Benjamins.

Eigen, E., & Winkler, R. (1983). *Laws of the game: How the principles of nature govern chance*. New York: Alfred A. Knopf.

Ellis, N. C. (2008). The dynamics of language use, language change, and first and second language acquisition. *Modern Language Journal, 92*(2), 232–249.

Ellis, N. C., & Robinson, P. (Eds.). (2008). *Handbook of cognitive linguistics and second language acquisition*. Hillsdale, NJ: Lawrence Erlbaum Associates.

Ellis, R. (1994). *The study of second language acquisition*. Oxford: Oxford University Press.

Evans, V., & Green, M. (2006). *Cognitive linguistics: An introduction*. Edinburgh: University Press Edinburgh.

Geeraerts, G. (2006). *Cognitive linguistics: Basic readings*. Berlin: Mouton de Gruyter.

Gibbs, R. W. (1994). *The poetics of mind: Figurative thought, language, and understanding*. Cambridge: Cambridge University Press.

Goldberg, A. (1995). *Constructions*. Chicago: University of Chicago Press.

Goldberg, A. (2006). *Constructions at work: the Nature of generalization in language*. Oxford: Oxford University Press.

Huong, N. T., & Verspoor, M. (2008). Cognitive grammar and teaching english articles to Asian students. In J. R. Lapaire (Ed.), *From gram to mind: Grammar as cognition*. Presses Universitaires de Bordeaux: Bordeaux.

Kövecses, Z. (1986). *Metaphors of anger, pride, and love: a Lexical approach to the structure of concepts*. Amsterdam: Benjamins.

Kövecses, Z., & Szabó, P. (1996). Idioms: A view from cognitive semantics. *Applied Linguistics, 17,* 326–355.

Krashen, S. (1981). *Second language acquisition and second language learning*. Oxford: Pergamon.

Lakoff, G. (1987). *Women, fire and dangerous things*. Chicago: University of Chicago Press.

Lakoff, G., & Johnson, M. (1980). *Metaphors we live by*. Chicago: University of Chicago Press.

Langacker, R. W. (1987). *Foundations of cognitive grammar Vol. 1: Theoretical prerequisites*. Stanford: Stanford University Press.

Langacker, R. W. (1991). *Foundations of cognitive grammar Vol. 2: Descriptive applications*. Stanford: Stanford University Press.

Larsen-Freeman, D. (1996). The role of linguistics in language teacher education. In J. Alatis, C. Straehle, B. Gallenburger, & M. Ronkin (Eds), *Proceedings of the 1995 Georgetown Roundtable*. Washington, DC: Georgetown University Press.

Laufer, B. (1997). What's in a word that makes it hard or easy: Some intra lexical factors that affect the learning of words. In N. Schmitt & J. McCarthy (Eds.), *Vocabulary: Description, acquisition and pedagogy* (pp. 140–155). Cambridge: Cambridge University Press.

Lee, D. (2001). *Cognitive linguistics: An introduction.* Oxford: Oxford University Press.

Lindstromberg, S. (1997). *English prepositions explained.* Amsterdam: John Benjamins.

MacLennan, C. H. G. (1994). Metaphors and prototypes in the teaching and learning of grammar and vocabulary. *IRAL, 32,* 97–110.

Pütz, M., Niemeier, S., & Dirven, R. (Eds.). (2001a). *Applied cognitive linguistics, Vols I and II: Theory and language acquisition.* Berlin: Mouton de Gruyter.

Pütz, M., Niemeier, S., & Dirven, R. (Eds.). (2001b). *Applied cognitive linguistics Vol II. Language pedagogy.* Amsterdam: Benjamins.

Radden, G., & Dirven, R. (2007). *Cognitive english grammar.* Amsterdam: Benjamins.

Riddle, E. (1985). The meaning and discourse function of the past tense in English. *TESOL Quarterly, 20,* 267–286.

Rosch, E. (1975). Cognitive reference points. *Cognitive Psychology, 7,* 532–547.

Rudzka-Ostyn, B. (2003). *Word power: Phrasal verbs and compounds, a cognitive approach.* Berlin: Mouton de Gruyter.

Rumelhart, D. E., & McClelland, J. L. (Eds.). (1986). *Parallel distributed processing: Explorations in the microstructure of cognition. Vol. 2: Psychological and biological models.* Cambridge, MA: MIT Press.

Rumelhart, D. E., & Norman, D. (1981). Analogical processes in learning. In J. R. Anderson (Ed.), *Cognitive skills and their acquisition.* Hillsdale, NJ: Erlbaum.

Schmitt, N. (2000). *Vocabulary in language teaching.* Cambridge: Cambridge University Press.

Schmitt, N., & McCarthy, J. (Eds.). (1997). *Vocabulary: Description, acquisition and pedagogy.* Cambridge, England: Cambridge University Press.

Sweetser, E. (1990). *From etymology to pragmatics: Metaphorical and cultural aspects of semantic structure.* Cambridge: Cambridge University Press.

Talmy, L. (1981, May). *Force dynamics.* Paper presented at conference on Language and Mental Imagery, University of California, Berkeley.

Talmy, L. (2000). *Toward a cognitive semantics.* Cambridge, MA: MIT Press.

Tannen, D. (Ed.). (1993). *Framing in discourse.* Oxford: Oxford University Press.

Taylor, J. R. (2002). Introduction. In R. W. Langacker (Ed.), *Cognitive grammar.* Oxford: Oxford University Press.

Taylor, J. (2003). *Linguistic categorization* (3rd ed.). Oxford: Oxford University Press. 1st ed.: 1989, 2nd ed.: 1995.

Tyler, A. (2008). Applying cognitive linguistics to second language learning. In N. Ellis & P. Robinson (Eds.), *Handbook of cognitive linguistics and second language acquisition* (pp. 456–546). Hillsdale, NJ: Lawrence Erlbaum Associates.

Tyler A., & Evans V. (2001). The relation between experience, conceptual structure and meaning: Non-temporal uses of tense and language teaching. In M. Pütz, S. Niemeier, & R. Dirven (Eds.), *Applied cognitive linguistics* (Vol. I, pp. 63–108). Berlin: Mouton de Gruyter.

Tyler, A., & Evans, V. (2003). *The semantics of english prepositions.* Cambridge: Cambridge University Press.

Tyler, A., Kim, Y., & Takada, M. (Eds.). (2008). *Language in the context of use: Cognitive and discourse approaches to language and language learning*. Berlin: Mouton de Gruyter.

Ungerer, F., & Schmid, H.-J. (1996). *An introduction to cognitive linguistics*. London: Longman.

Verspoor, M., & Lowie, W. (2003). Making sense of polysemous words. *Language Learning, 53*, 547–587.

Wilson, P. T., & Anderson, R. C. (1986). What they don't know won't hurt them: The role of prior knowledge in comprehension. In J. Orasanu (Ed.), *Reading comprehension: From research to practice* (pp. 31–48). Hillsdale, NJ: Lawrence Erlbaum Associates.

# COMPONENTS OF LINGUISTIC REPRESENTATION AND PROCESSING IN SECOND LANGUAGE ACQUISITION

## INTRODUCTION TO PART III

This part of the volume reviews recent research on the SLA of the major components of linguistic knowledge—lexicon, morphosyntax, phonology, and pragmatics. Reviews of research on sentence processing and on the roles of implicit and explicit learning in SLA are also included here.

Knowledge of the lexicon of a language is generally seen as the core of knowledge of that language, since lexical items contribute centrally not only to the meaning of a sentence but to aspects of its form as well. Chapter 9 ("Second Language of the Lexicon") by Alan Juffs reviews recent research in this important area. As is clear from part II of this volume, research on SLA is conducted within a variety of research traditions in psychology, linguistics, and language pedagogy, and research on the lexicon in SLA is no exception. Juffs brings all of these traditions to bear in his review. After a basic overview of treatments of the contents of the lexicon within the generative, pedagogical, and Vygotskian points of view, Juffs reviews the psycholinguistic research on the acquisition and use of the form–meaning relationship in the lexicon conducted primarily by Judith Kroll and her colleagues. He then looks at the central issue of verb argument structure and the semantics of verbs in SLA. Finally, Juffs suggests some pedagogical implications and future directions for research.

Roger Hawkins (chapter 10—"Second Language Acquisition of Morphosyntax") surveys recent work on the relation between morphology and syntax in SLA, including a number of issues regarding proposals having to do with the learner's grammar at the apparent initial state of acquisition, the grammars that appear at stages in the subsequent process of acquisition, the nature of L2 grammars in their apparently final form, what properties of these grammars are traceable to the grammar of the first language and what properties derive from universal grammar, and finally, what role experience or input plays in the course of acquisition.

Chapter 11 by John Archibald ("Second Language Phonology") reviews research in the study of the SLA of phonology within the generative tradition. After a discussion of some general issues in the study of second language phonology, Archibald addresses specific questions in the study of the SLA of segments, of syllable structure, and finally, of higher-level prosodic phenomena. He is concerned throughout with the issues of transfer, critical period, and so on, as they arise in the study of second language phonology.

Chapters 9–11 cover areas of the SLA of the *form* of linguistic expressions; Gabriele Kasper's chapter 12 ("L2 Pragmatic Development") addresses issues in research on the systems of knowledge that determine the *situated use* of those forms—that is, of pragmatic knowledge. Kasper first places the study of pragmatics in general in relation to research traditions in cognitive and cultural–historical psychology, linguistic anthropology, and sociology. She then addresses the problem of the learning of pragmatics in the individual—first, the learner's comprehension of the pragmatics of the native speaker of the second language, then the production of the speech acts by the learner, and subsequently, in terms of the learning process itself. Finally, she turns to work within a number of research traditions including Vygotskian sociocultural theory, language socialization, and finally, conversational analysis.

In addition to systems of linguistic knowledge (or linguistic competence, in the technical sense), the learner must internalize systems that put that knowledge to use in perception (sentence parsing) and production. In chapter 13 ("Sentence Parsing in L2 Learners: Linguistic and Experience-based Factors"), Paola E. Dussias and Pilar Piñar review research in this area of linguistic ability as it is found in second language learners. For a variety of methodological reasons (including the possibility of tracking eye movements), the problem of sentence parsing in the process of reading constitutes an excellent site for the study of sentence parsing by second language users, and this is the area on which Dussias and Piñar focus their discussion. Their treatment distinguishes between linguistic factors in comprehension (those having to do with the text such as its syntactic and semantic properties) and participant factors such as the proficiency, immersion experience, and working memory and reviews the research in each area. In order to add a new perspective on the variable of input in SLA, Dussias and Piñar review the literature on sentence parsing in the reading of deaf learners of English in view of the fact that, for most deaf learners, English is a second language.

An important distinction is drawn in the research literature of psychology—and in SLA research as well—between implicit and explicit knowledge. Implicit knowledge is that which affects behavior but is below the level of awareness, whereas explicit knowledge is that of which the actor is aware. John N. Williams's chapter 14 ("Implicit Learning in Second Language Acquisition") addresses the issues and research surrounding this distinction as it applies to SLA. After a discussion of implicit learning in general based on the psychological literature—most prominently the artificial grammar literature—Williams applies the distinction specifically to the case of language and, more specifically, to the features of language that can be both implicitly and statistically learned (e.g., chunking and form–meaning connections). He also notes results that show that certain aspects of grammatical knowledge do not lend themselves to learning that is both statistical and implicit (e.g., long-distance dependencies). He then addresses the questions of the role of attention in implicit learning, the interface between implicit and explicit knowledge, and individual differences.

CHAPTER 9

# SECOND LANGUAGE ACQUISITION OF THE LEXICON

Alan Juffs

## I. INTRODUCTION

No matter one's theoretical perspective, the lexicon is a key component of language. Jackendoff's (2002a) review of different stages in the development of Chomsky's (1965, 1981, 1995) generative grammar over 30 years shows that the one *enduring* element is the lexicon. This stability may be somewhat surprising given such evolution, but Jackendoff (2002a, p. 130) also suggests that almost all theories of language can agree that lexical items consist of "a long-term memory association of phonological, syntactic and semantic features." In some cases, for example concrete objects, the lexicon may also contain a visual–spatial structure. The lexicon has become a unifying part of the grammar, and as such, he argues that the lexicon as a whole is part of the interface components (see White, this volume). The lexicon is *central* to the whole grammar because it encodes a combination of phonological and morphological information that is vital in establishing *meaning contrasts*; in addition, it is the place of storage for syntactic categories and verb argument structure. Last, but certainly not least, it stores concepts. Given this central role, connected to all areas of language, understanding the lexicon is vital to any theory of SLA.

Although an understanding of the lexicon is crucial, it is not easy to achieve precisely because the lexicon, like language itself, is not an undifferentiated whole. It can, therefore, be understood only by investigating its different parts separately. The many strands of research on the lexicon reflect its complex nature: psycholinguists, generative SLA researchers, connectionist researchers, and pedagogical researchers all have different interests and methodologies. Psycholinguists such as Kroll and her colleagues (De Groot & Kroll, 1997; Kroll, 1993; Kroll & Sunderman, 2003) and Jiang (1999, 2002) focus on the relationship between L1 and L2 forms, meaning storage,

*The New Handbook of Second Language Acquisition*

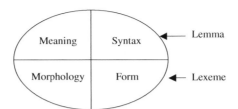

**Figure 1**   Levelt's (1989) model of the lexical entry.

and processing. Researchers interested in verb meaning and morphosyntax have concentrated more on the conceptual structure of verbs and how crosslinguistic differences in the lexicalization of concepts can affect morphosyntax (e.g., Hirakawa, 1995, 2001, 2006; Inagaki, 2001; Juffs, 1996, 2000; Montrul, 1999, 2001; Toth, 2000; White et al., 1998; White, 2003, chapter 7; Yuan, 1999; Zyzik, 2006). Researchers such as Ellis (2002, 2005) approach the lexicon from connectionist viewpoint and emphasize the role of frequency in acquisition of words, collocations, and morphosyntactic patterns. Researchers interested in word learning in instructional contexts focus much more on frequency of words and their collocations in corpora and less on the representation and processing of richer semantic representations (e.g., Cobb's website, the Compleat Lexical Tutor ⟨ http://www.lextutor.ca/⟩ McCarthy, 1994; Nation, 2001). Idioms and chunks are important in connectionist models, and are being recognized as more important in pedagogical SLA research in general (Steinel, Hulstijn, & Steinel, 2007; Wray & Perkins, 2000). Finally, sociocultural researchers point out the need to understand concept development from the point of view of participation in a culture (Lantolf & Thorne, 2006; Pavlenko, 2000; Vygotsky, 1986).

Because SLA researchers have written about the L2 lexicon from so many different viewpoints, an overview is needed that juxtaposes the different threads. Although a true synthesis is not possible, bringing together these different strands may help move the field forward. The chapter's structure, therefore, follows two main themes suggested by Gregg (1996) for any theory of SLA. Section II focuses on a sketch of the content of the lexicon. Section III addresses the psycholinguistic research into form–meaning correspondence, while section IV focuses on verbs and morphosyntax. Section V addresses some pedagogical issues. Section VI suggests some potential future research topics with reference theoretical developments and interdisciplinary connections which L2 researchers have so far left relatively unexplored.

## II. WHAT IS IN THE LEXICON?

### A. A Basic Model

A lexical entry consists of at least four parts. These four aspects of a lexical item's structure are reflected in Levelt's (1989, 2001) model in Figure 1, adapted by Jiang (2002, p. 619) and in other publications.[1]

---

[1]Levelt (2001) presents a summary of a series of experiments of how his model explains speech production. If conceptual semantics (meaning), syntax, and form were not separated, the data in his experiments could not be explained.

Beyond this basic model, disagreements remain on what is, in fact, *in* the lexicon and how the internal structure of each cell in Figure 1 is represented and learned. Until the 1990s, generative theory treated the lexicon as somewhat uninteresting because it was assumed that the lexicon contained idiosyncratic elements that could not be handled by rules and constraints. To some extent, this view of the lexicon as a store of arbitrary labels is correct. Obviously, form–meaning phonological labels must be learned from input, can be learned throughout the life span, and can be easily forgotten. This situation contrasts with the combinatorial mechanisms such as "merge," "movement" (Chomsky, 1995), and constraints on interpretation of semantic scope in quantification and negation (e.g., Crain & Pietroski, 2002), which cannot be learned from input (alone).

However, when one considers the internal structure of the cells in Figure 1, it is clear that what we call the "meaning" and "syntax" of a word must be defined in a complex and abstract system. Jackendoff (2002a, 2002b) has been particularly influential in discussing the details of each cell in Figure 1. Jackendoff (2002b, p. 27) suggests that information in a lexical entry will be distributed across at least *three* structures, linked by a "subscript," a fourth, morphology, must also be included, shown in (2). It is worth repeating and emphasizing that a lexical entry is not a single, indivisible "slot" or chunk in a list. That is, for "sit," each of the four elements in (1) and (2) can be stored, manipulated, and learned separately.

(1)  Lexical entry for "sit"
   a. Phonology:/sɪt/: [Note <u>contrast</u> with other words:/**h**ɪt/,/sɪ**n**/, etc.]
   b. Syntax: category [V], intransitive: unaccusative: V__⟨1⟩ ([PREP: in/on/down/ down on]); (transitive—somewhat rarer, e.g. "he sat the baby in the high chair.").
   c. Type: (Concept): go from standing or lying down to a seated position (intrans); to place something in a seated position (trans.).
(2)  Morphology:/sɪt/: related words:/sæt/past;/sɪtɪŋ/-progressive/gerund

The claim that the lexical entry consists of a linking of these independent structures is important for theories of language, language development, and language processing that permit the separation of the syntactic–semantic component from the phonological component (Hawkins, this volume; White, this volume). Quite simply, it allows for cases where a form can be recognized, but not linked to a fully elaborated meaning and vice versa. In specific theoretical models, the split allows "incorrect" phonological forms to be inserted into syntactic trees that have the correct morphosyntactic features (Embick & Noyer, 2006). Moreover, this claim is central to research of psycholinguists such as Levelt, Kroll, and Jiang, who assume that L2 and L1 lexical forms (phonological and written) can be stored independently of syntax and conceptual structure. Acquisition of the lexicon can, therefore, be stated in terms of creating, reinforcing, and making automatic the links between these components in production and comprehension.

With regard to the morphology in (2), notice that for the word "sit," English has an *irregular* past form and a *regular* progressive/gerund form. Jackendoff argues that these two kinds of elements are stored differently: "sat" will be a form that is listed in the lexicon as one of about 180 irregular past tenses in English, but "sitting" is a form that is produced by affixation. Jackendoff (2002b) uses the term "free combination" or "unify" for morphology instead of "rule"; grammatical "unification" will depend on the subcategorial properties of the stem. For example, "-ing" would "select" an appropriate [V], to "unify" with and create "sitting." In this way, word formation would take place in much the same way as syntactic operations such as "merge" in the Minimalist approach to language (Chomsky, 1995). Such operations do *not* occur "in the lexicon" but are created online by the computational system.[2] The assumption that morphological forms can be separate from syntactic structure is also crucial to discussions of second language errors in inflectional morphology (Hawkins, this volume).

Jackendoff makes the important point that lexical items are not *words*. Some lexical items are *smaller* than words, for example, affixes that are both inflectional (e.g., /d/-[past]) and derivational, for example, [/-nɛs/[a property]/ADJ -/]. Although Jackendoff (2002b) suggests that English may store many frequently occurring affixed forms, in highly inflected languages, such as Turkish and Navajo, it would be absurd to propose that all forms of *all* verbs are stored in *all* of their inflected forms. The point here is that *some* regular inflected forms may be stored, but others are created via the computational module. Some evidence for this position comes from Alegre and Gordon (1999), who showed that even in English only regular inflected forms with frequencies of over 6 per million in a corpus showed effects for storage. (They suggest that modified connectionist models were also compatible with their data for English.) Silva and Clahsen (2008) provide a recent overview and references to the debate over storage and computation with morphology.

The lexicon also contains elements that are *larger* than words. These elements are also lexical items. The classic examples are set phrases ("right to life," "tax and spend," "easy does it," "all mouth and trousers") and idioms ("a stitch in time saves nine," "his goose is cooked," "spill the beans." Jackendoff (2002b) argues that such items are stored in the lexicon. Constituents that make up parts of idioms can be moved, proving that idioms and set phrases are stored with complete morphosyntactic information, and not as unanalyzable chunks as previously suggested (Nunberg, Sag, & Wasow, 1994).

On the basis of this overview of lexical phenomena, Jackendoff argues that a theory of what is in the lexicon must be heterogeneous. In other words, one has to allow for both storage and free combination of items, with what he calls a "cline" from storage to free combinatorial production. This is an elaborated version of the dual mechanism approach articulated by Pinker and others (e.g., Clahsen, 1995).

It is important to add that applied linguists who have carried out in depth research on corpora and classroom instruction have also gone beyond the quartet of "(phonological) form," "syntax," "morphology," and "concept." Corpus linguists in particular have made important contributions to the question "how the lexicon is learned" through frequency analysis. Nation (2001, p. 27) suggests the following list of what is means to know a word, emphasizing both receptive and productive knowledge.
e.g., /kæt/, in (3)

(3)   a. Form Pronunciation (how it is spoken, what it sound like):
        /kæt/ → [kʰæt]
        Written (spelling) "cat"
        Word parts   (Morphological forms that do not change class)
                     Cat-s, but presumably not "catty."

---

[2]Naturally, this claim is controversial and not accepted by connectionists.

"Catty" is derived from "cat," but means something different, that is, "spiteful" or "mean-spirited." This is typical of the difference between inflected and derived forms of a word, where derived forms may involve "semantic drift" away from the core meaning of a word. Such drift may be culturally specific; for example, some cultures may not associate qualities such as "mean" and "spiteful" with cats.

b. Meaning
    (i)   What meaning does the word signal: feline
    (ii)  What is included in the concept: domestic feline and wild feline.
    (iii) Associations: which other words does it make us think of?
        e.g., dog, tiger, lion, tabby, kitten, etc.
c. Use
    (i)   Which patterns does the word occur in?
        e.g., the cat; a cat; etc. "rain cats and dogs," "cat-call," "big cat," "alley cat," etc.
    (ii)  Which words of other types of words occur with this word?
        e.g., cats and dogs; domestic cat; wild cat, etc.
    (iii) Constraints
        e.g., register: feline creature versus cat; region: kitty versus moggy, etc.

Nation's list of knowledge components for a lexical item makes clear that there is a lot more to know about a word than just its phonology, semantics, morphology, and syntax. Nation's description is useful for a teacher, but the "shopping" list of features is not as useful as more theoretical approaches in understanding the *stages* through which learners go in assembling the information in the cells in Figure 1 into a complete lexical entry and making that assembly a robust learned set of associations. Linguistic theory offers more detailed accounts of some Nation's categories, with the exception of the important collation and word association components. Nation's list also includes connotations and polysemy that are issues linguistic theory still struggles with.

## B. Representation of Forms

The theory of forms belongs of course to phonology and sound-spelling mappings. We will not discuss those theoretical issues in any great detail in this chapter, since an adequate discussion belongs in part to a theory of acquisition of phonemic contrasts. Essentially, the acquisition of forms involves the mapping of sound sequences or spellings to the rest of the lexeme/lemma structure. The internal representation of these sound strings is the topic of phonology (see Archibald, this volume; Jackendoff, 2002b, chapter 1).

## C. Representation of Morphology

Morphology is an issue that has been the center of linguistic theorizing over the past several years. One very influential, but controversial proposal, is Distributed Morphology (Embick & Noyer, 2006). The relevance of these issues in SLA are discussed at greater depth in Hawkins (this volume).

## D. Representation of Links between Meaning and Syntax

One of the most challenging parts of the lexicon is the lemma—the semantics and syntax in the top two cells in Figure 1. Where conceptual semantics is concerned, Fodor and Lepore (1996, p. 267) state that "A theory of concepts has two things to explain: how concepts function as categories, and how a finite mind can have an infinite conceptual capacity." This opinion is echoed by Jackendoff (1992) and Pustejovsky (1995). However, although linguists may agree on the problem, they cannot agree on a solution, even though philosophers of language and cognitive linguists have written at length on this issue (Cruse, 1986; Croft & Cruse, 2004; Fodor, 1998; Jackendoff, 2002b). Fodor (1998) insists that decomposing word meaning into "features" cannot be sustained, whereas Pustejovsky and Jackendoff insist that decomposition is the only way to account for knowledge of meaning.

Among semanticists who advocate decomposition, a consensus seems to be emerging among both generative and functional linguists that decompositional theories of meaning for nouns and verbs are going to be somewhat different (Jackendoff, 2002b; Landau, 2000, p. 321, footnote. 2; Pustejovsky, 1995; Van Valin & La Polla, 1997, p. 184). This separation is important because both generative and functional researchers hold that the semantic structure of a verb has important implications for syntax. Section IV elaborates this idea in some detail, showing how the meaning of a verb influences the number of noun phrases and prepositional phrases that occur in the sentence. The result is that even if decompositional analysis for nouns may not work (very well), a decompositional theory for verbs does seem to be necessary. We shall return to some of debates on decompositional semantics in section VI.

## E. Language, Culture, and Concepts

Linguists make a distinction between semantic structure that is relevant to computational aspects of morphosyntax and encyclopedic knowledge that does not affect computation. The boundary between these two aspects remains somewhat unclear and is a focus of on-going research. In the encyclopedic part of the lexicon, the conceptual store encodes how a culture labels artifacts and events; this information about *culture* must is created and learned through interaction with members of that culture (Vygotsky, 1986, chapter 4). For example, the noun phrase "the party" or "dang" will mean something very different to a member of the Chinese Communist Party and a member of the Republican Party in the United States. Even relatively simple words such a "chair" in English and "chaise" in French can cover different aspects of "chairness." In English, the word "chair" can include "armchair," "dining chair," among others, but in French it is necessary to say "fauteuil" when referring to an "armchair," because "chaise" is limited to unupholstered chairs. Vygotsky emphasizes three aspects of concept formation. First, he made a distinction between a child and an adult sharing a form, but not having the same "meaning." This position should be familiar by now from Figure 1. Second, the development of what we would now call child's lexeme to lemma links depends on refinement of sets of terms that Vygotsky called "complexes" but which we might call words related through taxonomic groups and the need for the concept to be related to "word" in order to complete goals in a task. Interestingly, he rejects simple form–meaning mapping by mere frequency of association (see also Bley-Vroman (2002) for a thought-provoking piece that addresses frequency and meaning acquisition). Lantolf and Thorne (2006, p. 108) summarize Vygotsky's position thus: "Vygotsky argued that words do not have meanings that stand independently from other words; rather, word meanings are organized into networks that, taken together, form concepts." The *precise* details of how networks are created (beyond (social) interaction), what their sublexical features might be, and how they are represented remains unclear, but modern Vygotskians' approach is clearly compatible with some version a decompositional, feature network.

Section II has discussed in some detail the content of a lexical entry. In the next two sections, we will focus on research that has focused on form–meaning learning in general, and then turn to research that has focused on verbs.

## III. ACQUIRING FORM–MEANING RELATIONS

Psycholinguistic research on the acquisition of form–meaning links has been largely restricted to psychologists who work on bilingualism and to pedagogical researchers. This section focuses on the work of those experimental psychologists who have worked on form–meaning mappings and the role of L1 forms in influencing performance in tasks that involve the L2. The nature of lexical features of nouns is also touched on. The section concludes with some recent experimental research that explores derivational morphology.

### A. Psycholinguistic Research on the Relationship between L1 and L2 Word Forms and Meaning

Psycholinguists who are interested in the bilingual lexicon have carried out some of the most influential research on the relationship between L1 and L2 forms. Most stimuli in these experiments seem to be nouns and adjectives. This program of research began with adult bilinguals who had learned both languages as children. The original question was whether bilinguals organize their lexicon in a coordinate structure (i.e., two separate lexicons), or in a compound structure, where the lexicon of the second language is dependent on, and linked to, the L1 lexicon (Weinreich, 1953). Adult learners of a second language have also been the focus of subsequent studies. Following the model in Figure 1, researchers assume that a form can be dissociated from its meaning (see papers in Kroll & De Groot, 1997; Kroll & Sunderman, 2003; Kroll & Tokowicz, 2001 for recent overviews and discussion).

The experimental methodology used to investigate form–meaning links consists of a variety of tasks, for example, speak a word associated with a picture out loud; translate a word into, or from, another language; decision tasks of various kinds in which the participant in the experiment must rapidly decide whether a word is a possible word in the language or not. Typically, a computer presents images to name, words to translate, or words to make a decision about, and also records the time taken to carry out these tasks. Inferences about storage and processing are then made based on accuracy and reaction time data. Many investigations of semantic links use the "masked" priming task (e.g., Forster & Jiang, 2001). For example, in a French–English bilingual experiment in the procedure would be as shown in (10). The first screen presented on the computer is a "mask" of nonsense characters, often "########." This is followed by a 30–80 ms "prime" of a word that the participant does not consciously perceive, but may "see" subliminally; this "flash" of a word is then followed by the "target" word. The target word is always in a different form (upper vs. lower case) in order to counteract the effect of exactly the same forms (Forster & Jiang, 2001). Finally, the participants must make a "lexical decision," that is, they must decide whether the target word is a word or not. Control words in these experiments are often nonsense words, so "no" is an appropriate answer in the experiment.

(10) Hypothetical masked priming experiment (without control stimuli for nonwords)

| Fixation 500 ms | Invisible Prime 50 ms | Target 1000 ms | Is this a word? Predicted RT |
|---|---|---|---|
| a. ######## | house | maison Primed word | Faster RT *semantic* prime |
| b. ######## | mason | maison Primed word | Faster RT *form* prime |
| c. ######## | stick | maison Unrelated word | No effect/control |

Notice that in this case, the *form* of "house" is not similar to "maison." The prediction is that if the L1 word "house" is related semantically to the L2 word "maison," then the decision about whether "maison" is an French word or not should be faster than the other conditions. However, words that are similar in form, such as "mason," may also prime the target. A totally unrelated word, such as "stick" should not prime the target "maison" and is used as a control. Some important studies using this and other methods in the past decade are summarized in Table I.

Some important conclusions of this research program have been as follows. First, in the representation and processing of lexemes, fluent bilinguals activate lexical forms in both languages; the activation is bidirectional in that L2 can affect L1 and vice versa. Jared and Kroll (2001) found that once an L2 is activated through a simple naming task, the L2 triggers activation of closely related items in the L1. For example, in the following language pairs, words that share forms by chance, would activate their "false" friend forms, even though they are not related in meaning at all.

(9)  a. English: room   Dutch: room (cream)
     b. English: red    Spanish: red (net)
     c. English: net    German: nett (nice)

This activation *increases* with proficiency, presumably because the L2 lexicon is more robustly represented the higher one's proficiency. One might conclude from these results that L1 and L2 forms are stored according to similarity of form and not meaning. However, links in form do not preclude semantic links.

TABLE I

**Selected Psycholinguistic Bilingual Lexicon Studies**

| Authors (year) | Participants | Task | Main result |
|---|---|---|---|
| De Groot and Poot (1997) | 60 Dutch-English; 3 groups: low, medium, and high proficiency | Translation task: words varied according to "imageability," cognate status and frequency | Same pattern across groups |
| Talamas et al. (1999) | 16 Spanish-English 34 English-Spanish | Translation manipulates Closeness of forms, for example, man-hambre versus hombre | Less fluent bilinguals show more form interference; more fluent bilinguals show more meaning interference |
| Kroll, Michael, Tokowicz, and Dufour (2002) | Experiment 1 Beginning versus fluent L1 English learning L2 French (59) Experiment 2: 18 L2 Spanish 13 L2 French | Word naming Translation | Less fluent learners slower in L1 word naming: not mediated by working memory More fluent rely less on forms Translation asymmetry lower for fluent bilinguals |
| Jiang (2002) | 18 Chinese-English (+controls) | Lexical decision of semantic relatedness of word pairs, e.g. problem-question = *wenti* in Chinese | Learners' lexicons are affected by the L1 lemma since semantic decisions for English words with same translations result in longer reaction times and higher error rates. |
| Jiang (2004) | 15 Korean-English | | 2004 replicates 2002 findings |
| Sunderman and Kroll (2006) | 63 low proficiency 44 medium proficiency English learners of Spanish | Translation equivalent decision task, cara = face with distractors, for example cara-card cara-fact cara-head | Beginning learners showed more interference from competing *forms* New: All learners showed effects for word class, that is, form interference is modulated by grammatical class, N, V, etc. |

Second, findings suggest that form–meaning links are stronger for words that are concrete rather than abstract (e.g., "stone" vs. "trust") and for words that share similar forms in the L1 and L2. For example, cognates such as "tomato" in English and "tomate" in French will prime each other more reliably than forms that share less phonological material such as "forest" and "forêt." However, results of translation to and from pairs of languages have shown that as proficiency increases, there appears to be a shift from *form* activation to *meaning* activation. In other words, in the early stages, "flesh" would activate "flèche" for a beginning francophone learner of English because of lexical links, but the prediction is that more proficient bilinguals will show effects of "arrow" for "flèche." In adult native speakers, semantic links are more effective primes than form links. The L2 research suggests that learners shift from form focus to semantic organization as proficiency increases, suggesting the development of native-like lexical processing.

Third, in terms of semantics, some investigators claim that the L1 semantically primes the L2, but not vice versa (Jiang, 1999). This result has lead to the conclusion that the L2 lexicon is dependent on the L1 lexicon at the early stages in development, and perhaps even permanently for some aspects of word syntax and morphology. However, in a recent paper, Wang (2007) has suggested that in masked priming experiments, increasing the duration of the first stimulus up to 80 ms may results in effects being found for semantic priming of L2–L1.

The finding that "form" acquisition precedes lemma (semantic) acquisition is consistent with research by Schmitt and Meara (1997) who found that beginning learners are more likely to associate words even within the L2 based on form only, associations they call "clang associates." For example, Juffs et al. (2006) report the errors in (11). Arabic-speaking learners were asked to write a sentence using the word "cease," which was a word they had seen during reading exercises. The learners misidentified the word "cease" as "scene," "case," and "sees," which are all "clang" associates.

(11)  a. I watch the last cease of the movie and i didnt undersand it. [scene]
      b. I am investigation in very difficault cease [case]
      c. My boss geive me a important cease, he will I can finish that. [case]
      d. He cease me at midnight [sees]

As a result of earlier research, Kroll and colleagues have suggested the lexical mediation model in Figure 2 to account for such results. The model claims that beginning learners access concepts via the L1 forms, but as proficiency increases direct links from L2 forms to concepts are established. In other words, L2 lexical entries are initially just lexemes (cf., Jiang, 2000), without the lemma semantic and syntactic content listed in Figure 1. Only later do direct L2 form–concept meaning links become established (Talamas, Kroll, & Dufour, 1999).

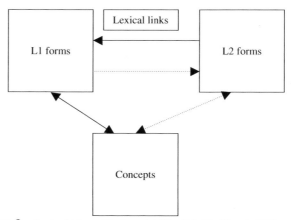

**Figure 2**   Revised hierarchical model (Kroll & De Groot, 1997, p. 178).

However, this model requires some refinement due to variation in the nature of the lexical items and concepts themselves. De Groot and colleagues suggest that although the revised hierarchical model accounts for much of the data, within the lexicon different features of words may make representation in the L2 easier or harder, regardless of level of proficiency or stage in L2 development. De Groot and Poot (1997) manipulated fairly coarse conceptual categories of imageabilty, frequency, and cognate status in Dutch–English bilinguals. For example, "hand" and "hand" are highly imageable, very frequent, and exact cognates, whereas "compulsion" and "dwang" have very low imageability, low frequency, and zero cognate relationship, even though they "mean" the same. In a study of forward (L1→L2) and backward (L2→L1) translation, findings showed effects for imageability at all levels of proficiency, with more concrete nouns being translated more easily than more abstract nouns, and more frequent nouns being translated more easily than less commonly occurring nouns. In addition, cognate status showed a reliable main effect. Naturally, the more lexical forms shared by words, the easier it is to translate them. Contrary to the revised hierarchical model, however, findings suggested that L1–L2 translation was easier than backward translation from L2–L1. Kroll and Tokowicz (2001, p. 61) responded that this might be because for abstract L2 words several L1 equivalents exist that might compete, causing reaction times to be slower. Hence, for each lexical entry, a set of form features will be matched with a set of conceptual features. The greater the overlap, the greater the ease of semantic and lexical representation will be. Discrepancies among studies may therefore be due to the materials used and variation in the type of lexical and conceptual features involved. Progress in this area may be made by a more detailed theory of concepts and concept acquisition than is currently being assumed in this research program (see also, Pavlenko, 2000), perhaps along the lines of *qualia* theory described suggested in section VI. As we have seen, the concept for even simple items, such as "chair" and "chaise" in French, may not be as straightforward as some of this research has assumed. The basic point is of course that some words are harder than others and that a more precise semantic theory is necessary to account for that fact.

In this regard, Jiang (2002, 2004) points out that it is often assumed that L2 meanings (concepts) are acquired at the same time as L2 forms (phonological entry), but as we have seen this is unlikely to be true except perhaps for the most common nonabstract terms that share meaning, for example, "stone." For example, "marry" in English can be translated into Chinese as "jiehun," but also has two other translations which express the point of view of the "giving" and "receiving" family of the woman: "jia" is used when marrying a daughter *out* of the family and "qu" is used when a daughter marries *into* a family. (These two terms are falling into disuse as Chinese culture changes among urban dwellers.) Jiang (2002, 2004) conducted two experiments based on translations of single Chinese and Korean words that, in English, must be translated into two words (e.g., expense-cost, doubt-suspect). Chinese and Korean learners judged pairs (over 20) that have one translation only more quickly than pairs that have two translations in the L1. Jiang interprets his findings as evidence for the continuing influence of L1 mediation of the L2 lexicon at the level of semantics.

These experimental results are consistent with the research on conceptual development of more "encyclopedic" knowledge, summarized by Lantolf and Thorne

(2006), that suggests that conceptual information transfers from the L1 even when an L2 form has been acquired. Research by Pavlenko (2002) that suggests Russian speakers transfer their understanding of the word "privacy" to their L2 English, but immigrants eventually develop this concept once they have participated in US culture. Pavlenko (2000) also suggests a need to separate semantic from conceptual knowledge, with the latter being more culturally rooted. This notion recapitulates the point made by earlier lexicon researchers, for example, Pinker (1989), that some aspects of meaning are more relevant to computation (core) and others more culturally determined (see also Pavlenko, 2008, and commentaries for recent developments on terms of emotion). Surprisingly, experimental studies of L2 concept development remain rare, inspite of Kellerman's (1986) well-known seminal work in which he showed that very marked, or unusual, polysemous meanings are not transferred even when the L1 and L2 share those marked meanings. As Lantolf and Thorne (2006) point out, much remains to be done in this area of L2 learning.

A new thrust in the area of *form* acquisition is in the area of derivational morphology, the somewhat neglected bottom left quadrant of Figure 1. Schmitt and Meara (1997) reported poor development of derivational morphology in their study of Japanese learners of English. More recently Silva and Clahsen (2008) have conducted masked priming research into derivational and inflectional morphology. One may assume that relationships among less frequent derived forms such as "hostile" and "hostility," and inflected forms like "induce" and "induced" is recorded in the lexicon or created online. Indeed, in masked priming experiments, it has been shown for native speakers that derived and inflected forms prime each other when compared to control stimuli. However, Silva and Clahsen found that advanced Chinese-speaking and German-speaking learners of English L2 showed reduced priming effects. Silva and Clahsen interpret these findings to mean that L2 learners have a morphological processing problem, which makes adult L2 learners rely more on storage than processing. In addition to inflectional forms, Silva and Clahsen looked only at two derivational affixes, -*ness* and -*ity*, so further experiments are needed to confirm or refine this finding.

To summarize this section, learners seem to go through stages in which forms in the L1 and L2 are closely related even if these links are the wrong ones to make such as in "false friends." Except perhaps for some basic words, forms are acquired earlier to, and separate from, fully developed semantic and conceptual information, although properties of the words themselves influence this general pattern of development. More complex encyclopedic entries for nouns are elaborated through participation in the L2 culture, and need to be refined through encountering the word in numerous contexts for the form–conceptual mappings to be firmly established.

## B. Collocation and "Arbitrary" Word Associations

McCarthy (1990) points out that there are some totally idiosyncratic facts concerning which words are used with which other words. For example, "strong" can be used with "tea" and "argument" but not with "car"; instead, we talk of a "powerful car." We have seen already in section II that generative researchers such as Jackendoff have conceded the need for knowledge of language to include constructions and not just rules for combination of items chosen from the lexicon. For example, "dance" is typically not transitive except with nouns like "tango" and "waltz," but it can be used in the structure "dance the night away" (Jackendoff, 1997). This fact about language has led some to claim that **all** there is to knowledge of language is sets of chunks and links between those chunks in a connectionist network (Ellis, 2002, 2005). Ellis (2002) maintains that frequency is the key to understanding the nature of the acquisition from everything from lexis to morphosyntax. Unfortunately, for reasons of space, this aspect of the lexicon cannot be discussed further at this point. Readers are referred to an extended summary in DeKeyser and Juffs (2005), and to the papers that are in the same volume of *Studies in Second Language Acquisition* as the Ellis (2002) paper.

## IV. SYNTAX–SEMANTICS CORRESPONDENCES WITH VERBS

### A. Theoretical Background

A form of semantic feature analysis been central to research on the acquisition of verb meaning and clause structure in first and second language acquisition. The basic idea is that verbs' meanings are made up of semantic primitives which combine to create the lexical conceptual structure (LCS) of a verb. Juffs (1996, 2000) summarized how this might work, based on proposals by Jackendoff (1990), Pinker (1989), and Talmy (1985).

Table II lists a set of semantic functions that make up a possible verb meaning. These main functions can be modified by a set of features that are motivated

TABLE II
**Building Blocks of Lexical-Conceptual Structure for Verbs**

| Building block | Event types | Example |
|---|---|---|
| *Main Functions* | | |
| ACT(+effect) | Causative events. Adds an external argument. | John filled the glass. The sun melted the ice. |
| ACT(−effect) | Noncausative transitives. Unergatives | Mary saw a ghost. Jane laughed. |
| GO+STATE | Unaccusatives (change of state) | The ice melted. |
| GO+PATH | Unaccusatives (motion) | The ball slid. |
| BE+STATE | Statives | A theory exists. John knows the answer. |
| | | |
| Features | Function that the feature is most commonly linked to. | |
| ±Effect | ACT | Kill, (+effect); see (−effect) |
| ±Manner | GO | Pour, splash, spill. |
| Property of the Theme/ Agent | THING | Ooze: whatever oozes must be liquid but sticky. See Talmy (1985, p. 73). |
| ±Polarity | BE+STATE | *Believe*. vs. *doubt* |
| ±Factivity | BE+STATE | *Regret* vs. *hope* |

through crosslinguistic semantic and morphological analysis. Languages may vary in the way they that combine the major building blocks of verbs, but these patterns tend to be tendencies rather than absolute rules (Juffs, 1996, 2000). The lexicalization of semantic functions (e.g., ACT with GO and STATE) into a single verb is called "conflation." One of the most frequently cited examples is that Romance languages have a tendency to "conflate" motion and PATH in a verb. For example, in French the verbs *entrer* "go in," *sortir* "go out," *monter* "go up," *descendre* "go down" include direction/path, whereas Germanic languages tend to put the PATH outside the core morpheme in a preposition. Instead, Germanic verbs tend to include MANNER, for example, "dance," "swim" with movement, which is not typically permitted by French. For example, in English one can say "John swam the river" meaning John crossed the river by swimming, whereas the equivalent French sentence is ungrammatical "*Jean a nagé la rivière"; instead, French uses the equivalent of the English paraphrase: "Jean a traversé la rivière à la nage."

Hence, the conceptual structure of a verb can have an influence on the number of noun phrases and prepositional phrases that may occur in a clause containing that verb. Most theories assume an intermediate level of representation between LCS to predicate argument structure (PAS), which dictates the number of noun phrases and prepositional phrases (arguments) that may appear in a clause. Languages may vary as to how these arguments are realized: in addition to NP and PP, some may be bound morphemes or zero morphemes. Table III provides an example of some crosslinguistic patterns of argument realization.

TABLE III

**Patterns of Lexical Conceptual Structure, Argument Structure, and Argument Projection for the Verb "Break" and Disappoint**

| Verb | To break casser (French) (da) po (Chinese) | Disappoint deçevoir shiwang |
|---|---|---|
| LCS | $[ACT+eff \; x \; [GO \; y \; [STATE]]$ | $[ACT+eff \; x \; [GO \; y \; [STATE]]$ |
| PAS | ↓    ↓ | ↓    ↓ |
| | V    $\underline{X}$    $<Y>$ | V    $\underline{X}$ |
| | ↓    ↓ | ↓    ↓ |
| | English: NP    NP | English: NP    NP |
| | French: 'se' if no $\underline{X}$ argument | French: NP    NP |
| Morphology | Chinese: no morphology with | Chinese: causative morpheme 'shi' |
| | alternation. | with transitive version is required to |
| | | license $\underline{X}$ |

Table III shows that although LCS may be similar because basic verbs ought to have close meanings—morphological operations mediate the expression of LCS and PAS in the syntax. For French, the intransitive version of a change of state verb requires the morpheme "se" "la fenêtre s'est cassée" = "the window broke," whereas in Chinese it is the addition of a causative morpheme that is required for the transitive "disappoint," "Zhang San shi wo shiwang" = "ZS made me disappointed" or "Zhang San disappointed me." Crosslinguistic differences in verb meaning and morphosyntax and the effects on the acquisition of the lexicon are the topic of a number of SLA studies.

Pinker refers to rules that combine the major "functions" such as ACT and STATE into lexical items, as "broad range rules" (BRR). These rules determine the semantics of NPs and PPs associated with the major functions them, for example, an NP associated with ACT is usually an agent. Pinker (1989) proposed other features that can affect narrow range rules (NRR), that is, rules that limit alternations inside and outside VP. To illustrate a narrow range rule, some locative verbs (verbs that describe caused movement to a location) may alternate in their LCS and therefore their syntax; for example, in (12) "spray" permits a conversion of the LCS [ACT [GO [PATH] to [ACT [GO [STATE] because of a narrow class feature "ballistic spatial distance along a trajectory" feature.

(12)   a. The hose sprayed insecticide on the tree. [ACT [GO [PATH]
       b. The hose sprayed the tree with insecticide. [ACT [GO [STATE]

However, "spew" in (13), which also applies to a liquid, does not permit alternation, because of a narrow range class feature "mass expelled from inside an entity."

(13)   a. The hose spewed insecticide on the tree. [ACT [GO [PATH]
       b. *The hose sprewed the tree with insecticide. [ACT [GO [STATE]

Juffs (1996, pp. 225–227) argues that patterns of difference among BRR, their morphology, and constraints on them, might be part of universal grammar (UG). In contrast, NRR are so specific and idiosyncratic that knowledge of them cannot be evidence for or against access to UG. Very recent theoretical work seems to support this division, because Embick and Noyer (2006) include the feature CAUSE ( = ACT) in their features in the vocabulary (form-based phonology), but do not include such features as detailed as "mass expelled from inside an entity," which are more likely in the encyclopedia in their framework.

Early SLA work on verbs drew attention to learnability and markedness with the dative alternation in English, which at the time was seen as a syntactic operation constrained by semantics and morphology (White, 1987). White showed that English-speaking learners of French as a second language overgeneralized the English double object dative to French, as shown in (14), where English allows double objects for animate recipients (14b, c), in contrast to French, (15), which does not.

(14)   a. Mary sent a letter to John.
          [X CAUSE Y TO GO TO Z]—Prepositional dative
       b. Mary sent John a letter.
          [X CAUSE Z TO HAVE Y] Double object dative
       c. Mary sent a package to the house/?? Mary sent the house a package.

(15)   a. Henri a donné des fleurs à Lucie.
          Henri AUX given some flowers to Lucie
          "Henri gave some flowers to Lucie."
       b. *Henri a donné Lucie des fleurs.

A key concept in this analysis is that English is a more general grammar than French, since it allows two syntactic patterns with the dative, but French only allows one. English is thus said to be a superset of French. Several learning contexts have been investigated in which differences between languages, or overgeneralizations with verb classes, means that learners have to make their grammar narrower. This means that a learner has to determine that certain sentences are not possible in the target language. The "unlearning" required here is thought be harder than expanding a grammar because it requires (overt) negative evidence if some other facet of the grammar does not preempt the erroneous representation. (A frequency account would allow the errors to disappear through nonoccurrence in the input; some researchers have suggested this as "indirect negative evidence," but it is considered a weak argument, Pinker, 1989, p. 14).

## B. Current Issues in Verb Meaning, Verb Argument Structure, and Morphology

Juffs (2000) and White (2003) provide extensive reviews which should be consulted for important foundational concepts and earlier work. This section concentrates on some more recent topics of discussion. The first issue concerns the "initial state" of the lexicon for verbs and the role of transfer. This question is important for the theory of full transfer/full access because Schwartz and Sprouse (1996) argue that it is the whole of the L1 that transfers. In an important series of papers, Montrul (1999, 2000, 2001) argues that learners begin not by transferring argument structure (by which I assume she means PAS and not LCS because she does not work in a framework that clearly defines an elaborated LCS separate from a syntactic representation), but by assuming a default pattern of argument structure for any verb, for example, SVO in English. This default PAS results in an overgeneralization pattern in which L2 learners, like children, think sentences such as "the dentist cried the patient" and "the magician disappeared the rabbit" are possible in their L2, even though the equivalent sentences in the L1 are also ungrammatical. Helms-Park (2001) also found that Vietnamese and Hindi-speaking learners of ESL overgeneralized in this way. Although Montrul argues against full transfer of argument structure at the beginning stages, she argues for the transfer of morphology that relates to argument structure. The basis of this claim comes from Montrul's Spanish-speaking learners of ESL who judged sentences such as "the glass broke" as less acceptable than sentences such as "the glass got broken." The latter type of sentence allows the Spanish-speakers to morphologically mark a semantic undergoer (object) that appears in a syntactic subject position, satisfying a morphological constraint in Spanish by equating "got" with the Spanish morpheme "se." Similarly, Montrul notes that Turkish-speaking learners of English rate sentences with "make" more acceptable than Spanish-speakers because the morphological causative in Turkish is "transferred" to the "the wind made the glass break" sentence type, even though the Turkish morpheme is a bound suffix rather than a free morpheme. Montrul's results are consistent with data and analyses by Hirakawa (1995) and Juffs (1996) in their studies which show overgeneralization of transitive structures and morphological crosslinguistic influence.

Advocates of complete full transfer/full access have challenged the failure of argument structure transfer (Whong-Barr, 2006). Their counterargument is that PAS transfers at the very early stage, but mismatches in morphology causes the system to overgeneralize in some verb classes. In considering this question, several lines of argument need to be clarified. Given the complex nature of linking of forms to concepts discussed in section III, it is necessary to establish that an L2 learner at the beginning stage of language learning is able to accurately recognize an L2 form and then associate it with an appropriate L1 concept/PAS. This semantic L1 influence may be filled in only later when L1 form–L2 form mappings are stable, so what a learner does at the very early stage may not mean much for either side of this argument. Advocates of full transfer/full access with verbs, then, must show that LCS is transferred—that is the conceptual content. Their position is consistent with findings in section III in that L2 forms are initially routed through the L1 to access concepts, and that L2 complete lexeme–lemma complexes are hard to achieve (Jiang, 2004).

Next, supporters of full transfer/full access much show that PAS is derived from the L1 LCS. A learner may get LCS wrong, but still get PAS right; for example, intransitive verbs vary crosslinguistically as to whether they are unaccusative or unergative (Rosen, 1984; Sorace, 1995). However, intransitive verbs all take one argument, so it will be hard to know if the L1 LCS has been transferred in a very such as "blush." Hence, errors at the level of PAS are not necessarily fatal to the full transfer account. Finally, the mapping from PAS into the morphosyntax can be influenced by the L1, as Montrul shows. From this discussion, it appears that full transfer can be maintained at LCS. This transfer of LCS leads to some over-generalization errors in PAS, with mapping affected by L1 morphosyntax.

Other challenges to early work in this area are now appearing. For example, Stringer (2006, 2007) takes another look at research by Inagaki (2001, 2002) in the acquisition of verbs that conflate motion and PATH and motion and MANNER. Inagaki assumed that a "parametric" conflation difference exists between English and Japanese in lexical "syntax," which is a framework adapted from Hale and Keyser (1993) (see Juffs, 1996, pp. 72–73, for problems with this *syntactic* approach to conceptual structure.) Inagaki argues that in English BRR incorporate PLACE into PATH, but in Japanese this incorporation is not possible. This difference explains the fact that the English sentence "John swam under the bridge" is ambiguous between being locational ( = John was swimming under the bridge) and directional ( = John swam from open water to a place under the bridge) in English. The equivalent Japanese sentence can only be locational. English-speaking learners of Japanese L2, therefore, have to narrow their grammar to one that allows only a locational meaning for prepositional phrases with motion verbs. Ingaki shows that even advanced English-speaking learners of Japanese make errors in allowing motion interpretations with sentences such as "John wa gakko-ni aruita," ≠ "John walked to school." Stringer argues that L1 acquisition data by Japanese-speaking children undermine the claim by Inagaki that Japanese does not allow a directional meaning for PPs with motion verbs. His data reveal strong tendencies along the lines suggested by Inagaki, but 15.7% of the motion events with PPs in his Japanese data show evidence of a directional meaning for the prepositional phrase with manner of motion verbs, for example, "sotto e hashitta" (outside to run-PAST) = "he ran outside." Stringer thus reverts to the more classic "conservative" item learning approach, suggesting that many words are acquired one-by-one (Baker, 1979). He also advocates the position that the whole of the L1 transfers, including the L1 lexicon, "with all its idiosyncratic combinations of sound (phonemes, phonological features) and meaning (lexemes [sic], and semantic features). This position would seem to be too strong given the experimental work of Kellerman (1986), which was part of the move away from full transfer to a more nuanced theory of "crosslinguistic influence". Once again, it seems important to recall Jackendoff's suggestion regarding storage, frequency and computation. Stored examples, even exceptions, need not undermine claims regarding computational regularity.

Evidence against full LCS transfer emerges in recent work on locatives. Recall that the LCS of verbs comprises both broad range conflation rules, and narrow range constraints. In this context, Bley-Vroman and Joo (2001) and Joo (2003) investigated the acquisition of locative verbs in English by Korean-speaking learners. They show that Pinker's BRR are acquired along with constraints on wholistic interpretation; for example, in the sentence "John sprayed the door with paint," the door is understood to be fully covered, whereas in the "John sprayed paint on the door" the door is not necessarily fully covered. However, they also show that learners have not acquired the narrow range constraints on locative alternation, that is, the difference between such features "ballistic trajectory" and "mass forcefully expelled." Hence, Joo (2003) does not deny that some aspects of verb meaning–syntax correspondences are driven by LCS–PAS rules, but her data do show that it is the refinement of narrow range constraints that is highly problematic for learners and that an item-by-item LCS–PAS link is not made. Crucially, the learners do not transfer L1 NRR into the L2 representations, a result which contradicts the strongest version of full transfer/full access hypothesis. The results are, however, consistent with NRR being part of encyclopedic knowledge, thus heavily dependent on input and context. Juffs' (1996, pp. 225–227) pointed out that narrow range constraints are unlikely to be part of UG, but rather language specific and learned from input. Juffs also suggests that where overgeneralizations do occur and can be preempted in the grammar, it is more likely to be the result of a broader underlying BRR conflation pattern that has an impact across verb classes.

The results of SLA research in this domain point to success in establishing the conceptual structure—PAS—syntax links in the L2 after adequate exposure. However, fine-grained distinctions in both nouns (e.g., question vs. problem) and verbs (e.g., spray vs. spew) seems much harder. These results do not necessarily make L2 learning in this domain fundamentally different from L1 acquisition (see Naigles, 1991, critique of Pinker's NRR). These findings suggest that an explanation for L2 lexical learning needs both UG-based verb class information and frequency/exposure information. Recent L1 research reflects this theme: Ambridge, Pine, Rowland, and Young (2008, p. 35) investigate how children learning directed motion (fall/tumble), appearing/disappearing, and verbs of semivoluntary emotion (laugh/giggle). They conclude that item learning and learning by verb class is important: "..., our findings have provided compelling evidence in support of both the semantic verb class hypothesis

(Pinker, 1989) and the entrenchment hypothesis (Braine & Brooks, 1995). However, our findings have also demonstrated that neither hypothesis on its own is sufficient to account for the pattern of data observed, and that the answer to the question of how children learn to restrict their argument-structure overgeneralization errors will necessarily include elements of both proposals." Some learners can probably acquire new narrow range constraints over time, but it is important to acknowledge that the process of acquisition will take frequent exposure. Future research will need to look once again to the more sophisticated methods of first language acquisition researchers.

## V. THE LEXICON AND SECOND LANGUAGE PEDAGOGY

This chapter is not designed as a review of pedagogical issues concerning the lexicon, but it is important to understand some concerns of language teaching, especially for the importance that frequency in various L1 corpora raise for learning. An understanding of the importance of corpora is essential if we are to fully understand the influence of input on refining LCS.

There are several book-length treatments of the lexicon and pedagogy. One important and comprehensive reference on the topic of vocabulary, semantics, and instruction is Hatch and Brown (1995).[3] Schreuder and Weltens (1993) contains some papers on pedagogy and psycholinguistics, and Folse (2004) is a very accessible guide for teachers of second language vocabulary.

However, Paul Nation (e.g., Nation, 2001) has been one of the most influential researchers in establishing, for English as a second or foreign language, how many words and which words a learner needs to know in order to be able to successfully read texts in English (see also McCarthy, 1990, 1994; see Biber et al., 2004 for words and structures occurring in written and spoken academic discourse). It is generally accepted that a learner needs to know between 2000 to 3000 word families in order to be able to read most texts. (Nation, 2001, p. 8) defines a word family as "a head word, its inflected forms, and its closely related derived forms"). Thus, the grouping of words into word families does not really address the fact that for some learners morphological variants are not well-understood and recognized (see also Jiang, 2007; Schmitt & Meara, 1997; Silva & Clahsen, 2008), and that there is more to word learning than frequency measures (Meara, 2005).

The task of vocabulary learning for adults is best understood by comparing what L1 learners achieve and the time it takes them. It is estimated that children learn approximately 1000 words a year and know about 8000 words by the time they are 8 (Carey, 1978, cited in Jackendoff, 2002b), and well over 15,000 by the time they reach age 18. This rate of learning implies that children learn approximately 5 words per day from ages 2–8. The task faced by the adult L2 learner for the lexicon is, therefore,

---

[3]Given its coverage, it is surprising that this book is not cited more. In a search of 100 citations in *Google Scholar*, Hatch and Brown (1995) is not once cited by mainstream researchers in the second language psycholinguistics literature. Strangely, Nation (2001) does not refer to their work either, even though his book is specifically on the same subject and published by the same company, Cambridge University Press.

daunting. Indeed, it is rare for second language learners to acquire so many words. Although applied linguists believe that knowledge of approximately 3000 word families is enough for most reading tasks, Cobb (2006) notes that even these basic 3000 word families may not be adequately learned by many learners in foreign language contexts. West (1953) developed a list of 2000 essential words known as the General Service List. Knowledge of this list is supposed to be a prerequisite for progress in learning other words, since these words are the key to understanding about 80% of texts in an L2. The academic word list (Coxhead, 2001) provides a further 570 word families that occur frequently in texts in the humanities and social sciences.

All the work on corpora has been particularly informative for teachers developing curricula. However, the suggestions do not really attack the problems that the psychology and linguistics literature bring up. A new phonology for the L2 learner means that sound labels for items must be processed and matched with new items. Whether words are in fact associated with lemmas in a way similar to the L1 remains an issue of research. Jiang (2004) has suggested that L2 learners may never develop lexical entries that are more than "episodic" memory traces of words, without full linguistic specification in the L2. However, the research on lexicalization in verbs indicates that this may be a rather too pessimistic a view, since learners do seem to be able to acquire new patterns of lexicalization. Moreover, Ellis (2005) also suggests that implicit knowledge can be developed from input after multiple exposures. Current applied linguistic research is focused on the quality, in terms of depth of processing, and quantity of exposure that is needed for successful learning of both recognition and production (Folse, 2006; Hulstijn & Laufer, 2001). All too often learners make only weak form–meaning links that enable them to pass a test of recognition, but their knowledge of morphological variants, concept, and use in syntax (what is traditionally called "usage"!) is lacking. A key to further progress in this field will be research that incorporates detailed theories of concepts, morphology, and processing (including frequency) in addition less complicated form–meaning links.

## VI. FUTURE RESEARCH

Recent research in a variety of fields has not yet influenced L2 research on the lexicon. Future L2 research might benefit from considering these developments.

### A. Neurolinguistic Evidence for Conceptual Organization and New Avenues of Research

Caramazza and Mahon (2006) describe several conceptual deficits that a theory of semantics must account for and which should influence thinking about lexical research. This research strongly suggests that the potential for conceptual development is language specific, part of UG, and therefore not part of some general learning mechanism. First, patients with semantic deficits may be unable to name living animate objects, but are able to name living inanimate objects and vice versa. Second, these deficits are unrelated to any perceptual or sensory impairment. Third, patients may have a "conspecific" (same species) impairment, which means that they may suffer from a deficit that affects their perceptions only of other humans; for example, a patient may be unable to recognize very famous people, but be able to recognize faces in general. Taken together, these three properties have led Caramazza and colleagues to endorse a theory of conceptual organization that is based not on a correlation between the real world and object properties, but rather on representational constraints that are domain-specific to semantic organization, and rely on conceptual categories such as living animate, living inanimate, same species features (including emotion), and tools. (They suggest that superior sensitivity to these categories may be related to natural selection. For example, presumably, knowing whether some larger member of your species is angry and aggressive may be useful.) Moreover, recent fMRI studies suggest that nouns and verbs are represented neurally in different localities, with verbs being represented in the left frontal cortical network and nouns more in *bilateral* temporal areas of the brain (Shapiro et al., 2004). Not surprisingly, given their location in the traditional "language" areas, verbs are more susceptible to impairment in aphasia (Bi, Han, Shu, & Caramazza, 2005). The point of these comments is that future research might explore these issues directly in order to address whether the second language lexicon can be similarly "deficient" or not. Research that is focused on the four categories discussed by Caramazza and Mahon could go a long way to addressing issues in the L2 lexicon for nouns that goes beyond the categories discussed so far in the L2 literature. One might imagine linking Caramazza's work with the existing L2 literature on psych verbs and emotion (e.g., White et al., 1998).

## B. Cognitive Linguistic Approaches to Word Meaning

Functional linguists have also addressed issues of lexical semantics in considerable detail (e.g., Cruse, 1986). Croft and Cruse (2004), who do not adopt a decompositional approach, nevertheless implicitly invoke semantic features in their discussion of how native speakers of English understand taxonomic subdivisions. Typological and taxonomic work is important if we are to understand connotations and associations, which are important aspects of word knowledge mentioned in section I. For example, Croft and Cruse (2004, p. 149) discuss various "horse" terms. They ask why the sentence "a mustang is a kind of horse" sounds fine, but "a stallion is a kind of horse" sounds odd (to some people). They conclude that a good taxonym must have as its core a specification of the core of the hyponym. Since MALE is not part of the core specification of horse, stallion cannot be a good example type. Note that in fact this analysis tacitly assumes some decompositionality. Cruse and Croft advocate a view that the *perspective* for stallion is SEX (e.g., male horse), whereas for mustang the perspective is "kind of horse." It is not clear what theoretical status "perspective" has other than the judgment for this distinction is necessarily based on participation in a "horse" culture. Although, I agree with their intuitions, among six other native speakers who I consulted, only one agreed with the view that "a stallion is a kind of horse" was worse than the phrase "a mustang is a kind of horse." This person also was knowledgeable about horses. In this context, one must invoke, as Jackendoff (2001, p. 375), Lantolf and Thorne (2006), and Pavlenko (2000, 2008) do, the key role of social frames. However, if decompositionality—features such as SEX and ANIMACY—are important, one should have a more detailed theory of concepts than typologists currently offer, which is the strength of more formal approaches. Such a theory is described in the next section.

### C. *Qualia* Theory

Pustejovsky (1995, 1998) addresses the problem of a finite mind having an infinite conceptual capacity by proposing a decompositional theory that makes use of "*qualia*" rather than binary features. His theory seeks to address our knowledge of meaning and relatedness. *Qualia* are features that relate to the "real world" in some sense and were originally discussed in work by Aristotle. Pustejovsky (1995, p. 76) suggests that *qualia* structure specifies four aspects of a word's meaning, listed in (16):

(16)  a. CONSTITUTIVE: relation between object and constituent parts.
           e.g., material, weight, parts
        b. FORMAL: that which distinguishes it from a larger domain.
           e.g., orientation, magnitude, shape, color, position
        c. TELIC: its purpose and function.
           e.g., purpose, function
        d. AGENTIVE: factors involved in its origin or "bringing it about"
           e.g., creator, artifact, natural kind, causal chain

For example, in (17) Pustejovsky suggests the following basic structure for the noun "novel":

(17)

| Novel |
| --- |
| . . . |
| -         *Qualia* = CONST     = **narrative** |
|                     FORMAL = **book** |
|                     TELIC     = **reading** |
|                     AGENT    = **writing** |

For Pustejovsky, a verb would also consist of an event structure and an argument structure. For all lexical entries, Pustejovsky allows such templates to be filled by culturally specific information. The combination of noun and verb *qualia* structures can explain the various "compositional" meaning of phrases. For example, he contrasts the meanings of "enjoy" in: "Mary enjoyed the movie last night," "John enjoys his morning coffee," and "Bill enjoyed Steven King's last book," where the meanings of "enjoy" involve respectively "watching," "drinking," and "reading" because of the noun complement in each sentence (see also Harley (2004) and Yoshimura and Taylor (2004) for interesting applications of decomposition and *qualia* theory for verb subcategorization). Both Jackendoff (2002b) and Van Valin and La Polla (1997) adapt some version of this approach. Hence, *qualia* structure provides a detailed framework with which to describe word meaning. While these proposals for the organization of concepts have not influenced any second language acquisition research, they do provide a framework that encompasses UG, cognitive, and culturally specific aspects of meaning that address some of Pavlenko's (2000) concerns.

This program of research will be a challenge, however. Although decomposition seems to provide insights in some cases, failures of finer-grained analysis in providing complete sets of distinctive features have led Fodor (2001) to reject *any* theory of concepts for nouns that is based on componential analysis or even prototypes. Instead, Fodor (2001) and Fodor and Lepore (1996, 1998) advocate a theory of concepts as indivisible or as "atomic" monads. (In philosophy, "monad" means an absolutely simple entity.) If we can understand meaning without having access to component parts, features or semantic components may not be part of a mental representation of a word (Fodor, 1998; Landau, 2000). Since decompositional features are a key part of theory of polysemy, etc., researchers who deny such features find it hard to account for intuitions about word-relatedness (synonmy, polsemy, taxonomic relations, etc.). Their position forces them to dismiss intuitions about how words are related as uninteresting. For example, Fodor and Lepore assert (1998, p. 287):

> We do not have a theory of polysemy beyond the suggestion, implicit in the preceding, that where it is sensitive to the syntactic structure of the context, polysemy belongs not to the theory of content but to the theory of logical form. That leaves many residual cases like lamb ('meat' vs. 'animal'), window ('the opening' vs. 'what fills the opening'), newspaper ('the thing that is read' vs. 'the organization that publishes it'). We suspect that there is nothing interesting to say about such cases; the meanings of words can partially overlap in all sorts of ways, so there are all sorts of ways in which polysemous terms can differ from mere homonyms. Nothing in the literature convinces us that there are powerful generalizations to state.

It seems that Fodor's stance puts many of the "facts" that need to be accounted for into the realm of real-world knowledge and out of the *linguistic* ( = formal) lexicon and into what Embick and Noyer (2006) label the "encyclopedia." This conclusion does *not* mean that linguists do not have to be concerned about the acquisition of such meanings; it just means that a restricted *formal* theory of the kind we are familiar with in morphosyntax will not be available where concepts such as these are concerned. Cultural aspects of language knowledge remain a vital part of L2 lexical learning.

In a view of language that is modular, that is one that separates the specific language module from general cognition, parts of the problem of word meaning not relevant to syntax are outside the formal linguistic module, but must interface with it (Pinker, 1989, p. 166). Yet, As Jackendoff (2002b, p. 376) pointed out over 10 years after Pinker drew attention to this distinction, the problem is that no *principled* division between this narrowly "linguistic" and "encyclopedic" meaning has been made. Some of the second language acquisition literature has lagged behind in even recognizing that these problems exist, in part because no one source brings research on these aspects into contact where they can inform one another.

## VII. CONCLUSION

The lexicon is a complex field of study that requires a heterogeneous set of theoretical constructs. Some of these constructs may be formal, other may not be stable in these theoretical terms. As for the process of lexical development, in both early and later bilinguals, L1 and L2 forms clearly have a significant influence on one another. Lemmas in the form of conceptual features, conflation patterns, and projection of clause structure seems to rely heavily but not exclusively on the L1 early in development for adult SLA, but need not fossilize into L1 transferred patterns. We have seen that at the lemma level, "meaning" needs to be separated into those parts of conceptual structure that can affect clause structure, and those aspects that are more "encyclopedic" in nature and may create subset/superset learning challenges for learners. Decompositional theories of nouns will need more careful analysis so that more fuzzy notions such as "abstractness" (e.g., stone vs. compulsion) can be broken down into more carefully defined properties, perhaps suggested by *qualia* structure.

Until the 1990s, formal linguists treated the acquisition of the lexicon and concepts as uninteresting. Lantolf and Thorne (2006) suggest that this view has its roots in the development of linguistic theory in the 20th century from Saussure through Bloomfield to Chomsky, who by separating semantics from syntax, drew attention away from meaning. Presently, the lexicon is has returned to center stage. However, the complexity is daunting and can be frustrating, even for someone who has worked as long as Jackendoff on this topic: "It should be recognized that there are fundamental methodological and expository difficulties in doing lexical semantics. ... Perhaps there is no way out: there are just too many goddamned words, and so many parts to them. ... *Next to lexical semantics, the acquisition problem for grammar pales by comparison.*" (italics by the author). (Jackendoff, 2002b, p. 377).

The task ahead will involve creating an interface between theoretical advances from psycholinguistic experiments and linguistic research with scholars who are involved with pedagogy and testing. Erwin-Tripp (2000, p. 10) agrees that researchers who look at form–meaning mappings are going to need to focus more on the contexts in which words are encountered and in some cases the cultural knowledge that goes along with it. As we develop a more elaborated theory of the "*what*" of learning the lexicon—which set of words and how they might be psychologically represented—we can provide a more solid basis for the *how* of learning and instruction. Given the domain that this chapter has surveyed, we will be looking for many answers, not an answer, to these questions.

## ACKNOWLEDGMENTS

This research was supported in part by a grant from the National Science Foundation, award number SBE-0354420 to the Pittsburgh Science of Learning Center.

## REFERENCES

Alegre, M., & Gordon, P. (1999). Frequency effects and the representational status of regular inflections. *Journal of Memory and Language, 40*, 41–61.

Ambridge, B., Pine, J. M., Rowland, C., & Young, C. R. (2008). The effect of verb semantic class and verb frequency (entrenchment) on children's and adults' graded judgments of argument-structure overgeneralization errors. *Cognition, 106*, 87–129.

Baker, C. L. (1979). Syntactic theory and the projection problem. *Linguistic Inquiry, 10*, 533–581.

Bi, Y., Han, Z., Shu, H., & Caramazza, A. (2005). Are verbs like inanimate objects? *Brain and Language, 95*, 28–29.

Biber, D., Conrad, S. M., Reppen, R., Byrd, P., Helt, M., Clark, V., et al. (2004). *Representing language use in the university: Analysis of the TOEFL 2000 spoken and written academic language corpus*. Princeton, NJ: Educational Testing Services.

Bley-Vroman, R. (2002). Frequency in production, comprehension, and acquisition. *Studies in Second Language Acquisition, 24*, 209–213.

Bley-Vroman, R., & Joo, H.-R. (2001). The acquisition of interpretation of English locative constructions by native speakers of Korean. *Studies in Second Language Acquisition*, 207–220.

Braine, M. D. S., & Brooks, P. J. (1995). Verb argument structure and the problem of avoiding an overgeneral grammar. In M. Tomasello & W. E. Merriman (Eds.), *Beyond names for things: Young children's acquisition of verbs* (pp. 352–376). Hillsdale, NJ: Erlbaum.

Caramazza, A., & Mahon, B. Z. (2006). The organization of conceptual knowledge in the brain. The future's past and some future directions. *Cognitive Neuropsychology, 23*, 13–38.

Carey, S. (1978). The child as word learner. In M. Halle, J. Bresnan, & G. Miller (Eds.), *Linguistic theory and psychological reality* (pp. 264–293). Cambridge, MA: MIT Press.

Chomsky, N. (1965). *Aspects of the theory of syntax*. Cambridge, MA: MIT Press.

Chomsky, N. (1981). *Lectures on government and binding*. Dordrecht, The Netherlands: Foris.

Chomsky, N. (1995). *The minimalist program*. Cambridge, MA: MIT Press.

Clahsen, H. (1995). German plurals in adults second language development: Evidence for a dual mechanism model of inflection. In L. Eubank, M. Sharwood-Smith, & L. Selinker (Eds.), *The current state of interlanguage: Studies in honour of William Rutherford* (pp. 123–138). Philadelphia, PA: John Benjamins.

Cobb, T. (2006). *The old vocabulary, the new vocabulary and the Arabic learner*. Paper presented at the A TESOL Symposium on vocabulary. Words matter: The importance of vocabulary in English Language Teaching and Learning, Dubai Men's College, Dubai, United Arab Emirates.

Cobb, T. Compleat lexical tutor. http://www.lextutor.ca/. Retrieved May 22, 2007.

Crain, S., & Pietroski, P. (2002). Why language acquisition is a snap. *The Linguistic Review, 19*, 163–184.

Croft, W., & Cruse, D. A. (2004). *Cognitive linguistics*. Cambridge: Cambridge University Press.

Cruse, D. A. (1986). *Lexical semantics*. Cambridge: Cambridge University Press.

Coxhead, A. (2001). A new academic word list. *TESOL Quarterly, 34*, 213–238.

De Groot, A. M. B., & Kroll, J. (1997). Lexical and conceptual memory in the bilingual: Mapping form to meaning in two languages. In A. M. B. De Groot & J. Kroll (Eds.), *Tutorials in bilingualism*. Mahwah, NJ: Erlbaum.

De Groot, A. M. B., & Poot, R. (1997). Word translation at three levels of proficiency: The ubiquitous involvement of conceptual memory. *Language Learning, 47*, 215–264.

DeKeyser, R. M., & Juffs, A. (2005). Cognitive considerations in L2 learning. In E. Hinkel (Ed.), *Handbook of research in second language teaching and learning* (pp. 437–454). Mahwah, NJ: Lawence Erlbaum Associates.

Ellis, N. C. (2002). Frequency effects and language processing: Investigating formulaic use and input in future expression. *Studies in Second Language Acquisition, 24*, 143–188.

Ellis, N. C. (2005). At the interface: Dynamic interactions of explicit and implicit language knowledge. *Studies in Second Language Acquisition, 27*, 305–352.

Embick, D., & Noyer, R. (2006). Distributed morphology and the syntax-morphology interface. In Ramchand & C. Reiss (Eds.), *The Oxford handbook of linguistics interfaces* (pp. 289–324). New York: Oxford University Press.

Erwin-Tripp, S. (2000). Bilingual minds. *Bilingualism: Language and Cognition*, *3*, 10–12.

Fodor, J. A. (1998). *Concepts: Where cognitive science went wrong*. Oxford: Clarendon.

Fodor, J. A. (2001). Language, thought, and compositionality. *Mind and Language*, *16*, 1–15.

Fodor, J. A., & Lepore, E. (1996). The red herring and the pet fish: Why concepts can't be prototypes. *Cognition*, *58*, 253–270.

Fodor, J. A., & Lepore, E. (1998). The emptiness of the lexicon: Reflections on James Pustejovsky's The Generative Lexicon. *Linguistic Inquiry*, *29*, 269–288.

Folse, K. S. (2004). *Vocabulary myths: Applying second language research to classroom teaching*. Ann Arbor, MI: University of Michigan Press.

Folse, K. S. (2006). The effect of type of written exercise on L2 vocabulary retention. *TESOL Quarterly*, *40*, 273–293.

Forster, K. I., & Jiang, N. (2001). The nature of the bilingual lexicon. In J. Nicols (Ed.), *One mind, two languages* (pp. 72–83). New Malden, UK: Blackwells.

Gregg, K. (1996). The logical and developmental problems of second language acquisition. In W. C. Ritchie & T. K. Bhatia (Eds.), *Handbook of second language acquisition* (pp. 50–84). New York: Academic Press.

Hale, K., & Keyser, S. J. (1993). On argument structure and the lexical expression of syntactic relations. In K. Hale & S. J. Keyser (Eds.), *The view from Building 20: Essays in linguistics in honor of Sylvain Bromberger* (pp. 53–110). Cambridge, MA: MIT.

Harley, H. (2004). Wanting, having and getting: A note on Fodor and Lepore 1998. *Linguistic Inquiry*, *35*, 255–267.

Hatch, E., & Brown, C. (1995). *Vocabulary, semantics, and language education*. Cambridge: Cambridge University Press.

Helms-Park, R. (2001). Evidence of lexical transfer in learner syntax. The acquisition of English causatives by speakers of Hindi–Urdu and Vietnamese. *Studies in Second Language Acquisition*, *21*, 71–102.

Hirakawa, M. (1995). *L2 acquisition of English unaccusative constructions*. Paper presented at the Proceedings of the 19th Boston University Conference on Language Development, Somerville, MA.

Hirakawa, M. (2001). L2 acquisition of Japanese unaccusative verbs. *Studies in Second Language Acquisition*, *23*, 221–246.

Hirakawa, M. (2006). More evidence on the knowledge of unaccusativity in L2 Japanese. In S. Unsworth, T. Parodi, A. Sorace, & M. Young-Scholten (Eds.), *Paths of development in L1 and L2 acquisition* (pp. 161–186). Philadelphia, PA: John Benjamins.

Hulstijn, J. H., & Laufer, B. (2001). Some empirical evidence for the involvement load hypothesis in vocabulary acquisition. *Language Learning*, *51*, 539–558.

Inagaki, S. (2001). Motion verbs with goal PPs in L2 acquisition of English and Japanese. *Studies in Second Language Acquisition*, *23*, 153–170.

Inagaki, S. (2002). Japanese learners' acquisition of English manner-of-motion verbs with locational/directional PPs. *Second Language Research*, *18*, 3–27.

Jackendoff, R. S. (1990). *Semantic structures*. Cambridge, MA: MIT Press.

Jackendoff, R. S. (1992). What is a concept? In A. Lehrer & E. F. Kittay (Eds.), *Frames, fields, and contrasts*. Mahwah, NJ: Erlbaum.

Jackendoff, R. S. (1997). Twistin' the night away. *Language*, *73*, 534–559.

Jackendoff, R. S. (2002a). What's in the lexicon? In S. Nooteboom, F. Weerman, & F. Wijnen (Eds.), *Storage and computation in the language faculty* (pp. 23–58). Dordrecht, The Netherlands: Kluwer.

Jackendoff, R. S. (2002b). *Foundations of language*. New York: Oxford University Press.

Jared, D., & Kroll, J. F. (2001). Do bilinguals activate phonological representations in one or both of their languages when naming words? *Journal of Memory and Language, 44*, 2–31.

Jiang, N. (1999). Testing processing explanations for the asymmetry in masked cross-language priming. *Bilingualism: Language and Cognition, 2*, 59–75.

Jiang, N. (2000). Lexical representation and development in a second language. *Applied Linguistics, 21*, 47–77.

Jiang, N. (2002). Form–meaning mapping in vocabulary acquisition in a second language. *Studies in Second Language Acquisition, 24*, 617–638.

Jiang, N. (2004). Semantic transfer and its implications for vocabulary teaching in a second language. *Modern Language Journal, 88*, 416–432.

Jiang, N. (2007). Selective integration of linguistic knowledge in adult second language learning. *Language Learning, 57*, 1–33.

Joo, H.-R. (2003). Second language learnability and the acquisition of the argument structure of English locative verbs by Korean speakers. *Second Language Research, 19*, 305–328.

Juffs, A. (1996). *Learnability and the lexicon: Theories and second language acquisition research*. Amsterdam: John Benjamins.

Juffs, A. (2000). An overview of the second language acquisition of the links between verb semantics and morpho-syntax. In J. Archibald (Ed.), *Second Language Acquisition and Linguistic Theory* (pp. 187–227). Oxford: Blackwells.

Juffs, A., Eskenazi, M., Wilson, L., Callan, J., Heilman, M., Collins-Thompson, K., et al. (2006). *Robust learning of vocabulary: investigating the relationship between learner behaviour and the acquisition of vocabulary*. Paper presented at the American Association of Applied Linguistics, Montreal, QC, Canada.

Kellerman, E. (1986). An eye for an eye: Crosslinguistic constraints on the development of the L2 lexicon. In E. Kellerman & M. Sharwood-Smith (Eds.), *Crosslinguistic influence in second language acquisition* (pp. 35–38). New York: Pergamon.

Kroll, J. (1993). Accessing conceptual representations for words in a second language. In R. Schreuder & B. Weltens (Eds.), *The bilingual lexicon*. Amsterdam: Benjamins.

Kroll, J., & De Groot, A. M. B. (Eds.) (1997). *Tutorials in bilingualism: Psycholinguistic perspectives*. Mahwah, NJ: Erlbaum.

Kroll, J., Michael, E., Tokowicz, N., & Dufour, R. (2002). The development of lexical fluency in a second language. *Second Language Research, 18*, 137–171.

Kroll, J., & Sunderman, G. (2003). Cognitive processes in L2 learners and bilinguals. In M. Long & C. Doughty (Eds.), *Handbook of second language acquisition* (pp. 104–129). New Malden, UK: Blackwell.

Kroll, J. & Tokowicz, N. (2001). Representation for words in a second language. In J. Nicol (Ed.). *One mind, two languages: Bilingual language processing* (pp. 49–71). New Malden, UK: Blackwell.

Landau, B. (2000). Concepts, the lexicon, and acquisition: Fodor's new challenge. *Mind and Language, 15*, 319–326.

Lantolf, J., & Thorne, S. (2006). *Sociocultural theory and the genesis of second language development*. Oxford: Oxford University Press.

Levelt, W. (1989). *Speaking: From intention to articulation*. Cambridge, MA: MIT Press.

Levelt, W. (2001). Spoken word production: A theory of lexical access. *Proceedings of the National Academy of Sciences USA, 98*, 13464–13471.

McCarthy, M. (1990). *Vocabulary*. Oxford: Oxford University Press.

McCarthy, M. (1994). A new look at vocabulary in EFL. *Applied Linguistics*, *5*, 12–22.

Meara, P. M. (2005). Lexical frequency profiles: A Monte Carlo analysis. *Applied Linguistics*, *26*, 32–47.

Montrul, S. (1999). Causative errors with unaccusative verbs in L2 Spanish. *Second Language Research*, (15), 191–219.

Montrul, S. (2000). Transitivity alternations in L1 acquisition: Toward a modular view of transfer. *Studies in Second Language Acquisition*, *22*, 229–273.

Montrul, S. (2001). First language constrained variability in argument structure changing morphology with causative verbs. *Second Language Research*, *17*, 144–194.

Naigles, L. (1991). Review of Pinker 1989. *Language and Speech*, *34*, 63–79.

Nation, I. S. P. (2001). *Learning vocabulary in another language*. Cambridge: Cambridge University Press.

Nunberg, G., Sag, I., & Wasow, T. (1994). Idioms. *Language*, *70*, 438–491.

Pavlenko, A. (2000). New approaches to concepts in bilingual memory. *Bilingualism: Language and Cognition*, *3*, 1–4.

Pavlenko, A. (2002). Bilingualism and emotions. *Multilingua*, *21*, 45–78.

Pavlenko, A. (2008). Emotion and emotion laden words in the bilingual lexicon. *Bilingualism: Language and Cognition*, *11*, 147–164.

Pinker, S. (1989). *Learnability and cognition: The acquisition of argument structure*. Cambridge, MA: MIT Press.

Pustejovsky, J. (1995). *The generative lexicon*. Cambridge, MA: MIT Press.

Pustejovsky, J. (1998). Generativity and explanation in semantics: A reply to Fodor and Lepore. *Linguistic Inquiry*, *29*, 289–311.

Rosen, C. (1984). The interface between semantic roles and initial grammatical relations. In D. M. Perlmutter & C. Rosen (Eds.), *Studies in relational grammar* (Vol. 2, pp. 38–80). Chicago: Chicago University Press.

Schmitt, N., & Meara, P. (1997). Researching vocabulary through a word knowledge framework. *Studies in Second Language Acquisition*, *19*, 17–36.

Schreuder, R., & Weltens, B. (Eds.) (1993). *The bilingual lexicon*. Amsterdam: John Benjamins.

Schwartz, B. D., & Sprouse, R. (1996). L2 cognitive states and the full transfer/full access model. *Second Language Research*, *12*, 40–72.

Shapiro, K. A., Mottaghy, F. M., Schiller, N. O., Poeppel, T. D., Flü, M. O., Müller, H.-W., et al. (2004). Dissociating neural correlates for nouns and verbs. *Neuroimage*, *24*, 1058–1067.

Silva, R., & Clahsen, H. (2008). Morphologically complex words in L1 and L2 processing. Evidence from masked priming experiments in English. *Bilingualism: Language and Cognition*, *11*, 245–260.

Sorace, A. (1995). Acquiring linking rules and argument structures in a second language: The unaccusative/unergative distinction. In L. Eubank, L. Selinker, & M. Sharwood-Smith (Eds.), *Current trends in interlanguage* (pp. 153–176). Amsterdam: Benjamins.

Steinel, M. P., Hulstijn, J., & Steinel, W. (2007). Second language idiom learning in a paired associate paradigm. Effects of direction of learning, direction of testing, Idiom Imageability and Idiom Transparency. *Studies in Second Language Acquisition*, *29*, 449–484.

Stringer, D. (2006). The development of PATHS. In S. Unsworth, T. Parodi, A. Sorace, & M. Young-Scholten (Eds.), *Paths of development in L1 and L2 acquisition* (pp. 135–158). Philadelphia, PA: John Benjamins.

Stringer, D. (2007). *Motion events in L2 acquisition: A lexicalist account*. Paper presented at the Boston University Conference on Language Development. Boston, MA (November 2006).

Sunderman, G., & Kroll, J. (2006). First language activation during second language lexical processing: an investigation of lexical form, meaning and grammatical class. *Studies in Second Language Acquisition, 28*, 387–422.

Talamas, A., Kroll, J., & Dufour, R. (1999). Form to meaning: Stages in the acquisition of second language vocabulary. *Bilingualism: Language and Cognition, 2*, 45–58.

Talmy, L. (1985). Lexicalization patterns: Semantic structure in lexical patterns. In T. Shopen (Ed.), *Language typology and syntactic description* (Vol. III: Grammatical Categories and the Lexicon, pp. 57–149). Cambridge: Cambridge University Press.

Toth, P. D. (2000). The interaction of instruction and learner internal factors in the acquisition of L2 morphosyntax. *Studies in Second Language Acquisition, 22*, 169–208.

Van Valin, R., & La Polla, R. (1997). *Syntax: Structure, meaning and function.* Cambridge University Press.

Vygotsky, L. (1986). *Thought and language.* Cambridge, MA: MIT Press.

Wang, X. (2007). *Chinese–English bilinguals' 'semantic awareness' of masked primes in lexical processing.* Paper presented at the American Association of Applied Linguistics, Costa Mesa, CA.

Weinreich, U. (1953/1974). *Languages in contact: Findings and problems.* The Hague: Mouton.

West, M. (1953). *A general service list of English words.* London, UK: Addison-Wesley Longman.

White, L. (1987). Markedness and second language acquisition: The question of transfer. *Studies in Second Language Acquisition, 9*, 261–286.

White, L. (2003). *Second language acquisition and universal grammar.* New York: Cambridge University Press.

White, L., Montrul, S., Hirakawa, M., Chen, D., Bruhn de Garravito, J., & Brown, C. (1998). Zero morphology and the T/SM restriction in the L2 Acquisition of Psych verbs. In M.-L. Beck (Ed.), *Morphology and interfaces in second language knowledge* (pp. 257–282). Philadelphia, PA: John Benjamins.

Whong-Barr, M. (2006). What transfers? In S. Unsworth, T. Parodi, A. Sorace, & M. Young-Scholten (Eds.), *Paths of development in L1 and L2 acquisition* (pp. 197–199). Philadelphia, PA: John Benjamins.

Wray, A., & Perkins, M. R. (2000). The functions of formulaic language: An integrated model. *Language and Communication, 20*, 1–28.

Yoshimura, K., & Taylor, J. R. (2004). What makes a good middle? The role of qualia in the interpretation and acceptability of middle expressions in English. *English Language and Linguistics, 8*, 293–321.

Yuan, B. (1999). Acquiring the unaccusative/unergative distinction in a second language: Evidence from English-speaking learners of L2 Chinese. *Linguistics, 37*, 275–296.

Zyzik, E. (2006). Transitivity alternations and sequence learning: Insights from L2 Spanish production data. *Studies in Second Language Acquisition, 28*, 449–486.

CHAPTER 10

# SECOND LANGUAGE ACQUISITION OF MORPHOSYNTAX

Roger Hawkins

## I. INTRODUCTION

An issue that has dominated the recent investigation of morphosyntactic properties in second language acquisition (SLA) is the interpretation to be given to L2 speakers' use of forms/constructions in speech (and writing) and their underlying knowledge of the associated grammatical properties. Consider a sample of the transcribed speech of an L2 speaker, 'Patty', taken from Lardiere (2007, p. 23). Patty is a native speaker of two varieties of Chinese (Mandarin and Hokkien), who has been immersed in English in the United States for over 18 years. Here she is describing a period when she lived in Indonesia.

(1)  So I ... well uh, when I was thirteen, from thirteen to fourteen there's political change in Indonesia. So my school, which is Indonesian school, was closed. [ ... ] And uh, I eventually also get into the Chinese school for maybe six month. And then school was close.

In this short transcript there are past-tense-marked verb forms (*was*), but also an apparently intended past tense verb that is not inflected for past (*get*). The inflected participle *closed* is used on one occasion with *was*, but in a second use the non-inflected form appears (*was close*). Nouns requiring determiners for native speakers have them in two cases (*my school, the Chinese school*), but not in a third ( ... *then school was close*). There is no plural marking on *month* in *six month*.

Where such divergence from expected native speaker patterns is systematic in the speech of L2 learners (i.e. does not represent temporary 'slips of the tongue/pen'), does it directly reflect the speaker's mental grammatical representations, or do L2 learners know more about the morphosyntactic properties of the target language than is

*The New Handbook of Second Language Acquisition*

apparent from their performance? The responses these questions receive are central to hypotheses about a number of aspects of SLA:

- What L2 learners' mental grammars are like at the start of L2 acquisition (the initial state)
- How those grammars change with time and exposure to samples of the L2 (transition)
- What the nature of L2 grammars is when L2 speaker performance appears to stabilise (the steady state)
- What role properties of the L1 might play in these stages
- How properties of universal grammar (UG) are involved
- What role input plays in driving the development of L2 knowledge

This chapter examines different interpretations that have been given to the relation between L2 performance and L2 competence, and how this has affected hypotheses about the initial state, transitional states and so on. It is necessarily selective in the studies reported. The aim is to give an overview of some of the issues that are being addressed in the investigation of morphosyntax in SLA.

## II. EXAMPLE OF THE MORPHOSYNTACTIC REPRESENTATION OF A LINGUISTIC EXPRESSION

It is worth starting with a concrete illustration of a surface string and a proposed underlying morphosyntactic representation for that string, and the possible ways in which the relation between surface string and structural representation could be interpreted. This will allow easier comparison of different hypotheses subsequently. Figure 1 is a structural representation of the native version of an expression found in example (1): *I eventually also got into the Chinese school.*

It is not a complete representation of all the relevant morphosyntactic properties (this would have been unwieldy for illustrative purposes), but is sufficient to give an idea of the problem of interpreting the relation between performance and competence.

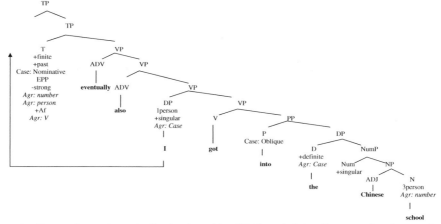

**Figure 1**  Proposed morphosyntactic structure (simplified) underlying 'I eventually also got into the Chinese school'.

The representation consists of heads (N, ADJ, D, P, ...) that are bundles of morphosyntactic features. These heads have merged with other constituents (heads or phrases) to produce labelled phrases. The feature make-up of heads is open to theoretical debate and empirical testing. It is possible that the features chosen and their distribution in Figure 1 are wrong and that better hypotheses and empirical evidence will subsequently show this to be the case. At present, however, the representation assumed in Figure 1 is within the spirit of recent work in syntactic theory.

The tense head (T) consists of some features that are relevant to the semantic interpretation of the expression: finiteness and tense. Specifically, the expression is finite and is intended to have past tense reference. T also has features that are not relevant to semantic interpretation but are relevant to determining the grammaticality of the expression. T assigns nominative case to the subject, ensuring that the form *I* rather than *me* will surface. The so-called extended projection principle (EPP) feature (Chomsky, 1995) forces the subject *I* to move from its position as argument of *got* in the VP to merge with TP. T in English does not require main verbs to raise to merge with it, in contrast to languages like French and German where main verbs do raise to T. This is represented here as a 'strength' feature with a [–strong] value. T also 'agrees with' the person and number of the subject. In relevant cases this shows up phonologically, distinguishing the grammatical *I get/she gets* from the ungrammatical (in standard English) *\*I gets/\*she get*. While the person and number features of the subject D are relevant to semantic interpretation, the person and number agreement features of T are not, but they are relevant to the grammaticality of the expression. In recent work within the 'Minimalist Program' for syntactic theory (Chomsky, 1995, 1998, 2001), the person and number features of nouns and pronouns are referred to as *interpretable*, while the features of T that agree with those features are referred to as *uninterpretable*. Uninterpretable features are represented here as '*Agr: x*', where *x* is a variable for a type of feature (person, number, Case, V) that is assigned a value by an interpretable feature from another category. Note that D and N also have uninterpretable features in Figure 1. Finally, T is affixal, indicated by the feature [+Af], and needs to adjoin to a head that has a verbal feature; this is the reason for the uninterpretable [*Agr: V*] feature. Both [+Af] and [*Agr: V*] are relevant to the grammaticality of the expression, not its interpretation, and are uninterpretable features. At the surface, then, T must have a verbal host, either through lowering to the main verb or through the merging of another kind of verb (copula, auxiliary or modal) directly with T.

*Eventually* and *also* are adverbs that merge with (and modify) VPs. The pronoun *I* is represented here as a DP because it probably involves the merger of D with an empty NP that provides the interpretable person and number features (Panagiotidis, 2002). It has an uninterpretable Case feature that is valued by the nominative case feature of T. V has features, but none that are important for the purposes of illustration here. The preposition *into* has an oblique case feature to assign. The determiner D has an uninterpretable Case feature that will be valued by the Case feature of P and a semantically interpretable [+definite] feature. The number property that determines whether nouns are singular or plural is assumed to be an independent head here (following Bernstein, 1991; Ritter, 1993). The justification for this is that in some languages, nouns raise to Num, placing the N to the left of adjectives (as in French *l'école chinoise*, lit. 'the school Chinese'). This suggests that Num also has a strength feature (although this is not represented here). The N, then, has an interpretable person feature and an uninterpretable number feature that is valued by the Num head.

## III. INTERPRETING THE RELATIONSHIP BETWEEN FORM IN L2
## PERFORMANCE AND UNDERLYING REPRESENTATION

Consider how a string of forms produced by an L2 speaker might be associated with the representation in Figure 1. In the case of Patty, the string she produced is very close to the expected native string, with one exception. It appears she intended this expression to have past tense reference, but produced the form *get* rather than *got*. How should this be interpreted? One possibility is that her representation for T lacks the feature [+Af]. This would mean that although her grammar determines the expression as [+past], there is no requirement for T to merge with V; hence the form that appears as an exponent of V is *get*, rather than *got*. A second possibility is that her representation for T lacks [+past]. This would mean that although T merges with V, there is no feature to prompt the selection of the form *got*, so *get* appears. A third possibility is that the feature representation for T is as indicated in Figure 1 for Patty, but that she has a post-syntactic problem in selecting the appropriate form of 'get' to insert into the V position. There are probably other options.

The first two interpretations described assume a *feature deficit* account in relation to the expected native representation. Since [+Af] is not relevant to the semantic interpretation of the expression, but is relevant to its grammaticality, this account suggests that divergence between Patty and native speakers might be located in the *uninterpretable feature system*. By contrast, [+past] is interpretable; if this is where divergence from the expected representation occurs, divergence might appear in the *interpretable feature system*. The third case assumes no deficit in the representation, but instead a problem *mapping* the underlying representation to a surface exponent.

Where less proficient speakers' performance is more divergent from the expected native speaker pattern, there could be other possibilities. An early L2 learner of English who produces *She get into Chinese school for six month* and systematically uses verb stem forms like *get* in the context of third person subjects (for the native *gets* or *got*) as well as systematically not producing articles and number marking on count nouns might be claimed to have no functional category structure at all, so that the T, D and Num of Figure 1 are all absent from such a speaker's grammar. Alternatively, it might be proposed that the functional categories and their features are present (perhaps coming from the L1) but that the learner has yet to acquire the forms that realise these functional elements; essentially they have phonologically empty forms realising T, D and Num. In the following sections of this chapter, the way that such differences in interpretation have informed different hypotheses about early and later stages of L2 development will be discussed. We start with hypotheses about the initial state.[1]

---

[1]The discussion in the rest of the chapter excludes a number of hypotheses about the initial and subsequent stages of L2 acquisition that can be found in the literature: the 'Valueless Features' hypothesis of Eubank (1994), the 'Local Impairment' hypothesis of Beck (1998), the 'Global Impairment' hypothesis of Meisel (1997), the 'Fundamental Difference' hypothesis of Bley-Vroman (1990), the 'Initial State of UG' hypothesis of Epstein, Flynn, and Martohardjono (1996), and various hypotheses that fall under the umbrella of the 'Emergentist Program' (see, e.g., Ellis, 2006; MacWhinney, 2004; O'Grady, 2008). The reason for this is space restrictions. For an overview of some of these other theories, see White (2003b, chapters 3 and 4).

## IV. THE INITIAL STATE

Early L2 learners' productions often have missing target forms, are formulaic or just different from the target L2:

(2)  a. girl play with toy (missing target forms: Ionin & Wexler 2002, p. 106)
        Mary so funny
      b. Comment t'appelles-tu le garçon? (formulae in L2 French: Myles, 2004)
        lit. How yourself call you the boy?
        Intended: What is the boy's name?
        Mon petit garcon euh où habites-tu?
        lit. My little boy umm where live you?
        Intended: Where does your little boy live?
      c. I'm something eating (non-target word order: Haznedar, 2001, pp. 9, 22)
        Not I got two bicycles

Performance of this kind is unsurprising. Learners have encountered only a small sample of the language, and even in this small sample there will be properties that they have not yet identified as relevant to the grammar of the target L2. What is the relationship between productions like these and morphosyntactic representations in the grammars of the speakers in question?

### A. Restricted Trees in the Initial State

One hypothesis is that the earliest L2 grammars identify only a limited range of morphosyntactic categories, perhaps just the lexical categories (N, V, ADJ, P) in the input they encounter, and these are the basis for production. An early learner therefore produces an utterance like *girl play with toy* because this involves only merging lexical categories:

(3) [N girl] [VP [Vplay] [PP [Pwith] [N toy]]]

On this view, the functional category projections illustrated in Figure 1 (TP, DP, NumP), as well as other functional projections like C(omplementiser)P, are simply absent from early representations. The radical form of this view, where no functional categories are present in the initial state, is known as the *minimal trees* hypothesis and is associated with the work of Vainikka and Young-Scholten (1994, 1996, 1998a).[2] The rationale for the hypothesis is as follows. The grammars of mature native speakers vary in the range of functional categories they instantiate. For example, native grammars of English instantiate D and Num to accommodate the articles *the/a* and grammaticalised plural on nouns (*books/children*). By contrast, native grammars of Japanese have neither D nor Num; there are no articles and there is no productive, grammaticalised number marking. Different target grammars for language learners therefore have their own

[2]In more recent work, to overcome certain misunderstandings of their model, they refer to the hypothesis as *Organic Syntax* (Vainikka & Young-Scholten, 2007). Since 'Minimal Trees' is the term that has been widely used in the work reported in this chapter, that is the preferred description here. For other 'restricted trees' proposals, see Bhatt and Hancin-Bhatt (2002) and Prévost and White (2000a).

'master tree that includes all possible projections occurring in the language' (Vainikka &
Young-Scholten, 2007, p. 321). Given such variation between languages, an economical
language learning mechanism would not, from the outset, expect that all functional
categories project in the language. Unambiguous triggering evidence from the input is
required to select a functional category and its features.

The evidence that Vainikka and Young-Scholten adduce in support of this
hypothesis can be illustrated from their early (1994) study of L1 speakers of Korean,
Turkish, Spanish and Italian learning German as adults under immersion conditions.
Nine informants were identified as being at the earliest stage of acquisition. Their
speech showed the following characteristics:

(i) Main verbs were rarely raised over adverbs and negation (raising is obligatory in
matrix clauses in German):

**L2 utterance**                              **Native German**
Nein in matina nix *essen*                    Morgens *esse* ich nicht(s)
No in morning not eat
'I don't eat in the morning'

Für mei Junge immer vo mir *schimpfe*   Mein Junge *schimpft* immer mit mir
For my boy always from me scold
'My boy always scolds me'

(ii) Correct subject–verb agreement with main verbs was produced in only
11%–36% of cases (varying from individual to individual). Non-target
subject–verb agreement is illustrated in the examples of (i).

(iii) Auxiliary and modal verbs were produced only by some of the subjects, and
then infrequently.

(iv) There were no embedded clauses or uses of the complementiser *dass* in any
utterance.

On the minimal trees interpretation, the relation between L2 speech and the
underlying morphosyntactic representations is direct: if a form or construction is
missing in speech, the relevant property is absent from the grammar.

Observe, however, that in cases (i)–(iii), forms associated with functional categories
are nevertheless represented: there is some main verb raising, some subject–verb
agreement and some use of auxiliaries/modals. Vainikka and Young-Scholten treat this
as 'noise' in the data, that is, forms that have been learned as part of lexical items, but
which as yet have no morphosyntactic significance. A different view is that these forms
are not noise. If they are used productively, they must in some sense be represented in
the grammar. Such representation presupposes that functional categories are present.

## B. Functional Categories in Initial State Representations

Schwartz (1998a, p. 44) asks the question:

> Can absence of verbal inflection and overt complementizers be considered sufficient for
> considering that the *categories* Infl and C themselves are non-existent? It seems equally

plausible to say that functional categories are indeed there – and even fully specified as in the L1 grammar – but just not overtly filled ... initially (*Infl is equivalent to T in the present discussion*).

Proponents of this position use other kinds of evidence to support it. For example, Prévost and White (2000b) show that the distribution of finite and non-finite verb forms in the speech of two L1 speakers of Moroccan Arabic (Zahra and Abdelmalek) acquiring L2 French naturalistically indicates that their grammars have a T with the feature [+/–finite]. At the time of first sampling, these subjects were judged to have very limited proficiency. In native French, infinitives are marked by an infinitive affix, for example *cherch-er* 'look for', *sort-ir* 'leave' and *prend-re* 'take'. Finite forms inflect differently, for example *sort* '(he/she) goes out', *sortons* '(we) go out' and *sortez* '(you) go out'. Zahra and Abdelmalek both use finite and non-finite verb forms in finite main clauses (where native speakers would use only finite forms), as illustrated in (4) (from Zahra's description of a Charlie Chaplin film):

(4)  a. après 10 jours charlie i chercher    li fille     (non-finite form)
        after 10 days Charlie he looks for the girl
     b. après charlie i monte ...     la maison    (finite form)
        after Charlie he goes up (to) the house

From the minimal trees perspective, such optionality in the use of finite and non-finite forms in finite contexts would be interpreted as absence of T and random use of verb forms in a VP projection. Prévost and White, however, show that while both finite and non-finite verb forms appear in finite contexts in the speech of Zahra and Abdelmalek, finite verb forms rarely appear in non-finite contexts (following an auxiliary, a modal or a preposition, that is, few cases of *il veut cherche la fille* 'He wants to look for the girl'). The distribution of forms is shown in Table I.

Because the two speakers are making a clear distinction in the distribution of finite and non-finite forms in production, their grammars must be representing this distinction. That is, they are distinguishing T[+finite] from T[–finite]. Their use of forms to realise this distinction, however, is quite different from the use of forms by native speakers. Specifically, they seem to be allowing forms like *chercher*, *monter* and *sortir* to realise both feature values. Why they might be doing this is discussed in section V.

Furthermore, when Zahra and Abdelmalek use finite verb forms in finite contexts, they are almost always appropriate to the subject. They produce expressions like *il sort* 'he goes out' and *nous sortons* 'we go out', but rarely *\*nous sort* or *\*il sortons*. The distribution of appropriate and inappropriate finite forms is shown in Table II.

TABLE I
**Distribution of Finite and Non-Finite Verb Forms (Based on Prévost & White, 2000b, p. 119)**

|            | Non-Finite V in Finite Contexts | Finite V in Non-Finite Contexts |
|------------|---------------------------------|---------------------------------|
| Zahra      | 224/755 (23%)                   | 2/156 (1%)                      |
| Abdelmalek | 243/767 (24%)                   | 17/278 (6%)                     |

TABLE II

**Appropriateness of Finite Verb Forms to Subject (Based on Prévost & White, 2000b, p. 120)**

|                  | Zahra          | Abdelmalek     |
|------------------|----------------|----------------|
| Main verbs       | 552/591 (93%)  | 447/472 (95%)  |
| être, avoir, aller | 156/158 (99%)  | 264/270 (98%)  |

This suggests that both speakers have not only T with the feature [+/–finite] represented in their grammars, but also the uninterpretable *Agr: person* and *Agr: number* features that are valued by the interpretable person and number features of the subject. It is the association of the finite forms of verbs with these features that gives rise to their use with appropriate subjects.

In a different study with native English speakers learning French, Prévost (2003) further observes that his subjects typically use nominative-case-marked subject clitic pronouns in finite clauses, even where the verb has a non-finite form, for example *Il prendre des vêtements* 'He takes some clothes' and *Il se réveiller à 7 heures* 'He wakes at 7 o'clock'. French also has strong pronouns, but utterances like *Lui prendre des vêtements* (lit. Him take some clothes) rarely appear in the speech of his informants. This suggests that these informants have represented the [Case] feature of T in their grammars.

Haznedar (2001), investigating the L2 English of a child L1 Turkish speaker (Erdem) over an 18-month period from his first productions, also found highly consistent use of pronouns; in fact there were no Case errors in his use of pronouns at all. Additionally, she found few null subjects in his speech, even though Turkish is a null-subject language. Given the representation assumed in Figure 1, the presence of overt, appropriately Case-marked subjects presupposes a T not only with a [Case] feature but also with an [EPP] feature that requires overt subjects in the specifier of TP.

To summarise, while 'restricted trees' hypotheses (of which minimal trees is a radical extreme) interpret the low frequency of suppliance of overt phonological exponents of functional categories, and apparent absence of syntactic operations associated with functional categories, to imply absence of those categories in underlying morpho-syntactic representations in the initial state, the hypothesis that functional categories are present focuses on the distribution of finite/non-finite verb forms, appropriateness of agreement inflections when used and the Case and obligatoriness of subject pronominals. From this perspective, where phonological exponents are absent, this is the result of either insufficient learning of those forms or the failure to map the features of the underlying representation consistently to their phonological exponents. For discussion of these cases, see section V.B.

## C. L1 Influence on Initial State Morphosyntactic Representations

Vainikka and Young-Scholten (1994, 1998a) provide evidence that the headedness of the VP in the early grammars of L2 learners of German is influenced by the L1. Their least proficient L1 speakers of Turkish and Korean (in both languages the verb is clause final, following an object) produce early utterances that have an XV (head final) structure in over 95% of cases (1998a, p. 20). By contrast, their least proficient L1 speakers of Spanish and Italian (both head-initial languages where the verb precedes an object) produce early utterances that have VX order in over 65% of cases. Other things being equal, this suggests that the L1 influences the word order of the earliest lexical representations of L2 learners.

One version of the hypothesis that functional categories are present in the initial state—the Full Transfer (Full Access) hypothesis of Schwartz and Sprouse (1994, 1996) and Schwartz (1998a)[3]—proposes that they are 'fully specified as in the L1 grammar' (1998a, p. 44). In relation to Figure 1, this means that features have the value they have in the L1. If T in the L1 has a [+strong] feature, this is the value it will have in the L2 initially.

In support of this claim, Schwartz (1998b) cites a study by Hulk (1991) of L1 Dutch speakers learning French in a classroom setting. Dutch, like German, requires finite verbs in main clauses to appear in second position (V2) and non-finite parts of verbs to appear in clause-final position, as in *Gisteren heeft Jan de aardbeien gegeten* (lit. Yesterday has Jan the strawberries eaten) 'Yesterday Jan ate the strawberries'. This pattern is assumed to arise from a basic underlying SOV structure for clauses, where finite V raises to C at the beginning of the sentence (C would have a [+strong] feature in declarative clauses in Dutch and German), and a topic constituent raises to the specifier of CP. French, by contrast, like English, has an underlying SVO order and no [+strong] feature on C in declarative clauses: *Hier Jean a mangé les fraises* (lit. Yesterday Jean has eaten the strawberries).

Hulk asked learners of different proficiency from beginner to high intermediate/ advanced to judge the grammaticality of French sentences, some of which showed Dutch word order properties. She found that the beginners accepted Dutch word order to a large extent and rejected grammatical French word order. The more proficient groups showed increasing acceptance of French word order and decreasing acceptance of the Dutch word order sentences. These results would seem to suggest that the earliest learners studied have a C category in their grammars, transferred from Dutch, to which finite verbs move, and this is why they behaved as they did on the test.

A potential problem for this account, however, is that the form of the test itself might be producing the results, rather than the subjects' L2 grammars. The test sentences involved compound verb forms, as well as subjects, objects and adverbs. These are complex sentences for beginning learners, and it could be that they identified the French words involved, but treated the task as if it were testing their knowledge of Dutch syntax. That is, the task may simply have been beyond their competence. If this were the case, then the results do not tell us anything about their initial grammars for French.

A study by Bohnacker (2006) does not appear to suffer from this problem, but still shows both the presence of a C category and the transfer of properties from a previously acquired language in the earliest grammars. Bohnacker's informants were

---

[3]Here 'Full Access' refers to full availability of the resources of UG in the subsequent development away from the initial state—see section V.B for discussion.

TABLE III

**Verb Position in the German Utterances of Four Swedish Speakers (Based on Bohnacker, 2006, p. 461)**

|              |       | SVX   | XVS   | XSV   | VSX |
|--------------|-------|-------|-------|-------|-----|
| German L2    | Märta | 58/82 | 42/82 | 0     | 0   |
|              | Algot | 43/62 | 19/62 | 0     | 0   |
| German L3    | Rune  | 35/64 | 16/64 | 13/64 | 0   |
|              | Gun   | 58/78 | 11/78 | 9/78  | 0   |

four Swedish speakers acquiring German as a second or third language. Swedish (like Dutch and German) is a V2 language requiring finite verbs to appear in second position in main clauses. For two of the informants (Märta and Algot), German was the first language other than Swedish that they had learned; the other two informants (Rune and Gun) had learned English as an L2 before German as an L3.[4] Data were collected four months after informants had started *ab initio* German classes, and again after nine months, from a task where they had to speak about 'what I do or would like to do in my spare time' in German. The frequency of word orders in utterances that contained a finite verb, an overt subject and some other constituent (object or adverbial) is presented in Table III.

The speakers for whom German is an L2 are only producing utterances consistent with V2. Since V2 is an effect of raising a verb to T, and then raising T to C, this suggests that these speakers have these categories in their early grammars with the feature [+strong]. The speakers for whom German is an L3 show optionality: they allow both V2 and V3. This suggests that they have been influenced by their knowledge of English, where C with a [–strong] feature is grammatical. Taken together, these results indicate early grammars that contain functional categories influenced by the features of already acquired languages.

While the results from Bohnacker's study are impressive, speech is still a problematic source of evidence for underlying morphosyntactic representations in the initial state. This is because much of what early learners produce may be formulaic, rote-learned chunks. Such chunks do not necessarily reflect the nature of underlying morphosyntactic representation. Myles (2004) has examined the early L2 French of English adolescent classroom learners with a view to separating the productive from formulaic uses of forms. Focusing on the early uses of the contracted subject pronoun *j'* 'I', she observes that of 332 uses by her subjects, 329 appear to be part of the formulaic use of *j'aime* 'I like', *j'adore* 'I really like' and *j'habite* 'I live'. There are only three uses of *j'* with other verbs. In early speech production, then, what looks like evidence for functional categories and their features may instead be an unanalysed, associatively learned pattern.

Studying very early L2 learners' interpretations of sentences, rather than their speech, appears to be one of the most promising ways of investigating the nature of morphosyntactic knowledge in the earliest stages. This does not require the heavy

---

[4]Because English has been a compulsory school subject in Sweden for decades, Bohnacker selected her informants from a group of people in their late 60s, some of whom had not learned any other L2 before.

processing demands of planning propositional content and retrieving lexical items required for speech. Nor does it involve asking learners to judge the grammaticality of sentences that may be beyond their competence (as in the Hulk study). Rather, learners judge whether sentences that are all grammatical differ in the way they are interpreted. Dekydtspotter, Schwartz, Sprouse, and Liljestrand (2005) report such a study by Garcia (1998), testing whether very early L2 learners are sensitive to the presence of a CP projection in embedded clauses. Garcia used biclausal sentences like the one in (5a) and PP modifiers like the one in (5b), combined in the different ways illustrated in (5c–e):

(5)  a. Charles told Anne (that) he played tennis
     b. in the winter
     c. Charles told Anne in the winter he played tennis
     d. Charles told Anne in the winter that he played tennis
     e. Charles told Anne that in the winter he played tennis

In each of (5c–e) *in the winter* can potentially modify either the main clause (when Charles told Anne) or the embedded clause (when Charles played tennis). For native speakers, when the complementiser *that* is absent, as in (5c), both possibilities are available. However, when the complementiser is present, it appears to limit the scope of the PP: in (5d) the strongly preferred reading is for it to modify the main clause; in (5e) the strongly preferred reading is for it to modify the embedded clause. If early L2 learners have a CP layer of structure in their grammars, they should show the same preferences as natives. If they do not, it might be predicted that they would treat all of (5c–e) in the same way.

Using a picture verification task, where informants were shown three cartoons, heard one of the sentences (5c–e) and had to decide which of the cartoons was appropriate to the sentence they had heard, Garcia (1998) found that her Arabic- and Chinese-speaking informants, who were all of 'quite rudimentary proficiency' (Dekydtspotter et al., 2005, p. 14), broadly made similar selections to the native speaker controls. They preferred the cartoon corresponding to PP modification of the embedded clause in the case of *that*-PP sentences (5e) and were less likely to choose that cartoon in the case of PP-*that* sentences (5d). When *that* was absent, they chose the cartoon corresponding to PP modification of the embedded clause at a rate in between these two. This suggests that these early L2 learners are assigning a structural representation to the sentences they are hearing that contains a CP projection in the embedded clause.

## D. Methodological Issues Concerning the Initial State

A major problem in investigating the nature of the initial state is determining where it ends. It is not always clear that evidence purporting to be relevant to the initial state is in fact relevant or whether it results from a grammar that is already beyond the initial state. For example, a closer examination of Haznedar's (2001) data (whose work is one of the most careful attempts in the current literature to track a learner from the beginning of L2 acquisition through early development) shows that the properties cited as support for initial functional structure are not reliably present until at least samples 7 or 8 (i.e. at least five months after the subject, Erdem, was first exposed to

English at nursery school) and much later for certain properties. Haznedar's early samples show the following:

- 9/10 missing copulas from obligatory copula contexts in samples 1–7 (at sample 8 there are suddenly 17/18 copulas present in obligatory contexts)
- 11/17 missing auxiliary *be*'s in samples 1–9
- Five null subjects and only three overt pronouns in samples 1–7
- no modal verbs in samples 1–14, 3 in sample 15 and a sudden leap to 20 in sample 16
- 4/44 irregular past tense forms in obligatory contexts in samples 1–15
- 1/19 regular past tense verb forms in samples 1–15
- 4/52 realisations of third person *–s* in obligatory contexts in samples 1–22

There is, then, an early period in the samples of speech from Erdem where his production of exponents of functional categories could be construed as 'noise' (forms acquired along with other lexical items, but having no morphosyntactic significance in his grammar). Then, in some cases, there is a sudden leap in functional exponents, for example the sudden increase in copula forms at sample 8 and a sudden leap in modals at sample 16, suggesting an important change in his grammar. This looks more consistent with the minimal trees hypothesis than the later data do.

The evidence discussed above from Prévost and White (2000b) is a powerful argument that their early L2 learners of French have fully specified functional categories in their grammars. A problem with these data, though, is that they are aggregated across samples collected over a three-year period, from learners who, like Erdem, may already have been beyond the initial state from the start of data collection. As discussed above, a methodology that asks informants to focus on differences in the meanings of sentences determined by morphosyntactic properties, rather than asking them to determine their grammatical status, is highly promising for investigating in more detail the nature of initial state grammars.

## V. HOW L2 MORPHOSYNTACTIC REPRESENTATIONS CHANGE: THE TRANSITION PROBLEM

### A. Minimal Trees

The assumption of the minimal trees hypothesis is that the initial state grammar changes when learners identify non-lexical properties of the input that are associated with the features of functional categories: *operations* like verb raising to T and T raising to C in questions; *free morphemes* like copulas, auxiliaries and modals; and *bound morphemes* like affixal tense, number marking and subject–verb agreement.[5]

---

[5]Vainikka and Young-Scholten (1998b) propose that of the three types of evidence available, free forms like copula *be* play a leading role in triggering the projection of functional structure. If correct, this implies that morphology drives change in L2 grammars, a perspective that White (2003b, p. 182) refers to as 'morphology before syntax'.

Input triggers the selection of functional features from UG, and these are integrated into the underlying morphosyntactic representation. Furthermore, the evidence that Vainikka and Young-Scholten (1994, 1996, 1998a) consider suggests that triggering is incremental. For example, in the acquisition of L2 German, the first functional stage following the lexical initial state is the projection of a finite phrase (FP)—in terms of Figure 1, a T specified [+finite] and [+strong], but not specified for other features. The result is that learners at the FP stage raise main verbs over negation and VP adverbs 'about half the time' (1998a, p. 25) and use auxiliaries and modals productively, but main verbs do not show consistent agreement or tense marking; they appear either as bare stems or with an –n (non-finite) ending.

The work by Prévost and White (2000b) discussed in section IV casts some doubt, however, on whether an FP stage exists independently of a stage where T is also specified for Case, an EPP feature and uninterpretable *Agr: person* and *Agr: number*. If subjects are obligatorily overt and appropriately Case marked and finite verb forms, when used, are used with appropriate subjects and are consistent with intended tense, it is likely that the learner has an underlying representation for the features in question.

## B. Change in Grammars with Functional Categories

In contrast to the minimal trees hypothesis, the hypothesis that functional structure is already present in the initial state appears to assume that change in L2 grammars takes two forms: (a) association of phonological exponents with underlying morphosyntactic features and (b) changes in the values of underlying morphosyntactic features transferred from the L1.

### Association of Phonological Exponents with Underlying Morphosyntactic Features

As learners gain more experience of the target L2, some phonological exponents appear to be supplied more frequently in their speech than others. The results in Table IV from a study by Ionin and Wexler (2002) show the distribution of copula and auxiliary *be*, regular past tense –ed and third person singular –s in the speech of 20 child learners of L2 English with L1 Russian. Their ages range from 3;9 to 13;10, and their exposure to English ranges from under a year to three years.

TABLE IV

**Tense/Agreement Morphology in Obligatory Contexts (Based on Tables 1 and 2 in Ionin & Wexler, 2002, pp. 106–107)**

|  | Copula *be* | Auxiliary *be* | Regular Past –ed | Third Person Singular –s |
|---|---|---|---|---|
| Suppliance | 329/431 (76%) | 300/479 (63%) | 73/174 (42%) | 67/321 (21%) |
| Bare v | 69/431 (16%) | 158/479 (33%) | 101/174 (58%) | 250/321 (78%) |
| Tense/agreement mismatch | 33/431 (8%) | 21/479 (4%) | 0/174 (0%) | 4/321 (1%) |

Three things should be observed about these results. First, forms of *be* are supplied more frequently than the affixal forms of regular past tense and third person singular *–s*. Secondly, as in the Prévost and White (2000b) study, there are few cases of inappropriate subject–verb agreement or *–ed* in non-past contexts. Thirdly, the differential patterns of suppliance of *be* forms and affixal forms are characteristic of individual subjects and not a group effect (i.e. they are not the result of combining individuals who always mark *–s* and individuals who never mark *–s*). Analysis of the individual subjects in the Ionin and Wexler corpus shows that individual performance is similar to group performance.[6]

Although *–ed* and *–s* are infrequent, their presence and appropriate use by the subjects in Ionin and Wexler's study suggest that the features [+finite], [±past], [*Agr: number*], [*Agr: person*], [+Af] and [*Agr: V*] are all present. But if these L2 learners have functionally specified underlying morphosyntactic representations, and there is evidence that they know the appropriate phonological exponents of abstract functional features, why do they not supply these forms all the time? One proposal to deal with this characteristic pattern of speech of L2 learners in transitional stages of development draws on the 'separation hypothesis' (Beard, 1995) that is implicit in Figure 1. The organisation of the grammar is such that the output of syntactic operations is terminal strings consisting of bundles of morphosyntactic and semantic features, but lacking phonological exponents. The phonological exponents are stored separately, for example in a 'vocabulary' component as proposed by distributed morphology (Embick & Marantz, 2005; Embick & Noyer, 2007; Halle & Marantz, 1993; Harley & Noyer, 1999).

Phonological exponents have entries in the vocabulary, which specify their *contexts of insertion*. For example, native speakers of English might have entries like the following:

(6)  $/(\iota)z/ \leftrightarrow$   [T, BE, –past, *Agr: +sing, Agr: 3p*]
     $/s/ \quad \leftrightarrow$   /[V, –past, *Agr: +sing, Agr: 3p*]+ ___
     $/d/ \quad \leftrightarrow$   /[V, +past]+___
     $/\emptyset/ \leftrightarrow$   /[V]+ ___

The entry for the third person singular form of *be*, $/(\iota)z/$, specifies that it can be inserted in a terminal T node if it has the features indicated. The entry for the third person singular agreement marker, /s/, specifies that it can be inserted in the context of a verb to the left ('/X' means 'in the context of X'; '+ ___' means 'put the form to the right of X') if it has the features indicated, and so on. Insertion occurs through feature matching between the exponent and the terminal node. Matching does not require full feature identity; hence vocabulary entries may be underspecified by comparison with syntactic terminal nodes. The vocabulary entry /d/ in (6) would be inserted into a terminal V node specified not only for [+past] but also for [*Agr: number*] and [*Agr: person*] (features required for the insertion of /s/). No phonological exponent can be inserted into a terminal node where one of its features clashes with a feature in the

---

[6]The informant data used by Ionin and Wexler are from the Ionin corpus on the CHILDES database (MacWhinney, 2000).

terminal node; /s/ cannot be inserted in the context of a terminal V node with the feature [+past], because that would clash with its own [-past] feature. Similarly, /d/ cannot be inserted in the context of a terminal V node with the feature [-past].

Since some vocabulary entries are underspecified with respect to the features of syntactic terminal nodes, more than one phonological exponent may be available for insertion. The phonologically null affix /Ø/ could be chosen with any terminal V node, hence competes with /s/ and /d/. For native speakers, the exponent with the largest number of features matching those of the terminal node is the one that is inserted. This ensures that /Ø/ appears only where V is not specified [+past] or [-past, *Agr: +sing*, *Agr: 3p*]; for example it is inserted in cases like *I walk-Ø*, *they walk-Ø* and *she must walk-Ø*, but not in cases like *He walk-Ø every day* or *Yesterday he walk-Ø to work*. There is, then, what might be called a *competition condition* on the insertion of forms for native speakers[7]: insert the form whose features maximally match those of the terminal node.

One account of observations like those of Ionin and Wexler is that L2 speakers lack the competition condition. They allow a phonological form with fewer features to be inserted where a form with more features is also available. This has come to be known as the *Missing Surface Inflection Hypothesis* (MSIH) (Haznedar & Schwartz, 1997; Prévost & White, 2000b). The implication of this is that when L2 speakers use affixal inflections like the regular past tense and third person singular /s/ in English, they will use them appropriately, as observed above. At the same time, they will allow verbs with a phonologically null affix /Ø/ to appear in the same environments because they lack the competition condition on insertion of vocabulary items. This claim neatly captures the observations of Prévost and White (2000b) concerning the distribution of finite and non-finite verb forms in L2 French discussed in section IV.B. The reason why non-finite forms like *chercher* 'look for' appear in finite contexts, while finite forms like *cherche* are less likely to appear in non-finite contexts, follows if *chercher* is an entry in the vocabulary that is underspecified by comparison with *cherche*, and hence is likely to be inserted where *cherche* should be inserted, if L2 speakers lack the competition condition on vocabulary insertion. For some potential empirical problems for the MSIH, see section VI.

If the MSIH is correct, L2 learners develop by identifying phonological forms in the target L2 that map onto features in the 'vocabulary' component. The organisation of entries in the vocabulary is similar to the organisation in native grammars, but a difference is that in speech, L2 speakers lack the competition condition, at least in early development.

An alternative to the MSIH is proposed by Ionin and Wexler (2002) (following earlier work by Zobl & Liceras, 1994). Observing that *be* forms are exponents of a verb that raises to T (copula or auxiliary), whereas the affixal forms /d/ and /s/ are exponents of a T that has lowered to V, they propose that 'L2 learners initially consider morphological agreement to be a reflex of verb raising' (2002, p. 117) and that this follows from a general principle of UG that if a category raises overtly for feature valuing, then it is expressed by phonological exponents. Where categories do not raise,

---

[7]Halle (1997) refers to this condition as a 'Subset Principle'.

overt phonological expression is language specific and may or may not be realised. This idea implies that once an L2 learner has identified a category as raising to T, he/she will expect this to be expressed phonologically and hence will identify forms of *be* rapidly. The non-raising relationship between T and V involving tense and agreement with main verbs will not lead to the expectation of phonological expression, and learners will take time to identify this from the input. One problem with this account, however, as observed by White (2003b, p. 201) is that it predicts that in the L2 acquisition of a language where all verbs raise (copula, auxiliaries, main verbs), like French, there should be no difference in the phonological expression of inflection across all verb types. However, in the Prévost and White (2000b) study, their subjects were more accurate on the use of the copula/auxiliary forms than on inflected main verbs.

### Changes in the Values of Features Transferred from the LI

If an initial state grammar is the set of morphosyntactic features transferred from the L1, as predicted by the Full Transfer hypothesis, what enables the L2 learner to converge on the target grammar? Schwartz (1998b, p. 147) proposes that development occurs when input cannot be assigned a structural description by the transferred grammar: 'input that cannot be ... accommodated ... can cause the system to restructure; hence, syntactic development is "failure-driven." In some cases this revision may occur rapidly; in others, much more time may be needed'.

Assuming this scenario, differences in the rapidity with which grammars restructure can be illustrated from two studies concerned with verb raising. Evidence for verb raising/lack of verb raising is potentially offered by the contexts in which verbs occur. In French, the raising of a main verb to finite T is visible in the location of the verb to the left of negation (*mange pas* 'eats not'), location of the verb to the left of VP-modifying adverbs (*mange souvent des crêpes* 'eats often pancakes') and T-to-C movement in some forms of interrogatives, where the main verb is carried to the front of the sentence (*mange-t-elle des crêpes?* 'eats she pancakes?'). In English, the lack of main verb raising is signalled by the location of the verb to the right of VP-modifying adverbs and by *do*-support in negation and questions.

White (1992—summarised in White, 2003b) gave a grammaticality preference task involving pairs of English grammatical and ungrammatical sentences (like *Linda always takes the metro*/*Linda takes always the metro*) to 72 Canadian-French-speaking adolescent learners of English after one or two years of classroom English. Her results show that informants accurately chose the non-raised verb option in 86% of questions and 85% of negatives (i.e. those involving *do*-support), but made the right choice only in 23% of the adverb cases. This suggests that the English input they encounter gives rise to only partial restructuring of their transferred grammars, at least at the stage of development investigated by White.[8]

---

[8]For an account of why informants differ in responding to sentences involving questions and negatives, on the one hand, and adverbs, on the other, see White (1992).

Two studies by Yuan (2001, 2003) of L2 Mandarin Chinese show different results on verb raising with adverbs. Like English, main verbs in Mandarin do not raise over negation or VP-modifying adverbs, suggesting that T has a [–strong] feature: *Zhangsan bu kan shu* (lit. Zhangsan not read book) 'Zhangsan doesn't read books' and *Ta changchang he pijiu* (lit. He often drink beer) 'He often drinks beer'. Yuan tested speakers whose L1s were French, German (verb-raising languages) and English (no main verb raising) at different proficiency levels. Fifty-two of them were beginners. Using an oral production task and a grammaticality judgement task, Yuan found that all groups, including beginners, categorically produced/accepted S Adv V X word order in over 90% of cases and produced/accepted *S V Adv X order in hardly any cases. Similar results were obtained for negation (where only French and English informants were compared).

In contrast to the results of White's study, then, Mandarin input gives rise to rapid restructuring where adverbs are involved. Mandarin appears to be quite limited in where adverbs can be located, either between the subject and the verb or in sentence initial position. In English, on the other hand, adverbs can appear in a number of positions: *Often he drinks beer*, *He often drinks beer*, *He drinks beer often* and *He is often drinking beer*. It is possible that evidence provided about lack of verb raising with adverbs in English is rather ambiguous for speakers of verb-raising L1s. Chinese, on the other hand, may provide speakers of any language with clear evidence that verbs do not raise over adverbs.

The Full Transfer hypothesis also proposes that there will be occasions when a transferred feature from the L1 never changes, even though the target L2 has a different feature value. This can occur where the transferred grammar accommodates or misanalyses the input, as illustrated in another study by Yuan (2007). Chinese and Japanese form wh-questions by merging a wh-word in a position where an ordinary noun phrase would appear and merging a question particle with an interrogative C (which in both languages happens to be to the right of the clause) as illustrated in (7). (In Chinese the particle can be overt—*ne*—or null):

(7)  a. Ni xiang chi shenme (ne)? (Chinese)
         You want eat what Q
         'What would you like to eat?'
     b. Mary-ga nani-o katta no? (Japanese)
         Mary-Nom what-Acc buy-past Q
         'What did Mary buy?'

An interesting difference between the two languages is that in Japanese a wh-word cannot be c-commanded by a quantifier like 'everyone', although this is possible in Chinese:

(8)  a. *Daremo-ga nani-o katta no?
         Everyone-Nom what-Acc buy-past Q
         'What did everyone buy?'
     b. Meigeren dou mai-le shenme?
         Everyone all buy-perf what
         'What did everyone buy?'

Yuan assumes that the reason for this difference is that in Japanese a phonologically null operator attached to the wh-word raises to adjoin to *no* and that a higher quantifier blocks this movement. By contrast, there is no such movement in Chinese, and (8b) is grammatical. Yuan asked L1 Japanese and L1 English learners of Chinese to rate sentences like (7) and (8) for grammaticality on a scale ranging from –2 (completely unacceptable) to +2 (completely acceptable). While advanced proficiency English speakers gave sentences like (8b) a mean rating of 1.21 (similar to the native speaker controls' mean rating of 1.33), the Japanese speakers rated them at only 0.01, suggesting that they do not know whether they are grammatical or not. This was not a general problem with quantifiers for the Japanese speakers; they rated sentences where a wh-word was not present (*Meigeren dou mai-le yixie shu* 'Everyone bought one book') like the native controls. Yuan suggests that the Japanese speakers have taken the Chinese question particle *ne* as corresponding to *no* in Japanese. Since their transferred L1 grammar can accommodate most uses of the Chinese *ne* particle, they persistently misanalyse it when a quantifier is involved. Because the properties of English wh-questions are very different from those of Chinese, English-speaking learners' grammars have restructured.

## VI. WHEN PERFORMANCE STABILISES: THE STEADY STATE

'Steady state' grammars are those where it is assumed that underlying morpho-syntactic representations are unlikely to change further, following a speaker's long immersion in the target language.[9] A striking observation about the performance of L2 speakers with steady state grammars is that it can diverge considerably from the performance of native speakers. To illustrate, consider the use in Patty's speech (the L2 speaker studied by Lardiere, 2007) of five properties in obligatory contexts of use for native speakers: overt subjects in finite clauses, nominative Case marking of subject pronouns in finite past tense contexts, appropriate agreement marking with the subject of copula/auxiliary *be*, past tense marking (regular and irregular combined) in intended past tense contexts and third person singular –*s* marking of main verbs. Table V summarises the results (Lardiere, 2007, pp. 74–80). There were three points at which Patty's speech was sampled: the first after 10 years of immersion in English and two more after 18½ years (separated by a few months).

Patty's performance on some of these properties converges on the expected native pattern: use of overt subjects, Case marking of pronouns and suppliance of forms of copula and auxiliary *be* that agree with the subject. However, performance on past tense marking and third person singular agreement marking on main verbs diverges dramatically from the expected native pattern. This is not directly attributable to morphosyntactic features in Patty's L1s, Mandarin and Hokkien. These two varieties allow null subjects, do not distinguish pronouns for Case (e.g. the form *ta* in Mandarin is the equivalent of both *he/she* and *him/her*) and lack subject–verb agreement on copula/ auxiliary verbs. Her performance on the English counterparts is highly target-like. These

---

[9]For a discussion of the issues involved in determining the steady state, see Long (2003).

TABLE V

**Use of Target Forms in Obligatory Contexts in the Speech of Patty (Based on Lardiere, 2007, pp. 74–80)**

|  | Data Collection Point | | |
|---|---|---|---|
| Property | 1 | 2 | 3 |
| Overt subjects | 362/364 (99%) | 788/805 (98%) | 329/336 (98%) |
| Nominative case subjects (in [+past] contexts) | 49/49 (100%) | 378/378 (100%) | 76/76 (100%) |
| Correct form of *be* | 57/69 (83%) | 50/53 (94%) | 59/63 (94%) |
| Correct past tense forms | 24/69 (35%) | 191/548 (35%) | 46/136 (34%) |
| Correct third person –*s* | 2/42 (5%) | 0/4 (0%) | 1/22 (5%) |

TABLE VI

**Suppliance in Obligatory Contexts of Past Tense and Third Person Singular –*s* on Main Verbs by SD (Based on White, 2003a, p. 134)**

|  | Sample after 10 years | Sample after 11 ½ years |
|---|---|---|
| Past forms of main verbs | 192/226 (85%) | 126/166 (76%) |
| Main verbs+–*s* | 145/185 (78%) | 70/86 (82%) |

varieties also lack past tense marking and subject–verb agreement, but here she is highly non-target-like. At the same time, divergence from native English on these last two properties appears considerably less likely for L2 speakers whose L1 marks past tense and subject–verb agreement on main verbs. White (2003a), investigating the steady state grammar of a Turkish speaker, SD, after 10 years and again after 11½ years of immersion in English in Canada, found that she was supplying both tense and agreement marking on main verbs in speech most of the time, as shown in Table VI.

The same question arises here about how to interpret the observed performance of Patty and SD in relation to underlying morphosyntactic representations that arose in interpreting performance in the initial state and in transitional states. One interpretation of Patty's performance offered by Lardiere's early work (1998a, 1998b) is that her grammar has the relevant functional representation for English, but she has a mapping problem of the kind proposed by the MSIH. This is compounded by a problem producing word-final consonant clusters, an effect of persistent influence of phonotactic constraints in Chinese. Chinese allows only a vowel or vowel–consonant combination in word-final position; regular inflected forms of main verbs in English often involve consonant–consonant final clusters like *walks* /-ks/ or *walked* /-kt/, and these remain difficult to produce.

In more recent work, Lardiere (2007, pp. 138–139) observes that Patty uses past tense marking in a number of ways that native speakers do not: double marking of T and V (*I was still wrote to my friend*), marking of T rather than V (*I was have a breakthrough*), marking of V when T should be marked (*We don't spoke that much English*), marking of an infinitive rather than the main verb (*He or she have to spoke uh, English*) and displacement of the contracted form of *had* or *would* (*I decided on Monday that we better booked it*). On the basis of this, Lardiere suggests that Patty may have a 'breakdown at some point in the correspondence rules or algorithms that guide the mapping from morphosyntactic feature to phonological form', and this may be influenced by L1 knowledge 'at various levels of representation, including phonological, lexico-semantic, and discourse-pragmatic' (2007, pp. 138–139). In other words, there is a more general problem with re-mapping morphosyntactic, semantic and discourse-related features that have been assigned to a set of phonological exponents in the L1 to different phonological exponents in the L2. The underlying morphosyntactic features required to produce derivations appropriate to the L2, of the kind illustrated in Figure 1, are fully available through UG, but a persistent problem for L2 learners is establishing the correct mappings to forms in the vocabulary. If this is correct, then the challenge for L2 research is to identify what kinds of mapping are unproblematic for L2 learners (at least Case marking and finiteness for Patty) and what kinds are problematic (at least tense and agreement marking on main verbs for Patty) and to determine whether these are natural kinds and can be used to explain the behaviour of other L2 learners.

A different interpretation of the relation between underlying morphosyntactic features and phonological exponents in cases of persistent divergence in performance from the target L2 is offered by Hawkins and Liszka (2003). They examined the use of English past-tense-marked main verbs in the elicited speech of two Chinese and five Japanese speakers, all of comparable advanced proficiency in English. Two of their observations are as follows. First, the Chinese speakers were less likely to omit the final consonant in clusters like /-kt/ and /-nd/ when the word in question was an uninflected mono-morpheme like *fact* or *kind* or an inflected participle like *(is) sliced* or *(is) released* than when it was a main verb in the regular past (although the frequencies of forms produced were small, so caution is required in generalising from this). Secondly, the Japanese speakers did not omit the final consonant of a cluster when the form involved was a regular past tense main verb (or a monomorpheme or participle); the regular past tense affix was supplied in 137/149 (92%) of obligatory contexts by the informants studied. What is striking here is that Japanese is like Chinese in disallowing word-final consonant clusters, but differs from Chinese in having an overt past tense marker –*ta*.

Hawkins and Liszka argue that if these observations are generalisable to the larger population of Chinese and Japanese learners of L2 English, they are problematic for the MSIH and cast doubt on the persistent influence of L1 phonotactic constraints on L2 acquisition. If the MSIH is correct, then all L2 learners should, presumably, have difficulty with the competition condition for the insertion of phonological exponents, tending to choose V-Ø in English where V-d is required. The fact that Japanese speakers do not do this means that the extent to which the competition condition is impaired may be influenced by whether an L1 has phonological exponents in the vocabulary component that are counterparts to forms in the L2. The persistence of L1 influence on phonotactic constraints is also doubtful since word-final consonant clusters appear not to be problematic for the Japanese speakers, nor are they problematic for the Chinese speakers studied, in monomorphemes and participles.[10]

---

[10]It should be pointed out that Patty, in contrast to the two subjects studied by Hawkins and Liszka (2003), did not differ in her treatment of clusters across past tense, monomorphemes, and participles. Lardiere (2007, pp. 107–108) reports absence of final -t/-d in clusters in nearly all monomorphemes and participles.

TABLE VII

**Contexts in Which –s Was Supplied (Based on Goad et al., 2003, p. 259)**

| Contexts | Example | Suppliance (%) |
|---|---|---|
| (i) VC-*s* | fill-s | 68% |
| (ii) VCC-*s*-C | builds for | 9% |
| (iii) VCC-*s*-V | builds on | 75% |

Hawkins and Liszka's proposal is that the [+Af] and [*Agr: V*] features of Figure 1 are missing from the grammars of Chinese speakers.[11] This follows from the Interpretability Hypothesis of Tsimpli and Dimitrakopoulou (2007). This proposes that there is a critical period in the development of grammatical knowledge specifically for the selection of uninterpretable features. At birth, all features required for acquisition of any human language are made available through UG. If particular uninterpretable features are not selected for a grammar during early life, they disappear from the UG inventory of features. Older L2 learners may then have to acquire an L2 without the benefit of particular uninterpretable features. Hawkins and Liszka's claim is that Chinese has not selected the uninterpretable features required to realise past tense marking on main verbs, and that is why their performance diverges from that of native speakers. Japanese, in contrast, has selected such features, and the acquisition of past tense marking in English is unproblematic for them.

A third interpretation of performance like that displayed by Patty is offered by Goad, White, and Steele (2003). They assume, as Lardiere does, that L2 learners have available the full set of underlying morphosyntactic features appropriate for the target L2, but transfer the prosodic constraints of the L1, which limit the production of certain word forms. Although their study deals with 12 L1 Mandarin speakers of intermediate/low-advanced proficiency in English, their proposal is extendible to L2 speakers with steady state grammars. Focusing on the suppliance of third person singular –*s*, they find that six of their informants supply –*s* on average 10% of the time and six of them on average 49% of the time. The group who supplied –*s* in 49% of contexts did so differentially, as shown in Table VII. Here C = 'consonant' and V = 'vowel'.

Goad et al. argue that in case (ii), the prosodic representation for *builds* involves three syllables, with the third one adjoined to a prosodic word (PWd) to meet universal constraints on prosody (see Goad et al. for details):

(9)  [PWd [PWd bɪl.dø] zø]
          1    2    3

They claim that adjunction of this type is not possible in Mandarin, only adjunction to a phonological phrase (PPh). Chinese speakers can potentially accommodate clusters (which are not possible in Chinese) through adjunction to the PPh:

(10) [$_{PPh}$ [$_{PWd}$ ftl] zø]

However, this is the maximal adjunction structure possible for them. They cannot attach a further syllable, hence their failure to realise *–s* in a word like *builds* followed by a consonant, or at the end of a phrase. However, when *builds* is followed by a word beginning with a vowel, the *–s* can be treated as part of the following syllable, and hence is pronounceable: [$_{PPh}$[$_{PWd}$ bɪl ] dø] [$_{PWd}$ zon]. Note that although Chinese speakers have the potential for accommodating word-final clusters in this way, some speakers may not take advantage of it. Six of the informants in their study barely accommodate at all, supplying *–s* on average in only 10% of contexts.

If this account is along the right lines, it suggests that divergence between L2 learners and native speakers of the kind displayed by Patty may arise at the interface between the output of morphosyntactic/morphophonological representation and the assignment of prosodic structure. For discussion of interface relations between grammatical representation and other modules in SLA, see chapter 3.

## VII. CONCLUSION AND FUTURE DIRECTIONS

Much of the debate about the nature of L2 speakers' knowledge of morphosyntax results from different interpretations that researchers have given to the relation between performance and underlying representation. Controversy about whether initial state grammars contain functional categories and their features remains unresolved. Although some aspects of production data suggest the presence of functional categories, those data may relate to a stage of development that is already beyond the initial state, or they may represent associatively learned formulae rather than analysed properties. Studies of the earliest learners' interpretations of meaning contrasts associated with functional category distinctions are a promising line of enquiry for resolving this issue.

Evidence from studies of speakers with developing grammars points strongly to two conclusions: first, that the relationship between speech production and underlying morphosyntactic representation in the grammar of an individual L2 learner is indirect; secondly, that the feature values of functional categories are L1 influenced. The second conclusion militates against the idea that functional categories and their features develop solely on the basis of triggering by input from the target L2. However, the nature of input clearly plays a role, in that some L2s allow learners to restructure rapidly while others give rise to much slower restructuring. We need more comparative studies of learners acquiring cognate properties in different L2s to determine precisely what the role of input is, as in the case of French speakers encountering lack of verb raising in English and in Chinese, and the different apparent effects on their grammars.

The debate about the nature of morphosyntax in L2 steady state grammars is ongoing. Should cases of divergence in performance from native speakers be explained as a representational deficit (where one or more features are missing), as a problem with mapping morphosyntactic features to phonological forms or as problems involving mapping to more peripheral properties of the grammar (like prosodic structure) or even other modules of mind? Future research will almost certainly attempt to explicate the nature of the mapping between levels of linguistic representation.

## ACKNOWLEDGEMENTS

I thank Kholoud Al-Thubaiti, Carol Jaensch, and Yunju Jeon for very helpful comments on an earlier version of this chapter.

## REFERENCES

Beard, R. (1995). *Lexeme-morpheme base morphology*. Albany, NY: SUNY Press.

Beck, M.-L. (1998). L2 acquisition and obligatory head movement: English-speaking learners of German and the local impairment hypothesis. *Studies in Second Language Acquisition, 20,* 311–348.

Bernstein, J. (1991). DPs in French and Walloon: Evidence for parametric variation in nominal head movement. *Probus, 3,* 101–126.

Bhatt, R., & Hancin-Bhatt, B. (2002). Structural minimality, CP and the initial state in second language acquisition. *Second Language Research, 18,* 348–392.

Bley-Vroman, R. (1990). The logical problem of foreign language learning. *Linguistic Analysis, 20,* 3–49.

Bohnacker, U. (2006). When Swedes begin to learn German: from V2 to V2. *Second Language Research, 22,* 443–486.

Chomsky, N. (1995). *The minimalist program*. Cambridge, MA: MIT Press.

Chomsky, N. (1998). Minimalist inquiries: the framework, *MIT Working Papers in Linguistics* (15, pp. 1–56). Also published. In R. Martin, D. Michaels & J. Uriagereka (Eds.). (2000). *Step by step: Essays on minimalist syntax in honor of Howard Lasnik* (pp. 89–155). Cambridge, MA: MIT Press.

Chomsky, N. (2001). Derivation by phase. In M. Kenstowicz (Ed.), *Ken hale: A life in language* (pp. 1–52). Cambridge, MA: MIT Press.

Dekydtspotter, L., Schwartz, B. D., Sprouse, R., & Liljestrand, A. (2005). Evidence for the C-domain in early interlanguage. *Eurosla Yearbook, 5,* 7–34.

Ellis, N. C. (2006). Selective attention and transfer phenomena in L2 acquisition: contingency, cue competition, salience, interference, overshadowing, blocking, and perceptual learning. *Applied Linguistics, 27,* 164–194.

Embick, D., & Marantz, A. (2005). Cognitive neuroscience and the English past tense: Comments on the paper by Ullman et al. *Brain and Language, 93,* 243–247.

Embick, D., & Noyer, R. (2007). Distributed morphology and the syntax/morphology interface. In G. Ramchand & C. Reiss (Eds.), *The Oxford handbook of linguistic interfaces*. Oxford: Oxford University Press.

Epstein, S., Flynn, S., & Martohardjono, G. (1996). Second language acquisition: Theoretical and experimental issues in contemporary research. *Brain and Behavioral Sciences, 19,* 677–758.

Eubank, L. (1994). Optionality and the initial state in L2 development. In T. Hoekstra & B. D. Schwartz (Eds.), *Language acquisition studies in generative grammar* (pp. 369–388). Amsterdam: John Benjamins.

Garcia, B. (1998). *The L2 initial state: Minimal trees or full transfer/full access?* Unpublished MA dissertation, University of Durham, England.

Goad, H., White, L., & Steele, J. (2003). Missing inflection in L2 acquisition: Defective syntax or L1-constrained prosodic representations? *Canadian Journal of Linguistics, 48,* 243–263.

Halle, M. (1997). Distributed morphology: Impoverishment and fission. *MIT Working Papers in Linguistics, 30,* 425–449.

Halle, M., & Marantz, A. (1993). Distributed morphology and the pieces of inflection. In K. Hale & S. J. Keyser (Eds.), *The view from building 20* (pp. 53–109). Cambridge, MA: MIT Press.

Harley, H., & Noyer, R. (1999). Distributed morphology. *Glot International, 4,* 3–9.

Hawkins, R., & Liszka, S. (2003). Locating the source of defective past tense marking in advanced L2 English speakers. In R. van Hout, A. Hulk, F. Kuiken & R. Towell (Eds.), *The lexicon–syntax interface in second language acquisition* (pp. 21–44). Amsterdam: John Benjamins.

Haznedar, B. (2001). The acquisition of the IP system in child L2 English. *Studies in Second Language Acquisition, 3,* 1–39.

Haznedar, B., & Schwartz, B. D. (1997). Are there optional infinitives in child L2 acquisition? In E. Hughes, M. Hughes, & A. Greenhill (Eds.), *Proceedings of the 21st Annual Boston University Conference on Language Development* (pp. 257–268). Boston: Cascadilla Press.

Hulk, A. (1991). Parameter setting and the acquisition of word order in L2 French. *Second Language Research, 7,* 1–34.

Ionin, T., & Wexler, K. (2002). Why is 'is' easier than '-s'? Acquisition of tense/agreement morphology by child second language learners of English. *Second Language Research, 18,* 95–136.

Lardiere, D. (1998a). Case and tense in the 'fossilized' steady state. *Second Language Research, 14,* 1–26.

Lardiere, D. (1998b). Dissociating syntax from morphology in a divergent L2 end-state grammar. *Second Language Research, 14,* 359–375.

Lardiere, D. (2007). *Ultimate attainment in second language acquisition: A case study.* Mahwah, NJ: Lawrence Erlbaum Associates.

Long, M. H. (2003). Stabilization and fossilization in interlanguage development. In C. J. Doughty & M. H. Long (Eds.), *Handbook of second language acquisition* (pp. 487–535). Oxford: Blackwell.

MacWhinney, B. (2000). *The CHILDES project: Tools for analyzing talk* (3rd ed.). Mahwah NJ: Lawrence Erlbaum.

MacWhinney, B. (2004). A multiple process solution to the logical problem of language acquisition. *Journal of Child Language, 31,* 883–914.

Meisel, J. (1997). The acquisition of the syntax of negation in French and German: Contrasting first and second language acquisition. *Second Language Research, 13,* 227–263.

Myles, F. (2004). From data to theory: The over-representation of linguistic knowledge in SLA. *Transactions of the Philological Society, 102,* 139–168.

O'Grady, W. (2008). The emergentist program. *Lingua, 118,* 447–464.

Panagiotidis, P. (2002). *Pronouns, clitics and empty nouns: 'Pronominality' and licensing in syntax.* Amsterdam: John Benjamins.

Prévost, P. (2003). Root infinitives in adult L2 French: A longitudinal study. In A.-T. Pérez-Leroux & Y. Roberge (Eds.), *Romance linguistics: Theory and acquisition* (pp. 367–384). Amsterdam: John Benjamins.

Prévost, P., & White, L. (2000a). Accounting for morphological variation in L2 acquisition: Truncation or missing inflection? In M.-A. Friedemann & L. Rizzi (Eds.), *The acquisition of syntax* (pp. 202–235). London: Longman.

Prévost, P., & White, L. (2000b). Missing surface inflection or impairment in second language acquisition? Evidence from tense and agreement. *Second Language Research, 16,* 103–133.

Ritter, E. (1993). Where's gender? *Linguistic Inquiry, 24,* 795–803.

Schwartz, B. D. (1998a). On two hypotheses of 'transfer' in L2A: Minimal trees and absolute L1 influence. In S. Flynn, G. Martohardjono, & W. O'Neil (Eds.), *The generative study of second language acquisition* (pp. 35–59). Mahwah, NJ: Lawrence Erlbaum Associates.

Schwartz, B. D. (1998b). The second language instinct. *Lingua, 106,* 133–160.

Schwartz, B. D., & Sprouse, R. (1994). Word order and nominative case in nonnative language acquisition: A longitudinal study of (L1 Turkish) German interlanguage. In T. Hoekstra & B. D. Schwartz (Eds.), *Language Acquisition Studies in Generative Grammar* (pp. 317–368). Amsterdam: John Benjamins.

Schwartz, B. D., & Sprouse, R. (1996). L2 cognitive states and the full transfer/full access model. *Second Language Research, 12,* 40–72.

Tsimpli, I.-M., & Dimitrakopoulou, M. (2007). The interpretability hypothesis: Evidence from wh-interrogatives in second language acquisition. *Second Language Research, 23,* 215–242.

Vainikka, A., & Young-Scholten, M. (1994). Direct access to X'-theory: Evidence from Korean and Turkish adults learning German. In T. Hoekstra & B. D. Schwartz (Eds.), *Language acquisition studies in generative grammar* (pp. 265–316). Amsterdam: John Benjamins.

Vainikka, A., & Young-Scholten, M. (1996). Gradual development of L2 phrase structure. *Second Language Research, 12,* 7–39.

Vainikka, A., & Young-Scholten, M. (1998a). The initial state in the L2 acquisition of phrase structure. In S. Flynn, G. Martohardjono, & W. O'Neil (Eds.), *The generative study of second language acquisition* (pp. 17–34). Mahwah, NJ: Lawrence Erlbaum Associates.

Vainikka, A., & Young-Scholten, M. (1998b). Morphosyntactic triggers in adult SLA. In M.-L. Beck (Ed.), *Morphology and its interfaces in second language knowledge* (pp. 89–113). Amsterdam: John Benjamins.

Vainikka, A., & Young-Scholten, M. (2007). Minimalism vs. organic syntax. In S. Karimi, V. Samiian & W. Wilkins (Eds.), *Phrasal and clausal architecture: Syntactic derivation and interpretation. In honor of Joseph Emonds* (pp. 319–338). Amsterdam: John Benjamins.

White, L. (1992). Long and short verb movement in second language acquisition. *Canadian Journal of Linguistics, 37,* 273–286.

White, L. (2003a). Fossilization in steady state L2 grammars: Persistent problems with inflectional morphology. *Bilingualism: Language and Cognition, 6,* 129–141.

White, L. (2003b). *Second language acquisition and universal grammar.* Cambridge: Cambridge University Press.

Yuan, B. (2001). The status of thematic verbs in the second language acquisition of Chinese. *Second Language Research, 17,* 248–272.

Yuan, B. (2003). The syntax of clausal negation in French and English speakers' L2 Chinese. In J. M. Liceras, et al. (Eds.), *Proceedings of the 6th Generative Approaches to Second Language Acquisition Conference (GASLA 2002)*. *Cascadilla Proceedings Project* (pp. 352–360), Somerville, MA: Cascadilla Press.

Yuan, B. (2007). Japanese speakers' second language Chinese wh-questions: A lexical morphological feature deficit account. *Second Language Research, 23,* 329–357.

Zobl, H., & Liceras, J. M. (1994). Review article: Functional categories and acquisition orders. *Language Learning, 44,* 159–180.

CHAPTER II

# SECOND LANGUAGE PHONOLOGY

John Archibald

## I. INTRODUCTION

The acquisition of a second language (L2) is a complex task, which involves learning about many diverse phenomena. One component that must be acquired is the sound system of the target language; its *phonology*. It is important to recognize that the construct of phonology is much broader than the pedagogic notion of *pronunciation*. While pronunciation teachers are concerned with affecting the production and perception of L2 speech, here we are more concerned with the nature of the phonological competence of the learner.

This chapter is structured in the following way. I will begin by discussing some general issues from the field of second language acquisition (SLA) and show how the study of L2 phonology addresses these issues. Then, I will discuss the acquisition of (1) segments, (2) syllable structure, and (3) higher-level prosodic phenomena. By nature, such a survey is selective, and I have chosen to present works conducted within what we may call the generative tradition. For an overview of broader issues in second language phonology, see Archibald (1998) or Major (2001).

### A. Phonological Knowledge and Skill

A basic insight from cognitive theory helps us to understand that SLA in general involves the acquisition of both *knowledge* and *skill*. The knowledge that we store in our heads is a relatively stable trait. You either know the word *cat* or you don't. You either know that the sentence, "They was inable to speaked French" is ungrammatical or you don't. Clearly, you have to acquire knowledge of your L2, but you also have to acquire skills. You have to be able to comprehend fast speech, or carry on a conversation. Proficiency in a second language is a complex construct that includes a

237

range of knowledge (from grapheme to phoneme to sentence to text) and a range of abilities (from politeness routines to appropriate register).

The acquisition of L2 phonology also involves both knowledge and skill. The learner must acquire the knowledge (in the form of the appropriate mental representation for the target language) and the skills necessary to be able to accurately produce and perceive the relevant phonological contrasts. An obvious characteristic of L2 speech is that it is accented. Native speakers (NS) are able to recognize the characteristics of say French-accented English as being distinct from German-accented English. The first language (L1) of the speaker is one factor that can have quite a predictable influence on L2 speech. L2 learners can sound non-native-like for two reasons, Let's take an example from stress. Many languages mark certain syllables as prominent by stressing them. The second syllable in "banána" is more prominent than the first or third syllable. Languages vary in where they put the stress, so this is something that has to be learned. This, then, is one possible source of error, and hence, one way in which people can sound non-native-like; they can get the stress placement wrong and say "bánana." This would be a phonological problem. They could, however, put the stress on the right syllable but still not sound like a native speaker. In their L1, they may indicate stress by loudness or vowel length, whereas in English the main means of indicating stress is by a pitch change. Marking stress in English by loudness or vowel length rather than pitch would be an example of a phonetic marker of their accent.

## B. What Is Acquired?

From a linguistic point of view, the first thing to consider in looking at the acquisition of phonology in a second language is the question of what exactly is being acquired. That is, we must adopt a theory of phonological knowledge. The model in Figure 1 indicates some of the areas that will be addressed in this chapter. Second language learners must acquire features, segments, moras, syllables, and feet.

This is the kind of mental representation that learners are trying to acquire. Much of the core of L2 phonology research attempts to see whether L2 learners are setting up target-like representations. However, there is also much research that attempts to address

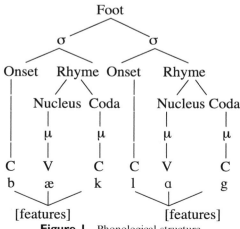

**Figure 1**  Phonological structure.

the question of which extralinguistic factors (e.g., age, motivation, learning style) may be influencing the learner's proficiency. Due to space limitations, I will only consider one such factor here as it is known to affect L2 production—that is, the age of the learner.

## C. Age Effects

Many in the SLA field (e.g., Birdsong 1999; Hyltenstam & Abrahamsson, 2000) have investigated the question of whether adults can attain native-like proficiency in a second language. Often this question is investigated under the rubric of the *critical period hypothesis* (see Singleton, 1989). There are undeniably some age-related effects in second language learning. For example, people who start acquiring their L2 early are less likely to have a strong non-native accent than those who start learning later in life. However, we must always remind ourselves that pronunciation is a small part of L2 communicative competence (see Bachman, 1990). White and Genesee (1996) have demonstrated that some non-native speakers who started their L2 learning later in their lives *can* evidence grammatical knowledge and performance that is statistically indistinguishable from native speakers when it comes to aspects of syntax. But what about L2 phonology? Bongaerts (1999) provides a summary of a number of projects, which demonstrate that late L2 learners can attain native-like performance in pronunciation as well. Bongaerts, van Summeren, Planken, and Schils (1997) showed that there were some instructed second language learners who were not significantly different from native speakers in terms of their production. Bongaerts, Mennen, and van der Slik (2000) demonstrate that this is also true of uninstructed learners as well. Thus, we note that while there is still a definite connection between age of acquisition and degree of foreign accent, it is not the case that it becomes impossible for adults to acquire phonological ability that is indistinguishable from native speakers. However, the question that remains unanswered is this: If there are some people who are able to achieve this, what factors contribute to their success?

The givens of our field of study, then, appear to be the following:

(1) L2 learners of phonology are attempting to acquire a complex system of knowledge.
(2) The learner's L1 influences his/her interlanguage grammar considerably.
(3) Extralinguistic factors such as age also exert an influence on elements of the learner's grammar.

Even accepting these facts, though, does not mean that all researchers agree on how best to explain these facts.

## D. Diverse Theoretical Approaches

Broadly speaking, in the field of SLA, we are trying to answer the question: why do second language learners sound different than native speakers do? In the phonological domain, we might ask: why do some learners master some sounds but do not master others? Obviously, one could tackle these questions from a variety of theoretical perspectives (see Archibald (2002) for more discussion).

- Accents are social constructs brought about by the fact that people use language in a social context (Schumann, 1976).

- Accents are the result of universals reflected in language typology (Eckman & Iverson, 1993, 1994).
- Accents are the result of phonetic phenomena either articulatory or perceptual (e.g., Flege, 1995).
- Accents are the result of phonological phenomena.

Oversimplifying slightly, in this chapter, I am going to explore the research program that suggests that the final approach has been the most productive. The stance I am going to take is that much of second language accent can be explained by linguistic theory.

## E. The Deficit Hypothesis

Elsewhere in the field of SLA, we have witnessed a debate between those who argue that certain linguistic properties (e.g., some functional category features) may be unable to be acquired by adult speakers (e.g., Hawkins & Chan, 1997; Hawkins, this volume) and those (such as White, 2003) who argue that adult learners *are* able to acquire these features. The first line of thought is what we can call the *Deficit Hypothesis*. The deficit hypothesis holds that if element $x$ is not found in the first language then it will be unlearnable in adult SLA. So, from a deficit perspective it would be argued if a speaker's L1 lacks a morphosyntactic [±past] feature then it will be impossible for that learner to acquire the feature [±past] in an L2. The opposing view would hold that the lack of surface inflection in production does not entail the lack of the appropriate linguistic feature in the grammar. Lardiere (1998) argued that a Chinese L1 subject who was consistently omitting tense markers in her English L2 production also showed evidence of having acquired the abstract feature related to finiteness in her grammar (see White, this volume, and Hawkins, this volume, for further discussion).

Let us return to the field of L2 phonology. In many second language learning scenarios, we may find that someone from a given L1 is attempting to acquire an L2 which has some different phonological properties. Perhaps a feature may be lacking, or the onsets don't branch, or the codas don't project moras, or the feet are iambic rather than trochaic. The empirical question is: will second language learners be able to acquire structures that are not found in their first language? A classic treatment of this question can be found in the work of Brown (1997, 2000). We will begin our analysis of L2 features by discussing Brown's model.

## II. PHONOLOGICAL FEATURES

Brown (2000) argues that if featural representations are lacking from the L1, then they will be unacquirable in the L2. She looked at the acquisition of English /l/ and /r/ by speakers of Japanese and Mandarin Chinese (neither of which contrasts /l/ and /r/ phonemically). The Japanese situation is diagrammed in Figure 2, where SV stands for sonorant voice:

In Japanese, [l] and [ɾ] are allophones of a single phoneme. This phoneme may appear only in a simple onset in Japanese. Mandarin Chinese also lacks the contrast

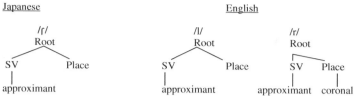

**Figure 2**   Feature geometry of liquids.

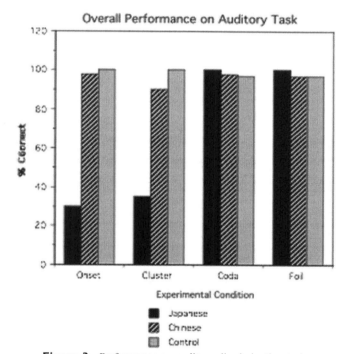

**Figure 3**   Performance on auditory discrimination task.

(and hence the structure is the same as shown in Figure 2). If the *segment* is taken to be the level of explanation, then we might predict that both Mandarin and Japanese speakers should be unable to acoustically discriminate /l/ from /r/ (given their L1 feature geometries).

The graph in Figure 3 shows the overall performance of the subjects on an auditory discrimination task. Such a task demands that a listener hear two stimuli (e.g., "rip/ lip" or "lip/lip") and judge whether they are the same or different (known as an AX discrimination task).

This graph demonstrates that the Japanese speakers were unable to discriminate /l/ from /r/ in an acoustic task, whereas the Chinese speakers discriminated the contrast successfully. The same results were obtained in a task that demanded the subjects access lexical representations (i.e., they saw a picture of a "rake" and of a "lake" and, when hearing a single word, had to point out the picture of the word that they heard.

(a)

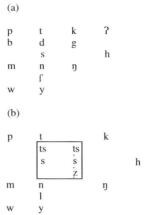

(b)

**Figure 4**  Chinese and Japanese inventories. (a) Japanese inventory; and (b) Mandarin Chinese inventory.

The initial hypothesis that speakers of both languages would be unable to perceive the /l-r/ distinction because one of the members of the contrast is an L1 *phoneme* is not supported by the Chinese subjects. So, what aspect of the L1 could be accounting for this difference? Brown suggests that a speaker may be able to perceive a non-native contrast if the *feature* that distinguishes the two segments is present in the L1 feature geometry (even if the feature is not utilized for the contrast in question). Under her analysis, it is the feature [coronal] that distinguishes /l/ from /r/. Chinese requires the coronal node for some features but Japanese does not. The inventories are given in Figure 4.

Regardless, then, of the L1 liquid inventory, the Chinese speaker will have a representation for the feature [coronal] somewhere in the phonological inventory (i.e., to contrast alveolar from postalveolar segments shown in the box). The Japanese inventory, on the other hand, does not contrast any coronal phonemes and will, therefore, lack a coronal node. Thus, Brown concludes that L2 speakers cannot build representations for segments that require features not present in their L1. They can, however, combine the features of their L1 in new ways to yield new segments.

## A.  A Nondeficit Stance

There may be reason to believe, however, that this deficit model is too strong. There are a number of studies suggesting that circumstances exist where adult second language learners can acquire phonological contrasts even when the relevant feature is inactive in their L1.

Larson-Hall (2004) is one such study. She looks at the perceptual abilities of Japanese speakers learning Russian. Remember that Brown argued that the Japanese subjects were unable to acquire the English [l]/[r] contrast in onsets because they lacked the relevant phonological feature in their L1. The graph in Figure 5 clearly shows that the Japanese learners of Russian were able to perceive the contrast successfully.

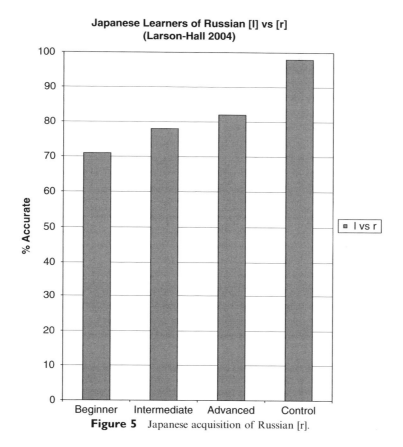

**Figure 5** Japanese acquisition of Russian [r].

Even the beginners were accurate more than 70% of the time (contrasted with the 30% accuracy of Brown's learners of English [ɹ]). One possible explanation for this is that the Russian [r] is a trilled sound, which makes it very salient in the input to the L2 learners. When the phonetic cues are robust, it is possible to override the effects of the L1 filter (see Wright 2004 of a discussion of robust cues).

Additional complexities are revealed in work by Curtin, Goad, and Pater (1998). They document a case study where English speakers learning Thai are able to acquire a feature that is not present in their L1. The property in question is aspiration, which is most likely represented by the feature [spread glottis]. English does not make use of the phonetic feature of aspiration contrastively in its lexical items. Ignoring some complexities, suffice it to say that English has aspirated stops at the beginning of stressed syllables (e.g., "top" [tʰɑp]) but lacks aspiration after an [s] (e.g., "stop" [stɑp]). Aspiration, then, in English is predictable from the phonetic context and does not have to be memorized as part of the word. Thai, on the other hand, utilizes aspiration contrastively. For example, the word [pet] means "duck" and the word [pʰet] means "spicy." English speakers learning Thai, then, would have to learn how to store the feature of aspiration as part of the lexical entry. Curtin et al. (1998) argued that English speakers *did* show the ability over time to lexicalize this phonological feature. That is to say that while their initial structures were transferred from the L1, they *were* able to trigger new knowledge.

Gonzalez (in preparation) also provides evidence of a situation where L2 learners are able to acquire a contrast based on a feature absent from their L1. He looks at the acquisition of Yucatec Maya ejectives by Spanish speakers. Spanish lacks the [constricted glottis] feature required for the phonological structure of ejectives. He conducted both an auditory discrimination task and a force-choice picture selection task. The results of the auditory discrimination task are shown in Figure 6.

In onset position, the Spanish speakers were not performing significantly differently from the native Yucatec Maya speakers; they were able to acquire the contrast in that position. In the coda position, however, they were not behaving in a native-like range. One explanation for this goes back to the notion of robust phonetic cues. The transitional cue from the ejective in onset position to the vowel is much more robust than the phonetic cue found when an ejective is at the end of a word. Learners appear to be sensitive to such distinctions. Gonzalez found the same basic results in his picture-selection task, but there are added complications that prevent full explication here. Suffice it to say that there were confounds with word familiarity in the subjects.

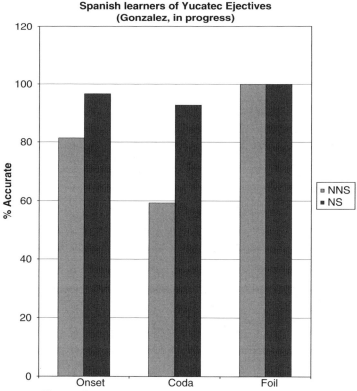

**Figure 6**  Spanish acquisition of Yucatec Maya ejectives.

For words that they knew quite well, they were very good at detecting the contrast. However, in less familiar lexical items, they were not as accurate.

LaCharité and Prévost (1999) proposed a refinement of Brown's model. In looking at French speakers acquiring English, they proposed a hierarchy of difficulty for new sounds. Whereas Brown argued that if a feature was lacking from the L1 then any contrast dependent on that feature could not be acquired, LaCharité & Prévost argued that a missing articulator node would be more difficult to acquire than a missing terminal node. French learners of English have to acquire the sounds [h] and [θ]. They propose the representations of Figure 7 for these sounds:

The features in boldface are the ones absent from the French inventory. They predict that the acquisition of [h] will be more difficult than the acquisition of [θ] because [h] requires the learner to trigger a new articulator node. On a discrimination task, the learners were significantly less accurate identifying [h] than identifying [θ]; however, on a word identification task (involving lexical access) there was no significant difference between the performance on [h] versus [θ]. Mah (2003) conducted an event-related potential (ERP) study, which looked at English speakers acquiring French and Spanish "r" sounds. Under her analysis, English lacks a pharyngeal node ([h] being laryngeal) while French [R] is analyzed as pharyngeal. Spanish [r], on the other hand, is coronal. The acquisition of both French and Spanish "r" will require English speakers to activate a new terminal node, which Mah defines as [vibrant]. In her analysis of the processing of these two "r" sounds, Mah did not find any differences between the perception of a French "r" as opposed to the Spanish "r." This is an argument against the LaCharité & Prévost position.

## B. The Speech Learning Model

No discussion of second language phonology would be complete without even a brief mention of the Speech Learning Model of Flege. Flege is a very prolific researcher, but his (1995) chapter provides a good overview of the model. He is primarily concerned with phonetic aspects of L2 speech. Many of his empirical studies have attempted to answer the question *why are some sounds harder to learn than others?* His explanation centers on the comparison between L1 and L2 sounds. There are three possible relationships between these sounds: (1) the L2 sound is *identical* to the L1 sounds, (2) the L2 sound is *similar* to the L1 sound, and (3) the L2 sound is *new*. He predicts that (1) will be a case of ease of learning as the L2 sound is mapped directly onto the L1 category. A case might be the [m] of English and the [m] of German. These

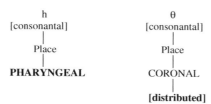

**Figure 7**   Articulator versus terminal nodes in English.

sounds are virtually identical and appear to propose no difficulty for second language learners. Cases such as (3) are also predicted to result in ease of learning because the new L2 sound is so different from any existing L1 category that a new category can be set up. An example of this might be the learning of Yucatec Maya ejectives ([p'], [t'], and [k']). However, the case of (2) is predicted to cause learning difficulty. An English alveolar [t] is quite similar to a French dental [t̪], and this similarity may block the formation of a new phonetic category. The interested reader is recommended to consult the original works of Flege, many of which are available online at: http://www.jimflege.com/.

## III. SYLLABLES

Let us turn now to another example of hierarchical structure at a higher level: the syllable. A common model of syllable structure is shown in Figure 8.

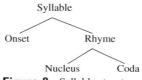

**Figure 8**  Syllable structure.

The languages of the world vary according to such things as whether syllabic nodes can branch. Some languages (e.g., Japanese) do not allow branching onsets or codas. A common phenomenon in second language learning involves modifying an L2 word so that it fits the L1 syllable structure. Consider the words given in (1) spoken by someone whose L1 is Arabic (these examples come from Broselow, 1988):

(1)  | English target | Non-native speaker's version |
     |----------------|------------------------------|
     | plant          | pilanti                      |
     | Fred           | Fired                        |
     | translate      | tiransilet                   |

Arabic does not allow branching onsets or codas, so an English word like *plant* cannot be mapped onto a single Arabic syllable.

As this example helps show, we can explain why Arabic speakers pronounce English words in the way that they do by investigating the principles of syllabification in the L1. Especially at the beginning levels of proficiency, the structure of the interlanguage (IL) is influenced by the structure of the L1. This would suggest that learners are clearly transferring the L1 principles of syllabification.

Now let us look more closely at the acquisition of consonant clusters. Most of the consonant clusters in the world's languages obey what is known as the Sonority Sequencing Generalization (diagrammed in Figure 9), which captures the fact that the nucleus of a syllable is the most sonorous element (that is, the vowel), and sonority diminishes toward the edges, [p] and [t] being less sonorant than [l] and [n]:There are,

**Figure 9**   The Sonority Sequencing Generalization.

however, sequences of consonants that violate this generalization, and they tend to involve the phoneme /s/.

In English some s-clusters violate sonority sequencing (e.g., "st" since the fricative [s] is more sonorous than the stop [t]) while some do not (e.g., "sn" where the fricative [s] is less sonorous than the nasal [n]).

The analysis of the structure of s-clusters is a complex and problematic area of phonological theory, and I will not go into the details here. Many researchers argue that [s] is what is known as *extrasyllabic*. In other words, it is not really part of the syllable, but somehow outside it. The interesting fact, bringing all this back to SLA, is that L2 learners are aware of this.

Carlisle (1997) looked at how Spanish speakers deal with English onset clusters. He notes that three-consonant clusters are changed significantly more often than two-consonant clusters. Carlisle (1991), in a study on two-segment onsets, found that Spanish speakers modified onsets that violated the Sonority Sequencing Generalization (e.g., st-) significantly more often than they modified those that did not (e.g., sn-).

Broselow (1992) shows that Arabic speakers treat s-clusters that violate the Sonority Sequencing Generalization differently than those that do not as shown in (2):

(2)   sweater → [siwɛtar]      study → [istadi]
       slide → [silayd]          ski → [iski]

Singh (1985) demonstrates the same pattern for Hindi speakers as shown in (3):

(3)   fruit → [fırut]           school → [ıskul]
       please → [pılız]          spelling → [ıspɛliŋ]

Samarajiwa and Abeysekera (1964) show the same pattern by native speakers of Sinhalese speaking Sanskrit, given in (4).

(4)   Sanskrit         Sinhalese
       tyage →          [tiyage]        'gift'
       sriyavə →        [siriyavə]      'grace'
       stri →           [istiri]        'woman'

These data suggest that L2 learners have full access to the principles of sonority sequencing regardless of their L1 experience. A recent paper by Cardoso (2007) also addresses this issue. He looks at Portuguese learners of English (Portuguese lacks onset clusters) and investigates two hypotheses as to the developmental path that the learners will follow. Hypothesis A is that the learners will acquire the less marked clusters (e.g., [sl]) before the more marked clusters (e.g., [st]). Hypothesis B is that the learners will acquire the most frequent clusters in the input ([st]) before the less frequent ones ([sl]). Analyzing the production of his subjects demonstrated that the

Portuguese learners followed the path predicted by markedness. Even though the [st] clusters were *much* more frequent in the input to the learners, they still acquired the [sl] cluster before the [st] cluster.

The work of Eckman and Iverson (1993, 1994) also clearly demonstrate that syllable structure can be changed in L2 learning. People can learn to pronounce new clusters that are not found in their L1.

Abrahamsson (2003) provides one of the best overviews of the studies into the SLA of syllable structure. He focuses on the patterns of acquisition in coda position. Abrahamsson looks at the different types of repair strategies that are available to a learner whose L1 does not sanction coda consonants. Two strategies that are covered are epenthesis and deletion. Consider the examples in (5):

(5)  | **Target Word** | **Deleted Form** | **Epenthesized Form** |
|---|---|---|
| *when* | [wɛ] | [wɛnə] |
| *wet* | [wɛ] | [wɛtə] |
| *went* | [wɛ] | [wɛntə] |

As the above example illustrates, the *deleted* forms are much more difficult to recover for the listener than are the *epenthesized* forms. Abrahamsson hypothesizes that the proportion of epenthesis to deletion repairs will increase as a subject's overall proficiency increases.

He looks at speakers of Chinese (who allow at most one consonant in the coda) learning Swedish (which allows, or as Abrahamsson puts it, has a "pain threshold of," five consonants at the end of a word). Subjects were recorded nine times with 3–5 weeks between recordings. The first recording took place 10–24 days after their arrival in Sweden. The tenth recording took place one year after the ninth. For all three subjects, the proportion of epenthesis to deletion increased over time (Figure 10).

Furthermore, Abrahamsson showed that subjects modified (epenthesis and deletion) inflected forms significantly more often that monomorphemic lexical forms. In addition, subjects used epenthesis as a repair strategy more on monomorphemic lexical items than they did on inflected items, as shown in the graph in Figure 11.

They also used inflection more often on open class lexical items than closed class lexical items. Abrahamsson proposes a functional explanation for this: there is a greater possibility for ambiguity in open class words than closed class words, and therefore recoverability will be enhanced for the listener by epenthesizing the open class words. As there are fewer lexical competitors for closed class words, the subjects are freer to delete sounds from them and the message will still be conveyed.

Lin (2001) presents another take on the syllable simplification strategies used by second language learners. Lin looks at the effects of different tasks, or different register as stimulated by a given task, on the accuracy of consonant cluster production. S/he argues that more formal registers do not lead to greater accuracy, as had been suggested in other studies (e.g., Tarone, 1983), but rather that the formality of the register correlates with the *type* of repair strategy used. S/he suggests that epenthesis is used relatively more often in more formal contexts (where focus is on the form of the utterance, rather than on the content). Conversely, deletion and substitution will be used relatively more often in less formal contexts.

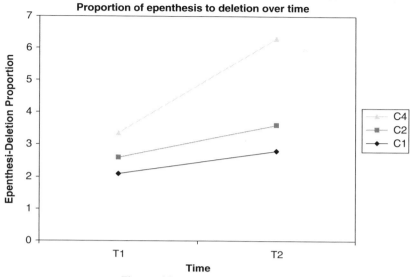

**Figure 10**   Modification strategies.

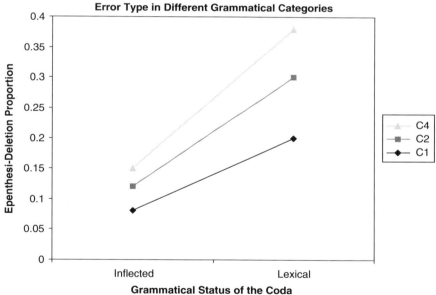

**Figure 11**   Effect of grammatical category.

In this study, Lin looked at 20 Chinese speakers producing a variety of two-consonant onset clusters (e.g., [pj], [dr], [fl], [sn]) in English monosyllables. Subjects were taught the meanings of a variety of words (and pseudowords) and were given 15 min to learn them and practice pronouncing them. The four tasks were: (1) reading minimal pairs with normal orthography *and* phonetic transcription, (2) reading randomized list of target words in normal orthography, (3) reading two sentences out loud in a grammaticality judgment task, and (4) controlled conversation, or structured interview. Task (1) was assumed to be the most formal, moving down the scale to task (4), which was assumed to be the most casual.

There were no significant differences in overall error *rates* between the four tasks, as shown in Figure 12.

However, as predicted, there was a significant decrease in the amount of epenthesis as the task formality decreased, as shown in Figure 13.

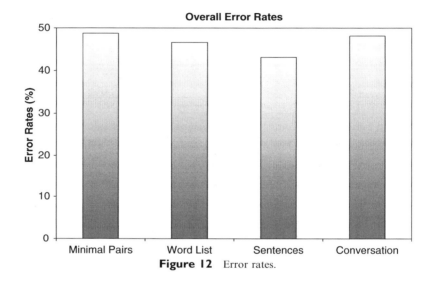

**Figure 12**   Error rates.

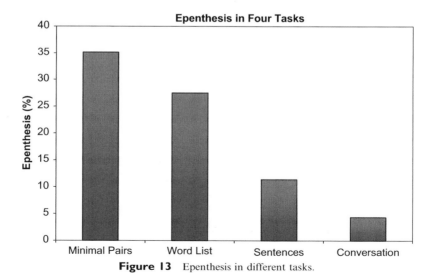

**Figure 13**   Epenthesis in different tasks.

## IV. MORAS

At another level of phonological structure, the moraic level, we also see that learners are transferring their L1 phonological structures as shown by Broselow and Park in their paper on mora conservation in L2 phonology.

Broselow and Park (1995) began by presenting the data given in (6) from native speakers of Korean who were learning English:

(6)  a. bitʰɨ      "beat"       b. bit       "bit"
       čipʰɨ      "cheap"          tʰip      "tip"
       pʰikʰɨ     "peak"           pʰik      "pick"
       rutʰɨ      "route"          gut       "good"
       khotʰɨ     "coat"           buk       "book"

Note that the Korean speakers insert an epenthetic [ɨ] at the end of the words in column (a), but not at the end of the words in column (b). Each of the words in the two columns ends in the same consonant, so it cannot be triggered by the final consonant in the English word. Broselow and Park suggested that it is the quality of the vowel in the English root that determines whether epenthesis takes place. The epenthetic vowel is added to words that have long (bimoraic) vowels and not to words that have short (monomoraic) vowels. What would cause this difference in behavior?

Broselow and Park (1995) assumed coda obstruents are nonmoraic in Korean. Syllabic nuclei must be monomoraic in Korean (contrasted with English, in which they may be either mono- or bimoraic). In their view, the L2 learner begins by perceiving the L2 English input of a word like "beat," and setting up a representation that includes a bimoraic vowel, as shown in (7):

(7)   μ μ
       \/
      b i t

Because this is an illicit structure in Korean, the second mora is delinked from the vowel as in (8):

(8)   μ μ
       \×
      b i t

This triggers epenthesis, which fills the empty mora, and then onset formation occurs as in (9):

(9)    σ   σ
       |   |
       μ   μ
       |   |
       b i t i

They argue, then, that what the Korean learners are doing is attempting to preserve the mora count of the original English word (which has two moras attached to the vowel). Because this is an illicit structure in Korean, they set up a new syllable that allows the bimoraic structure to be preserved.

Work by Summerell (2007) also looks at the acquisition of moraic structures. She looked at the acquisition of Japanese length contrasts (in both consonants and vowels) by native speakers of English. Japanese has minimal pairs based on length shown in (10).

(10) *kite* (wear)
 *kiite* (listen)
 *kitte* (stamp)

English has a contrast between tense vowels (which are bimoraic) and lax vowels (which are monomoraic), but the difference is manifested as quality (e.g., [i] vs. [ɪ]) not length (e.g., [ii] vs. [i]). English does not have a phonemic length distinction when it comes to consonants. Will English speakers be able to acquire Japanese length? Summerell (2007) conducted both an auditory discrimination task and a forced-choice picture selection task. The results of the auditory discrimination task are shown in Table I.

The non-native speakers were not performing significantly differently than the native speaker control group. This is true for the groups with beginner, intermediate, and advanced levels of proficiency. The results from the picture selection task are given in Table II.

Here we note that there is a significant difference between the native speakers and the non-native speakers. However, this difference is due to differential performance between groups. The beginners were significantly different from the control group, but both the intermediate and advanced groups were performing at native-like levels of

TABLE I
**Results from Discrimination Task**

| Contrast | Group | % Correct | Mann–Whitney U | Probability |
|----------|-------|-----------|----------------|-------------|
| V vs. VV | L1 English | 95.58 | 187.00 | 0.290 |
|          | L1 Japanese | 96.88 | | |
| C vs. CC | L1 English | 95.08 | 223.50 | 0.677 |
|          | L1 Japanese | 94.63 | | |

TABLE II
**Results from Picture Selection Task**

| Contrast | Group | % Correct | Mann–Whitney U | Probability |
|----------|-------|-----------|----------------|-------------|
| V vs. VV | L1 English | 94.96 | 137.50 | 0.011* |
|          | L1 Japanese | 100 | | |
| C vs. CC | L1 English | 89.23 | 114.50 | 0.005* |
|          | L1 Japanese | 99.13 | | |

* Significant difference.

accuracy. Under one interpretation, then, English speakers (who lack consonantal length) are able to acquire this feature in their second language. See Summerell (2007) for a more extended discussion on how the English speakers are redeploying their L1 property of weight-by-position (where coda consonants are moraic) to acquire Japanase geminate consonants (which are also moraic).

## V. STRESS

A number of papers have addressed the question of L2 learners acquiring stress. Table III below illustrates how languages may differ in their parameter settings with respect to stress. When the parameter settings are different in the first and the second language, we have the potential for transfer. Often, the L1 parameter settings transfer into the L2.

Archibald (1993) showed that L2 learners were able to reset their existing parameters to new values. (see Van der Pas & Zonneveld, 2004 for counter-arguments.) In other words, if your L1 is quantity-sensitive to the nucleus (i.e., a long vowel attracts stress) you will be able to acquire the English setting of having your stress system sensitive to the rhyme (where a closed syllable can also attract stress). What this study revealed was that a simplistic view of stress assignment is not supported. A simple proposal would follow these lines: Hungarian has a rule of initial stress assignment which will transfer into English; Polish has a rule of penultimate stress assignment which will transfer into English. The adoption of this parameter-setting analysis reveals that both what transfers into the interlanguage grammar, and the nature of the interlanguage grammar is much subtler. Our representations must include constructs like quantity-sensitivity, extrameticality and the like.

Pater (1997) examined the acquisition of English stress by French speakers. Under his analysis, Quebec French is a quantity-insensitive language with unbounded feet (unlike English's trochaic binary feet). He had subjects produce nonce forms in English which were designed to reveal whether the French speakers had acquired English foot structure and quantity sensitivity. Pater argued that they had. Once again, it seems that the acquisition of stress shows that learners can reset their L1 grammatical settings.

### TABLE III
### Metrical Parameters

|  | Spanish | Polish | Hungarian | English |
|---|---|---|---|---|
| P1 (word tree) | Right | Right | Left | Right |
| P2 (foot type) | Binary | Binary | Binary | Binary |
| P3 (strong on) | Right | Right | Left | Right |
| P4 (built from) | Left | Left | Left | Left |
| P5 (Quantity sensitive) | Yes | No | Yes | No |
| P6 (sensitive to) | Rhyme | NA | Nucleus | Rhyme |
| P8 (extrametrical) | Yes | No | No | Yes |
| P8A (extrametrical on) | Right | NA | NA | Right |

However, we must also ask the question of whether subjects whose first languages did not have stress accent but rather had tone or pitch accent were able to trigger these metrical representations. Archibald (1997a) argued that Chinese and Japanese subjects learning English did not compute metrical representations but rather stored stress placement for each lexical item. Ou and Ota (2004) argue that Chinese learners of English show sensitivity to syllable weight in a perception test of English words and hence that these subjects are able to engage in a computational process to generate stress placement. This would be further evidence that second language learners are able to create new representations that are not found in their L1. Similarly, Kawagoe (2003) argues that Japanese learners of English *are* able to acquire a computational system for English metrical properties building on their L1 system of loanword phonology adaptation. This would be another example of how L1 knowledge in one phonological domain can be redeployed to acquire new knowledge in an L2.

## VI. RHYTHM

While pedagogic treatments of L2 rhythm abound (primarily focusing on the differences between so-called stress-timed and syllable-timed languages), there have been relatively few empirical studies of this phenomenon. Guilbault (2002) investigates the acquisition of French rhythm by English L2 learners. French has been argued to be a language where there is much more equal duration of syllables (syllable-timed) than in English (stress-timed). He argues that advanced L2 learners of French have modified the temporal properties of their speech to approximate its rhythmic patterns. See also Archibald (1997b) for an investigation of the L2 acquisition of phrasal stress.

## VII. INTONATION

There are very few studies on the acquisition of L2 intonation carried out within a generative framework. To understand why this would be the case, we need merely go back to the question posed at the beginning of this chapter: what is being acquired? In order to understand how syllable structure is acquired, we need to have a model of what syllable structure *is*. In order to understand how people arrive at knowledge of intonation in a second language, we need to have a model of what exactly native speakers of a language know when they can produce and perceive intonation patterns in their first language. And this is where we find relatively little agreement in the generative literature (see Ladd, 1996 for a discussion).

One exception is the work of Jilka (2000). Working within the ToBI system, Jilka demonstrates that a non-native intonation pattern is a robust cue to non-native-like phonology. Native speakers of English were recorded speaking German, and native speakers of German were recorded speaking English. All subjects were assessed as having high levels of proficiency and high levels of segmental accuracy. For all subjects, the non-native utterances were "corrected" by an automated program.

Both raw and corrected versions of the sentences were played (non-sequentially) to native speaker judges. A significant number of the native-speaking judges judged the corrected versions to be more native-like than the raw versions.


## VIII. WORK WITHIN OPTIMALITY THEORY

The advent of Optimality Theory has spawned much work in the fields of both first and SLA of phonology. Escudero's (2005) thesis provides a good overview of many of the current issues within this framework. However, I will focus on a discussion of the work of Broselow, Chen, and Wang (1998) and Broselow (2004), as I believe it is accessible without getting caught up in too many details of theoretical machinery. Optimality theory (Prince & Smolensky, 1993) is a theory of phonological competence, which invokes a ranked set of violable constraints that guide the output of the speaker. Constraints that are highly ranked are violated at great cost, while lower-ranked constraints can be violated quite easily. Constraint rankings are specific to each language and, therefore, the goal in learning a second language is to acquire the appropriate constraint rankings.

Broselow et al. (1998) look at the acquisition of English coda consonants by native speakers of Mandarin. Mandarin allows only glides and nasals in coda position, while English allows a range of sonorants *and* both voiced and voiceless obstruents. The data presented show that the Mandarin speakers tended to devoice their final voiced obstruents in English. The question that immediately arises is "where does this pattern come from?" There is nothing in L1 grammar that says to devoice obstruents, since no coda obstruents are allowed. There is nothing in the L2 input to reveal this pattern either, as English speakers produce both voiced and unvoiced obstruents. Broselow et al. note that universally voiceless codas are less marked than voiced codas. Therefore, a markedness constraint would exist which would favor voicelss codas and disfavor voiced codas. This constraint is part of the universal constraint set found in universal grammar. The L1 grammar does not allow us to see the evidence for this constraint, but as we chart the developmental path of the interlanguage grammar we can see the emergence of the unmarked coda pattern. The behavior of these L2 learners, then, provides an example of what is called in the Optimality Theory literature *the emergence of the unmarked*. Studies such as these show us that linguistic theory can help to explain learner behavior, but that studies in SLA can also be very useful for construction and testing of new linguistic theories.


## IX. SUMMARY

When we probe the construct of second language accent, we can demonstrate the complexity of the phonological grammars of language learners. Linguistic theory and the field of SLA combine to explain the nature of the mental representations that underlie second language speech.

## REFERENCES

Abrahamsson, N. (2003). Development and recoverability of L2 codas. *Studies in Second Language Acquisition, 25*, 313–349.

Archibald, J. (1993). *Language learnability and L2 phonology: The acquisition of metrical parameters.* Dordrecht: Kluwer.

Archibald, J. (1997a). The acquisition of English stress by speakers of non-accentual languages: Lexical storage versus computation of stress. *Linguistics, 35*(1), 167–181.

Archibald, J. (1997b). The acquisition of L2 phrasal stress: A pilot study. In S. J. Hannahs & M. Young-Scholten (Eds.), *Focus on phonological acquisition.* Amsterdam: John Benjamins.

Archibald, J. (1998). *Second language phonology.* Amsterdam: John Benjamins.

Archibald, J. (2002). Models of phonological acquisition. In B. Swierzbin, et al. (Eds.), *Selected Proceeding of the Second Language Research Forum 2000.* Somerville, MA: Cascadilla Press.

Bachman, L. (1990). *Fundamental considerations in language testing.* Oxford, UK: Oxford University Press.

Birdsong, D. (Ed.). (1999). *Second language acquisition and the critical period hypothesis.* Mahwah, NJ: Lawrence Erlbaum.

Bongaerts, T. (1999). Ultimate attainment in L2 pronunciation: The case of very advanced late L2 learners. In D. Birdsong (Ed.), *Second language acquisition and the critical period hypothesis* (pp. 133–159). Mahwah, NJ: Lawrence Erlbaum.

Bongaerts, T., Mennen, S., & van der Slik, F. (2000). Authenticity of pronunciation in naturalistic second language acquisition: The case of very advanced learners of Dutch as a second language. *Studia Linguistica, 54*(2), 298–308.

Bongaerts, T., van Summeren, C., Planken, B., & Schils, E. (1997). Age and ultimate attainment in the pronunciation of a foreign language. *Studies in Second Language Acquisition, 19*, 447–465.

Broselow, E. (1988). Prosodic phonology and the acquisition of a second language. In S. Flynn & W. O'Neil (Eds.), *Linguistic theory in second language acquisition* (pp. 295–308). Dordrecht: Kluwer.

Broselow, E. (1992). Transfer and universals in second language epenthesis. In S. Gass & L. Selinker (Eds.), *Language transfer in language learning* (pp. 71–86). Amsterdam: John Benjamins.

Broselow, E. (2004). Unmarked structures and emergent rankings in second language phonology. *International Journal of Bilingualism, 8*(1), 51–66.

Broselow, E., Chen, S.-I., & Wang, C. (1998). The emergence of the unmarked in second language phonology. *Studies in Second Language Acquisition, 20*, 261–280.

Broselow, E., & Park, H.-B. (1995). Mora conservation in second language prosody. In J. Archibald (Ed.), *Phonological acquisition and phonological theory* (pp. 151–168). Mahwah, NJ: Lawrence Erlbaum.

Brown, C. (1997). *Acquisition of segmental structure: Consequences for speech perception and second language acquisition.* Ph.D. dissertation, McGill University.

Brown, C. (2000). The interrelation between speech perception and phonological acquisition from infant to adult. In J. Archibald (Ed.), *Second language acquisition and linguistic theory* (pp. 4–63). Malden, MA: Blackwell.

Cardoso, W. (2007). *The development of sC onset clusters in interlanguage: Markedness versus frequency effects.* Paper presented at GASLA 9, University of Iowa.

Carlisle, R. S. (1991). The influence of environment on vowel epenthesis in Spanish/English interphonology. *Applied Linguistics*, *12*, 76–95.

Carlisle, R. S. (1997). The modification of onsets in a markedness relationship: Testing the Interlanguage Structural Conformity Hypothesis. *Language Learning*, *47*, 327–361.

Curtin, S., Goad, H., & Pater, J. (1998). Phonological transfer and levels of representation: The perceptual acquisition of Thai voice and aspiration by English and French speakers. *Second Language Research*, *14*(4), 389–405.

Eckman, F., & Iverson, G. (1993). Sonority and markedness among onset clusters in the interlanguage of ESL learners. *Second Language Research*, *9*, 234–252.

Eckman, F., & Iverson, G. (1994). Pronunciation difficulties in ESL: Coda consonants in English interlanguage. In M. Yavas (Ed.), *First and second language phonology*. San Diego: Singular Publishing Group.

Escudero, P. (2005). *Linguistic perception and second language acquisition: Explaining the attainment of optimal phonological categorization*. LOT Dissertation Series 113, Utrecht University.

Flege, J. E. (1995). Second-language speech learning: Theory, findings, and problems. In W. Strange (Ed.), *Speech perception and linguistic experience: Issues in cross-language research* (pp. 229–273). Timonium, MD: York Press.

Gonzalez A. (in preparation). *The acquisition of Yucatec Maya ejectives by native speakers of Spanish*. Ph.D. dissertation, University of Calgary.

Guilbault, C. (2002). *The acquisition of French rhythm by English second language learners*. Ph.D. dissertation, University of Alberta.

Hawkins, R., & Chan, Y.-H. C. (1997). The partial availability of Universal Grammar in second language acquisition: The 'failed functional features hypothesis'. *Second Language Research*, *13*, 187–226.

Hyltenstam, K., & Abrahamsson, N. (2000). Who can become native-like in a second language? All, some or none? *Studia Linguistica*, *54*(2), 150–166.

Jilka. M. (2000). *The contribution of intonation to the perception of foreign accent*. Ph.D. dissertation, University of Stuttgart.

Kawagoe, I. (2003). Acquisition of word stress by Japanese learners. In Juana M. Liceras et al. (Eds.), *Proceedings of the 6th Generative Approaches to Second Language Acquisition Conference (GASLA 2002)*, pp. 161–167.

LaCharité, D., & Prévost, P. (1999). The role of L1 and of teaching in the acquisition of English sounds by Francophones. In A. Greenhill, H. Littlefield, & C. Tano (Eds.), *The Proceedings of BUCLD 23* (pp. 373–385). Somerville, MA: Cascadilla Press.

Ladd, R. (1996). *Intonational phonology*. Cambridge, UK: Cambridge University Press.

Lardiere, D. (1998). Case and tense in the 'fossilized' steady state. *Second Language Research*, *14*, 1–26.

Larson-Hall, J. (2004). Predicting perceptual success with segments: A test of Japanese speakers of Russian. *Second Language Research*, *20*(1), 33–76.

Lin, Y.-H. (2001). Syllable simplification strategies: A stylistic perspective. *Language Learning*, *51*(4), 681–718.

Mah, J. (2003). *The acquisition of phonological features in a second language*. M.A. thesis, University of Calgary.

Major, R. (2001). *Foreign accent: The ontogeny and phylogeny of second language phonology*. Mahwah, NJ: Lawrence Erlbaum.

Ou, S.-C., & Ota, M. (2004). *Metrical computation in L2 stress acquisition: Evidence from Chinese–English interlanguage*. Paper presented at Laboratory Phonology 9.

Pater, J. (1997). Metrical parameter missetting in second language acquisition. In S. J. Hannahs & M. Young-Scholten (Eds.), *Focus on phonological acquisition* (pp. 235–262). Amsterdam: John Benjamins.

Prince, A., & Smolensky, P. (1993). *Optimality theory*. Rutgers manuscript.

Samarajiwa, C., & Abeysekera, R. M. (1964). Some pronunciation difficulties of Sinhalese learners of English as a foreign language. *Language Learning, 14*, 45–50.

Schumann, J. (1976). Social distance as a factor in second language acquisition. *Language Learning, 26*(1), 135–143.

Singh, R. (1985). Prosodic adaptation in interphonology. *Lingua, 67*, 269–282.

Singleton, D. (1989). *Language acquisition: The age factor*. Clevedon, UK: Multilingual Matters.

Summerell, F. (2007). *The L2 acquisition of Japanese length contrasts*. M.A. thesis, University of Calgary.

Tarone, E. (1983). On the variability of interlanguage systems. *Applied Linguistics, 4*, 142–163.

Van der Pas, B., & Zonneveld, W. (2004). L2 parameter resetting for metrical systems: An assessment and a new interpretation of some core literature. *The Linguistic Review, 21*(1), 125–170.

White, L. (2003). *Second language acquisition and Universal Grammar*. Cambridge, UK: Cambridge University Press.

White, L., & Genesee, F. (1996). How native is near-native? The issue of ultimate attainment in adult second language acquisition. *Second Language Research, 12*, 233–265.

Wright, R. (2004). A review of perceptual cues and cue robustness. In B. Hayes, et al. (Eds.), *Phonetically based phonology* (pp. 34–57). Cambridge, UK: Cambridge University Press.

CHAPTER 12

# L2 PRAGMATIC DEVELOPMENT

Gabriele Kasper

## I. INTRODUCTION

According to one of its many definitions, pragmatics is "the study of language from the point of view of the users, especially of the choices they make, the constraints they encounter in using language in social interaction, and the effects their use of language has on the other participants in an act of communication" (Crystal, 1997, p. 301).

Pragmatics made its entrance to second language (L2) research 30 years ago, mainly under the influence of curricular interests in teaching and testing language for communication and sociolinguistic concerns with intercultural discourse. A few notable precursors in the 1980s aside, studies of how L2 pragmatics is learned first started to slowly gain momentum in the 1990s (Bardovi-Harlig, 1999, 2001b; Kasper & Rose, 2002; Kasper & Schmidt, 1996). In the same period, metatheoretical debates from across the social sciences made their way into second language acquisition (SLA), where they introduced new ontological and epistemological perspectives to the discipline (Zuengler & Miller, 2006). Several of these perspectives have influenced research on L2 pragmatic development as well.

At the time of writing, the most prevalent theoretical and methodological orientations in developmental L2 pragmatics come from cognitive and cultural–historical psychology, linguistic anthropology (language socialization), and sociology (conversation analysis, CA). Although cognitive and cultural–historical psychology share their interest in the development of mind and language, their ontological outlook contrasts markedly and aligns cultural–historical psychology more with language socialization and CA. Cognitive-psychological theories conceptualize L2 learning as the operation of internal cognitive processes, located in the individual learner's mind,

259

and operating on externally available data as well as internal knowledge stores to establish new L2 knowledge. To the extent that social context is accorded a role in L2 acquisition, it is typically conceptualized as a constellation of learner-external factors that may influence learner-internal learning processes and outcomes. In contrast to theories that share the view of SLA as individual cognition, cultural–historical psychology, or, as it is better known in applied linguistics, sociocultural theory (SCT), language socialization, and CA, propose (or are compatible with) L2 learning as a socially constituted—not merely socially influenced—interindividual process, situated in and intertwined with social activities. Theories that share the general ontological premise of L2 learning as socially constituted may differ substantially in other regards, as will be seen later in this chapter.

On the face of it, pragmatics would seem to align itself most readily with the concept of socially constituted SLA. But in tandem with SLA research at large, L2 pragmatics has been strongly influenced by cognitivist perspectives. In analogy to interlanguage grammar, interlanguage phonology, and the interlanguage lexicon, learners' developing L2 pragmatic competence has come to be conceptualized as interlanguage pragmatics (henceforth, ILP) (Bardovi-Harlig & Hartford, 2005; Kasper & Blum-Kulka, 1993). Consistent with the interlanguage concept more broadly, ILP researchers have given particular attention to the differences and similarities between learners' ILP knowledge and use in comparison with those of native speakers of the L1 and the L2, and to the cognitive and interactional processes that may shape learners' pragmatics. A central concern has been pragmatic transfer, the influence of already existing pragmatic knowledge from other languages on the interlanguage (Kasper, 1992; Takahashi, 1996).

Recent comprehensive reviews of L2 pragmatic learning (Bardovi-Harlig, 2001a, 2001b; Kasper & Rose, 2002) have covered such topics as the relationship between L2 grammar and pragmatics (Bardovi-Harlig, 1999, 2006; Niezgoda & Röver, 2001; Schauer, 2006), developmental trajectories (Achiba, 2003; Bardovi-Harlig & Salsbury, 2004; Barron, 2003), social-affective factors (Takahashi, 2005b), and the influence of the learning environment, including pragmatic learning during study abroad (Barron, 2003; Cook, 2008; DuFon & Churchill, 2006), in institutional settings outside of classrooms (Bardovi-Harlig & Hartford, 2005) and under formal instruction (Alcón & Martínez Flor, 2005; Jeon & Kaya, 2006; Kasper, 2001; Rose, 2005; Rose & Kasper, 2001). With the exception of two influential studies by Schmidt (1983) and Schmidt & Frota (1986), the earlier research in particular was largely descriptive rather than theory guided, charting the development of a pragmatic object longitudinally or inferring developmental paths from cross-sectional data (Kasper & Rose, 2002). While the learning *object* was often explicitly conceptualized according to speech act theory (predominantly Searle, 1969, 1976) or politeness theory (Brown & Levinson, 1987), the learning *process* remained untheorized for the most part, or theoretical explanations of the research findings were offered post hoc rather than motivating or guiding the study from the outset.

In the remainder of this chapter, I will review research on L2 pragmatics conducted explicitly under one or more of the theoretical perspectives introduced earlier: individual-cognitive theories, sociocultural theory (SCT), language socialization, and CA.

## II. PRAGMATIC LEARNING AS INDIVIDUAL COGNITION

A productive line of research engages cognitive theories to explain how individual learners develop their ability to comprehend and produce pragmatic meaning in an L2 and their awareness of L2 pragmatics. Not all of this research is developmental, but as comprehension and production processes are seen as constitutive of L2 learning, I will cast the net more widely in this section.

### A. Pragmatic Comprehension

Early research on the comprehension of pragmatic meaning was generated by a processing model according to which the syntactic form of indirect requests determines ease and difficulty of processing in adult (Clark & Lucy, 1975) and child native speakers of English (Carrell, 1981a). Applying the model of syntactically determined processing hierarchies to ESL learners at different proficiency levels, Carrell (1981b) found the same ranking of difficulty across learners. For instance, lower proficiency learners were less successful in understanding syntactically more complex requests incorporating interrogatives and negatives (e.g., "Why color the circle blue?," "Should you color the circle blue?," "You shouldn't color the circle blue"), suggesting an interaction between grammatical and pragmatic knowledge that has come to the fore as a research topic more recently (Bardovi-Harlig, 1999, 2006).

Other theoretical sources for examining how indirect speech acts are understood originated in ordinary language philosophy and made their way into the psychology of L1 and L2 comprehension research. Bringing Grice's (1975) theory of conversational implicature to bear on the examination of how L2 learners comprehend indirect answers, Carrell (1979) found that intermediate and advanced ESL learners' understanding of the target utterances differed significantly from that of an English native speaker group, although within the latter group too, not all of the implicatures were interpreted as expected.

The theme of learners' comprehension of implicature was further developed in a series of studies by Bouton, who examined whether successful implicature interpretation hinges on the type of implicature. Based on an initial cross-sectional study, Bouton conducted the first investigations that charted ESL learners' comprehension of implicature longitudinally. While the students initially showed discrepant interpretations of several implicature types, after four and half years of exposure, the only remaining problematic implicatures related to idiosyncratic and culture-specific content rather than implicature type. However, a group tested after 17 months of residence in the United States had remaining difficulties understanding indirect criticism, sequence implicature, formulaic implicature, and irony, a finding that has been taken to indicate that implicature comprehension should be explicitly taught (Bouton, 1994).

As an alternative to theorizing indirectness in terms of Gricean implicature, a few studies draw on relevance theory (Sperber & Wilson, 1995) in order to account for learners' comprehension of indirectness. In the same vein as Grice's Cooperative Principle, relevance theory underwrites a rationalist account of action, conceptualizing comprehension as a recipient's recognition of the speaker's intention. Relevance theory collapses Grice's four conversational maxims (quality, quantity, relation

(=relevance), and manner) into one, arguing that in interpreting utterances, a recipient selects the most relevant of many candidate meanings in the given context. An inferred meaning is optimally relevant when it has the greatest contextual effect and requires the least processing effort. In a case study on pragmatic inferencing in interactions in a psychiatric ward between a nonnative English speaking nurse and her native English speaking patients and supervisor, Cameron and Williams (1997) find that despite her linguistic limitations, the nurse competently brings relevant cognitive environments to bear on indeterminate utterances, resolves ambiguities, and successfully discharges her professional expertise in the setting.

In contrast to this naturalistic study, and building on Bouton's earlier work, Taguchi (2002) investigated in relevance-theoretical perspective how a small group of L2 learners at two proficiency levels understood indirect answers given as relevance implicatures. Her study introduced two methodological innovations to the researcher-controlled investigation of pragmatic inferencing: the tasks were designed for listening rather than reading comprehension and, in addition to prompting for the result of the comprehension process, a consecutive verbal report component was added to obtain information about the inferential strategies used. Participants arrived at the same, overwhelmingly successful implicature interpretation, suggesting for Taguchi that the predictions of relevance theory extend to L2 listeners regardless of L2 proficiency. Both groups reported using the same categories of inferential strategies and deployed the same number of self-identified strategies in total, but the more advanced group professed more reliance on paralinguistic cues, the adjacency pair rule, and a motivational analysis of speaker intention. The less proficient listeners, on the other hand, reported more frequent inferences based on background knowledge and keywords, an outcome consistent with research on lexical inferencing (Ross, 1997). The findings thus support the view that (socially and cognitively mature) L2 users and learners bring with them universal pragmatic knowledge, including inference heuristics, as an enabling condition for L2 use and learning; however, the current state of L2 grammatical knowledge can inhibit the universal pragmatic knowledge from fully unfolding (Kasper & Rose, 2002). Although Taguchi's study is very small, it opens interesting perspectives for more large-scale investigations of pragmatic inferencing.

A different though related thread of research on pragmatic inferencing takes its cues from Searle's (1975) proposal about how conventionally indirect speech acts are understood. Searle suggested that a recipient starts by understanding the literal meaning of another speaker's utterance first. Upon recognizing that the literal meaning is incoherent in the context, the recipient will invoke the Cooperative Principle and bring the Gricean implicature machinery to bear on the contextualized utterance, identify which of the conversational maxims has, or have, been violated, and through a stepwise inferential process arrive at the conventional utterance meaning. The theory spawned a comprehensive research program in cognitive psychology, exploring the process by which recipients assign meaning to indirect speech acts and nonliteral language use more broadly. Specifically, psychologists have tested three competing models. The "literal meaning first" model reflects Searle's serial theory: the recipient recognizes the literal meaning first, evaluates it as a contextual misfit, and recovers the contextualized conventional meaning through implicature. The multiple meaning model holds that recipients process literal and conventional meanings concurrently and evaluate through contextual information which of the candidate meanings is relevant. Finally, according to the conventional meaning model, the recipient draws on context information to directly assign the conventional meaning to the utterance, without deriving the literal meaning also (Gibbs, 1983).

Early work on pragmatic comprehension in interaction had shown that child L2 speakers were able to infer the meanings of indirect requests in conventional contexts (Ervin-Tripp, Strage, Lampert, & Bell, 1987), and that adult EFL speakers tended to give literal interpretations to indirectly conveyed speech acts (Kasper, 1984). But the methodologies of these studies did not shed light on the processes by which the L2 speakers arrived at their interpretations and were therefore not capable of testing the three processing models. In the first study to undertake just that, Takahashi and Roitblat (1994) probed into advanced ESL readers' online processing of conventionally indirect requests, using a reaction time task with written scenarios. The results support the multiple meaning model of pragmatic comprehension for the advanced L2 English readers as well as for the group of native English readers. The main difference between the two groups was processing speed, with the native readers responding consistently faster. As the authors note, while the results indicate that advanced ESL readers process conventionally indirect requests in the same manner as native English recipients, they raise the question of whether readers with less well developed L2 proficiency infer indirect speech act meaning differently. In addition, the study also raises an issue of stimulus modality: if the scenarios were delivered aurally, how would this affect L2 recipients' comprehension?

Some of these questions were taken up by Taguchi (2005), who investigated Japanese EFL students' listening comprehension of indirectly conveyed meaning in reaction time experiments. In addition to theories of pragmatic comprehension (Grice, 1975; Sperber & Wilson, 1995), the theoretical framework also incorporates from SLA research and cognitive psychology the "accuracy–speed trade-off," the prediction that high accuracy requires more time and high speed is error prone (Skehan, 1998). The study examined how fast and accurate the EFL listeners understood three types of implicature with different degrees of conventionality, indirect requests and indirect refusals (more conventionalized) and implied statements of opinion (less conventionalized), whether speed and accuracy were related, and the effect of L2 proficiency on both. In contrast to a group of L1 English listeners, who understood the more and less conventionalized implicatures equally fast and accurately, the EFL listeners comprehended the more conventionalized implicatures significantly faster and more accurately. Increased proficiency predicted higher accuracy but not speed, and there was no significant relationship between the two dimensions. While the L2 listeners' superior comprehension of the more conventionalized utterances is of a piece with theory and research purporting that conventionality aids successful and rapid comprehension (Röver, 2005), the counterevidence to the accuracy–speed trade-off suggests that accuracy and speed are independent dimensions in L2 pragmatic comprehension and follow separate developmental paths.

A more recent study confirmed and expanded these findings. Taguchi (2007a) examined how the pragmatic listening comprehension of EFL students in the same population changed over a seven-week intensive course in academic English that did not have a pragmatic focus. At the end of the course, the students' listening comprehension of indirect refusals and expressions of opinion had improved significantly, and again comprehension of the more highly conventionalized refusals was better than that of the lesser conventionalized indirect expressions of opinion. The gains were greater in comprehension accuracy than speed, and the two processing dimensions were related to different L2 abilities but not to each other: comprehension speed correlated with speed of lexical access, while accuracy correlated with general L2 proficiency. The findings lend further support to models according to which L2 knowledge and processing are distinct capacities (Bachman & Palmer, 1996; Bialystok, 1993).

Theories addressing how indirect speech acts are understood, and the role of conventionality of action, form, and context in the process, have afforded productive outlooks on L2 pragmatic comprehension. Compared to the earlier studies, which centered on reading comprehension by design, more recent work has turned to examining pragmatic comprehension in listening. In this effort, the theoretical framework has been enriched by theories addressing key topics in L2 processing more generally, notably conceptualizations of accuracy and speed, and their interrelation. By combining pragmatic theories with general processing theories, studies of L2 pragmatic comprehension can readily be aligned with proposals to conceptualize and study L2 listening and processing more generally. While these advancements bode well for future research, studies on L2 pragmatic listening comprehension in real time have not yet much to say about the developmental paths through which L2 listeners progress in the comprehension of indirectly conveyed speech acts. A fruitful research program would therefore incorporate longitudinal studies of L2 pragmatic listening with multiple data collection points in naturalistic and experimental settings, using technologies that enable researchers to infer—or even better, observe—processing characteristics at the microlevel and their changes over time.

## B. Speech Act Production

Research on learners' production of action in an L2 conducted under cognitive-psychological perspectives is extremely rare. It is true that a significant portion of acquisitional studies, and even more so the larger literature on ILP from the perspective of language use, is based on production data of some sort, but the production of speech acts in L2 is not the actual research focus. Rather, production serves as a window to learners' ILP *knowledge*, consistent with the prevalent view that the focal object of SLA is the learner's developing L2 knowledge, not use (Long, 1997). Although rarely acknowledged in the ILP literature, the centrality of knowledge and the subservient role of production are grounded in the competence–performance distinction and the privilege accorded to competence as the proper object of SLA research, even if "competence" is expanded to pragmatic competence and communicative competence more broadly. If ILP competence is defined as an abstract underlying capacity, it follows that what is theoretically interesting about learners' production of speech acts is the strategies and linguistic structures serving to implement illocutionary acts and their selection according to theory-derived factors of social contexts. Consequently, the process dimension of speech act production in real time and the conditions that may facilitate or impede it did not receive more than cursory attention.

This situation—unsatisfactory from an SLA perspective that views speech production itself as a central ability whose development warrants specific investigation (Kormos, 2006)—has recently changed with the advent of studies that merge SLA research on task difficulty and fluency with pragmatic theory and research on speech acts and politeness. Drawing on earlier proposals on variable competence (Ellis, 1985; Tarone, 1988) and discourse domains (Douglas, 2004, for a recent update) as well as speech act and politeness theory, Fulcher and Márquez-Reiter (2003) found that test-takers assessed their own role-play performance of requests as less successful in high imposition and high power differential contexts. Although Fulcher and Márquez-Reiter's study does not indicate a consistent relationship between social context factors and perceived task difficulty, it does call into question constructs of task difficulty defined exclusively in abstract cognitive terms (Skehan, 1998). Taguchi (2007b) unfolds the construct of task difficulty in speech act production into a knowledge dimension, the sociopragmatic and pragmalinguistic appropriateness of speech act strategies, and a processing dimension, composed of pretask planning time and speech rate as a fluency measure. Echoing Fulcher and Márquez-Reiter's (2003) findings, the study shows that in contexts where social power (P), social distance (D), and imposition (R) were high, the participants produced requests and refusals less appropriately, at a lower speech rate, and after spending more preplanning time than in contexts where the values of these variables were low, irrespective of L2 proficiency. However, pretask planning time and speech rate were not related, nor did the longer time spent on preplanning and producing the speech acts in the PDR-high contexts result in greater appropriacy.

As Taguchi notes, these outcomes depart from prior research showing that preplanning benefits accuracy and fluency. It also underscores the need for research on tasks in L2 learning to systematically incorporate sociopragmatic dimensions into task design and performance measurement. The greater appropriateness and speed, and shorter advance planning, by which the participants produced requests and refusals in the PDR-low contexts suggests that such contexts are both socially less demanding and pragmatically easier to manage as the speech acts can be adequately produced with formulaic structures. By integrating the temporal dimension of speech production and pragmatic theory, Taguchi's study exemplifies a research strategy that benefits ILP as well as long-standing SLA concerns with the conceptualization and effective design of language learning tasks. Future research can usefully expand on these efforts by incorporating further temporal and prosodic characteristics of speech production in order to afford a more complex view of how learners produce speech acts in real time. It also remains to be seen what changes learners' speech act production undergoes as part of their overall L2 pragmatic development.

## C. Learning

Studies that expressly conceptualize L2 pragmatic development from a cognitive-psychological perspective have predominantly drawn on three theoretical sources: the two-dimensional model of L2 proficiency development (Bialystok, 1993), the noticing hypothesis (Schmidt, 2001), and notions of implicit and explicit instruction (DeKeyser, 1995; Williams, this volume). These models and concepts have been of special interest to ILP researchers partly because their extensions to ILP were already available

(Bialystok, 1993; Schmidt, 1993), or because they afford a conceptual handle on the learning of pragmatics through instruction that may inform pedagogical practice.

The noticing hypothesis is concerned with the initial phase of input processing and the attentional conditions required for input (the L2 data available in the learner's environment) to become intake (the subset of the input that the learner appropriates to build the interlanguage). In order to distill intake from input and make it available for further processing, relevant input features have to be "noticed," that is registered under attention, or detected under awareness. Global alertness to target language input is not sufficient, rather attention has to be allocated to specific learning objects. Schmidt (1995) further distinguished noticing from understanding. Noticing is defined as the "conscious registration of the occurrence of some event," while understanding implies "the recognition of some general principle, rule, or pattern. Noticing refers to surface-level phenomena and item learning, while understanding refers to deeper level(s) of abstraction related to (semantic, syntactic, or communicative) meaning, system learning" (p. 29). Whereas the noticing hypothesis accounts for initial input selection, the two-dimensional model explains the development of already available knowledge along the dimensions of analyzed representation and control of processing. Bialystok's model contends that children's primary learning task in pragmatics is to develop analytic representations of pragmalinguistic and sociopragmatic knowledge, whereas adult L2 learners mainly have to acquire processing control over already existing representations. Since the noticing hypothesis and the two-dimensional model address different phases of the L2 learning process, researchers have occasionally joined them together in a common theoretical framework (Barron, 2003, 2006; Hassall, 2006).

### Two-Dimensional Model

Support for the two-dimensional model's prediction that adult learners primarily have to gain control over how to allocate attentional resources effectively comes from observations of learners' speech production and conversational participation, such as the temporal and prosodic structuring of their turns at talk, and the lack of elliptical turn constructions when this would be sequentially indicated. Hassall (2001) observed that L2 learners of Indonesian had yet to develop sufficient control of processing over available sociolinguistic resources, as could be seen in their indiscriminate use of address terms in interaction. Conversely, progress toward greater control was registered in the increased use of conversational routines by L2 learners of German (Barron, 2003) and appropriate and well-synchronized leave-taking routines in Indonesian (Hassall, 2006). As control of processing in oral production encompasses both contextually appropriate selections of linguistic resources and fluently delivered utterances, these findings align well with Taguchi's (2007b) work on pragmatic production. But whether, for adults, the need to develop control of processing takes precedence over establishing new pragmatic knowledge is another matter. The literature shows conclusively that beginning adult L2 learners are able to participate in interaction, which has been taken as evidence of universal pragmatic knowledge (Blum-Kulka, 1991; Kasper & Rose, 2002) and positive transfer of prior local pragmatic knowledge (Hassall, 2001; Kasper, 1992). But the contention that "pragmatic competence in interlanguage does not have to develop *conceptually* in a developmental continuum from simple/basic to the elaborate/complex forms" (Koike, 1989, p. 286) appears to underestimate the need for learners to establish new L2-specific pragmatic knowledge. For example, pragmatic routines transferred from Irish English to German, resulting in nontarget-like usages of such formulaic expressions as *Kein Problem* (from *no problem*) or *Ich wundere mich* (from *I wonder*) (Barron, 2003), learners' difficulties with the reciprocal use of address forms in German (Barron, 2006), mitigating resources in requests (Hassall, 2001), and formulae for preclosings and leave-taking specific to Indonesian (Hassall, 2006) would seem to contradict the claim that requisite knowledge representations are largely in place for adult learners. Indeed, the large literature documenting negative pragmatic transfer at all stages of the learning process supports the view that the task of forming new pragmatic knowledge—whether of pragmalinguistic resources or their sociopragmatically effective deployment in context—presents a significant challenge to adult L2 learners.

## Noticing Hypothesis

Difficulties in establishing new pragmatic knowledge can reportedly persist even where ample input opportunities are available in the environment, such as in immigration and study abroad contexts. In the absence of negative feedback, widely reported in the study abroad literature (Churchill & DuFon, 2006; Kasper & Rose, 2002), learners may not "notice the gap" (Schmidt & Frota, 1986) between their own production and target practices (Barron, 2003). Hassall's (2006) self-study of learning how to take leave in Indonesian, conducted during an in-country sojourn, supports the critical role of noticing new linguistic resources and interactional practices, as documented in the researcher–participant's diary. Recurrent cognitive strategies associated with the learner's production were to evaluate the effectiveness of his leave-taking conduct after the fact and to preplan upcoming leave-takings by incorporating previously noticed material. Hassall also registers the impact of affective factors on his learning process and its outcome, noting that his motivation to learn Indonesian pragmatics was not sufficiently strong to consistently seek out social interactions with speakers of the language.

While Hassall (2006) does not address a possible link between his motivation, or lack thereof, and his noticings of leave-taking practices, Takahashi (2005b) examined how type and strength of motivation affect EFL students' attention to request strategies and linguistic resources in an implicit learning task. It appeared that motivational profiles were related, in variable degree, to the categories of pragmalinguistic resources that students paid attention to. In particular, intrinsic motivation was implicated in the extent to which students noticed bi-clausal requests in question format (*Is it possible*) and L2-specific idiomatic expressions. Takahashi notes that her findings have broader implications for the cognitive subsystems engaged in attention. Whereas Tomlin and Villa (1994) had argued that detection, but not alertness, and orientation are critically involved in attention, the relationship between motivation and noticing suggests that alertness and orientation also participate as key factors in attention, lending support to the view that alertness, orientation, and detection operate in attention synergistically (Schmidt, 2001).

## Explicit and Implicit Instruction

Research has repeatedly shown that pragmatic ability does not develop in tandem with L2 grammatical knowledge or exposure to L2 pragmatics in the social environment (Bardovi-Harlig, 1999, 2001a; Kasper & Rose, 2002, for review). The observation that even advanced learners' pragmatics often lags behind their grammar, or that their pragmatic ability progresses slowly, has been taken to indicate that learners' L2 pragmatic knowledge and ability will develop better through instructional intervention (Bardovi-Harlig, 2001a; Bouton, 1994). Although research on the effect of instruction in pragmatics goes back to the early 1980s (Kasper, 2001), the advent of the noticing hypothesis supplied a compelling theoretical rationale that is widely accepted in research on instructed L2 learning generally and pragmatics specifically.

Under the noticing hypothesis, the problem for instruction is how to facilitate students' allocation of attention to the learning target. A vigorous line of research on instruction in pragmatics therefore examines the effectiveness of different instructional arrangements, especially those commonly referred to as "implicit" and "explicit," respectively. Based on approximately 40 studies available to date, reviews (Kasper, 2001; Rose, 2005) and a meta-analysis of 13 quantitative studies (Jeon & Kaya, 2006) suggest that explicit instruction is generally superior to implicit instruction. However, Rose (2005) notes that the outcomes of several comparative investigations were inconclusive, and Jeon and Kaya (2006) caution that the small sample size of studies that met the criteria for inclusion in their meta-analysis is prone to error.

In addition, there are concerns of how "explicit" and "implicit" conditions are conceptualized and operationalized. Writers on the topic agree that instruction is explicit if it involves rule explanation (DeKeyser, 1995; Jeon & Kaya, 2006; Norris & Ortega, 2000; Schmidt, 1994). Whereas Schmidt (1994) limits explicit instruction to presenting metalinguistic rules to the learner deductively, Norris and Ortega (2000) follow DeKeyser (1995) by also including inductive arrangements that directly request learners to attend to specific forms and draw their own metalinguistic generalizations. Norris and Ortega (2000) recommend that deductive and inductive explicitness should be understood as a continuum rather than a dichotomy, with different instructional treatments ranging more or less toward the one pole or the other.

The inclusive notion of explicit instruction has its problems. Effect of instruction studies in pragmatics consistently include explicit rule explanation as part of explicit instruction, but some explicit treatments feature deductive metapragmatic presentation only (e.g., Rose & Kwai-Fong, 2001; Takahashi, 2001), whereas others include one or more further activities (Alcón, 2005; Koike & Pearson, 2005; Martínez Flor & Fukaya, 2005; Tateyama, 2001; Yoshimi, 2001). It is not possible, in the cases of multiple-component treatments, to evaluate the contribution of each component to the outcome. What is more, as Jeon and Kaya's (2006) useful table shows (p. 186), "consciousness raising" figures as a component of explicit instruction in some studies (Bouton, 1996; Lyster, 1994) and of implicit instruction in others (Rose & Kwai-Fong, 2001; Tateyama, 2001; Wildner-Bassett, 1984), further muddying the waters of what "explicit instruction" entails and consequently in what ways it may contribute to the instructed learning of pragmatics.

Implicit instruction comprises similarly heterogeneous components. The construct is most consistently defined *ex negativo*, that is, by excluding deductive metapragmatic explanation and explicit induction of pragmatic patterns. Jeon and Kaya (2006) also register learner-initiated data collection or observation exclusively as a component of *explicit* instruction. One study that demonstrates how critical it is to separate different treatment forms in order to assess their effectiveness is Takahashi's (2005a) comparison of two implicit activities, form search and form comparison. In the form comparison task, students compared their own production of requests in response to a discourse completion task with transcripts of native speaker requests in comparable contexts. In the form search condition, students compared native and nonnative requests in transcripts and were asked to list request expressions that were different in the native speaker transcripts. Retrospective reports indicated that the form comparison students noticed the target request forms, mitigation and directness, and the sequential structure of the requests significantly more than the form search group did. It remains a matter of speculation whether the two conditions might direct attention in different ways, but it appears from the quoted verbal reports that the students were more personally engaged in the task that required a comparative analysis of their own request production. Heightened interest may have resulted in greater alertness and facilitated detection, echoing the connection between affect and attention shown in Takahashi (2005b).

This section has examined how theories and concepts from rationalist pragmatics, cognitive psychology, and SLA have shed light on how learners comprehend, produce, and learn a range of pragmatic objects in an L2. As several of the studies show, these research efforts have not only contributed to theoretical and methodological insights in ILP but also to central topics in SLA at large. They pull into view the role of social context and pragmatic meaning as critical factors in accuracy and speed of utterance comprehension and production, and thereby indicate the need for a more complex notion of task difficulty, with attendant implications for task-based instruction and language testing. They confirm the linkage between motivation and attention, and supply further evidence for the need to coherently and consistently define and operationalize notions of explicitness and implicitness in instructed L2 learning. In consequence, the traffic between pragmatics, studied as a matter of individual cognition, and SLA is bidirectional, with ILP contributing to several key SLA topics.

## III. SOCIOCULTURAL THEORY

Originating in the work of Vygotsky, cultural–historical psychology—commonly referred to as Sociocultural Theory in the Anglo-American literature—conceptualizes cognitive development and learning as historically constituted and situated in social practice. As such, SCT's ontological stance contrasts markedly with the individual-centered intrapsychological perspective prevalent in SLA. As an alternative psychology in SLA, SCT has the longest history among socially grounded theories of L2 learning (Frawley & Lantolf, 1985; Lantolf & Poehner, this volume; Lantolf

& Thorne, 2006). The approach first appeared in pragmatics in the mid 1990s, about the same time that it started to make a growing impact on the field at large (Zuengler & Miller, 2006). Vygotsky's fundamental tenet is that human activity and cognitive development are mediated by culturally significant physical and semiotic artifacts, among which language has a special status. Whereas in Vygotskyan psychology, language serves a central mediational role in children's development of higher-order thinking, in SCT research on L1 and L2 learning, language has the dual function of a mediating tool and learning object. SCT research on L2 development incorporates numerous elaborations and transformations of Vygotskyan theory. Of these, situated learning theory (Lave & Wenger, 1991) has been particularly influential in applied and educational linguistics. As a perspective on L2 pragmatic development, SCT has guided studies on conversational ability in English and Spanish, polite requests, interactional routines, listener responses and modality in Japanese, and address forms in French and German.

Researchers applying SCT to pragmatic development have mainly appealed to the most widely known construct in Vygotskyan theory, the zone of proximal development (ZPD). In Vygotsky's definition, the ZPD refers to "the distance between the actual developmental level as determined by independent problem solving and the level of potential development as determined through problem solving under adult guidance or in collaboration with more capable peers" (1978, p. 86). As Donato (2004) clarifies, "collaboration" is not to be taken as synonymous with "interaction." Interaction lead by the teacher, and even activities involving a native speaker classroom guest, may not necessarily be structured in developmentally productive ways (Hall, 2005; Mori, 2002). Collaboration implies a sense of shared purpose, social and affective relationships, and epistemic stances that the co-participants create together. Through collaboration, new knowledge and abilities are jointly constructed.

Research on how L2 learners achieve pragmatic competencies in the ZPD shows how in collaboration between L2 learners and teachers or native speakers of the target language, the expert participants may offer assistance through scaffolding, metapragmatic comments, and other forms of guidance that make pragmatic resources and their use in context salient to the learner. For instance, Ohta (2001) observed that teachers of Japanese as a foreign language (JFL) explicitly reminded students in peer activities to provide listener responses and even prompted choral response (*minasan itte kudasai yo:: aa soo desu ka::* "Everyone please say 'oh really?'" 2001, p. 197). In IRF (initiation–response–follow-up)-structured classroom interaction, teachers modeled listener responses in third turn and thereby gave students repeated opportunities to observe this interactional practice, whether as direct or peripheral participants (Ohta, 2001). In this way, the IRF makes salient for students the sequential contexts for acknowledgments and assessments, and the linguistic resources by which such actions in third turn can be implemented. However, the teacher-controlled IRF routine does not offer students the opportunity to produce third turn responses themselves.

Environments that charge learners with more interactional control include computer-mediated communication that offers students in foreign language classes opportunities to interact with native target language speaking peers (Kinginger, 2000; Bhatia & Ritchie, this volume). Belz and Kinginger (2002) examined different forms of telecollaboration (email and synchronous chat) between students in French and

German courses at a North American university and students in intact English classes at universities in France and Germany. Over a one-year period, they observed how the students gradually came to develop interactional competence in the use of *tu/Du* forms of address. As social indexicals, *tu/Du* can be associated with dimensions of power or solidarity, yet classrooms do not usually provide the sociolinguistically diverse contexts that would enable students to sort out the pragmatic ambiguity of these forms. In the authentic online conversations, the native speaker co-participants offered models, corrections, and metapragmatic comments that helped the students understand the sociopragmatic complexities of the address terms.

While Belz and Kinginger's analysis highlights the benefits of authentic interactions outside of regular classroom settings, Shea's (1994) study sounds a note of caution. From observations of advanced ESL speakers in various types of social encounter outside of the classrooms, Shea concludes that interaction with a more capable native speaker co-participant itself does not necessarily benefit learners' conversational L2 ability. In developmentally productive interactions, the co-participants succeed in achieving a shared referential perspective and social affiliation, precisely the conditions that transform an interaction into a collaboration, according to Donato (2004). Belz and Kinginger's (2002) study supports this view, finding that the telecollaborators became increasingly more attuned to using affiliative forms of address as their social relationships developed. However, socially comfortable conversation with native speakers is not a sufficient condition to instantiate ZPDs. One recurrent observation from the literature is that when it comes to L2 speakers' pragmatic and sociolinguist conduct, native speaker interlocutors often shy away from providing feedback, corrections, or other forms of developmentally useful guidance (Barron, 2003; Kasper & Rose, 2002, for review). Without drawing L2 speakers' attention to specific pragmatic objects and their use in context, interactions with native speakers may not sufficiently unfold their potential as mediators of pragmatic development.

Conversely, there is evidence to suggest that L2 learners' ZPDs are not contingent on mediation by native speaker interlocutors, or even pragmatically more competent peers. Ohta (1995, 1997) examined how JFL students at different proficiency levels used polite Japanese request strategies in a role-play activity. Different from the expert–novice constellation prescribed by Vygotsky, both students shifted between taking the roles of expert or novice during the activity. Through their collaboration, the students were able to produce requests beyond their current individual stage of pragmatic development.

The observations from Ohta's studies would seem to support Donato's (1994) suggestion that expertise is distributed between collaborating students. In light of these studies and similar findings relating to L2 grammar, Ohta proposed to modify the concept of ZPD in the context of instructed L2 learning: "the ZPD is the distance between the actual developmental level as determined by individual linguistic production and the language produced collaboratively with a teacher or peer" (2001, p. 9).

In yet another examination of the ZPD, Ohta (2005) critiqued the revised version as still too narrow. She argued that the construct has to be expanded to settings and social relationships outside of classroom contexts, and even beyond (copresent) social interaction. As literary adults arrange for themselves assistance through mediational tools such as print and electronic resources, the ZPD would have to be rethought to encompass both an interpersonal space to enable other-management and an intrapersonal space to afford self-management (Ohta, 2005, p. 506).

As a conceptual tool to examine how pragmatics is learned in language classrooms, the ZPD, and SCT more broadly, has been put to use in observational but not interventional studies of classroom interaction and learning (Kasper & Rose, 2002). But as Ohta (2005) shows, planned instruction in pragmatics under different theoretical frameworks may be reinterpreted in the light of the ZPD. Taking as examples Takahashi's (2001) conditions of input enhancement and their effect on students' noticing of bi-clausal requests, Samuda's (2001) study on the effect of teachers' intervention in small group work on English modals, and Yoshimi's (2001) multiple-component program to teach Japanese discourse markers in conversational storytelling, Ohta evaluates the effectiveness of these instructional arrangements from the perspective of whether they afforded the type and amount of assistance necessary for the students to notice or produce the targeted pragmatic objects. Her reanalysis suggests that the notion of ZPD is helpful to assess when and how to best provide and withdraw assistance, evaluate the effectiveness of different forms of mediation— artifacts such as handouts, teacher's lectures, or peer collaboration—during different phases in the learning process, and how various types of assistance may best work together synergistically. From this perspective, it could be asked, for instance, whether the implicit conditions in Takahashi's (2001) study might structure noticing and learning more effectively if they were designed as peer collaborations instead of individual work.

SCT focuses on the material and sociohistorical conditions of development and its path on different timescales. At the ontogenetic level, this perspective requires longitudinal studies (Brooks, Donato, & McGlone, 1997). In pragmatics, longitudinal SCT research has exhibited developmental patterns in the collaborative production of requests (Ohta, 1997), listener responses (Ohta, 2001), and address pronouns (Belz & Kinginger, 2002; Kinginger, 2000), and drawn attention to developmentally productive forms of assistance at different stages as well as individual variation between learners. At the microgenetic level, SCT research aims to "grasp the process in flight" (Vygotsky, 1978, p. 68), that is, to observe how new abilities emerge while learners collaborate on an activity. Microgenesis of L2 pragmatic ability is documented in research on address pronouns (Belz & Kinginger, 2002; Kinginger, 2000) and modal expressions in Japanese (Ishida, 2006). Translating SCT's theoretical interest in microgenesis into research methodology requires a microanalytic approach that exhibits the mediating socio-interactional processes. Discourse analysis or CA are therefore standard analytical methods in SCT research.

SCT studies of L2 pragmatic development confirm and further elaborate several significant insights from SCT research on L2 learning more broadly. Among them is a changed understanding of the role of "expertise" in L2 learning and pragmatic development. From an intrapsychological perspective, expertise adheres to persons as a static trait. SCT research makes a dynamic and fundamentally socio-interactional view of expertise available. It documents that expertise shifts contingently during collaborative activities (Ohta, 1995), and that participants' individual expertise coalesces into a collective expertise that is more than the sum of its parts

(Donato, 1994). By bringing the ZPD construct to bear on different configurations of classroom interaction, SCT studies have highlighted the developmental value of peer collaborations, whether between L2 and L1 speakers (Belz & Kinginger, 2002; Kinginger, 2000) or L2 students. Although IRF sequences can provide opportunities for L2 pragmatic learning, peer activities were shown to enable higher levels of performance for all participants than individual work, teacher-fronted classroom interaction, or displayed performance in front of the class (Ohta, 2001). As assistance can encompass mediating objects other than interaction, an important task for future research is to examine how the interplay of different forms of assistance may support pragmatic development (Ohta, 2005).

## IV. LANGUAGE SOCIALIZATION

In the preceding section, I noted that under an SCT perspective of L2 development, language serves the dual role of a mediating tool and goal of the learning process. The dual function of language in human development is the premise of language socialization, an approach that investigates how cultural and linguistic competencies are acquired—more or less successfully—through language and language-mediated practices. While incorporating SCT in its theoretical framework, language socialization has its disciplinary home in linguistic anthropology rather than psychology. As Kulick and Schieffelin (2004) note, early language socialization research (Schieffelin & Ochs, 1986a, 1986b) was driven by the desire to overcome two theoretical gaps in research on child development: the absence of culture from the study of child L1 acquisition in developmental psychology and the absence of language from the sociological and anthropological investigation of socialization. Studies in the 1980s concentrated on child language socialization predominantly in non-Western societies and communities outside of the North American white middle class "mainstream." This work highlighted how children jointly acquire linguistic resources and cultural values, views of the world, and community practices through participation in interactional routines and other forms of discourse. It showed how interactional and pragmatic competencies emerge from interactions between children and adults or older children, including children's ability to understand and perform language-mediated social acts, politeness, register variation, and participation in conversation. In this process, children learn to associate linguistic forms and manners of their production with dimensions of situational context (Kulick & Schieffelin, 2004). Such conventional associations of forms and contextual meanings index social actions and activities, identities and relationships, status, roles, and affective and epistemic stance (Ochs, 1996). Predominantly, language socialization operates implicitly through caregivers' use of indexical expressions and the discursive arrangements in which children participate directly or as observers. But caregivers also engage in explicit socialization, for instance, by providing metapragmatic comments on normative interactional conduct (Blum-Kulka, 1997). Both implicit and explicit socialization practices and targets are community specific to some extent, yet they also comprise universal categories of semiotic resources and fundamental structures of social organization that are cross-culturally shared and locally elaborated (Ochs, 1996).

From the outset, the framework insisted that language socialization is a life-long process and consequently extends to novices to any setting. It also acknowledged that socialization processes are multidirectional, encompassing not only efforts by experts to induct novices to community membership but also mutual ways of shaping social roles, relationships, and identities through interaction. Initially, however, the life span trajectory and multidirectionality of language socialization remained programmatic. The L1 socialization studies of the first generation examined socialization processes and resources involving young children who were learning their first language in monolingual family and community settings, focusing on how socio-cultural organization, interpretive frameworks, language-mediated activities, and linguistic resources are intergenerationally reproduced and perpetuated.

When researchers began to investigate L2 socialization in the early 1990s, they adopted a perspective equivalent to the emphasis on continuity and reproduction in the study of L1 socialization. The overarching question that the early L2 language socialization studies addressed was how children and adults learning an L2 come to develop interactional competencies that enable them to participate in L2 environments appropriately and effectively. Unlike the L1 research, the early L2 studies examined language socialization processes in formal educational settings. Several studies describe how teachers index social status relationships through their choice and realization of speech acts. Poole (1992) found that ESL teachers in Californian college classrooms avoided overt displays of status differences between them and their adult students by soliciting suggestions (e.g., *How should we fix this room*) and mitigating directives through inclusive pronouns and verb forms (e.g., *Let's do our journals*). In contrast, Falsgraf and Majors (1995) observed that teachers' directives in JFL immersion classes and elementary school classes in Japan were significantly more direct than those in English-medium classes. While the high directness style can be taken to index teachers' authority and the asymmetry of teacher–student relationships, Falsgraf and Majors argue that it also constructs the rapport between teachers and their young students as close and informal.

L1 research had shown that interactional routines are powerful socialization tools in domestic and community contexts (Schieffelin & Ochs, 1986b). Compared to less prestructured interaction, interactional routines facilitate novices' participation because the same routines occur frequently in particular settings, their sequential components are predictable, and they are often associated with fixed participant roles, actions, or linguistic forms. In foreign language education, interactional routines play an equally important part. Kanagy (1999) described how over the course of a school year, children in a JFL immersion kindergarten came to participate increasingly more independently in daily "morning routines." The students' actions were guided and facilitated through verbal and nonverbal modeling, repetition, praise, corrective feedback, and scaffolding, provided by both teacher and peers. In a series of studies, Ohta (1999, 2001) showed that interactional routines are just as critical in college-level JFL instruction. As noted earlier in this chapter, IRF-structured interaction affords students the opportunity to repeatedly observe how teachers offer acknowledgements and assessments in third turn. The teachers in Ohta's studies also structured the interaction so that students were able to take sequential slots for producing *ne*-marked assessments, to which the teacher then aligned herself in next turn. Over time, some of the focal students produced *ne*-marked assessments in unscripted peer activities. Ohta's research shows how the participation opportunities associated with differently configured classroom activities hold the potential to socialize students into interactional competencies that are highly valued and indeed necessary for appropriate participation outside of the classroom interaction, such as expressing affect through aligning assessments.

Although studies conducted from different theoretical perspectives have cautioned repeatedly that classroom routines, and classroom interaction more broadly, may be specific to the classroom setting and in fact prevent students from developing pragmatic competencies needed for participation in nonclassroom activities (Hall, 2005; Kasper, 2001), the language socialization studies reviewed in this section assert that the reported interactional practices both socialize students to become competent classroom members and to participate effectively in interactions outside of the classroom. Studies of pragmatic socialization in (predominantly foreign) language classrooms emphasized collaborative assistance, facilitation, and uncontested acceptance of "appropriate" L2 use, defined by the pragmatic norms of target language native speakers. Differences in learning rates and outcomes were registered but rarely further interrogated (but see Yoshimi, 1999), and although socialization processes were shown to evolve slowly and over multiple steps, they displayed for the most part the linear developmental trajectories of cooperative L2 students.

Recent reviews of language socialization theory and research (Duff & Hornberger, 2008; Garrett & Baquedano-López, 2002; Kulick & Schieffelin, 2004; Watson-Gegeo, 2004; Watson-Gegeo & Nielsen, 2003; Zuengler & Cole, 2005) note that under the influence of constructionist, post-structuralist, and critical theory, and a broader and more complex range of language socialization contexts, the framework has been elaborated and shifted emphasis. Based on her studies of English-medium programs in Hungary, high school mainstream classes, and workplace-oriented programs for immigrants in Canada, Duff observes that "the social contexts of learning tend to be much more complicated, fluid, dynamic, competitive, multilingual, and potentially unwelcoming. People are concurrently negotiating and maintaining membership and identities in many different communities, in their L1, L2, and even L3, or a mixture of these at any given time, and their degree of affiliation with each community and language may vary, waxing and waning over time" (2003, p. 24). Increasingly, studies of L2 pragmatic socialization (Blum-Kulka, 1997) and discourse socialization (Duff, 1996; Morita, 2000, 2004) emphasize these complexities and contradictions as well.

The literature published within the last decade has expanded the scope of L2 pragmatic socialization studies in several ways. They span a larger variety of settings, including multiethnic work places (Li, 2000); dinner table conversations in multilingual families (Blum-Kulka, 1997) and between students and their host families during homestay (Cook, 2006, 2008; DuFon, 2006; Iino, 2006); ceremonial speech events (Siegal, 1995); and diverse educational contexts, including public high schools (Talmy, 2008, in press), English-medium high schools (Duff, 1996), heritage language classrooms (He, 2000, 2003b, 2004; Lo, 2004), graduate courses (Morita, 2000, 2004), university office hours (Siegal, 1995), and arranged learner–native speaker peer conversations (Yoshimi, 1999).

Rather than focusing on how novices become gradually socialized to stable community practices, some of this work highlights how language socialization in multilingual societies becomes a vehicle for pragmatic change. Two studies are illustrative of such transformations in very different settings. Blum-Kulka (1997) describes how in dinner table conversations in Israeli-American families, hybrid pragmatic styles emerged as a result of linguistic and cultural contact. Duff (1996) documents that reform of educational institutions in the wake of political change may render established speech genres dysfunctional and give rise to new forms of classroom activity. In the English immersion programs in Hungary after the political shift in the early 1990s that Duff studied, the traditional impromptu exam of a nominated student (*felelés* "recitation") gave way to a new type of student presentation that redistributed expertise and reconfigured the institutional identities of teacher and students. Expertise in language socialization does not necessarily rest with the older, more senior, higher-ranking participants, or those with more long-standing community membership. Because the student presentation as a speech genre was new to all classroom members, becoming competent participants in the activity was a joint, multidirectional project that implicated teacher and students alike.

Li (2000) highlighted the multidirectionality of pragmatic socialization in her case study of Ming, a Chinese college-educated woman participating in an immigrant job-training program in Canada. In a longitudinal study of Ming's request development, Li showed that at first Ming's directives were too implicit and unassertive to accomplish her goals in the workplace interaction. Over time, Ming's colleagues successfully encouraged her to state her directives more explicitly and firmly by using conventionally indirect (polite and clear) request forms. Conversely, her expanded pragmatic competence enabled Ming, together with other nonnative English speaking colleagues, to overtly resist, criticize, and correct discriminating remarks made by white native English speaking co-workers, explicitly instructing them to be more respectful toward their immigrant colleagues, and asserting her human dignity in the multicultural workplace.

Mutuality and resistance are often interconnected in recent studies of L2 pragmatic and discourse socialization. Cook (2006) and Iino (2006) describe that in homestay interactions, the foreign students contested, but also conspired in, ideological discourses, such as ideologies about "Japaneseness" (*nihonjinron*). Through various actions, the students resisted their hosts' identity attributions and generated counter-socializing discourse. For instance, they would refute stereotypical contrasting assumptions about "American" or "Japanese" ways of life through counterexamples, or disagree with categorizations and judgments in matters of food (DuFon, 2006). As the authors note, the conflicting positions taken by hosts and students created an opportunity for all parties to question their own cultural beliefs and contribute to rendering the homestay a transformational process for all participants.

These recent studies continue a central focus of the earlier work, that is, to show how language socialization operates through the use of linguistic resources and practices. For example, Cook (2006) analyzes how the hosts discursively construct cultural beliefs as taken for granted through the epistemic stance marker *no*, and

DuFon (2006) shows how a native speaker dinner guest models the timely placement of food compliments for the guest student. Some studies make the important observation that L2 discursive practices themselves can become objects of resistance. Siegal (1995) reports how two Western women on sojourn in Japan substituted the polite *desu/masu* style and the incorrectly used modal *deshoo* for normative honorific usage (but over time, one of these women did take on board the formal speech style required for a ceremonial speech event). DuFon (1999) notes that some learners of Indonesian during study abroad registered but decided not to adopt the complex system of address terms, opting for the generalized and often incorrectly used form *anda* instead. In both cases, the learners' resistance to target pragmatic practices appears to be grounded in pragmatic ideologies that prioritize social equality over context-sensitive social differentiation.

The theme of resistance has become especially prominent in recent work on language socialization in schools. Several studies have observed students' more or less persistent opposition to the line of conduct laid out for them by the teacher. While it would be easy to discount students' uncooperative actions as simply unruly behavior, this would miss the possibility that the conflicts between teacher and students may have deeper sociopolitical significance. Language heritage classes, an increasingly more widespread type of educational institution, can be a platform for this kind of struggle. In a series of studies, He closely examines the interactions between four Chinese L1 speaking teachers with their young English dominant students. She shows how, through directives (He, 2000), pragmatic markers (Chen & He, 2001), structuring of participation statuses (He, 2003b), and sequence organization (He, 2004), the teachers built a cultural space, conveyed norms of acceptable conduct, and assigned identities to students that differed from the children's experience in their daily lives. Similarly, Lo (2004) reports from Korean heritage language classes that the teacher recurrently deployed grammatical resources that jointly indexed epistemic stances and moral judgments which contrasted with the students' social world outside of Korean class. In both heritage language schools, the students on occasion contested the teachers' moral ideologies and the identities assigned to them.

The reported instances of students' resistance to the teachers' socialization agenda bring to mind Kulick and Schieffelin's (2004) observation that novices who persistently "deviate" from socially sanctioned manners of conduct fit the category of "bad subjects" (Althusser, 1971, p. 169), that is, actors who refuse to conform to expected subject positions. An educational setting that demonstrably produced "bad subjects" in this sense was the high school ESL classes studied by Talmy (2004, 2008, 2009, in press). Talmy (2008) describes the ESL students at the school as "generally uninvested, unwilling incumbents of a stigmatized identity category" (p. 2). In the ESL classes that the nonnative speakers of English were forced to take irrespective of their actual English abilities (which were not tested, and which were native-like in the case of some of the ESL students), students had to work with children's books for L1 readers far below the ESL students' age and grade level. Some of the teachers had no training in ESL and were junior staff at the school. In this environment, the ESL students developed a shared repertoire of practices that sabotaged the teachers' efforts to deliver instruction according to the official curriculum. Among the pragmatic practices were "bargaining for reduced requirements on classwork and extended time to complete it; refusal to participate in instructional activities; teasing students who did participate; and the often delicate negotiations with teachers that resulted" (2008, p. 13). Together with nondiscursive modes of resistance, they were practices through which the students asserted oppositional identities to that of the school-sanctioned ESL student.

As argued in this section, contemporary developments in language socialization research bring into focus the reciprocity of L2 socialization, the agency and subjectivity of all parties, the multiplicity and contestability of identities, and the contingency of language socialization processes. They make visible how macrostructures— institutional settings and roles, ideologies, ethnic and language affiliations—become procedurally consequential (Schegloff, 1991b) in interaction. In turn, it is in situated interactions, whether in classrooms, at the family dinner table, or at the workplace, that social categories and organizational structures are reproduced, contested, and transformed. Linguistic resources and discursive practices play a critical role in this process, both as vehicles of pragmatic and discourse socialization and as its— sometimes contested—objective. Language socialization serves as a pivot that reflexively interconnects macro- and microstructural processes in a developmental trajectory. In this perspective, learning L2 pragmatics cannot be separated either from the wider sociopolitical context or from the interactions in which novices participate.

## V. CONVERSATION ANALYSIS

While in SCT and language socialization, certain forms of interaction are the medium through which pragmatic and discourse competence are acquired, interaction itself is the central concern of CA. Originating in sociology and closely linked to ethnomethodology, CA contends that talk-in-interaction in practical quotidian activities is the fundamental site where sociality is constituted and reproduced. Its project is to elucidate the methods through which social members accomplish coordinated actions in an organized and orderly fashion through their verbal and nonverbal conduct. CA shares with pragmatics its concern with *actions* mediated by language and other semiotic resources. But especially in comparison to speech act pragmatics, actions are conceptualized very differently in CA (Kasper, 2006). In Searle's version of speech act theory—the version that is most influential in L2 pragmatics—speech acts are categories of speaker's intentions expressed by means of linguistic conventions. Speakers are seen as individual rational actors who balance their pragmatic intentions against principles of cooperation (Grice, 1975) and politeness (Brown & Levinson, 1987), and encode their mental action plans in conventionalized linguistic forms that can then be readily transmitted to a recipient. Against the mentalist view, CA holds that the habitat of action is not an individual speaker's mind but social *inter*action in which co-participants accomplish action jointly in organized sequences. Pragmatic meanings are not transmitted between individual minds but emerge from the recipient's response to what the co-participant produced in a prior turn—for the most part, in the immediately prior turn. They do not inhere in linguistic conventions but result from participants' ongoing, contingent interpretive work during jointly pursued practical activities. In CA perspective, pragmatic competence is interwoven with the interactional competencies that sustain shared understanding, or intersubjectivity. As Mehan (1979) notes, interactional competence is "a competence that is available in interaction" (p. 129), specifically in the organization of turns and sequences. For CA, interaction is the site where intersubjectivity is achieved and cognition constituted as a socially shared phenomenon (Schegloff, 1991a).

Compared to the three approaches to L2 pragmatic development discussed earlier, and despite a history that predates that of language socialization by roughly two decades, CA is a late arrival as a perspective on SLA generally (Firth & Wagner, 1997, 2007; Markee, 2000, 2004) and developmental L2 pragmatics specifically. Among many possible reasons, the most obvious is that CA is primarily concerned with locating, and providing detailed analytical accounts of, interactional competencies in the discursive practices of social members, but less with the development of interactional competence. One of the few exceptions is a series of studies by Wootton, which investigate the development of pragmatic competence in young children acquiring English as their first language. These studies demonstrate what a CA perspective on pragmatic development has to offer and provide a transferable model.

Wootton (1997) investigated how Amy, between 10 months and three years of age, made requests to her parents in a range of domestic situations. Using standard conversation-analytic methods (ten Have, 2007), Wootton shows that from age two onward, Amy's requests display a critical sensitivity to sequential organization, that is, knowledge about the orderly production of turns and actions in situated discourse. Amy's sequential knowledge, her "understandings" displayed in the request sequences, shows several properties. It is particular to the present event rather than trans-situational; it is public in that it shows Amy's orientation to events that were overtly manifested in the earlier discourse, and it is moral in that it grounds Amy's normative expectations of how the discourse should develop. Amy's selection of request forms such as imperatives becomes increasingly attuned to interactional contingencies, exhibiting her expectations of how the request might be responded to. At age three, two new request forms emerge, *can I/you do X?* and *shall I/we do X?*, each with a different developmental history. The conventionally indirect request form *can I/you do X?* replaces the earlier imperative in contexts where the child has no evidence to assume that her parents will go along with the course of action formulated in the request. Here, an already existing interactional meaning becomes associated with a better fitting form. In contrast, by using *shall I/we* the child not only deploys a new form but displays a new sequential orientation as well, that is a concern that all parties be jointly involved in the activity. In this case, the linguistic resource and its interactional meaning emerge simultaneously.

In a recent follow-up study, Wootton (2005) examines Amy's *can you* requests at age five. At this stage of development, the usage of the form has stabilized. In contrast to other request forms, Amy regularly deploys *can you* in interactional environments where she has reason to expect her recipient to opt for an alternative course of action. In this fashion, the *can you* formula indexes a distinct way of partitioning the request domain based on interactional contingencies that are not predicted by such interaction-external factors as status, power, or culturally determined imposition. Pragmatic meaning is grounded, first and foremost, in the sequential environment in which particular actions and their linguistic formats are situated.

Unlike young children whose interactional competencies are under construction, adult L2 speakers are interactionally and pragmatically competent in one or more languages. For them, it has been argued, interactional competence is both a resource and a goal of L2 learning. For the most part, the rapidly growing CA literature on L2 talk has provided detailed evidence of L2 speakers' available interactional competence (Gardner & Wagner, 2004). Based on accumulated research evidence, CA researchers recognize L2 speakers as competent social beings rather than deficient communicators. Their fundamental stance on L2 speakers' interactional competence contrasts markedly with that of cognitivist SLA and ILP. Lee (2006), for instance, proposes to reinterpret Hymes's notion of communicative competence in an ethnomethodological and conversation-analytic perspective in order to examine the interactional competencies that enable L2 teaching and learning. Sequential analysis of students' and teachers' interaction in class reveals how repair and error correction—commonly taken as evidence of students' knowledge deficits—are enabled by students' competence to monitor how the talk is developing, locate trouble, and initiate or respond to modifications that are specifically tailored to deal with the problem at hand. SLA research under the interactionist hypothesis, for instance, treats learners' interactional competence as a resource that does not warrant further examination. Lee demonstrates how in the details of the classroom members' production of relevant next turns, their ongoing analysis and understanding of the prior sequence becomes visible. While the interactional competencies to make the classroom discourse mutually intelligible are a resource for the participants, analysts need to treat them as a topic of investigation in order to explicate interactional competence as an enabling condition for L2 learning.

Lee's call to give more analytical attention to interactional competence as a participants' resource and condition for L2 learning is well taken, but parallel efforts to examine how L2-specific pragmatic competencies emerge do not seem to be premature. This literature is still small, but the few existing studies affirm the potential of CA as an approach to L2 pragmatic development and offer valuable pointers for future research directions.

The CA studies on L2 pragmatic learning available to date examine several pragmatic phenomena that have been investigated in the pragmatic and discourse-analytical literature inside and outside of CA: discourse connectives (Kim, 2009), modal resources to express epistemic and affective stance (Ishida, 2006, 2009), telephone openings (Huth & Taleghani-Nikazm, 2006; Taleghani-Nikazm, 2002), and speech act sequences (Félix-Brasdefer, 2006; Golato, 2002; Huth, 2006). This research has begun to trace pragmatic development in cross-sectional, longitudinal, and microgenetic perspective, examine the role of pragmatic transfer in L2 interaction, and explore the application of CA to interventional classroom research on the instructed learning of L2 pragmatics.

Although cross-sectional comparison is a very common method in ILP, there is only one study to date that adopts a cross-sectional design in a CA study on L2 pragmatic development. Kim (2009) analyzed how five learners of L2 Korean at different proficiency levels used the connective -*nuntey* in ordinary conversations with L1 speakers of Korean. In proficient Korean interaction, -*nuntey* is a multifunctional marker. Depending on its placement in the turn structure, it serves to establish background information, preface dispreferred action, or set up an accountability relevance point. The developmental pattern that emerged from the analysis shows that the novice-high speaker displayed understanding of the marker; however, with the exception of a single incorporation from the previous speaker's turn, did not use -*nuntey* productively. The intermediate speakers used the marker as a clausal connective in turn-medial position, and the advanced speakers deployed -*nuntey* both as a clausal connective and as an interactional marker in turn-final position, in the same way as L1 Korean speakers. In addition, Kim registered that the observed developmental trajectory paralleled the grammaticalization process that -*nuntey* underwent diachronically. Her study shows that CA's detailed attention to sequential organization and turn-construction is able to provide evidence of acquisitional grammaticalization (Giacalone Ramat, 1992), a process in individual language development that corresponds to diachronic grammaticalization.

Adopting a microgenetic perspective, Ishida (2006) observes how the participants in a decision-making activity conducted in Japanese constructed several decision episodes through the use of modal expressions such as *ne, jaa, ja nai?*, and –*yoo*. These markers are critical resources in the co-construction of decisions as they set up the next step after an agreement to a prior proposal and manage the absence of a sequentially relevant agreement. The analysis shows that even within the short 10-minute period, the L2 speaker came to understand the interactional import of agreeing overtly to *ne*-marked assessments and *jaa*-initiated prior turns, anticipate the interactional trajectory, and use modal markers to move a decision in progress to completion. The shared objective to come to a joint decision at several points in the interaction oriented the L2 speaker to the sequential contexts in which her co-participant used modal resources, and the co-participant's repeated use of the modal expressions in particular sequential environments made their pragmatic meanings salient for the L2 speaker. The study illustrates well the dual role of interactional competence as an enabling condition and an objective in L2 interaction, and how the competence to engage linguistic resources to coordinate joint action develops at the microgenetic level.

In longitudinal perspective, Ishida (2009) followed up on previous research examining L2 Japanese speakers' use and learning of the particle *ne*. In eight conversations with a variety of interlocutors, videorecorded over a 10-month period in Japan, the focal study abroad student expanded his use of *ne* to different sequential contexts and so was able to engage more actively and effectively in developing the talk. His growing interactional competence was also evident in his use of the response formula *soo desu ne*, which had a poor fit to the prior turn at first, but later became an effective resource for conversational alignment. In the later conversations, the L2 speaker provided accounts following assessments and so further affiliated himself with the co-participants while moving the talk along.

Ishida's study qualitatively expands previous research on the development of *ne* as a resource in L2 Japanese speakers' interactional competence. It widens the scope of interactional environments from classrooms, interviews, and arranged conversations to a broader variety of ordinary conversations with diverse co-participants.

Accordingly, a wider range of sequential environments and pragmatic-interactional functions becomes available for analysis, showing the use of *ne* as a turn-management device and marker of epistemic and affective stance. The study also highlights the gains of CA's analytical methods, such as to inspect the sequential development of the talk prior and subsequent to the focal analytical object. By paying close attention to the details of the interactional context, Ishida was able to see that some instances of the L2 speaker's *ne* or *soo desu ne* that at first seemed sequentially misplaced turned out to make interactional sense when the further development of the talk was considered. Finally, the longitudinal perspective affords a view on how L2 speakers' interactional competences may or may not develop in concert. One topic to pursue in future research is the manner in which L2 speakers' available interactional competences in other languages organize their participation in L2 talk, and what developmental changes may be seen in that regard.

Despite a large research literature on pragmatic transfer, the topic has not received much scrutiny under the theoretical approaches discussed earlier in this chapter (notable exceptions are Takahashi, 1996 and Yoshimi, 1999). One of the traditional questions in ILP is (a) which of their pragmatic practices learners transfer from their native language (or any other language than the language of interaction), (b) what the conditions for such transfers may be, and (c) what interactional consequences negative transfers may have. Outside of interactional sociolinguistics (Gumperz, 1982), there is little research examining these questions in natural interaction.

Studies of telephone openings and compliment responses demonstrate CA's potential to get a distinct analytical and theoretical handle on the phenomenon. In a comparative analysis of telephone openings between L1 speakers of Farsi and L1 speakers of German, Taleghani-Nikazm (2002) found that extended reciprocal ritual inquiries after the health of the co-participant and his or her family members are normative in Iranian openings of phone calls. By contrast, in German opening exchanges, ritual inquiries are possible but not normative, they are shorter, and not normatively reciprocal. In telephone openings between advanced Iranian L2 speakers of German and German L1 speakers, the Iranian L2 speakers but not the German L1 speakers produced extended ritual inquiries. These ostensible pragmatic transfers derailed the interaction, as was evident in inter-turn gaps and repair initiations. On occasion, the German interlocutor oriented to the ritual inquiry as a topic initiation, showing that the co-participants diverged in their understanding of what the activity at hand was. Such contingently arising sequential misunderstandings were also observed in earlier research on contextualization and inferencing from an interactional sociolinguistic perspective (Gumperz, 1982). Several studies in that tradition identify "frame conflicts" in intercultural interaction (Ross, 1998; Tyler, 1995) that become visible through contextualization cues and sequential misalignments. The strength of Taleghani-Nikazm's study is that she was able to show, through comparative analysis of German and Iranian L1 telephone openings, what the interactional source of the misalignments appeared to be.

The outcomes of Taleghani-Nikazm's analysis are paralleled by an instance of pragmatic transfer reported by Golato (2002) in a comparative study of compliment responses in German and American English. In a conversation conducted in English, a German L1 speaker responds to a compliment with a same strength assessment (adjective) and a response pursuit (tag) (*D: that's the best tea I think I've ever had. C: great, right?* (Golato, 2002, p. 566, simplified). This type of response is one of the standard compliment responses in German but not in American English. Upon hearing the response, D's vocal and nonvocal conduct shows that he is taken aback by this form of uptake. For the next few turns, the interaction is hearably uneasy. The German interlocutors show no sign of recognition that in D's North American pragmatics, the response was misplaced.

As Taleghani-Nikazm's study and Golato's example show, CA can refuel the research agenda on pragmatic transfer by examining what pragmatic practices L2 speakers transfer in situated interaction, whether and how the co-participants orient to pragmatic transfer in their subsequent vocal and nonvocal conduct, and how interactional misalignments are resolved. Because CA examines natural interaction rather than self-reports, it also specifies possible sources of pragmatic transfer that are yet unknown. With its focus on sequential organization and close attention to minute interactional detail, CA is capable of identifying pragmatic transfer as a participant concern, that is, as an interactional event that the participants themselves orient to.

Finally, incipient efforts are under way to apply CA to instruction in pragmatics (Félix-Brasdefer, 2006; Huth, 2006; Huth & Taleghani-Nikazm, 2006; Liddicoat & Crozet, 2001). These proposals build on CA in several ways. First, at the most general level, they adopt the notion of learning as socially shared cognition that is grounded in students' sequential knowledge (Wootton, 1997). Secondly, teaching materials are based on CA research on the instructional target (such as compliments or telephone openings). Thirdly, CA is applied to analyze records of students' interaction in activities involving the pragmatic object. The initial studies suggest that CA supplies an effective resource for instruction in L2 pragmatics and opens a new direction for interventional classroom research.

Although CA research on L2 pragmatic development has only just begun, the start is promising. It lays to rest the concern that CA, while demonstrably the most compelling approach to L2 interaction, may not be equipped to deal with L2 learning.

As the literature reviewed above documents, (L2) speakers' interactional competencies enable their participation in joined activities. "Participation" implies that the speakers orient to the unfolding interaction moment by moment, making sense of the co-participants' actions, and fitting their own contribution to the sequential context. The understandings that emerge through the co-participants' orientation to sequence organization and turn progression are also what enable the participating L2 speakers to notice and understand new pragmatic meanings and forms, and to register how the co-participant understands the L2 speaker's contributions. In this way, L2 pragmatic development is located in socially shared cognition as a practical accomplishment.

## VI. CONCLUSION

It is common in SLA to combine several theories and research methods in a joined theoretical framework to guide a study or as a source for testable hypothesis. In the context of this chapter, the question arises whether the four perspectives on pragmatic development are equipped for such joint enterprises. The three approaches that conceptualize L2 pragmatic development as socially constituted, and others that share their ontological stance on L2 learning (Zuengler & Miller, 2006), have been engaged in various combinations. Language socialization incorporated Vygotskyan theory as one of its main intellectual antecedents and has more recently taken situated learning theory on board (Ohta, 1999). He (2003a, 2004) explicitly argues that in order to document learning in interaction and also to provide a theoretical resource that can incorporate learning events outside of interaction, language socialization and conversation analysis have to join forces. For Mondada and Pekarek Doehler (2004), SCT's epistemological focus on the development of mind supplies a number of theoretical resources to complement CA's emphasis on the accomplishment of order in interaction.

While the productive research outcomes can be taken to support the various combinations of perspectives on socially constituted learning, there is also a risk that they may gloss over metatheoretical differences that are not easy to bridge. For instance, Lantolf and Thorne (2006) argue that Vygotsky's unified, non-reductionist theory is not compatible with the "upward reductionism" enshrined in constructionism. A note of caution may be sounded regarding the proposal to link conversation analysis with other theories because a joined framework runs the risks of violating the conversation-analytic policy of "unmotivated looking." This risk is minimized, however, if an interpretive perspective is brought to bear on the outcomes of a completed CA. An example of how a supplementary perspective can be added subsequent to the analysis is Kim's (2009) proposal to interpret the developmental pattern found for the connective –*nuntey* in light of acquisitional grammaticalization.

Compared with the relationship of theories of L2 pragmatic development as individual cognitive and socially constituted process, the differences between various theories in the latter group may seem quite subtle. And yet, it has recently been proposed that the dichotomous divide into cognitivist and social practice approaches to L2 learning is unhelpful and in need to be overcome by a Hegelian synthesis of sorts. Some approaches that may have this capacity have been proposed— emergentism, originating in a cognitivist tradition, being one (Larsen-Freeman, 2006), language socialization another (Watson-Gegeo, 2004; Gregg, 2006, for a vigorously opposing view). While possible confluences are a promising project for future exploration, they are not yet visible in research on L2 pragmatics. At this stage, it appears most helpful to bring out the specific contributions of different approaches to L2 pragmatics in sharp relief, to better enable researchers to evaluate their merits and drawbacks and prepare the ground for potential syntheses in the work ahead.

## REFERENCES

Achiba, M. (2003). *Learning to request in a second language: Child interlanguage pragmatics.* Clevedon, UK: Multilingual Matters.

Alcón, E. S. (2005). Does instruction work for learning pragmatics in the EFL context? *System, 33*, 417–435.

Alcón, E. S., & Martínez Flor, A. (Eds.). (2005). *Pragmatics in instructed language learning. Special issue, System* 33: 3 (September).

Althusser, L. (1971). Ideology and ideological state apparatuses. In L. Althusser (Ed.), *Lenin and philosophy and other essays* (pp. 127–188). London: Monthly Review Press.

Bachman, L., & Palmer, A. (1996). *Language testing in practice: Designing and developing useful language tests.* Oxford: Oxford University Press.

Bardovi-Harlig, K. (1999). Exploring the interlanguage of interlanguage pragmatics: A research agenda for acquisitional pragmatics. *Language Learning, 49,* 677–713.

Bardovi-Harlig, K. (2001a). Empirical evidence of the need for instruction in pragmatics. In K. R. Rose & G. Kasper (Eds.), *Pragmatics in language teaching* (pp. 13–32). New York: Cambridge University Press.

Bardovi-Harlig, K. (2001b). Pragmatics and second language acquisition. In R. Kaplan (Ed.), *Handbook of applied linguistics* (pp. 182–192). Oxford: Oxford University Press.

Bardovi-Harlig, K. (2006). On the role of formulas in the acquisition of L2 pragmatics. In K. Bardovi-Harlig, C. Félix-Brasdefer, & A. Omar (Eds.), *Pragmatics and language learning* (Vol. 11). Honolulu, HI: National Foreign Language Resource Center, University of Hawaii at Manoa.

Bardovi-Harlig, K., & Hartford, B. (Eds.). (2005). *Interlanguage pragmatics. Exploring institutional talk.* Mahwah, NJ: Lawrence Erlbaum.

Bardovi-Harlig, K., & Salsbury, T. (2004). The organization of turns in the disagreements of L2 learners: A longitudinal perspective. In D. Boxer & A. D. Cohen (Eds.), *Studying speaking to inform second language learning* (pp. 199–227). Clevedon, UK: Multilingual Matters.

Barron, A. (2003). *Acquisition in interlanguage pragmatics: Learning how to do things with words in a study abroad context.* Amsterdam: Benjamins.

Barron, A. (2006). Learning to say 'you' in German: The acquisition of sociolinguistic competence in a study abroad context. In M. A. DuFon & E. Churchill (Eds.), *Language learners in study abroad contexts* (pp. 59–88). Clevedon, UK: Multilingual Matters.

Belz, J. A., & Kinginger, C. (2002). The cross-linguistic development of address form use in telecollaborative language learning: Two case studies. *Canadian Modern Language Review/ Revue Canadienne des Langues Vivantes, 59,* 189–214.

Bialystok, E. (1993). Symbolic representation and attentional control in pragmatic competence. In G. Kasper & S. Blum-Kulka (Eds.), *Interlanguage pragmatics* (pp. 43–59). New York: Oxford University Press.

Blum-Kulka, S. (1991). Interlanguage pragmatics: The case of requests. In R. Phillipson, E. Kellerman, L. Selinker, M. Sharwood Smith, & M. Swain (Eds.), *Foreign/second language pedagogy research* (pp. 255–272). Clevedon, UK: Multilingual Matters.

Blum-Kulka, S. (1997). *Dinner talk.* Mahwah, NJ: Erlbaum.

Bouton, L. F. (1994). Conversational implicature in the second language: Learned slowly when not deliberately taught. *Journal of Pragmatics, 22,* 157–167.

Bouton, L. F. (1996). Pragmatics and language learning. In L. F. Bouton (Ed.), *Pragmatics and language learning, monograph series, volume 7* (pp. 1–20). Urbana-Champaign, IL: Division of English as an International Language, University of Illinois, Urbana-Champaign.

Brooks, F. B., Donato, R., & McGlone, J. V. (1997). When are they going to say 'it' right? Understanding learner talk during pair-work activity. *Foreign Language Annals, 30,* 524–541.

Brown, P., & Levinson, S. D. (1987). *Politeness: Some universals in language usage.* New York: Cambridge University Press.

Cameron, R., & Williams, J. (1997). Senténce to ten cents: A case study of relevance and communicative success in native–nonnative speaker interactions in a medical setting. *Applied Linguistics, 18,* 415–445.

Carrell, P. (1979). Indirect speech acts in ESL: Indirect answers. In C. Yorio, K. Perkins, & J. Schachter (Eds.), *On TESOL '79: The learner in focus* (pp. 297–307). Washington, DC: TESOL.

Carrell, P. (1981a). Children's understanding of indirect requests: Comparing child and adult comprehension. *Journal of Child Language, 8,* 329–345.

Carrell, P. (1981b). Relative difficulty of request forms in L1/L2 comprehension. In M. Hines & W. Rutherford (Eds.), *On TESOL '81* (pp. 141–152). Washington, DC: TESOL.

Chen, Y., & He, A. W. (2001). *Dui bu dui* as a pragmatic marker: Evidence from Chinese classroom discourse. *Journal of Pragmatics, 33,* 1441–1465.

Churchill, E., & DuFon, M. A. (2006). Evolving threads in study abroad research. In M. A. DuFon & E. Churchill (Eds.), *Language learners in study abroad contexts* (pp. 1–27). Clevedon, UK: Multilingual Matters.

Clark, H. H., & Lucy, P. (1975). Understanding what is meant from what is said: A study in conversationally conveyed requests. *Journal of Verbal Learning and Verbal Behavior, 14,* 56–72.

Cook, H. M. (2006). Joint construction of folk beliefs by JFL learners and Japanese host families. In M. A. DuFon & E. Churchill (Eds.), *Language learners in study abroad contexts* (pp. 120–150). Clevedon, UK: Multilingual Matters.

Cook, H. M. (2008). *Japanese speech-style shifts among learners of Japanese and their host families.* Amsterdam: Benjamins.

Crystal, D. (1997). *Dictionary of linguistics and phonetics* (4th ed.). Oxford: Blackwell.

DeKeyser, R. (1995). Learning second language grammar rules: An experiment with a miniature linguistic system. *Studies in Second Language Acquisition, 17,* 379–410.

Donato, R. (1994). Collective scaffolding in second language learning. In J. P. Lantolf & G. Appel (Eds.), *Vygotskyan approaches to second language research* (pp. 33–56). Norwood, NJ: Ablex.

Donato, R. (2004). Aspects of collaboration in pedagogical discourse. *Annual Review of Applied Linguistics, 24,* 284–302.

Douglas, D. (2004). Discourse domains: The cognitive context of speaking. In D. Boxer & A. D. Cohen (Eds.), *Studying speaking to inform second language learning* (pp. 25–44). Clevedon, UK: Multilingual Matters.

Duff, P. A. (1996). Different languages, different practices: Socialization of discourse competence in dual-language school classrooms in Hungary. In K. M. Bailey & D. Nunan (Eds.), *Voices from the classroom* (pp. 407–433). New York: Cambridge University Press.

Duff, P. A. (2003). New directions in second language socialization research. *Korean Journal of English Language and Linguistics, 3,* 309–339.

Duff, P. A., & Hornberger, N. H. (Eds.). (2008). *Encyclopedia of language and education, 2nd edition, volume 8: Language socialization.* New York: Springer Science.

DuFon, M. A. (1999). *The acquisition of linguistic politeness in Indonesian as a second language by sojourners in naturalistic interactions.* Unpublished Ph.D. dissertation, University of Hawaii at Manoa.

DuFon, M. A. (2006). The socialization of taste during study abroad in Indonesia. In M. A. DuFon & E. Churchill (Eds.), *Language learners in study abroad contexts* (pp. 91–119). Clevedon, UK: Multilingual Matters.

DuFon, M. A., & Churchill, E. (Eds.). (2006). *Language learners in study abroad contexts*. Clevedon, UK: Multilingual Matters.

Ellis, R. (1985). Sources of variability in interlanguage. *Applied Linguistics, 6*, 118–131.

Ervin-Tripp, S., Strage, A., Lampert, M., & Bell, N. (1987). Understanding requests. *Linguistics, 25*, 107–143.

Falsgraf, C., & Majors, D. (1995). Implicit culture in Japanese immersion classroom discourse. *Journal of the Association of Teachers of Japanese, 29*(2), 1–21.

Félix-Brasdefer, J. C. (2006). Teaching the negotiation of multi-turn speech acts: Using conversation-analytic tools to teach pragmatics in the FL classroom. In K. Bardovi-Harlig, J. C. Félix-Brasdefer, & A. Omar (Eds.), *Pragmatics and language learning* (Vol. 11). Honolulu, HI: National Foreign Language Resource Center, University of Hawaii at Manoa.

Firth, A., & Wagner, J. (1997). On discourse, communication, and (some) fundamental concepts in SLA research. *The Modern Language Journal, 81*, 285–300.

Firth, A., & Wagner, J. (2007). Second/foreign language learning as a social accomplishment: Elaborations on a reconceptualized SLA. *The Modern Language Journal, 91*, 798–817.

Frawley, W., & Lantolf, J. P. (1985). Second language discourse: A Vygotskyan perspective. *Applied Linguistics, 6*, 19–44.

Fulcher, G., & Márquez-Reiter, R. (2003). Task difficulty in speaking tests. *Language Testing, 20*, 321–344.

Gardner, R., & Wagner, J. (Eds.). (2004). *Second language conversations*. London: Continuum.

Garrett, P. B., & Baquedano-López, P. (2002). Language socialization: Reproduction and continuity, transformation and change. *Annual Review of Anthropology, 31*, 339–361.

Giacalone Ramat, A. (1992). Grammaticalization processes in the area of temporal and modal relations. *Studies in Second Language Acquisition, 14*, 297–322.

Gibbs, R. (1983). Do people always process the literal meanings of indirect requests? *Journal of Experimental Psychology: Learning, Memory, and Cognition, 9*, 524–533.

Golato, A. (2002). German compliment responses. *Journal of Pragmatics, 34*, 547–571.

Gregg, K. R. (2006). Taking a social turn for the worse: The language socialization paradigm for second language acquisition. *Second Language Research, 22*, 413–442.

Grice, P. (1975). Logic and conversation. In P. Cole & J. Morgan (Eds.), *Syntax and semantics, volume 3: Speech acts* (pp. 41–58). New York: Academic Press.

Gumperz, J. J. (1982). *Discourse strategies*. Cambridge: Cambridge University Press.

Hall, J. K. (2005). "Practicing speaking" in Spanish: Lessons from a high school foreign language classroom. In D. Boxer & A. D. Cohen (Eds.), *Studying speaking to inform second language learning* (pp. 68–87). Clevedon: Multilingual Matters.

Hassall, T. (2001). Modifying requests in a second language. *International Review of Applied Linguistics, 39*, 259–283.

Hassall, T. (2006). Learning to take leave in social conversations: A diary study. In M. A. DuFon & E. Churchill (Eds.), *Language learners in study abroad contexts* (pp. 31–58). Clevedon, UK: Multilingual Matters.

He, A. W. (2000). The grammatical and interactional organization of teacher's directives: Implications for socialization of Chinese American children. *Linguistics and Education, 11*, 119–140.

He, A. W. (2003a). Linguistic anthropology and language education. In S. Wortham & B. Rymes (Eds.), *Linguistic anthropology of education* (pp. 93–119). Westport, CT: Praeger.

He, A. W. (2003b). Novices and their speech roles in Chinese heritage language classes. In R. Bayley & S. R. Schecter (Eds.), *Language socialization in bilingual and multilingual societies* (pp. 128–146). Clevedon, UK: Multilingual Matters.

He, A. W. (2004). CA for SLA: Arguments from the Chinese language classroom. *The Modern Language Journal, 88*, 551–567.

Huth, T. (2006). Negotiating structure and culture: L2 learners' realization of L2 compliment response sequences in talk-in-interaction. *Journal of Pragmatics, 38*, 2025–2050.

Huth, T., & Taleghani-Nikazm, C. (2006). How can insights from conversation analysis be directly applied to teaching pragmatics? *Language Teaching Research, 10*, 53–79.

Iino, M. (2006). Norms of interaction in a Japanese homestay setting: Toward two-way flow of linguistic and cultural resources. In M. A. DuFon & E. Churchill (Eds.), *Language learners in study abroad contexts* (pp. 151–173). Clevedon, UK: Multilingual Matters.

Ishida, M. (2006). Interactional competence and the use of modal expressions in decision-making activities: CA for understanding microgenesis of pragmatic competence. In K. Bardovi-Harlig, J. C. Félix-Brasdefer, & A. Omar (Eds.), *Pragmatics and language learning* (Vol. 11). Honolulu, HI: National Foreign Language Resource Center, University of Hawaii at Manoa.

Ishida, M. (2009). Development of interactional competence: Changes in the use of ne in L2 Japanese during study abroad. In H. t. Nguyen & G. Kasper (Eds.), *Talk-in-interaction: Multilingual perspectives* (pp. 351–385). Honolulu, HI: National Foreign Language Resource Center and University of Hawaii Press.

Jeon, E. H., & Kaya, T. (2006). Effects of L2 instruction on interlanguage pragmatic development: A meta-analysis. In J. M. Norris & L. Ortega (Eds.), *Synthesizing research on language learning and teaching* (pp. 165–211). Amsterdam: Benjamins.

Kanagy, R. (1999). Interactional routines as a mechanism for L2 acquisition and socialization in an immersion context. *Journal of Pragmatics, 31*, 1467–1492.

Kasper, G. (1984). Pragmatic comprehension in learner-native speaker discourse. *Language Learning, 34*, 1–20.

Kasper, G. (1992). Pragmatic transfer. *Second Language Research, 8*, 203–231.

Kasper, G. (2001). Classroom research on interlanguage pragmatics. In K. R. Rose & G. Kasper (Eds.), *Pragmatics in language teaching* (pp. 33–60). New York: Cambridge University Press.

Kasper, G. (2006). Speech acts in interaction: Towards discursive pragmatics. In K. Bardovi-Harlig, C. Félix-Brasdefer, & A. Omar (Eds.), *Pragmatics and language learning* (Vol. 11). Honolulu, HI: National Foreign Language Resource Center, University of Hawaii at Manoa.

Kasper, G., & Blum-Kulka, S. (1993). Interlanguage pragmatics: An Introduction. In G. Kasper & S. Blum-Kulka (Eds.), *Interlanguage pragmatics* (pp. 3–17). New York: Oxford University Press.

Kasper, G., & Rose, K. R. (2002). *Pragmatic development in a second language*. Oxford: Blackwell.

Kasper, G., & Schmidt, R. (1996). Developmental issues in interlanguage pragmatics. *Studies in Second Language Acquisition, 18*, 149–169.

Kim, Y. (2009). Korean discourse markers in L2 Korean speakers' conversation: An acquisitional perspective. In H. t. Nguyen & G. Kasper (Eds.), *Talk-in-interaction: Multilingual perspectives* (pp. 317–350). Honolulu, HI: National Foreign Language Resource Center and University of Hawaii Press.

Kinginger, C. (2000). Learning the pragmatics of solidarity in the networked foreign language classroom. In J. K. Hall & L. S. Verplaetse (Eds.), *Second and foreign language learning through classroom interaction* (pp. 23–46). Mahwah, NJ: Erlbaum.

Koike, D. A. (1989). Pragmatic competence and adult L2 acquisition: Speech acts in interlanguage. *The Modern Language Journal*, *73*, 279–289.

Koike, D. A., & Pearson, L. (2005). The effect of instruction and feedback in the development of pragmatic competence. *System*, *33*, 481–501.

Kormos, J. (2006). *Speech production research and second language acquisition*. Mahwah, NJ: Erlbaum.

Kulick, D., & Schieffelin, B. (2004). Language socialization. In A. Duranti (Ed.), *A companion to linguistic anthropology* (pp. 349–368). Malden, MA: Blackwell.

Lantolf, J. P., & Thorne, S. L. (2006). *Sociocultural theory and the genesis of second language development*. Oxford: Oxford University Press.

Larsen-Freeman, D. (2006). The emergence of complexity, fluency, and accuracy in the oral and written production of five Chinese learners of English. *Applied Linguistics*, *27*, 590–619.

Lave, J., & Wenger, E. (1991). *Situated learning: Legitimate peripheral participation*. New York: Cambridge University Press.

Lee, Y-A. (2006). Towards respecification of communicative competence: Condition of L2 instruction or its objective? *Applied Linguistics*, *27*, 349–376.

Li, D. (2000). The pragmatics of making requests in the L2 workplace: A case study of language socialization. *The Canadian Modern Language Review/La Revue Canadienne des Langues Vivantes*, *57*, 58–87.

Liddicoat, A., & Crozet, C. (2001). Acquiring French interactional norms through instruction. In K. R. Rose & G. Kasper (Eds.), *Pragmatics in language teaching* (pp. 125–144). New York: Cambridge University Press.

Lo, A. (2004). Evidentiality and morality in a Korean Heritage language school. *Pragmatics*, *14*, 235–256.

Long, M. (1997). Construct validity in SLA research: A response to Firth and Wagner. *The Modern Language Journal*, *81*, 318–323.

Lyster, R. (1994). The effect of functional-analytic teaching on aspects of French immersion students' sociolinguistic competence. *Applied Linguistics*, *15*, 263–287.

Markee, N. (2000). *Conversation analysis*. Mahwah, NJ: Erlbaum.

Markee, N. (Ed.). (2004). Classroom talks. *The Modern Language Journal*, *88* (4).

Martínez Flor, A., & Fukaya, Y. J. (2005). The effects of instruction on learners' production of appropriate and accurate suggestions. *System*, *33*, 463–480.

Mehan, H. (1979). *Learning lessons*. Cambridge, MA: Harvard University Press.

Mondada, L., & Pekarek Doehler, S. (2004). Second language acquisition as situated practice: Task accomplishment in the French second language classroom. *The Modern Language Journal*, *88*, 501–518.

Mori, J. (2002). Task-design, plan and development of talk-in-interaction: An analysis of a small group activity in a Japanese language classroom. *Applied Linguistics*, *23*, 323–347.

Morita, N. (2000). Discourse socialization through oral classroom activities in a TESOL graduate program. *TESOL Quarterly*, *34*, 279–310.

Morita, N. (2004). Negotiating participation and identity in second language academic communities. *TESOL Quarterly*, *38*, 573–603.

Niezgoda, K., & Röver, C. (2001). Pragmatic and grammatical awareness: A function of learning environment? In K. R. Rose & G. Kasper (Eds.), *Pragmatics in language teaching* (pp. 63–79). Cambridge: Cambridge University Press.

Norris, J., & Ortega, L. (2000). Effectiveness of L2 instruction: A research synthesis and quantitative meta-analysis. *Language Learning*, *50*, 417–528.

Ochs, E. (1996). Linguistic resources for socializing humanity. In J. J. Gumperz & S. L. Levinson (Eds.), *Rethinking linguistic relativity* (pp. 407–437). New York: Cambridge University Press.

Ohta, A. S. (1995). Applying sociocultural theory to an analysis of learner discourse: Learner–learner collaborative interaction in the zone of proximal development. *Issues in Applied Linguistics*, *6*, 93–121.

Ohta, A. S. (1997). The development of pragmatic competence in learner–learner classroom interaction. In L. F. Bouton (Ed.), *Pragmatics and language learning, monograph series, volume 8* (pp. 223–242). Urbana-Champaign, IL: Division of English as an International Language, University of Illinois, Urbana-Champaign.

Ohta, A. S. (1999). Interactional routines and the socialization of interactional style in adult learners of Japanese. *Journal of Pragmatics*, *31*, 1493–1512.

Ohta, A. S. (2001). *Second language acquisition processes in the classroom: Learning Japanese*. Mahwah, NJ: Lawrence Erlbaum.

Ohta, A. S. (2005). Interlanguage pragmatics in the zone of proximal development. *System*, *33*, 503–517.

Poole, D. (1992). Language socialization in the second language classroom. *Language Learning*, *42*, 593–616.

Rose, K. R. (2005). On the effects of instruction in interlanguage pragmatics. *System*, *33*, 385–399.

Rose, K. R., & Kasper, G. (Eds.). (2001). *Pragmatics in language teaching*. New York: Cambridge University Press.

Rose, K. R., & Kwai-Fong, C. (2001). Inductive and deductive teaching of compliments and compliment responses. In K. R. Rose & G. Kasper (Eds.), *Pragmatics in language teaching* (pp. 145–170). New York: Cambridge University Press.

Ross, S. (1997). An introspective analysis of listener inferencing on a second language listening task. In G. Kasper & E. Kellerman (Eds.), *Communication strategies: Psycholinguistic and sociolinguistic perspectives* (pp. 216–237). London: Longman.

Ross, S. (1998). Divergent frame interpretations in oral proficiency interview interaction. In R. Young & A. W. He (Eds.), *Talking and testing. Discourse approaches to the assessment of oral proficiency* (pp. 333–353). Amsterdam: John Benjamins.

Röver, C. (2005). *Testing ESL pragmatics*. Frankfurt am Main: Lang.

Samuda, V. (2001). Guiding relationships between form and meaning during task performance: The role of the teacher. In M. Bygate, P. Skehan, & M. Swain (Eds.), *Researching pedagogic tasks* (pp. 119–140). Harlow, England: Longman/Pearson Education.

Schauer, G. A. (2006). Pragmatic awareness in ESL and EFL contexts: Contrast and development. *Language Learning*, *56*, 269–318.

Schegloff, E. A. (1991a). Conversation analysis and socially shared cognition. In L. B. Resnick, J. M. Levine, & S. D. Teasley (Eds.), *Perspectives on socially shared cognition* (pp. 150–171). Washington, DC: American Psychological Association.

Schegloff, E. A. (1991b). Reflections on talk and social structure. In D. Boden & D. H. Zimmerman (Eds.), *Talk and social structure* (pp. 44–71). Cambridge: Polity Press.

Schieffelin, B. B., & Ochs, E. (1986a). Language socialization. *Annual Review of Anthropology*, *15*, 163–191.

Schieffelin, B. B., & Ochs, E. (1986b). *Language socialization across cultures*. Cambridge: Cambridge University Press.

Schmidt, R. (1983). Interaction, acculturation and the acquisition of communicative competence. In N. Wolfson & E. Judd (Eds.), *Sociolinguistics and second language acquisition* (pp. 137–174). Rowley, MA: Newbury House.

Schmidt, R. (1993). Consciousness, learning and interlanguage pragmatics. In G. Kasper & S. Blum-Kulka (Eds.), *Interlanguage pragmatics* (pp. 21–42). Oxford: Oxford University Press.

Schmidt, R. (1994). Deconstructing consciousness in search of useful definitions for applied linguistics. *AILA Review, 19*, 11–26.

Schmidt, R. (1995). Consciousness and foreign language learning: A tutorial on the role of attention and awareness in learning. In R. Schmidt (Ed.), *Attention and awareness in foreign language learning* (pp. 1–63). Honolulu, HI: University of Hawaii, Second Language Teaching and Curriculum Center.

Schmidt, R. (2001). Attention. In P. Robinson (Ed.), *Cognition and second language instruction* (pp. 3–33). New York: Cambridge University Press.

Schmidt, R., & Frota, S. N. (1986). Developing basic conversational ability in a second language: A case study of an adult learner of Portuguese. In R. Day (Ed.), *Talking to learn* (pp. 237–326). Rowley, MA: Newbury House.

Searle, J. R. (1969). *Speech acts: An essay in the philosophy of language*. Cambridge: Cambridge University Press.

Searle, J. R. (1975). Indirect speech acts. In P. Cole & J. Morgan (Eds.), *Syntax and semantics, volume 3: Speech acts* (pp. 59–82). New York: Academic Press.

Searle, J. (1976). A classification of illocutionary acts. *Language in Society, 5*, 1–23.

Shea, D. P. (1994). Perspective and production: Structuring conversational participation across cultural borders. *Pragmatics, 4*, 357–389.

Siegal, M. (1995). Individual differences and study abroad: Women learning Japanese in Japan. In B. F. Freed (Ed.), *Second language acquisition in a study abroad context* (pp. 225–244). Amsterdam: Benjamins.

Skehan, P. (1998). *A cognitive approach to language learning*. Oxford: Oxford University Press.

Sperber, D., & Wilson, D. (1995). *Relevance: Communication and cognition* (2nd ed.). Cambridge: Cambridge University Press.

Taguchi, N. (2002). An application of relevance theory to the analysis of L2 interpretation processes: The comprehension of indirect replies. *International Review of Applied Linguistics, 40*, 151–176.

Taguchi, N. (2005). Comprehension of implied meaning in English as a second language. *The Modern Language Journal, 89*, 543–562.

Taguchi, N. (2007a). Development of speed and accuracy in pragmatic comprehension in English as a foreign language. *TESOL Quarterly, 41*, 313–338.

Taguchi, N. (2007b). Task difficulty in oral speech act production. *Applied Linguistics, 28*, 1.

Takahashi, S. (1996). Pragmatic transferability. *Studies in Second Language Acquisition, 18*, 189–223.

Takahashi, S. (2001). The role of input enhancement in developing pragmatic competence. In K. R. Rose & G. Kasper (Eds.), *Pragmatics in language teaching* (pp. 171–199). New York: Cambridge University Press.

Takahashi, S. (2005a). Noticing in task performance and learning outcomes: A qualitative analysis of instructional effects in interlanguage pragmatics. *System, 33*, 437–461.

Takahashi, S. (2005b). Pragmalinguistic awareness: Is it related to motivation and proficiency? *Applied Linguistics, 26*, 90–120.

Takahashi, S., & Roitblat, H. (1994). Comprehension process of second language indirect requests. *Applied Psycholinguistics, 15*, 475–506.

Taleghani-Nikazm, C. (2002). A conversation-analytic study of telephone conversation opening between native and nonnative speakers. *Journal of Pragmatics, 34*, 1807–1832.

Talmy, S. (2004). Forever FOB: The cultural production of ESL in a high school. *Pragmatics, 14*, 149–172.

Talmy, S. (2008). The cultural productions of the ESL student at Tradewinds High: Contingency, multidirectionality, and identity in L2 socialization. *Applied Linguistics, 29*, 619–644.

Talmy, S. (in press). Achieving distinction in ESL: A critical pragmatics analysis of classroom talk. In G. Kasper, H. t. Nguyen, D. Yoshimi, & J. K. Yoshioka (Eds.), *Pragmatics & language learning* (Vol. 12). Honolulu, HI: National Foreign Language Resource Center.

Talmy, S. (2009). Resisting ESL: Categories and sequence in a critically "motivated" analysis of classroom interaction. In H. t. Nguyen & G. Kasper (Eds.), *Talk-in-interaction: Multilingual perspectives*, (pp. 181–213). Honolulu, HI: National Foreign language Resource Center and University of Hawaii Press.

Tarone, E. (1988). *Variation in interlanguage*. London: Arnold.

Tateyama, Y. (2001). Explicit and implicit teaching of pragmatic routines: Japanese sumimasen. In K. R. Rose & G. Kasper (Eds.), *Pragmatics in language teaching* (pp. 200–222). New York: Cambridge University Press.

ten Have, P. (2007). *Doing conversation analysis* (2nd ed.). London: Sage.

Tomlin, R., & Villa, V. (1994). Attention in cognitive science and second language acquisition. *Studies in Second Language Acquisition, 16*, 183–203.

Tyler, A. (1995). The coconstruction of cross-cultural miscommunication. *Studies in Second Language Acquisition, 17*, 129–152.

Vygotsky, L. S. (1978). *Mind in society: The development of higher psychological processes.* Cambridge, MA: Harvard University Press.

Watson-Gegeo, K. A. (2004). Mind, language, and epistemology: Toward a language socialization paradigm for SLA. *The Modern Language Journal, 88*, 331–351.

Watson-Gegeo, K. A., & Nielsen, S. (2003). Language socialization in SLA. In C. Doughty & M. Long (Eds.), *Handbook of second language acquisition* (pp. 155–177). Oxford: Blackwell.

Wildner-Bassett, M. (1984). *Improving pragmatic aspects of learners' interlanguage*. Tübingen: Narr.

Wootton, A. (1997). *Interaction and the development of mind*. Cambridge: Cambridge University Press.

Wootton, A. (2005). Interactional and sequential configurations informing request format selection in children's speech. In A. Hakulinen & M. Selting (Eds.), *Syntax and lexis in conversation* (pp. 85–207). Amsterdam: Benjamins.

Yoshimi, D. R. (1999). L1 socialization as a variable in the use of ne by L2 learners of Japanese. *Journal of Pragmatics, 31*, 1513–1525.

Yoshimi, D. R. (2001). Explicit instruction and JFL learners' use of interactional discourse markers. In K. R. Rose & G. Kasper (Eds.), *Pragmatics in language teaching* (pp. 223–244). New York: Cambridge University Press.

Zuengler, J., & Cole, K. (2005). Language socialization and L2 learning. In E. Hinkel (Ed.), *Handbook of research in second language teaching and learning* (pp. 301–316). Mahwah, NJ: Lawrence Erlbaum.

Zuengler, J., & Miller, E. R. (2006). Cognitive and sociocultural perspectives: Two parallel SLA worlds? *TESOL Quarterly, 40*, 35–58.

# CHAPTER 13

# SENTENCE PARSING IN L2 LEARNERS: LINGUISTIC AND EXPERIENCE-BASED FACTORS

Paola E. Dussias and Pilar Piñar

When we read in our second language, we face many uncertainties about how the people or objects referred to in the text are connected to one another. This is so because when our eyes move along the printed text in a left-to-right fashion, the information needed to establish correct dependencies between word strings is not yet available. So what does the second language (L2) reader do under these conditions of uncertainty? Because learners who are relatively proficient in two or more languages have access to the grammar and lexicon of each language when they comprehend written sentences, one critical question concerns whether the specific semantic and syntactic subprocesses engaged during L2 language comprehension are different when monolingual speakers and second language learners process input in the target language.

Experimental work in sentence comprehension by L2 learners has investigated this question using an array of psycholinguistic methods, ranging from behavioral tasks that measure reaction times or provide records of eye movements to electrophysiological responses recorded through the scalp while participants are exposed to stimuli (e.g., Kroll, Gerfen, & Dussias, 2008 and references therein). This rapidly growing body of work suggests that L2 learners' performance on reading tasks is sometimes strikingly close to that of native speakers, but not always. Evidence comes from studies that examine different aspects of L2 sentence processing, such as morphological processing (e.g., Hahne, Müller, & Clahsen, 2006), morphosyntactic processing (e.g., Hawkins, this volume), syntactic ambiguity resolution (e.g., Frenck-Mestre & Pynte, 1997), and the processing of syntactic dependencies (e.g., Lieberman, Aoshima, & Phillips, 2006). In this chapter, we will delimit the area of sentence comprehension to those aspects of sentence comprehension, be it sense–semantic information, syntactic-category-based

*The New Handbook of Second Language Acquisition*

information, or structurally driven parsing principles, that are drawn upon to derive a syntactic analysis and interpret an input word string (Pickering, 1999). We will also discuss how the learners' characteristics and specific linguistic experience may determine their performance in reading comprehension tasks. Thus, we will see how factors such as the learner's type of experience with the target language (e.g., immersion vs. non-immersion experience), competence, proficiency level, and previous linguistic knowledge all play a role in comprehension processes. Given that the learner's experience and learning style is an important variable to be considered in L2 sentence processing, we include a discussion of a particular group of L2 learners, namely deaf individuals. We will discuss whether their learning experience is qualitatively different from that of hearing learners and will examine some of the variables that affect their reading comprehension success.

As will become evident, there are currently too many gaps in the available literature for researchers to be able to construct the set of complete and detailed specifications that are used in the various stages of L2 sentence comprehension. However, existing empirical evidence from hearing and deaf L2 learners can be used to tell us something about the kinds of information that would need to be incorporated in such a set. Some of this evidence is outlined in the next paragraphs.

## I.  FACTORS INFLUENCING SENTENCE COMPREHENSION IN L2 LEARNERS

A number of variables have been demonstrated to influence sentence comprehension in L2 learners. For ease of exposition, we will divide them into two categories: Linguistic variables, which refer to properties that are particular to the input, and participant variables, which denote qualities of the learners themselves.

### A.  Linguistic Variables

#### "Sense–Semantic" Information

It is widely accepted that sense–semantic information (e.g., information about thematic relations, lexical semantics, and plausibility information) is useful when resolving syntactic ambiguity resolution. For example, the verb *fly* can be transitive or intransitive. In the sentence fragment *While the plane flew the man ...*, the transitive analysis (in which a plane is the agent of the act of flying) is implausible. The parser might take this plausibility information into consideration to determine that the verb *fly* is probably intransitive and might use this information to make certain decisions when parsing the input (Pickering, 1999).

Numerous experiments have investigated whether L2 speakers select among different candidate structures by relying on the same type of sense–semantic information that influences sentence processing during native language reading. Although there is some variability in the results, largely owing to effects of proficiency, the findings are generally consistent with the interpretation that proficient L2 speakers are guided by semantic information during sentence processing, and indeed parse sentences in their L2 in accordance with the semantic constraints of the L2 (for reviews, see Clahsen & Felser, 2006; Kroll & Dussias, 2004).

## Lexical-Semantic Information

A number of studies have reported effects of lexical-semantic features on the assignment of thematic roles during sentence comprehension. The early work on this domain is grounded in the *Competition Model* (Bates & MacWhinney, 1982), which aims at explaining how learners determine semantic relationships (e.g., agent, patient, goal, etc) among elements in a sentence. Sentence processing is seen as the convergence or competition among various cues, each contributing to a different resolution in sentence interpretation. Cues are said to converge when they concomitantly designate the same thematic relation, and to compete when they point to different relations. For example, in the English sentence *The girl sees the plant*, three cues converge to assign *the girl* the function of agent: word order, subject–verb agreement, and animacy. However, in *The pencil kicks the donkey,* word order and agreement enter into competition with animacy.

Studies involving a variety of typologically different languages have shown the existence of crosslinguistic variation in the way forms map onto semantic functions, as well as in the weights associated with different form–function mappings. Given this, researchers have asked whether L2 learners are able to learn the mappings and weights that are specific to the L2. Gass (1987) and Harrington (1987) found evidence that learners who favored semantic-based cues (i.e., noun animacy) as the primary source of information in their L1 were dependent on these cues when assigning thematic roles in English, a language where word order provides the strongest cue. In contrast, Gass (1987) and Sasaki (1991) found that L1 English learners of Italian and Japanese were able to abandon their reliance on word order and to employ animacy as the primary cue in interpreting Japanese and Italian sentences. In addition, a recent study by Su (2001) reports that L2 learners tune into the parsing strategies that are more consonant with the structure of the L2 (i.e., rely more on either lexical-semantic or syntactic cues for the L2 rather than those for the L1) as they become more proficient.

The properties of certain words with respect to assigning a thematic role have also been shown to affect learners' choices during syntactic ambiguity resolution. For instance, the decision to interpret a temporarily ambiguous relative clause as referring to one of two noun-phrase host sites preceding it is influenced by the lexical-semantic properties of the preposition linking the two noun phrases (cf., Fernández, 2003; Papadopoulou & Clahsen, 2003). In "... the *psychiatrist with the actress who was having a glass of wine*," the preposition *with* introduces a thematic role, so the attachment domain becomes *with the actress*, and attachment of the relative clause to the noun phrase *the actress* is predicted. This outcome has been consistently observed in L1 and L2 speakers alike. Conversely, in the case of "...the *psychiatrist of the actress who was having a glass of wine*," the linking preposition does not introduce a thematic role. Hence, the relative clause is construed in relation to the whole complex noun phrase *the psychiatrist of the actress*. The decision to attach the relative clause to the first NP (NP1) or to the second NP (NP2) is a matter of debate in the literature. Some accounts explain it in terms of universal discourse-based principles that interact with language-specific rules (Frazier & Clifton, 1996), whereas other explanations are based on structurally based parsing strategies (e.g., Gibson, Pearlmutter, Canseco-Gonzalez, & Hickock, 1996). The relevant finding for our purposes is that in this linguistic context, L2 speakers have sometimes not shown any preference for NP1 or

NP2 attachment. This finding has been taken by some to indicate that L2 speakers are not influenced by structurally-based parsing strategies, but rather are mainly guided by lexical cues (e.g., Clahsen & Felser, 2006 and references therein).


## Plausibility

Recently, a number of studies have also investigated how learners use plausibility information to recover from garden paths online. These studies have produced empirical evidence demonstrating the rapid influence of plausibility information during L2 sentence processing, and have shown that in this respect, nonnatives can behave in a native-like way.

Frenck-Mestre and Pynte (1997) investigated how advanced English learners of French and French native speakers resolved prepositional-phrase attachment ambiguities in sentences such as *They accused the ambassador of espionage (of Indonesia) but nothing came of it*. Eye-movement records revealed that both groups of speakers were influenced by plausibility information in that they were more likely to attach the prepositional phrase to the verb phrase if it was a plausible verbal argument, but to the noun phrase when it was a plausible NP modifier. In addition, Felser and Roberts (2004) found that Greek learners of English were strongly influenced by plausibility and had difficulty recovering from misanalysis when deciding if a postverbal NP functioned as a direct object or as an embedded subject. In particular, participants experienced processing difficulty if the initial analysis of the ambiguous NP as a direct object led to an implausible semantic interpretation.

The role of plausibility during L2 syntactic parsing has also been investigated in filler-gap structures. Williams, Möbius, and Kim (2001) explored differences between native and nonnative readers of English by asking whether the semantic plausibility of a potential filler modulated the postulation of a gap during parsing. Their study included native English speakers and advanced learners of English whose first languages had overt Wh-movement, such as German, or nonovert Wh-movement, such as Korean and Chinese. They compared the processing of sentences like (1) and (2) using a self-paced, plausibility judgment task:


(1) Which girl did the man push the bike into late last night?
(2) Which river did the man push the bike into late last night?


For the native and nonnative English groups alike, when the *wh*-filler was a plausible direct object of the verb, as in (1), it was more costly to discard it as the actual gap filler. Conversely, when it was an implausible direct object, as in (2), there was less resistance to reanalysis and, therefore, reading times were faster at the position of the actual filler (*the bike*). This indicates that adult learners of English use plausibility information in a manner that is very similar to that of native speakers, even when the parallel structures in their native languages look very different. Taken together, the findings in the studies presented above indicate that the L2 parser can behave very similarly to the L1 parser with respect to the use of sense–semantic information to resolve syntactic ambiguity.

## Syntactic Category and Subcategorization Information

The category information of words (i.e., whether words are verbs, nouns, or adjectives) is part of their lexical entry. Subcategorization information, or information about whether a verb is transitive or intransitive, for example, is also assumed to be part of the lexical entry of a word. An important question in the L1 processing literature is whether the processor bases initial decisions solely on category information or whether subcategorization information is also used initially. In this respect, a number of experiments have shown that native comprehenders keep track of the relative frequencies of a verb's different subcategorization alternatives and use this information to resolve syntactic ambiguity during reading (e.g., Garnsey, Pearlmutter, Myers, & Lotocky, 1997; Wilson & Garnsey, 2009). This leads us to ask whether nonnative readers also use this same type of information in their second language.

In an early study conducted by Frenck-Mestre and Pynte (1997), French-dominant and English-dominant bilinguals read sentences in both their L1 and their L2 containing temporary subject/object ambiguities, as in *Every time the dog obeyed the pretty girl showed her approval.* In English, *obey* is optionally transitive. Therefore, it is ambiguous whether the NP *the pretty girl* is the object of *obeyed* or the subject of the ensuing clause. In French, however, this syntactic ambiguity does not exist because the French equivalent of *obey* must be interpreted as an intransitive verb. Eye-movement records from both groups failed to show any qualitative differences between the native and second language speakers at the point of disambiguation, indicating that L2 speakers were able to activate the correct lexical representation of the L2 verbs, even when these lexical representations were different in each language.

Recently, Dussias, and Cramer Scaltz (2008) examined the degree to which structural commitments made while Spanish–English L2 learners read syntactically ambiguous sentences in their L2 were constrained by the verb's preferred structural environment (i.e., subcategorization bias). The temporary ambiguity arises because an NP immediately following a verb could be parsed as either the direct object of the verb "*The CIA director confirmed the rumor when he testified before Congress*," or as the subject of an embedded complement "*The CIA director confirmed the rumor could mean a security leak.*" In a monolingual experiment with English participants, the authors replicated the findings reported in previous monolingual literature (e.g., Wilson & Garnsey, 2001) demonstrating that native speakers are guided by subcategorization bias. In a bilingual experiment, they then showed that L2 learners also keep track of the relative frequencies of verb-subcategorization alternatives and use this information when building structure in the L2.

## Structure-Driven Parsing Principles

Whether or not L2 parsing involves structure-driven parsing principles is a matter of debate. These principles have been postulated to explain the parser's preference for initially computing a certain syntactic analysis over others. A classic example of this is given in (3) below:

(3) Molly said that she will go to New Jersey yesterday.

In this case, the ambiguous constituent (yesterday) can be linked either to the higher clause or to the lower clause. If linked to the higher clause, the sentence means "it was yesterday that Molly said that she would go to New Jersey." Linking it to the lower clause results in the mistaken interpretation that "Molly will go to New Jersey yesterday." For the vast majority of readers, the tendency is to link the ambiguous constituent to the lower clause. The realization that the outcome yields an incorrect interpretation forces reanalysis of the ambiguous site.

Two of the principles that have been proposed to explain the parser's initial attachment preferences (i.e., Recency and Predicate Proximity) will be introduced later in our discussion of the role of proficiency in L2 sentence comprehension. Others include parsing heuristics such as *Minimal Attachment* and *Late Closure*, which have been proposed within the framework of the *Garden-Path Model* of Frazier (1978). *Minimal attachment* ensures that when faced with ambiguity, the parser will initially select the simplest—and therefore the quickest—structure to build. *Late closure* (which is equivalent to the notion of low attachment or NP2 attachment discussed earlier) allows incoming material to be structured more rapidly, by immediately incorporating it to already processed material.

We saw in our discussion on the role of thematic information that when L2 learners parse ambiguous relative clause constructions for which no lexical-semantic information is available to guide the parsing process, some learners do not show any preference for one attachment site over the other. Based on this and other evidence suggesting the lack of intermediate gap effects during second language reading, Clahsen and Felser (2006) have recently argued that the structure-building processes during online L2 sentence comprehension are fundamentally different from the representations built by native speakers of the target language. According to their *shallow structure hypothesis*, the syntactic representations that second language learners construct while processing input in their L2 are "shallower" and less detailed than those computed by adult L1 speakers. In their view, whereas L1 speakers prioritize on structure-driven strategies and syntactic information, second language speakers privilege lexical-semantic and pragmatic information.

As stated above, some of the data that Clahsen and Felser (2006) use in favor of shallow processing come from two studies that contrast the behavior of L1 and L2 speakers while reading syntactically ambiguous relative clauses (*The dean liked the secretary of the professor who was reading a letter*). For example, Papadopoulou and Clahsen (2003) asked native speakers of high-attaching languages to read ambiguous constructions in their L2 Greek, a language where high attachment is also the preferred strategy. They found that proficient L2 speakers showed no particular preference for high or low attachment when processing an L2 that, like their L1, also favored high attachment. This finding, coupled with evidence that clear attachment preferences were observed when lexical cues guided attachment decisions, was interpreted as evidence that L2 speakers do not use structure-based information but rather are guided by lexical-semantic cues (see Felser, Roberts, Gross, & Marinis, 2003 for similar findings; but Frenck-Mestre, 1997, 2002; Dussias, 2003; Dussias & Sagarra, 2007; Miyao & Omaki, 2006 for counterevidence).

One might speculate that the absence of an attachment preference arises not because of an inability to use structure-based parsing principles, but rather as the result of group averaging. In other words, it may be that some learners displayed nonlocal attachment preferences while others attached locally, and averaging across the subjects produced no clear preference (cf., Frenck-Mestre, 2005). Omaki (2005), who also found no attachment preferences when Japanese learners of English read ambiguous relative clause constructions, carried out individual analyses to rule out this possibility. Germane to our discussion, when examined individually, some learners displayed target-like relative clause attachment preferences while others transferred their Japanese preferences. Because Papadopoulou and Clahsen (2003) did not carry out such analyses, it is difficult to rule out group averaging effects as a possible account of their results.

There is, in addition, some indication in the literature that the difficulties L2 speakers experience while parsing temporarily ambiguous structures could be explained by universal, structure-based principles of parsing. For example, Frenck-Mestre and Pynte (1997) showed that the L2 parser can operate on the basis of structure-based parsing principles such as Late Closure. These authors investigated the way in which advanced English-speaking learners of French and native French speakers resolved attachment ambiguities involving prepositional phrases. Records of eye movements revealed that the L2 speakers momentarily experienced greater difficulty than native speakers with verb phrase attachment (i.e., high attachment) of the prepositional phrase in sentences such as *He rejected the manuscript on purpose because he hated its author*. No such difficulty was observed when they read structures in which the correct analysis required attachment of the prepositional phrase to the noun phrase immediately preceding it (i.e., low attachment or late closure), as would be the case in *He rejected the manuscript on horses because he hated its author*. In other words, L2 speakers temporarily adopted a strategy of attaching the ambiguous prepositional phrases low, to the most recently processed constituent. This analysis resulted in an incorrect interpretation in the first example, but not in the second example. To account for this finding, Frenck-Mestre and Pynte proposed that nonnative readers may have a general preference for a low attachment strategy.

As our previous discussion indicates, it seems indisputable that the evidence discussed in earlier sections is rather tilted in support of the claim that L2 speakers are guided by sense–semantic information during L2 sentence parsing. However, the need for more research in this area is clear, given that the claim that L2 speakers never adopt structure-based parsing principles has not been convincingly challenged. As we will discuss later, the extent to which L2 learners utilize structure-based information might vary according to proficiency level.

## B. Participant Variables

### Proficiency

Research seems to indicate that the effect of level of proficiency on L2 sentence comprehension varies as a function of the type of information (semantic vs. syntactic) being processed. For example, results from event-related brain potential (ERP) studies on the processing of semantic violations point to similar brain response patterns between L1 speakers and high- and low-proficiency L2 learners, with differences consisting mainly in a decrease in the efficiency of semantic processing mechanisms. Perhaps the most direct empirical evidence comes from Ojima, Nakata, and Kakigi (2005), who compared ERPs recorded from a group of adult native English speakers and two groups of adult Japanese learners who attained either high or intermediate proficiency in English. For all the groups, semantically anomalous English sentences (*This house has ten cities in total*) produced the so-called N400, which has been associated with difficulty during semantic integration (Kutas & Hilliard, 1983). Many other studies have consistently found an N400 in the ERPs of nonnative speakers when processing semantic violations (see Hahne, 2001; Hahne & Friederici, 2001 and references therein), providing strong evidence that semantic aspects of sentence processing are not severely affected by differences in language proficiency (cf., Kotz & Elston-Güttler, 2004).

In contrast to semantic processing, some data suggest that the degree to which L2 learners utilize other types of information during L2 sentence comprehension varies along the proficiency dimension, with only the proficient learners resembling native speakers. One such type of information involves the use of structure-based locality principles, which are assumed to be operative during monolingual sentence parsing. Two of these principles are what Gibson et al. (1996) have termed *Recency*—which refers to a tendency by the parser to reduce the distance between a potential host site and a modifier within the sentence—and *Predicate Proximity*—or the preference to attach a modifier as close as possible to the head of a predicate phrase. These principles have been proposed to explain crosslinguistic differences in attachment preferences. Specifically, preferences reflecting the application of recency have been found in languages such as English, Brazilian Portuguese, and Arabic, but the application of predicate proximity has been reported in other languages like Spanish, Dutch, German, or French (cf., Carreiras & Clifton, 1999 and references therein). To illustrate, consider the temporarily ambiguous sentence *The man called the daughter of the psychologist who lives in California*, in which the modifier *who lives in California* can be interpreted as referring to *the daughter* or *the psychologist* (hence the temporary ambiguity). Empirical evidence suggests that in English recency dominates over predicate proximity, so the preferred resolution of the ambiguity is to "attach" the relative clause to the noun closest to it (i.e., NP2 attachment or *low attachment*). This results in an interpretation in which *the psychologist lives in California*. Contrary to this, in Spanish, predicate proximity is strong enough to dominate over recency. In this case, the ambiguity is resolved in favor of NP1 attachment or *high attachment*, resulting in an interpretation in which *the daughter lives in California*.

Frenck-Mestre (1997) examined the processing of this construction in less proficient learners of French—a language in which NP1 is the preferred attachment site—by considering whether the general attachment preferences in the L1 and the L2 were congruent or incongruent. In the congruent case (i.e., L1 Spanish–L2 French), learners showed a preference for NP1 attachment. In the incongruent case (i.e., L1 English–L2 French), the trend was toward NP2 ambiguity resolution. That is, the L2 readers only followed the target language's general attachment preference when it was congruent with the general preference in their L1. Frenck–Mestre attributed this pattern of results to the influence of the native language on L2 processing.

A subsequent study (Frenck-Mestre, 2002), however, found that English-French learners who were more proficient in their L2 French resolved the ambiguity in favor of NP1 attachment, the same pattern found in the French monolingual group. Frenck-Mestre suggested that the parsing preferences observed in the first group of nonnative French learners were due to their low level of proficiency in the L2. In contrast, the learners in Frenck-Mestre (2002) were more proficient. This suggests that proficiency modulates the degree to which L2 learners are guided by phrase-structure-based parsing principles of the type that are evidenced during L1 processing.

Other findings also indicate that proficiency modulates the ability to access and use syntactic information as well as plausibility information during L2 sentence comprehension. Hopp (2006), for instance, found that advanced learners of German displayed the same processing preferences as native Germans when reading subject–object ambiguities, but they did not show differences in response latencies found in native syntactic reanalysis. The near-native speakers, however, reliably used syntactic features in phrase-structure reanalysis, and also showed evidence of incremental reanalysis patterns typically found in native speakers. Finally, studies investigating theta-role assignment under the Competition Model generally find that L2 learners use parsing strategies that are more consonant with the structure of the L2 as they become more proficient (Su, 2001).

Taken together, these findings suggest that the extent to which L2 learners are able to exploit various sources of information during L2 sentence comprehension may depend on proficiency level. This may be, in part, because lower proficiency confers a processing disadvantage to second language learners, as the increased effort required to process lower-level information in the second language detracts from the cognitive resources needed to carry out higher-level comprehension processes. By contrast, higher proficiency levels free up cognitive resources needed to carry out higher-level computations involving the rapid access and integration of information, resulting in processing that is similar to that of native speakers. Some recent evidence from the L2 production literature indicates that this may, in fact, be the case. For example, Hoshino, Dussias, and Kroll (Accepted) found that only Spanish–English speakers who were highly proficient in their L2 were sensitive to conceptual number and grammatical number in the computation of subject–verb agreement, replicating in behavior the performance of native English speakers with high memory span. However, low-proficiency L2 learners showed sensitivity to only the grammatical number, much like the native speakers with low-span scores. This result, together with the findings discussed above, suggests that only at near-native levels of proficiency do nonnatives converge on native-like processes.

## Immersion Experience

Previous literature on adult native speakers has raised the possibility that the sentence parser is experience based, and that initial parsing choices are made on the basis of the experience that the individual readers or listeners have with the language spoken in their environment (e.g., Cuetos, Mitchell, & Corley, 1996). Although this claim has been subjected to much empirical testing in the monolingual literature, few studies have examined whether immersion experience impacts L2 sentence comprehension, and whether, in fact, learners immersed in their L2 tune in to linguistic variations of the environment and use this information to resolve syntactic ambiguity.

One such experiment is reported in Fernández (2003). A pencil-and-paper questionnaire was employed to investigate relative clause attachment preferences in Spanish learners of English living in an English-speaking environment and Spanish monolingual controls. Participants read stimulus materials in Spanish and English, in which the important linguistic variable was the manipulation of the length of the relative clause—a factor known to influence relative clause ambiguity resolution in monolingual sentence parsing (Fodor, 1998). Accordingly, sentences either had short relative clauses (e.g., *The nephew of the teacher that was divorced*) or long relative clauses (e.g., *The nephew of the teacher that was in the communist party*). Consistent with the proposal advanced in Fodor that the parser has a tendency to equalize the prosodic weight size of constituents (so, long RCs should "attract" NP1 attachment and short relative clauses should attract NP2 attachment), Fernández found overall higher rates of NP1 attachment with long versus short relative clauses for monolingual Spanish controls. However, the Spanish learners of English were sensitive to the length of the relative clause when reading in English, but failed to exhibit length effects with Spanish materials, despite the fact that Spanish was their dominant language. To explain the findings, Fernández hypothesized that sensitivity to length emerges more clearly in the language that the participants read more frequently. In the case of the Spanish–English speakers, the fact that they were immersed in an English environment and were, therefore, more frequent readers of English, may have contributed to the lack of a length effect in Spanish, their own native language.

Similar findings were reported in Dussias (2003) who also tested Spanish–English speakers in their two languages. As in previous studies, the construction examined contained a complex noun phrase followed by a relative clause. Findings for the control groups (i.e., Spanish and English monolinguals) showed the conventional bias for NP1 and NP2, respectively, reported in the literature. However, for the Spanish-dominant bilinguals, the prevailing strategy was NP2 attachment regardless of whether they were reading Spanish or English materials. To account for the findings, Dussias suggested that the amount of exposure to the second language by these learners could have played a role. The Spanish–English participants had lived in the second language environment for approximately 8 years and had been under intense contact with English. It could have been that exposure to a large number of English ambiguous constructions resolved in favor of NP2 may have rendered this interpretation more available, ultimately resulting in the preference for NP2 attachment observed in the results.

More recently, Dussias and Sagarra (2007) compared the performance of monolingual Spanish speakers with that of Spanish–English bilinguals who had limited or extensive immersion experiences in the L2 environment. Participants read temporarily ambiguous constructions in Spanish, their dominant language, again consisting of a complex NP followed by a relative clause. The findings showed that the Spanish–English speakers with limited immersion experience in the L2 environment resolved the ambiguity using the same strategies employed by monolingual Spanish readers. Conversely, the Spanish–English speakers with extensive exposure to English parsed the ambiguous construction using strategies associated with English, their second language. Importantly, the results were apparent after proficiency between the two groups of bilinguals was matched, showing that the difference was not due to proficiency in the L2, but rather to immersion experience.

These results taken together suggest that amount of immersion in the L2 language can alter the processing strategies of the L2 learners and counteract the influence of L1 processing patterns when processing the L2. Moreover, the above studies also suggest that L2 immersion can have the effect of altering processing patterns in the bilingual's L1.

## Working Memory

In the L1 sentence processing literature, working memory has been hypothesized to play a central role in language comprehension. During reading, comprehenders must recognize words, compute syntactic structure, and assign thematic roles to phrases. They must also quickly retrieve the representations of previously processed words and phrases to integrate them with newly processed phrases in the text. In addition, they need to store other information, such as explicit text propositions and inferences based upon those propositions, which are implicated in the construction of a functional, coherent representation of the text in memory (Kintsch & Van Dijk, 1978). During the execution of these processes, working memory is important in storing the inter-mediate and final products of a reader's successive computations. This allows for the construction and integration of different types of information from the text (cf., Just & Carpenter, 1992).

A number of studies in the monolingual literature support the view that individual differences affect parsing behavior. For example, high-span individuals have shown a speed advantage for integrating pragmatic information, but a speed disadvantage when resolving certain types of syntactic ambiguity (MacDonald, Just, & Carpenter, 1992). Other studies examining the influence of working memory resources in the resolution of relative clause ambiguities of the type discussed above, suggest that high-span speakers have sufficient cognitive resources to keep both the nonlocal NP1 and the local NP2 active in working memory when resolving the ambiguity, but low-span individuals can only encode the nonlocal NP in working memory (Mendelsohn & Pearlmutter, 1999). These findings raise the question of whether the observed differences in sentence processing between L2 speakers and monolingual speakers could be explained under a cognitive load account. This question is even more relevant when considering that studies in the L2 domain indicate that even for relatively proficient bilinguals, processing the L2 requires additional cognitive resources compared to L1 processing (e.g., Michael & Gollan, 2005).

The available findings generally show no relationship between availability of cognitive resources, as measured by reading span tests, and L2 sentence comprehension. For example, Juffs (2004, 2005) failed to find a correlation between reading times and span scores when high- and low-span L2 learners read sentences that are known to cause a garden-path effect in monolingual speakers. Although these results suggest a dissociation between working memory capacity and L2 sentence processing behavior, one major challenge to the findings involves the type of working memory measure employed. Studies that have used Daneman and Carpenter's (1980) reading span test, or a variant of the test (as is the case in Juffs, 2004, 2005), may have found no correlations because the test is potentially invalid as a measure of working memory capacity (see Omaki, 2005 for a similar argument). In the Daneman and Carpenter span test, participants are asked to read sentences aloud while remembering the last word of each sentence for a subsequent recall task. Because reading aloud does not guarantee that participants process sentences for meaning, it has been argued that the processing component of working memory is not taxed in the manner that it normally is during language comprehension (Waters & Caplan, 1996).

To address this limitation, Omaki (2005) used a modified version of the Waters and Caplan (1996) reading span test to examine whether ambiguity resolution was associated with working memory capacity when Japanese learners of English read ambiguous relative clauses in English (e.g., *The doctor said that the sister of the bishop who injured himself (herself) last summer was concerned about the infection*). Once again, no relation was found between reading span and attachment preferences. However, as Omaki suggests, the lack of a relationship is expected if the Japanese-English learners had failed to learn that English is a subset of Japanese with respect to the scope of the interpretation that a modifier phrase (e.g., a relative clause) has over the two nouns in the genitive phrase. In other words, English is like Japanese in that its genitive construction contains two noun phrases separated by a genitive marker. The two languages differ, however, in that Japanese genitive constructions allow a relative clause to modify either one of the two nouns in the genitive phrase, but the English genitive only permits attachment of the relative clause to the local noun. This means that Japanese L2 learners of English must know, minimally, that a relative clause following a genitive construction in English can only be construed as referring to the syntactically closer (i.e., local) noun phrase before this knowledge can interact with availability of cognitive resources. Because Omaki did not explicitly test whether the learners favored only the local, more restricted interpretation of the modifier, it is difficult to interpret the lack of an effect between cognitive resources and L2 sentence comprehension reported in his study.

Contrary to the empirical evidence reviewed above, some other studies suggest that L2 speakers employ processing resources to the degree that is necessary to perform the task at hand. In Williams (2006), participants were required to perform one of two tasks: (1) To press a button as soon as they thought that a sentence displayed on a computer screen had stopped making sense, (2) to perform a memory task that required the completion of a sentence using a word that had appeared in a previously displayed sentence. The results showed that L2 speakers processed the input incrementally, just as native speakers did, when the task encouraged such type of processing (i.e., in the stop-making-sense task). However, when the task imposed memory demands, the nonnative readers did not process the input incrementally, most likely because they were not able to allocate sufficient resources to perform such processing. This suggests that availability of processing resources plays a role during L2 sentence comprehension; it also indicates that L2 readers may be able to overcome processing limitations under the appropriate task conditions. In a similar vein, Dussias & Piñar (in press) found that although higher working memory resources did not prevent an initial misparse for Chinese-English speakers reading *wh*-subject and *wh*-object extraction structures in English, only the participants with higher working memory scores, like the native English speakers, were able to use semantic plausibility cues to recover from misanalysis, with implausible analyses facilitating recovery.

## The Nature of the Language Input: The Case of Deaf Learners

As we discussed above, the learner's individual linguistic experience can interact with both semantic and structural factors and determine the outcome of the parsing process. Given that the experience of deaf learners is different from that of hearing learners, a review of some of the issues that affect reading processing among deaf individuals can inform our understanding of second language processing in general. The following discussion can apply to deaf readers in any language, but for the purpose of this chapter we will focus on deaf Americans reading English. (See also Berent, this volume.)

For most deaf Americans, English is considered to be a second language. Although only 10% of deaf people are born to deaf parents and are thus exposed to a sign language from birth (American Sign Language in this case), most deaf children learn ASL (or some form of sign language) at school, and most deaf adults use ASL as their primary form of communication (Musselman [Reich] & Reich, 1976). With few exceptions, profoundly deaf children, including those from hearing families, have a very limited knowledge of English by the time they start going to school and learning how to read. In contrast to hearing children, who typically learn how to read after they have acquired the spoken language, deaf children learning how to read in English have to learn the skill of reading at the same time as they learn English (cf., Berent, this volume). Additionally, deaf children who have not been exposed to sign language at home (about 90%) most typically have to learn how to read in an L2 before they have even fully developed an L1. To the above circumstances, one must add the fact that written language is a representation of the spoken language, to which deaf individuals do not have direct access. For all these reasons, deaf people's experiences with print pose interesting questions for the study of written language parsing. One question that arises is whether reading is qualitatively different for hearing and for deaf individuals. Research addressing this issue will be reviewed and discussed within the wider context of second language processing in general. We will focus on three selected variables, competence in the L2, cognitive resources, and knowledge in an L1.

### The Role of Competence in the Target Language

Some studies have found a relation between deficiencies in knowledge of English grammar and vocabulary and low reading comprehension among some deaf readers (e.g., LaSasso & Davey, 1987; Quigley, Wilbur, Power, Montanelli, & Steinkamp, 1979). However, in spite of the identified gaps in grammatical knowledge that some deaf individuals may have, other studies reveal that grammatical competence in English cannot completely explain reading comprehension differences between skilled and not skilled deaf readers, or even between deaf and hearing readers.[1] For example,

---

[1] Competence is understood here as the internalized knowledge of a language (Chomsky, 1965). In this sense, competence must be understood as different from actual performance in the language. It is, therefore, different from level of proficiency, which incorporates the notion of performance.

Lillo-Martin, Hanson, and Smith (1992) conducted a study on deaf reader's competence in relative clause structures. They compared two groups of college deaf students with different levels of independently measured reading comprehension skills. A difference between the two groups in the syntactic processing of complex structures, such as relative clauses, would have indicated that specific syntactic deficits might underlie the difference in reading comprehension skills between the higher and the lower-skilled readers. Their subjects completed a battery of tests to determine their knowledge of relative clause structures in written English, ASL, and Signed English. No significant group effect was found in any of the three language conditions. Interestingly, for the English sentences, both high- and low-skilled readers displayed the same pattern of errors depending on the pragmatic felicity conditions of the relative clause type, thus showing similar competence and similar processing patterns for both groups across different types of relative clauses. This suggests that the independently measured differences in the reading skill levels of the two groups were not due to differences in knowledge of complex structures.

In a more recent study, Kelly (2003) also found that deaf readers with very different levels of reading comprehension skills did not differ qualitatively in how they processed relative clause structures. Although only the less skilled group showed a significant decline in relative clause comprehension in contrast to the control sentences, the reading pattern was similar for both groups of subjects. For example, both groups showed markedly slower reading times for the main verb in relative clause structures as compared to the same verbs in the control sentences. This is the expected reading pattern for relative clause sentences, since the main verb is the point at which the reader first identifies a syntactic gap, as in "She is the woman who__kissed the man." The same processing pattern has been consistently found among L1 readers in the sentence processing literature. The reading patterns obtained in this study suggest strongly that, in spite of the comprehension differences between the high- and low-skilled groups in the relative clause structure condition, both groups displayed a clear command of relative clauses and processing patterns that were consistent with that of L1 readers.

On the basis of these findings, both Lillo-Martin et al. (1992) and Kelly (2003) conclude that differences in reading comprehension skills between skilled and nonskilled readers cannot be accounted for simply on the basis of differences in syntactic competence of complex structures. More generally, we might add that, given that the deaf readers in the above-mentioned studies showed processing patterns that were equal to those found among L1 hearing readers, differences in reading comprehension among hearing and deaf subjects do not seem to be solely attributable to differences in syntactic knowledge. Interestingly, the literature on L2 sentence processing has come to the same conclusion regarding the comprehension performance of hearing L2 learners. A case in point, for example, is Juffs & Harrington's (1995) discussion of the processing of English long-distance *wh*-questions. In their study, L2 learners displayed evidence of knowing the *wh*-structure, yet differed significantly in their comprehension performance when compared to L1 subjects. A wider range of syntactic structures needs to be methodically tested in order to clearly determine the role of grammatical competence in sentence comprehension. But if, as the cited research suggests, grammatical competence alone cannot account for differences in comprehension skills among the different groups of readers, what else might be driving the subjects' performance? Below we discuss how the nature of the L2 input (namely, written only) and the deaf reader's general linguistic experience may influence the amount of cognitive resources he or she brings into the task of performing higher-level reading operations.

## Cognitive Resources

Readers use different decoding mechanisms to perform basic reading operations, such as identifying words and other basic text units and relating them to one another. For example, it is widely assumed that phonological coding (or the mapping from print to sound) is one strategy used by hearing readers to identify basic text units and keep them in short-term memory. Since deaf readers do not have access to the phonological aspects of English, are their lexical retrieval and storage strategies different from those utilized by hearing readers? And how might different strategies affect cognitive resources while reading?

There is no consensus on which decoding or short-term memory strategies deaf readers are more likely to use. Some studies have found that they use a variety of strategies available to them: visual strategies (such as grapheme or whole word recognition, as well as cheremic associations with signs) and also speech-based strategies (developed through articulation, visual cues, and finger spelling, e.g., Hanson & Fowler, 1987; Padden & Hanson, 2000). Lichtenstein (1998), for example, observed that the subjects in his study could not be classified into groups that used one strategy versus another. He concluded, however, that speech-based recoding was the most effective system for temporarily storing information—given its higher correlation with scores in the sequential recall of word lists—but that it was not likely to be the strategy used to help with lexical retrieval. Similar conclusions were drawn in an earlier study by Hanson (1982). From the results of these studies, it might seem that effective deaf readers use a more visual strategy for basic reading operations such as word identification, and a more sequentially based strategy for storing information in short-term memory. The role of phonological awareness, or speech-based recoding, in reading among deaf individuals, however, is rather controversial. First, evidence establishing a relationship between reading skill level and the use of phonological coding in word recognition and recall tasks is mixed and unclear (cf., Musselman, 2000 for a review). Second, even those studies claiming that there is a relation have not been able to establish a causal direction.

Investigating decoding and short-term memory strategies is, nevertheless, important because shortcomings in either one would take up cognitive resources while reading and overburden working memory. One of the goals of the above-mentioned experimental design by Kelly (2003) was precisely to tease out whether reading processing differences among higher and lower-skilled deaf readers could be attributable either to differences in processing automaticity for basic reading tasks, such as word identification, or to short-term storage capacity. In order to isolate automaticity as the variable that might distinguish between high- and low-skilled readers, Kelly administered the working memory test designed by Daneman and Carpenter (1980) twice in a row to two groups of college-age deaf students with different levels of reading comprehension skills. The logic was that the readers' familiarity with the vocabulary and the sentences would make the basic reading tasks more automatic the second time around and, thus, reduce any possible initial reading automaticity differences between the two groups. Administering the test a second time, however, would not affect the storage capacity demands of the task. As expected, the less skilled readers performed lower than the more skilled readers in the first test administration. However, both groups performed more similarly on the second test administration, after any possible initial automaticity differences between the two groups were reduced by enhancing familiarity. Kelly concluded that this result points to automaticity and not to storage capacity as the factor that differentiates reading performance between the two groups.

To isolate the short-term storage capacity variable, Kelly administered sentence reading tasks in which the demands on processing and storage were experimentally manipulated. Specifically, the subjects had to read relative clause structures and their simpler controls in a whole sentence condition and in a word-by-word presentation condition in which subjects only saw one word of the sentence at a time. Arguably, the word-by-word presentation condition imposed a heavier burden on storage capacity. Interestingly, Kelly found that neither group showed any significant comprehension differences in the whole sentence versus the word-by-word presentation condition, which suggests that a difference in storage capacity did not make a difference in comprehension for either group. Since short-term storage is the variable that has been linked to type of decoding strategy in the literature, it would seem that the comprehension differences in this study did not stem from whether the subjects made use of phonological decoding or not.

The less skilled readers in Kelly's study, however, were overall much slower than the skilled readers, even in the simple sentence condition—with speed being a sign of processing automaticity. Additionally, in contrast to the higher-skilled group, the lower-skilled group was not only slower, but also showed significantly lower comprehension in complex structures. This suggests that automaticity had a significant effect on the lower-skilled group's comprehension performance. That is, as automaticity decreased due to structure complexity, comprehension also decreased for the lower-skilled group. Interestingly, in spite of these differences, recall that both groups showed the expected processing pattern for relative clause structures (i.e., both groups' reading times were significantly higher at the site of the main clause verb). On the basis of these results, Kelly concluded that sentence comprehension differences between the two groups was not due to deficient knowledge of the relative clause structure on the part of the lower-skilled group or to storage capacity differences, but rather to a difference in processing automaticity. Arguably, low automaticity taxed cognitive resources and derailed sentence comprehension for the slower readers.

In sum, just as has been found in the L1 and L2 processing literature, differences in cognitive resources among deaf subjects may affect their comprehension performance. More specifically, the previous discussion suggests that automaticity in decoding and recognizing the basic units of printed texts may be an important factor in accounting for differences in comprehension performance between different groups of readers. The question is what produces low automaticity and how do skilled readers acquire the necessary automaticity to efficiently comprehend written text? As Kelly (2003) points out, the causal relation between automaticity and reading experience might, in fact, be reciprocal. Thus, while automaticity seems to influence the quality of the reading experience, successful experiences with reading might also enhance automaticity in recognizing and establishing relations among basic text units.

Bottom-up reading components, such as automaticity in recognizing basic text units and their syntactic relationship to each other normally interact with the so-called top-down aspects of the reading process, such as application of context and topic knowledge and stored linguistic knowledge. One factor, not yet discussed, that seems to be key in enabling the mapping between print and meaning for deaf learners, is the quality of stored linguistic knowledge. Below, we discuss the relationship between sign language skills and reading skills and the role that the development of a first language might play in the development of literacy skills in a written language.

## Stored Linguistic Knowledge and Deaf Literacy

The role of the L1 in the acquisition of an L2 has been a topic of hot debate in the second language learning literature (cf., see Gass, 1996 for a review). Interestingly while knowledge of an L1 is assumed for hearing L2 learners, deaf learners present a wide range of variation regarding their previous linguistic knowledge in an L1 by the time they start learning written English. Since not all deaf learners come to the task of learning English with a fully formed L1, deaf people's experiences in acquiring English literacy can inform the debate on language transfer in interesting ways. For example, research in deaf literacy can provide insight into the question of how Universal Grammar and the L1 interact in the development of an L2. Specifically, how much previous knowledge is enough, and to what extent can Universal Grammar principles compensate for gaps in L1 experience?

The relationship between signing skills and the acquisition of English literacy has also been a source of controversy in the history of deaf education. The proliferation of oral programs before the 1970s was based on the assumption that ASL would interfere with the acquisition of English. More current approaches adopt Cummins' (1981, 1989) model of linguistic interdependence as a model for bilingual education for deaf students. Based on Cummins' tenet that there is a common proficiency underlying the two languages of a bilingual person, it is argued that development of cognitive and academic skills in ASL will translate into the development of similar skills in English.

It has been shown that deaf children of deaf parents attain higher reading achievements, on average, than deaf children of hearing parents—who are less likely to experience early exposure to sign (cf., Kampfe & Turecheck, 1987 for a review). Signing skills, however, are only one variable in the dynamics of hearing versus deaf families. In order to isolate the role of ASL in the academic achievement of deaf children, Strong and Prinz (2000) investigated whether the deaf versus hearing family effect would persist if the ASL skills of the children were held constant. They studied a group of children, ages 8–15, from the same deaf residential school and found an overall statistically significant relation between ASL skill level and English literacy skills. Moreover, they found that the students within the highest ASL skill-level groups performed equally well on English literacy tasks regardless of family hearing versus deaf status. They conclude that this result confirms the hypothesis that the reported academic performance difference between deaf children of hearing versus deaf families is due to linguistic knowledge of ASL. The same kind of relation between ASL and

English literacy has been found in other studies, such as those of Hoffmeister (2000) and Padden and Ramsey (2000).

The evidence from the studies above indicates that knowledge of ASL facilitates English literacy. At the same time, it is important to understand that ASL is a *bona fide* language with grammar and vocabulary that are completely different from English (Klima & Bellugi, 1979; Stokoe, 1960). Given the lack of a one-to-one correspondence between printed English and ASL, much remains unknown about how exactly sign language might be used to bridge the gap between print and meaning (Chamberlain & Mayberry, 2000; Hirsh-Pasek & Treiman, 1982; Padden & Hanson, 2000). The reported facilitatory effect of ASL, however, may well be an important factor for the establishment of the reciprocal relationship between automaticity and reading experience.

## II. CONCLUDING REMARKS

The field of L2 sentence comprehension has reached an exciting point. The number of findings involving different types of syntactic structures is rapidly growing, and explanations are beginning to emerge that attempt to characterize the type of processing in which L2 learners engage while constructing a syntactic parse. The framing question underlying the studies discussed in this chapter is to what extent L2 processing is qualitatively similar or different from L1 processing. In addressing this question, we have discussed a number of variables that appear to affect reading processing among L2 learners. Some of these variables are linguistic in nature in that they are concerned with the specific sources of linguistic information that L2 learners access and use during L2 sentence comprehension. We have seen that, just as in L1 processing, "sense–semantic" information appears to have very rapid effects on L2 comprehension and, under some circumstances, influences incremental sentence processing. However, it is much less clear whether the L2 processor takes into account structure-driven parsing principles of the type proposed in the L1 sentence processing literature. We have also discussed other variables that are related to the characteristics of learners or to their linguistic experience. We saw, for example, how learners' characteristics, such as proficiency and type of linguistic experience, often interact with linguistic aspects of the input in producing a parsing outcome.

In order to arrive at an accurate representation of L2 language processing, more interdisciplinary collaboration is needed that examines a wider variety of L2 learners and use a range of methodological tools. A case in point, which was highlighted in this chapter, is deaf learners. The case of deaf L2 learners is particularly interesting because the written language constitutes their primary access to the L2. As we saw, this raises important questions about the nature of the decoding mechanisms they use and about whether those mechanisms ultimately affect their syntactic processing and render their reading experience qualitatively different from that of hearing L2 readers. Their unique language and learning experience can inform the field of second language processing in insightful ways. At the same time, the study of deaf written literacy can be enriched when looked at in the context of the experiences of other second language learners.

Recent research efforts are also trying to incorporate other learner groups that have heretofore been excluded from the literature on L2 processing. One example of this is Juffs (2007) study on what he terms "low-educated learners." As we examine a wider range of learners, we will have a more complete picture of the factors that are implicated in second language processing and will find ourselves in a better position to identify the crucial variables that lead to successful second language comprehension.

## ACKNOWLEDGMENTS

The research reported in this paper was supported in part by NIH Grant HD50629 and NSF Grant BCS 0750347.

## REFERENCES

Bates, E., & MacWhinney, B. (1982). Functionalist approaches to grammar. In E. Wanner & L. Gleitman (Eds.), *Language acquisition: The state of the art* (pp. 173–218). New York: Cambridge University Press.

Carreiras, M., & Clifton, C. (1999). Another word on parsing relative clauses: Eyetracking evidence from Spanish and English. *Memory and Cognition, 27,* 826–833.

Chamberlain, C., & Mayberry, R. (2000). Theorizing about the relation between American Sign Language and reading. In C. Chamberlain, J. Morford, & R. I. Mayberry (Eds.), *Language acquisition by eye* (pp. 221–259). Mahwah, NJ: Lawrence Erlbaum Associates.

Chomsky, N. (1965). *Aspects of the theory of syntax.* Cambridge: The MIT Press.

Clahsen, H., & Felser, C. (2006). Grammatical proceeding in language learners. *Applied Psycholinguistics, 27,* 3–42.

Cuetos, F., Mitchell, D., & Corley, M. (1996). Parsing in different languages. In M. Carreiras, J. Garcia-Albea, & N. Sebastian-Galles (Eds.), *Language processing in Spanish* (pp. 145–187). Mahwah, NJ: Erlbaum.

Cummins, J. (1981). The role of primary language development in promoting educational success for language minority students. *Schooling and language minority students: A theoretical framework* (pp. 3–50). Los Angeles: California State University, Evaluation, Dissemination and Asssessment Center.

Cummings, J. (1989). A theoretical framework for bilingual special education. *Exceptional Children, 56*(2), 111–119.

Daneman, M., & Carpenter, P. (1980). Individual differences in working memory and reading. *Journal of Verbal Learning and Verbal Behavior, 19,* 450–466.

Dussias, P. E. (2003). Syntactic ambiguity resolution in L2 learners. *Studies in Second Language Acquisition, 25,* 529–557.

Dussias, P. E., & Cramer Scaltz, T. R. (2008). Spanish-English L2 speakers' use of subcategorization bias information in the resolution of temporary ambiguity during second language reading. *Acta Psychologica, 128,* 501–513.

Dussias, P. E., & Piñar, P. (in press). Effects of Working Memory and plausibility in the reanalysis of *wh*-gaps by Chinese-English bilinguals. *Second Language Research, 25.*

Dussias, P. E., & Sagarra, N. (2007). The effect of exposure on syntactic parsing in Spanish-English L2 speakers. *Bilingualism, Language and Cognition, 10,* 101–116.

Felser, C., & Roberts, L. (2004). Plausibility and recovery from garden paths in second language sentence processing. Poster presented at AMLaP, Aix-en-Provence, September.

Felser, C., Roberts, L., Gross, R., & Marinis, T. (2003). The processing of ambiguous sentences by first and second language learners of English. *Applied Psycholinguistics, 24*, 453–489.

Fernández, E. M. (2003). *Bilingual sentence processing: Relative clause attachment in English and Spanish*. Amsterdam: John Benjamins.

Fodor, J. D. (1998). Learning to parse? *Journal of Psycholinguistic Research, 27*, 285–319.

Frazier, L. (1978). *On comprehending sentences: Syntactic parsing strategies*. Unpublished PhD dissertation, University of Connecticut, Storrs, CT.

Frazier, L., & Clifton, C. (1996). *Construal*. Cambridge, MA: MIT Press.

Frenck-Mestre, C. (1997). Examining second language reading: An on-line look. In A. Sorace, C. Heycock, & R. Shillcok (Eds.), *Proceedings of the GALA 1997 Conference on Language Acquisition* (pp. 474–478). Edinburgh: Human Communications Research Center.

Frenck-Mestre, C. (2002). An on-line look at sentence processing in the second language. In R. Heredia & J. Altarriba (Eds.), *Bilingual sentence processing* (pp. 217–236). New York: Elsevier.

Frenck-Mestre, C. (2005). Ambiguities and Anomalies: What can eye movements and event-related potentials reveal about second language sentence processing? In J. F. Kroll & A. M. B. de Groot (Eds.), *Handbook of bilingualism* (pp. 268–281). Oxford: Oxford University Press.

Frenck-Mestre, C., & Pynte, J. (1997). Syntactic ambiguity resolution while reading in second and native languages. *Quarterly Journal of Experimental Psychology, 50*, 119–148.

Garnsey, S. M., Pearlmutter, N. J., Myers, E., & Lotocky, M. A. (1997). The contributions of verb bias and plausibility to the comprehension of temporarily ambiguous sentences. *Journal of Memory and Language, 37*, 58–93.

Gass, S. (1987). The resolution of conflicts among competing systems: A bidirectional perspective. *Applied Psycholinguistics, 8*, 329–350.

Gass, S. (1996). Second language acquisition and linguistic theory: The role of language transfer. In W. C. Ritchie & T. K. Bhatia (Eds.), *Handbook of second language acquisition* (pp. 317–340). San Diego, CA: Academic Press.

Gibson, E., Pearlmutter, N., Canseco-Gonzalez, E., & Hickock, G. (1996). Recency preferences in the human sentence processing mechanism. *Cognition, 59*, 23–59.

Hahne, A. (2001). What's the difference in second-language processing? Evidence from event-related brain potentials. *Journal of Psycholinguistic Research, 30*, 251–266.

Hahne, A., Müller, J., & Clahsen, H. (2006). Morphological processing in a second language: Behavioral and ERP evidence for storage and decomposition. *Journal of Cognitive Neuroscience, 18*, 121–134.

Hahne, A., & Friederici, A. (2001). Processing a second language: Late learners' comprehension mechanisms as revealed by event-related brain potentials. *Bilingualism, Language and Cognition, 4*, 123–141.

Hanson, V. (1982). Short-term recall by deaf signers of American Sign Language: Implications of encoding strategy for order recall. *Journal of Experimental Psychology, 8*, 572–583.

Hanson, V. L., & Fowler, C. A. (1987). Phonological coding in word reading: Evidence from hearing and deaf readers. *Memory and Cognition, 15*, 199–207.

Harrington, M. (1987). Processing transfer: Language-specific processing strategies as a source of interlanguage variation. *Applied Psycholinguistics, 8*, 351–377.

Hirsh-Pasek, L., & Treiman, R. (1982). Recoding in silent reading: Can the deaf child translate print into a more manageable form? *The Volta Review, 84,* 71–72.

Hoffmeister, R. (2000). A piece of the puzzle: ASL and reading comprehension in deaf children. In C. Chamberlain, J. Morford, & R. I. Mayberry (Eds.), *Language acquisition by eye* (pp. 143–166). Mahwah, NJ: Lawrence Erlbaum Associates.

Hopp, H. (2006). Syntactic features and reanalysis in near-native processing. *Second Language Research, 22,* 369–397.

Hoshino, N., Dussias, P. E., & Kroll, J. K. (Accepted). Processing subject–verb agreement in a second language depends on proficiency. *Bilingualism, Language and Cognition.*

Juffs, A. (2004). Representation, processing, and working memory in a second language. *Transactions of the Philological Society, 102,* 199–225.

Juffs, A. (2005). The influence of first language on the processing of *wh*-movement in English as a second language. *Second Language Research, 21,* 121–151.

Juffs, A. (2007). Working memory, second language acquisition, and low-educated second language and literacy learners. In I. van de Craats, J. Kurvers, & M. Young-Scholten (Eds.), *Low-Educated Second Language and Literacy Acquisition: Proceedings of the Inaugural Symposium*-Tilburg 05 (Vol. 6, pp. 89–104), LOT Occasional Papers. The Netherlands: Netherlands Graduate School of Linguistics.

Juffs, A., & Harrington, M. (1995). Parsing effects in second language processing: Subject and object asymmetries in wh-extractions. *Studies in Second Language Acquisition, 17,* 483–516.

Just, M. A., & Carpenter, P. (1992). A capacity theory of comprehension: individual differences in working memory. *Psychological Review, 99,* 122–149.

Kampfe, C. M., & Turecheck, A. G. (1987). Reading achievement of prelingually deaf students and its relationship to parental method of communication: A review of the literature. *American Annals of the Deaf, 132,* 11–15.

Kelly, L. (2003). The importance of processing automaticity and temporary storage capacity to the differences in comprehension between skilled and less skilled college-age deaf readers. *Journal of Deaf Studies and Deaf Education, 8,* 230–249.

Kintsch, W., & Van Dijk, T. A. (1978). Toward a model of text comprehension and production. *Psychological Review, 85,* 363–394.

Klima, E. S., & Bellugi, U. (1979). *The signs of language.* Cambridge, MA: Harvard University Press.

Kotz, S. A., & Elston-Güttler, K. (2004). The role of proficiency on processing categorical and associative information in the L2 as revealed by reaction times and event-related potentials. *Journal of Neurolinguistics, 17,* 215–235.

Kroll, J. F., & Dussias, P. E. (2004). The comprehension of words and sentences in two languages. In T. K. Bhatia & W. C. Ritchie (Eds.), *Handbook of bilingualism* (pp. 169–200). Cambridge, MA: Blackwell.

Kroll, J. F., Gerfen, C., & Dussias, P. E. (2008). Laboratory designs and paradigms in psycholinguistics. In L. Wei & M. Moyer (Eds.), *The Blackwell guide to research methods in bilingualism and multilingualism* (pp. 108–131). Cambridge, MA: Blackwell.

Kutas, M., & Hilliard, S. A. (1983). Event-related. Brain potentials to grammatical errors and semantic anomalies. *Memory and Cognition, 11,* 539–550.

LaSasso, C., & Davey, B. (1987). The relationship between lexical knowledge and reading comprehension for prelingually, profoundly hearing-impaired students. *Volta Review, 89,* 211–220.

Lichtenstein, E. (1998). Reading in deaf children. *Journal of Deaf Studies, 3,* 1–55.

Lieberman, M., Aoshima, S., & Phillips, C. (2006). Native-like biases in generation of *wh*-questions by non-native speakers of Japanese. *Studies in Second Language Acquisition, 28,* 423–448.

Lillo-Martin, D., Hanson, V., & Smith, S. (1992). Deaf readers' comprehension of relative clause structures. *Applied Psycholinguistics, 13,* 13–30.

MacDonald, M. C., Just, M. A., & Carpenter, P. A. (1992). Working memory constraints on the processing of syntactic ambiguity. *Cognitive Psychology, 24,* 56–98.

Mendelsohn, A., & Pearlmutter, N. J. (1999). Individual differences in relative clause attachment preferences. Poster presented at the Twelfth Annual CUNY Conference on Human Sentence Processing, New York.

Michael, E. B., & Gollan, T. H. (2005). Being and becoming bilingual: Individual differences and consequences for language production. In J. F. Kroll & A. M. B. De Groot (Eds.), *Handbook of bilingualism: Psycholinguistic approaches* (pp. 389–410). Oxford, UK: Oxford University Press.

Miyao, M., & Omaki, A. (2006). No ambiguity about it: Korean learners of Japanese have a clear attachment preference. In D. Bamman, T. Magnitskaia, & C. Zaller (Eds.), *Proceedings of the 30th Annual Boston University Conference on Language Development Supplement.* Available at: http://www.bu.edu/linguistics/APPLIED/BUCLD/proc.htm

Musselman, C. (2000). How do children who can't hear learn to read an alphabetic script? A review of the literature on reading and deafness. *Journal of Deaf Studies and Deaf Education, 5,* 9–31.

Musselman [Reich], C., & Reich, P. A. (1976). Communication patterns in adult deaf. *Canadian Journal of Behavioral Science, 8,* 56–67.

Ojima, S., Nakata, H., & Kakigi, R. (2005). An ERP study of second language learning after childhood: Effects of proficiency. *Journal of Cognitive Neuroscience, 17,* 1212–1228.

Omaki, A. (2005). *Working memory and relative clause attachment in first and second language processing,* M.A. thesis, University of Hawaii.

Padden, C., & Hanson, V. (2000). Search for the missing link: The development of skilled reading in Deaf children. In K. Emmorey & H. Lane (Eds.), *The signs of language revisited: An anthology to honor Ursula Bellugi and Edward Klima* (pp. 435–447). Mahwah, NJ: Lawrence Erlbaum Associates.

Padden, C., & Ramsey, C. (2000). American sign language and reading ability in Deaf children. In C. Chamberlain, J. Morford, & R. I. Mayberry (Eds.), *Language acquisition by eye* (pp. 165–189). Mahwah, NJ: Lawrence Erlbaum Associates.

Papadopoulou, D., & Clahsen, H. (2003). Parsing strategies in L1 and L2 sentence processing: A study of relative clause attachment in Greek. *Studies in Second Language Acquisition, 25,* 501–528.

Pickering, M. J. (1999). Sentence comprehension. In S. C. Garrod & M. J. Pickering (Eds.), *Language processing* (pp. 123–153). Hove, UK: Psychology Press Ltd.

Quigley, S., Wilbur, R., Power, D., Montanelli, D., & Steinkamp, M. (1979). *Syntactic structure in the language of deaf children.* Urbana, IL: Institute for Child Behavior and Development, University of Illinois.

Sasaki, Y. (1991). English and Japanese interlanguage comprehension strategies: An analysis based on the Competition Model. *Applied Psycholinguistics, 12,* 47–73.

Stokoe, W. C. (1960). Sign Language Structure: An outline of the visual communication systems of the American Deaf. *Studies in Linguistics, Occasional papers 8,* Silver Spring, MD: Linstock Press.

Strong, M., & Prinz, P. (2000). Is American sign language skill related to English literacy? In C. Chamberlain, J. Morford, & R. I. Mayberry (Eds.), *Language acquisition by eye* (pp. 131–141). Mahwah, NJ: Lawrence Erlbaum Associates.

Su, I.-Ru (2001). Transfer of sentence processing strategies: A comparison of L2 learners of Chinese and English. *Applied Psycholinguistics, 22*, 83–112.

Waters, G. S., & Caplan, D. (1996). The measurement of verbal working memory capacity and its relation to reading comprehension. *Quarterly Journal of Experimental Psychology: Human Experimental Psychology, 49*, 51–79.

Williams, J. N. (2006). Incremental interpretation in second language sentence processing. *Bilingualism: Language and Cognition, 9*, 71–88.

Williams, J. N., Möbius, P., & Kim, C. (2001). Native and non-native processing of English *wh*-questions: Parsing strategies and plausibility constraints. *Applied Psycholinguistics, 22*, 509–540.

Wilson, M., & Garnsey, S. M. (2001). Making simple sentences harder: Verb bias effects and direct objects. Poster presented at the CUNY Conference on Human Sentence Processing, Philadelphia, PA.

Wilson, M. P., & Garnsey, S. (2009). Making simple sentences hard: Verb bias effects in simple direct object sentences. *Journal of Memory and Language, 60*, 368–392.

# CHAPTER 14

# IMPLICIT LEARNING IN SECOND LANGUAGE ACQUISITION

John N. Williams

## I. INTRODUCTION

We constantly use implicit knowledge in everyday action and perception. The father who tries to teach his child to ride a bicycle immediately realises that, despite riding to work every day, he cannot explain how to turn a corner. A tennis player's backhands might always land out despite their conscious efforts to aim them in. When we listen to music we will instantly recognise a note that violates the principles of musical structure to which we have become accustomed in our culture, even if we have never had any musical training. People have fluent and productive command of their native language and are able to instantly detect grammatical irregularities, without being able to explain the underlying rules. Implicit knowledge 'can be causally efficacious in the absence of awareness that this knowledge was acquired or that it is currently influencing processing' (Cleeremans, Destrebecqz, & Boyer, 1998, p. 406). Examples of the use of explicit knowledge are when a student selects a particular theorem to solve a geometry problem, when the learner driver follows their instructor's step-by-step commands in order to change gear or when the language learner consults a grammar book in order to find the first person singular form of a particular verb. Explicit knowledge is knowledge that we know that we know (Dienes & Perner, 1999) and that we are aware of using.

Within second language acquisition (SLA), the contrast between implicit 'acquisition' and explicit 'learning' was brought to the fore by Krashen (1981, 1994), but his Acquisition–Learning Hypothesis is compatible with any theory of the putative implicit learning mechanism. At one extreme, generative linguists would appeal to processes that operate with reference to universal grammar (UG). At the other, emergentists would appeal to domain-general principles of associative learning, as exemplified perhaps by connectionism. All studies of 'acquisition' are studies of implicit learning.

*The New Handbook of Second Language Acquisition*

What appears to define 'implicit learning research' is a type of methodology, rather than a theoretical orientation. It involves control over the learning task, control over the input, measurement of learning and, in the best cases, rigorous attempts to establish whether test performance is a reflection of a properly operationalised concept of implicit knowledge. But this is simply the methodology one needs in order to unambiguously establish acquisition, in Krashen's sense, of anything, whatever one's theoretical orientation. Thus, although researchers with a more emergentist view of learning are naturally drawn to implicit learning research, this is a field within which it is possible to rigorously explore all learning processes. Indeed, evidence of limitations on implicit learning can, in principle, provide a firmer basis for an appeal to innate constraints on learning than the traditional and, for some, questionable (e.g. Elman et al., 1996) theoretical arguments from learnability theory.

In this overview we will consider a number of theoretical and methodological issues. First, how are implicit and explicit knowledge to be operationalised so that they can be measured, and what is the evidence for implicit second language knowledge according to these criteria? We then consider the learning process, what can be learned and what cannot, and what this might tell us about the nature of the implicit learning mechanism. This raises the issue of constrains on implicit learning, which we consider further in the context of the influence of attention.

But first some terminology. As noted by Hulstijn (2003), it is important to maintain a distinction between incidental learning and implicit learning. In its strictly methodological sense, *incidental learning* refers to an experimental arrangement in which the participants are not informed that there will be a test of learning. This is also true of implicit learning experiments. Within SLA research, the term *incidental* has also come to be used in relation to the actual learning process to mean that people learn something without intending to. For example, they might learn a rule of grammar in the course of performing a meaning-focused task, or they might learn some regularity in the sequencing of forms whilst performing a short-term memory task. The term *implicit learning* refers to the above situations, with the added condition that there is no awareness of the regularity to be learned at the point of learning. In contrast, *explicit learning* involves an intention to learn (which may or may not result from advance warning of a test of learning) as well as the use of conscious knowledge at the point of learning. For example, the learner might engage in hypothesis formation and testing in an attempt to discover underlying structure.

The learning process itself can be characterised as either inductive or deductive. *Inductive* learning involves forming generalisations on the basis of examples, whereas *deductive learning* is guided or constrained by additional knowledge (e.g. parametric options provided by UG). Implicit learning is usually regarded as inductive, but if UG is involved, it could be regarded as deductive (DeKeyser, 2003).

It is useful to distinguish the nature of the learning process from the status of the resulting knowledge as assessed by a test of learning. Implicit learning could lead to explicit knowledge, since a person may become spontaneously aware of regularities in the input. To borrow a term from the problem-solving literature, this might be referred to as 'insight'. At the same time, explicit learning might result in implicit knowledge. With increased practice, explicit knowledge may become automatised and may come to influence behaviour without awareness. Thus, the issue of the existence of implicit or explicit knowledge in the mind of the learner is distinct from the issue of how it got there. We start with a discussion of how implicit and explicit knowledge may be measured, regardless of how it was acquired.

## II. IMPLICIT AND EXPLICIT KNOWLEDGE

As Ellis (2005) remarks, there is a 'data problem' in SLA research. Although there are competing theories of the acquisition process, it is difficult to adjudicate between them because of the difficulty of accurately measuring acquisition, as opposed to learning. 'Thus, SLA as a field of inquiry has been characterized by both theoretical controversy and by a data problem concerning how to obtain reliable and valid evidence of learners' linguistic knowledge' (Ellis, 2005, p. 142). What criteria might be used to determine whether a person's behaviour is determined by implicit knowledge?

### A. Influences Behaviour Without Awareness

Awareness is the most commonly used criterion of implicitness within psychology. Explicit knowledge is knowledge that a person knows that they know (Dienes & Perner, 1999). If we characterise a first-order state as simply having knowledge of something, a person can be said to have explicit knowledge when they are in a higher order state of knowing that they know something. They should be able to intentionally use this higher order knowledge to control actions, including verbal report. Conversely, implicit knowledge is defined as knowledge that a person has without knowing that they have it.

Two commonly used implicit learning paradigms in psychology make use of verbalisation as an operationalisation of implicit knowledge. The artificial grammar (AG) learning paradigm was introduced by Reber (1967). The learning materials consist of letter sequences such as VXXVS and TPPPTS that are generated by a finite state grammar.[1] Participants are typically exposed to these sequences in the context of what appears to be a short-term memory test. They are then told that the letter sequences, in fact, followed a rule system, and they perform a grammaticality judgement test (GJT) on new grammatical and ungrammatical letter strings. Their performance is above chance, yet they are completely unable to verbally describe the underlying system (Reber, 1967; Reber & Allen, 1978). Reber and Allen (1978) conclude that it is possible to implicitly acquire an abstract representation of the structure of the grammar. Whilst some disagree that the knowledge acquired can be properly described as abstract, or that it is wholly unconscious (see below), there is no doubt that such experiments demonstrate incidental acquisition of statistical properties of stimulus sequences.

In serial reaction time (SRT) tasks, a stimulus moves between different screen positions (typically 4 or 6) and the participant indicates each position using corresponding response keys. What the participant is not told is that the majority of the sequences

---

[1]Strings are produced by tracing a path through a state diagram. Starting from an initial state, each transition to a subsequent state generates a specific letter. Some states can lead to a variety of alternative states. Strings are grammatical if a path can be traced through the diagram from the start state to the end state. The grammar generates a finite set of strings.

follow a regular pattern, generated by either a finite state grammar (e.g. Cleeremans & McClelland, 1991) or, more simply, a repeating sequence of positions (Curran & Keele, 1993; Destrebecqz & Cleeremans, 2001, 2003). With practice, responses to stimuli in the regular sequences gradually get faster, but if the stimuli suddenly appear in random sequences, responses slow down markedly, indicating sensitivity to the structure of the regular sequences. Yet when asked afterwards if they noticed any pattern to the sequences, participants can provide only minimal valid information (Cleeremans & McClelland, 1991; Norman, Price, Duff, & Mentzoni, 2007). In Cleeremans and McClelland (1991), they even felt that explicit knowledge was detrimental to their performance and so avoided using it. Subjects may also fail to distinguish fragments of the trained sequence from novel fragments in a recognition memory test (Destrebecqz & Cleeremans, 2003; Norman et al., 2007). Thus, it appears that the slowdown for random sequences is due to the violation of expectancies based on implicit knowledge.

Green and Hecht (1992) showed a striking dissociation between verbal report and a sentence correction task within naturalistic SLA. They found that the ability to correct grammatical errors lagged well behind the ability to provide explanations for the corrections and that correct corrections were often associated with incorrect explanations. They argue that the ability to correct sentences is driven by implicit knowledge and that whilst explicit knowledge provided through instruction might facilitate the development of implicit knowledge, learners rely on the latter in the correction task.

The above studies appear to demonstrate sensitivity to regularities in the absence of verbalisable knowledge. But do they demonstrate the existence of implicit knowledge? According to critics such as Shanks and St. John (1994) the evidence is not compelling. AG and SRT experiments tend to use regularities that are intrinsically difficult to verbalise; there is a delay between training and debriefing and a lack of detailed questioning. Therefore, verbal reports are not a reliable indicator of awareness.

An alternative to verbal report is to require participants to make subjective judgements of their mental state when making each decision. For example in a GJT, learners might be asked to rate their confidence in each judgement that they make. If the accuracy of their decisions is above chance when they say they are guessing, then they can be said to be using implicit knowledge. In an AG experiment, Dienes and Scott (2005) found exactly this, providing compelling evidence of implicit learning of letter sequences. But they also found that the average confidence level of correct decisions was significantly higher than that of incorrect ones, suggesting that people were basing some of their decisions on conscious knowledge.

But do correct high-confidence judgements necessarily imply explicit knowledge? Not necessarily. Consider making grammaticality judgements in one's native language. One may well be highly confident, even though the judgements might be based on implicit knowledge. In such cases, judgements appear to be a reflection of *intuition*. Dienes and Scott (2005) therefore argue that we must separate out the part of the mental state concerned with whether the judgement is based on a conscious intention (i.e. confidence) from the part concerned with conscious knowledge of the structure of the domain (i.e. structural knowledge). Intuition would be when one has conscious judgement knowledge (not guessing), but no conscious structural knowledge. Norman et al. (2007) refer to this state as 'fringe consciousness' and define it as 'A situation in which behaviour is driven in a flexible manner by consciously accessible feelings, but where there is no conscious access to the antecedents of those feelings' (p. 833).

How can we assess this state of intuition? In Dienes and Scott's (2005) AG learning experiment, in addition to making confidence judgements, subjects were also asked to say whether each judgement was based on a guess, intuition, memory (for items received in training) or rule. Judgements based on memory and rule were above chance in accuracy, reflecting explicit knowledge; so too were judgements based on guess and intuition, suggesting a contribution of implicit knowledge. Rebuschat (2008) also used a GJT supplemented with confidence and source judgements in a study of learning German verb position rules under different training conditions. Under incidental training conditions involving a focus on meaning, there was a correlation between confidence and accuracy, and responses based on memory and rule were significantly above chance, indicating a contribution of explicit knowledge. But whilst guess responses were at chance, moderately confident responses based on intuition were significantly above chance, indicating a contribution of unconscious structural knowledge. Interestingly, under training conditions that required participants to intentionally search for rules, there was rather stronger evidence for unconscious knowledge since above-chance responding was even found for guess responses. Thus, even intentional induction can lead to implicit knowledge.

We can draw two conclusions from this work on the assessment of subjective mental states. First, no test of knowledge is likely to be process pure. Grammaticality judgements will reflect contributions of both implicit and explicit knowledge, perhaps depending on the specific item involved. For example, in an AG experiment, ungrammatical items that contain violations in the salient beginning and end positions might lead to high-confidence judgements based on memory or rule, whereas violations in the middle part of the string might lead to moderately confident responses based on intuition, or even guesses. In SLA studies, combining such measures with a linguistic analysis of test structures could provide valuable information about the kinds of regularities that are more or less likely to be associated with explicit and implicit knowledge.

Second, limiting our interest to situations in which knowledge is applied completely unconsciously is perhaps too severe and unrealistic. Indeed, for some sceptics there are no such situations in any case, and all claims to the contrary are based on flawed methodology (Lovibond & Shanks, 2002; Shanks & St. John, 1994). Knowledge structures conscious perception, and learning involving cognitive representations will usually lead to changes in conscious experience of one kind or another (Perruchet & Gallego, 1997; Perruchet & Vinter, 1998). For example, in a GJT, grammatical items might be processed with greater perceptual fluency than ungrammatical ones, and awareness of this fact can bias towards judging them as grammatical (Buchner, 1994; Kinder & Shanks, 2003). Or learners may come to consciously perceive the input as segmented into chunks, such as bigrams in AG experiments or words and phrases in natural language. The underlying learning mechanisms producing these effects may be implicit, but their effect is to structure conscious perception. Therefore, we should not be surprised that it is difficult to isolate cases where knowledge has absolutely no conscious effects and behaviour is a result of guessing. What is perhaps more important is that in the moment of use, knowledge influences behaviour in the absence of conscious or intentional recollection of previous experiences or explicit rules. This leads us towards measures of awareness that allow for confident responses based on intuition. But it also opens the way to other diagnostics of implicit knowledge, such as automaticity.

## B. Influences Behaviour Automatically

Explicit knowledge guides intentional actions, whereas implicit knowledge is deployed automatically (Cleeremans & Jiménez, 2002; Dienes & Perner, 1999). Thus, automaticity can be used as a diagnostic of implicitness. Of course, how automaticity is to be identified is an issue in itself (Segalowitz, 2003). Within SLA a speed diagnostic is prevalent, presumably because it relates to the notion of fluency, and fluency is seen as a reflection of acquisition, as opposed to learning (consider Krashen's, 1981, Monitor Hypothesis).

Ellis (2005) examined the correlations between performance by learners of English on 17 target structures in five language tests: oral imitation, oral narrative, a timed GJT (responding before a deadline), an untimed GJT and a metalinguistic knowledge test. A principal components factor analysis showed that the two oral tests and the timed GJT loaded on one common factor, whilst the untimed GJT and metalinguistic tests loaded on a second.[2] In terms of Ellis's task analysis, the factor that distinguishes the oral and timed GJT is time pressure. Assuming that speeded performance primarily reflects implicit knowledge, these two sets of tasks distinguish implicit and explicit knowledge. Considering the very different tasks involved, it is impressive that such a clear division between them emerged. In a detailed by-item analysis of the timed and untimed GJTs, Ellis (2006) found no relationship between the level of performance for individual structures on the two tasks, reinforcing the idea that they tap different types of knowledge.

The Ellis (2005, 2006) studies clearly show a distinction between knowledge that can be applied quickly and knowledge that takes longer to access. But this need not correspond to any differentiation in the form of the underlying knowledge because the same (explicit) knowledge could just be used more quickly with practice. Another approach is to combine various aspects of automaticity within one test, such as speed and freedom from attentional control. Oral production and imitation tasks are often regarded as relatively good measures of implicit knowledge because they divert attention away from form whilst imposing time pressure. Ellis (2005) found that out of his battery of tasks, elicited imitation loaded most heavily on the 'implicit' factor. Erlam (2006) developed a version of an elicited imitation task that involved hearing a statement (that may or may not involve a grammatical error), judging its truth value and repeating it in *correct* English. Performance correlated moderately well with an oral narration task and fairly strongly with IELTS listening and speaking scores. However, it is unclear just how critical time pressure is in such tasks. Hulstijn and Hulstijn (1984) found that accuracy in a story-retelling task was not affected by time pressure, only by focus on form. As Erlam (2006, p. 487) notes, the most direct evidence for the use of implicit knowledge in elicited imitation would come from

---

[2]See Isemonger (2007) for a critique of the statistical procedures used by Ellis (2005), and Ellis and Loewen (2007) for an even clearer separation of the two factors when more appropriate procedures are employed.

spontaneous, fluent and unconscious corrections of ungrammatical sentences in the input. Unfortunately, her study did not contain a rigorous assessment of awareness, but the idea is reminiscent of the notion of 'fluent restoration' in speech shadowing (Marslen-Wilson & Welsh, 1978). Whilst shadowing speech in their native language, subjects will often spontaneously correct mispronounced words with no disfluency. The ability to fluently restore grammatical errors in shadowing tasks that also involve a meaning-based component would perhaps provide a more stringent test of implicit grammatical knowledge than imitation.

Neurological measures perhaps provide the most promising approach to the identification of automatic processing. Event-related potential (ERP) responses like the P600, N400 and especially the early left anterior negativity (ELAN) are produced within a few hundred milliseconds of semantic and syntactic violations and so are not likely to be the result of conscious thought processes. This is especially true of the ELAN, which is assumed to reflect immediate and automatic structure-building operations (for a review, see Friederici, 2002). Friederici, Steinhauer, and Pfeifer (2002) found the characteristic ERP signatures of syntactic processing in learners of Brocanto, an artificial language that was learned under intentional induction in the context of a board game. It is perhaps surprising to find such native-like processing in an artificial-language-learning experiment involving relatively little exposure when studies on naturalistic learners fail to find such effects, particularly with regard to the ELAN (Hahne & Friederici, 2001). Friederici et al. (2002) argue that their participants can simply be regarded as having achieved a very high level of proficiency in a very small language. Morgan-Short (2007) replicated these results, but also found that there were no ERP effects for participants who were given explicit instruction in the rules of Brocanto prior to playing the board game, even though final GJT performance was similarly high for the instructed and uninstructed groups. Thus, ERPs can reveal differences in underlying processing that are not reflected in behaviour. Also there appears to be a big difference between being told rules and working them out for oneself, with (intentional) induction being more likely to lead to native-like processing than instruction, even when the amount of practice is held constant. As in the case of Rebuschat (2008), we see that intentional induction can lead to implicit knowledge.

There is also evidence for native-like brain responses after very little exposure in classroom settings (Osterhout, McLaughlin, Pitkanen, Frenck-Mestre, & Molinaro, 2006), suggesting rapid assimilation of the L2 into the learners' comprehension system. Particularly impressive are cases that show dissociations between brain responses and more 'direct' behavioural tests. McLaughlin, Osterhout, and Kim (2004) found that after only 14 h of instruction, learners of French showed different ERP responses to words and nonwords, yet they were unable to distinguish them in a lexical decision task. Tokowicz and MacWhinney (2005) studied beginner learners of Spanish and found strong ERP responses to gender violations in online processing despite low sensitivity to gender violations in an offline task. As we will see below, we must be cautious in interpreting these task dissociations as evidence for different implicit and explicit knowledge systems. But these experiments do appear to show very rapid assimilation of some aspects of second languages, resulting in automatic and native-like brain responses.

## C. Different Brain Systems

Another way of distinguishing implicit and explicit knowledge may be in terms of the brain regions that support them. Amnesics show dissociations between implicit and explicit memory in that they perform normally on 'indirect' tests of implicit memory, but relatively poorly on 'direct' tests of explicit memory (see Gabrieli, 1998, for a review). After being exposed to a list of words, they will show poor recognition memory, but intact priming (Haist, Musen, & Squire, 1991). Or in AG learning experiments, they will show normal levels of performance on GJT, but impaired recognition for the training items compared to controls (Knowlton & Squire, 1996). An obvious conclusion from such dissociations is that implicit and explicit memories are subserved by different brain regions (N. C. Ellis, 1994; Gabrieli, 1998; Squire, 1992).

But despite what appears to be compelling evidence for dissociations between implicit and explicit knowledge, it is still possible to defend a single system view in which performance on different tasks, such as recognition and priming, simply reflects the differential accessibility of the same knowledge. What determines conscious accessibility is not where the knowledge is stored in the brain, but its level of 'analysis' (Bialystok, 1982) or more generally its 'quality' as defined in terms of stability, strength and distinctiveness (Cleeremans & Jiménez, 2002). The further the knowledge has progressed along these dimensions, the more likely it is to become amenable to conscious control and to enter into the 'global workspace' where it becomes available to other cognitive systems (Dehaene & Naccache, 2001). It has also been shown through computational modelling that dissociations between tasks can even be obtained when the underlying knowledge is of the same level of analysis or quality (Kinder & Shanks, 2003). Retrieving a specific learning episode in, say, a recognition memory task is relatively difficult because it involves a fine discrimination between memory traces, whereas making an intuitive judgement about well-formedness is relatively easy because it can utilise information that is aggregated over all training items. We should bear in mind, therefore, that demonstrations that learners' brain responses show effects that are not evident in behavioural measures (McLaughlin et al., 2004; Tokowicz & MacWhinney, 2005) may reflect differential sensitivity of the tasks to the same underlying knowledge. The moral is that we should be very cautious in interpreting dissociations between tasks as evidence for dissociations between implicit and explicit knowledge systems.

Nevertheless, within SLA there is a strong preference for a multiple systems perspective. For example, Paradis (1994, 2004) distinguishes the kind of procedural knowledge acquired in learning a motor skill, or one's first language, from the kind of declarative knowledge acquired in a geography lesson or the metalinguistic knowledge acquired in a foreign language lesson. Obviously, given the radically different form of representation involved, we would expect these types of knowledge to be represented in different brain regions. Ullman (2001, 2004) also draws a distinction between different memory systems in his declarative–procedural (DP) model and argues specifically that the rule-governed aspects of language (across syntax and morphology) are supported by the procedural system (rooted in frontal/basal ganglia circuits) and item-based aspects are supported by the declarative system (rooted in medial and lateral temporal lobe structures).

From a single system perspective, the fact that different types of knowledge are represented in different brain regions is irrelevant to the issue of conscious availability. What is relevant is the level of analysis/quality of the knowledge (indeed, for Cleeremans & Jiménez, 2002, all knowledge is ultimately represented in the same subsymbolic form). In contrast, Paradis (1994, 2004) appears to equate declarative and procedural knowledge with explicit and implicit knowledge, respectively, such that any aspect of language that is known implicitly must be assumed to be represented in the procedural system. However, there is evidence that contradicts such a strong association between memory systems and conscious accessibility. For example, damage to the declarative system can impair certain forms of implicit learning (Chun & Phelps, 1999), and damage to the procedural system does not necessarily impair implicit AG learning (Reber & Squire, 1999; Witt, Nuhsman, & Deuschl, 2002). Such findings can be accommodated by the DP model since here the terms 'procedural' and 'declarative' are used primarily to refer to differing forms of knowledge (and associated brain systems). The model does not assume an isomorphic relation between declarative/procedural memory and explicit/implicit knowledge and assumes that declarative memory underlies implicit and explicit knowledge, while the procedural system is one of several brain systems underlying different types of implicit knowledge (Ullman, personal communication; see Ullman, 2005, for discussion). Just because some knowledge is known implicitly does not necessarily imply that it is represented in the procedural system, although if there is anatomical evidence that it is represented in the procedural system, the prediction would be that it should also bear the hallmarks of implicit knowledge.

### D. Conclusion

Following the definition of implicit knowledge as knowledge that a person does not know that they know (Dienes & Perner, 1999), implicitness can be operationalised only through assessments of subjective mental states, that is, through measurements of awareness. When automaticity is used as a diagnostic, we must recognise that we are *assuming* that conscious knowledge could not have been used in the moment of generating the behaviour that we are measuring. The more converging lines of evidence there are, such as speed, independence from attention and native-like brain responses, the more convincing this assumption will be. An advantage of this approach is that we can accept that learners might have conscious knowledge, as assessed by unspeeded tasks and yet still be producing automatic behaviour using implicit knowledge.[3] Having said this, the most convincing evidence for implicit knowledge will always come from subjective measures.

To date, few language studies have attempted to establish that implicit knowledge was acquired according to any of the above criteria. The term *implicit learning* is often simply used to refer to a mode of learning that is incidental and inductive.

---

[3]Morgan-Short's (2007) study provides an example. Given that GJT performance was around 80% correct, it seems likely that both instructed and uninstructed groups had conscious knowledge of the rules of Brocanto, yet only the uninstructed group showed evidence of implicit knowledge according to an automaticity criterion.

This is presumably a reflection of a concern with the effectiveness of particular modes of learning rather than the status of the resulting knowledge. So in the remainder of this review we shall be essentially concerned with the nature of incidental inductive learning, treating this as 'implicit learning', even if the implicitness of the resulting knowledge was not actually established. Ideally, though, the term *implicit learning* ought to be used to refer to situations where implicit knowledge was acquired, as established by the awareness criterion, or as assumed by virtue of automaticity.

## III. THE NATURE OF WHAT CAN BE LEARNED IMPLICITLY

### A. Chunking and Statistical Learning in Orthography, Phonology and Syntax

Research using the AG and SRT paradigms consistently shows evidence for chunk learning, that is, short sequences of letters or stimulus positions that frequently occur in the input. For example, the test item XXVXJ contains the bigrams XX, XV, VX and XJ and the trigrams XXV, XVX and VXJ. Participants may simply learn these bigrams and trigrams, perhaps also being sensitive to which occur at the beginnings and ends of strings. The more of these bigrams and trigrams a test item contains, the greater the likelihood that it would be classified as grammatical (Johnstone & Shanks, 1999; Perruchet & Pacteau, 1990; Servan-Schreiber & Anderson, 1990).

Chunking is just one instantiation of what, more recently, has come to be referred to as 'statistical learning', a strongly empiricist and emergentist approach that sees acquisition as the absorption of statistical regularities in the environment through implicit learning mechanisms. For example, it has been shown that when people are played what appears at first to be a random sequence of syllables such as *ba-bu-pu-du-ta-ba-bu-pa-da-du-ta-ba-tu-ti-bu-ba-bu-pu-tu-ti-bu*, they rapidly acquire a sense of recurring sequences that could be regarded as constituting lexical items, that is *babupu dutaba bupada dutaba tutibu babupu tutibu* (Saffran, Newport, & Aslin, 1996b). The dominant interpretation of this result is that people unconsciously 'tally' the transition probabilities (Aslin, Saffran, & Newport, 1998), or more precisely contingencies (N. C. Ellis, 2006a) between syllables. Because the predictability of syllables is higher within words than between them, dips in transitional probability signal lexical boundaries (but see Perruchet & Vinter, 1998, for an alternative account in terms of chunking effects in memory and perception). This effect has been demonstrated in adults after 20 min of exposure (Saffran et al., 1996b), in eight-month-old infants (Saffran, Newport, & Aslin, 1996a) and even in cotton-top tamarins (Hauser, Newport, & Aslin, 2001). Mirman, Magnuson, Graf Estes, and Dixon (2008) demonstrate that it actually feeds into vocabulary learning.

Implicit statistical learning effects have also been demonstrated in phonology and orthography. Dell, Reed, Adams, and Meyer (2000) investigated learning of artificial phonotactic constraints. For example, the fact that within the experimental materials [f] always occurred as an onset and [s] as a coda influenced the speech errors that were produced. The learning effect was assumed to be implicit because there was no difference between participants who were initially informed about the constraints and those who were not and because in any case, speech errors are produced unintentionally and automatically. Even more impressively, Dell et al. (2000) and Warker and Dell (2006) demonstrate implicit learning of second-order constraints; for example, if the vowel is [ae], [g] must occur as an onset and [k] as a coda, but if the vowel is [I], [k] must occur as an onset and [g] as a coda.

Following from research showing that statistical information can be used to break syllable streams into words, a number of experiments have explored whether it can help learners break streams of words into phrases. These experiments involve presenting meaningless strings of words that are generated by a phrase structure grammar and seeing if participants incidentally acquire sensitivity to the underlying phrasal groupings. One statistical cue to phrase structure is what is referred to as 'predictive dependencies'. For example, in English, an article requires a noun to be present, but a noun can occur with or without an article. Artificial languages that respect this structure are learned better than ones that do not (Saffran, 2001; Saffran et al., 2008). In addition, transition probabilities between words are high within phrases and low at phrasal boundaries, and this can be made more evident by including optional, repeated and moved phrases. Even though such features increase the complexity of the language, they do improve sensitivity to underlying phrasal structure (Morgan, Meier, & Newport, 1989; Thompson & Newport, 2007). However, one problem with these studies is that they do not convincingly show that test performance reflects abstract grammatical categories as opposed to surface similarity to training items, so the generalisability of what is learned is not clear. Nevertheless, they do suggest that low-level statistical information could feed into the process of learning phrase structure.

If one is to develop a theory of statistical learning, one needs a theory of what is learned. Currently, the dominant approach is to regard statistical learning as contingency learning, which, broadly speaking, refers to associative learning of the predictability of outcomes given cues (Shanks, 1995). N. C. Ellis (2006a, 2006b) provides an extensive discussion of the possible role of contingency learning in SLA. Although probability theory provides formal methods for calculating contingency, this does not tell us how this is achieved in human brains. Connectionist models provide one indication of how contingency could be computed in a psychologically, if not neurally, plausible way (Shanks, 1995). An especially interesting type of connectionist model is the 'simple recurrent network' (SRN), which is specialised for the kind of sequence learning that is assumed to occur in the procedural system. The details of such models need not concern us here (see Elman, 1990, for examples); suffice it to say that such models treat sequence learning as a prediction task. For any particular training item, say the string ABCD in an AG experiment, the network is taught to predict the next element in the string, taking into account not only the current element, but also its context (e.g. it is trained to predict B from A, and C from B in the context of A). The network essentially learns the context-dependent contingencies between elements in training strings. SRNs have been used to successfully model implicit learning in lexical segmentation (Christiansen, Allen, & Seidenberg, 1998; Elman, 1990), AG and SRT experiments (Cleeremans & McClelland, 1991; Kinder & Shanks, 2001) and, using a somewhat different architecture, phonotactic constraints

(Warker & Dell, 2006). See Cleeremans and Dienes (2008) for a review of computational models of implicit learning.

## B. Abstraction and Transfer in Statistical Learning

One obvious limitation of chunking and connectionist approaches is that responses to test items are a function of what appears to be surface similarity to training items. The response to novel test items is determined by how well they reflect the probabilistic structure of the training set. But in the case of natural language learning, we assume that learners internalise abstract grammatical representations that can be applied to word combinations that bear no similarity to previous utterances (e.g. we can appreciate the sense in which the sentence *Green ideas sleep furiously* is syntactically well-formed). Is there evidence that representations of sufficient abstraction to support this kind of generalisation can be learned implicitly by humans or connectionist networks?

Research within the AG tradition has examined the abstraction issue by simply changing the letter set between training and test (e.g. the string AABCAB in training would correspond to the string DDEFDE in test). Typically, GJT performance for changed letter sets is lower than that for same letter sets, although still significantly above chance (Knowlton & Squire, 1996; Matthews et al., 1989). More impressive are demonstrations of transfer to different modalities, as for example when the grammar used to generate letter sequences in training is used to generate tone sequences at test (Altmann, Dienes, & Goode, 1995), although here too performance is lower than for same modality test items. The question then is what kind of knowledge supports this limited generalisation? Is it knowledge of the abstract structure of the grammar, as argued originally by Reber (1967)? The current consensus appears to be that this is not strictly the case; rather people pick up 'some rules about permissible locations of letter repetitions, alternations, or dependencies between different parts of the letter strings' (Knowlton & Squire, 1996, p. 179). Sensitivity to abstract patterns of alternation and doubling in syllable strings has been demonstrated in seven-month-old infants (Marcus, Vijayan, Bandi Rao, & Vishton, 1999) and even in tamarin monkeys (Hauser, Weiss, & Marcus, 2002). It appears that human and primate perceptual mechanisms code events in terms of change. It would not be unreasonable to assume that such codings could form part of the input to an associative learning system. When this is done, transfer problems of the type explored by Marcus become trivial for connectionist networks and hence do not pose a challenge to connectionist and other associative learning approaches (Dominey & Ramus, 2000; McClelland & Plaut, 1999). In a natural language context, Pacton, Perruchet, Fayol, and Cleeremans (2001) show implicit learning of constraints on consonant doubling in French and that the results can be modelled by an SRN.

What about transfer to sentences with new lexis in natural language grammar? Robinson (2005) examined incidental learning of Samoan by Japanese participants, targeting rules for ergative marking in transitive sentences (*ave e le tama le taavale* = drive ERG the boy the car), an incorporation rule (*inu-pia le tama* = drink-beer the boy) and locative (*taalo le tama i le paka* = play the boy IN the park). Performance on an immediate GJT showed high accuracy on old grammatical sentences, but poor performance on new grammatical and ungrammatical sentences (except for the locative, which corresponds to an English structure). Thus, there was an almost complete failure to transfer the knowledge of the novel trained structures to new sentences. However, it must be noted that there were only nine different training sentences, each of which was repeated 50 times. Each verb occurred in only one context during training, and so individual verbs were strongly associated with specific word order patterns. These results are therefore best explained in terms of learning of the kinds of item-based constructions that are characteristic of the early stages of first language acquisition (FLA) (Lieven & Tomasello, 2008; Tomasello, 2000), which here is encouraged by overlearning of a very small training set.

In an earlier study, Robinson (1996) did show a degree of transfer of a rule for forming pseudo-clefts of location (e.g. *Where my parents vacation is in Europe, Where LA is is in California*). After exposure to sentences illustrating this structure in an implicit (memory) task, learners of English were above chance on a GJT using sentences that contained different content words from the training sentences, despite being unable to state the rule in a debriefing. Whilst this might appear to show implicit learning of abstract structure, Robinson points out that it could also be based on memory for doubling of the verb *to be* (which was repeated from training as either an *is is* or *are is* pattern) along with patterns of plural and tense marking. One could go further and argue that the participants learned word order templates or 'constructions' (Goldberg, 1995, 2006) using a combination of specific lexis and abstract categories, such as *Where* N-PL V *is* PP and *Where* N *is is* PP, which then transfer to sentences with new lexis.

More direct evidence for learning of word order templates that generalise to new lexis comes from the studies of incidental learning of German word order by Rebuschat (2008, Experiment 3) that were mentioned earlier (see also Rebuschat & Williams, 2006). A unique aspect of these studies was that the materials used English lexis but German word order. Participants performed a semantic plausibility judgement task on 120 training sentences, 40 for each of three German structures (examples of each structure: V2, *In the evening ate Rose excellent dessert at a restaurant*; VF-V1, *Since his teacher criticism voiced, put Chris more effort into his homework*; V2-VF, *George repeated today that the movers his furniture scratched*). Participants then received a surprise GJT on sentences containing new lexis. Sentences that repeated grammatical patterns encountered in training were accepted at levels well above chance (and better than a control group who had received no training), whilst performance on ungrammatical sentences was at chance. Thus, there was rapid incidental learning of abstract word order patterns, but judging by performance on ungrammatical items, no learning of the actual verb placement rules (see below). Acceptance of grammatical items was likely to reflect template representations using categories that were sufficiently abstract to support transfer to new lexis (e.g. categories such as subject, verb and time adverbial). Williams and Kuribara (2008) obtained similar results in a study of incidental learning of Japanese word order. We also performed connectionist (SRN) simulations in which the input was coded as sequences of grammatical categories rather than words. The simulations accounted well for the relative difficulty of most of the test items, suggesting that the participants were learning sequences of abstract categories in much the same way as they learn the sequences of letters in AG experiments. These studies demonstrate incidental learning of word order patterns represented at a sufficient level of abstraction to support transfer to sentences with new lexis.

## C. Implicit Learning of Grammatical Form–Meaning Connections

All of the demonstrations of implicit learning effects that have been mentioned so far essentially involve learning contingencies between representations within the same domain—be they letters, phonemes, syllables or grammatical categories. But what about learning associations between forms and meanings? After all, from functionalist and usage-based perspectives, form–meaning mappings lie at the heart of language processing and learning (Bates & MacWhinney, 1989; Goldberg, 1995; Tomasello, 2003). According to the Competition Model (Bates & MacWhinney, 1989), learners track the probabilities with which input cues in the domains of word order, morphology and meaning are associated with specific interpretations. Basic principles of associative learning such as cue competition, salience, interference, overshadowing and blocking can be used to explain first and second language learning phenomena such as morpheme acquisition orders, fossilisation, transfer and interference (N. C. Ellis, 2006b). Clearly, knowledge of the cue-interpretation contingencies underlying language is implicit. We have no awareness of these contingencies or of the process by which they are constantly updated through usage.

However, it has been argued that whilst the tuning of existing form–meaning connections may proceed implicitly, establishing new connections requires explicit learning processes. This is because of the requirement to integrate information across different cognitive systems, and such 'relational encoding' (Eichenbaum, Otto, & Cohen, 1994) requires declarative memory systems such as the hippocampus (N. C. Ellis, 1994; N. C. Ellis, 2005). The main line of evidence for this argument is that vocabulary acquisition is impaired in amnesia (Gabrieli, Cohen, & Corkin, 1988). However, the kind of hippocampus-dependent relational encoding that is assumed to be required for learning form–meaning connections does not appear to be confined to explicit learning. It is important for certain types of implicit learning as well, as suggested by the research on 'contextual cuing' that will be described later (Chun & Phelps, 1999; Park, Quinlan, Thornton, & Reder, 2004). The fact that amnesics cannot learn form–meaning connections does not mean that explicit memory is necessary, but only that this kind of learning depends on an intact hippocampus. Thus, it may be possible to obtain implicit learning of form–meaning connections in the normal population.

There have been few empirical investigations of implicit learning of novel form–meaning connections. DeKeyser (1995) employed a miniature artificial language with rich inflectional morphology for marking biological gender, number and object role. Some sample sentences are *Bep-on warufk-at rip-us* (Worker-PL build-PL house-OBJ; 'The workers are building a house') and *Hadeks-on wulas-in-it melaks-is-on* (Queen-PL peel-FEM-PL apple-OBJ-PL; 'The queens are peeling apples'). During training participants had to indicate whether a given sentence correctly described a picture, and in the test phase, they were required to describe pictures using the artificial language. When it was possible to use stem–inflection combinations that had occurred in training, performance was very good, but when tested on items that required novel stem–inflection combinations, performance was at chance, indicating no learning of the semantic correlates of the inflectional morphemes. This was despite extensive training of 20 learning sessions of 25 min.

More positive evidence has come from a series of studies by myself (Williams, 2005) and Janny Leung (Leung, 2007; Leung & Williams, 2006; Leung & Williams, in preparation). These studies all had a much narrower focus than DeKeyser's, involving fewer novel forms and fewer meaning distinctions. The training tasks also involved greater attention to the relevant forms and meanings and test procedures that were potentially more sensitive to implicit knowledge than the production task used by DeKeyser. In all cases, the participants were taught just four novel grammatical morphemes (*gi, ro, ul* and *ne,* which might be introduced as determiners) and told that they encoded a certain meaning dimensions (e.g. *gi* and *ro* occurred with near objects, *ul* and *ne* with far objects). The aim was to see if the participants would spontaneously induce a correlation with another, hidden, meaning dimension (e.g. that *gi* and *ul* were used with animate nouns and *ro* and *ne* with inanimate nouns). The novel forms were embedded in English carrier phrases or sentences (e.g. *I was terrified when I turned around and saw gi lion right behind me*) upon which the participants had to perform tasks that forced them to process the novel determiners in relation to the meaning dimension they had been taught. After training, Williams (2005) found significantly above-chance selection of determiners according to the non-instructed meaning dimension (in this case animacy) in entirely novel sentences even for participants who reported no awareness of the relevance of that dimension to determiner usage.

Extending this work, Leung (2007) developed a novel reaction time methodology that hinged on the use of form–meaning connections to direct attention. For example, suppose a person knows that the determiner *gi* always occurs with animate objects. If presented with a display containing a picture of a lion and a clock, on hearing the phrase 'gi lion', they would be able to orient their attention to the lion on hearing *gi,* that is, even before hearing the word *lion.* Their time to respond to this object in a reaction time task would therefore be facilitated. If the knowledge of the animacy correlation were implicit, then this orienting effect would occur outside of awareness, providing an online measure of the automatic use of implicit knowledge in comprehension. The experiments provided evidence for such effects across a range of form–meaning correlations: animacy, thematic role (agent/patient) and, in a case where the novel forms acted as reflexive pronouns, reflexivity.

Constructionist approaches stress the acquisition of linking rules between word order and a verb's argument structure. Can these be learned implicitly? Casenhiser and Goldberg (2005) provide evidence for rapid acquisition of the mapping between SOV word order and novel verbs encoding appearance (e.g. *The spot the king mooped* was paired with a video of a spot appearing on a king's nose). English-speaking children between age 5 and 7 simply observed pairings of videos of sentences over a 3 min training period. In the test phase, a sentence containing a new verb had to be matched with either of two videos. If the sentence had SOV order the children tended to choose the video depicting a scene of appearance, whereas if it had the familiar SVO order they tended to choose a scene depicting a transitive action. This learning effect was claimed to be implicit because the children were unable to articulate the meanings of the novel verbs. Whilst it would be interesting to see whether above-chance responding would still be obtained using more sensitive measures of awareness (such as subjective ratings of guessing and intuition), this experiment does provide impressive evidence of rapid inductive learning of linking rules involving both a novel argument structure and a novel word order.

When considering what is implicitly learnable we must obviously bear in mind the possibility of interactions with prior linguistic knowledge. In the case of learning grammatical form–meaning connections there may be involvement of grammatical processes (e.g. in searching for a basis for agreement) or the search space for possible meanings may be constrained by biases towards the kinds of distinctions that are likely to be encoded in natural language grammars (Bickerton, 1999). In fact, Williams (2004, 2005) found that implicit learning effects were greater in participants who knew languages with grammatical gender systems, suggesting that prior linguistic knowledge facilitated learning. On the other hand, the novel appearance meaning that was learned in Casenhiser and Goldberg (2005) is not encoded in English and may even fall outside the scope of whatever universal linking rules have been proposed (see Goldberg, 2006, p. 83). The way in which prior knowledge influences implicit learning is clearly an important issue in SLA and arises again in relation to determining what is learnable, as we shall see below.

### D.  Limitations of Implicit Learning

There is a tendency to believe that a statistical learning approach implies that any regularity in the environment can be acquired. For example, Hayes and Broadbent (1988) characterise implicit learning as involving 'the unselective and passive aggregation of information about the co-occurrence of environmental events and features' (ibid., p. 251), and Cleeremans and Jiménez (2002), following O'Reilly and Munakata (2000), characterise it as 'model learning', the goal of which is to 'enable the cognitive system to develop useful, informative models of the world by capturing its correlational structure' (ibid., p. 18). However, it is becoming increasingly apparent that not all environmental regularities are equally learnable by implicit means. The question is though, do these limitations reduce the significance of implicit learning to language, or, as some believe, do they help us understand how the form of language might be constrained by our human cognitive capacities?

### Long-Distance Dependencies

An important feature of natural languages is that they contain long-distance, or non-adjacent, dependencies, both in phonology and in syntax. Saffran et al.'s (1996b) work on segmentation of syllable sequences suggested that people rapidly learn associations between adjacent syllables. Newport and Aslin (2004) went on to examine learning non-adjacent dependencies in syllable sequences; for example, the frame ba_te recurred in the sequence, but with random intervening syllables. Over a series of seven experiments manipulating exposure, language size and task, they were unable to obtain any learning effects. These null results reveal a surprising limitation on statistical learning. However, learning effects were obtained when the dependencies concerned individual consonants and the intervening segment was a vowel; for example, the consonant frame p_t could be learned even though it occurred with random intervening vowels. This latter situation is more like that found in Semitic languages where words are formed from consonant frames. The learnability of the more natural system may derive from Gestalt principles of perceptual organisation, which group elements of a common type together (where 'type' is defined here in terms of different phonological tiers for consonants and vowels). Thus, even if statistical learning is limited to adjacent elements, this constraint can be overcome by bringing non-adjacent elements into adjacency at a common level of linguistic representation. Interestingly, tamarin monkeys show the converse pattern, being able to learn non-adjacent dependencies between syllables but not consonants (Newport, Hauser, Spaepen, & Aslin, 2004). Whilst it is not clear what kind of representation the monkeys impose on the input that makes this possible, it appears that the form of the coding provided by prior knowledge determines what is learnable (just as in the case of learning patterns of alternation or doubling mentioned earlier).

AG research provides another example of the problem of learning long-distance dependencies. In 'biconditional grammars', letter sequences such as TPPV.XCCS and TPVP.XCSC are formed by substituting letters (in this example any T on the left is substituted by an X on the right, any P with a C and any V with an S). This kind of grammar is not learnable under incidental training conditions (Johnstone & Shanks, 2001; Matthews et al., 1989). Given Newport & Aslin's (2004) failure to find learning of associations between non-adjacent syllables, this is hardly surprising.

Embedding in natural language syntax is another domain where long-distance dependencies are critical. The ability to understand and produce such structures depends on a grasp of the principle of recursion, which it has been claimed is uniquely human (Hauser, Chomsky, & Fitch, 2002). Fitch and Hauser (2004) compared a context-free grammar with 'centre embedding' of the form $A^n B^n$ (e.g. AAABBB) with a finite state grammar of the form $(AB)^n$ (e.g. ABABAB), where A and B stand for different categories of syllables, spoken by male and female speakers, respectively. Both grammars were learnable by humans (under incidental conditions), but only the finite state grammar was learnable by tamarin monkeys. It was subsequently found that only the $A^n B^n$ grammar activates Broca's area (Friederici, Bahlmann, Heim, Schubotz, & Anwander, 2004). However, it is important to note that the ability to distinguish, say, an AAABBB string from an ungrammatical AAABBA string does not necessarily entail sensitivity to centre embedding. It could just reflect an understanding that there has to be an equal number of A items followed by an equal number of B items. Indeed, it has been found that the ability to reject ungrammatical AAABB items after training on the $A^n B^n$ grammar is confined to subjects who reported using a counting strategy (Hochmann, Azadpour, & Mehler, 2008). Starlings have also been shown to perform this kind of discrimination (Gentner, Fenn, Margoliash, & Nusbaum, 2006), but again this is more likely to be due to their counting (or more probably subtising) abilities than an appreciation of recursion (Corballis, 2007). None of these experiments test the essential characteristic of embedding, which is that there are long-distance dependencies between specific elements. That is, for the case of English the relevant structure is not AAABBB but $A_1 A_2 A_3 B_3 B_2 B_1$. When an AG is constructed along these lines, it turns out to be unlearnable even by humans under incidental training conditions (Perruchet & Rey, 2005), again pointing to problems learning long-distance dependencies.

Does this line of research necessarily pose problems for an implicit, associative learning account of natural language? Not necessarily. First, the unlearnability of non-adjacent dependencies has generally been demonstrated when the intervening stimuli are randomly generated. In contrast, SRT research shows that people are sensitive to the predictiveness of elements up to three stimuli back in the sequence (Cleeremans & McClelland, 1991). The difference here is that the intervening material is structured according to a finite state grammar, a situation that is more like long-distance dependencies in natural language syntax than the systems studied by Newport et al. (2004). Second, whether effects are obtained probably depends on whether the separated items can be brought into adjacency through Gestalt principles of perceptual organisation, that is, through attentional processes (Pacton & Perruchet, 2008, see below). The existence of a common underlying representation provides an underlying motivating force towards perceptual grouping, as shown by Newport et al.'s (2004) contrasting results for syllable and consonant frames. In the case of long-distance dependencies in syntax, meaning provides a level of representation at which disparate forms can be related to each other. For sentences such as *The mouse the cat chased escaped*, the knowledge that the cat is likely to have done the chasing and the mouse the escaping would surely aid the learner in bringing the relevant words into adjacency at the level of meaning. Thus, just because statistical learning at the level of form cannot solve this problem does not mean that such structures are unlearnable.

## Learning Grammatical Categories by Distributional Analysis

It has been argued that abstract lexical and grammatical categories can be learned by distributional analysis of forms, that is, by analysing patterns of lexical co-occurrence (Maratsos, 1982; Redington & Chater, 1998). The idea is that forms that show similar patterns of co-occurrence with other forms come to constitute a category. Grammatical gender classes provide a simple example, where nouns of different classes might occur with different sets of articles. However, there is little evidence that abstract grammatical categories can be formed through implicit/ incidental learning when those categories are 'arbitrary', that is, when they are not also correlated with semantic or phonological properties of the words. Even when people have good memory for the specific items they have been trained on, their behaviour on tests of generalisation shows no learning of the underlying noun class distinction (Braine, 1987; Braine et al., 1990; Brooks, Braine, Catalano, & Brody, 1993; Frigo & McDonald, 1998; Gerken, Wilson, & Lewis, 2005).[4] Frigo and McDonald (1998) argue

---

[4]Thompson and Newport (2007) claim to demonstrate learning of phrase structure based on word classes that are defined purely distributionally. But, as they themselves admit, their experiment did not permit a proper test of generalisation. Mintz (2002) found learning of a word class that was signalled by two surrounding markers (rather than the one marker used in previous studies) and when there was only one withheld example of the paradigm in training. These factors may have provided sufficiently strong distributional cues to permit construction of the class, but one must wonder whether they are representative of natural language.

that models of noun class learning that depend on pure distributional analysis are 'too powerful' (*ibid.*, p. 237). However, the power of connectionist networks to learn arbitrary noun classes may depend on the specific architecture that is adopted. A network that modelled the kind of passive, and unsupervised, model learning occurring in incidental learning situations was indeed unsuccessful at learning the same system that had been shown to be unlearnable by humans (Williams, 2003). Connectionist models are not necessarily too powerful in this respect.

Of course, in natural languages, distributional information is just one of the possible cues to grammatical classes since there are also phonological and semantic correlates of varying predictiveness in different languages (Kelly, 1992). The same studies that showed no learning on the basis of distributional information also showed high levels of learning when such correlates were included, even if they were present only for a subset of category members (Braine, 1987; Brooks et al., 1993; Frigo & McDonald, 1998; Gerken et al., 2005). However, even here the picture is not so clear because in some studies generalisation to nouns without the relevant cues is at best marginally significant (Brooks et al., 1993) or not significant at all (Frigo & McDonald, 1998), suggesting that in these cases the nouns were not actually represented as belonging to different abstract grammatical classes (see Williams, 2003, for discussion).

Do these limitations on implicit (or rather incidental) learning limit its relevance to SLA? Not necessarily. Gender classes are notoriously difficult for learners to master (Carroll, 1999; Holmes & Dejean de la Batie, 1999), and processing of gender agreement is impaired in the second language (Guillelmon & Grosjean, 2001; Sabourin & Stowe, 2008). Furthermore, in contrast to first language learners, second language learners are overly sensitive to phonological cues to gender in languages such as French (Holmes & Dejean de la Batie, 1999) and Russian (Taraban & Kempe, 1999), in line with the above research on artificial languages. What we see in these experiments, therefore, could be just a reflection of a limitation of the adult implicit learning mechanism. See Blom and Polisenská (2008) and accompanying articles for recent research on gender in SLA and FLA.

## Other Grammatical Rules

Studies that have examined other kinds of natural language regularities have failed to find implicit learning effects. Ellis (1993) examined the soft mutation rule in Welsh. A word like *trwyn* (nose) would appear in its citation form in isolation or in a context such as *blae mae trwyn* (where is a nose), but the initial /t/ mutated to /d/ in contexts such as *ei drwyn o* (his nose). Not all initial consonants displayed mutation, however. After receiving examples in an implicit (Welsh-to-English translation) task, there was no evidence that the soft mutation rules had been learned. Well-formedness decision on items that had been received in training was 82% (in the 'yoked random' condition), whereas on incorrect items such as *ei trwyn o*, it was 50%. Subjects clearly knew that *ei trwyn o* was different from any training items; what they did not feel confident about was whether it was well-formed or not. Given that each of the five different mutation patterns was only exemplified by two different examples in training, it is quite possible that the quantity of input fell short of the 'critical mass' required to move beyond individual items to generalisations (Marchman & Bates, 1994). But the system itself may be beyond the scope of implicit learning. What appears to be required is that certain contexts be identified as triggering an abstract notion of 'mutation' that then selects an alternate form of the noun which is derived according to phonological rules (such as addition of voicing). As in the case of noun classes, it is not obvious how a connectionist network simulating unsupervised learning could acquire this kind of system. Also bear in mind that we do not know whether soft mutation rules are acquired (as opposed to learned) in SLA.

Robinson (1997) examined learning of a phonological constraint on the dative alternation, such that monosyllabic verbs could take both prepositional (PO) and double-object (DO) datives, whereas disyllabic verbs took only the PO dative. After implicit (memory for form) and incidental (focus on meaning) training, there was no evidence for generalisation of this rule to new verbs. Once again, this is a difficult learning problem. Learners would presumably have to unconsciously 'realise' that certain verbs that would have otherwise been expected to appear with both PO and DO in fact only occur with PO (Goldberg, 2006, refers to this as 'statistical pre-emption'). The next step would be to make a form-level generalisation across these verbs. But each verb in training was associated with only one structural alternative, making statistical pre-emption impossible. It should also be noted that most analyses assume that it is the semantics of verbs, rather than their form, that determines their argument structure possibilities (Goldberg, 1995; Pinker, 1989), and so it is not even clear that this system would be learnable under naturalistic conditions. Thus, as in the case of Ellis (1993), it is rather difficult to draw conclusions about what may or may not be learnable because it is not clear whether the input that was provided licensed the generalisations that were tested.

With regard to learning syntactic rules, as described earlier, Rebuschat (2008) examined incidental learning of German word order rules using materials that combined English lexis with German word order patterns (e.g. *Yesterday scribbled David a long letter to his family*). Whilst patterns that had been received in training were accepted in a GJT, performance on ungrammatical items showed that the underlying word order rules had not been learned. For example, there was high endorsement of single-clause verb-final structures (e.g. *\*After dinner Susan an old car with her savings bought*). It appeared that whilst participants had learned possible verb positions at clause level (verb-second, verb-first, verb-final), they had not learned how verb position was determined by clause type and clause sequence.

Williams and Kuribara (2008) adopted a similar methodology in order to examine the acquisition of Japanese scrambling. From a generative perspective, scrambling is an optional syntactic operation that moves a phrase in the direction opposite to the head direction (Saito & Fukui, 1998). So in a right-headed language like Japanese, scrambling takes place to the left. The materials employed English lexis combined with Japanese word order and case markers (e.g. *John-ga pizza-o ate*). The training set contained a majority of simple and embedded canonical SOV structures and a minority of scrambled structures, but only scrambled structures involving movement of the direct object occurred in training (e.g. OSV). The training task was to perform plausibility judgements on a total of 194 sentences, and learning was assessed by a surprise GJT on sentences with new lexis. There was evidence of learning canonical structures, confirming the incidental acquisition of abstract grammatical patterns.

With regard to scrambling, 44% of participants showed a general preference for canonical structures and did not reliably endorse even the scrambled structures they had been trained on. The remaining 56% of participants accepted these structures and even generalised to certain, but not all, scrambled structures that they had not been trained on (involving fronting of an indirect object). However, they also failed to reliably reject structures that manifested the word orders reflecting a head-initial (i.e. English) parameter setting (e.g. SVO). We concluded that even amongst these participants there was no learning of scrambling defined in terms of optional movement constrained by head direction. On the other hand, a connectionist simulation (using an SRN trained on sentences coded as sequences of grammatical categories) provided a good fit to the GJT data, taking into account that performance was also affected by a general preference for canonical structures in some participants, as well as processing difficulties involved in embedded structures. It appeared that GJT performance on both grammatical and ungrammatical items was strongly influenced by their similarity to training sentences (as determined by context-dependent contingencies in the sequences of grammatical categories). Note that the failure to obtain evidence for incidental learning of scrambling is consistent with reported problems acquiring scrambling in adult SLA (Iwasaki, 2003) and contrasts with the apparent ease with which scrambling is acquired in FLA, despite its rarity in the input (Murasugi & Kawamura, 2005).

## E.  Conclusions

The studies reviewed in the first part of this section show that it is possible to obtain implicit learning of linguistically relevant regularities. Humans possess a powerful learning mechanism that can absorb the statistical structure of the environment, defined as the contingencies between events. This type of learning is successful in the areas of lexical segmentation, phonological and orthographic structure, phrase structure and grammatical form–meaning connections. It may also support the rapid absorption of word order patterns (templates, schemas or constructions), represented at a sufficient level of abstraction to be independent of lexical content. But there appear to be limits to what can be learned in this way. There is evidence that implicit learning is temporally constrained, so that associations between events are only learned if they are adjacent or brought into adjacency through some other means (by attention or by virtue of the way they are represented). Whether this causes a problem for learning long-distance dependencies in language is debatable. But there also seem to be problems in going beyond the statistical properties of the input to deeper regularities that depend on abstract notions, as exemplified by the above studies on word classes, scrambling and possibly soft mutation. In the case of word classes and scrambling, there is evidence for similar difficulties in naturalistic SLA.

A common feature of many studies is that whilst there is good learning of trained items, and even transfer to new sentences with familiar underlying structures, there is poor rejection of ill-formed items in GJTs. In fact the simulations in Williams and Kuribara (2008) showed that performance on ungrammatical items could be explained largely by their similarity to trained items. This is not a phenomenon confined to laboratory studies. R. Ellis (2005) found that whereas performance on grammatical items in a speeded GJT loaded on the same factor as other speeded tasks assumed to tap implicit knowledge, performance on ungrammatical items in an unspeeded GJT loaded on the same factor as metalinguistic knowledge. Ellis concluded that whereas acceptance of grammatical items can be driven by implicit knowledge, reliable rejection of ungrammatical items is dependant on explicit knowledge. Similarly, Roehr (2008) suggests that implicit knowledge of a second language is exemplar –based, leading to prototype and similarity effects, whereas categorical, and context-independent, performance can be achieved only by using explicit metalinguistic knowledge.

Yet in the case of FLA, reliable rejection of ungrammatical sentences appears to be possible using implicit knowledge, and grammatical gender and Japanese scrambling are acquired with ease. Whether such divergences between FLA and SLA can be explained purely within an associative learning framework is at present unclear. For the moment it appears that what is currently known about the limitations of associative learning makes it a more promising approach to explaining SLA than FLA.

## IV. THE ROLE OF ATTENTION IN IMPLICIT LEARNING

Implicit learning was characterised earlier as a form of incidental learning, that is, an automatic form of learning that occurs without intention. Given that a characteristic of automaticity is that it makes relatively few, if any, demands on attentional resources, the implication is that implicit learning can occur without attention. This is important in the context of SLA because it would mean that, for example, acquisition of one aspect of form could occur even if the learner's attention is focused on some other aspect of form or on meaning.

A common way to address this question is by using dual-task paradigms. For example, whilst performing an SRT task, participants might also be required to indicate whether tones are of low or high pitch. It has been found that learning is still obtained, sometimes being equivalent to that obtained under single-task conditions (Jiménez & Méndez, 1999) and sometimes reduced, but still significant (Shanks & Channon, 2002). Clearly, the demands of the secondary tasks prevent participants from actively trying to work out the underlying regularities of the system, and yet learning effects are still obtained. This is enough to suggest that learning is largely independent of the kinds of attention-demanding processes assumed to underlie explicit learning (for reviews, see Goschke, 1997; Shanks, 2005).

However, even granted that learning is incidental, we can still ask whether attention needs to be paid to the relevant stimuli for learning to occur. In dual-task situations, responses are required to stimuli in both tasks, and so it is obvious that participants are attending to the relevant stimuli, even if they do not have the resources to engage in additional explicit learning. What is the evidence for learning from unattended stimuli? Within SLA we may wonder whether learning about a particular form can occur when attention is directed to meaning or other aspects of form.

It is widely assumed that learning is dependent on focal attention (Cowan, 1999; Logan & Etherton, 1994; Perruchet & Gallego, 1997). Only attended content, or more specifically, content that is in 'access' (as opposed to 'phenomenal') consciousness (Block, 1990) is remembered;[5] an assumption that within SLA is encapsulated by the 'noticing hypothesis' (Schmidt, 2001). For example, Leow (2000) found that only learners whose think-aloud protocols suggested that they had noticed certain verb forms during the training task showed learning of those forms in a post-test. Pacton and Perruchet (2008) showed that non-adjacent dependencies can be learned only if the subjects actively maintain the to-be-associated items in focal attention as part of the task they are set. As Pacton and Perruchet (2008) put it, 'associative learning is an automatic process that links together all the components that are present in the attentional focus at a given point' (*ibid.*, p. 82).

Whilst noticing may be necessary for encoding instances of language use in memory, extraction of regularities across instances might still occur unconsciously (Robinson, 1995). We must separate awareness at the level of noticing instances of language from awareness at the level of understanding generalisations across them (Schmidt, 2001). For example, Rosa and Leow (2004) found evidence for learning a generalised rule in participants whose think-aloud protocols revealed awareness at the level of noticing but not at the level of understanding. Thus, attention facilitates memory encoding, but learning of generalisations may still be implicit.

However, we should not be too hasty in assuming that focal attention is always a necessary condition for implicit learning. There is evidence that associations can be learned between attended stimuli and ambient stimuli that are not focally attended. Such a mechanism might be relevant to implicit learning of associations between attended words and non-attended contextual information.

Vision research suggests that a certain amount of semantic processing occurs for even complex stimuli, such as natural scenes and faces, that are presented outside of the focus of attention (Koch & Tsuchiya, 2007). The phenomenon of 'contextual cuing' demonstrates implicit learning of the association between such stimuli and a focally attended target (Chun, 2000). In a visual search task, participants might be asked to locate a rotated T amongst a number of distracting rotated L's. What they do not know is that displays are repeated, such that certain spatial configurations of distracters are always paired with certain target positions. It is found that targets are located more quickly on these repeated trials than on trials where the distracter positions are determined randomly. In a subsequent recognition task, participants are unable to distinguish repeated arrays from random ones, suggesting that the learning effect is implicit.[6] Similar effects have been obtained when the target location is predicted by the shapes of the distracters, as opposed to their position (Chun, 2000), or even by aspects of their meaning (Goujon, Didierjean, & Marmèche, 2007). Thus, an

---

[5]Content that is in access consciousness is available to other cognitive systems via the global workspace and so, for example, can be reported. Phenomenal consciousness refers to sensations, such as the difference between red and green. Content that is only phenomenally conscious is assumed to be rapidly forgotten (Lamme, 2003).

[6]Contextual cuing effects are absent in amnesics, suggesting that an intact hippocampus is involved in implicit as well as explicit learning (Chun & Phelps, 1999; Park et al., 2004).

attended stimulus can pick up correlations with ambient stimuli, even if those stimuli are not focally attended. Seitz and Watanabe (2005) refer to this as 'task irrelevant learning' and report studies which show that it can occur even when the task-irrelevant stimuli are presented subliminally. Here, then, we have cases of learning without noticing. The target item is noticed, but the stimuli with which it comes to be associated are not.

In the domain of verbal learning, Logan and Etherton (1994) studied similar effects in situations where pairs of words were presented for semantic categorisation. For example, in their Experiment 5, participants were asked to respond when the member of a word pair cued by an arrow was a metal. Certain specific word pairings were repeated (e.g. *Gold* might always be paired with *Sky*), and response times to those pairings became faster than non-repeated pairings. Although subjects were clearly learning these associations incidentally, there was no test of whether learning was implicit. But as in the contextual cuing situation, a non-attended stimulus that is part of the context when a target response is made becomes associated with the target.

Seitz and Watanabe (2005) suggest that task-irrelevant learning is due to the alerting function of attention. When a task-relevant stimulus is detected there is a general alerting response (a release of neurotransmitters) that allows currently processed ambient stimuli to be associated with that target. This view stresses simultaneity; the target and non-target stimuli have to simultaneously activate mental representations for learning to occur. The importance of temporal contiguity in implicit learning of associations is also evident from research on verbal learning in amnesia (Gabrieli, Keane, Zarella, & Poldrack, 1997; Goshen-Gottstein & Moscovitch, 1995).

However, there is an important constraint on this kind of learning apart from timing. In situations where there is prior orientation of attention to a target, there is no learning of task-irrelevant associations. In another condition of Logan and Etherton's (1994) Experiment 5, the arrow appeared half a second before the word pair. Now subjects did not learn the repeated word pairings. Similarly, Toro, Sinnett, and Soto-Faraco (2005) found that lexical segmentation of syllable sequences by statistical learning (Saffran et al., 1996b) is completely eliminated when the subjects performed a demanding distracting task, for example monitoring a rapid stream of line drawings for repetitions. These results should not be surprising when we consider that there appears to be a lack of perceptual processing for stimuli when sustained attention is directed elsewhere (Dupoux, Kouider, & Mehler, 2003; Naccache, Blandin, & Dehaene, 2002). Returning to the issue of learning form–meaning connections, what these studies suggest is that if the task encourages sustained attention to form alone, then contextual associations will not be learned.

When considering the influence of attention on learning, we must also consider the fact that attention not only is directed to discrete stimuli in space or time, but also can be directed to different dimensions of the same stimulus. Here too, sustained attention to one dimension will eliminate learning effects related to another dimension. Toro et al. (2005) showed that no learning of lexical segmentation occurred when subjects had to monitor the syllable stream for pitch changes. Attention was focused on the syllables, but not on the relevant dimension. Jiménez and Méndez (1999) used an SRT task in which the sequence of positions was generated in the usual way by a finite state grammar. However, they also built in a separate regularity such that the identity of the characters that were used as stimuli also predicted the position of the next stimulus (e.g. a * predicted position A, whereas a ? predicted position C). Using the standard SRT procedure in which subjects simply indicate at which position each stimulus occurred, only the position-based regularity was learned. But when they also had to keep a running count of how often certain characters (x or *) occurred, learning of the second, identity-based, regularity was obtained. Both regularities were learned implicitly. Thus, awareness at the level of noticing stimulus identity led to learning without understanding its predictiveness. Together, these experiments also illustrate the importance of attending to the appropriate stimulus dimensions for learning the regularities that relate to them, even when attention is always apparently directed to the same stimuli.

Work on task-irrelevant learning and contextual cuing suggests that an attended, and noticed, word might implicitly, and unselectively, acquire associations to contextual information that is outside the focus of attention. However, based on the above, we can hypothesise that this will occur only under specific conditions: the word and the contextual information have to be simultaneously active, and attention must not be oriented in advance to either the word or the context, or to some irrelevant dimension of either. If the word and the contextual information are not simultaneously active, then unitisation through joint attention will be necessary. Clearly, implicit learning is highly sensitive to attentional effects. Only by working through the microstructure of learning processes at this level of detail will we be able to understand the precise conditions under which implicit learning is likely to occur.

## V. CONCLUSION

Even though there is a long tradition of research on implicit learning dating back to Reber's seminal 1967 publication, one senses that the study of implicit language learning is still in its infancy. On the positive side, there are now clearly developed ideas on how to measure subjective states and technologies that can provide indications of the automaticity and nativelikeness of brain responses, so we are in a good position to at least identify when implicit knowledge has been acquired. There are also clearly developed ideas about how attention is involved in learning processes, and these should give a good indication of the task conditions under which implicit learning is most likely to occur. Whilst of practical relevance in themselves, these advances also provide important methodological groundwork for the investigation of the crucial theoretical issues concerning the nature of the implicit learning process itself and the nature of what is learnable. Here there is much more that could be done. When investigating what is learnable we need to consider how characteristics of the hypothesised learning mechanism might determine learnability (perhaps following the example of research on non-adjacent dependencies). Ideally, computational modelling will be used to explore the learnability of different regularities, helping us to make explicit what exactly a wholly empiricist and associative view of implicit learning predicts.

Certain areas of potentially important implicit learning research have been curiously neglected. We need to know far more about the influence of prior knowledge and where that knowledge comes from (L1, L2 or UG?). The issue of the interface between implicit and explicit knowledge is remarkably under-researched in both psychology and SLA. N. C. Ellis (2005) provides a theoretical framework for thinking about this issue, but there is a need for hard experimental evidence. We must consider not only how explicit knowledge can influence implicit learning, but also how implicit knowledge can become explicit (see Haider & Frensch, 2005, for an intriguing suggestion). The issue of individual differences has been dominated by Reber's (1989) hypothesis that implicit learning should be relatively immune to factors such as IQ and age. Whilst this appears to be true (for recent evidence, see Don, Schellenberg, Reber, DiGirolamo, & Wang, 2003; Gebauer & Mackintosh, 2007), does this mean that implicit learning is completely independent of all dimensions of individual differences? Robinson (2005) found no relationship between the Modern Language Aptitude Test (MLAT) and incidental learning of a natural language, but suggests that the component skills measured by the MLAT are probably more relevant to explicit than implicit learning. Given that implicit learning is a memory-driven process, one would expect it to be related to memory ability. There is some evidence for this connection in AG learning (Karpicke & Pisoni, 2004), but as yet there is no evidence from implicit learning of natural language.

Clearly, much more needs to be known about these issues before the exact role of implicit learning in SLA can be specified. However, given that we are clearly endowed with a powerful associative learning mechanism for unintentionally picking up aspects of the statistical structure of the environment, it would surely be absurd to argue that it makes no contribution to language learning. The goal is to specify exactly what that contribution is.

## ACKNOWLEDGMENTS

Thanks to Peter Robinson, Michael Ullman, Chieko Kuribara and Patrick Rebuschat for their comments on portions of this chapter.

## REFERENCES

Altmann, G. T. M., Dienes, Z., & Goode, A. (1995). Modality independence of implicitly learned grammatical knowledge. *Journal of Experimental Psychology: Learning Memory, and Cognition, 21*, 899–912.

Aslin, R. N., Saffran, J. R., & Newport, E. L. (1998). Computation of conditional probability statistics by 8-month-old infants. *Psychological Science, 9*, 321–324.

Bates, E., & MacWhinney, B. (1989). Functionalism and the competition model. In B. MacWhinney & E. Bates (Eds.), *The crosslinguistic study of sentence processing* (pp. 3–73). Cambridge: Cambridge University Press.

Bialystok, E. (1982). On the relationship between knowing and using forms. *Applied Linguistics*, *3*, 181–206.

Bickerton, D. (1999). Creole languages, the language bioprogram hypothesis, and language acquisition. In W. C. Ritchie & T. K. Bhatia (Eds.), *Handbook of child language acquisition*. San Diego, London: Academic Press.

Block, N. (1990). Consciousness and accessibility. *Behavioral and Brain Sciences*, *13*, 596–598.

Blom, E., & Polisenská, D. (2008). The acquisition of grammatical gender in Dutch. *Second Language Research*, *24*, 259–265.

Braine, M. D. S. (1987). What is learned in acquiring word classes: A step towards an acquisition theory. In B. MacWhinney (Ed.), *Mechanisms of language acquisition* (pp. 65–87). Hillsdale, NJ: Lawrence Erlbaum Associates.

Braine, M. D. S., Brody, R. E., Brooks, P. D., Sudhalter, V., Ross, J. E., Catalano, L., & Fisch, S. M. (1990). Exploring language acquisition in children with a miniature artificial language: Effects of item and pattern frequency, arbitrary subclasses, and correction. *Journal of Memory and Language*, *29*, 591–610.

Brooks, P. J., Braine, M. D. S., Catalano, L., & Brody, R. (1993). Acquisition of gender-like noun classes in an artificial language: The contribution of phonological markers to learning. *Journal of Memory and Language*, *32*, 76–95.

Buchner, A. (1994). Indirect effects of synthetic grammar learning in an identification task. *Journal of Experimental Psychology: Learning, Memory, and Cognition*, *20*, 550–565.

Carroll, S. E. (1999). Input and SLA: Adults' sensitivity to different sorts of cues to French gender. *Language Learning*, *49*, 37–92.

Casenhiser, D., & Goldberg, A. E. (2005). Fast mapping of a phrasal form and meaning. *Developmental Science*, *8*, 500–508.

Christiansen, M. H., Allen, J., & Seidenberg, M. S. (1998). Learning to segment speech using multiple cues: A connectionist model. *Language and Cognitive Processes*, *13*, 221–268.

Chun, M. M. (2000). Contextual cueing of visual attention. *Trends in Cognitive Sciences*, *4*, 170–178.

Chun, M. M., & Phelps, E. A. (1999). Memory deficits for implicit contextual information in amnesic subjects with hippocampal damage. *Nature Neuroscience*, *2*, 844–847.

Cleeremans, A., Destrebecqz, A., & Boyer, M. (1998). Implicit learning: News from the front. *Trends in Cognitive Sciences*, *2*, 406–417.

Cleeremans, A., & Dienes, Z. (2008). Computational models of implicit learning. In R. Sun (Ed.), *Cambridge handbook of computational psychology* (pp. 396–421). Cambridge: Cambridge University Press.

Cleeremans, A., & Jiménez, L. (2002). Implicit learning and consciousness: A graded, dynamic perspective. In R. M. French & A. Cleeremans (Eds.), *Implicit learning and consciousness* (pp. 1–40). Hove: Psychology Press.

Cleeremans, A., & McClelland, J. L. (1991). Learning the structure of event sequences. *Journal of Experimental Psychology: General*, *120*, 235–253.

Corballis, M. C. (2007). Recursion, language, and starlings. *Cognitive Science*, *31*, 697–704.

Cowan, N. (1999). An embedded-processes model of working memory. In A. Miyake & P. Shah (Eds.), *Models of working memory: Mechanisms of active maintenance and executive control* (pp. 62–101). Cambridge: Cambridge University Press.

Curran, T., & Keele, S. W. (1993). Attentional and nonattentional forms of sequence learning. *Journal of Experimental Psychology: Learning, Memory, and Cognition*, *19*, 189–202.

Dehaene, S., & Naccache, L. (2001). Towards a cognitive neuroscience of consciousness: Basic evidence and a workspace framework. *Cognition*, *79*, 1–37.

DeKeyser, R. (2003). Implicit and explicit learning. In C. Doughty & M. Long (Eds.), *Handbook of second language acquisition* (pp. 313–348). Oxford: Blackwell.

DeKeyser, R. M. (1995). Learning second language grammar rules: An experiment with a miniature linguistic system. *Studies in Second Language Acquisition, 17*, 379–410.

Dell, G. S., Reed, K. D., Adams, D. R., & Meyer, A. S. (2000). Speech errors, phonotactic constraints, and implicit learning: A study of the role of experience in language production. *Journal of Experimental Psychology: Learning Memory, and Cognition, 26*(6), 1355–1367.

Destrebecqz, A., & Cleeremans, A. (2001). Can sequence learning be implicit? New evidence with the process dissociation procedure. *Psychonomic Bulletin & Review, 8*, 343–350.

Destrebecqz, A., & Cleeremans, A. (2003). Temporal effects in sequence learning. In L. Jimenez (Ed.), *Attention and implicit learning* (pp. 181–213). Amsterdam: John Benjamins.

Dienes, Z., & Perner, J. (1999). A theory of implicit and explicit knowledge. *Behavioural and Brain Sciences, 22*, 735–808.

Dienes, Z., & Scott, R. (2005). Measuring unconscious knowledge: Distinguishing structural knowledge and judgment knowledge. *Psychological Research, 69*, 338–351.

Dominey, P. F., & Ramus, F. (2000). Neural network processing of natural language: I. Sensitivity to serial, temporal and abstract structure of language in the infant. *Language and Cognitive Processes, 15*, 87–127.

Don, A. J., Schellenberg, E. G., Reber, A. S., DiGirolamo, K. M., & Wang, P. P. (2003). Implicit learning in children and adults with Williams syndrome. *Developmental Neuropsychology, 23*(1–2), 201–225.

Dupoux, E., Kouider, S., & Mehler, J. (2003). Lexical access without attention? Explorations using dichotic priming. *Journal of Experimental Psychology: Human Perception and Performance, 29*, 172–184.

Eichenbaum, H., Otto, T., & Cohen, N. J. (1994). Two functional components of the hippocampal memory system. *Behavioral and Brain Sciences, 17*, 449–518.

Ellis, N. C. (1993). Rules and instances in foreign language learning: Interactions of explicit and implicit knowledge. *European Journal of Cognitive Psychology, 5*, 289–318.

Ellis, N. C. (1994). Vocabulary acquisition: The explicit ins and outs of explicit cognitive mediation. In N. C. Ellis (Ed.), *Implicit and explicit learning of languages* (pp. 211–282). London: Academic Press.

Ellis, N. C. (2005). At the interface: Dynamic interactions of explicit and implicit language knowledge. *Studies in Second Language Acquisition, 27*, 305–352.

Ellis, N. C. (2006a). Language acquisition as rational contingency learning. *Applied linguistics, 27*, 1–24.

Ellis, N. C. (2006b). Selective attention and transfer phenomena in L2 acquisition: Contingency, cue competition, salience, interference, overshadowing, blocking, and perceptual learning. *Applied Linguistics, 27*, 164–194.

Ellis, R. (2005). Measuring implicit and explicit knowledge of a second language: A psychometric study. *Studies in Second Language Acquisition, 27*, 141–172.

Ellis, R. (2006). Modelling learning difficulty and second language proficiency: The differential contributions of implicit and explicit knowledge. *Applied Linguistics, 27*, 431–463.

Ellis, R., & Loewen, S. (2007). Confirming the operational definitions of explicit and implicit knowledge in Ellis (2005): Responding to Isemonger. *Studies in Second Language Acquisition, 29*, 119–126.

Elman, J. L. (1990). Finding structure in time. *Cognitive Science, 14*, 179–211.

Elman, J. L., Bates, E. A., Johnson, M., Karmiloff-Smith, A., Parisi, D., & Plunkett, K. (1996). *Rethinking innateness: A connectionist perspective on development*. Cambridge, MA: MIT Press.

Erlam, R. (2006). Elicited imitation as a measure of L2 implicit knowledge: An empirical validation study. *Applied Linguistics, 27*, 464–491.

Fitch, W. T., & Hauser, M. D. (2004). Computational constraints on syntactic processing in a nonhuman primate. *Science, 303*, 377–380.

Friederici, A. D. (2002). Towards a neural basis of auditory sentence processing. *Trends in Cognitive Sciences, 6*, 78–84.

Friederici, A. D., Bahlmann, J., Heim, S., Schubotz, R. I., & Anwander, A. (2004). The brain differentiates human and non-human grammars: Functional localization and structural connectivity. *Proceedings of the National Academy of Sciences, 103*, 2458–2463.

Friederici, A. D., Steinhauer, K., & Pfeifer, E. (2002). Brain signatures of artificial language processing: Evidence challenging the 'critical period' hypothesis. *Proceedings of the National Academy of Science, 99*, 529–534.

Frigo, L., & McDonald, J. L. (1998). Properties of phonological markers that affect the acquisition of gender-like subclasses. *Journal of Memory and Language, 39*, 218–245.

Gabrieli, J. D. E. (1998). Cognitive neuroscience of human memory. *Annual Review of Psychology, 49*, 87–115.

Gabrieli, J. D. E., Cohen, N. J., & Corkin, S. (1988). The impaired learning of semantic knowledge following medial temporal lobe resection. *Brain and Cognition, 7*, 157–177.

Gabrieli, J. D. E., Keane, M., Zarella, M. M., & Poldrack, R. A. (1997). Preservation of implicit memory for new associations in global amnesia. *Psychological Science, 8*, 326–329.

Gebauer, G. F., & Mackintosh, N. J. (2007). Psychometric intelligence dissociates implicit and explicit learning. *Journal of Experimental Psychology: Learning, Memory, and Cognition, 33*, 34–54.

Gentner, T. Q., Fenn, K. M., Margoliash, D., & Nusbaum, C. (2006). Recursive syntactic pattern learning by songbirds. *Nature, 440*, 1204.

Gerken, L., Wilson, R., & Lewis, W. (2005). Infants can use distributional cues to form syntactic categories. *Journal of Child Language, 32*, 249–268.

Goldberg, A. E. (1995). *Constructions: A construction grammar approach to argument structure*. Chicago: Chicago University Press.

Goldberg, A. E. (2006). *Constructions at work*. Oxford: Oxford University Press.

Goschke, T. (1997). Implicit learning and conscious knowledge: Mental representation, computational mechanisms, and brain structures. In K. Lamberts & D. Shanks (Eds.), *Knowledge, concepts, and categories*. Hove: Psychology Press.

Goshen-Gottstein, Y., & Moscovitch, M. (1995). Repetition priming effects for newly formed associations are perceptually based: Evidence from shallow encoding and format specificity. *Journal of Experimental Psychology: Learning, Memory, and Cognition, 21*, 1249–1262.

Goujon, A., Didierjean, A., & Marmèche, E. (2007). Contextual cueing based on specific and categorical properties of the environment. *Visual Cognition, 15*, 257–275.

Green, P., & Hecht, K. (1992). Implicit and explicit grammar: An empirical study. *Applied Linguistics, 13*, 168–184.

Guillelmon, D., & Grosjean, F. (2001). The gender marking effect in spoken word recognition: The case of bilinguals. *Memory and Cognition, 29*, 503–511.

Hahne, A., & Friederici, A. D. (2001). Processing a second language: Late learners' comprehension mechanisms as revealed by event-related brain potentials. *Bilingualism: Language and Cognition, 4*, 123–141.

Haider, H., & Frensch, P. A. (2005). The generation of conscious awareness in an incidental learning situation. *Psychological Research, 69*, 399–411.

Haist, F., Musen, G., & Squire, L. (1991). Intact priming of words and nonwords in amnesia. *Psychobiology, 19*, 275–285.

Hauser, M. D., Chomsky, N., & Fitch, W. T. (2002). The faculty of language: What is it, who has it, and how did it evolve? *Science, 298*, 1569–1579.

Hauser, M. D., Newport, E. L., & Aslin, R. N. (2001). Segmentation of the speech stream in a non-human primate: Statistical learning in cotton-top tamarins. *Cognition, 78*, B53–B64.

Hauser, M. D., Weiss, D. J., & Marcus, G. (2002). Rule learning by cotton-top tamarins. *Cognition, 86*, B15–B22.

Hayes, N. A., & Broadbent, D. E. (1988). Two modes of learning for interactive tasks. *Cognition, 28*, 249–276.

Hochmann, J. R., Azadpour, M., & Mehler, J. (2008). Do humans really learn $A^n B^n$ artificial grammars from exemplars? *Cognitive Science, 32*, 1021–1036.

Holmes, V. M., & Dejean de la Batie, B. (1999). Assignment of grammatical gender by native speakers and foreign language learners. *Applied Psycholinguistics, 20*, 479–506.

Hulstijn, J. H. (2003). Incidental and intentional learning. In C. Doughty & M. Long (Eds.), *Handbook of second language acquisition* (pp. 349–381). Oxford: Blackwell.

Hulstijn, J. H., & Hulstijn, W. (1984). Grammatical errors as a function of processing constraints and explicit knowledge. *Language Learning, 34*, 23–43.

Isemonger, I. M. (2007). Operational definitions of explicit and implicit knowledge: Response to R. Ellis (2005) and some recommendations for future research in this area. *Studies in Second Language Acquisition, 29*, 101–118.

Iwasaki, N. (2003). L2 acquisition of Japanese: Knowledge and use of case particles in SOV and OSV sentences. In S. Karimi (Ed.), *Word order and scrambling* (pp. 273–300). Oxford: Blackwell.

Jiménez, L., & Méndez, C. (1999). Which attention is needed for implicit sequence learning? *Journal of Experimental Psychology: Learning, Memory, and Cognition, 25*, 236–259.

Johnstone, T., & Shanks, D. R. (1999). Two mechanisms in implicit artificial grammar learning? Comment on Meulemans and Van der Linden (1997). *Journal of Experimental Psychology: Learning, Memory, and Cognition, 25*, 524–531.

Johnstone, T., & Shanks, D. R. (2001). Abstractionist and processing accounts of implicit learning. *Cognitive Psychology, 42*, 61–112.

Karpicke, J. D., & Pisoni, D. B. (2004). Using immediate memory span to measure implicit learning. *Memory and Cognition, 32*, 956–964.

Kelly, M. H. (1992). Using sound to solve syntactic problems: The role of phonology in grammatical category assignments. *Psychological Review, 99*, 349–364.

Kinder, A., & Shanks, D. R. (2001). Amnesia and the declarative/nondeclarative distinction: A recurrent network model of classification, recognition, and repetition priming. *Journal of Cognitive Neuroscience, 13*, 648–669.

Kinder, A., & Shanks, D. R. (2003). Neuropsychological dissociations between priming and recognition: A single-system connectionist account. *Psychological Review, 110*, 728–744.

Knowlton, B. J., & Squire, L. R. (1996). Artificial grammar learning depends on implicit acquisition of both abstract and exemplar-specific information. *Journal of Experimental Psychology: Learning, Memory, and Cognition, 22*, 169–181.

Koch, C., & Tsuchiya, N. (2007). Attention and consciousness: Two distinct brain processes. *Trends in Cognitive Sciences, 11*, 16–22.

Krashen, S. (1981). *Second language acquisition and second language learning.* London: Pergamon.

Krashen, S. D. (1994). The input hypothesis and its rivals. In N. C. Ellis (Ed.), *Implicit and explicit learning of languages.* London: Academic Press.

Lamme, V. A. F. (2003). Why visual attention and awareness are different. *Trends in Cognitive Sciences, 7*, 12–18.

Leow, R. P. (2000). A study of the role of awareness in foreign language behavior. *Studies in Second Language Acquisition, 22*, 557–584.

Leung, J. (2007). *Implicit learning of form–meaning connections.* Ph.D. thesis, University of Cambridge, Cambridge.

Leung, J., & Williams, J. (2006). Implicit learning of form–meaning connections. In R. Sun & N. Miyake (Eds.), *Proceedings of the annual meeting of the cognitive science society* (pp. 465–470). Mahwah, NJ: Lawrence Erlbaum Associates.

Leung, J., & Williams, J. N. (in preparation). *Implicit learning of grammatical form–meaning connections in semi-artificial languages.*

Lieven, E., & Tomasello, M. (2008). Children's first language acquisition from a usage-based perspective. In P. Robinson & N. C. Ellis (Eds.), *Handbook of cognitive linguistics and second language acquisition* (pp. 168–196). New York: Routledge.

Logan, G. D., & Etherton, J. L. (1994). What is learned during automatization? The role of attention in constructing an instance. *Journal of Experimental Psychology: Learning, Memory, and Cognition, 20*, 1022–1050.

Lovibond, P. F., & Shanks, D. R. (2002). The role of awareness in Pavlovian conditioning: Empirical evidence and theoretical implications. *Journal of Experimental Psychology: Animal Behavior Processes, 28*, 3–26.

Maratsos, M. (1982). The child's construction of grammatical categories. In E. Wanner & L. R. Gleitman (Eds.), *Language acquisition: The state of the art* (pp. 240–266). Cambridge: Cambridge University Press.

Marchman, V. A., & Bates, E. (1994). Continuity in lexical and morphological development: A test of the critical mass hypothesis. *Journal of Child Language, 21*, 339–366.

Marcus, G. F., Vijayan, S., Bandi Rao, S., & Vishton, P. M. (1999). Rule learning in 7-month-old infants. *Science, 283*, 77–80.

Marslen-Wilson, W., & Welsh, A. (1978). Processing interactions and lexical access during word recognition in continuous speech. *Cognitive Psychology, 10*, 29–63.

Matthews, R. C., Buss, R. R., Stanley, W. B., Blanchard-Fields, F., Cho, J.-R., & Druhan, B. (1989). The role of implicit and explicit processes in learning from examples: A synergistic effect. *Journal of Experimental Psychology: Learning, Memory, and Cognition, 15*, 1083–1100.

McClelland, J. L., & Plaut, D. C. (1999). Does generalization in infant learning implicate abstract algebra-like rules? *Trends in Cognitive Sciences, 3*, 166–168.

McLaughlin, J., Osterhout, L., & Kim, A. (2004). Neural correlates of second language word learning: Minimal instruction produces rapid change. *Nature Neuroscience, 7*, 703–704.

Mintz, T. H. (2002). Category induction from distributional cues in an artificial language. *Memory and Cognition, 30*, 678–686.

Mirman, D., Magnuson, J. S., Graf Estes, K., & Dixon, J. A. (2008). The link between statistical segmentation and word learning in adults. *Cognition, 108*, 271–280.

Morgan, J. L., Meier, R. P., & Newport, E. L. (1989). Facilitating the acquisition of syntax with cross-sentential cues to phrase structure. *Journal of Memory and Language, 28*, 67–85.

Morgan-Short, K. (2007). *A neurolinguistic investigation of late-learned second language knowledge: The effects of explicit and implicit conditions.* Ph.D. thesis, Georgetown University, Washington.

Murasugi, K., & Kawamura, T. (2005). On the acquisition of scrambling in Japanese. In J. Sabel & M. Saito (Eds.), *The free word order phenomenon: Its syntactic sources and diversity* (Vol. 69). Berlin/New York: Mouton de Gruyter.

Naccache, L., Blandin, E., & Dehaene, S. (2002). Unconscious masked priming depends on temporal attention. *Psychological Science, 13*, 416–424.

Newport, E. L., & Aslin, R. N. (2004). Learning at a distance I. Statistical learning of non-adjacent dependencies. *Cognitive Psychology, 48*, 127–162.

Newport, E. L., Hauser, M. D., Spaepen, G., & Aslin, R. N. (2004). Learning at a distance II. Statistical learning of non-adjacent dependencies in a non-human primate. *Cognitive Psychology, 49*, 85–117.

Norman, E., Price, M. C., Duff, S. C., & Mentzoni, R. A. (2007). Gradations of awareness in a modified sequence learning task. *Consciousness and Cognition, 16*, 809–837.

O'Reilly, R. C., & Munakata, Y. (2000). *Computational explorations in cognitive neuroscience: Understanding the mind by simulating the brain.* Cambridge, MA: MIT Press.

Osterhout, L., McLaughlin, J., Pitkanen, I., Frenck-Mestre, C., & Molinaro, N. (2006). Novice learners, longitudinal designs, and event-related potentials: A means for exploring the neurocognition of second language processing. *Language Learning, 56*, 199–230.

Pacton, S., & Perruchet, P. (2008). An attention-based associative account of adjacent and nonadjacent dependency learning. *Journal of Experimental Psychology: Learning, Memory, and Cognition, 34*, 80–96.

Pacton, S., Perruchet, P., Fayol, M., & Cleeremans, A. (2001). Implicit learning out of the lab: The case of orthographic regularities. *Journal of Experimental Psychology: General, 130*, 401–426.

Paradis, M. (1994). Neurolinguistic aspects of implicit and explicit memory: Implications for bilingualism and SLA. In N. C. Ellis (Ed.), *Implicit and explicit learning of languages* (pp. 393–419). San Diego: Academic Press.

Paradis, M. (2004). *A neurolinguistic theory of bilingualism.* Amsterdam/Philadelphia: John Benjamins.

Park, H., Quinlan, J., Thornton, E., & Reder, L. M. (2004). The effect of midazolam on visual search: Implications for understanding amnesia. *Proceedings of the National Academy of Sciences, 101*, 17879–17883.

Perruchet, P., & Gallego, J. (1997). A subjective unit formation account of implicit learning. In D. C. Berry (Ed.), *How implicit is implicit learning?* (pp. 124–161). Oxford: Oxford University Press.

Perruchet, P., & Pacteau, C. (1990). Synthetic grammar learning: Implicit rule abstraction or explicit fragmentary knowledge? *Journal of Experimental Psychology: General, 119*, 264–275.

Perruchet, P., & Rey, A. (2005). Does the mastery of center-embedded linguistic structures distinguish humans from nonhuman primates? *Psychonomic Bulletin & Review, 12*, 307–313.

Perruchet, P., & Vinter, A. (1998). PARSER: A model for word segmentation. *Journal of Memory and Language, 39*, 246–263.

Pinker, S. (1989). *Learnability and cognition.* Cambridge, MA: MIT Press.

Reber, A. S. (1967). Implicit learning of artificial grammars. *Journal of Verbal Learning and Verbal Behavior, 6*, 855–863.

Reber, A. S. (1989). Implicit learning and tacit knowledge. *Journal of Experimental Psychology: General, 118*, 219–235.

Reber, A. S., & Allen, R. (1978). Analogic and abstraction strategies in synthetic grammar learning: A functionalist interpretation. *Cognition, 6*, 189–221.

Reber, P. J., & Squire, L. R. (1999). Intact learning of artificial grammars and intact category learning by patients with Parkinson's disease. *Behavioral Neuroscience, 113*, 235–242.

Rebuschat, P. (2008). *Implicit learning of natural language syntax.* Ph.D. thesis, University of Cambridge, Cambridge.

Rebuschat, P., & Williams, J. N. (2006). Dissociating implicit and explicit learning of natural language syntax. In R. Sun & N. Miyake (Eds.), *Proceedings of the annual meeting of the cognitive science society* (p. 2594). Mahwah, NJ: Lawrence Erlbaum.

Redington, M., & Chater, N. (1998). Connectionist and statistical approaches to language acquisition: A distributional perspective. *Language and Cognitive Processes, 13*, 129–191.

Robinson, P. (1995). Attention, memory, and the "noticing" hypothesis. *Language Learning, 45*, 283–331.

Robinson, P. (1996). Learning simple and complex second language rules under implicit, incidental, rule-search, and instructed conditions. *Studies in Second Language Acquisition, 18*, 27–67.

Robinson, P. (1997). Generalizability and automaticity of second language learning under implicit, incidental, enhanced, and instructed conditions. *Studies in Second Language Acquisition, 19*, 223–247.

Robinson, P. (2005). Cognitive abilities, chunk-strength, and frequency effects in implicit artificial grammar and incidental L2 learning: Replications of Reber, Walkenfeld, and Hernstadt (1991) and Knowlton and Squire (1996) and their relevance for SLA. *Studies in Second Language Acquisition, 27*, 235–268.

Roehr, K. (2008). Linguistic and metalinguistic categories in second language learning. *Cognitive Linguistics, 19*, 67–106.

Rosa, E., & Leow, R. P. (2004). Awareness, different learning conditions, and second language development. *Applied Psycholinguistics, 25*, 269–292.

Sabourin, L., & Stowe, L. (2008). Second language processing: When are first and second languages processed similarly? *Second Language Research, 24*, 397–430.

Saffran, J. R. (2001). The use of predictive dependencies in language learning. *Journal of Memory and Language, 44*, 493–515.

Saffran, J. R., Hauser, M., Seibel, R., Kapfhamer, J., Tsao, F., & Cushman, F. (2008). Grammatical pattern learning by human infants and cotton-top tamarin monkeys. *Cognition, 107*, 479–500.

Saffran, J. R., Newport, E. L., & Aslin, R. N. (1996a). Statistical learning in 8-month-old infants. *Science, 274*, 1926–1928.

Saffran, J. R., Newport, E. L., & Aslin, R. N. (1996b). Word segmentation: The role of distributional cues. *Journal of Memory and Language, 35*, 606–621.

Saito, M., & Fukui, N. (1998). Order in phrase structure and movement. *Linguistic Inquiry, 29*, 439–474.

Schmidt, R. (2001). Attention. In P. Robinson (Ed.), *Cognition and second language instruction* (pp. 3–32). Cambridge: Cambridge University Press.

Segalowitz, N. (2003). Automaticity and second languages. In C. Doughty & M. Long (Eds.), *Handbook of second language acquisition* (pp. 382–408). Oxford: Blackwell.

Seitz, A., & Watanabe, T. (2005). A unified model for perceptual learning. *Trends in Cognitive Sciences, 9,* 229–234.

Servan-Schreiber, D., & Anderson, J. R. (1990). Learning artificial grammars with competitive chunking. *Journal of Experimental Psychology: Learning, Memory, and Cognition, 16,* 592–608.

Shanks, D. R. (1995). *The psychology of associative learning.* Cambridge: Cambridge University Press.

Shanks, D. R. (2005). Implicit learning. In K. Lamberts & R. Goldstone (Eds.), *Handbook of cognition* (pp. 202–220). London: Sage.

Shanks, D. R., & Channon, S. (2002). Effects of a secondary task on 'implicit' sequence learning: learning or performance? *Psychological Research, 66,* 99–109.

Shanks, D. R., & St. John, M. (1994). Characteristics of dissociable human learning systems. *Behavioral and Brain Sciences, 17,* 367–447.

Squire, L. (1992). Memory and the hippocampus: A synthesis from findings with rats, monkeys, and humans. *Psychological Review, 99,* 195–231.

Taraban, R., & Kempe, V. (1999). Gender processing in native and nonnative Russian speakers. *Applied Psycholinguistics, 20,* 119–148.

Thompson, S. P., & Newport, E. L. (2007). Statistical learning of syntax: The role of transitional probability. *Language Learning and Development, 3,* 1–42.

Tokowicz, N., & MacWhinney, B. (2005). Implicit and explicit measures of sensitivity to violations in second language grammar: An event-related potential investigation. *Studies in Second Language Acquisition, 27,* 173–204.

Tomasello, M. (2000). The item-based nature of children's early syntactic development. *Trends in Cognitive Sciences, 4,* 156–163.

Tomasello, M. (2003). *Constructing a language.* Cambridge, MA: Harvard University Press.

Toro, J. M., Sinnett, S., & Soto-Faraco, S. (2005). Speech segmentation by statistical learning depends on attention. *Cognition, 97,* B25–B34.

Ullman, M. T. (2001). A neurocognitive perspective on language: The declarative/procedural model. *Nature Reviews: Neuroscience, 2,* 717–726.

Ullman, M. T. (2004). Contributions of memory circuits to language: The declarative/procedural model. *Cognition, 92*(1–2), 231–270.

Ullman, M. T. (2005). A cognitive neuroscience perspective on second language acquisition: The declarative/procedural model. In C. Sanz (Ed.), *Mind and context in adult second language acquisition: Methods, theory, and practice* (pp. 141–178). Washington, DC: Georgetown University Press.

Warker, J. A., & Dell, G. S. (2006). Speech errors reflect newly learned phonotactic constraints. *Journal of Experimental Psychology: Learning, Memory, and Cognition, 32,* 387–398.

Williams, J. N. (2003). Inducing abstract linguistic representations: Human and connectionist learning of noun classes. In R. van Hout, A. Hulk, F. Kuiken, & R. Towell (Eds.), *The interface between syntax and the lexicon in second language acquisition* (pp. 151–174). Amsterdam: John Benjamins.

Williams, J. N. (2004). Implicit learning of form-meaning connections. In B. VanPatten, J. Williams, S. Rott, & M. Overstreet (Eds.), *Form meaning connections in second language acquisition* (pp. 203–218). Mahwah, NJ: Lawrence Erlbaum Associates.

Williams, J. N. (2005). Learning without awareness. *Studies in Second Language Acquisition, 27,* 269–304.

Williams, J. N., & Kuribara, C. (2008). Comparing a nativist and emergentist approach to the initial stage of SLA: An investigation of Japanese scrambling. *Lingua, 118,* 522–553.

Witt, K., Nuhsman, A., & Deuschl, G. (2002). Intact artificial grammar learning in patients with cerebellar degeneration and advanced Parkinson's disease. *Neuropsychologia, 40,* 1534–1540.

# NEUROPSYCHOLOGY AND COGNITIVE DEVELOPMENT

## INTRODUCTION TO PART IV

Part IV treats the neurological substrate of second language acquisition (SLA) and use and, in addition, the related questions of the effects of age on SLA.

Chapter 15 ("Neuropsychology of Second Language Acquisition") by Cosimo Urgesi and Franco Fabbro provides an overview of neurological factors in SLA. After a brief introduction to basic facts about the relationship between brain damage and language—particularly in bi-/multilinguals—the authors review the literature on a variety of issues in the field, including the representation of implicit and explicit knowledge of language in the brain, the neurological correlates of sensitive period phenomena, the results of cortical stimulation and neuroimaging studies of bilinguals, pathological switching and mixing of languages, and finally, brain plasticity and language acquisition.

In relation to age and SLA, Usha Lakshmanan reviews the literature on child SLA in chapter 16 ("Child Second Language Acquisition"). Lakshmanan first addresses central theoretical issues in the field including strong versus weak continuity hypotheses as well as the variety of positions on the place of transfer in child SLA. Methodological issues in the study of child SLA are somewhat different from those in the study of adult SLA, and Lakshmanan discusses these differences in detail. The chapter then turns to a specific treatment of the development of phonology, lexicon, and morphosyntax in child SLA.

Research on critical/sensitive period effects in language acquisition is the topic of chapter 17 ("Age and the End State of Second Language Acquisition") by David Birdsong. The author takes on a number of conceptual and methodological issues and then discusses at length a range of possible sources of the well-known fact that, in general, adults are not as adept at SLA as children are. Among the sources he discusses are the neurobiological and neurocognitive differences between children and adults, aspects of cognitive development, and L1 entrenchment. A number of additional methodological issues arise in the study of age effects in SLA having to do with age of onset or age of arrival and the adoption of the native speaker as a standard for determining success in SLA, and Birdsong discusses these as well. After a treatment of some of the ways in which second language acquirers actually achieve native-like knowledge of the second language, the author raises the central questions in this area of research (Is there a critical period? Are critical period effects maturational in nature? How is the available data to be analyzed with respect to these questions?) and provides what answers are possible at this time.

One question in connection with SLA and age that is not often addressed in the literature is: What is the fate of the results of SLA (i.e., of bi-/multilingualism) in advanced age? Kees de Bot takes up this issue in chapter 18 ("Multilingualism and Aging"). He sets the central problems in this area of research in terms of his dynamic systems theory, which is intended to capture language as a skill that is constantly changing in the individual. In the case under discussion, these changes can be understood in terms of three dimensions: the biological, the psychological, and the social. As might be expected, many of the changes that occur in the languages of the elderly are concerned with reductions of various sorts—reduction in short-term or working memory, and so on. Some of the more dramatic changes occur in dementia in the elderly and, in particular, a variety of forms of code switching. An interesting observation that comes out of this work is that bi-/multilingualism appears to "protect" elderly people against dementia.

CHAPTER 15

# NEUROPSYCHOLOGY OF SECOND LANGUAGE ACQUISITION

Cosimo Urgesi and Franco Fabbro

Brain injuries may cause language impairments that impact one or more of the languages that the patient uses. One main question of neurolinguistics is whether the first (L1) and the second language (L2) of a bilingual (or the several languages of a multilingual) have similar or different brain representations. One way to study the cerebral organization of L1 and L2 is to assess the pattern of impairment and recovery following brain lesions. These types of clinical studies have shown that bilingual aphasics do not necessarily manifest the same type of disorders and the same degree of severity in both languages. The patterns of impairment and recovery in bilingual aphasics, however, are largely variable, suggesting that the neural representations of bilingualism may vary according to several factors that may differently influence the subcomponents of language. Experimental investigations by means of neurophysiologic and neuroimaging techniques have provided strong contributions to the investigation of the variables that influence the neural activations during L2 processing in bilinguals. Those studies have shown that several variables, such as the age and modality of acquisition, the degree of exposure and use of the two languages, and the level of proficiency affect the way in which the two languages are represented in the bilingual brain. This chapter discusses some of the main findings of studies on the cerebral organization of languages in bilinguals who acquired L2 subsequently to L1.

## I. BILINGUAL APHASIA

The main aim of clinical studies of bilingual aphasia is to identify the similarities and the differences between the impairment and recovery of L1 and L2 knowledge after brain damage. The logic underlying this approach is that if the patient is impaired in or

*The New Handbook of Second Language Acquisition*

recovers both languages to the same extent and at the same time, it can be assumed that they have the same macroanatomical representations. If the patient is selectively impaired in one language but not in the other or shows a differential recovery, then the hypothesis of a different cerebral representation and/or organization may be advanced.

## A. Clinical Aspects of Aphasia in Bilinguals

Several clinical studies have shown that bilingual aphasics do not necessarily manifest the same language disorders with the same degree of severity in both languages (Fabbro, 1999, 2001a). The clinical features of bilingual aphasics may be very different and vary according to the different temporal phases after stroke. Three different phases should be taken into account: (1) the *acute phase*, generally lasting for one month after onset, (2) the *lesion phase*, which lasts for several weeks and perhaps even up to 4–5 months after onset; and (3) the *late phase*, beginning a few months after onset and continuing for all the patient's life.

During the acute phase a regression of the functional impairment effects occurs in brain areas that are structurally unaffected but functionally connected to the damaged area, the so-called regression of *diaschisis*. In this period, language impairments have a dynamic quality in that they may evolve and resolve according to the regression of the diaschisis. Studies have reported, for example, temporary mutism with preserved comprehension in both languages, thus showing a parallel pattern of impairment. On the other hand, other cases showed severe word-finding difficulties in one language with concurrent relative fluency in the other language and good comprehension in both; as the impaired language may alternate, this pattern has been referred to as *alternating antagonism*. Finally, cases of selective aphasia have been described, in which severe impairment of the language acquired during childhood was observed with complete preservation of the one learned at school.

In the lesion phase, the language disorders are more strictly related to the functionality of the lesioned tissue and may affect mainly the comprehension of language (fluent, Wernicke's aphasia), the production of language (nonfluent, Broca's aphasia), or both (global aphasia). The impairments in the two languages are generally typical of a single aphasic syndrome, though with different degrees of symptomatic severity in the two languages (Fabbro & Paradis, 1995).

## B. Language Recovery in Bilingual Aphasia

When bilinguals or polyglots lose the ability to use all the languages they knew following a brain injury affecting language areas (Figure 1) and exhibit the same type of aphasia in all their languages, the pattern of subsequent recovery of their languages may be *parallel* or *nonparallel*. The most common pattern of recovery is parallel recovery from aphasia, in which the patient recovers all his/her languages in a similar way. According to recent studies (Fabbro, 2001a; Paradis, 2004), the percentage of polyglot aphasics showing a parallel recovery of their languages is higher than 60%. The fact that the typical pattern of language recovery after brain lesion is parallel recovery of all languages would be suggestive for an *Extended System Hypothesis*, according to which the neural representations of subsequently learned languages are

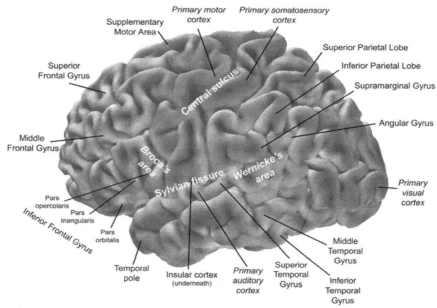

**Figure I**   Lateral surface of the left hemisphere of the standard brain. The locations of the main gyri and sulci of the brain are approximately indicated.

superimposed on the neural representations of the first-acquired language (Paradis, 2004). A minority of polyglot aphasics, however, present with a nonparallel pattern of recovery of the languages they know.

Different patterns of nonparallel recovery have been discussed.

1. *Differential recovery* occurs when languages recover differentially relative to their premorbid levels.
2. *Selective recovery* occurs when the patient recovers only one language, while the other languages are not recovered.
3. *Blended recovery* occurs when the patient inappropriately mixes his/her languages.
4. *Successive recover* occurs when the temporal dynamics and the rate of recovery vary between languages. For example, two languages may eventually recover, but recovery of the second language may only begin after the first has been recovered.
5. *Antagonistic recovery* pattern occurs in exceptional cases, when one language recovers to a certain extent first and then starts regressing when the other language begins to recover.

The existence of nonparallel recovery from aphasia may support a *Dual System Hypothesis*, according to which the different learned languages are represented in separate and distinct neural structures. The large variability of impairment and recovery patterns, however, cannot be explained by a unified view of language representations in bilinguals. For this reason, Paradis (2004) has proposed a model that may explain both parallel and nonparallel impairments and recovery of languages in polyglot aphasics.

According to this model, referred to as *Subsystem Hypothesis*, there is a redundant representation of the languages. It posits, indeed, the existence of a unified neurofunctional cognitive system as well as of language-specific subsystems. The interaction between the interindividual differences in the neurocognitive representations of languages before injury determined by the age of acquisition and by the way in which languages were learned and used, and in the microanatomical nature of the lesion may explain the variability of the patterns of impairment and recovery of languages.

## C. Factors Accounting for Differential Language Recovery

Several factors have been proposed to explain parallel language recovery versus nonparallel recovery in bilinguals. Albert Pitres (1895, in Paradis, 1983) was the first to draw attention to the fact that the dissociation of the languages affected by aphasia was not an exceptional phenomenon, but rather ordinary. Pitres described seven clinical cases of patients exhibiting differential recovery of the two languages they spoke. On the basis of the frequency of dissociation, Pitres put forward hypotheses on the causes that might determine a better recovery in one language, thus reaching the conclusion that patients tend to recover the language that was most familiar to them prior to the insult. This hypothesis was subsequently called *Pitres' rule*. In proposing his theory, Pitres referred to a work by Ribot (1882) in which it was claimed that, in the case of memory diseases, the general rule held that the later acquired language deteriorates earlier than the old, the so-called *Ribot's rule*. In his work, Pitres maintained that the recovery pattern could occur only if the lesion had not destroyed the language centers, but only temporarily inhibited them through *pathological inertia*. In Pitres' opinion, the patient generally recovered the most familiar language because the neural elements subserving it were more firmly associated. If the patient had become aphasic owing to *functional inertia* of the language areas, these inhibitory pathological phenomena should have affected to a greater extent the languages that exhibited weaker associations between the neural elements subserving them.

Several scholars have suggested that when a language is not available, it is not because its neural substrates have been physically destroyed, but because its system has been weakened (cf., Fabbro, 1999). This weakening can be explained in terms of increased inhibition, raised activation threshold or unbalanced distribution of resources among the various languages. However, in some cases, stable dissociations in the recovery of the two languages observed in the intermediate or in the late phase cannot be ascribed to neurofunctional impairments only, but also to the consequences of the destruction of cortical and/or subcortical neural substrates (Fabbro, 1999, 2001a). Actually, in the late phase dynamic phenomena have hardly ever been described. This seems to suggest that after one or two years from onset, the recovery pattern remains stable as a result of pathological phenomena that are partly due to neurofunctional impairments and partly due to the loss of cerebral tissue originally involved in the organization of linguistic functions.

Subsequently, numerous neurologists compared and contrasted the Pitres' rule (recovery of the most familiar language) with Ribot's rule (recovery of the mother tongue). However, neither the native language, nor the most familiar to the patient at

the time of the insult, nor the most socially useful or the most affectiv
still, the language of the environment recovers first or best. Nor does i
matter of whether the two languages were acquired and used in the same conte..
opposed to different contexts or at different times of development (Paradis, 2004).
Still, neither the type of aphasic syndrome nor the type of lesion (tumor, infarction, or
cerebral hemorrhage) nor the site of the lesion (cortical versus subcortical, frontal
lobe versus temporal lobe, etc.; Figure 1) seem to be directly responsible for parallel
language recovery versus nonparallel recovery. So far, empirical studies have not
provided tenable explanations for the presence of parallel recovery in some bilingual
aphasic patients and of differential recovery in others.

## D. Lateralization of Languages

The hemisphere that is dominant for language in most right-handed (and also left-
handed) monolinguals is the left hemisphere. Indeed, patients present with aphasia
mainly after left hemisphere lesions, while cases of so-called *crossed aphasia*, that
is aphasia following right hemisphere lesion in right-handed individuals, are rare.
Several claims have been made in the past in favor of greater participation of the
right hemisphere in language processing in bilinguals. In an analysis of the
literature on bilingual aphasics, Albert and Obler (1978) suggested that almost 10%
of bilingual aphasics had suffered a lesion in the right hemisphere, whereas crossed
aphasia in monolinguals was generally less than 5%. On the basis of these results,
Albert and Obler concluded that in bilinguals more often than in monolinguals
linguistic functions are represented in the right hemisphere. Several studies have
been carried out on the cerebral organization of language in bilinguals (Vaid & Hull,
1991). These studies were generally performed using typical techniques of experimental
neuropsychology, namely, dichotic listening, tachistoscopic technique, and reaction
times paradigm. However, as the degree of cerebral dominance emerging with these
techniques may vary according to several variables—for example exposure time,
participants expectancies, etc.—their results are controversial (Paradis, 2004). On the
other hand, the analysis of a large number of cases of bilingual aphasics showed that
the incidence of aphasia following a lesion to the right hemisphere (crossed aphasia) is
as high in monolinguals as in bilinguals (Karanth & Rangamani, 1988).

However, it is known that the right hemisphere is crucially involved in the
processing of pragmatic aspects of language use. It is, thus, possible to conceive that
the greater involvement of the right hemisphere in verbal communication processes
during the first stages of second language learning, both in children and adults, may
be due to the fact that beginners try to compensate with pragmatic inferences for the
lack of implicit linguistic competence in L2. The greater involvement of the right
hemisphere during verbal communication in L2, however, does not necessarily imply a
greater representation of language processes (phonology, morphology, and syntax) in
the right hemisphere (Paradis, 2004). In conclusion, neurolinguistic studies suggest
that the sheer linguistic aspects (phonology, morphology, and syntax) of both L1 and
L2 are organized in the language-dominant hemisphere (the left hemisphere). The
hypothesis of a greater involvement of the right hemisphere in the organization of L2
linguistic aspects has therefore not been confirmed.

## II. IMPLICIT AND EXPLICIT LEARNING OF LANGUAGE

### A. Unexpected Recovery of L2

A few cases of aphasic patients with *unusual* recovery of one of the languages they knew premorbidly have been described. Their peculiarity is that these patients had either never spoken or used this language for communicative purposes before (e.g., the so-called *dead* languages, such as classical Greek and Latin). For example, Adhemar Gelb (1937, in Paradis, 1983) described the case of a professor of classical languages who became aphasic after a left hemisphere lesion and was unable to use his mother tongue but could still correctly express himself in Latin. On this basis, Gelb concluded that aphasic syndromes tend to affect the most automatized (i.e., unconsciously used) languages more severely, whereas the foreign languages or dead languages are best preserved since they require conscious effort and reflection.

The clinical features of E.M., an aphasic patient described by one of the authors (F.F.) and Salvatore M. Aglioti, demonstrated a peculiar case of recovery of L2 (Aglioti & Fabbro, 1993; Aglioti, Beltramello, Girardi, & Fabbro, 1996). The peculiarity of this clinical case is that the patient did not believe she could speak her second language as well after the insult. E.M. had the Veronese dialect, a variant of Venetian, as her mother tongue and almost exclusively used Veronese in everyday life. As a child she had attended elementary school for three years only, where she learnt to read and write Standard Italian (SI). Before the insult her husband made sure that she spoke SI at least 2 or 3 times a year. On these occasions, the patient said only a few words in SI and switched back to her dialect.

In November 1990 E.M. suffered an injury to the left hemisphere with consequent aphasia. She was admitted to hospital and remained completely mute for two weeks. Magnetic resonance imaging revealed a lesion localized in some left subcortical structures only (mainly the caudate nucleus and the putamen; Figure 2). When she did start speaking, much to her own and her family's amazement, she expressed herself in SI instead of the Veronese dialect, even though in the hospital ward the staff mainly spoke Veronese. When she was discharged from hospital a month after the insult, the patient's condition had improved: she understood both her dialect and SI, but only expressed herself in SI. E.M. had to use SI to communicate with her family, which sounded rather artificial. E.M. expressed herself in SI, whereas adults replied in Veronese dialect and her younger nephews in SI. On these latter occasions, E.M. noticed that she understood SI better than Veronese dialect. She had communication difficulties with her acquaintances and friends who addressed her in Veronese dialect, whereas she could only reply in SI. Consequently, E.M. decided to apply to the speech therapy service of the University of Verona to rehabilitate Veronese, a language that to her was socially more important than SI. Unlike most Venetians, when speaking SI, E.M. did not have a Venetian accent. On the contrary, her verbal output in L2 was characterized by a foreign accent. This phenomenon, known as *foreign accent syndrome*, is characterized by the onset, following an acquired lesion, of a strong foreign accent in the first language and is generally associated with a lesion to the basal ganglia. In this patient, the linguistic deficit in mother tongue production was observed in spontaneous speech and in cross-linguistic translation tasks, which showed an

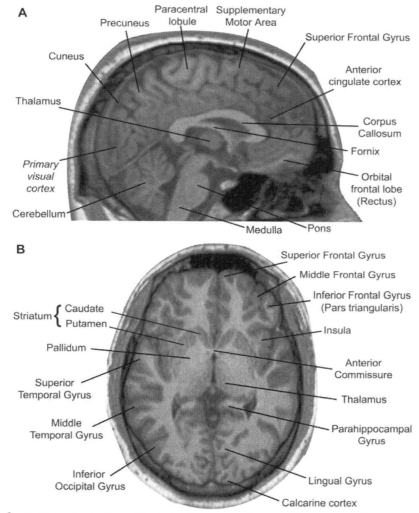

**Figure 2**  Sagittal and axial slices of the brain of a young male scanned throw structural magnetic resonance imaging (MRI). (A) Midsagittal view of the left hemisphere showing cortical and subcortical structures on the medial surface of the brain. (B) Axial view of the brain at the level of the anterior commissure. Basal ganglia are visible along with the thalamic nuclei and the frontal and occipito-temporal cortex.

asymmetrical paradoxical performance. Indeed, unlike neurollogically intact subjects E.M. presented more difficulties when translating into her mother tongue than into her second language.

## B. Implicit and Explicit Memory Systems

Recent studies on long-term memory may provide an explanation for the reason why some patients exhibit a better recovery of the second language as opposed to the mother tongue, and hence of unexpected recovery. The distinction between explicit and implicit memory is of crucial importance. Explicit memory refers to learnt knowledge of which individuals are aware and consists of semantic memory and autobiographical memory. Implicit memory concerns learnt knowledge of which people are not aware, even though they use it (see also Williams, this volume).

The two memory systems are organized in distinct brain structures. Implicit memory involves subcortical structures, such as the basal ganglia and the cerebellum (Figure 2), and specific cortical areas; explicit memory is represented diffusely in the cerebral cortex (Tulving, 1987). The claim that the two different types of memory are subserved by separate cerebral structures is supported by the double dissociation between the symptoms of patients with amnesia following medial temporal lobe lesions and patients with Parkinson's disease, a degenerative disease mainly affecting the basal ganglia (Saint-Cyr, Taylor, & Lang, 1988). Indeed, patients suffering from a pure amnesic syndrome are still capable of procedural learning, and they are still able to learn a foreign language (Hirst, Phelps, Johnson, & Volpe, 1988). Cases of patients suffering from Parkinson's disease have been described in which explicit memory or working memory was intact, whereas their capacity to learn procedures had been damaged.

## C. Memory Systems and Language Acquisition

According to recent models (Paradis, 1994; Ullman, 2001) the lexical knowledge, that is, the mental representation of memorized word-specific knowledge, depends on explicit or declarative memory, which underlies the storage and use of knowledge of facts and events. In contrast grammatical knowledge, which subserves the rule-governed combination of lexical items into complex representations, depends on the implicit or procedural memory system. While lexical knowledge is represented in the implicit or declarative memory system for both L1 and L2, grammatical representation of L2 may rely upon explicit or implicit memory system depending on the age and way of acquisition (Paradis, 1994; Ullman, 2001). In particular, grammatical knowledge of L2 acquired late in life is explicit rather than being implicit as for L1. Paradis (1994) advanced the hypothesis that the mother tongue, being acquired unconsciously and in informal contexts through constant repetition, is mainly stored in implicit memory systems. Therefore, the mother tongue seems to be mainly organized in the subcortical structures involved in linguistic functions and in limited areas of the cerebral cortex, whereas the second language and hence all other languages of a polyglot, being acquired through explicit strategies, seem to be more diffusely represented in the cerebral cortex.

A case in point for languages being acquired and stored in the explicit memory systems is that of *dead* languages. They are generally learnt at school, through reading, and their use requires a conscious knowledge of their grammar. However, many people also use conscious learning strategies based on explicit rules to learn modern languages. Since it has been claimed that aphasic syndromes mainly affect the implicit memory systems of language, it is not surprising that some bilingual aphasics show a better recovery of the languages that they spoke least well premorbidly, or that they recover the languages that they had mainly learnt and used through explicit strategies.

The fact that E.M., who became aphasic following a lesion of the basal ganglia and recovered SI better than Veronese, would support this view. Furthermore, a recent study (Zanini et al., 2004) has showed that patients with Parkinson's disease are especially impaired in syntactic processing of L1 as compared to L2. Thus, in keeping with the different involvement of explicit versus implicit memory systems in L1 and L2 grammatical knowledge, the study showed that patients with Parkinson's disease are especially impaired in accessing implicit, procedural grammatical knowledge of L1.

Differences in age and manner of learning and language use seem to influence the way languages are stored in the brain. When a second language is learnt formally and is mainly used at school, it apparently tends to be more widely represented in the cerebral cortex than the first language, whereas if it is acquired informally, such as it usually happens with the first language, it is more likely to involve subcortical structures (basal ganglia and cerebellum) (Paradis, 1994; Fabbro & Paradis, 1995). The degree of involvement of these structures in the production of a less automatized language, such as the second language, may be different from the degree of involvement in the production of the native language. Age and way of acquisition or learning of L2 can therefore determine a greater or reduced involvement of implicit memory and subcortical structures (e.g., basal ganglia and cerebellum) in the organization of L2 versus L1.

## III. SENSITIVE PERIOD FOR LANGUAGE ACQUISITION

### A. Acquired Aphasia in Children

Aphasia in childhood refers to acquired language disorders due to cerebral lesions (cranial trauma, tumor, hemorrhage, and cerebral infarction) that occur after language acquisition. Therefore, it is to be distinguished from developmental language disorders, namely, neurological disturbances affecting language acquisition (specific language impairment).

Acquired childhood aphasia presents typical features. Independently of the site of the cerebral lesion, mutism emerges immediately post-onset, or children speak little; in either case, acquired childhood aphasia is nonfluent as opposed to numerous cases of fluent aphasia in adults. This symptom persists for weeks. In addition, children recover most of their linguistic abilities rapidly. However, lifelong they will continue to have mild word-finding difficulties and exhibit an impoverished lexicon as against normal subjects of their age. They often have a simplified syntax and exhibit writing and calculation disorders. Mutism and articulatory disorders are generally associated with lesions to the left frontal lobe or the left Rolandic structures, whereas phonemic comprehension disorders are more frequently associated with lesions to the left temporal lobe. One of the most intriguing aspects of acquired childhood aphasia is the extent and the rapidity with which aphasic children recover language. In the past, neurologists were baffled by the quality and rapidity of language recovery in aphasic children as opposed to aphasic adults. In more recent times, however, it was observed that lifelong most children continue to exhibit more or less severe linguistic deficits.

None of them generally succeeds in following a normal progression through school (cf., Fabbro, 2004).

## B. Age of Language Acquisition

The extent and rapidity of language recovery in aphasic children as compared to acquired aphasia after puberty has been interpreted as suggestive for the existence of a sensitive period for language acquisition. Eric Lenneberg claimed that, if a lesion affects a child before puberty, language recovery may be complete, because the linguistic functions damaged by the left hemisphere lesion reorganize in the corresponding area of the right hemisphere (Lenneberg, 1967). In Lenneberg's opinion, a similar reorganization of linguistic functions is possible only before the 10th year of age, since children have not yet passed the critical period when it is still possible to transfer language from the left hemisphere to the right hemisphere.

Numerous hypotheses have been advanced in the attempt to explain language recovery in aphasic children. Some neurologists have claimed that before a given age the two cerebral hemispheres organize language almost in the same manner. However, with growth language is preferably represented in the left hemisphere, whereas the right hemisphere specializes in other cognitive functions. Therefore, if the left hemisphere is affected by a lesion during the first years of life, language will develop in the right hemisphere. According to another hypothesis, a child's brain, like a neonate's brain, contains redundant neural circuits, some of which would normally be lost with growth owing to a selection process influenced by the natural and cultural environment. When a lesion affects a child's brain, some of the circuits that would have decayed because they would have been redundant are recycled and activated in order to reorganize the damaged function.

In keeping with the existence of a critical or sensitive period for language acquisition are the cases of dramatic deprivation of language experience in childhood, the so-called *Wild Children,* like the famous case of Genie (Curtiss, 1977). In these cases, language acquisition after the early years of life is very limited, with mainly defective speech production, grammar, and phonology. Furthermore, in the United States, deaf-born children learn the American Sign Language first and American English as a second language later during special courses. They usually have a huge vocabulary in English, but they do not master grammar perfectly (Berent, this volume). In a similar vein, syntax acquisition of the second language is more difficult and rarely reaches very good levels when the language is learnt after a critical age, which more or less coincides with the age of 6–8 years (Johnson & Newport, 1989; Birdsong, this volume).

The notion that the time window crucial for language acquisition closes after about the first six years of life has been partially challenged by late onset of speech development after left hemispherectomy. For example, Alex, a nine-year-old boy suffering from Sturge-Weber Syndrome affecting the left hemisphere and with deep deficit in language production and comprehension, began to acquire speech and language after left hemispherectomy (Vargha-Khadem et al., 1997). Interestingly, Alex not only has learned a sizable vocabulary, but his verbal production is grammatically correct, thus suggesting that the sensitive period for normal, or nearly normal, acquisition of grammatical knowledge extends beyond the first six years till puberty.

It should be noted, however, that, unlike Wild Children, Alex had been exposed to language before surgery although the nonfunctioning left hemisphere may have been inhibiting the development of language functions sustained by the right hemisphere.

## C. Electrophysiological Studies

A series of studies carried out by Helen Neville and associates (Neville, Mills, & Lawson, 1992; Neville et al., 1997; Weber-Fox & Neville, 2001) by means of Event Related Potentials (ERPs) revealed possible differences in the cerebral cortical organization of languages according to the age of acquisition and way of learning. In early bilinguals, closed-class words of both languages tend to be represented in the left frontal lobe, whereas open-class words tend to involve post-rolandic cortical structures (Figure 1). On the other hand, in bilinguals who learnt their second language after the sensitive period, closed-class words of L2 versus L1 do not seem to be represented in left frontal areas but together with open-class words in post-rolandic areas.

A recent study (Friederici, Steinhauer, & Pfeifer, 2002) has challenged the view that later learned languages are processed in different neural structures than L1. The authors trained adults in an artificial language so that all participants reached a high level of proficiency and fluency in the miniature language. By recording ERPs while adults listened to syntactic errors and correct control sentences in the learned miniature language, they showed that with a high level of proficiency the brain mechanisms involved in L1 and L2 processing are similar even when the L2 has been learned late.

This study points out to the fact that the neural representation of L1 and L2 is affected not only by the age of acquisition, but also by the level of proficiency as well as by complex interaction between these two factors. Furthermore, while considering the effect of the age of acquisition on the neural representation of L2, one should consider that speech production and comprehension rely upon several linguistic abilities with their own developmental courses and with different timing and duration of their sensitive periods (Dussias & Piñar, this volume; Sakai, 2005).

## IV. CORTICAL STIMULATION STUDIES

During neurosurgical operations the need might arise to delimit specific language areas so as not to damage them. To this aim, cortico-electrical stimulation can be carried out in conscious patients under local anesthesia because the brain is insensitive to pain. Weak electrical stimulations are applied to inhibit transiently the functional activity of given portions of the cortex. If the stimulated area is crucial for the task being performed, the patient is temporarily no longer able to perform the task of naming objects. George Ojemann and associates have mapped both L1 and L2 neural representations by using identical object-naming stimuli in 25 bilingual patients (Lucas, McKhann, & Ojemann, 2004). The authors found that stimulation of some sites caused interference with naming in L1 but not in L2 or vice versa. Along with these language-specific sites, shared sites were identified whose stimulation caused interference with naming in both languages. These results would suggest the existence of both shared and separate neural representations of L1 and L2. However, the spatial resolution of this technique does not allow us to exclude the possibility that subsequent stimulations were performed on the same site. Furthermore, differential effects of stimulation on the two languages may derive from intensity threshold differences and not from spatial separation of L1 and L2 neural structures. Thus, results of direct cortical electrical stimulation of the bilingual brain are still controversial.

## V. NEUROIMAGING STUDIES IN BILINGUALS

Over the past few years many studies have used advanced functional neuroanatomical techniques such as PET and functional fMRI, which allow visualization of the functioning (bilingual) brain (Fabbro, 2001b; Perani & Abutalebi, 2005). These investigation techniques certainly present advantages, but they also show some limitations due to their low temporal resolution, the difficulty of interpreting subtractive comparisons that depend on the control task used, and to the fact that they cannot establish whether neural activity is crucial—rather than epiphenomenal—to task performance. PET and fMRI studies that investigated language organization in the brain of bilinguals will be discussed according to the linguistic stimuli that were used: (1) word processing, (2) sentence processing, and (3) short story processing (see Figures 1 and 2 for the locations of the brain areas referred to in the text).

### A. Word Processing

Neuroimaging studies in monolinguals suggest that auditory phonological processing of words is associated with activation in the posterior superior temporal gyrus and inferior frontal gyrus areas, while lexico-semantic processing involves activations in the left extra-sylvian temporo-parietal regions and, less consistently, the left inferior frontal gyrus (Price, 2000; Sakai, 2005).

One of the first neuroimaging (PET) studies on bilinguals compared cerebral activations during word repetition in L1 and in L2 learned after the age of 5 years (Klein, Zatorre, Milner, Meyer, & Evans, 1994). The authors found that repeating words in L2 yielded increased activations in the left putamen. In keeping with the clinical evidence that the foreign accent syndrome may occur after damage to the basal ganglia (see the case of E.M.), they suggested that higher activation of left putamen may reflect the increased articulation demands in speaking a second language. The involvement of the striatum in word articulation has been recently confirmed by a PET study (Klein, Watkins, Zatorre, & Milner, 2006) that has compared neural activations during repetitions of words and nonwords in L1 and in L2 in English–French bilinguals. Word repetition in L1 and L2 involved the left insular cortex, the ventral premotor region, and the left striatum, which showed increased activity with the increased articulatory demands in speaking L2. Furthermore, nonword repetition in L2 as compared to L1 engendered higher activations in the left ventral premotor region and in the cerebellum, whose activity may reflect the increased complexity of motor control to produce novel sequences.

In a further PET study (Klein, Milner, Zatorre, Meyer, & Evans, 1995), the neural activations during word repetitions in L1 and L2 were subtracted from those arising during tasks requiring the generation of words either in L1 and in L2 based on phonological cues (rhyme generation) or on semantic cues (synonym generation). Irrespectively of the retrieval cues and languages, word generation produced activations of the left inferior frontal gyrus, along with activations in left parietal and inferior temporal regions, thus suggesting the involvement of the left inferior frontal gyrus in lexical search in L1 and L2.

Other neuroimaging studies have used tasks of word generation (Klein, Milner, Zatorre, Zhao, & Nikelski, 1999), word stem completion (Chee, Tan, & Thiel, 1999b), semantic judgments on words (Illes et al., 1999), and semantic priming (Klein et al., 2006) to compare lexico-semantic representations of L1 and L2 in late bilinguals. Irrespective of the task used, all these studies reported similar activations during lexico-semantic processing in L1 and in L2. These effects were independent of the structural distance and of the different writing of L1 and L2 and were similar for both early and late bilinguals (Chee et al., 1999b). On the other hand, the extent of activations seems to be influenced by the level of proficiency in L2 in polyglot individuals, with increased activated volume for the less-mastered language (Briellmann et al., 2004).

## B. Processing Sentences

Understanding the meaning of sentences does not rely only on lexico-semantic information for each word, but also on the meaning conveyed by the syntactic structures (Dussias & Piñar, this volume). The selection and integration of lexico-semantic information into sentence meaning seem to be subserved by the pars triangularis and orbitalis of the inferior frontal gyrus (Sakai, 2005).

An fMRI study (Kim, Relkin, Lee, & Hirsch, 1997) compared cortical areas activated during silent sentence generation tasks in L1 and L2 in early versus late bilingual subjects. For both languages they found a similar activation of Broca's and Wernicke's areas in early bilinguals, while in late bilinguals they found a similar activation of Wernicke's area but a significant difference in the activation of Broca's area between L1 and L2. In late bilinguals the authors found in the left Broca's area two distinct but adjacent centers, separated by approximately 8 mm, subserving language production in L1 versus L2. They thus concluded that the anatomical separation of the two languages in Broca's area depended on their different acquisition age. However, the differences in functional organization in Broca's area between early bilinguals and late bilinguals could also be correlated with the poorer L2 competence of late bilinguals. Unfortunately, the authors did not describe the phonologic (presence of foreign accent) and syntactic skills (presence of syntactic errors) of the late bilinguals. They only reported that these participants showed a high standard fluency in L2.

Another fMRI study (Chee et al., 1999a) investigated the cortical areas activated during a sentence-processing task in fluent early Chinese (Mandarin)–English bilinguals. Participants were asked to judge whether the visually presented sentences were "true" or "false". The most activated areas were the inferior and middle prefrontal cortex (more extensive on the left side), the left temporal region, the left angular gyrus, the anterior supplementary motor area (more activated on the left side), and the bilateral superior parietal and occipital regions, without any difference between the two languages. The authors concluded that in early fluent bilinguals common macroscopic areas are activated by syntactically complex sentences in L1 and L2. However, the fact that only proficient bilinguals, exposed to both languages early in life, were studied did not allow the authors to exclude the possibility that different neural representations are used for processing L1 and L2 in late and less proficient bilinguals.

Furthermore, a recent fMRI study (Yokoyama et al., 2006) showed that although processing of simple sentences in L1 and L2 elicited a similar pattern of activation in late bilinguals, processing of structurally complex (passive) sentences in L2, but not in L1, elicited greater activation in the left front-parietal circuits involved in language processing. Thus, also the complexity of the linguistic task at hand must be taken into account when investigating the neural representations of L1 and L2.

## C. Processing Short Stories

The neural representations of semantic processing of short stories have been investigated in a series of studies by Daniela Perani and associates, who have systematically investigated the effects of the age of acquisition and the level of proficiency in L2. In their first studies (Dehaene et al., 1997; Perani et al., 1996), neural activation during listening to short stories in L1 and L2 was investigated in bilingual volunteers with moderate command of L2. While in L1 the most activated areas were the classical perisylvian language areas (inferior frontal gyrus, the superior and middle temporal gyri, the temporal pole, and the angular gyrus) and the right cerebellum, in L2 the number of active language areas was significantly reduced and only left and right superior and middle temporal areas remained active (Perani et al., 1996). Furthermore, while processing stories in L1 engendered a similar pattern of activations in all participants, listening to stories in L2-activated networks that varied greatly from subject to subject, with six subjects showing dispersed active pixels in the left temporal lobe and the remaining two only in the right temporal lobe (Dehaene et al., 1997). However, the groups tested in both studies were exposed to L2 only later in life and mastered L2 to a moderate level of competence. Thus, the different patterns of activations in L1 and L2 could be ascribed both to age of acquisition and to the level of proficiency.

Perani et al. (1998) used PET to investigate brain activation during short story listening tasks in two groups of bilinguals with high proficiency in L2 but with different ages of acquisition. Indeed, the first group was composed of Italian native speakers who had learned English after the age of 10 years (late acquisition high proficiency, LAHP), while the second group was composed of Spanish-born individuals who were exposed to both Spanish and Catalan very early in life and used both languages in their everyday life (early acquisition high proficiency, EAHP). The pattern of activations during processing of stories in L1 and in L2 was similar in both the LAHP and EAHP groups and included foci in the left temporal pole, superior temporal sulcus, middle temporal gyrus, and hippocampal structures. These results led the authors to conclude that representation of languages in the bilingual brain seems to be dependent on proficiency in the two languages and to be independent of the acquisition age.

Interpreting the results of functional anatomical studies with bilinguals performing short story listening tasks, however, is very difficult. Indeed, knowledge of the different linguistic and pragmatic levels involved in a story-processing task is still scant. Therefore, the linguistic and pragmatic complexity of the task is most probably responsible for the complexity and the variety of the brain activation patterns shown by these studies.

## D. Age of Acquisition and Level of Proficiency in L2

The cerebral representations and processing of grammar and lexico-semantics seem to rely on implicit–procedural and explicit–declarative memory systems, respectively (Paradis, 1994; Ullman, 2001), and these two components of language competence may be differently affected by age of acquisition and level of proficiency in L2.

A systematic fMRI investigation of the effect of age of acquisition and proficiency level in L2 on the neural representation of L2 has been recently conducted (Wartenburger et al., 2003). The authors compared neural activation of three groups of Italian–German bilinguals during semantic and grammatical judgments of sentences in L1 and in L2. The first group was composed of individuals with high level of proficiency and who acquired L2 from birth (EAHP). The second group was composed of individuals who acquired L2 later in life (on average at the age of 18 years), but who had a comparable high level of proficiency in L2 (LAHP). The third group was composed of individuals who acquired L2 late (on average at the age of 20 years) and had a low level of proficiency in L2 (late acquisition low proficiency, LALP).

Comparing the EAHP and LAHP groups allowed the authors to investigate the effect of the age of acquisition without the confounding effect of the level of proficiency. No difference between the two groups was observed during the semantic judgments of L2 sentences. In contrast, grammatical judgments in L2 elicited higher activation of the inferior frontal gyrus in the LAHP group as compared to the EAHP group. Furthermore, in the LAHP, but not in the EAHP group, activation of the inferior frontal gyrus was higher during grammatical judgments of sentences in L2 than in L1.

By comparing high- and low-proficiency individuals who acquired L2 late, the authors explored the effect of the level of proficiency independently of the age of acquisition. During the semantic judgment task, the LALP group showed more extensive activations in the Broca's area and right middle frontal gyrus as compared to the LAHP group. In contrast, the LAHP groups showed higher activations in left middle frontal and right fusiform gyrus as compared to the LALP group. During grammaticality judgments, more extensive activity in posterior temporo-parietal areas were observed in the LALP than in the LAHP group, thus suggesting that while the level of proficiency affects the neural representation of both semantic and grammatical knowledge, age of acquisition is more crucial than proficiency for grammar representation in Broca's area.

## VI. SELECTION OF LANGUAGES IN THE BRAIN

Cerebral lesions may alter the capability of bilingual subjects to separate their languages and use each language in appropriate contexts. Many neurologists have supported the hypothesis of the existence of a center responsible for the ability to switch between languages (cf., Fabbro, 1999). A lesion to the switching mechanism causes a patient either to speak only one language or to switch repeatedly from one language to another. A distinction between pathological switching and pathological mixing phenomena has been made. Patients who show pathological mixing intermingle different languages within a single utterance (a self-contained segment of speech that stands on its own and conveys its own independent meaning). By contrast, patients affected by pathological switching alternate their languages across different utterances. Additional studies have established that pathological mixing typically occurs in bilingual aphasia and is mainly due to lesions in the parieto-temporal structures of the left hemisphere, whereas the nervous structures responsible for switching between languages have not been clearly described so far (Fabbro, 1999). Fabbro and associates have described a 56-year-old bilingual patient (L1 Friulian, L2 SI) with a lesion to the left anterior cingulate and to the prefrontal lobe who presented with compulsive switching between languages in the absence of any other linguistic impairment (Fabbro, Skrap, & Aglioti, 2000). The lack of aphasic symptoms in the case described suggests that the system responsible for switching between languages is independent of language, being part of a more general system underlying the selection of different behaviors.

Recent neuroimaging studies have contributed to the understanding of the neural mechanism that subserves selections between languages. Naming pictures alternating between languages elicited higher activation of the dorsal prefrontal cortex as compared to naming in only one language (Hernandez, Martinez, & Kohnert, 2000). This result is in keeping with previous neuropsychological data (Fabbro et al., 2000) that language switching is a part of a general executive attentional system. On the other hand, language may be considered as a series of behavior patterns and their selection may be subserved by the basal ganglia (Abutalebi, Miozzo, & Cappa, 2000). Price, Green, & von Studnitz (1999) showed that translations between languages activated anterior cingulate cortex, the putamen, and the head of the caudate nucleus. The role of the left caudate nucleus in language control has been demonstrated in a recent fMRI study (Crinion et al., 2006). The authors have compared the adaptation of neural responses for sequential presentation of semantically related words (semantic priming) within or across languages. They found that while the left anterior temporal region showed adaptation for semantic priming both within and across languages, thus suggesting common neural representation of L1 and L2 lexicons, activations of the left caudate was sensitive to changes in languages, thus suggesting a role for the left caudate in monitoring and controlling the language in use.

## VII. BRAIN PLASTICITY AND LANGUAGE ACQUISITION

Recent neuroimaging studies have shown that the acquisition of grammatical competencies in late bilinguals is achieved through the same neural systems for processing L1 grammar. Broca's area in the left inferior frontal gyrus seems to be involved in grammatical processing in both L1 and L2 as well as in the acquisition of L2 (Sakai, 2005). Sakai, Miura, Narafu, & Muraishi (2004) trained 13-year-old Japanese twins to conjugate verbs in English. The pre- versus post-training increase of activity in the left dorsal inferior frontal gyrus was correlated with the individual performance improvements. Interestingly, both neural activation changes and performance improvement were highly consistent within each pair of twins (Sakai et al., 2004). Furthermore, the Broca's area has been shown to be involved in the acquisition of rules from a foreign language in adulthood only when they are consistent with natural language (Musso et al., 2003). Thus, Broca's area in the left inferior frontal gyrus seems to be a cortical mechanism for the acquisition of L1 and L2 grammar, which strongly depends on both genetic and environmental factors.

Direct evidence for the plasticity effect of experience on brain structure involved in language processing has been recently demonstrated by using voxel-based morphometry (Mechelli et al., 2004), a technique that allows the noninvasive measuring of the density of gray and white matter. As compared to monolinguals, bilinguals had an increased gray-matter density in the inferior parietal lobe, which was higher for individuals with higher level of proficiency in L2 and with earlier age of acquisition of L2. Thus, learning or acquiring L2 alters the structure of the brain, and the extent of these structural changes are higher when children learn L2 early in life and master L2 with high level of competence.

## VIII.  CONCLUSIONS

At the microanatomical level, that is, at the level of neuronal circuits, it is reasonable to assume that the two languages are represented in completely or partially independent neuronal circuits. On the other hand, the question whether at the macroanatomical level L1 and L2 are represented in common or different cerebral structures is still under debate. Recent neuroimaging studies have shown that L1 and L2 are represented in the same cortical circuitry. Indeed, when people master L2 with high proficiency, although their learning started later in life, the cortical representations of L2 tend to overlap with that of L1 (the so-called convergence hypothesis; Green, 2003). Although these studies have separated the effects of the level of proficiency and of the age of acquisition on the cortical representations of L2, the age of acquisition strongly affects the level of competence that one can reach. Thus, although LAHP individuals may have the same cortical representations of L2 as the early acquisition individuals, the probability of becoming highly proficient in L2 and to represent L2 in the same cortical structures involved in L1 processing is lower for late beginners.

## REFERENCES

Abutalebi, J., Miozzo, A., & Cappa, S. F. (2000). Do subcortical structures control 'language selection' in polyglots? Evidence from pathological language mixing. *Neurocase, 6,* 51–56.

Aglioti, S., Beltramello, A., Girardi, F., & Fabbro, F. (1996). Neurolinguistic and follow-up study of an unusual pattern of recovery from bilingual subcortical aphasia. *Brain, 119*, 1551–1564.

Aglioti, S., & Fabbro, F. (1993). Paradoxical selective recovery in a bilingual aphasic following subcortical lesions. *Neuroreport, 4*, 1359–1362.

Albert, M. L., & Obler, L. K. (1978). *The bilingual brain.* New York: Academic Press.

Briellmann, R. S., Saling, M. M., Connell, A. B., Waites, A. B., Abbott, D. F., & Jackson, G. D. (2004). A high-field functional MRI study of quadrilingual subjects. *Brain and Language, 89*, 531–542.

Chee, M. W. L., Caplan, D., Soon, C. S., Sriram, N., Tan, E. W. L., Thiel, T., et al. (1999a). Processing of visually presented sentences in Mandrian and English studied with fMRI. *Neuron, 23*, 127–137.

Chee, M. W. L., Tan, E. W. L., & Thiel, T. (1999b). Mandarin and English single word processing studied with functional magnetic resonance imaging. *Journal of Neuroscience, 19*, 3050–3056.

Crinion, J., Turner, R., Grogan, A., Hanakawa, T., Noppeney, U., Devlin, J. T., et al. (2006). Language control in the bilingual brain. *Science, 312*, 1537–1540.

Curtiss, S. (1977). *Genie: A psycholinguistic study of a modern-day 'Wild Child'.* New York: Academic Press.

Dehaene, S., Dupoux, E., Mehler, J., Cohen, L., Paulesu, E., Perani, D., et al. (1997). Anatomical variability in the cortical representation of first and second language. *Neuroreport, 8*, 3809–3815.

Fabbro, F. (1999). *The neurolinguistics of bilingualism.* Hove, UK: Psychology Press.

Fabbro, F. (2001a). The bilingual brain: Bilingual aphasia. *Brain and Language, 79*, 201–210.

Fabbro, F. (2001b). The bilingual brain: Cerebral representation of languages. *Brain and Language, 79*, 211–222.

Fabbro, F. (Ed.). (2004). *Neurogenic language disorders in children.* Amsterdam: Elsevier.

Fabbro, F., & Paradis, M. (1995). Differential impairments in four multilingual patients with subcortical lesions. In M. Paradis (Ed.), *Aspects of bilingual aphasia* (pp. 139–176). Oxford: Pergamon Press.

Fabbro, F., Skrap, M., & Aglioti, S. (2000). Pathological switching between languages following frontal lesion in a bilingual patient. *Journal of Neurology, Neurosurgery, and Psychiatry, 68*, 650–652.

Friederici, A. D., Steinhauer, K., & Pfeifer, E. (2002). Brain signatures of artificial language processing: Evidence challenging the critical period hypothesis. *Proceedings of the National Academy of Sciences of the United States of America, 99*, 529–534.

Gelb, A. (1937). On medical psychology and philosophical anthropology. In M. Paradis (Ed.), *Readings on aphasia in bilinguals and polyglots* (pp. 383–385). Didier, Montreal, 1983.

Green, D. W. (2003). The neural basis of the lexicon and the grammar in L2 acquisition. In R. van Hout, A. Hulk, F. Kuiken, & R. Towell (Eds.), *The interface between syntax and the lexicon in second language acquisition* (pp. 197–208). Amsterdam: John Benjamins.

Hernandez, A. E., Martinez, A., & Kohnert, K. (2000). In search of the language switch: An fMRI study of picture naming in Spanish–English bilinguals. *Brain and Language, 73*, 421–431.

Hirst, W., Phelps, E. A., Johnson, M. K., & Volpe, B. T. (1988). Amnesia and second language learning. *Brain and Cognition, 8*, 105–116.

Illes, J., Francis, W. S., Desmond, J. E., Gabrieli, J. D. E., Glover, G. H., Poldrack, R., et al. (1999). Convergent cortical representation of semantic processing in bilinguals. *Brain and Language, 70*, 347–363.

Johnson, J. S., & Newport, E. L. (1989). Critical period effects in second language learning: The influence of maturational state on the acquisition of English as a second language. *Cognitive Psychology, 21*, 60–99.

Karanth, P., & Rangamani, G. N. (1988). Crossed aphasia in multilinguals. *Brain and Language, 34*, 169–180.

Kim, K. H. S., Relkin, N. R., Lee, K. M., & Hirsch, J. (1997). Distinct cortical areas associated with native and second languages. *Nature, 388*, 171–174.

Klein, D., Milner, B., Zatorre, R. J., Meyer, E., & Evans, A. C. (1995). The neural substrates underlying word generation: A bilingual functional-imaging study. *Proceedings of the National Academy of Sciences of the United States of America, 92*, 2899–2903.

Klein, D., Milner, B., Zatorre, R. J., Zhao, V., & Nikelski, J. (1999). Cerebral organization in bilinguals: A PET study of Chinese–English verb generation. *NeuroReport, 10*, 2841–2846.

Klein, D., Watkins, K. E., Zatorre, R. J., & Milner, B. (2006a). Word and nonword repetition in bilingual subjects: A PET study. *Human Brain Mapping, 27*, 153–161.

Klein, D., Zatorre, R. J., Chen, J. K., Milner, B., Crane, J., Belin, P., et al. (2006b). Bilingual brain organization: A functional magnetic resonance adaptation study. *Neuroimage, 31*, 366–375.

Klein, D., Zatorre, R. J., Milner, B., Meyer, E., & Evans, A. C. (1994). Left putaminal activation when speaking a second language: Evidence from PET. *Neuroreport, 5*, 2295–2297.

Lenneberg, E. H. (1967). *Biological foundations of language.* New York: Wiley.

Lucas, T. H., 2nd, McKhann, G. M., 2nd, & Ojemann, G. A. (2004). Functional separation of languages in the bilingual brain: A comparison of electrical stimulation language mapping in 25 bilingual patients and 117 monolingual control patients. *Journal of Neurosurgery, 101*, 449–457.

Mechelli, A., Crinion, J. T., Noppeney, U., O'Doherty, J., Ashburner, J., Frackowiak, R. S., et al. (2004). Neurolinguistics: Structural plasticity in the bilingual brain. *Nature, 431*, 757.

Musso, M., Moro, A., Glauche, V., Rijntjes, M., Reichenbach, J., Buechel, C., et al. (2003). Broca's area and the language instinct. *Nature Neuroscience, 6*, 774–781.

Neville, H. J., Coffey, S. A., Lawson, D. S., Fischer, A., Emmorey, K., & Bellugi, U. (1997). Neural systems mediating American Sign Language: Effects of sensory experiences and age of acquisition. *Brain and Language, 57*, 285–308.

Neville, H. J., Mills, D. L., & Lawson, D. S. (1992). Fractionating language: Different neural subsystems with different sensitive periods. *Cerebral Cortex, 2*, 244–258.

Paradis, M. (1983). *Readings on aphasia in bilinguals and polyglots.* Montreal: Didier.

Paradis, M. (1994). Neurolinguistic aspects of implicit and explicit memory: Implications for bilingualism and SLA. In N. Ellis (Ed.), *Implicit and explicit language learning* (pp. 393–419). London: Academic Press.

Paradis, M. (2004). *A neurolinguistic theory of bilingualism.* Amsterdam: John Benjamins.

Perani, D., & Abutalebi, J. (2005). The neural basis of first and second language processing. *Current Opinion in Neurobiology, 15*, 202–206.

Perani, D., Dehaene, S., Grassi, F., Cohen, L., Cappa, S. F., Dupoux, E., et al. (1996). Brain processing of native and foreign languages. *Neuroreport, 7*, 2439–2444.

Perani, D., Paulesu, E., Galles, N. S., Dupoux, E., Dehaene, S., Bettinardi, V., et al. (1998). The bilingual brain. Proficiency and age of acquisition of the second language. *Brain, 121,* 1841–1852.

Pitres, A. (1895). Aphasia in polyglots. In: M. Paradis (Ed.), *Readings on aphasia in bilinguals and polyglots* (pp. 26–49). Didier, Montreal, 1983.

Price, C. J. (2000). The anatomy of language: Contributions from functional neuroimaging. *Journal of Anatomy, 197,* 335–359.

Price, C. J., Green, D. W., & von Studnitz, R. (1999). A functional imaging study of translation and language switching. *Brain, 122,* 2221–2235.

Ribot, T. A. (1882). *Diseases of memory: An essay in the positive psychology.* New York: Appleton.

Saint-Cyr, J. A., Taylor, A. E., & Lang, A. E. (1988). Procedural learning and neostriatal dysfunction in man. *Brain, 111,* 941–959.

Sakai, K. L. (2005). Language acquisition and brain development. *Science, 310,* 815–819.

Sakai, K. L., Miura, K., Narafu, N., & Muraishi, Y. (2004). Correlated functional changes of the prefrontal cortex in twins induced by classroom education of second language. *Cerebral Cortex, 14,* 1233–1239.

Tulving, E. (1987). Multiple memory systems and consciousness. *Human Neurobiology, 6,* 667–680.

Ullman, M. T. (2001). A neurocognitive perspective on language: The declarative/procedural model. *Nature Reviews Neuroscience, 2,* 717–726.

Vaid, J., & Hull, D. G. (1991). Neuropsychological perspectives on bilingualism: Right, left, and center. In A. G. Reynolds (Ed.), *Bilingualism, multiculturalism, and second language learning* (pp. 81–112). Hillsdale: Erlbaum.

Vargha-Khadem, F., Carr, L. J., Isaacs, E., Brett, E., Adams, C., & Mishkin, M. (1997). Onset of speech after left hemispherectomy in a nine-year-old boy. *Brain, 120,* 159–182.

Wartenburger, I., Heekeren, H. R., Abutalebi, J., Cappa, S. F., Villringer, A., & Perani, D. (2003). Early setting of grammatical processing in the bilingual brain. *Neuron, 37,* 159–170.

Weber-Fox, C., & Neville, H. J. (2001). Sensitive periods differentiate processing of open- and closed-class words: An ERP study of bilinguals. *Journal of Speech, Language, and Hearing Research, 44,* 1338–1353.

Yokoyama, S., Okamoto, H., Miyamoto, T., Yoshimoto, K., Kim, J., Iwata, K., et al. (2006). Cortical activation in the processing of passive sentences in L1 and L2: An fMRI study. *Neuroimage, 30,* 570–579.

Zanini, S., Tavano, A., Vorano, L., Schiavo, F., Gigli, G. L., Aglioti, S. M., et al. (2004). Greater syntactic impairments in native language in bilingual Parkinsonian patients. *Journal of Neurology, Neurosurgery, and Psychiatry, 75,* 1678–1681.

CHAPTER 16

# CHILD SECOND LANGUAGE ACQUISITION

Usha Lakshmanan

## I. INTRODUCTION

Child second language acquisition (SLA) is the successive acquisition of a second language (L2) during childhood, where the initial exposure to the target language typically occurs beyond the age of three years, that is, after the first language has already been established (for the most part), but prior to the onset of puberty. Some scholars also assume an intermediary cutoff point of seven years to distinguish between younger and older child L2 learners.

In the 1970s, when SLA had begun to be established as a field in its own right, the child L2 learner was at the center of debates concerning the processes characterizing SLA and whether they were similar to or different from the processes in child first language acquisition (Hatch, 1978; Lakshmanan, 1995; McLaughlin, 1978). The 1970s witnessed a spate of studies on the child L2 learner, many of which were primarily longitudinal studies of individual children and a few cross-sectional studies of groups of children from different first language (L1) backgrounds acquiring the same L2 (mostly English). The impetus for this research stemmed from a reaction against the contrastive analysis position that the learner's L1 plays a primary role in SLA, and that errors in the L2 were owing to interference from the L1. An additional impetus for these early child L2 studies came from findings emerging from research on monolingual child L1 English, that children traverse through common developmental paths in acquiring grammatical morphemes and various syntactic structures such as negation and interrogatives. Child L2 learners, like adult L2 learners, have prior knowledge of another language (i.e., the L1). If the developmental sequences in L2 acquisition mirror the sequences observed for monolingual child L1 acquisition, this would serve to weaken the contrastive analysis position that ascribes a primary role for the L1 in L2 acquisition and would strengthen the role of universal developmental mechanisms in L2 acquisition. A common belief is that child L2

377

learners, in contrast to adults, are typically successful in acquiring the target L2. Additionally, while child L2 acquisition often takes place naturalistically, through immersion in the target language environment, adult L2 acquisition typically takes place in a more formal instructed setting. The evidence from child L2 acquisition was, therefore, crucial for refuting arguments based upon a strong contrastive analysis position. The overall findings of these early studies on child L2 served to emphasize the role of developmental universals vis a vis L1 transfer in L2 acquisition (Dulay & Burt, 1974). However, the influence of the L1 was not entirely discounted as some of the findings suggested a secondary or a more selective role for L1 influence, evidenced as temporary detours from universal or common developmental sequences (Ravem, 1978; Wode, 1978).

Despite their concern with developmental universals, the early studies were largely descriptive in nature and their characterization of developmental universals was rather general and not sufficiently precise (Lakshmanan, 1995). In the 1980s, advances in linguistic theory within the Chomskyian framework of principles and parameters began to exert considerable influence on SLA research. The focus of this research in the 1980s was largely on the adult L2 learner, specifically the issue of whether or not adult L2 learners, like child L1 learners, have access to universal grammar (UG) and whether they can reset parameters that are not fixed in the same way as in the L1 and the L2. As child L2 acquisition was assumed to be similar to child L1 acquisition in relation to the access to UG issue, evidence from child L2 was not viewed as being directly pertinent to the question of whether L2 acquisition is fundamentally different from child L1 acquisition. A direct outcome of this was that child L2 acquisition began to take a back seat in SLA research during the 1980s and the early 1990s. In the mid-1990s, this situation began to change as researchers became less engrossed with the issue of whether or not adult L2 learners have access to UG and began to focus on the mental representation of L2 grammars. With this shift in focus, SLA researchers became more and more interested in child L2 acquisition. Since then, the number of studies on child L2 acquisition has steadily grown; child L2 acquisition is now on its way to becoming established as a field in its own right. In what follows, I discuss key terminological, theoretical, and methodological issues in the emerging field of child SLA and review major advances in our understanding of child L2 development.

## II. WHAT IS CHILD SECOND LANGUAGE ACQUISITION?

In many countries around the world, exposure to and acquisition of two languages occurs sequentially during childhood, after exposure to and acquisition of the L1 has already begun. A cutoff point of three years has generally been used in the L2 literature in order to distinguish between simultaneous acquisition of two languages and successive acquisition of L2 in early childhood (McLaughlin, 1978). While the cutoff point of age three is somewhat arbitrary, the assumption underlying the distinction is that by three years or sometime shortly thereafter, the L1 has, for most part, been acquired. A complicating factor, of course, is that even in the case of simultaneous acquisition of two languages, there can be variation in relation to the onset of exposure of the two languages; exposure to one language may begin right from birth and another only later, but before the age of three. This type of bilingual acquisition, where exposure to one of the two languages is delayed (i.e., takes place sequentially), may be more similar to child L2 acquisition than to child L1 acquisition, or it may share similarities with both (for a discussion of the differences between simultaneous and sequential bilingualism, see Bhatia & Ritchie, 1999). Another complicating factor in determining the lower boundary for child L2 acquisition is that not all aspects of the L1 are acquired by the age of three. Some aspects of the L1, especially certain complex properties (e.g., passives, constraints on the interpretation of reflexives and pronouns), may emerge in late childhood. Therefore, the child L2 learner at a given stage in the acquisition process may exemplify successive L2 acquisition with respect to certain linguistic properties and also at the same time exemplify simultaneous acquisition of two languages with respect to other linguistic properties (Lakshmanan, 1995).

In the L2 literature, the onset of puberty is generally used to distinguish between child L2 acquisition and other forms of successive L2 acquisition. Exposure to and acquisition of an L2 (after the age of three years) but prior to the onset of puberty constitutes child L2 acquisition. Exposure to and acquisition of an L2 after the onset of puberty is either adolescent or adult L2 acquisition. However, even within the period representing child L2 acquisition, there can be variation in relation to the onset of exposure to the L2. The onset of exposure to and acquisition of the L2 may occur prior to age seven or later. Schwartz (2003) proposed that age seven (not puberty) is the upper boundary distinguishing child L2 acquisition from other forms of successive L2 acquisition. Schwartz based the upper cutoff point on the findings from retrospective studies on L2 ultimate attainment (Johnson & Newport, 1989), which found that only those L2 speakers of English whose exposure to English had begun after the age of seven differed significantly in their performance on grammaticality judgment tests from monolingual native speakers of English; whereas, those who had been exposed to English prior to the age of seven performed similar to native speakers. However, there may have been other factors that could have contributed to the results, such as whether or not the L1 was maintained and continued to develop, language dominance and language use (L1 and L2). As Susan Foster-Cohen has observed, global cutoffs at the boundaries typically used in language acquisition research are in the long run not very helpful given the evidence that different parts of language appear to exhibit discontinuities at different times. Foster-Cohen (2001, pp. 341–342) recommends the use of a "sliding window" in addressing questions in L1 and L2 acquisition.

> Instead of trying to divide L1 discretely from L2, and early L2 from later L2, we need to look through the window at one or a series of ages and stages and ask, with reference to properly theoretically motivated hypotheses about the nature of language, what an infant/child/adolescent/adult knows or can do ... If we approach the L1/L2 questions in this way, we focus on the continuum between L1 and L2 and within L2. And if you focus on the continuities, the discontinuities take care of themselves.

## III. WHY STUDY CHILD L2 ACQUISITION?

The study of child L2 acquisition is important to gain an understanding of language development in early and late childhood and the capacity of the human mind to acquire multiple languages during this period. Theories of the *how* and *why* of language acquisition in children must explain the patterns of language development observed not only in monolingual children but also in simultaneous bilingual learners as well as child L2 learners.

Learnability theories within language acquisition research have been driven by the logical problem of language acquisition, stemming from a consideration of the poverty of the stimulus. How do learners, through the course of language acquisition, attain complex knowledge states that are underdetermined by the input available to them? As Yip and Mathews (2007) observe, the knowledge states attained by simultaneous bilingual children pose an even greater challenge for the logical problem of language acquisition. Simultaneous bilingual children receive input in two languages; in terms of the overall quantity of the input, they may be no different from monolingual children. However, the quantity of the input available to bilingual children in *each* of their two first languages is inevitably greatly reduced compared to the total quantity of the input available to their monolingual child counterparts. Similarly, the knowledge states attained by child L2 learners also serve to exacerbate the logical problem of language acquisition. Take for example, a typical scenario involving minority language children who are exposed to the L2 after the age of three years (outside the home) and who continue to be exposed to the L1, but only within the home environment. Subsequent to the onset of exposure in the L2, the quantity of the input available to a child L2 learner, in each of his or her two languages (i.e., the L1 and the L2) is greatly reduced, as in the case of simultaneous bilingual children (or perhaps even more so). It is, of course, conceivable that as in the case of simultaneous bilingual children, the steady-state knowledge that child L2 learners attain in their two languages (i.e., the L2 *and* the L1) may not necessarily be *exactly* the same as that attained by monolingual children (Lakshmanan, 2006). However, from a learnability perspective, what crucially needs to be explained is how child L2 learners in the course of acquisition attain L2 knowledge states that go beyond the input available to them, which, as stated earlier, is also greatly reduced in quantity compared to the input available to the monolingual child L1 learner.

Child L2 acquisition is also important in that it can bring new empirical evidence to bear upon questions being debated within linguistic theory, child L1 acquisition (monolingual and bilingual) and adult L2 acquisition (Lakshmanan, 1989, 1994, 2006; Schwartz, 2003). A fairly uncontroversial assumption is that the genetic or biological blueprint for language (UG) that constrains child L1 acquisition also constrains child L2 acquisition. Compared to the child L1 learner, however, the child L2 learner is cognitively more mature. The greater cognitive maturity of the child L2 learner renders child L2 developing grammars as a valuable testing ground for theoretical proposals regarding the universal status of a linguistic principle. For the same reason, evidence from child L2 acquisition may also be useful in helping us decide between purely linguistic-based explanations versus processing-based accounts of children's speech production in the early stages of L1 acquisition. Additionally, evidence from child L2 acquisition can also shed light on debates within L1 acquisition research regarding the role of inherent maturational factors. For example, some researchers (e.g., Radford, 1990) have proposed that children below the age of 23 months lack knowledge of certain universal grammatical properties and principles that characterize the adult grammar, but that such knowledge matures or becomes available only later (i.e., above the age of 23 months). Assuming that the maturational account is correct, we would not expect children who begin acquiring an L2 at age four, for example, to go through an initial stage (in the L2), where they lack knowledge of the universal properties or principles that are believed to be maturationally triggered at an earlier point in the course of L1 acquisition. If the evidence from children acquiring an L2 reveals that child L2 development patterns differently from child L1 development in relation to these properties, then it would bolster maturation-based explanations of child L1 developing grammars. Alternatively, if child L2 development patterns in the same way as child L1, then it would serve to weaken maturation-based accounts.

Research on the simultaneous acquisition of two first languages has focused on the issue of whether the bilingual child's two systems, developing in tandem, are differentiated in the course of acquisition, as well as the issue of the cross-linguistic influences exerted by each developing system onto the other. While such cross-linguistic influences can be potentially bidirectional, Yip and Mathews (2007) propose that the directionality of transfer effects may be determined by language dominance. In other words, they predict that transfer will take place from the bilingual child's more dominant language to the less dominant language rather than from the less dominant language to the more dominant one. As the two languages develop in tandem from birth or very early in simultaneous bilingual acquisition, determining which of the bilingual child's two languages is dominant at any given point is bound to be difficult. Yip and Mathews propose mean length utterance (MLU) as an appropriate measurement of language dominance in simultaneous bilingual acquisition. However, they also acknowledge that MLU as a measure can be more readily applied in those cases where the bilingual child's two languages are of the same morphological type than in those cases where they are of different morphological types (e.g., one isolating and the other richly inflectional). In the case of child L2 acquisition, the onset of exposure to the L2 typically occurs after age three, when the L1 has become established for the most part. In other words, during the initial stages of child L2 acquisition, it is the L1 that is undoubtedly the child's dominant language. Later on during the course of acquisition, depending on individual patterns of exposure to the two languages, it is conceivable that the L2 child, particularly in L2 immersion contexts, may become more dominant in the L2. A comparison of the pattern of development in child L2 acquisition with the pattern of development in simultaneous bilingual acquisition, keeping the two languages constant across the two comparisons, can shed light on the role played by language dominance in the directionality of transfer effects.

An issue that has been fraught with much controversy within the adult L2 literature is whether the biological blueprint for language (i.e., UG) is still available for acquisition of an L2 in adulthood (White, 2003). In the child L2 acquisition literature, in contrast, a fairly uncontroversial assumption is that UG is available for the successive acquisition of an L2 during childhood. Child L2 learners are cognitively less mature than adult L2 learners. However, like adult L2 learners, but unlike the monolingual child L1 learner, child L2 learners also have prior knowledge of another language (i.e., the L1), which, however, may be less firmly established or less developed at the onset of exposure to the L2, than in the case of the adult learner. If child L2 and adult L2 developing grammars pattern in the same way, but differently from child L1, and if the L1–L2 differences stem from L1 transfer, and both the adult and the child

L2 learner are shown to attain knowledge states that are undetermined by the input, then this would strengthen arguments in favor of the position that the biological blueprint for language remains available for acquisition of an L2 in adulthood (Schwartz, 2003). Another scenario is one where although L1 influence causes the child L2 learner and adult L2 learner to initially hypothesize a grammar that is larger than the target L2 grammar, only the child L2 learner is able to successfully retract from this overgeneralization in the course of acquisition. Such a scenario would not necessarily point to adult L2–child L2 differences in the availability of UG per se. Instead, all else being equal, it may point to adult L2–child L2 differences in relation to processing the L2 input, specifically the ability to use implicit or indirect negative evidence for grammar restructuring (Lakshmanan, 2006).

The study of child L2 acquisition is of direct relevance in educational and clinical settings. In many countries around the world, there has been a steady increase in the number of minority language children growing up in a majority language culture who acquire an L2 sequentially. Parents as well as professionals such as teachers and clinicians, involved in the care and education of such children, need to be well informed about the stages in development that typically developing children go through in acquiring the target L2. Information about L2 development in typically developing children is crucial for the identification and the treatment of language learning difficulties in children acquiring an L2 sequentially. In the absence of such information, typically developing minority language children are liable to be mistaken as being language impaired; likewise, minority language children with language impairment may be mistaken for a typically developing child L2 learner. Comparative studies of the patterns of development in normally developing child L2 learners and monolingual children with specific language impairment (SLI) could lead to the development of selective criteria to distinguish between normal L2 learners and impaired language learners (Paradis, 2005).

## IV. THEORETICAL ISSUES IN CHILD SLA RESEARCH

Much of the recent and current research on child SLA has been couched within the framework of UG. As noted above, the general assumption is that the innate biological endowment for language (UG) continues to be available for acquisition of an L2, at the very least, during childhood. At the same time, however, an issue that has been debated in the child L2 acquisition literature is whether UG is operative at the early stages of child L2 development in its entirety or only partially.

According to proponents of the Strong Continuity Hypothesis, UG in its entirety constrains child L2 acquisition throughout the course of acquisition (Epstein, Flynn, & Martohardjono, 1996; Grondin & White, 1996; Haznedar, 2001; Lakshmanan, 1994; Schwartz, 2003). Under the Strong Continuity account, the child L2 learner possesses the grammatical categories and features that characterize the grammar of the mature native speaker of the target L2, although these may not be readily discernible in a simple fashion from the child's surface productions. The Strong Continuity account does not predict a direct relationship between the development of syntax and overt grammatical morphology in the child's L2. Instead, the child L2 learner's knowledge of overt grammatical morphology may lag behind his or her knowledge of the abstract morphosyntactic properties of the target L2.

According to proponents of the Weak Continuity Hypothesis (Vainikka & Young-Scholten, 1996), UG is only partially accessed during the earliest stages of child L2 grammar construction. In other words, child L2 grammars are initially underspecified in relation to the representation of certain grammatical categories and features that characterize the mature grammars of native speakers of the target L2. The evidence generally cited in support of the underspecification account of child L2 grammars is children's omission of overt morphological elements associated with the grammatical properties or categories in question. According to the Weak Continuity account, child L2 grammar building takes place gradually (in a stepwise fashion), driven by the interaction of UG and the L2 input. Specifically, under the Weak Continuity account, the trigger for moving from an underspecified representation of the target L2 to a full blown adult-like grammatical representation is the presence of overt morphological cues in the L2 input. Likewise, evidence that the child's underlying representation of the L2 grammar is no different from that of the mature native speaker would, under this account, hinge on the child's consistent suppliance of overt morphology associated with the abstract grammatical properties. Under this view, syntax and grammatical morphology are predicted to develop in tandem in child L2 acquisition. The Weak Continuity position has, however, found little support in the child L2 domain.

Another controversial issue in current debates within child L2 acquisition research is the role of the L1 in child L2 acquisition. Does the L1 grammar impinge on the child's L2 grammar development in the course of acquisition? If L1 transfer is operative in child L2 acquisition, does it impinge on L2 grammar development in its entirety or only partially? According to one variant of the Strong Continuity account, the child L2 learner constructs the L2 grammar based solely on an interaction between UG and the incoming L2 input, similar to child L1 (Epstein et al., 1996). According to another variant of the Strong Continuity account, the L1 grammar in its entirety (excluding the phonetic matrices of lexical–morphological items) determines the child L2 initial state (Schwartz & Sprouse, 1996). Subsequent restructuring of the L2 grammar takes place through an interaction of UG with the L2 input. Under this full-transfer view, the pattern of development in child L2 acquisition may be more similar to the pattern of development in adult L2 acquisition than in child L1 acquisition, especially in the initial stages of L2 acquisition and perhaps in relation to the steady-state L2 grammar as well. The full-transfer account also predicts that at the initial stages, the L1 and the L2 systems of the child L2 learner, as in the case of the adult, are not differentiated. L2 acquisition from this perspective can be viewed as a process whereby the child L2 learner gradually moves from a unitary system to a dual system, where the L2 grammar is differentiated from the L1 grammar. In contrast, proponents of the partial L1 transfer position argue that L1 transfer is restricted to certain but not all aspects of L2 grammar development. A partial L1 transfer position coupled with the Weak Continuity view (e.g., Vainikka & Young-Scholten, 1996) predicts that in the child L2 initial state, the L1 impinges only upon the child's L2 representation of lexical categories but not on the functional/grammatical categories.

Several researchers have argued that the full-transfer account applies equally to both adult and child L2 acquisition (Haznedar, 2001; Schwartz, 2003); however, there is an obvious distinction between the status of the L1 in the two forms of L2 acquisition, which is often ignored in the L2 literature. In the case of adult L2 acquisition, it may be assumed that the L1 is fully established prior to onset of exposure to the L2. However, in the case of child L2 acquisition, where exposure to the L2 occurs, for example, at age four, the L2 develops alongside the continued development of the child's L1 (assuming, of course, continued and consistent exposure to it). Whether or not the L1 grammar impinges upon child L2 acquisition in its "entirety" depends on the child's internalized knowledge as represented by his or her current grammar of the L1. Crucially, at the onset of exposure to the L2, child L2 learners, unlike adult L2 learners, are unlikely to have acquired all the grammatical properties instantiated in their L1. This means that, even assuming the full-transfer position, child L2 development and adult L2 development cannot be predicted to pattern in the same way for all aspects of the L2. Another possibility regarding the role of the L1 in child L2 acquisition is that in those cases where the L1 continues to develop alongside the development of the L2, the L1 may not impinge in any major way on L2 grammar construction. Instead, its role in child L2 development may be a relatively minor one. Language transfer may be governed by the principle "procrastinate" (as opposed to "haste") such that it becomes operative only when required—as a last resort—to ensure that the derivation that is the output of the underlying L2 representation converges in real time (Lakshmanan, 2000).

Recent research on child L2 acquisition has tended to focus on the underlying mental representation of L2 learner's grammatical knowledge in the course of L2 acquisition. Not much attention has been given to the study of the role of internal procedural mechanisms that motivate a change in the mental representation from one stage to the next in L2 development. In those cases where the child L2 learners' initial hypothesis in relation to a particular property P generates a smaller grammar than the one instantiated in the L2, restructuring can take place on the basis of positive evidence and convergence on the L2 grammar is the predicted outcome. However, in some cases, the child L2 learner may overgeneralize (i.e., hypothesize a grammar that is larger than that instantiated in the L2), either on the basis of contradictory or ambiguous L2 input and/or based on influence from the L1. Such a scenario exemplifies the poverty of the stimulus problem, and restructuring of the learner's initial hypothesis on the basis of positive evidence would not be predicted. However, even in situations exemplifying the poverty of the stimulus, child L2 learners often do succeed in converging on the target L2 grammar, in the absence of negative evidence; this would indicate that their internal mechanisms entail the use of a learning procedure that is able to process the absence of evidence in the input (i.e., indirect negative evidence) for grammatical mapping from UG onto their developing L2 grammar (Lakshmanan, 2006; Lakshmanan & Selinker, 1994). Recently, there have been a spate of studies that have investigated sentence processing in adult L2 learners, which reveal quantitative and qualitative differences between L2 adults, L1 adults, and L1 children. With the sole exception of a study by Marinis (2007), research on real-time processing in child L2 learners has not hitherto been addressed. Research on this aspect of child L2 acquisition should shed light on the procedural aspects of L2 development.

A growing trend within current child L2 acquisition research has been to conduct comparative studies of monolingual child L1 learners, child L2 learners, and adult L2 learners. The impetus for this research stems from the view that the child L2 learner bridges the gap between adult L2 and child L1 (Schwartz, 2003). A major issue addressed within this line of research is whether the child L2 learner is more similar to the adult L2 learner or to the monolingual child L1 learner in regard to grammar building, or whether the nature of the relationship to both is dependent on the specific linguistic domain (morphology vs. syntax). In this regard, comparing child L2 acquisition with simultaneous bilingual acquisition (as opposed to monolingual child L1 acquisition) may be a more appropriate approach and could be more revealing about key issues in child L2 development.

The theoretical issues addressed within the domain of child L2 acquisition have focused on the development of the child's L2; in contrast, issues such as the status of universal constraints in child L2 code switching and the patterns of L1 (and L2) loss or attrition have received little attention. In order to fully comprehend the nature of child L2 acquisition, evidence from these neglected aspects also need to be included and brought to bear on learnability theories in child L2 acquisition.

## V. METHODOLOGICAL ISSUES IN CHILD SLA RESEARCH

A problem that language acquisition researchers have to grapple with in investigating what learners know at any given stage in their language development is that information about their competence can only be determined indirectly by examining performance data. As is true of other acquisition contexts as well, care needs to be taken to ensure that the methodology used in collecting and analyzing data from child L2 learners neither underestimates nor overestimates what the child L2 learner knows. In order to characterize the language learner's linguistic competence in the L2 accurately, the interlanguage system must be analyzed in its own terms, independently of both the target language system as well as of the L1 system. However, this is not an easy task to accomplish, and L2 research (both past and present) has often succumbed to the "comparative fallacy" inherent in L2 research (for discussion of this issue, see Lakshmanan & Selinker, 2001).

A majority of the existing child L2 studies have been based on oral production data, especially spontaneous speech. A number of these studies are longitudinal case studies of one or more individual children, and only a few of them are based on experimentally elicited production data gathered from a large group of children. Examining children's speech output alone is problematic. Child L2 learners, like learners in other forms of language acquisition, have been observed to omit grammatical morphemes. However, their surface productions may not necessarily reflect their underlying grammatical representation. In other words, child L2 learners may know more than what is revealed by their speech output. Therefore, studies examining children's L2 comprehension, as well as their real-time processing, would be helpful in ascertaining the extent to which the evidence from children's speech output can be supported. In the adult L2 literature, grammaticality judgment tasks (or variants of these) have been widely used in assessing adult's L2 linguistic competence. They have rarely been used in child L2 studies other than in retrospective L2 studies on age effects in ultimate attainment, where the learners are adults when they are tested. An exception is a recent study by Whong-Barr and Schwartz (2002) who successfully used an oral grammaticality judgment task with child L2 learners in their study of verb argument structure. Other methods, widely used in the child L1 acquisition literature, such as the truth-value judgment task, the sentence picture matching task, and the act-out task, which elicit intuitional data, have been used in a few child L2 studies as well.

As discussed earlier, unlike in the case of the adult L2 learner, the child L2 learner's L1 may still be in the process of development, and not fully established at the onset of exposure to the L2. In addressing the role of language transfer in child L2 acquisition, it is important to ascertain the learner's knowledge of the L1 as well, although this is not common practice in the child L2 literature. Additionally, child L2 studies that have investigated transfer effects in child L2 have typically been unidirectional (i.e., learners with typologically different L1s learning the same L2, usually English or another major European language). Child L2 studies where the L1 is kept constant and the L2s are varied are rare.

Other methodological issues concern the choice of an appropriate measure of language proficiency as well as language dominance. There is typically considerable variation in the child L2 population in relation to the age of onset of exposure and the length of exposure to the target L2. MLU, a measure commonly used in tandem with age in child L1 acquisition (and simultaneous bilingual acquisition), would not be feasible or appropriate in the child L2 context, particularly in the case of children who are beyond age five. Other measures, such as verbal density or mean number of verbs and arguments per utterance, may need to be used instead when determining language proficiency and language dominance.

Studies comparing the pattern of development in children and adult L2 learners need to ensure that the experimental tasks used are cognitively appropriate for both age groups. Studies comparing child L2 development and child L1 development have typically considered only monolingual child L1 development. As noted above, in addressing key issues in child L2 acquisition, it would be relevant to compare child L2 acquisition with simultaneous bilingual acquisition as well.


## VI. DEVELOPMENTAL ASPECTS OF CHILD L2 ACQUISITION

Children acquiring an L2 have been observed to go through an initial "silent period" during which they do not produce any utterances in the L2 (for discussion, see Lakshmanan, 1994). The initial silent period corresponds to their initial exposure to the L2 in the target milieu. Silent periods have been reported in the literature only for children but not for adult L2 learners. Additionally, children have been observed to differ in relation to the length of the silent period; it could be as brief as one month or longer (e.g., six months). It is possible, of course, that the typological distance between the L1 and the L2 may be a factor determining the duration of the silent period, although individual differences have also been observed in cases involving a common L1 (and L2). During the silent period, acquisition of the target L2 has likely already been set in motion; the individual variation with respect to the duration of the silent period poses an obvious methodological problem when addressing questions regarding the knowledge states characterizing the initial child L2 state. To the child, the silent period may also be helpful in preempting any potential language transfer effects resulting from their producing utterances in the L2 before they are ready for it, thereby facilitating the use of L1 borrowing as a strategy to meet the communicative demands. The silent period may also be a way for the child to attend to the ambient input without being hampered by his or her own productions in the L2.

Another phenomenon characterizing the early stages of child L2 acquisition is the use of formulas or prefabricated routines, which constitute nonproductive unanalyzed language use, which are, nevertheless, a valuable communicative resource to the child L2 learner during the early stages of acquisition (Lakshmanan, 1995; Wong-Fillmore, 1976). As in the case of silent periods, there are individual differences in the use of such formulas in child L2 acquisition. According to Wong-Fillmore (1976), formulas facilitate language acquisition in that they provide the learner with accessible data for segmentation and analysis of the internal structure of the unit. The process of such segmentation and analysis may aid the learner in discerning the morphosyntactic properties of the target language. In what follows, I discuss advances in our understanding of child L2 acquisition in the domains of phonology, lexis, morphology, and syntax.

## A. Child L2 Phonological Acquisition

A popular belief is that children, but not adults, acquire the phonology of the L2 with relative ease and typically attain native-like pronunciation abilities in the L2. To date, there have been a number of studies on the effect of age of exposure on L2 pronunciation abilities. These studies have typically used a retrospective methodology, which involves testing the subjects when they are older. A consistent finding of these studies is that one of the strongest factors influencing the degree of perceived L2 foreign accent is age of first exposure to the L2, as indexed by the learners age of arrival (AOA) in the L2 speaking country. Late learners, who arrived in the L2 speaking country when they were older (e.g., as adults), are more likely to be perceived as having a strong foreign accent than early learners, who arrived in the L2 speaking country when they were children. Some researchers have attributed the age effects on L2 pronunciation to a critical period for phonological acquisition (Scovel, 1988). However, the proposed connection between neurological maturation and the degree of L2 foreign accent is a tenuous one and has yet to be clearly established (Flege, 1999). Additionally, age of exposure to the L2 (i.e., AOA) has been observed to co-vary with other factors that impact L2 phonological acquisition, including factors such as L1 phonological development and language use (L1 and L2). Contrary to popular belief, early learners are not always able to escape foreign accent detection. Their success in doing so has been shown to be inversely related to their frequency of L1 and L2 use; the less frequent their use of the L1 (and the more frequent the use of the L2), the more likely they are to be perceived as having native-like pronunciation abilities in the L2 (MacKay, Flege, & Imai, 2006).

To date, there have been very few studies that have child L2 phonological development as their specific focus. The few studies that have examined L2 phonological acquisition in young children indicate that the acquisition of a new phonological system is largely similar to that of child L1 learners. At the same time, differences in patterns of development, primarily stemming from transfer of sound segments already acquired in the L1, have also been observed (Hecht & Mulford, 1982; Piper, 1984). In their recent study of the development of English speech patterns of a seven-year-old Polish-speaking child, Winitz, Gillespie and Starcev (1995) found that the child L2 learner (AO) had acquired native-like pronunciation patterns about one year after his arrival in the United States. AO remained silent (i.e., in the L2) in the first six months, and Winitz et al. propose that his silent period experience may have contributed significantly to his development of English speech patterns. Anderson (2004) studied the English L2 phonological development of children from varied L1 backgrounds. Unlike earlier studies, she assessed the children's phonological skills in their L1s as well. Her longitudinal study found that the children, who were acquiring the L2 via immersion, were able to acquire the L2 phonology with relative ease. Additionally, the study found that the children use their articulatory knowledge from their L1 to aid their learning of the L2 phonological system, evidenced largely by their use of shared sounds across both languages. Although language transfer (from the L1 to L2) did occur, the children's error patterns and the phonetic inventories in both the L1 and L2 suggest that they are able to maintain two distinct or separate phonological systems. This was observed even in the case of the children who had been exposed to the L2 for a very short period of time.

However, a recent study by Yavas (2002), on the acoustic analysis of consonantal sounds produced by Spanish-speaking child L2 learners of English, found that differences at the acoustic level (e.g., voice-onset-time) distinguish child L2 learners from monolingual native speakers of Spanish and English. Harada (2006) found that English-speaking children exposed to Japanese via L2 immersion are able to acquire the Japanese contrast between single and geminate stop consonants, which is not present in their L1. However, the new phonetic categories acquired were far from being identical to that of monolingual native speakers of Japanese (or that of the immersion teachers). Crucially, evidence of interaction between the new categories with the closest sound in the children's L1 was observed, which may in turn stem from frequent use of the L1.

## B. Child L2 Lexical Acquisition

Lexical acquisition has been extensively investigated in child L1 research; in contrast, child L2 research on this issue has been surprisingly sparse. Although a few studies have addressed this issue in passing, only two studies, to date, have lexical development as their specific focus (Rescorla & Okuda, 1984; Yoshida, 1978). At the onset of exposure to the L2, the child L2 learner, unlike the child L1 learner, will already have a relatively fully developed conceptual system in his or her L1, as well as more developed memory skills. The relatively greater cognitive maturity of the child L2 learner may have a positive impact on vocabulary acquisition. In their longitudinal study of Atsuko, a five-year-old Japanese child who acquired English in the United States, Rescorla and Okuda (1984) found that Atsuko's data evidenced a different pattern of lexical acquisition from that commonly observed in child L1 learners.

Atsuko's lexical acquisition (at the earliest stages) was rapid in comparison to child L1 learners, which Rescorla and Okuda partly attribute to the presence of Japanese–English cognates or English loanwords in her L1 lexicon. Overextensions, typical of child L1 development, were not very frequent; a majority of the overextensions were either analogical–metaphorical extensions (as opposed to categorical extensions) or were presyntactic strategies for encoding propositional relationships between referents. Atsuko resorted to very little object labeling in the L2 and focused instead on commenting on a large variety of referents using a small set of words that she had acquired. Rescorla and Okuda describe Atsuko as using an expressive style or strategy; however, although her general nominal percentage was typical of expressive learners, her L2 lexicon at the early stages included a high proportion of closed-class words (pronouns, lexical and auxiliary verbs, conjunctions, and prepositions), which is not typical of early L1 acquisition. Unlike Atsuko, Yoshida's (1978) three-year-old Japanese boy, Miki, used a referential or nominal strategy. Approximately 60% of the 300 words he learned in the first seven months of his acquisition were nominals, and lexical verbs were rare. His early utterances were characterized by use of the copula *be* (realized as /iz/ or *am* or *are*) instead of a lexical verb (e.g., *Miki is submarine!* [ = I saw a submarine in Disneyland]; *I am jacket* [ = I bought a jacket today]). Verbless utterances, where the lexical/thematic verb is missing, have been reported for other child L2 learners, as well, during the early stages of L2 acquisition (Lakshmanan, 1993/1994, 1998). The omission of lexical verbs is not unique to child L2 acquisition and has also been observed for child L1 learners (Radford, 1990). However, unlike in the case of the verbless utterances attested for child L1 learners, which are typically binominal expressions such as *Kendall bath* ( = Kendall takes a bath), the verbless utterances produced by child L2 learners contain elements such as *for*, *with*, and *and*, which Lakshmanan (2000) analyzed as overt realizations of a lexico-functional category, that heads the "minimal" maximal projection of the early verbless utterances (e.g., *The girl for the tamboron* [ = The girl is playing the tambourine]; *Boy and ball* [ = The boy is kicking the ball]).

The verb is the nucleus of relevant structural information about a language. In addition to acquiring the phonological form and the meaning of the verb, the learner will have to figure out the semantic roles associated with it, the number of arguments that it can take, and how these arguments are mapped onto the overt syntax. Although the issue of lexical argument structure has been extensively researched in relation to the adult L2 learner, with the exception of a study by Whong-Barr and Schwartz (2002), there are no studies that have researched this issue in the child L2 context. Whong-Barr and Schwartz used an oral grammaticality judgment task to compare the acquisition of English *to* and *for*-dative alternation by L1 English, L1 Korean, and L1 Japanese children (e.g., *give a book to someone/give someone a book; buy a book for someone/buy someone a book*). They found that the child L2 learners, like the child L1 learners, overgeneralized the *to*-dative alternation to verbs in English that can take only the prepositional dative form but not the double-object variant. However, it was only the Japanese children, but not the Korean and the English children, who overgeneralized the *for*-dative alternation to verbs that do not permit the double-object variant. Japanese allows only prepositional datives and not the double-object variant. Korean allows the double-object form only in relation to *for*-datives, provided the lexical verb is marked by the benefactive suffix. Whong-Barr and Schwartz attributed the Korean children's success in rejecting the illicit double-object *for*-datives to their L1 grammar, which requires an overt morphological licensor for the grammatical double-object benefactive datives.

## C. Child L2 Morphosyntactic Acquisition

In comparison to the relatively few studies on phonological and lexical acquisition, child L2 research (since the 1990s), as in the case of the early child L2 studies (in the 1970s), has focused largely on the acquisition of morphosyntax. A substantial body of this recent research on morphosyntactic acquisition has been couched within the Chomskyian framework of UG. The central issues addressed include the status of functional categories and phrase/clause structure in the child L2 initial state; the relationship between overt grammatical morphology, such as verb inflections, and the underlying representation of the abstract categories/features and syntactic operations associated with them; the role of L1 transfer in morphosyntactic acquisition; and the similarities and differences between child L2 learners and learners in other acquisition contexts, including adult L2 learners, typically developing monolingual child L1 learners, and monolingual child L1 learners with SLI.

In relation to the status of functional or grammatical categories in the early stages of child L2 acquisition, a growing body of morphological and syntactic evidence, largely based on longitudinal case studies, suggests that child L2 learners do not go through an initial lexical/thematic-only stage where functional categories associated with the inflection phrase (e.g., tense and agreement), the determiner phrase, and complementizer phrase are absent. Instead, the findings lend support to the Strong Continuity position in relation to child L2, namely, that once functional categories and their projections have emerged for L1 acquisition (i.e., prior to the age of three years), they are operative from the very beginning for successive acquisition of an L2 during childhood (see, e.g., studies by Gavruseva & Lardiere, 1996; Grondin & White, 1996; Haznedar, 2001, 2003; Kakazu & Lakshmanan, 2000; Lakshmanan, 1993/1994; Lakshmanan & Selinker, 1994). As stated above, within child L1 acquisition research, proposals for the maturational triggering of functional categories have been put forth (e.g., Radford, 1990). Assuming that the maturational account is correct for child L1, the findings from child L2 acquisition suggest that child L2 learners do not regress to an earlier lexical–thematic stage of development in the course of L2 acquisition, where functional categories and their projections are absent. In relation to clause structure, the availability of functional categories entails a fully articulated clause structure, involving not only the lexical layer of the verb phrase (VP) but also the higher grammatical layers represented by the inflection and complementizer projections. As stated earlier, Vainikka and Young-Scholten (1996) and Paradis, Corre and Genessee (1998) have argued in favor of a Weak Continuity account in relation to the status of functional categories and clause structure in the early stages of child L2 developing grammars. Specifically, they have claimed that similar to child L1 grammars, child L2 learners' early clauses are maximally VPs and that the higher functional projections of the inflection phrase and the complementizer phrase are built up gradually, in a stepwise fashion, based on the interaction between UG and L2 input.

Gradual structure building accounts tend to emphasize the overt suppliance of functional/grammatical morphemes at relatively high criterial levels in determining the availability of the abstract functional categories and projections associated with them. On the other hand, proponents of the Strong Continuity position argue that the absence of overt functional morphology at high criterial levels does not necessarily imply a deficit in the representation of abstract functional properties. Rather, the omission of grammatical morphemes, such as verb inflections, stems from performance difficulties encountered by children in the overt mapping of the abstract functional categories in the target L2 (Haznedar & Schwartz, 1997). In other words, the strong continuity position predicts a mismatch between the child's speech output and the underlying representation, in that the former underdetermines the latter.

The mapping problem in child L2 acquisition is more apparent in the case of bound functional morphemes compared to independent functional morphemes. For example, a consistent finding in relation to child L2 learners of English is that it is free or suppletive inflectional morphemes, such as the copular *be* and the auxiliary *be* that are supplied from the very early stages of L2 acquisition, whereas the affixal inflectional morphemes such as the past tense *–ed* and the third singular *–s* tend to be omitted during the same period (Haznedar, 2001; Ionin & Wexler, 2002; Kakazu & Lakshmanan, 2000; Lakshmanan, 1993/1994, 2000; Zobl & Liceras, 1994). This contrasts with child L1 grammars of English, where affixal verbal inflectional elements are developmentally prior to the suppletive forms such as the copula and the auxiliary. At the same time, however, the evidence from longitudinal case studies indicate that similar to child L1 English, but different from adult L2 English, child L2 learners do succeed in mastering or come close to mastering the affixal verb inflectional morphology by approximately the 10th month of exposure (Kakazu & Lakshmanan, 2000; Lakshmanan, 1994).

Overall, the developmental relationship between overt morphology and syntax in child L2 appears to be an indirect rather than a direct one. For example, child L2 learners of English, whose L1s are null-subject languages, appear to know from early on that English is not a null-subject language, even though they may continue to produce uninflected lexical verbs (i.e., nonfinite forms), where inflected (i.e., finite) verb forms would be required in the target (Haznedar & Schwartz, 1997; Lakshmanan, 1994). Likewise, regardless of whether there is overt representation of finiteness or not, the subject pronouns of root clauses in child L2 grammars tend to occur only in the nominative case form and non-nominative case-marked subjects, observed in child L1 English, have rarely been attested (Haznedar, 2001; Kakazu & Lakshmanan, 2000; Lakshmanan, 1994; Lakshmanan, 2000). These child L2 English developmental facts are very different from child L1 English, where a developmental relationship between verb inflections and overt subjects, as well as a correlation between non-nominative subjects and the absence of finite verb inflection in root contexts have been observed (Guilfoyle, 1984; Schütze & Wexler, 1996).

Most of the studies on the status of functional categories in child L2 grammars have examined production data. However, this situation has begun to change as researchers have begun to examine children's comprehension as well. Grüter (2005) investigated the comprehension and production of French object clitic pronouns by English-speaking children. English, unlike French, does not have any clitic pronouns.

Grüter found that the children showed a low rate of suppliance in clitic production but performed well in the comprehension task. Herschensohn and Stevenson (2003) compared the comprehension and production of verb inflectional morphology by English-speaking children acquiring Spanish in an immersion setting. They found that the children's comprehension of verb inflectional forms in Spanish was substantially higher than their production, suggesting that the problems encountered by the children in their production does not stem from a deficit in morphosyntactic competence. Additionally, they also found that syntax and overt verb morphology develop separately and not in tandem, contrary to what would be predicted by the Weak Continuity account.

UG-based approaches on child L2 acquisition of verb inflections have largely focused on the development of tense and agreement features; aspectual properties, including the inherent aspectual semantics of lexical verbs, have largely been ignored. An exception to this trend, but couched within a non-UG framework, is the bidirectional study of child L2 learners of English and child L2 learners of Italian by Rocca (2002). Rocca found that in both child L2 English and child L2 Italian, distinctions based upon verbal semantic aspect are developmentally prior to distinctions based upon tense alone.

The role of the L1 in child L2 morphosyntactic acquisition continues to be debated and the issue is far from being settled. Proponents of a full-transfer account propose that child L2 learners, like adult L2 learners, initially transfer their L1 representations and the properties associated with them to the developing L2 grammar. Under this scenario, child L2 learners' clause structure in the initial state is expected to pattern in the same way as their L1, with respect to both lexical projections (i.e., VP) as well as the higher functional projections of inflection and complementizer. However, the evidence in support of the full-transfer position in relation to the word order properties of VPs and the higher functional projections is sparse. Haznedar (1997) in her study of a Turkish child L2 learner of English argued that head-final properties of the lexical projection of VP and inflectional projection of negation phrase in Turkish are initially transferred by the child to English, a head-initial language. However, the data on which Haznedar based her conclusions are open to other analyses, which weaken a transfer-based account in this domain (for discussion, see Lakshmanan & Selinker, 2001). Additionally, the evidence from longitudinal studies of other child L2 learners of English with head-final languages as L1s does not support the full-transfer account (Lakshmanan, 2000). In other words, in relation to the word order of VPs and the higher functional projections, child L2 learners are able to acquire the target orders at the earliest stage in their L2 development. Lakshmanan and Selinker (1994) show that Spanish-speaking and French-speaking child L2 learners of English go through a fairly long stable stage where they treat the complementizer *that* in tensed biclausal declaratives as being obligatorily null, even though in these learners' L1s, the +tense complementizer is obligatorily overt, suggesting that children are able to override potential L1 transfer effects. As stated earlier, child L2 learners of English, whose L1s are null-subject languages, appear to know early on that English requires subjects of tensed clauses to be obligatorily overt, indicating nontransference of the null-subject property from their L1s to the L2. Some null-argument languages such as Korean also permit null objects. However, Park (2004) reports an asymmetry between the overt suppliance of subjects and objects in relation to the English L2 grammars of Korean children. Park argues that of the two types of argument omission, it is the property of null objects, but not the property of null subjects, that is transferred to the children's English L2. A similar asymmetry has been observed in the case of Chinese-speaking adult L2 learners of English as well (Yuan, 1997).

As stated earlier, a potential difficulty in examining the role of L1 transfer in child L2 acquisition is that the L1 may still be in the process of development. It is therefore necessary to assess the child L2 learners' knowledge of the L1 as well. This procedure has been rarely adopted in previous child L2 studies. An exception is a study by Yip, Mathews and Huang (1996) who conducted a cross-sectional study of Cantonese children's knowledge of the Binding Principles A and B, which constrain the interpretation of reflexives and pronouns, respectively, in their L1 (Cantonese) and L2 (English). The children were three years old when they began to be exposed to English and ranged in age from 3;4 to 6;4 at the time of testing. By ages five to six (i.e., within a comparatively *shorter* period of time since their onset of L2 acquisition), they had reached a level of competence in the domain of binding similar to monolingual English children of the same age. An apparent developmental delay of Principle B relative to Principle A in their L2 English was observed, comparable to what has been observed in the case of monolingual English children (for similar results in relation to Korean child L2 learners of English, see Lee & Schachter, 1997). Surprisingly, in relation to Binding Principle A, the child L2 learners were conservative in relation to the choice of antecedents for reflexives, not only in English, but in Cantonese as well, accepting only local antecedents in the case of both, even though their L1 allows local as well as long-distance binding of reflexives. This contrasts with the interpretation of the reflexive by Cantonese speaking children whose onset of exposure to English occurred at the age of six years, and who were also tested when they were older (Yip & Tang, 1998). In the case of these older child L2 learners, Yip and Tang found evidence of transference of the long-distance binding properties from their L1 to English, although the findings suggested that learners were able to revise their initial hypothesis and restructure their L2 grammar in line with the binding properties of English.

Studies on the effects of age on L2 acquisition of morphosyntax, such as those of Johnson and Newport (1989, 1991), have focused on the L2 end state rather than child–adult differences in the pattern of development. Recently, within child L2 research, there has been a shift in focus from a concern solely with the end-state knowledge attained to a systematic comparison of the L1 child, L2 child, and adult L2 patterns of development evidenced in the course of acquisition. Within this more recent line of research, there has been a fair amount of controversy as to whether child L2 learners show a similar pattern of development to child L1 or adult L2 learners. According to one account, L2 children are predicted to show a similar pattern of development to L1 children. An alternative account is that L2 children should show a similar pattern of development to L1 children in relation to the development of inflectional morphology, whereas their development of syntax, as a result of L1 transfer, should resemble the pattern attested in L2 adults. The issue is far from being resolved as evidence supporting both positions has been attested. Weerman, Bisschop and Punt (2003) have shown that in relation to the acquisition of adjectival inflection in Dutch, child L2 is like child L1 acquisition and that both are distinct from adult L2 acquisition. Blom and Polisenská (2005) in their study of the development of verb inflections and verb placement in Dutch found age effects in relation to both domains, with the child L2 learners patterning like the child L1 learners but differently from the adults. They also found L1 transfer effects only in the case of the adults and not in the child L2 learners. In contrast, Tran (2005) found that in relation to both verb inflectional morphology and verb placement, child L2 learners of German exhibited different developmental patterns from child L1 learners of German. Unsworth (2005) compared the status of direct object scrambling in the developing grammars of child L1, child L2, and adult L2 learners of Dutch. She found that the L2 children and adults followed the same developmental path, with an initial stage characterized by L1 influence, thus distinguishing both groups from L1 children.

Studies on real-time sentence processing in adult L2 learners have reported quantitative and qualitative differences between L2 adults, L1 adults, and L1 children (Clahsen & Felser, 2006). Surprisingly, with the sole exception of a study by Marinis (2007), the issue of how children process sentences in real time has not hitherto been addressed. Marinis investigated the processing and comprehension of reversible passives (and actives) by monolingual English children and Turkish-English L2 children using an online and an offline task. He found that the L2 children's performance on the offline task was poor in comparison to the performance of the monolingual English children. However, the results of the online task showed that L2 children, similar to L1 children, were able to make use of morphological cues (progressive –*ing* and the passive participle suffix –*ed*) in processing reversible actives and passives and reassign thematic roles (i.e., assign the *theme/patient* semantic role to the subject of passives). As Marinis has argued, online measures may more accurately reveal children's morphosyntactic knowledge in the L2 than offline measures standardized on monolingual populations.

In previous studies comparing child L2 with child L1 development, the point of comparison has nearly always been with monolingual child L1 learner. An exception is the study by Lakshmanan and Ito (2000) who compared the development of verbal inflection, overt subjects, and nominative subjects in the simultaneous bilingual L1 acquisition of English and Japanese; sequential bilingual L1 acquisition of two languages prior to age three (Japanese from birth and English from age two); and successive child L2 acquisition of English by a native speaker of Japanese, whose onset of exposure occurred beyond age four. They found that successive child L2 acquisition of English and sequential bilingual acquisition of English patterned similarly, and differed from simultaneous bilingual acquisition in relation to all three properties. Crucially, only the child who acquired English and Japanese simultaneously went through an initial stage in both languages where only nonfinite verb forms were present, and subjects were always omitted. When overt subjects began to emerge, they were often in the non-nominative case form in both languages (objective and genitive pronouns in English and genitive case-marked nouns in Japanese).

Recently, some researchers have reported remarkable similarities between the spontaneous speech production of child L2 learners and monolingual children with SLI—see, for example, Hakansson's (2001) study on the acquisition of word order in Swedish and Paradis and Crago's (2000) study on the acquisition of verb inflectional morphology and object clitics in French. However, production data cannot help address the issue of whether or not the developmental problems experienced by the two groups of children stem from a deficit in the underlying representation or are purely due to processing/performance related factors. Grüter (2005) addressed the gap in the research by examining production as well as comprehension data in relation to the acquisition of object clitic pronouns in French. Her analysis of the group results indicated that the L1 French children with SLI, like the child L2 learners of French, showed a low rate of clitic suppliance on the production task but performed well on the comprehension task. However, her analysis of individual results showed that there was a correlation between performance and production in the case of the L2 children but not the children with SLI.

## VII. CONCLUSION

In conclusion, with the renewal of interest in the child L2 learner since the 1990s, child L2 acquisition is now on its way to becoming established as a field in its own right. Major advances have been made in our understanding of how an L2 is acquired during the childhood years, particularly in relation to morphosyntax and to a lesser extent in relation to phonology. Further research in these two areas as well as in other sparsely researched areas such as lexical acquisition and the real-time sentence processing in L2 children should lead to a fuller understanding of the developmental paths traversed by children in their acquisition of an L2 beyond the first. Research on L2 children has typically focused on the acquisition of the L2; future studies on child L2 attrition, as well as the development of the child's L1 alongside the L2, should also enhance our understanding of the capacity of the human mind to acquire and sustain multiple languages in childhood. Finally, the phenomenon of language mixing or code switching has been largely ignored in child L2 research (but see Arias & Lakshmanan, 2005).  Future investigations of L2 children's code mixing should shed light on how children are able to draw on their knowledge of the L1 and L2 grammar and vocabulary as they converge upon the constraints that characterize adult code switching.

## REFERENCES

Anderson, R. (2004). Phonological acquisition in pre-schoolers learning a second language via immersion: A longitudinal study. *Clinical Linguistics and Phonetics, 18*, 183–210.

Arias, R., & Lakshmanan, U. (2005). Code-switching in a Spanish-English bilingual child: A communication resource? In J. Cohen, K. T. McAlister, K. Rolstad, & J. Macswan (Eds.), *ISB4: Proceedings of the 4th International Symposium on Bilingualism* (pp. 94–109). Somerville, MA: Cascadilla Press.

Bhatia, T., & Ritchie, W. (1999). The bilingual child: Some issues and perspectives. In T. Bhatia & W. Ritchie (Eds.), *Handbook of child language acquisition* (pp. 569–643). San Diego, CA: Academic Press.

Blom, E., & Polisenská, D. (2005). Verbal inflection and verb placement in first and second language acquisition. In *Proceedings of the 29th Linguistic Colloquium*. Amsterdam: Vrij Universiteit.

Clahsen, H., & Felser, C. (2006). Grammatical processing in language learners. *Applied Psycholinguistics*, *27*, 3–42.

Dulay, H., & Burt, M. (1974). Natural sequences in child second language acquisition. *Language Learning*, *24*, 37–53.

Epstein, S., Flynn, S., & Martohardjono, G. (1996). Second language acquisition: Theoretical and experimental issues in contemporary research. *Brain and Behavioral Sciences*, *19*, 677–714.

Flege, J. (1999). Age of learning and second-language speech. In D. Birdsong (Ed.), *Second language acquisition and the critical period hypothesis* (pp. 101–132). Hillsdale, NJ: Erlbaum.

Foster-Cohen, S. (2001). First language acquisition…second language acquisition: What's Hecuba to him or he to Hecuba? *Second Language Research*, *17*, 329–344.

Gavruseva, L., Lardiere, D. (1996). The emergence of extended phrase structure in child L2 acquisition. In A. Stringfellow, D. Cahana-Amitay, E. Hughes, & A. Zukowski (Eds.), *Proceedings of the Annual Boston University Conference on Language Development* (pp. 225–236). Somerville, MA: Cascadilla Press.

Grondin, N., & White, L. (1996). Functional categories in child L2 acquisition of French. *Language Acquisition*, *5*, 1–34.

Grüter, T. (2005). Comprehension and production of French object clitics by child second language learners and children with specific language impairment. *Applied Psycholinguistics*, *26*, 363–391.

Guilfoyle, E. (1984). The acquisition of tense and the emergence of thematic subjects in child grammars of English. *The McGill Working Papers in Linguistics*, *2*, 20–30.

Hakansson, G. (2001). Tense morphology and verb-second in Swedish L1 children, L2 children, and children with SLI. *Bilingualism: Language and Cognition*, *4*, 85–99.

Harada, T. (2006). The acquisition of single and geminate stops by English-speaking children in a Japanese immersion program. *Studies in Second Language Acquisition*, *28*, 601–632.

Hatch, E. (Ed.). (1978). *Second language acquisition: A book of readings*. Rowley, MA: Newbury House Publishers.

Haznedar, B. (1997). L2 acquisition by a Turkish-speaking child: Evidence for L1 influence. In E. Hughes, M. Hughes, & A. Greenhill (Eds.), *Proceedings of the 21st Annual Boston University Conference on Language Development* (pp. 245–257). Somerville, MA: Cascadilla Press.

Haznedar, B. (2001). The acquisition of the IP system in child L2 English. *Studies in Second Language Acquisition*, *23*, 1–39.

Haznedar, B. (2003). The status of functional categories in child second language acquisition: Evidence from the acquisition of CP. *Second Language Research*, *19*, 1–41.

Haznedar, B., & Schwartz, B. D. (1997). Are there optional infinitives in child L2 acquisition? In E. Hughes, M. Hughes, & A. Greenhill (Eds.), *Proceedings of the 21st Annual Boston University Conference on Language Development* (pp. 257–268). Somerville, MA: Cascadilla Press.

Hecht, B. F., & Mulford, R. (1982). The acquisition of a second language phonology: Interaction of transfer and developmental factors. *Applied Psycholinguistics*, *3*, 313–328.

Herschensohn, J., & Stevenson, J. (2003). Failed features or missing inflection? Child L2A of Spanish morphology. In B. Beachley, A. Brown, & F. Conlin (Eds.), *Proceedings of the 27th*

*Annual Boston University Conference on Language Development* (pp. 299–310). Somerville, MA: Cascadilla Press.

Ionin, T., & Wexler, K. (2002). Why is 'is' easier than '-s'?: Acquisition of tense and agreement morphology by child second language learners of English. *Second Language Research, 18*, 95–136.

Johnson, J., & Newport, E. (1989). Critical period effects in second language learning: The influence of maturational state on the acquisition of English as a second language. *Cognitive Psychology, 21*, 60–99.

Johnson, J., & Newport, E. (1991). Critical period effects on universal properties of language: The status of subjacency in the acquisition of a second language. *Cognition, 39*, 215–258.

Kakazu, Y., & Lakshmanan, U. (2000). The status of IP and CP in Child L2 acquisition. In B. Swierzbin, F. Morris, M. Anderson, C. Klee, & E. Tarone (Eds.), *Social and cognitive factors in second language acquisition: Selected proceedings of the 1999 second language research forum* (pp. 201–221). Somerville, MA: Cascadilla Press.

Lakshmanan, U. (1989). *Accessibility to universal grammar in child second language Acquisition.* Doctoral dissertation, University of Michigan, Ann Arbor, MI.

Lakshmanan, U. (1993/1994). The boy for the cookie: Some evidence for the non-violation of the Case Filter principle in child second language acquisition. *Language Acquisition, 3*, 55–91.

Lakshmanan, U. (1994). *Universal grammar in child second language acquisition.* Amsterdam: John Benjamins.

Lakshmanan, U. (1995). Child second language acquisition of syntax. *Studies in Second Language Acquisition, 17*, 301–329.

Lakshmanan, U. (1998). Functional categories and related mechanisms in child second language acquisition. In S. Flynn, G. Martohardjono, & W. O'Neil (Eds.), *The generative study of second language acquisition* (pp. 3–16). Mahwah, NJ: Lawrence Erlbaum.

Lakshmanan, U. (2000). Clause structure in child second language grammars. In A. Juffs, T. Talpas, G. Mizera, & B. Burtt (Eds.), *Proceedings of the 1998 GASLA IV* (pp. 15–40). University of Pittsburgh.

Lakshmanan, U. (2006). Child second language acquisition and the fossilization puzzle. In Z. Han & T. Odlin (Eds.), *Studies of fossilization in second language acquisition* (pp. 100–133). Clevedon: Multilingual Matters Ltd.

Lakshmanan, U., & Ito, Y. (2000). *Root Infinitives and non-nominative subjects in the bilingual first language acquisition of Japanese and English.* Paper presented at the GASLA conference, MIT, Cambridge, March 2000.

Lakshmanan, U., & Selinker, L. (1994). The status of CP and the tensed complementizer *that* in the developing L2 grammars of English. *Second Language Research, 10*, 25–48.

Lakshmanan, U., & Selinker, L. (2001). Analysing Interlanguage: How do we know what learners know? *Second Language Research, 17*, 393–420.

Lee, D., & Schachter, J. (1997). Sensitive period effects in binding theory. *Language Acquisition, 6*, 333–362.

Mackay, I., Flege, J., & Imai, S. (2006). Evaluating the effects of chronological age and sentence duration on degree of perceived foreign accent. *Applied Psycholinguistics, 27*, 157–183.

Marinis, T. (2007). On-line processing of passives in L1 and L2 children. In A. Belikova, L. Meroni, & M. Umeda (Eds.), *Galana 2—Proceedings of the Conference on Generative Approaches to Language Acquisition—North America.* Somerville, MA: Cascadilla Press.

McLaughlin, B. (1978). *Second language acquisition in childhood.* Hillsdale, NJ: Erlbaum.

Paradis, J. (2005). Grammatical morphology in children learning English as a second language: Implications of similarities with specific language impairment. *Language, Speech and Hearing Services in the Schools, 36*, 172–187.

Paradis, J., Corre, M., & Genessee, F. (1998). The emergence of tense and agreement in child L2 French. *Second Language Research, 14*, 227–256.

Paradis, J., & Crago, M. (2000). Tense and temporality: A comparison between children learning a second language and children with SLI. *Journal of Speech and Hearing Disorders, 43*, 834–848.

Park, H. (2004). A minimalist approach to null subjects and objects in second language acquisition. *Second Language Research, 20*, 1–31.

Piper, T. (1984). Phonological processes in ESL five-year-olds. *TESL Canada Journal, 1*, 71–80.

Radford, A. (1990). *Syntactic theory and the acquisition of English syntax*. Oxford: Blackwell.

Ravem, R. (1978). Two Norwegian children's acquisition of English syntax. In E. Hatch (Ed.), *Second language acquisition: A book of readings* (pp. 148–154). Rowley, MA: Newbury House.

Rescorla, L., & Okuda, S. (1984). Lexical development in second language acquisition: Initial stages in a Japanese child's learning of English. *Journal of Child Language, 11*, 689–695.

Rocca, S. (2002): *Child Second Language Acquisition of Tense Aspect Morphology: A Bidirectional Study of English and Italian*. Unpublished Ph.D. dissertation, University of Edinburgh.

Schütze, C., & Wexler, K. (1996). Subject case licensing and English root infinitives. In A. Stringfellow, D. Cahana-Amitay, E. Hughes, & A. Zukowski (Eds.), *Proceedings of the 20th Annual Boston University Conference on Language Development* (pp. 670–681). Somerville, MA: Cascadilla Press.

Schwartz, B.D. (2003). Why child L2 acquisition? In J. van Kampen & S. Baauw (Eds.) *Proceedings of GALA 2003* (Vol. 1, pp. 47–66). Utrecht: Netherlands Graduate School of Linguistics.

Schwartz, B. D., & Sprouse, R. (1996). L2 cognitive states and the full transfer/full access model. *Second Language Research, 12*, 40–72.

Scovel (1988). *A time to speak: A psycholinguistic inquiry into the critical period for human speech*. Rowley, MA: Newbury House.

Tran, J. (2005). Verb position and verb form in English-speaking children's L2 acquisition of German. In A. Brugos, M.R. Clark-Cotton, & S. Ha (Eds.), *Proceedings of the 29th Annual Boston University Conference on Language Development* (pp. 592–603). Somerville, MA: Casacadilla Press.

Unsworth, S. (2005). *Child L2, adult L2, child L1: Differences and similarities: A study on the acquisition of direct object scrambling in Dutch*. Ph.D. dissertation, Utrecht University.

Vainikka, A., & Young Scholten, M. (1996). Gradual development of L2 phrase structure. *Second Language Research, 12*, 7–39.

Weerman, F., Bisschop, J., & Punt, L. (2003). *L1 and L2 acquisition of Dutch adjectival inflection*. Paper presented at the generative approaches to language acquisition 2003, Utrecht, the Netherlands.

White, L. (2003). *Second language acquisition and universal grammar*. Cambridge, UK: Cambridge University Press.

Whong-Barr, M., & Schwartz, B. D. (2002). Morphological and syntactic transfer in child L2 acquisition of the English dative alternation. *Studies in Second Language Acquisition, 22*, 579–616.

Winitz, H., Gillespie, B., & Starcev, J. (1995). The development of English speech patterns of a 7-year-old Polish-speaking child. *Journal of Psycholinguistic Research*, *24*, 117–143.

Wode, H. (1978). Developmental sequences in naturalistic L2 acquisition. In E. Hatch (Ed.), *Second language acquisition: A book of readings* (pp. 101–117). Rowley, MA: Newbury House.

Wong Fillmore, L. (1976). *The second time around: Cognitive and social strategies in second language acquisition.* Unpublished doctoral dissertation, Stanford University, Stanford, CA.

Yavas, M. (2002). Voice onset time in bilingual phonological development. In F. Windsor, M. L. Kelly, & N. Hewlett (Eds.), *Investigations in clinical phonetics and linguistics* (pp. 341–350). Mahwah, NJ: Erlbaum.

Yip, Y., & Mathews, S. (2007). *The bilingual child: Early development and language contact.* Cambridge: Cambridge University Press.

Yip, V., Mathews, S., & Huang, Y.Y. (1996). *Knowledge of binding in Hong Kong bilingual children.* Paper presented at the Second Language Research Forum, 24–27 October 1996, University of Arizona, Tucson, AZ.

Yip, V., & Tang, G. (1998). Acquisition of English reflexive binding by Cantonese learners. In M. Beck (Ed.), *Morphology and its interfaces in second language knowledge* (pp. 165–193). Amsterdam: John Benjamins.

Yoshida, M. (1978). The acquisition of English vocabulary by a Japanese child. In E. Hatch (Ed.), *Second language acquisition: A book of readings* (pp. 91–100). Rowley, MA: Newbury House.

Yuan, B. (1997). Asymmetry of null subjects and null objects in Chinese speakers' L2 English. *Studies in Second Language Acquisition*, *19*, 467–497.

Zobl, H., & Liceras, J. (1994). Functional categories and acquisition orders. *Language Learning*, *44*, 159–180.

CHAPTER 17

# AGE AND THE END STATE OF SECOND LANGUAGE ACQUISITION

David Birdsong

In contrast to child first language acquisition (L1A), the typical outcome of postadolescent second language acquisition (L2A) is nonnativelike attainment. However, some adult learners at the L2A end state perform like natives in psycholinguistic experiments. A number of age-related factors are thought to influence learners' potential for nativelike attainment in L2A. Data from L2 learners at the end-state figure prominently in major themes in L2A research, such as the critical period hypothesis for L2A (CPH/L2A), L1 influence, neurocognitive and neurobiological aging, and L1 versus L2 processing.

## I. THE L2A END STATE

### A. The Construct of End State

The outcome of language acquisition is often referred to as the *end state*. This term should not be understood in an absolute sense. In the native language, there is no "end" to the accumulation of vocabulary items (including regionalisms, neologisms, slang, and idiomatic expressions) over the course of a person's lifetime. Among L2 users, the pronunciation, lexis, and syntax of the L1 are subject to ongoing assimilation to the L2, as is also conspicuously the case with L1 intrusions into the L2 (see discussion in section V regarding L1–L2 reciprocal influence).

While such examples indeed illustrate the dynamic nature of linguistic systems, linguists commonly posit an idealization of finality with respect to the development of the underlying grammatical system of a language. On this view, most of the abstract features of L1 syntax, phonology, and morphology are stably represented in the minds

*The New Handbook of Second Language Acquisition*

of speakers at some point prior to adulthood. It is this knowledge that many linguists refer to when they use the term end state or its synonyms *steady state* or *final state*. Psycholinguists often use the terms *asymptote* or *asymptotic attainment* to accommodate the idea that there may be a practical end, but no absolute finality, in the development of linguistic knowledge and language processing ability.

In the L2A context, the term *ultimate attainment* is commonly substituted for end state attainment. Though sometimes erroneously used in reference to nativelikeness, ultimate attainment refers to any and all L2A end points, up to and including nativelikeness.

## B. Studying the L2A End State

In the literature on late L2A (defined in this contribution as immersion in the L2 around adolescence), the traditional emphasis is on "failure." Failure is understood as an L2A end state that is measurably different from the end state of L1A. Studies too numerous to mention have revealed L1–L2 differences; however, many studies showing differences do not target learners at the L2A end state.

Another perspective emphasizes the variety of L2A outcomes among individual learners. These range from telegraphic speech, to functional adequacy in everyday situations, to sounding like native speakers. Bley-Vroman (1989) points out that a primary goal in L2A research is to explain why there is such uniformity of outcome at the L1A end state and such diversity at the L2A end state.

A third perspective focuses on learner potential. What are the upper limits of L2 attainment? Despite well-studied impediments to learning, late L2 acquisition is not doomed to result in failure. Nativelike levels of proficiency in pronunciation, morphosyntax, and processing have been documented in the literature, and some adult L2 learners attain nativelikeness across multiple challenging tasks (see section VI).

An individual learner's potential is not directly revealed by pace of acquisition (e.g., the length of training required to reach a learning goal). Nor is potential necessarily seen in descriptions of stages or processes involved in learning. It is only with end-state data that one can begin to determine the upper limits of L2 learner attainment.

The most commonly used benchmark for studying L2 learner attainment is the performance of monolingual native speakers (in section V, the limitations of this methodology are discussed). Comparisons of the outcomes of L1A and L2A allow researchers to hypothesize and test possible constraints on L2A. Similarities and differences are discerned in tasks involving auditory perception, judgments of acceptability, elicited sentence production and imitation, sentence- and word-level processing, ambiguity resolution, global-level and segmental-level pronunciation, to name some of the more frequently employed tasks. Comparisons may involve behavioral data (e.g., accuracy in acceptability judgments, degree of accent in elicited pronunciation, etc.) as well as brain-based data (e.g., electrophysiological patterns for processing syntactic and semantic anomalies; localization of brain function during sentence comprehension and production).

## C. Operationalizing the End State

The construct of ultimate attainment applies locally, not globally. That is, it is not assumed that proficient L2 learners at a given point in time have effectively reached asymptote across the entire range of features of L2 linguistic knowledge, language production, and language processing. Even within a narrow domain such as constituent movement in syntax, a hypothetical learner may have reached the asymptote of attainment with respect to *wh*-movement but not with respect to verb raising. In light of this uncertainty, selecting subjects who may be at the L2A end state involves intelligent guesswork in the form of generous residency requirements. It is not uncommon to find residence minima of 10 years or more. Because it is possible for a person to reside in the L2 context and yet be isolated from contact with the L2, the residency requirement should be accompanied by stringent criteria (or statistical controls) for L2 exposure and use.

In case studies such as Lardiere's work with Patty (Lardiere, 2006), longitudinal observations in a local domain such as inflectional morphology might be expected to reveal stability of performance. Arguably, long-term stability would suggest finality of attainment in this domain. However, observable stability in production may not always be a reasonable expectation. For example, longitudinal analyses of individuals' production of overt features of morphosyntax (e.g., use of definite versus indefinite articles, past tense morphology for irregular verbs) reveal that stability in production may not ever occur (Long, 2003).[1] Indeed, even native speakers do not display unwavering stability in idiolectal performance and evaluations of acceptability (Birdsong, 2005a).

## II. THE END STATE, THE INITIAL STATE, AND AGE

The concept of end state is often juxtaposed with the complementary notion of *initial state*. In L1A, the initial state is the mental apparatus, be it dedicated to language learning or to learning more generally, that the neonate brings to the task of acquiring the ambient language. For L2A, the initial state is equated with postnatal development at the cognitive, neurological, and linguistic (L1) levels.

The L2A initial state and age go hand in hand. Consider the initial state of a child who begins learning the L2 at age 3, and the initial state of an 18-year old. The initial state of the child reflects a still-developing knowledge of the L1, and relatively little cumulative use of cognitive systems for perceiving, processing, and producing the L1. Unlike this infant, the postadolescent L2 learner has in place a fully developed neurological representation of the L1 grammar, along with automatized neuromuscular routines for pronouncing the L1, and a finely tuned auditory system that enables accurate perception of L1 sounds. (Here we consider only initial-state differences in terms of development of the L1; other dimensions of initial-state differences are discussed in section III.) As this example and common sense suggest, differences in age of L2 learning imply differences in the initial state of acquisition, and vice versa.

For this reason, age of acquisition is understood to be a proxy for the initial state of L2 acquisition. Operationally, age of acquisition is a quantitative measure that

---

[1]A lack of stability at the end state is one reason some researchers avoid use of the term fossilization. Critiques of the concept of fossilization are found in Birdsong (2005a), Long (2003), and MacWhinney (2005).

represents the initial state, a complex "metavariable" (which includes prior linguistic knowledge, the state of neural and cognitive development, education, attitudes toward L2 learning, etc.) that is difficult to quantify. L2A researchers use age of acquisition in regressions as a predictor variable for performance at the L2A end state. In the literature, age of acquisition usually emerges as the strongest predictor of end-state performance of all biographical variables. "Earlier is better" is a convenient if simplistic rule of thumb that suggests this relationship.[2]

In much of the literature, "age" is shorthand for the point in a learner's life where immersion in the L2 begins. *Age of acquisition* is frequently substituted for *age of immersion*, and is abbreviated AoA.

## III. SOURCES OF AGE-RELATED EFFECTS

End-state differences between child L1A and adult L2A (and between early L2A and late L2A) are linked to AoA and are commonly chalked up to the "age factor." However convenient and however pervasive the label, the age factor is an omnibus term that under-specifies the range of neural, cognitive, attitudinal, and experiential variables that distinguish adult L2A from child L1A. It is inappropriate to lump together, for example, neurobiological changes over increasing AoA with qualitative and quantitative changes in linguistic exposure, or with changes in attitude toward native speakers of the target language (Klein, 1995).

In the interest of conceptual granularity, when there are observed differences in ultimate attainment between early and late L2 learners, it is more accurate to speak of age-*related* effects rather than age effects. Indeed, because much of the literature explores the relationship between ultimate attainment and age of immersion, it is even more accurate to refer to *AoA*-related effects. (Because researchers do not usually split this terminological hair, the two terms will be used interchangeably in this chapter.)

The literature abounds with discussion of underlying sources of AoA-related effects in L2A. It is not possible here to summarize this literature adequately. Thorough reviews are offered by Herschensohn (2007) and Singleton and Ryan (2004).

The varied sources of age-related effects can be broken down into four major classes, which are discussed below: neurobiological, neurocognitive, cognitive-developmental, and linguistic-experiential. (Other influences on ultimate attainment are attitudinal and biographical in nature; they are considered in section VI.F.)

### A. Neurobiology

Increases in neurofunctional specificity (i.e., progressive dedication of neural circuitry to a given mental operation) lead to system-level declines in plasticity. These changes over age result in difficulty in representing new linguistic knowledge. They may also speed the processing of the L1 but slow the processing of the L2. At the

---

[2]It is widely recognized that the potential upside of L2 learning is not reached merely by classroom study or by incidental naturalistic contact with the L2. It is also known that age of first incidental exposure and age of beginning formal study of the L2 study are at best weak predictors of ultimate attainment.

macro level of observation, Lenneberg (1967) cites eventual lateralization of function over age as an impediment to new language learning. In a similar argument, Seliger (1978) cites localization of mental function.

With respect to the cellular level, Long (1990) and Pulvermüller and Schumann (1994) identify the process of myelination as a possible impediment to postpubertal L2A. Myelin is a phospholipid contained in glial cells. Insulating axons in a sheath of myelin speeds up electrical transmission. However, this efficiency comes at a cost: synaptic plasticity is reduced in areas of the brain that are densely myelinated. During the process of myelination, glial cells also produce substances that inhibit axonal growth in neighboring neurons, reducing the likelihood of formation of new synapses. According to Pulvermüller and Schumann, the insulating and inhibiting effects of myelination may impede the establishment of new circuitry in brain areas that are associated with language learning.

de Bot (2006) suggests that the neural plasticity required for new language learning may be related to the extent and timing of synaptic pruning. As a function of language use (particularly the use of more than one language) individuals differ in the degree to which synapses are maintained or pruned.

Pinker (1994) proposes a "use it then lose it" account of the decline of language learning ability, whereby the organism is genetically programmed to dismantle the neural circuitry required for language learning once it has served its purpose, that is, once the L1 has been acquired.

## B. Neurocognition

A collection of papers edited by Cabeza, Nyberg, and Park (2005) reveals the effects on cognition of age-related neurological changes, such as shrinking brain volume, hemispheric organization, functional connectivity, and declining levels of dopamine and other neurotransmitters. It is known that neurologically based declines in processing speed, cued and free recall, and working memory take place over age. A synthesis of the literature carried out by Park (2000) indicates that these declines begin at around age 20. Bialystok and Hakuta (1999) relate such life span neurocognitive changes to the ability to acquire and use an L2.

Likewise for the L2A context, Schumann et al. (2004) explore the connection between age-related declines in nigrostriatal dopamine and declines in attention, motoric sequencing, and working memory, all of which are essential to language use. Schumann et al. also implicate dopamine in motivation to learn, learning reinforcement, and suppressing L1 influence.

Ullman (2005) suggests that the neural structures subserving procedural memory (which allows for coordination of syntactic and motoric gestures in real time) are more affected by age than the neural structures responsible for declarative memory (which permits acquisition of lexical and idiosyncratic information, along with facts such as dates and lists and names). Among low-proficiency L2 users, the declarative system is a repository of memorized surface forms, whether these forms are irregular (e.g., *ran*, the past tense of *run*) or regular (e.g., *talked*, the past tense of *talk*). In low-proficient L2 use, both regular and irregular forms are retrieved from declarative memory. At high levels of L2 proficiency, however, the combinatorial aspects of language production (e.g., affixation of the regular -*ed* past tense morpheme to verb stems: *talk+ed ⇒ talked*) are assumed by the procedural system, while the declarative system remains responsible for irregulars. Ullman argues that this dualistic system mirrors that of native speakers. Paradis (2004) provides a comprehensive account of the memory systems and neural structures involved in L1 and L2 use.

## C. Cognitive Development

Newport (1991) proposes that postadolescents, with a large memory bandwidth, take in and try to process so much linguistic information at once that acquisition ends up incomplete. By comparison, children have a smaller short-term memory capacity; this limits them to processing fewer bits of information (i.e., fewer morphemes) at a time, with the result that acquisition becomes a tractable problem. In this sense, "less is more" in language learning.

In the Chomskyan tradition, linguists have taken varied positions on the possibility that access to Universal Grammar (UG) declines with age, with resultant nonnative-like attainment for certain abstract features of the L2. One position is that UG limits the hypothesis space of L2 learners, with the result that features of learner grammars (from initial state to end state) fall within the finite range of possibilities specified by UG (Schwartz & Sprouse, 1996; White, 2000). On another view, resetting parameters becomes increasingly difficult with age (Towell & Hawkins, 1994). A specific instantiation of this idea is the claim that L2 learners with AoA > 7 are unable to properly set parameters of certain functional categories in cases where the L1 values and the L2 values for these parameters are different (Tsimpli & Roussou, 1991). In a similar vein, Hawkins and Hattori (2006) and Tsimpli and Dimitrakopoulou (2007) claim that the ability to correctly represent L2 uninterpretable features (i.e., formal features that are devoid of strictly semantic content, such as case in English) that are not present in the L1 is lost after the closure of a critical period. However, the ability to acquire interpretable features such as [+/−past] in English is not affected. See Han (2003) and Hardin (2001) for discussion of theories of L2A initial-state UG and their relevance to the L2A end state.

Bridging UG and mainstream developmental constructs, Bley-Vroman (1989) argues that late L2 learners have no access to UG, nor to acquisition mechanisms specific to language learning; these are replaced, respectively, by knowledge of the L1 and by domain-general learning mechanisms.

## D. L1 Entrenchment

With advancing AoA, there is a concomitant increase in the cumulative use of the L1 for speaking and processing. Generally speaking, as L1 representations become progressively entrenched over age, learning an L2 becomes more difficult, and the likelihood of persistent effects at the L2A end state increases.

Concerning pronunciation, Flege (1992) proposes that, with accumulated years of speaking and hearing the L1, the phonetic categories for L1 sounds become better defined. The result is that L2 vowels and consonants that are acoustically close to corresponding L1 segments are likely to assimilate into the preexisting (L1) categories.

According to Flege's "unfolding hypothesis," the degree to which L2A end-state pronunciation is accented is positively correlated with the degree of development of the L1 phonetic system when L2A begins.

With respect to syntax and sentence interpretation, Brian MacWhinney's Competition Model (MacWhinney, 2005) predicts that, for example, L2 learners whose L1 canonical word order is subject-initial (Subject–Verb–Object or Subject–Object–Verb) will tend to interpret the first noun in an L2 string as the agent, even if the L2 is itself not subject-initial. MacWhinney attributes this tendency to a progressive strengthening, over increasing AoA, of the association that links noun position to noun function.

Consistent with the spirit of this proposal are results of connectionist simulations (e.g., Elman et al., 1996; Marchman, 1993) that may relate to the L2A context. As L1 representations become progressively entrenched in neural networks, rerepresentation or "unlearning" becomes progressively difficult. In other words, L2 learning is impeded with advancing AoA as a consequence of learning itself, not because of any change in the learning mechanism.

### E.  Discussion

A single presumed source of age effects cannot adequately account for the textured facts of end-state attainment in L2A. For example, accounts that emphasize biology over other factors and which predict zero or little incidence of nativelikeness (e.g., Hyltenstam & Abrahamsson, 2003; Johnson & Newport, 1989; Long, 1990) do not match up well with the sizable incidence of nativelike performance.

However, in light of the multifactorial nature of age effects in L2A, Birdsong (2006) suggests not discounting out of hand any empirically supported sources of age-related effects in L2A. This includes sources relating to the biology of the species, which may play out in declines in some areas of cognition (e.g., phonological working memory) and in increases in others (e.g., processing "bandwidth"). Along with this assumption of face validity, it may also be reasonably assumed that some factors and mechanisms account for more variance than others, and that the proportional effects of each of the sources on L2 processing and acquisition will vary to some extent from individual to individual (Bowden, Sanz, & Stafford, 2005; Dewaele, this volume; Dörnyei & Skehan, 2003).

### IV.  STUDYING AOA AND THE L2A END STATE

In L2A research, there are several possible ways of determining if there are AoA-related effects on ultimate attainment. The most frequently used procedure is regression of predictor variables onto outcome measures, or correlations that partial out covariants such as education.

Studies using regression methods normally report significant negative correlations of performance over the range of sampled AoA, hence the "earlier is better" rule of thumb. Some studies disaggregate the results into two distributions, one for early arrivals and one for late arrivals, and perform separate correlations for each distribution. This procedure produces differing slopes and correlation coefficients for each set of results.

Another approach is to compare performance of two or more participant groups (e.g., early and late arrivals). If the sample size is sufficiently large and the data are normally distributed, ANOVA or similar statistical models can be employed. In the most basic application of ANOVA in this context, the independent variable is AoA with two or more levels, and the dependent variable is quantified performance on an attainment measure.

For intergroup comparisons, learner and control groups are shown schematically below.

| *Learner group* | *Learner group* | *Controls* |
|---|---|---|
| Late (postadolescent) L2 | Early (preadolescent) L2 | Monolingual L1 |
| | | Simultaneous L1–L2 |

AoA studies may involve three-way comparisons (early vs. late learners; each learner group vs. controls). One-way comparisons of late learners versus controls are also common.

In several recent studies of brain function in L2 processing (and in a few behavioral studies as well), the variable of L2 proficiency is considered along with AoA. The basic between-group designs are as follows:

| *Learner group* | *Learner group* | *Controls* |
|---|---|---|
| Late (postadolescent) L2 | Early (preadolescent) L2 | Monolingual L1 |
| High L2 proficiency | High L2 proficiency | Simultaneous L1–L2 |
| Low L2 proficiency | Low L2 proficiency | |

(In some cases, L1–L2 comparisons within a learner group are carried out, i.e., performance in the L2 is compared with performance in the L1 for the same subjects.)

Especially when proficiency is not controlled, it is typical to find that the performance of late L2 groups is inferior to performance of earlier-exposed groups, which are in turn inferior to performance of monolinguals and simultaneous L1–L2 bilinguals. These differences have been interpreted as indicating that the AoA-defined learner groups differ in terms of their potential for learning.

Group designs such as these set performance criteria and informatively integrate the age and proficiency variables. However, a limitation of pure between-group comparisons is that by definition they do not adequately capture the range of performance within groups. As we will see in section VI, there are individuals in late-arriving groups who perform within the range of performance of controls. Such findings are an essential complement to between-group comparisons, inasmuch as performance data from individuals contribute to our understanding of the upper limits of end-state attainment.

## V. THE NATIVE SPEAKER STANDARD

Comparisons of L2 learners with monolingual native speakers are instructive. The benchmark is readily established empirically, and referencing learner performance to that of natives provides an easily understood metric of the potential for learner attainment.

The native standard is not predetermined. That is, researchers do not stipulate what is native speaker performance and what is not. In the experimental context, the native standard is considered to be the performance of a sample of a relevant population of native speakers. Natives' performance is not uniform, but is inclusive of a range of outcomes.

In L2A research, nativelikeness is often operationalized as L2 learner performance that falls within the range of performance of native controls. In other cases, the criterion for nativelikeness is performance within 1 or 2 standard deviations of the native mean.

The native standard permeates research that relates age to ultimate attainment. In the context of evidence for the CPH/L2A, for example, Long (1990) maintains that the CPH/L2A could be falsified by one L2 learner whose competence is indistinguishable from that of a native speaker. Johnson and Newport (1989) assert that biological constraints associated with maturation deterministically prevent late learners from becoming nativelike. Hyltenstam and Abrahamsson (2003) claim that it is impossible for a late learner to display nativelikeness across the complete range of language performance, and the researchers link nonnativelikeness to a loss of learning ability over age. In all three examples, the criterion is understood to be monolingual nativelikeness.

However instructive and however widespread the use of this standard, there is an inherent problem in stipulating monolingual-likeness as the criterion for success in L2A. Consider the nature of bilingualism. Among bilinguals (i.e., people who routinely use both the L1 and the L2, irrespective of AoA and irrespective of proficiency in the two languages), the L1 and the L2 exert reciprocal influences on one another. Influences of the L1 on the L2 are widely recognized. Less well known are influences of the L2 on the L1, which have been observed in such varied areas as syntactic processing, judgments of acceptability for middle voice, voice onset time, and sentence-level pronunciation (see Birdsong, 2006). As Grosjean (1989) famously put it, the result of these reciprocal influences is that a bilingual is "not two monolinguals in one." Assuming that the learner is using both languages actively, the reciprocal influences in bilingualism appear to operate across all ages of immersion in the L2 (Harley & Wang, 1997).

Such observations suggest that comparisons with monolingual natives, while revealing, may not be an altogether appropriate criterion for falsifying the CPH/L2A, since the L2 of a bilingual cannot be expected to resemble, down to the most trivial detail, the language of a monolingual. In the context of AoA research more generally, what may be more illuminating than flushing out minute departures from monolingual likeness are comparisons of late and early L2 learners with bilinguals from birth. This approach has the potential for revealing how the reciprocal influences of L1 and L2 differ among the three groups.

Reciprocal effects in the two languages are a reminder that not all L1–L2 differences should be linked to the idea that language learning mechanisms deteriorate over age. A simple causal logic underscores this point. In the L1, departures from monolinguals' performance cannot possibly be the result of compromised learning of that L1; instances of nonmonolingual-likeness in the L1 are reflexes of the L2 on the fully developed L1. By the same token, in the L2, at least some observed departures from monolingual standards can be attributed to processes inherent in multiple language use, rather than to declines in language-learning ability.

## VI. NATIVELIKE ATTAINMENT

This section highlights behavioral and brain-based studies that reveal that some postadolescent L2 learners are capable of nativelike attainment. In most studies, nativelikeness is not tested across multiple domains. But a small number of studies summarized here do examine diverse areas of linguistic performance, and they reveal that postadolescent L2 learners are capable of attaining broad nativelikeness.

Recall that comparisons of performance of groups of native controls with groups of L2 learners almost invariably reveal intergroup differences. However, the upper limits of attainment are not established by between-group comparisons but by examining the performance of individuals.

Given that use of both the L1 and the L2 inhibits the attainment of complete monolingual nativelikeness, and given the questionable appropriateness of the monolingual standard, an exploration of nativelike attainment might appear to be unwarranted. In the discussion at the end of the section, we will consider how observed nativelike attainment might be reconciled with the nature of bilingualism.

### A. Pronunciation

In the area of pronunciation, differences from native controls are found among subjects with AoAs as early as 1 or 2 years of age (Flege, 1999). A typical result is seen in Flege, Munro, and MacKay (1995). Two hundred forty Italian immigrants to Canada, with English as their L2, were asked to read aloud five short English sentences. A linear decline in accent ratings was observed over increasing AoA. The earliest AoA at which L2 learners began to fall out of the native range was age 2. Among postadolescent learners, 6 of the 120 subjects performed in the native range; all 6 had AoAs in the lower range of postadolescent subjects.

A higher rate of nativelike pronunciation is reported by Oyama (1973). On a task involving telling a personal anecdote, 6 of 36 native Italian speakers who had immigrated to the United States with AoAs at or beyond adolescence received pronunciation ratings that fell within the range of ratings received by native speakers. A still higher incidence of nativelike pronunciation emerges from the research of Bongaerts (1999). Bongaerts sampled the French pronunciation of nine Dutch-speaking subjects who were highly proficient in French. Of the nine late learners, three received ratings within the range of ratings for native controls. To obtain a more generalizable idea of the incidence of nativelikeness, Birdsong (2007) studied the pronunciation of learners who had not been screened for L2 proficiency. The sample consisted of 22 Anglophones with late AoA ($\geq 18$ years) residing in the Paris area.

On two subtle acoustic measures (vowel length and VOT), as well as in global-level pronunciation, 2 of the 22 subjects were indistinguishable from native controls.

## B. Perception

Kuhl (2000) and Werker (1994) are among the researchers who have identified the constraining effects of the mother tongue on infants' perception of speech sounds in a new language. With exposure and training, these initial perceptual deficiencies in the L2 can be tempered or eliminated (Werker & Tees, 2005). For example, significant improvements with training have been observed with respect to Japanese speakers' difficulty perceiving the /r/-/l/ distinction in English (Bradlow, Akahane-Yamada, Pisoni, & Tohkura, 1999; McClelland, Fiez, & McCandliss, 2002). Nevertheless, the phenomenon of "listening to a second language through the ears of a first" can persist into adulthood (Cutler, 2001).

An example of nativelike perception is provided in a study by Darcy, Peperkamp, and Dupoux (2007). In English, assimilation of coronals to following labials or velars involves a shift of place of articulation. For example, if "sweet" (ending in the coronal/t/) is followed by "melon" (ending in the bilabial/m/), the resulting pronunciation is "swee[pm]elon." Similarly, "grapes" (beginning with the velar/g/) would alter the final segment of "sweet," producing "swee[kg]rapes." In contrast, with respect to obstruent clusters in French, assimilation involves the feature of voice. Thus *botte* 'boot' with final /t/ is produced with a final voiced [d] if it is followed by an adjective beginning with a voiced obstruent, such as *grise* ('gray'). The resulting sequence is pronounced 'bo[dg]rise.' Can native speakers of one language detect appropriately assimilated words in the other, or do they interpret the L2 as they do the L1? In Darcy et al.'s word detection task, English subjects with low French L2 proficiency mapped their L1 assimilation routine onto perception of sequences in French; the same L1-to-L2 mapping was found for French subjects who were low-proficiency learners of English. At high proficiency levels, however, learners of both languages were able to adjust their perception of assimilation and performed like natives when listening to L2 stimuli.

## C. Morphosyntax

In an influential study of French L2A, Coppieters (1987) found that no late-learning participants (who were from varied L1 backgrounds) came close to the performance of native controls in judgments of subtle syntactic contrasts in French. In the landmark study of Johnson and Newport (1989) not one of the 23 late-arriving Chinese or Korean subjects performed in the range of native controls on a test of knowledge of L2 English morphosyntax.

Birdsong (1992) carried out a partial replication of the Coppieters (1987) study and found that 15 of the 20 late-arriving Anglophone subjects performed in the range of native controls. Less impressive results were found by Birdsong and Molis (2001) in a strict replication of Johnson and Newport (1989). The 61 subjects were native speakers of Spanish. Only 1 of the 32 late arrivals scored in the native range. However, 13 late arrivals scored above 92% accuracy. Van Wuitswinkel (1994) asked Dutch speakers who had begun learning English after age 12 to judge the acceptability of a subset of the Johnson and Newport items, along with items exemplifying additional structures in English. In one group of learners, 8 of 26 participants performed like natives; in another group, 7 of 8 performed like natives.

To what can the divergent results be attributed? In the case of Birdsong (1992), there were certain procedure and materials differences from those in Coppieters (1987) that may have contributed to the divergence. In this instance, the high rate of nativelikeness could not be attributed to the fact that Birdsong's participants were Anglophones, because several of Coppieters's subjects were Anglophones and their performance, like that of the other subjects, fell outside the native range. However, we cannot exclude the possibility that the L1 of the experimental subjects influenced the rate of nativelikeness in the van Wuitswinkel (1994) and Birdsong and Molis (2001) replications of Johnson and Newport (1989). An L1 influence is also suggested by the results of Cranshaw (1997). Cranshaw examined the acquisition of tense-aspect features in English by 20 Francophone and 20 Sinophone late learners of English. While 3 of the Francophones performed like native controls, only 1 Sinophone performed like the natives.

Nativelikeness in L2 morphosyntax is not uncommon among highly proficient L2 users. For example, White and Genesee (1996) looked at the ability of Francophone late learners of English to produce and judge examples of *wh*-extraction in English. Sixteen of 45 highly proficient learners performed like natives across all tasks. In a study of the acquisition of aspectual features in Spanish, Montrul and Slabakova (2003) administered two interpretation tasks to late-learning Anglophones. Among their sample of highly proficient learners, 70% performed like natives on all sentence types in both tasks.

## D. Multiple Domains

Hyltenstam and Abrahamsson (2003), Long (1990), and Scovel (2000) contend that attained nativelikeness, if observed at all, will not equal that of natives across several domains of performance. For example, an L2 user may be competent in the surface morphological features of the language, but misassign stress on polysyllabic words like "hypothesis" and "octopus." While this is certainly the typical case, there are notable exceptions.

Marinova-Todd (2003) studied 30 highly proficient postadolescent learners of English, who had resided in the Boston area for 5 years or more. The learners and native controls performed nine tasks, which covered lexical knowledge, language use in narratives and discourse, pronunciation in spontaneous speech and read alouds, and morphosyntax in off-line and online tasks. Three of the late learners performed like native controls over all nine tasks.

Ioup, Boustagui, El Tigi, and Moselle (1994) published a case study of two Anglophones who were highly proficient late learners of Cairene Arabic. Nativelike performance was revealed in two tests involving identification of dialects of Arabic, three tasks relating to grammatical knowledge (English-to-Arabic translation, judgments of grammaticality, and interpretation of anaphora), and a free-form description task which was rated for pronunciation accuracy. With a few minor exceptions, the two subjects were indistinguishable from natives.

## E. Brain-Based Studies

Examinations of brain activity reveal the degree of functional similarity between processing in the L1 and processing in the L2 (and in some cases, between early and late bilingual processing). For recent reviews, see Abutalebi, Cappa, and Perani (2005); Birdsong (2006); Stowe and Sabourin (2005).

The locus of language processing is studied with imaging techniques such as functional magnetic resonance imaging (fMRI) and positron emission tomography (PET). Electrophysiological components of language processing are investigated with event-related brain potential (ERP) methodologies, a variant of electroencephalography. The timing of language processing events, such as reactions to semantic and syntactic anomalies, is revealed by measurements of brain activity through the scalp.

Brain-related research in L2A has focused on AoA and L2 proficiency as predictors of degree of similarity. Production studies using fMRI reveal that high-proficiency learners, even those with late AoA, tend to resemble monolingual natives in terms of regional brain activity during such tasks as word repetition, cued word generation, and sentence generation (see Birdsong, 2006). In a PET study involving listening to a story, Perani et al. (1998) compared the brain activity of late and early bilinguals (there was no comparison with monolinguals in this study). Subjects in both groups were highly proficient in the L2. The researchers found overlapping patterns of brain activity for the early and late bilinguals.

In general, the ERP literature suggests that, for high-proficient L2 users, reactions to syntactic anomalies (the P600 effect) and to semantic anomalies (the N400 effect) take place at the same poststimulus latencies as L1 users. Overlooking many details, this generalization extends to late-arriving learners (see Birdsong, 2006)

The relevance of proficiency is demonstrated in a study done by Sabourin (2003). Subjects were only fairly proficient late learners of Dutch and were native speakers of German, English, or a Romance language. All three groups performed slightly below natives on grammaticality judgments relating to verb agreement. However, on ERP readings taken concurrently with the behavioral task, none of three groups were identical to Dutch controls (although the German natives showed roughly nativelike N400 and P600 responses).

An emerging pattern in both imaging work (which relates to the "where" of language processing) and electrophysiological work (which relates to the "when" of processing) is that L2 proficiency is a more robust and reliable predictor of functional similarity than AoA. By and large, brain-based data reveal that processing in the L1 and processing in the L2 begin to converge with increasing L2 proficiency (Green, Crinion, & Price, 2006). Exceptions to this tendency are discussed in Clahsen and Felser (2006); see also section VI.F.

## F.  Discussion

Given the nature of bilingualism (see section V), how can we explain attained nativelikeness? There are two main approaches to reconciling nativelikeness with L1 effects in bilingualism.

One approach is to suggest that nativelikeness is observed because the tasks subjects perform are not sufficiently challenging. For example, off-line tasks such read alouds and unpaced judgments of grammaticality may not put a sufficiently heavy cognitive load on subjects to reveal learner-native differences. This argument is not consistent, however, with results of online tasks in Juffs and Harrington (1995) and Marinova-Todd (2003). Relatedly, it may be that the experimental tasks employed do not tap subtleties in grammatical knowledge. This possibility is countered by results of Birdsong (1992) and Ioup et al. (1994).

However, the argument that nativelikeness is restricted to certain types of processing and linguistic knowledge finds support in research by Clahsen and Felser (2006) and Sorace (2003). The results of experiments reported by Clahsen and Felser suggest that, in sentence parsing, both monolinguals and highly proficient late L2 learners use lexical and semantic cues for interpretation. However, compared to natives, learners tend to rely less on syntactic information. Both behavioral and brain-based evidence suggests that L1 processing involves detailed structural representations, whereas L2 processing is comparatively shallow. Consistent with the idea that L2–L1 differences are revealed in processing tasks are results from studies of lexical retrieval, structural ambiguity resolution, and detection of acoustic features of speech (see Birdsong, 2006). Sorace's research focuses on the interface between semantics and syntax. Languages like Italian do not require overt subjects when there is no shift of topic in the discourse; conversely, overt subjects are required when there is a shift of topic. English, however, requires subjects whether there is a shift of topic or not. Sorace proposes that English L1 learners of Italian L2 do not recognize the abstract relationship between topic and occurrence of overt subjects. Rather, they consider the realization of overt subjects to be optional in Italian, and not governed by the Italian rule that specifies the conditions under which subjects are required.

Another approach to reconciling nativelikeness with obstacles to learning involves the possibility that nativelike attainers distinguish themselves in terms of a cluster of attributes that favor high levels of attainment. For example, nativelikeness may not be possible without motivation to learn and to assimilate psycho-socially into the L2 linguistic culture (Klein, 1995). Education is another learner variable that affects L2A outcomes. For example, education in the L2 environment predicts attainment of regular features of inflectional morphology (Flege, Yeni-Komshian, & Liu, 1999). Along the same lines, amount of L2 use is predictive of degree of nativelikeness in L2 pronunciation (Flege & Liu, 2001). Especially in the area of pronunciation, training (formal or informal) may be required for attainment of nativelikeness (Birdsong, 2007; Bongaerts, 1999).

The distinction between necessary and sufficient conditions applies here. Strengths in these affective and experiential dimensions are not sufficient in themselves to guarantee high levels of attainment or nativelikeness. At the same time, in the absence of such strengths, nativelikeness is unlikely.

A more complex picture emerges from studies of aptitude and L2A ultimate attainment. Aptitude in language learning (which typically takes place in structured classroom environments) is predictive of ease of certain types of L2 learning (Robinson, 2001). However, the literature on the relation of foreign-language aptitude to ultimate L2 attainment is mixed.

DeKeyser (2000) administered a test of English morphosyntactic knowledge to L1 Hungarian subjects at the end state of English L2A. Among the late AoA subjects, three of the four best performers had received high scores on a test of foreign language-learning aptitude/talent. However, many of the high-aptitude subjects in the DeKeyser study did not score well on the measure of morphosyntactic knowledge. The finding that one of the best performers did not have high aptitude raises further questions about the predictive value of this trait.

Schneiderman (1991) compared the foreign-language learning aptitudes of a group of near-nativelike attainers and a group of learners with somewhat lower attainment. Across a battery of measures, both groups showed modest aptitude levels, suggesting that the association between aptitude and outcome is weak. The evidence further suggests that freakishly high levels of aptitude may not be necessary for high attainment in L2A.

It is likely that more granular approaches will better establish the connection between aptitude and proficiency at the end state. For example, Winke (2005) found that, of the various components of the Defense Language Aptitude Battery, only phonological working memory was predictive of advanced attainment.

One additional learner attribute to considered in the context of nativelike attainment is L2 dominance. For some L2 learners, including late L2 learners, the second language learned is more often spoken (and heard, read, and written) than the first. Relative frequency of use is one dimension of dominance. Another dimension of dominance is psycholinguistic in nature. Psycholinguistically, language dominance is operationalized in such tasks as speeded picture and number naming, and recall of words heard under noise. The L2 is considered dominant if it is processed with greater accuracy and speed than the L1.

By either definition, dominance is a matter of degree. That is, L2-dominants differ quantitatively in their relative use of the L2 and in their performance on the psycholinguistic tasks.

A proficient L2 learner is not necessarily L2-dominant. A study by Flege, MacKay, and Piske (2002) suggests that the distinction between proficiency and dominance may play out in observed nativelikeness. Their study involved three groups of Italian L1/English L2 bilinguals: one group was English (L2) dominant, one was Italian dominant, and a third group was composed of individuals who were highly proficient in both languages. While the latter two groups had detectable accents, the L2-dominants were indistinguishable from natives. The authors speculate that effects of the L1 diminish with increased L2 dominance.

What if contact with the L1 were eliminated altogether? The findings of a study by Pallier et al. (2003) are suggestive in this regard. Subjects were eight Korean adoptees who were brought to Paris at ages ranging from 3 to 8 years. On informal behavioral measures as well as on experimental tasks tapping implicit knowledge of French (Ventureyra, 2005), the adoptees were indistinguishable from monolingual French natives. The same was true for regional brain activity while listening to French, as revealed by fMRI. Behavioral as well as brain-based evidence revealed no trace of knowledge of Korean: the adoptees appeared to have completely "forgotten" their L1. Under conditions of extreme L1 loss, the neural substrates for language learning appear plastic enough to acquire an L2 to monolingual-like levels.

To summarize, high levels of motivation, linguistic training, and education in the L2 milieu are likely to characterize individuals who attain a high level of nativelikeness in the L2. However, these traits alone cannot be expected to suppress L1 effects in the L2. The key to overcoming bilingualism effects may reside in L2 use and L2 dominance. L1 effects are mitigated if the L1 is infrequently used. The intrusion of the L1 is perhaps more minimized if the L2 is dominant in terms of processing and use, even more so if the L1 is not used at all.

Thus we can speculate with some degree of confidence that nativelikeness is not out of the question for individuals with high levels of motivation, education, L2 use, and L2 dominance, and (possibly) foreign-language learning aptitude. However, further testing along the lines of Clahsen and Felser (2006) and Sorace (2003) will determine the empirical adequacy of this speculation.

## VII. THE AOA FUNCTION

### A. Is There a Critical Period for L2A?

The function that relates AoA to end-state attainment has been interpreted as evidence for and against a critical period in L2A. The AoA function is the best-fitting line through points in a distribution of L2 learner performance (e.g., grammatical accuracy, accentedness, etc.). Observable declines in the function reveal the effects of AoA, or, more precisely, the effects of factors that covary with AoA.

The most commonly observed AoA function is a straight line that begins at early childhood and continues over the AoA span. Since in this instance AoA effects are not confined to a circumscribed temporal span (i.e., a period), a straight-line function is not compatible with the notion of a critical period. However, it is consistent with the literature on neurological and cognitive aging (Birdsong, 2006).

Three AoA functions that contain a period are presented in crude and idealized form here. On one view, declines in end-state attainment begin at a very early AoA and then level off. After the point of articulation that marks the start of the leveling, there are no further performance declines over AoA. The resulting geometry resembles a stretched "L" which is represented by the image in Figure 1A.

On another view, the function is flat and performance is at ceiling in preadolescent AoA, after which begin declines in end-state attainment. The AoA function roughly resembles a stretched "7" and is represented in Figure 1B. On the left, a flat segment

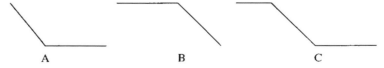

A                                    B                                    C

**Figure 1**   Three patterns of bounded age effects. (A) Stretched "L" shape; (B) stretched "7" shape; and (C) stretched "Z" shape. *Note*: To simplify visualization, the vertical axis (representing performance, or level of end-state attainment) and the horizontal axis (representing AoA) have been removed from all three figures.

signifies a null effect for AoA. The absence of a performance decrement in this segment corresponds to the idea of a circumscribed window of opportunity for nativelike attainment. On the right end of the function, the AoA effects persist indefinitely.

A third version is a hybrid of the first two, and is shown in Figure 1C. This stretched "Z"-shaped figure is composed of a finite window of opportunity, the onset and end of a decline, and a leveling off of the function. As in Figure 1A, after the rightmost articulation in the AoA function, there is no further performance decline over increasing AoA.

Note that in Figure 1A, the decline with increasing AoA is confined to a period. In Figure 1B, it is the lack of decline with increasing AoA that is confined to a period. Figure 1C incorporates two periods. The first is a finite null effect for AoA, followed by a finite AoA effect.

Thus, a common feature of each of these figures is at least one finite span, conforming to a strict interpretation of a "period" that is deemed optimal or critical for L2 mastery. (The same logic can apply to the term *sensitive period*, which is often associated with a function whose declines are less steep and their timing more variable than those of a critical period. In the present contribution, *critical period* will be used as a cover term for both phenomena. For further discussion, see Knudsen, 2004.)

## B.  Are Critical Period Effects Maturational in Nature? (1)

The highly schematic figures given here represent critical periods in the AoA function. These periods can be interpreted as reflecting maturational influences if their span coincides with biologically specified maturational epochs in development. That is to say, maturational effects would be suggested if the points of articulation coincide with the end of maturation. Thus, in the functions represented by Figures 1A and C, a case for maturational effects could be made if the span of age-related decline terminates around the end of maturation. For the function in Figure 1B, maturational effects would be suggested if the decline begins around the end of maturation; that is, if the closure of the window of opportunity coincides with the end of maturation.

Note that the presumed end of maturation apparently coincides, on the one hand, with the beginning of age-related declines (Figure 1B), and on the other hand, with the end of age-related declines (Figure 1A and C). The literature is unclear about whether the role of maturation is to delay declines or end declines, or both. This is a fundamental conceptual and theoretical issue that awaits a principled resolution.

## C.  Are Critical Period Effects Maturational in Nature? (2)

Let us now consider functions whose points of articulation do not line up with the end of maturation. Suppose the flat segments on the left of the functions in Figure 1A and C terminate at a point prior to the end of maturation, for example, at an AoA of 7 years as observed by Johnson and Newport (1989). How can one explain the onset of the decline that does not match up with the end of maturation? One possible explanation is that the timing of the decline is unrelated to maturation. For example, the onset of declines might reflect a threshold after which the effects of L1 entrenchment begin to cascade. It could also be that individuals who begin learning at age 7 immerse themselves less in the L2 than their earlier-AoA counterparts. An AoA of 7 years might coincide with a decline in motivation to learn the L2 or to assimilate with native speakers of the L2.

However, maturational explanations cannot be ruled out. It is possible that biological mechanisms contributing to attainment declines assert themselves at ages prior to the end of maturation. In other words, on this view not all maturational effects have to be keyed to the point at which (neuro)biological maturation ceases. Thus, for example, Scovel (1988) posits a brief window of opportunity for nativelike pronunciation relative to nativelike morphosyntax, owing to the early onset of declines in the neuromuscular coordination of articulators in the vocal apparatus.

Along these lines, Moyer (1999) and Singleton and Ryan (2004) point out that the observed duration of the window of opportunity is likely to depend on what domain of linguistic attainment is being tested. Observed differences in the timing of declines support the notion of "multiple critical periods" for different components of linguistic knowledge and processing (Seliger, 1978).

The same type of argument can be applied to the onset of declines in the L-shaped and Z-shaped functions. Some factor(s) other than biological aging (e.g., the onset of L1 effects) could trigger the declines. The effects may run their course and stop at a point prior to adolescence, after which no further declines would be expected. However, as with prematurational declines in the seven-shaped figure, biology cannot be ruled out. Some unspecified biological factor may exert its influence prior to the end of maturation, and not thereafter. No biological explanation suggests itself, however, if the point of articulation in the L-shaped figure appears after the end of maturation.

Clearly, if a case is to be made for any of these possibilities, it is necessary to identify the nature of the presumed sources of the effects and to specify their relationship to timing parameters of the AoA function.

## D. Approaches to Analysis (1)

Birdsong (2005b) reviews the published L2 behavioral evidence relating to the three functions presented above. Analyses of pooled data (performance of learners across the full span of AoA) are to be distinguished from analyses of disaggregated data, where separate analyses are performed on early-arriving and late-arriving subjects.

With respect to pooled data, all studies reveal declines in ultimate attainment persisting beyond the end of maturation. The AoA function that best fits the pooled data is roughly a straight line, with no distinct prematurational window of opportunity feature or postmaturational leveling off feature. (It should be noted the number of data points is usually low, and the data have typically not been subjected to nonlinear modeling.)

A slightly more mixed picture emerges when data from early and late arrivals are disaggregated. For early learners, there is some evidence of declines of ultimate attainment. These results are thus roughly consistent with Figure 1A and with the middle segment of Figure 1C, with the exception that, in these studies, the end of maturation does not mark the beginning of an orderly leveling off of the function, but rather a random dispersion of performance.

For late learners, several studies reviewed reveal ultimate attainment declines that persist beyond the end of maturation. Though the onset of declines varies, such results nevertheless reveal an ongoing decline in ultimate attainment over increasing AoA (see Figure 1B).

In the context of disaggregated analyses, two sets of data are worthy of note. Johnson and Newport (1989) relate their results to the notion that declines in ultimate attainment level cease around AoA = 16. Their results unambiguously indicate a decline in ultimate attainment up to AoA of about 16 years. They argue that this decline is followed by a leveling off and no further decline (Figures 1A and C). This would be in line with their view that age effects should cease at the end of maturation (see also Pinker, 1994; Pulvermüller & Schumann, 1994). While the decline over AoA is uncontroversial, the leveling-off feature, so crucial to this particular maturational account, has been called into question. Bialystok and Hakuta's (1994) reanalysis indicates that the declines actually persist past the end of maturation. Birdsong's (2005b) analysis of the late-arrivals' results reveals no orderly flattening of the function, but random performance. With respect to the window of opportunity geometry (Figure 1B), Birdsong and Molis (2001), using the same materials and procedures as Johnson and Newport (1989), found a flat segment at the top of the function (i.e., a ceiling effect) among their early-arriving subjects that persisted until an AoA of 27.5 years. Because the span of null AoA effects extends well into adulthood, the period cannot be construed as maturational in nature.

## E. Approaches to Analysis (2)

A minimal criterion for maturational effects is an articulation in the AoA function, a point where the slope of the function changes. The reasoning here is that a significant departure from linearity would suggest the onset of a qualitative change in learning ability. (Note that a departure from linearity might also be consistent with other age-related phenomena. For example, as mentioned above, it might signal a threshold after which L1 entrenchment effects are manifest in ultimate attainment.)

With respect to pooled data, there is little decisive evidence of nonlinearity or discontinuity that would suggest the onset of a decline in learning ability. This said, there is considerable controversy regarding the appropriate statistical and sampling measures for demonstrating departures from linearity. Also considered are the separation of length of residence, chronological age, and AoA effects; the timing along the AoA function of any putative elbow; and the possibility that an elbow might exist for attainment of L2 morphosyntax but not for pronunciation (Flege et al., 1999; Hakuta, Bialystok, & Wiley, 2003: Stevens, 2006).

It should be noted that nonlinear models applied to large numbers of data points are more revealing than simple regressions applied to the small data sets that are common in L2A research. Note too that the disaggregation procedure invariably produces departures from linearity. This is so because, in any distribution that does not yield a correlation equal to exactly +1 or −1, two separate functions account for more variance than a single function. Minor slope differences between two linear functions (imagine a slight bend in a drinking straw) can be simple artifacts of disaggregation, and thus may not represent a qualitative change in language learning.

## VIII. CONCLUSION

In this contribution, a central concern was the impact of age-related factors on end-state attainment in L2A. We considered this question from diverse methodological, analytic, and theoretical perspectives. The topics addressed include the monolingual standard, the attainment of nativelikeness in the face of obstacles to learning, and the adequacy of maturational accounts of age effects.

Another recurrent theme in this chapter is the upper limits of attainment among late L2 learners. The past 15 years have witnessed an expansion of research that investigates learner potential. The goal of these efforts goes beyond inventorying what late L2 learners are capable of doing. Rather, the goal is to produce an unbiased, composite picture of late learner attainment, a picture that integrates models of acquisition, external constraining and enabling factors, learner variables, facts of neurocognition over the life span, and features of processing and knowledge at the end state. It is in these rich and varied dimensions that the upper limits of attainment are explored.

## REFERENCES

Abutalebi, J., Cappa, S. F., & Perani, D. (2005). What can functional neuroimaging tell us about the bilingual brain? In J. F. Kroll & A. M. B. DeGroot (Eds.), *Handbook of bilingualism: Psycholinguistic perspectives* (pp. 497–515). New York: Oxford University Press.

Bialystok, E., & Hakuta, K. (1994). *In other words: The science and psychology of second-language acquisition.* New York: Basic Books.

Bialystok, E., & Hakuta, K. (1999). Confounded age: linguistic and cognitive factors in age differences in second language acquisition. In D. Birdsong (Ed.), *Second language acquisition and the critical period hypothesis* (pp. 161–181). Mahwah, NJ: Lawrence Erlbaum.

Birdsong, D. (1992). Ultimate attainment in second language acquisition. *Language, 68,* 706–755.

Birdsong, D. (2005a). Why not fossilization. In Z.-H. Han & T. Odlin (Eds.), *Studies of fossilization in second language acquisition* (pp. 173–188). Clevedon, UK: Multilingual Matters.

Birdsong, D. (2005b). Interpreting age effects in second language acquisition. In J. F. Kroll & A. M. B. DeGroot (Eds.), *Handbook of bilingualism: Psycholinguistic perspectives* (pp. 109–127). New York: Oxford University Press.

Birdsong, D. (2006). Age and second language acquisition and processing: a selective overview. *Language Learning, 56*(Suppl. 1), 9–49.

Birdsong, D. (2007). Nativelike pronunciation among late learners of French as a second language. In O.-S. Bohn & M. J. Munro (Eds.), *Language experience in second language speech learning* (pp. 99–116). Amsterdam: John Benjamins.

Birdsong, D., & Molis, M. (2001). On the evidence for maturational effects in second language acquisition. *Journal of Memory and Language, 44,* 235–249.

Bley-Vroman, R. (1989). What is the logical problem of foreign language learning? In S. Gass & J. Schachter (Eds.), *Linguistic perspectives on second language acquisition* (pp. 41–68). Cambridge, UK: Cambridge University Press.

Bongaerts, T. (1999). Ultimate attainment in L2 pronunciation: The case of very advanced late learners. In D. Birdsong (Ed.), *Second language acquisition and the critical period hypothesis* (pp. 133–159). Mahwah, NJ: Lawrence Erlbaum.

Bowden, H. W., Sanz, C., & Stafford, C. A. (2005). Individual differences: Age, sex, working memory, and prior knowledge. In C. Sanz (Ed.), *Mind and context in adult second language acquisition: Methods, theory, and practice* (pp. 105–140). Washington, DC: Georgetown University Press.

Bradlow, A. R., Akahane-Yamada, R., Pisoni, D. B., & Tohkura, Y. (1999). Training Japanese listeners to identify English/r/and/l/: long-term retention of learning in perception and production. *Perception & Psychophysics, 61*, 977–985.

Cabeza, R., Nyberg, L., & Park, D. C. (2005). *Cognitive neuroscience of aging: Linking cognitive and cerebral aging.* New York: Oxford University Press.

Clahsen, H., & Felser, C. (2006). Grammatical processing in language learners. *Applied Psycholinguistics, 27*, 3–42.

Coppieters, R. (1987). Competence differences between native and near-native speakers. *Language, 63*, 544–573.

Cranshaw, A. (1997). *A study of Anglophone native and near-native linguistic and metalinguistic performance.* Unpublished doctoral dissertation, Université de Montréal.

Cutler, A. (2001). Listening to a second language through the ears of a first. *Interpreting, 5*, 1–23.

Darcy, I., Peperkamp, S., & Dupoux, E. (2007). Bilinguals play by the rules: Perceptual compensation for assimilation in late L2-learners. In J. Cole & J. I. Hualde (Eds.), *Laboratory Phonology 9* (pp. 411–442). Berlin: Mouton de Gruyter.

de Bot, K. (2006). The plastic bilingual brain: Synaptic pruning or growth? Commentary on Green, et al. *Language Learning, 56*(Suppl. 1), 127–132.

DeKeyser, R. M. (2000). The robustness of critical period effects in second language acquisition. *Studies in Second Language Acquisition, 22*, 499–533.

Dörnyei, Z., & Skehan, P. (2003). Individual differences in language learning. In C. J. Doughty & M. H. Long (Eds.), *The handbook of second language acquisition* (pp. 589–630). Malden, MA: Blackwell.

Elman, J. L., Bates, E. A., Johnson, M. H., Karmiloff-Smith, A., Parisi, D., & Plunkett, K. (1996). *Rethinking innateness: A connectionist perspective on development.* Cambridge, MA: MIT Press.

Flege, J. E. (1992). Speech learning in a second language. In C. Ferguson, L. Menn, & C. Stoel-Gammon (Eds.), *Phonological development, models, research, and applications* (pp. 233–273). Parkton, MD: York Press.

Flege, J. E. (1999). Age of learning and second language speech. In D. Birdsong (Ed.), *Second language acquisition and the critical period hypothesis.* (pp. 1–22). Mahwah, NJ: Lawrence Erlbaum, pp. 101–131.

Flege, J. E., & Liu, S. (2001). The effect of experience on adults' acquisition of a second language. *Studies in Second Language Acquisition, 23*, 527–552.

Flege, J. E., MacKay, I. R. A., & Piske, T. (2002). Assessing bilingual dominance. *Applied Psycholinguistics, 23*, 567–598.

Flege, J. E., Munro, M., & MacKay, I. (1995). Factors affecting degree of perceived foreign accent in a second language. *Journal of the Acoustical Society of America, 97*, 3125–3134.

Flege, J. E., Yeni-Komshian, G. H., & Liu, S. (1999). Age constraints on second-language acquisition. *Journal of Memory and Language, 41*, 78–104.

Green, D. W., Crinion, J., & Price, C. J. (2006). Convergence, degeneracy, and control. *Language Learning, 56*(Suppl. 1), 99–125.

Grosjean, F. (1989). Neurolinguists, beware! The bilingual is not two monolinguals in one person. *Brain and Language, 36*, 3–15.

Hakuta, K., Bialystok, E., & Wiley, E. (2003). Critical evidence: A test of the critical-period hypothesis for second-language acquisition. *Psychological Science, 14*, 31–38.

Han, Z.-H. (2003). *Fossilization in adult second language acquisition.* Clevedon, UK: Multilingual Matters.

Hardin, C. A. (2001). *Initial state and end state in second language acquisition theory.* Unpublished MA thesis, University of Texas at Austin.

Harley, B., & Wang, W. (1997). The Critical Period Hypothesis: where are we now? In A. M. B. de Groot & J. F. Kroll (Eds.), *Tutorials in Bilingualism: Psycholinguistic perspectives* (pp. 19–51). Mahwah, NJ: Lawrence Erlbaum.

Hawkins, R., & Hattori, H. (2006). Interpretation of English multiple *wh*-questions by Japanese speakers: A missing uninterpretable feature account. *Second Language Research, 22*, 269–301.

Herschensohn, J. (2007). *Language development and age.* Cambridge, UK: Cambridge University Press.

Hyltenstam, K., & Abrahamsson, N. (2003). Maturational constraints in SLA. In C. J. Doughty & M. H. Long (Eds.), *The handbook of second language acquisition* (pp. 539–588). Malden, MA: Blackwell.

Ioup, G., Boustagui, E., El Tigi, M., & Moselle, M. (1994). Reexamining the critical period hypothesis: A case study of successful adult SLA in a naturalistic environment. *Studies in Second Language Acquisition, 16*, 73–98.

Johnson, J. S., & Newport, E. L. (1989). Critical period effects in second language learning: The influence of maturational state on the acquisition of English as a second language. *Cognitive Psychology, 21*, 60–99.

Juffs, A., & Harrington, M. (1995). Parsing effects in L2 sentence processing: subject and object asymmetries in Wh-extraction. *Studies in Second Language Acquisition, 17*, 483–516.

Klein, W. (1995). Language acquisition at different ages. In D. Magnusson (Ed.), *The lifespan development of individuals: Behavioral, neurobiological, and psychosocial perspectives: A synthesis* (pp. 244–264). Cambridge, UK: Cambridge University Press.

Knudsen, E. I. (2004). Sensitive periods in the development of the brain and behavior. *Journal of Cognitive Neuroscience, 16*, 1412–1425.

Kuhl, P. K. (2000). A new view of language acquisition. *Proceedings of the National Academy of Science, 97*, 11850–11857.

Lardiere, D. (2006). *Ultimate attainment in second language acquisition: A case study.* Mahwah, NJ: Lawrence Erlbaum.

Lenneberg, E. H. (1967). *Biological foundations of language.* New York: Wiley.

Long, M. H. (1990). Maturational constraints on language development. *Studies in Second Language Acquisition, 12*, 251–285.

Long, M. H. (2003). Stabilization and fossilization in interlanguage development. In C. J. Doughty & M. H. Long (Eds.), *The handbook of second language acquisition* (pp. 487–535). Malden, MA: Blackwell.

MacWhinney, B. (2005). A unified model of language acquisition. In J. F. Kroll & A. M. B. DeGroot (Eds.), *Handbook of bilingualism: Psycholinguistic perspectives* (pp. 49–67). New York: Oxford University Press.

Marchman, V. A. (1993). Constraints on plasticity in a connectionist model of the English past tense. *Journal of Cognitive Neuroscience, 5*, 215–234.

Marinova-Todd, S. (2003). *Comprehensive analysis of ultimate attainment in adult second language acquisition.* Unpublished doctoral dissertation, Harvard University.

McClelland, J. L., Fiez, J. A., & McCandliss, B. D. (2002). Teaching the/r/-/l/discrimination to Japanese adults: Behavioral and neural aspects. *Physiology & Behavior, 77*, 657–662.

Montrul, S., & Slabakova, R. (2003). Competence similarities between native and near-native speakers: an investigation of the Preterite/Imperfect contrast in Spanish. *Studies in Second Language Acquisition, 25*, 351–398.

Moyer, A. (1999). Ultimate attainment in L2 phonology: The critical factors of age, motivation and instruction. *Studies in Second Language Acquisition, 21*, 81–108.

Newport, E. L. (1991). Contrasting conceptions of the critical period for language. In S. Carey & R. Gelman (Eds.), *The epigenesis of mind* (pp. 111–130). Hillsdale, NJ: Lawrence Erlbaum.

Oyama, S. C. (1973). *A sensitive period for the acquisition of a second language.* Unpublished doctoral dissertation, Harvard University.

Pallier, C., Dehaene, S., Poline, J.-B., LeBihan, D., Argenti, A.-M., Dupoux, E., et al. (2003). Brain imaging of language plasticity in adopted adults: Can a second language replace the first? *Cerebral Cortex, 13*, 155–161.

Paradis, M. (2004). *A neurolinguistic theory of bilingualism.* Amsterdam: John Benjamins.

Park, D. C. (2000). The basic mechanisms accounting for age-related decline in cognitive function. In D. C. Park & N. Schwarz (Eds.), *Cognitive aging: A primer* (pp. 3–21). Philadelphia, PA: Psychology Press.

Perani, D., Paulesu, E., Sebastian-Galles, N., Dupoux, E., Dehaene, S., Bettinardi, V., et al. (1998). The bilingual brain: Proficiency and age of acquisition of the second language. *Brain, 121*, 1841–1852.

Pinker, S. (1994). *The language instinct: How the mind creates language.* New York: Morrow.

Pulvermüller, F., & Schumann, J. H. (1994). Neurobiological mechanisms of language acquisition. *Language Learning, 44*, 681–734.

Robinson, P. (2001). Individual differences, cognitive abilities, aptitude complexes and learning conditions: An aptitude complex/ability differentiation framework for SLA research. *Second Language Research, 17*, 368–392.

Sabourin, L. (2003). *Grammatical gender and second language processing.* Groningen Dissertations in Linguistics, 42, GLCG, Groningen.

Schneiderman, E. (1991). *Some neuropsychological characteristics of talented adult language learners.* Paper presented at the Second Language Research Forum University of Southern California.

Schumann, J. H., Crowell, S. E., Jones, N. E., Lee, N., Schuchert, S. A., & Wood, L. A. (2004). *The neurobiology of learning: Perspectives from second language acquisition.* Mahwah, NJ: Lawrence Erlbaum.

Schwartz, B. D., & Sprouse, R. A. (1996). L2 cognitive states and the full transfer/full access model. *Second Language Research, 12*, 40–72.

Scovel, T. (1988). *A time to speak: A psycholinguistic inquiry into the critical period for human speech.* Rowley, MA: Newbury House.

Scovel, T. (2000). A critical review of the critical period research. *Annual Review of Applied Linguistics, 20*, 213–223.

Seliger, H. W. (1978). Implications of a multiple critical periods hypothesis for second language learning. In W. Ritchie (Ed.), *Second language acquisition research: Issues and implications* (pp. 11–19). New York: Academic Press.

Singleton, D., & Ryan, L. (2004). *Language acquisition: The age factor* (2nd ed.). Clevedon, UK: Multilingual Matters.

Sorace, A. (2003). Near-nativeness. In C. J. Doughty & M. H. Long (Eds.), *The handbook of second language acquisition* (pp. 130–151). Malden, MA: Blackwell.

Stevens, G. (2006). The age-length-onset problem in research on second language acquisition among immigrants. *Language Learning, 56*, 671–692.

Stowe, L. A., & Sabourin, L. (2005). Imaging the processing of a second language: Effects of maturation and proficiency on the neural processes involved. *International Review of Applied Linguistics in Language Teaching, 43*, 329–353.

Towell, R., & Hawkins, R. (1994). *Approaches to second language acquisition.* Clevedon, UK: Multilingual Matters.

Tsimpli, L.-M., & Dimitrakopoulou, M. (2007). The interpretability hypothesis: Evidence from *wh*-interrogatives in second language acquisition. *Second Language Research, 23*, 215–242.

Tsimpli, I.-M., & Roussou, A. (1991). Parameter-resetting in L2? *UCL Working Papers in Linguistics, 3*, 149–169.

Ullman, M. T. (2005). A cognitive neuroscience perspective on second language acquisition: The declarative/procedural model. In C. Sanz (Ed.), *Mind and context in adult second language acquisition: Methods, theory, and practice* (pp. 141–178). Washington, DC: Georgetown University Press.

Van Wuitswinkel, K. (1994). *Critical period effects on the acquisition of grammatical competence in a second language.* Unpublished BA thesis, Katholieke Universiteit, Nijmegen.

Ventureyra, V. A. (2005). *À la recherche de la langue perdue: Étude de l'attrition de la première langue chez des Coréens adoptés en France.* Unpublished doctoral dissertation, Ecole des Hautes Etudes en Sciences Sociales, Paris.

Werker, J. F. (1994). Cross-language speech perception: developmental change does not involve loss. In J. C. Goodman & H. C. Nusbaum (Eds.), *The development of speech perception* (pp. 93–120). Cambridge, MA: MIT Press.

Werker, J. F., & Tees, R. C. (2005). Speech perception as a window for understanding plasticity and commitment in language systems of the brain. *Developmental Psychobiology, 46*, 233–251.

White, L. (2000). Second language acquisition: From initial state to final state. In J. Archibald (Ed.), *Second language acquisition and linguistic theory* (pp. 130–155). Oxford, UK: Blackwell.

White, L., & Genesee, F. (1996). How native is near-native? The issue of ultimate attainment in adult second language acquisition. *Second Language Research, 12*, 233–265.

Winke, P. (2005). *Individual differences in adult Chinese second language acquisition: the relationships among aptitude, memory, and strategies for learning.* Unpublished doctoral dissertation, Georgetown University.

CHAPTER 18

# MULTILINGUALISM AND AGING

Kees de Bot

In this chapter multilingualism and aging will be discussed from a Dynamic Systems Theory (DST) perspective. It will be argued that language development continues over the life span but that development, which can be growth or decline, is dependent on different types of resources. Aging is defined in terms of changes in physical, social, and psychological resources that interact over time. A DST perspective allows us to integrate a sociolinguistic and a psycholinguistic approach to develop language in the elderly.

The overview presented in De Bot and Makoni (2005) will be taken as a starting point. In this book, we tried to gather all relevant research on language and aging, including research on multilingualism. Here we present the main findings from the literature from about 2004 onwards and discuss some of the more recent additions in more detail.

## I. DEFINING MULTILINGUALISM AND AGING

It is now generally accepted that for the larger part of the world population, some form of multilingualism is the norm rather than the exception (see, e.g., Bhatia & Ritchie, 2004). It is also true that many countries in the world, in particular western ones, are confronted with an increasingly aging population. The United Nations report on world population ageing 1950–2050 (2001) presents compelling data on demographic developments in various parts of the world. In both the developed and the developing countries the total number of elderly and percentage of elderly people in the population will grow dramatically. The data show that by 2050, for the first time in human history the number of elderly people (60 years or older) will exceed the number of young people. Given that the larger part of the world population is multilingual and a considerable portion is aging, it is remarkable that so little research has been done on multilingualism and aging. Language and aging is now a topic that

425

attracts quite some attention, and there are several very active research groups around the world working on this topic, though they have not yet made the step to include multilingualism in their work. The main reason probably is that the two communities have few links: only a handful of researchers in applied linguistics and multilingualism have an interest in aging, and similarly, few researchers working on aging are interested in multilingualism.

Before a description of research in this topic can be given, we need to define the two core concepts: aging and multilingualism. As indicated by De Bot and Makoni (2005, p. 1):

> It is probably best to define aging as a change on three interacting dimensions: biological, psychological and social. No one is denying that there are physical changes in our body over time, but they have their impact in different ways in different individuals. The risk of mental and physical decline increases more or less with age in the larger population, but strictly speaking grouping of individuals on the basis of age in order to learn more about aging is inappropriate.

So "aged" is not a state in itself, but a conglomerate of changes of functions and variables over time. Development is a continuous process, and this also applies to language after middle age. In contrast to language development in childhood, there are no clear phases (e.g., one word/two words) that are related to certain ages. Variation is the rule, even when general trends can be found.

Also multilingualism, and accordingly language, needs to be defined here. Language is seen as a dynamic system at both the individual and the societal level. It is a set of variables (patterns, words, conventions) that changes over time through use; it is not a fixed set of rules and words. This view is expressed very adequately by Larsen-Freeman (2002, p. 42):

> Grammar is regarded as epiphenomenal, a by-product of a communication process. It is not a collection of rules and target forms to be acquired by language learners. Language, or grammar, is not about having; it is about doing: participating in social experiences.

This means that also in old age, language is defined by its use at the individual and the social level. And this is also a main point of this contribution: the social and the psychological cannot be separated completely since they interact with individual systems influencing the language system at the social level and the other way around.

Multilingualism then refers to the existence of separate but interconnected subsystems in the larger language system. These subsystems interact constantly and continue to change due to variation in use and contact among the languages.


## II. A DST APPROACH TO LANGUAGE AND AGING

There is a growing body of literature on language as a dynamic system and language development as a dynamic process. It is beyond the scope of the present contribution to deal with DST in detail. For a detailed treatment of these issues the reader is referred to De Bot, Lowie, and Verspoor (2005) and peer commentaries thereon in *Bilingualism: Language and Cognition* (2007, p. 1), as well as the contributions in a special issue of *The Modern Language Journal* (2007, 91, p. 4), Van Dijk and van Geert (2005), and Larsen-Freeman and Cameron (2008).

The main characteristics of DST are the following:

- Complex systems are sets over variables that interact over time.
- Dynamic systems are typically nested in the sense that each system is both part of a larger system and dividable into smaller subsystems. For example, language can be seen as a dynamic system that is both part of the larger cognitive system and in itself consists of subsystems like the lexicon and the phonological system.
- Systems interact with each other, and changes in one system or subsystem have repercussions on other parts of the system.
- Because the interaction over time between variables cannot be predicted fully, development may be—but is not necessarily—chaotic and nonlinear.
- The development of dynamic systems is highly dependent on initial conditions: a small difference in initial conditions may have large effects in the long run.
- Development is dependent on resources. Language development is dependent on internal resources, such as memory capacity, motivation to learn or use a language, word knowledge, and on external resources, such as opportunities for contact with the language, amount and type or quality of language input, and willingness of other people to interact.
- Development has no inherent goal and takes place due to external input and internal reorganization.

A DST perspective on language development is closely linked to a life-span developmental perspective on language. Language is constantly changing, both as a communication system between users and as a system of knowledge within an individual. If there is a real beginning, it is in very early childhood, if not in the womb. From then on, language development continues and is dependent on various internal resources, such as memory capacity and hearing acuity, and external resources, such as the caretaker's attention and the richness of the linguistic environment. The assumption is that languages are always developing, but not necessarily growing in the sense of more words or patterns. The language continues to develop even with cognitive decline. Due to nonuse, which in a way is a lack of resources, the language system can reorganize itself and make language elements that have not been used for some time, less readily available. This is typically what happens in nonpathological language attrition (cf., De Bot & Weltens, 1995; Schmid & Köpke, 2004). All languages of a multilingual go through phases of growth and decline due to more or less use of the language. For the first language the pattern may show little variation when it is used regularly, but on a larger time span moving from childhood to adulthood, it will clearly show changes over time, with a creative period in adolescence, a growth of specific language skills due to professional use, hobbies, migration, and so on. Foreign language skills will show variation over time depending on learning and use.

The unpredictability of development also applies to language and aging: it is likely that with decline of physical resources, such as memory, hearing, and vision, language skills will decline. But that is not necessarily the case: many factors interact in aging and some of them seem to prevent or delay decline, such as physical exercise, healthy nutrition, a high level of education, continued intellectual activity, and, as we will discuss in more detail below, multilingualism.

In the introduction it was pointed out that aging implies changes at the biological or physical level, the psychological level, and the social level. Linguistic decline may have its basis in biological changes, but the interaction between psychological and social changes will affect the rate of decline. These changes are in fact changes in the resources for different systems: the cardiovascular system, the hearing system, the motor system, and the cognitive system. All of these play a role and interact in language production and perception. The interaction between biological, psychological, and social changes is presented as a model with different interconnected modules in Figure 1.

Biological or neuropsychological changes lead to a reduction of resource capacity, in particular with respect to working memory, which then leads to changes in behavior and appearance. This may or may not be decline. Decline suggests difference from a norm, which basically doesn't exist. What is important is that these changes are generally *interpreted* as decline, and this interpretation leads to changes in behavior in interactions with this less competent person. The elderly person is confronted with a style of interaction that is less demanding, less complex, easier to understand, and more easy to engage in. There is also social pressure on the elderly person to accommodate in this respect, even when the perception of cognitive decline is totally wrong. This is where social stereotypes with respect to elderly people come in. Such stereotypes tend to be very strong and persistent (Ryan, Hamilton, & See, 1994). Elderly people are forced into a type of language use that robs them of opportunities to use the language in all its complexity. Given the "skills" character of language, nonuse of a part of the sets or registers, words, and constructions may lead to a decline in the use of these skills. If that happens, a catastrophic negative spiral sets in: changes in behavior are interpreted as decline, and these lead to simplified language use. The lack of exercise of more advanced linguistic skills that results from this simplified language use leads to a decline of these skills, and accordingly the language used

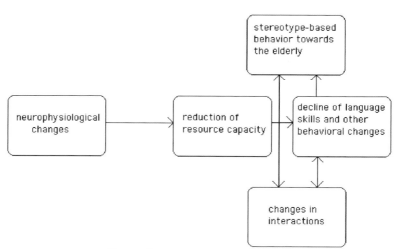

**Figure 1**   Language and aging model.

becomes less elaborate and complex, suggesting a decline in cognitive abilities, which will lead to further adaptations and simplifications in linguistic input and a reduction of the quality of the interaction.

At the cognitive level, the core of the problem in language decline is most likely in the functioning of the working memory component. Different types of buffers and short-term storage systems are needed for language production and perception, and the decline of the capacity of these systems may be detrimental to our language skills. But working memory is more than just a storage system; it is also the workbench where information is prepared for the next processing step. And the tool used with the workbench is language. So, memory and language interact in an interesting way: better language skills enhance memory performance, and accordingly, declines in working memory capacity can be compensated for by high levels of linguistic skills (Miyake & Friedman, 1999).

The validity of the model as presented still needs to be established. There is as yet no research that has looked at the impact of a change of interaction patterns on linguistic skills in elderly people. In a study by Barresi, Obler, Au, and Albert (1999), one of the main findings was that naming performance of elderly participants was negatively related to amount of hours spent on watching TV. Additional analyses of the data show that the subjects who watched more TV and spent less time on other activities, in particular those requiring active language use, such as writing, computer work, or conversation, exhibited loss in naming performance. This supports the idea that active language use is needed to maintain skills like naming. More passive activities like watching TV appear to have a negative effect. Whether that negative effect is caused by the reduction of the time available for active language use or by the poor quality of the input from TV is another matter.

## III. MULTILINGUALISM AND HEALTHY AGING

There are two possible perspectives on multilingualism and healthy aging. One is how the languages of multilinguals develop with age and whether the type of development that is seen in monolinguals also emerges in multilinguals. The second is what the impact of multilingualism is on cognitive functioning in aging. This latter issue will be discussed in section V. We will start with a review of some of the literature on multilingual proficiency in the elderly. The number of studies on foreign/second-language proficiency and its decline in the elderly is remarkably small. Weltens's (1989) review of the literature on foreign-language attrition shows that attention has merely been focused on age groups under 25, especially former secondary-school pupils and university students. Empirical data on foreign/second-language proficiency in the elderly are available from several studies by Michael Clyne (1977; 1982) and from the investigation by Harry Bahrick (1984).

Clyne's work on language loss and language maintenance in Dutch and German migrants in Australia has been pioneering in this respect. He recorded spontaneous speech in English of 200 postwar Dutch migrants and their children and 600 German–English bilinguals (half of them migrants, the other half Australian-born), and analyzed the patterns of switching and interference in their respective languages.

One of the outcomes of his research was that a number of elderly migrants tended to become less fluent in the second language, while the number of transfers and switches into the first language increased (1982, p. 27). Clyne lists a number of explanations for this "reversion" to the first language. The most likely explanation is the change in social setting, retirement, the absence of children, and the decreased socio-economic value of English, but "the phenomena described are not restricted to the retired or those whose children live away from home. They are even found in elderly migrants active in the work force who are married to English speakers" (Clyne, 1977, p. 50).

The most extensive study in the field of foreign-language attrition is Bahrick's (1984) study. In this study the retention of Spanish learned in school was tested throughout a 50-year period for 733 individuals. Each individual was tested on a large number of aspects of language proficiency. The data show that memory curves for Spanish decline exponentially for the first 3–6 years of the retention interval. After that retention remains stable for periods of up to 30 years. Then the memory curves show what Bahrick calls a "final decline" (1984, p. 1).

Here we want to look more closely at the oldest informants in Bahrick's study who were tested 50 years (on average) after the completion of the acquisition process (categorized in the study as "group 8"). In the analyses these subjects show a remarkable drop in their scores when compared to younger groups, in particular with regard to grammar recognition, word order, reading comprehension, and Spanish–English and English–Spanish vocabulary recall. No decline was found for grammar recall, idiom recall, and Spanish–English and English–Spanish vocabulary recognition. Bahrick himself refrains from speculating about possible explanations for the different scores in group 8 in his study. In his comments on Bahrick's study, Neisser (1984, p. 34) says: "It is too early to tell whether this downturn is universal or particular; whether it is an age effect, a cohort effect, a time-in-storage effect, or a result of some other factor yet unknown." Information about age is not provided in Bahrick's study, but a post-training interval of 50 years suggests that these subjects are at least 65 years old, so there is some ground for assuming an age effect or a cohort effect. Although Bahrick wanted to investigate the amount of rehearsal needed to maintain a particular level of performance, he failed to accomplish this goal because his informants rehearsed so little that no correlations could be found between retention and rehearsal variables.

Another study that looked at the retention of *foreign* language skills is a study by De Bot and Lintsen (1986) on German and French in the Netherlands. This study looked at language skills in highly educated, independently living, healthy men. The main purpose of this study was to investigate to what extent the data on language proficiency in the elderly support Bahrick's findings. The data for German as a foreign language show that the elderly informants (mean age 75+) made slightly more grammatical and lexical errors in spontaneous speech than the informants in the 65–75 age range. One of the tests used was a verbal fluency task. In this task participants had to list as many items as possible within a minute from a specific set, such as "words beginning with a T" or "vegetables." For verbal fluency the elderly outperformed the younger group on two out of three letters, and their error rates were also lower. No differences between age groups were found on a range of other measures.

As in many other studies on language attrition a self-evaluation instrument was used to study reported change over time. The participants had to rate their proficiency on a number of can-do statements (conversing with friends on an everyday topic) for three moments in their lives: at the end of secondary education, at the peak of the command of the foreign language, and at present. Interestingly, there was a clear pattern for improvement after school and hardly any change between "peak" and "at present." This is in clear contrast with the finding in the language attrition literature of a general feeling of having lost the language over time.

These data also contrast with Bahrick's findings. Although the informants were at least the same age as Bahrick's informants (group 8), there are important differences in initial training level and in the amount of rehearsal. In Bahrick's study there were 33 subjects in group 8, most of them (27) with a training level of 2–4, that is, 2–4 years of high-school Spanish instruction or 2–4 one-semester college courses or combinations of high-school and college courses (one year high school = one term or semester in college). So, the initial training level of Bahrick's informants was not very high. The remaining six subjects had a training level comparable to that of the informants in the study by De Bot and Lintsen: 3–6 years of foreign-language instruction. Bahrick suggests that the amount of loss is independent of the initial level of training. The Dutch data could be explained by postulating that higher initial levels of training suffer less attrition, both in relative and in absolute terms.

Another difference is the amount of rehearsal. The informants in the Dutch study did not stop using the foreign language after the acquisition period. Significant differences between the (self-reported) knowledge of the foreign language at the end of secondary school and the peak of their command indicate that the informants had additional contact with the foreign language. Craik (1977, pp. 402–403) cites a number of studies to show that memory performance in the elderly tends to remain fairly stable for tasks that are ecologically valid, that is, tasks that test the retention of knowledge that has been acquired and maintained in meaningful activities. The use of foreign languages was a meaningful activity for the participants in the Dutch study, which may explain the retention found.

In the USA the focus has been on English and Spanish as the main languages of multilinguals. Rosselli et al. (1999) compared the performance of an English monolingual group and a Spanish–English bilingual group on a number of tests, including verbal fluency, sentence repetition, and picture description. In both groups, subjects' ages range from 55 to 84. The monolinguals showed higher scores on semantic verbal fluency ("name as many fruits and vegetables as you can in one minute") than the bilinguals, while the bilinguals had a higher number of connected words in spontaneous speech. For the bilingual subjects higher numbers of words in the English picture description test were found. Since the groups were very small (7 and 8 subjects), no effects of age could be measured. Also, the range of the subjects' ages was large, making it difficult to consider such results as providing useful information about elderly in different age ranges.

In a follow-up study, Rosselli et al. (2000) looked at verbal fluency and sentence repetition in a group of English–Spanish bilinguals and monolingual controls for the two languages. The mean age of the group was 61.8. Overall, bilinguals showed lower scores in the two languages than monolinguals. Only for the semantic verbal fluency an effect of age of acquisition was found: early bilinguals had a score similar to that of the monolinguals, while the late bilinguals had a lower score. A much larger study was done by Acevedo et al. (2000) on verbal fluency norms in Spanish and English speakers over 50 years of age. The results show that age, education, and gender are the most important factors predicting scores for both groups regardless of primary language.

So far, the effects of structural and conceptual differences between languages have not received much attention in research. Kempler, Almor, and MacDonald (1998) compared performance on a semantic verbal fluency task in a group of elderly subjects including Chinese, Hispanic, and Vietnamese immigrants as well as white and Afro-American English speakers. In this study, there were differences for age and education, but here we want to focus on the differences between ethnic groups. Language differences appear to play a major role: the Vietnamese subjects produced many more animal names than the Spanish subjects. This is attributed to the fact that in Vietnamese, animal names are short (mostly one syllable) while in Spanish animal names are longer, which points to one of the problems in comparing data between languages: the same test may lead to different scores within the same individual because of differences between the linguistic systems.

Another aspect of language proficiency that has recently attracted researchers' attention is the so-called tip-of-the-tongue (TOT) phenomenon—the inability to find the word form for a word one knows. TOTs are typically elicited by giving a definition (someone who collects stamps) for the word to be given (philatelist). Gollan and Brown (2006) present an overview of research on TOTs in bilingualism and aging. They found opposite trends for the two groups: increased age seems to lead to more TOTs for difficult but not for easy targets, while bilinguals show more TOTs for easy targets than monolinguals but fewer for difficult targets. One of the problems with studying TOTs in bilinguals is that speakers in this group generally have smaller lexicons for a specific language than monolingual speakers of that language, and so they may have fewer TOTs because they simply do not know the word required. Gollan and Brown suggest a two-step approach to TOTs to deal with this type of problem in studying lexical access through the study of TOTs. The most widely accepted explanation for an increase in TOTs with aging is that the connections between elements in the lexicon decrease in strength, probably caused by a reduction in the use of those words due to a change in social settings.

All in all, the research available does not seem to support the idea of second-language attrition with aging, though it should be kept in mind that the research that has been done was not set up to test the specific predictions of this theory and that the empirical evidence so far is very limited.

## IV. MULTILINGUALISM AND DEMENTIA

Again, the number of studies on multilingualism and dementia is very small, and most of them are concerned with variants of the verbal fluency task and various types of code switching (CS). Also various batteries for measuring aphasia, such as Paradis's Bilingual Aphasia Test (BAT) (Paradis & Libben, 1987), have been used to test multilingual performance in dementia. While most of the patients discussed show signs of Alzheimer's disease, dementia is used here as an overall term for cognitive decline.

De Picciotto and Friedland (2001) investigated verbal fluency abilities in healthy and demented English–Afrikaans bilinguals. In contrast to most research on verbal fluency and aging, no effect of aging was found for the healthy bilinguals when they were tested in their bilingual mode, that is, when they were allowed to use both languages. Pattern of use of the languages had no effect on the fluency data.

Until the mid-1980s the trend was to discuss language problems in bilinguals within the bilingual aphasia framework (e.g., Albert & Obler, 1978, who briefly refer to two cases of involuntary CS in patients with senile dementia). Some researchers have studied bilingualism in the elderly from an aphasia perspective and have defined the patterns of language decline along the line of aphasia qualifications. Meguro, Senaha, and Caramelli (2003) studied a group of Japanese/Portuguese patients with dementia. Three of their patients were classified as anomic in both languages, while a fourth was classified as anomic in Portuguese and Wernicke in Japanese. In particular this last finding supports the idea that bilingual patients should be tested in all their languages to see what is still there and can be used for diagnosis and treatment.

More recently, language and dementia has developed as a separate subfield in language pathology. The literature on CS and dementia is discussed by Friedland and Miller (1999). The research focuses on two main issues: language choice and language separation. The distinction between these two issues is not always properly made, and they may show overlap; in cases of CS it is not always exactly clear what causes the switch in a conversation. There is anecdotal evidence suggesting a higher incidence of CS in dementia patients, but the research done is not in all aspects convincing. Levels of proficiency of the patients and information on switching behavior before the onset of cognitive decline are, more often than not, absent as is information on patterns of CS in the community the patients come from. Friedland and Miller make a plea for using conversational analysis as the better approach, because it is better suited to defining to what extent CS is or is not appropriate in a given situation. At the same time they have to admit that such analyses do not tell us much about the mechanisms that govern CS, and in particular with dementia patients guessing motives is hazardous. For instance, what may be perceived as inappropriate CS for healthy speakers may be perceived as very appropriate by patients, who may interpret the situation differently. This is supported by Hyltenstam's (1995) analysis of cases of CS reported in the literature. He also notes that, on the basis of the information given in the older (pre-1960s) cases in the literature, it is hard to say to what extent CS was a part of normal language use of the patients. His analysis shows that it is not always the case that speakers with dementia have more problems keeping their languages apart and choosing the right language in conversations: "In conclusion, it is probably safe to say that neither CS problems nor language choice problems are necessary consequences of all stages of deterioration in dementia for bilingual speakers" (Hyltenstam 1995, p. 318). On the basis of data from patients tested, Hyltenstam makes the suggestion that a second language learned in adulthood is "probably more affected by the limited processing capacity which is a typical effect of dementia, so that the patients would generally—partly or totally—revert to their first language when interacting with speakers of their first language, but not the other way around" (Hyltenstam, 1995, p. 319).

From the literature on the cases mentioned, the conclusion is that there does not seem to be a relation between severity of dementia and amount of CS, while there is an effect of level of proficiency in the sense that more CS takes place from the dominant language into the nondominant language than in the other direction (Ludérus, 1995). This has been found in many studies of healthy speakers too. It is obvious that the general finding of lack of control and disinhibition, which is normally seen as characteristic of dementia patients, does not simply lead to lack of control over languages in conversations. In the literature on dementia and bilingualism a number of cases have been described that show involuntary mixing of languages. In their overview, Albert and Obler (1978) refer to several historical cases, and De Vreese, Motta, and Toschi (1988 in Meguro et al., 2003) also describe a case of a multilingual who involuntary mixed English, French, and Italian. So, in more advanced stages of dementia a lack of control can lead to a mix of languages used involuntarily. Van de Ven (1987) describes a fascinating case of an 81-year-old multilingual who had a stroke leading to right hemisphere brain damage, and who, after the stroke, showed extensive language switching between Dutch, Italian, and English. Another interesting aspect of this case is that the patient never finished primary education and acquired all of his foreign languages working as an acrobat in a circus touring through various European countries, and that he was basically illiterate, which turned out to be a problem when administering the BAT. He was tested with parts of the BAT and showed a pattern of aphasia with serious production problems and word-finding problems in particular. His score on a mental status test suggests heavy cognitive decline. When tested in Dutch, some switching to Italian and English occurred. When tested in Italian, probably his best second language, he had serious problems adhering to that language, mixing in words and morphemes from Dutch all the time. His case is similar to one reported by Perecman (1984), which also showed patterns of CS due to both confusion about the language required in the testing setting, and an inability to keep the two languages apart. Analyses of her test sessions made it clear that the two testers, who were pretending to be monolingual speakers of the two languages tested, were constantly interacting with each other about what to do next, thus creating confusion about the language to be used. The translation behavior of the patient was at first interpreted as some sort of a compulsive drive to translate spontaneously. This was in fact adequate from the perspective of the patient: two languages were used, and thus it was better to repeat what was said in the other language.

As Kemper, Vandeputte, Rice, Cheung, and Gubarchuk (1995) and various other authors have argued, loss of control, particularly disinhibition, is among the more prominent characteristics of various forms of dementia. In the cases reported on by Van de Ven and Perecman, inability to block the inappropriate language is probably the best explanation for these findings. The problem with the case described by Van de Ven is that there is an interaction between the effects of general cognitive decline as a result of global brain degeneration, and the impact of the more local impact of the stroke. According to the spouse of Van de Ven's patient, the switching between languages only began after the stroke. This suggests a link between particular right hemisphere damage and decline of language control in CS, but in the rest of the bilingual aphasia there is only one other case of involuntary switching involving the right/nondominant hemisphere (Gloning & Gloning, 1965, case 4)

One of the few longitudinal studies on dementia in multilinguals was carried out by Ludérus (1995). She presents three cases of women who grew up in a German-speaking environment and moved to the Netherlands. In those patients there was CS from German, their dominant language, into Dutch, but far less in the other direction. Her patients were able to intentionally switch languages, for example, in quotations from the other language, so the switching mechanism as such was still there, but she also mentions that the language-choice problems may have been (partly) caused by confusion and inadequate interpretation of the conversational setting. Because the patients appear to be able to use both languages at other occasions, Ludérus (1995) concludes "that it is not a language separation problem that underlies the inappropriate (base-) language use, but instead a language choice problem" (p. 124).

Most studies looked at CS in natural settings. Hernandez and Kohnert (1999) report on an experimental study on CS; they compared a group of college-age bilinguals with a group of older bilinguals (mean age 70.8) in an experiment with one condition in which only one language was used, a second condition in which the participants were cued to use one or the other language in naming pictures, and a third condition in which they had to switch language every next item. In the first condition no differences between young and older participants were found, whereas the older group made significantly more errors and showed much longer latencies in the other two mixed conditions. This suggests an effect of problems of task set shifting with age. In other words, older participants have more problems switching tasks and tend to show interference from previous task settings.

## V. THE IMPACT OF BILINGUALISM ON COGNITIVE FUNCTIONING IN THE ELDERLY

The most influential work on bilingualism and aging in recent years has no doubt been done by Ellen Bialystok and her colleagues. In a number of articles they have reported on a series of studies on the relation between attentional control and bilingualism. Bialystok, Craik, Klein, and Viswanathan (2004) report on a study in which they looked at possible advantages of lifelong bilingualism in aging. Building on earlier work showing that bilingual children perform better on various cognitively demanding tasks, they tested the hypothesis that such advantages could continue to play a role in adulthood and even help to counter cognitive decline. Their argument is basically this: bilinguals who use more than one language on a daily basis have to keep their languages apart all the time. It is generally accepted now that bilinguals cannot simply switch off languages in processing: while speaking one language, the other languages are processed as well, so there is competition between languages within the language production system (Francis, 1999; Hermans, Bongaerts, de Bot, & Schreuder, 1998). The inhibitory control mechanisms of bilinguals have to be well developed, which also has an effect on other cognitive tasks. In the experiments reported by Bialystok et al. (2004) younger (mean age = 40) and older (mean age = 71) monolingual and bilingual (English–Tamil) groups had to perform a nonlinguistic task requiring speeded reactions to congruent and incongruent information. The data show a clear effect of bilingualism in both age groups: they responded more rapidly to conditions that placed greater demands on working memory. In the older group the advantage of bilingualism was even greater than in the younger group. These findings suggest that the lifelong training of keeping languages apart has a positive effect on cognitive functioning not just for languages but also more generally.

A further extension of this research concerns the experiments reported on in Bialystok, Craik, and Ryan (2006). In the experiments, executive control is studied using a so-called anti-saccadic task. In this task the participants have to focus on a point on a screen. Then some distracting information is presented on the left or the right of the focal point and the task is NOT to look at this information, which would be a natural reaction, but to turn the gaze in the opposite direction. The experiment is further complicated by a manipulation in which in one condition the participants are to react, while in the other condition they are instructed not to react at all.

In the first experiment, in which eye movements were measured, older participants were slower and made more errors on the anti-saccadic trials than the younger participants, and no differences were found between the monolingual and the bilingual group. In the second experiment the same procedure was used, but this time the reaction to the presentation of the visual information was measured using key presses rather than eye movements. For the anti-saccadic items the participants had to push the left-side key when the information was presented on the right of the focal point, and the other way around. In this experiment a clear age effect was found, along with an effect of bilingualism. In the control conditions there were no differences between language groups, but in the other conditions the slowing down with age in the latencies was clearly less for the bilinguals than for the monolinguals, supporting the earlier findings of an advantage of bilinguals in executive control.

The difference between the two conditions, eye movements versus key strokes, sheds some light on the locus of the bilingualism effect. Eye movements are faster and more automatic and therefore less amenable to higher-level cognitive control. So the "training effect" in bilinguals may only manifest itself in tasks that take longer and are less automatized. It may also be that for the key stroke condition there is at least some symbolic mapping between stimulus and response, and it may therefore be the case that this translation process is more advanced in bilinguals. Bialystok et al. (2006) also suggest that "lifelong practice may increase the efficiency of the ventrolateral prefrontal cortex" (p. 1352), and that enhanced functioning of Broca's area may play a role, but why this should be and what causes it to happen is not yet clear.

While these experiments were done with participants without any signs of dementia, the line of argumentation is extended to dementia in the study reported in Bialystok, Craik, and Freedman (2007). In this study they tested 288 patients with cognitive complaints; 184 of these were diagnosed with dementia and half of this group was bilingual with a range of mother tongues. On the basis of Mini Mental State Examination (MMSE) data, it was found that the bilingual group showed symptoms of dementia about four years later than a monolingual control group. The data were controlled for level of education and level of occupation before onset. Remarkably, the average level of education of the bilingual group was significantly lower than that of the monolingual group, and level of education has been reported as one of the main factors explaining the onset and development of dementia. The authors assume that the data on educational level reflect opportunity and access to education rather than ability, because many of the patients came from Europe and their lives had been disrupted by World War II. Once the symptoms appeared, the rate of decline was the same for monolinguals and bilinguals.

For their explanation of the difference in onset, the authors use Valenzuela and Sachdev's (2006) distinction between "neurological brain reserve" and "behavioral brain reserve." The former refers to the effect of brain volume on cognitive decline: "peak brain volume can ameliorate the effects of brain pathology on cognitive performance and signs of dementia" (Bialystok et al., 2007, p. 459). The other type refers to the kind of sustained complex cognitive activities over the life span that seem to provide protection against dementia. Obviously, bilingualism is part of the latter type and in this sense contributes to cognitive reserve due to continued training of executive control.

The findings of Bialystok and her colleagues are based on well-designed and controlled experiments with different groups of bilinguals, many of them in fact multilinguals. The studies mentioned lead to a number of stimulating questions that are particularly relevant in an increasingly multilingual world. The first is a question about default settings. We assume that bilinguals have something "special," because in this line of thinking they have to switch tasks and attention much more than "normal" monolinguals. Given that the majority of the world's population is bilingual and probably has been so for ages, if we assume that the use of different styles and registers requires similar control mechanisms, we may wonder whether it is not the earlier onset of dementia in monolinguals that is the deviant case, rather than the later onset in the bilinguals. It could well be argued that the brain has developed primarily to process more than one language. The use of only one language may then lead to atrophy of a part of the brain that is "available" for the processing of multiple languages (see De Bot, 2006, for this argument based on synaptic pruning).

Another pertinent question is what type of bilingualism and how much bilingual use is needed for the protective effect to materialize. In the experiments a very high level of bilingualism was reportedly used: "The criterion for bilingualism was that patients had spent the majority of their lives, at least from early childhood, regularly using at least two languages" (Bialystok et al., 2007, p. 460). There are very few studies that relate to level of bilingualism and dementia. In a study conducted in Melbourne, Australia, LoGuidice, Hassett, Cook, Flicker, and Ames (2001) report on the incidence of dementia in a sample of 556 patients in a memory clinic. One hundred and forty eight of them were of a non-English-speaking background, mostly Italian. Although there was no extensive information about their level of proficiency of English before onset, this group showed the characteristic pattern of migrants from that generation. They came with little education and largely stayed within the ethnic community with few contacts outside of it, and accordingly had low levels of proficiency in the second language. The analyses in the LoGuidice et al. study show that those patients showing decline were less educated, younger, less likely to live alone, and had a higher incidence of depression. Also, patients from this group showed more advanced symptoms of dementia when they reported to the hospital than the English-speaking background group (which is not by definition monolingual). So, while this study suggests that the bilingual group is not better off than the monolingual group, several factors, such as education and professional activity, may have played a more prominent role. Zeid, Allain, and Pinon (2004) also present Stroop test data that are relevant for this discussion. They tested two groups of balanced and nonbalanced French–Arabic bilinguals: a younger group (mean age 30.7) and an older group (mean age 71.3). The data show that the nonbalanced bilinguals were slower and made more errors in their weaker language and that the older group was slower and less accurate generally. In contrast, the older balanced bilinguals had lower error rates and shorter latencies. This suggests that level of proficiency has an impact on attentional control with aging. Unfortunately, there were no monolingual control groups in this study, so it does not provide information on the effects of lower levels of proficiency on the enhancement of attentional control in aging.

So, the question remains what type of bilingualism will lead to the positive effects mentioned in the studies by Bialystok and colleagues. Is an early onset but limited use later on enough, with the attentional control mechanisms set in motion in early childhood, or is it indeed the continued use and inhibitory exercise that is the crucial issue? What about foreign languages learned at school or later and used frequently but not daily? The real question here is: how little is enough to get the protection against early onset of dementia? How about dialect speakers, who also have to select languages depending on the setting? What is the effect of CS? The logic of the argument would be that extensive CS lowers the effect of bilingualism, because the inhibitory activity in such settings is much more limited. Finally, how linguistic is this cause-and-effect relation: what if some one had to switch tasks constantly and select and inhibit different types of competing information, as in driving a bus, or operating the controls of an energy plant; is that type of attentional control effective too? As Bialystok has shown in recent years that the line of research she has introduced can and should be extended to answer this type of question, because if bilingualism has indeed such a profound effect on cognitive decline, the argument of language learning becomes even more compelling than it already is.

## VI. CONCLUDING REMARKS

As indicated in the introduction, most countries in the world will be faced with a growth of the elderly population and with advantages and disadvantages that come with that. Decline in language skills may happen to a part of the older population, not necessarily to all. As we have indicated, language development should be seen as a dynamic process that is only partly predictable. Development depends on many interacting resources that change with age, not only in the biological sense but also in the social and psychological sense. Physical changes leading to a decline of memory and sensory acuity, reduced mobility, and increased health risks interact with social changes such as a reshuffling of the social network due to retirement or a move to residential homes. Also, the physical changes lead to people being seen and treated as old and therefore dependent and fragile, even when this may not be the case at all. Psychological changes have to do with self-perceptions and other perceptions, a changing view on life, and so on. In this process, language plays a central role as the main mediational tool in communication and self-regulation.

Language as part of the cognitive system is in itself a dynamic system that combines many different subsystems, many of which are impacted by the changes with age. Some aspects of language production and perception will show decline, while other aspects such as narrative skills will improve with age. So far, multilingualism seems to be an asset in aging rather than a problem. The groundbreaking work by Ellen Bialystok and her colleagues on the cognitive advantages of bilingualism over the life span is highly relevant here, both for its outcomes and for the fascinating new directions in research it suggests. Research on language and aging is likely to become an important part of the language sciences in the future, not only because of the interest in decline but probably more importantly for the role language or rather languages are likely to play in maintaining life quality and social bounds.

One area in which basically no research has been done is the learning or relearning of foreign languages in the elderly. While there seems to be a relation between the ability to store information in long-term memory and aging, it does not necessarily mean that the ability to learn or refresh another language is beyond the reach of elderly people. The current problems of elderly migrants grappling with the language of the immigration country should not be seen as a sign of the inability of elderly people to learn a second language. In that particular setting the resources to learn that new language are simply lacking.

## ACKNOWLEDGMENT

The author is indebted to Sybrine Bultena for her help in finalizing the manuscript and the editors for helpful comments and suggestions.

## REFERENCES

Acevedo, A., Loewenstein, D., Barker, W., Harwood, D., Luis, G., Bravo, M., et al. (2000). Category fluency test: Normative data for English- and Spanish-speaking elderly. *Journal of the International Neuropsychological Society*, 6, 760–769.

Albert, M., & Obler, L. (1978). *The bilingual brain*. New York: Academic Press.

Bahrick, H. (1984). Fifty years of second language attrition: Implications for programmatic research. *Modern Language Journal*, 68, 105–118.

Barresi, B., Obler, K. L., Au, R., & Albert, M. (1999). Language-related factors influencing naming in adulthood. In H. Hamilton (Ed.), *Language and communication in old age: Multidisciplinary perspectives* (pp. 77–90). New York: Garland.

Bhatia, T., & Ritchie, W. (2004). *Handbook of bilingualism*. Oxford, UK: Blackwell.

Bialystok, E., Craik, F., & Freedman, M. (2007). Bilingualism as a protection against the onset of symptoms of dementia. *Neuropsychologia, 45*, 459–464.

Bialystok, E., Craik, F., & Ryan, J. (2006). Executive control in a modified antisaccade task: Effects of aging and bilingualism. *Journal of Experimental Psychology: Language, Memory and Cognition, 32*, 1341–1354.

Bialystok, E., Craik, I. M., Klein, R., & Viswanathan, M. (2004). Bilingualism, aging, and cognitive control: Evidence from the Simon Task. *Psychology and Aging, 19*, 290–303.

Clyne, M. (1977). Bilingualism in the elderly. *Talanya, 4*, 45–65.

Clyne, M. (1982). *Multilingual Australia: Resources, needs, policies.* Melbourne: River Seine Publishers.

Craik, F. (1977). Age differences in human memory. In J. Birren & K. W. Schaie (Eds.), *Handbook of the psychology of aging* (pp. 384–420). New York: Van Nostrand Reinhold.

De Bot, K. (2006). The plastic bilingual brain: Synaptic pruning or growth? Commentary on Green et al. In M. Gullberg & P. Indefrey (Eds.), *The cognitive neuroscience of second language acquisition* (pp. 127–132). Malden: Blackwell.

De Bot, K., & Lintsen, T. (1986). Foreign-language proficiency in the elderly. In B. Weltens, K. De Bot, & T. van Els (Eds.), *Language attrition in progress* (pp. 131–141). Dordrecht: Foris Publications.

De Bot, K., Lowie, W., & Verspoor, M. (2005). *Second language acquisition, an advanced resource book.* London: Routledge.

De Bot, K., & Makoni, S. (2005). *Language and aging in multilingual societies: A dynamic approach.* Clevedon: Multilingual Matters.

De Bot, K., & Weltens, B. (1995). Foreign language attrition. *Annual Review of Applied Linguistics, 15*, 151–166.

De Picciotto, J., & Friedland, D. (2001). Verbal fluency in elderly bilingual speakers: Normative data and preliminary applications to Alzheimer's disease. *Folia Phoniatrica et Logopaedica, 53*, 145–152.

De Vreese, L., Motta, M., & Toschi, A. (1988). Compulsive and paradoxical translation behavior in a case of presenile dementia of the Alzheimer type. *Journal of Neurolinguistics, 3*, 233–259.

Francis, W. S. (1999). Cognitive integration of language and memory in bilinguals: Semantic representation. *Psychological Bulletin, 125*, 193–222.

Friedland, D., & Miller, N. (1999). Language mixing in bilingual speakers with Alzheimer's dementia: A conversation analysis approach. *Aphasiology, 13*, 427–444.

Gloning, I., & Gloning, K. (1965). Aphasien bei Polyglotten. Beitrag zur Dynamik des Sprachabbaus sowie zur Lokalisationsfrage dieser Störungen. *Wiener Zeitschrift für Nervenheilkunde, 22*, 362–397.

Gollan, T., & Brown, A. (2006). From tip-of-the-tongue (TOT) data to theoretical implications in two steps: When more TOTs mean better retrieval. *Journal of Experimental Psychology: General, 135*, 462–483.

Hermans, D., Bongaerts, T., de Bot, K., & Schreuder, R. (1998). Producing words in a foreign language: Can speakers prevent interference from their first language. *Bilingualism: Language and Cognition, 1*, 213–229.

Hernandez, A., & Kohnert, K. (1999). Aging and language switching in bilinguals. *Aging, Neuropsychology, and Cognition, 6*, 69–83.

Hyltenstam, K. (1995). The code-switching behavior of adults with language disorders–with special reference to aphasia and dementia. In L. Milroy & P. Muysken (Eds.), *One speaker, two languages: Cross-disciplinary perspectives on code-switching* (pp. 302–343). Cambridge: Cambridge University Press.

Kemper, S., Vandeputte, D., Rice, K., Cheung, H., & Gubarchuk, J. (1995). Speech adjustments to aging during a referential communication task. *Journal of Language and Social Psychology*, *14*, 40–59.

Kempler, D., Almor, A., & MacDonald, M. C. (1998). Teasing apart the contribution of memory and language impairments in Alzheimer's disease: An online study of sentence comprehension. *American Journal of Speech-Language Pathology*, *7*, 61–67.

Larsen-Freeman, D. (2002). Language acquisition and language use from a chaos/complexity theory perspective. In C. Kramsch (Ed.), *Language acquisition and language socialization* (pp. 33–46). London: Continuum.

Larsen-Freeman, D., & Cameron, L. (2008). *Complex systems and applied linguistics*. Oxford: Oxford University Press.

LoGuidice, D., Hassett, A., Cook, R., Flicker, L., & Ames, D. (2001). Equity of access to a memory clinic in Melbourne? Non-English speaking background attenders are more severely demented and have increased rates of psychiatric disorders. *International Journal of Geriatric Psychiatry*, *16*, 327–334.

Ludérus, S. (1995). *Language choice and language separation in bilingual Alzheimer patients*. University of Amsterdam. Unpublished manuscript.

Meguro, K., Senaha, M., & Caramelli, P. (2003). Language deterioration in four Japanese–Portuguese bilingual patients with Alzheimer's disease: A trans-cultural study of Japanese elderly immigrants in Brazil. *Psychogeriatrics*, *3*, 63–68.

Miyake, A., & Friedman, N. (1999). Individual differences in second language proficiency: Working memory as language aptitude. In A. Healy & L. Bourne (Eds.), *Foreign language learning: Psycholinguistic experiments on training and retention* (pp. 339–362). Mahwah, NJ: Lawrence Erlbaum.

Neisser, U. (1984). Interpreting Harry Bahrick's discovery: What confers immunity against forgetting? *Journal of Experimental Psychology: General*, *113*, 32–35.

Paradis, M., & Libben, G. (1987). *The assessment of bilingual aphasia*. Hillsdale, NJ: Erlbaum.

Perecman, E. (1984). Spontaneous translation and language mixing in a polyglot aphasic. *Brain and Language*, *23*, 43–63.

Rosselli, A., Ardila, A., Araujo, K., Weekes, V. A., Caracciolo, V., Padilla, M., & Ostrosky-Solí, F. (2000). Verbal fluency and repetition skills in healthy older Spanish–English bilinguals. *Applied Neuropsychology*, *7*, 17–24.

Rosselli, M., Ardila, A., Araujo, , Weekes, V. A., Volk, L., & Caracciolo, V. (1999). The aging of language in Spanish–English bilinguals. *Archives of Clinical Neuropsychology*, *14*, 63–64.

Ryan, E., Hamilton, J., & See, S. (1994). Patronizing the old: How do younger and older adults respond to baby talk in the nursing home. *International Journal of Aging and Human Development*, *39*, 21–32.

Schmid, M., & Köpke, B. (2004). *First language attrition*. Amsterdam: John Benjamins.

UN Department of Economic and Social affairs: Population division. (2001). *World population ageing 1950–2050*. New York: United Nations.

Valenzuela, M., & Sachdev, P. (2006). Brain reserve and dementia: A systematic approach. *Psychological Medicine*, *36*, 441–454.

Van de Ven, H. (1987). *'Ha you capito?' Bilingual aphasia and code-switching*. Unpublished manuscript, University of Nijmegen.

Van Dijk, M., & van Geert, P. (2005). Disentangling behavior in early child development: Interpretability of early child language and the problem of filler syllables and growing utterance length. *Infant Behavior and Development, 28*, 99–117.

Weltens, B. (1989). *The attrition of French as a foreign language*. Dordrecht: Foris Publications.

Zeid, K., Allain, P., & Pinon, K. (2004). Bilingualism and adult differences in inhibitory mechanisms: Evidence from a bilingual stroop task. *Brain and Cognition, 54*, 254–256.

# MODALITY AND THE CONTRIBUTION OF THE ENVIRONMENT

## INTRODUCTION TO PART V

Part V contains five chapters about the contribution of the environment to the process and consequences of SLA and includes a discussion of the special position of the deaf and the input available to them as they acquire a second language—in the usual case, input from a spoken language. Finally, the Internet and other forms of electronic communication provide yet one more context for SLA and for related research, and this part of the volume includes a chapter on this topic.

In chapter 19 ("Input and Second Language Processing"), Kira Gor and Michael Long provide a review of research on the linguistic input to the learner and how the learner processes it as he/she acquires the second language. The authors establish the setting for their overview of recent work by giving historical background up to and including Long's 1996 exposition of his Interaction Hypothesis and the role of recasts in SLA in the first edition of the present volume. They then address the role of frequency of occurrence of forms in the input; in particular, they discuss the occurrence of inflectional forms in the input in two quite different cases—in English (a language with limited inflections) and Russian (a richly inflected language). On the basis of the results, they conclude that frequency plays a central role in natural acquisition with high-frequency forms predominating in the determination of what forms are acquired, but that, in classroom instruction, high-frequency forms do not predominate, since the learner has greater exposure to low-frequency forms than the acquirer in a natural setting.

Chapter 20 ("Second Language Acquisition in the Instructional Environment") by Teresa Pica provides an overview of research on classroom SLA. Pica begins by giving the reader some historical background. She then looks at modified input of various kinds as a starting point for her treatment of more recent work and proceeds to treatments of recasts, form-focused and processing instruction, as well as learner output and its instructional effects. After a discussion of teachability and readiness, she devotes considerable discussion to instructional tasks of several kinds, not only as instructional tools but as opportunities for classroom research as well.

Of course, SLA occurs outside the classroom as well, and chapter 21 ("Untutored Second Language Acquisition") by Wolfgang Klein and Christine Dimroth provides a treatment of the forms of language that result from this instance of SLA. More specifically, they describe "the Basic Variety," a language structure that they abstract from the learner varieties found in many cases of informal SLA.

Language acquisition in the deaf provides a case that resembles SLA in crucial respects, no matter whether it is acquisition of a first language or of a second— specifically, it typically occurs at a more advanced age than is normal for first language acquisition. Gerald Berent's chapter 22 ("The Interlanguage Development of Deaf and Hearing Learners of L2 English: Parallelism via Minimalism") summarizes research on the acquisition of a spoken language—English—by the deaf and interprets it in terms of the Minimalist Program. Berent observes that, because the deaf (unlike ordinary second language learners) lack a first spoken language, the variety that results from their acquisition of English provides direct access to the properties of universal grammar that are retained at more advanced stages of maturation, without the influence of transfer.

The rapid development of electronic communication has made it possible not only to extend SLA itself to new contexts, but also to expand the opportunities for SLA research. Chapter 23 ("Second Language Acquisition: Research and Application in the Information Age") by Tej K. Bhatia and William C. Ritchie summarizes current thinking in both computer-assisted language learning and research on SLA using the computer as an instrument for conducting such research.

CHAPTER 19

# INPUT AND SECOND LANGUAGE PROCESSING

Kira Gor and Michael H. Long

## I. FOREIGNER TALK, NEGOTIATION FOR MEANING, AND INPUT AS POSITIVE AND NEGATIVE EVIDENCE

From roughly 1970 to 1990, research on the linguistic environment for second language acquisition (SLA) was devoted primarily to descriptive studies of native speaker (NS) speech modifications to nonnative speakers (NNSs) in naturalistic, classroom, and laboratory settings during a process known as *negotiation for meaning*. The resulting input, together with any written texts that learners encounter, comprises *positive evidence*, samples of what is grammatical and/or acceptable in the target language, and the data from which learners must induce the rules of the new grammar. Under certain conditions, the environment also becomes a source of *negative evidence*, direct or indirect information about what is ungrammatical and/or unacceptable. Negative evidence may be explicit, for example, a grammatical explanation or overt, on-record error correction, or implicit, for example, communication breakdowns perceived as such by the learner, absence of items in the input, or corrective recasts (see below).

Findings on speech modifications to NNSs and the resulting input were broadly consistent across settings and, for the most part, echoed those on caretaker speech to young children. Adaptations to L2 acquirers, for example, shorter utterance length, a greater here-and-now orientation, and a preference for yes–no questions over wh-questions, were shown to be predominantly quantitative, resulting in a recognizably different, but grammatically well-formed, "foreigner register" (Arthur, Weiner, Culver, Young, & Thomas, 1980). Qualitative, or categorical, changes resulting in *un*grammatical

*The New Handbook of Second Language Acquisition*

speech of the kind usually referred to, following Ferguson (1975), as "foreigner talk" were rarely observed. (For review, see Gass, 1997, 2003; Long, 1996a).

## II. INPUT AND COMPREHENSION: SIMPLIFICATION AND ELABORATION

During *negotiation for meaning*, NSs were shown to exploit an extensive repertoire of *strategies* to avoid communication breakdowns and *tactics* to repair trouble when breakdowns occurred (Long, 1983a, 1983b). Such modifications in face-to-face communication mostly affect the *interactional structure of conversation*. Rather than linguistic *simplification*, with the exception of reduced mean length of utterance, comprehensibility is achieved primarily through *elaboration*, that is, use of a variety of modifications mostly at the discourse level. Some changes, for example, clearer articulation, fewer sandhi processes, and canonical word order, result in greater *regularity* and predictability. Modifications also provide increased *redundancy*. Devices employed to this end include slower rate of delivery, suppliance of contextually redundant optional constituents where NSs delete them (e.g., subject pronouns in pro-drop languages, and overt markers of grammatical and semantic relations, such as Japanese particles indicating topic, subject, object, directionals, and locatives) useful for the nonnative listener/reader, but which would be marked and considered inefficient communication among natives. Other examples resulting in useful redundancy are full NPs in place of anaphoric referents, exact and semantic repetition, synonyms and lexical switches, intra- and intersentential markers (*next*, *however*, *therefore*, *as a result*, etc.) of conceptual relationships within and across clauses, shifts from subject-predicate to topic-comment constructions, acceptance by NSs of unintentional topic switches by NNSs, parallelism between order of occurrence and order of mention, comprehension checks, clarification requests, confirmation checks, and a variety of subtle prosodic and other phonological cues, including word stress and pauses before and/or after key meaning-bearing lexical items.

Changes also increase the *saliency* of key information in messages. For example, a slower rate of delivery, left dislocation, stress, and one-beat pauses before and/or after can highlight key information-bearing words, such as "like" in (1):

(1) Did you (*pause*) *like* San Diego? . . . San Diego (*pause*) did you like it?

as can a more complex discourse-level modification, decomposition (Long, 1983a, 1996a). Interactional changes sometimes have knock-on effects on the input, for example, the shift from a subject-predicate construction to an equivalent topic-comment construction (Givon's presyntactic mode) producing an example of left dislocation in (1), above, and higher frequencies of canonical word order and yes–no questions. There is often no such impact, however. For instance, exact repetition, a frequently used device, again provides the same, not different, input.

While the research on NS–NNS conversation showed real-world NS modifications to L2 learners typically to be characterized by elaboration, commercially published language teaching materials continue to utilize linguistic simplification as the primary modification strategy. Compared with baseline NS–NS communication, simplified speech or written texts employ shorter; syntactically or propositionally less complex sentences, with little subordination or embedding; a restricted range of verb tenses; and avoidance of idiomatic usage and low-frequency vocabulary items.[1] The "graded readers," textbook dialogs, and pedagogic materials for teaching listening comprehension that result are usually more comprehensible to NNSs, but often constitute stilted, fragmented, unnatural, and psycholinguistically inappropriate target-language samples reminiscent of those found in many basal readers (Long, 1996b). Elaborated input, in contrast, retains much of the linguistic complexity and naturalness of native–native communication and constitutes richer input for acquisition.

Several experimental and quasi-experimental studies have demonstrated that simplification, elaboration, and a combination thereof all improve the *comprehensibility* of spoken and written input for language learners, as well as their perceived comprehensibility by language learners (see, e.g., Chaudron, 1983; Kim, 2003; Long, 1985; Oh, 2001; Yano, Long, & Ross, 1994). However, since simplification achieves that effect largely by removing from the input forms and structures as yet unknown to the NNS, the increased comprehensibility comes at a price: exposure to L2 samples largely bled of the very items to which learners must be exposed if they are to progress. Language development will be possible only if meaningful exposure is available to *un*known forms. For language acquisition, as opposed to pure comprehension of specific spoken or written texts, therefore, elaboration is more useful, and pedagogic materials produced specifically for some high-stakes instructional programs in the past few years have begun to reflect that realization (see, e.g., Chaudron et al., 2005). Simplification also tends to bleed input of semantic content, whereas elaboration can preserve all the information in a spoken or written text originally intended for NSs (Long & Ross, 1993). Along with improved comprehensibility, this is another potentially critical advantage. In educational settings, for example, simplification of language in teacher speech, written texts, homework assignments, and so on simultaneously tends to dilute curriculum content. The cumulative effect over years of instruction can have dire consequences for the educational achievement of nonnative children and adults educated through the medium of a second language.

## III. INPUT AND ACQUISITION: THE INTERACTION HYPOTHESIS

What has proven harder to demonstrate empirically has been a direct causal relationship between various characteristics of the linguistic environment and SLA. Krashen's Input Hypothesis (Krashen, 1985, and elsewhere) holds that adult SLA is fundamentally the same as first language acquisition by children—a subconscious process—incidental, while doing something else, and implicit, involving abstraction of patterns from input.

---

[1]The somewhat different results obtained by Crossley, McCarthy, Louwerse, and McNamara (2007) are due to their having compared simplified texts with authentic texts *simple enough to have been included in beginning level ESL texts*. The discussion here, in contrast, involves comparisons of simplified versions of original spoken and written NS–NS communications on the same topics that would be far too complex linguistically to include in anything but materials for learners already possessing advanced L2 proficiency, but communications, nevertheless, with which the learners in question will eventually have to grapple. For discussion, see Long (1996b). Application of Crossley et al.'s sophisticated computational analysis, using Coh-Metrix, of various dimensions of text cohesion to such corpora could make a very valuable contribution.

It requires only two things: comprehensible input samples (positive evidence) containing linguistic structures "one step ahead" of a learner's current developmental stage and a positive affective profile (a "low affective filter") on the learner's part that makes him or her receptive to that input. As noted elsewhere, however, the claim is difficult to sustain, for a number of reasons. For instance, documentation abounds of learners who have failed to achieve grammatical accuracy even after years of exposure under apparently favorable conditions, according to the Input Hypothesis, from French immersion students in Canada (Swain, 1991) to Italian waiters in Scotland (Pavesi, 1986), or who have achieved very little at all, for example, "Wes" (Schmidt, 1983). Also, some L2 rules cannot logically be learned by exposure to positive evidence alone because there simply is no positive evidence for them. Constraint on adverb placement between subject and direct object in English (*I drink every day coffee*) for NSs of languages like French that allow such placement (White, 1991) is one of many such examples, often the result of (L1) superset—(L2) subset relationships. Following Schmidt (1990, and elsewhere), many have argued that attention to form is required for acquisition and that rules and constraints of the French adverb-placement type can be acquired only if their operation is "noticed," either unaided, which is unlikely, or because brought to learners' attention by one or more forms of negative evidence.

While a facilitating effect for some kinds of input modification is a reasonable expectation, it is by no means given. Hatch (1978) suggested that rather than grammatical knowledge developing in order to be put to use in conversations at some later date (as assumed by most language teaching syllabi and "methods"), "language learning evolves out of learning how to carry on conversations" (1978, p. 404). She cautioned, however (Hatch, 1983), that some aspects of conversation might actually inhibit learning. For example, "(M)istakes in the marking of verbs ... would not be caught by when? questions. Such question corrections would more likely elicit a time adverb rather than a verb correction for morphology" (Hatch, 1983, p. 157).

A pioneering investigation of these issues was conducted by Sato (1986, 1988, 1990) as part of a larger longitudinal study of naturalistic L2 acquisition motivated by Givon's claims concerning the shift from presyntactic to grammaticized speech in language change (e.g., Givon, 1979). In addition to a series of laboratory-type elicitation tasks focusing on pronunciation and syllable-structure issues, Sato's data consisted of spontaneous conversations between NSs and two Vietnamese **children who are** brothers, Than and Tai, whose early naturalistic English development she observed each week for a year. In the area of emergent syntax, Sato found some examples comparable to those in L1 acquisition of collaborative complex propositions across utterances and speakers, as with the precursors to adverbial and relative clauses in (2) and (3):

(2)   Than: vitnam dei (bli) ka :
      '[In] Vietnam they (play) cards'

                              NS: They what?

      Than: plei ka :
      'play cards'

                              NS: They play cards?

      Than: yae wen wen krismes
      'Yeah, when [it's] Christmas

                                          (Sato, 1988, p. 380)

(3)   Tai: hi lok am am-
      'He's looking, urn'

                                        Than: ast masn
                                        'At [the] man

      Tai: ast masn hi hi smowkig
      'At the man [who is] smoking'

                                                    (Sato, 1988, p. 380)

Such cases were rare during the first year, however, perhaps due to the limited overall proficiency of the children, who were near beginners when the study began. When it came to inflectional morphology, Hatch's caution proved well founded. Sato showed how the brothers initially used conversational scaffolding, specifically their interlocutors' prior establishment of reference to a past event to compensate for their lack of overt inflectional past time marking. Even severe communication breakdowns failed to elicit learner attempts at the missing verbal morphology, as in (4):

(4)                                      NS: Oh, Mary said that you went to
                                            um—went to a game by the Fever?
      Tai: noy tan hi go yet
           no-Thanh-he-go-yet
                                        You didn't go yet? To the Fever?
      wat?
      What?
                                        Did you go to see the Fever play
                                        soccer?
      yes
      Yes
                                        When was that?
      nat nat nay
      not-not-now
                                        Oh. uh-later? Oh. I see. Who else is going?
      tan hi go in da pro
      Than-he-go-in-the [pro]

                                                    (Sato, 1986, p. 36)

Later, like adult learners of German (Meisel, 1987), the brothers moved to alternative surrogate systems of their own, such as the use of temporal adverbials (*Yesterday I go*) and order of mention, but neither boy progressed very far with past time inflectional morphology during the first year of the study.

In an explicit discussion of the issue, Sato (1986) proposed that conversation is *selectively facilitative* of grammatical development, depending on the structures involved. The beneficial effects of conversational scaffolding and situational knowledge on communication make overt past time marking on verbs expendable in most contexts, which may hinder acquisition by lessening the need to encode the function morphologically in speech. There is some limited evidence that conversation nourishes emergent L2 syntax, on the other hand (Sato, 1988), and most of the few attempts at complex syntactic constructions produced during the children's first year of English occurred in a conversational context. Studies of collaborative syntax across utterances and speakers in talk between NSs and adult beginners or more proficient learners remain serious lacunae in the L2 database.

Since Sato's work, studies that have sought evidence of a direct link between conversation and negotiation for meaning and acquisition have mostly been cross-sectional, conducted in the laboratory or classroom. Recent findings have been fairly consistent, generally supporting relationships embodied in an updated version of the Interaction Hypothesis (Long, 1981, 1983a, 1996a), which posited that

> environmental contributions to acquisition are mediated by selective attention and the learner's developing L2 processing capacity, and ... these resources are brought together most usefully, although not exclusively, during negotiation for meaning. Negative feedback obtained during negotiation work or elsewhere may be facilitative of L2 development, at least for vocabulary, morphology, and language-specific syntax, and essential for learning certain specifiable L1-L2 contrasts. (Long, 1996a, p. 414)

For example, in a study by Mackey (1999), students allowed to interact with NSs on a task-based activity improved more in their development of English question formation than students allowed to only observe the interactions and also performed better than others who received scripted premodified input on the same tasks, and the interactors maintained their advantage on delayed posttests. (For a sample of additional studies and discussion of the interactionist research agenda, see also Gass, 1997; Gass & Mackey, 2007; Mackey, 2007a, 2007b; Mackey & Gass, 2006; Pica, 1994, 1996).

Three statistical meta-analyses of interaction studies (Keck, Iberri-Shea, Tracy-Ventura, & Wa-Mbaleka, 2006; Mackey & Goo, 2007; Russell & Spada, 2006) have now reported significant positive effects on acquisition for interaction, in general, and corrective feedback, in particular. Extending findings of the two earlier surveys, Mackey and Goo (2007) concluded that while effects were larger for lexis than for grammar,

> Interaction plays a strong facilitative role in the learning of lexical and grammatical target items. The 28 interaction studies qualified for the present meta-analysis showed large mean effect sizes across immediate and delayed post-tests, providing evidence of short-term as well as longer-term effects on language acquisition. (Mackey & Goo, 2007, p. 405)

## IV. NEGATIVE FEEDBACK: RECASTS AND SLA

Contributing to the overall findings reported by Mackey and Goo were results from studies of one aspect of negotiation, in particular, negative feedback. Whereas most of the 1970s and 1980s work on the linguistic environment for SLA emphasized its role in providing the learner with *positive evidence* (models), more research since the early 1990s has attempted to ascertain the value of the *negative evidence* supplied, either directly or in the form of recasts, and the relative value of the two. One reason for the interest is that, if it works, recasting is a less intrusive procedure for delivering negative feedback to instructed learners (see Doughty & Williams, 1998, for a detailed review of other options) and can allow teachers and students to focus on nonlinguistic content (tasks, curricular subject matter, etc.) uninterrupted, while dealing with language problems incidentally.

*Corrective recasts* are defined as reformulations of all or part of a learner's immediately preceding utterance in which one or more non-target-like (lexical, grammatical, etc.) items are replaced by the corresponding target-language form(s) and where, throughout the exchange, the focus of both interlocutors is on meaning, not language as object. This is illustrated by the following excerpt from Sato's data, which contains two NS recasts (italicized), one of a learner utterance lacking in obligatory morphology and syntax for coding for negation and past time, and another of a lexical error:

(5)                                       NS: Oh, Mary said that you went to um—you went
                                               to a game by the Fever?
      Tai: nou tan hi go get
                                          NS: *You didn't go yet?* To the Fever?
      Tai: wat?
                                          NS: Did you go to see the Fever play soccer?
      Tai: Yes
                                          NS: When was that?
      Tai: nat nat nau
                                          NS: Oh uh, *later*? Oh I see. Who else is going?
                                                                          (Sato, 1986, p. 36)

Research on recasts has taken a variety of forms and been carried out in a variety of settings (for detailed reviews and discussion, see Doughty, 2001; Long, 1996a, 2007; Mackey & Goo, 2007; Nicholas, Lightbown, & Spada, 2001; Russell & Spada, 2006).

Recasts have been shown to be pervasive and usable by both children (Oliver, 1998) and adults (Ishida, 2004). Learners who are psycholinguistically ready to do so notice the linguistic information they contain (Mackey, 1999) and in some cases learn from it faster than they do from the same information contained in models (Long, Inagaki, & Ortega, 1998). Recasts can facilitate lexical, morphological, and syntactic development (Iwashita, 1999). Variable features of recasts can make them differentially effective in classrooms (Loewen & Philp, 2006). Importantly, they can produce pattern learning, that is, knowledge of rules, not just learning of the particular items that were recast (Choi, 2000).

These findings notwithstanding, recasts are no panacea. They often take the same form as teachers' (especially) and other NSs' repetitions of learners' correct utterances, resulting in potential functional ambiguity (confirmation of correctness or feedback on error) from the learners' perspective (Lyster, 1998). Also, while relatively little work has focused directly on these topics as yet, there is some suggestive evidence that recasts work better with lexical targets than with morphological or syntactic ones (Mackey, Gass, & McDonough, 2000; Trovimovich, Ammar, & Gatbonton, 2007) and with more salient linguistic features than with less salient ones (Long et al., 1998; Ono & Witzel, 2002), and that simple grammar and less salient targets may develop faster with more explicit corrective feedback (R. Ellis, 2007; Ellis, Loewen, & Erlam, 2006;

Norris & Ortega, 2000). Similarly, just as psycholinguistic properties of target forms may affect the success rate for recasts, so may individual differences among learners. While research in this area has only recently begun, several cognitive variables, including working and phonological memory, aptitude, attentional control, and analytic ability, seem capable of influencing the noticing and/or processing of recasts (Mackey & Oliver, 2002; Sagarra, 2007; Trovimovich et al., 2007).

Overall, results are encouraging. Based on their statistical meta-analysis, and echoing a similar conclusion by Russell and Spada (2006), Mackey and Goo find that "(R)ecasts seem to be developmentally helpful, with large effect sizes across all post-tests" (2007, p. 409). They caution, however, that there has as yet been an insufficient number of studies with which to evaluate the relative effectiveness of different types of negative feedback.

The effectiveness of recasts for at least some categories of linguistic target and with at least some types of learner should come as no surprise. As argued elsewhere (Doughty, 2001; Long, 1996a, pp. 452–453, 2007, pp. 77–78), information about the target language supplied in this manner has several potential advantages from a psycholinguistic perspective over the same information in noncontingent utterances, that is, as positive evidence, or models. Recasts convey needed information about the target language *in context*, when the interlocutors share a *joint attentional focus* and when the learner already has *prior comprehension* of at least part of the message, thereby facilitating form–function mapping. The learner is *vested* in the exchange, as it is his or her message that is at stake, and so will probably be *motivated* and *attending*, conditions likely to facilitate *noticing* of any new linguistic information in the input. The fact that the learner will already understand all or part of the interlocutor's response (because it is a reformulation of the learner's own) also means that he or she has additional freed-up *attentional resources* that can be allocated to the form of the response and, again, to the form–function mapping. Finally, the *contingency* of recasts on deviant learner output means that the incorrect and correct utterances are juxtaposed. This potentially allows the learner to compare the two forms side by side, so to speak, and to observe the contrast, an opportunity not presented by (noncontingent) models.

## V. FREQUENCIES AND PROBABILITIES IN L2 PROCESSING: THE ROLE OF INPUT

The work on the linguistic environment for SLA discussed so far has been an interest for researchers over the past three decades. More recently, an increasingly prominent focus of attention has been the role of input as the source of information to the learner on frequencies of individual lexical items or word forms (*token frequencies*), as well as frequencies of linguistic patterns or rules (*type frequencies*). This area of inquiry bears on debates between *nativists*, who hold linguistic knowledge to be computational, and *constructivists*, who view learning from the input as the main driving force in knowledge acquisition.

## VI. THE DEBATES BETWEEN NATIVISTS AND CONSTRUCTIVISTS

While both nativists and constructivists agree that input plays a role in language acquisition, they disagree on how much the learner infers directly from the input and to what extent inferences are constrained by innate knowledge. Initially, the debates were concerned with L1 acquisition and processing and used English past tense for testing predictions stemming from each approach. The agenda gradually broadened to include languages with richer inflectional morphology, such as German, Norwegian, Icelandic, Italian, and Russian, and turned to L2 acquisition. A thematic issue of *Studies in Second Language Acquisition* (2002, Vol. 24) was devoted entirely to the role of frequencies in L2 acquisition, with the position paper by N. Ellis promoting associative learning. The influence of *input frequencies* on SLA may manifest itself at two levels. First, more frequent items or patterns are likely to be noticed sooner and learned faster. Second, input frequencies shape L2 learners' probabilistic mechanisms, with the result that they prefer to use and expect more frequent forms or patterns.[2]

Since SLA has a long tradition of research into *explicit* and *implicit* aspects of L2 learning, including explicit and implicit memory, knowledge, processing, learning, and instruction, it is useful to situate the new research agenda within the existing framework (see Williams, this volume, for general discussion of explicit and implicit memory). In very general terms, in child L1 acquisition, both lexical items and rules are acquired implicitly.[3] In adult SLA, rules may be acquired and processed either explicitly or implicitly, while lexical items committed to memory tend to be processed implicitly. When processing L1 or L2, the built-in counters, for both words and rules or patterns, operate implicitly and subconsciously. We are not aware of the number of times a certain word, structure, or rule occurs in the input; thus, input frequencies belong almost entirely to the implicit domain.[4] However, it appears that unlike young children acquiring L1 or L2, adult L2 learners often require explicit triggers, for example, in the form of explicit rule explanations, in order to notice a rule or structure in the input and set the frequency counter. In this sense, the study of input frequencies provides insights into the way explicit and implicit L2 processing interact. Data collected on the processing of regular and irregular morphology by different populations of speakers—L2 learners with and without explicit training in rule application and of varying proficiency levels as well as NSs, children, and adults— indicate that two different aspects of L2 input, explicit instruction in rule application, on the one hand, and frequencies of various linguistic features, patterns, rules, and so on, on the other, interact in complex ways in adult L2 acquisition. Apparently, the need for explicit instruction in rule application is a property of L2 acquisition

---

[2]Frequencies of individual lexical items and patterns are different psycholinguistically, as patterns involve more abstract representations.

[3]This statement refers to preschool children and does not address the impact of literacy on L1 acquisition.

[4]This does not mean that speakers may not have reasonably accurate estimates of frequency ranges for individual lemmas. However, those estimates are often "contaminated" with real-world knowledge. For example, most people will agree that chicken is more frequent than lark, but such estimates may include both their linguistic and real-world experiences.

rather than L1 acquisition, while input frequencies play an important role in both (DeKeyser & Larson-Hall, 2005).

This section addresses the role of input frequencies and probabilities in L2 processing of inflectional morphology and is structured in the following way: First, debates surrounding the role of frequencies in L1 and L2 processing are briefly summarized. Then findings on the role of input frequencies in adult L2 processing in English and languages with rich inflectional morphology are reviewed. Finally, results of experiments on Russian verb generation by several kinds of speakers are compared: adult American learners of Russian of different levels of proficiency and different amounts of instruction and exposure to Russian, with native Russian children aged 4–6, and native Russian adults. Differences in the results obtained for each group are analyzed together with the kinds of input and input frequencies they received. We conclude by comparing the novel verb generation patterns of L2 learners and NSs of Russian, connecting the L2 response data with the amount of explicit instruction and implicit exposure, and evaluating the contributions of explicit and implicit input to the shaping of native-like probabilistic mechanisms in L2 learners.

## VII. DUAL-SYSTEM AND SINGLE-SYSTEM THEORIES OF LINGUISTIC PROCESSING

The influence of input frequencies on L1 and L2 processing has long been noted. High-frequency words leave stronger memory traces and are more quickly retrieved from memory. Input frequency was one of the leading factors hypothesized to determine the accuracy order of free and bound English morphemes (Larsen-Freeman, 1978) and later became one of the components of salience, the construct based on a meta-analysis of morpheme order studies (Goldschneider & DeKeyser, 2001). However, the role of input frequency has been reassessed within the context of debates among proponents of innate knowledge and associative learning. In fact, sensitivity to input frequency in the processing of inflectional morphology has been used in numerous studies as a litmus test of the computational or, alternatively, associative memory-based nature of the underlying mechanisms. Since the intricacies of those debates lie outside the main focus of this paper, we will keep the relevant information to an absolute minimum required to follow the discussion below.

The nativist position postulates innate knowledge of fundamental principles of language and of the ways languages vary and recognizes the role of input chiefly as a trigger for parameter setting. According to this position, language operates by symbolic rule computation, with symbolic rules applied regardless of input frequencies and probabilities. These principles underlie the *dual-system approach* to linguistic processing, with the focus on inflectional morphology the most clearly articulated in Words and Rules Theory (Pinker, 1999). The dual-system approach holds that linguistic processing is subserved by two systems: a computational system in charge of symbolic rule application and an associative memory that handles uninflected words and idiomatic expressions, but also irregularly inflected words with idiosyncratic forms. Thus, the main proposal of Words and Rules Theory is that words and rules are handled by two distinct mechanisms; for example, the past tense of regular verbs (*walk-walked*) is computed, whereas for irregular verbs (*bring-brought*), it is stored. The assertion that regularly inflected words are computed online, whereas irregularly inflected words are stored in memory, leads to testable predictions: input frequencies and probabilities will affect irregular, but not regular, inflection as far as individual lexical items are concerned.[5]

A question that immediately arises with regard to the dual-system position is whether any regularly inflected word forms are stored (and hence will show frequency effects) or all of them are computed online. The dual-system approach maintains that only the most high-frequency inflected words are stored, and this fact does not present a challenge to the theory. However, it has been found that English inflected words with a frequency above six per million word uses in a corpus of English show frequency effects and, therefore, are presumably stored undecomposed in their inflected form (Alegre & Gordon, 1999), which undermines the claims of the dual-system approach. A similar effect was found for inflected Swedish words, although the exact threshold for Swedish remains unclear (Lehtonen, Niska, Wande, Niemi, & Laine, 2006). Such low thresholds imply that a large number of words are stored in their inflected form.

The *single-system approach* shifts emphasis from the idea of innate knowledge to learning and views linguistic processing not as symbolic rule computation but as associative patterning in neural networks. It draws heavily on connectionist modeling of learning processes and maintains that an associative network uses the same mechanism for processing regular and irregular word forms. Associative learning is based on the input, as input frequencies determine the weight of connections in mappings between different word forms. The single-system approach also makes clear and testable predictions about the role of input frequencies—they will influence the processing of both regular and irregular word forms.

Several aspects of the single-system approach have also been challenged by its opponents. One of them is the claim that connectionist networks truly represent unconstrained learning from scratch. Indeed, the architecture of the network is controlled by the experimenter; it typically has a layer of hidden nodes, and the chosen settings, such as the number of nodes, initial weights, amount of training, and so on, work similarly to the priors, which are hypothesized to constrain human learning, and can be viewed as part of innate knowledge (Goldwater & Johnson, 2004; Hulstijn, 2002). Also, constructivists argue that successful modeling of human processing, for example, of inflectional morphology, in neural networks can be taken as proof that real linguistic processing does not make use of symbolic rule computation. Their critics point to the fact that connectionist networks do not have recording mechanisms, or "memory," built into them, yet humans store linguistic information in memory, presumably in some abstracted categorized form. The possibility exists, therefore, that patterns are stored (and eventually applied) as symbolic rules outside the associative

---

[5]Strictly speaking, the rationale developed in the Words and Rules Theory deals with token frequency effects in item-based storage, as opposed to online inflection, yet the idea that symbolic rules do not depend on type frequencies comes as an extension of this approach (see, e.g., Clahsen, 1999). It is true, nonetheless, that type frequency plays a role in modern computational parsing systems, and some accounts of morphological inflection (see, e.g., N. Ellis, 2002; Gor, 2003, 2004).

patterner, and thus, associative patterning in neural networks may be a step on the way to abstracting symbolic rules.[6]

Several attempts have been made to address problematic areas in the dual-system and single-system theories of regular and irregular processing and come up with more viable alternatives, one of them being the dual-route model (Baayen, Dijkstra, & Schreuder, 1997). The schemas in cognitive grammar supporting a usage-based approach to language and learning could be also viewed as "hybrid" constructs. In fact, Langacker (1987), founder of cognitive grammar, has warned against the exclusionary fallacy of supporting either computation or storage. For L1 acquisition, Yang (2002) has proposed the Rule Competition Model, according to which competing rules in a developing L1 linguistic system have probabilities shaped by input frequencies. A similar approach, claiming that rule application in regular inflection depends on probabilities, is used in the Rules and Probabilities Model, according to which both L1 and adult L2 regular morphological processing are affected by input frequencies (Gor, 2003, 2004). Both these models depart radically from the dual- and single-system approaches, in that they claim that rules are part of regular processing, *and* their application is affected by input frequencies.

The claims of the dual-system approach were mainly based on the data on English past-tense inflection, but were generalized as a universal aspect of linguistic processing (Pinker, 1999). Indeed, English past tense is perfectly suited to support the claims of the dual-system approach; it has a large regular class of verbs, which form their past tense by a concatenative rule "add -*ed* to the stem" and a small class of irregular verbs whose past-tense forms are idiosyncratic and have to be stored and processed in associative memory.

A reliance on this simple and transparent system for generalizations about universal language mechanisms has two disadvantages. First, languages with complex inflectional morphology often have several classes of verbs, nouns, and so on, displaying a range of regularity rather than a sharp regular/irregular dichotomy. Second, experimental data on novel verb generation have revealed the role of a default, a pattern with the most open schema that speakers choose "when all else fails" (Bybee, 1995). In English, it is impossible to make a distinction between regular and default processing, since the large regular verb class also happens to be the default class. Research on languages with complex morphology—Norwegian, Icelandic, Italian, and Russian—has demonstrated that regularity may, indeed, be a gradual parameter in terms of mental representations; thus, a clear distinction between rule-based and memory-based processing is often arbitrary. Regular verbs also show frequency and phonological similarity effects, and irregular conjugational patterns may be generalized to regular patterns (Gor, 2003; Gor & Chernigovskaya, 2001, 2005; Orsolini & Marslen-Wilson, 1997; Ragnasdóttir, Simonsen, & Plunkett, 1997; Simonsen, 2000). It turns out that a categorical distinction between regular and irregular processing may indeed impose an *ad hoc* structure on the data in these cases.

---

[6]Neural networks are used not only in connectionist modeling, but also in modeling computational processes.

## VIII. FREQUENCIES AND PROBABILITIES IN SLA

This section will be devoted to hypotheses and findings on the role of input frequencies and probabilities in L2 processing. It will demonstrate that while the research paradigm based on the categorical regular/irregular dichotomy and making predictions about frequency effects in regular versus irregular inflection may not find experimental support, this does not diminish the impact of input frequencies on L2 (or L1) acquisition. Indeed, this research often uses token frequencies, or the frequencies of word forms, to demonstrate frequency effects.[7] The underlying notion is that if a word is stored in memory in inflected form, the inflected form will be frequency sensitive. Conversely, if the inflected form is computed online, it will not show any frequency effects. There exists another possibility that it is type frequency, or the frequency of the rule or pattern, that influences linguistic processing. Research on the processing of Russian verbal morphology shows that this third possibility is, indeed, the case and connects the probabilistic aspects of L2 processing to properties of the input.

Research on L2 processing of regular and irregular inflection and the role of frequencies and probabilities in L2 has evolved in two main directions: The first tests the hypotheses advanced for L1-like processing in L2 acquisition with the goal of establishing whether the same mechanisms operate in SLA as in native processing (Beck, 1997; Hahne, Mueller, & Clahsen, 2006; Murphy, 2004). These studies typically show substantial differences between L1 and L2 data. A second, newly evolving direction, attempts to connect the issue of the role of frequencies in regular and irregular processing with more SLA-driven issues concerning the role of input and, in particular, explicit and implicit input, in L2 processing. This section will discuss these two directions, as they both are connected to our main topic.

Several proposals have been made regarding the processing of inflectional morphology by L2 learners, with predictions addressing two parameters, age of acquisition— late versus early learners—and proficiency level—high versus low. In his declarative/ procedural model, Ullman suggests that late and less proficient L2 learners will rely heavily on declarative memory, even in processing regularly inflected words, since their procedural memory is attenuated (Ullman, 2001, 2006). For example, *walk+ed* and *the+cat* would be computed in procedural memory in L1 speakers, but memorized as a chunk in declarative memory by late/less-proficient L2 learners (2006, p. 99). In terms of input and type of processing, this would mean that late/less-proficient L2 learners will depend more on, and show a stronger effect for, input frequencies and will have recourse to memorization of inflected forms.

While declarative and procedural mechanisms cannot be directly mapped onto explicit and implicit processing, it is obvious that memorization falls within the implicit domain. Unfortunately, there are practically no experimental data in direct support of the declarative/procedural model in L2, other than general findings on the critical period for SLA. Birdsong and Flege (2001) showed differences in the processing of English high- and low-frequency irregular, but not regular, past-tense verbs and plural

---

[7]Note, however, that the effects of stem-cluster (lemma) frequency may manifest themselves even in online computation, which makes the frequency-based argument much more nuanced.

nouns by advanced learners (in accordance with the dual-system hypothesis), NSs of Korean and Spanish, reporting only the accuracy data, while most studies use reaction times (RT) in an attempt to distinguish between storage/retrieval and online computation of inflected forms. Ullman cites the results of the Birdsong and Flege study in support of the declarative/procedural model, as it demonstrates similarities between advanced L2 and L1 processing (2006, p. 103). Paradoxically, Birdsong and Flege conclude exactly the opposite, namely, that the declarative system may be more prone to age effects than the procedural system (2001, p. 131).

The hypothesis that in the initial stage, learners memorize inflected words as whole chunks and start decomposing them later has received some experimental support (Ellis & Schmidt, 1998; Zobl, 1998). However, it is not clear what amount of exposure and/or proficiency level calls for a shift in processing mode, or how inflected forms are "erased" from declarative memory. Chunking and formulaic language use are typically observed at a very low level of L2 acquisition. Consequently, if declarative knowledge within the declarative/procedural model refers to this type of L2 processing, its scope is limited.

Several studies involving Swedish and Finnish clearly demonstrate that the morphological richness of L1 and L2 influences the way both L1 and L2 speakers deal with inflectional morphology. The first study employed a visual lexical decision task (LDT) to investigate the processing of complex Finnish words by two groups, monolingual (native) speakers of Finnish and early Finnish–Swedish bilinguals (Lehtonen & Laine, 2003).[8] The study used inflected Finnish words in three frequency ranges—high, medium, and low—and obtained different results for the two groups. While Finnish monolinguals processed low-frequency and medium-frequency inflected words by decomposition and high-frequency inflected words as whole words, Finnish–Swedish bilinguals used decomposition in all three frequency ranges. In other words, bilinguals with lower exposure to Finnish, a language with extremely rich inflectional morphology, do not develop whole-word representations even for high-frequency words. This result conflicts with predictions of the declarative/procedural model, which anticipates more reliance on storage in less proficient speakers. A follow-up study narrowed the range for whole-word processing in monolingual NSs of Finnish to very high frequency inflected words (Soveri, Lehtonen, & Laine, 2007).

A similar visual lexical decision study with Swedish as the target language and two groups of subjects, monolingual Swedes and early Finnish–Swedish bilinguals, demonstrated morphological decomposition only for low-frequency inflected words in both the monolingual and bilingual groups (Lehtonen et al., 2006). The comparison of these two studies suggests that morphological richness is a leading factor in determining which (regularly) inflected forms will be stored. At the same time, similarly to Alegre and Gordon (1999), the Swedish study indicates that many inflected Swedish words are stored undecomposed.

Another study (Portin et al., 2007) compared the performance of two groups of Finnish late learners of Swedish differing in their proficiency level on a Swedish LDT

---

[8]The way the study labels the monolingual group is somewhat controversial, since the participants also speak some Swedish, in addition to Finnish. However, it is reasonable to expect very little influence of Swedish as L2 on the processing of Finnish as L1.

and found the same effect as in the Lehtonen et al. (2006) study. This result is more in line with the predictions of the declarative/procedural model.

And finally, two groups of L2 learners of Swedish, NSs of Hungarian and Chinese, showed different decomposition patterns in experiments using the same set of Swedish monomorphemic and inflected words as in Lehtonen et al. (2006) and Portin et al. (2007). While Hungarian L1 speakers used decomposition to access medium- and low-frequency inflected words, and whole-word representations in the high-frequency range, Chinese L1 speakers used whole-word representations to access inflected words across all the frequency ranges (Portin, Lehtonen, & Laine, 2007). This finding demonstrates the role of L1 morphological structure in L2 processing of inflection. Additionally, a comparison of Hungarian and Finnish L2 processing of L2 Swedish inflected words reveals that Hungarian learners did not use whole-word representations for medium-frequency words, while Finnish learners did. Given that both Hungarian and Finnish are agglutinative languages with extremely rich inflectional morphology, these differences cannot be traced back to L1, and the explanation suggested in the study evokes differences in language-learning backgrounds. While Hungarian speakers had learned Swedish mostly by immersion, with little visual input, Finnish speakers had received formal instruction with intensive visual input (Portin et al., 2007). This conclusion can be broadened to the types of input received by the two groups, implicit in case of Hungarian learners and explicit in case of Finnish learners.

## IX. FREQUENCIES AND PROBABILITIES IN THE PROCESSING OF RUSSIAN VERBAL MORPHOLOGY

This section discusses data obtained in experiments on Russian verb generation by L2 learners with regard to the amount and kind of input they received. It shows that in regular verb conjugation, the choice of conjugational pattern in novel verb generation depends on the type of frequency, as well as the morphological complexity of the pattern. Furthermore, it shows that L2 learners receiving more explicit instruction in verb conjugation approximate native processing more than those who receive less instruction—again, with respect to the generation of novel verbs. And finally, it compares L2 learners with more informal exposure to Russian, but less formal training in verb conjugation, to those with limited, classroom-based exposure to Russian with focused explicit instruction in verb conjugation, and shows that the type of exposure and training, explicit or implicit, determines the properties of the internalized conjugational system and L2 processing.

The Russian verbal system has an advantage over the English system for studies of this kind, since Russian possesses 11 verb classes, some of them high-frequency productive and others low-frequency unproductive and with conjugational patterns varying in the degree of regularity.[9] As a result, it is possible to compare the processing

---

[9]We are exerting caution in labeling Russian inflectional patterns as regular and irregular, since they display a range of regular and irregular properties. Following the dual-system claim that regular inflection is always productive, we would need to categorize the unproductive patterns as irregular.

of regular default and non-default verbs, as well as that of high- and low-frequency regular classes.[10] Regularity here is viewed as systematic morphonological changes characterizing an inflectional pattern that can be predicted based on rules. This is a broader understanding corresponding to the more gradual nature of regularity in Russian. According to the dual-system view, regular inflection is productive and is processed by symbolic rule computation. The single-system approach associates regularity and high type frequency, or the number of members in an inflectional class (Bybee, 1995). The default inflectional pattern is used when all else fails, and is characterized by the most open schema (Bybee, 1995). Russian verbal inflection makes it possible to differentiate regular and default processing, while English regular past-tense inflection combines both. Russian language uses two main conjugational patterns, with the suffixes ending in a "j" (vowel+j) and in a vowel (vowel+ɸ), forming classes with different vowels, such as the -aj-, -a-, and -i- classes. The verb generation experiments made use of the following properties of Russian conjugation:

1. The "vowel+j" pattern (as in -aj-) is regular and productive. It does not include any nonautomatic morphonological processes in addition to the automatic truncation of the "j" before a consonant. This is the default pattern for Russian, with the -aj- being the largest class.
2. The "vowel+ɸ" pattern (as in -a-, -i-) is less regular and may be productive or unproductive, depending on the suffix vowel. The -i- class is high type frequency and productive, while the -a- class is low-frequency unproductive.
3. Automatic truncation of the "j" in the suffix results in ambiguous infinitives with unrecoverable stems. For example, an infinitive ending in -at' may belong to either an -aj- or -a- class verb.
4. These two main conjugational patterns are associated with the vowel of the suffix in probabilistic ways. For example, the infinitive in -at' is much more likely to belong to the -aj- than to an -a- class, while the infinitive in -it' is much more likely to belong to the -i- than to the (i)j- subclass.
5. The -ova- class has a rare feature, with the -ova- suffix alternating with -uj- in the nonpast tense, which results in the use of the "vowel+j" pattern in the nonpast paradigm and the "vowel+ɸ" pattern in the past paradigm.

Points 1–5 are illustrated in Table I with examples of the verbs included in the experiments reviewed below plus the (i)j- subclass to contrast the "vowel+j" and "vowel+ɸ" patterns competing in verbal processing.

A series of studies on Russian verbal morphology described below focused primarily on formal learners with highly structured explicit input in verb conjugation, including rule explanations and practice. For the beginning learners, after one year of study with a very rigorous curriculum, it was possible to produce a reasonable estimate of type frequencies of the verb classes, as well as the number of uses of each verb, by recording all class and homework activities in their set of instructional materials. For the learners

---

[10]The studies reported use the one-stem description of the Russian verbal system, in which all parameters of the conjugational pattern for each verb class are defined by its suffix, for example, -aj- and -a- (Jakobson, 1948).

TABLE I

**Examples of Russian Conjugational Patterns**

| Verb class/conjugation pattern | Frequency (based on Zaliznjak, 1980) Productivity | Stem/gloss | Infinitive | First person nonpast tense | Masculine past tense | Morphonological processes |
|---|---|---|---|---|---|---|
| -aj- 'vowel+j' | 11,814 Productive | chit-aj- 'read' | chitat' | chit-aj-+-u = chitaju | chit-aj-+-l = chital | Automatic consonant truncation |
| -a- 'vowel+φ' | 940 (Approx. 60 stems) | pis-a- 'write' | pisat' | pis-a-+-u = pishu; s→sh | pis-a-+-l = pisal | Automatic vowel truncation; consonant mutation |
| -i- 'vowel+φ' | 7,019 Productive | xod-i- 'go' | xodit' | xod-i-+-u = xozhu; d→zh | xod-i-+-l = xodil | Automatic vowel truncation; consonant mutation |
| -ova- 'vowel+j' 'vowel+φ' | 2,816 Productive | ris-ova- 'draw' | risovat' | ris-ova-+-u = risuju; ova→uj | ris-ova-+-l = risoval | Suffix alternation |
| (i)j- 'vowel+j' | 160 (seven stems) | pij- 'drink' | pit' | pij-+-u = p'ju | pij-+-l = pil | Vowel deletion |

*Note:* The table shows four classes used in the experiment and the additional subclass (i)j- to illustrate two main conjugational patterns in the Russian verb system: the 'vowel+j' pattern (as in the regular, default, high-frequency, productive -aj- class) and the 'vowel+φ' pattern (as in the semi-regular, non-default, low-frequency, unproductive -a- class). The infinitives of both these classes end in -at', and thus, the stem is unrecoverable. The -aj- class exhibits no truncation or consonant mutation in the nonpast tense, while the -a- class exhibits both vowel truncation and consonant mutation.

after two years of study, only type frequencies of verb classes were calculated, as the level of control over language use (and hence the frequency of occurrence of each individual verb) decreases in a more advanced classroom.[11] While the hierarchy of frequencies in native use and L2 input was the same, the differences between the sizes of verb classes are much smaller in the L2 input, which could be anticipated, given that the lexicon of beginning L2 learners is very small. The input to second-year learners mainly reveals increases in the type frequencies of the high-frequency -aj- and -i-classes, yet while the difference between high- and low-frequency classes grows, the increase is too small to approximate native frequency distributions. This led to the following predictions:

1. Generalization rates for different verb classes in L2 and L1 novel verb generation experiments will reflect the type frequencies of the classes in L2 input versus L1 use.
2. The system of probabilities in formal L2 learners will reflect the fact that input to L2 learners is much less than that to NSs, with the differences between type frequencies of different verb classes leveled out.
3. Consequently, the high-frequency default pattern will determine the choice of conjugational pattern less in formal L2 learners than in NSs.

The first experiment dealing with the role of input frequency and the degree of regularity (complexity of the paradigm) compared novel verb generation by L2 learners after one year of study with that of native Russian adults (Gor, 2004; Gor & Chernigovskaya, 2001, 2005). The verbs belonged to nine classes, which differed in regularity and type frequency; L2 learners received real verb stimuli, while NSs received matching nonce verbs created by manipulating the initial segment of the real verbs used with L2 learners. The verbs were presented in the past-tense form, and subjects were asked to generate the first and third person singular nonpast tense of those verbs. All the verbs were included in simple carrying sentences, which formed a quasi-dialog acted out orally by the experimenter with each subject and recorded.[12] The results of this experiment indicated that L2 learners' responses reflected their knowledge of the probabilities of different conjugational patterns, but at the same time, they were less influenced by the default pattern than were the responses of NS adults. Overall, the choice of conjugational pattern, the default "vowel+j" or the non-default "vowel+ɸ," as well as the other patterns, reflected the L2 input frequencies and the leveling of differences in type frequency among the classes compared to native use (Gor, 2004). This outcome is consistent with the kind of input received by the L2 learners—intensive explicit instruction in both default and non-default conjugational patterns.

The next series of experiments used the same data-collection instrument, mini-dialogs, which elicited the oral verb generation data, in different populations of L2 learners, with NS adults and children as controls (Chernigovskaya, Gor, & Svistunova,

---

[11]The first-year curriculum used the textbook: Davidson, Gor, and Lekic (1996).
[12]This procedure, adapted from Bybee and Slobin (1982), is widely used in verb-generation experiments.

2007; Gor & Chernigovskaya, 2003, 2004; Gor & Vdovina, forthcoming; Svistunova, Gor, & Chernigovskaya, 2007)[13]. The material included high-frequency, low-frequency, and nonce verbs belonging to four classes, -aj-, -i-, -a-, and -ova-, presented as infinitives. These four classes range in regularity from the most regular -aj- to the least regular -a- class.[14]

- Default high-frequency productive -aj- class, with only automatic truncation in the stem;
- Non-default high-frequency productive -i- class, with more changes in the stem, some of them nonautomatic;
- Low-frequency unproductive -a- class, with changes in the stem similar to the -i- class; and
- High-frequency productive -ova- class, with predictable suffix alternations, a rare feature in Russian.

The infinitives of the -aj- and -a- verbs both end in -at', meaning that the stem is unrecoverable and for novel verbs needs to be "guessed" based on probabilities and phonological similarity to existing (or known) verb(s). The situation is different for the -i- class, which is as irregular as the -a- class, with the difference that it is a high type frequency productive class. Its counterpart, the (i)j- subclass using the "vowel+j" pattern, contains only five verbs, all of which share the same idiosyncratic feature, stem vowel deletion, and are phonologically similar. Therefore, the choice of the -i- pattern in response to -it' verbs will reflect the knowledge of probabilities, whereas the choice of the (i)j- pattern will reflect the influence of the default "vowel+j" pattern.[15]

Two parameters of subjects' responses were obtained, correct stem and accuracy rates. The former takes into account only the choice of conjugational pattern; if the intended verb class is clear, but there is an error in the generated verb form, such responses are nevertheless accepted. The correct stem parameter makes it possible to assess the probabilities underlying the choice of the pattern. The latter parameter, accuracy rate, takes into account only the verb forms with all aspects of the conjugational pattern applied correctly, which for nonce verbs means that the conjugational pattern was correctly established or guessed, and then properly applied.

Three groups of L2 learners took part in the experiment: 15 university students after one year of intensive Russian with explicit instruction in verb conjugation (HILE 1, or high-instruction, low-exposure condition after one year), 16 students after two years of similar training (HILE 2), and 15 L2 speakers of Russian with an average of 5.3 years of study and use of Russian (range 3–13 years); in most cases this included immersion experiences and/or the use of Russian at the workplace or at home with a spouse,

---

[13]The child L1 experiment is a separate study (Chernigovskaya et al., 2007; Svistunova et al., 2007), whose results are used for comparisons with the L2 data.

[14]The -ova- suffix is an unambiguous cue to the verb class, while suffix alternation is, generally speaking, a rare feature in Russian conjugation. For the -ova- verbs, the choice of the pattern will demonstrate knowledge of the appropriate conjugational pattern for this class.

[15]The Rule Competition Model uses the term "free-rider effect" for a similar type of processing, when the high-frequency pattern is chosen for a low-frequency item.

but no focused explicit instruction in verb conjugation (LIHE, low-instruction, high-exposure condition).[16] The control group included 15 adult NSs of Russian. The HILE 2 group differed from the HILE 1 group in at least three respects: it was exposed to more native-like input frequencies, it knew more individual verbs, and it received more focused instruction and practice in verb conjugation. The LIHE group had more exposure and native-like input, but less structured explicit instruction in verb conjugation than either of the high-instruction groups.

The following predictions were made for the three L2 speaker groups:

1. Both correct stem and accuracy rates in the HILE 2 group will be closer to NS rates than those in the HILE 1 group.
2. The LIHE group will outperform the other L2 groups on the regular default high-frequency -aj- class.
3. The LIHE group will outperform the other L2 groups on all other classes in the processing of real verbs, at least, in the high-frequency condition.
4. The LIHE group will not outperform the other L2 groups on nonce verbs.

Since the testing material contained three categories of verbs—high- and low-frequency real and nonce verbs—it was hypothesized that real and nonce verbs would show different response patterns. The results of the study generally confirmed the above predictions; however, some unexpected effects were observed. Thus, contrary to predictions, in real verb generation, the LIHE group outperformed the HILE 1 group, but not the HILE 2 group.

The most interesting comparison involved the performance of different groups on nonce verbs, when the knowledge of the lexeme was not a factor in the choice of the conjugational pattern. The correct stem rates in verb generation are presented in Figure 1 and accuracy rates in Figure 2. In nonce verb generation, the HILE 1 group had the lowest scores and NSs the highest scores, in both correct stem and accuracy rates, which was an expected result. Another anticipated finding was that the HILE 2 group scored in between the HILE 1 group and NSs. The LIHE group was close to NSs on the default -aj- verbs and high-frequency -i- verbs in correct stem rate and only on the -aj- verbs in accuracy rate. These are the high-type-frequency classes, and consequently, the result seems to be input driven. On the -ova- verbs and accuracy rate for the -i- verbs, the LIHE group scored higher than the HILE 1 group, but lower than the HILE 2 group. And most remarkably, on the unproductive -a- verbs, the LIHE group scored the lowest of all the four groups. This suggests that high exposure with no focused explicit instruction leads to input-driven strategies in the processing of inflectional morphology, while the control of lower-frequency patterns lags behind.

---

[16]Note that explicit explanations and practice in verb conjugation, which involve systematic knowledge of the types of stem changes associated with different verb classes, are provided in very few academic programs. This was the kind of input our subjects received after one and two years of study. A traditional approach to teaching Russian verb conjugation treats combining the stem with the set of inflections and ignores the complexities of stem changes; thus, the majority of curricula combine reduced nonnative input with a lack of structured explicit training. Our third group of more advanced speakers received such training at the beginning of their study of Russian.

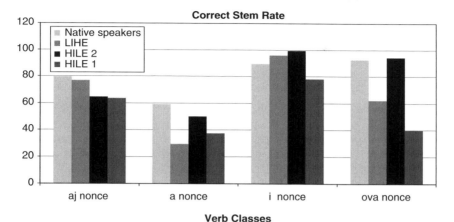

**Figure 1**  Correct stem rate for nonce verbs. The figure represents correct stem rates for four classes of nonce verb stems, as evidenced in a verb-generation task. Correct stem rate refers to the choice of the conjugational pattern based on analysis of the presented infinitive and does not necessarily imply that the generated verb form is correct. Native speakers had the highest correct stem rate for all classes, except the -i- class. The LIHE group outperformed the other two groups of American learners only on the -aj- class. The HILE 2 group outperformed the HILE 1 group on all three non-default classes.

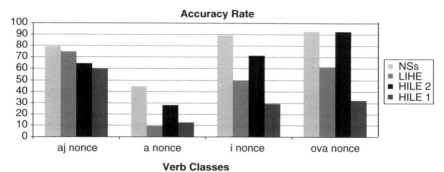

**Figure 2**  Accuracy rate for nonce verbs. The figure represents accuracy rates for nonce verbs belonging to four classes in a verb-generation task. These rates refer to completely accurate productions, and the percentages are either the same or lower than in Figure 1. Native speakers scored the highest on all four classes, while the rates for the LIHE group ranged from the highest of the three groups of American learners for the default -aj- class to the lowest for the semi-regular low-frequency -a- class. The HILE 2 group outperformed the HILE 1 group on all four classes.

And finally, comparison of the data on L2 verb generation with the data on L1 children aged four to six revealed similarities in L1 and high-exposure L2 response rates (Chernigovskaya et al., 2007; Svistunova et al., 2007). Children acquire the default -aj- conjugational pattern before the others, which points to an input-driven sequence, and high exposure to L2 produces a similar tendency in L2 learners, as observed in the LIHE group.

## X. CONNECTING INPUT AND PROCESSING

There are two main types of adult L2 learners shaped by two different kinds of learning experiences: naturalistic and formal classroom learners, as well as learners who have had different proportions of both experiences. Naturalistic learners receive input similar to that of native children. It is characterized by native frequencies and is completely implicit, with no explicit explanations. What consequences does this have for adult L2 acquisition of complex inflectional morphology? In the absence of explicit explanations, naturalistic learners internalize the most high-frequency regular default pattern, but have problems with less regular and frequent patterns. Apparently, high type frequency and regularity are the two conditions that enable adult L2 learners to derive the rule from the input and start applying it productively, regardless of whether they had focused formal instruction in that rule.[17] At the same time, less frequent or regular inflectional patterns are at a disadvantage in naturalistic L2 acquisition, but they can be successfully acquired with formal instruction. This conclusion is supported by two facts. First, adult L2 learners of Russian with intensive training in verb conjugation, which included both explicit explanations and practice, exhibited control of both high- and low-frequency conjugational patterns ranging in degree of regularity. Second, L2 learners with high exposure to Russian, but little formal instruction in verb conjugation, fared similarly to low-exposure high-instruction groups on the regular default pattern, especially with high-frequency verbs, but did poorly on non-default and less regular unproductive patterns, especially with nonce verbs. One property of the beginning formal classroom, as distinct from a naturalistic setting, is that it does not provide exposure to native-like linguistic frequencies; the magnitude of differences between high- and low-frequency conjugational patterns is greatly attenuated. As a result, lower-proficiency high-instruction learners develop a system of probabilities that reflects native probabilities only to the extent that the input frequencies they receive reflect native frequencies. In the case of L2 learners of Russian, this means that they apply and generalize conjugational patterns they have learned to recognize with L2 input-based probabilities instead of native probabilities.

## XI. CONCLUSIONS

The review of findings on languages with rich inflectional morphology and regularity as a gradual parameter suggests that both token and type frequency play a role in regular L2 processing. While token frequency effects are more predictable, given that vocabulary size and depth depend on L2 proficiency level, and lower-frequency items may not even be part of the mental lexicon of an individual L2 learner, the situation is less trivial with type frequencies. Indeed, the knowledge of type frequencies is implicit and based on the input, or in case of L2 learners, on the intake. While type frequencies

---

[17]The exact mechanisms underlying the documented differences in their suppliance of inflectional morphology in obligatory and non-obligatory contexts (Pica, 1983) are yet to be determined. Additionally, the default pattern is normally taught in any beginning Russian classroom.

affect L2, as well as L1, processing of more and less regular inflectional morphology, this does not necessarily mean that this processing is not based on abstract symbolic rules. In this sense, while the prediction of the dual-system approach that the processing of regular forms is not frequency sensitive does not receive support, a difference between storage and computation is not ruled out. For a given inflected form, two possibilities appear to exist: to be retrieved from the lexicon or generated online. Normally, both these routes would be activated, and the fastest would win. However, a number of factors will influence L2 processing of the inflected form using either route, including token and type frequencies, as well as the complexity of the conjugational pattern. Apparently, depending on proficiency level and the particular language concerned, more or fewer inflected forms will be stored, and the use of probabilities will be constrained by knowledge of linguistic frequencies acquired through L2 input. Beginning learners with a small vocabulary are unable to rely on associative patterning, but at the same time, their computational system is not fully developed either. More advanced L2 learners can potentially take advantage of associative patterning, as well as abstract rules, and in order to do so, adult L2 learners will make use of both implicit and explicit inputs on the way to successful mastery of inflectional morphology.

## ACKNOWLEDGMENT

We thank Colin Phillips for helpful comments on parts of this chapter.

## REFERENCES

Alegre, M., & Gordon, P. (1999). Frequency effects and the representational status of regular inflections. *Journal of Memory and Language, 40*, 41–61.

Arthur, B., Weiner, R., Culver, J., Young, M., & Thomas, D. (1980). The register of impersonal discourse to foreigners: Verbal adjustments to foreign accent. In D. Larsen-Freeman (Ed.), *Discourse analysis in second language acquisition research* (pp. 111–124). Rowley, MA: Newbury House.

Baayen, H., Dijkstra, T., & Schreuder, R. (1997). Singulars and plurals in Dutch: Evidence for a dual parallel route model. *Journal of Memory and Language, 37*, 94–119.

Beck, M.-L. (1997). Regular verbs, past tense and frequency: Tracking down a potential source of NS/NNS competence differences. *Second Language Research, 13*, 93–115.

Birdsong, D., & Flege, J. E. (2001). Regular–irregular dissociations in L2 acquisition of English morphology. *BUCLD 25: Proceedings of the 25th Annual Boston University Conference on Language Development* (pp. 123–132). Boston, MA: Cascadilla Press.

Bybee, J. L. (1995). Regular morphology and the lexicon. *Language and Cognitive Processes, 10*, 425–455.

Bybee, J. L., & Slobin, D. I. (1982). Rules and schemas in the development and use of the English past tense. *Language, 58*, 265–289.

Chaudron, C. (1983). Simplification of input: Topic restatements and their effects on L2 learners' recognition and recall. *TESOL Quarterly, 17*(4), 437–458.

Chaudron, C., Doughty, C. J., Kim, Y., Kong, D-K., Lee, J., Lee, Y-G., et al. (2005). A task-based needs analysis of a tertiary Korean as a foreign language program. In M. H. Long (Ed.), *Second language needs analysis* (pp. 225–261). Cambridge: Cambridge University Press.

Chernigovskaya, T., Gor, K., & Svistunova, T. (2007). Formirovanie glagol'noj paradigmy v russkom jazyke: Pravila, verojatnosti, analogii kak osnova organizacii mental'nogo leksikona (In Russian). In T. V. Chernigovskaya & V. D. Solov'jov (Eds.), *Kognitivnye issledovanija*. Moscow: Institut Psixologii.

Choi, M.-Y. (2000). *Effects of recasts on irregular past tense verb morphology in web-chat.* M.A. in ESL thesis, Department of Second Language Studies, University of Hawai'i, Honolulu, HI.

Clahsen, H. (1999). Lexical entries and rules of language: A multidisciplinary study of German inflection. *Behavioral and Brain Sciences, 22*, 991–1060.

Crossley, S. A., McCarthy, P. M., Louwerse, M. M., & McNamara, D. S. (2007). A linguistic analysis of simplified and authentic texts. *Modern Language Journal, 91*(1), 15–30.

Davidson, D. E., Gor, K. S., & Lekic, M. D. (1996). *Russian: Stage one: Live from Moscow!.* Dubuque, IA: Kendall/Hunt Publishing Company.

DeKeyser, R., & Larson-Hall, J. (2005). What does the critical period really mean? In J. Kroll & A. M. B. de Groot (Eds.), *Handbook of bilingualism: Psycholinguistic approaches* (pp. 88–108). USA: Oxford University Press.

Doughty, C. J. (2001). Cognitive underpinnings of focus on form. In P. Robinson (Ed.), *Cognition and SLA* (pp. 206–257). Cambridge: Cambridge University Press.

Doughty, C. J., & Williams, J. (1998). Pedagogical choices in focus on form. In C. J. Doughty & J. Williams (Eds.), *Focus on form in classroom second language acquisition* (pp. 197–261). Cambridge: Cambridge University Press.

Ellis, N. C. (2002). Frequency effects in language processing: A review with implications for theories of implicit and explicit language acquisition. *Studies in Second Language Acquisition, 24*, 143–188.

Ellis, N. C., & Schmidt, R. (1998). Rules or associations in the acquisition of morphology? The frequency by regularity interaction in human and PDP learning of morphosyntax. *Language and Cognitive Processes, 13*, 307–336.

Ellis, R. (2007). The differential effects of corrective feedback on two grammatical structures. In A. Mackey (Ed.), *Conversational interaction and second language acquisition. A series of empirical studies* (pp. 311–330). New York: Oxford University Press.

Ellis, R., Loewen, S., & Erlam, R. (2006). Implicit and explicit corrective feedback and the acquisition of L2 grammar. *Studies of Second Language Acquisition, 28*(2), 339–368.

Ferguson, C. (1975). Towards a characterization of English foreigner talk. *Anthropological Linguistics, 17*(1), 1–14.

Gass, S. M. (1997). *Input, interaction, and the second language learner.* Mahwah, NJ: Lawrence Erlbaum.

Gass, S. M. (2003). Input and interaction. In C. J. Doughty & M. H. Long (Eds.), *Handbook of second language acquisition* (pp. 224–255). Oxford: Blackwell.

Gass, S. M., & Mackey, A. (2007). Input, interaction and output in SLA. In B. VanPatten & J. Williams (Eds.), *Theories in SLA*. Mahwah, NJ: Lawrence Erlbaum Associates.

Givon, T. (1979). *On understanding grammar.* New York: Academic Press.

Goldschneider, J., & DeKeyser, R. (2001). Explaining the 'natural order of L2 morpheme acquisition' in English: A meta-analysis of multiple determinants. *Language Learning, 51*(1), 1–50.

Goldwater, S., & Johnson, M. (July 2004). Priors in Bayesian learning of phonological rules. *Proceedings of the Workshop of the Association for Computations Linguistics.* Barcelona: ACL Special Interest Group on Computational Phonology (SIGPHON).

Gor, K. (2003). Symbolic rules versus analogy in the processing of complex verbal morphology. *Regards Croisés sur L'Analogie. Revue d'Intelligence Artificielle, 17*(5–6), 823–840.

Gor, K. (2004). The rules and probabilities model of native and second language morphological processing. In L. Verbitskaya & T. Chernigovskaya (Eds.), *Theoretical problems of linguistics: Papers dedicated to 140 anniversary of the Department of General Linguistics, St. Petersburg State University* (pp. 51–75). St. Petersburg: Philological Faculty of St. Petersburg State University Press.

Gor, K., & Chernigovskaya, T. (2001). Rules in processing of Russian verbal morphology. In G. Zybatow, U. Junghanns, G. Mehlhorn, & L. Szucsich (Eds.), *Current issues in formal Slavic linguistics* (pp. 528–535). Frankfurt(Main): Peter Lang.

Gor, K., & Chernigovskaya, T. (2003). Mental lexicon structure in L1 and L2 acquisition: Evidence from Russian. *Glossos, 4,* 1–31. http://www.seelrc.org/glossos/issues/4/

Gor, K., & Chernigovskaya, T. (2004). Generation of complex verbal morphology in first and second language acquisition: Evidence from Russian. *Nordlyd, 31*(6), 819–833. http://www.ub.uit.no/munin/nordlyd/

Gor, K., & Chernigovskaya, T. (2005). Formal instruction and the acquisition of verbal morphology. In A. Housen & M. Pierrard (Eds.), *Investigations in instructed second language acquisition* (pp. 131–164). Berlin: Mouton De Gruyter.

Gor, K., & Vdovina, T. (forthcoming). Frequency, regularity, and input in second language processing of Russian verbal inflection. *Slavic and East European Journal, 54*(1).

Hahne, A., Mueller, J. L., & Clahsen, H. (2006). Morphological processing in a second language: Behavioral and event-related brain potential evidence for storage and decomposition. *Journal of Cognitive Neuroscience, 18,* 121–134.

Hatch, E. M. (1978). Discourse analysis and second language acquisition. In E. Hatch (Ed.), *Second language acquisition: A book of readings* (pp. 401–435). Rowley, MA: Newbury House.

Hatch, E. M. (1983). Input and interaction and language development. In *Psycholinguistics: A second language perspective* (pp. 152–187). Rowley, MA: Newbury House.

Hulstijn, J. H. (2002). What does the impact of frequency tell us about the language acquisition device? *Studies in Second Language Acquisition, 24*(2), 269–273.

Ishida, M. (2004). Effects of recasts on the acquisition of the aspectual form of *–te i (ru)* by learners of Japanese as a foreign language. *Language Learning, 54*(2), 311–394.

Iwashita, N. (1999). *The role of task-based conversation in the acquisition of Japanese grammar and vocabulary.* Unpublished Ph.D. thesis, Department of Linguistics and Applied Linguistics, University of Melbourne, Australia.

Jakobson, R. O. (1948). Russian conjugation. *Word, 4,* 155–167.

Keck, C., Iberri-Shea, G., Tracy-Ventura, N., & Wa-Mbaleka, S. (2006). Investigating the empirical link between task-based interaction and acquisition: A quantitative meta-analysis. In J. M. Norris & L. Ortega (Eds.), *Synthesizing research on language learning and teaching.* Philadelphia: John Benjamins.

Kim, Y. (2003). *Effects of text simplification and elaboration on EFL reading comprehension and vocabulary acquisition.* Unpublished Ph.D. dissertation, Department of Second Language Studies, Honolulu, HI.

Krashen, S. D. (1985). *The input hypothesis. Issues and implications.* Harlow, Essex: Longman.

Langacker, R. (1987). *Foundations of cognitive grammar. Theoretical prerequisites* (Vol. 1). Stanford, CA: Stanford University Press.

Larsen-Freeman, D. (1978). An explanation for the morpheme accuracy order of learners of English as a second language. In E. M. Hatch (Ed.), *Second language acquisition: A book of readings* (pp. 371–379). Rowley, MA: Newbury House Publishers.

Lehtonen, M., & Laine, M. (2003). How word frequency affects morphological processing in monolinguals and bilinguals. *Bilingualism, 6,* 213–225.

Lehtonen, M., Niska, H., Wande, E., Niemi, J., & Laine, M. (2006). Recognition of inflected words in a morphologically limited language: Frequency effects in monolinguals and bilinguals. *Journal of Psycholinguistic Research, 35,* 121–146.

Loewen, S., & Philp, J. (2006). Recasts in the adult English L2 classroom: Characteristics, explicitness, and effectiveness. *The Modern Language Journal, 90,* 536–556.

Long, M. H. (1981). Input, interaction and second language acquisition. In H. Winitz (Ed.), *Native Language and Foreign Language Acquisition. Annals of the New York Academy of Sciences, 379,* 259–278.

Long, M. H. (1983a). Native speaker/non-native speaker conversation and the negotiation of comprehensible input. *Applied Linguistics, 4*(2), 126–141.

Long, M. H. (1983b). Linguistic and conversational adjustments to non-native speakers. *Studies in Second Language Acquisition, 5*(2), 177–193.

Long, M. H. (1985). Input and second language acquisition theory. In S. M. Gass & C. Madden (Eds.), *Input and second language acquisition* (pp. 377–393). Rowley, MA: Newbury House.

Long, M. H. (1996a). The role of the linguistic environment in second language acquisition. In W. C. Ritchie & T. K. Bhatia (Eds.), *Handbook of second language acquisition* (pp. 413–468). New York: Academic Press.

Long, M. H. (1996b). Authenticity and learning potential in L2 classroom discourse. In G. M. Jacobs (Ed.), *Language classrooms of tomorrow: Issues and responses* (pp. 148–169). Singapore: SEAMEO Regional Language Centre.

Long, M. H. (2007). Recasts in SLA: The story so far. In M. H. Long (Ed.), *Problems in SLA* (pp. 75–116). Mahwah, NJ: Lawrence Erlbaum.

Long, M. H., Inagaki, S., & Ortega, L. (1998). The role of implicit negative feedback in SLA: Models and recasts in Japanese and Spanish. *Modern Language Journal, 82*(3), 357–371.

Long, M. H., & Ross, S. (1993). Modifications that preserve language and content. In M. Tickoo (Ed.), *Simplification: Theory and application* (pp. 29–52). Singapore: SEAMEO Regional Language Centre.

Lyster, R. (1998). Recasts, repetition and ambiguity in L2 classroom discourse. *Studies in Second Language Acquisition, 20*(1), 51–81.

Mackey, A. (1999). Input, interaction and second language development. *Studies in Second Language Acquisition, 21*(4), 557–581.

Mackey, A. (2007a). Interaction and second language development: Perspectives from SLA research. In R. DeKeyser (Ed.), *Practice in second language learning: Perspectives from linguistics and psychology.* Cambridge: Cambridge University Press.

Mackey, A. (Ed.). (2007b). *Conversational interaction and second language acquisition. A series of empirical studies.* New York: Oxford University Press.

Mackey, A., & Gass, S. M. (2006). Pushing the methodological boundaries in interaction research: Introduction. *Studies in Second Language Acquisition, 28*(2), 169–178.

Mackey, A., Gass, S. M., & McDonough, K. (2000). How do learners perceive interactional feedback? *Studies in Second Language Acquisition, 22*(4), 471–497.

Mackey, A., & Goo, J. (2007). Interaction research in SLA: A meta-analysis and research synthesis. In A. Mackey (Ed.), *Conversational interaction and second language acquisition. A series of empirical studies* (pp. 377–419). New York: Oxford University Press.

Mackey, A., & Oliver, R. (2002). Interactional feedback and children's L2 development. *System, 30*(4), 459–477.

Meisel, J. M. (1987). Reference to past events and actions in the development of natural second language acquisition. In C. Pfaff (Ed.), *First and second language acquisition processes* (pp. 206–224). Cambridge, MA: Newbury House.

Murphy, V. A. (2004). Dissociable systems in second language morphology. *Studies in Second Language Acquisition, 26*(4), 433–459.

Nicholas, H., Lightbown, P. M., & Spada, N. (2001). Recasts as feedback to language learners. *Language Learning, 51*(4), 719–758.

Norris, J. M., & Ortega, L. (2000). Effectiveness of L2 instruction: A research synthesis and quantitative meta-analysis. *Language Learning, 50*, 417–528.

Oh, S. (2001). Two types of input modification and EFL reading comprehension: Simplification vs. elaboration. *TESOL Quarterly, 35*(1), 69–94.

Oliver, R. (1998). Negotiation of meaning in child interactions: The relationship between conversational interaction and second language acquisition. *Modern Language Journal, 82*(3), 372–386.

Ono, L., & Witzel, J. (2002). *Recasts, salience, and morpheme acquisition. Scholarly Paper.* Honolulu, HI: Department of Second Language Studies, University of Hawai'i.

Orsolini, M., & Marslen-Wilson, W. (1997). Universals in morphological representation: Evidence from Italian. *Language and Cognitive Processes, 12*, 1–47.

Pavesi, M. (1986). Markedness, discourse modes and relative clause formation in a formal and an informal context. *Studies in Second Language Acquisition, 8*(1), 38–55.

Pica, T. (1983). Adult acquisition of English as a second language under different conditions of exposure. *Language Learning, 33*, 465–497.

Pica, T. (1994). Research on negotiation: What does it reveal about second-language learning conditions, processes, and outcomes? *Language Learning, 44*(3), 493–527.

Pica, T. (1996). *Second language learning through interaction: Multiple perspectives.* University of Pennsylvania Working Papers in Educational Linguistics 12, pp. 1–22.

Pinker, S. (1999). *Words and rules: The ingredients of language.* New York: Basic Books.

Portin, M., Lehtonen, M., Harrer, G., Wande, E., Niemi, J., & Laine, M. (2007). L1 effects on the processing of inflected nouns in L2. *Acta Psychologica, 128*(3), 452–465.

Portin, M., Lehtonen, M., & Laine, M. (2007). Processing of inflected nouns in late bilinguals. *Applied Psycholinguistics, 28*(1), 135–156.

Ragnasdóttir, H., Simonsen, H. G., & Plunkett, K. (1997). Acquisition of past tense inflection in Icelandic and Norwegian Children. In E. V. Clark (Ed.), *Proceedings of the 28th Annual Child Language Research Forum*, Stanford.

Russell, J., & Spada, N. (2006). The effectiveness of corrective feedback for second language acquisition: A meta-analysis of the research. In J. M. Norris & L. Ortega (Eds.), *Synthesizing research on language learning and teaching.* Philadelphia, PA: John Benjamins.

Sagarra, N. (2007). From CALL to face-to-face interaction: The effect of computer-delivered recasts and working memory on L2 development. In A. Mackey (Ed.), *Conversational interaction and second language acquisition. A series of empirical studies* (pp. 212–228). New York: Oxford University Press.

Sato, C. J. (1986). Conversation and interlanguage development: Rethinking the connection. In R. R. Day (Ed.), *Talking to learn: Conversation and second language acquisition* (pp. 23–45). Rowley, MA: Newbury House.

Sato, C. J. (1988). Origins of complex syntax in interlanguage development. *Studies in Second Language Acquisition, 10*(3), 371–395.

Sato, C. J. (1990). *The syntax of conversation in interlanguage development.* Tubingen: Gunter Narr.

Schmidt, R. W. (1983). Interaction, acculturation, and the acquisition of communicative competence. In N. Wolfson & J. Manes (Eds.), *Sociolinguistics and second language acquisition* (pp. 137–174). Rowley, MA: Newbury House.

Schmidt, R. W. (1990). The role of consciousness in second language learning. *Applied Linguistics, 11*(2), 129–158.

Simonsen, H. G. (2000). Past tense acquisition and processing in Norwegian: Experimental evidence. *Language and Language Behavior, 3*(2), 86–101.

Soveri, A., Lehtonen, M., & Laine, M. (2007). Word frequency and morphological processing in Finnish revisited. *Mental Lexicon, 3*(2), 359–385.

Svistunova, T., Gor, K., & Chernigovskaya, T. (2007). Modular and network approaches to morphology: The experimental study of the acquisition of Russian verbal inflectional classes by children. *Vestnik Peterburgskogo Universiteta*, St. Petersburg University.

Swain, M. (1991). French immersion and its offshoots: Getting two for one. In B. F. Freed (Ed.), *Foreign language acquisition research and the classroom* (pp. 91–103). Lexington, MA: D.C. Health and Company.

Trovimovich, P., Ammar, A., & Gatbonton, E. (2007). How effective are recasts? The role of attention, memory, and analytic ability. In A. Mackey (Ed.), *Conversational interaction and second language acquisition. A series of empirical studies* (pp. 161–181). New York: Oxford University Press.

Ullman, M. T. (2001). The neural basis of lexicon and grammar in first and second language: The declarative/procedural model. *Bilingualism: Language and Cognition, 4*, 105–122.

Ullman, M. T. (2006). The declarative/procedural model and the shallow structure hypothesis. *Applied Psycholinguistics, 27*, 97–105.

White, L. (1991). Adverb-placement in second language acquisition: Some effects of positive and negative evidence in the classroom. *Second Language Research, 7*, 133–161.

Yang, C. D. (2002). *Knowledge and learning in natural language.* USA: Oxford University Press.

Yano, Y., Long, M. H., & Ross, S. (1994). The effects of simplified and elaborated texts on foreign language reading comprehension. *Language Learning, 44*(2), 189–219.

Zalizniak, A. A. (1980). *The grammatical dictionary of the Russian language.* Moscow: Russian Language Publishers.

Zobl, H. (1998). Representational changes: From listed representations to independent representations of verbal affixes. In M.-L. Beck (Ed.), *Morphology and its interfaces in second language knowledge.* Amsterdam: John Benjamins.

CHAPTER 20

# SECOND LANGUAGE ACQUISITION IN THE INSTRUCTIONAL ENVIRONMENT

Teresa Pica

## I. INTRODUCTION

The label, "instructional," applied to "environment" suggests a setting in which a content area or skill is organized, presented, and explained to the learner. The second language instructional environment (henceforth, IE) is unique in that it can offer the L2 as the content or skill that is instructed as well as the medium through which the instruction is offered. Through the IE, learners can access samples of L2 text and discourse. These can serve as evidence or information that learners can apply to their developing interlanguage system and use to modify and reconfigure its linguistic and communicative features. Understanding, describing, and predicting what makes the L2 accessible and the learner successful are central to the numerous studies that bear the label, "instructional." These include studies carried out in classroom settings as well as in controlled environments in which the label, "instructional" characterizes the treatments or conditions that make the L2 available for learning. Findings from these studies have informed the broader field of second language acquisition (SLA) at empirical and theoretical levels.

## II. HISTORICAL PERSPECTIVES ON THE IE IN L2 LEARNING AND RESEARCH

Languages, like all other objects of learning, are acquired in contexts. Among the contexts available to language learners, the IE is one that has been a source of curiosity and debate in the field of SLA since the early 1970s. Long before that, second languages were instructed (see, e.g., Howatt, 1984; Kelly, 1969) and their acquisition was researched (e.g., Leopold, 1939–1949; see also Hatch, 1980 for a detailed

473

overview). However, during the 1970s, the IE began to take on theoretical significance, as advances in psycholinguistics provoked questions and concerns about its role in SLA. Since the mind appeared capable of amassing, sorting, and synthesizing intricate grammatical operations and complex cultural rules, and of handling whatever ambient linguistic data it encountered, what was left for an IE to offer the L2 learner?

Initially, it appeared as though the IE had little to offer the learner. The features of rule provision and error feedback that made the IE distinctive (Krashen & Seliger, 1975) were believed to help build conscious knowledge of L2 forms and grammatical structures. What the learner needed, however, was to acquire a systematic interlanguage grammar that could be restructured unconsciously and accessed readily for spontaneous, unmonitored use. SLA was seen as a process of creative construction (Dulay, Burt, & Krashen, 1982) that resembled first language acquisition. It required an environment composed of meaningful input, made comprehensible through the familiarity of its topics, the visual cues that accompanied it, and the interaction that provided support. Such features were potentially available in the IE, but they could also be found in everyday settings, through informal L2 contact, as well as in classrooms not designed for language study but abundant with opportunities for language use (Krashen, 1976).

These reservations about the contributions of the IE began to shift in the 1980s, when Michael H. Long published a meta-analytical comparison of studies whose data on SLA had come from instructional, exposure, and combined environments (Long, 1983). Findings from these studies pointed to a superiority for the IE, particularly in the acquisition rate and level of attainment of instructed learners. Although the meta-analysis was not able to pinpoint the factors responsible for this result, Long raised the possibility that the discourse of the IE, particularly its linguistic complexity and markedness, might have played a role.

Since the time of Long's meta-analysis, research on SLA in the IE has burgeoned in size and scope. This research has embraced dozens of questions, topics, and themes, some of which are described in this chapter. The IE itself has been analyzed, in descriptions of instructional moves, interaction structures, and participation patterns, and through comparisons of experienced and novice instructors, form—and meaning—based approaches, and input-oriented and production-driven methods. (See Chaudron, 1988; Lightbown & Spada, 2006 for overviews.) In attempting to link these components with SLA, researchers have gone beyond describing the complexity, markedness, and other features of instructional discourse, to discovering the interaction structures that draw attention to L2 form and meaning and make the L2 available as input for learning (see, e.g., Doughty & Williams, 1998). Features of rule provision and corrective feedback are no longer viewed as limited to the formation of conscious L2 knowledge. They have taken on greater theoretical importance as vital contributors to cognitive processes and learning outcomes (see, e.g., DeKeyser, 2003; R. Ellis, 2005).

An update of Long's original meta-analysis by Norris and Ortega (2001) has lent further insight and raised additional issues regarding the IE and SLA. Through a comparison of 51 studies whose data came from four distinct types of IEs, Norris and Ortega found that explicit, form-focused IEs resulted in more accurate and advanced SLA outcomes than those that followed implicit approaches. Appearing at a time of considerable evidence and convincing argument that implicit L2 knowledge is the basis for communicative L2 use, (N. Ellis, 2003), the findings of the meta-analysis have suggested the need to consider how explicit learning might contribute to the implicit knowledge that learners eventually come to use (see, e.g., DeKeyser, 2003).

These findings have also posed methodological challenges to SLA research. This is because so many of the analyzed studies obtained their results through short-term treatments, and documented learning through discrete point tests. These methodological approaches are known to favor the learner's demonstration of explicit over implicit knowledge. Implicit knowledge takes a long time to acquire and its acquisition is not always obvious on isolated test items. The findings of the meta-analysis thus underscore the need for long-term treatments and for measures and tests more sensitive to the acquisition of implicit L2 knowledge and the demonstration of its outcomes (Norris & Ortega, 2003, 2006; see also Doughty, 2003).

These methodological issues reveal one of the many ways in which concerns about SLA in the IE resonate across the broader field of SLA. Questions on the contributions of input, interaction, production, and correction are relevant to all SLA environments and remain at the forefront of SLA theory and research (Gor & Long, this volume). The relationship of explicit to implicit features, whether about learning, instruction, or knowledge, continue to perplex and fascinate scholars throughout the field (Williams, this volume). This chapter will, therefore, look at research on SLA in the IE as it bears on broader theoretical concerns of the field at large and contributes to its methodological needs.

The chapter first highlights research from the IE that has introduced theoretical constructs to SLA and tested their claims about input, interaction, feedback, and output processes. It then describes ways in which task-based activities that originated in the IE have contributed to this research and proposes strategies through which they might do likewise for outcomes-oriented projects. The chapter ends with a brief discussion of the ways in which the classroom can serve as an environment in which instruction and research can thrive, by providing an optimal context for the implementation of task-based activities and by offering time as a commodity greatly needed to address current questions on SLA.

## III. CONTRIBUTIONS AND CONCERNS

The IE has served as a source of SLA data beginning with early studies that compared the morpheme accuracy order of learners from different instructional backgrounds (Dulay & Burt, 1974; Pica, 1983) and has remained so to date. Initially, there was a need for descriptive data on L2 classrooms. Studies uncovered similarities and differences between teacher-fronted and student group interaction (Pica & Doughty, 1985a, 1985b); communicative and grammar-focused activities (Long & Sato, 1983); and high and low levels of student turn taking and participation (Allwright, 1980). Over the years, the IE has taken on a much broader role in the field of SLA, contributing research that has informed SLA theory about "notice the gap," (Schmidt & Frota, 1986), "focus on form," (Long, 1991), and "modified, comprehensible output," (Swain, 1985), and validated theoretical claims about the role of negative evidence (L. White, 1991), the importance of recasts in meaning focused contexts (Doughty & Varela, 1998), and language "teachability" (Pienemann, 1989).

rch has been carried out in intact classrooms, but a good deal has
d in controlled environments in which the label, "instructional"
reatments or the conditions under study rather than the setting of
s have been noted about the "ecological validity" of this approach
has required the isolation and comparison of instruction-related
atments (DeKeyser, 2003; Doughty, 2003). As will be revealed
throughout this section, however, findings from this research have demonstrated a
good deal of external validity to instructional and informal environments alike. In
addition, results of a recent study that compared task-based interaction in classrooms
and laboratory conditions suggest that setting type might not be as critical as other
instructional dimensions in addressing questions on the IE (Gass, Mackey, & Ross-
Feldman, 2005). The study found striking similarities in learner behavior across the
two settings. Differences appeared to be a function of the types of tasks in which the
learners engaged rather than the settings in which they worked.

Methodologically, the isolation and comparison of instruction-related variables and
treatments has been an important and necessary step toward understanding their role
in the SLA process and their contributions to successful L2 outcomes. Together,
studies carried out across a range of IEs and activities have informed the field about
learners' needs to obtain input and evidence, to participate in form-focused
interaction, to be given form-focused feedback and instruction, and to produce and
modify their output.

## IV. INPUT, EVIDENCE, AND SLA IN INSTRUCTIONAL PERSPECTIVE

That L2 learners need to access comprehensible, meaningful input for their learning
is fundamental to SLA theory. One of the most comprehensive discussions of input
appeared in a chapter of the original *Handbook of Second Language Acquisition*
(Long, 1996), and has been updated by Long for the current volume (Gor & Long, this
volume). According to Long, learners need access to input that supplies positive
evidence of relationships between message meaning and the form in which that
meaning is encoded. Such input is found in the texts they read and hear, and in the
responses they receive to their questions and comments. When the input is repeated,
reformulated, and modified to insure comprehensibility, its form and meaning
relationships become more perceptually salient and available to the learner. Since
learners often need to have messages made comprehensible, modified input provides
an excellent source of positive data on L2 morphology, syntax, and lexis.
Unfortunately, it is not a guaranteed source, nor is it always sufficient, particularly
for providing access to L2 forms and features that are low in salience or lack
communicative transparency. In English, for example, forms such as articles and
determiners, with their elusive rules and patterns of use, are difficult for learners to
notice on their own. Researchers have explored alternative ways to promote access
to them.

One approach has been to enhance or enrich the input in which these forms appear.
However, studies in which such forms have been highlighted visually (Izumi, 2002;

J. White, 1998), or made more abundant through "flooding" in written and spoken texts (Trahey & L. White, 1993) have had disappointing results. While some degree of noticing appeared to occur, its interlanguage application was incomplete. Thus, in the Izumi study, the enhanced forms were not sufficiently noticed to affect learners' ability to use them in text reconstruction. In the J. White study, even though learners were given texts with italics, bold, enlargement, and underlining, these enhancement devices did not make a significant difference in their learning of possessive determiners. In the study of Trahey and L. White, learners were able to add correct forms to their interlanguage, but were not able to substitute them for older, incorrect versions, which remained in the interlanguage as well.

A related approach has been to make learners more aware of low-salience forms through "consciousness-raising" experiences that range from providing them with texts in which the forms are highlighted and to offering explicit instruction and explanation on form application (Rutherford & Sharwood Smith, 1985), to deciding among and discussing form choices in grammar-based activities (Fotos, 1994; Fotos & R. Ellis, 1991). Although some success has been reported with respect to learners' ability to notice these forms in future contexts (e.g., Fotos, 1994), questions remain about the extent to which these interventions promote the kind of implicit L2 knowledge learners need in order to make form generalizations and apply to productive use (see Doughty & Williams, 1998, pp. 239–240).

To help them notice items that are low in salience and to manage and overcome the errors that ensue, learners appear to benefit from input that supplies negative evidence about what is *not* in the L2. As Schmidt found from self-study of his own learning processes (Schmidt & Frota, 1986), even frequent exposure to forms that were low in perceptual salience was not sufficient for him to detect what he needed to develop and change them in his own production. Only when he was able to notice the "gap" between his own, and target versions, was he able to move on in his development and application of these forms. Schmidt identified the importance of negative evidence through an IE that included formal classroom learning, everyday social interaction, and informant consultation. His experience has inspired the study of negative evidence across a broad range of contexts.

Much of what is known about negative evidence has come from studies that examined its role at process and short-term outcome levels, using actual or adapted instructional materials or instructor intervention to deliver treatments and collect data. These studies first identified L2 forms and structures whose limited saliency or relative complexity made them difficult for learners to master, but whose development was underway. Negative evidence was then provided through "negative" or corrective feedback to learner misproductions or incorrect selections of these forms and structures, and its usefulness for error revision and L2 development was tracked. These studies revealed important findings on the role of negative evidence in the modification, development, and in some instances, retention, of linguistic items that had heretofore defied the learner's mastery.

Thus, in studies on English language learners, Carroll and Swain (1993) found that a combination of instruction and negative feedback promoted gains for dative constructions. Williams and Evans (1998) found that such a combination also helped learners with participial adjectives, but not passives, apparently because they had better control over the participial forms to begin with, and thus were more ready to make gains in their acquisition. Negative evidence (L. White, 1991) was able to assist French learners with English L2 adverb placement rules whose tiny differences with French had defied the learners' grasp. Mackey and Philp (1998) and Spada and Lightbown (1993) and found that negative evidence helped students progress through the stages of question formation, each an important step toward mastery of this complex construction. Doughty and Varela (1998), whose treatment was more lengthy and intensive than others carried out in the IE, found that feedback presented through repetition and recasting of past tense and aspect errors had a positive and lasting effect on students' learning.

With respect to languages other than English, Long, Inagaki, and Ortega (1998) found that negative evidence, delivered through interlocutor recasts immediately after a learner's misproduction made a difference in adjective ordering in Spanish and adverb placement in Japanese, especially when compared with an instructional modeling treatment provided right before the learner's attempts at production. Finally, Tomasello and Herron (1988, 1989) found that when errors were induced and feedback was immediate, learners were better able to revise grammatical features in French L2 that were prone to errors from English L1 transfer and overgeneralization.

Many of these studies were implemented under controlled conditions, in which actual or adapted instructional materials were used to deliver treatments and collect data (see again, Carroll & Swain, 1993; Iwashita, 2003; Leeman, 2003; Long et al., 1998; Mackey, 1999; Mackey & Philp, 1998; Oliver, 1995; Williams & Evans, 1998). Others were carried out in intact classrooms with researcher intervention (e.g., Doughty & Varela, 1998; Lyster & Mori, 2006; Lightbown & Spada, 1990; Oliver, 2000; Oliver & Mackey, 2003; Tomasello & Herron, 1988, 1989; L. White, 1991). These studies have revealed that negative evidence can be provided through formal instruction, and explicit corrective feedback, as well as from feedback that arises when interaction is modified in order to achieve mutual comprehension. This latter, known as the negotiation of meaning, has been shown to occur frequently during conversational interaction with learners engaged, and to provide an especially rich resource for input and evidence adjusted to their linguistic and communication needs.


## V. MODIFIED INTERACTION AS A SOURCE OF EVIDENCE

When interaction is modified by the negotiation of meaning, teachers, classmates, and other interlocutors request clarification or confirmation from the learner through utterances that attempt to understand the learner's intended meaning. These brief, but frequent interludes help the learner to *focus on form* (Doughty & Williams, 1998; Long & Robinson, 1998) by shifting the learner's attention to the form of the message and to possible problems with its encoding. Simple signals such as "What did you say?" or "Please repeat" are often used as well as linguistically elaborated responses. When an interlocutor seeks to confirm the learner's message, and thereby reformulates it, this helps the learner to notice the gap between the interlanguage encoding of its meaning and the encoding of that meaning in the interlocutor's request. This is shown in the following brief exchange:

1.  Learner: My grass broken
    Interlocutor: Your glasses? Are your glasses broken?

The importance of mutual comprehension and message comprehensibility becomes especially acute when interaction is goal oriented and requires learners and interlocutors to exchange and integrate information they hold individually in order to solve a problem or complete a task (see, e.g., classroom-based studies of Pica, Lincoln-Porter, Paninos, & Linnell, 1996; Pica, 2002; Pica & Washburn, 2003). Such a focus on message form is incidental, however, as learners' attention is necessarily devoted to repairing and resolving impasses in message communication in order to reach their goal. In many cases, the attention paid to a message is not directed at the accuracy of its grammatical form, but rather the preciseness of its content. Below is an example of what frequently occurs when an interlocutor is asked to reproduce a picture based on directions from a learner:

2.  Learner: Two book. Draw two book.
    Interlocutor: Two? Did you say two?
    Learner: Yes

Thus, one of the concerns about negotiation is that its inexactness for drawing attention to form and meaning limits its sufficiency for L2 learning. Nevertheless, its frequency of occurrence during goal-oriented interaction makes it a useful, if inexact source of negative evidence for the learner.

When comprehensibility is not at issue, as often happens when teachers are familiar with their students' interlanguage errors and are engaged with them in classroom routines and lessons, the teachers may use negotiation signals to promote accuracy, through what has been referred to by Lyster (1998) and Lyster and Ranta, (1997) as the negotiation of form. They found this signaling technique to be particularly effective for learners in correcting their lexical errors and many of their syntactic errors as well. To modify their phonological errors, however, learners in their studies appeared to benefit from another kind of intervention, known as recasts. These responses, known to be abundant in classroom and caregiver settings, have been the subject of numerous studies in the IE. Results of the studies have not been uniform, but their further analysis has shed light on the conditions of time and setting in which recasts work best.

## VI. RECASTS: VARIATION ACROSS THE IE

When interlocutors respond to a learner by recasting the learner's message they restate what they believe to be the meaning of the message, but recode its errors into an accurate form. This recoded message provides positive evidence as input for learning. Its timely proximity to the learner's error provides negative evidence that helps the learner to notice the gap in form between the original message and the recast one.

There has been a considerable amount of debate about recasts as an intervention in the learning process. While acknowledging the effectiveness of the recast in drawing the learner's attention to form and meaning, some researchers question whether it is the positive, negative, or combined evidence that makes the recast an effective response to the learner. Other researchers point to studies in which recasts were not effective, presumably because their preservation of the message meaning had made their minor corrective properties difficult for learners to notice.

In attempting to resolve this theoretical debate, several studies (Ayoun, 2001; Doughty & Varela, 1998; Leeman, 2003) together with reviews of recast studies and comparisons of their methods by Doughty (2001) and Nicholas, Lightbown, and Spada (2001) have shed considerable light on the ways in which recasts can best help the learner. These works reveal that both the positive and the negative evidence in a recast can be useful. Because recasts are encoded as immediate, semantically contingent response moves, their formal and functional properties are made more salient to the learner, so that they can be noticed and applied to the developing grammar. Thus, it is the immediacy in timing and saliency of positioning of recasts that make useful to the learner (see also Gor & Long, this volume).

Beyond settling a theoretical debate, the analysis of recasts has revitalized the role of positive evidence in the L2 learning process. Meaningful, comprehensible input works best when given in responses, rather than initiation moves, to the learner. Lending further support to this perspective is a study by Long et al. (1998), and a review by R. Ellis (1999). Together, they emphasize that where positive evidence does not make a difference for the learner, the evidence has been supplied in the form of enhanced texts, premodified on the basis of interlocutor judgments about the learner's abilities and needs. In studies where positive evidence does make a difference, the evidence has come from immediate interlocutor responses that incorporate or reformulate the learner's very own message. This form of adjusted input is far more direct and individualized than its premodified counterpart.

Several studies have pointed out the fact that recasts are not always practical. First, the limited salience of their reformulation makes them less likely to be noticed by learners, compared, for example with explicit corrections or even confirmation checks, which also reformulate, but do so through a shift toward rising intonation. Even those recasts that are noticed have been found to have little impact in the immediate term (see, e.g., Mackey & Philp, 1998; Philp, 2003). Findings on recasts in the classroom setting have been subject to these same concerns, as it is difficult for teachers to recast errors of form when they are engaged in meaningful instruction. As Lyster (1998) and Lyster and Ranta (1997) have noted, when recasts are used in controlled research conditions, their function is restricted to that of responses to errors. However, during classroom interaction they can be serve as reinforcements to student contributions of accurate content and as expressions of approval or acceptance. These noncorrective, pedagogical functions of classroom recasts tend to obscure the negative evidence they contain. Thus, Lyster and Ranta (1997) found that classroom learners were less likely to notice or "uptake" negative evidence that was encoded in their teacher's recasts, and were more responsive to their teacher's explicit corrections and form-focused instruction.

A recent study by Lyster and Mori (2006) has pointed out the role played by context and setting in determining the effectiveness of recasts in getting the learner to uptake and repair their errors. Though recasts were abundant and predominant in the two very distinct immersion environments they compared, learners in the environment with a lower communicative orientation responded to them more frequently than learners in a more communicative program, where the learners were more responsive to prompts. Accordingly, Lyster and Mori advanced their "counterbalance hypothesis," that instruction and feedback are more likely to be effective when they are counterbalanced, rather than congruent, with a classroom's predominant communicative orientation.

## VII. FORM-FOCUSED INSTRUCTION

During form-focused instruction, learners are provided with information and corrective feedback about language forms and rules within the context of communicative activities, through either immediate, extemporaneous intervention within a communicative activity or in follow-up work shortly thereafter (Lightbown & Spada, 1990; Spada & Lightbown, 1993). Instructional features such as display or evaluation questions, metalinguistic statements, and explicit evaluations provide relevant information on what the learner can understand and produce in the L2. In form-focused instruction, whether immediate or delayed, there is usually a reference to the learner's problems with form, especially the ways in which such problems can interfere with the communication of meaning.

Functional grammar instruction (Harley, 1989), is also form-focused, but is implemented through materials and activities preplanned from the classroom curriculum. These instructional tools integrate a form-focused component into a content-oriented classroom. Students are provided with opportunities to practice specific forms that they have not been able to learn from subject content alone, by engaging in a range of classroom experiences, including role plays, class projects, problem solving grammar tasks, and board, card, and picture games. These additions to their curriculum facilitate access to L2 forms through the communicative functions and meanings that they serve.

Research on functional grammar instruction, carried out predominantly in Canadian French immersion programs, has revealed positive outcomes for students' learning of French L2 conditionals (Day & Shapson, 1991); verb tense and aspect markers (Harley, 1989); noun gender marking (Harley, 1998); and *tu-vous* distinctions (Lyster, 1994). Aside from revealing the value of functional grammar instruction to L2 learners, these studies have shown researchers that it is possible to carry out studies on SLA in authentic classroom environments. Not only did the classrooms provide cohorts of learner participants, they also allowed for an extended period of instructional treatment, data collection, and testing as well as all-too-rare outcomes data on SLA.

## VIII. PROCESSING INSTRUCTION

As another type of instruction oriented toward drawing attention to form, processing instruction, has been successful in helping learners to identify sentence constituents and understand message meaning (e.g., VanPatten & Cadierno, 1993). Learners are given explicit instruction on how to process L2 input whose word order is different from that of their first language or is a marked alternative in the L2. Passive constructions in English are good candidates for processing instruction that identifies sentence agents and objects to learners who are used to relying on the unmarked, "default" SVO patterns they have already mastered in their L1. After instruction, learners better equipped to understand the correct meaning of "The dog was chased by the cat" than they would, had they relied on predictable SVO order and real world experience to believe that it was the dog who was chasing the cat.

Processing instruction appears to be especially effective for assisting learners' comprehension of sentences with marked constituent order. As several studies have revealed, however, not all rules, forms, and structures are amenable to this approach. As was illustrated by Allen's work on French causative verbs (Allen, 2000) and DeKeyser and Sokalski's studies on Spanish morphosyntax (DeKeyser & Sokalski, 2001), rule-focused and practice-oriented instruction can be just as effective for aiding learners' sentence comprehension and interpretation and more effective in facilitating production of most grammatical forms and constructions.

## IX. OUTPUT PRODUCTION AND ADVANCEMENT IN SLA

In addition to the positive and negative evidence that comes from modified input, feedback, and instruction, learners' own production can serve as a resource for evidence, as well as a mechanism for important learning processes. Some of the most compelling arguments about the role of output have come from Swain (1985, 1998), and originated with her review of test data on long-term French immersion learners. Her analysis revealed scores that were considerably lower in production accuracy than in the receptive areas of reading and listening, despite the learners' access to input that was meaningful, copious, and comprehensible. To explain the data, Swain turned to the IE of the immersion classroom. Its emphasis on content transmission necessarily reduced students' opportunities to produce spontaneous L2 output and to adjust what might be a comprehensible, but grammatically inaccurate message into a syntactically more successful one. She proposed that if all learners, not just those in classroom settings, were given opportunities to modify their message production toward greater comprehensibility or accuracy, they might be able to move from an interlanguage characterized by semantic processing and juxtaposition of constituent features, to one distinguished by syntactic processing and message organization.

From her initial argument about "comprehensible output" as a necessary mechanism in SLA (Swain, 1985, p. 252), Swain went on to propose that learners' production, especially their modified production of their responses during collaborative undertakings, would be a source of feedback and a basis for their hypothesis testing. It could also help them notice the insufficiencies of their own grammatical and lexical repertoires, and motivate them to listen more carefully for needed structures and words in new contexts in which such features might be found. Over the years, many of Swain's proposals have been confirmed through studies in authentic and controlled classroom settings (see, e.g., He & Ellis,1999; Izumi, 2002; Linnell, 1995; McDonough, 2005; Paninos, 2005; Pica, Holliday, Lewis, & Morgenthaler, 1989; Shehadeh, 1999, 2001; Swain, 1993; Swain & Lapkin, 1998).

Some of the research has shown that output production prior to opportunities to hear input and notice its features is more effective for SLA than input noticing activities alone (Izumi, 2002; Paninos, 2005). Other studies have shown that interlocutor feedback can affect the learner's ability to produce syntactically complex and accurate structures (Linnell, 1995) and to advance through the stages of question formation (McDonough, 2005). These and other studies have revealed ways in which the impact of output on the learning process is heightened when it is produced in response to feedback. While feedback has long been viewed as a means whereby learners can seek additional input (see, also, Krashen, 1976), and more recently as a source of negative evidence, it appears equally important as a trigger for learners to modify their production of output and thereby advance their interlanguage development.

An increasing number of researchers have focused on learner production within the theoretical perspective of information-processing theory, which views SLA as the acquisition of a complex cognitive skill, and therefore responsive to direct instruction and practice (Altarriba & Basnight-Brown, this volume). The most convincing studies have used artificial languages, assisted through monitored, computer interaction, which allowed the researchers to control instructional treatments and track learning over time (e.g., DeGraaff (1997); DeKeyser, 1997). Learners were first given explicit instruction of linguistic rules, which was followed by opportunities for practice. This combination was shown to greatly aid the learner's ability to apply the rules to subsequent activities. Although there have been theoretical concerns as to whether the resultant learning revealed skill demonstration only and not implicit, generalizable knowledge, one of the most carefully implemented studies (DeKeyser, 1997) found that production practice might best be viewed within the framework of rule automaticity. Accordingly, DeKeyser has argued that a sequence of explicit rule learning followed by opportunities for practice and application can lead to highly automatized L2 knowledge, readily available for a range of communicative uses.

## X. L2 TEACHABILITY AND LEARNER READINESS

The importance of readiness for instruction has been a theme with considerable resonance in the field of SLA for several decades. Early on, in advancing his "input hypothesis," Krashen (1981), looked to the importance of the learner's readiness for what he considered optimal and sufficient input. As such, the input would need to be meaningful, comprehensible, and encoded slightly beyond students' current level of language development. Because these features were difficult to operationalize for empirical study, the construct remained acknowledged, but untested, until Manfred Pienemann's studies on developmental stages in German L2 and his "teachability hypothesis" on the role of instructional intervention in speeding up the learner's rate of passage through them (Pienemann, 1985, 1989). His findings revealed that learners could not skip any stages in their sequence of L2 development, but that appropriately timed instruction in features that were teachable, that is, at the stage just beyond their current stage could help them go through intermediate steps more quickly than they would have if left on their own.

Thus, Pienemann (1989) and R. Ellis (1989) were able to show that learners at the "particle" stage in their German L2 development, benefited from instruction on the next, "inversion," stage when given instruction on particle movement. This enabled them to extend their ability for separating particles from other constituents within phrases and for moving them to sentence final position, to the ability to separate and move particles internally, within a sentence as well. Learners at stages below "particle," who could not yet separate particles from other constituents in phrases, were not yet ready and able to benefit from "inversion" instruction. Recently, Pienemann has advanced his theory of "processability," through which he has been able to predict cross-linguistically the syntactic structures that learners are ready to process at particular stages in their development. His studies of English, Japanese, and Swedish have provided empirical support to his claims (Pienemann, 1998).

Several other studies have expanded the construct of learner readiness by connecting it with instructional features. For example, Mackey and Philp (1998) found that learners who were ready to advance to the next stage of English question formation did so successfully if their question errors were recast. However, other "ready" learners, whose question errors were not recast, did not advance as consistently as the recast group. "Unready" learners were not able to benefit from the recasts of their questions. Similar findings were reported by Han (2002) and Oliver (1995), although their research questions addressed recasts, not readiness. In trying to explain why some of the learners were not able to take advantage of the recasts used in responses to their errors, Oliver, for example, argued that the errors had emanated from spontaneous, conversational interaction, and included misproduced features and structures that were well beyond the developmental level of the students. Together these studies suggest that it is the combination of readiness for instructional treatment and the treatment type that can make a difference in the learner's progression across the sequences of L2 development.

Lightbown (1998) has raised important issues regarding readiness, within a classroom perspective. Acknowledging the variation in readiness that is likely within a given classroom of learners, she has proposed that form-focused, L2 input, tailored to the more advanced students, can also serve at least some of the input needs of students at lower levels (Lightbown, 1998). Supportive findings from her work with Spada (Spada & Lightbown, 1999) have shown that across the sequences of question formation, even low-level students can begin to display knowledge of advanced features, albeit not as consistently as peers who are closer to the stage where these features might next be anticipated. R. Ellis (1989) has provided an additional perspective on variation in readiness, reflected in the higher and lower levels found within each stage of individual learner development. He has suggested ways in which instructional interventions can be tailored to the more advanced dimensions of each stage (R. Ellis, 1995; 2003).

In addition to the issues raised by Lightbown with respect to ~~the~~ feasibility of applying **the** constructs of teachability and readiness within the classroom are concerns about the scope of its application (Pica, 2007), as teachability applies to stage-related forms and constructions, and these constitute only a portion of the L2 forms that learners need to know and be able to use for communication. In English, for example, many L2 forms are acquired, not in developmental sequences, but vary on an individual basis, due to learner orientations toward functional or formal accuracy, and learner age, perceptual acuity, and access to input. Their learning trajectory is less predictable, and their mastery less likely than is the case for forms acquired in a developmental sequence. Grammatical inflections for verb tense and noun number, and functors such as the copula, for example, neither align with developmental sequences, nor fall into a predictable order of acquisition.

Because these variational features often have limited perceptual salience or communicative value for learners, they are seldom mastered on their own (see Harley, 1989, 1993; Long, 1996). Yet, indications of readiness for their learning appear quite early in L2 development, as functions arise for their application, contexts for their use, and as the forms themselves begin to emerge, as target-like items as well as misformations. The nonsyllabic past -*ed*, as in, *we liked*, might appear in the base form, *we study*, or with a past adverbial, as in *before we studied*. Similarly, the connector *but* might appear as *and*, thus filling its function as a connector, albeit a misformed one.

Interventions that draw the learner's attention to features whose functions are already apparent might, therefore, begin early during the acquisition process, as soon as contexts for their use appear in the learner's messages, when form omission and misformation alternate with form suppliance. Such interventions would need to be sustained throughout the course of L2 development, to allow for the time needed for mastery by the learner. In addition to assisting the learner, this approach would also enable researchers to track the learner's increasing accuracy in using these features and to account for the factors behind their variation in the interlanguage.

The learning of variational, low-salience forms and the study of their acquisition require a longer stretch of time than that used in most of the studies on SLA. As simple as this seems, its actualization is difficult. It is not easy to locate learners who can commit their time and patience to the research rigors of a long-term project, even if results of the project might lead to information that could assist their learning. The IE can play a crucial role in this long-term endeavor in two distinctive ways, through the design and implementation of task-based activities as tools for L2 instruction, acquisition, and research, and in the use of the classroom as a research site.

## XI. TASKS AS INSTRUMENTS FOR L2 TEACHING, LEARNING, AND RESEARCH

Tasks that engage language learners in meaningful, goal-oriented communication in order to solve problems, complete projects, and reach decisions have been used for a broad range of instructional purposes They have served, for example, as units of course syllabi, activities for structure or function practice, and language focusing enhancements to content-based curricula. Connections between task activity and communicative uses of the L2 inside and outside the classroom have made tasks attractive to educators and their students.

Tasks have had great and growing appeal to researchers as well. Demands on learners' attention, comprehension, and production as they carry out a task can lead them to obtain feedback, draw inferences, and test hypotheses about L2 forms and features, and produce more accurate and developmentally advanced output. Observing and measuring these task behaviors provide researchers with further insight into the processes of implicit learning.

Many of the tasks used in research have been taken directly or adapted from professional references (e.g., Brumfit & Johnson, 1979; Ur, 1988), scholarly publications (e.g., R. Ellis, 2003; Nunan, 1989), and student textbooks (e.g., Harmer & Surguine, 1987; Helgesen, Brown, & Mandeville, 2000). Among the tasks most widely used are those which require learners to exchange information, either by drawing from the same initial pool they are given, or by transferring and sharing their initially unique contributions (see Pica, Kanagy, & Falodun, 1993 for an overview and examples). These latter are often referred to as information gap tasks (see Doughty & Pica, 1986; Pica, 2005; Pica, Kang, & Sauro, 2006 for individual studies). Information-exchange tasks have been used primarily to ground instructional treatments or interventions that generate opportunities for modified interaction, support provision of modified input, and stimulate feedback and the production of modified output. Table I displays the studies cited in this chapter that have used tasks in these ways.

TABLE I

**Studies that used Information Exchange Tasks as Contexts for Instructional Interventions and Treatments and for Data Collection on them**

| Task purposes | Studies |
| --- | --- |
| Generate opportunities for modified interaction | Doughty and Pica (1986), Doughty and Varela (1998), de la Fuente (2002), Gass and Alvarez Torres (2005), Kowal and Swain (1994), Leeman (2003), Long (1981), Mackey and McDonough (2000), Mackey et al. (2003), Oliver (1995, 2000), Pica (1991), Pica and Doughty (1985a, 1985b), Pica et al. (2006), Pica et al. (1996), Porter (1986), Smith (2005), Swain (1998), Swain and Lapkin (2001) |
| Support provision of meaningful, comprehensible, and/or modified input | Doughty and Pica (1986), Gass and Alvarez-Torres (2005), Iwashita (2003), Izumi (2002), Long (1981), Pica and Doughty (1985a, 1985b), Porter (1986), Spada and Lightbown (1999) |
| Stimulate feedback, including explicit correction and recasts | Doughty and Varela (1998), Iwashita (2003), Leeman (2003), Long et al. (1998), Mackey and McDonough (2000), Mackey and Oliver (2002), Mackey and Philp (1998), McDonough (2005), Muranoi (2000), Nobuyoshi and Ellis (1993), Oliver (1995, 2000), Philp (2003), Pica et al. (1996), Takashima and Ellis (1999) |
| Stimulate production of modified output | Izumi (2002), Kowal and Swain (1994), McDonough (2005), Newton and Kennedy (1996), Swain (1998), Swain and Lapkin (2001) |

Among the studies listed in Table I, Pica, Lincoln-Porter, Paninos, and Linnell (1996) used information-exchange tasks to study the ways in which opportunities for modified interaction on these tasks helped the learners extend modified input and request clarification to each other. The tasks required the learners to choose pictures as their partners narrated a story line. Gass and Alvarez-Torres (2005) used information gap tasks as a way to generate different sequences of input and interaction that could then be studied for their role in vocabulary learning. Tasks designed by Iwashita (2003) for both information transfer and information exchange provided a way to deliver modified input and feedback to learners, which, in turn allowed her to compare the effects of these interventions on Japanese L2 learning. The picture description and drawing tasks used by Nobuyoshi and Ellis (1993), generated clarification requests to learners' attempts at production, which provided data for their study of the modified output in the learners' responses.

Although the language used to carry out a task need not be pre-specified, a task can be designed so that the information exchanged in attaining its goal favors the use of specific grammatical forms (e.g., Loschky & Bley-Vroman, 1993; R. Ellis, 2003). Many of the studies listed in Table I employed such form-focused tasks for variational forms of limited communicative transparency and low salience, as well as for sequential features with considerable operational complexity. These linguistic and communicative properties made forms and features difficult to master despite learners' readiness to do so. Table II provides short summaries of the design and results of these studies.

In the study of Doughty and Varela (1998), for example, students' reports of their science experiments provided contexts for them to produce past time morphology. When they made errors of suppliance, the researchers repeated and recast their utterances, and then tracked the results of this intervention over time. This commonly used classroom task, which was part of the everyday curriculum, thus turned into an effective learning tool for the students, as well as a helpful means of data collection for the researchers.

Pica et al. (2006) applied the structures of three widely used information gap tasks, *Spot the Difference*, *Jigsaw*, and *Grammar Communication*, to the reading passages of a film appreciation course. The resulting tasks were then used to generate learners' modified interaction, noticing, and awareness of English articles and verb morphology in the passage. These were the linguistic features that had been difficult to learn from course content alone. Pairs of learners read the same original passage, and then were given slightly modified versions of the passages, with sentence-level differences in articles or verb forms. For example, a sentence in the original passage might have *the table*. The same sentence in one student's version might be modified with *a table*, while the other student's version would retain *the table* from the original. Each pair had a mix of some of the original and modified sentences.

Without looking at each other's versions, they were asked to work together to locate differences between the sentences (for *Spot the Difference*), and/or reorder the sentences to match the original (for *Jigsaw*), or fill in blanks to make the sentences complete (for *Grammar Communication*). They then had to choose what they believed were the "better" versions of their sentences, justify their choices for selection, and recall the selected sentences in order to jointly reconstruct the original. All three tasks

TABLE II

**Subset of Table I Studies, which used Information Exchange Tasks in the Study of Specific L2 Forms, Features, and Operations**

| Study | Focus | Tasks | Treatments | Treatment intensity, duration | Total length of study | Findings |
|---|---|---|---|---|---|---|
| Doughty and Varela (1998) | Effect of recasts and meaning focused interaction on past form learning | Oral and written reports of classroom science experiments | Corrective recasting of oral errors, circling of written errors on English L2 simple and conditional past formation | Five sessions/week/4 weeks | Twenty-two weeks, due to delayed posttesting after treatment | Large, significant and durable effect for past formation |
| de la Fuente (2002) | Effects of negotiation with and without pushed output on L2 receptive, productive vocabulary acquisition, and retention | Follow directions for map placement of pictures of targeted vocabulary | Combinations of negotiation with and without pushed output for English vocabulary acquisition and retention | Two 20-min sessions | Three weeks, due to 1 week and 3 week delayed posttesting after treatment | Positive effects for negotiation on vocabulary comprehension and for negotiation with pushed output on vocabulary acquisition and productive retention |
| Gass and Alvarez Torres (2005) | Possible ordering effects of input and interaction on vocabulary and rule learning | Jigsaw and information gap tasks | Task generated input, interaction, feedback on vocabulary, gender agreement, verb (*estar*)+location | Two 20-min sessions | Forty minutes | Positive effects for vocabulary learning across all ordering; "interaction then input" significantly better than other conditions for *estar*+location |
| Iwashita (2003) | Impact of negative feedback and positive evidence on morphosyntax in NS–NNS task-based interaction | Jigsaw and one-way information gap tasks | Task generated recasts and negotiation moves, and positive evidence in completions, translations, continuation moves on Japanese locative-initial constructions and verb morphology | One session | One week, due to delayed posttest 1 week after treatment | Positive evidence beneficial for learners with above average pretest scores. Negative feedback, especially recasts, beneficial for all learners. Treatment effects not apparent on delayed posttest |

| Study | Focus | Task | Treatment | Session | Duration | Results |
|---|---|---|---|---|---|---|
| Izumi (2002) | Effects of output and visually enhanced input on noticing for relative clause formation | Computer-assisted passage reading and reconstruction tasks | Enhanced reading and output for passages with English relative clauses | Six 30-60-min sessions/2-week period | Three weeks, including posttest | Positive effect on relative clause reception and production for output; no effect for input enhancement |
| Leeman (2003) | Differential contributions of positive and negative evidence within recasts on morphosyntactic processes and outcomes | Information gap tasks | Negative evidence, with and without recasts, and stress-enhanced positive evidence for Spanish noun–adjective agreement | One 20-min session | One week including delayed posttest | Positive effect for recasts and positive evidence; no effect for negative evidence alone |
| Long et al. (1998) | Relative utility of models and recasts on morphosyntax and rule formation | Object description, picture description, giving instructions for matching task | Recasts and models of utterances for Japanese: adjective ordering and locatives; Spanish topicalization and adverb placement | One 40-min session | One day | Positive effects for recasts on adverb placement |
| Mackey and McDonough (2000) | Effect of communication tasks on triggering negotiation and recasts for form learning | Spot the difference; information transfer through picture description and drawing; collaborative story sequencing | Participation in tasks designed to promote negotiation and form noticing for noun classifiers and questions | Three 50-min sessions per week for 1 week | One week | Tasks triggered negotiation and recasts, which promoted noticing for noun classifiers. No negotiation or recasts for question forms |
| Mackey and Oliver (2002) | Effect of feedback on question formation | Spot the difference, story completion, picture placement, picture sequencing, picture description, picture drawing, meet your partner | Feedback through recasts, negotiation, clarification requests in response to question formation | Three 30-min sessions/eek | Three weeks | Positive effect for feedback on question formation, immediate, sustained |

TABLE II. (*Continued*)

| Study | Focus | Tasks | Treatments | Treatment intensity, duration | Total length of study | Findings |
|---|---|---|---|---|---|---|
| Mackey and Philp (1998) | Effect of recasts on immediate uptake and question development | Picture drawing, story completion, story sequencing | Negotiated interaction, with or without recasts, and incorporation into responses, for English L2 question formation | Three 15–25-min sessions/week | Three sessions | Short-term, positive effect for recasts on question development |
| McDonough (2005) | Impact of negative feedback and modified output on question development | Information exchange and gap tasks | Four different combinations of negative feedback and modified output for English L2 question formation | Three 10-min sessions | Eight weeks— posttests after treatment, and weeks 2, 5, 8 | Positive effects for modified output in response to negative feedback on question development |
| Muranoi (2000) | Impact of interaction enhancement through implicit feedback on L2 articles | Problem solving role play tasks | Interaction enhancement through implicit feedback; form versus meaning focused debriefing | Three 30-min sessions during weekly regular class meeting time | Eight weeks, due to delayed posttesting 5 weeks following first posttest | Positive effects for interaction enhancement on article use, especially when followed by form focused debriefing |
| Newton and Kennedy (1996) | Possible relationships between task type form-function encoding | Split and shared information to use for persuasion in resolving medical dilemma and description of zoo layout | Small-group assigned tasks with conjunctions and prepositions as linguistic foci | One 120-min session/group | One session | More prepositions on split information tasks, especially for description task; more conjunctions on shared information tasks |
| Nobuyoshi and Ellis (1993) | Immediate and long term effects of clarification requests on learners' pushed output on past-tense forms | Description of pictures with past time contexts | Specific, "pushing" clarification requests for learner correction of past-verb errors versus general requests for meaning clarification | One session/week for 2 weeks | Two weeks, with 8 days between the first and second sessions | "Pushing" clarification requests more effective for structurally-oriented learners (who paid more attention to form) than functionally-oriented (who focused on communication of meaning) |

| Study | Purpose | Task | Treatment | Frequency | Duration | Findings |
|---|---|---|---|---|---|---|
| Oliver (1995) | Existence and patterns of corrective feedback in child NS/NNS dyads | Picture description jigsaw picture comparison tasks | Task served as treatment | One 30-min session per week/2 weeks | Two weeks | Feedback and negotiation strategies influenced by error type and complexity |
| Pica et al. (2006) | Role of information gap tasks in generating modified interaction, noticing, and awareness for low salience noun and verb phrase forms | Text based spot the difference, jigsaw, grammar communication tasks with sentence level differences in articles and verb morphology | Identify and describe sentence differences, make correct selections and recall them for text reconstruction | Three days of one 2-h session and different task/day | Three days | Learners able to identify and describe form differences, and make correct selections and recall them for text reconstruction through modified and unmodified interaction |
| Smith (2005) | Role of negotiation and uptake in vocabulary acquisition | Jigsaw and decision-making tasks conducted through text chat | Computer-mediated negotiation | One 30-min task session/week/4 weeks | Six weeks, due to final delayed post test given 1 week after final treatment | Uptake rare; had no effect on successful acquisition of target lexical items |
| Spada and Lightbown (1999) | Effects of level of instruction, implicit instruction and L1 on developmental stages in question formation | Oral production, scrambled question preference task, picture-cued written question task | "Input flood" of questions with stage 4 and 5 inversion to ready to learn (stage 3) and unready (stage 2) learners | Four 60-min sessions/week/2 weeks | Six weeks, including pretest, 8 days intervention, and posttest; delayed posttest after 4 weeks | Acceptance of questions with Stage 4 and 5 inversion of pronoun subjects by both ready and unready learners possibly due to L1 influence |
| Swain (1998) | Effects of modeling metalinguistic talk before a dictogloss task on learners' talk and attention to form during task implementation | Dictogloss task | Pretask metalinguistic talk | One dictogloss/week/3 weeks | Four weeks, including posttest | Greater attention for L2 form with pretask metalinguistic talk than no pretask metalinguistic talk |

TABLE II. (*Continued*)

| Study | Focus | Tasks | Treatments | Treatment intensity, duration | Total length of study | Findings |
|---|---|---|---|---|---|---|
| Swain and Lapkin (1998) | Effects of collaborative dialogue on L2 learning and communication | Jigsaw task (collaborative story building through pictures) | Minilesson followed by pair task implementation | Two sessions | Five weeks, including pretest; 2 weeks treatment and posttest | Collaborative dialogue effective for resolving communication breakdowns and providing assistance with SLA |
| Takashima and Ellis (1999) | Effects of clarification requests on immediately reformulated output and on past tense over time | Story reconstruction and presentation | Focused *vs.* nonfocused clarification requests in response to utterances with nontarget past-verb forms | One 45-min session/week for 3 weeks | Six weeks, due to posttests and delayed posttests following treatment | Clarification requests effective for self-correction; mixed results for verb tense accuracy |

were effective in drawing students'attention to the targeted forms and retaining them during text reconstruction over the short duration of the study.

Muranoi (2000) also focused on English articles through problem solving tasks that required article suppliance for their completion. She used the tasks to look for ways in which learners produced and modified their production as they negotiated their plan for solving the problems. Similar design and implementation of tasks that drew learners' attention to low-salience features were shown by Iwashita (2003) for particles in Japanese; Leeman (2003) for features of Spanish agreement; Long et al. (1998) for Japanese adjective ordering and locatives and Spanish adverb placement; Mackey and McDonough (2000) for Thai noun classifiers; Newton and Kennedy (1996) for English prepositions and conjunctions; and Nobuyoshi, and Ellis (1993) for English past time markers. Researchers have also customized tasks to draw learners' attention to sequentially acquired, complex forms such as English questions and relative clauses. Some of their studies (e.g., Izumi, 2002; Mackey & Oliver, 2002; Mackey & Philp,1998; McDonough, 2005; Spada & Lightbown 1999) are also shown in Table II.

Socioculturally oriented, information-exchange tasks are designed to promote collaborative interaction through which learners can support and guide each other's L2 learning. Swain and Lapkin (2001), for example, have used the "dictogloss" to provide a basis for the process of "scaffolding," whereby learners can support each other when confronted with task components they cannot yet accomplish on their own (see also Kowal & Swain, 1994). Working independently, learners take notes while listening to a teacher-delivered text. Next they meet in pairs or groups, using their notes to coconstruct the text, which they then present orally to their classmates. The task appears to be especially effective for vocabulary learning. Table II displays design and outcome information from Swain (1998) and Swain and Lapkin (2001), and from de la Fuente (2002); Gass and Alvarez Torres (2005); and Smith (2005), who also used tasks to study vocabulary learning.

As Table II makes evident, task methodology has been effective in helping learners with forms that they are ready to learn, but are challenged to do so. At the same time, it provides researchers with an effective approach to data collection on important L2 processes and outcomes. As Table II also makes evident, however, task methodology has been employed largely in short-term research. Even when durations of several weeks time were reported, these durations included delayed post-testing, carried out after the actual treatment was over (see, e.g., de la Fuente, 2002; Doughty & Varela, 1998; Iwashita, 2003; Izumi, 2002; Smith, 2005; Spada & Lightbown, 1999; Takashima & Ellis, 1999).

Just as extending the period of time for post-testing is important for addressing questions on L2 retention, so too is extending the period of treatment time important for questions on learning processes and L2 outcomes, especially for those areas of SLA that defy short-term intervention. Ideally, a controlled environment would allow for the isolated study of key factors of input, interaction, feedback, and output in SLA. The use of tasks would surely provide a good deal of relevant data in these areas. Realistically, though, finding learners willing to participate in a controlled study, over an extended time, is not an easy enterprise for SLA researchers. Opportunities to compensate through funding or through tutoring or teaching services, though possibly effective, are usually not feasible, due to cost and time constraints. This is where intact classrooms might play an important role. Although they do not allow for random selection and assignment, they can provide large cohorts of learners, who are likely to be available for weeks or months of treatment time. Most learners and their teachers would be familiar with the kinds of information-exchange tasks that have originated from, and can be accommodated to, their current, familiar classroom curriculum. The combination of tasks and classroom settings can play a role in the methodology needed to address questions on SLA within and beyond the IE.

## XII. TASKS AND CLASSROOMS: EXPANDING THEIR ROLE IN SLA RESEARCH

L2 classrooms are first and foremost environments for teaching and learning. Although they also serve as environments for research, much of the research in classrooms to date has been aimed at describing instructional practices rather than testing the effects of instructional interventions on SLA. Studies that expanded the role of the classroom as an SLA research environment (e.g., Day & Shapson, 1991; Doughty & Varela, 1998; Harley, 1989, 1998; Lyster, 1994) are instructive in the design of future studies. All used activities and tasks that were consistent with the curriculum, schedule, and format of the classrooms where they carried out their studies, and were therefore not intrusive to the work of teachers and students.

Information-exchange tasks add an additional component to research in the classroom, however, due to their dual role as tools for data collection and instructional interventions. As learners work together to reach task goals, their L2 exchanges provide interaction-based data that can address questions on evidence, its accessibility through input, interaction, feedback, and output, and its relationship with cognitive processes such as noticing and attention, However, when designed with research concerns in mind, such tasks also **carry the** risk of appearing like tests to classroom participants, as indeed was found by Pica et al. (2006). Their attractiveness for communication can be offset by their inconsistency with the content of the classroom curriculum. Learners might be willing to carry them out over the short term, but are likely to lose interest in **them** over time.

To enhance their authenticity and insure their long-term use, research tasks first need to be integrated into curriculum texts, topics and assignments, and have enough variety to warrant sustained participation. With this in mind, Pica et al. (2006) based their research tasks on the texts students were asked to read and discuss in their daily classroom life. In keeping with the course emphasis on academic English, task directions began with a purpose statement, that is, the task would help the students become "more accurate and precise" in their speaking and writing in areas such as reviewing, editing, organizing and reporting information. The tasks were simple to implement for long-term application by the teacher, as the researchers could not be on hand on a daily basis. Teacher, researcher, and student involvement was ongoing in task design, piloting, and revision. Directions were reworded and revised frequently, based on numerous pilot runs. Such preparation, though labor intensive, was considered an investment by the researchers, affording both the opportunity to carry out more than one study, and to collaborate, present, and publish their work over time.

Early in this chapter, methodological issues were raised regarding the IE from the point of view of L2 teaching and learning, as well as research on the SLA that occurs there. A meta-analysis by Norris and Ortega (2001) had found that explicit, form-focused IEs resulted in more accurate and advanced SLA outcomes than those that had followed implicit approaches. However, as they argued, this was largely because so many of the analyzed studies had used short-term treatments, and documented L2 learning through discrete point tests. These two characteristics reduced the possibility for a valid comparison, as implicit approaches are claimed to promote implicit knowledge. Such knowledge takes a long time to acquire and is ill-served by isolated test items.

The findings of the meta-analysis suggested several new directions for the field. One direction involved the tracking of the ways in which explicit learning might contribute to the implicit knowledge that learners eventually come to use. Research on this front is well underway (e.g., DeKeyser, 2003; Williams, 2009). Another direction was to lengthen the treatment and research time for both individual studies and multistudy comparisons. Any number of controlled settings would be ideal for such projects, but it is difficult to imagine many participants able and willing to commit to this effort. The classroom, with a cohort of learners in place over time, offers a site worth considering, not only for its promise in responding to issues on the consequences of implicit L2 teaching, but also for its ecological validity in informing questions on evidence, input, feedback, and output. From its introduction of theoretical constructs such as "notice the gap," "focus on form," and "teachability," to its contributions of task-based activities and classrooms sites, the IE has made many contributions to the study of SLA. The richness of these resources for responding to current methodological needs and addressing broader research goals bodes well for contributions of an even greater magnitude through future studies.

## REFERENCES

Allen, L. (2000). Form-meaning connections and the French causative: An experiment in processing instruction. *Studies in Second Language Acquisition, 22*, 69–84.

Allwright, R. (1980). Turns, topics, and tasks: Patterns of participation in language learning and teaching. In D. Larsen-Freeman (Ed.), *Discourse analysis in second language research* (pp. 165–187). Rowley MA: Newbury House.

Ayoun, D. (2001). The role of negative and positive feedback in the second language acquisition of the passé composé and imparfait. *The Modern Language Journal, 85*, 226–243.

Brumfit, C., & Johnson, K. (Eds.). (1979). *The communicative approach to language teaching.* Oxford: Oxford University Press.

Carroll, S., & Swain, M. (1993). Explicit and implicit feedback: An empirical study of the learning of linguistic generalizations. *Studies in Second Language Acquisition, 15*, 357–386.

Chaudron, C. (1988). *Second language classrooms.* Cambridge: Cambridge University Press.

Day, E., & Shapson, S. (1991). Integrating formal and functional approaches in language teaching in French immersion: An experimental study. *Language Learning, 41*, 21–58.

DeGraaff, R. (1997). The eXperanto experiment: Effects of explicit instruction on second language acquisition. *Studies in Second Language Acquisition, 19,* 249–276.

DeKeyser, R. (1997). Beyond explicit rule learning: Automatizing second language morpho-syntax. *Studies in Second Language Acquisition, 19,* 195–221.

DeKeyser, R. (2003). Implicit and Explicit Learning. In C. Doughty & M. Long (Eds.), *The handbook of second language acquisition* (pp. 313–347). Malden, MA: Blackwell Publishing Ltd.

DeKeyser, R. M., & Sokalski, K. J. (2001). The differential role of comprehension and production practice. *Language Learning, 51*(Suppl. 1), 81–112.

de la Fuente, M. J. (2002). Negotiation and oral acquisition of L2 vocabulary: the roles of input and output in the receptive and productive acquisition of words. *Studies in Second Language Acquisition, 24,* 81–112.

Doughty, C. (2001). Cognitive underpinnings of focus on form. In P. Robinson (Ed.), *Cognition and second language instruction* (pp. 206–257). Cambridge: Cambridge University Press.

Doughty, C. (2003). Instructed SLA: Constraints, compensation, and enhancement. In C. Doughty & M. Long (Eds.), *The handbook of second language acquisition* (pp. 256–310). Malden, MA: Blackwell Publishing Ltd.

Doughty, C., & Pica, T. (1986). "Information gap tasks": An aid to second language acquisition? *TESOL Quarterly, 20,* 305–325.

Doughty, C., & Varela, E. (1998). Communicative focus on form. In C. Doughty & J. Williams (Eds.), *Focus on form in classroom second language acquisition* (pp. 114–138). Cambridge: Cambridge University Press.

Doughty, C., & Williams, J. (1998). Pedagogical choices in focus on form. In C. Doughty & J. Williams (Eds.), *Focus on form in classroom second language acquisition* (pp. 197–261). Cambridge: Cambridge University Press.

Dulay, H., & Burt, M. (1974). Natural sequences in child second language acquisition. *Language Learning, 24,* 253–278.

Dulay, H., Burt, M., & Krashen, S. (1982). *Language 2.* New York: Oxford University Press.

Ellis, R. (1989). Are classroom and naturalistic second language acquisition the same? A study of the classroom acquisition of German word order rules. *Studies in Second Language Acquisition, 23,* 305–328.

Ellis, R. (1995). Interpretation tasks for grammar teaching. *TESOL Quarterly, 29,* 87–105.

Ellis, R. (1999). Input-based approaches to the teaching of grammar. In W. Grabe (Ed.), *Annual review of applied linguistics.* New York: Cambridge University Press.

Ellis, N. (2003a). At the interface: Dynamic interactions of explicit and implicit language knowledge. *Studies in Second Language Acquisition, 27,* 305–352.

Ellis, R. (2003b). *Task-based language learning and teaching.* Oxford: Oxford University Press.

Ellis, R. (2005). Measuring implicit and explicit knowledge of a second language: A psychometric study. *Studies in Second Language Acquisition, 27,* 141–172.

Fotos, S. (1994). Integrating grammar instruction and communicative language use through grammar consciousness-raising tasks. *TESOL Quarterly, 28,* 323–351.

Fotos, S., & Ellis, R. (1991). Communicating about grammar: A task-based approach. *TESOL Quarterly, 2,* 605–628.

Gass, S., & Alvarez Torres, M. (2005). Attention when? An investigation of the ordering effect of input and interaction. *Studies in Second Language Acquisition, 27,* 1–31.

Gass, S., Mackey, A., & Ross-Feldman, L. (2005). Task-based interactions in classroom and laboratory settings. *Language Learning, 55,* 575–611.

Han, Z. (2002). A study of the impact of recasts on tense consistency in L2 output. *TESOL Quarterly*, *36*, 543–572.

Harley, B. (1989). Functional grammar in French immersion: A classroom experiment. *Applied Linguistics*, *10*, 331–359.

Harley, B. (1993). Instructional strategies and SLA in early French immersion. *Studies in Second Language in Acquisition*, *15*, 245–260.

Harley, B. (1998). The role of focus-on-form tasks in promoting child L2 acquisition. In C. Doughty & J. Williams (Eds.), *Focus on Form in Classroom Second Language Acquisition* (pp. 156–174). Cambridge: Cambridge University Press.

Harmer, J., & Surguine, H. (1987). *Coast to coast*. London, UK: Longman.

Hatch, E. (1980). *Second language acquisition: A book of readings*. Rowley, MA: Newbury House.

He, X., & Ellis, R. (1999). Modified output and the acquisition of word meanings. In R. Ellis (Ed.), *Learning a second language through interaction* (pp. 115–132). Amsterdam: John Benjamins.

Helgesen, M., Brown, S., & Mandeville, T. (2000). *English firsthand*. Hong Kong: Longman Asia ELT.

Howatt, A. (1984). *A history of English language teaching*. Oxford: Oxford University Press.

Iwashita, N. (2003). Negative feedback and positive evidence in task-based interaction: Differential effects on L2 development. *Studies in Second Language Acquisition*, *25*, 1–36.

Izumi, S. (2002). Output, input enhancement, and the noticing hypothesis. *Studies in Second Language Acquisition*, *24*, 541–577.

Kelly, L. G. (1969). *25 centuries of language teaching: An inquiry into the science, art, and development of language teaching methodology, 500B.C.–1969*. Rowley, MA: Newbury House Publishers.

Kowal, M., & Swain, M. (1994). Using collaborative language production tasks to promote students' language awareness. *Language Awareness*, *3*, 73–93.

Krashen, S. (1976). Formal and informal environments in language acquisition and language learning. *TESOL Quarterly*, *10*, 157–168.

Krashen, S. (1981). *Second language acquisition and second language learning*. Oxford: Pergamon.

Krashen, S., & Seliger, H. (1975). The essential characteristics of formal instruction. *TESOL Quarterly*, *9*, 173–183.

Leeman, J. (2003). Recasts and second language development: Beyond negative evidence. *Studies in Second Language Acquisition*, *25*, 37–63.

Leopold, W. F. (1939–1949). Speech development of a bilingual child: A linguist's record, 1939, 1947, 1949, Vol. 1, vocabulary growth in the first two years. Vol. 2, sound learning in the first two years. Vol. 3, grammar and general problems in the first two years. Vol. 4, diary from age 2. Northwestern University Press, Evanston, IL.

Lightbown, P. (1998). The importance of timing in focus on form. In C. Doughty & J. Williams (Eds.), *Focus on form in classroom second language acquisition* (pp. 177–196). Cambridge: Cambridge University Press.

Lightbown, P., & Spada, N. (1990). Focus on form and corrective feedback in communicative language teaching: Effects on second language learning. *Studies in Second Language Acquisition*, *12*, 429–448.

Lightbown, P., & Spada, N. (2006). *How languages are learned* (3rd ed.). London, UK: Oxford University Press.

Linnell, J. (1995). *Negotiation as a context for learning syntax in a second language.* Unpublished doctoral dissertation, University of Pennsylvania, Philadelphia, PA.

Long, M. (1981). Input, interaction, and second language acquisition. In H. Winitz (Ed.), *Native and foreign language acquisition* (Vol. 379). New York: Annals of the New York Academy of Sciences.

Long, M. (1983). Native speaker/non-native speaker conversation and the negotiation of comprehensible input. *Applied Linguistics, 4,* 126–141.

Long, M. (1991). Focus on form: A design feature in language teaching methodology. In K. deBot, R. Ginsberg, & C. Kramsch (Eds.), *Foreign language research in cross-cultural perspective* (pp. 39–52). Amsterdam: John Benjamins.

Long, M. (1996). The role of the linguistic environment in second language acquisition. In W. C. Ritchie & T. K. Bhatia (Eds.), *Handbook of language acquisition, Vol. 2: Second language acquisition* (pp. 413–458). New York: Academic Press.

Long, M., Inagaki, S., & Ortega, L. (1998). The role of implicit negative feedback in SLA. *The Modern Language Journal, 82,* 357–371.

Long, M., & Robinson, P. (1998). Focus on form: Theory, research, and practice. In C. Doughty & J. Williams (Eds.), *Focus on form in classroom second language acquisition* (pp. 15–41). New York: Cambridge University Press.

Long, M., & Sato, C. (1983). Classroom foreigner talk discourse: Forms and functions of teachers' questions. In H. W. Seliger & M. H. Long (Eds.), *Classroom oriented research in second language acquisition* (pp. 268–285). Rowley, MA: Newbury House.

Loschky, L., & Bley-Vroman, R. (1993). Creating structure-based communication tasks for second language development. In G. Crookes & S. Gass (Eds.), *Tasks and language learning* (Vol. 1). Clevedon, Avon, UK: Multilingual Matters.

Lyster, R. (1994). The role of functional-analytic language teaching on aspects of French immersion students' sociolinguistic competence. *Applied Linguistics, 15,* 263–287.

Lyster, R. (1998). Negotiation of form, recasts, and explicit correction in relation to error types and learner repair in immersion classrooms. *Language Learning, 48,* 183–218.

Lyster, R., & Mori, H. (2006). Interactional feedback and instructional counterbalance. *Studies in Second Language Acquisition, 28,* 269–300.

Lyster, R., & Ranta, L. (1997). Corrective feedback and learner uptake: Negotiation of form in communicative classrooms. *Studies in Second Language Acquisition, 19,* 37–66.

Mackey, A. (1999). Input, interaction, and second language development. *Studies in Second Language Acquisition, 21,* 557–588.

Mackey, A., & McDonough, K. (2000). Communicative tasks, conversational interaction and linguistic form: An empirical study of Thai. *Foreign Language Annals, 33,* 82–91.

Mackey, A., & Oliver, R. (2002). Interactional feedback and children's L2 development. *System, 30,* 459–477.

Mackey, A., Oliver, R., & Leeman, J. (2003). Interactional input and the incorporation of feedback: an exploration of NS-NNS and NNS-NNS adult and child dyads. *Language Learning, 53,* 35–66.

Mackey, A., & Philp, J. (1998). Conversational interaction and second language development: Recasts, responses, and red herrings? *The Modern Language Journal, 82,* 338–356.

McDonough, K. (2005). Identifying the impact of negative feedback and learners' responses on ESL question development. *Studies in Second Language Acquisition, 27,* 79–103.

Muranoi, H. (2000). Focus on form through interaction enhancement: Integrating formal instruction into a communicative task in EFL classrooms. *Language Learning, 50,* 617–673.

Newton, J., & Kennedy, G. (1996). Effects of communication tasks on the grammatical relations marked by second language learners. *System*, *24*, 309–322.

Nicholas, H., Lightbown, P., & Spada, N. (2001). Recasts as feedback to language learners. *Language Learning*, *51*, 719–758.

Nobuyoshi, J., & Ellis, R. (1993). Focused communication tasks and second language acquisition. *ELT Journal*, *47*, 203–210.

Norris, J., & Ortega, L. (2001). Does type of instruction make a difference? Substantive findings from a meta-analytic review. *Language Learning*, *51*, 157–213.

Norris, J., & Ortega, L. (2003). Defining and measuring SLA. In C. Doughty & M. Long (Eds.), *The handbook of second language acquisition* (pp. 717–761). Malden, MA: Blackwell Publishing Ltd.

Norris, J., & Ortega, L. (2006). The value and practice of research synthesis for language learning and teaching. In J. Norris & L. Ortega (Eds.), *Synthesizing research on language learning and teaching* (pp. 3–50). Amsterdam: John Benjamins Publishing Co.

Nunan, D. (1989). *Designing tasks for the communicative classroom*. Cambridge: Cambridge University Press.

Oliver, R. (1995). Negative feedback in child NS-NNS conversation. *Studies in Second Language Acquisition*, *17*, 459–481.

Oliver, R. (2000). Age differences in negotiation and feedback in classroom and pairwork. *Language Learning*, *50*, 119–151.

Oliver, R., & Mackey, A. (2003). Interactional context and feedback in child ESL classrooms. *The Modern Language Journal*, *87*, 519–533.

Paninos, D. (2005). *The role of output in noticing of input for second language acquisition*. Unpublished doctoral dissertation, University of Pennsylvania, Philadelphia, PA.

Philp, J. (2003). Constraints on "noticing the gap": Nonnative speakers' noticing of recasts in NS-NNS interaction. *Studies in Second Language Acquisition*, *25*, 99–126.

Pica, T. (1983). Adult acquisition of English as a second language under different conditions of exposure. *Language Learning*, *33*, 465–497.

Pica, T. (1991). Classroom interaction, participation, and negotiation: Redefining relationships. *System*, *19*, 437–452.

Pica, T. (2002). Subject matter content: How does it assist the interactional and linguistic needs of classroom language learners? *The Modern Language Journal*, *86*, 1–19.

Pica, T. (2005). Classroom learning, teaching, and research: A task-based perspective. *The Modern Language Journal*, *89*, 339–352.

Pica, T. (2007). Time, teachers, and tasks in focus on form instruction. In S. Fotos & H. Nassaji (Eds.), *Form-focused instruction and teacher education* (pp. 161–176). Oxford: Oxford University Press.

Pica, T., & Doughty, C. (1985a). Input and interaction in the communicative language classroom: A comparison of teacher-fronted and group activities. In S. Gass & C. Madden (Eds.), *Input in second language acquisition* (pp. 115–132). Rowley, MA: Newbury House.

Pica, T., & Doughty, C. (1985b). The role of group work in classroom second language acquisition. *Studies in Second Language Acquisition*, *7*, 233–248.

Pica, T., Holliday, L., Lewis, N., & Morgenthaler, L. (1989). Comprehensible output as an outcome of linguistic demands on the learner. *Studies in Second Language Acquisition*, *11*, 63–90.

Pica, T., Kanagy, R., & Falodun, J. (1993). Choosing and using communication tasks for second language instruction. In G. Crookes & S. Gass (Eds.), *Tasks and language learning* (Vol. 1). Clevedon, Avon, UK: Multilingual Matters.

Pica, T., Kang, H., & Sauro, S. (2006). Information gap tasks: Their multiple roles and contributions to interaction research methodology. *Studies in Second Language Acquisition*, *28*, 301–338.

Pica, T., Lincoln-Porter, F., Paninos, D., & Linnell, J. (1996). Language learners' interaction: How does it address the input, output, and feedback needs of L2 learners? *TESOL Quarterly*, *30*, 59–84.

Pica, T., & Washburn, G. (2003). Negative evidence in language classroom activities: A study of its availability and accessibility to language learners. *ITL Journal of Applied Linguistics*, *141*, 301–344.

Pienemann, M. (1985). Learnability and syllabus construction. In K. Hyltenstam & M. Pienemann (Eds.), *Modeling and assessing second language acquisition* (pp. 23–75). Clevedon, Avon, UK: Multilingual Matters.

Pienemann, M. (1989). Is language teachable? Psycholinguistic experiments and hypotheses. *Applied Linguistics*, *10*, 52–79.

Pienemann, M. (1998). *Language processing and second language development: Processibility theory*. Amsterdam: John Benjamins.

Porter, P. (1986). How learners talk to each other: Input and interaction in task-centered discussions. In R. R. Day (Ed.), *Talking to Learn: Conversation in Second Language Acquisition* (pp. 200–222). Rowley, MA: Newbury House Publishers, Inc.

Rutherford, W., & Sharwood Smith, M. (1985). Consciousness-raising and universal grammar. *Applied Linguistics*, *6*, 274–282.

Schmidt, R., & Frota, S. (1986). Developing basic conversational ability in a second language: A case study of an adult learner of Portuguese. In R. Day (Ed.), *Talking to learn: Conversation in second language acquisition* (pp. 237–336). Rowley, MA: Newbury House.

Shehadeh, A. (1999). Non-native speakers' production of modified comprehensible output and second language learning. *Language Learning*, *49*, 627–675.

Shehadeh, A. (2001). Self- and other-initiated modified output during task-based interaction. *TESOL Quarterly*, *35*, 433–457.

Smith, B. (2005). The relationship between negotiated interaction, learner uptake, and lexical acquisition in task-based computer-mediated communication. *TESOL Quarterly*, *39*, 33–58.

Spada, N., & Lightbown, P. (1993). Instruction and the development of questions in L2 classrooms. *Studies in Second Language Acquisition*, *15*, 205–224.

Spada, N., & Lightbown, P. (1999). Instruction, first language influence, and developmental readiness in second language acquisition. *The Modern Language Journal*, *83*, 1–22.

Swain, M. (1985). Communicative competence: Some roles of comprehensible input and comprehensible output in its development. In S. M. Gass & C. G. Madden (Eds.), *Input in second language acquisition* (pp. 235–253). Rowley, MA: Newbury House.

Swain, M. (1993). The output hypothesis: Just speaking and writing aren't enough. *The Canadian Modern Language Review*, *50*, 158–164.

Swain, M. (1998). Focus on form through conscious reflection. In C. Doughty & J. Williams (Eds.), *Focus on form in classroom second language acquisition* (pp. 64–81). Cambridge: Cambridge University Press.

Swain, M., & Lapkin, S. (1998). Interaction and second language learning: Two adolescent French immersion students working together. *The Modern Language Journal*, *82*, 320–337.

Swain, M., & Lapkin, S. (2001). Focus on form through collaborative dialogue: Exploring task effects. In M. Bygate, P. Skehan, & M. Swain (Eds.), *Researching pedagogic tasks: Second language learning, teaching and testing* (pp. 99–118). New York: Longman.

Takashima, H., & Ellis, R. (1999). Output enhancement and the acquisition of the past tense. In R. Ellis (Ed.), *Learning a second language through interaction* (pp. 173–188). Amsterdam: John Benjamins.

Tomasello, M., & Herron, C. (1988). Down the garden path: Inducing and correcting overgeneralization errors in the foreign language classroom. *Applied Psycholinguistics, 9,* 237–246.

Tomasello, M., & Herron, C. (1989). Feedback for language transfer errors: The garden path technique. *Studies in Second Language Acquisition, 11,* 385–395.

Trahey, M., & White, L. (1993). Positive evidence and preemption in the second language classroom. *Studies in Second Language Acquisition, 15,* 181–204.

Ur, P. (1988). *Grammar practice activities.* Cambridge: Cambridge University Press.

VanPatten, B., & Cadierno, T. (1993). Explicit instruction and input processing. *Studies in Second Language Acquisition, 15,* 225–243.

White, L. (1991). Adverb placement in second language acquisition: Some effects of positive and negative evidence in the classroom. *Second Language Research, 7,* 122–161.

White, J. (1998). Getting the learners attention: A typographical input enhancement study. In C. Doughty & J. Williams (Eds.), *Focus on form in classroom second language acquisition* (pp. 85–113). Cambridge: Cambridge University Press.

Williams, J. (2009). Implicit learning in second language aquisition. In W. C. Ritchie & T. K. Bhatia (Eds.), *New handbook of second language acquisition* (2nd ed., pp. 319–353). Bingley: Emerald Group Publishing Limited.

Williams, J., & Evans, J. (1998). Which kind of focus on which kind of forms? In C. Doughty & J. Williams (Eds.), *Focus on form in classroom second language acquisition* (pp. 139–155). Cambridge: Cambridge University Press.

CHAPTER 21

# UNTUTORED SECOND LANGUAGE ACQUISITION

Wolfgang Klein and Christine Dimroth

## I. INTRODUCTION

Many millennia ago, some genetic changes endowed our species with the ability

- to construct highly complex linguistic systems (natural languages),
- to copy such systems, once created, from other members of the species, and
- to use them for the exchange of thoughts, wishes, feelings between members of the species.

These three capacities—the *construction capacity*, the *copying capacity*, and the *communication capacity*—are closely interconnected, and they draw largely on the same cognitive resources, such as memory, perception, and reasoning. But they are not the same. Our ancestors, when creating the first linguistic systems, had little to *copy*; they had to build linguistic systems, in a way which we can only speculate about. This process, in whichever way it was achieved, is surely neither momentaneous nor done by a single person, and therefore, it also involved a great deal of *copying* from others. Nowadays, people are rarely confronted with the need to *construct* a new linguistic system; but everybody is confronted with the need to *copy* at least one existing system. This process is what we call language acquisition. It involves the copying capacity, it involves the construction capacity, it also involves—and dramatically changes—the capacity to communicate by linguistic systems. Normally, we all experience this transition in childhood, with no or little guided intervention on the part of the social environment, but it can also happen at a later age, with or without systematic intervention. Language acquisition is a natural process; it does not need tutoring. But its study is deeply shaped by a certain view that is naturally invited by the context in which

503

we are first confronted with it—the classroom. This is a very natural view; but it risks missing crucial aspects of what really happens when our language capacities are at work.

## II. TWO VIEWS ON SECOND LANGUAGE ACQUISITION

At present, there are at least 6000 languages and about 200 states on earth. So, there are about 30 languages per state on average. Surely, this does not mean that every inhabitant of a state is faced with the need to learn 30 languages. But it means that the acquisition of a single linguistic system is not the normal case. The normal case, from which any investigation of language acquisition should start, is rather that human beings, equipped with certain cognitive capacities, set out to copy the ways in which others (a) pair sounds and meanings to elementary expressions and (b) build complex expressions from simpler ones; they set out to copy the *lexicon* and the *grammatical rules* of some existing system, and they do this with varying success. They develop what one might call learner varieties—that is, linguistic systems which initially are quite simple and which can already be used for communication. This process continues, and under specific conditions, it is pushed to a degree where the learners competence to speak and to understand does not saliently differ from that of their social environment. Then, we speak of perfect mastery of a language. This perfect mastery is thus a special case of mastering a learner variety; similarly, a real language is just a special case of a learner variety. Perfect mastery reflects that case in which neither the learner nor those around him notice any difference they would consider noteworthy.

This process is what has happened in the history of mankind ever since the first linguistic systems were created, and this is what happens right now all over the earth. It is a natural, species-specific process which exhibits a number of regularities, but which may also vary in many dimensions. We may sum up this way to view language acquisition as follows (Klein & Perdue, 1997, p. 307):

A. Learners pass through a series of increasingly complex linguistic systems— learner varieties. The internal structure of each variety at a given time as well as the transition from one variety to the next are not random but characterized by certain principles.

B. The structure of learner utterances results from the interaction of several organizational principles. With successive input analysis, the interaction changes. For example, picking up some component of noun morphology from the input may cause the learner to modify the weight of other factors to mark argument status. From this perspective, learning a new feature is not like adding a new piece to a puzzle which the learner has to put together. Rather, it leads to sometimes minor, sometimes substantial reorganization of the whole variety.

C. Learner varieties are not imperfect imitations of a "real language" but linguistic systems in their own right, characterized by a particular lexical repertoire and by a particular interaction of structural and functional principles. In fact, fully developed languages, such as English, German, French, are nothing but special cases of learner varieties. They represent a relatively stable state of language acquisition—that state where the learner stops learning because there is no perceivable difference between his variety and the variety of his social environment.

Thus, the process of language acquisition is characterized by a twofold systematicity: the inherent systematicity of a learner variety at any given time and the way in which such a variety evolves into another one. If we want to understand the very nature of acquisition, we must uncover this twofold systematicity; precisely, this is the core task of language acquisition research, be it first or second.

Additionally, we might also want to know how and why learners often miss the target, and what could be done to help them. But if we consider language acquisition as the natural achievement of certain species-specific capacities, then these are secondary questions, though of eminent practical importance. In the history of mankind, systematic intervention into this natural process—that is, second language teaching in a classroom—comes in very late. But these practical concerns have deeply influenced our view on languages and how they are learned. As a result, the dominant view on second language acquisition is rather what one might label the target deviation perspective:

A. There is a well-defined *target* of the acquisition process—the language to be learned. As any real language is a clearly fixed entity—perfectly mastered by those who have learned it in childhood and who are thus competent to judge—and is more or less correctly described in grammars and dictionaries.

B. Second language learners usually *miss* this target to varying degrees—they make errors in production as well as in comprehension, or they process the language in ways different from those of native speakers.

Both assumptions seem very natural. After all, it is the teacher's natural task to minimize or even erase deviations from the target. As a consequence, it seems to be the researcher's natural task to investigate which errors occur when and for which reasons, and why some of them are so robust that they can hardly be overcome after a certain age. Therefore, the learner's production and comprehension are not so much studied in their own right, as an independent manifestation of their language capacities, but in relation to a set norm, not in terms of what learners do but in terms of what they fail to do. Learners, within this perspective, desperately try to do what the native speaker does, but as a rule, they do it less well. These deficiencies must be described, and they must be explained. This is the first reason why this perspective seems so self-evident: it is the way in which the *teacher* looks at what happens.

There is a second reason. It is also the natural perspective of all of those who had to *learn* a language in the classroom—and thus of some language researchers. Here, as in so many other cases, our way to look at certain everyday phenomena is less shaped by the nature of these phenomena themselves than by the contexts which first confront us with them as objects of reflection. Children normally speak one or several languages at school age. But they hardly think about what a language is, unless they are confronted with certain linguistic rules in school settings. It is very difficult to get rid of the perspective which the teachers' red ink burned into our mind: there is a language to be learned, it is very well defined, and you missed it!

Third, this perspective provides the researcher with a straightforward research design. There is a yardstick against which the learners' performance can be measured: the target language, or what grammar books and dictionaries say about it. What is measured is the differences between what learners do and what the set norms demand. Therefore, the research design is essentially an elaboration of the red ink method: errors are counted and statistically analyzed. One may count, for example, how often Spanish and Dutch learners of English omit the subject pronoun in a test, and if there is a substantial difference, then this may be attributed to the influence of the first language. Alternatively, one might also look at the individual error and try to find out what led to it, that is, quantitative analysis and hypothesis testing can be replaced or complemented by more qualitative, interpretive approaches. The guiding idea is always: We analyze how well learners reproduce a certain regularity, as defined by the researcher or the teacher, and we try to explain why they are able or not able to do this.

This way to look at second language acquisition has many merits. But it hardly informs us about the principles of second language acquisition—that is, how the human language capacities construct and copy linguistic systems. At the very best, it tells us to which extent and why the results of the acquisition process deviate from certain norms. This is useful for anyone who wants to overcome these problems, or wants to help others to overcome them—that is, for students and teachers. But even for these practical purposes, it would be useful if we understood the very nature of the process that we want to optimize. To this end, we must investigate what our genetically given language capacities do when they try to do their job. In other words, we must investigate language acquisition in its natural habitat—outside the classroom, without the influence of systematic intervention.

First attempts in this direction are reflected in notions such as interlanguage (Selinker, 1972), approximate systems (Nemser, 1971), and related ones. But they still assume that the real things—the target language and the source language—are on both sides, whereas what is in-between is some imperfect hybrid. The more radical learner variety perspective sketched above goes back to early attempts to analyze the language of adult migrants who have no or very limited teaching and are thus bound to their genetically given, though perhaps no longer fully vital construction and copying capacities. An early example is Schumann's study of how a Spanish-speaking migrant acquires and uses American English (Schumann, 1978). Schumann's work is primarily interested in the sociopsychological factors which push the learner to stick to a particular, reduced system. It is less concerned with the inherent structural systematicity of this system and how it evolves over time. Precisely, these questions are in the focus of some larger projects on the language of foreign workers, which began at about the same time in Germany (Clahsen, Meisel, & Pienemann, 1983; Heidelberger Forschungsprojekt Pidgin-Deutsch, 1975; Klein & Dittmar, 1979; von Stutterheim, 1986). In section IV, we shall consider some findings from more recent endeavors that are based on these early attempts. First, however, we will examine a number of parameters, along which language acquisition with and without systematic intervention varies.

## III. TUTORED VERSUS UNTUTORED

The opposition between tutored and untutored is a bold simplification. Tuition is always an attempt to intervene into a natural process, in order to optimize it.

This intervention is highly variable in amount, type, and consequences (Doughty, 2003; Hulstijn and Ellis, 2005; Pica, this volume). Labor immigrants, for example, primarily learn by daily interaction, but this does exclude a certain amount of tuition (as is even mandatory in some countries). Classroom learning, on the other hand, can be interrupted or complemented by communicative interaction with a target language community. Some teaching methods can be more grammar oriented or more communication oriented. In what follows, we will discuss a few core dimensions, along which the learning conditions and the final outcome of tutored and untutored acquisition may vary.

## A. Learning Conditions

Outside and inside the classroom, language acquisition constructs linguistic systems, which are partly or wholly copied from some input and already can be, and often are, used for communication. It always involves all three language capacities, but their relative weight varies sharply. Three factors are of particular importance here.

### Access to the Linguistic System

In untutored acquisition, the learner has access to the target language by everyday communication. The sounds (or graphic representations) of the language are embedded in a relevant context, and from this material, the learner derives how sound and meaning are coupled and how complex expressions are formed from simple ones. In tutored acquisition, such material is preprocessed in different ways. In the extreme case, the learner is initially offered only a metalinguistic description and some illustrative examples. The other extreme is a carefully guided imitation of actual communication, with very little explicit grammar. There are many intermediate stages between these extremes. In each case, preprocessing does not only affect the *way* but also the *order* in which the learner has access to the linguistic system to be learned. This order depends mainly on the estimated degree of difficulty and relevance of various portions of the material. It is an interesting and still unsettled question to which extent the teaching order should adopt the order in which the human language capacities would proceed without intervention: should teaching follow the natural sequence? (for discussion see Diehl, Christen, Leuenberger, Pelvat, & Studer, 2000).

### Communicative Pressure

Unlike students in the classroom, immigrant workers rapidly find themselves in situations in which they cannot wait for the relevant structures to be acquired in the exact target language way. Instead, the copied raw material has to be used immediately for communicative purposes, and the expressive means of a rather limited repertoire have to be extended as far as possible. A silent period like the one encountered in first language acquisition might be beneficial for language learning (Krashen, 1981; Slobin, 1993), but is often no option for adult immigrant learners who have to survive in the second language speaking community. In such a situation, the communication capacity of older learners must somehow bridge the gap between what is needed and what the copying and construction capacities are able to achieve. For the sake of early communication, untutored second language learners have to find ways to put their words together, and they have been shown to do this in a way that is partly independent of the source and target language regularities.

### Systematic External Control

Outside the classroom, the learner has two ways to control his or her success: (a) Do I understand, am I understood? (b) Do I have the impression that my way of speaking is exactly like that of the others? In the classroom, there is a teacher who permanently checks to which extent the learners' performance agrees with the target norms. Clearly, this gives the copying faculty a much higher weight than in untutored acquisition. As a consequence, one should expect that—everything else being equal—tutored learners are better in copying than untutored learners, and if ultimate attainment is measured in this way, then classroom learners should have an advantage here.

## B.  Outcome

What is more successful, tutored or untutored acquisition? No one really knows, but there are two popular convictions, strongly rooted in everyday experience:

A.  If you want to learn a second language perfectly well, you must go to the country where they speak it.
B.  In contrast to children, adults cannot learn a second language perfectly well.

The first of these convictions reflects strong doubts on the efficiency of classroom teaching, when compared to untutored acquisition, but there is hardly any reliable investigation of this issue (but see Diehl et al., 2000). Much in contrast, the second conviction has been, and still is, the object of much research and heated debates, especially in connection with the Critical Period Hypothesis (see, e.g., Birdsong, 1999, 2005; Long, 2005; Pagonis, 2007; Marinova-Todd, 2003; Singleton & Ryan, 2004). There is clear evidence that B, in its radical form, is false: there are adult second language learners whom native speakers cannot tell apart from native speakers on all sorts of tasks (see, e.g., Bongaerts, 1999; van Boxtel, 2005). Interestingly, by far most of these learners had undergone extensive teaching. But they also had a lot of practical experience and thus have probably learned a lot outside the classroom, and there is at least one study (Ioup, Boustagui, El Tigi, & Moselle, 1994) which gives evidence that untutored acquisition alone might lead to perfect mastery.

The entire discussion of age effects in acquisition is perhaps too much obsessed with the question to which extent learners produce 100% copies of how other speakers handle a given linguistic system, and thus, by potential changes in the copying faculty. But acquiring a second language, and a language in general, also means constructing a linguistic system and using it for communicative purposes. And if we want to understand the nature of human language, these aspects are perhaps much more important than potential age-related changes and individual differences in the ability to copy a system perfectly well.

## IV. THE STRUCTURE OF LEARNER VARIETIES

Systematic, and in particular longitudinal, investigation of how adults learn a second language outside the classroom began only in the early 1970s. This has changed, and although second language research is still dominated by work on tutored acquisition, a full survey is beyond the scope of this paper. We will therefore concentrate on the most comprehensive study so far, the project second language acquisition of adult immigrants, and some follow-up work. Funded by the European Science Foundation (Strasbourg), it was coordinated by the Max-Planck-Institut für Psycholinguistik in Nijmegen and took place from 1981 to 1988 in five European countries—France, Germany, Great Britain, the Netherlands, and Sweden; a comprehensive account is found in Perdue (1993). Numerous other studies followed, partly with the same, partly with parallel data but other language pairs, such as Chinese–Italian, Polish–German or Polish–French. Good surveys of this work are found in a number of volumes, such as Giacalone Ramat and Crocco Galeas, eds. (1995); Dittmar and Giacalone Ramat, eds. (1999); and Wegener, ed. (1998).

The project was longitudinal and crosslinguistic. It examined the productions of 40 adult learners of Dutch, English, French, German, and Swedish. All were recently arrived immigrants and in daily contact with the language of their new social environment. The following combination of source language (SL) and target language (TL) was chosen:

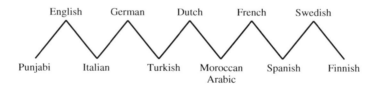

All learners were observed and recorded over about 30 months. Data-collection techniques ranged from free conversation to more controlled methods, such as film retellings, personal narratives, instructions (stage directions), and picture descriptions. All techniques were ordered into three data-collection cycles, such that each task was performed at least three times. Data were transcribed and computerized (see http://corpus1.mpi.nl/ds/imdi_browser). Analysis concentrated on six major themes: the structure of utterances (see Klein & Perdue, 1992), the expression of temporality (Dietrich, Klein, & Noyau, 1995), the expression of spatiality (Becker & Carroll, 2005), the lexicon, the misunderstandings and how they are corrected, and the feedback. In several follow-up studies, researchers have focused on the acquisition of finiteness and scope bearing elements like adverbials, negation, and focus particles (Benazzo, 2003; Bernini, 2005; Dimroth, 2002).

In what follows, we shall first discuss how learners structure their utterances at some intermediate level and then discuss how they manage to express temporality and negation.

## A. Utterance Structure

As one might predict, the learners utterances and the way they evolved over time varied in many respects. But there are also many similarities, the most striking of which is the existence of a special language form called the *basic variety* (Klein & Perdue, 1997). It was developed and used by all learners, independent of SL and TL. About one-third of the learners remained at this level; small changes aside, they only extended their lexical repertoire and learned to make more fluent use of the basic variety (henceforth BV).

As for any linguistic system, the BV consists of a set of elementary units—the lexemes and rules which allow the speakers to construct more complex expressions—the (morpho)syntactic rules of composition.

### The Lexicon

There is no inflection in the BV, hence no morphological marking for case, number, gender, tense, aspect, or agreement. Typically, a lexeme corresponds to the bare stem, the infinitive, or the nominative of the TL, but it can also be a form that would be an inflected form in the TL. Sometimes a word appears in more than one form. Such variation does not seem to have a function; the learners simply try out phonological variants.

The lexicon grows steadily during the acquisition process. The main source for the lexicon is the TL, but there are also many borrowings from the SL. The composition of the lexicon is remarkably constant among all learners. It essentially consists of a repertoire of noun-like and verb-like words as well as a few adjectives and adverbs. The pronoun system is extremely reduced. It includes minimal means to refer to speaker, listener, and a third person (functioning deictically and anaphorically). There are a few quantifiers and determiners (mainly demonstratives), a negator, and a few prepositions with over-generalized lexical meanings. There are no subordinating conjunctions. In other words, the repertoire consists mainly of open-class items and a few closed-class items with lexical meaning. There are no semantically empty elements, such as existential *there*.

### The Rules of Composition

How do BV speakers build more complex expressions? The complete absence of inflectional morphology, one of the favorite domains of classroom acquisition, reduces the possibilities for the combination of words, in the form of noun–noun compounds (rarely) and in the form of utterances. The structure of these utterances is determined by the interaction of three types of constraints. First, there are absolute "phrasal" constraints on the form and relative order of phrases. Second, there are "semantic" constraints relating to the case-role properties of arguments. Third, there are "pragmatic" constraints relating to the organization of information in connected text. The main phrasal constraints observed in the BV allow three basic utterance patterns with some subvariants (the NP subscripts correspond to different types of noun phrases, discussed below):

P1a.      $NP_1 - V$

P1b.      $NP_1 - V - NP_2$

P1c.      $NP_1 - V - NP_2 - NP_2$

P2.      $NP_1$ - COPULA - $\left\{ \begin{array}{l} \text{ADJECTIVE} \\ NP_2 \\ \text{PREPOSITIONAL PHRASE} \end{array} \right\}$

P3.      $\left\{ \begin{array}{l} \text{V} \\ \text{COPULA} \end{array} \right\}$ - $NP_2$

All patterns may be preceded or followed by an adverbial or by the conjunction *and*. There are also some scopal particles, in particular negators.

Note that a pattern such as NP–V–NP does not mean that the first NP is the "subject" and the second NP is the "object." In fact, it is not easy to define these notions *within* the BV, rather than in terms of their closest TL or SL counterparts. So which argument takes which position? We found that the control asymmetry between the two noun phrases, and thus a semantic feature, is crucial here. One can rank each argument of a verb by the greater or lesser degree of control that its referent exerts or intends to exert over the referents of the other argument(s). In the English sentence "Nick sliced the ham," for example, Nick ranks higher on the control hierarchy than the ham. The semantic constraint is as follows:

SEM1. The NP Referent with the Highest Control Comes First (Controller First)

Some verbs, notably verbs of saying and giving, take three arguments. These verbs are regularly of the "telic" type, that is, their lexical meaning involves two distinct states (see Klein, 1994, pp. 79–97). It is crucial that the control relation between the various arguments is not the same in both states. In an utterance like "Miriam gave Eva a book," there is a first state (the "source" state) in which Miriam is "in control of" the book and is active in bringing about a distinct state (the target state). In the target state, Eva rather than Miriam is "in control of" the book. The control status of the NP, which refers to the gift, is low in both states. The principle "controller first" thus requires that this argument does not come first. It does not prescribe, however, whether the controller of the source state or the controller of the target state comes first. "Controller first" must therefore be supplemented by an additional constraint which defines the relative weight of source and target state in determining word order.

SEM2. Controller of Source State Outweighs Controller of Target State

This principle applies analogously to verbs of saying if we assume that the control of information changes in both states. There is one referent in control of the information in both states, and another referent who controls the information in the target state, but not in the source state. Thus, the speaker comes first, the hearer comes second, and what is said comes last.

The two control constraints are not always operative, either because there is no asymmetry between the NP referents, or because the verb has only one argument. In these cases, the NP's position depends on how information is distributed across an utterance in context—that is, by pragmatic factors. The BV has two types of pragmatic constraints. They relate to information status—given versus new—or to the topic–focus structure. These two factors must be kept distinct, although in practice they often go together. The topic–focus structure reflects the fact that part of the utterance defines a set of alternatives (the topic) and selects the appropriate one (the focus). For example, the utterance "Eva ate an apple" can answer at least three different questions: (1) Who ate an apple? (2) What did Eva eat? (3) What did Eva do? In (1), the alternatives are the persons who could have eaten an apple (the topic) and the person specified by the NP *Eva* (the focus). In (2), the topic is the set of things that Eva could have eaten, and *the apple* specifies one of them (the focus). In (3), the set of alternatives comprises all the events involving Eva that could have occurred on that occasion, and the verb phrase specifies the one selected from this set (the focus). Full-fledged languages can mark an expression as a focus or topic expression by specific devices that include intonation, clefting, and special particles. BV mainly uses word order.

PRAG. The Focus Expression Comes Last (Focus Last)

If there is only one argument, then there is no control asymmetry, and so the controller constraints cannot apply. Hence, only PRAG and phrasal constraints interact. If the referent of the NP is topic, then one of the three patterns P1a, P1b, or P1c is used; if it is in the focus, then pattern P3 is used. The same constraint stipulates the NPs' position in copula constructions. In this way, word order can be accounted for without resorting to ill-defined notions like "subject" or "object."

The second pragmatic factor is the "given-new distinction": is what an expression refers to maintained from a preceding utterance or is it new? This distinction does not result in a simple word-order rule like PRAG, but rather in different types of NPs. These, in turn, are restricted to certain positions indicated by the numbers in the phrasal rules P1 to P3 noted above. Here, we find some variation within the BV. In particular, there are some numerals and (rarely) a definiteness marker, usually a demonstrative. We indicate this in the following diagram by optional DET. Typically, however, nouns are unadorned. This gives us the following main types:

|  $NP_1$  |  $NP_2$  |
|---|---|
| proper name | proper name |
| (DET) (adjective) noun | (DET) (adjective) noun |
| pronoun | |
| Zero (i.e., without phonological features) | |

The choice among these forms depends on whether a referent is new or given and whether the referring expression is in topic or focus. The most general opposition is between use of noun (or name) and pronoun or zero. Zero is used exclusively to maintain reference in the context of a controller moving from topic to topic in successive utterances. Maintaining semantic role and position (controller first) is thus not in itself sufficient to license zero where there are two potential controllers in the previous utterance (and is a further indication that "subject of" is not a BV function). With names and lexical nouns, position is the sole indicator of the referent's topic–focus status. It follows from the observed distribution that reference maintenance in focus cannot be achieved by pronominal means. So there are clear constraints on how things can be expressed in the BV, and where its speakers might run into problems. These problems are a major source of structural complexities.

## Complications

In comparison to real languages, the BV has something to offer. For instance, it lacks irregular verbs and other nuisances that are so much cherished by linguists and detested by learners. But problems arise when its neat principles come into conflict.

Consider the following case from a task in which the learners had to watch and describe scenes from Chaplin's *Modern Times*. In one of these scenes, a girl is accused of stealing a loaf of bread. In the "German" version of the BV, this can be easily described by the utterance *Mädchen stehle Brot* (girl steal bread).

There are two nominal arguments. The first is the controller and the second is focused. These three rules taken together result in *Mädchen stehle Brot*. But the film's plot becomes more convoluted. The speaker now has to express that Charlie (not the girl) stole the bread. The speakers produced *Charlie stehle Brot* as well as *Brot stehle Charlie*. But in *Charlie stehle Brot*, PRAG is violated because *Charlie* is focused and so should be in final position. In *Brot stehle Charlie*, the speaker violates SEM1 because Charlie is the controller and so should be in first position. In such cases, the BV breaks down. There are two solutions. First, the two principles could be ranked, for example, as follows.

### Semantic Constraints Outweigh Pragmatic Constraints

Native speakers of English would probably opt for such a ranking principle and thus consider the first argument to be the controller. A sentence like *Bread steal Charlie* would seem bizarre to a native speaker of English much more than *Brot stehle Charlie* to native speakers of German, because in German the controller might easily be in final position. Hence, if there is ambiguity, they tend to follow the opposite ranking. Nevertheless, one of the constraints is violated no matter which ranking is chosen. If we adopt the English strategy, it is not clear which argument is in focus. If we adopt the German strategy, it is not clear which element is the controller (though here, it is unlikely that the bread is the controller).

The other way to solve the problem is to create an additional device that allows the speaker to mark either what is the focus or what is the controller. Two options which the construction capacity offers here are prosody and grammatical (free or bound) morphemes. Both solutions to the conflict are indeed observed (see Klein & Perdue, 1997, p. 330). Many learners use the order *Charlie stehle Brot* and mark the first argument by pitch as focus. Some learners of French use a particle [se] to mark an element in initial position as focused. This free morpheme is apparently a precursor of the cleft construction *c'est ... que*. In both cases, it is the focus constituent that gets special marking and thus allows this element to be in a different position than the one required by PRAG. Alternatively, one could mark the controller, for example, by a special suffix; the noncontroller by a different suffix; the nonfocus by still another suffix (thus indicating something like "topic-hood"); and so on. It may be that the relevant marking only occurs when at least two arguments are present (otherwise no confusion arises), but it is also possible that the case role is marked in all occurrences regardless of whether there is a second argument with which it can be confused. At this point, it may be interesting to compare the situation of a language learner and a language inventor. Each of these possibilities just mentioned is within the range of the human language construction capacity. But a learner cannot freely choose between them and build his own—perhaps very simple and elegant—system. Eventually, he or she has to copy what the social environment does, no matter how complicated and idiosyncratic this may be. Adult learners may be somewhat reluctant to do this if they find it difficult and if they do not see the point. This may be one of the reasons why they often get stuck at a certain stage of proficiency. Children normally do not get stuck. This may be because they are better or more willing imitators of things they do not understand.

## B. The BV at Work

### The Expression of Temporality

The BV exhibits a very transparent form–function structural organization, which may get into trouble in some cases. In general, however, it is a remarkably efficient instrument for the communicative capacity. In this subsection, we shall see how it is used to encode time. All human languages have developed elaborate means to express it. The best studied of these are (grammatical) tense and aspect, which are normally encoded by the finite verb. Hence, with each normal sentence, the speaker has to refer to time, whether he wants to or not—something not everybody would consider to be desirable. The BV is much more elegant here. Essentially, its way to express temporality can be summed up in four points:

1. There is no inflection. This means that the BV lacks the usual grammatical means to express tense and aspect.
2. The lexical meaning of verbs allows a differentiation between various situation types—events, states, processes, etc. In other words, whereas the BV has neither (grammatical) aspect nor tense, it has aktionsarten or lexical aspect.
3. There is a rich repertoire of temporal adverbials, including (a) calendaric type adverbials (*Sunday*, *in the evening*); (b) anaphoric adverbials expressing the relation AFTER (*then*, *after*), and also typically an adverbial which expresses the relation BEFORE; (c) some deictic adverbials such as *yesterday*, *now*; (d) a few frequency adverbials, notably *always*, *often*, *two time*, etc.; (e) a few durational adverbials, normally as bare nouns, such as *two hour*, etc. Temporal adverbials involving two reference points such as *again*, *still*, *already* do not belong to the standard repertoire of the BV.
4. There are some markers for temporal boundaries; they allow the learner to express the beginning and the end of some situation, as in constructions like *work finish*, "after work is/was/will be over."

Compared to the tools for temporality in real languages, this seems to impose strong restrictions on what can be said. But at this stage, learners are often extremely good storytellers, a task that requires the expression of all sorts of temporal information. How is this possible?

The BV allows its speakers to specify temporal relations such as BEFORE, AFTER, SIMULTANEOUS, etc. In particular, it allows the specification of some time span t (in relation to some other time span s, for example, the time of utterance). It can also express duration and frequency of time spans. Suppose that some time span t, about which the speaker wants to say something, is introduced. Such a time span will be called "topic time" (abbreviated TT). The TT is simply the time about which the speaker wants to make an assertion—in contrast to the "time of the situation" (abbreviated Tsit)—that is, the time at which the event, process, or state described by the sentence happens or obtains. All that the speaker has to do is to introduce and, if there is need, to shift TT, and to relate Tsit to it. More systematically, the functioning of the BV is described by the following three principles:

I. At the beginning of the discourse, a time span $TT_1$ is fixed, either
   (a) by explicit introduction on the learner's part, usually by a temporal adverbial in initial position; or
   (b) by explicit introduction on the native speaker's part (e.g., *what happened last Monday?*); or
   (c) by implicitly taking the "default topic time"—the time of utterance, in this case, nothing is explicitly marked.

$TT_1$, once introduced, serves as a point of departure for all subsequent TTs.

II. If $TT_i$ is given, then $TT_{i+1}$ is either maintained or changed. If it is maintained, nothing is marked. If it is changed, there are two possibilities:
   (a) The shifted TT is explicitly marked by an adverbial in initial position;
   (b) The new TT follows from a principle of text organization. For narratives, this is the classical principle of chronological order. "Unless marked otherwise, the order of mention corresponds to the order of events" (von Stutterheim, 1986). In other words, $TT_{i+1}$ is some interval more or less right adjacent to $TT_i$.

This particular principle does not obtain in all text types. It is only characteristic of narratives and other texts with a similar temporal organization. Even in these texts, it only applies to foreground sequences. In other text types, such as descriptions or arguments, the principle of chronological order does not apply, nor does it hold for side structures in narratives, that is, those sequences which give background information, evaluations, comments, etc. For those cases, change of TT must be marked by adverbials.

Principles I and II provide the temporal scaffold of a sequence of utterances—the time spans about which something is said. The "time of situation," Tsit, is then given by a third principle:

III. The relation of Tsit to TT in the BV is always "more or less simultaneous." TT can be contained in Tsit, or Tsit can be contained in TT, or TT and Tsit are contained in each other.

Thus, the various aspectual distinctions often observed in fully fledged languages are collapsed in the BV.

This system is very simple but extremely versatile. It allows the learner to express what happens when—provided that (a) there are enough adverbials and (b) it is cleverly managed. Therefore, one way the learner has of improving his expressive power is simply to enrich his or her vocabulary, especially by adding temporal adverbials, and to perfect his or her technique on this instrument.

When compared to English, French, or German, one might deplore the absence of the verbal categories tense and aspect in the BV—categories which, to judge from the research tradition and from grammar books, are for many almost tantamount to temporality in human languages. Now, if the core function of tense is indeed to localize the situation on the time axis, this can easily be done by temporal adverbials. In fact, they allow a much more precise localization; no known human language has a verbal inflection which differentiates between *last week* and *three weeks ago*. So, one wonders how important grammatical tense marking really is. In contrast to this, it is not so easy to express aspectual differentiations (e.g., between *he slept* and *he was sleeping*) by adverbials. But note, first, that German or Dutch have no grammatical aspect, either. Second, the human construction capacity offers simpler methods, for example, a few aspectual particles, as in Chinese. BV speakers could use this simple option, if they intend to differentiate between various ways to present a situation. In fact, they never do, since they *must copy* the particular ways in which this differentiation is encoded in the TL. Two-thirds of the 40 learners investigated indeed try this—they begin to mimic the idiosyncrasies of German, English, French regular and irregular verbs. About one-third prefer not to go beyond the BV. But they steadily improve it in two respects—more words, better practice, thus avoiding any further, and largely unnecessary, complications. Speakers of such a linguistic system can say what they want to say about temporal relations—not what the structure of the language forces them to say. But they do not sound like a speaker of German, English, or French.

## The Expression of Negation

Just as all languages have devices to express temporality, they have devices to express negation, the most important of which are particles, such as *not*, *ne ... pas*, *nicht*, etc. (see Horn, 2001; Payne, 1992). These particles are syntactically optional, but there are strong interactions between the particle and the syntactic structure, reflected in positional constraints and in a close relation to finiteness. This relation is particularly salient in the English *do*-support, in which the finite component of the verb only surfaces in the lexically empty element *do*, which in turn is combined with the negation. In the classroom, learners are told that the form *don't* consists of two words, the carrier of finiteness and the negator itself. Outside the classroom, learners have to figure this out on their own, and this leads to complicated learning problems for finiteness as well as for negation.

There is considerable work on the acquisition of negation via communication alone (e.g., Cancino, Rosansky, & Schumann, 1978; Felix, 1982; Meisel, 1997; Parodi, 2000; Stauble, 1984; Wode, 1981). Most of this work is primarily interested in how the target structures—for example, preverbal or postverbal position—are imitated. But there are also some more recent studies that try to uncover the way in which negation is rooted in the inherent structure of learner varieties and how it evolves over time as a part of this structure (Becker, 2005; Bernini, 2000; Dimroth, 2002; Giuliano, 2003; Silberstein, 2001). In what follows, we shall first see how negation is integrated into the BV and then have a brief look on how it develops afterward.

Finiteness has strong consequences for the overall organization of sentences—in most Indo-European languages, the basic word order is crucially linked to the finite element. It also has consequences for the expression of tense and assertion (Klein, 2006). This becomes rapidly clear if the finite element in a sentence such as *John WAS here* is highlighted: this highlighting can indicate a tense contrast (*he is not here, but he was here*); it can also highlight the assertion (*He WAS here, in contrast to He was NOT here*). In other words, there is a close connection between finiteness, assertion, and negation. There is no finiteness in the BV. In the preceding sections, we have seen what this means for the basic utterance structure and for the expression of temporality. What does it mean for negation?

The Focus Last Principle of the BV (see section IV.B) divides the utterance into a focus part and a topic part. In the BV, the relation between these two components is not explicitly marked: they are simply juxtaposed, with the topic component first:

| Topic component | Focus component |
|---|---|
| *Adverbials, first argument* | *Nonfinite verb + other argument(s)* |

The topic component specifies what the assertion is about—a place, a time, an entity—and the focus component assigns some properties, the comment, to these topical elements.

We now must slightly differentiate the structure description from section IV.B. There, it was assumed that the two components are simply juxtaposed. This is correct in general, but whenever the way in which the prediction expressed by the focus component applies to the topic needs to be qualified in some way, BV speakers can use a number of linking expressions (Dimroth, Gretsch, Jordens, Perdue, & Starren, 2003). These are lexical precursors of finiteness, which are drawn from the TL category of modal and temporal adverbs and particles (like *perhaps*, *again*), focus particles (like *also*), and negation. These linking expressions typically occur in a position between the topic and the focus component.

| Topic component | Linking element | Focus component |
|---|---|---|
| *Adverbials, first argument* | *Modal adverbs, particles, negation* | *Nonfinite verb + other argument(s)* |

This tripartite structure allows the speaker to modify or qualify the way in which the predication expressed by the focus component relates to the agent and/or the particular spatiotemporal anchor point identified in the topic component. The linking expressions have scope over the focus component. The most straightforward way of expressing (sentence-) negation at the BV therefore consists of putting the negator in the position of the linking element (Becker, 2005; Dimroth, 2008). Negative linking expressions are mainly taken from the TLs inventory of negative particles (including anaphoric ones like English *no*), but unanalyzed auxiliary clusters (e.g., *don't*) are attested as well (Silberstein, 2001). In this position, negation directly precedes the focused constituents whereas the topic component is kept out of its scope. The majority of negated BV utterances belong to this type, but it is not the only one.

Under particular information structural conditions, learners use replacive negations of the type *not X, but Y.* In this case, the correction of the negated constituent is indicated by a rectification added behind and by intonational prominence of both, the negator and the focus (Becker, 2005). In the BV, this type of negation only shows up when the negation has narrow scope, that is, when it does not affect the whole verb complex but only some part of it. As before, the negator directly precedes the elements in its scope. Such a replacive negation is not possible with the topical (agent) argument, since a negator preceding the topic would contradict the basic linearization principle (topic linking focus), whereas moving the agent argument to the right (into the scope of negation) would contradict the BV mapping between word order and argument structure: controller first). There is, however, another possibility to negate topic elements at the BV. In order to express that a given state of affairs does not apply to a particular topic (in contrast to another one), learners can use a special intonation contour (so called bridge accent, see Büring, 1995). As a rule, these utterances consist only of the topic expression, realized with a rising accent, and the negator following it, carrying a falling accent (e.g., /jetzt nein\).

What happens beyond the BV? The crucial step here is the acquisition of finiteness marking. Parodi (2000) has argued that the acquisition of postverbal negation is directly related to the emergence of productive finite verb morphology. However, the evidence is not uncontroversial. Ideally, one would want to see that finite lexical verbs appear with postverbal negation, whereas nonfinite verbs come with preverbal negation, but the picture is not as clear. The acquisition of tense marking and subject–verb agreement in untutored adult learners is a gradual and slow process and the outcome often stays fragile and error prone for a long time. Pointing to the high degree of variation, other researchers (Meisel, 1997) therefore deny that there is a causal relationship between the target-like realization of verbal morphology and the placement of negation.

After the BV stage, we also note more and more modals and auxiliaries which combine with nonfinite lexical verbs. These modals and auxiliaries are typically finite from their first occurrence onward (Parodi, 2000). They play a crucial role for the grammaticalization of assertion marking in the developing learner varieties (Giuliano, 2003; Jordens & Dimroth, 2006; Verhagen, 2005). This is particularly clear for lexically empty auxiliary verbs whose only function is the expression of features of finiteness (assertion and tense). The acquisition of the auxiliary system entails a syntactic reorganization of the utterance structure in terms of a functional category system. It helps the learner to establish both a relation of morphological agreement between the auxiliary verb and the agent argument, and a head-complement relation between the auxiliary and the nonfinite lexical verb.

Importantly, however, auxiliaries also allow the learner to separate the encoding of finiteness on the one hand and of the lexical content of verbs on the other. This means that the negation scope can still be marked in a transparent way, since the negator precedes all elements (including the lexical verb) in its scope. These advantages seem to determine the order of acquisition of finiteness and negation in untutored adult learners of Germanic languages in which auxiliaries seem to be a necessary intermediate step before morphosyntactic finiteness marking becomes productive with lexical verbs.

When finite lexical verbs with postverbal negation finally come to be used in TLs like French or German, the transparent separation of finite and nonfinite forms has to be given up in favor of the fusion of functional and lexical information. Unlike the BV and the first developmental steps beyond it, learner utterances then have a syntactic structure in which scope and information structure can no longer be directly mapped onto surface word order. In other words, the learners are forced to sacrifice a simple and elegant learner variety in favor of a real language with all its idiosyncrasies.

## V. CONCLUDING REMARKS

Untutored second language acquisition is not something exotic, it is the normal case, and if we want to understand the very principles according to which the human mind constructs, copies, and uses linguistic systems, then we must study how human beings cope with this task when not under the influence of teaching. This does not render the study of second language acquisition in the classroom uninteresting—quite the opposite. But if one wants to interfere with a natural process in order to optimize it, it is helpful to know the principles that govern this process.

## REFERENCES

Becker, A. (2005). The semantic knowledge base for the acquisition of negation and the acquisition of finiteness. In H. Hendriks (Ed.), *The structure of learner varieties* (pp. 263–314). Berlin, NY: de Gruyter.

Becker, A., & Carroll, M. (2005). *The acquisition of spatial relations in a second language.* Amsterdam: Benjamins.

Benazzo, S. (2003). The interaction between verb morphology and temporal adverbs of contrast. In C. Dimroth, & M. Starren (Eds.), *Information structure and the dynamics of language acquisition* (pp. 187–210). Amsterdam: John Benjamins.

Bernini, G. (2000). Negative items and negation strategies in non-native Italian. *Studies in Second Language Acquisition, 22,* 399–438.

Bernini, G. (2005). The acquisition of negation in Italian L2. In H. Hendriks (Ed.), *The structure of learner varieties* (pp. 315–354). Berlin, NY: de Gruyter.

Birdsong, D. (Ed.). (1999). *Second language acquisition and the critical period hypothesis.* Mahwah, NJ: Lawrence Erlbaum.

Birdsong, D. (2005). Interpreting age effects in second language acquisition. In J. Kroll & A. DeGroot (Eds.), *Handbook of bilingualism: Psycholinguistic perspectives* (pp. 109–127). Oxford: Oxford University Press.

Bongaerts, T. (1999). Ultimate attainment in foreign language pronunciation: The case of very advanced late foreign language learners. In D. Birdsong (Ed.), *Second language acquisition and the critical period hypothesis* (pp. 133–159). Mahwah, NJ: Lawrence Erlbaum.

Büring, D. (1995). *The 59th Street Bridge Accent. On the meaning of topic and focus.* Ph.D. dissertation, Tübingen University.

Cancino, H., Rosansky, E., & Schumann, J. (1978). The acquisition of English negatives and interrogatives by native Spanish speakers. In E. Hatch (Ed.), *Second language acquisition: A book of readings* (pp. 207–230). Rowley, MA: Newbury House.

Clahsen, H., Meisel, J., & Pienemann, M. (1983). *Deutsch als Zweitsprache. Der Spracherwerb ausländischer Arbeiter.* Tübingen: Gunter Narr.

Diehl, E., Christen, H., Leuenberger, S., Pelvat, I., & Studer, T. (2000). *Grammatikunterricht: Alles für die Katz? Untersuchungen zum Zweitspracherwerb Deutsch.* Tübingen: Niemeyer.

Dietrich, R., Klein, W., & Noyau, C. (1995). *The acquisition of temporality in a second language acquisition.* Amsterdam: Benjamins.

Dimroth, C. (2002). Topics, assertions, and additive words: How L2 learners get from information structure to target language syntax. *Linguistics, 40*, 891–923.

Dimroth, C. (2008). German at different ages: Negation and finiteness in adult, adolescent and child second language learners. *Language Learning, 58*, 117–150.

Dimroth, C., Gretsch, P., Jordens, P., Perdue, C., & Starren, M. (2003). Finiteness in the acquisition of Germanic languages: A stage-model for first and second language development. In C. Dimroth, & M. Starren (Eds.), *Information structure and the dynamics of language acquisition* (pp. 65–94). Amsterdam: John Benjamins.

Dittmar, N., & Giacalone Ramat, A. (Eds.). (1999). *Grammatik und Diskurs; Grammatica e Discorsol.* Tübingen: Stauffenburg.

Doughty, C. J. (2003). Instructed SLA: Constraints, compensation, and enhancement. In C. J. Doughty & M. H. Long (Eds.), *The handbook of second language acquisition* (pp. 256–310). New York: Blackwell Publishing.

Felix, S. (1982). *Second language development: Trends and issues.* Tübingen: Narr.

Giacalone Ramat, A., & Crocco Galeas, G. (Eds.). (1995). *From pragmatics to syntax: Modality in second language acquisition.* Tübingen: Narr.

Giuliano, P. (2003). Negation and relational predicates in French and English as second languages. In C. Dimroth, & M. Starren (Eds.), *Information structure and the dynamics of language acquisition* (pp. 119–158). Amsterdam: John Benjamins.

Heidelberger Forschungsprojekt "Pidgin-Deutsch". (1975). *Sprache und Kommunikation ausländischer Arbeiter.* Kronberg: Scriptor.

Horn, L. R. (2001). *A natural history of negation* (2nd ed.). Chicago, IL: Chicago University Press.

Hulstijn, J. H., & Ellis, R. (Eds.). (2005). Implicit and explicit second-language learning. In *Studies in Second Language Acquisition, 27* (Thematic Issue).

Ioup, G., Boustagui, E., El Tigi, M., & Moselle, M. (1994). Reexamining the critical period hypothesis: A case study of successful adult SLA in a naturalistic environment. *Studies in Second Language Acquisition, 16*, 73–98.

Jordens, P., & Dimroth, C. (2006). Finiteness in children and adults learning Dutch. In D. Bittner & N. Gagarina (Eds.), *Acquisition of verb grammar and verb arguments* (pp. 173–200). Dordrecht: Kluwer.

Klein, W. (1994). *Time in language.* London: Routledge.

Klein, W. (2006). On finiteness. In V. van Geenhoven (Ed.), *Semantics in acquisition* (pp. 245–272). Dordrecht: Springer.

Klein, W., & Dittmar, N. (1979). *Developing grammars: The acquisition of German syntax by foreign workers.* Berlin, NY: Springer.

Klein, W., & Perdue, C. (1992). *Utterance structure*. Amsterdam: Benjamins.

Klein, W., & Perdue, C. (1997). The basic variety (or: Couldn't natural languages be much simpler?). *Second Language Research, 13*, 301–347.

Krashen, S. (1981). *Second language acquisition and second language learning*. Oxford: Pergamon Press.

Long, M. H. (2005). Problems with the supposed counter-evidence to the critical period hypothesis. *International Review of Applied Linguistics, 43*, 287–317.

Marinova-Todd, S. H. (2003). *Comprehensive analysis of ultimate attainment in adult second language acquisition*. Ph.D. dissertation, Harvard University.

Meisel, J. M. (1997). The acquisition of the syntax of negation in French and German. Contrasting first and second language development. *Second Language Research, 13*, 227–263.

Nemser, W. (1971). Approximate systems of foreign language learners. *International Review of Applied Linguistics, 9*, 115–123.

Pagonis, G. (2007). *Der Einfluss des Alters auf den Spracherwerb. Eine empirische Fallstudie zum ungsteuerten Zweitspracherwerb des Deutschen durch russische Lerner unterschiedlichen Alters.* Ph.D. dissertation, Universität Heidelberg.

Parodi, T. (2000). Finiteness and verb placement in second language acquisition. *Second Language Research, 16*, 355–381.

Payne, J. R. (1992). Negation. In T. Shopen (Ed.), *Language typology and syntactic description* (Vol. 3). Cambridge: Cambridge University Press.

Perdue, C. (Ed.). (1993). *Adult language acquisition*. Cambridge: Cambridge University Press.

Schumann, J. (1978). *The pidginization process*. Rowley, MA: Newbury House.

Selinker, L. (1972). Interlanguage. *International Review of Applied Linguistics, 10*, 209–231.

Silberstein, D. (2001). Facteurs interlingues et spécifiques dans lacquisition non-guidée de la négation en anglais L2. *Acquisition et Interaction en Langue Etrangère, 14*, 25–58.

Singleton, D., & Ryan, L. (2004). *Language acquisition: The age factor*. Clevedon: Multilingual Matters.

Slobin, D. (1993). Adult language acquisition: A view from child language study. In C. Perdue (Ed.), *Adult language acquisition: cross-linguistic perspectives* (Vol. 2, pp. 239–252). Cambridge: Cambridge University Press.

Stauble, A.-M. (1984). A comparison of a Spanish-English and a Japanese-English second language continuum: Negation and verb morphology. In R. W. Andersen (Ed.), *Second languages: A cross-linguistic perspective* (pp. 323–353). Rowley, MA: Newbury House.

Van Boxtel, S. (2005). *Can the late bird catch the worm? Ultimate attainment in L2 syntax.* Utrecht: LOT.

Verhagen, J. (2005). The role of the auxiliary 'hebben' in Dutch as a second language. *Zeitschrift für Literaturwissenschift und Linguistik, 140*, 99–127.

von Stutterheim, C. (1986). *Temporalität in der Zweitsprache*. Berlin, NY: de Gruyter.

Wegener, H. (Ed.). (1998). *Eine zweite Sprache lernen. Empirische Untersuchungen zum Zweitspracherwerb*. Tübingen: Narr.

Wode, H. (1981). *Learning a second language. Vol. 1, An integrated view of language acquisition*, Tübingen: Narr.

CHAPTER 22

# THE INTERLANGUAGE DEVELOPMENT OF DEAF AND HEARING LEARNERS OF L2 ENGLISH: PARALLELISM VIA MINIMALISM

Gerald P. Berent

## I. A BROADER CONTEXT FOR SECOND LANGUAGE ACQUISITION

In outlining the broad scope of inquiry of second language (L2) research, Doughty and Long (2003) emphasized the importance of L2 research not only in its own right, but also for informing many other domains of inquiry and application. For example, they noted the value of existing and potential implications of L2 research for theory testing in linguistics and psychology, for understanding topics of relevance to neuroscience, for teaching second and foreign languages, for managing bilingual and literacy education, for language intervention with special populations, and for understanding the acquisition of sign languages such as American Sign Language (ASL). A largely unnoticed domain that L2 research also informs is the acquisition of spoken language knowledge by deaf individuals, whose access to spoken language input is severely limited because of hearing loss. The goal of this chapter is to demonstrate that research into deaf learners' acquisition of spoken languages such as English belongs squarely in the mainstream of L2 research, where it can be as informative to L2 research as L2 research is to it.

In this regard, a premise advanced in this chapter is that, for many deaf learners, English *is* an L2, not on the basis of the cultural identification of ASL as the L1 of the Deaf community (see Parasnis, 1996), but on the grounds that English acquisition by deaf learners is largely the product of *later* language learning. Depending on the severity of restricted access to English language input in early childhood, many deaf learners of English can effectively be considered "L2 learners without an L1" (Berent & Kelly, 2008). Their acquisition of English begins at a time when L2 acquisition might typically begin for a hearing speaker of a given L1 and proceeds with

523

great variability in the degree of ultimate attainment. Consistent with this characterization, this chapter demonstrates that there are striking parallels between deaf and hearing L2 learners in their English interlanguage (IL) development. Therefore, logical questions arise regarding the relative contributions of universal grammar (UG) and L1 transfer in second language acquisition (L2A). What are the consequences for L2A when there is no L1 to transfer? And what are the consequences for L2A when learners with an L1 and learners without an L1 exhibit parallel IL development?

In this chapter it is assumed, though the question still requires focused research, that deaf learners of English or any spoken language have access to the principles of UG. Though research on deaf learners' acquisition of spoken language knowledge is extremely limited relative to mainstream L2A research on acquisition by hearing learners, the small body of research devoted to the topic offers evidence suggesting that deaf learners of spoken language knowledge indeed have access to UG (e.g., Berent & Samar, 1990; Lillo-Martin, 1998). The topics discussed in the chapter offer further evidence of UG access.

## II. DEFINING A DEAF LEARNER OF L2 ENGLISH

### A. Early Restricted Access to English Input

Based on audiometric assessment, there are four conventional categories of hearing loss tied to ranges of decibel loss in the better ear: mild, moderate, severe, and profound deafness (Levitt, 1989). On average it is severely and profoundly deaf individuals who experience the greatest challenge to the development of spoken language knowledge, that is, the acquisition of the lexical, morphological, syntactic, and discourse knowledge of the language (whether or not a deaf person develops or uses speech skills). The acquisition of spoken language knowledge must therefore be facilitated through any residual hearing a deaf person might have but especially through vision: lipreading, facial expression, signed English, cued speech, and (once a foundation is established) reading and writing. Because over 90% of deaf children are born to two hearing parents, who may not even detect that their child is deaf for a considerable period of time and who, in all likelihood, do not know a sign language, delayed access to English (and most likely sign language) input is virtually inevitable.

However, there are some deaf children who compensate well for restricted access to English input and ultimately develop native-level English language and literacy skills. Toscano, McKee, and Lepoutre (2002) interviewed profoundly deaf college students whose assessed English reading and writing skills were no different from their hearing peers'. Every student interviewed reported growing up in a communicatively rich home environment with persistent interaction among family members, irrespective of knowledge or use of sign language in the family. The experiences of these students underscore the fact that early, aggressive, and sustained intervention can provide sufficient compensatory English input to yield native-level attainment.

A deaf person can also be an L2 learner of English in the conventional sense. If a deaf child is born to two deaf parents and ASL is their L1, then the child's L1 from infancy is ASL (see Lillo-Martin, 1999). However, proportionately very few deaf children are born to two deaf parents, so true native signers of ASL comprise a very small percentage of the deaf population. Nevertheless, many deaf children learn ASL or English-based signing at some point during their education, and many attain high or near-native proficiency in ASL. Therefore, later-learned ASL can become a deaf person's preferred or better language, especially in view of the naturalness of its access and communication through the visual–spatial modality.

Despite all the variables described above, the focus of inquiry in this chapter is on the type of deaf learner of English whose access to English input was severely or totally restricted for an extended period of time from infancy, whose onset of English language learning was considerably delayed, and who did not have any L1, ASL or otherwise. In comparing the IL development of such L2 learners of English without an L1 with hearing L2 learners of English, individuals at the college level are the targeted age group in this chapter. Such older deaf learners are even more comparable to older hearing L2 learners in that they are beyond the stages of cognitive development in other domains that otherwise influence L1 acquisition or child L2 acquisition.

## B. Characteristics of Deaf Learner Interlanguage

Overviews of deaf students' English language development have been provided in Berent (1988, 1993, 1996a, 1996b), Quigley and King (1980), and elsewhere. With respect to deaf learners' IL characteristics observed in naturalistic (written) production, the data set provided in Figure 1 shows the extent to which deaf college students at a relatively low level of English proficiency (for deaf college students) successfully produced the nine structures referred to in the figure. The structures were targets for "mastery" in a grammar course associated with an academic writing course that these students were taking at the same time. The summary data provided in Figure 1 are based on the average successful productions of 68 students in short essays that they produced at the beginning of their grammar course.

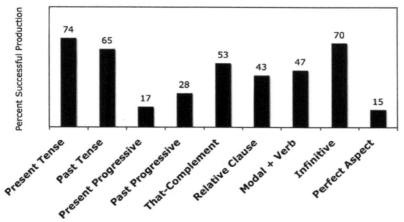

**Figure I**   Low-intermediate deaf learners' successful production of nine target structures in required discourse environments.

The percentages in Figure 1 were derived from the coding of each student's essay according to whether the student produced a given structure correctly in the student's own established discourse. Therefore, for each structure, the percentage reflects the number of successful productions of that structure out of the total attempted productions in required discourse environments (see Berent et al., 2007; Berent, Kelly, Schmitz, & Kenney, 2009). An unsuccessful production was either one that was attempted in the required discourse environment but produced incorrectly (e.g., *flied* for *flew*) or one that failed to occur as required by the discourse environment (e.g., *I fly to Washington last week*).

For each of the target structures assessed in Figure 1, sample sentences from the students' essays are included in (1)–(9) below as descriptive detail to this overview of deaf learners' IL development. The (a) examples illustrate successful productions of the target structures (italicized within the sample sentences), and the (b) examples illustrate unsuccessful productions of the target structures.

(1) Present tense
    a. They always *support* me ever if I *need* and concern about me.
    b. They *are care* about me and show me their love.
(2) Past tense
    a. Because they *thought* that we *didn't understand* about social with people.
    b. When we *hang out* one day, we had fun time.
(3) Present progressive
    a. I *am teaching* him how to play football to catch the ball and running.
    b. When my friends *doing* something else. My friends do not want to hang out and have a good time.
(4) Past progressive
    a. He said I *was doing* a good job helping.
    b. We *were* always *be playing* baseball in fall, spring, and summer every years.
(5) *That*-complement
    a. I thought *the tow truck will pick me up in about half hour* but it turn out *that they never came till three hours*.
    b. They wanted *that go to college*.
(6) Relative clause
    a. I will not forget some embrassing things *I did at work* or some mistakes *I made*.
    b. I have another best friend *that I know her for a long time*.
(7) Modal + verb
    a. Hopefully we *can meet* soon again.
    b. She *would happy* alway my best friend.
(8) Infinitive
    a. Most of the people like *to have* average one to 3 best friends.
    b. I love *to talked* people about swimming, play water game, and other.
(9) Perfect aspect
    a. When she moved to my apartment, we clicked and *have been* a great friends ever since.
    b. I *know* him for 3 years.

The data summarized in Figure 1 and exemplified in (1)–(9) provide a mere snapshot of deaf learners' IL development. These data obviously motivate the same kinds of theoretical questions as those posed in the context of hearing learners' IL development with respect to the acquisition of lexical and morphological features, syntactic projections, ultimate attainment, and so on.

## III. AN INPUT MODEL INCORPORATING VISUAL COMPENSATION

In proposed models of L2A (e.g., Gass, 1997, Figure 1.1), the first step in the process is the "apperception," or *noticing*, of the L2 input. Once noticed, the input is available for "comprehension," "intake," and "integration," ultimately yielding L2 "output." Figure 2 is an illustration of the fundamental difference between deaf and hearing L2 learners in accessing, and noticing, L2 spoken language input. The figure indicates the availability of auditory L2 input (the uppermost solid arrows) to the hearing learner, which is unavailable to the deaf learner, under an assumption of no audition whatsoever. The dotted arrow represents compensatory visual L2 input in the form of lipreading, facial expression, signed renditions of the spoken language, the reading of print, and so on. This visual input will obviously vary greatly in its accessibility and quality. What is not reflected in Figure 1 is that *hearing* learners also have access to visual L2 input, which can play a major facilitative role in L2 acquisition (e.g., through reading) and even the primary role in instances of classroom foreign language learning. Nevertheless, the focus here is on the availability of spoken L2 input and the consequences of its absence for deaf learners of L2 English. Once the L2 input is "received" by the learner, it is filtered by whatever cognitive and other factors are at play and, if it is noticed, proceeds to subsequent stages of L2A.

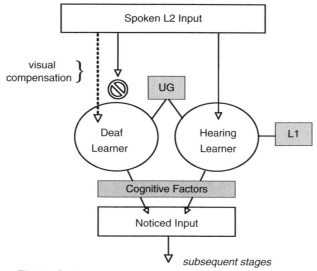

**Figure 2**  Deaf and hearing L2 learners' access to L2 input.

In addition to the differences by which deaf and hearing learners receive L2 input, Figure 2 also indicates that it is hearing, but not deaf, learners who have access to an L1 in L2A. In the broader context, this distinction motivates a rethinking of the issue of the relative roles of UG access and L1 transfer in L2A. If there are, as defined, L2 learners who have no L1 to access, then the source of their L2A is presumably UG alone. To the extent that this assumption holds, deaf learners' ILs should provide a clearer window into UG instantiation in later (i.e., L2) acquisition, "uncontaminated" by the effects of an L1. In addition to the value of this view into UG in its own right for understanding deaf learners' language acquisition, this situation creates new options for assessing L1 transfer in hearing L2A. Schwartz and Sprouse (2000) argued that "the key to investigating the extent of [L1] transfer is comparative interlanguage research" (p. 181). They maintained that, where the IL development of a particular target language phenomenon diverges between L2 learners with typologically distinct L1s, this is evidence that L1 transfer is at play; IL convergence implies no transfer. The addition of deaf learners' L2 ILs to the mix introduces the opportunity to evaluate hearing learners' ILs against a "purer" comparative standard in the search for L1 effects. Simplistically, if $IL_{DEAF} = UG$ and $IL_{HEARING} = UG + L1$ transfer, then $IL_{HEARING} - IL_{DEAF} = L1$ transfer. Under this assumption, the inclusion of deaf learners' ILs as a baseline in comparative interlanguage research could prove highly rewarding.

## IV. A MINIMALIST ACCOUNT OF INTERLANGUAGE PARALLELS

The Minimalist Program (MP) in linguistic research (Chomsky, 1995, 2000) maintains that the human language faculty follows *principles of economy* in that there are "no extra steps in derivations and no extra symbols in representations beyond those that are necessary for the system to function at all in connecting sound (or, in the case of signed languages, gesture) and meaning" (Bošković & Lasnik, 2007, p. 1). Although theory building and testing within the MP are largely assessed via theory-internal analyses and constructs, it is also assumed that economy principles strongly influence language acquisition (e.g., Platzack, 1996; Roberts, 1999), including L2A *per se* (Hawkins, 2001; Yusa, 1998). The scenarios detailed below suggest that economy principles of the MP exert pressures on L2A and, at least in the case of the first two scenarios, are responsible for the observable IL parallels between deaf and hearing learners.

### A. Interpretation of English Universal Quantifier Sentences

Hearing and deaf L2 learners of English were shown by Berent, Kelly, and Schueler-Choukairi (2009) to exhibit remarkable parallels in their interpretation of English sentences containing the universal quantifiers *each*, *every*, and *all*. The authors administered a 50-item multiple-picture judgment task (Berent, Kelly, Porter, & Fonzi, 2008) to deaf students and L2 learners at the college level, along with a control group of L1 English-speaking college students. The deaf students comprised a lower-English-proficiency group pursuing no higher than an associate's degree and a higher-English-proficiency group pursuing bachelor's degree. The mean scores of the lower- and higher-English-proficiency deaf groups on the Michigan Test of English Language Proficiency (1977) were 59.5 and 76.6, respectively. The two hearing L2 groups included a lower-English-proficiency group and a higher-English-proficiency group of students enrolled in ESL courses in preparation for university matriculation. The two L2 groups exhibited mean Michigan Test scores of 50.5 and 74.2, respectively. The L2 groups included speakers of 12 different L1s.

The picture task included sentences containing a universal quantifier phrase (QP) in subject position and an indefinite noun phrase (i.e., *determiner phrase*, or DP) in object position (*subject QP sentences*), as well as sentences exhibiting the opposite order (*object QP sentences*). For example, for the quantifier *every*, two target sentences on the picture task are shown in (10).

(10)    a. Every boy is climbing a tree.
        b. A woman is smelling every flower.

Each picture task item contained a target sentence accompanied by five professional drawings designed to assess learners' interpretations of the sentence. For example, with reference to (10a), the five pictures depicted the following different scenes: (i) four boys standing around and no tree in the picture; (ii) three boys, each climbing a different tree, but one boy not climbing any tree; (iii) four boys, each climbing a different tree; (iv) four boys, each climbing a different tree, and a fifth tree not being climbed; and (v) four boys, all climbing the very same tree. For each task item, participants were instructed to read the sentence, to study each picture, and to circle YES or NO under each picture depending on whether they thought that picture represented a *possible* interpretation of the target sentence.

The response patterns of both the deaf and L2 learners verified that they each had firm knowledge of the lexical properties of English universal quantifiers and the constraints on the interpretation of sentences in which these quantifiers occur (i.e., evidence of UG access). Of relevance to the present discussion are the learners' acceptance patterns of *collective* and *distributive* interpretations of the target sentences. For a sentence like (10a), acceptance of the collective interpretation is apparent in the acceptance of the picture described in (v) above, in which all members of the set of boys distribute to one specific tree. The collective depiction of sentence (10b) is a picture in which one specific woman is smelling all members of a set of flowers. For the distributive interpretation of (10a), the relevant picture is described in (iii) above, in which all members of the set of boys distribute to different trees. The distributive depiction of (10b) shows four women, each smelling a different flower. The results of the collective/distributive analysis revealed remarkably parallel performance between the deaf and hearing learner groups. Figure 3 reveals that, overall, the four groups accepted significantly more collective interpretations (the first and third bars in each grouping) than distributive interpretations (the second and fourth bars). Of the latter, the groups accepted very few of the object QP distributive interpretations (the fourth bars). That is, the groups more frequently accepted the depiction of a sentence like (10a) in which four boys are each climbing a different tree, than the depiction of (10b) in which four women are each smelling a different flower.

The conventionally accepted mechanism of quantifier sentence interpretation has been May's (1977) *Quantifier Raising* (QR). QR involves *covert* movement of

530 Gerald P. Berent

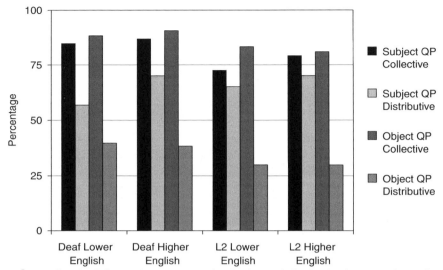

**Figure 3** Deaf and L2 learners' acceptance of collective and distributive interpretations of English sentences containing universal quantifiers.

constituents to account for interpretations that cannot be "read off" of the *overt* order of constituents. For example, the two interpretations of the ambiguous sentence (10a) result from the application of QR to both the universally quantified (∀) expression *every boy* and the existentially quantified (∃) expression *a tree* to positions outside the sentence core. The collective meaning results when *a tree* raises to the left of *every boy*, in which case ∃ "takes scope over" ∀. However, when *every boy* (∀) raises and takes scope over *a tree* (∃), the distributive meaning is derived in which the members of a universal set of boys distribute to members of a set of trees.

Within the MP, QR has become problematic because it violates economy principles (e.g., *shortest move*) that otherwise apply to sentence derivations. To address this problem, Fox (2000) proposed a principle of *scope economy*, according to which the interpretation of quantifier sentences like those in (10) is derived from their *surface scope* orders without QR. Accordingly, (10a) by default is assigned the distributive interpretation, whereas (10b) is assigned the collective interpretation. However, because (10a) is capable of receiving a collective interpretation and (10b) a distributive interpretation, QR can apply to yield those *inverse scope* readings in violation of scope economy. Under this analysis, movement is reduced in conformity with the goals of the MP, restricted only to those derivations that force QR.

Building on Fox's (2000) scope economy, Berent et al. (2009) incorporated proposals by Schwarzschild (2002) and Reinhart (2006) into the analysis of their results. According to Schwarzschild's *singleton indefinites* analysis, the interpretation of a singular indefinite DP can always be limited to a singleton (one-member) set, in which case the DP is "free" in scope. That is, the DP is interpreted in place, without QR, and refers to a specific entity. Alternatively, when a singular indefinite DP is not restricted to a singleton set, it is interpreted within the scope of the universal quantifier. Reinhart argued that QR is a *last resort* "rescue operation," very costly in minimalist terms, required only to obtain the distributive interpretation of a sentence like (10b). Synthesizing these proposals, the collective and distributive derivations of sentence (10a) are shown, without structural detail, in (11a) and (11b), respectively, and the collective and distributive derivations of sentence (10b) are shown in (12a) and (12b), respectively. The subscript *(sg)* denotes a singleton set, and $t_i$ marks the position from which *every flower$_i$* has moved via QR in (12b). The order of these sentences parallels the order of the histogram bars per group, from left to right, in Figure 3.

(11)  a. Every boy is climbing a tree$_{(sg)}$.
　　 b. Every boy is climbing a tree.
(12)  a. A woman$_{(sg)}$ is smelling every flower.
　　 b. [every flower$_i$ [a woman is smelling t$_i$]].

In (11a), the domain of *a tree* is restricted to a singleton set. It is therefore free from the scope effects of *every boy* and refers to one specific tree. Because *every boy* is a universal QP, all members of the relevant set of boys are understood to distribute to the one specific tree. In (12a), the singleton indefinite *a woman* denotes one specific woman who is smelling all members of the relevant set of flowers. As singleton indefinites, *a tree* and *a woman* in these collective representations are both morphologically and semantically singular. In addition to this isomorphism, these collective representations exhibit economy of derivation, requiring no application of QR. From Figure 3 it is seen that the deaf and L2 learner groups, at both lower- and higher-English-proficiency levels, accepted subject QP and object QP collective interpretations with high frequency. This IL knowledge is to be expected if ease of acquisition parallels the maximal economy exhibited in these derivations.

However, participants accepted fewer subject QP distributive interpretations (the second bars). Although derivation (11b) involves no QR, because the singular indefinite DP *a tree* is not restricted to a singleton set, it must receive its domain restriction within the scope of the universal QP *every boy*. Accordingly, even though it is morphologically singular, it is semantically plural. Thus, in (11b), all members of a set of boys distribute to two or more members of a set of trees. This greater derivational complexity appears to have a negative acquisitional reflex in learners whose access to the target language input is constrained by factors associated with hearing loss and/or later language learning.

Of the four derivations in (11) and (12), the object QP distributive derivation (12b) is very costly in minimalist terms. It is the only derivation requiring QR, specifically the movement of *every flower* from its object position after *is smelling* to an adjoined position higher than *a woman* from which it takes scope over *a woman*. Accordingly, *a woman* denotes a plural set, and the sentence is interpreted to mean that two or more members of a set of women are smelling every member of a set of flowers. Reinhart (2006) argued that such QR is in fact an "illicit" operation, nevertheless one that must be invoked as a rescue operation for deriving the distributive interpretation of these sentences. She maintained, therefore, that QR creates a computational burden and explains why such interpretations are often difficult to obtain, even by native speakers. Consistent with these proposals, the cost of deriving object QP distributive interpretations is apparent in their very low acceptance by the deaf and L2 learner groups in the results of Berent et al. (2009), as seen in Figure 3. Even the hearing participants in the study accepted fewer of these interpretations than the other interpretations.

It was concluded that this parallelism observed in the ILs of the deaf and hearing L2 learners of English is the acquisitional reflex of minimalism. Learner judgments of the four interpretive options depicted on the picture task, involving the matching of sentences with pictorial discourses, paralleled the relative degree (or violation) of economy proposed in the context of the MP. Therefore, group performance in that study suggests that, in the interpretation of English universal quantifier sentences like those in (10) (and similar sentences containing *each* and *all*), $IL_{HEARING}-IL_{DEAF} = UG$, with no evidence of L1 transfer.

## B. English Infinitive Complement Interpretation

Another English phenomenon on which research has revealed that deaf and hearing L2 learners exhibit parallel performance is the interpretation of sentences containing infinitive complements. Berent (1983) assessed 51 deaf students and 103 hearing L2 students at the college level on their interpretation of the logical subjects of infinitives in sentences like (13a), (14a), and (15a) using related questions with two choices as shown in (13b), (14b), and (15b). The (c) representations are discussed further below. The deaf students were enrolled in remedial English courses and represented three levels of English proficiency, ranging roughly from low intermediate to low advanced. The hearing L2 learners were speakers of 12 different L1s and also spanned a range from low-intermediate to low-advanced overall English proficiency.

(13)  a. Tom reminded George to do the homework.
      b. Who will do the homework?                          Tom    George
      c. Tom reminded George$_i$ [PRO$_i$ to do the homework]
(14)  a. Tom asked Bill what to buy.
      b. Who will buy something?                            Tom    Bill
      c. Tom$_i$ asked Bill [what PRO$_i$ to buy]
(15)  a. Alice explained what to do.
      b. Who will do something?                             Alice  another person
      c. Alice explained [what PRO$_{arb}$ to do]

For each sentence, students circled their choice of who they thought would perform the action expressed by the infinitive. In some cases, the logical subject of the infinitive is the closer of two names (*George* in 13a), in some cases the more distant name (*Tom* in 14a), and in some instances an implied external logical subject (*another person* for 15a).

The results of that study yielded markedly parallel performance by the deaf and L2 learners (an overall significant Spearman rho rank order correlation coefficient of 0.90). Performance was examined in the context of the *control theory* module of government-binding theory (Chomsky, 1981), as articulated at that time. In this chapter, the data from Berent (1983) are reanalyzed in the context of minimalist proposals. Within the government-binding analysis, the results of Berent (1983) revealed that learners overextended the *Minimal Distance Principle* (MDP) in interpreting the reference of the PRO subject of the infinitive. The MDP stipulated that the *controller* (antecedent) of PRO in sentences containing an infinitive complement is the structurally closest DP to PRO as, for example, in (13c) where $PRO_i = George_i$; *George* is interpreted as the doer of the homework. Some verbs, such as *ask* followed by a *wh*-infinitive complement as in (14a), permitted a "violation" of the MDP, whereby the more distant DP is interpreted as the antecedent of PRO. $PRO_i = Tom_i$ in (14c). Learners frequently misinterpreted such sentences, assuming that the MDP also applied in the interpretation of those sentences. Sentences like (15a) were also frequently misinterpreted because, as indicated in (15c), $PRO_{arb}$ receives "arbitrary" reference determined by the discourse. The MDP is violated there in view of the absence of a controller.

Hornstein (1999) proposed a minimalist analysis of infinitive complement interpretation in his *movement theory of control*. His account enables the elimination of PRO and therefore the entire control theory module from the theory of grammar. This move is a significant simplification consistent with the goals of the MP. Hornstein proposed that, among other features, verbs possess "θ-features" that encode the *thematic roles* (*θ-roles*) associated with them. θ-roles are the semantic functions assigned to a verb's arguments such as the *agent, theme, experiencer,* and so on. For example, in (13), *George* has a θ-role associated with the semantics of *remind* that can be informally stated as the "reminde*e*" (where *Tom* is the "reminde*r*"), but PRO must have its own distinct θ-role, which is the "doer" of the homework. Hornstein proposed that a DP can "absorb" more than one θ-role in the course of a sentence derivation as it combines with other constituents and moves to positions in which it can "check off" morphological features (to be illustrated below). The basic idea is that, in the minimalist derivation of a sentence like (13a), as constituents merge and move, *George* combines with the infinitive verb *do* and assumes its "doer" θ-role and later combines with *reminded* and assumes its "reminde*e*" θ-role. By virtue of its "doer" θ-role, *George* serves as the "subject" of *to do*, eliminating the need for the existence of PRO.

Table I provides a reanalysis of the sentences targeted in Berent (1983), consistent with Hornstein's movement theory of control (as refined in Boeckx & Hornstein, 2003, 2004). The left column of the table includes the 15 target sentences. Underneath each sentence is an abbreviated minimalist representation. Only the relevant feature-checking movement is indicated and constituent labeling is excluded. Copies of moved DPs are shown between angled brackets. The highest, italicized copy of a moved DP is understood as the logical subject of the infinitive in the sentence because, as explained above, the DP has assumed the θ-role associated with the θ-feature of the infinitive. In the center column of Table I, the θ-roles of the italicized DP are specified informally. Under the θ-role specifications are syntactic and/or lexical codes (for discussion) that relate to the sentence derivation. The right column of Table I shows the percentage correct scores of the hearing and deaf L2 student participants. Sentences (a) through (o) appear in the overall success order that was exhibited by the hearing L2 learners in the study.

As illustration, the derivation of sentence (a) in Table I starts with *Bill* merging with *stay* and assuming the θ-role of "stayer." *Bill* moves to the next higher available position in the derivation and ultimately to the sentence subject position, merging with *chose* and assuming its "chooser" θ-role. Accordingly, *Bill* serves as the overt subject of the main verb *choose* and the covert subject of the infinitive *to stay*. A dash in the center column of the table signifies that the sentence has an active main verb and that

TABLE I

**A Minimalist Reanalysis Based on Hornstein (1999) and Boeckx and Hornstein (2003, 2004) of Target Sentences from Berent (1983) with Percentage Correct Scores for Hearing and Deaf L2 Learners**

| | θ-role(s) of infinitive subject | Percentage correct | |
| Sentence and minimalist derivation | Structural and lexical codes | Hearing | Deaf |
|---|---|---|---|
| a. Bill chose to stay at home. | *Bill*: "chooser"/"stayer" | 99 | 100 |
|    *Bill* chose [<Bill> to [<Bill> stay at home]] | | | |
| b. John told Mary to close the door. | *Mary*: "tellee"/"closer" | 98 | 100 |
|    John told *Mary* [<Mary> to [<Mary> close the door]] | — | | |
| c. Linda chose Mary to answer the question. | *Mary*: "chosen"/"answerer" | 96 | 98 |
|    Linda chose *Mary* [<Mary> to [<Mary> answer the question]] | — | | |
| d. George asked Tom to buy a newspaper | *Tom*: "askee"/"buyer" | 93 | 98 |
|    George asked *Tom* [<Tom> to [<Tom> buy a newspaper]] | — | | |
| e. Tom reminded George to do the homework. | *George*: "remindee"/"doer" | 91 | 88 |
|    Tom reminded *George* [<George> to [<George> do the homework]] | — | | |
| f. Mary asked to see the teacher. | *Mary*: "asker"/"seer" | 88 | 86 |
|    *Mary* asked [<Mary> to [<Mary> see the teacher]] | | | |
| g. Jim showed Larry where to go. | *Larry*: "showee"/"goer" | 87 | 96 |
|    Jim showed *Larry* [where [<Larry> to [<Larry> go <where>]]] | WH | | |
| h. Larry told John what to do. | *John*: "tellee"/"doer" | 86 | 100 |
|    Larry told *John* [what [<John> to [<John> do <what>]]] | WH | | |
| i. Bill promised George to wash the dishes. | *Bill*: "promiser"/ "washer" | 84 | 65 |
|    *Bill* promised [P$_{null}$ George] [<Bill> to [<Bill> wash the dishes]] | LEX, P$_{null}$ | | |
| j. Mike was reminded by George to answer the question. | *Mike*: "remindee"/ "answerer" | 81 | 78 |
|    *Mike* [was reminded <Mike> [$_{PP}$by George] [<Mike> to [<Mike> answer the question]]] | PASS | | |
| k. Alice explained what to do. | *pro*: "doer" | 71 | 59 |
|    Alice explained [what [*pro* to do <what>]] | WH, pro | | |
| l. Jim was told whom to visit. | *Jim*: "tellee"/"visiter" | 68 | 57 |
|    *Jim* [was told <Jim> [whom [<Jim> to [<Jim> visit <whom>]]]] | PASS, WH | | |
| m. Tom asked Bill what to buy. | *Tom*: "asker"/"buyer" | 56 | 26 |
|    *Tom* asked [P$_{null}$ Bill] [what [<Tom> to [<Tom> buy <what>]]] | LEX, P$_{null}$, WH | | |
| n. Larry was asked where to sit. | *pro*: "sitter" | 46 | 20 |
|    Larry [was asked <Larry> [where [*pro* to sit <where>]]] | PASS, LEX, WH, pro | | |
| o. John said to come at 7:30. | *pro*: "comer" | 41 | 49 |
|    John said [*pro* to come at 7:30] | LEX, pro | | |

*Note:* θ-roles are expressed informally with reference to specific verbs. Codes: LEX = an exceptional lexical feature or lexical ambiguity; WH = the sentence contains a *wh*-infinitive complement; PASS = the finite verb is passive; P$_{null}$ = a DP is the object of a null preposition; pro = the null pronominal is inserted as subject of the infinitive.

the DP possessing the θ-role of the infinitive verb has not crossed a different DP in raising to its overt (italicized) position. Thus, the sentences (a) through (f) all reflect the minimalist principle of shortest move, in which the DP that merges with the infinitive verb subsequently moves only as far as required for the derivation to *converge* ( = succeed). Both the hearing and deaf learners were highly successful in interpreting these unexceptional sentences. Performance on sentence (f) shows only a slight drop in the percentage correct scores, which may be attributable to the lexical confusion associated with English *ask*, which is discussed below. Although (f) abides by shortest move, when *ask* has the meaning of "request action," learners may have an expectation of the inclusion of an "askee," like *Tom* in sentence (d), in addition to only an "asker" as in (f); that is, an "askee" is implied.

With the presence of other elements, such as a *wh*-phrase in sentences coded with WH in Table I, another layer of complexity is introduced. For example, the derivations of sentences (g) and (h) involve not only merger and movement of the DP, but also *wh*-movement of *where* and *what*, respectively, to the front of the infinitive complement. The movement of *Larry* and *John* still follows shortest move, though the DPs cross a *wh*-phrase. The ceiling-level percentages of the deaf learners on these sentences versus the slightly lower percentages for the hearing learners merely raise the suspicion that, in the range of relative proficiency levels of the two groups, the L2A knowledge of the derivation of English *wh*-infinitive complements may be less firm within the hearing group.

The L2 derivation of English passive sentences (indicated by the symbol PASS in Table I) also had a noticeable impact on the interpretation of the target sentences. The impact was not so significant for sentence (j) because the presence of the explicit agent *by*-phrase, *by George*, likely facilitates the noticing of passive verb morphology required for the successful interpretation of the sentence. Furthermore, although *George* appears to intervene between two of the copies of "*Mike*," the prepositional phrase *by George* is too low in the structural representation of (j) to allow a DP to merge with and move through it. Therefore, the derivation of (j) in fact follows shortest move because the position of the highest copy of "*Mike*" is the closest available position to which the next lower copy of "*Mike*" can move. These UG-established facts are "free" once the learner firmly acquires passive morphology. Passive sentence (l) received much lower correct scores by the two learner groups no doubt because there is no facilitating *by*-phrase to establish an agent θ-role and the sentence also has the added complexity of *wh*-movement.

The remaining sentences exhibit more exceptional lexical properties (indicated by the symbol LEX), and the learners' performance on them is enlightened considerably by Hornstein and Boeckx's movement theory of control. Sentence (i) is the classic case of the interpretation of an infinitive complement in a structure containing the verb *promise*. In such sentences it is the more distant main clause subject that is interpreted as the logical subject of the infinitive; as noted in Table I, *Bill* is both the "promiser" and the "washer." This long-noted violation of the MDP in such sentences was attributed to the exceptional lexical properties of *promise*. However, in this regard, Hornstein and Boeckx proposed that the object of *promise* in (i) is really a prepositional phrase headed by a *null preposition*, as illustrated. If so, *Bill* abides by shortest move because, just as in (j), a DP cannot move through a prepositional phrase. Therefore, a derivation that moved *George* from within the infinitive complement to its current position would crash. Whether or not the null preposition proposal is tenable, the hearing learners were almost 20 percentage points more successful than the deaf learners on sentence (i), which is not passive and which does not contain a *wh*-phrase. This difference raises the suspicion that this might be an instance of L1 lexical transfer by the hearing learners, unavailable to the deaf learners. Other languages (e.g., Russian) have *"promise* sentences" parallel to English in structure and interpretation. Specific hearing learners' transfer of a parallel "lexical template" could account for a more rapid acquisition of sentences like (i).

A novel proposal by Hornstein (1999) relates to sentences like (k) and (o), which have been called "non-obligatory control" sentences. In other words, these sentences are not required to (and cannot) have an internal DP that serves as the logical subject of the infinitive. The interpretation of sentence (o) requires that the "comer" not be *John* but rather some sentence-external discourse-determined person or persons. With PRO eliminated from the theory, there is no covert or overt subject constituent for the infinitive in the derivation of (o). To account for such sentences, Hornstein proposed that the UG-available empty subject *pro* (not to be confused with PRO) is inserted as a last resort rescue operation that keeps the derivation from crashing. The constituent *pro* is the uncontroversial "null subject" in languages such as Spanish in sentences like ***pro*** *fué* "(he/she/it) went," for which an overt subject pronoun need not occur when its reference is obvious.

Hornstein compared *pro*-insertion as a rescue operation to the widely recognized rescue operation of *do*-insertion in English, which saves the derivations of questions and negative sentences from crashing by allowing *do* to carry and raise tense features for checking. As discussed above with respect to QR in the derivation of universal quantifier sentences, last resort operations are derivationally costly, as also noted by Hornstein. This derivational cost is clearly apparent in Table I in the learners' low percentage scores for sentence (o). The derivation of sentence (k) also involves *pro*-insertion, but scores on that item were somewhat higher. The reason for the difference may be tied to the fact that the verb *say* has semantic ambiguity that *explain* does not have. The verb *say* is ambiguous between "speak" or "convey information" when followed, for example, by a *that* clause, but a meaning akin to "command" in sentences like (o). The meaning of *explain*, on the other hand, straightforwardly implies an "explainee," which is noticeably absent in (k).

Finally, sentences (m) and (n) were highly problematic for both the hearing and the deaf learners. First of all, the ambiguity of the verb *ask* contributes to confusion in acquisition. In sentences (d) and (f) of Table I, *ask* has the meaning of "request action"; however, when *ask* is followed by a *wh*-infinitive complement as in (m) and (n), it has the meaning of "request information." Most languages use two distinct verbs for these different meanings, for example, Spanish *pedir* and *preguntar*, respectively. A derivational distinction becomes apparent in a sentence like (m), in which it is the sentence subject *Tom* that is both the *asker* and the intended *buyer*. In other words, unlike the structurally parallel sentence (h), with the main verb *told*, the derivation of sentence (m) appears to violate shortest move, which accounts for the high degree of selection of *Bill*, rather than *Tom*, as the "buyer." As in *promise* sentences, Hornstein would propose that *Bill* in (m) is the object of a null preposition, difficult to perceive in acquisition, but which would enable the derivation of (m) to follow the principle of shortest move.

In view of the complexity of sentence (n), as indicated by the list of symbols for that item in the center column of Table I, it was the overwhelmingly most difficult task sentence to interpret. It contains lexically ambiguous *ask*, confounding passive morphology, and the need for last resort insertion of *pro*.

In conclusion, Hornstein and Boeckx's movement theory of control establishes a theoretical context in which the results of Berent (1983) receive a more adequate and detailed explanation. Their minimalist account articulated explicit derivational processes associated with the meanings and lexical features of specific verbs, which in turn determine the syntactic projections that DPs merge with and move through. As a simpler theory following minimalist goals, the account formalizes rescue operations like last resort *pro*-insertion associated with discourse interpretations that were left vague in association with the control module of government-binding theory.

The observed similarity in deaf and hearing learners' success orders is another example of "parallelism via minimalism." However, unlike the parallelism observed above in learners' IL knowledge of universal quantifier sentences, lexical acquisition, including the likelihood of some transfer of L1 lexical features by the hearing L2 learners, appears to interact with minimalist pressures in the acquisition of English sentences containing infinitive complements. Most notably, as with QR in the derivation of object QP quantifier sentences, derivations requiring costly *pro*-insertion, proposed as a last resort rescue operation, appear to resist acquisition by both deaf and hearing L2 learners.

## C. Resumptive Pronouns in English Relative Clauses

The occurrence of *resumptive pronouns* (RPs) in L2 relative clause acquisition has received considerable attention in research on IL development but remains poorly understood. Whereas many languages do not employ RPs in relative clauses (e.g., English, Spanish, Swedish), some languages do (e.g., Chinese, Farsi, Romany). For example, whereas English permits only a gap in the relative clause *who Mary likes* in (16a), which targets the direct object position, other languages permit or require a pronominal element in that position (and other positions), yielding structures equivalent to the ungrammatical English sentence (16b).

(16)   a. We met the boy who Mary likes ____.
       b. *We met the boy *who* Mary likes *him*.

The issues are very complex. In the L2A literature focusing on the acquisition of English relative clauses, the production and/or acceptance of relative clauses containing (illicit) RPs as in (16b) has been observed among both speakers of L1s that permit RPs and speakers of L1s that do not (e.g., Gass, 1979). Although speakers of L1s in which RPs occur in relative clauses appear to produce more IL RPs than speakers of L1s in which RPs do not occur, speakers of all types of L1 tend to produce IL RPs. It is assumed that L2 learners deploy RPs as an available UG option even if the L2 input provides no evidence of RPs in the language. Like hearing L2 learners, deaf learners sometimes produce RPs in English relative clauses, as documented in the "unsuccessful" production provided in (6b): *I have another best friend that I know her for a long time*.

Among various analyses of RPs in the linguistics literature, Shlonsky (1992) argued with respect to Hebrew that RPs are a last resort mechanism in cases where traces (gaps) are not permitted for language-internal reasons. That is, these traces are "spelled out" as RPs to rescue certain derivations. In studying the English L1 production and acceptance of relative clauses containing RPs by young children, McKee and McDaniel (2001) adopted a minimalist analysis based on competition among derivations. They developed arguments that the derivations of sentences like (16a) and (16b) start with the same numeration (lexical array) under the view, similar to Shlonsky's, that RPs are spell-outs of traces; that is, traces and RPs are not differentiated in the lexicon. Both derivations involve *wh*-movement, leaving a trace in the vacated position. The derivations are identical until the point of spell-out (Chomsky, 1995), where, if the trace is illicit for language-internal reasons, it is spelled out as an RP. Because that requires an additional operation, McKee and McDaniel argued that the trace-as-gap derivation, as in English, is the more economical of the two competing derivations.

Eckman (2004) reached a different conclusion about RP production in acquisition in his analysis of the results of Hyltenstam (1984). Hyltenstam had observed that learners of L1s that both do and do not permit RPs produced RPs in L2 Swedish, a language that does not have RPs in relative clauses. In analyzing Hyltenstam's data in the context of Optimality Theory, Eckman concluded that L2 RP production is an instance of "the emergence of the unmarked" as a strategy in IL grammars. The implication is that derivations yielding RPs are *more* economical than derivations yielding gaps. This assumption would seem to account for the overproduction of RPs in Hebrew by young deaf children relative to their hearing peers. Friedmann and Szterman (2006) observed that the later the intervention to provide assistive hearing (e.g., via hearing aids) to a deaf child, the more RPs that child produced in relative clauses. However, the situation is confounded by the fact that Hebrew permits RPs in relative clauses.

In view of the diversity of perspectives on RPs in both the linguistics and acquisition literature, an examination of the relative clause acquisition of older deaf learners identified as L2 learners without an L1 might shed light on the complex issue of RPs in L2A. With respect to economy of derivation, if RP-insertion is in any sense a costly last resort operation like *do*-insertion, one would expect not to observe their frequent occurrence in the ILs of learners experiencing restricted access to target language input. The discussion below is based on the identification of relative clauses in short essays produced by 38 deaf learners of L2 English at the college level. Based on mean scores on the Michigan Test of English Language Proficiency (1977), three learner groups were chosen: a high group ($M = 84$), a mid-group ($M = 68$), and a low group ($M = 49$).

The overwhelming majority of relative clauses produced (91% of 99 relative clauses identified) were discernible "*wh*-relative clauses" such as in *I like some of my friends who was nice to me*, "*that* relative clauses" as in *I was so unhappy with my roommate because she was not the right roommate that I always want*, and "zero relative clauses" (lacking the complementizer *that*) as in *Of course there are people I dislike*. With acknowledgment that nonoccurrence in a sample does not imply lack of acquisition or

TABLE II
**Deaf Learners' Production of English Relative Clauses by Type and Position at Three Proficiency Levels**

| Relative clause type/position | Group | | |
| --- | --- | --- | --- |
| | High | Mid | Low |
| *wh*-relative | | | |
| Subject | 17.8 | 13.3 | 3.3 |
| Direct object | — | — | — |
| *that* relative | | | |
| Subject | 7.8 | 6.7 | 2.2 |
| Direct object | 14.4 | 5.6 | 7.8 |
| zero relative | | | |
| Subject | — | — | — |
| Direct object | 13.3 | 3.3 | 4.5 |

*Note:* Data are reported as percentages. The table values total to 100%.

usage, not a single relative clause was produced containing an RP. However, the sample of production data revealed other IL behavior that implies pressure to defer to derivational economy.

For example, there was virtually no evidence of explicit *wh*-movement of a *wh*-phrase to clause initial position, leaving a trace. Table II shows the distribution of relative clauses based on type (*wh*-, *that*, or zero) and targeted position within the relative clause (subject, direct object). In addition, three relative clauses were produced that targeted the object of preposition position, one of which was *My adventures that I have been through are the program called Summer Vestible* [Vestibule] *Program* .... These three relative clauses are not included in the Table II statistics.

Table II reveals that all of the deaf learners' *wh*-relative clauses targeted the subject position within the relative clause. It has been argued that the occurrence of a *wh*-phrase in subject position implies absence of *wh*-movement of a *wh*-phrase because there is no overt evidence of movement out of the subject position. In contrast, with relativization of a nonsubject position, the *wh*-phrase clearly moves to the left of the clausal subject, as in (16a). If we accept that analysis, no *wh*-movement was observed in the groups sampled. The derivations of *that* relatives and zero relatives have been argued to involve the movement of a *wh*-feature to the front of the clause rather than lexical material. Therefore, the data in Table II suggest that deaf learners at the English proficiency levels identified have IL grammars that lack relative clause derivations involving the less economical *wh*-movement of explicit lexical material. Where nonsubject positions are relativized, from the sample it appears that deaf learners opt for more economical derivations involving only feature movement as in *that* relatives and zero relatives.

Importantly, the deaf learners at all three levels were capable of explicit *wh*-movement in nonrelative clause structures for which there is no alternative derivation. There is no nonmovement alternative to the derivation of embedded *wh*-clauses in the sentences *Sometimes I confused what I am doing* (low Michigan group), *That is what I expect* (mid-group), and *You can also learn more about college program like what kind of major I like and want to learn* (high group). The production of such sentences suggests that the ILs of the targeted learners do not lack *wh*-movement *per se* but that the learners default to intrinsically more economical derivational options when they are available, as with English relative clauses.

These data underscore the need for comparative IL studies that further delve not only into issues related to IL RP production, but also into the L2 acquisition of different types of relative clauses. Although *wh*-, *that*, and zero relative clauses in English involve different derivational processes, they tend not to be differentiated in the research on hearing L2A. There is a need for further research on L2 relative clause acquisition that focuses on distinct relative clause types at the same time that IL RP production is examined. Comparative deaf/hearing IL research in this context may provide clearer answers regarding the relative roles of UG and L1 transfer in this domain of inquiry.

## V. CONCLUSION

This chapter has provided both an overview of aspects of deaf learners' English IL development and a demonstration of some of the close parallels that exist between the ILs of deaf and hearing L2 learners. The parallels were explained in terms of access to UG in L2A and specifically the constraints associated with UG as articulated in the MP. The observed IL parallels were shown to result from the influence of economy principles on acquisition, especially the consequences of more costly last resort operations. To the extent that deaf and hearing IL development is shown through further research to exhibit similarities in other target language domains, the more support there is that those similarities are more the product of direct UG access than of L1 transfer. To the extent that deaf learner and hearing learner ILs diverge in a specific target language domain, the greater is the likelihood that L1 transfer is influencing the hearing learners' IL development.

From the discussion in this chapter, it has been assumed that it is restricted access to target language input in L2A, whether the consequence of hearing loss or cognitive constraints on later language learning, that induces over-economical IL development in specific domains. A common misconception about deaf learners of English is that they exhibit "disordered" language learning. As in the hearing population, the deaf population includes a percentage of individuals who have language-related learning disabilities or other disorders that negatively impact language acquisition (see Berent, Samar, & Parasnis, 2000). Although the study of deaf learners' acquisition of spoken language knowledge might well inform certain issues related to disordered language learning, it more directly provides a window into the products of language acquisition, presumably guided by UG, under conditions of severely restricted access to target language input. For this reason, within the broader context of L2A research, comparative deaf/hearing IL research can be highly informative to distinguishing the roles of UG and L1 transfer in L2A along with the characterization of acquisition by specific learner populations.

# REFERENCES

Berent, G. P. (1983). Control judgments by deaf adults and by second language learners. *Language Learning, 33,* 37–53.

Berent, G. P. (1988). An assessment of syntactic capabilities. In M. Strong (Ed.), *Language learning and deafness* (pp. 133–161). Cambridge: Cambridge University Press.

Berent, G. P. (1993). Improvements in the English syntax of deaf college students. *American Annals of the Deaf, 138,* 55–61.

Berent, G. P. (1996a). The acquisition of English syntax by deaf learners. In W. Ritchie & T. Bhatia (Eds.), *Handbook of second language acquisition* (pp. 469–506). San Diego, CA: Academic Press.

Berent, G. P. (1996b). Learnability constraints on deaf learners' acquisition of English *wh*-questions. *Journal of Speech and Hearing Research, 39,* 625–642.

Berent, G. P., & Kelly, R. R. (2008). The efficacy of visual input enhancement in teaching deaf learners of L2 English. In Z.-H. Han (Ed.), *Understanding second language process* (pp. 80–105). Clevendon, UK: Multilingual Matters.

Berent, G. P., Kelly, R. R., Aldersley, S., Schmitz, K. L., Khalsa, B. K., Panara, J., & Keenan, S. (2007). Focus-on-form instructional methods promote deaf college students' improvement in English grammar. *Journal of Deaf Studies and Deaf Education, 12,* 8–24.

Berent, G. P., Kelly, R. R., Porter, J. E., & Fonzi, J. (2008). Deaf learners' knowledge of English universal quantifiers. *Language Learning, 58,* 401–437.

Berent, G. P., Kelly, R. R., Schmitz, K. L., & Kenney, P. (2009). Visual input enhancement via essay coding results in deaf learners' long-term retention of improved English grammatical knowledge. *Journal of Deaf Studies and Deaf Education, 14*(2), 190–204.

Berent, G. P., Kelly, R. R., & Schueler-Choukairi, T. (2009). Economy in the acquisition of English universal quantifier knowledge: Sentence interpretation by deaf and hearing students and L2 learners at the college level. *Applied Psycholinguistics, 30,* 251–290.

Berent, G. P., & Samar, V. J. (1990). The psychological reality of the subset principle: Evidence from the governing categories of prelingually deaf adults. *Language, 66,* 714–741.

Berent, G. P., Samar, V. J., & Parasnis, I. (2000). College teachers' perceptions of English language characteristics that identify English language learning disabled deaf students. *American Annals of the Deaf, 145,* 342–358.

Boeckx, C., & Hornstein, N. (2003). Reply to 'control is not movement'. *Linguistic Inquiry, 34,* 269–280.

Boeckx, C., & Hornstein, N. (2004). Movement under control. *Linguistic Inquiry, 35,* 431–452.

Bošković, Ž., & Lasnik, H. (2007). *Minimalist syntax: The essential readings.* Malden, MA: Blackwell Publishing.

Chomsky, N. (1981). *Lectures on government and binding.* Dordrecht, The Netherlands: Foris Publications.

Chomsky, N. (1995). *The minimalist program.* Cambridge, MA: MIT Press.

Chomsky, N. (2000). Minimalist inquiries: The framework. In R. Martin, D. Michaels, & J. Uriagereka (Eds.), *Step by step: Essays on minimalist syntax in honor of Howard Lasnik* (pp. 89–155). Cambridge, MA: MIT Press.

Doughty, C. J., & Long, M. H. (2003). The scope of inquiry and goals of SLA. In C. J. Doughty & M. H. Long (Eds.), *The handbook of second language acquisition* (pp. 3–16). Malden, MA: Blackwell Publishing.

Eckman, F. R. (2004). Optimality theory, markedness and second language syntax: The case of resumptive pronouns in relative clauses. *Studies in Phonetics, Phonology and Morphology, 10*, 89–110.

Fox, D. (2000). *Economy and semantic interpretation*. Cambridge, MA: MIT Press.

Friedmann, N., & Szterman, R. (2006). Syntactic movement in orally trained children with hearing impairment. *Journal of Deaf Studies and Deaf Education, 11*, 56–75.

Gass, S. M. (1979). Language transfer and universal grammatical relations. *Language Learning, 29*, 327–344.

Gass, S. M. (1997). *Input, interaction, and the second language learner*. Mahwah, NJ: Lawrence Erlbaum Associates.

Hawkins, R. (2001). *Second language syntax: A generative introduction*. Oxford: Blackwell Publishers.

Hornstein, N. (1999). Movement and control. *Linguistic Inquiry, 30*, 69–96.

Hyltenstam, K. (1984). The use of typological markedness conditions as predictors in second language acquisition: The case of pronominal copies in relative clauses. In R. Andersen (Ed.), *Second languages: A cross-linguistic perspective* (pp. 39–58). Rowley, MA: Newbury House Publishers.

Levitt, H. (1989). Speech and hearing in communication. In M. C. Wang, M. C. Reynolds, & H. J. Walberg (Eds.), *Handbook of special education research and practice volume 3: Low incidence conditions* (pp. 23–45). New York: Pergamon Press.

Lillo-Martin, D. (1998). The acquisition of English by deaf signers: Is universal grammar involved? In S. Flynn, G. Martohardjono, & W. O'Neil (Eds.), *The generative study of language acquisition* (pp. 131–149). Mahwah, NJ: Lawrence Erlbaum Associates.

Lillo-Martin, D. (1999). Modality effects and modularity in language acquisition: The acquisition of American Sign Language. In T. K. Bhatia & W. C. Ritchie (Eds.), *Handbook of child language acquisition* (pp. 531–567). San Diego, CA: Academic Press.

May, R. (1977). *The grammar of quantification*. Unpublished dissertation, Massachusetts Institute of Technology, Cambridge, MA.

McKee, C., & McDaniel, D. (2001). Resumptive pronouns in English relative clauses. *Language Acquisition, 9*, 113–156.

Michigan Test of English Language Proficiency. (1977). English Language Institute, University of Michigan, Ann Arbor, MI.

Parasnis, I. (Ed.) (1996). *Cultural and language diversity and the deaf experience*. Cambridge, England: Cambridge University Press.

Platzack, C. (1996). The initial hypothesis of syntax. In H. Clahsen (Ed.), *Generative perspectives on language acquisition* (pp. 369–414). Amsterdam: John Benjamins.

Quigley, S. P., & King, C. M. (1980). Syntactic performance of hearing impaired and normal hearing individuals. *Applied Psycholinguistics, 1*, 329–356.

Reinhart, T. (2006). *Interface strategies: Optimal and costly computations*. Cambridge, MA: MIT Press.

Roberts, I. (1999). Verb movement and markedness. In M. DeGraff (Ed.), *Language creation and language change: Creolization, diachrony, and development* (pp. 287–327). Cambridge, MA: MIT Press.

Schwartz, B. D., & Sprouse, R. A. (2000). When syntactic theories evolve: Consequences for L2 acquisition research. In J. Archibald (Ed.), *Second language acquisition and linguistic theory* (pp. 156–186). Malden, MA: Blackwell Publishing.

Schwarzschild, R. (2002). Singleton indefinites. *Journal of Semantics, 19,* 289–314.

Shlonsky, U. (1992). Resumptive pronouns as a last resort. *Linguistic Inquiry, 23,* 443–468.

Toscano, R. M., McKee, B., & Lepoutre, D. (2002). Success with academic English: Reflections of deaf college students. *American Annals of the Deaf, 147,* 5–23.

Yusa, N. (1998). A minimalist approach to second language acquisition. In S. Flynn, G. Martohardjono, & W. O'Neil (Eds.), *The generative study of language acquisition* (pp. 215–238). Mahwah, NJ: Lawrence Erlbaum Associates.

CHAPTER 23

# SECOND LANGUAGE ACQUISITION: RESEARCH AND APPLICATION IN THE INFORMATION AGE

Tej K. Bhatia and William C. Ritchie

## I. INTRODUCTION

The Information Age has revolutionized the way in which language is used, transmitted, and taught around the world. The scope and magnitude of this revolution is unprecedented in the history of human communication. The Internet, telecommunication, and the forces of globalization have brought about tremendous change in the way language is used and communication is carried out in the rapidly globalizing society as a whole. Language use in e-mails, chat groups, and text messaging in computer-mediated communication (CMC) and the emergence of new forms of communication (bimodal, i.e., verbal and visual) are representative of new communication forms. Technological change in turn has impacted the conceptualization of learning, and the theory and practice of language teaching in a profound fashion. Concerning the nature and scope of its impact on the field of second language acquisition (SLA), the jury is still out. However, there is no doubt about the potential and promise of technology in shaping and reshaping the direction of research on SLA and in providing a potential testing ground for current theories of SLA.

The remainder of this chapter is divided into four sections. Section II deals with the new contexts and conditions created by the information and learning technology that have changed and continue to change the practice and scope of language teaching inside and outside the classroom. The magnitude of technological development is so compelling as to give rise to doomsday predictions for language teaching, the role of the teacher, and the reduction of the human linguistic stock. Sections III and IV explore issues pertaining to research and practice in SLA grounded in technology. Section III

*The New Handbook of Second Language Acquisition*

focuses specifically on fundamental issues in computer-assisted language learning (CALL) and the salient features of CMC. Research on the distinct promise that this modality holds for language instruction and consequently for SLA is presented. Section IV is devoted to issues surrounding the role of explicit and implicit learning in language acquisition by adults. What is the role of information technology in testing central theoretical claims about implicit and explicit learning? How does the positive and negative evidence provided by instructional technology contribute to language learning? What is the impact of computer-based learning on the acquisition of production and comprehension skills? These issues are discussed with reference to current research. Section V deals with theoretical and methodological problems stemming from the research-practice relationship prompted by CALL and SLA. The chapter ends with a presentation of new issues and directions in computer-assisted second language acquisition research (CASLAR). Conclusions are presented in section VI.

## II. NEW LANGUAGE LEARNING CONTEXTS AND CONDITIONS IN THE INFORMATION AGE

The introduction of computers has led to the emergence of CALL, which is used either as a supplementary or as an independent tool of traditional classroom language teaching, thus yielding two new options: hybrid (that is, human-machine) and computer-driven methodologies of language teaching. In qualitative terms, CALL facilitates language teaching at the pace and time of the learner's own choice, at the same time granting autonomy and flexibility to language professionals as well. On the research side, CASLAR presents a series of structured tasks which require learners to work on the target language interactively either with a computer program or through a computer-human interface.

The emergence of the Internet marks the beginning of a new period in the theory and practice of language instruction both inside and outside the classroom. Language learning materials now offer a considerable array of language teaching materials delivered through various modalities (e.g., CDs, DVDs, slides, audiotapes, film strips, CD ROMS, software packages, etc.) in addition to a large variety of printed material. The diversity of language teaching approaches, learning styles, intrinsic properties of different modalities (e.g., print, software, etc.), and the interface among modalities (multimedia) further determine the character of language learning materials and software development (for details, see Ur, 2002 and Blake, 2007).

I-Pods and MP3 portable devices have added a new dimension to delivery systems of language teaching materials. Developments in computer hardware, storage virtualization, and distributed computing have added to existing learning tools (Goodwin-Jones, 2008). The generation of pocket computers released in the latter part of 2008 have made materials more accessible to learners. While the potential application of technological development seems limitless for language teaching, this chapter will focus on certain technologies widely used in language instruction and learning—in particular the Internet and Web-based technology—and in research on SLA.

Within the classroom format, courses are organized from the perspective of either face-to-face delivery or computer-mediated delivery, for example, through

BlackBoard, Web CT (Siekmann, 2000). This new aspect of the delivery system has given rise to a distinct threefold organization—teacher, student, and material—where the choices within each of these components are quite free.

Technology allows distance learning, and e-learning or Web-based teaching. Laptops with Skype and classrooms equipped with video-conferencing facilities have made distance language learning a reality and has assured near-universal accessibility to language learning and e-communication despite the global digital divide. Learners today can contact a native speaker (NS) in any part of the world and receive highly individualized feedback in spoken and written language at the time or place of the learner's choice. The Web-based delivery of language material consists of spoken, written, and visual modalities and their combinations.

The impact of the Internet and new technology on language teaching is evident from the fact that computers, the Internet, and various electronic tools have become a permanent fixture in any language teaching program—whether long-distance or face-to-face. Technology has brought about a new generation of information and language learning tools. To take an example, the range of information and learning tools offered by the search engine Google have considerable potential for e-language learning. Notable resources include Web-based linguistic corpora and KWIC (key word in context). Google's corpus of language usage, and translational packages with e-dictionaries and other tools provide language learners opportunities that are "informative, productive, collaborative, communicative, and aggregative" (Chinnery, 2008, p. 4). The application of Google for language learning has just begun to be tapped.

Rich data collection is not only imperative for developing effective learning tools, but also the data collected from language learners serves as an important tool for research on SLA. The expansion of the Internet provides increased opportunities for collecting a wide variety of data that can contribute to CASLAR. Real-world data drawn from e-communication facilitates socially realistic language teaching. Authentic and task-based texts and large corpora have become important elements in contemporary language teaching/learning (see Crystal, 2001 for details).

Prior to the introduction of Internet-based teaching, the learning of foreign languages, particularly the teaching of the less commonly taught languages (LCTLs) and the almost never taught languages (ANTLs) of Asia and Africa, was subject to severe constraints due to demographics, cost, lack of pedagogical materials, and trained teachers. The teaching of LCTLs and ANTLs has particularly benefited from the Web-based approach to language teaching by overcoming important obstacles such as cost and lack of printed materials. Therefore, the democratization of language teaching has taken a major step with Web-based teaching.

The instantaneous availability of electronic dictionaries and the option of machine translation and synthesized speech call into question the traditional wisdom of language learning. One might wonder what place language learning has in a rapidly globalizing world. After all, spoken and written words and the ability to translate from one language into another are at one's fingertips. Furthermore, English is rapidly evolving as a global language. If at all one has to learn a language, the choice is reasonably clear; the most preferred language is English. The dominance of English, whether in the Internet arena or elsewhere, is the prime cause of language shift around the globe. Somewhat unexpectedly, globalization and the Internet have not downgraded the teaching of the major and minor languages of the world in spite of the fact that the Internet and globalization both still favor English (Crystal, 2001). Ironically, these two developments—the Internet and the global appeal of English—have turned out to contribute to the preservation and the transmission/teaching of the endangered languages of the world and for the teaching of ANTLs and LCTLs. Technology has increased language learning and the diversity of forms of human communication.

The developments brought about by globalization and technology have also had some impact on English teaching policy. A new report issued in mid-March 2007 by the Demos Institute, an important think tank in the United Kingdom that has played a considerable role in shaping the policies of the Labor government during the past decade, has been influential in the field of teaching English as a foreign or second language in the United Kingdom (Jones & Bradwell, 2007). The report recommended a new approach to teaching English as a global *lingua franca* (Graddol, 2006, p. 87). It asserted that the spread of English as a global language has led to the emergence of mixed languages referred to as "Chinglish," "Hinglish," and "Spanglish." According to this report, the practice of English teaching in the United Kingdom (or, for that matter, around the world) needs to respond to this global reality. The report advocated English teaching in the United Kingdom that accommodates speakers of, say, "Hinglish" rather than forcing the acquisition of Standard British English. This report led to widespread media attention and a strong reaction on the part of language teachers and publishing companies, resembling to some extent the response to the Ebonics debate in America in 1996–1997 (Pullum, 1997). Nevertheless, the report constituted an alert for researchers on SLA and practitioners of English language teaching that the era of new Englishes and language varieties has arrived. "The challenge that faces us is how we move beyond seeing such hybrid languages as Chinglish, Hinglish, Singlish, Spanglish, and multiple others as amusing corruptions. We should see them as varieties, rather than 'interlanguages', which bring with them their own distinct culture and provide equally distinct means of understanding their users" (Jones & Bradwell, 2007, p. 87). The report thus argued that current practice reflects an outmoded model of English language teaching. In short, in the view expressed in this report, the forces of globalization, in addition to naturalistic and language accommodation models, require a departure from the normative approach to language teaching.

One can sum up the new learning context as providing a wide range of choices of methodologies, approaches, languages, language materials, etc. Input is at the heart of SLA research; the e-generation of language learners are exposed to multiple norms and varieties, thus providing rich input and testing the limits of the learner's intake—that is, the learner's capacity to make sense of this rich and various input. The new options and potential of CALL pose challenges regarding the effectiveness of the new teaching practices and tools and, therefore, constitute an interesting opportunity for research.

## III. CALL: RESEARCH ON MERITS AND POTENTIALS

What is the attitude of language professionals and learners toward the use of computers in language instruction? What intrinsic merits of CALL can be tapped for effective language teaching? These two fundamental issues continue to pervade the field of CALL since its inception in the late 1970s. Innovations in technology have further added a new urgency to these issues.

Concerning the first question, current research shows that there is near-unanimous agreement among researchers that language professionals are open to using computers for language instruction. The same is true of language learners around the world (Chapelle, 2007). Besides learning materials and software, a positive attitude on the part of both instructors and learners is critical for ensuring any effective learning; CALL is capable of meeting this critical test. These attitudes have affected both teachers' and learners' knowledge and expectations about the role of technology in language teaching. While in the late 1970s, technology was viewed as an innovation in language teaching both by teachers and students, today it is viewed as a basic necessity of any teaching, including language teaching; computers are like the paper and pen of traditional pedagogy. How, then, can any teacher fail to respond to such a necessity? Besides agreement concerning the necessity of technology in the classroom, CALL requires a knowledge of technology and particularly of the theory of computer-assisted instruction, a means for exploring and evaluating new teaching tools. These new requirements pose a serious challenge to the professional engaged in language teaching (see Chapelle, 2003; Chapelle, 2007, pp. 588–589; Leloup & Ponterio, 2003 for details).

The second question of the merit of CALL has two parts: the first part concerns the intrinsic characteristics of the medium while the second part concerns its effectiveness. The advent of Web-based teaching through the Internet has changed the characteristics of language teaching. Research shows that anonymous communication—that is, communication that is not face-to-face—and multiple tasking have added a new dimension to human communication and processing. Consequently, interactivity and nonlinear learning (e.g., learning through Web-links) have become the two defining characteristics of language teaching and learning through technology (Crystal, 2001).

Interactivity is the defining feature of CALL. In addition to receiving highly-individualized instruction through NSs of (or non-native experts on) the target language, learners may engage in synchronous or asynchronous chats with an e-community of their choice by means of software, providing them an option of turn-taking and interacting with each other on an equal basis—unlike a classroom situation in which teacher–student, student–teacher, and student–student communication is usually unequal. As the discussion in section IV will indicate, interactivity offers a distinct potential that can be and is capitalized on by research in SLA and CALL.

The answer to the second part of the question (i.e., the effectiveness issue) is, however, still open to debate in part due to the lack of sufficient research devoted to the task of testing hypotheses about SLA in this context. Nevertheless, current empirical research showing CALL's effectiveness is notable in the following areas, which, in turn, reveal the distinct strength of the new medium.

## A. Decreasing Negative Affect

Any successful approach to language teaching has to take into account factors external to the learning of linguistic structure *per se* such as the learner's motivation, intelligence, economic benefits, and other determinants such as attitude toward the target language and culture. In addition, affective factors that have played an important role in SLA research since the 1960s (see, e.g., Gardner & Lambert, 1972) may either inhibit or promote the learning of a second or foreign language. Affective factors include negative influences such as anxiety, lack of self-confidence, and inadequate motivation, which can create serious obstacles to language learning.

Current research in CMC shows that CALL has a significant edge over classroom pedagogy in reducing negative affect in the learner. Nearly all studies reveal positive student attitudes toward technology that shows a lowering of anxiety levels, the creation of higher interest, and the stimulation of greater student participation. In terms of production, the ratio of language production on the part of learners increases more significantly than in a classroom setting. Learners express a preference for tasks that promote social interaction between and among NSs and non-native speakers (NNSs) (see Liu, Moore, Graham, & Lee, 2002). Language learners report an overall positive attitude toward computer use when they are engaged in language learning requiring cooperative tasks. Due to the increase in the interactivity between NSs and NNSs, learners' attitudes toward the target culture are found to be positive. Thus, through CALL, language learners perform more like integrative learners than they do like instrumental learners.

## B. Providing a Naturalistic Environment

There is also a unanimous consensus among researchers that CALL is well suited to providing a relatively informal environment for language learning (Crystal, 2001). Since in classrooms, learning takes place in a formal environment, the data obtained from classroom learning is less likely to be naturalistic than in informal conditions. Thus, CALL presents a good opportunity for facilitating language learning and for testing hypotheses in SLA research.

The intrinsic properties of technology led us to the conclusion that its potential is considerable; however the fundamental issue is how to tap that potential for language teaching and to optimize it in order to provide highly individualized instruction customized to the learner's needs. In other words, rather than configuring technology with a "one-size fits all" approach, the challenge of optimization of learning environments and learning resources is the fundamental challenge for the theory and practice of CALL. The discussion of Doughty and Long's (2003) 10 methodological principles in section IV.C reveals that research and practice based in these principles will add further strength to CALL.

More important than the use of technology *per se* is the quality of what is done with this medium. A badly conceived interactive task or activity is poor whether it is done on a computer or face-to-face teaching. Using technology is an important but not a sufficient condition for learning. In order to promote successful learning, pedagogical tasks must be meaningful and comprehensible with a built-in interactional capacity (Chapelle, 2003; Liu et al., 2002; Warschauer & Healey, 1998; see also Gor & Long, this volume). Accordingly, language assessment is another vital part of language teaching. Web-based learning has made comprehensive, and yet objective, language assessment possible. Consider the case of vocabulary learning; vocabulary learning can be a very labor-intensive task for a teacher in a traditional classroom setting, yet the results are unlikely to be as rewarding and objective as those rendered by computer-based language instruction. Thanks to computers, it is possible to carry out an evaluation of students' progress in vocabulary and grammar development practically on a daily basis, thus making assessment (and research) more objective, more accurate, and less labor-intensive.

Despite advances in the theory and the practice of SL teaching and technological innovation, effective teaching is as good as the tools used to deliver it. CALL has responded to this challenge by developing computer-driven software. The design features of instructional software provide an excellent opportunity for testing hypotheses about SLA. A body of work in CASLAR is devoted to comparison and evaluation of specific design features of instructional software based on implicit input to learners. Notable studies are those by Plass, Chun, Mayer, and Leutner (1998), Chun and Plass (1996), and Borrás and Lafayette (1994), all of which are aimed at comparing reading and listening software. This research reveals that software with vocabulary annotations tends to promote better learning of vocabulary than those without annotations. Similarly, the evaluation of software with more specific feedback versus that without feedback on learners' errors favors the former over the latter (Nagata, 1995). In short, the cognitive and learning benefits of these software features modeled after the Interaction Hypothesis (R. Ellis, 1997; Gass, 1997, 2003; Long, 1996; Pica, 1994) have been largely validated in research (Gass & Mackey, 2007; Sanz & Morgan-Short, 2004, 2005). These findings represent a major contribution to CALL and CASLAR.

## IV. CALL AND SLA RESEARCH

Technology has given researchers in SLA new options for testing their claims and present directions for teaching languages as well. According to Chapelle (2008, p. 99), CASLAR presents a degree of control over the instructional conditions that "far exceeds what can be obtained in classroom research where teachers are to teach in a particular way." Thus, technology is capable of furnishing researchers the data to evaluate the relative strength of modes of organizing input, thereby paving the way for researchers to challenge and refine their theories and to present fine-grained analysis of their theoretical constructs. In what follows, based on computer-mediated experimental and computer-networked discourse studies, we will show how tasks developed within CASLAR respond to key issues of second language learning.

### A. Implicit and Explicit Learning; Implicit and Explicit Knowledge

In current research on SLA (and in cognitive psychology in general) a distinction is made between implicit and explicit learning (see Williams, this volume). N. C. Ellis (1994) writes:

> Explicit learning is acquisition of knowledge about the underlying structure of a complex stimulus environment by a process which takes place naturally, simply, and without conscious operations. Explicit learning is a more conscious operation where the individual makes and test hypotheses in a search for structure. (p. 1)

In the paradigm cases, children acquire languages implicitly—almost entirely without explicit instruction. What is required is input (positive evidence) from parents, caretakers, and others in the child's environment. Explicit language learning is more typical of adults, who tend to require explicit teaching and conscious learning involving more effort and planning on the part of both teachers and learners. A central and common goal in CASLAR and research on SLA in general is to uncover the underlying mechanisms that determine the patterns of explicit and implicit learning and how best to integrate the two ways of learning for second language learners.

As mentioned above, children acquire language in a linguistic environment, which is termed "natural" (informal), whereas adults generally learn language under formal conditions such as in classroom settings. Consequently, in many cases explicit learning plays a central role in the adult's experience with the L2. The central question, then, is whether or not explicit learning is either necessary or sufficient for the adult to attain implicit knowledge of the L2. There is, of course, a vast research literature on this issue, and a full review is beyond the scope of this chapter. Nonetheless, we offer a few, limited observations. As will be seen, the evidence on this question is decidedly mixed.

With respect to the role of explicit and implicit learning in the attainment of implicit knowledge of the L2, consider the adult's attainment of the structures relevant to the operation of the Functional Head Constraint (FHC), a universal constraint on code-mixing (see chapter 25 for a more detailed discussion of the FHC). An experimental study by Bhatia and Ritchie (2001) explored the attainment of the FHC structures by English learners of Hindi as a second language. This study revealed that, without any explicit training, adult learners show evidence of the knowledge of the FHC, thus showing that it is possible for L2 learners to attain such complex knowledge on their own (as children do). Since these learners were not explicitly taught the FHC (but were, in fact, discouraged from code-mixing at all), this constitutes evidence against the necessity of explicit language instruction for the acquisition of unconscious knowledge of the structures that invoke the operation of a principle of Universal Grammar (UG), that is, the FHC.

With respect to the sufficiency of explicit learning for the attainment of implicit knowledge, the works of Rosa and O'Neill (1999) and VanPatten and Oikkenon (1996) indicate that explicit explanation has no beneficial effects on implicit learning. Even worse, some studies show negative effects of explicit learning (Pica, 1983; Robinson, 1996).

On the other hand, de Graaff (1997) and several experimental and quasi-experimental studies presented in Hulstijn (1997) were designed to induce a variety of pedagogical conditions. In contrast with the studies showing either the no-beneficial effect or negative effect of explicit learning, these studies (Alanen, 1995; DeKeyser, 1995; de Graaff, 1997; N. C. Ellis, 1994; Robinson, 1996, 1997) show that explicit learning can lead to implicit knowledge. de Graaff 's study showed the beneficial effects of explicit explanation in the acquisition of both simple and complex morphological and syntactic forms of the artificial language eXpranto. He employed computer-assisted instruction in his design to examine the effects of explicit rule presentation enhanced by practice rather than a mere exposure to instances of applications of the rule. Both the implicit input group and the explicit input group received immediate feedback, which included positive and negative evidence.

The differential factor was that the explicit input group received exposure to metalinguistic (explicit) rules and feedback, while the implicit input group rehearsed example sentences. The result showed that the explicit group did better than the implicit group in all sessions and tests involving complex syntactic structure.

Similarly, Sanz and Morgan-Short (2004), incorporating computer-assisted instruction in their experiment, studied the role of the variable presence or absence of grammar explanation and explicit feedback delivered through computers on the acquisition of Spanish word order. Extending the scope of CASLAR, Nagata (1993) and Nagata and Swisher (1995) examined the role of traditional (T-CALI) or intelligent (I-CALI) feedback in raising second language learners' awareness of linguistic structure in the process of computer-assisted learning instruction (CALI). The T-CALI group received feedback indicating what was wrong with their answers, whereas the I-CALI group received feedback with metalinguistic explanations in addition to an indication of what was wrong with their response. The results from a final achievement test showed that I-CALI outperformed T-CALI group on sentence-level grammatical complexity. The study concluded that "when a grammatical system is nontrivially complex, metalinguistic feedback by means of computer-aided instruction involving natural language processing is more effective than traditional CALI feedback" (Nagata & Swisher, 1995, p. 345). For more recent developments in the area of intelligent CALL (*i*-CALL), see Blake (2007). Doughty (1991) tested the effects of carefully varied input conditions for the acquisition of relative clauses in reading contexts.

The fundamental principle seems to be that explicit instruction works for the attainment of simple structures, but is not sufficient for complex structures. In either case, "withholding basic information from learners" (MacWhinney, 1997, p. 278) or providing overly simplified input is ineffective. Such input only leads to potentially harmful effects in language learning. Consider the case of Keki (Yang & Givon, 1997), a pidgin language. For teaching Keki, second language learners were placed in two separate groups: one group was exposed to the full language from the beginning, while the other was imparted a limited version of the language with certain rules during the first half of the learning period and the full version in the latter half of the learning session. The findings revealed that the latter group, which had to make a mid-course correction from limited input to full input did less well than the group that received full input from the start. This is particularly instructive for CALL.

In short, in search of the crucial features of input, explicit instruction delivered through computers has provided new opportunities to gain insights into the fundamentals of these features (e.g., input conditions, input mode, input time, input complexity, types of explicit input, positive and negative evidence, and practice, whether input-based, output-based, or task-based). Despite the fact that computer-aided SLA research is "notoriously difficult to design because the researcher tends to attempt to make the classroom and CALL learning conditions the same in order to detect any difference the computer makes" (Chapelle, 2007, p. 590), research stimulated by computer application in SLA holds promise for shedding more light on the constructs of implicit and explicit learning, bottom-up learning (i.e., explicit-to-implicit learning), and the continuum of input complexity (see Sanz & Morgan-Short, 2005, pp. 235–236). Current CASLAR shows that explicit input leads to explicit learning, which in turn yields some degree of implicit learning with practice. This finding about the interface of explicit–implicit learning is also supported by brain research showing that conscious knowledge is stored in the right brain before being transferred to the left brain with the knowledge gaining unconscious status (see Urgesi & Fabbro, this volume).

## B. Processing and Knowledge

Now let us turn to two other constructs of language learning: processing and knowledge. Studies by VanPatten and Oikkenon (1996), Benati (2004), and Wong (2004) show that learners change their processing strategies "when practice decoding structured input requires it, but not when they are only told how to decode the input" Sanz and Morgan-Short (2005, p. 248).

To conduct language-processing studies, computer technology has an undoubted edge over traditional classroom methodology. In addition to gaining insights into the qualitative (information) and quantitative (speed, etc.) aspects of language processing, and the learner's approach to the learning task, CASLAR reveals a number of aspects of learners' linguistic and cognitive skill. For instance, some learners may turn to an e-dictionary to look up a word while other learners might ask for a word from a NS/participant engaged in computer-mediated conversation. In both cases such differential behavior may provide a window to learners' noticing ability and desire to communicate (Hegelheimer & Chappelle, 2000).

In terms of differential cognitive behavior, Chun and Payne (2004) found that learners with lower working memory capacity favored the use of a built-in dictionary rather than social interaction as a basis for the learning of vocabulary. Data obtained from processing studies provides insight into the development of interlanguage communicative competence. Tavaossoli and Han's research (2001) involving Chinese–English bilinguals has identified language-based processing that impacts memory. Luna & Peracchio's (2005) computer-aided processing study reveals that code-mixing can activate association with language-specific domains, which constitute an integral part of the communicative competence associated with emergent or attained bilingualism.

## C. From Theory to Practice: SLA Research and CALL Pedagogy

Ritchie and Bhatia (2008) argue that both kinds of linguistic knowledge and learning (explicit and implicit) need to be exploited to the greatest extent possible in classroom interaction and material development, among other factors in SLA. This calls for the optimization of theoretical insights in the design of instructional strategies for computer-based and noncomputer-based learning materials and software. Pica (1998) reminds practitioners of language teaching and SLA researchers, "as a perspective on language learning, [the Interaction Hypothesis] holds none of the predictive weight of an individual theory. Instead, it lends its weight to any number of theories" (Pica, 1998, p. 10). The Interaction Hypothesis states that "negotiation work that triggers interactional adjustments by the NS or more competent interlocutor facilitates acquisition because it connects input, internal learner capacities, particularly selective attention, and output in productive ways" (Long, 1996, pp. 451–452). In other words, language teaching requires reliance not on a single theory but integration of insights abstracted from several SLA theories to optimize learning based on internal (innate) and external (input/environmental) factors.

The development of technology has given language teaching a number of choices. It is not the consideration of technological innovation but internal and external factors in language learning that should determine the choice of material/software for CALL. Doughty and Long (2003) have developed a set of methodological/guiding principles (MP) for task-based language teaching in order to provide directions for research-practice in CALL. These principles can be assigned to the following four categories:

(1) Learning: *MP1*: Use tasks, not texts, as a unit of analysis; *MP2*: Promote learning by doing.
(2) Input: *MP3*: Elaborate input (do not simplify; do not rely solely on "authentic" texts); *MP4*: Provide rich (not impoverished) input.
(3) Learning process: *MP5*: Encourage inductive (chunk) learning; *MP6*: Focus on form; *MP7*: Provide negative feedback; *MP8*: Respect learner syllabuses/develop mental processes; *MP9*: Promote a cooperative/collaborative environment.
(4) Learners: *MP10*: Individualize instruction (according to communicative needs, psycholinguistically).

These principles constitute a foundation of CALL and CASLAR tasks. Any instructional material based on these principles is capable of achieving the goal of "optimization" pointed out by Ritchie and Bhatia (2008).

One of the main pitfalls of CALL is the seductiveness of technological innovation. As pointed out in section II, language teachers and learners show remarkable openness to technology. For that reason, they may end up embracing software such as Praat, which is used by phoneticians for phonetic analysis. Learners are given model input (the sound wave of a teacher's token) as a target to be emulated. This exemplifies extremely negative potential for learning, since speech analysis software cannot filter out the nonsignificant variation found in speech, and hence may penalize learners for pronunciation that does not match that of the model's with respect to details that do not have linguistic significance. Similarly, the use of accent-reduction packages, particularly for learners of English as a foreign language, have potentially negative impact on language learning. Moreover, they can be exploitative and unethical (see Lippi-Green, 1997).

## D. The Interface of SLA and CALL Research: Discourse-Oriented Studies

Any cursory examination of child–parent interaction will reveal that children are smart interactionists. They often bombard their caretakers with wh-questions and thus induce even the most reluctant adult into interacting with them. The Interaction Hypothesis (Long, 1996) and sociocultural theories of SLA (e.g., Lantolf & Poehner, this volume; Lantolf & Thorne, 2007) aim at capturing the dynamic (de Bot, 2008) interaction aspect of second language learning.

The introduction of computers for communication and language teaching calls for an examination of the two modes of learning (face-to-face and CMC)—in particular, their shared and distinct characteristics, which can in turn be employed for SL teaching and research. In addition to psycholinguistic studies, research on CALL concerning L2 learners' language production and comprehension in CMC has been pursued following one of the three approaches or their combination—interactional, intercultural, and identity construction—within the framework of "critical discourse analysis." Rather than seeking evidence from an experimental or quasi-experimental approach, these methods seek evidence for language learning by studying linguistic strategies that learners use to interact with each other or with NSs. The fundamental assumption of the interaction approach is that language learning is facilitated when learners engage in interaction and negotiate meaning with NSs/NNSs. CMC provides ample opportunities for such interaction in synchronous (real time) or asynchronous (different time) chats and computer-based written communication.

Interaction-driven research on CMC (e.g., Abrams, 2006; Blake, 2005, 2006a, 2006b; Doughty & Long, 2003; Meskill, 2005; B. Smith, 2003) reveals how synchronous CMC (SCMC) stimulates negotiation of meaning as is evident in any form of communication including face-to-face communication. Comparative interaction studies show that learners in face-to-face communication are largely focused on meaning rather than form (e.g., Blake, 2000; Lee, 2001), while CMC provides more opportunities for focus on form as well (Blake, 2005; Pellettieri, 2000). The underlying reason for the relative advantage of CMC over face-to-face communication is that face-to-face communication progresses at a rapid pace, which is subject to the effects on limitations on memory storage/allocation. For this reason there is less opportunity for learners to focus on form. Accordingly, the consideration of meaning in negotiations overrides consideration of the accuracy of form in face-to-face communication. This explains why Jepson (2005) found more incidences of meaning-oriented repair moves in voice chat. However, negotiation of meaning in text chat is also evident (e.g., Fernández-Garcia & Martinez-Arbelaiz, 2003).

A common and fundamental source of miscommunication between L2 and L1/L2 learners involves lexical items. Consider a conversation between two interlocutors—an NS of English and an NNS learner of English. The NS sees two boxes of books ready to be shipped to China by the L2 learner of English. Observe the following exchange between L1 and L2 speakers of English.

> L2: I send two book to China today.
> L1: you mean two boxes.
> L2: Yes, two box.
> L1: ah... two boxes
> L2: Yes, two boxes.

This type of interaction (termed a "recast"; see Gor and Long, this volume) is significant for an L2 learner in that he/she takes notice of the lexical item which is the source of miscommunication and corrects it. This process of correction involves three steps: First, the L1 speaker provides a clue about the source of the problem using the linguistic frame: "(Do) you mean X (?)"; second, through a mid-course interruption of the conversation flow marked by a topic switch (a conversational shift from action to object); and third, the L1 speaker suggests a solution by providing explicit input. The negative evidence provided by the L1 speaker lends saliency to the lexical item to be corrected and grammatical form to be negotiated. This type of recasting feedback from an NS (with repair by a non-native interlocutor) facilitates the learning of lexicon. Vocabulary is now recognized as fundamental to language development and may be the most important component for language learners (Gass & Mackey, 2007; see Juffs, this volume). Computer-mediated negotiated synchronous interaction by L2 learners shows that lexicon thus negotiated and practiced is retained significantly better than lexical items in receptive and lagged production modes (B. Smith, 2004). This finding is also supported by De la Fuente (2003). Recent works (e.g., Peters, 2007) point out the role of task-based word relevance for retention.

How do learners go about seeking access to vocabulary? While some learners turn to electronic dictionaries, others turn to higher cognitive skills, using strategies such as attention-getters, paraphrasing, and summation in the process of retrieving a target vocabulary item (e.g., B. Smith, 2004). The choice of distinct approaches to lexical retrieval on the part of learners reflect not only distinct learning strategies but also differential learning capacity (e.g., memory). More importantly, findings of discourse research on vocabulary acquisition has provided further insights not only into the development of language ability, but has also provided a window into metalinguistic cognitive strategies.

Increasingly, CALL researchers are turning to discourse analysis for the investigation of comprehension and other topics as a framework to examine student interactions using bimodal or multimodal chatting (i.e., discourse with both text and audio channels and video in some cases; see Blake, 2005). Experimental intelligibility studies (e.g., L. Smith, 1992) of global Englishes suggest that communication between NNS–NNS pairs and NS–NNS pairs show that the incidence of intelligibility between members of NNS–NNS pairs is higher than within NS–NNS pairs, in part due to the absence of asymmetrical power relations in the NNS–NNS pair. NNSs show more accommodation than NSs. CMC studies by Blake and Zyzik (2003) and Lee (2004) also support this conclusion to some degree with a notable perspective on the beneficiary of communication breakdown or comprehension. The assumption that the only beneficiary of negotiation of meaning is the NNS/L2 learner group is challenged by these two studies and others. Blake and Zyzik explored the networked interaction between heritage speakers of Spanish (rather than NSs of Spanish) and L2 learners of Spanish. The results showed that both groups exhibited accommodation, and both groups turned out to be the beneficiaries of CMC exchanges. The finding concerning mutual beneficiaries in CMC is also confirmed by the positive mediating effects of NS/NNS face-to-face oral discussion (Pica, 1994; Mackey, 1999).

Language switching (from L2 to L1 or vice versa), language mixing, and modality mixing are other notable strategies to enhance input and employ repair strategies. For instance, Borrás and Lafayette (1994) provided video input with L2 subtitles. Kotter (2003) found that negotiation of meaning in synchronous written chats between German-speaking L2 learners of English and English-speaking L2 learners of German employed repair strategies similar to those found in CMC studies and face-to-face interaction studies. In addition, he observed a high incidence of code-switching for repairing communication gaps, which is also supported by studies on bilingual verbal behavior (see chapter 25). Research shows that whatever benefit accrues from engaging in CMC is not a function of the tools (e.g., Thorne, 2003; Zhao, Alvarez-Torres, Smith, & Tan, 2005), but rather the effective engagement in meaningful interactions and real intercultural reflections. Breakdowns can be frequent, but they also provide opportunities for tapping the emerging L2 system as well as new ways of conceiving of students' new bilingual identities (O'Rourke & Schwienhorst, 2003).

Sociocultural and pragmatic factors, which are viewed as peripheral in some theories of SLA, gain utmost prominence in sociocultural studies (e.g., Belz & Thorne, 2006; Darhower, 2007; Lomicka, 2006; Thorne, 2003; Ware & Kramsch, 2005; Lantolf & Poehner, this volume). Sociocultural researchers contend that any model of interaction that is divorced from the environment and context of its users is too narrow in nature (Byrnes, 2006). This perspective calls for a distinction between intracultural CMC and intercultural CMC (also termed, telecollaboration) or intercultural communication for foreign language learning (ICFLL; see Thorne & Payne, 2005) in order to gain insights into "the complex nature of humans as sociocultural actors and technological settings as artifacts and as mediators, rather than determiners of action and interaction" (O'Rourke, 2005, p. 435). Since technology is a new reality in human communication, the sociocultural studies aimed at studying distinct discourse styles and actors' identity construction (see Blake, 2007, pp. 78–79 for an overview; see de Bot, 2008 for the role agents) add yet a new emerging dimension to CMC (Darhower, 2007). For an excellent example of the implementation of telecollaboration, see the details of the *Cultura* project (Blake, 2007, p. 78).

## V. PROBLEMS AND FUTURE DIRECTIONS

The introduction of and the potential for technology in language learning and SLA research have opened a wide range of opportunities. In addition to serious gains registered in the areas of both practice and research, the breadth and depth of new opportunities and challenges rendered by technology are multifaceted. We turn now to some problems and future directions.

### A. Methodological Problems

Although the scope of empirical and evaluative studies concerned with the effects of technology on learning has increased, they do not go beyond correlational studies. Opinions concerning the causal effect of the use of the various new technologies on language learning are far from showing any kind of consensus.

A cursory examination of recent experimental studies devoted to exploring the effects of explicit input on language learning show a diversity of issues and research methodologies. Sanz and Morgan-Short (2005, pp. 254–258) sum up the wide array of methodologies employed in experimental studies during the past two decades; no methodology is free of limitations. The underlying problem is that language learning is a dynamic process, the management of which calls for an integration of theoretical and methodological approaches. Where methodology is concerned, the issue of the integration of qualitative and quantitative methodology is a challenging one as is evident from our discussion of work on negotiation of meaning. A good theory should explain a variety of seemingly unrelated phenomena, whether those phenomena are the result of applying quantitative methods or qualitative methods. With respect to the question of how to integrate online and introspective data from learning tasks, there is no unanimous agreement. In addition, there is an issue as to how to incorporate learning tasks effectively into software; this is yet another methodological problem confronting researchers. Often the material that is designed for classroom teaching is also used for CALL without consideration of the differences between the two settings.

The population of subjects tested is still very narrow. For instance, the overwhelming trend is to select university students. Little attempt is made to extend the population of subjects or the languages investigated; for example, secondary school students and nonwestern languages are seldom tested. Heavy reliance on self-reported data is yet another methodological problem. Similarly, many studies fail to control factors such as subjects with similar attitudes and proficiency with technology (word processing and information search ability) and the differential power of technology and other modalities.

The development of assessment criteria for computer software and computer-driven tools is still in its infant stage. Either through the media or through overzealous instructors, untested software is often introduced into classes or CMC settings without any serious consideration of their value for learning. A case in point is the recent introduction of a Hindi–English translation tool. Numerous newspapers in India and abroad commended Google for this innovation. The news appeared in the media about its potential use in classes; the product manager gave a sermon to the media about the product, and several newspaper articles followed the same theme. The South Asia language teachers' listserv drew attention to this system as an important instructional tool. However, a cursory examination of the software by the first-named author of this chapter revealed that the package has some fundamental flaws (e.g., in translating present tense or sentences such as "I like this"); if introduced as an instructional device in its present form, it can do tremendous damage to learners instead of facilitating learning. The methodology of exploring and assessing software has to be scrutinized.

## B. Theoretical Issues

There is a near-unanimous consensus among researchers that computers are better equipped than classroom instruction to control and simulate conditions under which second language learning takes place so that hypotheses about SLA can be tested. On the theoretical front, although gains have been registered pertaining to explicit and implicit learning and other key issues, Ortega (2007, p. 245) points out the following fundamental questions in SLA research that need to be pursued:

What constitutes explicit vs. implicit knowledge of L2?

How does each type of knowledge originate?

How and when do they interface with each other?

What is the relative contribution of each to L2 learning?

These questions, which are at the core of CALL and CASLAR, await answers. From the viewpoint of theory-practice, most theories do not attempt to offer any lead to instructional design for traditional classroom pedagogy or, particularly, for CALL. The basic constructs of mainstream SLA theories (including one key construct, input) are still hopelessly underspecified. Consider the notion of "complexity"; there is no set of objective criteria for determining complexity of structure. This poses a serious dilemma for the interpretation of research findings. Researchers agree that the role of complexity is critical in the development of implicit knowledge. However, how to define complexity is still very subjective. The following is instructive in this regard. DeKeyser, Salaberry, Robinson, and Harrington (2002) claim that the preverbal Spanish direct object clitic system "boils down to a *simple* [our emphasis] morphological alternation." In contrast, Sanz (1999) "treats it as an example of a complex, late-acquired rule" (both quotes from Sanz and Morgan-Short, 2005, p. 240). This poses a serious problem with testing theories and evaluating research results.

## C. Future Directions

Developments in instructional and information technology underlie new conditions and contexts for learning languages. Consequently, every facet of language instruction ranging from CALL, materials development, teacher education, and assessment is open to innovation and future research. The increase in opportunities for research and practice is now extensive. What remains to be seen is how researchers will respond to these opportunities by bridging the present research–practice divide in an optimal fashion. Learning conditions ("natural" in theoretical terms) and scope of learning languages (major or minor languages including mixed languages) provide a conducive environment for developing socially relevant and yet powerful theories. Learners have a choice of learning practically any language, tapping a vast pool of NSs around the globe and forming Internet-based language learning communities to accelerate learning.

This brings us to the core question of input and the mode of learning in SLA. The scope and diversity of input received through technology is tremendously rich. Whether this new input reality will spell cohesion or chaos for the learner's ability to translate it into implicit learning, future research awaits an answer to this fundamental question. Dynamic System Theory (de Bot 2008, this volume), which proposes to study SL development as a dynamic process by integrating chaos, complexity, and dynamic systems seems to provide a good fit for CALL and CASLAR. Whether the time has arrived for such theories, only future research will tell. Moreover, current CALL and SLA research is still concerned primarily with the learning of western languages and the monolingual grammar of the L2 serves as a target for L2 learners, future CALL and SLA research calls for developing more natural targets for L2 grammars drawn from bilingual learning models. Furthermore, CALL shows that the targets for L2 learners are not static but constitute a moving target.

Finally, future SLA and CALL research has to incorporate an ethical dimension. Technology and globalization has given rise to unethical practices, which can be witnessed in modern-day call centers and medical practices (e.g., performing tongue surgery to ensure the acquisition of a native accent) around the globe

(Bhatia, in press). Similarly, the innateness hypothesis is presented with religious overtones to market language software and courseware (Bhatia, forthcoming). The profession has to find ways to explore and respond to such unethical practices.

## VI. CONCLUSIONS

The introduction of technology has revolutionized every facet of human communication and language learning. It offers tremendous new opportunities and challenges for researchers and professionals engaged in imparting language education. Researchers can utilize the invaluable data received through computer-mediated instruction or hybrid (man–machine) instruction to test their theories and fine-tune them. It has opened up the new possibility of bilateral exchange between theoreticians and practitioners of CALL and SLA researchers in order to devise a new phase of integrated research and practice.

## REFERENCES

Abrams, Z. (2006). From theory to practice: Intracultural CMC the L2 classroom. In L. Ducate & N. Arnold (Eds.), *Calling on CALL: From theory and research to new directions in foreign language teaching, CALICO Monograph Series* (Vol. 5, pp. 181–209). San Marcos, TX: CALICO.

Alanen, R. (1995). Input enhancement and rule presentation in second language acquisition. In R. Schmidt (Ed.), *Attention and awareness in foreign language learning* (pp. 259–302). Honolulu, HI: University of Hawaii Press.

Belz, I., & Thorne, S. (Eds.). (2006). *Internet-mediated intercultural foreign language education.* Boston, MA: Heinle.

Benati, A. (2004). The effects of structured input activities and explicit information on the acquisition of the Italian future tense. In B. VanPatten (Ed.), *Processing instruction: Theory, research and commentary* (pp. 187–206). Mahwah, NJ: Lawrence Erlbaum.

Bhatia, T. (in press). Teaching language. In P. Hogan (Ed.), *The Cambridge encyclopedia of the language sciences.* Cambridge: Cambridge University Press.

Bhatia, T. (forthcoming). Religion and advertising in India. Manuscript.

Bhatia, T., & Ritchie, W. (2001). Language mixing, typology, and second language acquisition. In P. Bhaskararao & K. Subbarao (Eds.), *The yearbook of South Asian languages and linguistics 2001: Tokyo symposium on South Asian languages: Contact, convergence and typology* (pp. 37–62). London: Sage.

Blake, R. (2000). Computer mediated communication: A window on L2 Spanish interlanguage. *Language Learning and Technology, 4,* 120–136.

Blake, R. (2005). Bimodal chatting: The glue of a distance language learning course. *The CALICO Journal, 22,* 497–511.

Blake, R. (2006a). Two heads as better than one: C[omputer] M[ediated] C[ommunication] for the L2 Curriculum. In R. P. Donaldson & M. A. Haggstrom (Eds.), *Changing language education through CALL* (pp. 229–248). New York: Routledge.

Blake, R. (2006b). Computer-mediated communication: A window on L2 Spanish inter-language. *Language Learning and Technology*, *4*, 120–136.

Blake, R. (2007). New trends in using technology in the curriculum. *Annual Review of Applied Linguistics*, *27*, 76–97.

Blake, R., & Zyzik, B. (2003). Who's helping whom?: Learner/heritage speakers' networked discussions in Spanish. *Applied Linguistics*, *24*, 519–544.

Borrás, I., & Lafayette, R. C. (1994). Effects of multimedia courseware subtitling on the speaking performance of college students of French. *The Modern Language Journal*, *78*, 61–75.

Byrnes, H. (2006). Perspectives. *Modern Language Journal*, *90*, 244–246.

Chapelle, C. (2003). *English language learning and technology: Lectures on teaching and research in the age of information and communication*. Amsterdam: Benjamins.

Chapelle, C. (2007). Computer-assisted language learning. In B. Spolsky & F. M. Hult (Eds.), *Handbook of educational linguistics* (pp. 585–593). Malden, MA: Blackwell Publishing.

Chapelle, C. (2008). Technology and second language acquisition. *Annual Review of Applied Linguistics*, *27*, 98–114.

Chinnery, G. M. (2008). You've got some GALL: Google-assisted language learning. *Language Learning and Technology*, *12.1*, 3–11. [pdf pagination].

Chun, D. C., & Payne, J. S. (2004). What makes students click: Working memory and look-up behavior. *System*, *32*, 481–503.

Chun, D. C., & Plass, J. S. (1996). Effects of multimedia annotations on vocabulary acquisition. *The Modern Language Journal*, *80*, 183–198.

Crystal, D. (2001). *Language and the Internet*. Cambridge, UK: Cambridge University Press.

Darhower, M. (2007). A tale of two communities: Group dynamics and community building in a Spanish–English telecollaboration. *CALICO Journal*, *24*, 561–589.

de Bot, K. (2008). Introduction: Second language development as a dynamic process. *The Modern Language Journal*, *92*, 166–178.

de Graaff, R. (1997). The eXperanto experiment: Effects of explicit instruction on second language acquisition. *Studies in Second Language Acquisition*, *19*, 249–276.

DeKeyser, R. (1995). Learning second language grammar rules: An experiment with a miniature linguistic system. *Studies in Second Language Acquisition*, *17*, 379–410.

DeKeyser, R., Salaberry, R., Robinson, P., & Harrington, M. (2002). What gets processed in processing instruction? A commentary on Bill VanPatten's "Processing instruction: An update". *Language Learning*, *52*, 805–823.

De la Fuente, M. J. (2003). Is SLA interactionist theory relevant to CALL? A study of the effects of computer-mediated interaction in L2 vocabulary acquisition. *Computer-Assisted Language Learning*, *16*, 47–81.

Doughty, C. J. (1991). Second language instruction does make a difference: Evidence from an empirical study of SL relativization. *Studies in Second Language Acquisition*, *13*, 431–469.

Doughty, C. J., & Long, M. J. (2003). Optimal psycholinguistic environments for distance foreign language learning. *Language Learning and Technology*, *7.3*, 50–80. [Gale document No: A115245940, pp. 1–28].

Ellis, N. C. (1994). Introduction. In N. C. Ellis (Ed.), *Implicit and explicit learning of languages*. London: Academic Press.

Ellis, R. (1997). *SLA research and language teaching*. Oxford, UK: Oxford University Press.

Fernández-Garcia, M., & Martinez-Arbelaiz, A. (2003). Negotiation of meaning in nonnative speaker–nonnative speaker synchronous discussions. *CALICO Journal, 19,* 279–294.

Gardner, R. C., & Lambert, W. E. (1972). *Attitudes and motivation in second-language learning.* Rowley, MA: Newbury House.

Gass, S. (1997). *Input, interaction, and the second language learner.* Mahwah, NJ: Lawrence Erlbaum.

Gass, S. (2003). Input and interaction. In C. J. Doughty & M. H. Long (Eds.), *The handbook of second language acquisition* (pp. 224–255). Oxford, UK: Blackwell Publishing.

Gass, S., & Mackey, A. (2007). Input, interaction and output in second language acquisition. In B. VanPatten & J. Williams (Eds.), *Theories in second language acquisition* (pp. 175–199). Mahwah, NJ: Lawrence Erlbaum Associates.

Goodwin-Jones, R. (2008). Emerging technologies of elastic clouds and treebanks: New opportunities for content-based and data-driven language learning. *Language Learning and Technology, 12.1,* 12–18.

Graddol, D. (2006). *English next.* London: British Council.

Hegelheimer, V., & Chappelle, C. A. (2000). Methodological issues in research on learner–computer interactions in CALL. *Language Learning and Technology, 4,* 41–59.

Hulstijn, J. H. (1997). Second language acquisition research in the laboratory: Possibilities and limitations. *Studies in Second Language Acquisition, 19,* 131–143.

Jepson, K. (2005). Conversations—and negotiated interaction—in text and voice chat rooms. *Language Learning and Technology, 9,* 79–98.

Jones, S., & Bradwell, P. (2007). *As you like it: Catching up in an age of global English.* London: Demos Institute. < http://www.demos.co.uk/files/ >

Kotter, M. (2003). Negotiation of meaning and codeswitching in online tandems. *Language Learning and Technology, 7,* 145–172.

Lantolf, J. P., & Thorne, S. L. (2007). Sociocultural theory and second language learning. In B. VanPatten & J. Williams (Eds.), *Theories in second language acquisition* (pp. 201–223). Mahwah, NJ: Lawrence Erlbaum.

Lee, L. (2001). Online interaction: Negotiation of meaning and strategies used among learning Spanish. *ReCaLL Journal, 13,* 232–244.

Lee, L. (2004). Learners' perspectives on networked collaboration interaction with native speakers of Spanish in the U.S. *Language Learning and Technology, 8,* 83–100.

Leloup, J. W., & Ponterio, R. (2003). Second language acquisition and technology: A review of research. *ERIC Digest,* EDO-FL-03-11, December.

Lippi-Green, R. (1997). *English with an accent: Language ideology, and discrimination in the United States.* London: Routledge.

Liu, M., Moore, Z., Graham, L., & Lee, S. (2002). A look at the research on computer-based technology use in second language learning: A review of the literature from 1990–2000. *Journal of Research on Technology in Education, 34,* 250–273.

Lomicka, L. (2006). Understanding the other: Intercultural exchange and CMC. In L. Ducate & N. Arnold (Eds.), *Calling on CALL: From theory and research to new directions in foreign language instruction. Volume 1: Teaching with technology* Boston, MA: Heinle.

Long, M. (1996). The role of the linguistic environment in second language acquisition. In W. C. Ritchie & T. K. Bhatia (Eds.), *Handbook of second language acquisition* (pp. 413–468). New York: Academic Press.

Luna, D., & Peracchio, L. A. (2005). Sociolinguistic effects of code-switched ads targeting bilingual consumers. *Journal of Advertising, 34,* 43–56.

Mackey, A. (1999). Input, interaction and second language development: An empirical study of question formation in ESL. *Studies in Second Language Acquisition, 21*, 557–587.

MacWhinney, B. (1997). Implicit and explicit processes. *Studies in Second Language Acquisition, 19*, 277–281.

Meskill, C. (2005). Triadic scaffolds: Tools for teaching English language learners with computers. *Language Learning and Technology, 9*, 46–59.

Nagata, N. (1993). Intelligent computer feedback for second language instruction. *Modern Language Journal, 77*, 330–339.

Nagata, N. (1995). An effective application of natural language processing in second language processing in second language instruction. *CALICO Journal, 13*, 47–67.

Nagata, N., & Swisher, V. (1995). A study of consciousness-raising by computer: The effect of metalinguistic feedback on second language learning. *Foreign Language Annals, 28*, 337–347.

O'Rourke, B. (2005). Form-focused interaction in online tandem learning. *CALICO Journal, 22*, 433–466.

O'Rourke, B., & Schwienhorst, K. (2003). Talking text: Reflections on reflection in computer-mediated communication. In D. Little, J. Ridley, & B. Ushida (Eds.), *Learner autonomy in foreign language teaching: Teacher, learner, curriculum, assessment* (pp. 47–60). Dublin: Authentik.

Ortega, L. (2007). Second language learning explained? SLA across nine contemporary theories. In B. VanPatten & J. Williams (Eds.), *Theories in second language acquisition* (pp. 225–250). Mahwah, NJ: Lawrence Erlbaum.

Pellettieri, J. (2000). Negotiation of cyberspace: The role of chatting in the development of grammatical competence in the virtual foreign language classroom. In M. Warschauer & R. Kern (Eds.), *Network-based language teaching: Concepts and practice* (pp. 59–86). Cambridge, UK: Cambridge University Press.

Peters, E. (2007). Manipulating L2 learners' online dictionary use and its effects on L2 word retention. *Language Learning and Technology, 11*, 36–58.

Pica, T. (1983). Adult acquisition of English as a second language under different conditions of exposure. *Language Learning, 33*, 465–497.

Pica, T. (1994). Research on negotiation: What does it reveal about second-language learning conditions, processes and outcomes? *Language Learning, 44*, 493–527.

Pica, T. (1998). Second language learning through interaction. In V. Regan (Ed.), *Contemporary approaches to second language acquisition* (pp. 1–31). Dublin: University of Dublin Press.

Plass, J. L., Chun, D. M., Mayer, R. E., & Leutner, D. (1998). Supporting visual and verbal learning preferences in a second-language multimedia learning environment. *Journal of Educational Psychology, 90*, 25–36.

Pullum, G. (1997). Language that dare not speak its name. *Nature, 386*(March 27), 321–322.

Ritchie, W. C., & Bhatia, T. K. (2008). Psycholinguistics. In B. Spolsky & F. M. Hult (Eds.), *The handbook of educational linguistics* (pp. 38–52). Oxford, UK: Blackwell Publishing.

Robinson, P. (1996). Learning simple and complex language rules under implicit, incidental, enhanced, and instructed conditions. *Studies in Second Language Acquisition, 18*, 27–68.

Robinson, P. (1997). Generalizability and automaticity of second language learning under implicit, incidental, enhanced, and instructed conditions. *Studies in Second Language Acquisition, 19*, 223–247.

Rosa, E., & O'Neill, M. (1999). Explicitness, intake, and the issue of awareness: Another piece to the puzzle. *Studies in Second Language Acquisition, 21*, 511–556.

Sanz, C. (1999). What form to focus on? Linguistics, language awareness, and the education of L2 teachers. In J. F. Lee & A. Valdman (Eds.), *Meaning and form: Multiple perspectives* (pp. 3–23). Boston, MA: Heinle & Heinle.

Sanz, C., & Morgan-Short, K. (2004). Positive evidence versus explicit rule presentation and explicit negative feedback: A computer-assisted study. *Language Learning, 54,* 35–78.

Sanz, C., & Morgan-Short, K. (2005). Explicitness in pedagogical intervention: Input, practice, and feedback. In C. Sanz (Ed.), *Mind and context in adult second language acquisition* (pp. 234–263). Georgetown, Washington, DC: Georgetown University Press.

Siekmann, S. (2000). CALICO software report: Which web course management system is for me? A comparison of WebCT 3.1 and Blackboard 5.0. *CALICO, 18,* 590–617.

Smith, B. (2003). Computer-mediated negotiated interaction: An expanded model. *The Modern Language Journal, 87,* 38–54.

Smith, B. (2004). Computer-mediated negotiated interaction and lexical acquisition. *Studies in Second Language Acquisition, 26,* 365–398.

Smith, L. E. (1992). Spread of English and issues of intelligibility. In B. B. Kachru (Ed.), *The other tongue: English across cultures* (pp. 75–90). Urbana, IL: University of Illinois Press.

Tavaossoli, N., & Han, J. (2001). Scripted thought: Processing Korean Hancha and Hangul in a multicultural context. *Journal of Consumer Research, 28,* 482–494.

Thorne, S. L. (2003). Artifacts and cultures-of-use in intercultural communication. *Language Learning and Technology, 7,* 38–67.

Thorne, S. L., & Payne, J. (2005). Evolutionary trajectories, Internet-mediated expression, and language education. *CALICO Journal, 22,* 371–397.

Ur, P. (2002). *A course in language teaching: Practice and theory.* Cambridge, UK: Cambridge University Press.

VanPatten, B., & Oikkenon, S. (1996). Explanation versus structured input in processing instruction. *Studies in Second Language Acquisition, 18,* 495–510.

Ware, P. D., & Kramsch, C. (2005). Toward an intercultural stance: Teaching German and English through telecollaboration. *The Modern Language Journal, 89,* 190–205.

Warschauer, M., & Healey, D. (1998). Computers and language learning: An overview. *Language Teaching, 31,* 57–71.

Wong, W. (2004). Processing instruction in French: The role of explicit information and structured input. In B. VanPatten (Ed.), *Processing instruction: Theory, research and commentary* (pp. 187–206). Mahwah, NJ: Lawrence Erlbaum.

Yang, L. R., & Givon, T. (1997). Benefits and drawbacks of controlled laboratory studies of second language acquisition. *Studies in Second Language Acquisition, 19,* 173–193.

Zhao, Y., Alvarez-Torres, M. J., Smith, B., & Tan, H. S. (2005). The non-neutrality of technology: A theoretical analysis and empirical study of computer mediated communication technologies. In Y. Zhao (Ed.), *Research in technology and second language learning: Developments and directions* (pp. 281–316). Greenwich, CT: Information Age.

# SOCIAL PSYCHOLOGY AND SECOND LANGUAGE ACQUISITION

## INTRODUCTION TO PART VI

That social factors play a major role in SLA—whether in the classroom or out—is a given. In addition, there are many ways in which individuals differ in their approach to the task of SLA, some of these consisting in social attitudes. These factors are the topic of the chapters in this part of the volume.

Chapter 24 ("Language Contact and Second Language Acquisition") by Jeff Siegel surveys the research on the phenomena of languages in contact, including the process and consequences of SLA under these circumstances. He begins by introducing the field of contact linguistics to SLA researchers and then reviews work on features of SLA in pidgin and creole formation, including a discussion of the notions of fossilization and "imperfect" language learning in this context.

It is well known that one aspect of being bilingual, the consequence of SLA, is the ability to code-switch and code-mix. Less known is that certain conditions on intra-sentential code-switching that are, arguably, part of universal grammar (UG) show up in second language learners' grammaticality judgments of code-switched utterances when they have had no experience that bears on these conditions, thus providing evidence not only that the conditions are, in fact, part of UG but also that UG is accessible to the second language learner. These facts and others about code-switching and code-mixing are treated in chapter 25 ("Language Mixing, Universal Grammar, and Second Language Acquisition") by Tej K. Bhatia and William C. Ritchie.

The highly complicated and difficult area of individual differences in SLA is reviewed in Jean-Marc Dewaele's chapter 26 ("Individual Differences in Second Language Acquisition"). Dewaele surveys every aspect of individual difference from aptitude to personality factors to the interaction between learner-internal and learner-external factors such as social context, motivation, and pedagogical context.

Finally, issues surrounding social identity and SLA are treated by Kimberly A. Noels and Howard Giles in chapter 27 ("Social Identity and Language Learning"). As in many other areas of the study of SLA, there is a wide variety of approaches to the questions addressed in this chapter. The authors distinguish between what they refer to as intergroup/social-psychological perspectives, on the one hand, and sociocultural perspectives, on the other. Under the former, they include a treatment of identity in relation to additive and subtractive bilingualism, the notion of integrativeness in the socioeducational model, the sociocontextual model, the intergroup model, and finally, the acculturation model. Under sociocultural perspectives, they include Vygotskian sociocultural theory, language socialization, Bakhtin and dialogism, and imagined communities. They then discuss three themes that are found across these different sets of perspectives: the assumption of a multiplicity of a given individual's group memberships, changeability of his/her social identity, and conflict among groups.

CHAPTER 24

# LANGUAGE CONTACT AND SECOND LANGUAGE ACQUISITION

Jeff Siegel

## I. INTRODUCTION

Languages are said to come into contact when their speakers interact with one another. The linguistic and sociolinguistic consequences of long-term contact between languages are studied in the subfield of linguistics called 'contact linguistics'. Two of the major concerns of contact linguistics are contact-induced language change and the formation of new contact varieties such as new dialects, pidgins and creoles. However, the actual site of language contact is in the minds of individuals using more than one language (Weinreich (1970) [1953]). Thus, second language acquisition (SLA), an individual psycholinguistic process involving two languages, is by definition a kind of language contact. Changes that occur in languages, or the new varieties that emerge, must have originated in individuals' ways of speaking. This chapter examines the role of processes of SLA in individuals that may ultimately lead to the outcomes of language change or the emergence of new contact varieties in communities of speakers.

## II. CONTACT-INDUCED LANGUAGE CHANGE

When languages come into contact, one language may be influenced by the other in its phonology, morphosyntax and/or lexicon. The language that is affected is often called the 'recipient language', and the language that is the origin of the influence is called the 'source language' (see van Coetsem, 1988; Winford, 2003). Often the effect is conceived of as one language importing or duplicating linguistic material from another, and referred to by labels such as replication (Heine & Kuteva, 2005) and

569

code copying (Johanson, 2002). Thus, following Weinreich (1970), the terms replica language and model language are also used (Heine & Kuteva, 2005).

It is generally agreed in contact linguistics that there are basically two kinds of contact-induced language change, depending on the agents of the change, the dominant language, and the degree of maintenance of the languages in contact. In the first kind of contact-induced change, speakers of the recipient language are the agents of change, and the change usually begins with the lexicon—for example, English speakers using Hindi words in their English, as the British did in India (van Coetsem, 1988, p. 3). This kind of language change is often referred to as 'borrowing' (Thomason, 2001; Thomason & Kaufman, 1988); another, more specific, term is 'adoption' (Johanson, 2002). In this kind of contact-induced change, the recipient language is dominant in terms of the speakers' proficiency and fluency. Heine and Kuteva (2005, p. 237) refer to this as 'L2 > L1 replication', where the L2—the second, less dominant language—influences the L1—the first, dominant language. In this kind of change, the L1 (here, the recipient language) is generally maintained. An example of adoption—that is language change with recipient language agentivity—is what occurred when English was influenced by French after the Norman invasion.

In the second kind of contact-induced language change, speakers of the source language are the agents of change, and the change usually begins with phonology and syntax—for example, Hindi speakers using the phonology of their language when speaking English (van Coetsem, 1988, p. 3). This kind of change is often called 'interference'; another, more specific, term is 'imposition' (Johanson, 2002; van Coetsem, 1988). In this kind of language change, the source language is dominant. Heine and Kuteva (2005, p. 237) refer to this as 'L1 > L2 replication', where the L1 influences the L2. Since in such cases the L1 is considered the substratum language, this is commonly known as 'substratum influence' or 'substratum interference'. Furthermore, in such cases, the L1 is often not entirely maintained, as its speakers shift to the L2 completely, or partially in particular domains. Thus, this kind of change is often referred to as 'shift-induced interference' (Thomason, 2001; Thomason & Kaufman, 1988). Examples of imposition—that is language change with source language agentivity—are found in the development of Irish English and South Asian English. The emergence of Irish English involved complete language shift to English for the majority of the population in Ireland, with the L1 (Irish) affecting the L2 (English) in phonology and some aspects of morphosyntax. South Asian English emerged with partial shift to English for substantial numbers in the Indian subcontinent in domains such as education and government, in this case with typologically similar L1s (various Indo-Aryan languages) affecting the L2 (English).

SLA strategies are considered to be among the mechanisms of contact-induced change in general (Thomason, 2001, p. 129); however, they are recognized as being more important in imposition (or shift-induced interference) than in adoption (or borrowing). This is because in imposition, the agents of change have been engaged in learning the recipient language as a second language. As pointed out by Heine and Kuteva (2005, p. 238), in L1 > L2 replication, the replica (or recipient) language is the L2, which is acquired as a second language and thereby influenced by the L1, the model (or source) language. On the other hand, in L2 > L1 replication, the replica language is the L1, and while the model language (L2) influences the L1, it is not necessarily learned as a second language. However, according to Thomason and Kaufman (1988), it is not simply second language learning that leads to shift-induced interference, but rather 'imperfect learning' of a second language or target language (TL).

According to Thomason (2001, p. 75), the process through which L1 features are introduced by a group of learners into a TL involves at least two components or strategies:

> First, learners carry over some features of their native language into their version of the TL, which can be called the $TL_2$. Second, they may fail (or refuse) to learn some TL features, especially marked features, and these learners' errors also form part of the $TL_2$.

The first strategy includes 'gap-filling'—that is 'using material from the native language, while speaking the target language, to plug holes in knowledge of the TL' (Thomason, 2001, pp. 146–147). In addition to lexical items, both phonological and syntactic features, such as word order, can be carried over from the native language into the TL—often by 'projecting L1 structure onto TL forms' (p. 147). A second strategy used by second language learners is 'to ignore distinctions, especially marked distinctions, that are present in the TL but opaque to learners at early to middle stages of the learning process' (p. 148).

Those familiar with the SLA literature will recognize these strategies as transfer and simplification. However, in works on contact-induced language change, the term 'transfer' is generally used to refer to the results of material from one language being adopted by another, rather than to an individual psycholinguistic process in SLA where learners use features of their L1 when speaking the L2. It is worth noting that while many other scholars of contact-induced language change refer to the importance of processes of SLA, they do not discuss these processes with reference to the SLA literature or relevant research in SLA. An exception is Winford (2003), who first discusses changes that occur in the interlanguage (IL) of particular speakers as a result of individual SLA, as described in the SLA literature, and then goes on to demonstrate how these are relevant to changes that occur in the language of an entire community, as a result of group SLA or shift. Winford (2003, p. 236) notes that 'we would expect that the various kinds of innovation and creative restructuring found in individual SLA would have their counterparts in the outcomes of group shift as well'. However, he points out that the two situations are not identical because 'contact-induced changes in individual production are variable and ephemeral, while such changes in language are fixed and permanent'.

Winford (2003, p. 209) discusses three kinds of changes in individual production in SLA that are related to group language change: '(a) L1 or substratum influence on the learner version of the TL or "interlanguage"; (b) various kinds of simplification of TL structures ...; and (c) changes that are internal to the interlanguage system'. L1 influence is again what is usually labelled in SLA as language transfer or cross-linguistic influence. Simplification includes the development of IL that is reduced in lexicon and structure in comparison to the TL. Changes internal to the IL system include regularization or overgeneralization of rules. Examples of these changes are given in the following section on language contact varieties.

## III. THE DEVELOPMENT OF NEW CONTACT VARIETIES

### A. Types of Contact Varieties

Processes of SLA are also relevant to the other concern of contact linguistics, the development of new contact varieties: especially pidgins, creoles, indigenized varieties and language shift varieties.

Pidgins and creoles are new languages that develop out of a need for communication among people who do not share a common language—for example, among plantation labourers from diverse geographical origins. Most of the forms in the lexicon of the new language come from one of the languages in the contact situation, called the 'lexifier' (or sometimes the 'superstrate')—usually the language of the group in control of the area where contact occurs. However, the meanings and functions of the lexical forms, as well as the phonology and grammatical rules of the pidgin or creole, are different to those of the lexifier, and may sometimes resemble those of one or more of the other languages in contact, usually referred to in pidgin and creole studies as the 'substrate languages'.

An example is the following sentence from Fitzroy Valley Kriol, a creole spoken in the Kimberley region of Western Australia (Hudson, 1983, p. 66):

(1)  *Dei*       *bin*   *stab-am-bat*       *orla*   *kid*       *from*   *taka.*
     3PL        PST     starve-TR-ITER       PL       CHILD       ABL      food
     'They denied the children a meal (as punishment).'

All the lexical forms in this sentence are derived from English, but with changes that conform to the phonology of the substrate languages, such as Walmajarri—for example, *dei* from *they* and *stab* from *starve*. Some of the words have meanings different from English—for example, *stab* does not really mean 'starve'. And *taka* does not mean 'food' in general, as *tucker* does in Australian English, but rather 'vegetable food' as opposed to 'game', which in Fitzroy Kriol is *mit* (from *meat*). This reflects a distinction in Walmajarri between *miyi* 'edible vegetable product' and *kuyi* 'game or meat bought in a store' (Hudson, 1983, p. 137). Furthermore, some forms from English have taken on grammatical functions: *bin* (from *been*) as a past tense marker, -*am* (from *him* and/or *them*) as a suffix indicating the verb is transitive, -*bat* (from *about*) as a suffix marking repeated or continuing action, and *orla* (from *all the*) indicating plural.

Such contact languages begin to emerge when people first develop their own individual ways of communicating, often by using words and phrases they have learned from other languages (most often from the lexifier) that they know others might be familiar with. The combination of these individualized ways of communicating is called a 'jargon' or 'pre-pidgin'. If the groups remain in contact, certain communicative conventions may develop, resulting in a new language—a pidgin. Once a stable pidgin has emerged, it is generally learned as an auxiliary language and used only when necessary for intergroup communication. Its vocabulary remains small, and it has little, if any, grammatical morphology. This is called a 'restricted pidgin'. Examples are Chinese Pidgin English, Pidgin French of Vietnam and Pidgin Delaware (Native American).

In some cases, the use of a restricted pidgin is extended into wider areas—for example, as the everyday lingua franca in a multilingual community and even as a language used in religion and government. As a result, the language expands lexically and grammatically, and is fittingly called an 'expanded pidgin'. An example is Melanesian Pidgin, which developed on plantations in Queensland and Samoa, and expanded when it became an important lingua franca after labourers brought it back to their home countries.

In another scenario, people in a newly emerging mixed community use a pidgin on a daily basis, and some of them shift to it as their primary language, which they speak to their children. Because of this extended use, the pidgin would already be expanded or in the process of expanding. Thus, children growing up in this context acquire the expanded pidgin as their mother tongue (or first language), and it becomes their community language. At this stage it is then called a 'creole'. Like any other vernacular language, a creole has a full lexicon and a complex set of grammatical rules, and is not at all restricted in use, having a complete range of informal functions. Examples are Hawai'i Creole and Jamaican Creole.

In contrast to pidgins and creoles, indigenized varieties are new dialects, rather than new languages. They arise in colonies where the colonial language has had widespread use in the education system and has been learned as a second language by a large proportion of the population. Like expanded pidgins, indigenized varieties are used in a multilingual environment and function as a lingua franca for daily interactions. Also, like creoles, some aspects of their lexicon, phonology and morphosyntax are influenced by the indigenous substrate languages (thus, indigenized). Unlike expanded pidgins and creoles, however, the grammatical rules of an indigenized variety are much closer to those of the lexifier (the colonial language). The indigenized varieties that have been most studied are based on English and are often called 'New Englishes' or 'World Englishes'—for example, Singapore English, South Asian English and Fiji English. Here is an example from Fiji English (Siegel, 1987, p. 236):

(2)  *I can't give you us two's money because us two poor.*
     'I can't give you our money because we are poor.'

This illustrates two features: the use of *us two* for first person dual (instead of *we* or *our*) and the optional absence of the copula.

Another kind of new dialect is a 'language shift variety'. This type of contact variety emerges when a whole population shifts to another language, most often the language of the colonizers or conquerors. However, the way the population speak that language has been strongly affected by their original language, through substratum interference (Thomason & Kaufman, 1988). Examples are South African Indian English and Irish English. Here is an example from South African Indian English (Mesthrie, 1992, p. 76):

(3)  *You can't beat Vijay's-planted tomato.*
     'You can't find better tomatoes than those which Vijay planted.'

This illustrates a relative clause similar to the participial strategy of the Indic substrate languages and the optional absence of overt plural marking on nouns.

## B. Simplification in Pidgin Development

Linguistically, restricted pidgins are characterized by morphological simplicity—that is the absence of productive bound morphology and very few, if any, grammatical markers. Things that are expressed grammatically in other languages are expressed lexically in restricted pidgins. For example, adverbs rather than any kind of tense, modality or aspect (TMA) markers are used to indicate temporal and aspectual relationships. In addition, in comparison to their lexifier, they have a smaller number of prepositions and pronouns and a limited lexicon, a single preverbal negative marker and no complementizers. Except for the fact that they are not stabilized, pre-pidgins are generally similar to restricted pidgins in morphological simplicity.

The origin of this morphological simplicity in restricted pidgins and pre-pidgins is a matter of great controversy (see Siegel, 2006), However, clear evidence now exists that adult second language learners in naturalistic contexts produce varieties of IL very similar to pre-pidgins and restricted pidgins in terms of morphological simplicity. First, there are studies comparing ILs and pidgins with the same language as the target or the lexifier. Schumann (1978) reported on a longitudinal study of six native speakers of Spanish learning English outside the classroom setting. One of the learners, Alberto, remained in the early stages of development with regard to the linguistic features being studied. His IL productions resembled pidgins generally in terms of simplicity and English-derived pidgins specifically in particular features, such as the following (Schumann, 1978, p. 66):

a) negatives formed by *no* preceding the verb
b) absence of inversion in questions
c) no auxiliaries
d) unmarked possessives
e) absence of *-ed* past tense marking

Schumann's claim was not that Alberto spoke a pidgin, but that this simplification was evidence of a process similar to that involved in pidginization. On the basis of a study of the speech of Alberto compared to the speech of speakers of a variety of pidgin English spoken in Hawai'i, Andersen (1980, p. 274) concluded that 'SLA and individual pidginization are really the same phenomenon viewed from different perspectives and often, although not always, occurring under different circumstances'.

More recently, Kotsinas (1996) illustrated numerous similarities between the features of the IL of Swedish immigrants where Swedish is the L2 and those of Russenorsk, a pidgin which has closely related Norwegian as a lexifier—for example, extended use of the preposition *på*. A later work (Kotsinas, 2001) shows similarities between the simplified features of L2 versions of Swedish and those typical of pidgin languages.

A good indication of IL features in general came out of one of the largest studies ever done of naturalistic adult SLA: the European Science Foundation (ESF) project which took place in the 1980s. This was a longitudinal study of 40 adult immigrants with various first languages: Arabic, Italian, Finnish, Spanish and Turkish. The TLs were Dutch, English, French, German and Swedish. In an article about the results of the study, Klein and Perdue (1997) report that all the learners went through a stage, which they call the 'Basic Variety' (BV), and that approximately one-third of the learners went no further. They summarize the structural features of this variety as follows: 'Strikingly absent from the BV are ... free or bound morphemes with purely grammatical function' (p. 332). For example, instead of TMA markers, lexical items, such as adverbs, are used. However, they also demonstrate that the BV is characterized by a small set of organizational principles based on pragmatic constraints which govern its structure—for example, 'focus expression last' (p. 317) (see also Klein and Dimroth, this volume). In a survey of studies on the acquisition of tense and aspect, Bardovi-Harlig (2000) describes similar pragmatic and lexical means, rather than morphological means, used to express temporality in the early stages of second language learning. Also, van de Craats, Corver, and van Hout (2000, pp. 228–230) describe three stages or states of knowledge for SLA. The first is the 'content-word state', in which learners use content words for generation of what is normally a grammatical construct in the TL—for example, in Dutch:

(4)    *vriend*      *huis*
      friend      house
      'my friend's house' (van de Craats et al., 2000, p. 229)

While there have been many criticisms of the BV as a theoretical construct, what is important here is the inventory of surface features of this variety, as mentioned in the article:

a) no inflections
b) lexical items used in invariant form (multifunctionality)
c) invariant forms generally infinitive or nominative (but also some inflected forms)
d) lexical items [mostly] noun-like and verb-like words with some adjectives and adverbs
e) most lexical items from the L2 but some from the L1 and other languages
f) minimal pronouns to refer to speaker, hearer and a third person
g) no anaphoric pronouns referring to inanimates
h) only a few quantifiers
i) a single word for negation
j) only a few prepositions
k) no complementizers
l) no expletive elements (e.g. *there is*)
m) use of temporal adverbs, rather than grammatical TMA markers, to indicate temporality
n) 'boundary markers' to express the beginning or end of some situation, such as *work finish* 'after work is/was/will be over' (p. 321)
o) no L1 influence except occasionally for word order.

The striking similarities between these features of the early IL of adult L2 learners and those of restricted pidgins strongly suggest that processes involved in early SLA are the source of morphological simplicity in both.

### C. Simplification and Regularization in Creole Development

Creoles are by definition more complex grammatically than restricted pidgins. However, in some specific linguistic areas—such as in verbal inflection—creoles still exhibit morphological simplicity in comparison with their lexifiers. One explanation is that SLA is responsible (e.g. Wekker, 1996). Evidence can be found in a few studies comparing creoles with L2 varieties of their lexifiers. Véronique (1994) describes several formal similarities between features found in the early ILs of Moroccan Arabic-speaking learners of French as a second language and what are considered simplified features of French-lexified creoles. Similarly, in an examination of L2 varieties of West African Ewe-speaking learners of French, Mather (2000, 2006) finds some features similar to those of French-lexified creoles which he concludes were the result of the process of simplification in second language learning. In another study, Muysken (2001) uses data from several studies of learning Dutch as a second language to compare features of learners' L2 varieties with features of the now extinct Dutch-lexifier creole, Negerhollands. He reports many similarities in formal simplicity, including the absence of inflections on verbs.

Creoles are normally acquired as a first language. Therefore, if SLA was responsible for their morphological simplicity, it must have been involved in an earlier stage of development. There are two very different views on the nature of this earlier stage. The first is that creoles developed from 'radically reduced pidgins' (McWhorter, 2000, p. 106) and therefore their morphological simplicity was inherited from this earlier restricted pidgin stage. And as we have seen, the morphological simplicity of restricted pidgins appears to be the result of initial stages of SLA.

The opposing point of view is that creoles developed gradually as the lexifier language was incrementally changed or 'restructured'. This restructuring occurred when newly arrived slaves learned only 'approximations' of the colonial language from other slaves: 'Creolization is thus a consequence, or the ultimate result, of approxima-tions of approximations of the lexifier' (Chaudenson, 2001, p. 305). According to this view, creoles should be treated as versions of their lexifiers that developed according to the usual processes of historical language change. As shown in section II, these include processes of SLA. For example, Mufwene (2001, p. 60) notes that the process of creole formation through gradual restructuring is 'a by-product of imperfect acquisition of the target by second-language learners'. In this light, proponents of this view refer to the stripped-down nature of early IL, as found in the results of the ESF project (Klein & Perdue, 1997), mentioned earlier.

DeGraff (2005, p. 316) also refers to the Klein and Perdue article, and in this and earlier work (DeGraff, 1999), he argues that SLA (or L2A) in the context of language contact is a crucial factor in language change. For example, he says (2005, p. 316) that 'the output of L2A by adults—under "duress," in many cases—has a crucial role in language change, particularly in the context of language contact'. According to DeGraff, the simplification found in creoles is a result of adult second language learning, and he states: 'What seems particularly affected in L2A is the learning of inflectional paradigms ...' (DeGraff, 2005, p. 316). Later, he mentions 'the inflectional erosion that seem typical of language change (via L2A in contact situations)' (p. 335).

From the preceding discussion it is clear that those who emphasize the restructuring of the lexifier, like those who emphasize a pidgin predecessor, view the morphological simplicity that exists in creoles ultimately as a consequence of processes of SLA and exposure to second language versions of the lexifier.

There is also evidence of other processes of SLA in the development of creoles. Klein and Perdue (1997) report that two-thirds of the adult learners in the ESF study eventually did go past the BV to the 'Post-Basic Variety' and acquired various grammatical features of the TL. The grammatical features of some creoles provide evidence of such targeted acquisition of the lexifier, demonstrating typical SLA phenomena such as overgeneralizaton. For example, in Hawai'i Creole, the pronoun system is primarily modelled on English; however, the first person singular independent possessive pronoun is *mainz* (*mines*), indicating overgeneralization of the final -*s* in other persons (i.e. *yours, his, hers, ours, theirs*). Also, the reflexive forms show overgeneralization of the singular suffix -*self*, as in forms such as *ourself* and *demself*.

The point must be stressed, however, that a large proportion of the morphology in an expanded pidgin or creole is generally not derived from the lexifier in both form and function. The form often comes from a lexical item in the lexifier, but the function appears to be derived from the L1. This brings us to a discussion of transfer.

## D.  Transfer

The term transfer is used in both historical linguistics and SLA with a variety of interpretations (see Odlin, 1989, 2003; Winford, 2003). But here it refers particularly to a psycholinguistic process that occurs in which the linguistic features of one language are used in learning or using another language (Færch & Kasper, 1987, p. 112). The transferred features may be phonemes, grammatical rules or meanings or functions of particular words. However, the focus here is on the transfer of morphosyntactic and semantic properties or structure.

This kind of transfer is hypothesized to have resulted in substrate influence found in pidgins and creoles—especially in the use of forms from the lexifier with grammatical functions from the substrate languages, which I call 'functional transfer' (Siegel, 2006). For example, in Bislama (spoken in Vanuatu) the lexicon is mainly from English, but many of the morphosyntactic features are not—such as the subject referencing pronoun and the transitive marker on the verb illustrated in the following examples:

(5)  a. Bislama: *Man     ya     i     stil-im   mane.*
              man    DET    3SG    steal-TR  money
              'This man stole the money.'
    b. Bislama: *Ol     woman  oli    kat-em  taro.*
              PL     woman  3PL    cut-TR   taro
              'The women cut the taro.'

These features, however, are typical of the Eastern Oceanic substrate languages—for example, Arosi and Kwaio:

(6)  a. Arosi:    *E     noni    a     ome-sia   i     ruma.*
              ART   man    3SG   see-TR.3SG  ART  house
              'The man saw the house.'

b. Kwaio:    *Ta'a*      *geni*       ***la***    *a'ari-**a***     *go'u*.
             people   female    3PL    carry-TR      taro
             'The women carried taro.'

Thus in Bislama, forms originally from English—*he, all he* and *him* or *them*—function as subject referencing pronouns and transitive markers in patterns similar to those in the substrate languages.

### Transfer in L2 Acquisition

The most common position in pidgin and creole studies is that substrate features were transmitted to expanded pidgins and creoles through transfer in SLA. This assumes that speakers of the substrate languages subconsciously transferred features of their first languages (L1) in attempting to acquire the lexifier (L2).

In the field of SLA, transfer refers to the form of cross-linguistic influence that involves 'carrying over of mother tongue patterns into the target language' (Sharwood Smith, 1996, p. 71) or, more accurately, into the IL. In other words, learners use linguistic features of their first language (L1)—phonemes, grammatical rules or meanings or functions of particular words—when learning the second language (L2). This is either to provide a basis for constructing the grammar of the L2 or because the learner has not yet recognized differences between the L2 and the L1.

Transfer may be positive (when features of L1 match those of the L2) or negative (when features do not match). The evidence of positive transfer is when learners who have a particular structure in their L1 are able to acquire a similar structure in the L2 more quickly than learners who do not have that structure in their L1. This has been shown, for example, with the acquisition of articles (Odlin, 1989, pp. 33–34). The evidence of negative transfer is when a learner uses rules of the L1 in speaking the L2—for example, in the transfer of English word order to French IL, as in the following example:

(7)   L1 English, L2 French:    \**Louise toujours mange du pain.*
      English:                 'Louise always eats bread.'
      French:                  *Louis mange toujours du pain.*

(Odlin, 2003, p. 460)

The first clear statement about the connection between the process of transfer in SLA and substrate influence in pidgins and creoles is made by Mufwene (1990, p. 2):

> Transfers apply putatively in the speech of multilingual speakers and/or at the stage of SLA; substrate influence is observed in a language as a relatively crystallized system. Once transfers have been replicated by different speakers, repeated by most of them, and established in the contact situation's new linguistic system (even as variable features), they may be characterized genetically as substrate influence. The latter need not be associated synchronically with multilingual speakers and/or SLA.

Later, Wekker (1996, p. 144) describes the process of creolization as 'one of imperfect second-language acquisition, predominantly by adults, involving the usual language transfer from the learners' L1'. Other creolists emphasizing the role of transfer in creole development include Winford (2003) and Migge (2003).

Writing about Haitian Creole, Lefebvre (1998) and Lumsden (1999) refer to the process of 'relexification' to explain substrate influence. This is a process in which the creators of a creole retain the abstract grammatical properties of the lexical entries of their L1 but replace the overt phonological shapes of these entries with those based on lexical items from the lexifier. The result is that the lexical entry of the creole has semantic and syntactic properties from the substrate but a form from the lexifier.

TMA marking in creoles is one important grammatical area where relexification is thought to have played a role in development. For example, the Haitian Creole definite future marker *ap* (from French *après*) has the properties of the definite future marker *ná* in the substrate language Fongbe, as illustrated below (Lefebvre, 1998, pp. 124–125):

(8)  Haitian Creole:     *Mari*        *ap*         *prepare*     *pat.*
     Fongbe:             *Mari*        *ná*         *ɖà*          *wǒ*
                         *Mary*        DEF-FUT      prepare       dough
                         'Mary will prepare dough.'

Lefebvre also provides evidence of relexification in many other grammatical markers, including definite determiners, plural markers, personal pronouns, possessives, reflexives and complementizers.

Both Lefebvre and Lumsden relate relexification to L1 transfer. For example, Lefebvre (1998, p. 34) makes it clear that 'the type of data claimed to be associated with the notion of transfer in creole genesis corresponds to the result of the process of relexification ... That is, it is claimed that substratal features are transferred into the creole by means of relexification'. Lumsden (1999, p. 226) says that relexification 'plays a significant role in SLA in general' and uses the term 'negative transfer error' to refer to an example of the process. More recently, relexification has been defined as 'a particular type of transfer' (Lefebvre, White, & Jourdan, 2006, p. 5).

But can transfer in SLA really account for such features in creoles? In order to answer this question, we need to see whether there is evidence of this kind of transfer actually occurring in SLA.

Debates about the nature of the initial state of L2 acquisition have revolved around two questions. The first is whether the principles of universal grammar (UG) are still available to second language learners; the second is whether transfer from the L1 plays a significant role in SLA. The 'full access' hypothesis (Epstein, Flynn, & Martohardjono, 1996) emphasizes access to UG but plays down the role of transfer— in this context viewed as the use of prior linguistic knowledge in the construction of the L2 grammar. However, other hypotheses or models accept continuing access to UG as well as allowing a major role for transfer. The strongest of these is the 'Full Transfer/ Full Access' (FT/FA) Hypothesis (Schwartz & Sprouse, 1996; Schwartz, 1998), in which the L2 initial state comprises the entirety of the L1 grammar along with UG, both therefore constraining IL development. Thus, all the abstract properties of the L1 grammar are thought to be initially transferred. Progress towards the L2 takes place when input from the L2 that cannot be accommodated to the L1 grammar causes the system to restructure.

With regard to creoles, the relexification view sees the substrate language as the L1, and therefore the abstract properties of its lexical entries make up the initial state. But according to this view, input from the L2 (here the lexifier) is restricted in the context of creole formation. Creators of creoles have enough input from the lexifier to acquire overt forms of its lexical items but not enough input to be aware of its abstract properties; thus, the L1 system does not restructure (Sprouse, 2006). Consequently, the abstract grammatical properties of the L1 (the substrate language) remain in the creole, even though the forms that express these properties may come from the L2—that is there is relexification, or functional transfer.

The problem, however, is that examples of this kind of transfer are extremely difficult to find in the SLA literature (see Siegel, 2006). The FT/FA Hypothesis is supported by many studies showing negative transfer of basic word order in both IL and acceptability judgements and positive transfer as well, for example from French in acquiring dative experience subjects in Spanish (Montrul, 1998). However, it is not supported by examples of functional transfer of TMA markers or any of the other grammatical markers Lefebvre examines to illustrate relexification. Furthermore, in the studies of the IL of learners of Dutch and Swedish mentioned earlier, there is no evidence of transfer of grammatical features of the kind found in pidgins or creoles with the same lexifier. Creolists who have specifically looked at learners' L2 versions of French and French-lexified creoles (e.g. Véronique, 1994; Mather, 2000, 2006) have found few, if any, similarities that could be attributed to functional transfer, except perhaps for the postnominal determiner *la*. Although it has been claimed that this kind of transfer is responsible for the TMA systems of expanded pidgins and creoles, there is no evidence that it occurs in the IL of L2 learners. On this point, Mather (2000, p. 258) refers to 'the mystery' of TMA markers in French creoles appearing to be similar to those of the substrate languages, while 'there is very little evidence of TMA markers in any French or other European interlanguage variety'. In fact, Bardovi-Harlig (2000, p. 411) observes: 'No significant L1 effect has been identified in the longitudinal studies of the acquisition of temporal expression'.

Thus, the fact that functional transfer is hardly ever attested in the IL of L2 learners seems to be evidence against the commonly held view that substrate-related features in creoles are a consequence of transfer in SLA in an earlier stage of development. It may also be evidence against FT/FA Hypothesis (Kouwenberg, 2006, p. 216).

## Transfer in L2 Use

Another context in which transfer can occur is second language *use*—which according to many scholars (e.g. Ellis, 1994, p. 13; Kasper, 1997, p. 310) is distinct from second language *acquisition*. L2 acquisition as opposed to L2 use is concerned with the gradual attainment of linguistic competence in the L2—in other words, with the learning of the L2 grammar. L2 use as opposed to L2 acquisition looks at how learners make use of their existing L2 knowledge, and other knowledge as well, when trying to communicate in the language.

Some researchers in the wider field of SLA think of transfer primarily as a strategy of L2 use rather than acquisition. L1 knowledge is considered as a resource in communication, used unconsciously to compensate for insufficient L2 knowledge (e.g., Kellerman, 1995; Jarvis & Odlin, 2000). Transfer is thought to occur as learners (or former learners) fall back on their L1 knowledge when their knowledge of the L2 is inadequate to express what they want to say or to interpret what is being said to them. Sharwood Smith (1986, p. 15) says that cross-linguistic influence (i.e. transfer) typically occurs in two contexts: (1) 'overload' situations or 'moments of stress' when the existing L2 system cannot cope with immediate communicative demands and (2) 'through a desire to express messages of greater complexity than the developing control mechanisms can cope with'. Thus, according to this view, transfer is considered to be a means for overcoming communication problems.

This point is related to another important difference between L2 acquisition and L2 use regarding the existence of a TL. In acquisition, the goal is to acquire the grammar of the L2; therefore, the L2 is clearly the target. L1 structures may be retained or utilized in an attempt to approximate the perceived norms of the L2, but are abandoned when they do not match input from the L2. In use, however, the goal is to communicate in the L2. L1 structures are called upon to compensate for a perceived shortage of the linguistic resources needed for successful communication. If they lead to successful communication, they do not have to be abandoned. Therefore, in L2 use, there is not really a TL as such because the desired outcome is not grammatical acquisition but rather successful communication. With regard to contact varieties, we are talking about L2 use that occurs before the emergence of an expanded pidgin or creole. Thus, the grammar of the lexifier is not the target, and the developing pidgin predecessor is actually the L2, since it, rather than the lexifier, is the language used for communication.

Various communication strategies have been described in the SLA literature (e.g., Tarone, 1981; Poulisse, 1996). One of these is 'transfer from the native language' (Tarone, Cohen, & Dumas, 1983, p. 5, 11). Blum-Kulka and Levenston (1983, p. 132) characterize this strategy as 'attributing to a lexical item of the second language all the functions—referential and conceptual meaning, connotation, collocability, register restriction—of its assumed first-language equivalent'. This, of course, is similar to what I have been calling functional transfer. But are there examples of this kind of functional transfer in studies of second language use? To answer this question, I examine data from three areas of research: (1) SLA, (2) indigenized and language shift varieties and (3) bilingualism.

## SLA

In a study in the field of SLA, Helms-Park (2003) shows that causative serial verb constructions occur in the English of Vietnamese-speaking learners, but not in the English of Hindi-Urdu-speaking learners. Since Vietnamese has such serial verb constructions but Hindi-Urdu does not, their occurrence in the English spoken by Vietnamese speakers is attributed to language transfer. The author considers this transfer to be the result of a communication strategy, or

> a compensatory L1-based strategy used by learners to manage a situation in which they are compelled to produce TL constructions before adequate information about the grammatical behavior of the targeted verbs has been noted in the input ... (Helms-Park, 2003, p. 230)

This is the result of the 'communication stress' caused by 'the elicitation of data through a tightly constrained test' (p. 230) in the study. (These findings are significant because similar serial verb constructions occur in creoles, such as Haitian Creole and Saramaccan, that have serializing substrate languages.)

Andersen (1980) presents several examples of functional transfer from Spanish-speaking 'learners/users of English'. Interestingly, these are the same as some of the features found in Hawai'i Creole thought to have been modelled on features from Portuguese, and Spanish and Portuguese share these particular features. Some examples are as follows:

a)    *for* as a complementizer modelled on Spanish *para*:
(9)    *Jennifer, put your clothes on **for** decorate the Christmas tree.* (p. 277)

b)    *have* as an existential marker modelled on Spanish *hay, había*:
(10)    *And then **have** another one in back they used to rent, too.*
        'And there was another one ...' (p. 282)

### Indigenized and Language Shift Varieties

Since studies that focus specifically on L2 language use are rare, more evidence for functional transfer in L2 use comes indirectly from features of indigenized varieties of English and language shift varieties, which emerged from individuals' use of English as an L2.

In Singapore Colloquial English, *already* serves as a completive aspect marker, as in the following examples:

(11)    a. *I only went there once or twice **already**.* (Platt and Weber, 1980, p. 66)
        b. *I work about four months **already**.* (Bao, 1995, p. 182)

These and other aspectual categories in Singapore Colloquial English have striking parallels with the Sinitic substrate. For example, Platt and Weber (1980, p. 66) show that the use of *already* is analogous to the use of the particle *liaú* in Hokkien:

(12)    *Gún        tháùke        tńg        chhù        **liaú**.*
        our        boss        return        home        already [PFT]
        'Our boss has returned home.'

In Fiji English, the word *full* is used as a preverbal marker indicating an extreme or excess quality or action (Siegel, 1987, p. 237):

(13)    a. *The boy just **full** shouted.*
        'The boy shouted really loudly.'
        b. *The fella **full** sleeping over there.*
        'The guy's sound asleep over there.'

This closely parallels the Fijian use of *rui* as a preverbal marker with the same function, as in the following example (from Schütz, 1985, p. 272):

(14)    *au        sā        **rui**        loma-ni        koya        vaka-levu.*
        I        ASP        EXT        care.for-TR        her        MANNER-big
        'I care for her very much.'

Another source of indirect evidence is substratum influence in language shift varieties, which are also thought to be a consequence of second language use. A well-known example is the recent past construction using *after* in Irish English (Harris, 1984, p. 319):

(15)  Irish English:   She is after selling the boat.
                       'She has (just) sold the boat.'
      Irish:           *Tá*        *sí*     *tréis*     *an*      *bád*      *a dhíol.*
                       be.NONPAST  she      after       the       boat       selling

## Bilingualism

Since speakers of a developing pidgin are bilingual in one of the substrate languages, another potential source of evidence is studies of language change resulting from bilingualism. Weinreich (1970) gives many examples from European and Asian languages of what could be interpreted as the results of functional transfer—for example, the future tense in Swiss Romansh formed with *vegnir* 'come' modelled on Swiss German and 'the new Breton perfect with *am euz* based on the French indefinite past with *avoir*' (p. 41).

Other examples are found in South America. Klee and Ocampo (1995) describe how bilingual speakers of Quechua and Spanish in Peru express evidentiality (an obligatory category in Quechua) with forms from Spanish. For example, the Spanish past perfect is used to indicate that the speaker has not witnessed or was not aware of the action or state described by the verb (p. 62). Another method is to use the Spanish word *dice* 'it is said' with the present perfect or preterite (p. 63). Sánchez (2003, pp. 99–100) shows that in the Quechua of Quechua–Spanish bilinguals (also in Peru), prenominal demonstrative adjectives such as *kay* 'this' and *huk/suk* 'one' have developed into indefinite determiners, presumably on the model of Spanish.

Aikhenvald (2002) gives many instances of language change in northwestern Amazonia that most probably originated from functional transfer among bilinguals. For example, in Tariana (an Arawak language), a nominal modifier *-sini* 'also' became a plural marker and the verb *-sita* 'finish' became a perfect aspect marker, both based on models in the East Tucanoan languages (pp. 98–99, 139–140). Aikhenvald (2002, pp. 315–316) also describes how the Portuguese spoken by indigenous people in this region includes four lexical expressions of evidentiality—for example, *eu vi* 'I saw' and *diz que* 'it is said'. These reflect the obligatory grammatical marking of evidentiality in both Tariana and East Tucanoan languages.

## Motivation for Transfer

As shown in the preceding discussion, the kind of functional transfer that appears to be responsible for substrate influence in expanded pidgins and creoles is frequently found in second language use and bilingualism. With regard to pidgin and creole development, increased second language use in wider contexts also provides the rationale for the occurrence of this kind of transfer. The key is in Sharwood Smith's (1986, p. 15) characterization of transfer, quoted above, where he says that it occurs when the existing L2 system cannot cope with immediate communicative demands and when there is a need to express messages of greater complexity than the developing system can cope with. This is similar to the 'gap-filling' strategy described earlier. In the case of a restricted pidgin that is being used in wider contexts, it is not just the learners' knowledge of the language that cannot cope, but the language itself. Thus, an important motivation for transfer in the emergence of contact varieties is to meet the needs of the language when it starts being used for widening functions.

## E. New Dialects

In the formation of new dialects, as opposed to pidgins and creoles, the role of SLA is much more straightforward because it is clear that the colonized population learned the language of the colonizers, most often through formal education. Most scholars who have written about new dialects specifically refer to the role of processes of SLA in their development (e.g. Mesthrie, 1992; Platt, Weber, & Ho, 1984; Schneider 2003). Some emphasize the role of transfer, as shown above, in the 'nativization' or indigenization of the new dialects (e.g. Ritchie, 1986). Others emphasize properties common to new dialects that could not be a consequence of transfer, but rather come under the heading of simplification (e.g. variable omission of copulas and past tense marking) or overgeneralization (e.g. invariable question tags, lack of distinction between count and non-count nouns and extension of the use of progressive aspect to stative verbs). Here are some examples of these kinds of overgeneralization from Singapore Colloquial English (Williams, 1987):

(16) The new committee has been formed, isn't it? (p. 171)

(17) (There's) something with my hairs. (p. 172)

(18) I'm having a business. (p. 173)

According to Williams (1987), these similarities are the result of the common production principles that occur in SLA—that is psycholinguistic strategies used by learners in acquiring or using a second language. These principles are discussed under two headings. The first is 'economy of production', which includes regularization and selective production of redundant markers. The second is 'hyperclarity' or the reduction of ambiguity by maximizing transparency and salience.

## IV. FOSSILIZATION AND 'IMPERFECT' SECOND LANGUAGE LEARNING

A general view of the development of indigenized varieties goes back to the notion of 'imperfect' SLA. Transfer, simplification and overgeneralization can be found in the IL of all second language learners, but for some, 'fossilization' occurs. In SLA theory, this refers to the cessation of learning or the halting of progress towards the acquisition of the L2 grammar. It is thought that new dialects are the result of a combination of learners' 'errors' or individual fossilized L2 varieties that have become institutionalized in ex-colonial settings.

However, as pointed out before (Siegel 2003), research in SLA has been done predominantly with English and in monolingual settings—for example, in Britain, the

USA and Australia—rather than in multilingual settings where indigenized varieties are spoken. This has led to a skewed view of the nature of the L2 and its speakers. First of all, even though the majority of speakers of English in the world are bilingual and speak indigenized varieties, only monolingual speakers of English are considered to be 'native speakers'. With regard to the target, the goal is most often to be able to use the L2 effectively not with 'native speakers' but with other mostly 'non-native speakers'. Thus, the target is actually the particular indigenized variety of the country, such as Singapore Colloquial English, not a native variety, such as British or American English. In addition, most of the input comes from the indigenized variety, not from a native variety, and most of it is obtained in the classroom or in interactions with other non-native speakers, not with native speakers. Finally, learners use the English they acquire alongside the other languages of their verbal repertoires which are already used for particular functions. Thus, they do not need to acquire English for as wide a range of functions as learners in monolingual settings have to.

Because of these factors, Sridhar and Sridhar (1986, p. 12) observe that 'SLA theory has been counter-intuitive and limited in explanatory power with regard to a very substantial segment of the second language learner population'. This is especially true with regard to transfer being seen negatively as L1 interference and to the notion of fossilized IL. Kachru and Nelson (1996) point out that considering the 'nonstandard' features of indigenized varieties to be the result of these notions relies on two assumptions: (1) learners who developed the indigenized varieties wanted to emulate a 'standard' monolingual variety and (2) models of this variety were available in the environment. In most cases, however, both of these assumptions are unfounded (see also Bhatt, 2001).

More recent perspectives in the SLA literature do not view a variety which differs from that of an idealized native speaker as necessarily representing its speakers' failure in attaining L2 competence. As Rampton (1997, p. 294) observes, 'People are not always concerned with improving their L2 interlanguage'. An 'imperfect' variety may be used to express a particular identity of the speaker, to show solidarity with a peer group, or to indicate attitudes towards society in general. For example, Sridhar and Sridhar (1986, p. 10) emphasize the positive use of transfer in communication: 'Given that transfer features are not idiosyncratic to learners but shared by speakers with the same substratal languages, they serve as effective simplification strategies, modes of acculturation ... and as markers of membership in the community of speakers of a given indigenized variety.' Lowenberg (1986) also observes that phonological transfer, especially in stress and intonation patterns, is often associated with group identity (see also Schneider, 2003). Furthermore, the decision not to use 'standard' L2 forms may represent a form of resistance, which alongside achievement and avoidance is one kind of communication strategy (Rampton, 1991, p. 239). It follows, then, that in many situations, native-like proficiency is not the goal of language learning.

These perspectives are also relevant to the emergence of pidgin and creole languages, whose features are often attributed to 'lack of success' or 'failure' in acquiring the lexifier. For example, Sebba (1997, p. 79) notes: 'A more pragmatic view would be that pidgins represent *successful* second language learning from the point of view of their learners—who learn just enough to communicate what they want to communicate and no more.' (italics in original).

## V. CONCLUSION

This chapter has shown that processes of SLA are relevant to both contact-induced language change and the emergence of new dialects and other contact varieties such as pidgins and creoles. A language is chosen for learning as a second (or additional) language by a group of people who speak another language, or several groups who speak different languages. But the purpose of learning this language is not for integration into the society of its speakers. Rather it may be at first for limited communication with these speakers and later predominantly for communication with other learners or former learners. In either case, the goal is not necessarily to acquire the language as it is spoken by its original speakers. Therefore, the learners go through the normal processes of SLA but acquire only as much as they need and adopt alterations to the language that suit their own purposes and reflect their own identities. As a result of a community adopting alterations made by individual learners, a new language or dialect may emerge, or the original language itself may change. Thus, in language contact, linguistic consequences can be the result of SLA that is not so much imperfect as it is strategic or adaptive.

## REFERENCES

Aikhenvald, A. Y. (2002). *Language contact in Amazonia.* Oxford: Oxford University Press.

Andersen, R. W. (1980). Creolization as the acquisition of a second language as a first language. In A. Valdman & A. Highfield (Eds.), *Theoretical orientations in creole studies* (pp. 273–295). New York: Academic Press.

Bao, Z. (1995). Already in Singapore English. *World Englishes, 14,* 181–188.

Bardovi-Harlig, K. (2000). *Tense and aspect in second language acquisition: Form, meaning, and use.* Oxford: Blackwell.

Bhatt, R. M. (2001). World Englishes. *Annual Review of Anthropology, 30,* 527–550.

Blum-Kulka, S., & Levenston, E. A. (1983). Universals of lexical simplification. In C. Færch & G. Kasper (Eds.), *Strategies in interlanguage communication* (pp. 119–139). London: Longman.

Chaudenson, R. (2001). *Creolization of language and culture (revised in collaboration with Salikoko S. Mufwene).* London: Routledge.

DeGraff, M. (1999). Creolization, language change, and language acquisition: An epilogue. In M. DeGraff (Ed.), *Language creation and language change: Creolization, diachrony, and development* (pp. 473–543). Cambridge, MA: The MIT Press.

DeGraff, M. (2005). Morphology and word order in "creolization" and beyond. In G. Cinque & R. S. Kayne (Eds.), *The Oxford handbook on comparative syntax* (pp. 293–372). Oxford: Oxford University Press.

Ellis, R. (1994). *The study of second language acquisition.* Oxford: Oxford University Press.

Epstein, S. D., Flynn, S., & Martohardjono, G. (1996). Second language acquisition: Theoretical and experimental issues in contemporary research. *Behavioral and Brain Sciences, 19,* 677–714.

Færch, C., & Kasper, G. (1987). Perspectives on language transfer. *Applied Linguistics, 8,* 111–136.

Harris, J. (1984). Syntactic variation and dialect divergence. *Journal of Linguistics*, *20*, 303–327.

Heine, B., & Kuteva, T. (2005). *Language contact and grammatical change*. Cambridge: Cambridge University Press.

Helms-Park, R. (2003). Transfer in SLA and creoles: The implications of causative serial verbs in the interlanguage of Vietnamese ESL learners. *Studies in Second Language Acquisition*, *25*, 211–244.

Hudson, J. (1983). *Grammatical and semantic aspects of Fitzroy Valley Kriol*, Work papers of SIL-AAB A/8, Darwin.

Jarvis, S., & Odlin, T. (2000). Morphological type, spatial reference, and language transfer. *Studies in Second Language Acquisition*, *22*, 535–556.

Johanson, L. (2002). Contact-induced change in a code-copying framework. In M. C. Jones & E. Esch (Eds.), *Language change: The interplay of internal, external and extra-linguistic factors* (pp. 285–313). Berlin: Mouton de Gruyter.

Kachru, B. B., & Nelson, C. L. (1996). World Englishes. In S. L. McKay & N. H. Hornberger (Eds.), *Sociolinguistics and language teaching* (pp. 71–102). Cambridge: Cambridge University Press.

Kasper, G. (1997). "A" stands for acquisition: A response to Firth and Wagner. *The Modern Language Journal*, *81*, 307–312.

Kellerman, E. (1995). Crosslinguistic influence: Transfer to nowhere? *Annual Review of Applied Linguistics*, *15*, 125–150.

Klee, C. A., & Ocampo, A. M. (1995). The expression of past reference in Spanish narratives of Spanish-Quechua bilingual speakers. In C. Silva-Corvalán (Ed.), *Spanish in four continents* (pp. 52–70). Washington, DC: Georgetown University Press.

Klein, W., & Perdue, C. (1997). The basic variety (or: Couldn't natural languages be much simpler?). *Second Language Research*, *13*, 301–347.

Kotsinas, U.-B. (1996). Aspect marking and grammaticalization in Russenorsk compared with immigrant Swedish. In E. H. Jahr & I. Broch (Eds.), *Language contact in the Arctic: Northern pidgins and contact languages* (pp. 123–154). Berlin: Mouton de Gruyter.

Kotsinas, U.-B. (2001). Pidginization, creolization and creoloid in Stockholm, Sweden. In N. Smith & T. Veenstra (Eds.), *Creolization and contact* (pp. 125–155). Amsterdam: Benjamins.

Kouwenberg, S. (2006). L1 transfer and the cut-off point for L2 acquisition processes in creole formation. In C. Lefebvre, L. White, & C. Jourdan (Eds.), *L2 acquisition and creole genesis* (pp. 205–219). Amsterdam: Benjamins.

Lefebvre, C. (1998). *Creole genesis and the acquisition of grammar: The case of Haitian creole*. Cambridge: Cambridge University Press.

Lefebvre, C., White, L., & Jourdan, C. (2006). Introduction. In C. Lefebvre, L. White, & C. Jourdan (Eds.), *L2 acquisition and creole genesis* (pp. 1–14). Amsterdam: Benjamins.

Lowenberg, P. H. (1986). Non-native varieties of English: Nativization, norms, and implications. *Studies in Second Language Acquisition*, *8*, 1–18.

Lumsden, J. S. (1999). The role of relexification in creole genesis. *Journal of Pidgin and Creole Languages*, *14*, 225–258.

Mather, P.-A. (2000). Creole genesis: Evidence from West African L2 French. In D. G. Gilbers, J. Nerbonne, & J. Schaeken (Eds.), *Languages in contact (Studies in Slavic and General Linguistics 28)* (pp. 247–261). Amsterdam: Rodopi.

Mather, P.-A. (2006). Second language acquisition and creolization: Same (i-) processes, different (e-) results. *Journal of Pidgin and Creole Languages*, *21*, 231–274.

McWhorter, J. H. (2000). Defining "creole" as a synchronic term. In I. Neumann-Holzschuh & E. W. Schneider (Eds.), *Degrees of restructuring in creole Languages* (pp. 85–123). Amsterdam: Benjamins.

Mesthrie, R. (1992). *English in language shift: The history, structure and sociolinguistics of South African Indian English.* Cambridge: Cambridge University Press.

Migge, B. (2003). *Creole formation as language contact.* Amsterdam: Benjamins.

Montrul, S. (1998). The L2 acquisition of dative experiencer subjects. *Second Language Research, 14,* 27–61.

Mufwene, S. S. (1990). Transfer and the substrate hypothesis in creolistics. *Studies in Second Language Acquisition, 12,* 1–23.

Mufwene, S. S. (2001). *The ecology of language evolution.* Cambridge: Cambridge University Press.

Muysken, P. (2001). The origin of creole languages: The perspective of second language learning. In N. Smith & T. Veenstra (Eds.), *Creolization and contact* (pp. 157–173). Amsterdam: Benjamins.

Odlin, T. (1989). *Language transfer.* Cambridge: Cambridge University Press.

Odlin, T. (2003). Cross-linguistic influence. In C. J. Doughty & M. H. Long (Eds.), *The handbook of second language acquisition* (pp. 436–486). Malden, MA: Blackwell.

Platt, J., & Weber, H. (1980). *English in Singapore and Malaysia: Status, features, functions.* Kuala Lumpur: Oxford University Press.

Platt, J., Weber, H., & Ho, M. L. (1984). *The new Englishes.* London: Routledge & Kegan Paul.

Poulisse, N. (1996). Strategies. In P. Jordens & J. Lalleman (Eds.), *Investigating second language acquisition* (pp. 135–163). Berlin: Mouton de Gruyter.

Rampton, B. (1997). A sociolinguistic perspective on L2 communication strategies. In G. Kasper & E. Kellerman (Eds.), *Communication strategies: Psycholinguistic and sociolinguistic perspectives* (pp. 279–303). London: Longman.

Rampton, M. B. H. (1991). Second language learners in a stratified multilingual setting. *Applied Linguistics, 12,* 229–248.

Ritchie, W. C. (1986). Second language acquisition research and the study of non-native varieties of English: Some issues in common. *World Englishes, 5,* 15–30.

Sánchez, L. (2003). *Quechua-Spanish bilingualism.* Amsterdam: Benjamins.

Schneider, E. W. (2003). The dynamics of new Englishes: From identity construction to dialect birth. *Language, 79,* 233–281.

Schumann, J. H. (1978). *The pidginization process: A model for second language acquisition.* Rowley, MA: Newbury House.

Schütz, A. J. (1985). *The Fijian language.* Honolulu: University of Hawaii Press.

Schwartz, B. D. (1998). The second language instinct. *Lingua, 106,* 133–160.

Schwartz, B. D., & Sprouse, R. A. (1996). L2 cognitive states and the full transfer/full access model. *Second Language Research, 12,* 40–72.

Sebba, M. (1997). *Contact languages: Pidgins and creoles.* New York: St Martin's Press.

Sharwood Smith, M. (1986). The competence/control model, crosslinguistic influence and the creation of new grammars. In M. S. Smith & E. Kellerman (Eds.), *Crosslinguistic influence in second language acquisition* (pp. 10–20). Oxford: Pergamon Press.

Sharwood Smith, M. (1996). Crosslinguistic influence with special reference to the acquisition of grammar. In P. Jordens & J. Lalleman (Eds.), *Investigating second language acquisition* (pp. 71–83). Berlin: Mouton de Gruyter.

Siegel, J. (1987). *Language contact in a plantation environment: A sociolinguistic history of Fiji.* Cambridge: Cambridge University Press.

Siegel, J. (2003). Social context. In C. J. Doughty & M. H. Long (Eds.), *The handbook of second language acquisition* (pp. 178–223). Malden, MA: Blackwell.

Siegel, J. (2006). Links between SLA and creole studies: Past and present. In C. Lefebvre, L. White, & C. Jourdan (Eds.), *L2 acquisition and creole genesis* (pp. 15–46). Amsterdam: Benjamins.

Sprouse, R. A. (2006). Full transfer and relexification: Second language acquisition and creole genesis. In C. Lefebvre, L. White, & C. Jourdan (Eds.), *L2 acquisition and creole genesis* (pp. 169–181). Amsterdam: Benjamins.

Sridhar, K. K., & Sridhar, S. N. (1986). Bridging the paradigm gap: Second language acquisition theory and indigenized varieties of English. *World Englishes, 5,* 3–14.

Tarone, E. (1981). Some thoughts on the notion of communication strategy. *TESOL Quarterly, 15,* 285–295.

Tarone, E., Cohen, A. D., & Dumas, G. (1983). A closer look at some interlanguage terminology: A framework for communication strategies. In C. Færch & G. Kasper (Eds.), *Strategies in interlanguage communication* (pp. 4–14). London: Longman.

Thomason, S. G. (2001). *Language contact: An introduction.* Washington, DC: Georgetown University Press.

Thomason, S. G., & Kaufman, T. (1988). *Language contact, creolization, and genetic linguistics.* Berkeley: University of California Press.

van Coetsem, F. (1988). *Loan word phonology and the two transfer types in language contact.* Dordrecht: Foris.

van de Craats, I., Corver, N., & van Hout, R. (2000). Conservation of grammatical knowledge: On the acquisition of possessive noun phrases by Turkish and Moroccan learners of Dutch. *Linguistics, 38,* 221–314.

Véronique, D. (1994). Naturalistic adult acquisition of French as L2 and French-based creole genesis compared: Insights into creolization and language change. In D. Adone & I. Plag (Eds.), *Creolization and language change* (pp. 117–137). Tübingen: Max Niemeyer.

Weinreich, U. (1970 [1953]). Languages in contact: Findings and problems. The Hague: Mouton.

Wekker, H. (1996). Creolization and the acquisition of English as a second language. In H. Wekker (Ed.), *Creole languages and language acquisition* (pp. 139–149). Berlin: Mouton de Gruyter.

Williams, J. (1987). Non-native varieties of English: A special case of language acquisition. *English World-Wide, 8,* 161–199.

Winford, D. (2003). *An introduction to contact linguistics.* Malden, MA: Blackwell.

CHAPTER 25

# LANGUAGE MIXING, UNIVERSAL GRAMMAR AND SECOND LANGUAGE ACQUISITION

Tej K. Bhatia and William C. Ritchie

## I. INTRODUCTION

Following Chomsky (e.g., 1963, 1986, 2005), we consider the central questions in the study of language to be the following four: What constitutes knowledge of a particular language? How is this knowledge put to use in the production, processing, and comprehension of speech? How is it acquired? How is it represented in the brain? Though these are generally conceived of as questions about monolinguals, we ask them with respect to bilinguals as well: How are the bilingual's two (or more) systems of linguistic knowledge organized both separately and in relation to each other? How does possession of two systems of linguistic knowledge affect the mental processes that underlie speech recognition and production? How do the two systems interact at various stages in the attainment of bilinguality? How are the two systems represented in the brain as indicated by the ways in which various forms of brain damage affect linguistic performance in the two languages? In addition to these questions, research on bilingualism must address the problems of the effects of bilingualism on cognitive functioning and of the social determinants of various forms of bilingual linguistic behavior.

In spite of a view of bilingualism as somehow deviant or pathological—held by many early researchers—investigation of these questions has proceeded intensively (particularly since the 1960s), and some degree of understanding has been achieved, although much remains to be done. (For a general account of the many facets of bilingualism, see Bhatia & Ritchie, 2004/2006.)

All of these issues come together in the study of the way in which bilinguals mix (or alternate) and integrate their two linguistic systems in their day-to-day verbal interaction. In many bi- or multilingual communities, this is not a peripheral, idiosyncratic, or "strange" phenomenon. On the contrary, it is such a common and natural part of

*The New Handbook of Second Language Acquisition*

bilingual linguistic behavior that speakers in such communities are largely unaware of mixing and do not react to it unless they are made aware of it by listeners, nor is their fluency hampered in any way, nor is there any evidence that suggests that the speaker is not understood by his or her bilingual listeners. In addition, whether bilingualism is grounded in a widely spoken European language on one hand and, say, one of the aboriginal languages of Australia or New Guinea on the other, one conclusion that seems to be inescapable is that language mixing is widespread if not universal among bilinguals.

In this chapter, we will use the term code mixing (CM) to refer to the alternation of the bilingual's two languages within the same sentence (i.e., intrasentential alternation) and the term code switching (CS) to refer to alternation between sentences (i.e., intersentential alternation). Whether there is a significant difference between CM and CS is controversial and we return to a more detailed discussion below. Since CM and CS share many properties—for example, their social motivation—we will have occasion to refer to both without distinguishing between them. In such cases, we will use the abbreviation CM/CS.

The study of CM/CS in fluent, balanced bilinguals has led to the discovery of strong morphosyntactic restrictions on the occurrence of CM in particular. It is generally agreed that these restrictions are due to principles of universal grammar (UG), the central element in the child's innate capacity for language acquisition. A general, central issue in the study of second language acquisition (SLA) in adults is whether the adult retains (or "has access to") the principles of UG. It is therefore a matter of some interest to determine whether these same restrictions apply to CM in cases where the second of the bilingual's languages was clearly acquired in adulthood. We turn to a direct discussion of this issue in section V of the chapter after general discussion of CM/CS in sections II–IV.

The study of CM/CS owes much to sociolinguistics for its origins and has subsequently been the subject of investigation by linguists and nonlinguists, including sociologists, anthropologists, psychologists, speech therapists, and computer scientists, and for a number of reasons: First, it appears to hold one key to the understanding of bilingual language processing and the treatment of certain speech disorders (see Ritchie & Bhatia, 2008; Ijalba, Obler, & Chengappa, 2004). Second, it sheds light on the deeper principles of human communication, namely the creativity and optimization in as well as complex social and psychological motivations for verbal communication. Third, it is of rapidly growing interest to linguistic theory (see, e.g., MacSwan, 2009). And fourth, it is increasingly the case that "mixed languages"— whether "second language varieties" like those of Indian English or the CM/CS-rich speech of many balanced bilinguals—are recognized as "legitimate" forms of language and language use (see, e.g., Jones & Bradwell, 2007).

This chapter presents a state-of-the-art overview of research on CM/CS and its relevance to the problem of the accessibility of UG to adult second language learners. Section II draws a distinction among several phenomena related to language mixing in general, thereby isolating CM/CS for further discussion. Section III discusses the formal constraints on CM referred to above, while section IV covers sociopsychological motivations for CM/CS. Based on the discourse and interactional analysis of CM/CS, including the social identities of interlocutors, further distinctions are drawn among the types of CM/CS. As noted above, section V reviews recent research on CM/CS at different stages of SLA and presents a model based on that research. Finally, section VI deals with some residual problems, and section VII is a conclusion.

The body of research on this topic has increased exponentially since the publication of our previous work (Bhatia & Ritchie, 1996). Only those works have been selected for review here that are important according to one or more of the following criteria: historicity, theoretical frameworks, impact on subsequent research, and relevance to the issue of the development of constraints in SLA. The restrictions on the scope of the chapter are as follows: A full discussion of speech processing in bilinguals is beyond the scope of this chapter (see, e.g., Kroll & Dussias, 2004 for discussion). No attempt is made to give an array of definitions of bilingualism or bilinguals (see Edwards, 2004 for an in-depth discussion). With the exception of the discussion of second language learners in section V, the chapter deals with the speech of the balanced or fluent bilingual. Furthermore, it should be stressed that the question of multiple mixing is not addressed here either (see Bhatia, 2006 for details).

## II. DEFINITIONS OF CM AND CS, BORROWING, AND OTHER RELATED PHENOMENA

We begin by cautioning that not all cases of the mixing of two languages qualify as either CM or CS in our sense. CM/CS constitutes a special type of language mixing in the speech patterns of balanced bilinguals exemplified in (1) and (2). The word "balanced" is central to our discussion at this point.

(1) *Spanish*–English (Valdés-Fallis, 1978, p. 1).
   a. No, *yo si' brincaba en el trampoline* when I was a senior.
      "No, I did jump on the trampoline when I was a senior."
   b. *La consulta era* eight dollars.
      "The office visit was eight dollars."
   c. Well, I keep starting some. *Como, por un mes todos los días escribo y ya dejo.*
      "Well, I keep starting some. For about a month I write everything and then I stop."
(2) *Hindi*–English
   a. Train *mẽ* seat *mil jaae to* ...
      "If one gets a seat in the train, then ... "
   b. Third class *kaa Dibbaa* ...
      of compartment
      "A third-class compartment" (lit.: compartment of third class)
   c. *buund*-ify *kar-naa* "to liquefy"
      "liquid-ify do-to"

As indicated by these examples (and as suggested earlier), language mixing can be either intrasentential (i.e., CM) as in examples (1a and 1b) and (2a–c) or intersentential (CS) as in example (1c). More specifically, the two terms will be applied in the following fashion:

(3)  a. CM refers to the mixing of various linguistic units (morphemes, words, modifiers, phrases, clauses, and sentences) primarily from two participating grammatical systems within a single sentence. It is constrained by grammatical principles and may be motivated by sociopsychological factors.

b. CS refers to the mixing of various linguistic units (words, phrases, clauses, and sentences) primarily from two participating grammatical systems across sentence boundaries within a speech event. It may be subject to discourse principles. Like CM, it is motivated by social and psychological factors.

In an actual discourse, the interaction between CS and CM often becomes so complex and fused that it is quite difficult to draw a clear line between them. In addition, such a distinction (or lack of distinction) is motivated by approaches and theoretical goals underlying research on this topic (for details, see Bhatia & Ritchie, 1996, pp. 630–631).

## A. Matrix and Embedded Language

A distinction that is often drawn in any discussion of CM/CS and related phenomena (e.g., Myers-Scotton, 1993) is that between the matrix (host, base) language and the embedded (guest) language in a particular case of language alternation. The matrix language is the language that gives the sentence its basic character, and the embedded language is the language that contributes the "imported" material. For example, in (1), Spanish–English bilinguals will claim on intuitive grounds that in (1b), the matrix language is Spanish, the embedded language is English; similarly, Hindi–English bilinguals will report that in example (2a), the matrix language is Hindi and the embedded language is English.

Though many researchers adopt this distinction, it is, as noted above, still problematic and has come under fire, particularly from researchers interested in uncovering underlying principles of the grammar of CM/CS. A number of criteria have been proposed to identify the matrix language in code-mixed or code-switched discourse. These criteria can be classified as follows—the matrix language is: the language of INFL in the government and binding framework (i.e., "inflection," the element that functions as head of the sentence) (Klavans, 1985; Treffers-Daller, 1991); the language that determines the overall structural properties of the sentence such as topic–comment versus subject–predicate structure (Nishimura (1986)); the language in which the speaker is most proficient; the speaker's mother tongue; the language intuited as most prominent in the utterance/discourse by the speaker; the language most frequently used by the speaker (Kamwangamalu & Lee, 1991).

The Matrix Language Frame (MLF) model (and its newer version the 4-M model) of Jake, Myers-Scotton, and Gross (2005) and extensive additional works by Myers-Scotton and others (henceforth, the MLF model) utilize the distinction between matrix and embedded language to capture the differential role of participating languages in the grammar and discourse of CM/CS. According to the MLF model, one language (i.e., the matrix language) plays a critical role in supplying the morphosyntactic frame for a mixed utterance.

The works of MacSwan (2005a, 2005b) reject Myers-Scotton et al.'s claim and the MLF model generally on both empirical and conceptual grounds. MacSwan shows convincingly that the notion of "matrix" language carries neither descriptive nor explanatory adequacy with respect to accounting for constraints on CM/CS.

According to his theoretical account of CM/CS within Chomsky's Minimalist Program, there is no room for a mechanism specific to CM/CS; CM can best be characterized by independently motivated principles of grammar, which are shared by monolingual as well as bilingual grammar. In what follows, the distinction between the matrix and embedded language is employed as a descriptive device rather than a theoretically/explanatorily motivated linguistic construct. Such a device is useful in describing the bilingual's perception and language labeling of a code-mixed utterance. In other cases, the matrix/embedded distinction is synonymous with the distinction between host and guest language in the context of borrowing.

## B. Borrowing and CM/CS

One of the theoretical assumptions that underlies most (if not all) studies of CM and CS is the distinction between borrowing on one hand and CM/CS on the other. Borrowed or loan words have the following characteristics that separate them from code-mixed or code-switched elements. First, they primarily serve the linguistic function of filling a gap in the lexicon of the borrower language, or they are prompted by nonlinguistic factors such as modernization or both, whereas CM/CS is motivated by sociopsychological factors, such as social identity and differential language domains (see section IV). Second, borrowed items are restricted to specific lexical items of the guest language, whereas such a restriction is not applicable in CM/CS where lexical items from both participating languages are freely chosen. Romaine (1989, p. 63) points out that most scholars accept the view that lexical items are most easily borrowed (with nouns more easily borrowed than verbs), followed by derivational morphological material, followed by inflectional material with syntactic structures the least likely to be borrowed. Third, borrowed items are assimilated into the host language by regular phonological and morphological processes of either the guest or the host language. In contrast, CM/CS material is generally unassimilated to the phonological and morphological processes of the matrix language. Fourth, borrowed material is part of the lexicon of monolingual as well as bilingual members of the community, whereas CM/CS is limited to bilinguals in the speech community.

It is worth mentioning that there is some disagreement among scholars about the phonological and morphological assimilation of loan words. For instance, Sobin (1976, p. 42) claims that some phonologically adapted items must be considered switches rather than borrowings for speakers of Spanish in Texas. Elias-Olivarés (1976, p. 187) contends that nouns of a dominant embedded language in business and other functional domains (English, in this case) often remain morphologically and syntactically unintegrated into the matrix language (Spanish) and yet must be treated as part of the Spanish lexicon of some Chicanos. It seems that prestige together with functional domains allow the borrowed lexicon to remain unassimilated into the matrix/host language. Adding one more layer of complexity to the issue of phonological adaptation, Bullock and Toribio (in press) show that the phonetic reflexes in bilingual CM/CS utterances are not predetermined or uniform. "The interlingual influence can be asymmetric, affecting only one language, or it can be bidirectional, affecting both".

As regards the criterion of morphological integration, not all scholars recognize it as a reliable basis for distinguishing between borrowing and CM/CS. Myers-Scotton (1988) rejects both morphological and syntactic integration as a reliable yardstick for distinguishing between CM/CS and borrowing. Pfaff (1979, p. 298) refers to differing degrees of morphological integration for various syntactic categories, particularly verbs. Verbs need to be morphologically integrated in terms of tense and aspect, whereas other categories such as adjectives or nouns do not have to undergo such a rigorous process of adaptation to attain borrowed status. Yet another dimension is added to the problem by the concept of nonce borrowing. Poplack, Wheeler, and Westwood (1989) distinguished between the well-established notion of borrowing discussed above and a notion of nonce borrowing. They state that the entire nominal lexicon of English is subjected to nonce borrowing by Finnish–English bilinguals. Thus, borrowing represents a continuum. For more details, see Bhatia and Ritchie (1996, pp. 632–634).

## C. CM/CS and Pidgin and Creoles

In addition to CM/CS, three types of other mixed linguistic systems—pidgin, creole, and diglossic systems—are quite widespread in human societies, but they are also quite distinct both on qualitative and quantitative grounds from CM/CS.

A pidgin language is a mixed language, usually with material from two languages exhibiting a socially dominant–subordinate relationship—a high-prestige language such as English or French and a more local, low-prestige language. Pidgins have very restricted functional domains primarily having to do with business. They are not native languages for anyone. Their lexicon is very limited (1000–2000 words) and their grammars are "simplified." Furthermore, the mixture of the two languages involved is uneven, tilted more in favor of the prestige language. CM/CS, on the other hand, is employed by children and, in that respect, is considered to be virtually part of the mother tongue of code mixers. As we will show in the following section, CM also involves a complex grammar, and CM/CS performs a wide variety of socio-psychological functions that cannot be fulfilled by means of the employment of the two "pure" linguistic systems that serve as the source languages for CM and CS (see section IV).

A creole language is the result of a pidgin language becoming the mother tongue of the children of the community in which the pidgin is used. There is, therefore, a difference between the input language in the acquisition of a creole and the inputs in the acquisition of the languages that enter into CM/CS. The input in the former case is a pidgin language, whereas in the later case, the input comes from two "full" languages. The evolutionary and developmental phase of a creole language is therefore different from that of bilinguals who engage in CM/CS. As shown in the tree diagram below, creole languages undergo either the process of decreolization (i.e., elaboration toward the prestige language) or intense creolization (hypercreolization). In that respect then creolization marks language shift or even language death. However, CM/CS does not affect bilingualism in an adverse fashion (i.e., it does not lead to monolingualism) as long as one language does not die out for a host of reasons different from language use.

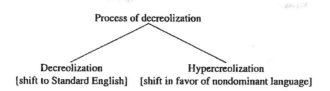

Process of decreolization

Decreolization                              Hypercreolization
[shift to Standard English]      [shift in favor of nondominant language]

## III. CONSTRAINTS ON CM

A number of different sets of factors that determine the occurrence and character of CM (i.e., intrasentential code alternation) can be studied more or less independently of factors in the occurrence of CS (intersentential alternation); the most important of these are formal, functional, and attitudinal factors.

Studies of formal factors in the occurrence of CM attempt to tap the unconscious knowledge of bilinguals about the internal structure of code-mixed sentences by postulating constraints or deeper principles to account for the grammaticality judgments and production and nonproduction of particular types of code-mixed sentences by fluent bilinguals. These studies differ from each other depending upon the theoretical goal and the level of explanation they seek and the predictions they make.

Studies of the social function of CM claim that the phenomenon of CM can best be studied not just by examining the internal structure of code-mixed sentences, but by seeking the sociopsychological and discourse-related factors that trigger mixing in a bilingual setting.

Finally, the third type of study investigates the ways in which societal factors such as a speech community's attitude towards CM determines the usage of CM. These attitudes explain why in some communities mixing is as natural as speaking in a mother tongue, although in other communities, even ones with widespread native-like control over the two languages, bilinguals employ CM with some level of hesitancy and apology.

In this section, we will examine the attempts made to capture formal constraints on CM within different frameworks and approaches. These approaches can be broadly classified into three groups (1) typological, (2) categorical (i.e., grammatical categories), and (3) constituency relationships grounded in different theoretical models, such as the Minimalist Program and its ancestral versions. We will discuss social functions in section IV.

### A. Is CM a Random Phenomenon?

If one takes a cursory look at the forms in (1) and (2) and, in fact, the data given throughout this chapter, one would be tempted to conclude that almost any kind of constituent or grammatical category can be mixed within a sentence—bound morphemes, lexical items, phrases, clauses, idioms, and so on. The mixing of such a wide array of linguistic elements of different types led the earlier researchers in the

1970s to conclude that CM is either not subject to syntactic constraints (Lance, 1975, p. 143) or, equivalently, is subject only to "irregular mixture" (Labov, 1971, p. 457). Labov went on to claim that the mixing of Spanish and English on the part of the New York Puerto Rican bilingual speaker is a "strange mixture of the two languages." He argued that "no one has been able to show that such rapid alternation is governed by any systematic rules or constraints." On the other hand, Gumperz (1982, p. 72) argued that although CM/CS is not a totally random phenomenon, the motivation for (and hence restrictions on) CM/CS in general seems to be "stylistic and metaphorical rather than grammatical."

The view of the grammar of CM as strange and random became outmoded when, in the late 1970s and early 1980s with Chomskyan linguistics, attempts were made to capture grammatical constraints on CM in particular. Not only did these attempts change fundamental assumptions about the verbal behavior of bilinguals, but they also altered a certain outmoded conception of bilinguals as individuals with "split personality" (see Hakuta, 1986, p. 14). Furthermore, it unveiled a complex aspect of CM that has occupied many CM researchers since then. Let us now turn our attention to some constraints on CM that have been posited in the linguistic literature.

## B. The Search for Universals

Some of the earliest restrictions on CM were proposed primarily as language-specific constraints. Proposals such as the size-of-constituent constraint of Gumperz and Hernandez-Chavez (1975) and Poplack (1980) and conjunction or complementizer constraints (Gumperz, 1977; Kachru, 1978) made no explicit claims either about their crosslinguistic applicability or their universality.

The constraint on the size of constituents was motivated by the observation that the higher the level or size of the constituent, the more was its probability of mixing. Essentially, this constraint states that mixing applies at the phrasal level and constituents smaller than a phrase are not subject to mixing. As examples (1a–b) and (2a–c) indicated, mixing of terminal constituents (e.g., Adj, N, V) and inflections is fully acceptable; in fact, such CM is widely found. We will return to the conjunction or complementizer constraints shortly during our discussion of a more recently proposed principle, the functional head constraint (FHC).

## C. Formal Constraints on CM

The following constraints were proposed as general syntactic constraints on CM inspired by the notion of constraints on transformational rules in generative linguistic theory and they are among the most widely cited constraints in the literature.

### The Free Morpheme Constraint (FMC)

> A switch may not occur between a bound morpheme and a lexical form unless the latter has been phonologically integrated into the language of the bound morpheme. (Sankoff & Poplack, 1981, pp. 5–6)

It is intended to account for the ill-formedness of expressions such as *run-*eando* "running." The Spanish-bound morpheme -*eando* violates the restriction against the mixing of a bound morpheme and a free morpheme from two different languages. This constraint shows that CM is rule governed and not random. However, languages with agglutinative elements (such as Bantu and Arabic) and non-agglutinative languages (such as Hindi) both violate this constraint, as shown by the following sentences:

(4)   *Arabic*–English (El-Noory, 1985)
    *?ana*     *ba*-cope      *ma?a*      *l-lahja.*
    I         pres-cope     with       the-dialect
    "I cope with the dialect."

In (4), the present tense marker bound morpheme occurs with the verb *cope*. Myers-Scotton (1993) proposed that the violations of the FMC are limited to agglutinative languages like Swahili. However, example (2c) shows that switches in a non-agglutinative language (Hindi) also violate the FMC. In addition, the stipulation attached in the "unless clause" phonologically integrated items qualify as instances of borrowing rather than CM.

Now, observe the following examples:

(5)  *Spanish*–English
    a. *el* old man
    b. the *hombre viejo*
       "the old man"
(6)  *Spanish*–English
    a. *El *viejo* man
    b. *the old *hombre*
    c. *the *viejo hombre*

Why are (5a–b) grammatical, while (6a–c) are ungrammatical? Poplack attempted to explain the grammaticality contrast between the two sets by the equivalence constraint (EC).

## The Equivalence Constraint

> Code-switches will tend to occur at points in discourse where the juxtaposition of L1 and L2 elements does not violate a syntactic rule of either language (i.e., at points around which the surface structures of the two languages map on to each other). (Poplack, 1980, p. 586; Sankoff & Poplack, 1981, p. 5)

The EC implies that CM will tend to take place only at those positions that are common to both languages and dissimilar points will not yield mixing. For instance, Spanish and English differ from each other in terms of the placement of adjectives within a noun phrase (i.e., in Spanish, the adjective is positioned after the noun whereas in English, it is placed before the noun). However, they share similar behavior with reference to the placement of noun and determiner (i.e., in both languages, the determiner precedes the noun). The EC predicts that mixing will be permissible between noun and determiner, whereas it will be blocked between noun and adjective.

Thus, the EC will make the right prediction that the phrases (5a–b) will be well formed in *Spanish*–English mixing. However, noun phrases such as those in (6a–b) will be ungrammatical.

Now, let us consider some examples of *Hindi*–English mixing. The phrase structure rule for noun phrases (NPs) in English and Hindi are identical (i.e., NP → (Det) (Adj) N). This will predict that the mixing between *Hindi* and English at the NP level should be free.

(7)   a. the old man
      b. *the *buuRaa* man
      c. *the *buuRaa aadmii*
(8)   a. *vo buuRaa aadmii*
      b. *vo* old *aadmii*
      c. *vo* old man

A comparison of (7a–c) and (8a–c) shows that although (8b) and (8c) allow mixing "that old man" with English in the adjectival and nominal positions, (7b) and (7c) show that Hindi mixing is not permitted in these two positions. The underlying source of the ungrammaticality of (7b) and (7c) is apparently that Hindi lacks articles. Berk-Seligson (1986, p. 328) found a similar situation in Hebrew–Spanish CM. Hebrew lacks the indefinite article. To fill the gap created by the absence of English articles in Hindi, the Hindi-speaking bilingual will employ one of the following two strategies: Either the demonstrative pronoun *vo* "that" is used instead of the article, or the definite article is dropped as in the code-mixed phrase "old *aadmii*." The result thus produced is well formed. The presence of the English article with a Hindi adjective and a noun is totally unacceptable.

The fundamental problem of EC is that it overlooks the absence of a neat mapping of grammatical categories crosslinguistically. However, what is even more interesting is that even if the EC is met both in terms of grammatical category and word order, it does not guarantee well-formed output as we will observe later in the case of the negative marker and verb mixing in Spanish and Nahuatl. (For more discussion and examples of asymmetry of grammatical categories, see Bhatia & Ritchie, 1996, pp. 642–643.)

Similarly, the EC fails to subsume the clitic pronoun constraint.

## The Clitic Pronoun Constraint

> Clitic pronoun objects are realized in the same language as the verb to which they are cliticized, and in the position required by the syntactic rule of that language. (Pfaff, 1979, p. 303)

Because both English and Spanish are SVO, one would predict by the EC that mixing will be possible in the verb and the object position and even the subject position. However, the clitic pronoun constraint rules out sentences such as the following:

(9)   English–*Spanish*
      *She sees *lo*
               him
      "She sees him"

Similarly, it has been observed that in the subject position, mixing with pronouns is banned while mixing with full noun phrases is not.

Finally, we consider Joshi's closed class constraint.

## The Closed Class Constraint

> Closed Class items (e.g., determiners, quantifiers, prepositions, possessive, Aux, tense, helping verbs, etc.) cannot be switched. (Joshi, 1985, p. 194)

Although it is observationally accurate for a wide range of cases, the closed class constraint (like the other constraints addressed in this section) carries less explanatory power than the constraints to be discussed in the next subsection.

The constraints discussed so far are inadequate on empirical grounds—as we have seen, they fail to make correct crosslinguistic predictions. The underlying problems are several, but most importantly (1) most of them are limited to surface and linear word order of the language pairs and some fail to make use of the hierarchical character of linguistic structures, although others are rooted in the classification of the lexicon and (2) the stipulation concerning phonological integration in the FMC has been criticized as a "third grammar" constraint by Pfaff, that is, a separate system or mechanism to mediate between the two languages involved in CM. We will return to this issue. In spite of the shortcomings of these constraints, they certainly represent important gains in dispelling the conception that CM is a "strange" and "irregular" phenomenon.

## D. Theoretical Models and Constraints on CM

In the light of this progress, the real challenge is not whether or not CM is subject to constraints but how best to capture those constraints, and how to make deeper claims about human language in general and bilinguals' mixing competence and their language acquisition in particular—that is, how to achieve a theoretical understanding of language mixing and its place in linguistic knowledge and behavior. In what follows, we will consider five such attempts, which are largely driven by deeper theoretical considerations and, thus, have serious implications for the study of UG and language acquisition as well as linguistic performance.

## Woolford's Model

Using Spanish and English as the two languages involved in CM, Woolford (1983) proposed a model to show how two monolingual grammars cooperate to generate code-mixed sentences. Under the proposed model, similar to assumptions underlying the EC, the grammars of the two languages are not altered in any way; no special hybrid rules of any sort are created for language mixing. The intersecting portion of the two grammars represents those phrase structure rules that are common to both languages and, thus, permits mixing rather freely from the two languages. "The two grammars operate during code switching just as they do during monolingual speech, except that each grammar generates only part of the sentence" (Woolford, 1983, p. 522). This finding that no separate new system is created is to be expected, since speakers are competent in two related languages which often have a high degree of similarity. Thus, the conception of the grammar of CM proposed by Woolford (1983) and Pfaff (1979) was powerful in terms of stating the goals of CM/CS research (i.e., no special mechanism or a third grammar mechanism), but their models either over- or under-generate mixed utterances (see Bhatia 1989 for a discussion of verb formation, adjectival agreement, and head deletion) and presented no objective basis of separating the two lexicons (see section VI).

## The Government Constraint

Di Sciullo, Muysken, and Singh (1986) attempt to capture the constraints on CM, in terms of the government constraint—formulated in terms of GB theory—given below:

(10)   a.  X governs Y if the first node dominating X also dominates Y, where X is a major category, N, V, A, P and no maximal boundary intervenes between X and Y.
       b.  If $L_q$ carrier has [language] index q, then $Y_q^{max}$
       c.  In a maximal projection $Y^{max}$, the $L_q$ carrier is the lexical element which asymmetrically c-commands the other lexical elements or terminal phrase nodes dominated by $Y_q^{max}$
       d.  At least the $L_q$ carrier of a governed category must have the same $L_q$ index as its governor.

Because under Di Sciullo et al.'s definition of government, only N, V, A, and P are potential governors, the constraint claims that in the structure (11), the $L_q$ carrier of the governed category $Y_{maxq}$ (i.e., $Z_q$) must have the same $L_q$ index as $X_q$, where $X_q$ is N, V, A, or P.

(11)        X′

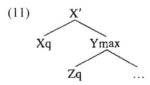

The government constraint is noteworthy on two grounds: First, the assignment of language indices results from the process of lexical insertion and not from the phrase structure rules as proposed by Woolford (1983); second, the phenomenon of syntactic integration is explained by an underlying principle that is valid not just for CM or for a single language but for linguistic structure in general and for all languages. It predicts that because a verb governs its complement clauses, direct and indirect objects and complement pre- and postpositional phrases, they must be in the same language as the verb and similarly for the other major categories.

The government constraint can capture some previously proposed constraints such as those of Kachru (1978) and Singh (1981), predicting that the complementizer of a complement clause will be in the same language as the matrix verb. However, Bentahila and Davies (1983) (French and Arabic), Romaine (1989), Bhatia and Ritchie (1996, pp. 649–651) (particularly mixing with English in Hindi light verbs), and Belazi, Rubin, and Toribio (1994), drawing from a wide array of language pairs, argued convincingly against the constraint. On conceptual grounds, the language index/label added a CM-specific constraint to which we will return in the discussion of the FHC below.

## The Functional Head Constraint

To remedy the inadequacy of the government constraint and other constraints such as the FMC, Belazi et al.(1994) proposed the FHC, as stated below:

(12)   The language feature of the complement f-selected by a functional head, like all other relevant features, must match the corresponding feature of that functional head.

Based on X-bar syntax, the FHC is grounded in the system of syntactic categories of Chomsky (1986) as modified by Abney (1987) to distinguish between categories that are functional: [+F] (e.g., C(omplementizer), I(nflection), D(eterminer), K( = case), Deg(ree), Agr(eement), Neg(ative), Modal, and Num(ber)), and those that are thematic ([−F], including N(oun), V(erb), A(djective), P(reposition), Adv(erb), Q(uantifier). The FHC extends the scope of f-selection—an independently motivated notion—to language indexing, that is, the language feature of a functional head must match the language feature of its complement in the same way a functional head must match other features of its complement. Constraints on language switching are thus understood to be local and hierarchical, limited to heads and their complements (or internal domains)—more specifically to a (functional) head and the head of its complement.

In contrast to the restriction against mixing between the functional head and its complement, the mixing between a lexical head and its complement occurs quite freely. The government constraint, which blocks mixing between a verb and its complement and between a pre- or postposition and its complement NP, is permitted by the FHC, and Belazi et al.'s data support this prediction as well. In addition, the FHC is the basis for an insightful account of the syntax of the complex/light verb constructions in South Asian languages referred to by Di Sciullo et al. (1986) as the "nativization" of verbs. Consider the two sets of examples below:

(13)   *Hindi*–English
    a. *mãĩ*     *yah*     *dikhaa*     *saktaa*     *hũũ*
       I          this       show       can       am
       "I can show (prove) this"
    b. *\*mãĩ*     *yah*     prove     *saktaa*     *hũũ*

(14)   *Hindi*–English
    a. *\*mãĩ*     *yah*     *dikhaa*     *kar*     *saktaa*     *hũũ*
       I          this       show       do        can       am
       "I can show (prove) this"
    b. *mãĩ*     *yah*     prove     *kar*     *saktaa*     *hũũ*

In each of these four examples, the (functional) modal element *saktaa* f-selects the position immediately preceding it, which, by the FHC, must therefore be in the same language as *saktaa*. This prediction is borne out as shown by the grammaticality of (13a) and the ungrammaticality of (13b). Hindi includes a rule that inserts *kar* "do" (which is not a functional head) in derivations that contain such verbs (as in [14b]), so that the FHC is circumvented, hence allowing such sentences to surface. In accordance with the notions of economy of derivation and representation discussed in Chomsky (1995), this rule does not apply when the verb is in the language of the f-selecting element, hence the ungrammaticality of (14a).

This case is typical of a wide range of other instances of f-selected mixed verbs in Hindi–English sentences as well as those in many other language-mixing combinations including the following (matrix language given first): Punjabi–English (Romaine, 1989), Tamil–English (Annamalai, 1978), Spanish–English (Pfaff, 1976), Philippine Creole Spanish–Tagalog/English (Molony, 1977), Japanese–English (Stanlaw, 1982), Turkish–Dutch (Boeschoten & Verhoeven, 1985), Warlpiri–English (Bavin & Shopen, 1985), and Navajo–English (Canfield, 1980) (see Bhatia & Ritchie 2001, for details).

Although the FHC is quite successful in accounting for a wide range of data on language mixing, it does face some challenges on universal and crosslinguistic grounds (see Dussias, 1997; MacSwan, 1999; Mahootian and Santorini, 1996; Nishimura, 1997; for a defense, see Toribio, 2001). More importantly, as pointed out by MacSwan (2006, p. 290), the operation of the constraint requires a language feature such as [+Spanish] or [+English] which is not independently motivated. "In particular, to evaluate the FHC, particular hypotheses are needed regarding which features of English, being distinct from features of Spanish, result in a conflict. Unfortunately, no such hypotheses are developed" (MacSwan, 2006, p. 291) (MacSwan's concern is addressed by Toribio, see section V).

## A Minimalist Approach to CM

Recent research by MacSwan within the Chomskyan Minimalist Program provides a new direction for theoretically driven research on CM. In addition to offering a new analysis to some nagging problems in CM research, his work (with his colleagues) also brings a new promise to a research agenda set by work carried out within the generative framework.

The main strength of the Minimalist Program (henceforth, MP), as the term indicates, is the elimination of all mechanisms that are not required on conceptual grounds to account for linguistic data. In other words, in the new treatment of CM, there are no statements, rules, or principles of grammar which are particular to CM, such as a "third grammar" constraint posited by some earlier research. In other words, the emphasis is on evaluation in terms of simplicity, naturalness, etc.

The main assumption of MP as it is operationalized for CM is stated in (15).

(15)   Nothing constrains code switching apart from the requirements of the mixed grammars

The word "constrains" requires explanation. It is being used in a technical sense (not in a descriptive sense to mean that there are no unacceptable code-mixed sentences— the prevalent view of CM before the onset of sociolinguistic research on the topic). Specifically, it is being used here in such a way that (15) claims that there are no requirements or statements which are specific to CM such as language specificity in the FHC and government constraints. In other words, the phenomenon of CM may be explained "in terms of principles and requirements of the specific grammars used in each specific utterance" and nothing more (MacSwan, 2006, p. 298).

The minimalist framework for CM is shown diagrammatically below (Figure 1).

In order to extend the scope of the general MP to account for CM phenomena, MacSwan lays out the following two modifications: first, a one-language input lexicon is naturally replaced by a two-language lexicon ($L_x$) and ($L_y$), as at least two languages are involved in CM. Second, the union of two language phonologies at the PF level instead of one is built into the program. All other aspects remain unchanged. The PF refers to phonetic form (parallel to "surface structure" in Chomsky's *Aspects* model and S-structure in the government-binding model) and LF to logical form (i.e., the interpretive level).

There are two central components of the syntax in MP: (1) $C_{HL}$, a computational system for human language, which is invariant across languages and (2) a Lexicon, which is responsible for variation and idiosyncratic differences across languages. In other words, MP claims, for example, that word-order differences among human languages are primarily due to differences among the lexicons of languages and are the result of movement operations, triggered by morphosyntactic features coded into the lexicon. Thus, the lexicon is central to this framework right from the outset in the derivation (as shown by its place on the top in Figure 1). This is a departure from the earlier version of generative linguistics; in the early frameworks of generative grammar, lexicon was peripheral and lexical items were inserted at the end of the derivation.

Within MP, three operations are needed for the derivation of structures leading to the numeration level: (1) <u>Select</u> picks up lexical items from a given language and introduces them into a *numeration* or *lexical array*, an assembled subset of the lexicon

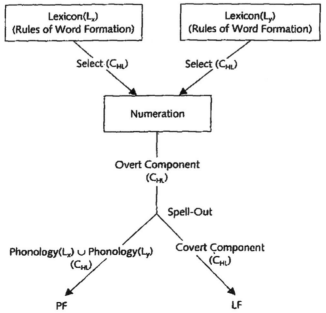

**Figure 1**   Organization of the bilingual language faculty (reproduced from Bhatia & Ritchie, 2004/2006, p. 301 with permission from Blackwell).

as required for a derivation. For CM, the lexicon is drawn from at least two languages; their features are introduced into the lexical array, which must then be checked for convergence in the same way as monolingual features must be checked. (2) <u>Merge</u> takes items from the lexical array and merges them into new, hierarchically arranged syntactic forms or phrases. (3) <u>Move</u> applies to syntactic objects/forms configured by merge to build new structures. Hence, phrase structure trees are built derivationally by the operations <u>merge</u> and <u>move</u>, constrained only by the condition that lexically encoded features match in the course of a derivation.

Movements within the structure are driven by feature checking (case, number, and gender), and may be of two types: A head may undergo *head movement* and adjoin to another head, thus forming a complex head, or a maximal projection may move to the specific position of a maximal projection (XP movement). Both types of movement are motivated by checking morphological features of case, number, person, and gender. Movement may be *overt* or *covert*. Overt movements are driven by strong features and are visible at both PF and LF levels. Covert movements are visible only at LF and are determined by weak features. For more details and examples concerning how feature checking, movement, and merge operate within the MP in relation to CM, see MacSwan (2006, 2009).

At some point in the derivation, generated by the merge and move operations, it is subjected to the operation "spell-out." The spell-out operation extracts from the derivation those elements relevant only to PF; the remaining features are mapped to LF by a subsystem of $C_{HL}$ called the *covert component*. The elements relevant only to PF are mapped to PF by operations which comprise the *phonological component*, another subsystem of $C_{HL}$. The subsystem of $C_{HL}$ which maps the lexicon to spell-out is the *overt component*. Note that the various components (*overt*, *covert*, and *phonological*) are all part of $C_{HL}$ the computational system for human language.

According to MacSwan, the difference between the syntactic and the phonological component of the grammar is particularly important for the grammar of CM. The phonological rules are ordered with respect to each other and vary across languages. Since CM is based on the union of two lexically encoded grammars, variation in rule ordering across languages naturally creates a paradoxical situation and yields no ordering of rules, a requirement that the PF components (i.e., language-pair PF components in CM) are unable to meet. Consequently, CM is not permissible at PF. This requirement is stated in the PF Disjunction Theorem below in (16).

(16)  **PF Disjunction Theorem** (MacSwan, 2006, p. 300)
   (i)   The PF component consists of rules/constraints which must be (partially) ordered/ranked with respect to each other, and these orders vary crosslinguistically.
   (ii)  Code switching [our CM—WCR and TKB] entails the union of at least two (lexically encoded) grammars.
   (iii) Ordering relations are not preserved under union.
   (iv)  Therefore, code switching [CM] within the PF component is not possible.

The PF Disjunction Theorem sets the stage for an "interface condition" for CM, which is further developed in MacSwan (2009) for the purpose of further explaining the prohibition of CM at PF.

As pointed out earlier, a "third grammar" (CM-specific) mechanism such as the one posited under non-lexicalist generative treatments of CM (e.g., FMC, government constraint) is done away with within the lexicalist approach. There is no special mechanism which mediates between the contradictory requirements of the two input linguistic systems. Thus, the new approach is stronger on descriptive as well as on explanatory grounds while offering powerful evaluationary tools.

When CM is blocked due to interlingual incongruency, it is not totally unexpected. However, what is interesting—as we have already observed to some extent in the discussion of constraints such as government and FHC—is that interlingual congruency shows the same pattern in CM, that is, renders an ungrammatical output in some cases. A case in point is the placement of negation in CM utterances in Spanish and Nahuatl which have the same basic word order with respect to negation. Spanish negation does not permit a Nahuatl verb in its complement position, while Nahuatl negation followed by a Spanish verb is well formed. One possible explanation for the differential behavior of negation in CM is that negation is a clitic in Spanish whereas it is a verb in Nahuatl.

Let us examine the reanalysis of some of the classics in the CM literature. Recall Poplack's (1980) restriction on word-internal mixing as exemplified in (17).

(17)    *Juan está eat-iendo
        Juan be/ISs eat-DUR
        "Juan is eating"

CM restrictions, as in (17), can be captured by a generalization that CM is not permissible within a single syntactic head as in (17a).

(17a)    X⁰

                Word

What about the different behavior of CM between a subject pronoun and a verb, and between a lexical DP (i.e., a full noun phrase) and a verb. In the former case, CM is not permissible, while CM is permitted in the latter case. According to van Gelderen and MacSwan (2008), CM is not permitted between a subject pronoun and a verb because pronouns undergo D-to-T movement in order for a subject pronoun to check features with T. The result of this head movement is the formation of a complex head as shown in (18). Whereas nouns do not have an option of head formation, they (lexical DP) check features in [Spec, TP].

(18)        X⁰

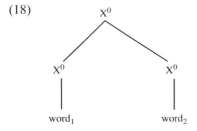

        word₁            word₂

Similarly, in a reanalysis of other classic cases such as "restructuring" verbs (e.g., modal, aspectual, and movement verbs) in CM, MacSwan (2009) shows that restructuring verbs show a different behavior from other verbs. CM is not permissible when it involves restructuring verbs. His analysis shows that restructuring verbs, like pronouns, involve head movement yielding a complex head (18). That explains why they do not permit CM.

Statements such as "A switch may not occur between a bound morpheme and a lexical form, head-internally, or in the cases of complex head" can capture a generalization on descriptive grounds but it falls short on explanatory grounds. Recall the prediction of the PF Disjunction Theorem that CM within the PF component is not possible. Also, recall in Figure 1 the spell-out point, where a derivation is split, with features relevant only to PF are sent directly to PF. CM below $X^0$ is not possible since $X^0$ are inputs to PF. Similarly, head movements generally show affiliation with the phonological component rather than the narrow syntax (Chomsky, 2000, 2001); essentially head movement is a phonological operation aimed at building a complex set of phonological features obtained from both adjoined heads and then subjecting them to the phonological processing of a single word-like unit. In other words, the PF interface condition in these cases can account for restrictions on CM on the grounds of independently motivated principles of the grammatical system. The interface condition on morphophonology and syntax thus is central to grammar itself and, naturally then, to the grammar of language mixing/CM.

### More Recent Developments in Myers-Scotton's Matrix Language Frame Model

As noted above, in recently published work, Myers-Scotton and Jake (2001) and Jake, Myers-Scotton, and Gross (2002) proposed a comprehensive revision of their MLF model. As is true of their earlier work, it merits acknowledgment as an effort to go beyond description to provide a genuine explanation of the phenomena of CM, this time within "a modified minimalist approach."

The revised model argues that MP in its present form is monocentric in nature and the minimalist approach toward CM offered by MacSwan and his colleagues cannot succeed without the incorporation of the MLF. MacSwan (2005a, 2005b) has challenged this claim by identifying significant theoretical problems with the MLF model and has argued persuasively that the model is invalid on both conceptual and empirical grounds. Moreover, the matrix versus embedded language distinction suffers from the same inadequacies as the "third grammar" constraints—that is, it lacks explanatory force.

## IV. SOCIOPSYCHOLOGICAL, LINGUISTIC, AND PRAGMATIC MOTIVATIONS FOR CM/CS

The search for new approaches to CM/CS continues in the new millennium. The challenge that research on the topic has to meet is to separate systematic restrictions on CM/CS that are prompted by grammatical constraints from those that are motivated or triggered by pragmatic factors/competence, such as social and psychological motivations for CM and CS, and then develop a unified and integrated approach. This will in turn provide researchers with a holistic view of the *what*, *how*, and *why* aspects of CM/CS. Though the question of monolingual language use is complex, that of language mixing is even more so (see Ritchie and Bhatia, 2004, pp. 338–340 for a detailed discussion of language choice).

Language mixing is largely prompted by the language user's implicit perceptions of the social/linguistic identities of his/her interlocutors and by the desire to accommodate his/her speech in accordance with these perceptions. Sociopsychological factors such as these motivate language mixing and are critical for developing a holistic view of SLA as well (see Noels & Giles, this volume), and are therefore relevant to the study of both CM/CS and SLA.

The rule of thumb is that CM/CS is triggered by a change in the language user's sociopsychological perception of a situation. This change could be prompted by the presence of an out-group member, by dynamic social relations or perceived identities of interlocutors, or by the deeper creative needs of the speaker (in terms of sociopsychological, stylistic effects) within the sentence or beyond the sentence. The following four factors determine language choice and mixing on the part of bilinguals: (1) the social roles and relationships of the participants; (2) situational factors (discourse topic and language allocation); (3) message-intrinsic considerations; and (4) language attitudes including social dominance and security. These four factors are interrelated in determining the character of a speech event; nonetheless, they do not represent watertight compartments. We will now address each of these factors.

## A. Participants' Roles and Relationships

Participants' roles and the dynamics of their relationships play a crucial role in bilinguals' unconscious agreement or disagreement on language choice. Based on a mutual understanding of the obligations and rights of participants (see Myers-Scotton, 1993, p. 84; 2002, pp. 43–46), agreement leads to language matching as determined by their perceived relationship.

### Dual/Multiple Identities, Social Distancing, and Speech Accommodation

Language matching or mismatching is not a static notion; it is subject to pragmatic conditions and group dynamics. In a mixed group, in-group language matching can lead to the exclusion of another group, so in-group language matching can naturally result in language mismatching from the view of an excluded group. Language mismatching does not necessarily reflect a failure of language negotiation. On the contrary, it may signal an accommodation to circumstances.

Consider now the exchange in (19), in which language mismatching (divergent accommodation) occurs in the middle of an interaction, and conflict resolution (convergent accommodation) takes place afterward. Four young office workers in the same government ministry in Nairobi are chatting. Interestingly, the languages are mismatched in the middle of the interaction. Among the participants, two are Kikuyu speakers, one is a Kisii speaker, and one is a Kalenjin speaker; neither one of the latter two speaks Kikuyu. All four also speak English and Swahili.

(19)   Kikuyu–*Swahili*–English (Myers-Scotton, 1989, p. 338)
       (The conversation up to this point has been in English and Swahili—the expected choices under the circumstances.)

       Kikuyu speaker I:        Andu amwe niméndaga kwaria maundu maria matari na ma namo.
                                "Some people like talking about what they're not sure of."
       Kikuyu speaker II:       Wira wa muigi wa kigina ni kuiga mbeca. No tigucaria mbeca.
                                "The work of the treasurer is only to keep money, not to hunt for money."
       Kisii speaker:           *Ubaya wenu ya kikuyu ni ku-*assume *kila mtu anaelewa kikuyu.*
                                "The bad thing about Kikuyus is assuming that every one understands Kikuyu."
       Kalenjin speaker:        *Si mtumie lugha ambayo kila mtu hapa atasikia? . . .*
                                "Shouldn't we use the language which everyone here understands?"
                                . . . (said with some force). We are supposed to solve this issue.

As noted, Swahili and English have been the unmarked choice up to the switch to Kikuyu. The conversation about setting up a group "emergency fund" has been proceeding, when the two Kikuyus switch to Kikuyu to make a negative comment on what has been said, a marked choice communicating solidarity between the two Kikuyus through convergent accommodation, but distancing them from the others (a case of divergence from the non-Kikuyu speakers). At this point, the Kisii complains in Swahili and English and the Kalenjin makes a switch from Swahili to a sentence entirely in English, a marked choice, to return the discussion to a more business-like plane, and thus conflict resolution (convergence) takes place. The marked choice on the part of two Kikuyus is an in-group language match but, at the same time, constitutes a language mismatch from the point of view of the two non-Kikuyu speakers in the group.

Of course, in those societies in which language identity ranks highest in the range of identities accessible to bilinguals (e.g., among Bengali speakers in South Asia, French speakers, or Japanese speakers), in a diverse group setting, convergent accommodation may not take place, thus diminishing the incidence of language switching.

## B. Situational Factors

In bi-/multilingual societies, languages generally do not duplicate each other's discourse domain. The pie of domains is cut up by the various languages used in such societies into mutually exclusive pieces. Consequently, some languages are viewed as more suited to particular participant/social groups, settings, or topics than others. For instance, very often bilinguals organize their two languages according to their public versus their private world. The public language often serves as the "they" code and the private language as the "we" code. The "they" code can be used to perform a range of functions from creating distance, asserting authority, and expressing objectivity to suppressing the tabooness of an interaction. The "we" code conveys a range from in-group membership, informality, and intimacy to emotions.

Richard Rodriguez (1982) notes that Spanish was the language of his private world. His Spanish voice insisted, "We are family members. Related. Special to one another," whereas English sounded loud, booming with confidence. The day the family decided to use English at home, family intimacy was not the same. In professional domains such as advertising, different languages carve their topical, target audience, and sociopsychological domains.

Social variables such as class, religion, gender, and age determine the pattern of CM/CS in both qualitative and quantitative terms. For example, a Hindi–English bilingual will tend to mix more Perso-Arabic while talking to a Muslim and will pepper their Hindi with Punjabi with a Sikh. (For more example of the role of social variables, see Ritchie and Bhatia (2004, pp. 343–345).)

## C. Message-Internal Factors

Linguistic and pragmatic functions of CM/CS are exemplified below:

### Quotations

Direct quotation or reported speech triggers CM/CS among bilinguals cross-linguistically. This function has been attested by a wide variety of empirical studies. The following examples illustrate this function:

(20)  *Spanish*–English (Gumperz, 1982, p. 76)
      From a conversation between two Chicano professionals. While referring to her baby-sitter, the speaker says the following:
      She doesn't speak English, so, *dice que la reganan: "Si se les va olvidar el idioma a las criaturas."*
      She does not speak English. So, she says they would scold her: "The children are surely going to forget their language."

### Addressee Specification

Another function of mixing or switching is to direct the message to one of several possible addressees. Consider the exchange among four graduate students in Singapore given in (21). The background of the participants is as follows: A is a computer science graduate who has just found a job and a speaker of Teochew, one of the seven mutually unintelligible "dialects" of Chinese spoken in Singapore; B is an accountancy graduate, is looking for a job and speaks Hokkien, another of the Chinese varieties of Singapore; and D is an arts graduate and speaks Teochew and Hokkien. Also present but not included at this point in the conversation is C, an accountancy graduate, who has been working for a week and speaks Cantonese, another of the varieties of Chinese

TABLE I
**Motivations for Code-Mixing/Switching**

| Participants | Situational factors | Sociopsychological factors | Linguistic/pragmatic considerations |
|---|---|---|---|
| Indexical (speaker/ addressee's social class, gender, age, etc.) | Formality, settings, private versus public world, etc. | Dominance, group membership neutrality, speech accommodation | Repetition, clarification, contrast, quotation, paraphrase, message qualification, deep-rooted cultural knowledge, topic–comment, hedging, language trigger |

spoken in Singapore. All four participants speak English in addition to one or more varieties of Chinese. Now observe the following piece of conversation among them.

(21)   English–*Hokkien*–**Teochew** (Tay, 1989, p. 416)
       D to B:   Everyday, you know *kào taim*
                 "Everyday, you know at nine o'clock"
       D to A:   **li' khi a'**
                 "You go."

In the above conversation, D addresses B in Hokkien but speaks to A in Teochew.

### Sentence Particles

Another function of language mixing or switching is to mark the pragmatic force of a sentence. Bilinguals in Singapore are well known to exploit this function by mixing a number of sentence particles such as *la* in (22). Interlocutors A, C, and D are as described for (21) above.

(22)   English–*Hokkien* (Tay, 1989, p. 416)
       D:   Do what?
       A:   System analyst *la*
            "System analyst, what else?"
       C:   *hà*
            "Is that so?"
       A:   Programmer *la*.

Other motivations include reiteration, tags, hedging, message qualification, topic–comment, idiom, and deep-rooted cultural wisdom. The determinants of CM are summarized in Table 1.

## V. CONSTRAINTS ON CM AND SECOND LANGUAGE ACQUISITION

From the discussion in sections III and IV, it is self-evident that (intrasentential) CM is perhaps the single most "colorful" and strategic feature of bilingual linguistic competence. It is the ultimate test of a high degree of bilingual linguistic competence, yet ironically it is the feature despised and stigmatized most by society—particularly by language educators. The following remarks of Poplack best sum up the paradox of bilingual mixing: Instances of intrasentential mixing (i.e., of CM) are "precisely those switch types which have traditionally been considered most deviant by investigators and educators" (Poplack, 1980, p. 615).

CM is constrained by general principles of grammatical competence such as the government constraint, the FHC, and constraints on mixing below $X^0$. Such constraints are interpreted as being subsumed by UG. For instance, Rubin and Toribio (1995) and Toribio (2001) propose that language mixing/CM follows naturally from Chomsky's MP because f-selection dictates independently that functional heads must be matched by the corresponding features of their complements and one such feature to be matched is the feature of language index. The notion of language index, as proposed within the GB framework, needs clarification. MacSwan's objection that language labels are sociopolitical distinctions is certainly valid. For this reason, Toribio (2001, p. 214) points out that her proposed notion of language refers to a language system which may "make reference to a subclass of lexical items" with a set of distinct features. When language labels are viewed in this way, they carry more objectivity, which can address MacSwan's objection.

Because the FHC (or for that matter, any other constraint on CM) is best viewed as a part of UG, the central question is what its role in language acquisition might be. In particular, in view of the centrality of the general question of UG accessibility in adult L2 learners, the question arises whether or not the FHC plays a role in the adult's acquisition of an L2 and of the ability to judge the grammaticality of utterances that involve CM between his or her two languages. If the answer to this question turns out to be positive, this would then constitute a test of the accessibility of UG to adult second language learners, since CM/CS is not part of L2 instruction for adults and, in fact, is generally condemned in the formal language learning situation as well as the social environment in which adult L2 learning takes place.

Below, we explore this central question with special reference to the FHC. Reasons for the choice of this constraint are as follow: (1) despite some objections to the efficacy of the FHC, it represents the most widely attested constraint crosslinguistically and it is operative both in monolinguals (in the form of f-selection) and in bilinguals; (2) research on bilingual children's early language development reveals that the development of functional categories plays a critical role in the development of grammatical constraints on CM (e.g., see Koppe & Meisel, 1995; Meisel, 1994 hypothesis concerning the emergence of functional categories) which in turn explains the distinct nature of children's early (unsystematic) language mixing and later adult-like language mixing. In other words, as Toribio (2001, p. 217) maintains, "as soon as the feature specifications referenced by FHC are in place in children, the systematic CM grammar begins to emerge"; and (3) empirical research on the acquisition of FHC have been carried out in SLA.

Toribio and Rubin (1996) set out to explore the question of UG accessibility by way of testing the following two competing hypotheses:

1. *The null hypothesis*—If the FHC is not accessible to adult L2 learners, their CM and CS behavior will be random with respect to the operation of the FHC.

2. *The FHC availability hypothesis*—If the FHC is available to adult learners as a part of UG, learners' verbal behavior will be parallel to that of balanced bilinguals.

Using a methodology similar to that employed extensively by Lust and others in the study of L1 acquisition, Toribio, Lantolf, Roebuck, and Perrone (1993) asked beginning, intermediate, and advanced learners of Spanish to imitate Spanish–English code-mixed utterances that were both "legal" and "illegal" with respect to the FHC. Analysis of the results obtained from this elicited imitation task revealed that the beginning students showed a wide range of random processing errors, leading to the conclusion that they had general difficulty with the task. Intermediate learners could repeat well-formed as well as ill-formed sentences with great fluency, indicating they had not yet acquired the tacit linguistic knowledge to differentiate the sentences that were well formed with respect to the FHC from those that were not. The advanced students either showed symptoms of disfluency in producing the token sentences or "corrected" them in their repetitions when the sentence violated the FHC and repeated it without change when it obeyed the FHC. These findings lead Toribio et al. (1993) to suggest that the beginning and intermediate adult learners had not acquired the necessary aspects of the system of the L2 to allow them to separate the ungrammatical code-mixed sentences from the grammatical ones. According to their analysis of the data, the beginning and intermediate students reinterpreted the Spanish segment of the sentence into their L1, English, and therefore judged their grammaticality in terms of English. Their failure to distinguish between grammatical and ungrammatical code-mixed utterances on independent grounds (i.e., a system of knowledge distinct from the L1, e.g, UG) points to the fact that these subjects did not show the effects of UG. However, the advanced subjects showed the emergence/operation of a universal principle, the FHC, to some degree.

These findings were supported in a study carried out by Bhatia and Ritchie (1996, 1998) in which intermediate and advanced adult English-speaking learners of Hindi judged code-mixed sentences that violated the dependency. The findings revealed that the intermediate students accepted ungrammatical sentences containing CM while that was not the case with learners with advanced bilingual competence. The advanced learners mirrored responses of competent Hindi–English bilinguals whose behavior obeys the FHC.

On the basis of the research findings of Toribio and Rubin (1996) and Bhatia and Ritchie (1996, 1998), we have proposed (1996) the following stages that bilinguals go through in the process of acquiring the mixed linguistic system:

1. *Stage I*: During this stage, the process of borrowing takes place but the borrowed as well as the native lexicon is treated as though they were stored in a single lexicon.
2. *Stage II*: The two lexicons are separate and firmly grounded and the process of translation or reinterpretation from the L1 becomes a part of language processing.
3. *Stage III*: The third stage can be characterized as the period of duality. The functional domains of the two participating linguistic systems begin to separate.

The process of domain allocation goes hand in hand with the process of reinterpretation and translation, which is complex and bidirectional in nature.
4. *Stage IV*: Emergence/operation of UG constraints—general principles such as the FHC or $X^0$ heads take effect.

We claimed then that bilingual children and adult learners will pass through these stages with some degree of uniformity. The Spanish–English and our Hindi–English language development data lend support to the stages posited above. The evidence of these stages can also be found in the language development of a bilingual child. The stages are in accord with Meisel's (1994) "grammatical deficiency" hypothesis and the unsystematic nature of language mixing in incipient bilingualism.

In a follow-up study, Toribio (2001) aimed at testing the correlation between language proficiency and the acquisition of the FHC with 104 bilinguals distributed over the three levels of proficiency—beginner ($N = 44$), intermediate ($N = 26$), and advanced ($N = 34$)—English-speaking learners of Spanish as a second language further provided strong experimental support to the FHC for CM and its correlation with varying language proficiency which in turn attests the stages identified in order for the FHC to become operative in adult second language learners. The methodology employed in this study included seeking appropriateness and acceptability judgments on the part of the learners. The beginners employed strategies such as the type of translation associated with Stage II. Intermediate learners' responses were somewhat similar to both the beginner and advanced, though statistically indistinguishable from the former. In short, their mastery of the FHC was still not fully realized.

Advanced learners' reports on task performance were found to be most candid both in terms of the operation of the FHC and conscious awareness of the negative social evaluation of CM. What is interesting is that the findings of these empirical studies lead to the same conclusion that adults have access to UG despite learning language in an environment in which they do not receive any evidence—either positive or negative evidence. Although teaching methodologies attempt to suppress the acquisition and use of mixed systems in view of the negative social evaluation of mixed speech, the systemic knowledge of the underlying principles of CM emerges. Furthermore, the stages identified are also attested to a large degree.

## VI. PROBLEMS

In this section, we will briefly review the issues and problems that the CM/CS research has encountered in the past three decades. Some of the problems can be attributed to the theoretical assumptions and analytical frameworks, the methodological procedures, and the level at which researchers attempt to seek explanations of CM/CS phenomena. These problems have affected the research findings on one hand and the direction of research on the other.

### A. Theoretical and Analytical Problems

As the discussion in section III demonstrates, with the change in researchers' conception of bilingual verbal behavior came some significant changes in our understanding of the grammar of CM. It is clear that CM involves the integration and the interdependence of a language pair; however, there is little consensus among researchers concerning the level at which such integration takes place either implicitly or explicitly. Most of the studies have assumed, at least for quite some time, that such an integration takes place at the level of the sentence and phrase, and not at the level of lower constituents, particularly inflections. That is the reason that models of CM still shy away from the question of morphological mixing. For a long time, mixing at the morphological level in particular was seen as "random" (Valdés-Fallis, 1978, p. 16). The interface of levels (semantic, syntactic, morphological, and phonological or phonetic) still awaits research on CM, although important progress has been made in the works carried on within the MP—particularly in MacSwan's work. The nagging problem of language indices and constraints on CS is close to being resolved.

We pointed out in section II the lack of consensus concerning the distinction between borrowing and CM. Related to that issue is the question of the matrix language of CM/CS discourse. Finally, as MacSwan rightly points out, recent developments in the field of CM/CS have permitted us to go beyond traditional battles and work toward the common goal of proposing "increasingly better theories about the nature of the bilingual language faculty as a reflection of the facts of CS [CM], informing the field of bilingualism as well as general theory."

## B. Methodological Problems

Of course, CM/CS research is not free from methodological issues or shortcomings. One such issue is where to draw a line between performance- and competence-based data. According to Beardsmore (1991, p. 44), the whole issue of bilingualism is a performance question, thus implying the irrelevance of the strict dichotomy between competence and performance. For others, though, the issue cannot be settled easily even at the level of borrowing and CM/CS (Poplack & Sankoff, 1988). Some researchers (notably, Bokamba, 1988) go so far as to propose that the attempt to discover such constraints be abandoned. Bokamba and others (Myers-Scotton, 1989; Pakir, 1989; Tay, 1989) argue that the distinction between intersentential and intrasentential code alternation and attempts at capturing formal constraints on CM are of considerably less consequence than functional—that is, social and pragmatic— constraints. Therefore, a new functional approach is more suited to the phenomenon of CM/CS.

In our view, there are a number of reasons why the search for universal principles of CM has not met with the success that it might have. First, mixed speech data fails to take into account the semantic equivalence criterion. An otherwise monolingual sentence is subjected to the substitution of a lexical item from a second language and the mixed sentence thus achieved is subjected to grammaticality judgments without giving any serious thought to the semantics of the mixed output. For the discussion of such cases, see section V of Bhatia and Ritchie (1996). In addition, as MacSwan points out, "researchers have given too little attention to the specific phonological, morphological, and syntactic characteristics of the examples cited to determine whether they are in fact violations" of constraints posited in the literature.

In short, theoretical, analytical, and methodological problems of the type discussed above have blurred our previous attempts to arrive at universals of language mixing.

## VII. CONCLUSION

CM/CS reflects a natural and universal aspect of bilingual verbal behavior. Jakobson claims that bilingualism poses a special challenge to linguistic theory. This claim is particularly true of CM/CS. Although remarkable progress has been registered in our understanding of language CM/CS over the past three decades, many challenges still need to be met. The long history of prescriptivism and foreign language teaching have resulted in the severe negative societal evaluation of this speech form, which, ironically, can contribute to the unlocking of new dimensions of human linguistic creativity; therefore, its value to an understanding of the human language capacity can hardly be underestimated. Furthermore, a phenomenon that was and in some circles still is seen as ad hoc, random, and inconsequential to language use seems to have a natural role in Chomsky's MP. Language matching is similar to Chomsky's CASE/feature checking, which is central to studies of language contact in general and language mixing in particular.

## REFERENCES

Abney, S.P. (1987). The English noun phrase in its sentential aspect. Unpublished doctoral dissertation, MIT, Cambridge, MA.

Annamalai, E. (1978). The anglicized Indian languages: A case of code-mixing. *International Journal of Dravidian Linguistics, 7*, 239–247.

Bavin, E., & Shopen, T. (1985). Warlpiri and English: Languages in contact. In M. Clyne (Ed.), *Australia, meeting place of languages* (pp. 81–94). Canberra: Department of Linguistics, Australian National University.

Beardsmore, H. B. (1991). *Bilingualism: Basic principles* (2nd ed.). Philadelphia, PA: Multilingual Matters.

Belazi, H. M., Rubin, E. J., & Toribio, A. J. (1994). Code switching and X-bar theory: The functional head constraint. *Linguistic Inquiry, 25*, 221–237.

Bentahila, A., & Davies, B. B. (1983). The syntax of Arabic-French code-switching. *Lingua, 59*, 301–330.

Berk-Seligson, S. (1986). Linguistic constraints on intersentential code-switching: A study of Spanish-Hebrew bilingualism. *Language in Society, 15*, 313–348.

Bhatia, T., & Ritchie, W. (2001). Language mixing, typology, and second language acquisition. In P. Bhaskararao & K. Subbarao (Eds.), *The Yearbook of South Asian Languages and Linguistics 2001: Tokyo Symposium on South Asian Languages: Contact, Convergence and Typology* (pp. 37–62). London/Delhi: Sage.

Bhatia, T. K. (1989). Bilingual's creativity and syntactic theory: Evidence for emerging grammar. *World Englishes, 9*(3), 265–276.

Bhatia, T. K. (2006). World Englishes in global advertising. In B. B. Kachru, Y. Kachru, & C. Nelson (Eds.), *Handbook of world Englishes* (pp. 601–619). Oxford: Blackwell Publishing.

Bhatia, T. K., & Ritchie, W. C. (1996). Bilingual language mixing, universal grammar, and second language acquisition. In W. C. Ritchie & T. K. Bhatia (Eds.), *The handbook of second language acquisition* (pp. 627–688). New York: Academic Press.

Bhatia, T. K., & Ritchie, W. C. (1998). Code switching, grammar, and sentence production: The problem of light verbs. In E. Klein & G. Martohardjono (Eds.), *The development of second language grammars: A generative approach* (pp. 273–291). Amsterdam: John Benjamins.

Bhatia, T. K., & Ritchie, W. C. (Eds.). (2004/2006). *Handbook of bilingualism*. Oxford: Blackwell Publishing.

Boeschoten, H. E., & Verhoeven, L. (1985). Integration niederlandischer lexicalischer elemente ins Turkische: Sprachmischung bei immigranten der ersten und zweiten generation. *Linguistische Berichte*, *98*, 347–364.

Bokamba, E. (1988). Code-mixing, language variation and linguistic theory: Evidence from Bantu languages. *Lingua*, *76*, 21–62.

Bullock, B. E., & Toribio, A. J. (in press). Trying to hit a moving target: On the sociophonetics of code-switching. In L. Isurin, D. Winford, & K. de Bot (Eds.), *Multidisciplinary approaches to code switching* (pp. 189–206). Amsterdam: John Benjamins Publishing.

Canfield, K. (1980). A note on Navajo-English code-mixing. *Anthropological Linguistics*, *22*, 218–220.

Chomsky, N. (1963). Formal properties of grammars. In R. D. Luce, R. R. Bush, & E. Galanter (Eds.), *Handbook of mathematical psychology* (pp. 323–418). New York: Wiley.

Chomsky, N. (1986). *Knowledge of language*. New York: Praeger.

Chomsky, N. (1995). *The minimalist program*. Cambridge, MA: MIT Press.

Chomsky, N. (2000). Minimalist inquiries: The framework. In R. Martin, D. Michaels, & J. Uriagereka (Eds.), *Step by step: Essays on minimalist syntax in honor of Howard Lasnik* (pp. 89–155). Cambridge, MA: MIT Press.

Chomsky, N. (2001). Derivation by phase. In M. Kenstowicz (Ed.), *Ken Hale: A life in language* (pp. 1–52). Cambridge, MA: MIT Press.

Chomsky, N. (2005). Three factors in language design. *Linguistic Inquiry*, *36*, 1–22.

Di Sciullo, A., Muysken, P., & Singh, R. (1986). Government and code-mixing. *Journal of Linguistics*, *22*, 1–24.

Dussias, P. E. (1997). *Switching at no cost: Exploring Spanish-English code switching using the response-contingent sentence matching task*. Ph.D. dissertation, University of Arizona.

Edwards, J. (2004). Foundations of bilingualism. In T. K. Bhatia & W. C. Ritchie (Eds.), *The handbook of bilingualism* (pp. 7–31). Oxford, UK: Blackwell.

Elias-Olivarés, L. (1976). *Ways of speaking in a Chicano community. A sociolinguistic approach*. Unpublished doctoral dissertation, University of Texas, Austin, TX.

El-Noory, A. (1925, March 21–23). *Code-switching and the search for universals: A study of (Egyptian) Arabic/English bilingualism*. Paper presented at the 16th annual Conference on African Linguistics, Yale University, New Haven, CT.

Gumperz, J. J. (1977). The sociolinguistic significance of conversational code-switching. *RELC Journal*, *8*, 1–34.

Gumperz, J. J. (1982). Conversational code-switching. In J. J. Gumperz (Ed.), *Discourse strategies* (pp. 233–274). Cambridge, UK: Cambridge University Press.

Gumperz, J. J., & Hernandez-Chavez, B. (1975). Cognitive aspects of bilingual communication. In E. Hernandez-Chavez, A. Cohen, & R. L. Whitehead (Eds.), *El Lenguaje de los Chicanos* (pp. 154–164). Arlington, VA: Center for Applied Linguistics.

Hakuta, K. (1986). *Mirror of language: The debate on bilingualism*. New York: Basic Books.

Ijalba, E., Obler, L. K., & Chengappa, S. (2004). Bilingual aphasia. In T. K. Bhatia & W. C. Ritchie (Eds.), *The handbook of bilingualism* (pp. 71–89). Oxford, UK: Blackwell.

Jake, J. L., Myers-Scotton, C. M., & Gross, S. (2002). Making a minimalist approach to code switching work: Adding the matrix language. *Bilingualism: Language and Cognition, 5*, 69–91.

Jake, J. L., Myers-Scotton, C. M., & Gross, S. (2005). A response to MacSwan (2005): Keeping the matrix language. *Bilingualism: Language and cognition, 8*, 271–276.

Jones, S., & Bradwell, P. (2007). *As you like it: Catching up in an age of global English* London: Demos Institute. http://www.demos.co.uk/files/

Joshi, A. (1985). Processing of sentences with intrasentential code switching. In D. Dowty, L. Kartunnen, & A. M. Zwicky (Eds.), *Natural language parsing: Psychological, computational and theoretical perspectives* (pp. 190–205). Cambridge, UK: Cambridge University Press.

Kachru, B. B. (1978). Toward structuring code-mixing: An Indian perspective. *International Journal of the Sociology of Language, 16*, 28–46.

Kamwangamalu, N. M., & Lee, C. L. (1991). Mixers and mixing English across cultures. *World Englishes, 10*, 247–261.

Klavans, J. L. (1985). The syntax of code-switching: Spanish and English. In L. D. King & C. A. Maley (Eds.), *Selected Papers from the XIIIth Linguistic Symposium on Romance Languages* (pp. 213–231). Amsterdam: John Benjamins, .

Koppe, R., & Meisel, J. (1995). Code-switching in bilingual first language acquisition. In L. Milroy & P. Muysken (Eds.), *One speaker, two languages* (pp. 276–301). Cambridge: Cambridge University Press.

Kroll, J., & Dussias, P. (2004). The comprehension of words and sentences in two languages. In T. K. Bhatia & W. C. Ritchie (Eds.), *Handbook of bilingualism* (pp. 169–200). Oxford, UK: Blackwell.

Labov, W. (1971). The notion of "system" in creole languages. In D. Hymes (Ed.), *Pidginization and creolization of languages* (pp. 447–472). Cambridge, UK: Cambridge University Press.

Lance, D. (1975). Spanish-English code-switching. In E. Hernández-Chavez, A. U. Cohen, & A. F. Beltramo (Eds.), *El lenguaje de los Chicanos: Regional and social characteristics used by Mexican Americans* (pp. 138–153). Arlington, VA: Center for Applied Linguistics.

MacSwan, J. (1999). *A minimalist approach to intrasentential code switching*. New York: Garland Press.

MacSwan, J. (2005a). Code-switching and generative grammar: A critique of the MLF model and some remarks on "modified minimalism". *Bilingualism: Language and Cognition, 8*, 1–22.

MacSwan, J. (2005b). Remarks on Jake, Myers-Scotton and Gross's response: There is no "matrix language". *Bilingualism: Language and Cognition, 8*, 277–284.

MacSwan, J. (2006). Code switching and grammatical theory. In T. K. Bhatia & W. C. Ritchie (Eds.), *The handbook of bilingualism* (pp. 283–311). Oxford, UK: Blackwell.

MacSwan, J. (2009). Generative approaches to codeswitching. In B. Bullock & A. J. Toribio (Eds.), *The Cambridge handbook of linguistic code-switching* (pp. 336–357). Cambridge: Cambridge University Press.

Mahootian, S., & Santorini, B. (1996). Code-switching and the complement/adjunct distinction. *Linguistic Inquiry, 27*, 464–479.

Meisel, J. (1994). Code-switching in young bilingual children: The acquisition of grammatical constraints. *Studies in Second Language Acquisition, 16*, 413–439.

Molony, C. H. (1977). Recent relexification processes in Philippine Creole Spanish. In B. G. Blount & M. Sanches (Eds.), *Sociocultural dimensions of language change* (pp. 131–159). New York: Academic Press.

Myers-Scotton, C. M. (1988). Code-switching and types of multilingual communities. In R. Lowenberg (Ed.), *Language spread and language policy* (pp. 61–82). Washington, DC: Georgetown University Press.

Myers-Scotton, C. M. (1989). Code-switching with English: Types of switching, types of communities. In T. K. Bhatia & W. C. Ritchie (Eds.), *Code-mixing: English across languages* (pp. 333–346). New York: Pergamon Press.

Myers-Scotton, C. M. (1993). *Social motivations for code-switching: Evidence from Africa.* Oxford: Clarendon Press.

Myers-Scotton, C. M. (2002). *Contact linguistics: Bilingual encounters and grammatical outcomes.* Oxford: Oxford University Press.

Myers-Scotton, C., & Jake, J. L. (2001). Explaining aspects of code-switching and their implications. In J. Nicol (Ed.), *One mind two languages: Bilingual language processing* (pp. 84–116). Oxford: Blackwell.

Nishimura, M. (1986). Intrasentential code-switching: The case of language assignment. In J. Vaid (Ed.), *Language processing in bilinguals: Psycholinguistic and neuropsychological perspective* (pp. 123–143). Hillsdale, NJ: Erlbaum.

Nishimura, M. (1997). *Japanese/English code-switching: Syntax and pragmatics.* New York: Peter Lang.

Pakir, A. (1989). Linguistic alternants and code selection in Baba Malay. In T. K. Bhatia & W. C. Ritchie (Eds.), *Code-mixing: English across languages* (pp. 379–388). New York: Pergamon Press.

Pfaff, C. (1976). Functional and structural constraints on syntactic variation in code-switching. In S. B. Steever, C. A. Walker, & S. S. Mufwene (Eds.), *Papers from the parasession on diachronic syntax* (pp. 248–259). Chicago, IL: Chicago Linguistics Society.

Pfaff, C. (1979). Constraints on language mixing: Intrasentential code-switching and borrowing in Spanish/English. *Language, 55,* 291–318.

Poplack, S. (1980). Sometimes I'll start a sentence in Spanish and termino en Espanol: Toward a typology of code-switching. In J. Amestae & L. Elias-Olivares (Eds.), *Spanish in the United States: Sociolinguistic aspects* (pp. 230–263). Cambridge, UK: Cambridge University Press.

Poplack, S., & Sankoff, E. (1988). Code-switching. In U. Ammon, N. Dittmar, & K. J. Mattheier (Eds.), *Sociolinguistics: An international handbook of language and society* (pp. 1174–1180). Berlin: de Gruyter.

Poplack, S., Wheeler, S., & Westwood, A. (1989). Distinguishing language contact phenomena: Evidence from Finnish–English bilingualism. In T. K. Bhatia & W. C. Ritchie (Eds.), *Code-mixing: English across languages* (pp. 389–406). New York: Pergamon.

Ritchie, W. C., & Bhatia, T. K. (2004). Social and psychological factors in language mixing. In T. K. Bhatia & W. C. Ritchie (Eds.), *Handbook of bilingualism* (pp. 336–352). Oxford: Blackwell Publishing.

Ritchie, W. C., & Bhatia, T. K. (2008). Psycholinguistics. In B. Spolsky & F. M. Hult (Eds.), *The handbook of educational linguistics* (pp. 336–352). Oxford, UK: Blackwell Publishing.

Rodriguez, R. (1982). *Hunger of memory.* New York: Bantam Books.

Romaine, S. (1989). *Bilingualism.* Oxford, UK: Basil Blackwell.

Rubin, B. L., & Toribio, A. J. (1995). Feature checking and the syntax of language contact. In S. Amastae, G. Goodall, M. Montalbetti, & M. Phinney (Eds.), *Contemporary research in Romance linguistics* (pp. 177–185). Amsterdam: John Benjamins.

Sankoff, D., & Poplack, S. (1981). A formal grammar of code-switching. *Papers in Linguistics: An International Journal of Human Communication, 14,* 3–46.

Singh, R. (1981). Grammatical constraints on code-switching. *Recherches linguistics Montreal, 17,* 155–163.

Sobin, N. (1976). Texas Spanish and lexical borrowing. *Papers in Linguistics, 9,* 15–47.

Stanlaw, S. (1982). English in Japanese communicative strategies. In B. B. Kachru (Ed.), *The other tongue: English across cultures* (pp. 168–197). Urbana, IL: University of Illinois Press.

Tay, M. W. J. (1989). Code switching and code mixing as a communicative strategy multilingual discourse. In T. K. Bhatia & W. C. Ritchie (Eds.), *Code mixing: English across languages* (pp. 407–417). New York: Pergamon Press.

Toribio, A. J. (2001). On the emergence of bilingual code-switching competence. *Bilingualism: Language and Cognition, 4,* 203–231.

Toribio, A. J., Lantolf, J., Roebuck, R, & Perrone, A. (1993). Syntactic constraints on code-switching: Evidence of abstract knowledge in second language acquisition. Unpublished manuscript, Cornell University, Ithaca, NY.

Toribio, A. J., & Rubin, E. (1996). Code-switching in generative grammar. In J. Jensen & A. Roca (Eds.), *Spanish in contact* (pp. 203–226). Somerville, MA: Cascadilla.

Treffers-Daller, J. (1991). French–Dutch language mixture in Brussels. Unpublished doctoral dissertation, University of Amsterdam, Amsterdam.

Valdés-Fallis, G. (1978). *Code switching and the classroom teacher, language in education: Theory and practice* (Vol. 4), Arlington, VA: Center for Applied Linguistics.

van Gelderen, E., & MacSwan, J. (2008). Interface conditions and code switching: Pronouns, lexical DPs, and checking theory. *Lingua, 118,* 765–776.

Woolford, E. (1983). Bilingual code-switching and syntactic theory. *Linguistic Inquiry, 14,* 520–536.

CHAPTER 26

# INDIVIDUAL DIFFERENCES IN SECOND LANGUAGE ACQUISITION

Jean-Marc Dewaele

## I. INTRODUCTION

Human beings are both similar and unique. They belong to the same species, which means they share the same anatomy, and yet they vary enormously within certain parameters. While many individual differences (IDs) are highly visible, others can only be inferred through systematic observation of behavior. One common observation is that some people seem to be better at learning and using second languages than others. The intriguing question is *why*? Traditional ID researchers tried to pin down internal characteristics of a person as the cause of the observed differences. A more dynamic perspective is emerging that acknowledges the complexity of second language acquisition (SLA). Internal characteristics may play a role, but only in interaction with the context. People are never in the same context from the start and their previous histories shape their future trajectories. The aim of this chapter is to provide an overview of the emerging answers to that single question from different strands of research into IDs in SLA. The epistemological and methodological diversity in IDs research in SLA has too often been described in terms of opposition and conflict (nature vs. nurture, quantitative vs. qualitative, etic vs. emic). The latest trends in IDs research indicate a growing consensus about the situated and dynamic nature of SLA.

Brains, like fingerprints, are unique. The reasons for this uniqueness are both genetic and epigenetic (Schumann, 2004). However, contrary to fingerprints, brains keep changing and adapting through a lifetime. This plasticity means that within anatomic, physiological, and genetic limits, skills and behavior can change. It also means that a person's actions affect the shape and the connections in that person's brain. A striking illustration of this phenomenon was provided by Maguire, Woollett, and Spiers (2006). The researchers discovered that black-cab drivers in London have a greater gray matter volume in the posterior hippocampus (i.e., the store for spatial memories) compared to control subjects, and the longer they had been on the job, the larger the gray matter volume. This difference is attributed to constant use and updating of spatial representations. The changes to the brain of second language (L2) learners may be less spectacular, but they seem real nonetheless. Mechelli et al. (2004) found increased gray matter density in the left inferior parietal region of the brain of bilinguals compared to monolingual controls. This particular region has been shown by functional imaging to become activated during verbal-fluency tasks.

To recapitulate, it thus seems that the brains of individuals starting to learn an L2 are different from each other, that the learning process will cause a physical change to the brains, and that IDs in the neural substrate may be responsible for IDs in the rate of development of the L2, in levels of fluency in the first language (L1) and the L2 and, finally, in ultimate linguistic attainment.

## II. ON VARIANCE AND INVARIANCE

Feldman Barrett recently defined the goal of human psychology as the discovery of "the scientifically viable constructs or categories that will characterize what is variant and invariant in the working of the human mind" (2006, p. 35). One could rephrase this definition for the investigation of language acquisition, that is, the search for scientifically viable constructs or categories that will characterize what is variant and invariant in the acquisition and use of language. Linguists in the Chomskyan tradition may favor what is invariant in language (i.e., common to all human minds), while sociolinguists typically focus on what is variant (i.e., "human minds reliably differ from one another, and how a mind functions differently in different situations" Feldman Barrett, 2006, p. 36; see also Preston and Bayley, this volume). SLA researchers who are typically also foreign language teachers will know from experience that equal exposure to a foreign language will not result in equal levels of competence in the L2. They may therefore be more interested in the causes of this variation in order to manipulate them and stimulate the development of the foreign language.

The present chapter will propose a short overview of IDs research in SLA in its widest sense. The first part will discuss some general issues and concerns in the field. The second part will present factors that have been linked to IDs in SLA. The factors have been grouped according to their status as "learner-internal," that is, intrinsic abilities and personality dimensions, a combination of learner internal and learner external factors, and purely "learner-external" factors. Given the constraints of space, some typical IDs variables such as learning styles and learning strategies have been left out.

## III. INDIVIDUAL DIFFERENCES RESEARCH IN SLA: THE QUEST FOR THE HOLY GRAIL?

Psychologists working in the field of IDs refer to personality dimensions shared by all people, but where every individual occupies a specific position on a dimension. This biological source of IDs interacts with social factors resulting in specific behavior for every individual. The idea that particular behaviors, dictated by underlying personality dimensions, are more conducive to the learning of foreign languages seems intuitively appealing. Indeed, it is easy to imagine the model foreign language learner: a good communicator with an excellent memory, eager and motivated, talkative and studious, creative and courageous, inclined both to take risks and to be cautious. Yet, many applied linguists who have set out to identify the sources of IDs in SLA have come back from a long journey with relatively little to show. There are many reasons why this quest for the sources of IDs in SLA has turned into a kind of search for the Grail. Researchers, like Arthur's knights, stumbling through the night, guided by a stubborn belief that something must be there, glimpsing tantalizing flashes of light from a distance, only to discover that their discoveries looked rather pale in the daylight. Part of the difficulty of investigating IDs in SLA is that the topic is highly interdisciplinary and requires a considerable amount of theoretical knowledge and methodological skill: a thorough understanding of the independent variables is necessary (personality and educational psychology, social psychology), as well as a good grasp of the dependent variables (applied linguistics, educational psychology, sociolinguistics, psycholinguistics).

So far, nobody has yet come up with the Grand Unified Theory of Individual Differences. One possible reason for this is that IDs are still conceptualized as largely learner-internal and that there cannot be one unified theory of something one-sided. As Pavlenko pointed out (personal communication), we are not even sure we will ever have a unified theory of Factors Mediating Second Language Learning Outcomes.

## IV. FACTORS THAT HAVE BEEN LINKED TO IDS IN SLA

### A. Learner-Internal Factors: Ability

#### Language Learning Aptitude

Gardner (2006) writes about "ability" (both intelligence and language aptitude) as one of the two primary ID variables involved in language learning (the other one being motivation). Gardner predicts that learners with higher levels of ability will be more successful language learners (2006, p. 241). For neurobiologists, variation in abilities and aptitudes are caused by differences in physical and chemical structures of the brain (Schumann, 2004, p. 9). However, the hypothesis has not yet been empirically demonstrated. The definition of the concept of language aptitude and its link with intelligence has evolved over the years. Skehan (1989) defined language-learning aptitude as a "talent for learning languages that is independent of intelligence" (p. 276). Dörnyei and Skehan (2003) revised Skehan's earlier definition of language-learning aptitude dropping the link with intelligence and inserting a reference to IDs: language-learning aptitude is a "specific talent for learning [...] languages which exhibits considerable variation between learners" (p. 590). In a recent paper, Dörnyei (2006) wondered whether such a thing as "language aptitude" actually exists, and whether it is just a number of cognitive factors making up a composite measure that can be referred to as the learner's overall capacity to master a foreign language (p. 46). This description comes quite close to Gardner's general term of "ability."

One hotly debated issue in this research area is the possible link between L1 learning aptitude and L2 learning aptitude. Skehan (1989) found a significant positive correlation between the rate of L1 acquisition in young children and their performance in L2 acquisition at age 13. Skehan (1989) argues that this is evidence of an innate aptitude for languages. Could this capacity to learn an L2 be related to an individual's L1 learning skills, and could the L2 learning difficulties be linked in part to L1 difficulties? This is the hypothesis put forward by Sparks and Ganschow (1991, 2001) and Sparks, Javorsky, Patton, and Ganschow (1998). An individual's language aptitude would be linked to a single factor, namely "linguistic coding" which refers to L1 literacy skills. These abilities would be fundamental for learning an L2, and an insufficient level of development in linguistic coding skills would limit the ultimate attainment in the L2. In a recent study, Dewaele (2007a) found that language grades obtained by high school students for the first language were highly correlated with their grades in the second, third, and fourth languages. These higher scores in language classes could be linked to cognitive or social factors, or a combination of both. In the former perspective one could argue that some participants had higher levels of verbal intelligence, in the latter perspective one could argue that the higher scores were the consequence of a rich literacy home environment.

Miyake and Friedman (1998) have suggested that capacity in working memory (WM) is the central component of language aptitude. They point to the literature showing a link between IDs in L1 WM capacity, and both L2 WM capacity and L2 language comprehension skills. A higher WM capacity was also found to stimulate L2 acquisition. Their own empirical study with native speakers of Japanese who were advanced learners of English showed that a higher WM capacity is linked to the acquisition of appropriate linguistic cues and better comprehension of complex sentence structures in the L2 (1998, p. 361). The role of attention and attentional capacity in the development of the L2 has been the object of intense research (Robinson, 2003). Robinson defined language aptitude as the sum of lower-level abilities (aptitude complexes), which can be grouped into higher-order cognitive abilities (e.g., noticing the gap) and stimulate SLA in various learning contexts (see also the chapters by Gor and Long, and by Pica in this edition).

Sternberg (2002) agrees that memory and analytic abilities play an important role in SLA, but only in combination with creative and practical abilities, constituting "successful intelligence." Success depends on the match between instructional conditions and pattern of abilities. In other words, "when students are taught in a way that fits how they think, they do better at school" (2002, p. 34).

Other abilities may play a role in SLA. Musical ability has been found to predict accuracy in perception and production of L2 sounds (Slevc & Miyake, 2006).

## B. Learner-Internal Factors: Personality Traits

### Extraversion–Introversion

This dimension, described by Eysenck (1967), is the first one of the "Giant 3". It has been described as "a truly psychological concept, slotting in between phenomena at the biological and social levels and providing an explanatory link between them" (Wilson, 1977, p. 213). Eysenck (1967) suggested that variation on this dimension is biologically based: extraverts are underaroused, introverts overaroused. As people operate ideally with a moderate level of cortical arousal, extraverts compensate for their suboptimal arousal levels by tending toward activities that involve greater sensory stimulation. Because introverts have higher baseline levels (tonic) of cortical arousal as well as more reactivity (phasic) to individual stimuli than extraverts, they do not need this external stimulation and will thus rather try to avoid overarousing situations. Introverts reach their tolerance levels much faster when exposed to strong stimuli. The extraverts' low autonomic arousability and the insensitivity to punishment signals make them more stress-resistant.

Psychological studies have consistently showed that extraverts are superior to introverts in short-term memory (STM) and WM (Lieberman, 2000). The causes for the reported differences in STM capacity/efficiency between introverts and extraverts are of a neurochemical nature. Introverts have higher levels of the neurotransmitter dopamine (the neurochemical precursor for norepinephrine). Stress releases extra dopamine, which might push them over the very narrow range of optimal innervation in the dorsolateral prefrontal cortex and impair performance. Lieberman and Rosenthal (2001) argue that both dopamine and norepinephrine affect the functioning of the prefrontal cortex following an inverted U-pattern: "too little or too much of either norepinephrine or dopamine disrupts attentional and working memory processes" (Lieberman & Rosenthal, 2001).

Applied linguists and educationalists have focused their attention on the possible effect of extraversion on success in L2 learning, the expectation being that the more talkative extraverted learners would have a natural advantage in the acquisition of the foreign language compared to their more introverted peers. However, studies where extraversion scores were correlated with language test scores revealed inconsistent results. In their overview of applied linguistic research that had included extraversion as an independent variable, Dewaele and Furnham (1999) concluded that the results "varied in how the personality trait was measured (i.e., self-report vs. others' ratings), the language that was being learnt, the nationality of the learners but most importantly which language variables were measured and how" (p. 523).

One striking finding was that researchers who had investigated the link between extraversion scores and measures based on written language found little or no significant correlations. The most influential study in this area was Naiman, Fröhlich, Stern, and Todesco (1978). The authors had hypothesized that extraversion might be a characteristic of the "good language learner." They collected written data from Canadian high school students learning French as L2. Contrary to their expectations they failed to find a correlation between extraversion and test scores, and questioned the construct validity of the introversion/extraversion dimension (Naiman et al., 1978, p. 67). This particular observation seriously tainted the reputation of the extraversion variable (Dewaele & Furnham, 1999).

However, extraversion scores have been found to correlate positively with measures of oral fluency in the L2, especially in stressful situations (Dewaele & Furnham, 2000). One possible explanation for this is that the heavier reliance on declarative knowledge in L2 production requires an important amount of STM capacity (Dewaele, 2002b). This could cause a STM overload in introvert L2 users in stressful situations. As a result, fragments of linguistic information would have to queue, resulting in slower processing and speech production.

The extraverts' inclination to take risks seems to extend to linguistic behavior: extravert L2 learners tend to use more colloquial words than their more introvert peers (Dewaele, 2004). Extraverts were also found to use more emotion words in their L2 production, which suggests they were less reluctant to talk about potentially more "dangerous" emotion-laden topics (Dewaele & Pavlenko, 2002). MacIntyre and Charos (1996) found that introvert L2 learners suffered more from foreign language anxiety (FLA) and were less willing to communicate in their French L2 than their extravert peers. van Daele (2007) on the other hand, did not find a link between extraversion and FLA.

Marin-Marin (2005) found very few significant relationships between extraversion and vocabulary learning strategies or vocabulary test results from Mexican EFL learners. However, a small subgroup of introverts obtained significantly higher end-of-semester English grades than a group of extraverts (2005, p. 273). MacIntyre, Clément, and Noels (2007) looked at the effect of learning situation on vocabulary test scores of introvert and extravert Canadian French L2 learners. Introverts were found to perform best after having studied in a very familiar situation, while the extraverts performed best in conditions involving a moderate degree of novelty (p. 296). The researchers also found an interaction between person and situation in trait willingness to communicate (trait WTC), which showed that extraverts are not always more willing to communicate.

Oya, Manalo, and Greenwood (2004) investigated the relationship between personality variables of Japanese students and their oral performance in English. The participants were native speakers of Japanese who were studying English in New Zealand. No significant correlations emerged between extraversion and oral fluency, accuracy, and complexity. However, extraverts produced better global impressions during their oral performance. Some significant effects of extraversion were uncovered by van Daele, Housen, Pierrard, and Debruyn (2006) in their longitudinal study on the development of fluency, complexity, and accuracy of Dutch-speaking secondary school students' L2 English and French in Flanders. Extraversion scores were found to be positively correlated with lexical complexity in both foreign languages, but with neither accuracy nor syntactic complexity at the first data collection point. The effect of extraversion faded over the following year. The author suggests that this may be a methodological artifact, namely that the extraverts grew bored with the task over time and made less of an effort (2006, p. 227).

Finally, Dewaele (2007) found negative, but nonsignificant, correlations between extraversion and language grades in the Dutch L1, French L2, English L3, and German L4 of Flemish high school students.

## Neuroticism–Emotional Stability

Neuroticism is the second factor of the "Giant 3" (Eysenck, 1967). People who score high on this scale tend to suffer from "anxiety, phobia, depression and hypochondriasis" (Furnham & Heaven, 1998, p. 326). Those with low scores can be described as calm, contented, and unemotional. Williams (1971) administered a battery of personality and language tests to Anglophone students who had been divided into three groups according to their participation in the classroom: active, intermediate, or nonparticipation. The group of nonparticipating students had the highest scores on insecurity and neuroticism, and the lowest scores on self-esteem and intellectual productivity. There is every reason to believe that this relation holds for the foreign language class. Dewaele (2002a) found a link between neuroticism and FLA in his study on Flemish learners of French and English (cf., *infra*). However, neuroticism did not correlate with foreign language grades (Dewaele, 2007a).

## Psychoticism

Psychoticism is the third major personality domain in Eysenck's model and measures tough-mindedness (Furnham & Heaven, 1998, p. 230). It is seen as being composed of Agreeableness and Conscientiousness in the "Five Factor Model." Persons scoring high on the psychoticism scale "tend to be hostile, cold, aggressive, and have poor interpersonal relations" (p. 327). Furnham and Medhurst (1995) found that individuals with low scores on the psychoticism scale were more likely to have good oral and written expression, were more motivated, and participated more actively in seminars. Dewaele (2002a) also found that high-psychoticism Flemish learners of English L3 suffered less than low-psychoticism participants from FLA in English (cf. *infra*). One explanation put forward was that a higher level of hostility is linked to a more limited concern about the reaction of the interlocutor(s) to one's speech production in the foreign language, hence a lower level of FLA for the speaker. Dewaele (2007a) found that his Flemish participants who scored high on psychoticism tended to have lower grades in French L2, but not in Dutch L1, English L3, or German L4.

## Conscientiousness

Conscientiousness is associated with striving for persistence, self-discipline, and achievement (Busato, Prins, Elshout, & Hamaker, 2000), characteristics which may be logically expected to increase a learner's success in SLA. Wilson (2008) found that open university students enrolled in French L2 courses who scored higher on Conscientiousness—measured through the OCEAN Personality Assessment—were more likely to complete the course successfully.

## Openness to Experience

Openness encompasses aspects of intellectual curiosity, creativity, imagination, and aesthetic sensibility. Individuals with high scores on Openness would have "a greater predisposition to engage in intellectually stimulating activities that lead to higher knowledge acquisition" (Furnham & Chamorro-Premuzic, 2006, p. 81).

This dimension is similar to "Open-mindedness," which refers to an open and unprejudiced attitude toward out-group members and toward different cultural norms and values (van der Zee & van Oudenhoven, 2001). According to Van Oudenhoven and Van der Zee (2002), individuals in a foreign context who show an interest in local people are likely to be exhibiting open-mindedness: it also necessitates a degree of freedom from prejudice toward out-group members. Young (2007) found that open-mindedness was a good predictor of foreign language learning achievement.

### Emotional Intelligence

In the last few years, emotional intelligence (EI) has been the object of intensive research in personality psychology. The construct of EI posits that "individuals differ in the extent to which they attend to, process, and utilize affect-laden information of an intrapersonal (e.g., managing one's own emotions) or interpersonal (e.g., managing others' emotions) nature" (Petrides & Furnham, 2003, p. 39). Trait EI is measured via self-report questionnaires and is located at the lower levels of personality hierarchies (Petrides & Furnham, 2003). In a recent study, Dewaele, Petrides, and Furnham (2008) investigated the link between levels of trait EI and levels of communicative anxiety (CA) in the L1, L2, L3, and L4 of adult multilinguals. A significant negative relationship emerged between trait EI and CA in the different languages. This was interpreted as an indication that participants with higher levels of trait EI are better at regulating stress levels and emotional reactions in communicative interactions. The capacity to express oneself clearly, and the ability to read an interlocutor's emotional state will lead to lower levels of CA. What remains to be investigated is whether higher levels of trait EI could also be an advantage in long-term L2 development.

## C.  Interaction of Learner-Internal and Learner-External Variables

### Social, Educational, and Political Contexts

MacIntyre, Clément, Dörnyei, and Noels (1998) have demonstrated that individual contexts are inextricably linked to social contexts, that is, the intergroup climate in which interlocutors evolve. Research into IDs need to take into account all enduring influences (e.g., intergroup relations, learner personality, gender, social class) which represent "stable, long-term properties of the environment or person that would apply to almost any situation" (1998, p. 546).

The importance of the context can be illustrated through a few simple examples. Students from countries like France, Poland, Hungary, or China realize that to succeed and compete in the global market they have to be proficient in at least one foreign language, because the rest of the world does not speak their language. In officially multilingual countries like Belgium or Canada, state employees are expected to master at least two of the national languages. They may not be overly enthusiastic about this requirement, given some antagonisms between the linguistic groups. However, since getting a job or obtaining promotion typically depends not only on the mastery of the second official language but also on the knowledge of English, and preferably some fourth or fifth language, students understand that they have no choice.

The situation is radically different in the United States or the United Kingdom where there is no market pressure for foreign language learning. It is not surprising therefore that not even half of 15- to 24-year olds in the United Kingdom reported having working knowledge of an L2, and that nearly 40% declared no interest in learning an L2. These results stand in sharp contrast with those from other EU countries where interest in foreign language learning is much higher (European Report on the Quality of School Education, 2001). The implication of this finding is that while learner-internal variables would mediate the outcomes of individual learners, their effect on overall levels of foreign language achievement in the society at large would undoubtedly pale compared to the effects of social and political contexts shaping language prestige and marketability.

## Cultural and Intergroup Empathy

Cultural Empathy (CE), one of the five subscales of the Multicultural Personality Questionnaire[1] (MPQ), refers to the ability to clearly project an interest in others, as well as to reflect a reasonably complete and accurate sense of the thoughts, feelings, and experiences of members of a different cultural group (van der Zee & van Oudenhoven, 2000, 2001). Young (2007) found that the MPQ's CE subscale was highly predictive of language learning ability and achievement of learners of English from 30 different nationalities. He also developed a new subscale called "Intergroup Cultural Empathy" in which 13 items from the original CE scale of the MPQ were transformed to make them more specifically about empathy toward members of a different cultural group. This new subscale was slightly better at predicting both number of languages spoken and self-rated linguistic ability (Young, 2007).

## International Posture

A relatively similar construct to Young's Intergroup Cultural Empathy was proposed by Yashima (2002), namely International Posture, which was based on Norton's (2001) concept of "imagined community." Included in the concept are interest in foreign or international affairs, willingness to go overseas to stay or work, and a readiness to interact with intercultural partners. It thus reflects students' desire to join an "imagined international community."

Yashima (2002) used structural equation modeling with a sample of Japanese university students enrolled in an EFL program in the United States. She found that international posture, hypothesized as a latent variable, predicted motivation, which, in turn, significantly predicted proficiency in English. A significant path also emerged between international posture and willingness to communicate in L2 English. Later studies showed that Japanese students who studied abroad acquired a higher level of international posture (Yashima, 2009; Yashima, Zenuk-Nishide, & Shimuzu, 2004; Yashima & Zenuk-Nishide, 2008).

## Communicative Anxiety and Foreign Language Anxiety

In their exploratory study of the relations between language anxiety and other anxieties in speaking English as L1 and French as L2, MacIntyre and Gardner (1989) found two different anxiety dimensions: "General Anxiety" and "Communicative Anxiety", respectively. Only the latter was found to be negatively correlated with French L2 vocabulary recall.

---

[1]The other subscales are open-mindedness, emotional stability, flexibility, and social initiative.

The authors later considered CA, of which FLA is a specific manifestation, as "a stable personality trait, among experienced language learners" (MacIntyre & Gardner, 1994, p. 297). The authors define CA as a feeling of tension and apprehension linked to L2 speech production and reception. Performance in the L1 was not linked to levels of CA in that language (1994, p. 301). One possible explanation for this is that L1 production and reception is typically largely automatized, based on implicit knowledge, hence requiring relatively little STM capacity. L2 production and reception, as was pointed out earlier, puts much more strain on the STM. Moreover, Dewaele (2002b) argued that the effect of introversion on the catecholamine system is similar to that generated by anxiety. Anxiety seems to be linked to levels of norepinephrine, which also seems to affect the capacity and/or efficiency of the STM. Excessive levels of dopamine and norepinephrine impair performance. Introverts have been found to be more anxious, which could further reduce the available processing capacity of WM (Gershuny, Sher, Rossy, & Bishop, 2000).

The cumulated effects of both introversion and anxiety could seriously affect fluency in L2 production. CA tends to co-occur with high stress, STM overload, and breakdown in automatic processing. Dewaele (2002b) compared the situation to a fire spreading through an overstretched airport control center. The combination of high anxiety and high introversion thus seems to reinforce the effects on speech production in the L2, especially in stressful interpersonal situations.

Reviews of the literature on FLA conclude that a moderate negative relationship exists between FLA and various measures of language achievement (Horwitz, 2001). However, van Daele's (2007) longitudinal study on the effects of psychological variables on the SLA of English and French by Dutch L1 students showed differential effects of FLA on both languages, and a lack of stability in its effects: FLA correlated negatively with lexical richness in English and French, and positively with grammatical accuracy in English at the start of the study. FLA was not significantly linked to lexical and grammatical accuracy in French, nor to syntactical complexity or fluency in both foreign languages. Interestingly, the effects were strongest for English, the language for which participants reported lower levels of FLA than French. The effects of FLA completely disappeared at the last data collection point after 22 months.

Dewaele (2002a) also demonstrated that patterns of interindividual variation in levels of FLA were quite different in the French L2 and English L3 of Flemish high school students. Participants from lower social classes were found to suffer more from FLA in French, but not in English. This social effect appeared to be a stronger predictor of FLA in French than that of the global personality traits. Psychoticism, extraversion, and, to a lesser extent, neuroticism, did however significantly predict levels of FLA in English L3 production. Extraverts, high-psychoticism, and low-neuroticism participants reported lower levels of FLA in English and French where it was nonsignificant. Rodriguez and Abreu (2003) examined general foreign language classroom anxiety construct in English and French and found them to be stable across the foreign languages. They suggest that levels of FLA may be linked to motivation, culture, and aptitude.

Dewaele and Thirtle (2009) found that FLA was linked to the decision of dropping further foreign language study among 14-year-old students in a London school.

Sparks et al. (1998) have suggested that variation in language skills in the L1 (e.g., reading, vocabulary) may be linked to variation of FLA levels. Individuals with a deficit in the L1 would consequently suffer more from FLA.

Pavlenko (2005) has argued that SLA researchers should not overemphasize FLA in classroom contexts. She points out that the more serious FLA is the one that occurs outside the classroom, when the L2 users encounter real threats, when they are discriminated against and need to stand up for themselves.

Dewaele et al. (2008) heeded Pavlenko's call for more FLA research in authentic interactions and investigated the relationships between levels of FLA reported by adult multilinguals and psychological and sociobiographical factors. The main finding was that participants with higher levels of trait EI suffered less from CA in the L1 and less from FLA in the L2, L3, and L4. This was interpreted as evidence that self-confidence in one's ability to read the emotional state of an interlocutor lowers one's FLA. Participants who started learning the L2 and L3 at a younger age tended to suffer less from FLA. Purely classroom-based language instruction was found to be linked to higher levels of FLA compared to instruction that also involved extracurricular use of the language. A higher frequency of use, a stronger socialization in a language, a larger network of interlocutors, and a higher level of self-perceived proficiency in a language were also linked to significantly lower levels of FLA. The authors conclude that FLA is linked to a myriad of interacting psychological, situational, cultural, and social factors.

## Language Attitudes

Gardner (1985) defined attitude as "an evaluative reaction to some referent or attitude object, inferred on the basis of the individual beliefs or opinions about the referent" (1985, p. 9). His socioeducational model of L2 acquisition is generally considered to be the seminal research paradigm for investigating the role of attitudes and motivation in SLA. It focused on the link between attitudes toward the learning situation, integrativeness, and motivation. Attitudes toward foreign languages have been found to be shaped by different sociocultural, historical, and political factors, as well as by purely didactic and personal factors (MacIntyre et al., 2007). These attitudes are the crucial antecedent of motivation to learn a language. Some languages sound sexy and attractive to the ears of potential learners. Piller (2002) coined the term "language desire" to describe the attraction for speakers of English. In her study of linguistic practices of bilingual couples, Piller (2002, p. 269) notes that some participants were in love with English or German as an L2 long before they actually met their partners. However, languages may have completely different effects on different people. Natasha Lvovich wanted to become "a woman" when she first heard her teacher speak French (Lvovich, 1997). For the American academic Richard Watson, French sounded "syrupy" and "effeminate" and a language that "Real Men" would not speak (Pavlenko, 2005, p. 67). He learned to read French very well, but attributed his limited success in speaking it to his attitude toward the language (Pavlenko, 2005).

Attitudes toward foreign languages in general are not as stable as some early studies have seemed to suggest. This error originated from the fact that most early SLA research into attitudes considered a single foreign language (typically French L2 in the

Canadian context). However, recent studies have shown that learners may have widely different attitudes toward the different foreign languages they are studying (Gardner & Tremblay, 1998). Lasagabaster (2005) considered the attitudes of university students toward three languages (i.e., Basque, Spanish, and English). He found that participants showed a very positive attitude toward English and toward their own L1 (Basque or Spanish). The Spanish L1 participants had more favorable attitudes toward English than those with Basque as L1. Dewaele (2005a) analyzed attitudes toward French L2 and English L3 among Flemish high school students. Attitudes toward English were found to be much more positive than those toward French, despite the fact that the participants had enjoyed a longer and more intense formal instruction in French. Participants who felt more Flemish (i.e., their regional identity) than Belgian displayed more negative attitudes toward French. This negative attitude toward French is the result of tense socio-political relations between Dutch and French speakers in Belgium. Higher levels of self-perceived competence, higher frequency of use of the target language (TL), and lower levels of CA were found to correlate positively with attitudes toward the TLs.

## Language Learning Motivation

Language learning motivation has been one of the most intensely investigated variables in SLA (cf. Gardner, 2006; Dörnyei, 2005; Dörnyei & Ushioda, 2009; Lasagabaster & Huguet, 2006; Masgoret & Gardner, 2003; Noels, 2003; Ushioda, 2008). Yet, motivation remains "one of the most elusive concepts in the whole of social sciences" (Dörnyei, 2001, p. 2). It could be described as a complex, composite construct, with some components that are more trait-like and others that are more state-like and situation-specific (Dörnyei, 2006, p. 50). Motivation is supposed to explain why people opt for certain actions, and how long and how hard they are willing to go on with certain activities (Dörnyei and Skehan, 2003, p. 614).

According to Gardner (1985), levels of motivation are influenced and maintained by attitudes toward the learning situation and integrativeness, that is, "an openness to the TL group and other groups in general linked to one's sense of ethnic identity" (Gardner, 2006, p. 236). Motivation can also be supported by instrumentality, that is, "conditions where the language is being studied for practical or utilitarian purposes" (2006, p. 249).

Research has shown stronger correlations between the level of integrativeness and SLA outcomes and somewhat weaker relationships between the level of instrumentality and foreign language measures (Dörnyei, 2001; Gardner, 2006).

In his recent work, Dörnyei has suggested leaving the term "integrative" completely behind and focusing more on the identification aspects and on the learner's self-concept (Dörnyei, 2005). An individual imagines an "Ideal L2 Self," which is the representation of all the attributes that that person would like to possess, including the mastery of an L2. Dörnyei also postulates a second dimension, the "Ought-to L2 Self," that is, the attributes that one believes one *ought to* possess. L2 motivation can then be defined as the desire to reduce the perceived discrepancies between the learner's

actual self and his/her ideal or ought-to L2 selves (Dörnyei, 2006, p. 54). The third dimension is labeled "L2 Learning Experience," which concerns situation-specific motives related to the immediate learning environment and experience. Dörnyei ponders about the interface of the Ideal L2 Self and the actional phase of motivation. He refers to Norton's (2001) concept of "imagined communities" agreeing with her that learners' motivation will relate to both real and imagined belongings within communities of practice (Dörnyei, 2006, p. 54).

Autobiographies by bilinguals contain numerous illustrations of the effect of imagination on individuals' motivation to learn an L2. Lvovich, for example, even though she resided in the Soviet Union, created an imaginary French identity for herself. She immersed herself in different aspects of both popular and "high" French culture, learned to speak with a Parisian accent, and even dipped "the imagined croissant into coffee" (Lvovich, 1997, p. 2).

Ushioda (2001) and Shoaib and Dörnyei (2005) have focused on motivational change over time or "emergent motivation" (Ushioda, 2009). Ushioda (2001) identified a number of sources of IDs in Irish learners' motivation to learn French. She found that successful learners engaged in intrinsic motivational processes more often, reminding themselves about their past and future successes and their aspirations. Less successful learners focused more on external incentives and blamed factors beyond their control for their lack of progress.

Shoaib and Dörnyei (2005) identified a number of salient recurring temporal patterns and episodes in the participants' lives that transformed their motivational disposition.

## Age of Onset of Acquisition

The debate on the Critical Period Hypothesis is still going strong (see DeKeyser & Larson-Hall, 2005, Muñoz, 2006; Singleton & Ryan, 2004; Birdsong, this volume). Paradis (2004) has argued that CP effects are caused by the decline of procedural memory for late L2 learners, which forces them to rely on explicit learning instead of implicit learning. The upper age limit is thought to be variable according to the component of the implicit language system that is being acquired through exposure to language interaction. This is, in chronological order, prosody, phonology, morphology, and syntax (Paradis, 2004, p. 59). There seems to be broad agreement in the SLA community that there are "general age factors" (Singleton & Ryan, 2004), but there is disagreement on the existence of cutoff points and on the effect of confounding variables. Birdsong (2005), for example, rejects the idea of "critical" period or maturational milestones, arguing that the decline in attained L2 proficiency is progressive rather than decisive and is spread over the age spectrum (2005, p. 125). In a recent study, Trofimovich and Baker (2006) found that Korean adult naturalistic learners' age at the time of first extensive exposure to English L2 (all in their 20s) was negatively linked to fluency measures. Dewaele (2007b) found similar patterns in a large-scale study of adult multilinguals. Participants who started learning English (as an L2) at a younger age rated their oral proficiency much higher than late starters.

## Residence in TL Country: Contact with the TL

Research on immersion education and study abroad has shown that increased contact with the L2 typically boosts the acquisition of different areas of the L2, including sociolinguistic competence (Mougeon, Rehner, & Nadasdi, 2004; Regan, 2005), sociopragmatic competence (Kinginger, 2004), and grammatical competence (Howard, 2005; Nadasdi, Mougeon, & Rehner, 2003). However, as Kinginger (2008) pointed out, study abroad may create the potential for rapid SLA, but it is insufficient in itself.

Yashima et al. (2004) showed that frequency and amount of L2 communication by Japanese students who participated in a study abroad program in the United States related to satisfaction in the sojourn experience, and satisfaction in friendship with hosts. A higher perceived quality of human relationship with host family members was linked to more interest in intercultural communication and/or international affairs. This in turn motivated students to put in more effort in learning the L2, which led to a further improvement in communicative skills and self-confidence.

Trofimovich and Baker (2006) found that length of residence (ranging from a few months to more than 10 years) had no significant effect on fluency measures in the English L2 in a group of adult Koreans. Only one suprasegmental, stress timing, correlated with amount of experience in the L2.

Dewaele (2007b) found that self-rated proficiency scores in English L2 from his adult multilinguals were linked to the amount of authentic interaction in English L2 both during the learning phase (on average 25 years before data collection) and at the time of data collection.

## Pedagogical Context

The language teacher's personality, ideology, and pedagogical approach clearly affects the learners' attitudes and motivation toward the TL (Dörnyei, 2001; Gardner, 1985), although not always in the expected direction. Pavlenko (2003) refers to her own experience in a Ukrainian school in 1975, when as a fifth grader she chose her foreign language, English, and attended her first class where their teacher welcomed them with a passionate speech explaining to them that the knowledge of English would be crucial in the event of a war with the West and the students would need their linguistic skills to help defeat the enemy. Pavlenko asked to be transferred to the French class where the teacher was politically more relaxed and where she made rapid progress.

The progress of an L2 learner could be linked between the chemistry that develops between the learner, the group of learners, and the their teacher. Borg (2006) investigated the specific traits exhibited by effective language teachers. One crucial trait was "an ability to communicate freely and to radiate positive feeling" (2006, p. 23). An ability to develop close relationships with students was also reported as a particular trait shared by effective language teachers (Borg, 2006). This finding reflects the conclusion of an earlier study on effective teachers of all subjects, namely their ability to create a caring emotional environment (Walls, Nardi, von Minden, & Hoffman, 2002).

## V. IDS RESEARCH IN SLA: OBSTACLES AND DIFFICULTIES

### A. IDs Research and Teaching Implications

While it undoubtedly makes sense to investigate the link between personality traits and language learning, one could wonder what Naiman et al's (1978) ultimate goal was. Had they been able to draw the psychological profile of the "good language learner," would this have had an effect on educational practices? Knowing that high scores on traits X or Y correlate with higher marks in the foreign language classroom is one thing, but what can the teacher do with that knowledge? Since personality traits are stable, they cannot be manipulated in any way. Should therefore potential language learners with low scores on certain personality dimensions be discouraged from enrolling? Should they be segregated and taught separately? This would rest on the very shaky assumption that a more efficient teaching method could be developed for this particular group. Schumann (2004) points out that because of IDs between learners, there is no "right way" to teach an L2: "brains vary, and therefore, people learn differently" (2004, p. 19). The author concludes that since there is no single method for teaching an L2 that can guarantee similar progress and uniform outcomes among learners, good teachers should simply provide "general guidelines and direction" (2004, p. 19).

No single personality trait has ever been shown to be a systematic and significant predictor of success in SLA. It remains to be seen whether this is the result of methodological difficulties in measuring "success" or whether success in SLA is just independent of personality traits. This is a fascinating question. Indeed, psychological research has shown that personality traits do affect complex cognitive performance, and since L2 production can be considered to be a complex cognitive task, IDs in production could be expected to be correlated with personality traits. Of course, there are complicating factors. Firstly, SLA typically lasts many years, which means it cannot easily (if at all) be replicated in laboratory conditions. Secondly, SLA and L2 production are both linked, but they are also independent. In other words, a slow learner is not necessarily also a slow speaker. Conversely, a fast learner is not automatically a fluent speaker. Obviously the amount of learning will affect the ease with which the L2 is produced. Mastery of morphology, for example, will depend on the grammar rules that the learner will have developed. The problem of previously acquired knowledge and its effect on performance makes IDs research in SLA much more difficult than in cross-sectional psychological studies where participants are typically required to perform a complex task (e.g., sorting cards) while some background variable is manipulated (e.g., noise level).

### B. Learners are More than Bunches of Variables

It has been argued that looking at an individual in terms of variables and neurons does not do justice to the uniqueness and richness of that individual's behavior and achievement. The argument comes not from neurobiologists working on SLA, some of whom include language learner autobiographies in search of longitudinal evidence (Schumann & Wood, 2004), but from postmodernist researchers.

Vygotskian sociocultural theorists see L2 learners as intentional human agents who play a defining role in shaping the qualities of their learning but who, at the same time, may be subject to variable positioning within specific settings and relations of power (Kinginger, 2008; Lantolf & Pavlenko, 2001; Lantolf and Poehner, this volume). Rejecting simplistic explanations of complex phenomena in SLA, sociocultural theorists adopt an emic perspective, that is, they take the perspective of participants considering them to be crucial witnesses of their own learning process, and use longitudinal case studies to understand differences in language learning achievement (cf. Pike, 1964). Kinginger (2008), for example, argues that variation in outcomes resulting from study abroad are not necessarily attributable only to the events or conditions characterizing the experience itself. Instead, she found links between outcomes and participants' life histories, aspirations, commitment, and self-image (Kinginger, 2004, 2008). IDs researchers acknowledge that a purely etic and quantitative approach does not "do full justice to the subjective variety of individual life" (Dörnyei, 2001, p. 193).

In his defense of a mixed epistemological approach, Dewaele (2005b) has argued that L2 learners are more than a bunch of variables, but that it is perfectly legitimate to look at them in those terms too. Such an approach allowed Dewaele (2008) to investigate IDs in 1459 adult multilinguals' perceptions of the emotional weight of the phrase "I love you" in their L1 and L2. Almost half of the participants felt "I love you" was strongest in their L1, a third felt it to be equally strong in their L1 and L2, and a quarter felt it to be stronger in their L2. Quantitative analyses showed that the perception of weight of the phrase "I love you" was significantly associated with self-perceived language dominance, context of acquisition of the L2, age of onset of learning the L2, degree of socialization in the L2, nature of the network of interlocutors in the L2, and self-perceived oral proficiency in the L2. An analysis of participants' comments revealed idiosyncratic variation linked to unique linguistic and cultural trajectories, identity issues, and metapragmatic awareness of the conceptual differences in emotion scripts of love in different languages.

## C. The Need for Context

Postmodernist researchers have also criticized the idealized and decontextualized nature of IDs research in SLA. The clear separation assumed in much SLA literature between social factors and the individual or psychological factors is untenable according to Pavlenko (2002). She argues that many individual factors, such as age, gender, or ethnicity, are also socially constituted, so that the understanding and implications of belonging to a particular ethnic group, generation, or gender are not the same across communities and cultures. Pavlenko points out that seemingly internal factors such as attitudes, motivation, or language learning beliefs have clear social origins and are shaped and reshaped by the social contexts in which the learners find themselves.

Dörnyei (2006) notes that a growing number of IDs researchers accept the situated nature of IDs variables. The notion that the various traits are context-independent and absolute is slowly being replaced by "new dynamic conceptualizations in which ID factors interact with the situational parameters rather than cutting across tasks and environments" (Dörnyei, 2006, p. 62).

## D. The Rejection of Static Categories

One of the main objections of postmodernist researchers against quantitative IDs research in SLA is the acceptance of stable, static, and homogeneous categories. Pavlenko (2002) points out that the causal, unidirectional, and stable nature attributed to constructs as attitudes and motivation is problematic given the continuous interaction between them. Initial success in SLA may strengthen a learner's motivation, but a series of failures may result in a diminished learning motivation (2002, p. 280). Gardner (2006) addresses this criticism by pointing out that the schematic representation of his model is a static representation of a dynamic forward moving process that is capable of change at any given point in time. Achievement can influence motivation (p. 244), and language anxiety is both influenced by and influencing language achievement (p. 245).

## E. The Danger of Oversimplification

Early IDs research in SLA often involved a single independent variable. Ackerman (2003) points out that isolated traits can have substantial impact on learning outcomes, but that combinations of traits could have more predictive power than traits in isolation (2003, p. 92). The danger with the exclusive focus on a single independent variable is the irresistible temptation to attribute causality when significant relationships are uncovered (Ellis, 2006). It is crucial to remember that the relationship might in fact be influenced by other variables of which the researcher is unaware. The decision on the number of independent variables to include in a single study is a delicate balancing act, given that too many variables may overly complicate the research design and hamper the statistical analysis, while too few may give a limited understanding of the complex interactions. One way forward is through the use of path analysis (e.g., MacIntyre & Charos, 1996), structural equation modeling (Csizér & Dörnyei, 2005), or cluster analysis (Yashima & Zenuk-Nishide, 2008) where the effect of multiple independent variables can be estimated quite accurately.

## F. The Limitations of Comparing Group Averages

SLA researchers who studied the effect of study abroad programs on development of the L2 have often been baffled by the amount of interindividual variation in their data (Howard, 2005; Regan, 2005). Because of an implicit assumption of homogeneity of the experimental and control groups, research designs tend to be overly simple: it typically involves two groups of participants: those who leave the home institution to study in the L2 environment, and a control group who continue their language study in the home university. Both groups are tested before departure of the first group (time 1), and tested again when they are reunited after a number of months (time 2). The averages for both groups on the same tests are compared at time 1 and time 2. The expectation is not to find significant differences between both groups at time 1, but any difference at time 2 is attributed to the treatment, namely the study abroad. The dangerous assumption in such designs is that every individual in the group goes through a similar experience and displays similar behavior. Those who stay at home are assumed not to seek extra exposure to the TL outside the language classes. Those who are abroad are assumed to constantly engage in interactions with native speakers. Both assumptions are intuitively appealing, but they do not correspond to reality. In fact, being abroad is only a potential cause for rapid development of the TL: some grab the opportunity, other participants, as Kinginger (2008) shows, do the opposite and avoid contact with TL speakers and the TL culture. The average performance of the study abroad group may be slightly higher than those who stayed at home (Howard, 2005), but some in the latter group may have made faster progress studying their grammar and reading books in the TL at home. It is therefore important to shelve the notion of the "monolithic prototypical faceless learner, whose identity is gross group averages" (Dewaele, 2005b, p. 367).

## VI. CONCLUSION

What I hope to have demonstrated in the present chapter is that the study of IDs is a very large and vibrant research area, and that SLA research on IDs has benefited from crossfertilization from neighboring disciplines. The field has witnessed many heated debates among researchers firmly defending their preferred epistemology and methodology. Encouragingly, the debates seem to have spurred a clear evolution in the field. The postmodernist view of the self as fluid and fragmented within a complex social context seems to have exerted a noticeable influence on the field of IDs research. Recent research stresses the situated nature of independent variables and the highly complex dynamic interactions between learner-internal and learner-external variables in SLA (Dörnyei, 2005, 2006; Dörnyei & Ushioda, 2009). Exciting links have been established between the neurological substrate (i.e., the brain) and the behavior (and ultimate attainment) of foreign language learners and users. The value of a combination of etic and emic perspectives is increasingly being recognized, with data from learners' personal experiences being collected through interviews, autobiographies, diaries, in addition to the quantitative analysis of corpora and traditional and holistic questionnaires (Kinginger, 2008; Lasagabaster, 2005; Pavlenko, 2005). Factors that previously tended to be ignored in IDs research, such as the sheer sex appeal of some languages, the power of imagination, and the relationship with the teacher, have been incorporated in the list of potential variables that drive SLA. Crucially, IDs researchers have recognized that it would be a folly to try to understand the incredible complexity of SLA by simplistic research designs (MacIntyre et al., 2007).

## REFERENCES

Ackerman, P. L. (2003). Aptitude complexes and trait complexes. *Educational Psychologist, 38,* 85–93.

Birdsong, D. (2005). Interpreting age effects in second language acquisition. In J. F. Kroll & A. M. D. de Groot (Eds.), *Handbook of bilingualism: Psycholinguistic approaches* (pp. 109–127). Oxford: Oxford University Press.

Borg, S. (2006). The distinctive characteristics of foreign language teachers. *Language Teaching Research*, *10*, 3–32.

Busato, V. V., Prins, F. J., Elshout, J. J., & Hamaker, C. (2000). Intellectual ability, learning style, achievement motivation and academic success of psychology students in higher education. *Personality and Individual Differences*, *29*, 1057–1068.

Csizér, K., & Dörnyei, Z. (2005). The internal structure of language learning motivation: Results of structural equation modeling. *Modern Language Journal*, *89*, 19–36.

DeKeyser, R., & Larson-Hall, J. (2005). What does the critical period really mean? In J. F. Kroll & A. M. D. de Groot (Eds.), *Handbook of bilingualism: Psycholinguistic approaches* (pp. 88–108). Oxford: Oxford University Press.

Dewaele, J.-M. (2002a). Psychological and sociodemographic correlates of communicative anxiety in L2 and L3 production. *The International Journal of Bilingualism*, *6*, 23–39.

Dewaele, J.-M. (2002b). Individual differences in L2 fluency: The effect of neurobiological correlates. In V. Cook (Ed.), *Portraits of the L2 user* (pp. 219–250). Clevedon: Multilingual Matters.

Dewaele, J.-M. (2004). Individual differences in the use of colloquial vocabulary: The effects of sociobiographical and psychological factors. In P. Bogaards & B. Laufer (Eds.), *Learning vocabulary in a second language: Selection, acquisition and testing* (pp. 127–153). Amsterdam: Benjamins.

Dewaele, J.-M. (2005a). Sociodemographic, psychological and politico-cultural correlates in Flemish students' attitudes toward French and English. *Journal of Multilingual and Multicultural Development*, *26*, 118–137.

Dewaele, J.-M. (2005b). Investigating the psychological and the emotional dimensions in instructed language learning: Obstacles and possibilities. *The Modern Language Journal*, *89*, 367–380.

Dewaele, J.-M. (2007a). Predicting language learners' grades in the L1, L2, L3 and L4: The effect of some psychological and sociocognitive variables. *International Journal of Multilingualism*, *4*(3), 169–197.

Dewaele, J.-M. (2007b). Interindividual variation in self-perceived oral communicative competence of English L2 users. In E. Alcón Soler & M. P. Safont Jordà (Eds.), *The Intercultural speaker. Using and acquiring English in the foreign language classroom* (pp. 141–165). Berlin: Springer Verlag.

Dewaele, J.-M. (2008). The emotional weight of 'I love you' in multilinguals' languages. *Journal of Pragmatics*, *40*, 1753–1780.

Dewaele, J.-M., & Furnham, A. (1999). Extraversion: The unloved variable in applied linguistic research. *Language Learning*, *49*, 509–544.

Dewaele, J.-M., & Furnham, A. (2000). Personality and speech production: A pilot study of second language learners. *Personality and Individual Differences*, *28*, 355–365.

Dewaele, J.-M., & Pavlenko, A. (2002). Emotion vocabulary in interlanguage. *Language Learning*, *52*, 265–324.

Dewaele, J.-M., Petrides, K. V., & Furnham, A. (2008). The effect of trait emotional intelligence and sociobiographical variables on communicative anxiety among adult polyglots. *Language Learning*, *58*(4), 911–960.

Dewaele, J.-M., & Thirtle, H. (2009). Why do some young learners drop foreign languages? A focus on learner-internal variables. *International Journal of Bilingual Education and Bilingualism*, 1747–7522, DOI 10.180/1367005080254965.

Dörnyei, Z. (2001). *Teaching and researching motivation*. Harlow: Longman.

Dörnyei, Z. (2005). *The psychology of the language learner. Individual differences in second language acquisition.* Mahwah, NJ: Lawrence Erlbaum.

Dörnyei, Z. (2006). Individual differences in second language acquisition. *AILA Review, 19,* 42–68.

Dörnyei, Z., & Skehan, P. (2003). Individual differences in second language learning. In C. J. Doughty & M. H. Long (Eds.), *The handbook of second language acquisition* (pp. 589–630). Oxford: Blackwell.

Dörnyei, Z., & Ushioda, E. (Eds.). (2009). *Motivation, language identity and the L2 self.* Bristol: Multilingual Matters.

Ellis, R. (2006). Individual differences in second language learning. In A. Davies & C. Elder (Eds.), *The handbook of applied linguistics* (pp. 525–551). Oxford: Blackwell.

European Report on the Quality of School Education (2001). European Communities, Brussels.

Eysenck, H. J. (1967). *The biological basis of personality.* Springfield: C. C. Thomas.

Feldman Barrett, L. (2006). Valence is a basic building block of emotional life. *Journal of Research in Personality, 40,* 35–55.

Furnham, A., & Chamorro-Premuzic, T. (2006). Personality, intelligence and general knowledge. *Learning and Individual Differences, 16,* 79–90.

Furnham, A., & Heaven, P. (1998). *Personality and social behavior.* London: Arnold.

Furnham, A., & Medhurst, S. (1995). Personality correlates of academic seminar behavior: A study of four instruments. *Personality and Individual Differences, 19,* 197–208.

Gardner, R. C. (1985). *Social psychology and second language learning: The role of attitudes and motivation.* London: Arnold.

Gardner, R. C. (2006). The socio-educational model of second language acquisition: A research paradigm. *Eurosla Yearbook, 6,* 237–260.

Gardner, R. C., & Tremblay, P. F. (1998). Specificity of affective variables and the trait/state conceptualization of motivation in second language acquisition. In R. Agnihotri, A. L. Khanna, & I. Sachdev (Eds.), *Social psychological perspectives on second language learning.* New Delhi: Sage.

Gershuny, B. S., Sher, K. J., Rossy, L., & Bishop, A. K. (2000). Distinguishing manifestations of anxiety: How do personality traits of compulsive checkers differ from other anxious individuals? *Behavior Research and Therapy, 38,* 229–241.

Horwitz, E. K. (2001). Language anxiety and achievement. *Annual Review of Applied Linguistics, 21,* 112–126.

Howard, M. (2005). On the role of context in the development of learner language: Insights from the study abroad research. *ITL Review of Applied Linguistics, 148,* 1–20.

Kinginger, C. (2004). Alice doesn't live here anymore: Foreign language learning and renegotiated identity. In A. Pavlenko & A. Blackledge (Eds.), *Negotiation of identities in multilingual contexts* (pp. 219–242). Clevedon: Multilingual Matters.

Kinginger, C. (2008). *Language learning in study abroad: Case studies of Americans in France.* Oxford: Blackwell.

Lantolf, J., & Pavlenko, A. (2001). (S)econd (L)anguage (A)ctivity theory: Understanding second language learners as people. In M. Breen (Ed.), *Learner contributions to language learning: New directions in research* (pp. 141–158). London: Longman.

Lasagabaster, D. (2005). Bearing multilingual parameters in mind when designing a questionnaire on attitudes: Does this affect the results? *International Journal of Multilingualism, 2,* 26–51.

Lasagabaster, D., & Huguet, A. (Eds.). (2006). *Language use and attitudes towards multi-lingualism in European bilingual contexts.* Clevedon: Multilingual Matters.

Lieberman, M. D. (2000). Introversion and working memory: Central executive differences. *Personality and Individual Differences, 28,* 479–486.

Lieberman, M. D., & Rosenthal, R. (2001). Why introverts can't always tell who likes them: Social multi-tasking and non-verbal decoding. *Journal of Personality and Social Psychology, 80,* 294–310.

Lvovich, N. (1997). *The multilingual self: An inquiry into language learning.* Mahwah, NJ: Erlbaum.

MacIntyre, P. D., & Charos, C. (1996). Personality, attitudes, and affect as predictors of second language communication. *Journal of Language and Social Psychology, 15,* 3–26.

MacIntyre, P. D., Clément, R., & Noels, K. A. (2007). Affective variables, attitude and personality in context. In D. Ayoun (Ed.), *French Applied Linguistics* (pp. 270–298). Amsterdam: Benjamins.

MacIntyre, P. D., Clément, R., Dörnyei, Z., & Noels, K. A. (1998). Conceptualizing willingness to communicate in a L2: A situational model of L2 confidence and affiliation. *Modern Language Journal, 82,* 545–562.

MacIntyre, P. D., & Gardner, R. C. (1989). Anxiety and second language learning: Towards a theoretical clarification. *Language Learning, 39,* 251–275.

MacIntyre, P. D., & Gardner, R. C. (1994). The subtle effects of language anxiety on cognitive processing in the second language. *Language Learning, 44,* 283–305.

Maguire, E. A., Woollett, K., & Spiers, H. J. (2006). London taxi drivers and bus drivers: A structural MRI and neuropsychological analysis. *Hippocampus, 16,* 1091–1101.

Marin-Marin, A. (2005). *Extraversion and the use of vocabulary learning strategies among university EFL students in Mexico.* Unpublished Ph.D. thesis, University of Essex.

Masgoret, A.-M., & Gardner, R. C. (2003). Attitudes, motivation, and second language learning: A meta-analysis of studies conducted by Gardner and associates. In Z. Dörnyei (Ed.), *Attitudes, orientations and motivations in language learning* (pp. 167–210). Oxford: Blackwell.

Mechelli, A., Crinion, J. T., Noppeney, U., O'Doherty, J., Ashburner, J., Frackowiak, R. S., et al. (2004). Structural plasticity in the bilingual brain. *Nature, 431,* 757.

Miyake, A., & Friedman, D. (1998). Individual differences in second language proficiency: Working memory as language aptitude. In A. F. Healy & L. E. Bourne (Eds.), *Foreign language learning: Psycholinguistic studies on training and retention* (pp. 339–364). Mahwah, NJ: Erlbaum.

Mougeon, R., Rehner, K., & Nadasdi, T. (2004). The learning of spoken French variation by immersion students from Toronto Canada. *Journal of Sociolinguistics, 8,* 408–432.

Muñoz, C. (Ed.). (2006). *Age and the rate of foreign language learning.* Clevedon: Multilingual Matters.

Nadasdi, T., Mougeon, R., & Rehner, K. (2003). Emploi du futur dans le français parlé des élèves d'immersion française. *Journal of French Language Studies, 13,* 195–219.

Naiman, N., Fröhlich, M., Stern, H. H., & Todesco, A. (1978). *The good language learner.* Toronto: Ontario Institute for Studies in Education.

Noels, K. A. (2003). Learning Spanish as a second language: Learners' orientations and perceptions of their teachers' communication style. In Z. Dörnyei (Ed.), *Attitudes, orientations, and motivations in language learning* (pp. 97–136). Oxford: Blackwell.

Norton, B. (2001). Non-participation, imagined communities and the language classroom. In M. P. Breen (Ed.), *Learner contributions to language learning: New directions in research* (pp. 159–171). Harlow: Longman.

Ocean Personality Assessment at www.testsonthenet.com/atctests/Ocean-Personality-Assessment-Specimen1.htm, accessed on 09/15/2008.

Oya, T., Manalo, E., & Greenwood, J. (2004). The influence of personality and anxiety on the oral performance of Japanese speakers of English. *Applied Cognitive Psychology*, *18*, 841–855.

Paradis, M. (2004). *A neurolinguistic theory of Bilingualism*. Amsterdam: Benjamins.

Pavlenko, A. (2002). Poststructuralist approaches to the study of social factors in L2. In V. Cook (Ed.), *Portraits of the L2 user* (pp. 277–302). Clevedon: Multilingual Matters.

Pavlenko, A. (2003). 'Language of the enemy': Foreign language education and national identity. *International Journal of Bilingual Education and Bilingualism*, *6*, 313–331.

Pavlenko, A. (2005). *Emotions and multilingualism*. Cambridge, New York: Cambridge University Press.

Petrides, K. V., & Furnham, A. (2003). Trait emotional intelligence: Behavioural validation in two studies of emotion recognition and reactivity to mood induction. *European Journal of Personality*, *17*, 39–57.

Pike, K. L. (1964). *Language in relation to a unified theory of the structure of human behaviour*. The Hague: Mouton.

Piller, I. (2002). *Bilingual couples talk: The discursive construction of hybridity*. Amsterdam: Benjamins.

Regan, V. (2005). From speech community back to classroom: What variation analysis can tell us about the role of context in the acquisition of French as a foreign language. In J.-M. Dewaele (Ed.), *Focus on French as a foreign language: Multidisciplinary approaches* (pp. 191–209). Clevedon: Multilingual Matters.

Robinson, P. (2003). Attention and memory during SLA. In C. J. Doughty & M. H. Long (Eds.), *The handbook of second Language acquisition* (pp. 631–678). Oxford: Blackwell.

Rodriguez, M., & Abreu, O. (2003). The stability of general foreign language classroom anxiety across English and French. *Modern Language Journal*, *87*, 365–374.

Schumann, J. (2004). The neurobiology of aptitude. In J. Schumann, S. E. Crowell, N. E. Jones, N. Lee, S. A. Schuchert, & L. A. Wood (Eds.), *The neurobiology of learning. perspectives from second language acquisition* (pp. 7–21). Mahwah, NJ: Erlbaum.

Schumann, J., & Wood, L. A. (2004). The neurobiology of motivation. In J. Schumann, S. E. Crowell, N. E. Jones, N. Lee, S. A. Schuchert, & L. A. Wood (Eds.), *The neurobiology of learning. Perspectives from second language acquisition* (pp. 23–42). Mahwah, NJ: Erlbaum.

Shoaib, A., & Dörnyei, Z. (2005). Affect in life-long learning: Exploring L2 motivation as a dynamic process. In P. Benson & D. Nunan (Eds.), *Learners' stories: Difference and diversity in language learning* (pp. 22–41). Cambridge: Cambridge University Press.

Singleton, D., & Ryan, L. (2004). *Language acquisition: The age factor*. Clevedon: Multilingual Matters.

Skehan, P. (1989). *Individual differences in second language learning*. London: Arnold.

Slevc, R., & Miyake, A. (2006). Individual differences in second-language proficiency. Does musical ability matter? *Psychological Science*, *17*, 675–681.

Sparks, R. L., & Ganschow, L. (1991). Foreign language learning differences: Affective or native language aptitude differences? *Modern Language Journal*, *75*, 3–16.

Sparks, R. L., & Ganschow, L. (2001). Aptitude for learning a foreign language. *Annual Review of Applied Linguistics*, *21*, 90–111.

Sparks, R. L., Javorsky, J., Patton, J., & Ganschow, L. (1998). Factors in the prediction of achievement and proficiency in a foreign language. *Applied Language Learning*, *9*, 71–105.

Sternberg, R. J. (2002). The theory of successful intelligence and its implications for language aptitude testing. In P. Robinson (Ed.), *Individual differences and instructed language learning* (pp. 13–43). Amsterdam: Benjamins.

Trofimovich, P., & Baker, W. (2006). Learning second language suprasegmentals: Effect of L2 experience on prosody and fluency characteristics of L2 speech. *Studies in Second Language Acquisition*, *28*, 1–30.

Ushioda, E. (2001). Language learning at university: Exploring the role of motivational thinking. In Z. Dörnyei & R. Schmidt (Eds.), *Motivation and second language acquisition* (pp. 91–124). Honolulu, HI: University of Hawaii Press.

Ushioda, E. (2008). Motivation and good language learners. In C. Griffiths (Ed.), *Lessons from good language learners* (pp. 19–34). Cambridge: Cambridge University Press.

Ushioda, E. (2009). A person-in-context relational view of emergent motivation, self and identity. In Z. Dörnyei & E. Ushioda (Eds.), *Motivation, language identity and the L2 self* (pp. 215–228). Bristol: Multilingual Matters.

van Daele, S. (2007). *Linguïstische vlotheid, accuraatheid en complexiteit in de verwerving en de verwerking van een tweede taal* [*Linguistic fluency, accuracy and complexity in the acquisition and processing of a second language*]. Unpublished Ph.D. dissertation, Free University of Brussels.

van Daele, S., Housen, A., Pierrard, M., & Debruyn, L. (2006). The effect of extraversion on oral L2 proficiency. *Eurosla Yearbook*, *6*, 213–236.

van der Zee, K. I., & van Oudenhoven, J. P. (2000). The multicultural personality questionnaire: A multidimensional instrument of multicultural effectiveness. *European Journal of Personality*, *14*, 291–309.

van der Zee, K. I., & van Oudenhoven, J. P. (2001). the multicultural personality questionnaire: Reliability and validity of self- and other ratings of multicultural effectiveness. *Journal of Research in Personality*, *35*, 278–288.

Van Oudenhoven, J. P., & Van der Zee, K. I. (2002). Predicting multicultural effectiveness of international students: The Multicultural Personality Questionnaire. *International Journal of Intercultural Relations*, *26*, 679–694.

Walls, R. T., Nardi, A. H., von Minden, A. M., & Hoffman, N. (2002). The characteristics of effective and ineffective teachers. *Teacher Education Quarterly*, *29*, 37–48.

Williams, R. L. (1971). Relationship of class participation to personality, ability, and achievement variables. *Journal of Social Psychology*, *83*, 193–198.

Wilson, G. (1977). Introversion/extraversion. In T. Blass (Ed.), *Personality variables in social behavior* (pp. 179–218). Hillsdale, NJ: Erlbaum.

Wilson, R. (2008). *"Another language is another soul": Individual differences in the presentation of self in a foreign language*. Unpublished Ph.D. dissertation, University of London, Birkbeck.

Yashima, T. (2002). Willingness to communicate in a second language: The Japanese EFL context. *Modern Language Journal*, *86*, 55–66.

Yashima, T. (2009). International posture and the L2 ideal self in the Japanese EFL context. In Z. Dörnyei & E. Ushioda (Eds.), *Motivation, language identity and the L2 self* (pp. 144–163). Bristol: Multilingual Matters.

Yashima, T., & Zenuk-Nishide, L. (2008). The impact of learning contexts on proficiency, attitudes, and L2 communication: Creating an imagined international community. *System*, *36*(4).

Yashima, T., Zenuk-Nishide, L., & Shimuzu, K. (2004). The influence of attitudes and affect on willingness to communicate and second language communication. *Language Learning*, *54*, 119–152.

Young, T. J. (2007). *Intercultural communicative competence and the teaching and learning of English as a foreign language*. Unpublished Ph.D. dissertation, University of London, Birkbeck.

# CHAPTER 27

# SOCIAL IDENTITY AND LANGUAGE LEARNING

Kimberly A. Noels and Howard Giles

For almost 50 years, identity has been a focal point for scholars interested in the social factors that influence second language (L2) learning.[1] Unlike other educational domains, the process of learning another language often has been argued to be influenced not only by the dynamics within the classroom, but also by the socio-political relations between ethnolinguistic groups in the broader societal context. Various frameworks have been proposed to better understand the interconnections between identification with these groups, termed social identity, and language learning. The purpose of this chapter is to outline some of these approaches and to discuss current controversies in the area. What we hope to demonstrate is that, regardless of ontological, epistemological, and methodological orientation, there is general agreement that developing competence in and using a nonnative language are intricately linked to the self and identity processes, power dynamics, and motivated effort and engagement in the learning process.

We do not claim to be exhaustive in our review; indeed this topic has garnered a great deal of academic attention, particularly in recent years. Rather, we concentrate on some representative research programs to underscore the diversity of scholarship in the area, and we do so in some detail in order to illustrate points of convergence and departure between them. We have organized this chapter with a historical structure, first outlining the early models that were developed primarily by social psychologists and then considering various critiques of these frameworks, followed by a review of more recent "sociocultural" frameworks. Through our exposition, we hope to capture the range of perspectives that inform the subject area and also to emphasize the benefit of multiple insights into the theme of language learning and social identity.

---

[1]For the purposes of the present article, "learning" and "acquisition" are used synonymously.

*The New Handbook of Second Language Acquisition*

## I. INTERGROUP/SOCIAL PSYCHOLOGICAL PERSPECTIVES[2]

The possibility that positive attitudes toward and social relations between members of different language groups might influence language-learning outcomes received some sporadic attention in the early part of the 20th century (see Gardner, 2001, for overview of early studies). For example, Whyte and Holmberg (1956, p. 13) claimed that American businesspersons' capacity to establish "sympathetic interest" and to identify with Latin American partners was the key to language learning, and hence commercial success. Nida (1956) suggested that two motivational forces, a desire to communicate and sensitivity toward the outgroup, were important considerations in language-learning achievement. Systematic research programs, however, began to develop only in the 1960s, and in this section we will focus on theoretical frameworks that were proposed between then and the 1990s, many of which have sustained productive research programs up to the present.

### A. Identity and Additive and Subtractive Bilingualism

Perhaps the earliest programmatic investigation of the link between social identity and language learning was that of Lambert, whose extensive work on bilingualism laid the foundation for much of the social and cognitive psychological research that was to follow (see Dil, 1972). Lambert (1956) maintained that learning an L2 entailed not only the acquisition of a linguistic system but also the acquisition of cultural characteristics of the target language group. In his comparison of beginning and advanced learners of French and bilingual Francophones, Lambert identified two clusters of language variables that were differentially involved in the process of becoming bilingual. The first was a "vocabulary" cluster, relating to specific vocabulary differences between languages, and the second a "cultural" cluster, pertaining to differences in linguistic behavior that were culturally based. Lambert maintained that the latter cluster represented a set of barriers to bilingualism that are difficult to overcome, and he argued that to do so it is necessary to adopt certain characteristics of the cultural group, thereby making the language a part of the self (Gardner, 2006). Although such changes in identity may sometimes be associated with anomie (Lambert, Gardner, Barik, & Tunstall, 1963), it was only when language, thought, and the self-concept became intertwined that communication in the nonnative language would become automatic (Gardner, 2006).

Contrary to the opinion held by many at that time, Lambert (1978) was emphatic that there was "no basis in reality for the belief that becoming bilingual or bicultural necessarily means a loss or dissolution of identity" (p. 544). His research, which covered a variety of contexts in North America, revealed several identity profiles that

---

[2]We are reluctant to use the term "social psychological" in contrast with "sociocultural," although Dörnyei (2005) has used this term to describe the work of Gardner and related theorists. Our reluctance comes from the fact that many social psychologists work within sociocultural frameworks. We feel it is more important to emphasize that the intergroup models tend to focus on social identities relevant to sociopolitical groups (often, but not always, from a sociocognitive perspective), whereas sociocultural models tend to focus on social identities as they constructed through interpersonal dynamics.

described the experience of bilingual people. Lambert noted that Franco-American youths who were successful at being both French and American shared the conviction that knowing both languages was useful and valuable in their social world. This pattern, in which one acquired two languages and lived with two cultural reference groups in relative ease, he termed "additive biculturalism" or "additive bilingualism." Other youths felt some pressure to give up one aspect of their dual identity:

> ... some oriented themselves definitely toward their French background and tried to ignore their American roots; others were tugged more toward the American pole at the expense of their Frenchness; and still others apparently tried not to think in ethnic terms, as though they did not consider themselves as being either French or American. (p. 540)

This pattern Lambert termed "subtractive biculturalism" or "subtractive bilingualism." Over time, subtractive bilingualism came to refer particularly to cases in which acquisition of an L2 threatened the loss of the first language (L1) and culture (cf. Gardner, 1985; Swain & Lapkin, 1991).

Lambert posited that the value accorded by a society to an ethnic group and its language was fundamental to the development of an additive experience of biliguality and biculturality. He suggested that in communities where differential prestige exists between ethnolinguistic groups, both groups should focus on the development of skills in the nondominant language. In this way, subtractive experiences of bilingualism and biculturalism could be transformed into additive ones for all members of society. Lambert's theoretical ideas have been foundational for many scholars interested in bilingualism and language learning (see Reynolds, 1991, for an overview), including many of those we will discuss in greater detail below.

## B. Integrativeness and the Socioeducational Model

Extending his work as a student under Lambert's supervision, Gardner developed what was to become the most influential research paradigm in the social psychology of L2 learning (Gardner, 1985, 2006; Gardner & Lambert, 1972). The socioeducational model of language learning focuses on formal, classroom contexts, and much of its empirical research has centered on English-speaking Canadians learning French. The central variable, motivation, is comprised of a broad range of features linked to attitudinal, goal-directed, and effortful behavior (Gardner, 2001). Within the Attitudes and Motivation Test Battery, it is more concisely operationalized through self-report instruments roughly corresponding to behavior, cognitions, and affect: (a) motivational intensity, or the level of effort expended; (b) the desire to succeed in learning the language; and (c) positive attitudes toward learning the language.

Motivation is supported by positive attitudes toward the learning situation and integrativeness; it is integrativeness that is most germane to issues of social identity. Integrativeness encompasses the notion of identity in the sense that one has "a willingness to be like valued members of the language community" (Gardner & Lambert, 1972, p. 271), sometimes to the point of identifying with that language group (Masgoret & Gardner, 2003). In recent discussions, Gardner (2006) emphasizes that integrativeness refers more broadly to an openness to have contact with the L2 community and with other cultural communities.

Like motivation, integrativeness is a complex of constructs, and it is generally assessed in terms of general interest in foreign languages, positive attitudes toward the L2 community, and an integrative orientation (Gardner, 2005). The term "integrative orientation" refers to the goal of learning an L2 because one wishes to have contact with, and perhaps identify with, the target language community. Gardner and his colleagues emphatically point out that orientations are not particularly good predictors of eventual achievement—without active engagement and intense effort, an orientation remains a vague, disembodied notion. When integrativeness, positive attitudes toward the learning situation, and motivation are all evident, the complex is described as an "integrative motive." Gardner (2006) maintains that, across societal contexts, such a motive is necessary to achieve the degree of automaticity that is characteristic of native-like speech.

Considerable research over 40 years attests to the central role that motivation, and particularly the integrative motive, plays in predicting language-learning achievement. A recent meta-analysis of 75 investigations succinctly describes the major findings (Masgoret & Gardner, 2003). Notably, of all the social psychological variables described in the socioeducational model, motivational intensity is the key predictor of achievement. In response to suggestions that social identity and sociopolitical concerns might be more relevant in the L2 context than the foreign language context, Masgoret and Gardner also tested whether the association between variables indicating integrativeness and proficiency might be stronger in second versus foreign language context, defined in terms of how well the L2 group is represented demographically, and implicitly, how potentially available its members are for social interaction with the learner. Their results showed no strong evidence that context mattered: integrativeness variables predicted grades better in the L2 context, but predicted other proficiency measures better in the foreign language context. Elsewhere, Gardner (2005) demonstrated that the attitudinal and motivational variables predict proficiency (grades) in other national contexts, including Spain, Poland, Croatia, and Romania, as they do in Canada, thereby underscoring the potential validity of this model across national contexts.

## C. Contact, Confidence, and the Sociocontextual Model

Clément's (1980) sociocontextual model retains the notion of integrativeness from the socioeducational model, but gives more attention to the importance of the learning context and, in recent years, more explicitly articulates how identity processes might be involved in language learning. This framework proposes that dynamics in the broader societal context, particularly the relative sociostructural status, or ethnolinguistic vitality (see Giles, Taylor, & Bourhis, 1977), of ethnolinguistic groups initiates a dialectical motivational process involving a set of opposing attitudes. Integrativeness, or the "desire to become an accepted member of the other culture" (Clément, 1980, p. 149), corresponds closely with Gardner's notion. "Fear of assimilation" refers to the apprehension that learning an L2 will result in the loss of the first culture and language.

In relatively homogeneous cultural contexts with little opportunity for interethnic contact, the outcome of this attitudinal dialectic is expected to predict motivation to learn the language. In turn, motivation and the ensuing communicative competence in the L2 have implications for acculturative change within the cultural group. In line with Lambert's notions of subtractive and additive bilingualism, two patterns of identification are postulated. For members of a majority group, the strong vitality of their ethnolinguistic group is argued to ensure the continued viability of the language and cultural identity. Thus, these individuals might be expected to experience integration, whereby identities with both cultural groups would be incorporated into the self-concept (similar to "additive bilingualism"). For members of minority groups, their group's weaker vitality is less likely to support the L1 and culture, and these individuals might experience assimilation, whereby the acquisition of an L2 and its culture is accompanied with the loss of the original language and cultural identity (akin to "subtractive bilingualism"). These outcomes at the group level, in turn, play back into the identity attitudes of individual learners.

In multicultural contexts where there is the potential for regular interaction with members of the L2 community, a second motivational process is posited to complement the attitudinal one. With increasingly frequent and better quality intergroup contact, individuals develop a sense that they are competent in the L2, accompanied by low levels of anxiety. This linguistic confidence supports the learner's motivation to engage further in language learning, with the attendant possibilities of integration or assimilation. Several studies support this hypothesized pattern: Although linguistic confidence is generally associated with stronger identification with the L2 community across high and low vitality groups, its relation with the L1 identity differs depending on the group vitality. Confidence using the L2 is unrelated to identification with the L1 group in the case of higher vitality groups, such as most English learners of French in Canada, and linked to lower levels of L1 identity in lower vitality groups, such as minority Francophones and immigrants in Canada (e.g., Gaudet & Clément, 2005; Noels, Pon, & Clément, 1996).

In the sociocontextual model, then, attitudes regarding social identity are foundational to motivation and identity changes are linked to motivated engagement and confidence and competence in the L2. In elaborating on identity, Clément and Noels (1992) proposed a situated approach that takes into account aspects of the immediate social interaction. They argue that, because identities are negotiated between interactants, identities shift depending on with whom one interacts, the setting in which the interaction takes place, the activity or topic under consideration, along with a host of other considerations. Moreover, consistent with the notion that people often negotiate multiple identities, in any given situation a learner may potentially identify more strongly with one group than the other group, with both groups to the same degree, or with neither group if ethnicity and language are not relevant to the interaction. Investigations by Clément and his colleagues consistently point to a trend in which identity shifts across situations, corresponding with the language and ethnicity of the people one is with (see Clément, Noels, & MacIntyre, 2007, for a review); such findings parallel those reported in experimental or diary studies (e.g., Ross, Xun, & Wilson, 2002; Yip, 2005). Moreover, these situational patterns are moderated by one's self-confidence in their English skills, such that those who are confident in the L2 show greater situational variation than those who lack confidence (Noels, Clément, & Gaudet, 2004), suggesting that without L2 confidence, one cannot feasibly claim an L2 identity.

## D.  Social Identity, Ethnolinguistic Vitality, and the Intergroup Model

The intergroup model of L2 learning follows from Giles's earlier work on ethnolinguistic identity theory (e.g., Giles et al., 1977; Giles & Johnson, 1981), which examined the role of language in intergroup encounters in light of Tajfel's social identity theory (Tajfel, 1978). The intergroup model focuses on contexts in which minority group members (e.g., immigrants) learn the language of a more dominant, majority group (Garrett, Giles & Coupland, 1989; Giles & Byrne, 1982). It extends earlier discussions of identity and the power relations involved in language learning in at least two ways.

First, it uses a well-articulated model of social identity in which identity mechanisms and group dynamics have been clearly described and empirically tested. Social identity is construed as "that part of the individuals' self-concept that derives from their knowledge of their membership of [sic] a social group (or groups) together with the value and emotional significance of that membership" (Tajfel, 1981, p. 255). From this perspective, people have a predisposition to categorize information in the world, including their social world, into discrete categories. Social identity derives from knowing in which category (or categories) a person belongs and assuming the characteristics of that social group (Hogg, 1988). Identity becomes salient through comparison with other social groups, and this process of social comparison is colored by a motivational desire to see one's own group in a positive light, in order to enhance one's self-esteem as a member of a positively valued group. Language comes into play when a speech style (e.g., language, dialect, accent, etc.) is a valued component of identification and can be gainfully used to differentiate one's own group from other groups. It is noteworthy that ethnolinguistic identity is only one of a number of social identities that a person entertains (e.g., gender, age, socioeconomic status), and certain identities may be more salient in some conditions than in others. The strength of identification that one has with a language group is the prime determinant of the motivational processes to learn an L2.

Second, the model extends earlier models in that it offers a variety of predictions about the kinds of reactions that individuals may have when comparisons with a dominant language group are unsatisfactory; such insecure interethnic comparisons are considered a second determinant of motivation. In these circumstances, individuals may strategize to improve their situation. A first option, individual mobility, refers to the strategy whereby a person may try to pass out of the group into the positively valued one. To this end, various conditions permitting, the individual will attempt to acquire the relevant language characteristics of the desired group and abandon the original group.

For those who are less willing or able to put aside their original group membership, social creativity strategies may be utilized to redefine the element of comparison. Group members may decide to no longer compare themselves with a group that they have no possibility of joining and compare themselves with others within their social group (intragroup comparisons; e.g., comparing oneself with another individual from one's group) or with other subordinate groups against which they can achieve a favorable comparison (e.g., comparing one's ethnolinguistic group with another, more recently arrived immigrant group). A second social creativity strategy is to redefine the dimension of comparison in a more positive light (e.g., a stigmatized dialect may be redefined as a symbol of cultural pride). A third strategy involves comparing the in- and outgroups along a new dimension (e.g., if an accent is stigmatized, one might compare using another dimension along which a more favorable comparison can be made). A fourth strategy, social competition, refers to the strategy adopted by individuals and collectivities who wish to reverse the perceived status of in- and outgroups on the valued dimension. An example of social competition in the linguistic domain is the language reform movement in Québec, in which the dominance of English was successfully challenged by the francophone minority.

The selection of any of these options is constrained by various perceptions regarding the relations between the two language groups. Individuals are hypothesized to most likely acquire native-like proficiency in an L2 when (1) language is not an important dimension by which they define their ingroup and/or their identification with their L1 group is weak, (2) comparisons with the other group suggest that no alternatives to the existing power structure are available, (3) the ingroup ethnolinguistic vitality (i.e., social prestige, demographic representation, and institutional support) is perceived to be low, (4) the boundaries between groups can be readily crossed, and (5) other social identities (e.g., gender, religion, etc.) are strong and satisfactory. When the converse conditions exist, persons are unlikely to gain native-like competency in an L2.

Despite its extensive consideration of the sociopolitical relations between groups and social identity concerns, the intergroup model has not received as much research attention as some other models. Although some research has been less supportive (e.g., Hall & Gudykunst, 1986), other research has found support for the importance of identification for use of that group's language (e.g., Kelly, Sachdev, Kottsieper, & Ingram, 1993), and more recent formulations that take into account the immediate communication climate have provided stronger predictive power (Leets & Giles, 1995).

## E. The Acculturation Model

In his acculturation model, Schumann (1975) argued that social and affective factors are the major causes of successful L2 acquisition in informal learning contexts involving minority group members. He maintained that learners vary in the extent to which they are socially and psychologically distant from target language speakers and that this distance, or acculturation, directly predicts language learning. Two types of acculturation are differentiated. In the first, a person can be characterized as psychologically open to the target language and able to take on those characteristics, such as language. The second is more extreme, in that not only is the learner open to and receptive of the target language, the learner also regards the target language speakers as a reference group "whose life style and values he consciously or unconsciously desires to adopt" (Schumann, 1978, p. 380). Although Schumann does not expressly use the term identification, his discussion of reference groups is certainly akin to this construct.

Schumann posits a number of social (i.e., aspects of the relationship between two language groups in contact) and psychological factors (i.e., characteristics that differ between individuals). Like other models, the acculturation model suggests that the relative dominance of a group, its degree of institutional support (termed "enclosure"), and size and cohesiveness, among other things predict the extent of acculturation, and hence language learning. In discussing personal, affective factors, Schuman incorporates Gardner's notion of integrative motivation, suggesting that it may be more pertinent for language learning in situations where there is little opportunity for target language contact. Also, drawing on Guiora's (1972) notion of ego-permeability, he suggests that language learning becomes internalized into one's sense of self when a person feels that there are few inhibitions to learn the new language because the boundaries between languages are weak. The original empirical evidence for the acculturation model was drawn from a 10-month, single-case study (drawn from a somewhat larger study involving six participants). Schumann concluded that social and affective factors were more important than cognitive and age-related factors for explaining why the person's language was "pidginized" (i.e., did not attain native-like proficiency). Although it has garnered rather little subsequent research attention (see Schumann, 1990, for a review), the acculturation model nonetheless has galvanized recent critiques of power, identity, and language learning (e.g., Norton, 2001).

## II. CRITIQUE OF THE INTERGROUP/SOCIAL PSYCHOLOGICAL PERSPECTIVES

Beginning in the 1990s, a number of critiques were directed at the existing models, especially Gardner's socioeducational model. One set of critiques questioned the emphasis that these models placed on intergroup relations and social identity concerns (e.g., Crookes & Schmidt, 1991; Dörnyei, 2001; Oxford, 1996). Critics pointed out that these theoretical formulations were developed in specific societal contexts and that their particular circumstances limit the applicability of these conceptual models to other contexts. More specifically, with its policy of French–English bilingualism and the greater opportunity for face-to-face interaction with members of the target language group (at least in some parts of the country), the learning of French and English in Canada was argued to represent a learning situation that was not necessarily descriptive of ethnolinguistic dynamics elsewhere. Hence, intergroup relations and social identity concerns were argued to be more salient for learners in Canada than they would be in other countries where learners have little exposure to the target language community and little opportunity to form attitudes and identities in relation to it (cf. Dörnyei, 2005). In such foreign language contexts, other factors, related specifically to the dynamics within the local classroom, were suggested to play a more important role in learner motivation, and so some researchers turned to study other cognitive motivational models from educational and social psychology. Such models focused on how one's thoughts about one's abilities, goals and expectations, attributions about past performances, and so on are related to motivation and achievement (see Dörnyei, 2001, 2005, for reviews).

Elsewhere, Noels (2001) argued that intergroup social identity models might be usefully complemented by a consideration of other self-relevant concerns. Drawing from Self-Determination Theory (Deci & Ryan, 1985), Noels argued that a sense of autonomy and personal choice (along with perceptions of competence and relatedness) is an important precondition of engaged learning, as it contributes to the internalization of the learning activity into the self-concept. Noels's findings demonstrated that social identity concerns may be more relevant for motivation in particular contexts, such as heritage rather than foreign language learning (Noels, 2005).

Others agree that the dynamics of the broader societal context impact language learning, but feel this relation is not well captured by the notion of integrativeness. For instance, Lamb (2004) questioned its utility in the context of English as a global language. He pointed out that learners may not seek opportunities to speak with native speakers of English (e.g., British, American, Australian, etc.) but rather use English as a *lingua franca* for communicating with speakers with whom no other common language is shared. In such a case, a desire to integrate with a specific English community is irrelevant; instead one might wish to integrate into a "global-English" community, associated with technological advances, education, and occupational opportunities. Citing Arnett (2002), Lamb depicts a "bicultural identity in which part of [learners'] identity is rooted in their local culture while another part stems from an awareness of their relation to the global culture" (p. 15). Relatedly, Yashima (2002) suggested that rather than an integrative motive, Japanese learners of English may adopt an "international posture" in which they are seen by others and see themselves as persons who have a broad perspective on the relations between language and culture, are well-informed of global issues and international affairs, possess little ethnocentrism and are open to interaction with diverse others, and see themselves as eventually having an international career and/or enjoying a stay abroad. From this perspective, identity is important for language learning; however, it does not concern identification with a specific language group but with a sense of the self as connected to a more global community.

Elaborating on this critique, Dörnyei (2005, p. 97) suggests that integrativeness should be recast as "a virtual or metaphorical identification with the sociocultural loading of a language, and in the case of the undisputed world language, English, this identification would be associated with a non-parochial, cosmopolitan globalized world citizen identity." Dörnyei maintains that users of World English imagine themselves as possibly becoming members of a virtual language community, such that "the more vivid and elaborate the possible self, the more motivationally effective it is expected to be" (p. 100). Integrative motivation, he maintains, should be reframed as the desired integration into such an imagined language community. This ideal L2 self is one of two self-guides that make up the L2 motivational self-system and governs the desire to internalize the L2 into one's sense of self (see also Dörnyei & Ushioda, 2009).

Still other critiques assert that the existing work on social identity and language learning has not gone far enough in its discussion of identity and power (Pavlenko & Blackledge, 2004). Although constructs such as "ethnolinguistic vitality" highlight the power relations between groups in the larger society and suggest how individuals' perception of these relations are relevant to language learning and use, it is argued that not enough work has been done to understand how persons with differential access to power manage their identities in specific relationships. By looking at interpersonal interactions, it is possible to consider not only how control is exercised but also how and when people resist domination and act as autonomous agents in determining their language choices.

For some, the idea that identity is negotiated through social interactions is incongruous with a mentalistic metaphor of identity as an attribute in the mind of the individual. To illustrate the limitations of trait or dispositional models that have informed language learning, Norton and Toohey (2001, p. 309) critique descriptions of the "good language learner" as someone who has "a particular constellation of personality characteristics, cognitive styles, attitudes, motivations, or past learning experiences," and suggest rather that a "good learner" has the good fortune of being someone who has access to a community because of the particular practices of that community and through their ability to exercise agency in positioning themselves as persons with valuable resources, making them worth talking to and being incorporated into the community. Similarly, identity is not simply an inner attribute of a person, but a part of a social process that operates through interpersonal interactions. To reflect such social embeddedness, new vocabulary has been proposed to reframe concepts such as "identity," "motivation," "autonomy," and so on as "subjectivity," "investment," and "agency."

Another concern is the portrayal of L2 learning as typically involving a monolingual and monocultural learner who lives in a homogeneous, self-contained community with little opportunity for daily use of the L2 (cf. Pavlenko & Blackledge, 2004). For many people living in multilingual contexts, the line between learning and using a language is blurred. Moreover, the assumption of a one-to-one correspondence between language and identity is tenuous; for many reasons, people may use the languages of groups with which they do not identify. In addition, a language may be seen less as an indicator of identification with a specific ethnic group than as a means of denoting other identities, such as professional or educational background. It has also been suggested that some social identity models that concentrate on identity–language correspondences may account less readily for the hybridized identities experienced by some individuals in multilingual contexts (Hansen & Liu, 1997; Ricento, 2005).

## III. SOCIOCULTURAL PERSPECTIVES[3]

This last set of critiques stems from scholars who have developed their ideas regarding social identity and language learning in reference to a variety of socio-cultural paradigms (Zuengler & Miller, 2006). These approaches are similar in that they emphasize the social and cultural contexts of learning and focus on how language learning is not only a cognitive process, but also a social process of active participation and membership in specific language communities. In this growing body of work

---

[3]Many terms are used to describe the range of theorizing we have grouped into this domain, including postmodern, poststructuralist, constructivist, sociohistorical, sociocultural, and critical theory.

(e.g., Martin-Jones & Heller, 1996; Pavlenko, Blackledge, Pillar, & Teutsch-Dwyer, 2001), which includes a new journal created as a forum for scholarly work at this intersection (Ricento & Wiley, 2002), the social process of language learning is argued to be intrinsically connected to patterns of identity and language use in interpersonal relationships (defined primarily in terms of power).

Taking our lead from Zuengler and Miller (2006), we begin with a consideration of social identity from Vygotskian sociohistorical and language socialization perspectives, followed by Bakhtinian and critical theory points of view. These models act as a set of complementary frameworks, from which ideas are often combined in "hybrid interdisciplinarity" (Rampton, Roberts, Leung, & Harris, 2002, p. 373; cited in Zuengler & Miller, 2006).

## A. Vygotskian Sociohistorical Theory

Although identity has not been extensively discussed from this perspective, sociohistorical theory suggests that when people develop new sociocultural competencies through using a new language in their social interactions, the self and identity are also transformed.[4] Drawing on the work of Vygotsky and other developmental psychologists from the same tradition (e.g., Vygotsky & Luria, 1993), Lantolf (2007, p. 694) assumes that speech is "motivated and purposive," in the sense that it is oriented toward solving both social and cognitive problems (see also Lantolf and Poehner, this volume). Initially, speech is used to communicate with others to achieve various goals in the social and physical world. Over time, this interpersonal speech becomes internalized as "private speech," which guides action until the action becomes automatic. Learning, thus, is an interactive process between the individual and others in the sociocultural environment, carried out by imitating more expert speakers' ways of doing things and transforming these ways into one's own practices. These practices become internalized, until the learner is capable of carrying out the activity on their own, with no assistance from others.

The internalization of a new communication system affects how one thinks, including how one thinks about oneself. Pavlenko and Lantolf (2000) suggest that as learners interact with others in a new sociocultural context in a new language, they also construct an inner dialogue in the new language (i.e., a new way of thinking) that includes new ways of thinking about themselves (see also Norton & Toohey, 2002). To explain how this occurs, sociocultural theory assumes that humans have a propensity for self-regulation and independent action (Bronson, 2000; cited in Ushioda, 2006). Although the responsibility for an activity rests initially with the more experienced interactant, eventually the learner will "assume responsibility (self-regulation) for L2 performance by appropriating the assistance negotiated between herself and the expert" (Lantolf & Pavlenko, 1995, p. 115). For this internalization of

---

[4]We maintain that sociocultural frameworks are not necessarily antithetical to the notions of language learning portrayed in some of the intergroup/social psychological models. Indeed, Lambert found much inspiration in the papers of Vygotstky, which were published during the time Lambert carried out much of his foundational work (see Lambert, 1991).

responsibility to occur, the learner must come to view themself as a relatively autonomous agent in the activity.

The process of internalization and agency development depends on supportive interpersonal dynamics. Ushioda (2003) draws on Self-Determination Theory (Deci & Ryan, 1985) to specify the kinds of supportive interpersonal interactions and optimal learning conditions that are necessarily for autonomous action and internalization. She argues that the people in the learning context must provide a stimulating environment for the development of competence and support for the learner's eventual independence, combined with a sense of cohesion and relatedness that enables a sense of security in exploring new activities.

## B. Language Socialization and Situated Learning: Participation, Apprenticeship, and Power

Language socialization research centers on how individuals become socially and culturally competent members of a society by participating in various discourse practices and interactional routines (Zuengler & Miller, 2006; see also Schieffelin & Ochs, 1986). It is assumed that learners (i.e., novices) partake in activities with more experienced persons (i.e., experts), who tacitly or explicitly display expected ways of thinking, feeling, and acting (see Zuengler & Cole, 2005, for an overview). Through such exposure and participation, novices internalize these ways of being (which include principles of social order) until they too become experts in that context. This internalization of social order, community practice, and cultural knowledge takes place primarily through the use of language (Garrett & Baquedano-López, 2002, p. 339).

Included in this internalized belief system is the person's own identity and position within the community. According to Ochs (1993), social identity is "a cover term for a range of social personae, including social statuses, roles, positions, relations and institutional and other relevant community identities one may attempt to claim or assign in the course of social life" (p. 288). She maintains that speakers establish their social identities and those of other people by performing verbal acts and displaying particular stances, the meanings of which are conventionally recognized. Social identity, then, is not explicitly encoded in the verbal message, but inferred from one's understanding of the conventions that are associated with the linguistic construction.

Although not language socialization theorists *per se*, Lave and Wenger (1991; Wenger, 1998) usefully articulate the importance of identity in learning through their discussion of the role of communities of practice and legitimate peripheral participation. For Lave and Wenger, "community of practice" refers to patterns of mutual social interaction directed toward a joint enterprise, involving habitual ways of using material and symbolic resources in a specific context. At any point in time, a person belongs to multiple communities, the boundaries of which are permeable and dynamic. The conception of "legitimate peripheral participation" refers to the process of social engagement in particular social/learning practices. Participation in a community of practice necessarily entails learning, which is conceptualized as a process of evolving participation in numerous and overlapping communities of practice.

To understand what it is that people learn (including how well they learn a language), it is critical to understand the kinds of social interactions that are possible, given the power dynamics of a particular community. Within a community, a learner may have a more or less desirable or powerful position, and what is learned is shaped by the positions that the learner occupies. Identification (with a position) is important because it can restrict or extend a person's opportunities to fully engage in a range of conversations, especially those that are critical to acquiring a new language.

Toohey's (2000) research on children acquiring English within a western Canadian classroom illustrates these points well. Toohey notes that current practice in many classrooms involves ranking students on the basis of several criteria, including academic, physical, social, behavioral, and linguistic competencies, and she maintains that such practices place the students in identity positions (akin to roles) that have differential access to resources in the classroom. As a result, students have greater or fewer opportunities to participate in the activities and conversation in the classroom, which ultimately constrains the kinds of things, including language, that can be learned.

## C. Bakhtin and Dialogism: Appropriation and Voice

Rather than viewing language learning as the internalization of a rule system and vocabulary items, scholars interested in language learning from Bakhtin's (1981) dialogical perspective emphasize that learners appropriate the utterances of the people with whom they engage and transform them to serve their own needs. Interactants mutually construct a set of interrelated utterances (the "dialogue"), and in this process, learners "try on" the language of other people, assessing how well the turns of phrase and other aspects of style serve their needs (Toohey, 2000). Language from this perspective is not a neutral medium; it is packaged with particular histories of use by other people (Hall, 1995), and hence inherently ideological. Each utterance indicates one's perspective on and relationship with other interlocutors. Thus, when learners practice and eventually master others' language, they simultaneously acquire its various associations, including political ones.

The self, then, is a dialogic phenomenon. As Vitanova (2005) poignantly emphasizes, newcomers who are unable to use a target language proficiently are constrained in the way in which they can author their selves. Their lack of proficiency may undermine their prior self-conceptions, an experience often associated with a strong negative "emotional-volitional tone"—feelings, desires, and moral evaluations. As newcomers begin to better understand their environment and its constraints ("responsive understanding") along with their new "voice," they can be more agentic and creative in authoring themselves in ways that fit in with the contextual constraints ("creative answerability") or possibly contest others' voices and resist attempts to position them undesirably. "To be a person is synonymous with having a voice, being heard, addressed, and responded to" (Vitanova, 2005, p. 163). Day's (2002) ethnographic case study underscores the capacity of even very young learners to claim such an authoritative voice.

## D. Critical Theory: Imagined Communities, Investments, and Agency

Perhaps the best known treatise on social identity and language learning from a critical theory perspective is Norton's (2000) examination of immigrant women learning English in Canada. Norton draws on Weedon's (1987) notions of subjectivity to define identity as "how a person understands his or her relationship to the world, how that relationship is constructed across time and space, and how the person understands possibilities for the future" (p. 5). Identities such as gender, class, and so on overlap and intersect with one another, and hence it is necessary to take this multiplicity into account to explain language learning.

Along with multiple identities, people have multiple goals and desires. Often these can be in conflict with each other. For this reason, Norton questions the utility of construing motivation as a characteristic of an individual and describing them as more-or-less motivated (e.g., Norton & Toohey, 2001). Rather, she argues that the term "investment" better captures the idea that learners choose to distribute their efforts in relation to the options and constraints that are available. " ... Learners invest in a second language ... [in order to] acquire a wider range of symbolic [e.g., education, friendship] and material [e.g., money] resources, which will in turn increase their cultural capital [e.g., knowledge]" (Norton, 1995, p. 17; cf. Bourdieu & Passeron, 1977). People invest in language learning only if they believe that their efforts will bring about commensurate returns. Because it emphasizes that both costs and benefits must be weighed in any given interaction, the concept of "investment" captures well the ambivalence some learners experience about learning and speaking another language.

Investments are closely linked to social identity (Norton, 2000). When learners speak with different people, they are conscious of the types of investments to be made, and hence they continually organize and reorganize a sense of who they are in relation to the social world. For example, a woman may identify as immigrant, mother, and language learner, among other identities, some of which may be in conflict with one another and/or in conflict with others' imposed identities. Depending on the importance of that identity investment at that time and place, one may choose or refuse to use a new language. Moreover, Norton (2001; Pavlenko & Norton, 2007) further theorizes that identities are not necessarily restricted to the here and now, but include potential identities projected into the future. For example, a new immigrant may imagine herself as currently a language learner, but also as potentially belonging in a community of professionals.

Norton cautions, however, that learners cannot claim identities unilaterally. Other people, particularly those who might be construed as gatekeepers of that desired community (and hence identity), can dismiss or invalidate the image in which the learner is so deeply invested; even though the learner may believe she has a legitimate claim to status in the imagined community, she cannot take this status for granted because others may attempt to impose other identities that undermine that claim. Hence, depending on the extent of investment in particular identities, one may choose to speak or not speak, thereby accommodating, ignoring, or altogether resisting identity impositions. Social identity is thus often a "site of struggle," between competing interests within the person and others in the social context. Such an analysis underscores Norton's notion of agency not as a characteristic of the individual, but as how an individual utilizes her resources and power to access a community and, correspondingly, how community members offer or deny opportunities for that access.

## IV. SOME POINTS OF CONVERGENCE

We have presented several major approaches to the study of social identity and language learning in some detail to counteract the failure of several previous reviews to fully describe this field's diversity (e.g., Hansen & Liu, 1997). In other reviews, only nascent formulations are recounted, although these models have evolved through productive research programs over several decades (e.g., Ricento's [2005] critique of Gardner's socioeducational model). In other cases, early formulations have proven easy targets for critique because they received little examination since they were first proposed (e.g., Norton's [2000] critique of Schumann's acculturation model). Cursory summaries contain inaccuracies and misleading interpretations (e.g., Ricento's [2005] claims that social psychological models are "unwittingly assimilationist" when, in fact, beginning with Lambert, many earlier models clearly articulate that linguistic and cultural assimilation is not a necessary outcome of language learning).

Moreover, a detailed description of various approaches opens the possibility of seeing points of convergence between perspectives. Without such a consideration, we may leave behind issues and concerns that merit further analysis and/or reinvent formulations that have been already contributed by others. We thereby lessen our opportunities to achieve new insights into that which is our common pursuit. As stated by McNamara (1997, p. 566), some current work "simply misses the opportunity to connect with relevant work, like ships passing in the night."

We elaborate on three themes articulated by McNamara (1997) that demonstrate some commonalities across these different perspectives: "the notion of a repertoire of social identities, the transformation of social identity associated with changes in the intergroup contexts in which social identity is negotiated, and the conflict perspective on intergroup relations" (p. 565). The first theme refers to assumption of a multiplicity of group membership, including ethnicity, language, gender, and other identities. As noted earlier, these identities intersect in complex ways. In some circumstances, however, certain identities may be more salient than others, and for some individuals, particular identities may be more or less central to their sense of self.

The second theme concerns the changeability of social identity. An assumption, implicit or explicit, underlying most of the theorizing discussed in this chapter is that the sociopolitical context is interwoven into the fabric of identity and the self. Social psychological/intergroup schemes tend to portray context as the sociopolitical dynamics between groups in terms of objective or perceived societal indicators (e.g., "ethnolinguistic vitality"), although other contextual aspects are sometimes considered. From this perspective, general tendencies are surveyed in order to elucidate how individuals' choices relate back to large-scale, societal dynamics. Sociocultural theories focus on the immediate social interaction, providing a window on the dynamics in the more immediate context. This view reveals how people use various languages, including those with which they claim little or no affiliation, to create and contest identities. Common to both perspectives is the idea that because the context is potentially changeable, identity is also changeable. This emphasis on the dynamism of identity has done much to counteract conceptions of an "authentic" self as an immutable structure of particular attributes. At the same time, it should not be overlooked that some identities are experienced as relatively stable over time, an "existential fact" (Menard-Warwick, 2005). This often-noted dialectic between change and constancy merits further theorizing (cf. Noels, 2009).

The third theme revolves around the notion of conflict. As pointed out by Ricento (2005), Tajfelian definitions of social identity posit a conflict model of intergroup relations, such that the perception of threat accentuates differences between groups of people. This focus on conflict is also evident in recent sociocultural research concerning the importance of human agency in "the negotiation of identities which takes place only when certain identities are contested … [that is,] in instances where individuals resist, negotiate, change and transform themselves and others" (Pavlenko & Blackledge, 2004, p. 20). Although the emphasis on conflict serves to alert the reader to the need for social change, each of these approaches overlooks the day-to-day constructions, negotiations, and performances of identity that may be less discordant and controversial, and may thereby limit the range of identity experiences we articulate, including identity hybrids (see Dallaire & Denis, 2005).

Moreover, this focus on conflict and power struggles might well mask other issues that bear on social identity. For instance, we might wonder how affiliation and nurturance dynamics are involved in identity processes and how agency and autonomy are linked not only to self-assertion in interpersonal relationships, but also to personal growth through creative and curious exploration. What are we missing if the analytic focus is primarily on power as the defining characteristic of human relationships?

There has been some attempt to unify these two broad perspectives on identity. For instance, Dörnyei's (2005) discussion of the L2 self combines Gardner's notion of integrativeness with Norton's idea of imagined communities by drawing from Markus and Nurius' (1986) work on possible selves (see also Dörnyei & Ushioda, 2009). But there are limitations associated with borrowing in this way from the existing literature on the self, not the least of which is that this body of work is so large that it becomes difficult to choose and integrate the various self-related constructs (MacIntyre, MacKinnon, & Clément, 2009). Another promising approach is to celebrate the diversity of theoretical perspectives that can inform our understanding. In their analysis of language teacher identity, Varghese, Morgan, Johnston, and Johnson (2005) comply with Feyerabend's (1988) admonition to incorporate a multiplicity of theories and illustrate how social identity theory, situated learning theory, and poststructural notions of image-text highlight and hide different aspects of identity.

## V. FUTURE DIRECTIONS

### A. Importance of a Comparative Perspective

Ricento (2005) suggests that much L2 research from the 1960s through the 1980s presupposed conflict in the language contact situation, and indeed, many of these theories were developed in contexts in which there was considerable intergroup conflict. As a case in point, Lambert and Gardner first postulated their theories during the 1960–1970s in Canada during a period known as the Quiet Revolution, during which time Québécois asserted their civil rights in the face of an oppressive sociopolitical situation. Inspired by Tajfel and other European social psychologists whose ideas regarding intergroup relations and social identity were formulated in postwar Europe, Giles's notion of ethnolinguistic identity was forged in the light of Welsh–English conflicts. These examples underscore the fact that social scientific theorizing is framed by the context within which the theorist lives and works. Much of the recent scholarship on identity and language learning has been articulated in the context of immigration, colonization, and globalization, often with English as the focal language. This context would certainly bring to light themes that are less prominent in other contexts. For instance, work on immigration and the learning of English generally reflects a situation in which a learner is vested in becoming a part of a new society, and mastering the local language is crucial for acquiring capital of different kinds. The experience of integrating into a new society and developing a new, possibly hybrid, identity is likely quite different than the experience of Quebec Anglophones and Francophones caught in conflict during the 1970s.

This extension of scholarly inquiry to the ESL/EFL context has brought new momentum to the field: It brings to light new issues and makes salient the limitations of previous models. But it is also important that we not forget that these new understandings are likewise constrained by the specific language contact situation. For the field to develop, we need a cross-contextual perspective to better ascertain the applicability of conceptual frames outside the realm in which they were developed. Concurrently, we should resist the impulse to quickly dismiss frameworks that were developed in other contexts and hence lie outside the purview of our own experience and expertise. As we continue to compare language-learning experiences across a variety of contexts (e.g., those with transnational allegiances, those who live in borderlands, heritage language learners with different degrees of ancestral relatedness, advocates for the use of auxiliary and "dead" languages, foreign language students, and so on), likely new dynamics will present themselves, requiring us to draw from other frameworks and/or develop new theoretical perspectives to articulate the range of issues that learners in the various contexts face. Unlike Ricento (2005), then, we do not see this context specificity as a "bias" that plagued early models, but as an integral part of scholarly inquiry and an important consideration that must be taken into account in theory development.

## B. Multiple/Mixed Methods and Triangulation

An important development is the growing diversity of research methods used to analyze the issue of social identity and language learning. While questionnaires and interviews remain standard information-gathering tools, participant observations, personal narratives (see Pavlenko & Lantolf, 2000), collective stories (Lin, Wang, Akamatsu, & Riazi, 2002), and other qualitative methods are becoming increasingly common, and still others might prove useful. For instance, visual research methods (see Stanczak, 2007, for an overview) might not only facilitate communication between researchers and participants who do share not a common language background, but also broaden researchers' understanding of the contexts in which learners live and learn. Ethnographies have underscored the value of a long-term perspective, and certainly other research methods could benefit from longitudinal designs, particularly as quantitative analytic techniques in developmental science become more sophisticated (e.g., multilevel modeling and latent growth curve analysis). Apart from these qualitative methods, experimental and quasi-experimental designs, in which certain conditions are created or sampled to examine their effects on behaviors of interest, have been underutilized. Perhaps one of the most important methods by which we can understand better the dynamic and interactional aspect of language learning is through conversation and discourse analysis of dialogues between learners and significant others (e.g., teachers, peers, members of the L2 community) in dyads and groups, in and outside the laboratory setting.

This diversity in methodological approaches is important in a field that values both empirical and interpretive aspects of scholarly inquiry: empirical in the sense that knowledge is gained "from experience," through our senses, most often through observations of others, "measured" or otherwise; and interpretive, in the sense that we derive meaning from those observations. As stated by Brydon-Miller and Tolman (1997, p. 804), "multiple methods of research enable us to know through different sorts of experiences, and ideally these methods would comprise all social scientists' repertoire." In a less-than-ideal world, it is likely that many researchers will continue to work with those methods with which they are more comfortable and familiar. For some, their ontological and epistemological orientation prescribes a particular methodology; for others, restricted time and resources simply preclude developing an expert understanding of more than a limited number of techniques. Acknowledgment of such human limitations compels us to emphasize the importance of collaborative endeavors between researchers with different capacities and the value of regular review papers that synthesize collective understanding and articulate points of dispute.

## VI. CONCLUSION

The study of social identity and language learning combines robust theoretical approaches using traditional social psychological techniques with newer formulations that have benefited from the application of methods often used in other disciplines. This combination offers great potential for the generation of new ideas, new knowledge, and new practices in the study of language learning and social identity.

A cautionary note is perhaps in order. To our mind, the most worrisome impediment to such a prospect is not the incommensurability of different ontologies, epistemologies, and methodologies as much as the confrontational discourse that runs through some of the scholarship in the area. In our view, critique is an important part of developing new ways of understanding how the social world is implicated in language learning. But too often, such critique is dismissive of less preferred approaches, sometimes subtly and sometimes with open hostility. This tendency is not restricted to a "positivistic" old guard defending their dying empire; indeed, it is most disturbing to hear polemic positions advanced by constructivists, those who elsewhere would argue that essentialist, categorical descriptions of any human practice are problematic. While such positioning serves a rhetorical function of clearly demarcating differences, the confrontational style fails to recognize, acknowledge, and consider diversity within perspectives, and more regrettably potentially shuts down constructive discussion. An alternative approach is to engage in a dialogue that opens the possibility of collaboration and transformation. As we noted in our review of the broader area of the social psychology of language (Noels, Giles, & Le Poire, 2003), high-spirited discussion should make us all more sophisticated in our thinking about the nature of the "social," "identity," "power," "motivation," and "language." "Even if peaceful coexistence and complementarity prove elusive, and the transformation of knowledge appears distant, this condition of multiple perspectives is not an entirely undesirable state of affairs. Through their dialectic, each perspective can at least serve to keep the others honest and humble about their truth claims" (p. 247).[5]

## ACKNOWLEDGMENT

We are grateful to Richard Clément, Tracey Derwing, Bill Dunn, and Robert Gardner for their invaluable comments on portions of this chapter.

## REFERENCES

Bakhtin, M. M. (1981). *The dialogical imagination: Four essays* (Michael Holquist, Ed.). Austin, TX: University of Texas Press.

Bourdieu, P., & Passeron, J. (1977). *Reproduction in education, society and culture*. London: Sage.

Bronson, M. (2000). *Self-regulation in early childhood: Nature and nurture*. New York: Guildford Press.

Brydon-Miller, M., & Tolman, D. L. (1997). Engaging the process of transformation. *The Journal of Social Issues, 53*, 803–810.

Clément, R. (1980). Ethnicity, contact and communicative competence in a second language. In H. Giles, W. P. Robinson, & P. M. Smith (Eds.), *Language: Social psychological perspectives* (pp. 147–154). Oxford: Pergamon Press.

Clément, R., & Noels, K. A. (1992). Towards a situated approach to ethnolinguistic identity: The effects of status on individuals and groups. *Journal of Language and Social Psychology, 11*, 203–232.

Clément, R., Noels, K. A., & MacIntyre, P. D. (2007). Three variations on the social psychology of bilinguality: Context effects in motivation, usage and identity. In A. Weatherall, B. Watson, & C. Gallois (Eds.), *Language, discourse and social psychology* (pp. 51–80). Melbourne: Palgrave MacMillan.

[5]This admonition for humility must be attributed to a wise scholar whose name the first author has unfortunately lost track of.

Crookes, G., & Schmidt, R. W. (1991). Motivation: Reopening the research agenda. *Language Learning, 41*, 469–512.

Dallaire, C., & Denis, C. (2005). Asymmetrical hybridities: Youths at Francophone games in Canada. *Canadian Journal of Sociology, 30*, 143–168.

Day, E. M. (2002). *Identity and the young English language learner*. Clevedon, UK: Multilingual Matters.

Deci, E. L., & Ryan, R. M. (1985). *Intrinsic motivation and self-determination in human behavior*. New York: Plenum.

Dil, A. S. (1972). *Language, psychology and culture: Essays by Wallace E. Lambert*. Stanford, CA: Stanford University Press.

Dörnyei, Z. (2001). *Teaching and researching motivation*. Essex: Longman.

Dörnyei, Z. (2005). *The psychology of the language learner: Individual differences in second language acquisition*. Mahwah, NJ: Lawrence Erlbaum.

Dörnyei, Z., & Ushioda, E. (2009). *Motivation, language identity, and the L2 self*. Bristol: Multilingual Matters.

Feyerabend, P. (1988). *Against method*. London: Verso.

Gardner, R. C. (1985). *Social psychology and second language learning: The role of attitudes and motivation*. London: Edward Arnold.

Gardner, R. C. (2001). Integrative motivation and second language acquisition. In Z. Dornyei & R. Schmidt (Eds.), *Motivation and second language acquisition* (pp. 1–19). Honolulu: University of Hawai'i Press.

Gardner, R. C. (2005, May 30). *Integrative motivation and second language acquisition*. Canadian Association of Applied Linguistics/Canadian Linguistics Association Joint Plenary Talk.

Gardner, R. C. (2006). *Motivation and second language acquisition*. Paper presented at the Seminario Sobre Plurilingüismo: Las Aportaciones Del Centro Europeo de Lenguas Modernas de Graz, on December 15, 2006, Universidad de Alcalá, Spain. Retrieved July 10, 2007, from http://publish.uwo.ca/~gardner/SPAINTALK.pdf

Gardner, R. C., & Lambert, W. E. (1972). *Attitudes and motivation in second language learning*. Rowley, MA: Newbury House.

Garrett, P., Giles, H., & Coupland, N. (1989). The context of language learning: Extending the intergroup model of second language acquisition. In S. Ting-Toomey & F. Korzenny (Eds.), *Language, communication and culture (13th international and intercultural communication annual)* (pp. 201–221). Newbury Park: Sage.

Garrett, P. B., & Baquedano-López, P. (2002). Language socialization: Reproduction and continuity, transformation and change. *Annual Review of Anthropology, 31*, 336–361.

Gaudet, S., & Clément, R. (2005). Identity maintenance and loss: Concurrent processes among the Fransaskois. *Canadian Journal of Behavioral Science, 37*, 110–122.

Giles, H., Bourhis, R. Y., & Taylor, D. M. (1977). Towards a theory of language in ethnic group relations. In H. Giles (Ed.), *Language, ethnicity and intergroup relations* (pp. 307–348). London: Academic Press.

Giles, H., & Byrne, J. L. (1982). An intergroup approach to second language acquisition. *Journal of Multicultural and Multilingual Development, 3*, 17–39.

Giles, H., & Johnson, P. (1981). The role of language in ethnic group relations. In J. C. Turner & H. Giles (Eds.), *Intergroup behavior* (pp. 199–243). Chicago: University of Chicago Press.

Guiora, A. Z. (1972). The effects of experimentally induced changes in ego states on pronunciation ability in a second language: An exploratory study. *Comprehensive Psychiatry, 13*, 421–428.

Hall, B. J., & Gudykunst, W. B. (1986). The intergroup theory of second language ability. *Journal of Language and Social Psychology, 5*, 291–301.

Hall, J. K. (1995). (Re)creating our worlds with words: A sociohistorical perspective on face-to-face interaction. *Applied Linguistics, 10*, 206–232.

Hansen, J. G., & Liu, J. (1997). Social identity and language: Theoretical and methodological issues. *TESOL Quarterly, 31*, 567–576.

Hogg, M. A. (1988). The social identity approach: Context and content. In M. A. Hogg & D. Abrams (Eds.), *Social identification: A social psychology of intergroup relations and group processes* (pp. 6–30). New York: Routledge.

Kelly, C., Sachdev, I., Kottsieper, P., & Ingram, M. (1993). The role of social identity in second-language proficiency and use: Testing the intergroup model. *Journal of Language and Social Psychology, 12*, 288–301.

Lamb, M. (2004). Integrative motivation in a globalizing world. *System, 32*, 3–19.

Lambert, W. E. (1956). Developmental aspects of second-language acquisition: III. A description of developmental changes. *Journal of Social Psychology, 43*, 99–104.

Lambert, W. E. (1978). Cognitive and socio-cultural consequences of bilingualism. *Canadian Modern Language Review, 34*, 537–547.

Lambert, W. E. (1991). And then add your two cents' worth. In A. G. Reynolds (Ed.), *Bilingualism, multiculturalism, and second language learning* (pp. 217–249). Hillsdale, NJ: Lawrence Erlbaum.

Lambert, W. E., Gardner, R. C., Barik, H. C., & Tunstall, K. (1963). Attitudinal and cognitive aspects of intensive study of a second language. *Journal of Abnormal and Social Psychology, 66*, 358–368.

Lantolf, J. P. (2007). Sociocultural theory: A unified approach to L2 learning and teaching. In J. Cummins & C. Davison (Eds.), *International handbook of English language teaching: Part II* (pp. 693–700). New York: Springer.

Lantolf, J. P., & Pavlenko, A. (1995). Sociocultural theory and second language acquisition. *Annual Review of Applied Linguistics, 15*, 108–124.

Lave, J., & Wenger, E. (1991). *Situated learning: Legitimate peripheral participation.* New York: Cambridge University Press.

Leets, L., & Giles, H. (1995). Dimensions of minority language survival/non-survival: Intergroup cognitions and communication climates. In W. Fase, K. Jaspaert, & S. Kroon (Eds.), *The state of minority languages* (pp. 37–71). Lisse, the Netherlands: Swets & Zeitlinger.

Lin, A., Wang, W., Akamatsu, N., & Riazi, A. M. (2002). Appropriating English, expanding identities, and revisioning the field: From TESOL to teaching English for glocalized communication (TEGCOM). *Journal of Language, Identity, and Education, 1*, 295–316.

MacIntyre, P. D., MacKinnon, S., & Clément, R. (2009). The baby, the bathwater, and the future of language learning motivation research. In Z. Dörnyei & E. Ushioda (Eds.), *Motivation, language identity and the L2 self* (pp. 9–42). Bristol, UK: Multilingual Matters.

Markus, H., & Nurius, P. (1986). Possible selves. *American Psychologist, 41*, 954–969.

Martin-Jones, M., & Heller, M. (1996). Education in multilingual settings: Discourse, identities and power. *Linguistics and Education, 8*(Special Issue 1–2), 1–228.

Masgoret, A., & Gardner, R. C. (2003). Attitudes, motivation, and second language learning: A meta-analysis of studies conducted by Gardner and associates. *Language Learning, 53*, 123–163.

McNamara, T. F. (1997). What do we mean by social identity? Competing frameworks, competing discourses. *TESOL Quarterly, 31*, 561–567.

Menard-Warwick, J. (2005). Both a fiction and an existential fact: Theorizing identity in second language acquisition and literacy studies. *Linguistics and Education*, *16*, 253–274.

Nida, E. A. (1956). Motivation in second language learning. *Language Learning*, *7*, 11–16.

Noels, K. A. (2001). Learning Spanish as a second language: Learners' orientations and perceptions of their teachers' communication style. *Language Learning*, *51*, 107–144.

Noels, K. A. (2005). Orientations to learning German: Heritage background and motivational processes. *Canadian Modern Language Review*, *62*, 285–312.

Noels, K. A. (2009). The internalization of language learning into the self and social identity. In Z. Dörnyei & E. Ushioda (Eds.), *Motivation, language identity and the L2 self* (pp. 295–313). Bristol, UK: Multilingual Matters.

Noels, K. A., Clément, R., & Gaudet, S. (2004). Language and the situated nature of ethnic identity. In S. H. Ng, C. N. Candlin, & C. Y. Chiu (Eds.), *Language matters: Communication, culture, and identity* (pp. 245–266). Hong Kong: City University of Hong Kong Press.

Noels, K. A., Giles, H., & Le Poire, B. A. (2003). Language and communication processes. In M. A. Hogg & D. Cooper (Eds.), *The Sage handbook of social psychology* (pp. 232–257). London, England: Sage.

Noels, K. A., Pon, G., & Clément, R. (1996). Language, identity, and adjustment: The role of linguistic self-confidence in the acculturation process. *Journal of Language and Social Psychology*, *15*, 246–264.

Norton, B. (1995). Social identity, investment, and language learning. *TESOL Quarterly*, *29*, 9–31.

Norton, B. (2000). *Identity and language learning: Gender, ethnicity and educational change*. London: Longman/Pearson Education.

Norton, B. (2001). Non-participation, imagined communities and the language classroom. In M. P. Breen (Ed.), *Learner contributions to language learning: New directions in research* (pp. 159–171). London: Pearson Education.

Norton, B., & Toohey, K. (2001). Changing perspectives on good language learners. *TESOL Quarterly*, *35*, 307–322.

Norton, B., & Toohey, K. (2002). Identity and language learning. In R. B. Kaplan (Ed.), *The Oxford handbook of applied linguistics* (pp. 115–123). Oxford: Oxford University Press.

Ochs, E. (1993). Constructing social identity: A language socialization perspective. *Research on Language and Social Interaction*, *26*, 287–306.

Oxford, R. (1996). Toward a more systematic model of L2 learner autonomy. In D. Palfreyman & R. C. Smith (Eds.), *Learner autonomy across cultures: Language education perspectives* (pp. 75–91). New York: Palgrave MacMillan.

Pavlenko, A., & Blackledge, A. (2004). Introduction: New theoretical approaches to the study of negotiation of identities in multilingual contexts. In A. Pavlenko & A. Blackledge (Eds.), *Negotiation of identities in multilingual contexts* (pp. 1–33). Clevedon, UK: Multilingual Matters.

Pavlenko, A., Blackledge, A., Pillar, I., & Teutsch-Dwyer, M. (2001). *Multilingualism, second language learning, and gender*. The Hague: Mouton de Gruyter.

Pavlenko, A., & Lantolf, J. P. (2000). Second language learning as participation and the (re)construction of selves. In J. P. Lantolf (Ed.), *Sociocultural theory and second language learning* (pp. 155–177). Oxford: Oxford University Press.

Pavlenko, A., & Norton, B. (2007). Imagined communities, identity, and English language learning. In J. Cummins & C. Davidson (Eds.), *International handbook of English language teaching* (pp. 669–680). New York: Springer.

Rampton, B., Roberts, C., Leung, C., & Harris, R. (2002). Methodology in the analysis of classroom discourse. *Applied Linguistics*, *23*, 373–392.

Reynolds, A. G. (Ed.). (1991). *Bilingualism, multiculturalism, and second language learning: The McGill conference in honour of Wallace E. Lambert*. Mahwah, NJ: Lawrence Erlbaum.

Ricento, T. (2005). Consideration of identity in L2 learning. In E. Hinkel (Ed.), *Handbook of research in second language learning* (pp. 895–910). Mahwah, NJ: Lawrence Erlbaum.

Ricento, T., & Wiley, T. G. (2002). Editors' introduction: Language, identity, and education and the challenges of monoculturalism and globalization. *Journal of Language, Identity, and Education*, *1*, 1–5.

Ross, M., Xun, W. Q. E., & Wilson, A. E. (2002). Language and the bicultural self. *Personality and Social Psychology Bulletin*, *28*, 1040–1050.

Schieffelin, B. B., & Ochs, E. (1986). Language socialization. *Annual Review of Anthropology*, *15*, 163–191.

Schumann, J. H. (1975). Affective factors and the problem of age in second language acquisition. *Language Learning*, *25*, 209–235.

Schumann, J. H. (1978). The acculturation model for second language acquisition. In R. C. Gingras (Ed.), *Second-language acquisition and foreign language teaching*. Arlington, VA: Center for Applied Linguistics.

Schumann, J. H. (1990). Extending the scope of the acculturation/pidginization model to include cognition. *TESOL Quarterly*, *24*, 667–684.

Stanczak, G. C. (2007). *Visual research methods: Image, society and representations*. Thousand Oaks: Sage.

Swain, M., & Lapkin, S. (1991). Additive bilingualism and French immersion education: The roles of language proficiency and literacy. In A. G. Reynolds (Ed.), *Bilingualism, multiculturalism, and second language learning: The McGill conference in honour of Wallace E. Lambert* (pp. 203–216). Mahwah, NJ: Lawrence Erlbaum.

Tajfel, H. (Ed.). (1978). *Differentiation between social groups: Studies in the social psychology of intergroup relations*. London: Academic Press.

Tajfel, H. (1981). *Human groups and social categories: Studies in social psychology*. Cambridge: Cambridge University Press.

Toohey, K. (2000). *Learning English at school: Identity, social relations and classroom practice*. Clevedon, UK: Multilingual Matters.

Ushioda, E. (2003). Motivation as a socially mediated process. In D. Little, J. Ridley, & E. Ushioda (Eds.), *Learner autonomy in the foreign language classroom: Teacher, learner, curriculum and assessment* (pp. 90–102). Dublin: Authentik.

Ushioda, E. (2006). Motivation, autonomy and sociocultural theory. In P. Benson (Ed.), *Learner autonomy 8: Insider perspectives on autonomy in language learning* (pp. 5–24). Dublin: Authentik.

Varghese, M., Morgan, B., Johnston, B., & Johnson, K. A. (2005). Theorizing language teacher identity: Three perspectives and beyond. *Journal of Language, Identity, and Education*, *4*, 21–44.

Vitanova, G. (2005). Authoring the self in a non-native language: A dialogic approach to agency and subjectivity. In J. K. Hall, G. Vitanova, & L. Marchenkova (Eds.), *Dialogue with Bakhtin on second and foreign language learning: New perspectives* (pp. 149–169). Mahwah, NJ: Lawrence Erlbaum.

Vygotsky, L. S., & Luria, A. R. (1993). *Studies on the history of behavior: Ape, primitive, and child*. Hillsdale, NJ: Lawrence Erlbaum.

Weedon, C. (1987). *Feminist practice and poststructuralist theory*. New York: Basil Blackwell.

Wenger, E. (1998). *Communities of practice: Learning, meaning, and identity*. New York: Cambridge University Press.

Whyte, W. F., & Holmberg, A. R. (1956). Human problems of US enterprise in Latin America. *Human Organization, 15*, 1–40.

Yashima, T. (2002). Willingness to communicate in a second language: The Japanese EFL context. *The Modern Language Journal, 86*, 54–66.

Yip, T. (2005). Sources of situational variation in ethnic identity and psychological well-being: A palm pilot study of Chinese American students. *Personality and Social Psychology Bulletin, 31*, 1603–1616.

Zuengler, J., & Cole, K. (2005). Language socialization and second language learning. In E. Hinkel (Ed.), *Handbook of research in second language teaching and learning* (pp. 301–316). Mahwah, NJ: Lawrence Erlbaum.

Zuengler, J., & Miller, E. R. (2006). Cognitive and sociocultural perspectives: Two parallel SLA worlds. *TESOL Quarterly, 40*, 35–58.

# GLOSSARY

A

**Adjacency Pair (Chapter 12)** In social interaction, a two-part sequence whereby an initial action (first pair part), produced by speaker A, makes relevant a responding action (second pair part) in next turn, produced by speaker B; for example, question–answer, request–acceptance/rejection (Schegloff & Sacks, 1973).

**Age of Acquisition/Age of Onset (Chapter 6, 26)** The age at which an individual begins to learn a language; typically used to refer to the learning of a second or subsequent language.

**Age Effects (Chapter 17)** Influences on the outcome of learning that can be related to age of acquisition (AoA).

**Aging (Chapter 18)** The interacting physical, social, and psychological changes in humans after the age of 45.

**Agreement (Chapter 10)** *Syntax:* In general terms, a relationship between two elements in a sentence such as Subject–Verb, Modifier–Head, etc., whereby the lexical or syntactic properties of one of the elements requires a particular form for the other. Example: *that book* but *these books*. Within the Government-Binding theory of syntax, Agr(eement) is an element of the category I(nflection), which, among other things, determines agreement between the Subject of a sentence and the form of its Verb.

**Alternating Antagonism (Chapter 15)** A case of nonparallel recovery of languages in polyglot aphasics in which one language is impaired while the other is spared, but the affected language may alternate.

**AoA Function (Chapter 17)** The mathematical relationship of AoA to end-state attainment.

**Aphasia (Chapter 15, 18, 25)** Language impairments acquired as a result of stroke or other brain injury.

**Aptitude (Chapter 26)** Innate or learned component of a capacity to perform at a certain level.

**Attitudes (Chapter 26)** An evaluative reaction to some referent, based on the individual beliefs or opinions about the referent (based on Gardner, 1985)

**Automatic Processing (or Automaticity) (Chapter 6)** Mental processes that occur without intention, are fast acting, and consume few mental resources.

**B**

**Balanced Bilingual (Chapter 25)** A person with a near-native competence in two languages.

**Borrowing (Chapter 25)** A borrowing is a word or phrase taken from a language other than the one in which the word or phrase appears and serves the linguistic function of filling a gap in the lexicon of the borrower language, or they are prompted by nonlinguistic factors such as modernization or both. Borrowings do not influence the structure of the borrowing language.

**C**

**C-Command (Chapter 10)** *Syntax:* A particular relationship between two elements in a sentence—if A is dominated by a node which dominates B, then A c-commands B.

**Child L2 (Chapter 16)** Term used to refer to children whose initial exposure to a second language occurs beyond the age of 3 years, that is, after the grammar of the first language has already been established (for the most part), but prior to the onset of puberty.

**Code Mixing (CM) (Chapter 25)** Code Mixing consists in the occurrence of various linguistic units (morphemes, words, modifiers, phrases, clauses, and sentences) primarily from two participating grammatical systems within a single sentence. It is constrained by grammatical principles and may be motivated by sociopsychological factors (Bhatia & Ritchie, 1996).

**Code Switching (CS) (Chapter 25)** Code Switching refers to the mixing of various linguistic units (words, phrases, clauses, and sentences) primarily from two participating grammatical systems across sentence boundaries within a speech event. It may be subject to discourse principles. Like Code Mixing, it is motivated by social and psychological factors.

**Coding (Chapter 1)** Organizing data into a manageable, easily understandable, and analyzable base of information, and searching for and marking patterns in the data.

**Competition Condition (Chapter 10)** *Morphology*: In Distributed Morphology (q.v.), phonological forms are entered in a dictionary known as the "Vocabulary" with features that determine where those forms can be inserted in the derivation created by the syntax (the syntactic terminal nodes). In some cases more than one phonological form has features that match the same terminal node. In such cases, the form with the largest number of matching features is the one that is inserted (for native speakers). Example: both -$\emptyset$ and -*s* are forms that can be inserted in the context of plural nouns in English. However, the specification for -$\emptyset$ includes reference to a small number of nouns with which it can cooccur, and -*s* cannot, like *(three) sheep-$\emptyset$, (four) fish-$\emptyset$*. In such cases, it is the Competition Condition that determines that -$\emptyset$ is inserted, and not -*s*: *(three) \*sheeps, (four) \*fishes*.

**Complementizer (C) (Chapter 10)** *Syntax:* An element that functions as the Head of a Complementizer Phrase (CP). *Example:* The element *that* is a Complementizer in the sentence *John knows that Mary left*. Other Complementizers in English are *whether* and *if*.

**Computer-Mediated Communication (CMC) (Chapter 23)** Communication mediated by a computer whether in real time (synchronous) or deferred time (asynchronous).

**Cooperative Principle (Chapter 12)** A fundamental principle of conversation by which participants fit their contributions to the mutually recognized purpose of the interaction and the current direction of their talk, and understand each others' contributions in that way (Grice, 1975).

**Creole Language (Chapter 25)** A creole language is the result of a pidgin language becoming the mother tongue of the children of the community in which the pidgin is used.

**Critical Period Hypothesis (Chapters 3, 6, 10, 11, 14, 15, 17, 22, 26)** The period of time coinciding with maturation beyond that it is thought to be difficult to fully acquire a language.

**Cultural Empathy (Chapter 26)** The ability to empathize with the feelings, thoughts, and behaviors of individuals from a different cultural background (van der Zee & van Oudenhoven, 2000).

**D**

**Data Elicitation (Chapter 1)** Data collection is the process of accumulating information pertaining to a particular research question, problem, or area. Data elicitation is a subset of data collection, data elicitation refers to the process of directly eliciting information from individuals, for example, through an interview or a task.

**Dementia (Chapter 18)** A nonspecific illness syndrome in which areas of cognition including memory, attention and language are declined more than might be expected with normal aging.

**Descriptive Statistics (Chapter 1)** A way of summarizing or describing a set of data.

**Diglossia (Chapter 25)** Diglossia refers to the relationship between two or more varieties of a language when they are used in different functions in a speech community—a high variety that carries greater prestige than the other, low variety. The two varieties are not mixed. Tamil and Arabic are excellent examples of diglossic societies.

**Distributed morphology (DM) (Chapter 10)** *Morphology:* DM is a name for an organization of the grammar where the properties of lexical items are not all located in a single lexicon, but are distributed across several lexicons: one that contains morphosyntactic features, one that contains the phonological forms of lexical items (the "Vocabulary") and one that contains idiosyncratic conventional meanings associated with particular items (the "Encyclopedia"). DM is one version of the "separation hypothesis" that proposes that syntactic operations are dissociated from the forms that realize linguistic expressions on the surface.

***Do*-Support (Chapter 10)** *Syntax:* A phenomenon in the syntactic structure of English in which the semantically empty verb *do* carries the verb inflections in a sentence. Examples: *Did John turn out the lights?*, *John did not turn out the lights*, *Mary turned out the lights and John did, too.*

**Dual System Hypothesis (Chapter 15)** A neurocognitive model of languages representation in bilinguals that may explain the existence of nonparallel recovery of languages in polyglot aphasics. It posits that the different languages of bilinguals are represented in separate and distinct neural structures.

**Dynamic Systems Theory (Chapter 18)** The study of change over time of systems of interacting variables.

**E**

**Ecological Validity (Chapter 21)** A research property whereby setting, participants, language circumstance of data collection are consistent with those under study.

**Efficiency-Driven Processor (Chapter 4)** A processor that seeks to minimize the burden on working memory.

**Emergentism (Chapter 4)** The view that language in all its complexity is best understood in terms of the interaction of simpler and more basic nonlinguistic factors.

**Emergentism, Input-Based (Chapter 4)** Emergentist work that focuses on the role on the input in understanding the properties of language and how they are acquired.

**Emergentism, Processor-Based (Chapter 4)** Emergentist work that focuses on the role on processing in understanding the properties of language and how they are acquired.

**Emic (Chapter 26)** Research perspective where behavior, events, and situations are described using the language of participants (Pike, 1964).

**End State (Chapter 26)** The outcome of language acquisition. In the L2A context, the terms ultimate attainment and asymptote are also used in reference to the outcome of learning.

**Etic (Chapter 26)** Research perspective where behavior, events, and situations are described using the language of the researchers (Pike, 1964).

**Event-Related Potentials (ERPs) (Chapter 15)** A noninvasive neuroimaging technique for recording electrophysiological responses to an internal or external stimulus. Although the changes of the electroencephalographic signal induced by a stimulus are small with respect to the background noise, averaging several signal epochs, timely triggered to the stimulus onset, allows the investigator to cancel the noise and to detect only signal changes related to the stimulus.

**Evidence (Chapters 19, 20, 21, 23, 25)** Information for the language learner about presence or absence of linguistic and communicative properties and regularities of a language, either provided explicitly or made inferable from language samples. Positive evidence, available in texts and discourse, consists of information about the actual linguistic and communicative properties of a language. Negative evidence consists of information about what is not a linguistic or communicative property of a language; available through instruction, "negative," that is, corrective, feedback, and responses, which seek clarification of utterances or recast and reformulate them.

**Explicit Learning (Chapters 14, 15, 23)** Explicit learning is a relatively conscious operation where the individual makes and test hypotheses in a search for structure. Explicit language learning is more typical of adults, who tend to require explicit teaching and conscious learning involving more effort and planning on the part of both teachers and learners.

**Extraversion–Introversion (Chapter 26)** Basic personality dimension (one of the so-called Big Five super-traits) (Eysenck, 1967).

**F**

**Features (Chapter 10)** *Syntax/Morphology:* In recent syntactic theory, morphosyntactic features are said to divide into interpretable features that are relevant to the semantic interpretation of a linguistic expression, and uninterpretable features that are not. Instead, uninterpretable features are relevant to the grammaticality of a sentence. Uninterpretable features are typically involved in Agreement (q.v.) dependencies and in causing Movement (q.v.). *Example:* [third person] and [+singular] are interpretable features of the pronouns *he/she/it* distinguishing them from *I/you/we/they*. There are uninterpretable counterparts of [third person] and [+singular] associated with the verb that give rise to forms like *(she) walks, (he) eats*. These features are not relevant to semantic interpretation, but determine agreement with the subject.

**Finite Verb (Chapter 10)** *Syntax/ Semantics:* A verb that indicates occurrence of the situation described in the sentence at some definite time. Distinct from a Nonfinite or Infinitive verb. *Examples:* Finite—*John works, John worked*. Nonfinite—*John will try to work, John's working is welcome*.

**First Language Influence (Chapter 10)** Any feature of second language performance that is related to the subject's Native Language.

**Focus on Form (Chapter 21)** A brief redirection of attention to the form of message meaning within the context of a communication impasse in the transmission of that meaning.

**Foreign Language Anxiety (Chapter 26)** Feeling of tension and apprehension linked to FL use.

**Form-Focused Instruction (Chapter 21)** Instruction on L2 forms and rules, within the context of a communicative need for these items.

**Formulaic Implicature (Chapter 12)** A type of implicature built on a recurrent semantic or rhetorical pattern. For example, indirect criticism: "A: Did you like Fred's new book?—B: I like the cover design" (Bouton, 1994).

**Full-Access Hypothesis (Chapter 10)** The hypothesis that adult second language learners have full access to the principles and parameters of Universal Grammar.

**Functional Categories (Chapters 10, 16, 25)** Functional categories are grammatical categories such as Determiner, Inflection (Tense and Agreement), and Complementizer. Functional categories, unlike Lexical categories, are not associated with semantic roles such as Agent, Patient/Theme, and Experiencer.

**Functional Magnetic Resonance Imaging (fMRI) (Chapter 15)** A neuroimaging technique that measures regional cerebral blood flow by recording changes in the magnetic field of red blood cells, taken as an index of neural activity. Usually researchers use the blood-oxygen-level dependent (BOLD) fMRI, which detects the difference between the magnetic signals created by oxygenated blood and deoxyhemoglobin blood.

**G**

**Grammaticality Judgment (Chapter 10)** A judgment made about the well formedness of an utterance in either spoken or written form.

**H**

**Head-Initial/Head-Final Language (Chapter 10)** *Syntax:* A Head-initial language is one in which the Head precedes the Complement in all phrases; a Head-final language is one in which the Head follows the Complement in all phrases. *Example:* English is a Head-initial language and Japanese is a Head-final language.

**I**

**Imagined Communities (Chapter 26)** Real or imagined belongings within communities of practice (Norton, 2001).

**Implicature (Chapter 12)** Conversational inference. On the default assumption that the Cooperative Principle (Grice, 1975) is in effect, ostensibly uncooperative (incoherent) responses are interpreted as contextually meaningful (e.g., "A: Is Keiko back?—B: I just went to check her mail.")

**Implicit Learning (Chapters 14, 15, 23)** Implicit learning refers to the acquisition of unconscious knowledge of the structures that invokes the operation of a principle of UG. Implicit learning takes place unconsciously in a natural environment such as the acquisition of language by children.

**Indirect Speech Act (Chapter 12)** An utterance whose contextually meaningful illocutionary force (the action that the utterance is doing) cannot be read off its literal meaning and needs to be interpreted through inferential strategies (Searle, 1975).

**Inferential Statistics (Chapter 1)** A way of modeling data patterns to draw inferences of the population being studied taking into account the randomness of the data.

**Infinitive (Chapter 10)** *Syntax/Semantics:* A form of a verb that refers to the situation described in the sentence independent of any particular time. Distinct from a Finite verb. Examples: Infinitive—*John will try to work.* Finite—*John works, John worked.*

**Inflexion [INFL] (Chapter 10)** See Functional categories.

**Information Processing (Chapter 6)** The notion that knowledge is processed through a series of stages that include encoding storage, and retrieval.

**Initial State (Chapter 10, 17)** In a highly idealized view of language acquisition, the learner's cognitive state prior to any linguistic experience, at which point all of the potential terminal states of the acquisition process are represented. In the case of first language acquisition, the Initial State is characterized by Universal Grammar (q.v.) and the terminal state by the grammar of a particular language.

**Input (Chapter 10, others)** The linguistic stimuli to which the language learner is exposed.

**Intelligent Computer-Assisted Language Learning (*i*-CALL) (Chapter 23)** Intelligent computer-assisted language learning which "empowers students to engage in online activities with computer applications that provide at least limited levels of feedback" (Blake, 2007).

**Interactional Capacity/Approach (Chapter 23)** The interaction capacity/approach refers to "learning through the learner's exposure to language, production of language, and feedback on that production" (Gass & Mackey, 2007).

**International Posture (Chapter 26)** Interest in international affairs combined with a willingness to live overseas and interact with intercultural partners (Yashima, 2002).

**Interfaces, External (Chapter 3)** Connection points between the grammar and other cognitive systems.
Logical Form (LF) provides the interface between the grammar and the conceptual–intentional system (meanings). Phonetic form (PF) provides the interface between the grammar and the auditory–perceptual system (sounds).

**Interfaces, Internal (Chapter 3)** Connection points between different components of the grammar, including syntax with semantics, syntax with morphology, phonology with morphology, etc.

## L

**Language Attrition (Chapter 18)** The nonpathological decline of language skills over time in individuals.

**Language Development (Chapter 18)** The changes of language proficiency over the life span.

**Language Dominance (Chapter 16)** The notion of language dominance is commonly used to refer to situations in simultaneous bilingual acquisition contexts as well as in child L2 contexts, where one of the two languages is more advanced or developing faster than the other. In a majority of bilinguals (children as well as adults), one language is generally more dominant than the other, although the dominance pattern can shift or change over time.

**Language Transfer (Chapter 16)** The influence exerted by the internalized linguistic system of one of the two languages of a bilingual individual onto the internalized linguistic system of the other. When the influence is from the first or native language onto the developing second language, it is termed as L1 transfer or L1 influence.

**Learner-External Variables (Chapter 26)** Variables originating from the learners' environment such as learning context, social, and political climate.

**Learner-Internal Variables (Chapter 26)** Variables originating from the learners themselves.

**Lexical Categories (Chapter 16)** Lexical categories include categories that have semantic roles associated with them. The major lexical categories are Noun, Adjective, Verb (e.g., hit, like, give) Preposition, and Adjective.

**Lexical Decision Task (Chapter 6)** A task that involves judging whether or not a string of letters forms a word within a given language.

## M

**Matrix and Embedded Language (Chapter 25)** In code-mixed utterance, the matrix language is the language that gives the utterance in which the mix occurs its basic character, and the embedded language is the language that contributes the "imported" material.

**Maturational Effects (Chapter 17)** Age effects that can be traced to biological maturation, and therefore do not extend past the end of maturation.

**Memory Span (Chapter 6)** The number of items that can be correctly recalled in the proper order.

**Minimal Trees (Chapter 10)** *Syntax:* This is a hypothesis that in initial acquisition grammars do not project all of the structure that is required for the target language. Initially only lexical projections (NP, VP, AdjP, PP) are present.

**Minimalist Program/Minimalism (Chapter 23)** The framework advanced by Noam Chomsky and others within which an optimal design of human linguistic knowledge is sought that incorporates the fewest elements and operations needed to adequately explain the nature of language and language acquisition.

**Missing Surface Inflection Hypothesis (MSIH) (Chapter 10)** *Morphology:* This hypothesis claims that where L2 speakers optionally use two exponents for the same underlying syntactic terminal node (e.g., producing both *she walks* and *she walk*) this is because they lack the Competition Condition (q.v.) that regulates insertion of phonological exponents for native speakers. For native speakers only -s is an appropriate exponent with third person singular present tense verbs because it has more features consistent with this context than the null affix -$\emptyset$. L2 learners, however, may allow the less specified form -$\emptyset$ to be inserted.

**Motivation (Chapter 26)**  The combination of effort plus desire to achieve the goal of learning the language plus favorable attitudes toward learning the language (Gardner, 1985).

**Movement (Chapter 10)**  *Syntax:* In the Government-Binding theory of syntax, a rule that enters into the relationship between D-structure and S-structure that moves an element from one position in a sentence structure to another leaving a Trace *t* in its D-structure position. *Examples:* NP-Movement enters into the mapping of the (schematic) D-structure *e was seen John by Alice* to give the (schematic) S-structure *John was seen t by Alice.* Wh-movement enters into the mapping of the (schematic) D-structure *John might see who* to give the (schematic) S-structure *who John might see t.*

**Multilingualism (Chapter 18)**  The knowledge and use of more than one language on a regular basis.

**N**

**Nativelike Attainment (Chapter 17)**  Learner performance in an experimental context that falls within the range of performance by native controls.

**Negation (Chapter 10)**  *Syntax:* The form that a sentence takes in expressing the denial or contradiction of some or all of the meaning of another sentence. *Example:* The sentence

*John will not win the prize* is the Negation of the sentence *John will win the prize.*

**Negotiation (Chapter 21)**  Interaction modified for purposes of communication or instruction. During negotiation of meaning, interaction is modified to repair communication impasses and reach mutual understanding. During negotiation of form, interaction is modified by a teacher to achieve accurate production by a learner.

**Notice the Gap (Chapter 21)**  Cognitive process through which learners compare their interlanguage version of form with a version in the input and notice the difference between them.

**Noun Phrase (Chapter 10)**  *Syntax:* A phrase of which a Noun is the Head.

**P**

**Past Tense (Chapter 10)**  *Syntax/Semantics:* A form of time reference in which an event or situation is regarded as a whole and as having occurred at some point before the time of speaking.

**Pidgin Language (Chapters 24, 25)**  A pidgin language is a mixed language, usually with material from two languages exhibiting a socially dominant–subordinate relationship—a high-prestige language such as English or French and a more local, low-prestige language. Pidgins have very restricted functional domains primarily having to do with business. They are not native languages for anyone.

**Pitre's Rule (Chapter 15)**  An hypothesis put forward by Pitres (1983) on the causes that might determine a better recovery of one language in polyglot aphasics. It claims that patients tend to recover the language that was most familiar to them prior to the injury.

**Positron Emission Tomography (PET) (Chapter 15)** A neuroimaging techniques that measures the changes of the regional blood flow by recording the levels of regional metabolism, taken as an index of neural activity.

**Pragmatics (Chapter 12)** "[T]he study of language from the point of view of users, especially of the choices they make, the constraints they encounter in using language in social interaction and the effects their use of language has on other participants in the act of communication" (Crystal, 1997, p. 301).

**Prepositional Phrase (Chapter 10)** *Syntax:* A phrase of which a Preposition is the Head. Examples: *in the garage, on the table, into the wastebasket.*

**Processing Instruction (Chapter 21)** Instruction on how to process sentences by recognizing cues for constituent order and relationships; shown to assist L2 comprehension more than production.

**Projection (Chapter 10)** *Syntax:* Within X-bar Theory, the phrases that are associated with a given Head. *Example:* In an NP, the N' level and the full NP itself are projections of the Head N.

**Prosody (Chapter 10)** *Phonology/ Phonetics:* The pattern of relative pitch, loudness, rhythm, and tempo of elements in a linguistic expression.

## Q

**Quantifier Scope (Chapters 4, 23)** The domain of a sentence over which a quantifier such as *many, some, three, few,* or *all* exerts a stronger semantic influence on the interpretation of the sentence than other elements in its domain; a quantifier that occurs or moves to a structurally higher position in a sentence representation takes scope over a quantifier in a lower position.

## R

**Restricted Access to Input (Chapter 23)** A limitation on the ability of a language learner, because of cognitive, linguistic, or physical factors, to perceive the sentences of a target language produced in a communicative environment; deaf learners have restricted access to spoken language input because of hearing loss.

**Restructuring (Chapters 6, 10)** Reorganization of the learner's linguistic knowledge in the process of language acquisition.

**Resumptive Pronoun (Chapter 23)** A pronominal element that occurs in relative clauses in some languages in a position in which there is only a gap in other languages; for example, where English has a gap after *read* in *the book which I read ___,* another language might have the equivalent of *the book which I read it,* where *it* is the resumptive pronoun.

**Ribot's Rule (Chapter 15)** An hypothesis attributed to Ribot (1882) on the causes that might determine a better recovery of one language in polyglot aphasics. It claims that, in the case of memory diseases, the later acquired language deteriorates earlier than the old.

## S

**Scope (Chapter 4)** The relationship between "logical operators" such as negation and quantifiers.

**Sensitive Period (Chapter 15)** A limited time during development, during which the effect of experience on brainfunction is particularly strong.

**Sequence Implicature (Chapter 12)** Utterances implying an event sequence (Bouton, 1994), for example, "She finished the book and went on vacation" versus "She went on vacation and finished the book."

**Shortest Move (Chapter 23)** An economy principle of the Minimalist Program (q.v.) that favors sentence derivations in which elements move locally in short steps over derivations that require longer movement.

**Simultaneous Bilingualism (Chapter 16)** The acquisition of two languages from birth, or one language from birth and another sometime thereafter, but prior to age of 3 years. Some researchers use a lower upper age boundary (e.g., 1 year) to distinguish between simultaneous bilingualism and sequential bilingualism.

**Social Identity (Chapter 27)** That aspect of the self, negotiated in social interaction, that pertains to one's emotional and cognitive connection with one or more normatively defined social groups and its associated roles, status, and relations.

**Specifier (Spec) of a Phrase (Chapter 10)** *Syntax:* Within the X-bar Theory of phrase structure, the element in a given phrase that is external to the Head-Complement structure.

**Statistics (Chapter 1)** A science relating to the collection, analysis, interpretation/explanation of data. (Also see "Descriptive statistics" and "Inferential statistics.")

**Steady State (Chapter 10, others)** A stage of development where an L2 speaker's performance has stabilized, and it is assumed that underlying grammatical knowledge has stabilized as well. The clearest evidence for the steady state is provided when performance of a long-immersed speaker is measured at two points separated by an interval of at least a year. If performance is the same at these two points it is reasonable to assume that the speaker's grammar has reached a steady state.

**Subsystem Hypothesis (Chapter 15)** A neurocognitive model of language representation in bilinguals proposed by Paradis (2004) to explain both parallel and nonparallel impairments and recovery of languages in polyglot aphasics. It posits a redundant representation of the languages in bilinguals, with a unified neurofunctional cognitive system and language-specific subsystems.

**T**

**Target Language (Chapter 10)** The language that a given learner is acquiring.

**Task (Chapter 21)** Goal-based activity that requires the transfer, exchange, and/or pooling of information; in a form-focused task, goal attainment depends on the use of specific grammatical features or forms.

**Teachability Hypothesis (Chapter 21)** A testable claim that instruction can accelerate the acquisition of a particular feature if learners are at a stage of development where they are close to acquiring the feature without such intervention.

**Tense (General Semantic Category) (Chapter 10)** *Syntax/Semantics:* A form of time reference in which an event or situation is referred to as a whole and as occurring in relation to some other time, usually the time of speaking.

**Tense (Formal, Theory-Internal Category: T, Tns) (Chapter 10)** *Syntax:* In the Government-Binding theory of syntax, either an element of I(nfl) or a separate category that carries the semantic interpretation of semantic Tense (q.v.).

**Thematic Role (θ-role) (Chapter 23)** The semantic function of an argument (e.g., a noun phrase) in its relationship to a verb or other predicate, for example, when a noun phrase serves as the performer ("agent") of an action, the receiver ("patient") of an action, the "experiencer" of a mental state or emotion, and so on.

**Third-Person Singular (Chapters 3, 10)** The English suffix -*s* that represents the agreement of the Verb with a third-person singular Subject in the present Tense. Example: *John likes rutabaga.*

**Trait emotional intelligence or trait emotional self-efficacy (Chapter 26)** Lower-order personality trait encompassing a constellation of emotion-related dispositions and self-perceptions (Petrides & Furnham, 2003).

**Transfer (Chapter 10)** The influence of the Native Language of a language learner on his/her performance in the second language. Positive Transfer, which consists in characteristics of the two languages that are similar, is claimed to facilitate performance in the second language whereas Negative Transfer, respects in which the two languages differ, is claimed to interfere with performance.

**Trigger (Chapter 10)** Within the Principles and Parameter Approach, an aspect of the Input to the language learner that induces the setting of a Parameter in one of its values.

**U**

**Underlying Representation (Chapter 16)** An individual's mental representation or the internalized knowledge of the grammar of a language.

**Universal Grammar (Chapters 10, 16)** The biological/genetic endowment that humans have for language acquisition, which is believed to consist of a finite system of abstract linguistic principles and parameters.

**Universal Quantifier (Chapter 23)** A modifying word such as *each*, *every*, and *all* that refers to all members of a set of entities that it modifies; for example, *every* in *every student* denotes all members of the total set of students referred to.

**V**

**Variational Feature (Chapter 21)** A form that emerges gradually with varying degrees of accuracy within and across learners; contrasted with a sequential feature, which develops in a predictable stage-like pattern, over time.

**Verb Movement (Verb Raising) (Chapter 10)** *Syntax:* Within the Government-Binding theory of syntax, the Movement (q.v.) of a Verb from its D-structure position in the Verb Phrase to be adjoined to the Functional Category Agr(eement) or T(ense). Some languages (e.g., French) require Verb Movement, others (English) exclude it.

**Verb Movement Parameter (Chapter 10)** *Syntax:* The Parameter that accounts for the difference between, for example; French and English that determines whether a language exhibits Verb Movement (q.v.) or not.

**Visual Compensation (Chapter 23)** The use of vision to access nonvisual linguistic input, for example, a deaf learner's use of vision rather than audition (hearing) to perceive spoken language sentences; examples of visual compensation are lipreading, sign language representation of spoken sentences, the reading of text, etc.

**W**

***Wh*-Movement (Chapter 10)** *Syntax:* The Movement (q.v.) of a Wh-phrase to a position at the beginning of a clause.

***Wh*-Question (Chapter 10)** *Syntax:* A question that includes a Wh-phrase in it. Example: *Who did John see?*

**Working Memory (Chapters 4, 6)** The mental workspace that coordinates ongoing mental activities; equated with current consciousness.

## REFERENCES

Bhatia, T. K., & Ritchie, W. C. (1996). Bilingual language mixing, Universal Grammar, and second language acquisition. In W. C. Ritchie & T. K. Bhatia (Eds.), *The handbook of second language acquisition* (pp. 627–688). New York: Academic Press.

Blake, R. (2007). New trends in using technology in the curriculum. *Annual Review of Applied Linguistics*, *27*, 76–97.

Bouton, L. F. (1994). Conversational implicature in the second language: Learned slowly when not deliberately taught. *Journal of Pragmatics*, *22*, 157–167.

Bouton, L. F. (1996). Pragmatics and language learning. In L. F. Bouton (Ed.), *Pragmatics and language learning* (Monograph Series Vol. 7). Urbana-Champaign, IL: Division of English as an International Language, University of Illinois, Urbana-Champaign.

Crystal, D. (1997). *Dictionary of linguistics and phonetics* (4th ed.). Oxford: Blackwell.

Ellis, N. C. (1994). Introduction. In N. C. Ellis (Ed.), *Implicit and explicit learning of languages* (p. 1). London, UK: Academic Press.

Eysenck, H. J. (1967). *The biological basis of personality*. Springfield, MA: C. C. Thomas.

Gardner, R. C. (1985). *Social psychology and second language learning: The role of attitudes and motivation*. London, UK: Arnold.

Gass, S., & Mackey, A. (2007). Input, interaction and output in second language acquisition. In B. VanPatten & J. Williams (Eds.), *Theories in second language acquisition* (pp. 175–199). Mahwah, NJ: Lawrence Erlbaum Associates.

Grice, P. (1975). Logic and conversation. In P. Cole & J. Morgan (Eds.), *Syntax and semantics* (Vol. 3: Speech Acts). New York: Academic Press.

Norton, B. (2001). Non-participation, imagined communities and the language classroom. In M. P. Breen (Ed.), *Learner contributions to language learning: New directions in research* (pp. 159–171). Harlow, UK: Longman.

Paradis, M. (2004). *A neurolinguistic theory of bilingualism*. Amsterdam: John Benjamins.

Petrides, K. V., & Furnham, A. (2003). Trait emotional intelligence: Behavioural validation in two studies of emotion recognition and reactivity to mood induction. *European Journal of Personality*, *17*, 39–57.

Pike, K. L. (1964). *Language in relation to a unified theory of the structure of human behaviour*. The Hague: Mouton.

Pitres, A. (1885). Aphasia in polyglots. In M. Paradis (Ed.), *Readings on Aphasia in Bilinguals and Polyglots*. (pp. 26–49). Montreal, Canada: Didier.Original work published in 1885

Ribot, T. A. (1882). *Diseases of memory: An essay in the positive psychology*. New York: Appleton.

Schegloff, E. A., & Sacks, H. (1973). Opening up closings'. *Semiotica*, *8*, 289–327.

Searle, J. R. (1975). Indirect speech acts. In P. Cole & J. Morgan (Eds.), *Syntax and semantics* (Vol. 3: Speech Acts). New York: Academic Press.

van der Zee, K. I., & van Oudenhoven, J. P. (2000). The multicultural personality questionnaire: A multidimensional instrument of multicultural effectiveness. *European Journal of Personality*, *14*, 291–309.

Yashima, T. (2002). Willingness to communicate in a second language: The Japanese EFL context. *Modern Language Journal*, *86*, 55–66.

# AUTHOR INDEX

# SUBJECT INDEX

Printed in the USA/Agawam, MA
August 17, 2011

560697.004